Directory of Theatre Training Programs

Eleventh Edition: 2007-2009

Profiles of College and Conservatory Programs throughout the United States

Information on admissions, degrees offered, faculties, courses, facilities, productions and philosophy of training

PJ Tumielewicz & Peg Lyons, Editors

Copyright © 2007, by Theatre Directories Inc.

PO Box 159, Dorset, Vermont 05251-0159 PHONE: (802) 867-9333; FAX: (802) 867-2297

Visit our website at www.theatredirectories.com

ISBN 10: 0-933919-65-4; ISSN 1041-5211

ISBN-13: 978-0-933919-65-5

dedicated to ❋❋❋

Jill Charles (1948-2001) Founding Editor-in-Chief
Anne M. Gilbert, supporter and friend, (1950-2007)

❋❋❋❋❋❋❋❋❋❋❋❋**Acknowledgments**

Many thanks to:

Don Reiser and his crew at Express Copy, Manchester VT
Jay Perry for contributing his essay.
All the schools listed, for their cooperation.
The Drama Book Shop, for their continued encouragement and support.
Ernest Montgomery, and the dedicated staff of Theatre Directories, Inc.

Rehearsal photo (cover) courtesy of Green Mountain College, Poultney, VT

Directory of Theatre Training Programs

Eleventh Edition: 2007-2009

"Read This First"

    Making the Choice:

        Should you pursue a career in the performing arts?   ii

    To B.F.A. or not to B. F. A.: choosing a theatre program   iv

    "Something to fall back on" (parents: read this!)   vii

    Mind Your Own Business by Jay Perry   vii

How to Use this Directory   ix

    Interviewing Schools: you ask the questions!   x

Theatre Training Programs (alphabetically, by state)

Alabama ···1	Kentucky ···93	North Dakota ···198
Alaska ···5	Louisiana ···98	Ohio ···199
Arizona ···7	Maine ···104	Oklahoma ···210
Arkansas ···9	Maryland ···105	Oregon ···214
California ···11	Massachusetts ···109	Pennsylvania ···217
Colorado ···34	Michigan ···119	Rhode Island ···233
Connecticut ···38	Minnesota ···126	South Carolina ···236
Delaware ···46	Mississippi ···132	South Dakota ···238
District of Columbia ···47	Missouri ···133	Tennessee ···239
Florida ···50	Montana ···142	Texas ···244
Georgia ···59	Nebraska ···143	Utah ···258
Hawaii ···64	Nevada ···145	Vermont ···261
Idaho ···65	New Hampshire ···146	Virginia ···264
Illinois ···66	New Jersey ···149	Washington ···274
Indiana ···78	New Mexico ···153	West Virginia ···278
Iowa ···85	New York ···155	Wisconsin ···279
Kansas ···90	North Carolina ···185	Wyoming ···288

Studies Abroad

    Canada   290

    United Kingdom   291

Index

    Institutions, alphabetical by name, with degrees offered   A-1

Making the Choice:
Should you pursue a career in the performing arts?

-- WORKING as a teacher and director has brought me into contact with many young and talented people who are considering a career in the performing arts. I enjoy working with young and talented people, because it means watching them grow, and sharing their excitement as they make discoveries about themselves and about their art. It is a learning process for me too, which keeps my own art from stagnating. With many of my students or pre-professionals in our Apprentice Company, there comes a time when they ask me a terrifying question: "What do you think are my chances at a career in theatre?"

What they want to hear from me is "Go for it! You've got the talent! It might be tough, kid, but stick it out and you'll make it."

Even supposing I **do** feel the person is extremely talented, I can't say that, because of the unbearable responsibility it entails: I have visions of the student in ten years, penniless, wandering the streets of New York, muttering to any passer-by who can't get away fast enough, "But my teacher told me I could be a great actress..." Yet the opposite is almost as bad: the frustrated insurance salesman who could have been a wonderful actor, with the right encouragement at the right time.

Over the years, I have evolved an answer that will let me off the hook—but to my credit, the answer is honest, and in fact the only one I can give with any conscience. Always assuming that the person is relatively talented, and I truly could foresee the possibility of a performing career, my answer is this:

"If there is anything else in the world that you could do with your life that would make you happy, do it."

Let me repeat that.

If there is anything else in the world that you could do with your life that would make you happy, do it.

The problem, of course, is that many students I say that to don't believe it, don't even think I'm serious. They think I'm testing their dedication to their art, saying, in effect, "if theatre doesn't mean more to you than everything else in life, then you don't deserve to become part of the club."

On the contrary, however, I am **most serious** when I tell you that the romanticized view of the artist starving in a garret is expounded by people who never had to wait on tables 60 hours a week so they could afford to pay their rent while being turned down by agents, producers, directors and the casting person for the carpet warehouse commercial.

Just what is so awful about pursuing a career in the arts? I'll proceed to give you a list, which I imagine none of you will take seriously at this point in your lives. But that's all right—keep this article, so that 10 years down the road you can't say I didn't warn you. I'll explain the three basic problems with a career in the arts: money, security and psyche.

If your concept of making a living as a performer comes from movie magazines quoting the latest multi-million dollar picture deal made by this week's hottest young star, you have a very skewed understanding of reality. For the cold hard facts, we can turn to statistics from the three professional unions: Actors' Equity Association (stage actors); Screen Actors Guild and American Federation of Television and Radio Artists. According to the US Department of Labor, Occupational Outlook Handbook, 2008-2009 Ed, Bulletin 270, Bureau of Labor Statistics, the average income that SAG members earn from acting, less than $5,000/year, is low because employment is sporadic.

So the majority of union actors in this country are making incomes well below "poverty level." And remember that most of them live in New York or Los Angeles, two of the most expensive cities in the nation. An actor has to keep up an apartment, keep together a decent wardrobe, pay for cabs (or keep up a car, in L.A.), pay for voice and dance les-sons, acting classes, photo/resumes, postage and telephone, not to mention eating once in a while.

So, keeping body and soul together while you're trying to "make it" as an actor, singer or dancer means taking a "survival job" * waiting on tables, doing temporary office work or driving a cab to pay the bills while you try to orchestrate your "big break". And you must find a job with a flexible schedule, or an understanding boss, so that you can take a two hour lunch break to attend an audition, or switch from the dinner shift to the lunchtime shift if you get cast in a showcase that's rehearsing at night. (A showcase rarely pays more than carfare—actors are the only people in the world who would rather work for free than not work at all.)

What I'm trying to tell you is this: if every "professional actor" in the East were to disappear tomorrow, New York City would note with sorrow that a few hundred people who had been entertaining them were gone—but it would be thrown into much greater chaos by the disappearance of most of the waiters and waitresses in every restaurant from 14th to 72nd Streets. [*
(please read "Something to Fall Back On")

The importance of security is hard to explain to teen-agers, because most of you, fortunately, have not experienced terrible insecurity: i.e., not knowing where your next meal is coming from, or where you're going to find the rent money, or when your next job is going to turn up. **Insecurity is a way of life for performing artists.**

Psychologists will tell you that one of the most stressful situations in which you ever can find yourself is having lost a job, or looking for a new one. You've heard much in the news about corporate "downsizing," and about the traumas executives go through, loosing a job and looking for work. Performing artists are ALWAYS looking for work. A job that you land after months of auditioning may last three to six weeks. If you're really lucky you might be hired for an entire season at a regional theatre—maybe October through April. Even your "big break" may be over by the time you read the reviews—of the 20-30 shows which open on Broadway in an average season, only a handful will survive through the following summer; as many as half of them will close overnight or in a few weeks.

This insecurity makes it almost impossible to make long-term plans for your life. It presents great difficulties in personal relationships, like marrying or starting a family. Such obstacles may not seem critical at 18, but at 34, when you see your best friends with a house, car, family and investments, while you're still living from hand to mouth in a fifth floor walkup in a section of New York which your mother refuses to visit, the glamour of the Bohemian artist wears thin beside such luxuries as taking the kids to DisneyWorld on their winter break.

I've left the worst for last. Lack of money and security do bad things to one's personal psyche. But even above and beyond those two factors is the additional factor of constant rejection which a performing artist must be prepared to face.

Let's look at the personality of someone who wants to go into the performing arts. Here a lot of the old cliches about artists really do hold: yes, an actor is generally a sensitive person; many of them are very shy; even the most extroverted (in fact, frequently the most extroverted) are insecure, with a fragile self-image. They care deeply about their work, they are a part of their work and cannot separate themselves from it—literally or figuratively, because for dancers, singers and actors, the body is the instrument of their art. Furthermore, the performing artist is by nature a person who needs immediate and tangible recognition and approval. He or she is after applause at the end of two hours, not a gold watch after twenty years.

Now take this person, and drop him or her into a situation where every day brings another rejection. He/she is constantly being told: you're too young; too old; too tall; too dark; too inexperienced; we want someone who does tap, not jazz; someone who's shorter than the leading man; someone who can belt to a high A; someone who sings in Russian; someone who's in the union; someone who's not in the union; someone who's willing to spend the next 14 months on tour; someone who will promise not to leave town all year... it goes on and on. And the most depressing thing of all is that there are so many others like you around that if you're a 5'4 blonde and they want a 5'5" blonde, they're more likely to find and hire a 5'5" blonde than put you in 1" heels.

To get back to my original point:

If there is anything else in the world that you can do that would make you happy, do it.

"Breaking into show business" is just that—and you frequently come out bloodied, without ever really having gotten into anything at all. Many of my friends have, at age thirty, looked back at the last ten years of their life and realized they had tricked themselves into thinking they were a professional artist when in fact they were a professional waiter. They had sacrificed a stable family life for one of a nomad, had accumulated no savings or possessions, and had acquired an embittered outlook on life through years of endless frustrations.

Finally, let me assure you there is no stigma attached to saying "no" to an artistic career. Turning to something else does not make you a Philistine, it does not lessen your enjoyment or appreciation of the arts, and in many cases it does not even cut down very much on your ability to practice your art. You can be working at a profitable and enjoyable career and still have as much time to play the piano as you would have if you were holding down two shifts of waiting table to keep body and soul together until someone recognized your genius at an after hours piano bar. If you make a rational decision not to pursue a career in the arts, based on an intelligent assessment of your personal goals in life, you are in no way disappointing yourself or your family and friends; in fact, you'll probably have the time, energy and spirit to contribute much more to a family or a friendship.

I have now made the best case I could to encourage you all to run to your guidance counselor tomorrow morning and ask to see a list of the top business schools in the country. But I suppose I still owe something to those of you who, after due consideration of all I and others may say to you, and after some real soul-searching, decide that you truly are not meant to be happy in a simpler, more secure and very possibly more rewarding career. To you, I will now attempt to lay down a few guidelines that might help you avoid some of the worst frustrations facing young artists. In my more cynical moments I call them:

Ten suggestions to avert self-destruction

1. Decide what kind of training you need.

This usually involves a decision by the time you're 16 or 17 as to whether you're headed for a conservatory training program or for a liberal arts college degree with more specific training after that. There are advantages to either, so the choice is a difficult one, but only you can make it for yourself, after investigating both possibilities in depth. [read "To B.F.A. or not to B.F.A."]

2. Find the best place to get that specific kind of training.

Do as much research as you possibly can, to find the place that will offer you exactly what you want and need, with the best reputation you can possibly afford. You've already begun the process by buying this book—use it to narrow down your choices to a manageable number, then write for catalogues. Try to talk to people who have been through the program to get as objective a view of it as possible. Take the time and the trouble to assure yourself that the commitment you're going to make to an institution will be fulfilling and worthwhile. And when you get there, make use of it all.

3. Get as much experience as you can, as soon as you can.

Every exposure you can get will teach you something more about the art. Try to find ways of working with artists whom you respect, so that simply watching them will add to your experience. If you can possibly afford it, use the summers to apprentice with a professional com-

pany, or to take part in a training program of some kind. Be willing to "pay your dues"—work in any capacity you can find, so long as you're connected with a place and people where you can learn.

4. Try to gain and keep the support of your family and friends.

It often happens that parents are against the idea of their children entering the arts—usually because they are concerned about the problems posed under "Money" and "Security". If you feel you must go ahead against their wishes, it will be worth every effort you can give it, somehow to come to an understanding and avoid a break with your family. You're going to **need** support—frequently financial, always emotional. Make sure the people close to you understand that you're serious about your work, and try to explain to them what it means to you. If you are asking your family to make financial contributions to help you pursue your training, be responsible about pulling your weight where you can, and let them know you're aware of their sacrifices. And, having asked them to live through your anxiety and frustrations, make sure you share the exhilaration as well.

5. Learn the business as quickly and as early as you can.

Learn what professionalism means, learn what is expected of you in your field. Learn the ropes—how to put together a resume, how to audition, how to make and use contacts. You learn these things through classes and seminars, by putting yourself into professional companies at whatever level, and by talking to professionals. You'll find in general that actors are glad to help someone just starting out to avoid a few pitfalls where possible.

6. Never stop your training.

You can always improve on your art. After you leave school you must keep working to achieve higher levels. Wherever you live, search out training opportunities with artists you respect and can learn from. Accept the fact that it costs money—paying for your acting/singing/dancing/music lessons is as important as paying your rent. The performing arts take as much just plain hard work as professional sports, medicine, law or any other profession you care to name. Without self-discipline you simply will not succeed, because there are so many others like you who have as much talent and more will.

7. Love your art, but love other things too.

Remember there are other things in life—like people, sports, hobbies, intellectual pursuits. It's easy to fall into a very narrow framework as an artist—and it's dangerous, because it makes for narrow artists, and narrow art. Ideally, your performances should bring to others an increased enjoyment of life, and it's hard to accomplish that if you don't find enjoyment for yourself in your own life.

8. Keep your sense of humor.

It's easy to take yourself too seriously. You really should cultivate the ability to sit back once in a while and laugh at the silly way you've chosen to try and make a living.

9. Develop your own personal, artistic integrity.

Sometimes that is all you have to keep you going. You must know what is real and what is false in your art form, and in yourself. You learn this "quality control" by watching others and listening to others, but ultimately you must make the distinctions for yourself. And once you reach that understanding you must not compromise. This is NOT to say it's beneath you to do a TV commercial. It may not be the most gratifying role in the world, but it might keep your head above water for a few more months until you find something that is gratifying. But you must bring the same integrity to the TV commercial that you would bring to Othello, or you will find it harder and harder to make distinctions, until you bring to Othello no more than you brought to the TV commercial.

10. THE MINUTE YOU FIND THAT THERE IS SOMETHING ELSE YOU COULD DO WITH YOUR LIFE THAT WOULD MAKE YOU HAPPY, DO IT.

ORIGINAL EDITORIAL COMMENT: by Jill Charles (1948-2001): UPDATED BY PJ TUMIELEWICZ AND PEG LYONS, EDITORS

To B.F.A. or not to B.F.A.:
Choosing a theatre program by Jill Charles

(While this article is geared toward the High School student looking for an undergraduate program, it is just as useful for the student seeking postgraduate study.)

THE PROBLEM with picking a college program—in theatre or anything else—is that they come in various shapes and sizes, with strong and weak programs in each category. Before you can sort them qualitatively, you have to decide which category to sort through. Do you want a small private liberal arts school with a small theatre department, or a state university with a mammoth theatre department? Do you want to end up with a B.A. or a B.F.A.? And what's the difference, anyway?

The Bachelor of Arts in general theatre, offered by Liberal Arts colleges and universities of all sizes, is a broad-based academic program where the student takes classes in all subjects, but with an overall major in theatre. The Bachelor of Fine Arts is a more specialized program where you major in an area of theatre—acting, design, directing, etc.—and take fewer courses in subjects other than theatre. Usually you go through a selection process—an audition or portfolio review and interview—to get into the B.F.A. program, after you have been accepted into the university, and you may be subjected to a periodic review of your work in order to remain in the program.

It used to be that the B.F.A. was offered only by larger colleges and universities; in the last few years, however, the B.F.A. degree has proliferated and some fairly small schools offer it. Another wrinkle is that many schools offering a B.A. degree are now offering concentrations in the various areas of theatre, so in some cases it may be hard to differentiate between, for instance, a B.F.A. with a major in design and a B.A. with a concentration in design. In general, however, assume that a B.A. will mean a broader academic range, and a B.F.A. will approach conservatory training.

One of the great arguments for choosing a Liberal Arts B.A. degree over a B.F.A. is the importance of learning to think, and of being exposed to a variety of subjects and ideas. At age 20, it is hard to draw on life experience when working on a role—you just haven't had that much of it. Studying a broad range of subjects, considering different points of view, being exposed to different philosophies, all can enhance a student's understanding of the world, and thus his or her ability to bring truth to a wider variety of roles. And the liberal arts education can establish patterns of logic and a humanistic world-view that are necessary for a person of any age to make headway (speaking materially or personally) in an extremely complex society.

As the B.A. proponents contend, focusing exclusively on theatre for four of your most intellectually fertile years can be a narrowing experience. But if a student is determined to enter the profession and doesn't want to let those four years go by without accumulating essential skills, then a B.F.A. makes sense. It is the responsibility of a good B.F.A. program to ensure that its students are still challenged to think, to read and to acquire a world-view of some kind (even though these efforts may not earn the students' whole-hearted appreciation at the time). Graduate and conservatory programs have the luxury of assuming that those needs have already been met, either as an undergrad or in "the real world," so they can specialize without a twinge, but your first four years have to teach you things beside theatre. This is a point worth pursuing in a course catalogue, or discussing on a visit to campus. It's also a good selling point for your parents, if you can find a program that will literally teach you to think before you act.

Let's illustrate the initial decision about an undergraduate program with a few fictional examples:

Lisa is a seventeen-year-old who has known she was going to be an actress since she was eight. She's had eight years of private music and dance lessons, she's spent four summers at an arts camp, she has auditioned for and been cast in almost every play available since seventh grade. During her junior year in high school she started "making the rounds" of the

advertising agencies in the small city where she lives, and got cast in a local commercial and a couple of voice-overs, as well as getting extra work on a movie that was shot on location nearby. She plans to audition for summer stock so she will have a professional Apprenticeship under her belt when she goes to college. She knows she either wants to attend a Conservatory or go for a BFA degree at a college in a city that has an active professional theatre industry: New York, Boston, Chicago, etc. She plans to work as many summers of stock as she can afford while she's in school, and then go directly into the business when she graduates.

Jeffrey is a top-of-his-class student who has always had a strong interest in the arts—theatre and music especially. He's done leads in a few plays and musicals, and went on to state competitions with his drama club. He sees as much live theatre as he can, and is a bit of a movie fanatic. He can probably get into an Ivy League school, which is what his parents are hoping for, with heavy hints of pre-law being dropped around the house. He's not necessarily opposed to the idea of law school or maybe an M.B.A., but he's reluctant to give up his dream of seeing if he's got what it takes as an actor. He's going to look at the top private schools he thinks he can get into, with an eye to their offerings in theatre. He may not even major in theatre, but will audition for as many shows as he can manage, both departmental and student sponsored. He figures that by his junior year he'll have an idea as to which grad schools he's aiming for—business, law or theatre. In any case, he'll wind up with a liberal arts degree from a top school.

Beverly and Steve are a little less certain about what they want in a college. Both have been very active in all aspects of their high school drama programs. Beverly played some lead roles, but also enjoyed building sets and costumes, and did some assistant design work. Steve wrote and directed a one-act which won a regional competition. Beverly's parents are supportive but concerned that she have "something to fall back on" if she doesn't find work in theatre. Steve's parents think he should find a communications program, because there seem to be more opportunities in television and communications fields. Both of them have decent grades, but frankly spent more time working on shows than trying to make phenomenal scores on their SAT's.

Steve is extremely outgoing, and wants to work intensely but still have the opportunity for varied activities. He'll probably settle on a large university where he can take a B.F.A. in Directing or Playwriting, and manage to integrate some film courses from the communications department into his program as well. Beverly tends to work better in smaller, close-knit groups; she will pursue a B.A. in a smaller state or private school, with an intimate theatre department where she can do a lot of everything until she decides what she likes best. She might even double major, since she's also interested in Psychology. If she finds out she really wants to pursue design, she'll apply to M.F.A. programs.

You will consider similar factors in selecting the size and type theatre programs to investigate. But within a given size and type, how do you determine which program has the most to offer? If you are looking for a specific area of theatre such as design or stage management, start with the Index to help you find institutions which offer the degree and area you want. Next use those institutions' profiles, keeping the following key points in mind, to help you narrow down the possibilities to a manageable number of schools, then send for their catalogues. Using these same key points, with catalogue in hand you should be able to come up with an accurate assessment of the program and of how well it would meet your needs.

Start your investigation with the most crucial elements of a program: who's teaching and what's being taught. The first consideration is the size of the department—the number of faculty and of students. The programs in this book which have four or fewer full time faculty are noted as "Small Programs." While it is hard to determine an optimum size for a theatre department (obviously a department which offers a B.F.A. program will generally be larger than one offering a B.A.), a faculty where the full-time equivalent (combined full-and part-time faculty) is less than five generally means more limited course offerings and a narrower orientation. Generally, small departments will supplement their offerings with input from other departments like English, Dance and Music. With a faculty of five or more, at least two of the five are most likely acting/directing people, so you will be getting some diversity in acting technique. The optimum size of the student body, or the number of majors, is a very personal matter—you probably know whether you function better with smaller or larger groups.

Next, look at the qualifications of the faculty. Compare the number of Ph.D., M.F.A. and "Prof. w/o adv. degree" under "Faculty and Classes Offered" in the school's profiles. These numbers say a great deal about a department: a more academically oriented department will hire M.A.'s and Ph.D.'s, and expect their faculty to publish articles and books; a more professionally oriented department will hire M.F.A.'s, or people without higher degrees but with extensive experience as directors or designers, and expect their faculty to continue to work professionally while associated with the college. The attitude a department takes toward its faculty is reflective of the attitude it will take toward students, and its philosophy in general. Thus, if you are looking for a degree in theatre history or dramatic criticism, look for a long list of Ph.D.'s on the faculty. But, if your main concern is performing or design, if you plan to be working in the profession as soon as you get out of school, then a major consideration is the amount of practical, professional experience your teachers can draw on in their classes.

One of the ways departments can integrate working professionals is by bringing them on part-time, to teach one or two courses a semester—an effective way to get top-notch people who are too active to devote an entire year to teaching. The perspective that a working professional can bring to a college program is invaluable. The director, designer or actor who can illustrate her theory with examples onstage in a nearby theatre, or anecdotes from a recent production brings that theory to life in a classroom. These people can also of tremendous benefit to the students in providing connections into the profession while still in school: a designer might be impressed enough with a student to take him/her on as an assistant; or a guest director might open a door to an internship with a regional or summer company.

However, there can also be drawbacks to the use of part-time faculty. Small colleges in or near a major theatre center like New York can find a healthy supply of struggling actors eager to pick up extra money by teaching on an "adjunct" basis—they are paid per class, at a much lower rate than regular faculty. The detriment to the student is usually a lack of commitment on the part of the adjunct teachers. They know they're being paid on a much lower scale than regular faculty, and part of the arrangement is that they have no duties other than teaching. They are generally working or teaching elsewhere at the same time, and they sometimes don't even have a real office on campus; they come in to the college only to teach their classes, and feel no obligation to be available to students outside of those hours.

This type of situation can occur even with highly regarded professionals that come in as part-time teachers or guest artists—they may be so active in their own career that the time they devote to their class or to designing a show at the school is the absolute minimum required. Of course, it's by no means always the case; frequently professionals are tremendously excited by the prospect of teaching, and are very good at it—these are the people that a strong theatre department will seek out for part-time or guest positions as they fill out their curriculum. How can a prospective student differentiate between the two sides of this coin? It's hard to do so from a profile or a catalogue, but it is the type of thing you can get a feel for from a campus visit or from talking to students who have gone through the program.

After looking over the faculty, look carefully at the "Classes Offered" section of the profiles; this will indicate if a course is given on a yearly (Y) or occasional (O) basis, or if it is offered by another department (X). This will give you a pretty thorough idea of the types and number of classes offered and their frequency. When you look through actual course catalogues, take the time to translate all the symbols and "major course sequence" and determine exactly which courses are taught every year, and which courses you will take if you go through the full major program. This is important, because once a course description gets into a catalogue, it usually stays there until the professor who originated it leaves—or dies—even if it's only taught once every eight or ten years!

If you are looking at a B.A. in general theatre, you should see a pretty thorough grounding in all areas as the sequence of courses required for a major. It will probably start with your basic "Theatre 101", a general introduction to theatre studies. You will also see required courses and electives in theatre history and dramatic literature—some of the latter probably offered through the English Department.

Next consider the skills courses that are offered. Obviously, the bigger the department, the more there will be, but even a small department should offer more than simply "Acting". There should be some attempt at providing at least the basics of voice and movement technique; in smaller departments, this might be done by crossing over into classes in the dance or music department, or by bringing in a voice teacher on a part-time basis. Acting should go beyond a two-semester introductory course, offering at least electives on a more advanced level, and in areas like mime and improvisation. In large departments you will have the option of more specialized advanced courses like stage combat, commedia dell'arte, period style, non-naturalistic acting, etc.; in a B.F.A. or conservatory situation, such courses will be part of the major program, rather than electives. If you are pursuing an area other than acting, the same general principals apply, but of course the skills courses will be in directing, or design, management, etc.

A general B.A. will also require you to take a stagecraft course (or "scenography" which seems to be the current name), including a "lab period" in the scene shop, working on sets. Your major should also include at least the basics in scenic, costume and lighting design courses and in directing. Electives in stage management, arts management and the like should fill out the program. Most departments make an effort to cover special needs of their majors with "Independent Study" or "Advanced Seminar" or some type of catch-all course that seniors can tailor to their own needs. This might allow someone with a bent toward playwriting or directing to work on a special project, under the one-on-one supervision of a faculty member. This can be an excellent opportunity—providing of course that someone on faculty really can offer the guidance necessary to make it a meaningful experience.

Of course, the larger the department, the greater the number and diversity of course offerings. A large department with a B.F.A. program can offer a full complement of skills courses—voice, movement, mime, improv, stage combat, etc.—and also allow for much more specialization, especially in design and production areas. But at the same time, there are only so many courses you can take in four years, and it is possible to get a general B.A. in theatre from a relatively small department which gives you a really solid grounding in all aspects of your craft. The key is to find the best quality available in whatever size college you've decided is right for you.

After you've found some schools that seem to offer what you want in faculty and courses, consider their productions and facilities. What kind of building will you be spending most of your waking hours in, what are the projects you'll be working on, and who are the people who will be guiding this aspect of your college experience?

College theatres have some of the best facilities in the country, and use them as a selling point when recruiting students. It is important to remember, however, that the quality of your experience is going to depend more on the people than on the facilities. There are even times when state-of-the-art facilities can be detrimental, if that is the only theatre experience you ever have. The production student who is used to pneumatic tools, a welding shop, a computerized lighting board and a stage full of traps and turntables may be at a total loss when he hits his first off-off-Broadway or shoestring summer stock experience. While it is certainly an advantage in the marketplace to be fully aware of and able to work with modern theatre technology, there is also much to be said for learning how to work miracles with more ingenuity than money.

The profiles in this book list how many productions are done on each stage, whether they are student- or faculty-directed and designed, and the average production budget. This will give you some basis for comparison between programs, and an indication of students' opportunities. Once you begin contacting programs, you should do more research in this area. Look at a list of the Mainstage productions at the college for the last three or four years. Is it well balanced between contemporary and classical,

American and European? If you see nothing but Shakespeare, Brecht and Chekhov, where will your exposure to current American playwrights come from? Is there a studio series for more current work? Have they ever done a (gasp) musical? The point is, there should not be a huge discrepancy between the type of work you will be doing in college and the type of work you want to do when you leave school. Just as you want your theatre history and dramatic lit. courses to cover all areas, you want your production experience to expose you to all styles.

One indication of how well-rounded a program is may be the shows that are student-generated. The profiles in this book specify if there is a student drama organization separate from the department. If you talk to students who have been through the program, ask about this relationship: does the department support, with money and/or enthusiasm, the student group? Or are the two at odds, and seen as mutually threatening? Sometimes a student group can be born out of genuine frustration with a department's refusal to deal with contemporary or experimental works; of course, it can also be a repository for disgruntled students who weren't cast in a departmental show. In a "healthy" department, there is a crossover between student- and faculty-generated projects, with each group respecting and supporting the other's work.

Some programs have a connection with a professional theatre company, which shares the college facilities (these are noted in the profiles). This may be a summer company, or a regional theatre running a full season of plays, such as the Huntington at Boston University, or Syracuse Stage at Syracuse University. The benefits of such a connection are obvious, and parallel those mentioned before, of having working professionals on the faculty. The opportunity to observe or take part in a professional company in full swing before you graduate can put you ahead of students coming into the business from a more protected ivory tower. However, especially when the college facilities are shared during the school year, it is important to investigate the actual hands-on opportunity you as an undergraduate will have. Is all the real interaction reserved for the MFA students? Is there real interaction, or is the professional company a totally separate entity? Even the latter isn't necessarily bad—you still have the presence of live regional theatre right at home—but make sure your expectations are going to be met. Again, the two institutions—school and theatre—should be mutually supportive of each other's activities, not fighting over their shared space.

You're not only going to learn skills at your college, you're going to begin to acquire the attitudes toward your chosen art that will eventually form your own personal philosophy of theatre. This encompasses inquisitiveness, creativity, intellectual curiosity, professionalism and interpersonal skills. You want a healthy foundation to this life-long building process.

You will hear talk in college bulletins of the collaborative nature of the art and of a program instilling "professionalism" in its students. The fact is, some theatre professionals are wonderful, warm, creative human beings, and some of them are unbearable jerks. They may get paid to act, and they may know all the Equity rules, but they are jerks nonetheless. Now maybe they would be jerks in any other walk of life, but it's also possible that they were never taught not to be jerks—they became professionals without acquiring that elusive quality of "professionalism".

A department's overall philosophy can be stated at great length in promotional material, but the essence of its attitude is going to be obvious in every contact you have with the program: what you sense is what you get. A faculty that is open, curious and creative turns out students who are open, curious and creative. A faculty that is stuffy, snobbish and rigid in its opinions turns out students who are…you guessed it. When you look at the environment where you may be spending a crucial four years of your life, look for indications of people working very hard in an atmosphere of creativity, discipline that is self-imposed as a means of achieving quality work, and mutual respect among students and teachers, and for one's peers and colleagues.

This may sound like a lot to glean from one campus visit or some phone calls, but trust your instincts to pick up an accurate assessment through even simple contacts. A case in point from an encounter I once had with a prestigious acting conservatory in New York: It was almost Christmas, and students were in the midst of their final projects for the semester. A dozen of them were milling about the green room, which a janitor was decorating for the holidays. Amidst all the discussion of scene work and pre-performance jitters, not one student helped with the little Christmas tree, or even spoke to the man who was decorating their lounge. It's easy to become obsessed with acquiring those skills that can make you a professional—but it's not the same as "professionalism."

One question remains, after having assessed a program's value in developing your skills and attitude: how well will it prepare you to find the work that will let you exercise those skills on leaving school? You should look for evidence that you will be taught about the business of theatre during your time at college, and also that you will be well served by some sort of alumni network on leaving.

A B.A. program in general theatre is not necessarily training people to enter directly into the profession. Their unwritten contract with a student is to provide a well-rounded education in all areas of theatre, providing a firm foundation for further study in specific areas—an actor is not going to receive all the in-depth skills training necessary to pursue a professional career, and will have to make those up in graduate school, a conservatory or in private study. That lets the B.A. program off the hook somewhat, but not entirely. One must audition or present a portfolio to get into a graduate program, and a B.A. program that doesn't promise to make you ready to work, should at least make you ready to move on to a program that does. Learning to audition, then, is a must for any program, and counseling a student in looking for post-graduate training should be included.

A B.F.A. program's unwritten contract with a student does promise that he or she will be ready to work upon leaving. The term "Professional Theatre Training Program" has been attached to many B.F.A. as well as graduate programs, and if that's what they claim and that's what you're buying, then make sure you'll get it. The minimum you should expect is the equivalent of one full semester course concerning auditioning, putting together a picture/resume, and learning to approach the business of acting. If you're a designer, an equal amount of time should be devoted to putting together a portfolio, learning about union exams, etc. If such a course is not listed, ask if there are guest seminars, workshops or the like to cover this ground.

The most enlightened programs will go well beyond that minimum. A school connected to a professional theatre, summer or regional, may enable you to come out not only with a degree, but with reputable professional credits on your resume. (You may also get a start toward your Equity card, although this is by no means crucial to an undergraduate.) If a program does not have a direct connection with a professional theatre, they should encourage and support students in working summer stock or interning during the school year. Be wary of programs that take such an overly paternalistic attitude as to actively discourage students looking for professional work while they're in school (except as a legitimate protection of their students' time and concentration). Summer work should be encouraged and even credited, as an opportunity to put into practice the skills being taught in the classroom. No matter how "professionally oriented" a school is, it cannot (and should not) replicate the pressures of a working theatre company.

There is a good deal to learn beyond auditions and portfolios, and unfortunately few of even the best programs teach the business skills an actor needs: effective goal setting; marketing principles and strategies; financing and budgeting. Read the article following this, by Jay Perry, for further guidance on how to begin acquiring these skills.

When you're researching your choice schools, find out about the program's alumni. How many recent graduates are now working professionals? Is there a "network" in a major theatre city like New York or Chicago? Have any small theatre companies been formed by groups of alumni to offer a showcase for graduates? Everything you've ever heard about the importance of making contacts is true, and a school alumni network can form the basis for some of your first contacts in the profession. Yale,

Juilliard, Carnegie-Mellon and The Theatre School (formerly the Goodman) are all prime examples of places that look after their own. The networks that these schools have developed, on a national scale, can be invaluable for new graduates. The same thing can happen on a smaller scale with smaller programs. The essential point, when you are looking over schools, is that you feel assured the mutual commitment made between student and program will last beyond graduation day.

Of course, once you have your B.A. or B.F.A., rather than plunging right into the ocean of uncertainty that is "the business" or you may prefer to dive back into the alphabet soup of graduate degrees. The difference between an M.A. and an M.F.A. is analogous to the two Bachelor degrees in specialization and intensity of training. The M.F.A. was developed as a "terminal degree" (no pun intended, I assume) for practicing or performing artists—actors, directors, designers—for whom a scholarly Ph.D. didn't make much sense.

In addition to advanced degrees offered by colleges and universities, there are conservatory programs connected to theatre companies, like Trinity Square Rep., Circle in the Square and American Conservatory Theatre. These may lead to an M.F.A. degree, or to a "Certificate" of some kind from the institution. Some of these programs will accept students without a Bachelor's degree, but they may discourage applications directly out of high school, preferring students who have worked professionally for a few years, or who are switching careers. Whether you're searching for an undergraduate or graduate program, you now should have a clearer idea of how to find the perfect college theatre program for you. Use this book as a starting point, then take your list of top prospects to the library and start poring over catalogues. Talk to people, take some trips, make some phone calls. The next few years may not be, ultimately, the most critical years of your life, but they could be some of the best.

Something to fall back on
(Parents, Read This!)

IF YOU'RE a student planning to go off to theatre school, you've probably had a conversation with your parents in which they insisted, "but you can't just study acting—you need something to fall back on." They are absolutely right—and totally wrong. Actors don't need a skill to fall back on; they need a skill to support themselves.

Becoming an actor takes years of training and experience, then more years of building the foundation for a career. During this time of finding an agent, honing audition skills and building contacts, you need an alternative means of support. Having a second career to fall back on implies that you stop acting because you have not been able to make a living at it, and turn to your secondary choice—presumably something less gratifying than acting, but which will support you. But in fact, you need to find something that you like to do, that will bring in a decent income, and that you can do while you spend those years it takes to build a career. You don't want an alternative career; what you need is a parallel career.

Many actors wind up taking a job as a waiter or an office temp, because they offer decent pay and some flexibility. All goes well for a while, but if you're good at your job, before long it becomes harder and harder to leave. If you're a key member of the wait staff, the restaurant manager doesn't want to hear that you're doing a showcase, so you can't work weekends for the next month. And when the company where you're temping likes you so much they want you full time, then there you are, locked into "nine to five," which is just what you were trying to avoid by temping in the first place.

There is an emotional toll to pay, too. Most actors find their support jobs an under-use of their skills. They may be bored or frustrated, but they become so dependent on a steady income that they find themselves turning down acting work because it doesn't pay enough to risk losing their "day job."

The challenge for you as an actor is to create a support job which will be gratifying, will use your skills and intelligence, will provide enough income for rent, food, etc., and will still be flexible enough that you can continue to pursue your primary goal of becoming a working actor. For example, an L.A. actor who started his own accounting firm to do taxes for other actors as a means of creating a steady income for himself. He now has an established practice, with enough help in his office so that he can leave to do a film or theatre job.Or the New York actress who took her own data base of industry contacts and turned it into a business, maintaining industry mailing lists (casting directors, agents, etc.) and selling them on labels to other actors.

The good news is that the communications explosion which we're experiencing in the 21st century is a prime opportunity for creative solutions to the actor's perennial problem. If you are a young actor now entering college, you might be well advised to look over the business and computer courses in your college catalogue, in addition to its theatre offerings.

Some ideas to prime your imagination: Are you artistic? Learn graphic design and desktop publishing so you can create resumes and flyers for other actors and small theatre companies. Are you computer-friendly? There are freelance opportunities for consulting and website creation. What will it take to get a teaching degree? Substitutes are always in demand, usually contracted on a day-by-day basis. Want to put your undergrad degree in literature to use? Learn copy editing—with faxes and email, you could be editing a Minnesota hospital's newsletter from your studio apartment in Hoboken.

Taking a pro-active approach to the actor's need for additional support can eliminate the desperation over money which is a tremendous obstacle for so many actors. It will make a huge difference in your attitude, give you more confidence in auditions and at meetings, and help you enjoy creating your career.

Mind Your Own Business ∗ ∗by Jay Perry∗ ∗

(Jay Perry was a founder of Actors' Information Project, Inc. in NYC, an organization which trained actors in creative business skills. He is now a Personal Business Coach.)

THE MOST common thing I hear from actors in New York is "I got great acting training at college, but I wish they had taught me more about the business; about how to find work." It doesn't matter whether you attend Yale Drama School or Lower Slobovia Junior College, odds are that the program will not completely prepare you for a career as a professional actor.

Many schools have not seen business training as part of their job. Often faculties haven't had the skills or desire to teach anything about the business. Other schools insisted that they did prepare their students for the real world, but, in fact, they didn't. Even programs that have promised students placement upon graduation have sent their students off to work without the skills needed to get the next job or, more importantly, without the skills to design their careers. Throughout history actors have had to find and develop their audience, but actors in our culture are seen to be "artists/craftspeople," and the educational system still has not recognized that the skills needed to find and develop an audience are needed or trainable.

Once out of school, professional actors quickly come to realize that they are "artists/craftspeople/business people." So if you are to have some say as to the outcome of your career and the quality of your life as an actor, you will need to develop some degree of mastery in business skills. At Actors' Information Project in over ten years we trained more than 4,000 actors in creative business skills, and we saw a good deal of success. While many actors had bought into the conventional wisdom that, as artists, they just weren't any good at business, in almost all cases this turned out to be untrue.

With good training and support actors make excellent business people. The trouble is it takes hard work. Face it: It may actually seem attractive to avoid the responsibility and hard work that it takes to design your career, but consider the alternative. Performers often spend years in New York or Los Angeles living in hope; avoiding a full commitment to their careers, while not committing themselves to anything else in life. The cost is often high and can be measured in money lost, lifestyles sacrificed, and low self esteem. For your own sake, it is important that your decision to be a professional actor be supported by your commitment to give yourself the very best career shot you can. Then, perhaps sooner rather than later, you will be able to design the acting career you want, or freely choose to pursue something else in life.

Of course there are many things that you'll just have to learn out there in the school of hard knocks, but until acting training programs catch up with the need for complete actor training, here are some ideas for putting together

An Independent Study Course In Business Skills For The Actor:

1. DEVELOP A CLEAR STATEMENT OF PURPOSE.

Most actors unconsciously operate with a purpose called "to prove myself worthy." "To be proven worthy" constantly calls into question the validity of being an actor. It gives rise to envy, jealousy, depression, anger, and desperation. It is important for an actor to have a powerful purpose; a truly important and motivating force behind his or her acting business. Ask yourself, "If I were given the gift to have any impact on my audience that I chose, what would I choose?" Being clear about the impact you want to have on an audience can give you a conscious statement of purpose; it can give you a powerful alternative to proving your worth. Your purpose may be as simple as "to wake people up" or "to make people laugh." Other people are motivated by purpose on a larger scale like "to create world peace." Whatever your purpose may be, the point is for you to keep your attention on something larger than whether or not someone likes you. (SUGGESTED READING: *The Inner Game of Tennis* by W. Timothy Gallwey.)

2. DEVELOP YOUR INQUISITIVE MIND.

Most education in this country is concerned with learning facts and rules in order to get right answers. As an actor pursuing work, you'll find that there are no rules for success. A true desire to investigate and create will serve you in developing your art and your business. (SUGGESTED READING: *Using Your Brain - for a Change* by Richard Bandler; *Think and Grow Rich* by Napoleon Hill)

3. DEVELOP SUPPORT GROUPS.

The friends you develop in school could be some of your best partners in the business. Unfortunately, most of our friendships are based on an unspoken agreement that goes something like "Let's just have a good time. I won't bother you too much if you don't bother me." A good support group is based on people challenging each other to be true to their commitments. Your support group could help you keep up on your work, get what you want out of school, and see you through some rough emotional times. Those friendships and the support skills you learn will be incredibly valuable after school.

4. DEVELOP EXCELLENT AUDITION SKILLS AND APPROPRIATE AUDITION MATERIAL.

Use some time at school to develop audition material that is appropriate for your age and type in a major market. Auditioning is distinct from performing. In college you may stretch and play roles that you would not play in a competitive market like New York or Los Angeles where they can find a person who is exactly the age and type they need. Also look for material that is consistent with your stated purpose. Think of auditioning not as a chance to prove your worth as an actor, but rather to communicate something that is truly important to you. Monologues and songs are important audition tools, but many auditions for films, television, commercials and stage require you to be skilled at reading scripts or written copy with a minimum of preparation. Request cold reading and commercial copy coaching in class or practice with friends or on video. (SUGGESTED READING: *Audition* by Michael Shurtleff; *The Monologue Workshop* by Jack Poggi; *Auditioning for the Musical Theatre* by Fred Silver)

5. WORK ON THE OTHER SIDE OF THE DESK.

Whether at your school or as an intern over a vacation in an entertainment center like New York, work in casting or in an agent's office. Investigate what their needs are. See what mistakes actors make. See what actors do that gets the job done. (SUGGESTED READING: *The NY Agent Book* or *The L.A. Agent Book*, both by K .Callan)

6. TAKE A JOB IN SALES AND/OR TAKE A COURSE IN SALES.

Learn the basics of personal sales technique: dealing with different personality types, overcoming objections, handling rejections, closings, etc. (SUGGESTED READING: *Power Selling* by James H. Brewer, J. Michael Ainsworth and George E. Wynne)

7. HANDLE YOUR OWN FINANCES.

It's great to be supported by your parents, but start taking responsibility for your money now. Acquire a marketable skill like word processing, legal proof reading, or waiting on tables that can give you some flexibility and a high hourly wage. Start saving money now. (SUGGESTED READING: *MoneyLove* by Jerry Gillies; *Showbiz Bookkeeper* by Annie Chadwick and Wallace Norman)

8. TRAIN YOURSELF TO BE ORGANIZED.

One of the seemingly attractive things about being an actor is a freedom to be different. Sometimes people translate that into a freedom to be lazy and sloppy. Organizational skills including time management, record keeping and impeccability will serve you in good stead if you're serious about being a professional actor. To quote Gustave Flaubert, "Be regular and orderly in your everyday life, so that you can be wild and creative in your art." (SUGGESTED READING: *Taming the Paper Tiger* by Barbara Hemphill; *Getting Control of Your Time* and *Life* by Alan Lakein; *Organizing for the Creative Person* by Dorothy Lehmkuhl & Dolores Cotter Lamping.)

9. REQUEST GUEST SPEAKERS.

Let your department know that it is important that you meet alumni, casting directors, business people, etc. to keep you in touch with what's happening in the entertainment industry. Listening to a guest speaker won't replace all the other work (just as listening to one lecture by an acting teacher will not replace many hours of work on your craft), but it's still important.

10. STAY IN COMMUNICATION WITH PEOPLE WHO GRADUATE AHEAD OF YOU.

It will be incredibly valuable to have some people you know in New York, Los Angeles, or any other entertainment center. They may be able to offer you advice, show you around, or give you a place to stay when you need one.

YOU MAY see this independent study course as a lot to handle. It is! Do what you can. I promise you it will be worth it. Even if you choose to pursue a career other than acting, many of the suggestions on this list will serve you.

SUGGESTED GENERAL READING: *How to be a Working Actor 5th Edition* by Mari Lyn Henry and Lynne Rogers; *How to Sell Yourself as an Actor* by K Callan; *An Actor's Business* by Andrew Reilly; *Indecent Exposure* by David McClintock; *Final Cut* by Steven Bach; *Smart Actors, Foolish Choices,* by Katherine Mayfield.

How to use this directory

THESE PROFILES are meant to be a starting point in researching the theatre training program best suited to a particular individual's wants and needs. Once an individual has narrowed down the institutions to a manageable list of possibilities, he or she can obtain more detailed information directly from the school. Please note that the material included was submitted by the institution. Where sections are incomplete, the institution failed to provide all the requested information. In general, the material might be slightly dated, however college curricula tend to change slowly, so these listings can, for the most part, still be considered a reasonably faithful profile of the department.

The schools are listed by state, and within states in strict alphabetical order (i.e., Sarah Lawrence is listed under "S"). Profiles contain the following information:

CONTACT AND ADMISSIONS INFORMATION

Name of institution, in boldface.

The name and title of the theatre program head, with contact address, followed by phone and fax number(s): "DEPT" is the direct line to the theatre department; "ADM" is the number for the Admissions office. E-mail and website addresses are listed when provided (without the "http://" prefix on websites).

Total enrollment of the institution; followed by the degree of competitiveness for admission to the institution, ranked as "not competitive", "competitive" or "highly competitive"..

School calendar: semester, trimester or quarter system.

The number of majors in the department; followed by membership in NAST; U/RTA; ATHE, etc. (see explanation at end of this page).

Tuition: the figure given after "T:" is annual tuition, unless otherwise noted. "O-ST T:" is annual tuition for an out-of-state student. "R&B" is annual room and board, in addition to tuition. These figures may be used for general information and comparison, however, in considering a specific school, one should request exact fees from the school, as they are subject to change.

Some programs are noted "SMALL PROGRAM", indicating they have four (or less) full-time faculty members in the department.

DEGREES OFFERED

Type of degree, area(s) in which the degree is offered, followed in parenthesis by the number of students enrolled in that area for the school year 2007-2008 and the year in which students declare their major field of study.

Number of undergraduate (UG) and graduate (G) degrees granted in spring 2007.

ADMISSION & FINANCIAL INFORMATION

Admission requirements for the institution, and any special requirements, such as audition or portfolio review, for the program.Ratios of those accepted to those applying.Scholarship information, if provided.

FACULTY AND CLASSES OFFERED

Number of Full Time (FT) and Part Time (PT) faculty, broken down by degrees held: PhD; MFA/MA; Professional without advanced degree; Staff.

Classes offered are broken down into four different areas:

    A. Dramatic Literature, Criticism, Theatre History, Playwriting.
    B. Acting, Directing, Voice, Movement & other skills courses.
    C. Design (Set, Lighting, Costume), Production, Stage Mgmt.
    D. Theatre Management.

(Some general course titles were used, for instance: "Mime, etc." includes courses in Mask, Commedia, Clowning, etc.)

The numbers in parenthesis at the beginning of each area (A, B, C, D)

indicates the number of Full and Part Time faculty in that area. In cases where a full-time faculty member's duties are divided between two or more areas, the division is indicated with fractions such as 1/2 FT.

Each course title is followed by a number/letter, such as 1/Y. The number indicates the number of different classes offered in an area, whether advancing in difficulty or varying in style. The letter indicates the frequency with which at least one section of the course is offered, using the following code:

    Y   offered every year.
    O   offered occasionally (at least once in a 4-year period).
    X   offered by another department.

FACILITIES & PRODUCTIONS

For each stage, the number of seats, whether there is fly space, and the type of lighting system, electronic or computerized.

The number of productions each season in each space, and whether they are directed (dir) and designed (des) by faculty (fac), guest artists, graduate students (G) or undergraduates (UG); followed by the average production budget (per show, materials only) in each space.

Year the facility was built and/or renovated; followed by available facilities other than stage, such as scene shop, costume shop, dance studios, classrooms.

Whether there is a non-departmental, student-run producing organization, and how many productions per year it presents.

Whether there is a connection with a professional company, and if so, the type of company and a description of the arrangement.

DESCRIPTION

Noted Faculty: with their teaching area, within the past two years.

Guest Artists: practising professionals who have come into the department for a specific production or to teach a master class in the past two years.

A statement of the philosophy and thrust of the department, particularly noting the broadness or specificity of training, and whether the program is meant to prepare the student for further study or career entry.

NAST: National Association of Schools of Theatre, recognized by the U.S. Dept. of Ed. as the accrediting agency for institutions offering theatre disciplines. NAST, 11250 Roger Bacon Dr., Suite 21, Reston, VA 20190 (703) 437-0700 www.nast.arts-accredit.org   Email: info@arts-accredit.org

U/RTA: University/Resident Theatre Association, an alliance of professional training programs and producing companies. U/RTA holds national auditions for college seniors at many sites around the U.S., leading to acceptance by graduate programs or professional jobs. (Information available through college departments.) U/RTA, 1560 Broadway, Suite 712, NYC 10036 (212) 221-1130 www.urta.com   Email: info@urta.com

ATHE: Association for Theatre in Higher Education, holds annual conferences for theatre educators, including employment service for faculty positions. ATHE, P. O. Box 1290, Boulder CO, 80306 (303) 530-2167; fax: (303) 530-2168; www.athe.org; info@athe.org.

ACTF(KCACTF): this abbreviation is used in some descriptive paragraphs to refer to the Kennedy Center American College Theatre Festival, an organization which provides opportunities for college and university theatre departments to showcase their best work at regional and national festivals. Through awards and scholarships, ACTF honors excellence of overall productions and offers student artists individual recognition. www.kcactf.org

Notes:

Interviewing schools: <u>you</u> ask the questions!

The best way to pick a school is to visit it and see for yourself if you like the atmosphere, the people and the facilities. If that isn't possible, glean what you can from the catalogues, but don't be afraid to make a few phone calls. People connected with a good department should be enthusiastic about it and willing to talk. You should be able to get the names of some recent graduates. And if you want to know what's really happening, strike up a conversation with the departmental secretary. After all, you're investing four years of your life and perhaps as much as $120,000; you have the right to some answers before you send off that tuition check.

Ask the department:
- Who on the faculty is currently working professionally?
- Do you bring in guest directors and designers?
- Do you run a summer theatre, or encourage students to work at other summer theatres? Do you give credit for summer theatre work, or for internships with professional theaters during the school year?
- In how many productions per semester would I be involved?
- Are there any restrictions on first year students' participation in productions?
- What is the departmental casting policy?
- Are there opportunities in the department for students to direct, design, or write plays?
- Does the department encourage students to do projects on their own? Are any student productions given a budget by the department?
- Do you feel your graduates are prepared to enter the profession?
- Is there any sort of alumni network?
- What are your recent graduates doing now? Which grad schools did they get into? How many are working?

Ask their current students:
- Is the casting policy fair and even-handed?
- Have you been taught how to audition or prepare a portfolio?
- Do you feel prepared to get work once you graduate?
- Which areas do you feel are the strengths of the department? The weaknesses?
- Are the faculty members accessible to students?
- Did you get to know the guest artists they brought in?
- On how many productions have you worked since you entered the program?
- If you were looking for a program now, would you choose to come here again?

Ask their graduates:
- Are there any areas in which you feel you now have to make up for a lack of training in school?
- Did you apply to any grad schools? Were you accepted?
- Were you well prepared to start your career by the time you graduated?
- Has it been any advantage to your career that you're an alumni of this particular school?

Then ask yourself:
- Is this the program that will take me where I want to go in four years?
- Can I see myself working well in this environment?
- Do I sense a positive energy and enthusiasm in these people?

ALABAMA

Alabama Shakespeare Festival

See ad in back of book

Ray Chambers, Prog Director
Greta Lambert, Assoc. Dir.
Alabama Shakespeare Festival
1 Festival Drive
Montgomery, AL 36117
DEPT: (334) 271-5350
www.asf.net

21 Total Enr.; highly compet.

Semester System
20 Majors; U/RTA
T: Waived
ADM: (334) 271-5300

DEGREES OFFERED

MFA in Acting (16), Stage Management (2), and Theatre Management (3). 2001 granted 12 degrees.

ADMISSION & FINANCIAL INFORMATION

Program is offered through U of AL (total enr. 16,000). GPA of 2.5, audition, interview. Accept 8 out of 500 into acting program. All MFA students receive full tuition, tuition waiver & stipend.

FACULTY AND CLASSES OFFERED

5 FT, 11 PT: 2 PhD, 4 MFA/MA, 2 Prof. w/o adv. degree, 1 Staff

A. (1 FT) Dramatic Lit-5/Y; Theatre History-5/Y; Shakes-2/Y

B. (4 FT, 11 PT) Acting-6/Y; Voice/Speech-6/Y; Movement- 5/Y; Mask-2/O; Stage Combat-4/Y; Dialects-3/Y

C. Stage Management-1/Y

D. (5 FT) Arts Mgmt-5/Y; Marketing/Promotion-1/Y; Development/Grant Writing-1/Y; Legal-1/Y; Budgeting/Accounting-2/Y; Production Management-1/Y; Business of Acting-2/Y; General Management-1/Y

FACILITIES & PRODUCTIONS

MAINSTAGE: 808 seats, fly space, computerized & electronic ltg. 6 prods: 1 Fac dir/Guest des, 5 Guest dir/des

SECOND STAGE: 303 seats, computerized & electronic lighting 8 prods: 2 Fac dir/Guest des, 6 Guest dir/des

2 Fac dir/Guest des Workshops/Readings

Facility was built in 1986; includes scene shop, costume shop, props shop, sound studio, 2 dance studios, 2 rehearsal studios.

Students present productions and workshops, as well as perform in supporting roles and understudy with the Alabama Shakespeare Festival, a professional, Equity company.

DESCRIPTION

This program is both a professional and academic experience. All of the faculty are employed full time by Alabama Shakespeare Festival, and work with the program's students as well as teach their classes.

Noted Faculty: Ray Chambers, Greta Lambert, Susan Wills, Sarah Felder, Denise Gabriel, Kent Thompson,.

Guest Artists: Scot Mann, Rodney Clark, Sam Gregory, Paul Hebron, Sonja Lanzener, Kathleen McCall, Chris Mixon, Philip Pleasants, Greg Thornton, Colleen Kelly.

The University of Alabama and Alabama Shakespeare Master of Fine Arts program offers degrees in acting, stage management, and theatre administration. It is a 2-year program (24 consecutive months) spent on both the University of Alabama campus in Tuscaloosa and at the Alabama Shakespeare Festival in Montgomery. MFA in Acting spent entirely at ASF in Montgomery. All students must have successfully completed an undergraduate degree prior to acceptance into the program. Participants range from recent college graduates to professional actors who wish advanced training and degree. This program is designed to develop creative, multi-talented theatre professionals through classroom training and quality performance or work experiences. The highest standards of training are maintained to develop artists and to teach the business side of professional theatre.

Auburn University

Dan LaRocque, Chair
Dept. of Theatre
School of Fine Arts
Auburn University
Auburn, AL 36849
DEPT:: (334) 844-4154
www.auburn.edu/academic/liberal_arts/theatre
ADM: The Quad Center, Auburn Univiversity, AL 36849
(334) 844-6349   www.auburn.edu

24,137 Total Enr; competitive
Semester System
60 Majors; NAST, ATHE
T: $2,893/$3,733 R&B
O-ST T: $8,143/$3,733 R&B
FAX: (334) 844-2585

DEGREES OFFERED

BA in Theatre ; BFA in Performance; Theatre Design/Technology; Theatre Production/Management (4).BFA in Music Theatre Declare major in Freshman year; 2001 granted 12 UG degrees.

ADMISSION & FINANCIAL INFORMATION

1140 SAT or 23.2 ACT. 66% of applics accepted by inst. Theatre program generally admits all applicants. Two competitive awards given at on-site auditions/presentations. Held each Feb.-see website for on-line applic. Schol. awards, extremely selective.

FACULTY AND CLASSES OFFERED

9 Full-Time: 3 PhD, 6 MFA, 4 Staff.

A. (3 FT) Intro to Theatre-1/Y; Theatre History-2/Y; Shakes-1/Y; Dramatic Lit.1/Y; Dramatic Critisicm-1/Y; Playwriting-1/O

B. (3 FT) Acting-6/Y; Directing-1/Y; Voice/Speech-6/Y; Movemt/Dance-2/Y; Singing-1/X; Stage Combat-1/O; Musical Th-1/O; Mime, etc.-1/O

C. (3 FT) Principles of Design-2/Y; Set Des.-1/Y; Costume Des.-2/Y; Lighting Des.-1/Y; Tech. Production-2/Y; Cost. Construction-2/Y; Cost. History-1/O; Make-up-2/Y; Stage Management-1/Y

D. Arts Mgmt.-1/O

FACILITIES AND PRODUCTIONS

MAINSTAGE: 370 seats, fly space, computerized lighting 7 Fac dir, 5 Fac des, 2 UG des prods; budget $3,000-5,000

SECOND STAGE: 100 seats, computerized lighting. 4 Fac dir/UG des prods; budget $200

Facility was built in 1973; includes scene, costume & prop shops, dance & design studios, rehearsal studios, classrooms.

A non-departmental, student-run, producing organization presents 2 productions per year in which dept. majors participate.

DESCRIPTION

Noted Faculty: Faculty are all theatre professionals with union and professional affiliation who publish, perform, design and direct within and beyone the university.

Guest Artists: Monica Bell, Alabama Shakespeare Festival (acting); Colleen Kelly, Alabama Shakespeare Festival (stage combat); Michael Sims, (designer), Yale School of Drama.

Auburn University Theatre offers students a comprehensive theatre education with an opportunity to pursue rigorous specialized training in several clearly defined areas. All majors are introduced to every aspect of theatre, pursuing more specialized training only after experiencing and understanding the broader context that is the foundation of every theatre artist's success. As a theatre program devoted exclusively to undergraduates, Auburn's theatre program provides students the opportunity to learn and DO theatre from the moment they set foot in our facility. More importantly, Auburn theatre students develop a strong professional relationship with a dedicated theatre faculty helping students reach their fullest potential as creative artists of integrity, discipline and intelligence.

Auburn University Montgomery

Val Winkelman, Chair	4,300 Total Enr; competitive
Dept. of Comm & Dramatic Arts	Quarter System
P.O. Box 244023, 223E Liberal Arts	32 Majors
Auburn University Montgomery	T: $$5,010
Montgomery, AL 36124-4023	O-St T: $14,255
DEPT: (334) 244-3632	R&B:$3,050
http://www.aum.edu/	FAX: (334) 244-3740
ADMISSIONS:AdmitMe@mail.aum.edu	
P.O.Box 244023, Montgomery , AL 36124	
(334) 244-3615	FAX: (334) 244-3762

DEGREES OFFERED

BA in Communication and Dramatic Arts (32). Declare major any yr.

ADMISSION & FINANCIAL INFORMATION

ACT or SAT plus GPA on a sliding scale. Theatre program generally admits all applicants. Scholarships available by interview, audition and/or portfolio review, recommendations, GPA for incoming students.

FACULTY AND CLASSES OFFERED

3 Full-Time, 3 Part-Time: 1 PhD, 8 MFA, 1 Staff.

A. (1 5/6 FT, 3 PT) Intro to Theatre-1/Y; Theatre History-2/O; Shakes-3/X; Dramatic Lit.-2/O+2/X; Playwriting-1/O; Film-5/O

B. (1/3 FT, 2 PT) Acting-4/Y; Directing-1/O; Dance-O-2/Y; Singing-1/X; Stage Combat-1/O; Voice/Movement-1/O; Oral Interp.-1/O; Phonetics-1/O

C. (5/6 FT) Set Des.-1/Y; Costume Des.-1/O; Lighting Des.-2/Y; Tech. Production-1/Y; Cost. Construction-1/Y; Cost. History-1/O; Make-up-1/Y; Stage Management-1/Y; Practicum-1/O; Scene Painting-1/O; Rendering-1/O

D. (1 PT) Arts Mgmt.-1/Y

FACILITIES AND PRODUCTIONS

MAINSTAGE: 180 seats, fly space, computerized ltg., black box. 6 prods: 2 Fac dir/des, 3 guest dir, 1 UG dir/10 des; budget $2,000

Facility was built in 1979; includes scene, costume & prop shops,

sound studio, CAD facility, dance studio.

One student-written play produced in the last two years.

Connection with Alabama Shakespeare Festival (Equity). Internships are available for qualified students, some members of the company are on faculty at AUM.

DESCRIPTION

Guest Artists: Barbara LeBow, Playwright A Shayna Maidel; Ed De Latte, Dir. A Shayna Maidel; Michael Wilson, Playwright, The Kiddie Pool; Actors/Teachers: Steven Martin, Norbert Butz, Suzanne Irving; James N. Brown, Vocal & Stage Combat; Haynes Owens, Jazz Dance Instruction.

Auburn University Montgomery provides a broad background in all areas of theatre arts. The Theatre program prepares a student for either graduate school or a theatre career. Theatre AUM provides the training in practical theatre production that clarifies the principles laid down in the classrooms.

University of Alabama

Birmingham

Will York, Chair	16,561 Total Enr.; competitive
Department of Theatre	Semester System
ASC 255, 1200 10th Ave South	102 Majors
University of AL-Birmingham	T: $4,792/ $4,100r/$3,140/b
Birmingham, AL 35294-1263	O-St T: $10,732/$4,100r/$3,140/b
DEPT:.(205) 934-3236	FAX: (205) 934-8076
yorkwill@uab.edu	www.theatre.hum.uab.edu
ADMISSIONS: HUC 260, 1530 3rd Ave. S., B'ham AL 35294-1150	
undergradadmit@uab.edu	800-421-8743

DEGREES OFFERED

BA in Theatre-General Studies (54); Theatre Pre-Professional Performance (34), Theatre-Pre-Professional Design/Technical (14). Declare major in freshman year .2007 granted 15 degrees.

ADMISSION & FINANCIAL INFORMATION

GPA of 2.0 (4 pt. scale); Min. ACT 20 or SAT of 950. Program accepts 88% of apps. Dept. offers a variety of schols & stipends in performance, musical theatre & production. No special requirements for admiss to theatre program. UG 4 out of 5 accepted. Ruby Lloyd Aspey Scholarship, David Lloyd Memorial Scholarship, Theatre Blazer Scholarships. All scholarships awarded through audition.

FACULTY AND CLASSES OFFERED

14 Full-Time, 3 Part-Time: 2 PhD, 13 MFA/MA; 2 prof w/o adv degree; 5 Staff

A. (2 FT) Intro to Theatre-15/Y; Theatre History-2/Y; Dramatic Lit-1/Y; Dramatic Crit-2/Y; Playwriting-3/Y

B. (7 FT, 3 PT) Acting-11/Y; Voice/Speech-4/Y; Movement-1/Y; Directing-3/Y; Dance-4/Y; Stage Combat-1/Y; Acting for Camera-2/Y; Film Prod-1/Y; Pedagogy in Acting-1/Y; Play Dir (k-12)-1/Y

C. (5 FT) Principles of Design-2/Y; Set Des-1/Y; Cost Design-1/Y; Lighting Design-1/Y; Tech. Prod.-4/Y; Cost. Construct.-4/Y; Make-up-2/Y; Stage Mgt-1/Y; Scene Painting-1/Y

FACILITIES AND PRODUCTIONS

MAINSTAGE: 350 seats, fly space, comput. & electronic lgt

3 prods: 3 Fac dir; 11 Fac des, 1 UG des; budget $10,000-15,000

SECOND STAGE: 105 seats, comput. lighting & electronic lighting
2 prods: 2 Fac dir, 1 Fac des, 7 UG des; budget $10,000-15,000

THIRD STAGE: 300 seats, electron ltg.
6 Workshop/readings: 2 Fac dir, 4 UG dir, 6 UG des; budget $500-1,000

Facility was built in 1999; renovated in 2001, includes scene shop, costume & prop shops, sound studio, 1 movement/dance studio, 1 rehearsal studio, 1 design studio, 1 classroom and computer lab.

16 student written plays produced in last two years.

DESCRIPTION

Noted Faculty: Kelly Allison, Design Tech; Ward Haarbauer, History/Lit.; Ron Hubbard, Movement, Combat; Lisa Channer, Acting, Directing; Marlene Johnson, Voice, Movement; Dennis McLernon, Acting/Voice; Marc Powers, Acting/Voice/Movement; Kim Schnormeier, Costuming; Lee Shackleford, Playwriting; Will York, Acting/Voice; Ed Zuckerman, Tech.

Guest Artists: Michael Randleman, Comic Improv; Ryan Jones Welsh, Movement Specialist; Anna Brody, Costume Des; Richard Shawn Reeves, Costume Des; Karen Maness, Scenic Des; Joseph Payne, Sound Des; Homer Johnson, Des.

The philosophy of the Department is that classroom study and practical experience are of equal and complementary value. Production opportunities are available in all aspects of theatre in two state-of-the-art venues. The program prepares students on a pre-professional level in performance and design/technical theatre as well as for venue Theatre. The program prepares graduating students for continued study in graduate school as well as for professional work in their chosen field.

University of Alabama – Tuscaloosa

William Teague, Interim Chair	24,000 Total Enr.
Department of Theatre & Dance	Semester System
Box 870239	150 Majors; NAST, U/RTA
University of Alabama	(205) 348-5283
Tuscaloosa, AL 35487-0239	FAX: (205) 348-9048
www.as.ua.edu/theatre	T: $2.850/ O-ST T: $8259

ADMISSIONS: Box 870132, Tuscaloosa, AL 35487-0132
(800) 933-BAMA   FAX: (205) 348-9046
www.ua.edu/admission   uaadmit@enroll.ua.edu

DEGREES OFFERED

BA in Theatre (50), Dance (40); MFA in Acting (22), Directing (3), Management/Arts Admin. (6), Costume Design (3),Scene Design/Technical Production (3), Stage Mgmt. (4), Costume Design/Production (3)
Declare major as early as freshman year; 2001 granted 12 UG, 25 grad. degrees.

ADMISSION & FINANCIAL INFORMATION

No aud. req. for BA, meet Univ. requirements. Grad. programs require audition or personal interview and Grad School requirements.

FACULTY AND CLASSES OFFERED

8 Full-Time: 1 PhD, 7 MFA/MA; 4 Staff

A. (1 FT) Intro to Theatre-1/Y; Theatre History-11/Y; Shakes-X; Dramatic Lit-2/Y; Dramatic Criticism-2/Y;

B. (3 FT) Acting-13/Y; Voice/Speech-6/Y; Movement-3/Y; Singing-X; Musical Th-2/Y; Directing-3/Y; Children's Th-1/O; Creative Dramatics-1/O

C. (3 FT) Principles of Design-2/Y; Set Des-7/Y; Cost Design- 4/Y; Lighting Design-2/Y; Tech. Production-3/Y; Cost Construction-4/Y; Costume History-1/Y; Make-up-1/Y; Sound Production-1/Y

D. (1 FT) Arts Mgmt-2/Y; Box Office Procedure-1/Y; Marketing/Promotion-1/Y; Devel/Grant Writing-1/Y; Contracts/Copy-right-2/X; Budgeting/ Acctg Procedure-1/Y; Internship-2/Y

FACILITIES AND PRODUCTIONS

MAINSTAGE: 338 seats, fly space, comput. ltg.
4 prods: 4 Fac dir, 6 Fac des, 6 Grad des.

SECOND STAGE: 171 seats, electronic lighting
4 prods: 4 Grad dir/des, 8 UG des

THIRD STAGE: 750 seats, fly space
4 productions total for dance.

Main Facility was built in 1958; includes scene shop, costume shop, sound studio, CAD facility, reh. studio, design studio, 7 classrooms.

Many of our Master of Fine Arts programs are offered in conjunction with the Alabama Shakespeare Festival (Equity). These programs include Theatre Management/Arts Administration, Stage Management, Scene Design/Technical Production, Costume Design/Production. In most cases, assistantships are available. These programs are specifically designed to develop creative, multi-talented theatre professionals through classroom training and quality performance or work experiences. For further information about these programs, please refer to the Alabama Shakespeare Festival listing of this directory.

DESCRIPTION

The University of Alabama's Department of Theatre and Dance has offered undergraduate and graduate study in theatre for more than fifty years. Our goal is to provide both the professional training and broad educational background essential to attaining the highest standards in today's competitive artistic community. The UA Theatre at Tuscaloosa presents four productions on our mainstage, as well at six graduate productions on our second stage each season. Production is supported by fully equipped scenery and costume studios. In addition to traditional training on the main campus in Tuscaloosa, some graduate students may also have the unique opportunity for specialized study at the Alabama Shakespeare Festival in Montgomery. Our graduates will excite tomorrow's audience because we are committed to creating excellent theatre today!

University of Montevallo

Dr. David Callaghan, Dir of Theatre	3,000 Tot. Enr.; compet.
Theatre Station 6210	Semester System; ATHE
University of Montevallo	75 Majors
Montevallo, AL 33115	T: $173/cr. hr.
Dept: 205-665-6210	O-ST T: $346 Cr/Hr
Admissions(205) 665-6030	FAX: (205) 665-6211

Theatre Box Office: (205) 665-6200 www.montevallo.edu/thea
lucasp@montevallo.edu

DEGREES OFFERED

BA or BS in Acting/Technology (60); BFA in Acting/Directing & Design, Musical Theatre(15); BFA by audition only. Declare major in Freshman year; grant approx. 15 UG degrees.

ADMISSIONS & FINANCIAL INFORMATION

HS GPA, Transcript and SAT or ACT scores required. Ltrs of recommendation 60% applicants accepted. Required for Undergraduate Admission: Audition and Interview, portfolio for des, admit 7 out of 10 UG applicants, 5 out of 10 BFA candidates

FACULTY AND CLASSES OFFERED

5 Full-Time, 6 Part-Time: 1 Ph.D./DFA; 5 MFA; 1 Staff

A. (1 FT) Intro to Theatre-1/Y; Theatre History-1/O; Shakes- 1/O; Dramatic Lit-3/O; Dramatic Criticism-1/Y; Playwriting-1/O; Screenwriting-1/O

B. (2 FT, 2PT) Acting-4/Y; Voice/Speech-2/Y; Movement-2/Y; Mask-1/O; Singing-8/X;Musical Theatre-2/Y; Directing-3/Y; Stage Combat-1/Y; Dance-2/Y; Film-3/Y; Acting For Camera-1/Y.

C. (2 FT) Principles of Design-O; Set Design-3/Y; Cost. Design-2/Y; Ltg. Design-2/Y; Tech. Production-2/Y; Cost. Construction-2/Y; Make-up-1/O

D. Arts Man.-O; Box Office Procedure-O; Mrktng/Prom.-O; Development/Grant Wrtng.-O; Legal: Contracts/Copyright-O; Budgeting/Accounting Procedure-O.

FACILITIES AND PRODUCTIONS

MAINSTAGE: 165 seats w/ computerized lighting

3 Fac dir, 6 Fac des prods; budget $3,000-15,000 ea.

SECOND STAGE: 50 seats w/ electronic lighting

1Fac dir, 4-6 UG dir/des prods; budget $100 to $1,000

THIRD STAGE: 1200 seats, fly space, computerized lighting, workshop readings, 1 UG dir, 3 UG des

Facility was built in 1931, mainstage renovated in 2004; additional space house: scene shop, costume shop, sound studio, CAD facility.

A non-departmental, student-run organization presents two original muscials per year. Majors participate.

One student written play per school year.

DESCRIPTION

Noted Faculty: Dr. David Callaghan, Theatre History/Theory/Directing/Musical Theatre/Acting; Ms. Tammy Killian, Acting/Directing/ Playwriting; Mr. John Franklin, Costume Design/Construction/Makeup; Mr. Kel Laeger, Set & Lighting Design/Set Construction; Mr. Vladimir Ravinsky, Movement/Acting/Directing/Mask/Stage Combat; Cameron Watson, Film/TV Acting; Arnold Mungioli, Auditioning; Rebecca Luker, Danny Burstein, Musical Theatre.

Guest Artists: Mark Amitin, Director/Actor/Manager; Bob Clendenin, Film/TV Acting; Melanie Jeffcoat, Shakespeare/Acting; Mary Sames, Agent; Doug Berky, Mask/Movement.

At Montevallo, we provide first-rate theatre training within the context of a well-rounded liberal arts education.

Philosophically, we believe that "smaller is better." If you study theatre here, you will be part of a highly personal department of approximately 75 majors. You will get to know your teachers well and work closely with them both in and out of the classroom. Experienced faculty members teach all courses instead of graduate students, and enrollment in acting classes typically ranges from 8 to 16 pupils. We work hard to prepare students to directly enter the profession, and the expertise of our faculty allows us to offer a range of classes that can match the curriculum of much larger departments. Our diverse production season includes contemporary dramas, classics and musicals; as well as numerous independent projects.

University of North Alabama

Dr. Bill Huddleston, Chair
Dept. of Communications & Theatre
Box 5007
University of North Alabama
Florence, AL 35632
(256) 765-4247
www2.una.edu/theatre
ADM: UNA, Box 5011, Univ. of N. Alabama, Florence, AL 35632
(256) 765-4608

6200 Total Enr.; not compet.
Semester System
45 Majors, 10 Minors
T: $1764/sem. or $3528/yr.
R&B: $2665/sem. or $5330/yr.
FAX: (256) 765-4839
druebhausen@una.edu

FAX: (256) 765-4349

DEGREES OFFERED

BA or BS in Theatre Arts (40). Declare major in fresh. or soph. year; 2003 granted 7 degrees.

ADMISSION & FINANCIAL INFORMATION

HS Diploma, 18+ ACT composit or top 50% of graduating class, 2.0 GPA (4.0 scale), 80% of applicants accepted by institution. No special req. for admission to theatre program, usually admit all applicants to theatre program. Scholarships (range $500 to $2,000): 3 for incoming freshmen (given to 3-6 students) ACT 20 composite and 3.0 GPA; 2 for sophomores and jrs. (given to 2-4 students), 2.5 GPA and Dept. Service; 1 for senior planning to attend grad program (given to 1 student) & Dept. Service.

FACULTY AND CLASSES OFFERED

2 Full-Time, 2 Part-Time: 1 PhD, 3 MFA/MA; 2 Staff

A. (1/2 FT) Intro to Theatre-1/Y; Dramatic Lit.-2/O; Theatre Hist.-2/O; Dramatic Criticism-2/O; Shakes-1/X; Playwriting-1/O

B. (1/2 FT, 2 PT) Acting-3/O; Movement-1/O; Voice/Speech 1/Y; Directing-2/O; Singing 2/X; Mus. Th.-1/X; Oral Interp-1/O

C. (1/2 FT) Prins of Design-1/O; Costume Design-1/O; Tech Production-1/Y; Cost History-1/X; Set Design-1/O; Lighting Design-1/O; Make-up-1/O

D. (1/2 FT) Arts Management-1/O; Marketing/Promo-1/O; Legal: Contracts/Copyright-1/X; Budget/Accounting-1/X

FACILITIES & PRODUCTIONS

MAINSTAGE: 1700 seats, fly space, computerized & electronic lighting.. 2 prods: 2 Fac dir/des; budget $2,000-10,000

SECOND STAGE: 350 seats, computerized, electronic lighting. 2 prods: 1 Fac dir, 1 UG dir, 2 UG des; budget $500-2,000

2 UG dir/des Workshops/Readings; budget $0-100

Facility built in 1969; includes scene shop, costume shop, sound studio, video studio, design studio, outdoor amphitheatre, 2 classrooms.

DESCRIPTION

Noted Faculty: Dr. David Ruebhausen, Design/Management/Directing/Acting;History/Criticism/Acting; Angela Green Childrea, Acting/Movement/Voice.

Guest Artists: Ernest Borgnine, Acting; Steven Root, Acting; Chad Darnell, Casting, Donna Robinson, Stage Combat; Aquila Theatre Co., Acting & Movement.

The University of North Alabama Theatre Program is designed to provide a generalist theatre education to its students by providing and requiring studies in all areas of performance, history/theory/literature and arts management. UNA Theatre believes that students interested in professional careers in theatre need to build upon their undergraduate experience with further training in MFA and/or MA/Ph.D. programs. In our classes, workshops, seminars and productions, we strive to provide our students with the professional standards, practical experience and academic foundation that will prepare them for any graduate program. We also strive to provide students with a challenging educational environment that encourages creative and personal growth.

University of South Alabama

Dr. Leon van Dyke, Chairman
Dept. of Dramatic Arts
PAC 1052
University of South Alabama
Mobile, AL 36688-0002
(251) 460-6305
www.southalabama.edu/drama/
ADMISSIONS: Univ. of South Alabama, Mobile, AL 36688-0002
(251) 460-6141   www.southalabama.edu
admiss@usamail.usouthal.edu

14,000+ Total Enr.;
    not compet.
Semester System
55 Majors, ATHE
T: $4,256.00; $1,291 r&b
O-ST T: $8,610; $1,291 r&b
FAX: (251) 461-1511

DEGREES OFFERED

BA in Dramatic Arts (15); BFA in Theatre Arts (40)
Declare major in any year; 2001 granted 7 degrees.

ADMISSION & FINANCIAL INFORMATION

ACT 19. No special req. for admission to th. program. 10 assistantships in costuming or scene shop; 10 in performance. Grades, experience, references, auditions for actors.

FACULTY AND CLASSES OFFERED

4 Full-Time, 4 Part-Time: 2 PhD, 5 MFA/MA, 1 Prof. w/adv. degree; 2 Staff

A. (1/2 FT, 1 PT) Intro to Theatre-1/Y; Dramatic Lit.-2/O; Theatre Hist.-2/O; Shakes-2/X; Playwriting-1/O

B. (1 FT) Acting-4/Y; Directing-1/O; Singing 1/X; Movement-1/O; Voice/Speech 1/O

C. (2 FT) Costume Design-1/O; Tech Production-1/O; Cost History-1/O; Set Design-1/O; Lighting Design-1/O; Cost Construction-1/O; Make-up-1/O

D. (1/2 FT) Arts Management-1/O

FACILITIES & PRODUCTIONS

MAINSTAGE: 180 seats, computerized lighting. 4 prods:
    3 Fac dir/des, 1 Guest dir/des; budget $7,000-12,000

SECOND STAGE: 100 seats Lab theatre
    Various Workshops/Readings
Facility built in 1999; includes scene shop, costume shop, rehearsal studio, 2 classrooms.
5 student-written plays have been produced in the last two years.

DESCRIPTION

Noted Faculty: Leon van Dyke, Theatre History; Matt Ames, Acting, Director; Rebecca Britton, Costumer; Lyle Miller, Scene Designer.

Guest Artists: Jean Galloway, Director; Louis Courie, Director

The Department of Dramatic Arts provides a solid and well-rounded program in theatre with a curriculum that is at the same time basic and innovative. Its play productions range from the classics to modern musicals, from the intimate to the large scale, from student directed to faculty produced. Its philosophy and practice are totally professional. The purpose of the department is to give students a sound foundation in the theatre arts so that they may enjoy it as spectators or as participants, professionally or as a leisure activity. The B.A. degree is designed to give the student general knowledge and practice in theatre. Its requirements include basic and elective drama courses and a minor in another area. The B.F.A. degree is planned for those who intend to pursue a professional career in theatre. It requires the basic courses plus intensive theatre work and advanced classes.

ALASKA

University of Alaska Anchorage

Tom Skore, Chair
Dept. of Theatre and Dance
University of Alaska - Anchorage
3211 Providence Drive
Anchorage, AK 99508
DEPT: (907) 786-1792
www.uaa.alaska.edu/theatre
ADMISSIONS: Enrollment Services, University Center
www.uaa.alaska.edu/enroll/   (907) 786-1480

20,000 Tot. Enr.; not compet.
Semester System
50 Majors, ATHE
T: $82-93 cr. hr.
O-ST T: $256-267cr. hr.
FAX:(907) 786-1799

DEGREES OFFERED

BA in Theatre (50+); BA in Theatre w/ Dance Emphasis; Theatre Minor; Dance Minor; Honors Program.
Declare major in any year; 2004 granted 6 degrees.

ADMISSION & FINANCIAL INFORMATION

SAT of 550 or ACT of 26 required; UG generally admits 95% of applicants; no special req's. for theatre program. Dept. offers tuition waiver (semester) based on potential, student effort. College offers tuition waiver (limited) based on chair recommendation (limited).

FACULTY AND CLASSES OFFERED

7 Full Time, 7-8 Part Time: 2 PhD, 6 MFA/MA; 2 Staff

A. (1 FT) Intro to Theatre-1/Y; Theatre History-2/Y; Shakes-2/Y; Dramatic Lit-2/Y; Dramatic Criticism-1/O; Playwriting-1/O

B. (2 FT 2PT) Acting-5/Y; Voice/Speech-2/Y; Movement-1/Y; Directing 2/Y; Stage Combat-1/O; Dance-8/Y

C. (3 FT) Set Design-2/O; Cost. Design-2/Y; Lighting Design-1/O;

Tech. Production-2/Y; Stage Management-1/O; Costume Construction-2/Y; Make-up-1/O

FACILITIES AND PRODUCTIONS

MAINSTAGE: 199 seat thrust theatre, fly space, computerized lighting+sound 4 Fac dir/des prods; budget $5-25,000

SECOND STAGE: 99 seats, computerized lighting
prods. varies, student dir/des; budget $200-2000

Wendy Williamson: 900 seats, proscenium, computerized lights & sound

2 Guest dir Workshops/Readings; budget $800-1000

Facility was built in 1986; includes scene shop, costume shop, sound studio, 2 dance studios, rehearsal studio.

3-4 student-written plays produced in the last two years.

DESCRIPTION

Noted Faculty: Fran Lautenberger, Costume, Makeup, LightingDesign; Tom T. Skore, Acting, Voice; Frank Bebey, Scene Design, Stagecraft; David Edgecombe, Dramat. Lit., Theory & Criticism; Jill Crosby, Fund. Modern Dance, Jazz I & II, Afro-Haitian Dance; Brian Jeffery, Movement for Actors, Dance.

Guest Artists: Heather Cornell of Manhattan Tap, teacher & performer; Katherine Kramer, Tap dancer; Dan Z Abierta of Havana, Cuba.

The department takes as its focus the performance of art within the academic liberal arts setting. Production is at the core of our curriculum, and our aim is to produce art at the highest standard we can, even as we strive to provide quality theatre education to the students, faculty and greater Alaska community we serve. To that end, we teach a generalist degree which demands that each graduate develop and demonstrate knowledge and expertise in all areas of the theatre, theoretical as well as applied. It is our aim to graduate students who are capable of advanced study, who have the potential for professional work and, when faced with the necessity, who can create their own theatre in the community they serve.

University of Alaska - Fairbanks

Tara Maginnis, Chair
Theatre Dept.
University of Alaska/Fairbanks
P.O. Box 755700
Fairbanks, AK 99775-5700
DEPT: (907) 474-6590
FAX: (907) 474-7048
www.uaf.edu/theatre
ADM: Admissions & Records, UAF, PO Box 757480, Fairbanks, AK 99775-7480
www.uaf.edu/admissions

10,000 Total Enr.; not compet.
Semester System
30 Majors
T: $4,000.
O-ST T: $10,700.
R & B: $2,605
fythtr@uaf.edu

admissions@uaf.edu
(800)478-1823

DEGREES OFFERED

BA in Performance (12), Directing (4), Technical/Design (6), Film (8)
Declare major in 1st year; 2004 granted 5 BA degrees.

ADMISSION & FINANCIAL INFORMATION

Accept 95% to institution; H.S. degree with 2.0 or higher; theatre program generally admits all apps. after one year of study at Univerity of Alaska-Fairbanks. Scholarship of the Wood Talent Grant are awarded to incoming freshman based on talent application and desire to become a professional in theatre.

FACULTY AND CLASSES OFFERED

4 Full-Time; 3 Part-Time; 1 PhD, 3 MFA/MA; 3 Staff, 1 w/o Masters.

A. (1 FT) Intro to Theatre-1/Y; Theatre History-2/Y; Shakes-1/O; Dramatic Lit-2/O; Dramatic Criticism-X; Playwriting-1/OX

B. (2 FT) Acting-4/Y; Voice/Speech-2/O; Movement-1/O; Singing-1/O; Directing-3/Y; Dance-1/Y; Film-1/Y; Voice/Speech-2/O; Alaska Native Theatre-3/Y; Musical Theatre-1/Y

C. (1 FT, 2 PT) Principles of Design-1/O; Set Design-1/O; Cost. Design-1/O; Lighting Design-2/O; Costume Construction-1/Y; Costume History-1/O; Make-up-1/O; Stage Management-1/O

FACILITIES & PRODUCTIONS

MAINSTAGE: 480 seats, fly space, computerized lighting.
5 prods; 3 Fac dir/des, 2 GA dir; 1 GA des; budget $3,000-6,000

SECOND STAGE: 110 seats, fly space, computerized lighting.
6 prods; 6 UG dir, 10 UG des; budget $500-700
6 prods; 3 GA dir/workshops/readings, 3 UG dir workshops/readings; budget $100-300

Facility was built in 1968, minor improvements continuing; includes scene shop, costume shop, welding shop, sound studio, CAD facil., video studio, rehearsal studio, 1 classroom, 1 design studio, video editing facility, a student lounge, a box office, a dept. office, and a drafting loft.

A non-departmental, student-run organization presents 2 productions per year in which majors participate.

Five student written plays produced in the last two years.

Connection with Fairbanks Drama Associates & Children's Theatre and with Perseverance Theatre, Juneau, AK. Opportunities with local community theatres - for acting, directing, design and Fairbanks Shakespeare Theatre, Fairbanks Light Opera Theatre Summer Fine Arts Camp (employs students). Numerous summer 'tourist' shows produced locally, including Alaska Native shows.

DESCRIPTION

Noted Faculty: Tara Maginnis, Cost. Des. (largest costume web site in the world); Kade Mendelowitz, CD rom, multimedia theatre applications; Anatoly Antohin, Russian Theatre, Virtual Theatre, Film Directing. Currently hiring tenure track position in acting/performance/speech.

Guest Artists: Jerry Quickley, Performance Poetry; Claudia Lively, Musical Theatre, Timaree McCormick, Set Design.

Theatre UAF at the University of Alaska Fairbanks offers a B.A. in Theatre with an emphasis in performance, directing, design/technical, or film. Classes and productions are open to the community, and provide unique opportunities for creative expression. The Lee H. Salisbury Theatre seats 468, and hosts numerous shows a year including community productions, student shows, and University Main Stage. Emphasis on mulitmedia and distance education helps develop the University's mission of providing a quality education to all Alaskans. The farthest North theatre in America at the finest land, sea and space grant institution, Theatre UAF is Alaska's creative edge.

ARIZONA

Arizona State University

Linda Essig, Director
Herberger College
School of Theatre and Film
Arizona State University
P.O. Box 872002
Tempe, AZ 85287-2002
Dept: (480) 965-5337
www.theatrefilm.asu.edu/students
ADMISSIONS: P.O. Box 870112, Tempe AZ 85287-0112
(480) 965-4495   FAX: (480) 965-3610
www.herbergercollege.asu.edu/students

57,000 Tot. Enr.,not compet.

Semester System; NAST
515 Majors;
T: $2,486; O-ST T: $8,502
R&B: $3,344-4,180
FAX: (480) 965-5351

DEGREES OFFER

(247) BA in Film + Media, Prod, (269) BA Theatre, BA in Theatre in Acting, BA Theatre w/focus on Prod., MA in Theatre, MFA in Theatre, MFA Creative Writing w/Playwrighting, PhD in Theatre. Declare major in freshman yr.; (49 Grad Student)

ADMISSION & FINANCIAL INFORMATION

UG: HS min. GPA is 3.0. Residents in top 50% of class, or ACT 22, or SAT 1040. Non-residents top 25% of class, or ACT 24, or SAT 1110; interview, audition for actors, portfolio for des req'd. Admit all UG, 20 out of 50 Grad. Scholarship awards ($100-5,000); incoming students' awards based on letters of rec. and potential for success in department.

FACULTY AND CLASSES OFFERED

28 Full-Time, 5 Part-Time: 12 PhD, 14 MFA/MA, 2 Prof. w/o adv. degree, 11 Staff

A. (6 FT) Intro to Theatre-1/Y; Dramatic Lit-2/Y; Theatre History-6/Y; Dramatic Criticism-2/Y; Shakes-1-Y; Playwriting-10/Y; Ethnic Theatre-2/Y; Capstone/Applied Projects-2/Y

B. (9 FT, 2 PT) Acting-16/Y; Voice/Speech-3/Y; Movement-2/Y; ; Directing-5/X; Singing-3/Y; Stage Combat-1/Y; Theatre for Youth-4/Y; Theatre Education-8/Y; Film Production-25/Y

C. (7 FT) Set Design-2/Y; Cost Design-3/Y; Lighting Design-3/Y; Tech Production-4/Y; Cost Construction-1/Y; Stage Mgmt-2/Y; Sound Design-1/Y; Puppetry-2/Y; Media for live Performance-3/Y

D. (1 ft) Arts Mgmt-3/Y

FACILITIES & PRODUCTIONS

MAINSTAGE: 480 seats, fly space, computerized & electron. ltg. 2-3 prods: 3 Fac dir, 10 Fac des, 1 Guest dir, 2 Guest des, 4 Grad. des, 2 UG des; budget $5,000-9,000.

SECOND STAGE: 162 seats, fly space, computerized lighting 6 prods: 2 Fac des, 1 Guest dir, 3 Grad dir, 4 Grad des, 2 UG dir, 8 UG des; budget $500-1,000

THIRD STAGE: 70 seats. 2 Fac dir, 1 Fac des, 6 Grad dir, 3 Grad des, 8 UG dir, 12 UG des Workshops/Readings; budget $50-100

Mainstage facility built in 1989: scene shop, costume shop, props shop, welding shop, CAD facil., child. drama studio, voice studio, Univ. computing commons, rehearsal studio, movement studio, design studio.

A non-departmental, student-run org. in which majors participate presents 10 prod. per year. Approx. 12 student-written plays in last 2 years.

Connection with Actors Theatre at Phoenix, Phoenix Theatre Company : workshops and master classes and Childsplay, Inc. :

Internships as actors, dramaturgs, educational outreach to schools.

DESCRIPTION

Noted Faculty: Barbara Acker, Lisa Anderson, David Barker,Roger Bedard,Rachel Bowditch, David Coffman,Chris Danowski, Bonnie Eckard,Gus Edwards,Linda Essig,Stephani Woodson Etheridge, Connie Furr-Soloman, Lance Gharavi, Oscar Giner,C.A. Griffith,Brian Hall,Gitta Honegger, Margaret Knapp, Chris LaMont, Jeff McMahon, Carla Melo, Ron Newcomer, William Partlan, Jacob Pinholster, Guillermo Reyes, Johnny Saldaña, Jennifer Setlow, Pamela Sterling,Michael Switzer,Philip Taylor,Ronald Thacker, Jeffrey Thomson, Tamara Underiner, F. Miguel Valenti.

The Arizona State University Theatre's mission is to educate imaginative, knowledgeable, skilled and responsible artists, teachers, scholars, and audience members for the future of theatre and film arts. We work collaboratively to celebrate and confront our diverse artistic heritage and to examine and practice the complex process of constructing meaning in live performance and media. We emphasize the importance of ethics. We create new work and engage existing work to challenge, enrich and transform the university and community.

Northern Arizona University

Kathleen M. Chair
Dept. of Theatre
PO Box 6040 Building 37 Rm. 120
Northern Arizona University
Flagstaff, AZ 86011
DEPT: (520) 523-3781
http://www.cal.nau.edu/theatre/
ADM: Box 4103, Northern Arizona Univ., Flagstaff AZ 86011
(520) 523-5511   FAX: (520) 523-6023
www.nau.edu   undergraduate.admissions@nau.edu

17,000 Total Enr.; not compet.
130 Majors; ATHE
Semester System
T: $$4,916 /$6,572 r&b
O-ST T: $14,750/$6,572 r&b
FAX: (520) 523-5111

DEGREES OFFERED

Theatre Studies (7), Performance (16), Design and Technology (3), Education (3)

ADMISSION & FINANCIAL INFORMATION

ACT/SAT scores, GPA 2.5. Admissions open, but students audition/interview into emphasis areas. Theatre program admits all applicants. Both in state and out of state tuition waivers and a few cash award schols. each year. The theatre faculty awards these according to talent, program participation and need of the individual student.

FACULTY AND CLASSES OFFERED

7 Full-Time, 3 Part-Time: 2 PhD, 4 MFA/MA, 3 Prof. w/out adv. degree; 1 Staff

A. (1 FT, 1 PT) Intro to Theatre-2/Y; Dramatic Lit-1/Y; Dramatic Crit-1/X; Theatre History-2/Y; Shakes-2/X; Playwriting-1/O

B. (2 FT, 1 PT) Acting-4/Y; Voice/Speech-1/Y; Movement-2/Y; Directing-4/Y; Stage Combat-1/O

C. (4 FT) Principles of Design-1/Y; Costume Design-1/Y; Tech Production-2/Y; Set Design-1/Y; Lighting Design-1/Y; Costume History-1/Y; Costume Construction-2/Y; Make-up-1/Y; Stage Management-1/Y

FACILITIES & PRODUCTIONS

MAINSTAGE: 300 seats, fly space, computerized & electron. ltg.
   4 prods: 3 Fac dir, 4 Fac des, 1 Guest Dir, budget $4,000-8,000

SECOND STAGE: 100-120 seats, computerized & electron. lighting. 4
   prods: 1 Fac dir/des, 3 UG dir/des productions; budget $500-650

2 UG dir/des Workshops/Readings; budget $500-1,000

Facility was built in 1968, renovated in 1999, Second Stage built in
   1999; includes scene shop, costume shop, prop shop, design
   studio, complete dressing room/make-up for both theatres.
   Studio theatre (2nd Stage) is state of the art.

A non-departmental, student-run organization presents 1-2 productions per year in which majors participate. 8 student-written plays
   produced in the last two years.

Connection with Summer Arts (in-house), a professional project of
   NAU Theatre. Students are given a variety of opportunities in
   Acting, Production, Management and Stage Management. Credit
   and stipend.

DESCRIPTION

Noted Faculty: Buddy Combs, Lighting, Timothy Bryson,
   Scene Design; Carey B. Hansor, Costume Des, Robert
   Yowell, Acting, Directing;

Northern Arizona University Theatre is grounded in the
liberal arts tradition. Just as the liberal arts experience
seeks to prepare students through a breadth of knowledge
and experience in order that they may make informed
choices and compete successfully in life and their chosen
professions, the Theatre Division gives the undergraduate
student the broadest possible understanding of Theatre
as a discipline, craft and art form through the creative,
critical and applied practice of the theatre art. In order to
know theatre, one must do theatre, therefore, performance and production are essential to our teaching.
Beyond a common, liberal arts theatre core that includes
history, literature, critical analysis, performance, production and other courses designed to demonstrate the collaborative nature of theatre, students are expected to pursue individual strengths, preparation, and interests in
Theatre Education on the Secondary level, Design and
Technology, Performance and general Theatre Studies.
NAU Theatre stages 10 theatre productions annually: four
mainstage, fully supported events in both the Clifford E.
White Theatre, a fully renovated, proscenium theatre, and
in the new, state of the art, studio facility, a flexible space
seating 100-140 persons in a variety of configurations;
four second stage, minimally produced student and faculty work in the studio theatre designed to emphasize student opportunities; and, two At Random productions,
original and developing work given audience and facility
support only.

University of Arizona ··············

Albert D. Tucci, Director
School of Theatre Arts
Univ. of Arizona, POB 210003
Tucson, AZ 85721
www.uatheatre.org

34,000 Total Enr.; compet.
Semester System
350 Majors, NAST, U/RTA
DEPT: (520) 621-7008
FAX: (520) 621-2412
T: *$4,098/$7,108 r&b
O-ST T: *$13,078/$7,108 r&b

ADMISSIONS: UA, P.O. Box 210040, Tucson, AZ 85721

UG (520) 621-3237
Grad. (520) 621-3132
appinfo@email.arizona.edu
*12 or more units

FAX: (520) 621-9799
www.arizona.edu

DEGREES OFFERED

BA in Theatre Arts (217); BFA in Theatre Production (options in
Acting, Design & Tech, Theatre History and Dramaturgy (60), Theatre
Education & Outreach (12), Musical Theatre (35); MFA in Design &
Technology (15); MA in Theatre Arts (options in Theatre Studies &
Theatre Education & Outreach)(10).
Declare major in first year; 2005 granted 75 UG, 3 Grad degrees.

ADMISSION & FINANCIAL INFORMATION

See School of Theatre Arts website for details. Limited number of
theatre scholarships available to freshman. UG accepts 5 out of 10
applicants, need aud., interview & portfolio; Grad admits 7 out of 10
applicants.

FACULTY AND CLASSES OFFERED

23 Full-Time, 3 Part-Time: 7 PhD/DFA, 24 MFA/MA; 11 Staff

A. (3 FT, 3 PT) Intro to Theatre-4/Y; Theatre History-6/Y; Dramatic Lit-
   6-Y; Dramatic Criticism-2/Y; Dramaturgy-2/Y; Collaborative Play
   Development-1/Y.

B. (7 FT, 4 PT) Acting-11/Y; Movement-5/Y; Singing-2/XY; Directing-
   4/Y; Voice/Speech-5/Y; Stage Combat-2/Y; Dance-11/X; Musical
   Theatre-3/YO; Improv-1/Y.

C. (10 FT, 1 PT) Prins of Des-2/Y; Set Des-2/Y; Cost Des-3/Y; Ltg.
   Des-2/Y; Tech Prod'n-3/Y; Cost. History-1/Y; Make-up-1/Y; Stg
   Mgmt-1/Y; CAD-1/Y; Drafting-1/Y;Scenic Paint-1/Y

D. (3 PT) Arts Management-1/Y; Creative Drama-2/Y; Teaching
   Methods-1/Y; Mrktng./Promo.-1/Y; Theatre Ed/Outreach

FACILITIES AND PRODUCTIONS

MAINSTAGE I: Prosc.: 332 seats, fly space, computerized lighting.

MAINSTAGE: II: Flexible: 300 seats, computerized lighting.

DIRECTING STUDIO: 80 seats, computerized lighting

Dept. produces 6 season prods. in 2 spaces; budget $9-34,000

Workshops: 3.

Mainstage was built in 1957 renovated in 1992; 2nd Stage built in
   1994. Includes scene shop, costume shop, prop shop, welding
   shop, sound studio, CAD facility, 2 rehearsal studios, 2 dance
   studios, 2 design studio.

Connection with Arizona Theatre Company (Equity): Internships
   available.

DESCRIPTION

Noted Faculty: Brent Gibbs, Artistic Dir.; Peter Beudert,
   Scenic Designer; Richard Hanson, Musical Theatre;
   Jerry Dickey, Theatre Studies.

The mission of the School of Theatre Arts at the University
of Arizona is to provide professional training and education leading to careers in acting, musical theatre, theatre
design and technology, theatre education and outreach,
and theatre history and dramaturgy. The School is dedicated to educating students through a highly visible production program enriching the university and Tucson
communities. The Arizona Repertory Theatre is the professional training company of the School of Theatre Arts
and provides opportunities for students working in all
areas of study.

ARKANSAS

Lyon College

Dr. Michael L. Counts, Dir of Theatre
Theatre Dept.
Lyon College
P.O. Box 2317
Batesville, AR 72503
DEPT: (870) 793-1750
http://www.lyon.edu/departments/theatre/
ADMISSIONS: P.O. Box 2317, Batesville, AR 72503
1-800-423-2542

489 Total Enr.; compet.
Semester System
15 Majors; ATHE KCACTF
T: $15,960; R&B:$6,644
SMALL PROGRAM
FAX: (870) 698-4622

FAX: (870) 698-4622

DEGREES OFFERED

BA in Theatre (15). Declare major in soph. year;

ADMISSION & FINANCIAL INFORMATION

GPA 2.50; ACT 22; 85% accepted to institution; Accept 100% into Theatre program; Fine Arts schols awarded by audition and interview. The college also offers competitive scholarships which allows students to receive full scholarships and gives the the option of participating in theatre without majoring.

FACULTY AND CLASSES OFFERED

2 Full-Time: 1 PhD, 1 MFA

A. (1/2 FT) Intro to Theatre-1/Y; Theatre History-1/O; Dramatic Lit.-2/O; Playwriting-1/O; London Theatre Trip-1/O

B. (1/2 FT) Acting-2/Y; Voice/Speech-1/O; Directing-1/O; Improvisational Theatre-1/O, Film-1/O

C. (1 FT) Principles of Design-1/O; Costume Des-1/O; Set Design-1/O; Lighting Des.-1/O; Cost. Construct-1/O; Make-up-1/O; Stage Mgmt.-1/O; Tech Prod'n-1/Y

FACILITIES & PRODUCTIONS

MAINSTAGE: 200 seats, black box, computerized lighting & sound
4-6 prods: 2 Fac dir, 2 Fac des, 2 UG des; budget $3,000-4,500
SECOND STAGE: Various prods; budget $50-100
Various Workshops/Readings
Facility was built in 1991, renovated in 1999; includes scene shop, costume shop, prop shop, rehearsal studio, 2 classrooms.
3 one student-written play produced in the last two years.
Connection with Arkansas Repertory Theatre (Equity). Internships available.

DESCRIPTION

Guest Artists: National Shakespeare Company (performance and workshop).

Students study theatre as a liberal art at Lyon College. The academic and the practical are equally stressed. A Theatre major will study a variety of courses in acting, directing, design/technical, and historical/critical. Our goal is to prepare you for life. We believe that actors, directors, and designers who are well-educated have more successful careers. Theatre majors with a solid, liberal arts background will be welcomed by graduate programs and will be prepared to enter other fields. A small department at a small school offers you individual guidance. We can design your major to fit your individual needs. We especially welcome students who are uncertain of their career plans.

Southern Arkansas University

Mr.D David Murphy, Chair
Dept of Theatre & Mass Comm..
SAU Box 9203
Southern Arkansas University
100 E. University Magnolia, AR 71754-5000
DEPT: (870) 235-4257
Adm: 1-800-332-7286 or (870)235-4040,
E-mail: muleriders@saumag.edu
http://www.saumag.edu/

2,830 Total Enr.; not compet.
Semester System
ATHE
T: $4,890O-ST T: $7,080
R&B: $3,930
SMALL PROGRAM

DEGREES OFFERED

BA in Theatre (14). Declare major in first year; grant approx. 3 UG degrees.

ADMISSION & FINANCIAL INFORMATION

Unconditional Admission-ACT scores of 19 or higher on the English, Mathmatics, and reading parts of he ACT, High School grad, and 2.0 H.S. GPA. Conditional Admissions-ACT score of 16.
Liberal admission; 90+% Accepted to institution; Accept 100% into Theatre program; Theatre scholarships: 3-4/yr., full and half instate tuition, by audition and interview.

FACULTY AND CLASSES OFFERED

3 Part-Time: 2 MFA/MA, 1 MA

A. Intro to Theatre, -Theatre Practicum, Theatre History-1 and 2, American Th.-1/O; Creative Dramatics-Directed Study in Theatre,The American Theatre, Theatre Internship, Special Problems

B. Fundamentals of Acting, Advanced Acting, Voice and Diction-Dance and Stage Movement,Oral Interpretation, Studies in Theatre, Studies in Musicl Theatre, Directing

C. Design for the Theatre, Principles of Design-Stagecraft, Costume History

FACILITIES & PRODUCTIONS

MAINSTAGE: 480 seats, fly space, computerized lighting
4 Fac/Student dir/dis, budget $500-2,000
Facility was built in 1975; includes scene shop, costume shop, sound studio, rehearsal studio, classrooms.

DESCRIPTION

The SAU theatre program has many strengths, among them the interaction between students and faculty. Students receive extensive hands-on production experience in both performance and technical theatre which, combined with a solid underpinning of theoretical knowledge in the classroom, for a well-rounded education.

University of Arkansas/Fayetteville

D. Andrew Gibbs, Chair
Dept. of Drama
619 Kimpel Hall
University of Arkansas
Fayetteville, AR 72701
Dept. E-mail: cavern@uark.edu

(479) 575-2953

16,000 Total Enr.; not compet.
Semester System
75 Majors
T: $6,038
O-ST T:$14,492

R&B: $7,017
FAX: (479) 575-7602
Admissions: uofa@uark.edu

ADMISSIONS:232 Silas Hunt Hall, Fayetteville, AR 72701
(479) 575-5346   FAX: (479) 575-7515

DEGREES OFFERED

BA in General (75). MFA in Acting, Design, Directing, Playwriting (25 total). Declare major in fresh. year; 2006 granted 18 UG, 6 Grad degrees.

ADMISSION & FINANCIAL INFORMATION

UG: 2.75; ACT 20. Grad: 2.75, GRE varies. Interview, Audition, Portfolio for designers req. for Grad. program. 65% of applicants admitted to institution. UG Theatre program generally admits 9 out of 10, Grad 3 out of 10 applicants. Various schols.; competitive through interview, portfolio and/or audition.

FACULTY AND CLASSES OFFERED

9 Full-Time, 3 Part-Time: 4 PhD/DFA, 5 MFA/MA; 3 Staff

A. (1 FT, 1/2 PT) Intro to Theatre-2/Y; Theatre History-3/Y; Shakes-2/Y; Dramatic Lit-2/Y; Dramatic Criticism-1/Y; Playwriting-3/O

B. (4 FT) Acting-8/O; Movement-2/Y; Singing-1/Y; Directing-5/O; Voice/Speech-4/Y; Mime/Mask-1/O; Musical Theatre-4/O; Stage Combat-1/O; Dance-4/Y

C. (3 FT) Principles of Design-1/Y; Set Design-4/Y; Cost Design- 6/O; Tech. Production-2/O; Costume History-2/O; Stage Mgmt-2/O; Lighting Design-4/O; Cost. Construction-4/O; Make-up-2/O

D. (1/2 PT) Arts Management-1/O

FACILITIES AND PRODUCTIONS

MAINSTAGE: 315 seats, fly space, computerized & electronic ltg.. 8 prods: 2 Fac dir, 3 Fac des, 1 Guest dir/des, 2 Grad dir, 3 Grad des

SECOND STAGE: 1205 seats, fly space, comput. & electronic ltg. 7 prods: 5 Grad dir/des, 2 UG dir/des

THIRD STAGE: 75 seats, black box
4 prods: 2 Grad dir/des, 2 UG dir/des workshops/readings

Facility was built in 1950, Renovated 72 & 92; includes scene shop, costume shop, welding area, sound studio, dance studio, design studio, rehearsal studio, classrooms.

A non-departmental student-run organization presents a production in which dept. majors participate. 4 student-written plays produced in the last two years.

DESCRIPTION

Noted Faculty: D. Andrew Gibbs (Chair), Lighting, Thea. Architecture, Mgmt.; Amy Herzberg, Musical Th., Acting; Roger Gross, Shakespeare, Playwriting, Theory & Crit.; Michael Riha, Scene Design; Patricia Martin, Costume Design; C. Patrick Tyndall, History, Multi-Cultural Theatre; Mavourneen Dwyer, Voice, Acting; Chuck Gorden, Directing, Acting, Playwriting; Terry Brusstar, Dance.

Philosophy: A generalist undergraduate degree (BA) in a liberal arts setting, that stresses professional values through awareness of the field and individual growth. A pre-professional graduate degree (MFA) with specialization in design, performance, directing and playwriting. Emphasis is on professional standards, personal accountability and artistic integrity; collaboration and unified aesthetics. Preparation for teaching is considered as significant as preparation for professional practice.

University of Arkansas at Little Rock

D. David Murphy, Chair
Dept. of Theatre & Dance
2801 South University
Little Rock, AR 72204
DEPT: (501) 569-3291
ADM: (501) 569-3127

12,000 Total Enr.; not comp
Semester System
25 Majors, NAST, ATHE
T: $$5,510
O-ST T: $$12,726
www.ualr.edu

DEGREES OFFERED

BA in Theatre, Dance. Declare major in sophomore; 2003 granted 13 UG degrees.

ADMISSION & FINANCIAL INFORMATION

2.5 cumulative high school combined verbal/math SAT score of at least 800 or a composite ACT of at least 21; 8 out of 10 applicants admitted to theatre program; Talent Award Assistantship available by audition.

FACULTY AND CLASSES OFFERED

6 Full-Time, 7 Part-Time: 5 MFA/MA, 2 Prof. w/o adv. degree; 2 Staff

A. (2 FT) Intro to Th.-1/Y; Th. Hist.-2/Y; Shakes-1/Y; Dramatic Lit-1/Y; Dramatic Crit.-1/O; Playwriting-1/O; Creative Dramatics 1/O

B. (2 FT, 2 PT) Acting/Scene Study-2/Y; Voice/Speech-1/Y; Movement-2/Y; Directing-1/Y; Musical Theatre-1/O; Stage Combat-1/O; Theatre Dance-1/Y; Readers Theatre-1/O; Oral Interpretation-1/P; Experimantal Theatre-1/O

C. (2 FT) Set Design-1/Y; Cost Design- 1/Y; Lighting Design-1/Y; Tech. Production-1/Y; Cost Construction- 1/Y; Costume History-1/O; Stage Mgmt-1/O; Scene Painting-1/Y

D. (1 FT) Theatre Management-1/O

FACILITIES AND PRODUCTIONS

MAINSTAGE: 658 seats, computer. & electronic ltg, fly space
2 prods: 2 Fac dir; budget $2,500-6,000

SECOND STAGE: 140 seats, computer ltg.
2 prods: 2 Fac dir; budget $2,000-4,000

Facility includes scene shop, costume shop, 2 dance studios, 1 design studio, 2 classrooms.

DESCRIPTION

Connection with Arkansas Repertory Theatre, Arkansas Arts Center (Children's Theatre), Murray's Dinner Theatre. Senior level students are permitted internships in performance, technical theatre and performance.

University of Arkansas at Little Rock offers a BA degree. It is designed to offer a broad base of theatrical knowledge and skills for specialization and further study.

University of Central Arkansas

Greg Blakey, Director
P.O. Box 4942
University of Central Arkansas
Conway, AR 72035
DEPT: (501) 450-5608
FAX: (501) 450-3102
www.uca.edu/theatre
ADMISSIONS: Bernard Hall, 201 S. Donaghey
(501) 450-3128   1-800-243-8245
www.uca.edu/uca/admissions.php

12,000 Total Enr.; not compet.
Semester System
57 Majors; NAST
T: $5,053/$3,920 R&B
O-ST T: $8,609/$3,920 R&B
SMALL PROGRAM
gregb@uca.edu

DEGREES OFFERED

BA in Theatre GeneraList (55); BS in Theatre GeneraList (2). Declare major in Freshman year; 2006 granted 20 UG degrees.

ADMISSION & FINANCIAL INFORMATION

ACT 19 or 2.25 GPA or top 40% of graduating class. Accept 100% into theatre program. Performance schols avail., aud or portfolio presentation and interview required.

FACULTY AND CLASSES OFFERED

5 Full Time: 2 PhD, 3 MFA/MA; 1 Staff

A. (1 FT) Introduction to Theatre-1/Y; Theatre History-1/O; Shakes-2/X; Dramatic Lit.-1/O; Dramatic Criticism-1/O; Playwriting-1/O

B. (1 FT) Acting-4/Y; Voice/Speech-1/Y; Movement-1/O; Singing-1/X; Directing-1/Y

C. (2 FT) Prins. of Design-1/Y; Set Design-1/O; Cost. Des.-1/Y; Lighting Design-1/O; Make-up-1/Y; Tech. Production-1/Y; Stage Mgmt-1/O; Make-up-1/Y

FACILITIES & PRODUCTIONS

MAINSTAGE: 307 seats, computerized lighting, fly space.
    4 prods: 4 Fac dir, 8 Fac des; budget $3,000-15,000

SECOND STAGE: 1200 seats, computer lighting, fly space
    2 prods: 2 UG dir, 4 UG des; budget $100-2,000
    2 UG dir/des Workshops/Readings; budget $0-500

THIRD STAGE: 80-120 seats, black box, electronic lighting.

Facility was built in 1968, renovated 1996; includes scene shop, cost. shop, prop shop, CAD facil., video studio, 2 rehearsal studios, design studio, 5 classrooms.

Internships available with various professional companies.

DESCRIPTION

Guest Artists: Bruce Campbell, Actor/Author; Joan Schirle, Actor/Mime; Paul Steger, Combat Choreography

The UCA Theatre Program strives to: 1) Provide students and audiences with a creative, diverse, challenging academic and artistic environment that encourages risk taking and promotes an examination of human values, cultural differences and social questions; 2) produce theatre pieces of high quality, diverse styles and various genres to foster an understanding of aesthetic standards and broaden artistic tastes; 3) assimilate a talented and diverse group of faculty, students and staff; 4) teach the major components, general practices and opportunities found in the theatre; 5) provide students with a strong foundation in theatre history, dramatic theory and literature; 6) provide an active production program where students have an opportunity to learn and develop theatrical skills and participate in the broad spectrum of world drama; 7) aid students in constructing a foundation for a career as a theatre professional, graduate student, theatre educator or a professional in allied fields such as communications, psychology, marketing, or public relations.

CALIFORNIA

American Academy of Dramatic Arts/Los Angeles

Dr. Nina LeNoir, Dir. of Instruction
Am. Acad. of Dram. Arts/Hollywood

210 Total Enr.; competitive
Semester System

1336 N. LaBrea Ave.
Hollywood, CA 90028
(323) 464-2777
FAX: (323) 464-1250

NAST + WASC
T: $18,000
Professional Training Prog.
www.aada.org

DEGREES OFFERED

AA in Acting (208); Certificate of Advanced Studies in Actor Training for those who complete the 3rd year.

ADMISSION & FINANCIAL INFORMATION

Must have HS diploma or equivalent; Audition/Interview, two recommendations, health certificate and transcripts required; Approximately 50% of applicants accepted. Merit schols. awarded to deserving second and third year students. A limited number of grants are awarded to entering students based on audition performance.

FACULTY AND CLASSES OFFERED

28 Part-Time: 1 PhD, 5 MFA/MA, 22 Prof. w/o adv. degree.

A. (1 PT) Theatre History-1/Y

B. (26 PT) Acting/Scene Study-13/Y; Voice/Speech-3/Y; Movement-3/Y; Singing-2/Y; Stage Combat-1/Y; Career Management-1/Y

C. (1 PT) Make-up-1/Y

FACILITIES & PRODUCTIONS

The facilities movement includes movement studios, prop department/production workshop, scene & costume shops, library and student lounge.

DESCRIPTION

In 1974, the American Academy of Dramatic Arts established its west coast branch in Pasadena, California to offer the same conservatory training for actors it had been successfully providing in New York since 1884. The Academy now proudly bears the distinction of being the only major acting school located in both of America's most vital centers of theatrical activity. AADA/West offers the same program as the Academy in New York. (See listing under New York for further information.) Transferring between the two branches is permitted, so it is possible for an Academy student to train one year in New York and one year in southern California. Academy students are constantly working on performance projects throughout the first two years, culminating in fully produced "senior plays" at the end of the 2nd year. The third year program is offered to 18-24 selected graduates: the Academy Company. Emphasis is on advanced personalized development of each actor through performance of plays in Academy theatres, combined with career guidance and showcasing. 12-16 productions are mounted by professional directors between September and February which are attended by agents, casting directors and potential employers of actors. 2nd year students and alumni are cast as needed.

American Conservatory Theater

Melissa Smith, Director
American Conservatory Theatre
30 Grant Ave., 6th Floor
San Francisco, CA 94108-5800
DEPT: (415) 439-2350
www.actactortraining.org

48 Total Enr; h. compet.
Semester System
48 Majors
T: $15,776
FAX: (415) 834-3300
ADM: (415) 439-2350

DEGREES OFFERED

MFA in Acting (120). 16 degrees granted 2006.

ADMISSION & FINANCIAL INFORMATION

Audition and Interview required; 6% of applicants accepted; Generally admit 16 out of 400 applicants to MFA program. Tuition Schols.- merit only, A.C.T. Schol.- need only.

FACULTY AND CLASSES OFFERED

13 Core, 9 Adjunct

A. (1 1/2 FT, 1 PT) Theatre History-2/Y; Shakes-3/Y; Dramatic Lit-2/Y.

B. (6 1/2, 8 PT) Acting-6/Y; Voice/Speech-8/Y; Movement-4/Y; Singing-2/Y; Clown, etc.-3/Y; Stage Combat-1/Y; Dance-1/Y; Alexander-2/Y

D. (1 PT) No courses listed

FACILITIES & PRODUCTIONS

MAINSTAGE: 1,000 seats, fly space, computerized lighting
    8 Guest dir prods

STUDIO: 50 seats, black box. 16 prods: 8 Fac dir, 8 guest dir

2 Workshops/Readings: budget $250-25,000

Facility was built in 1910; include scene shop, costume shop, prop shop, sound studio, 3 dance studios, 5 rehearsal studios, 7 classrooms; second stage.

Connection with Tony Award winning American Conservatory Theater, an Equity theatre.

DESCRIPTION

Noted Faculty: Francine Landes, Movement; Jeff Crockett, Voice; Frank Ottiwel, Alexander; Deborah Sussel, Speech; Leslie Felbain, Mask; Melissa Smith, Gregory Wallace, Stephen Anthony Jones, Rene' Augusen, Acting.

Guest Artists: Elizabeth Banks, Giles Havergal, Joanna Merlin, Ellen Novak, Anika Noni Rose, Olympia Dukakis, Robin Williams, Eve Ensler, James Calder, Philip Kerr, Charles Randolph Wright, Tom Stoppard, Dennis Krausnik.

The American Conservatory Theater, among the nation's largest and most respected professional companies, has been a leader in actor training for more than 25 years. A.C.T.'s M.F.A. Program is a rigorous and progressive three-year course of study culminating in a year of public performances and an MFA in acting for qualified students. Vital to our mission is the link we provide between young and established theater artists. All classes are led by working professionals who practice what they teach. The Conservatory curriculum is compulsory, with no elective subjects, and is designed so that a full range of classes in acting, voice, movement, performance, humanities, and professional issues are taught continuously throughout the year by Core Faculty members and guest artists. A.C.T. also offers an intensive 9-week Summer Training Congress that provides a full range of actor training. Through challenging and innovative training, which includes contract with A.C.T.'s mainstage artists, the Conservatory hopes to inspire in its students the imagination and courage to build exciting and fulfilling careers as professional actors.

The American Musical and Dramatic Academy

LA and NYC (see listing in NY)

David Martin, Artistic Director
AMDA, 2109 Broadway
New York, NY10023
ADMISSIONS: (212) 787-5300
800-367-7908

800 Total Enr.; competitive
Semester Sys; NAST
T: $24,240/yr./H:$6700/yr.
FAX: (212) 799-4623
www.amda.edu

California Address 6305 Yucca St. LA 90028 (Call NYC campus for information) 1-323-469-3300 Fax 323-469-3350

DEGREES OFFERED

Certificate in Theatre (Musical Theatre and Acting). Declare major at Application and Audition.

ADMISSION & FINANCIAL INFORMATION

Adm. reqs-Applicants to AMDA include graduating HS seniors, college transfer students and college graduates. Applicants are required to submit application, $50 fee, all transcripts from HS and college, 2 ltrs of recommendation, student essays and to audition to be considered for acceptance to the school. A 2.5 QPA from HS is required. 50-55% of applicants are accepted. Scholaships are available. Scholarships are determined by audition and application. Scholarships offered for 2 yr program and open to first year students. Auditions are held monthly on campus in NY and LA as well as throughout the US and Canada. Auditions have been held in the following cities: Atlanta, Boston, Chicago, Cleveland, Columbus, Dallas, Denver, Houston, Kansas City, Las Vegas, LA, Minneapolis, Nashville, NY, Phoenix, Portland, Raleigh, SF, Seattle, St. Louis, Tampa, DC, Calgary, Montreal, Toronto and Vancouver. See Website for further information.

FACULTY AND CLASSES OFFERED

150 faculty of professional artists and accompanists. Part-Time: 6 PhD, 30 MFA/MA, the remaining with B.A.'s and/or professional training and certificates; 35 Staff

CURRICULUM FOR THE INTEGRATED PROGRAM: Musical Theatre I, II, III (Techniques, Performance Styles and Scene Work), Acting I, II, III (Scene Study and Technique, Scene Study and Rehearsal Projects), Theatre Dance I, II, III, Ballet I, II, III, Tap I, II, III, Jazz I, II, III, Voice Production and Speech I, II, III, Voice I, Individual Voice II, III, IV, Musicianship I, Musicianship/Sight Singing, II, Fourth Semester: Performance Project, Career Seminars, Aud. Portfolio Workshop, Musical Th. Prep. for Auds, Monologues and Cold Readings for Auds, Dance Combinations for Auds, Acting for Film and Television Workshops.

CURRICULUM FOR THE STUDIO PROGRAM:: Acting I, II (Techniques and Resources), Acting I, II (Scene Study), Voice Production and Speech I, II, III, Theatre Movement I, II, III, Stage Combat I, II, III), Improvisation I, II, III, Masterpieces of the Stage, I, II, Heroic Acting I, Acting for Film and TV II, III, Shakes, Singing Technique and Jazz Dance (electives) I. 4th semester: Performance Project, Career Seminars, Aud. Workshops, Monologues and Cold Readings for Auds., Auditioning for Film and TV; Dialects, Singing Techniques or Stage Combat (electives).

FACILITIES AND PRODUCTIONS

AMDA -NY has two locations in the upper West Side of Manhattan: the Ansonia location is at 2109 B'way at West 73rd St and the other location is at 211 West 61st St at Amsterdam Ave. Both locations in NY have a mainstage theatre, private voice studios, dance studios, rehearsal studios, scene shops, costume shops, prop rooms and classrooms. There are 12 studio spaces and mainstage theatre at West 73rd St. location and 22 studios and a mainstage theatre at the 61st St. location. These locations are a short 12 blocks apart.

AMDA-LA is located on two acres in historic Hollywood, the campus is one block north of the intersection of Hollywood Blvd & Vine at 6305 Yucca Street. there is a mainstage theatre and 9 studios which include private voice studios, dance studios, rehearsal studios, scene shop, prop room, and classrooms. There is also housing and parking on campus. AMDA provides housing for all who request it in both NYC and LA.

35 FACULTY DIRECTED PRODUCTIONS FOR STUDENTS IN MUSICAL THEATRE AND ACTING. ALL IN HOUSE PRODUCTIONS SERVE AS GRADUATION PERFORMANCES TO WHICH OUTSIDE PEOPLE ARE INVITED.

DESCRIPTION

The creation of the American Musical and Dramatic Academy in 1964 marked a new era in the training of performers for the American Theatre. AMDA, as it has come to be known, was the first school to address the critical need for training in both acting and musical theatre. Today, the versatile performer is the rule, not the exception. Respected actors move from the legitimate stage to the musical stage, from modern plays to the classics, and from the live theatre to film and television. AMDA graduates have successful careers and habe been doing this for 40 years. Continuing with this vision AMDA has opened a second campus in LA to provide opportunities to students who wish to study in the two entertainment centers of the US. AMDA's 2 Training Programs, the Integrated Program and the Studio Program are carefully planned to prepare the student for a career in the performing arts. The focus is proactical rather than academic and is rigorous and requires. strong discipline. The Integrated Program is designed to prepare the student to work as an actor, singer and dancer in the professional theatre as well as in film and television. The Studio Program is deisgned to prepare the student to work as an actor in the professional theatre, film and television. Each program is offered in both locations and is 4 semesters of training. Upon completion of the 1st year students return to the 2nd year by invitation only. Fulfillment of all course requirements entitles the student to a Certificate of Theatre. AMDA offers a joint degree program leading to a BFA in Musical Theatre for Integrated students and a BA for Studio students with New School University in NYC.

California Institute of the Arts

Erik Ehn, Dean
School of Theater
California Institute of the Arts
24700 McBean Parkway
Valencia, CA 91355
661.255.1050
ADMISSIONS: (800) 545-2787
admiss@calarts.edu

1,200 Total Enrollment;
    highly competitive
Semester System
240 Majors; NAST, U/RTA
T: $$31,865/$$8,530 r&b
FAX: (661) 255-0462
FAX: (661) 254-8352
www.calarts.edu

DEGREES OFFERED

BFA and MFA in Acting (110), Design (70), Management (18), Technical Direction (10); MFA in Directing (4), Playwriting (5); Producing (8), Scene Painting (6), Prop Design & Mgmt (6), 2001 granted 13 UG, 7 Grad Acting degs.

ADMISSION & FINANCIAL INFORMATION

Audition/Portfolio Review/Interview required; accept 40% to institu-tion; Theatre program admits 98 out of 450 UG applicants, 68 out of 250 Grad applicants; Scholarship assistance based on merit and need.

FACULTY AND CLASSES OFFERED

23 Full-Time, 20 Part-Time: 8 Staff

A. (2 FT, 3 PT) Intro Theatre-2/Y; Th History-4/Y; Dramatic Lit-5/Y; Playwriting-6/Y

B. (11 FT, 10 PT) Acting-16/Y; Voice/Speech-16/Y; Mvmt-20/Y; Singing-2/Y; Directing-6/Y; Stg Combat-2/Y; Dance-X

C. (10 FT, 7 PT) Principles of Design-7/Y; Set Design-7/Y; Costume Design-6/Y; Lighting Design-12/Y; Sound Design-8/Y; Technical Production-7/Y; Costume Construction-6/Y; Costume History-2/Y; Make-up-2/O; Stage Mgmt.-6/Y; Technical Direction-7/YO

D. Arts Management-2/O

FACILITIES & PRODUCTIONS

11 prods: 2 Fac dir, 6 Guest dir, 3 Grad dir, 36 Grad des, 11 UG des; budget $5,000-8,000

Mainstage: 300 seats; computerized lighting.

SECOND STAGE: 60-100 seats, computerized lighting budget $1,500-4,000

THIRD STAGE: 30-80 seats, black box, computerized lighting

Workshops/Readings: budget $100-800

Facility was built in 1971, renovated in 1994; includes scene shop, costume shop, prop shop, welding shop, sound studio, CAD facility, 5 rehearsal studios, 2 design studios, 3 classrooms.

A non-departmental, student-run organization presents 12+ New Plays Fest. productions per year in which majors participate. 20+ student-written plays produced in the last two years.

DESCRIPTION

Noted Faculty: Chris Barreca, Scene Design; Fran Bennett, Voice and Speech; Marissa Chibas, Acting; Janie Geiser, Puppetry; Jon Gottlieb, Sound Design; Travis Preston, Directing; Mary Lou Rosato; Acting; Susan Solt, Producing; Suzan-Lori Parks, Playwriting; Joan MacIntosh, Acting; Carol Bixler, Producing; Christopheer Akerlind, Lighting Design; Ellen McCartney, Costume Design; Mary Heilman, Scene Painting and Props.

Guest Artists: Robert Israel, Designer, Ed Harris, Actor; Don Cheadle, Actor; Roman Paska, Puppetry Artist; Lisa Kron, Performance Artist; Danny Hoch, Performance Artist; Jose Rivera, Playwright; Marie Irene Fornes, Playwrite; Phil Goldfarb, Producer/Production Mgr.; Brian Cox, Actor; Richard Foreman, Playwright/Director; Michael Counts, Director/Designer; David Hancock, Playwright; Brian Freeman, Playwright/Performance Artist; Ken Jacobs, Filmmaker/Performance Artist, Karin Coonrad, Director; Barry Edelstein, Director

The school has two main branches: the Programs in Performance and the Programs in Design and Production. Performance offers programs in Acting, Directing and Writing for Performance. Design and Production offers programs in Scene, Costume, Lighting and Sound Design, Technical Direction, Producing, Scene Painting and Props Management. Public performances, curricular projects, individual student works, and an annual New Plays

Festival are presented in our architecturally unique Walt Disney Modular Theatre, four black-box theatres, and at other on- and off-campus venues. The faculty consists of outstanding active professionals who carefully guide each student's artistic development. Innovative guest artists from around the world continuously expand existing visions and structures. Our aim is to train students who will bring to the theatre a sense of high artistic, social, and ethical purpose. While we help students acquire the skills necessary for professional life, our primary commitment is to develop a vision of the theatre as a dynamic cultural force.

California State Polytechnic University

W.H. Morse, Chair	19,500 Total Enr.; not compet.
Department of Theatre	Quarter System
3801 W. Temple Avenue	75 Majors
Calif. State Polytechnic Univ.	T: $1,023
Pomona, CA 91768	O-St T: $10,714
DEPT: (909) 869-3900	MAIN: (909) 869-3900
FAX: (909) 869-3184	www.csupomona.edu

DEGREES OFFERED

BA in Theatre w/options: Tech/Design, Acting, General, Dance, Education and Community. Students declare major 1st or 2nd year. 2006 granted 14 UG degs.

ADMISSION & FINANCIAL INFORMATION

Accept 40% of applicants to institution. High school degree required; no audition necessary for theatre dept. 9 out of 10 applics admitted to theatre program. Resident: minimum SAT of 2800 or ACT of 694; non-resident: minimum SAT of 3402 or ACT of 842; OR 3.00 grade point average. Interview required. All theatre program applicants are accepted at present. University scholarships avail. $200 - $2,000. Dept. of Theatre offers various scholarships for majors. 2 - $300 Incoming Freshman/Transfer Student by application.

FACULTY AND CLASSES OFFERED

5 Full-Time: MFA; 5 Staff

A. (1 FT) Intro to Theatre-1/Y; Dramatic Lit-1/Y; Theatre History-3/Y; Shakes-1/Y; Playwriting-1/Y

B. (2 FT) Acting-6/Y; Voice/Speech-2/Y; Movement-1/Y; Mime, etc.-1/Y; Directing-1/Y; Dance-1/Y; Stage Combat-1/Y

C. (2 FT) Principles of Design-2/Y; Set Design-1/Y; Costume Design-2/Y; Lighting Design-1/Y; Tech. Production-2/Y; Costume Construction-1/Y; Costume History-2/Y; Make-up-1/Y; Stage Management-2/Y

D. (1 FT) Theatre in Education & Community.

FACILITIES AND PRODUCTIONS

MAINSTAGE: 500 seats, fly space, computerized lighting
  3 Fac dir/des, 1 Guest des, 1 UG des prods; budget $5,000-20,000
SECOND STAGE: 99 seats, electronic lighting
  1 Guest, 9 UG dir prods; budget $300-500
Workshops/Readings: 2 Guest dir, 3 UG dir; budget $75-150
Facility was built in 1965 and last renovated (lights/sound) in 1998; includes scene, costume, prop, welding shops; sound studio, CAD facil, movement/dance studio, classroom.

Student-written one-act festival every other year.
Connection with Mark Taper Forum, South Coast Repertory., Cornerstone Theatre Co. Internships available, part time tech/design work.

DESCRIPTION

The Cal Poly Theatre Department has an undergraduate program that emphasizes production and experience in the "doing" of theatre. At the same time, the department offers courses in all aspects of the theatre and dance, both artistic and academic. The program stresses concern for students as artists and individuals; faculty, staff, and students work closely together to build for the student a solid foundation of knowledge of both the practical and artistic aspects of drama. Mainstage productions range from dramas to musicals, from realism to highly theatrical styles, from new plays to classics, and the department also offers an opportunity for experimentation in the smaller "black box" theatre, where student involvement is strongly encouraged and supported. In the classroom, students receive intensive training in acting, directing, stagecraft, make-up, stage lighting, costume and scenic design, playwriting, theatre management, and dance. Cal Poly Theatre students have been accepted at major graduate schools and professional training programs throughout the country. Graduates have gone on to theatre companies, film and television; university and secondary theatre education, community theatre and other professions where their drama skills support their careers.

California State University - Bakersfield

Anita DuPratt, Chair	N/A Total Enr.; not compet.
Theatre Arts Department	Quarter System
California State University, Bakersfield	25 Majors; ATHE
9001 Stockdale Highway	T: $3,591/$$6,043 R&B
Bakersfield, CA 93311-1099	O-St T: $13,761/$$6,043 R&B
DEPT: (661) 664-3093	SMALL PROGRAM
FAX: (661) 665-6901	adupratt@csubak.edu
ADM: (661) 664-3036	www.csub.edu
http://www.csub.edu/home/stuinfo/admiss/	

DEGREES OFFERED

BA in Theatre Arts. Students declare major in any year.

ADMISSION & FINANCIAL INFORMATION

3.0 GPA with any test scores; GPA 2.0 to 3.0 with 10-30 ACT or 410-1200 SAT; No special req's for theatre program; admit all to program. Various schols, all awarded by faculty based on ongoing work or on audition or portfolio.

FACULTY AND CLASSES OFFERED

4 Full-Time, 2 PT: 2 PhD, 4 MFA; 1 Staff.

A. (1 FT) Intro to Theatre-1/Y; Dramatic Lit-2/Y; Theatre History-2/Y; Dramatic Criticism-1/O; Shakes-3/X; Playwriting-1/O

B. (2 FT, 2 PT) Acting-3/Y; Voice/Speech-1/O; Movement- 1/O; Directing-1/O

C. (1 FT) Principles of Design-1/O; Set Design-1/O; Costume Design-1/O; Lighting Design-1/O; Make-up-1/O

FACILITIES & PRODUCTIONS

MAINSTAGE: 500 seats, fly space, computerized & electronic ltg.
   3 prods: 2 Fac dir/des, 1 Guest dir/Fac des; budget $6,000

SECOND STAGE: 100 seats, electronic lighting
   1 Fac dir/UG des; budget $500

Facility was built in 1980; includes scene shop, costume shop, rehearsal studio.

DESCRIPTION

The CSUB Theatre Program offers a complete undergraduate curriculum in performance, technical theatre and design, and theatre studies. All students, from their first year to their last, have ample opportunities to participate in our productions as actors, directors, designers and crew members. We produce a wide variety of material; recent main-stage offerings have included Our Country's Good, True West, The School for Scandal, Pippin, All My Sons, Getting Out, Camille, A Midsummer Night's Dream, Sherlock Holmes, Brighton Beach Memoirs and Top Girls. We keep class sizes small—usually only ten to fifteen in courses for Theatre Arts majors—and so are able to tailor the training to each student's needs. Throughout the program, we encourage both the production of theatre and the study of theatre. Every student finishes with a senior project which reflects his or her area of particular interest or expertise in acting, directing, design or playwriting, dramaturgy, dramatic literature, theatre history.

California State University, Dominguez Hills

Sydell Weiner, Ph.D., Chair
Department of Theatre
1000 East Victoria Street
Carson, CA 90747
(310) 243-3588
www.cla.csudh.edu/dnp/theatre_arts
ADMISSIONS: 1000 East Victoria Street, Carson CA 90757
(310) 243-3645   FAX: (310) 516-3609
www.cla.csudh.edu

10,000 Total Enr.; compet.
Semester System
62 Majors; NAST (A)
T: $3,377 in-state, $11,513 o-st
$8,690

DEGREES OFFERED

BA in Theatre Arts (24), Performance (20), Television Arts (12); Tech/Stage Design (6). Students declare major in 2nd or 3rd year; 2001 granted 10 degrees.

ADMISSION & FINANCIAL INFORMATION

The CSU system has a prescribed equation for the balance between GPA and SAT; 66% of applicants accepted to inst.; 7 out of 10 admitted to theatre program. 2 Theatre Guild Schols. go to outstanding Th. majors chosen each semester; also awards given to outstanding majors.

FACULTY AND CLASSES OFFERED

6 Full-Time, 3 PT; 3 PhD, 3 MA/MFA, 1 Prof. w/o adv. deg.; 4 Staff.
A. (1 FT) Intro to Th.-1/Y; Dramatic Lit.-1/O; Theatre History-2/Y; Playwriting-1/O
B. (2 FT, 3 PT) Acting-3/Y; Voice/Speech-1/Y; Movement-1/Y; Directing-1/Y
C. (1 FT) Prins. of Des-1/Y; Set Des-1/Y; Cost. Des-1/O; Ltg. Des-1/Y; Tech. Prod'n-1/O; Cost. Constr.-O' Make-up-1/O; Stg. Mgmt.-1/O

FACILITIES & PRODUCTIONS

MAINSTAGE: 475 seats, fly space, computerized & electronic lighting. 3 Prods: 2 Fac. dir/des, 1 Guest dir/des; budget $7-10,000.

SECOND STAGE: 80 seats.
   2 Prod., up dir/des.; budget $1,500-$2,000
   Workshops/Readings: 2 UG dir.; budget $50-100

Two student-written plays have been produced by the department in the last two years.

DESCRIPTION

Freshmen and sophomores receive a thorough liberal arts education. Their grounding in Theatre stresses breadth. Juniors and Seniors are more vocationally oriented and both our performance option and tech option majors receive stronger professional training. General option majors normally move on for MA's or PhD's.

California State University - Fresno

Melissa Gibson, Chair
Theatre Arts Department
California State Univ.
5201 N. Maple
Fresno, CA 93740-8027
DEPT: (559) 278-3987
http://csufresno.edu/Theatre
ADMISSIONS: 5150 N. Maple, Fresno, CA 93740-8026
(559) 278-2261

20,200 Total Enr.; not compet.
Semester System
118 Majors; NAST (A), ATHE, USITT
   T: (Full-Time) $1,650
O-ST T: $339 per unit
FAX: (559) 278-7215
mgibson@csufresno.edu

DEGREES OFFERED

BA in Theatre Arts (95), Acting (50), Design/Tech (10), General (22) Teaching Credentials (10), Theatre Arts/Dance Option (10). Declare major in freshman year; 2007 granted 24 UG degrees.

ADMISSION & FINANCIAL INFORMATION

Minimum high school GPA: 2.0 w/ACT of 28 or SAT of 1200; transfer students must have minimum of 2.0 on 4.0 scale; 80% of applicants admitted to institution; Theatre program generally admits all applicants; Financial aid and theatre scholarships/grants are available; reviewed by theatre faculty and selected based on academics, talent and performance.

FACULTY AND CLASSES OFFERED

14 Full-Time, 6 Part-Time; 2 PhD, 10 MFA/MA; 7 Staff
A. (3 FT, 1 PT) Intro to Theatre-1/Y; Theatre History-2/Y; Shakes- 1/X; Dramatic Lit-1/Y; Dramatic Criticism-1/Y; Playwriting-1/Y
B. (5 FT, 1 PT) Acting-5/Y; Voice/Speech-2/Y; Movement-1/Y; Directing-2/Y; Musical Theatre-1/Y
C. (3 FT) Principles of Design-1/Y; Set Design-2/Y; Cost Design- 1/Y; Lighting Design-2/Y; Tech. Production-1/Y; Cost Construction-1/Y; Costume History-1/Y; Make-up-1/Y; Stage Mgmt-1/O;

FACILITIES AND PRODUCTIONS

MAINSTAGE: 360 seats, fly space. 4 prods: 2 Fac dir/des, 1 Fac dir/Fac, 1 Fac dir/Fac & UG des; budget $2,500-3,500

SECOND STAGE: 200 seats. 2 prods: Fac dir/des, Fac dir/Fac & UG des; budget $100-1,000

THIRD STAGE: 100 seats
   4 prods: 4 UG dir/des; budget $300-400

Facility renovated in 1991; includes scene shop, costume shop, welding area, sound studio, 1 dance studio, 5 classrooms.

A departmental student-run organization presents 4 productions (2 theatre and 2 dance) per year.

DESCRIPTION

Guest Artists: Mark Booher, California Shakespeare Festival; Kenshaka Ali, Black Theatre Specialist; Roger DeLaurier, PCPA and Gregory Hoffman, Stage Combat Specialist. Rodrigo Duarte-Clark, Teatro Esperanza; Adam Noble, Acting & Movement Specialist; Tony Carriero, Actor; Roy and Dorothy Christopher, Design.

California State University, Fresno's national- and international-award-winning Theatre Arts program offers extensive professional and educational preparation in all aspects of theatre and dance. The broad curriculum, combined with an annual production schedule of more than 12 plays and several dance concerts, provides the opportunity for intensive training. To insure a rich and varied experience for students, the program makes extensive use of Guest Artists as master teachers in workshops and courses, as well as providing exposure to accomplished performers, directors and designers. At Fresno State opportunities for a variety of theatre experiences abound. In addition to the six-play major season, the Experimental Theatre Company and University Dance Theatre present several all-student productions. Theatre for Young Audiences produces plays for young people on campus and on a spring school tour throughout the valley. Playwright's Theatre is dedicated to original plays, and the Portable Dance Troupe is the resident dance company. The Black Theatre Contingent regularly presents plays from the African-American theatre.

California State University Fullerton

Susan Hallman, Chair
Department of Theatre
  and Dance
California State University,
  Fullerton
800 N. State College Blvd, PA 139
Fullerton, CA 92834
www.fullerton.edu
ADM: Admissions, CSUF, above address
(714) 278-7601

30,000 Total Enr.; compet.
Semester System
400 Maj; U/RTA, NAST, ATHE
T: $1,651/unit/$7,500 R&B
O-ST T: $1,990/unit/$7,500 R&B
DEPT: (714) 278-2638
FAX: (714) 278-7041

FAX: (714) 278-7549

DEGREES OFFERED

BA in General Theatre (100); BA in Technical Production/Design (50); Acting (100); Directing (50); BA in Dance (100); BFA in Musical Theatre (25); MFA in Acting (15), Design (10). Students declare majors in freshman year. 2007 granted 75 UG, 14 Grad degrees.

ADMISSION & FINANCIAL INFORMATION

(UG) GPA of 2.0, four years of college prep English, 2 years of Math. SAT score with 2.0 must be 1400. Requirements for Theatre Program: Audition, Interview, Portfolio for Designers. Program admits 7 out of 10 UG, 4 out of 10 Grad applicants. Schols. are available from department upon entry into program. Admission by CSUF and audition, contact department for info. Grad applicants must aud/interview, portfolio for des.

FACULTY AND CLASSES OFFERED

18 Full-Time, 16 Part-Time: 4 PhD, 25 MA/MFA, 6 Prof. w/o adv.

degree; 14 Staff

A. (3 FT, 5 PT) Introduction to Theatre-2/Y; Dramatic Lit-2/Y; Theatre History-8/Y; Dramatic Criticism-1/Y; Shakes-2/Y; Playwriting-2/Y; Drama into Film-2/Y

B. (8 FT, 8 PT) Acting-8/Y; Mime,etc.-1/Y; Voice/Speech-8/Y; Movement-4/Y; Singing-6/Y; Musical Theatre-4/Y; Directing-4/Y; Dance-50/Y; Acting for non-majors-2/Y, Stage Combat 1/Y

C. (6 FT,2 PT) Set Design-4/Y; Cost Des-2/Y; Lighting Design-2/Y; Technical Production-4/Y; Cost construction-2/Y; Make-up-2/Y; Stage Mgmt-2/Y; Principles of Des-2/Y; Advanced Make-up-1/Y; Advanced Set Des-1/Y; Advanced Lighting-1/Y

D. (1 FT, 1 PT) Arts Management-2/Y

FACILITIES & PRODUCTIONS

New Performing Arts Center opened in 2006.
MAINSTAGE: 500 seats, fly space, computerized lighting
  13 prods: 11 Fac dir, 8 Fac des, 2 Grad dir, 6 Grad des, 2 UG des; budget $8,000-22,000
SECOND STAGE: 250 seats. 9 prods: 8 Fac des,
  6 Guest dir, 1 Grad dir, 6 Grad des, 2 UG dir, 6 UG des; $1,000-1,500
THIRD STAGE (GRAND CENTRAL): 150 seats (new)
Fourth Stage: 75 seats. 6 prods: 6 Guest dir, budget $100
2 WORKSHOP THEATRES: 50 seats. 20 Workshops/Readings: 2 Fac dir, 2 Guest dir, 2 Grad dir, 6 Grad des, 14 UG dir, 8 UG des; budget $0-150
Facility was built in 1960's, New facility in 2006; includes scene shop, costume shop, welding shop, prop shop, 2 sound studios, video studio, 6 movement/dance studios, rehearsal studios, CAD facility, design studio, make-up lab and paint lab, classrooms. Aside from the four on-campus theatres, the Dept. also produces in an off-site theatre named Grand Central.

5 prods and 12 readings departmental student produced.

DESCRIPTION

Noted Faculty: Susan Hallman, Chair/Design; Svetlana Efremova, Acting; John Fisher, Design; Bruce Goodrich, Design; Joan Melton, Voice, Speech, Movement; Ann Sheffield, Design; James R. Taulli, Acting; Jim Volz, Shakespeare/Management; Abel Zeballos, Design; Deb Lockwood, Design; Eve Himmelheber, Acting; David Nevell, Voice/Movement/Acting; Evelyn Case, Voice/Movement/Acting; Mitch Hanlon, Musical Theatre; Bill Lett, Dance/Musical Theatre; John Short, Acting for the Camera.

Guest Artists: Debbie Allen, Actor, Choreographer; Ben Vereen, Actor, Choreographer; Joanna Gleason, Actor; Susan Egan, Actor; Faith Prince, Actor; Alice Ripley, Actor; James Whitmore, Actor; Peri Gilpin, Actor; Ming Cho Lee, Designer; Jeff Greenberg, Casting; Brian Stokes Mitchell, actor.

The Cal State Fullerton Theatre program is among the top 16 "Most Highly Recommended Undergraduate Programs" in the nation, according to the most recent Performing Arts Major's College Guide (Macmillan Books). ranked with such prestigious schools as Julliard, New York University, Boston University and Northwestern University, Cal State Fullerton is one of only four California universities to achieve this top ranking. Our programs focus on the development of the complete artist. While public performance is at the heart of our programs, we maintain a creative balance between academic courses and professional theatre training. In our quest to meet all of the needs of a theatre arts career, students have a choice of concentrations in the following areas: liberal arts; teaching and production/performance (includes emphases in the areas of acting, directing, playwriting, technical production/design and musical theatre).

California State University - Long Beach

Joanne Gordon, Chairman
Department of Theatre
California State University
Long Beach,CA 90840-2701
DEPT: (562) 985-5357
MAIN: (562) 985-4111

31,000 Tot. Enr.; compet. (G)
Semester System
300 Majors; NAST
T: $3,116 r&b $7,536
O-ST T: $13,286 r&b $7,536
FAX: (562) 985-2263
www.csulb.edu/

DEGREES OFFERED

BA in Performance, Technical/Design, General Theatre; MFA in Acting, Costume/Design, Theatre Management.

ADMISSION & FINANCIAL INFORMATION

Grad program highly competitive, UG program not competitive; 50% of apps. accepted by instit. (UG) GPA of 2.75, (G) GPA of 3.00; Audition/Interview/Portfolio required for Grad admission; Theatre program admits 50 out of 65 UG, 15 out of 250 Grad applicants. Several schols available to theatre majors, auditions/ application/portfolio reviews are available each semester for theatre majors only.

FACULTY AND CLASSES OFFERED

10 Full-Time: 4 PhD, 6 MFA/MA,7 1/2 Staff

A. Introduction to Theatre-1/Y; Dramatic Lit.-1/Y; Theatre His-tory-1/Y; Dramatic Criticism-1/Y; Shakes-1/Y; Playwriting-2/Y

B. Acting-4/Y; Voice/Speech-2/Y; Movement-2/Y; Musical Theatre-1/O; Directing-2/Y; Stage Combat-1/O

C. Principles of Design-1/Y; Set Design-2-3/Y; Cost Des-2/Y; Lighting Design-2-3/Y; Tech Production-2/Y; Cost Construction-2/Y; Costume History-1/Y; Make-up-2-3/Y; Stage Management-1/Y

D. Arts Management-2/Y; Marketing/Promotion-2/Y

FACILITIES & PRODUCTIONS

MAINSTAGE: 378 seats, fly space, computerized lighting

SECOND STAGE: 250 seats, computerized lighting

THIRD STAGE: 90 seats, computerized lighting

FOURTH STAGE: Downtown Stage, 99 seats, Edison Theatre.

Mainstage was built in 1952, Second stage was built in 1972; facilities were renovated in 1989; includes scene shop, costume shop, prop shop, welding shop, sound studio, movement/dance studio, 5 rehearsal studios, 3 design studios, classroom.

California Repertory Company, is the Graduate company, a 99 seat Equity (waiver) professional company.

DESCRIPTION

Noted Faculty: Alexander Buravsky (PT); Johnathan Mack, Danila Korogdsky, David Wheeler, visiting faculty.

California State University Northridge

Peter Grego, Chair
Department of Theatre
CSU, Northridge
18111 Nordhoff Street
Northridge,CA 91330-8320
(818) 677-3086
www.csun.edu/theatre

35,000 Total Enr.
Semester System
263 Majors; NAST,U/RTA,ATHE
T: $1,521
O-ST T: $339 per unit + fees
FAX: (818) 677-2080

ADMISSIONS: CSUN Admissions, Bayramian Hall, as above, 91330-8207
(818) 677-3700   www.csun.edu/admissions

DEGREES OFFERED

BA of Theatre and MA of Theatre. Declare major in any year.

ADMISSION & FINANCIAL INFORMATION

Accept over 80% to institution; no special req's for UG theatre program; Grad applic. req. 24 units of upper division theatre courses. Variety of schols. based on need w/GPA, course content, leadership; Theatre Dept. schols based on artistic promise, achievement and GPA.

FACULTY AND CLASSES OFFERED

12 Full-Time, 13 Part-Time: 5 PhD, 19 MFA/MA; 7 Staff

A. (2 FT, 1 PT) Intro to Theatre-4/Y; Dramatic Lit-7/X, 2/O; Th History-14/YO; Dramatic Crit.-2/X, 3/O; Shakes-2/X

B. (4 FT, 4 PT) Acting-3/YO; Voice/Speech-2/Y; Movement- 1/O; Mime, etc.-1/O; Singing-4/X; Musical Theatre-2/O; Directing-3/YO; Creative Drama/Theatre for Youth-8/YO; Activity/Tutorial-8/Y

C. (3 FT, 6 PT) Principles of Design-2/Y; Set Design-2/O; Costume Design-1/O; Lighting Design-1/O; Technical Production-3/YO; Make-up-1/O; Theatre Graphics-1/O; Activity/Tutorial-8/Y

D. (1 FT) Arts Management-1/O

FACILITIES & PRODUCTIONS

MAINSTAGE: 400 seats, fly space, computerized lighting, 4 prods

SECOND STAGE: 205 seats, 4 prods

THIRD STAGE: 100 seats, 2 prods

Facility was built in 1960; includes scene shop, costume shop, sound studio, video studio, rehearsal studio, design studio, classrooms, meeting/seminar room.computer lab.

Because California State University, Northridge is situated in Los Angeles, students regularly serve internships at the Mark Taper Forum, other professional theatres in L.A, and in the entertainment industry.

DESCRIPTION

Noted Faculty: Lillian Lehman, Garry Lennon, John Binkley, Barry Cleveland, Ah-Jeong Kim, Peter Grego, J'aime Morrison

Guest Artists: Laurie Metcalf, Lily Tomlin, Oh Tae-Sok

In addition to its commitment to practical experience through THEATRE CSUN, the Department of Theatre at the California State University, Northridge provides an academic curriculum of over 100 courses covering the history, literature and theory of theatre, studio courses in the acting, directing, design and technology of theatre as well as management, theatre education and theatre for youth. The department is also committed to outreach programs for the public schools in which primary and secondary students attend matinees on campus. It tours Theatre for Youth productions in the greater Los Angeles area. Its members conduct research in academic and practical areas of theatre and collaborate with the professional theatre. Finally, the department serves as a community arts resource. One of the largest and most successful educational theatre programs in the state, the California State University, Northridge Department of Theatre is providing leadership in university education, pre-professional training while preserving the heritage of arts in American culture.

California State University Sacramento

Dr. Linda Goodrich, Chair	23,500 Tot. Enr.
Dept of Theatre and Dance	155 Majors; NAST
6000 J. St.	Semester System
California State University	T: $3,284 R&B $7,966
Sacramento,CA 95819-6069	O-ST T: $$13,454 R&B $7,966
DEPT.: (916) 278-6368	FAX: (916) 278-5681
ADMISSIONS: P.O. Box 6048, Sacramento CA 95819	
http://www.csus.edu/	admin:(916) 278-3901

DEGREES OFFERED

BA in Theatre (101); MA in Theatre (6).
Declare major in any yr.

ADMISSION & FINANCIAL INFORMATION

Eligibility Index - 2900 SAT or 694 ACT or 3.00 avg and above GPA; UG admits all apps. to program; UG auditons for actors, interview & portfolio for designers; Grad: apply to dept, 80% accepted; special scholarship through appl/interview, writing sample & letters of recommendation.

FACULTY AND CLASSES OFFERED

12 Full-Time, 3 Part-Time: 5 PhD, 8 MFA/MA; 6 Staff

A. (2 FT, 1 PT) Intro to Theatre-1/Y; Dramatic Lit-9/Y; Theatre History-2/Y; Shakes-1/Y; Dramatic Criticism-2/Y; Playwriting-2/O; Film (special major)

B. (3 1/2 FT, 1 PT) Acting-3/Y; Voice/Speech-1/Y; Movement-1/Y; Musical Theatre-4/Y; Singing-2/Y; Directing-2/Y; Stage Combat-O; Dance-26/Y.; Mime, etc.-O

C. (2 1/2 FT) Principles of Des-3/O; Cost. Des-1/Y; Tech Production-3/Y; Set Des-2/Y; Ltg. Des-2/Y;Cost Const-3/Y; Make-up-1/O;

FACILITIES & PRODUCTIONS

MAINSTAGE: 438 seats, fly space, computerized lighting, elect light, 6 prods: 3 Fac dir, 3 Fac des, budget $7,000-16,000

SECOND STAGE: 200 seats, computerized lighting, elect light, 21 prods: 2 Fac dir, 1 Guest dir, 2 Grad dir,2 Grad des, 7 UG dir, 7 UG des; budget $800-3,000

THIRD STAGE: 75 seats, elect light, Workshops/Readings; budget $50-100

Facility was built in 1957, renovated in 1970, includes scene shop, costume shop, prop shop, welding, sound studio, CAD facil., dance/movement studio, 2 rehearsal studios, design studio, 3 classrooms, dance space-75 seats fully equipped.

2-3 student-written plays have been produced in the last two years.

DESCRIPTION

Noted Faculty: Brennan Murphy; Acting; Roberto D.

Pomo, Theory/Film; Haibo Yu, Scenography; Richard Bay, Puppetry.;

Guest Artists: Participants in the Past Festival of the Arts: Tim Miller, Actor, Dell Arte Players, Actor Michael Halifax, National British Theatre, Actor Travis Guba, Movement; Art Gruenberger, Puppeteer; Costume Designers Theresa Shea, Clare Henkel; P.J. Gibson, Playwright, Black Theatre; Edit Villareal, Playwright Chicano Theatre; Ellen Geer.

The Department of Theatre and Dance undergraduate and graduate program seeks to provide specific skill development appropriate to the discipline for the training of those who wish to teach theatre and dance, those who will seek advanced training or eventual professional employment, and those who will use their training in community settings and other cultural service areas. We discourage narrow specialization in favor of comprehensive scope and we balance theoretical courses with practical training. Our active and award winning production program works closely with the Music and Dance programs on campus. As a community arts resource we host one of the largest High School drama festival and workshops in the country and we have active and well established programs in African-American and Chicano Theatre. We also offer a unique program in Puppetry and Children's Theatre. A Film concentration has been added.

California State University Stanislaus

Clay Everett	8,000 Total Enr.; not compet.
Drama Dept	Semester System
801 W. Monte Vista Ave.	35 Majors; NAST, ATHE, KC/ACTF
Turlock,CA 95382-0299	T: $2,000/yr./7800 r&b
(209) 667-3451	O-ST T: add $282/unit
FAX: (209) 667-3782	www.csustan.edu
ADMISSIONS: 801 W. Monte Vista Ave, Turlock, CA 95382	
(209) 667-3152	

DEGREES OFFERED

BA in General Theatre—may emphasize in acting, directing, tech. or Grad school preparation (30). Declare major in first year; 2006-07 granted 10 UG degrees.

ADMISSION & FINANCIAL INFORMATION

Program admits all applicants. Scholarships up to $500/semester application to CSUS Financial Aid Dept.

FACULTY AND CLASSES OFFERED

6 Full-Time; 2 PhD, 5 MFA/MA; 2 Staff

A. (1 FT) Intro to Theatre-2/Y; Theatre History-5/Y

B. (2 1/2 FT) Acting-4/Y; Musical Th.-2/Y; Directing- 2/Y, Stage Movement

C. (3 FT) Prins of Des-2/Y; Cost Des-1/O; Ltg Des-1/O; Tech. Production-6/Y; Cost Constr-1/Y; Make-up-1/Y; Stage Mgmt-1/Y

D. (1/2 FT) Arts Management-1/Y; Box Office Procedure-1/Y, Stage Combat

FACILITIES AND PRODUCTIONS

MAINSTAGE: 300 seats, fly space, electronic lighting 2-3 Fac dir/des prods; budget $3,000-5,000

SECOND STAGE: 100 seats, electronic lighting
 3-4 prods: 2-3 Fac dir/des, 1 Student dir/des; budget $2,000-4,000. Variable number of workshops/readings each year.
Facility built in 1970; includes scene shop, cost. shop, welding shop, sound studio, rehearsal studio, design studio, 3 classrooms.

DESCRIPTION

The Department of Drama offers a Bachelor of Arts degree in Drama. The Department trains undergraduates as general practitioners in the art of theatre. The curriculum balances theoretical and practical work and features a close relationship between courses and production. Students and faculty work together on all aspects of production in a 300-seat mainstage theatre and a 100-seat studio. Upon completion of the drama major, a student should be able to collaborate with others in the operation of a theatre or to qualify for further professional training as an artist or as a scholar. Courses in the drama curriculum also provide aesthetic and cultural enrichment for the student in liberal arts.

Dell'Arte International School of Physical Theatre

Joan Schirle, School Director
Dell'Arte International School
 of Physical Theatre
P.O. Box 816
Blue Lake,CA 95525
(707) 668-5663

30-50 Total Enr.; competitive
Trimester Sys
33 Majors;7 MFA NAST (A), ATHE
Tuition, PTP.: $10,900.
MFA: $15,900.
www.dellarte.com

DEGREES OFFERED

MFA in Ensemble based Physical Theatre. Certificates in Acting/Physical Theatre. 2003 granted 33 certificates.

ADMISSION & FINANCIAL INFORMATION

Audition/Interview/Recommendations required; Video audition acceptable if no other option is available; Accepts up to 40 of 90 applicants to institution; Schols. are based on financial need and are in varying amts. from $500-1,700/yr. ALL eligible students will receive aid. Minority applicants are encouraged to apply.

FACULTY AND CLASSES OFFERED

8 FT, 23-29 PT: 6 MFA/MA, 26 w/o adv. degree; 7 Staff
A. (2 PT) Theatre History -1/Y; Playwriting-1/Y
B. (3 FT, 18-24 PT) Acting-3/Y; Voice/Speech-2/Y; Movement- 3/Y; Mime, etc.-3/Y; Singing-2/Y; Stage Combat-1/O; Yoga-2/Y; Mask Performance-1/Y; Principles of Physical Act.-1/Y; Clown Theatre-1/Y; Alexander Technique-1/O; Melodrama-1/Y; Dance-2/Y; Contemporary Applications-1/Y
C. (1 PT) Mask Making-1/Y
D. (2 PT) Marketing/Promotion-1/Y; Budgeting/Accounting Procedure-1/Y; Touring Practicum-1/Y

FACILITIES & PRODUCTIONS

MAINSTAGE: 113 seats, electronic lighting. Weekly presentation of student work; 1 prod, Fac dir; budget $3,000
AMPITHEATRE: 300 seats, electronic lighting
 1 prod: 1 Fac dir; budget $5,000
 Summer Theatre festival: 4 to 7 prods: budget $50,000
SECOND STAGE: 1 prod; prof. dir & prof. des, Alumni performers; budg-

et $21,000
Student performance possibilities in Mad River Festival at Dell'Arte Studio & Amphitheatre in Summer.
Facility was built in 1912, has been renovated to include costume shop, prop shop, 2 movement/dance studios, guest apartment, student production office, community kitchen, 2 management offices.
Dell'Arte Company, a professional Equity company, are in residence as faculty for a portion of each year. They also direct projects. In addition, graduates have the opportunity to audition for Players tours as season needs require added cast.

DESCRIPTION

Noted Faculty: Joan Schirle, Michael Fields, Ronlin Foreman, Joe Krienke, Stephanie Thompson.
Guest Artists: Joan Mankin, Geoff Hoyle, Jeff Raz, Andy Barnett, Cathy Butler, Evamarii Johnson, Alicia Martinez, Robert Maurer, Juanita Samuels, Giovanni Fusetti.

Dell'Arte School of Physical Theatre is the only institution in the United States offering full-time professional training programs in physical performance styles. These are intensive programs designed for those who have chosen acting or variety performance as their profession. Here is a wealth of American and European popular theatre forms in which the physical art of the performer reached full development — mask, silent comedy, farce, melodrama, vaudeville, clowning and commedia dell'arte. These forms are the basis of training at the School of Physical Theatre. Each of the School's programs has as its goal the expansion of the actor's present physical range and the development of physical imagination. In a supportive environment which encourages risk-taking and commitment, students receive rigorous training in the skills of physical theatre. The approach stresses that character, speech, thought and emotion are all expressed through the actor's sole instrument: the body. Students are encouraged to investigate their personal vision and to accept responsibility for the content and expression of their work as mature contributing members of society.

The Old Globe/ University of San Diego

Richard Seer, Director
The Old Globe,Univ. of San Diego
Box 122171
San Diego, CA 92112-2171
DEPT: (619) 231-1941 x 2131
ADMISSIONS: 5998 Alcala Park, San Diego CA 92110-2492
(619) 260-4524

7,000 Tot. Enr.; high. compet.
Semester System
14 Majors
$30,000*/yr
FAX: (619) 231-5879
www.globemfa.org

DEGREES OFFERED

MFA in Dramatic Arts (14); Program began in September, 1987
2007 granted 7 grad. degrees.

ADMISSION & FINANCIAL INFORMATION

Bachelors degree or equivalent from an accredited academic institution. 2% of applicants accepted by institution. Program requires audition/interview. *All students receive full tuition scholarships plus monthly educational stipends.

FACULTY AND COURSES OFFERED

6 FT, 3 PT: 3 PhD, 8 MFA/MA, 2 Staff

A. (3 FT) Theatre Hist.-1/O; Shakes-2/Y; Dramatic Lit-4/Y

B. (3 FT, 9 PT) Acting-4/Y; Voice/Speech-4/Y; Mvmt-12/Y; Mime, etc.-1/O; Singing-4/Y; Audition Technique-1/Y; Video/Film Wkshp.-1/Y; Stage Combat-1/Y; Prof. Co. Acting Assigns.-5/Y.

FACILITIES AND PRODUCTIONS

MAINSTAGE: 581 seats, proscenium

SECOND STAGE: 617 seats, outdoor
   3 Studio prods: 1 Fac dir, 2 Guest dir

THIRD STAGE: 225 seats, arena

OTHER: Black box: 99 seats

Facility built in 1984, renovated in 1992; includes scene shop, costume shop, prop shop, welding shop, sound studio, 1 dance studio, 3 rehearsal studios, 1 design studio, 2 classrooms.

In addition to The Globe Theatres being the primary source for the program's performance faculty, directors, designers, guest artists, and master teachers, first and second year students routinely receive casting assignments with the professional company. In fact, student actors spend summer sessions exclusively on the stages of the Globe.

DESCRIPTION

Noted Faculty: Richard Seer, Jan Gist, Liz Shipman, Sabin Epstein, Fred Miller Robinson, Dramatic Literature; Maria Carerra, Alexander Technique; Gerhard Gessner, Yoga.

Guest Artists: Cherry Jones, Hal Holbrook, Victor Garber, Roger Rees, John Goodman, Actors; Stephen Wadsworth, Daniel Sullivan, Tina Landau, Jack O'Brien, Directors. Dakin Matthews, Dramaturgy.

The Master of Fine Arts in Dramatic Arts nationally recruits seven students each year to participate in an intensive two-year, year-round course of study in classic theatre. The professional actor training program has been expressly designed to take advantage of training and performance opportunities made available by The Globe Theatres, one of America's largest and most prestigious regional theatres. The program is unique because students' performance work in Old Globe professional productions is much more than an added attraction. It is the centerpiece of their training. Also, with only seven actors in each class, an exceptional amount of personal attention is given to the training needs of each student. After graduation, in addition to having accumulated enough EMC credits to receive their Equity card, students perform in showcase auditions in NYC and LA. All graduate actors are awarded full tuition scholarships and stipends.

Humbolt State University ·········

Prof. Bernadette Cheyne, Chair
Dept. of Theatre, Film & Dance
Humboldt State University
#1 Harpst St.
Arcata,CA 95521
(707) 826-5491
www.humboldt.edu/~theatre

7,250 Tot. Enr.; not compet.
Semester System
120 Majors; ATHE
T: $1,128/$7,281 R&B
O-ST T: Same plus $282/unit
FAX: (707) 826-5494
bmc3@humboldt.edu

ADMISSIONS: Office of Enrollment Mgmt., Humboldt University
(707) 826-4402   FAX: (707) 826-6194
www.humboldt.edu/~records   hsuinfo@humboldt.edu

DEGREES OFFERED

MA in Th. Production(20); MFA in Scenography; BA in ISDS (Interdisciplinary Studies): Dance Studies; BA in Theatre Arts (89). Declare major in Soph.-Jr. year; 2004: 20 UG, 10 Grad degrees.

ADMISSION & FINANCIAL INFORMATION

Application form, non-refundable fee of $55, residence and/or financial aid forms, official transcripts, ACT or SAT, GPA ELM & EPT Placement Exams. 80-90% of applics accepted by institution. There are no special requirements for admission to the theatre program. Contact the theatre department for scholarship information.

FACULTY AND CLASSES OFFERED

8 FT, 7-8 PT, 10 MFA/MA; 6 Staff

A. (2 1/2 FT, 2 PT) Intro to Theatre-2/Y; Dramatic Lit-2/Y; Theatre History-2/Y; Shakes-X; Dramatic Criticism-2/Y; Playwriting-2/Y.

B. (3 1/2 FT, 4 PT) Acting-2/Y; Voice/Speech-2/Y; Movement-8-10/Y; Mime/Mask/Circus-2/O; Singing-X; Directing-2/Y; Musical Theatre-1/O; Stage Combat-1/O; Dance-16/Y; Film-16/Y

C. (3 FT) Principles of Design-2/Y; Cost Des-2/Y; Tech Production-2/Y; Set Des-2/Y; Lighting Des-2/Y; Cost Constr-2/Y; Make-up-1/Y; Stage Mgmt-2/Y

D. Arts Management-1/O; Marketing Promotion-O; Legal:Contracts/Copyright-O; Box Office Procedure-1/O; Development/Grant Writing-1/Y;Budgeting/Accounting Procedure-O; Film Prod & Cinematography

FACILITIES & PRODUCTIONS

MAINSTAGE: 750 seats, fly space, computerized lighting. 2 prods: 2 Fac dir, 6 Fac des; budget $10,000-12,000

SECOND STAGE: 140 seats, fly space, computerized lighting. 2-3 prods: 2-3 Fac dir, 6-9 Fac des; budget $4,000-5,000

THIRD STAGE: 125 seats, black box, electronic lighting. 6-10 Workshops/Readings, 4-6 Grad dir, 4-6 UG dir; budget $50-$100.

Facility built in 1959; included scene shop, costume shop, prop shop, welding shop, sound studio, CAD facility, 1 video studio, 2 movement/dance studios, 1 rehearsal studio, 1 design studio, 4-5 classrooms. Three theater facilities serve as classrooms for film editing, audio, make-up, Super-8, 16mm.

9 student-written plays produced in the last two years.

DESCRIPTION

Noted Faculty: Ann Alter, Documentary Film; Bernadette Cheyne, Acting; Margaret Thomas Kelso, Dramatic Writing; James McHugh, Ltg Design; David Scheerer, Film; Rae Robison, Costume/Makeup; Sharon Butcher, Dance. Six staff in theatre, film and dance.

Guest Artists: David K Atherton, makeup artist (Beetlejuice, Dances With Wolves; Face/Off, etc.; Daniel Curry, Visual Effects (Indiana Jones, Flash Dance, etc.); Jim Klein, Oscar nominated documentary filmmaker; Joanna Quin, film animator from Wales, U.K.; Laura Zam, Czechoslovakia-based performance artist.

Departmental Goals: 1. To experiment with the teaching of performance and its history and literature. 2. To provide the general education student with experiences different from others available in the curriculum—experiences which encourage the recognition and evaluation of feelings and promote the creative process. 3. To focus on the uniqueness of the individual and foster the courage required for bold personal, artistic expressions and judgements. 4. To provide a laboratory for aesthetic exploration which encourages the creative gamble. 5. To present a pattern of growth which is as richly individual and rewarding as the process of developing a work in the theatre arts. 6. To challenge the contemporary value accepted by the theatre arts. 7. To enrich all our artistic perspectives by encouraging and participation in the creation of new works.

Los Angeles Theatre Academy at Los Angeles City College

See Ad

Fred Fate, Theatre Academy Chair	14,000 Total Enr.; compet.
855 N. Vermont Ave.	Semester System
	75 Majors
Hollywood, CA 90029	T: $20/unit
Fax: (323) 953-4013	O-ST T: $150/unit
Main: (323) 953-4000x2971	ffate@lacitycollege.edu
www.theatreacademy.lacitycollege.edu	
Admissions: (323) 953-4000x2990	

DEGREES OFFERED

AA in Theatre (3); Acting Certificate (18); Advanced Acting Certificate (12). Declare major in first year; 2007 granted 12 UG degrees.

ADMISSION & FINANCIAL INFORMATION

Admission to college is competitive (50% admittance); Acting School Auditions, interview required; Interview for tech, costume. Grad audtion for actors. UG Theatre program admits 1 out of 2 applicants. Technical Theatre Program; Jerry Blunt Foundation Scholarship based on GPA standing and need.

FACULTY AND CLASSES OFFERED

9 Full-Time, 7 Part-Time; 1 PhD, 16 MFA; 1 Staff

A. (5 FT, 5 PT) Intro to Theatre-3/Y; Theatre History-1/Y; Shakes-2/Y

B. (4 FT, 2 PT) Acting-21/Y; Voice/Speech-10/Y; Movement-6/Y; Singing-2/Y; Directing-1/Y; Stage Combat-1/Y; Mask, etc.-1/Y; Dance-6/Y; Acting for Camera-1/Y; Orient to Acting Professionally-2/Y

C (4 FT, 2 PT) Principles of Design-3/Y; Cost Design-1/Y; Tech Production-4/Y; Set Des-1/O; Lighting Design-1/O; Cost Construction-4/Y; Make-up-2/Y; Stage Management-1/Y

D. B.O. Procedure-2/Y

FACILITIES & PRODUCTIONS

MAINSTAGE: 305 seats, fly space, computerized/electron lighting
     2 prods: 2 Fac dir; 4 Fac des; budget $2,500-4,000

SECOND STAGE: 99 seats, computerized/electronic lighting
     5 prods: 5 Fac dir; 10 Fac des; budget $1,500-2,500

THIRD STAGE: 69 SEATS

Facility was built in 1965, includes scene shop, costume shop, welding shop, sound studio. Theatres are used as classrooms and rehearsal space; womens' gym is used as dance studio for musicals or additional space. Also make-up studio & computer room.

DESCRIPTION

Noted Faculty: Fred Fate, Acting, Prod; Dr. Al Rossi, Acting, Directing; Louie Piday, Leslie Ferreira, Acting,Directing; Kevin Morrissey, Light & Set Des; Jim Moody, Light Des, TD; Eddie Bledsoe, Costume Des; Naila Aladdin-Sanders, Costume Des; Jennifer Rountree, Speech & Voice; Diane Sisko, Costume.

Guest Artists: Bruce Kimmel, Prod,Dir, Writer; April Audia, Actress; Jim Hurley, Actor; Kevin Spirtas, Actor/Singer; Linda Purl, Actress/Singer; Susan Egan, Actress/Singer; Heather MacRae, Actress/Singer; James Graae, Singer/Actor/Comedian

We are a training conservatory in Hollywood for Actors, Technicians, and Costumers. Established in 1929, the theatre training program at Los Angeles City College is one of the oldest and most respected training programs in the country. It has trained countless numbers of students who have gone on to successful careers in the entertainment industry in acting, directing, casting, producing, writing, production coordination, design in lighting, sound, costuming, and sets, technical production, technical direction, owners and directors of various theatre and theatre-oriented businesses and organizations, and numerous technician and costuming specializations. Congratulating the program that has been in existence for over 70 years, President Bill Clinton recently wrote concerning the excellence within the field of the performing arts, "The strength of your organization today exemplifies the ongoing commitment to professionalism that inspired your founders." Graduates from LACC have won numerous awards including recipients of the Academy Award, Emmy Award, Tony Award, and Bravo Award. Its teaching excellence has been heralded by the Kennedy Center/American College Theater Festival, the California Community College Academic Senate, the California Educational Theatre Assoc, the Los Angeles Community College District, the County of Los Angeles, and the City of Los Angeles. Further, the Los Angeles Drama Critics Circle gave LACC a Special Award for ""maintaining consistently high standards of programming and production.

Loyola Marymount University

Ron Marasco, Chair
Theatre Arts Dept.
Loyola Marymount University
Los Angeles,CA 90045
DEPT: (310) 338-2839
(800) 568-4636

3,800 Tot. enr.; competitive
160 Majors; NAST, ATHE
Semester System
T: 31,168
ADM: (310) 338-2750
www.lmu.edu

DEGREES OFFERED

BA in General Theatre (22).. Declare major in freshman year; 2001 granted 25 degrees.

ADMISSION & FINANCIAL INFORMATION

SAT - 1100 combined.

FACULTY AND CLASSES OFFERED

6 Full-Time, 8 Part-Time: 4 PhD, 2 MFA/MA; 3 Staff

A. (2 FT, 1 PT) Theatre History-5/Y; Dramatic Lit-1/Y' Dramatic Criticism-1/O; Shakes-1/O; Playwriting-1/O

B. (4 FT, 2 PT) Acting-5/Y; Voice/Speech-2/Y; Movement-1/Y; Singing-X; Directing-2/Y

C. (2 FT) Principles of Design-1/Y; Costume Design-2/Y; Set Design-2/Y; Lighting Design-2/Y; Cost Construction-Y; Make-up-1/Y

FACILITIES & PRODUCTIONS

MAINSTAGE: 174 seats, computerized lighting
   3 Fac dir/des, 1 Guest dir/des prods

SECOND STAGE: 100 seats, electronic lighting

Various number of productions.

Facility was built in 1961: scene shop, costume shop, 2 classrooms.

A non-departmental, student-run organization presents 4 productions per year in which dept. majors participate. 3 student-written plays produced in the last two years.

DESCRIPTION

The Theatre Arts curriculum is planned to provide a broad education in the humanities, and to develop in the student an appreciation of self and the universality of the human experience. Participation in the performing arts experience is central to this work. All students pursue a general theatre program. Some students may elect to emphasize work in the areas of acting, directing, playwriting, history/literature/ criticism or design/technical theatre. The Theatre Arts Program is accredited by the National Association of Schools of Theatre.

Occidental College

Susan Gratch, Chair
Department of Theatre
1600 Campus Road
Los Angeles,CA 90041-3314
DEPT: (323) 259-2771
beatrice@oxy.edu
ADMISSIONS: 1600 Campus Road
(800) 825-5262

1,600 Total Enr.; h. compet.
Semester System
50 Majors
T: $34,400/$9,500 R&B
FAX: (323) 341-4987
SMALL PROGRAM
www.oxy.edu
FAX: (323) 341-4875

DEGREES OFFERED

AB in Theatre Major (50). However students empasize specific areas of interest within the Theater major. Those are Acting, Directing, Playwriting, Design and Arts Administration.
Declare major in 2nd or 3rd year; 1997 granted 9 degrees.

ADMISSION & FINANCIAL INFORMATION

Contact admissions for requirements; admit 53% of applicants to instuitution. Financial aid and Occidental schols. available to the general student body.

FACULTY AND CLASSES OFFERED

6 Full-Time: 1 PhD, 5 MFA/MA; 1 Staff

A. (3 FT) Intro to Theatre-1/Y; Dramatic Lit-1/Y; Theatre Hist.-1/Y; Shakes-1/O; Playwriting-1/Y

B. (3 FT) Acting-4/X; Movement-1/O; Singing-X; Directing-1/Y; Stage Combat-1/O; Mus. Theatre-1/O; Dance-8/X

C. (2 FT) Principles of Des-1/Y; Set Des-1/Y; Tech Prod.-1/Y; Lighting Des-1/Y; Cost Des./Construct.-1/O; Scene Painting-1/O; Stage Mgmt-can be done as an independent study

D. (1 FT) Arts Management-2/Y

FACILITIES & PRODUCTIONS

MAINSTAGE: 400 seats, fly space, computerized lighting. 3 prods: 2 Fac dir/des, 1 Guest dir, 2 Guest des; budget $4-6,000

SECOND STAGE: 400+ seats, computerized lighting
   6 UG dir/des prods; budget $300-600
   1-4 UG dir/des Workshops/Readings; budget $100-200

Facility was built in 1988, includes scene shop, costume shop, 1 design studio, 1 rehearsal studio

A non-departmental, student-run organization presents 10 productions per year. 12 student-written plays produced in the last two years.

DESCRIPTION

Noted Faculty: John Bouchard, Directing, Acting, Shakespeare; Alan Freeman, Acting, Musical Theater, Playwriting; Susan Gratch, Design, Theatre History.

Guest Artists: Charlie Stratton, Director; Jamie Angell, Director; O-Lam Jones, Sound Des.; Bones Malone, Sound Design; A.C. Weary, Stage Combat + Choreog.; John Ivo Gilles, Scenic Des.; Danny Michaels, Choreographer, Alex Ebben, Cost. Design.

The Theater Department at Occidental College provides students one of the country's finest undergraduate theater programs, featuring indoor and outdoor facilities unrivalled in both beauty and flexibility. Students are challenged to become accomplished actors, directors, playwrights and designers; and, when possible, to master many disciplines. In addition to full-time faculty, guest professionals from various Los Angeles theaters, and from throughout the world, are brought to campus each year through the Benjamin H. Culley Fund for Theater. They complete the extended family of theater arts working each year with Occidental students. Students study theater at Occidental with great joy and seriousness, and over the years many Occidental graduates have gone on to successful careers in theater and film.

PCPA Theaterfest

Mark Booher, Conserv Dir,Actg
Michael Dempsey,Conserv Dir,Tech
PCPA Theatrefest
800 S College Dr
Santa Maria,CA 93454-6399
DEPT: (805) 928-7731x4115
www.pcpa.org

95 Total Enr.;high compet.
Semester System
95 Majors; U/RTA
T: $800/approx.
O-ST T: $6000/approx
FAX: (805) 928-7506

DEGREES OFFERED

Certificate in Actor Training (65), Certificate in Technical Theatre Training (25), Actor Intern (4), Technical Theatre Intern (15). Declare major in first year.

ADMISSION & FINANCIAL INFORMATION

Audition, interview, mission statement, letters of recommendation, transcripts, portfolio for technical students, callback for 2 yr. acting and tech programs. Admit 45 out of 500 to institution/yr.

FACULTY AND CLASSES OFFERED

3 Full Time, 28 Part-Time: 1 PhD, 22 MFA/MA, 8 Prof. w/out adv. degree.
Actor Training:
(1 FT) Theatre History-2/Y (1 FT. 16 PT) Acting-4/Y; Shakes-2/Y; Movement-2/Y; Voice/Speech-2/Y; Dance-2/Y; Stage Combat-2/Y; Musical Theatre-4/Y; Audtion-2/Y.
Technical Theater Training:
(1 FT) Theater History-1/Y; (1 FT, 10PT) Theater Tech: Scenic-2/Y; Costumes-2/Y; Lighting-2/Y; Sound-2/Y; Stage Mgmt-2/Y; Tech Prod-10/Y.

FACILITIES AND PRODUCTIONS

MAINSTAGE: 448 seats, computerized lighting. 3 prods: 2 Fac dir, 2 Fac des, 1 Guest dir,1 Guest des; budget $12,000-20,000

SECOND STAGE: 185 seats, black box,1- 2 prods,1-2 Fac Dir,1-2 Fac Des, budget $5,000-8,000

THIRD STAGE:(SUMMER ONLY) 712 Seat Outdoor Amphitheater, 5 Prods. 3-4 Fac Dir, 1-2 Guest Dir, 3-4 Fac. Des. 1-2 Guest Des; Budget $12,000-20,000.

Facility was built in 1970, renovated in 1998; includes scene shop, costume shop, prop shop, welding area, sound studio, dance studio, rehearsal studios, design studios, classrooms.

Affiliation with professional equity company (PCPA Theaterfest). Students appear on stage in productions with a core company of Artists-in-Residence and Guest Artists. Resident and Guest Actors, Directors, and Designers teach Conservatory classes from Sept-May.

DESCRIPTION

Noted Faculty: Patricia Troxel,Shakespeare; Mark Booher, Shakespeare/Stage Combat; Michael Dempsey, Theatre Tech; Roger DeLaurier, Acting Styles; Jack Shouse, Theatre History; Kevin Robison, Singing Technique; Judy Ryerson, Costuming; Walter TJ Clissen, Sound. Tim Hogan, Properties.

Guest Artists: Michael Gruber, Actor; Risa Brainin, Dir; Patrick Kerr, Actor; Michael Klaers, Lighting; Melinda Parrett, Actor; Jon Kretsu, Dir; David Carey Foster, Actor; Brian Herndon, Actor; Heidi Hoffer, Scenic Des; Erik Stein, Actor; Kitty Balay, Actor.

Located on California's Central Coast mid-way between Los Angeles and San Francisco, the Pacific Conservatory of the Performing Arts was founded in 1964 at Allan Hancock College in Santa Maria as a professional theater training program guided by the philosophy that the way to learn theater is to do theater. Students in both acting and technical theater disciplines work with professional artists-in-residence, who serve as mentors and colleagues, to present an average of 10-12 productions every year. PCPA Theaterfest productions are staged year-round in 448-seat Marian Theater and 180-seat Severson Theater in Santa Maria. The 5-month long summer season runs in the Marian Theater in Santa Maria, and an open-air 708-seat Festival Theater in Solvang, built in 1974. The award-winning regional theatre company consists of visiting theater professionals from around the U.S. and abroad, artists-in-residence, professional staff, and students who work together to produce winter and summer seasons that explore the full spectrum of theater, from classics and musicals to new works. In addition, PCPA's Outreach Tour project brings Theater to schools and community centers throughout the Central Coast region. Now celebrating its 40th anniversary, PCPA Theaterfest is, as the LA Times noted, "an essential landmark on the theatrical map" and attracts a national audience.

Pomona College

James Taylor, Chair
Dept. of Theatre and Dance
Pomona College
Claremont, CA 91711
www.pomona.edu
ADMISSIONS: Above address.
admissions@pomona.edu

1,545 Total Enr.; h. compet.
25 Majors/ATHE
T: $$33,932/$11,748 R&B
DEPT: (909) 621-8186
FAX: (909) 621-8780
(909) 621-8733

MAJORS & DEGREES OFFERED

BA in Liberal Arts (22). Theatre Major - 0 Musical Theatre, 5 Design, 5 General, 12 Performance. Declare major junior year.

ADMISSION & FINANCIAL INFORMATION

Avg. SAT of 1420; 30% of applicants are accepted to the institution; no special req's for theatre program. Admission to the Claremont College as a student lets you apply for summer internship assistance. The college gives no special theatre scholarship.

FACULTY AND CLASSES OFFERED

10 FT, 8 PT: 4 PhD, 3 MA/MFA, 6 Staff.
A. (4 FT, 1 PT) Dramatic Lit.-2/X; Dramatic Criticism-1/X; Playwriting-1/O; Theatre History-3/Y; Theory-1/Y; Women Playwrights-1/Y
B. (4 FT, 1 PT) Movement-3/Y; Mime, etc.-1/Y; Singing-X; Directing-1/Y; Stage Combat-1/O; Dance-15/Y
C. (2 FT, 6 PT) Set Design-1/Y; Cost Des-1/Y; Tech Prod'n-1/Y; Lighting Des-1/Y; Cost. Constr-1/Y; Visual Arts of the Theatre-2/Y

FACILITIES AND PRODUCTIONS

MAINSTAGE: 330 seats, fly space, computerized lighting.
  2 Fac dir, 4 Fac des, 4 Guest des prods: budget $6,000-9,000

SECOND STAGE: 150 seats, fly space, computer lighting; budget
  2 Fac dir, 4 Fac des, 4 Guest des prods; budget $3,000-5,000
  Workshops/Readings: 1 Fac dir, 1 Guest dir, 1 UG des

Facility was built in 1992, renovated in 1998; facilities include scene shop, costume shop, prop shop, welding shop, sound studio, movement/dance studio, rehearsal studio, design studio, classroom.

A non-departmental, student-run producing org. presents 4-6 productions during the school year; dept. majors generally participate.

DESCRIPTION

Noted Faculty: Betty Bernhard, Indian Theatre, Women Playwrights; Thomas Leabhart, Mime; Leonard C. Pronko, Asian Theatre and Dance; Carol Davis, Nepal & History; Jim Taylor, Lights & Scenery; Sherry Linnell, Costumes.

Guest Artists: San Francisco Mime Troupe; Simona Giurgea, Actress; Gail Shapiro, Actress; Kailash Pandya, Dir and Kottakal Sasidharan Nair, Choreographer from the Darpana Acad of Arts in India; Diosdado "Boots" Pascual, Actor/Dir.

The Department of Theatre and Dance embodies the liberal arts education. Through the synthesis of body, mind, and spirit, theatre and dance celebrate the community of world cultures. In an atmosphere of freedom, discipline, and passion, students, faculty, and staff encounter intellectually and artistically great creations of the human spirit both in the classroom and in production. Theatre at Pomona College serves students from the five undergraduate colleges at Claremont. It includes the study of performance, design and technology, directing, and theatre history/dramatic literature. Theatre students become proficient in devising creative solutions to complex problems; they also develop sensitivity to the interpersonal relationships inherent in the collaborative process. Thus, they are prepared for a wide variety of careers in organizations and enterprises that value these qualities. While encouraging such development in all its students, the department also prepares concentrators for further study on the graduate or professional level. Many graduates of the department have become successful members of the professional community as actors, directors, designers, writers, teachers, and administrators.

San Diego State University

Randy Reinholz, Interim Director
Department of Theatre
San Diego State University
San Diego, CA 92182-7455
DEPT: (619) 594-5091
FAX: (619) 594-7431
ADMISSIONS: 5500 Campanile Drive
admissions@sdsu.edu

35,000 Tot. Enr.; not compet.
Semester System
245 Majors; NAST; ATHE
T: $3,428; $10,904 R&B
O-ST T: add $339/unit

(619) 594-6336
www.sdsu.edu

MAJORS & DEGREES OFFERED

BA in Drama (245). Emphases in General Drama, Children's Drama, Performance, Design for Drama, Design for TV & Film, Single Subject Teaching Credential; MFA in Design and Technical Theatre, Musical Theatre. Declare major in first year;

ADMISSION & FINANCIAL INFORMATION

High school graduate, grades of C or better in all courses incollege prep subjects; 92% applicants accepted for UG; Audition (Portfolio)/Interview required for Grad admission; numerous institutional and theatre scholarships. A minimum 3.5 GPA is required. All applications are made through the campus Scholarship Office.

FACULTY AND CLASSES OFFERED

13 Full-Time, 14 Part-Time (several in Creative Drama/Children's Drama): 9 Ph.D/DFA, 18 MFA/MA; 8 Staff

A. (4 FT, 4 PT) Intro to Theatre-1/Y; Dramatic Lit-1/Y; Theatre History-2/Y; Playwriting-1/Y; Theatre & Western Civ.-1/Y; Children's Drama-4/Y; Creative Drama-2/Y.

B. (4 FT, 3 PT) Acting-4/Y; Voice/Speech-8/Y; Movement-5/Y; Singing-3/Y; Musical Theatre 7/Y; Directing-8/Y; Stage Combat-1/Y; Audition Techniques-1/Y; Accents/Dialects-2/Y

C. (5 FT) Prins of Des-6/Y; Set Des-8/Y; Cost Des-4/Y; Ltg Des-3/Y; Tech Prod'n; Cost Constr-2/Y; Cost Hist-2/Y; Make-up-1/Y; Stage Mgmt-1/Y; Des Communication-1/Y; Aesthetics for Stage-1/Y; Prod'n Synthesis-1/Y; Scene Painting-1/Y; Prop Design-1/Y

D. Arts Management-1/Y; Marketing Publicity for the Theatre

FACILITIES & PRODUCTIONS

MAINSTAGE: 500 seats, fly space, computerized lighting
4-5 prods: Dir./Des. by fac, guest, grad or UG; budget $7300-$8200

SECOND STAGE: 175 seats, computerized lighting
4 prods: Dir./Des. faculty, guest, grad or UG; budget $3300-$3800. 5 prods: 4 Fac dir,1 Gr dir; 1 Fac des, 4 UG des; budget $747-1125

Facility built in 1969; last renovated in 1989. Includes scene shop, costume shop, prop shop, welding shop, rehearsal studio, design studios, classrooms.

DESCRIPTION

Noted Faculty: Ralph Funicello, Scenic Designer.

Guest Artists: Edward Albee, Playwright; Martin Benson, Director; Ralph Funicello, Set Designer; A.R. Gurney, Playwright; Ming Cho Lee, Set Designer; Emily Mann, Director.

The BA program is based on a firm liberal arts foundation and provides Drama majors with initial experiences in the applied theatre arts. The MA program is based on studies in dramatic literature, theatre history, theory, aesthetics, and criticism, and prepares students for academic and research careers. The MFA program provides students with training in performance, directing, and design for the various theatre professions. The Drama Department seeks to provide students with tools that are invaluable to the thoughtful citizen and the well-rounded theatre artist alike. The department affirms a special commitment to the production of original works, to collaborative and interdisciplinary efforts, and to the teaching of applied skills enabling students to express themselves with fluency and eloquence in all areas of their chosen field — the theatre.

San Francisco State University

Yuki Goto, Chair
Dept of Theatre Arts
1600 Holloway Avenue
San Francisco State University
San Francisco, CA 94132
DEPT: (415) 338-1341
http://www.sfsu.edu/~tha/
ADMISSIONS: 1600 Holloway Ave.
UG: (415) 338-1113;

28,950 Total Enr.
Semester System
300 Majors; NAST, ATHE,U/RTA
T: UG $1,260/sem;
    Grad $1,573/sem
O-ST T: $339 per unit/sem
$9,320 (est.) R&B
Adm: (415) 338-2017
Grad (415) 338-2234

DEGREES GRANTED

BA in Theatre Arts (350); MA in Drama (9); MFA in Design(5). Declare major in first year; 2007 degrees granted 45 BA - 2 MA - 2 MFA.

ADMISSION & FINANCIAL INFORMATION

Generally admit 100% of UG applicants to theatre program, 20% to Grad program. SAT or ACT, high school degree, grades of C or better on average. MFA portfolio for des, no special requirements for UG.

FACULTY AND CLASSES OFFERED

13 Full-Time;10 PT, 5 PHD/DFA, 11 MA/MFA; 7 professionals w/o adv degree, 5 staff

A. (4 FT, 2 PT) Dramatic Lit; Dramatic Criticism; Playwriting; Theatre History
B. (6 FT, 3 PT) Acting; Movement; Directing; Voice/Speech
C. (3 FT, 4 PT) Design; Production; Stage Management
D. (1 PT) Theatre Management

FACILITIES AND PRODUCTIONS

MAIN STAGE (LITTLE THEATRE): 250 seats, fly space, computerized lighting
    4 prods: 3 Fac dir, 1 GA dir
STUDIO THEATRE: 95 seats, computerized lighting. All prod student designed; 4 prods: 2 Fac dir, 1 Grad dir
Brown Bag: 50 seats, black box theatre, weekly workshops. All prods student designed.
Facility includes scene shop, costume shop, props shop, 2 movement/dance studio, design studio, classrooms.
A non-departmental student-run organization presents 1 production per year in which majors participate. Several student-written plays have been produced in theatre workshop.

DESCRIPTION

Noted Faculty: Larry Eilenberg, Theatre Historian; Mohammad Kowsar, Joel Schechter, Critic, Historian; John Wilson, Scenic Designer; Camille Howard, Actress, Critic; Rhonnie Washington, Actor/Director; William Peters, Yuki Goto, Directors; Carlos Baron, Actor; Joan Arhelger, Light Design; Roy Conboy, Director & Playwright; Todd Roehrman, Costume Designer; Jo Tomalin, Actor/Dir; Barbara Damashek, Writer/Dir

Guest Artists: Jacie Wang, Beijing Opera performer; Mark Jackson, Writer/Dir; Tracy Ward, Director; Brandon Adams, Music Dir

The Department of Theatre Arts offers a comprehensive program of both practical and theoretical courses for undergraduate and graduate students whose interests center of various aspects of educational and professional theatre. The curriculum provides the student with a foundation for advanced study in the dramatic arts, for teaching, or for a career in professional theatre. As a center for the training of future theatre artists, the department is committed to introducing a diversity of theatrical traditions and cultures to students. The department employs its three dedicated theatre spaces and it's one shared theatre space as learning laboratories, in which students collaborate with faculty and guest professionals. Graduates of the program are prominent in professional theatre throughout the nation, with positions of leadership in theatre, television, film, and theatre education.

San Jose State University

Michael H. Adams, Chair
Department of Theatre Arts
San Jose State University
One Washington Square
San Jose, CA 95192-0098
(408) 924-4530
http://www.sjsu.edu
ADMISSIONS: Admission & Records, SJSU, SJ, CA 95192

27,000 Total Enr.; not compet.
Semester System
590 Majors; NAST, ATHE
T: $1,816 per sem.

FAX: 408-924-4574

DEGREES GRANTED

BA in Drama (90), Radio, TV, Film (370); MA in Theatre Arts (35); BA in Single Subject Teaching Cred. (20), Musical Theatre (minor) (15), Drama (minor), (60). Declare major in first year.

ADMISSION & FINANCIAL INFORMATION

High School Diploma, grade of "C" or better in college prep courses; 48% accepted by institution; Theatre Program admits 1 of 2 UG applicants, 1 of 5 Grad applicants; Interview is required for Grad applicants. The Theatre Arts Dept. has the largest scholarship program outside athletics. Special scholarships target new theatre majors, performers, technicians, and designers. Financial need and GPA are considerations. Dept. administers 20 scholarships which support student grants between $50 and $500 per semester. In addition, there are paid UG and Grad assistantships which pay $1,200-1,500.

FACULTY AND CLASSES OFFERED

13 Full-Time, 8 Part-Time: 6 PhD, 8 MFA/MA; 6 Prof. w/out adv. degree, 8 Staff

A. (5 FT, 1 PT) Introduction to Theatre-5/Y; Dramatic Lit- 2/Y; Dramatic Criticism-2/Y; Theatre History-3/Y; Shakes-4/X; Playwriting-2/Y; Screenwriting-3/Y
B. (3 FT, 5 PT) Acting-12/Y; Voice/Speech-3/Y; Mvmt-10/Y; Singing-4/Y; Musical Th.-4/Y; Directing-4/Y; Stage Combat-1/O; Mime, etc.-1/O; Storytelling-6/Y; Voice Over-2/Y; Acting for Media-4/Y
C. (3 FT, 1 PT) Principles of Design-2/Y; Set Design-2/Y; Lighting Design-4/Y; Tech Production-2/Y; Cost Construction-2/Y; Make-up-3/Y; Stage Mgmt-1/Y; TV + Vidoe Prod.-6/Y; Computer Graphic Design-2/Y.
D. (1 FT, 1 PT) Arts Management-3/Y; Marketing/Promotion-2/Y; Box Ofc. Procedure-2/Y

FACILITIES & PRODUCTIONS

MAINSTAGE: 400 seats, fly space, computerized lighting
    4 prods: 2 Fac dir 8 Fac des, 1 Guest dir, 3 Guest des, 1 UG dir, 5 UG des; budget $6,000-10,000

SECOND STAGE: 160 seats, computerized lighting
  5 prods: 1 Fac dir, 5 Fac des, 1 Guest dir/des, 3 UG dir, 5 UG des; budget $2,000-5,000

THIRD STAGE: 60 seats, black box electronic lighting. 9 Workshops/Readings; 1 Fac dir/des, 3 Guest dir/1 Guest des, 1 Grad dir/des, 4 UG dir, 8 UG des; budget $100-2,000

Facility was built in 1954. Includes scene shop, costume shop, prop shop, welding shop, sound studio, CAD facility, 2 video studio, 4 movement/dance studios, 3 rehearsal studios, 2 design studios, 8 classrooms, radio station.

A non-departmental, student-run, producing org. presents 3 prods. per year in which majors participate. 5 student-written plays produced in the last two years.

SJSU has active internship/apprentice programs with a number of Equity companies during the school year. Though required industry internships in the senior year, all theatre arts students work with professional companies including San Jose Repertory Theatre, Theatreworks, KQED, Paramount Great America, Sun Microsystems, American Musical Theatre, The Barn Theatre among many others.

DESCRIPTION

Noted Faculty: Robert Jenkins, Directing, Storytelling, Acting; David Kahn, Directing, Th. History, Scriptwriting; Ethel Walker, Th. Hist. & Lit.; Amy Glazer, Acting, Directing; Betty Poindexter, Cost. & Make-Up; Karl Toepfer, Th. Hist., Perfomance; Stanley Baran, Media Theory; Kim Massey, Media Production; Randy Earle, Lighting, Sound; Jim Culley, Scene Des.; Buddy Butler, Acting.

Guest Artists: Kelly, Lynch, Film Actress; Ruby Dee, Actress; Tony Taccone, Statge Director; Ronnie Gilbert, Actress; Ed Bullins, Playwright; Linda Hoy, Actress; Wendy Malick, Actress; Timothy Near, Director; Joe Ragey, Designer; Mitch Glazer, Screenwriter; Mike Adasm, Radio; Babak Sarrafan, Film.

The mission of the Theatre Arts Department is to prepare students for successful careers in performance and media. We see this as indistinguishable from our parallel mission: to nurture ethical, thinking, and compassionate human beings. To this end, and given our location in the heart of Silicon Valley, the Theatre Arts programs in drama, radio, television, film and multimedia are committed to the development of artists, educators and scholars of the highest caliber and offer strong pre-professional training supported by a broadly-based liberal arts education. Studying and producing dramatic performance in different media and in different cultural contexts prepares our students to participate in a highly complex society where their acquired skills in critical studies will serve their career objectives whether in the broadly defined fields of theatre and media or in other capacities.

Santa Clara University

Aldo Billingslea, Chair
Theatre and Dance Dept.
Santa Clara University
Santa Clara, CA 95053
DEPT: (408) 554-4989
E-mail: abillingslea@scu.edu

8,377 Total Enr.; h. competitive
Quarter System
89 Majors; ATHE
T: $30,900/$10,380 R&B
FAX: (408) 554-5199
www.scu.edu/theatre

ADMISSIONS: SCU Undergrad. Admissions, Varsi Hall, 500 El Camino Real, Santa Clara, CA 95053   www.scu.edu/ugrad
(408) 554-4700

DEGREES OFFERED

BA in Theatre Arts; Dance. Declare major in junior year; 2007 granted 17 degrees.

ADMISSION & FINANCIAL INFORMATION

HS transcript (3.6 Avg. GPA), SAT (1210 Avg.).No aud for Liberal Arts Program. Accept 65% to institution; Theatre and Dance Scholarships range from approx $10,000 to $15,000. Auditions and portfolio presentations on-site or by video tape in January prior to desired entrance term to the university. Scholarship auds Jan 12

FACULTY AND CLASSES OFFERED

13 Full-Time, 6 Part-Time: 3 PhD, 13 MFA/MA; 3 professionals w/o adv degree; 2 Staff

A. (3 FT. 1 PT) Intro to Theatre-1/Y; Theatre History-3/Y; Shakes-2/XY; Dramatic Lit-2/O; Dramatic Criticism-1/Y; Playwriting-3/Y

B. (5 FT, 5 PT) Acting-4/Y; Voice/Speech-2/Y; Musical Theatre-Y; Movement-1/Y; Singing-3/Y; Dance-4/Y; Mime, Mask, Commedia, Circus-1/O; Directing-1/O

C. (4 FT) Principles of Design-2/Y; Set Design-2/Y; Costume Design-2/Y; Ltg Des-2/Y; Costume Const-1/Y; Make-up-1/O; Stage Mgmt-1/O

D. (1 FT) Arts Management-1/O

FACILITIES AND PRODUCTIONS

MAINSTAGE: 500 seats, fly space, comput. ltg.
  3 prods: 2 Fac dir, 3 Fac des, 1 Guest dir

SECOND STAGE: 100 seats, computerized & electronic lighting. 1 prod: 1 Fac dir, 1 Fac des

Facility was built in 1975; includes scene shop, cost. shop, make-up room, sound studio, 2 dressing rooms with showers, welding shop, 2 dance studios, 2 rehearsal studios, 3 classrooms.

A non-departmental student run producing organization showing 2-3 shows per year in which majors participate.

DESCRIPTION

Noted Faculty: Barbara M. Fraser, Theatre and American Musical Theatre; Derek Duarte, MFA Lighting; Jerald Enos, MFA Scenic Des; Aldo Billingslea, MFA Acting; Fred Tolleni, Phd Theatre; Michael Zampelli, Phd Theatre; Barbara Murray, MFA Costume Des; David Sword, MFA Tech Theatre; Brian Thorstenson, MFA Playwriting

Guest Artists: Tracy Ward, Director; Michael X. Martin Acting; Tom Gough, Directing

The Department of Theatre and Dance celebrates creativity of the human spirit, offering a well-rounded education leading to a Bachelor of Art's degree in Theatre Arts. This study involves both academic disciplines and creative processes. These include practice and analysis of skills required in the performing arts; critical evaluation of literature, history, and theory of drama and dance; collaboration in production and public presentation of performance. Through lectures, studio courses, labs, and productions, students work closely with faculty and staff mentors. The Theatre program offers coordinated courses in acting, design, technical production, directing, dramatic literature, and theatre history. The Dance program emphasizes modern dance and choreography, with additional training in jazz and ballet. Students within the program will have a well-rounded foundation but may focus their study on any of the above areas.

Sonoma State University

Paul Draper, Chair	8,000; competitive
Theater Department	Semester System
Sonoma State University	65 Majors; ATHE
1801 E. Cotati Avenue	T: $3,946
Rohnert Park, CA 94928	O-ST T: $12,082
DEPT: 707-664-2235	R&B$9,730
	SMALL PROGRAM

www.sonoma.edu/Depts/PerformingArtsTheatre/Theatre.htm
ADMISSIONS: 1801 E. Cotati Ave. Rohnert Park, CA 94928
www.student.outreach@sonoma.edu
(707) 664-2474   (707) 664-2060

DEGREES OFFERED

BA in Theater Arts/Acting (47), Theater Arts Dance (14), Theater Arts/Technical Theatre (8), Theatre Generalist; Interdisciplinary Studies (Drama and Music) Declare major in first year.

ADMISSION & FINANCIAL INFORMATION

Res. Req's.: SAT 2900, ACT 694. Non-Res. Req's.: SAT 3502, ACT 842. Accept 85.2% to institution; No special req's. for program, but interviews are encouraged to meet w/applicants for assistance; Accept all applicants to program; University schols., $200-2,000, based on achievement, scholarship and narrative; Evert B. Person schols. $500-2,000 talent awards based on audition and interview.

FACULTY AND CLASSES OFFERED

5 Full-Time, 6 Part-Time: 8 MFA/MA, 5 Prof. w/o adv. degree; 6 Staff

General: (1 FT, 1 PT) Intro History of Drama and Dance; Art of Theatr; Woeld Theatre; History of Drama; Shakespeare; Contemporary Plays and Playwrights; Directing; Advanced Directing; Drama Ensemble; Thaatre in Acting; Perf. Analysis and Criticism; Research; Special Topics; teaching Assistantship.

Acting: Acting Levels I, II, III; Comedy Improv; Intermediate Acting Blcok (Physical Theatre, Shakespeare); Advanced Acting Block (20th Cen. Non-Realism/On-Camera and New Work Exposure); Voice and Speech for the Actor; Audition Technique; Musical Theatre Worekshop; Private Voice Tutorial.

Dance: (1 FT, 3 PT) Dance Fundamentals; Dance Styles; Beg. Ballet; Ballet for Modern Dance; Dance Technique; Choreography; Dance Ensemble; Inter. Dance Block; Adv. Dance Block; Anatomy for Dancers; Hist. of Dance; Dancers of the World; Teaching/Direction for Dancers; Dance for Children

Production/Management: (2 FT) Beg. Theatre: Stagecraft/Lighting/Costumes/Scenery; Stage Management; Scene Painting; Design for Stage; Theories; History of Ornament; Theatre Management

FACILITIES & PRODUCTIONS

MAINSTAGE: 500 seats, fly space, computerized lighting. 2 Fac dir, 1 Fac des, 2 Guest dir, 3 Guest des prods: $10-50,000

SECOND STAGE: 300 seats, electronic lighting
2 prods: 1 Fac dir, 1 Guest dir; $4,000-5,000

THIRD STAGE: 99 seats, black box . 20 UG dir/des Workshops/Readings; budget $250-700

Facility built in 1990, includes scene, costume, prop shops; sound studio, 2 dance studios, video studio, rehearsal studio, design studio.

A non-departmental, student-run organization presents 5-10 productions per year in which majors participate. 4 student-written plays produced in the last two years.

DESCRIPTION

Noted Faculty: Nancy Lyons, Modern Dance; Judy Navas, Theatre History/Dramatic Lit/Acting/Drama Ensemble. Assistant Professor: Anthony Bish, Design/Technical Theatre, Assoc Prof: Paul Draper, Acting/Dir/Hist/Crit./Dance Ensemble; Danielle Cain, Audition/Art of theatre Acting; Tori Truss, Acting/Art of Theatre/Dir/Dance Ensemble; Stephanie Hunt, Acting/Voice, Patrick Toebe, Design/Tech/Stagecraft.

Guest Artists: Migdalia Cruz, Clair Potter, Melissa Fenley, Andre Bernard, George Guim, Kwaku Daddy, Raquel Lopez, Eric Bentley, Peggy Hackney, Kathleen Hermesdorf, Marcella Lorca Kingman, Diablo Mundo, 15 Head: A Theatre Lab, Mary Coleman, Harry Watters, Jr., Roberto Varea, Amanda McTigue, Jason Sherbundy; Word for Word.

At Sonoma State University we are committed to creating, teaching, and learning about theatre that enlightens as well as entertains, that explores the values and ideas of many cultures and times, and that contributes to the artistic and personal growth of both participants and audience. We work to create a teaching/learning environment that is a model for the collaborative work of theatre and life, in which student and teacher are equally important and respected. Theatre artists—dancers, actors, directors, playwrights, choreographers, designers, and technicians—are all engaged in various ways of exploring, shaping, and communicating experience. We believe that theatre can be a crucible in which values and beliefs, both personal and societal, can be tested. As we enter into the small world of a theatrical production, temporarily assuming the reality of the experiences; personalities and beliefs of the characters and situations we are bringing to life, we are presented with unique opportunities to grow in empathy, compassion and understanding. Making theatre helps us discover who we are and what we truly believe, not just about theater, but about life. At SSU we respect tradition, but we also cultivate the newest and most innovative approaches to dance, drama and theatre technology. We actively encourage and support the development of new work by both students and faculty.

University of California - Davis

Peter Lichtenfels, Chair
Dept. of Theatre & Dance
22 Wright Hall, One Shields Ave.
UC/Davis
Davis, CA 95616
DEPT: (530) 752-0888
http://theatredance.ucdavis.edu
ADMISSIONS: Undergraduate Admissions and Outreach Services, 178
Mark Hall, UC/Davis, CA 95616
(530) 752-2971   FAX: (530) 752-1280
www.admissions.ucdavis.edu/
undergraduateadmissions@ucdavis.edu

24,866 Total Enr.. compet.
120 Majors; ATHE
Quarter System
T: $8,109 R&B $11,533
O-ST T: $$27,177 R&B $11,533
FAX: (530) 752-8818
nhmedovoy@ucdavis.edu

DEGREES OFFERED

BA in Dramatic Art (w/emphasis in Dance or Theatre); MFA in Acting,
Design, Dance, Directing; PhD in Performance and Culture; Declare
major in Jr. year.

ADMISSION & FINANCIAL INFORMATION

Min. GPA 3.3 plus SAT/ACT scores. Graduate students apply
through the department. 63% of applics accepted by instit. No spe-
cial req. for admission to UG program; Grad. req. audition, interview;
8-10 out of 150 applics. admitted to MFA program, 5 out of 30 to
Ph.D. All grad applics at least 3.0 GPA. Ph.D: GRE scores (no min.),
writing sample (15-25 pp).

FACULTY AND CLASSES OFFERED

12 Full-Time, 8 Part-Time:5 PhD,6 MFA; 11 Staff.

A. Performance and Culture-3/Y; Intro to Theatre-3/Y; Theatre
    History/Dramatic Lit-9/Y; Playwriting-2Y; Dance History-1/Y;
    Introduction to Dance-1/Y; African American Dance History-1/Y

B. Acting-7/Y; Voice/Speech-1/Y; Movement-3/Y; Singing-1/X;
    Directing-4/Y; Dance-12/Y; Choreography-5/Y

C. Principles of Design-2/Y; Costume Design-1/Y; Set Design-2/Y;
    Lighting Design-1/Y; Sound Design-1/Y; Make-up-1/Y; Stage
    Management-2/Y; Tech Prod-2/Y

FACILITIES & PRODUCTIONS

MAINSTAGE: 470 seats, prosc., fly space, computerized lighting
    8 prods: 4 Fac dir, 4 Guest dir, 6 Guest des, 2 UG des; budget
    $3,000-10,000

SECOND STAGE: 250 seats, arena stage, computerized lighting
    2 prods: 2 UG dir/des; budget $600-1,000

THIRD STAGE: Wyatt Theatre: 220 seats, thrust stage, light grid, sound,
    flexible.

FOURTH STAGE: 150 seats, black box, computerized lighting

FIFTH STAGE: 100 seats, flex stage

SIXTH STAGE: Small prosc., seats 54, lab

Facility built in 1967, constant upgrades as needed. Includes Scene,
    costume, prop shop, welding shop, sound studio, 3 rehearsal
    studios, design studio, 7 classrooms.

7 student-written plays produced in the last two years.

Connection with Sacramento Theatre Company (Equity), Tahoe
    Shakespeare Festival,(summers only) Magic Theatre, B Street
    Theatre. The department maintains associations with several
    local and area professional theatre companies. Opportunities are
    available for graduate student actors (usually third year intern-
    ships) and undergraduates (acting and stage managing).

Working with several companies allows us to place students in
significant roles/positions because we are not limited to the con-
straints of a single company.

DESCRIPTION

Noted Faculty: John Iacovelli; Maggie Morgan; Thomas
    Munn, Des; Sarah Pia Anderson, Peggy Shannon,
    Directing; Barbara Sellers-Young, Movement,
    Intercultural Body; Sheldon Deckelbaum, Peter
    Lichtenfels, Acting; Jade McCutcheon, playwriting;
    Jon Rossini, Lynette Hunter, Perf Studies; Della
    Davidson, David Grenke, Dance; Darrell Winn, State
    Mgmt.

Guest Artists: Ray Tadio, Dance; Marlies Yearby, Dance;
    Howard Brenton, Playwriting; Joseph Chaikin, Acting;
    Joan Holden, Playwriting; William Gaskill, Directing;
    Lea Anderson, Dance; Yvonne Brewster, Directing,
    Acting; Pip Simons, Acting.

The UC Davis Department of Theatre and Dance provides
students with an appreciation and understanding of per-
formance and its role in relationship to culture and socie-
ty, and also provides a strong foundation in all aspects of
drama, theatre, and dance performance and production.
Undergraduate students can build significant skills in
specific areas while achieving the broad goals of the
degree. The distinctive strengths of the faculty afford spe-
cial preparation for undergraduates who wish to pursue
advanced degrees at the M.A. or Ph.D. level and for those
who wish to enter M.F.A. programs or professional
apprenticeships. The graduate programs train highly
skilled and talented individuals to become professional
actors (MFA) or research scholars (PhD). Excellent theatre
and dance facilities support these programs. The
Grenada Visiting Artists program brings distinguished
professional British theatre artists to the campus each
year who teach and direct in residence. A diverse per-
formance season of ten productions provides several
opportunities for student involvement.

University of California - Irvine

Eli Simon, Chair
Drama Dept
249 Drama
Univ. of California
Irvine, CA 92697-2775
DEPT: (949) 824-6614
fax: (949) 824-3475
drama@uci.edu
ADMISSIONS: Office of Admissions, 204 Administration, University of
California, Irvine CA 92697-1075   (949) 824-6703
www.admissions.uci.edu

25,024 Tot. Enr.; h. compet.
Quarter System;
402 Majors,U/RTA
T: UG- $7,513; G-$9,669.
O-ST T: UG-$26,197; G-$24,630
R&B: $8,408-11,784
http://drama.arts.uci.edu

DEGREES OFFERED

BA in Drama (329); MFA in Acting (25); in Directing (6); in Stage
Management (9); in Scenic Design (6); in Costume Design (6); in
Lighting Design (6); Sound Des (3); Ph.D. in Theatre & Drama (12).
Declare major in first year; 2007 granted 82 UG, 15 Grad degrees.

ADMISSION & FINANCIAL INFORMATION

Combination GPA and ACT/SAT scores; 59.1% of applicants accepted by institution; Theatre program admits 58 out of 100 UG applicants, 26 out of 300 Grad applicants; Audition, Interview and Portfolio (for designers) required for Grad applicants; UCI sponsors scholarships based on need or academic or performance excellence, by department and/or university and/or community service. No special requirements for UG admittance. Interview/Portfolio for des/dir/stage mgrs.

FACULTY AND CLASSES OFFERED

23 FT, 2 PT: 11 PhD, 14 MFA/MA; 3 Staff

A. (6 FT) Intro. to Th. 3/Y; Dramatic Lit-6/Y; Th. History-3/Y; Drama Crit.-6/Y; Shakes-2/Y; Playwriting-1/Y; Other classes offered: 12/Y

B. (10 FT) Acting-10/Y; Voice/Speech-6/Y; Movement- 5/Y; Mime/Mask/Commedia/Circus-1/Y; Singing-3/Y; Musical Theatre-9/Y; Directing-4/Y; Stage Combat-3/Y; Dance-6/O; Film-3/O

C. (7 FT, 2 PT) Set Design-12/Y; Costume Design-12/Y; Lighting Design-12/Y; Technical Production-3/Y; Stage Management-8/Y

FACILITIES AND PRODUCTIONS

MAINSTAGE: 285 seats, fly space, computerized lighting
6 prods: 3 Fac dir, 2 Fac des; 1 GA dir; 10 Grad des; 2 UG des budget $10,000-80,000

SECOND STAGE: 230 seats, computerized lighting
6 prods: 6 Grad dir, 14 Grad des; 2 UG des; budget $5,000-9,000

THIRD STAGE: 165 seats, computerized lighting. 12 workshops/readings: 1 Fac dir, 2 Grad dir, 9 UG dir, 12 UG des; budget $500-$1,000

FOURTH STAGE: 80 seats, black box, computerized lighting

FIFTH STAGE: 60 seat cabaret stage, electronic lighting.

Facility was built in 1969, renovated in 2002; includes scene shop, costume shop, prop shop, sound studio, video studio, 2 dance studios, 2 rehearsal studios, 2 design studios, 4 classrooms. Other facilities are the Acting Studio and the UCI Barn.

Connection with South Coast Repertory (Equity) which operates during the school year. Students have opportunity to intern in the following areas with SCR: acting, design, directing and stage mgmt. Camps and conferences are available.

6-8 non-departmental, student-run productions per school year, majors generally participate.

1 student written play produced in the last two years.

DESCRIPTION

Noted Faculty: Richard Brestoff, Acting for Camera; Dennis Castellano, Musical Theatre; Robert Cohen, Acting Theory; Keith Fowler, Directing; Michael Hooker, Sound Des; Douglas-Scott Goheen, Scenic Design; Eli Simon, Acting; Ian Munro, Theory & Crit; Bryan Reynolds, Theory/Crit; Anthony Kubiak, Theory/Crit.

Guest Artists/Scholars: James Calleri, J.R. Sullivan, Bob Gunton, Terri Ralston, Richard Schechner, Bill Rauch, Catherine Fitzmaurie, Peter Maradudin, John Iacovelli, Joyce Kim Lee.

The mission of the undergraduate program is (1) to provide an atmosphere in which to discover and develop skills in performance-oriented disciplines, as well as in the collaborative artistic process by which performance events are conceived and executed, and (2) to participate in the broader educational mission of the campus in general, focusing on the development of skills in research, analysis, and criticism necessary as preparation for further education at the graduate level or for participation in the complexities of contemporary culture. The mission of the graduate program is (1) to provide intensive and comprehensive professional training enabling graduates to compete for placement in their respective fields (2) to focus and amplify intellectual and critical resources in and beyond theatre and drama studies to inform students' work and provide them with the basis for future careers and (3) to conduct research and experimentation in drama, at the highest levels.

University of California - Los Angeles

Sue-Ellen Case, Director, Chair
Center for Performance Studies
UCLA,102 E.Melnitz,Box 951622
Los Angeles, CA 90095-1622
DEPT: (310) 825-7008
FAX: (310) 825-3383

ADMISSIONS: 103 E. Melnitz
FAX: (310) 825-3383
www.tft.ucla.edu
info @tft.ucla.edu

35,000 Total Enr.; h. compet.
Quarter System
350 Majors
T: $$7,034;
O-ST T: $26,102
R&B $12,420
www.centerperform@ucla.edu
(310) 825-8787
E-mail: ugadm@saonet.ucla.edu

DEGREES OFFERED

BA in Theater (350). MFA in Acting (34); Directing (9); Design & Production (21); Playwriting (7); PhD (11).. Declare major in 1st yr; 2001 granted 53 Grad and 95 UG degrees.

ADMISSION & FINANCIAL INFORMATION

20% of applicants accepted into graduate theatre program, 6% into undergraduate program. UG: 3.0 GPA, audition, 2 letters of reference, interview, portfolio, personal essay required for admission to theater program. Grad: Completion of UG degree, 3 letters of reference, statement of purpose, portfolio, audition, B avg. in last 2 years. PhD: submit evidence of potential as a practicing scholar as indicated by (1) breadth and depth of advanced courseworks in history, theory, criticism, (2) the imagination and quality of scholarly writing and academic achievements, and (3) the grade-point average, GRE scores, awards, scholarships, and fellowships. General schols. based on need and merit.Theater schols. and awards are merit. Theater schols and awards are merit based and req. nominations and rec. by the faculty.

FACULTY AND CLASSES OFFERED

27 Full-Time, 8 Part-Time: 13 PhD, 13 MFA/MA, 15 profs. w/o degree, 60 staff

A. (8 1/2 FT, 3 PT) Intro. to Theatre-1/Y; Dramatic Lit-O; Theatre History-O; Shakes-X; Playwriting-19/O; Dramatic Criticism-5/O

B. (8 1/2 FT, 4 PT) Acting-14/O; Voice/Speech-8/O; Mvmt-8/O; Mus. Th.-X; Directing-20/O; Dance-X; Stage Combat-X; Mime, etc.-O

C. (9 FT, 1 PT) Principles of Design-X; Set Design-5/Y; Costume Design-8/Y; Lighting Design-8/O; Tech Prod.-6/Y; Cost. Constr.4/O; Cost. Hist-3/Y; Make-up-1/Y; Stage Mgmt-1/Y; Sound Design-2/O; Computer-Aided Design-1/O; Playhouse History-1/O; Research in Tech Theatre-1/O; Rendering-6/Y

D. (1 FT) Arts Management-7/O; Box Office Procedure-1/O; Marketing/Promotion-X, Development/Grant Writing-X; Legal-X; Budgeting/Accounting-X

FACILITIES AND PRODUCTIONS

MAINSTAGE: 589 seats, fly space, computerized lighting
  7 prods: 1 Fac dir/des, 3 Guest dir, 1 Guest des, 3 Grad dir, 5 Grad des; budget $7,000-20,000

SECOND STAGE: 200 seats, fly space, computerized lighting
  28 prods: 16 Grad, 12 UG; budget $100-2,500

THIRD STAGE: 100 seats, computerized lighting
  18 Workshops/Readings: 15 Grad, 3 UG; budget nil

Facility built in 1963, and has had constant electronic and computer systems renovation. Facilities include scene shop, costume shop, prop shop, welding shop, 4 rehearsal studios, design studio, 4 classrooms, computer lab.

A non-departmental student-run organization presents several productions per year in which majors participate.

DESCRIPTION

Noted Professors: Sue-Ellen Case, Critical Studied; Neil Peter Jampolis, Lighting Design; Dunya Ramicova, Cost. Des.; Jose Luis Valenzuela, Directing; Mel Shapiro, Acting.

Guest Artists: Ron Liebman, Acting; Salome Jens, Acting; Ellen Geer, Acting.

Theater Study in UCLA's School of Theater Film and Television is offered at both the graduate and undergraduate levels. The Bachelor of Arts in Theater provides a liberal education in a program combining courses in the arts, humanities and sciences with an exploration of the principle areas of theater practice: acting, musical theater, dramatic writing directing, design, technical theater, and the study of the theater's history and literature, including its place in contemporary society. The school's theater program is enriched by its association with the fully professional Geffen Playhouse which it owns and operates. The Master of Fine Arts degree is a professional training program with specializations in Acting, Design and Production, Directing, and Playwriting. M.A. degree is awarded only in conjunction with study in the Ph.D. degree program to students who have successfully completed one year of graduate work and all requirements for the M.A. degree and who do not wish to continue the Ph.D. program. The program is staffed by a faculty of outstanding professional artists and master teachers. UCLA enjoys close proximity to the rich arts and entertainment world of Los Angeles which offers significant opportunities for field studies and internships.

University of California - Riverside

Eric Barr, Chairperson
Dept. of Theatre
Univ. of California - Riverside
Riverside, CA 92521
DEPT: (951) 827-3343
FAX: (951) 827-4651
ADMISSIONS: 1138 Hinderaker Hall
FAX: (951) 827-3413
discover@ucr.edu

17,000 Total Enr.; competitive
75 Majors; ATHE, R/RTA
Quarter System
T: $7,355; O-ST T: $26,975
R&B: $10,800
www.performingarts.ucr.edu
(951) 827-4531
www.ucr.edu

DEGREES OFFERED

BA in Theatre. MFA in Writing for the Performing Arts

ADMISSION & FINANCIAL INFORMATION

75% of apps. accepted by institution. Combination GPA & ACT/SAT scotrs. Chancellor's Performance Award Schol. To apply, letter of intent and 2 letters of rec. submitted directly to Dept. of Theatre.

FACULTY AND CLASSES OFFERED

9 Full-Time, 2 Part-Time: 2 PhD, 11 MFA/MA; 10 Admin.; 6 Tech Staff

A. (3 1/2 FT, 1 PT) Intro to Theatre-2/Y&O; Drama. Lit.-3/Y; Th. Hist.-11/Y&O; Dramatic Crit.-4/Y; Playwriting-3/Y; Screenwriting-1/Y.

B. (2-1/2 FT, 1 PT) Acting-7/Y&O; Voice/Speech-2/Y&O; Movement-1/O; Mime/Mask/Circus-1/O; Directing-3/Y

C. (3 FT) Prins of Design-1/Y; Costume Design-2/Y; Tech Prod'n-3/Y; Cost History-2/Y; Lighting Des-2/Y; Cost Constr-1/Y; Make-up-1/Y; Computer Aided Design-1/O; Design for Theatre-2/Y

FACILITIES & PRODUCTIONS

MAINSTAGE: 500 seats, fly loft, computer & electronic lighting
  1 prods: 1 Fac dir/des, 1 Artist-in Res; budget $12,000

STUDIO THEATRE: 150 seats, all computerized & digital systems
  5 prods: 3 Fac dir/des, 5 Artist-in-Res; budget $7-9,000

THEATRE LAB: 120 seats, all computer & digital systems
  3 prods: 3 UG dir/des; budget $1,000

BARN THEATRE: 50 seats. 3 prods: 3 UG dir/des; budget $500

New $26.5 million ARTS complex, including scene shop, costume shop, prop shop, visual computing lab, music library, visual resource library, 5 performance venues, screening room, 3 dance studios, photography and video studios, 3 painting/drawing studios, 3 sculpture studios, audio recording studio, state-or-the-art computer and digital systems.

DESCRIPTION

Noted Faculty: Richard Hornby, Dramatic Lit. & Theory; Eric Barr, Acting/Directing; Rickerby Hinds, Playwriting; Robin Russin, Screenwriting; Haibo Yu, Design.

Guest Artists: Margo Whitcomb, Director; Martin Aronstein, Lighting Design; Liz Stillwell, Lighting Designer; Ben Tusher, Lighting Designer; Doreen Tighe, Lighting Designer; Jim Alexander, Director; Mark Valdez, Director.

The Department of Theatre at the University of California, Riverside, offers classes in both practical and academic theatre subjects, taught by award-winning faculty members. The Department's four theatres give students the opportunity to work in a wide variety of beautifully designed, well-equipped spaces. The staff includes professional artists in costume design, costume construction, sound design, lighting design, scenic design, and theatre technology, including the latest forms of digital design and pre-visualization. The faculty and staff have ongoing professional theatre, film, and television careers in acting, directing, design, playwriting and criticism. The Department is dedicated to the pedagogical functions of production, and students receive course credit for their work. Undergraduate majors act in, direct, design, stage manage and crew productions almost as soon as they arrive. The new MFA Writing for the Performing Arts is a joint effort with the Department of Creative Writing and applications are being accepted for admission. Graduate writers will have their dramatic works read in weekly public performances and selected works will be fully produced by professional artists and staff. The award-winning ARTS building, completed in 2001, integrates five arts departments into one 55,000 sq. ft. complex, creating a dynamic, creative environment. The interaction between the arts in designated interdisiplinary spaces is a vital element of the facility.

University of California - San Diego

Charlie Oates, Chair
Dept. of Theatre & Dance
U. of California, San Diego
La Jolla, CA 92093-0344
DEPT: (858) 534-3791
FAX: (858) 534-1080
www.theatre.ucsd.edu
ADMISSIONS: Above address.

22,000 Total Enr.; h. compet.
Quarter System
155 UG Majors/66 G; ATHE
Fees: $4,927
O-ST T. $10,704
$5,000 room only
grad-theatre@ucsd.edu
(858) 534-1046

DEGREES OFFERED

BA in Theatre (130), Dance (25); MFA in Acting (29), Directing (4), Design (13), Stage Management (8), Playwriting (4), PhD in Drama and Theatre (6). Declare major in 1st year; 2001 granted 22 MFA degs., 40 BA degs.

ADMISSION & FINANCIAL INFORMATION

MFA 3.0 GPA, audition/interview, 3 letters of recommendation, GRE req. for playwriting and PhD. emphases. UG admits all applics, Grad 25 out of 500. 5% of applics. accepted by institution. A small number of departmental scholarships are available to graduate students and selection is made by the admissions committee.

FACULTY AND CLASSES OFFERED

25 Full-Time, 15 Part-Time:7 PhD, 32 MFA/MA, 1 Prof. w/o adv. degree, 10 Admin. & 22 Tech. Staff
A. (7 FT, 3 PT) Dramatic Lit/Criticism-12/Y; Playwriting-10/Y
B. (11 FT, 10 PT) Acting-32/Y; Directing-8/Y; Voice-10/Y; Movement-11/Y
C. (7 FT, 2 PT) Principles of Design-3/Y; Set Design-4/Y; Costume Design-4/Y; Lighting Design-4/Y; Technical Prod-uction-3/Y; Drafting-2/Y; Drawing-2/Y; CAD-1/Y;Moving Light Tech-2/Y; Photoshop-1/Y; Storyboarding-1/Y; Stage Mgmt.-6/Y

FACILITIES & PRODUCTIONS

MAINSTAGE: Mandell Weiss Th.: 500 seats, fly space, comp. ltg. 5 prods: 1 Guest/2 Grad/2 Fac. dir, 4 Grad des/1UG des; Avg. budget $4,000-12,000.

2nd MAINSTAGE: Mandell Weiss Forum: 400 seats, 3/4 thrust, computerized lighting. 7 prods: 4 Grad/2 Fac dir, 1 Grad/2 UG des.; avg. budget $1000-6000.

3rd Mainstage: The Sheila and Hughes Potiker Theatre: flexible seating 250-450, flexible config, comp ltg, 4 prods, 1 Fac.dir/3 Grad dir, 4 Grad des, avg budget $4000-12,000.

BLACK BOX: Forum Studio Theatre: 100 seats, end seating, comp ltg, 4 prods: 3 Grad/1Fac dir, 4 Grad des; Avg. budget $4000

Studio Theatre: Theatre 157: 100 seats, 3/4 thrust, comp ltg,4 prods, 2 Fac dir/2 Grad dir, 4 Grad des, avg budget $2000.

Mainstage was built in 1982; second mainstage was built in 1991; third mainstage under construction (completion Fall 2004). Facilities include 2 scene shops, costume shop, props shop,

welding shop, 3 dance studios, 6 rehearsal studios, 2 design studios, 6 classrooms, 2 seminar rms,14 station CAD and graphics lab, and a 100-seat dance black box performance space.

Baldwin New Play Festival: annual spring festival featuring fall productioons of Grad playwrights' plays that have been in development for the prior year. Professional guests are brought to campus for the festival each year. 10 student plays have been produced as part of this festival in the last two years.

Tony Award winning, regional theatre, The La Jolla Playhouse (Equity), is in residence at UCSD, sharing facilities and technical staff with the Dept of Theatre and Dance. The UCSD/LJP residency program guarantees each MFA actor, director, designer, and stage manager at least one paid professional opportunity in the area of their specialty. Many students will have more than one professional experience at LJP before graduation.

DESCRIPTION

Noted Faculty: Acting: Kyle Donnelly, Jim Winker, Darko Tresnjak. Design: Andrei Both, Judy Dolan. Directing: Gabor Tompa. Playwriting: Allan Havis, Adele Shank, Naomi Iizuka. Stage Management: Steven Adler, Lisa Porter. PhD: Jim Carmody, Janet Smarr, Nadine George,Jorge Huerta, Marianne McDonald. Dance Theatre: Yolande Snaith, Allyson Green.

Guest Artists: Directors: Anne Bogart, Joseph Chaikin, Robert Egan, Daniel Fish, Michael Greif, Andrei Serban, Robert Woodruff, Brian Kulick. Designers: Annie Smart, James Ingalls, Desmond Heeley, Franco Colavecchia, Tony Walton. Playwriting/Drama Lit: Charles Mee, Jose Rivera, Amy Freed, Mac Wellman, Len Jenkin, Robert Brustein, Patrice Pavis, Eric Ehn.

Our goal is to train young artists to create new works that reflect contemporary America of the 1990's. We create an atmosphere of trust and adventure, of security and challenge; we balance our respect for tradition with our desire to explore new forms that give expression to the ideas and ideals, emotions and experiences of the emerging theatre artists who enter our program. We believe that we can educate well only if we admit a very limited number of students to our programs. Consequently our students have a great deal of contact with faculty. The permanent faculty in our department is made up of artists and scholars committed to teaching who, at the same time, maintain active, high-profile professional careers. Each year we strive to achieve the most productive synthesis of theory and practice, studio exercise and public performance. Throughout their time at University of California, San Diego, students study and work with visiting professional artists in both department productions and classes. They also make invaluable professional contacts during their residencies at the La Jolla Playhouse. Students are also regularly awarded travel grants which allow them to serve as assistants to faculty members at professional venues both in the US and abroad.

University of California - Santa Barbara

Simon Williams, Chair
Department of Theatre and Dance
University of California 552 Univ. Rd.
Santa Barbara, CA 93106

18,000 Total Enr.; h. compet.
Quarter system; ATHE
230 UG, 20 Grad Majors
T: 7,896 R&B $11,946

DEPT: (805) 893-4895
MAIN: (805) 893-3241
www.uscb.edu

O-ST T: $26,964 R&B $11,946
appinfo@sa.ucsb.edu

MAJORS & DEGREES OFFERED

BA in Design (20), Directing (10), General (120), Lit & Theory (20); BFA in Acting (60); MA (8) and PhD (12) in Lit, Theory & Criticism. Declare major 1st/2nd yr.; 2001 granted 60 UG, 5-6 Grad degrees.

ADMISSION & FINANCIAL INFORMATION

50% of pre-screened applicants accepted; Requirements: (UG) GPA 3.7, & SAT & achievement test scores. Th. Prog. accepts all apps for BA degree, 30 out of 70 apps for BFA Acting Program, 12-15 out of 50 apps to grad prog. Aud. req'd for advanced students transferring into BFA, written work as ug. 4-5 schols. of $1,000 ea, awarded to Seniors in the major.

FACULTY AND CLASSES OFFERED

14 Full-Time, 2 Part-Time: 8 PhD, 7 MFA/MA, 1 Prof. w/o adv. degree; 11 Staff

A. (5 FT) Intro to Theatre-4/Y; Theatre History-6/Y; Shakes- 2/Y; Dramatic Lit-10/Y; Dramatic Criticism-6/Y; Playwriting-3/Y

B. (6 FT) Acting-12/Y); Voice/Speech-8/Y; Movemt-8/Y; Mime, etc.- 2/Y; Singing-X; Musical Th-1/Y; Directing-6/Y; Stage Combat-1/O

C. (3 FT, 2 PT) Principles of Design-2/Y; Set Design-4/Y; Cost Des- 5/Y; Lighting Design-4/Y; Technical Prod-3/Y; Costume Constr- 2/Y; Costume History-1/Y; Make-up-1/Y; Shop Practicums-7/Y

FACILITIES AND PRODUCTIONS

MAINSTAGE: 340 seats, fly space, computerized lighting.
3 prods: 2 Fac dir/des, 1 Grad dir, 1 UG des; budget $7,000-12,000

SECOND STAGE: 110 seats, computerized lighting. 3 prods:
2 Fac dir/des, 1 Grad dir, 2 UG des; budget $1,500-2,000

THIRD STAGE: 100 seats, electronic lighting
14 workshops/readings: 10 UG dir, 4 Grad. dir

Facility was built in 1964; includes scene shop, costume shop, large prosc. theatre, intimate black box theatre, rehearsal studio, design studio, dept. offices. New facility built in 1996 houses modern dance studio, ballet studio/theatre black box theatre, rehearsal studio, dressing rooms, and faculty offices. 12 student-written plays produced in the last two years.

Connection with Theatre Artists Group (summer): TAG is the faculty theatre company in residence at UCSB. Students serve as apprentices to the company.

DESCRIPTION

Noted Faculty: Irwin Appel, Acting; Leo Carranes-Grant, Spanish/Latin-American Drama; Catherine Cole, Contemporary Theatre Theory, African Theatre; Jay Michael Jagim, Design; James Donlon, Movement; W. Davies King, American Drama/Theatre History; Tom Whitaker, Directing/Acting; Judith Olauson, Acting/Musical Theatre; Simon John Cynan Williams, Dramatic History/Criticism; Naomi Iizkua, Playwriting; Tom Whitaker, Director/Acting.

Guest Artists: Jerzy Grotowski, Polish director; Simon Trussler, British Author and Critic; Ladislav Vychodi, Czechoslovakian designer, Giles Havergal, Director; William Glover, Director; Albert Takazauckas, Director, Joseph Chaikin, Rachel Rosenthal.

Dedicated to the study and practice of theatre in all its phases, the Department of Dramatic Art offers a wide range of classes appropriate for non-majors pursuing a liberal arts education and for majors preparing for a professional or educational career. The department currently awards BFA and BA degrees on the undergraduate level and MA and PhD degrees on the graduate level. All degree programs emphasize the study of dramatic literature and history as well as studio courses and participation in the production program. The department's approximately 230 undergraduate majors and 20 graduate students reap the benefits of a department committed to excellence situated in a large university. The size of the department's faculty and their active involvement presents the student not only with an excellent student-teacher ratio on paper but frequent interaction in both the classroom and the production program. In a typical year, the department produces 5 mainstage drama productions, 2 modern dance concerts, numerous graduate- and undergraduate-directed one-act plays, one person shows, honors projects, original scripts workshops, dance studio presentations, and participation in special events.

University of LaVerne

Elizabeth Pietrzak
Dr. David Flaten, Chair
Univ. of LaVerne
1950 Third St.
LaVerne CA 91750
DEPT: (909) 593-3511 x 4550
www.ulv.edu/theatre
ADMISSIONS: Address above: Attn. Admissions
1-(800) 876-4858
www.ulv.edu/~admit

1,500 Tot. Enr.; compet.

Semester System;
32 Majors;
T: $24,000/$10,000 R&B
FAX: (909) 392-2787
theatre@ulv.edu

FAX: (909) 596-1451
admissions@ulv.edu

DEGREES OFFERED

BA in Acting (15), Directing (3), Design/Technical Theatre (4), General (4), Teaching/Liberal Studies (5), Playwriting (1). Declare major in 2nd year; 2006 granted 7 degrees.

ADMISSION & FINANCIAL INFORMATION

Avg. 3.3, 1050 SAT. 77% of applicants accepted by institution; Theatre program admits all. Theatre Scholarships are selected through audition or portfolio review. Most schols. also awarded by the univ. to freshmen & transfers.

FACULTY AND CLASSES OFFERED

5 Full-Time, 2 Part-Time: 1 PhD, 2 MFA/MA, 5 Prof. w/o adv. degree

A. (2 FT, 1 PT) Intro to Theatre-1/Y; Dramatic Lit-8/Y; Theatre History- 2/Y; Shakes-2/Y; Playwriting-2/Y

B. (2 1/2 FT, 1 PT) Acting-5/Y; Voice/Speech-2/Y; Singing-6/X; Dance- 1/X; Directing-1/Y; Creative Drama for Teachers-3/Y; Theatre Seminar-2/Y; Children's Theatre-1/Y

C. (1-1/2 FT) Principles of Design-1/Y; Set Design-2/Y; Technical Production-1/Y; Stage Mgmt.-1/Y; Lighting Design-1/O; Desktop Publishing for Th-2/Y

FACILITIES AND PRODUCTIONS

MAINSTAGE: 175-250 seats, computerized lighting
8 prods: 2 Fac dir, 4 Fac des, 1 Guest dir, 2 Guest des, 5 UG dir, 5 UG des; budget $500-12,500

SECOND STAGE: 70 seats, computerized lighting. 21 prods: 1 Fac die, 2 Fac des, 20 UG dir/des; budget $50-1,500

THIRD STAGE: 475 seats, electronic lighting, fly space

Facility was built in 1972, continuously renovated; includes scene shop, costume shop, prop shop, CAD facil., rehearsal studio, design studio, classrooms, dept. library - video, books.

Five student-written plays produced in the last two years.

DESCRIPTION

Noted Faculty: Dr. David Flaten, Chair, Design/Directing/Th. History; Prof. Sean Dillon, Playwriting; Asst. Prof. Steve Kent, Acting/Directing, Elizabeth Pietrzak, Design/Lighting/Tech. Theatre/CAD; Adjunct Prof. Georgij Paro, Dir. Croatian Nat'l Theatre.

Guest Artists: Michelle George, Voice, Singing; Tim Miller & Dan Kwong, Highways Performance Space-L.A.; Jeff McMahon, Dance, Movement-N.Y. Artist; Michael Kerk, Solo Performer; Rose Porollo, Acting; Michael Kerns, Activist, Actor-L.A.; Shishir Karup, Founder, Cornerstone Theatre; Jawolle Zollar, Director/Founder Urban Bush Women.

The ULV Theatre Program is performance-oriented and is designed for non-major participants as well as for majors with various career goals. Majors fulfill requirements in acting, directing and design as well as getting a solid background in theatre history, theory and dramatic literature. Students prepare for professional and teaching careers or for graduate work. The mission of the Theatre Arts Department is, through contact with theatre as participant or audience, to celebrate and reflect upon the values that enrich life, to increase awareness of dynamic human interrelationships and of different cultures and world views, and to encourage students and the community to view an use theatre as a resource where ideas may be explored creatively and find physical form. Unique opportunities at ULV include the Steven Kent Institute for Conscious Acting, a connection with The Guildford School of Acting in England, and The Split International Theatre Festival in Croatia.

University of the Pacific

Gary Armagnac, Dept. Chair	3,535 Total Enr.; compet.
Department of Theatre Arts	Semester System
Drama Building	18 Majors; U/RTA
University of the Pacific	T: $28,980/$9,210 R&B
Stockton, CA 95211	DEPT: (209) 946-2116
www.uop.edu/cop/theatrearts	FAX: (209) 946-2118
	SMALL PROGRAM
ADMISSIONS: 3601 Pacific Ave.	(209) 946-2211
www.uop.edu	FAX: (209) 946-2413

DEGREES OFFERED

BA in Theatre Arts (15), Musical Theatre.
Declare major in fresh/soph. year;

ADMISSION & FINANCIAL INFORMATION

Average GPA 3.7, avg. SAT 1150. 50% of applicants accepted by institution. 9 out of 10 applicants admitted to theatre program. Interview req.

FACULTY AND CLASSES OFFERED

4 Full-Time: 1 PhD, 3 MFA; 3 Staff

A. (4 FT) Intro to Theatre-1/Y; Dramatic Lit-1/Y; Theatre History-1/Y; Shakes-1/X; Playwriting-1/0

B. (1 1/2 FT) Acting-2/Y; Movement-1/Y; Singing-1/X; Directing- 1/Y; Dance-4/Y

C. (7 FT) Prins. of Design-1/Y; Set Design-1/O; Tech Prod.-1/Y; Make-up-1/Y; Set Des-1/O; Ltg. Des-1/O; Stage Mgmt-1/Y

D. (3 FT) Arts Management-1/Y; Budget/Acct'ng-4/X

FACILITIES AND PRODUCTIONS

MAINSTAGE: 400 seats, computerized lighting
3 Fac dir, 4 Fac des, 1 Guest dir prod; budget $1,500-7,000

SECOND STAGE: 80-120 seats, computerized lighting. 2 Fac dir, 3 Fac des, 1 Guest dir, 7 UG dir/des prods; budget $1,000-1,500. Workshops/Readings; budget $50-100

Facility was built in 1956, renovated in 1999; includes scene shop, costume shop, prop shop, welding shop, sound studio, CAD facility, dance studio, design studio, 3 classrooms, departmental theatre library (3,500 volumes).

16 student-written plays produced in the last two years.

DESCRIPTION

Noted Faculty: Gary Armagnac, Dept Chair, Acting, Directing; Randall Enlou, Design; William Wolak, Acting Theatre History; Cathie McClellan, Costume/Makeup.

The Department of Theatre Arts is dedicated to the philosophy that students are best trained in our discipline by experience in the classroom balanced with experience in actual productions. Students are also encouraged to experience the different disciplines of the theatre arts by selecting a cross section of courses and having a breadth of experiences in production. The production program is designed to allow the students to experience plays from the classical and modern repertory, various dance genres and participate in the various technical areas of theatre. The Department attempts to maintain a balance between theoretical and practical learning by encouraging students to seek internship and other opportunities that relate their academic experience to the real world. After graduating from UOP with a bachelor of arts degree in Theatre Arts, the student is able to apply his or her knowledge and is prepared to make choices regarding career to advanced training. The Minor in Theatre Arts allows training for students who are interested in the theatre arts as an avocation. The Department of Theatre Arts has a history of placing its graduates in rewarding careers which range from professional placement in theatre, film and television as actors or technicians, distinguished educators at all levels, to citizens who enjoy participation in the theatre arts as a community activity. We are proud that 100% of the students in recent memory who applied for graduate school were accepted and that 100% of them completed their degrees.

University of Southern California

Madeline Puzo, Dean	33,000 Total Enr.; h.compet.
School of Theatre	Semester System
Univ. of Southern California	476 Majors, U/RTA

Los Angeles, CA 90089-0791
Dept: (213) 821-2744
thtrinfo@usc.edu
ADMISSIONS: 1029 Child's Way, LA, CA 90089
(213) 740-1286
http://theatre.usc.edu

T: $35,212/$10,858 R&B
FAX: (213) 740-8888

FAX: (213) 740-8888
admissions@theatre.usc.edu

DEGREES OFFERED

BA in Theatre (357); BFA in Acting (71); Design (13); Stage Mgmt (15); Tech Dir (4); MFA in Acting & Dramatic Writing (16). Declare major in freshman yr.; 2007 granted 114 UG, 3 Grad degs.

ADMISSION & FINANCIAL INFORMATION

Required coursework, GPA, SATs, Activities Summary, essay, counselor/teacher recommendations, interview. The School of Theatre only offers merit scholarships for incoming students. Students are able to apply for this award by completing a university application by the competitive application date. There are two awards: Trustee Award - full tuition & Presidential Award - half tuition. Accept 230 out of 1700 to UG program, 15 out of 300 to Grad program. Aud/Int for actors, int/portfolio for des. Play submission for dramatic writing.

FACULTY AND CLASSES OFFERED

22 Full-Time, 45 Part-Time: 5 PhD, 11 MFA/MA; 51 profs w/o adv degree, 25 Staff

A. Intro to Theatre-1/Y; Theatre History-2/Y; Shakes-1/Y; Dramatic Lit-2/Y; Dramatic Criticism-1/Y; Playwriting-2/Y

B. Acting-7/Y; Voice/Speech-7/Y; Movement-2/Y; Musical Theatre-2/Y; Directing-2/Y; Dance-4/Y; Singing-X; Mime, etc-1/Y; Stage Combat-1/Y

C. Prins of Des-7/Y; Set Des-7/Y; Cost Des-5/Y; Ltg Des-5/Y; Cost Constr-2/Y; Make-up-2/Y; Stage Mgmt-2/Y; Tech Prod-3/Y

D. Arts Mgmt-2/Y; Marketing/Promo-2/Y; Box Office Procedure-2/Y; Legal: Contracts/Copyright-2/Y; Devel/Grants-2/Y; Budget/Accounting-2/Y

FACILITIES AND PRODUCTIONS

MAINSTAGE: 551 seats, fly space, computerized & electronic lighting. 7 prods: 7 Fac dir, 7 GA des; 11 UG des

SECOND STAGE: 99 seats, 8 prods, 5 Fac dir, 3 GA dir, 26 UG des

THIRD STAGE: 60 seats, computerized & electron lighting; 3 prods: 1 Fac dir, 2 GA dir, 1 GA des, 9 UG des

Facility was built in 1975; includes scene shop, costume shop, prop shop, movement/dance studios, design studio, rehearsal studios, classrooms. Village Gate Theatre seats 70.

Non-departmental, student-run org. presents 5-7 prods./yr in which majors participate. 6 student-written plays produced in the last two yrs.

CTG (Center Theatre Group), equity, offers internships in development, marketing, publicity, casting and production.

DESCRIPTION

Noted Faculty: Dr. Margo Apostolos, Dance; Dr. Sharon Carnicke, Theatre Studies; Casey Cowan Gale, Lighting Design; Velina Hasu Houston, Playwriting; James Wilson, Acting; Don Llewellyn, Design; Oliver Mayer, Playwriting; Dr. Meiling Cheng, Critical Studies; Angus Fletcher, Critical Studies; Andrew J. Robinson, Acting

Guest Artists: Luis Alfaro, Dramatic Writing; Philip G. Allen, Design; Stephanie Shroyer, Acting; Jason

Robert Brown, Director; Kelly Ward, Musical Theatre; Anita Dashiell Sparks, Actress; Regina Williams, Dance; Paula Holt, Producing; Gates McFadden, Actor; Brian Nelson, Director

The USC School of Theatre offers professional and scholarly training, stressing the interdependence of production experience with academic knowledge. Study in theatre requires a close working relationship among students, faculty and staff. In this atmosphere of collective effort, a special bond develops. Academic advisement and discussions of educational and professional aspirations are important concerns attended to by faculty and staff. The School provides students with training in their specific area of interest, building upon a broad foundation of study as required by the unversity. There is a focus on both the theory and practice of theatre by furnishing intellectual challenges and providing opportunities for performance and practical experience.

COLORADO

Metropolitan State College of Denver

Dr. Marilyn Hetzel, Dir. of Theatre
Dept. of Theatre, Campus Box 34
P.O. Box 173362
Metropolitan State College
Denver, CO 80217-3362
(303) 556-3033

22,000 Tot. Enr.; n. compet.
150 Th.Majors
Semester System
T: $190.35/cr. hr.
O-ST T: $438.35/cr. hr.
MEDIUM SIZED PROGRAM

DEGREES OFFERED

BA in Theatre with BFA concentration in Music Theatre and Applied Theatre Technology and Design.
Declare major in soph. year; 2001 granted 60 degrees.

ADMISSION & FINANCIAL INFORMATION

Assessment tests ACT/SAT. Interview required. Theatre BA/BFA program admits all applicant to BA program; BFA concentrations require auditions and interviews. Contact admissions and records or financial aid for handbook, Theatre has talent and merit schol. up to $500/semester.

FACULTY AND CLASSES OFFERED

5 Full-Time, 10 Part-Time: 4 PhD, 9 MFA, 1 MA; shared Staff; 1 Theatre Production Manager; 1 Shop Foreman; 1 Costumer

A. (1 FT, 3 PT) Intro to Theatre/Theatre Hist.-1/Y; Dramatic Lit-2/X; Shakes-2/X; Dramatic Criticism-1/X; Playwriting-1/X

B. (2 FT, 4 PT) Acting-3/Y; Voice/Speech-2/Y; Movement-1/Y; Musical Theatre-1/Y; Singing-1/X; Directing-1/Y; Production Analysis; Oral Interpretation

C. (2 FT, 1 PT) Principles of Design-1/Y; Tech Production-1/Y; Set Design-1/O; Lighting Design-1/O; Sound; Costume

D. (1 FT) Marketing/Promotion-1/X; Legal: Contracts/Copy-right-1/X; Budgeting/Accounting Procedure-1/X

FACILITIES & PRODUCTIONS

MAINSTAGE: 250 seats, computerized lighting. 4 prods: 2 Fac dir/des, 1 Guest dir/UG des; 1 stud prod (Student Stage Ensemble) on alternate years; budget $4,000-35,000
3-5 Fac dir/des Workshops/Readings

Kenneth King Center Academic and Performing Arts facility (opened

2001), with one 250 Eugenia Rawls Courtyard Theatre (shared) and one Black Box Theatre (designated to MSCD), plus additional performance/rehearsal/studio spaces, scene shop, sound studios.

One Black Theatre in Arts Building, 100 seats. 2 Fac directors, guest dirs as needed; budget$4,000-$35,000/prod

30 1-acts produced last year.

Connections and internships with Denver Center for the Performing Arts (LORT), Arvada Center, Opera Shop and other commercial enterprises. Active members of Entertainment Services Technology Association (ESTA), USITT, Rocky Mountain Theatre Association (RMTA), ATHE.

DESCRIPTION

Noted Faculty: Dr. Marilyn Hetzel, musical theatre, voice; workshops in voice (Aspen Music Festival), adjudications, directing, ensemble acting, basic masks.

The MSCD Theatre Program is housed within the Communication Arts and Sciences Department. A student who wishes to major in theatre will earn either a BA or BFA in theatre. Students may focus on stagecraft, acting, directing, and music-theatre. The MSCD Theatre Program consists of two basic components: 1. Academic (i.e., formal classwork) and 2. Theatre Produc-tions (i.e., plays, musicals, community collaborations). Our focus is on the Liberal Arts: our students have diverse goals, including professional theatre, teaching, broadcasting, and theatre as a part of one's total educational experience. We offer a range of basic theatre classes with opportunities for students to develop theatre internships and to pursue individual interests.

National Theatre Conservatory

Daniel Renner, Dean
National Theatre Conservatory
1101 13th St
Denver, CO 80204
FAX: (303) 623-0693
www.denvercenter.org

23 T. Enr., highly compet.
Semester System
1 Major
(303) 446-4855
ADMISSIONS: Same as above.
ntc@dcpa.org

PROGRAMS/DEGREES OFFERED

MFA in Acting; Certificate in Acting. [Certificate granted if no undergrad degree–program and course work is the same.] Declare major in 1st yr. 2007 granted 8 Grad. degrees.

ADMISSION & FINANCIAL INFORMATION

After the initial Audition and Interview the NTC's audition panel will review the candidates and invite the finalists to a Callback Workshop in Denver. The weekend workshops consist of classes and further interviews and auditions before an enlarged audition panel, which includes but is not limited to the artistic director of the Denver Center Theatre Company, Conservatory Faculty and the DCTC casting Director. Admit 8 out of 450 to Graduate program. All admitted students receive a full tuition scholarship.

FACULTY AND CLASSES OFFERED

5 Full-Time, 13 Part-Time: 3 PhD, 12 MFA/MA, 3 Prof. w/o advanced degree, 2 Staff

A. (1 PT) Theatre History-2/Y; Shakes-2/Y; Playwriting-1/Y

B. (5 FT, 12 PT) Acting-7/Y; Voice/Speech-8/Y; Movement-4/Y; Singing-4/Y; Stage Combat-2/Y

FACILITIES AND PRODUCTIONS

MAINSTAGE: 550 seats, fly space, computerized & electronic lighting.. 6 Guest dir prods; budget $18,000-25,000

SECOND STAGE: 420 seats, fly space, computerized & electronic lighting. 1 Fac dir, 6 Guest dir prods; budget $12,000-18,000

THIRD STAGE: 150 seats, fly space, computerized & electronic lighting.. 10 Workshops/Readings; budget $0-3000

Facility was built in 1979; includes scene shop, costume shop, props shop, sound studio, video studio, 2 dance studios, 4 rehearsal studios, design studio, 6 classrooms

Connection with the Denver Center Theatre Company (Equity): In the first two years of study, students attend classes and perform "projects" (full-length shows without many props or costumes). Third year students become full-time apprentice members of the company, cast in mainstage productions and working on the design and technical as-pects of the shows, in fulfillment of their final year of study.

DESCRIPTION

Noted Faculty: Kent Thompson, Larry Hecht.

Guest Artists: Terrence McNally, August Wilson, Patrick Stewart, John Barton, Sir Peter Hall, Edward Albee, Hal Holbrook.

The National Theatre Conservatory is an integral part of the Denver Center Theatre Company. The NTC's aim is to uphold, and to raise, the standards of the theatrical profession in the United States. To this end, the NTC trains its students to interpret, at the highest level, the great plays of the past and present, and to encourage with all their skill the development of new American drama. The NTC assists its students in developing the professional relationships necessary for a life in the theatre. The NTC fosters an ongoing teacher/student/collaborator relationship between its students and the professional artists of the Denver Center Theatre Company. This relationship, paramount to the 3-year training program, is designed to culminate in a maturation from apprentice to colleague.

University of Colorado at Boulder

Dr. Bud Coleman, Chair
Campus Box 261
University of Colorado at Boulder
Dept. of Theatre & Dance
Boulder, CO 80309-0261
www.cutheatre.org
(303) 492-7355

28,624 Total Enr.; h.compet.
225 Majors; ATHE
Semester System
T: $7,212 ug/yr; $3,830 g/sem
O-ST T: $23,045 ug/yr; $11,470 g/sem
$8,300 r&b
fax: (303) 492-7722

DEGREES OFFERED

BA in Theatre (165); BFA in Performance (34); Musical Theatre (15); Des/Tech (12). Declare major in first or second year; 2005-6 granted 40 degrees (6 Grad).

ADMISSION & FINANCIAL INFORMATION

Requirements for UG average: HS GPA 3.55; SAT 1200; ACT 26; BFA is selective based on audition/int-approx. 20% admitted to grad programs. UG admits 50% to BFA. Performance/Musical Theatre/Design Tech need aud/int. Theatre awards by department through aud/int. Applicants selected on the basis of written letter and portfolio/resume.

FACULTY AND CLASSES OFFERED

12 Full-Time, 4 Part-Time: 7 PhD, 9 MFA, 7 Staff

A. (4 FT, 1/2 PT) Intro to Theatre-1/Y; Dramatic Lit-5/XY; Th Hist-4/Y; Shakes-3/XY; Dramatic Crit.-1/O; Playwriting-1/Y

B. (3 FT, 1 PT) Acting-8/Y; Voice/Speech-2/Y; Movement-1/O; Musical Theatre-2/Y; Singing-1/XY; Directing-2/Y; Acting for the Camera-1/O; Stage Combat-1/O; Dance-10/Y

C. (5 FT, 1/2 PT) Prins of Des-1/Y; Cost Des-2/Y; Set Des-2/O; Ltg Des-2/O; Cost Constr-2/O; Make-up-1/Y; Stg. Mgmt-1/O; Props-1/O; Millinery-1.O

D. (1/2 PT) Arts Mgmt-1/O; Marketing/Promo-1/Y

FACILITIES & PRODUCTIONS

MAINSTAGE: 416 seats, fly space, computer. & electron. lighting 4 prods: 3 Fac dir, 3 Fac des, 1 Grad dir, 1 UG des; budget $2,000-3,000

SECOND STAGE: 140 seats, computer. & electron. lighting 2 prods: 1 Fac dir, 1 Grad dir; budget $1,500-2,500

THIRD STAGE: 1004 seats, computer. & electron. lighting

WORKSHOPS: 2 Grad dir, no design; 3 UG dir.

Facility was built in 1902, renovated in 1989, includes scene shop, costume shop, prop shop, welding shop, movement/dance studio, rehearsal studio, design studio, classrooms, dye room.

A non-departmental, student-run organization presents various productions in which dept. majors participate.

The dept. sponsors the Colorado Shakespeare Festival each summer. This is a repertory company which hires professional actors and designers, advanced grad students, undergrads in all areas. Our students have learning and practicum opportunities in all areas. Productions are indoors in the Mary Rippon 1004 seat theatre.

DESCRIPTION

Noted Faculty: James M. Symons, Dramatic Lit., Theory and Criticism; Oliver Gerland, Dramatic Lit; Bud Coleman, Musical Theatre & LGBT Studies.

Guest Artists: Lee Blessing, Playwright; Holly Hughes, Playwright/Performer; Qishu Fang, Peking Opera Performer; Tim Miller, Playwright/Performer; Karen Finley, Performer/Playwright; The Curious Theatre Co, Denver, CO; Patricia Elliot, Performer

The Department of Theatre and Dance offers undergraduate and graduate degrees in both theatre and dance. These programs combine traditional studies with practical training. Ambitious seasons of theatre productions and dance concerts feature student performers and student designers, directors, and choreographers. The following areas of knowledge are central to the undergraduate degrees in theatre: knowledge of the major works of dramatic literature that are representative of the most important eras in the development of theatre; knowledge of the history of theatrical production—its styles, conventions, and socially related mores; knowledge of various means through which a theatrical concept is realized; awareness of the aesthetic and intellectual relationship between theatre in its various twentieth-century modes and contemporary society.

University of Colorado at Denver

Chair, Dept. of Perf. Arts
Campus Box 162
University of Colorado at Denver
P. O. Box 173364
Denver, CO 80217-3364
DEPT: (303) 556-4797
ADMISSIONS: UC-Denver, Campus Box 167, P.O. Box 173364
(303) 556-2704   FAX: (303) 556-4838
www.cudenver.edu/cam/

8,000 Total Enr.; competitive
60 Majors; ATHE
Semester System
T: $118/credit hr.
O-ST T: $625/credit hr.
FAX: (303) 556-2335

DEGREES OFFERED

BA in Theatre, Film & Television, BFA in Theatre, Film & Television, emphases developing in Film/Television; Design; Production Development, Directing and Performance. Declare major in fresh. year; 2002 granted 20 degrees.

ADMISSION & FINANCIAL INFORMATION

A CCHE Admission Index of 92 (Approx. a GPA of 3.2 & SAT of 900, ACT 19). 80% of applicants accepted to institution. Theatre program admits 15 out of 25 applicants. Aud., Interview, Portfolio for designers. Full to partial schols. available to a maximum of $2,000/yr. scholarship awarded on talent and scholarship.

FACULTY AND CLASSES OFFERED

6 Full-Time, 6 Part-Time: 3 PhD, 9 MFA/MA; 1 Staff

A. (1 FT, 3 PT) Intro to Theatre-1/Y; Dramatic Lit-1/Y; Th Hist-1/Y; Shakes-1/X; Dramatic Crit.-1/Y; Playwriting-1/Y

B. (4 FT, 2 PT) Acting-3/Y; Voice/Speech-2/Y; Movement-2/Y; Directing-2/Y; Dance-1/X

C. (1 FT, 1 PT) Principles of Design-1/Y; Cost Des-1/Y; Tech Production-1/Y; Set Des-2/Y; Lighting Des-1/Y; Costume History-1/Y; Make-up-1/Y

FACILITIES & PRODUCTIONS

MAINSTAGE: 350 seats, computerized lighting, fly system, flexible staging options; materials and guest artist budgets $10,000-$25,000 per show part of the Kenneth King Center for the Performing Arts

SECOND STAGE: Studio Theatre Flexible staging, 100-120 seats, computerized lighting; tension grid; materials and guest artist budgets $6,00- $20,00 per show; prat of the Kenneth King Center for the Performing Arts.

ARTS BUILDING SECOND STAGE: classroom and student production facility, 40-60 seats, flexible staging, computerized lighting, pipe grid, venue for Senior projects, Directing class projects and other course work and project presentations.

KENNETH KING CENTER FOR THE PERFORMING ARTS: multiple venues including Mainstage and Studio Theatre listed above, a recital hall, and a Concert Hall. Also includes Scene shop, Costume Shop, Paint Deck, Design Studio, Lighting Lab, Recording Studio, Music and Dance Studio and Medium Productions Studio. Facility is shared by three academic institutions on the Auraria Campus.

DESCRIPTION

Noted Faculty/Prod Support Staff: Mark Alan Heckler, Acting, Directing, Musical Theatre; Kathryn Maes, Voice & Speech, Dialects, Directing; Laura Cuetara, Acting, Directing, Production Development; Brad Bowles, Theory & Criticism, Drama of Diversity and Social Responsibility; Carol Bloom, Intro to Theatre; ,

Acting, and Acting for Non-Theatre Majors; Frederic Lahey, Film and Television Prod and Post Prod; Craig Volk, Playwriting, Scriptwriting Screenwiting, Screenwriting; Janetta Pahel, Costume Design and Construction, Makeup Design; Tom Sheridan, Stage and Prod Mgmt, AEA.; Nate Thompson, Tech Dir, IATSE; Charles Smith, Asst Tech Dir, Welding IATSE.

Recent Guest Artists: Penny Cole, Directing, Dramatic Literature; Richard Finkelstein, Scenery and Lighting Design, Portfolio Web Design; Rick Barbour, Directing, Movement; Bill Curley, Scenery and Lighting Design; John Hill, Directing; Lee Stamitz, Musical Director; Debra Reshotko, Movement and Choreography; G. Scott Hay, Lighting Design; Scott Anderson, Sound Design.

Students wishing to study theatre choose the Theatre Option, leading to a Bachelor of Arts in Theatre with an emphasis in Acting, Design, Technology or Production Development in the College of Arts and Media. The emphasis in theatre is designed to train the diversified theatre artist—writer, director, performer, designer, teacher—and to provide opportunities for a broad range of production process and performance experiences in courses, laboratory workshops, full production, and field work in the Denver area. The goal of the Theatre program is an understanding of the potential of the theatre as an expressive medium in the context of its culture and as a collaborative art form in relationship to literature, fine arts, and music. Students are required to complete a series of core courses in theatre, and then concentrate in one area of focus. Participation in on-campus productions and off-campus internship is required as the practicum component of the program.

The Film and Video Production program at the University of Colorado at Denver is intended for students seeking professional preparation for careers in film, video and related industries.

University of Denver ·············

Rick Barbour, Interim Chair
Paula Sperry, Asst. Professor
Theatre Dept., MRH 104
University of Denver
Denver, CO 80208-0211
DEPT: (303) 871-2518
E-MAIL: thea01@denver.du.edu
www.du.edu/thea/
ADMISSIONS: Admissions, U of Denver, CO 80208-0132
(303) 871-2036 or 800 525-9495
www.du.edu/admission

8,000 Total Enr.; competitive
Quarter System
40 Majors; ATHE, KC/ACTF
T: $26,000/$8,400 r&b
SMALL PROGRAM

FAX: (303) 871-2505

DEGREES OFFERED

BA in General Theatre (45)
Declare major in any year

ADMISSION & FINANCIAL INFORMATION

$50 app. fee, 3.4 GPA (rec), 25 ACT (avg), 1147 SAT (avg). $50,000 in scholarships awarded each year, renewable for 4 yrs., auditions and portfolio reviews held at D.U. in Jan., Feb. & March Write for application or go online www.du.edu/thea

FACULTY AND CLASSES OFFERED

4 Full-Time, 16 Part-Time: 3 PhD, 5 MFA/MA, 8 Prof. w/o adv. degree; 1 Staff

A. (1 FT) Introduction to Theatre-3/Y; Theatre History-2/Y; Shakes-2/X; Dramatic Lit-3/Y; Dramatic Criticism-1/Y; Playwriting-1/Y

B. (1 FT, 3 PT) Acting-6/Y; Movement-3/Y; Mime, etc.-1/O; Musical Theatre-1/O; Directing-2/Y; Stage Combat-1/O

C. (1 FT, 1 PT) Set Design-1/Y; Costume Design-1/Y; Lighting Design-1/Y; Make-up-3/Y; Scene Painting-1/O

D. Arts Management-1/O

FACILITIES AND PRODUCTIONS

MAINSTAGE: New flexible theatre in performing art center, 200-450 seats, opened in May,2003, fly space, computerized lighting, electronic lighting
3 prods: 2 Fac dir, 12 Fac des, 1 Guest dir, 3 UG des; budget $3,000-6,000

SECOND STAGE: 50 seats, electronic lighting. 20 prods: 10 UG dir, 40 UG des; $100-400. 15 Workshops/Readings: 6 UG dir, 8 UG des

THIRD STAGE: 250 seats, fly space, computerized lighting.

Two facilities are used, one built in 1938 (and renovated in 1998) and one built in 2002. Both include scene shop, costume shop, prop shop, welding shop, sound studio, 4 rehearsal studios, 2 movement/dance studios, design studio, CAD facility, computer scenographic studio, acting studio, 4 classrooms.

A departmental, student-run organization presents 5-10 productions per year in which dept. majors participate. 6 student-written plays produced in the last two years.

Internships with the Denver Center Theatre Company (Equity) and Curious Theatre Company (Equity).

DESCRIPTION

Noted Faculty: Chip Walton, th. history, directing; William Temple Davis, scene and ltg. design; Kim Axline, Theatre History, Dramatic Lit; Erika Kaufman, movement; Rick Barbour, Acting; Terry Dodd, playwriting; Paula Sperry, acting, directing; Trish Stevens, costume designer.

Guest Artists: Kathryn Gray, Terry Dodd, Larry Hecht, directors; Paul Loper, choreographer, Joan Staniunus, director, Geoff Kent, stage combat.

The Theatre Department at the University of Denver offers an undergraduate theatre major resulting in a B.A. degree. Three productions are mounted in the flexible theatre each academic year. The Theatre Department emphasizes team and one-on-one teaching. The Theatre Programs's philosophy is to provide rigorous training in all areas of theatre, expecting all students to experience theatre fully before finding an area of specialization. Full-time faculty members provide extensive advising to students on all academic and theatre matters, including assisting students in finding internships which will be that "foot in the door."

University of Northern Colorado ······

David Grapes II, Director
School of Theatre Arts & Dance
Univ. of Northern Colorado
Greeley, CO 80639

13,000 Total Enr.; h. competitive
340 majors, 100 minors; ATHE
Semester System
T: $4,000/$6,832 r&b

(970) 351-2991   O-ST T. $11,856/$6,832 r&b
fax (970) 351-4897   www.unco.edu
Admissions: UNC,Campus Box 10, 501 20th St., Greely, CO 80639
(970) 351-2881   www.unco.edu/admissions/index/html

DEGREES OFFERED

BA in Acting (91), Musical Theatre (90), Design Technology (61), Theatre Educ (40)Theatre Studies (58). Declare major in freshman year; 2007 granted 75 UG degrees.

ADMISSION & FINANCIAL INFORMATION

Admission eligibility is based on a CCHE index, which is calculated from high school performance and standardized test scores. See UNC's website at: www.unco.edu/admissions for index chart. 60% of apps. admitted to institution. Talent schols. avail., must audition. Academic schols. avail. apply through Admissions. Aud.and/or interviews req. for all programs. Generally admit 100 out of 1500 applicants to UG theatre program.

FACULTY AND CLASSES OFFERED

14 Full-Time; 5 Part-Time; 13 MFA; 1 PhD; 9 Staff

A. (2 FT, 2 PT) Intro to Theatre-8/Y; Dramatic Lit-2/Y; Theatre History-2/Y; Shakes-4/X; Playwriting-1/O

B. (8 FT, 2 PT) Acting-12/Y; Voice/Speech-2/Y; Directing-2/Y; Musical Th-6/Y; Movement-4/Y; Singing-4/Y; Dance-8/Y; Mime, etc-1/O; Stage Combat-1/O

C. (4 FT, 1 PT) Cost Design-2/Y; Set Des-2/Y; Lighting Des-2/Y; Make-up-2/Y; Stage Mgmt-1/O; Principles of Des-1/Y; Tech Prod-2/Y; Costume Constr-2/Y

D. Arts Mgmt-1/O; Marketing-1/Y

FACILITIES & PRODUCTIONS

MAINSTAGE: 600 seats, fly space, comput & electronic lighting 13 Prods: 13 Fac dir, 28 Fac des, 4 GA des, 22 UG des.(includes second stage prods); budget $8,000-15,000

SECOND STAGE: 100 seats, computerized & electronic lighting budget $4,000-8,000

THIRD STAGE: 1,800 seats, fly space, comput & electron. lighting.

Facility includes scene shop, costume shop, sound studio, prop shop, welding shop, 2 rehearsal studios, 3 movement and dance studios, design studio, 2 classrooms.

7 student-written plays produced in the past 2 years.

1 non-departmental student run producing in which majors participate.

Connection with Little Theatre of the Rockies. Equity guest artists with student actors. Oldest summer stock in the area—since 1934.LTR produces 5 shows per summer.

DESCRIPTION

Noted Faculty: David Grapes II, Directing; Tom McNally, former MFA acting teacher at Penn State; Vance Fulkerson, Broadway tour director, former head MFA music/theatre at Univ. of Utah; Mary Schuttler, award-winning hs drama teacher; John Leonard, musical theatre; Karen Genoff Campbell, Monte Black, dance.

Guest Artists: Victoria Morris, Greg Germann, Brian O'Neal, Dave Clemmons, Jeff Whiting, Bill Bowers, Michael Donovan, Rachel Hoffman, Deb McWaters, Joan See

The UNC School of Theatre Arts and Dance is a strong and highly competitive pre-professional undergraduate training program. Areas of concentration include: Musical Theatre, Performance Studies, Theatre Education, Design/Tech, Theatre Studies and a Dance Minor. Our training combines classroom instruction and personal mentorship with an active production program that stages over 30 productions each year. Additional training comes from a highly active guest artist and master class program, professional internships and through participation in our professional summer stock program - The Little Theatre of the Rockies. The School also produces two annual "senior showcases" for industry professionals - one in NYC and one in LA. Our goal is to prepare students to successfully enter the profession or to attend one of the premiere graduate school programs. Our talented faculty and staff are both master teachers and working professionals.

CONNECTICUT

Central Connecticut State University

Prof. Lani B. Johnson, Chair   9,644Total Enr.; competitive
Department of Theatre   Semester System
1615 Stanley Street   85 Majors
Central Conn. State University   T: $$6,442/$7,890 r&b
New Britain, CT 06050   O-ST T: $13,570/$7,890 r&b
DEPT: (860) 832-3150   FAX: (860) 832-3164
e-mail: johnsonlani@ccsu.edu
ADMISSION: CCSU, 115 Davidson Hall, New Britain, CT 06050/ P.O. Box 4010
(860) 832-2278   FAX: (860) 832-2295
www.ccsu.edu   admissions@ccsu.edu

DEGREES OFFERED

BA and BFA in General Theatre (25); BFA in Acting (34), in Design/Technical Theatre (20), in Dance (6)
Declare major in fresh./soph. year

ADMISSION & FINANCIAL INFORMATION

Recommended minimum SAT of 800, top 50% of class, "C" average academic track courses (4 years); 55% accepted by institution; Theatre program admits all applicants to General Theatre Program; Acting Program (BFA) requires audition in soph. yr. Theatre Dept. offers $1,000 to sophomore in BFA acting program; one semester tuition Torp Memorial Schol. given to junior or senior, based on need and service. Acting scholarship $1,000 based on academics, need and service. Student help money avail. for prod. work.

FACULTY AND CLASSES OFFERED

7 FT, 2 PT; 7 MFA/MA; 1 Staff

A. (1 1/2 FT, 1 PT) Intro to Theatre-5/Y; Dramatic Lit-1/X; Dramatic Crit-1/Y; Theatre History-2/Y; Shakes-1/O; Playwriting-1/X; Fashion History-1/O

B. (2 1/2 FT, 1 PT) Acting-5/Y; Voice/Speech-2/Y; Movement-2/Y; Singing-2/X; Directing-2/O; Stage Combat-1/O; Dance-5/Y; Film-2/X

C. (2 1/2 FT) Prins of Des-1/Y; Set Design-1/O; Cost Des-2/O; Lighting Des-1/O; Tech Production (Scenog)-1/O; Costuming-1; Make-up 2/Y; Stage Management-1/O; Stagecraft-1/Y; Design Projects-4/Y; Lighting-1/Y.

D. (1/2 FT) Box Office Procedure-1/Y

FACILITIES AND PRODUCTIONS

MAINSTAGE: 130 seats, fly space, computerized lighting. 5-6 prods: 2 Fac dir, 3 Fac des, 2 GA dir; 1UG dir, 3 UG des, budget $4,000-10,000.

SECOND STAGE: 300 seats, computerized lighting. 1-4 prods: 1 Fac dir, 3 UG des; budget $4,000-8,000

THIRD STAGE: 80 seats, computerized lighting. 7 prods, 2 fac dir, 5 GA dir workshops/readings; budget $2,000-5,000

Facility was built in 1989; includes scene shop, costume shop, prop shop, sound studio, 2 movement/dance studios, 3 rehearsal studios, 4 classrooms, CAD.

A non-departmental, student-run producing organization presents one large musical plus other smaller productions per year in which majors participate. 2 student-written plays produced in the last two years.

Connection with Equity companies at the Hartford Stage, Goodspeed Opera, Newington Children's Theatre which operate during school year. Students have the opportunity to intern in management, technical theatre, choreography, acting and children's theatre.

DESCRIPTION

Noted Faculty: Lani Beck Johnson, Costume and Make-up Design; Josh Perlstein, Acting; Thom Delventhal, Acting; Jarek Strzemien, Acting; Tom Callery, Lighting/Sound; Ken Mooney, Scene Design.

Guest Artists: Actress Jill Clayburgh; Mark Olsen; Double Edge Theatre; Jennifer Muller Dance Workshop; Efraim Silva Capoeira workshop, Lion King dance workshop; Directors Susan Streater, Billy Johnstone, John DeNicola; Designer Nathan Aldrich.

Nestled in the Connecticut Hills, Central Connecticut State University is close to professional theatres and New York City. Our BFA and BA degrees draw students from around the country who major in Acting, Design/Technical, Dance or General Theatre. There are many opportunities to perform and design in our active program. An annual New York Theatre experience ends each year with a chance to present a workshop production in the heart of Broadway. Many of our alumni are currently working in a professional theatre and film as well as distinguishing themselves in prestigious graduate schools such as Yale and Carnegie-Mellon.

Connecticut College

Linda Herr, Chair
Theatre Department
Connecticut College
270 Mohegan Ave., Box 5512
New London, CT 06320-4196

1,700 T. Enr.; highly compet.
Semester System
40 Majors
SMALL PROGRAM
(860) 439-2606

DEGREES OFFERED

BA in Theatre (20). Declare major end of sophomore year; grants approx. 15 degrees/yr.

ADMISSION & FINANCIAL INFORMATION

1200+ SAT

FACULTY AND CLASSES OFFERED

3 Full-Time, 2 Part-Time: 2 PhD, 1 MA/MFA; 2 Staff

A. (1/2 FT) Intro to Theatre-1/Y; Dramatic Lit-2/Y; Theatre History-2/Y; Shakes-2/Y

B. (2 1/2 FT) Acting-6/Y; Directing-2/Y

C. (1 PT) Tech. Production-1/Y; Costume Construction-1/Y

FACILITIES AND PRODUCTIONS

MAINSTAGE: 1300 seats, fly space, electronic lighting 4 prods: 2 Fac dir/Guest des, 1 Guest dir/des, 1 UG dir/des

SECOND STAGE: Black Box Theatre, 130 Seats, built 1999

THIRD STAGE: 75 seats. 8-12 UG dir/des prods; 4 UG dir workshops/readings.

Facility was built in 1941; last renovated in 2000; includes scene shop, costume shop, rehearsal studio.

DESCRIPTION

Noted Faculty: Linda Herr, Leah Lowe. Adjunct Faculty: Anna Strasberg, David Hayes, George White, Richard Digby Day.

Guest Artists: Jay Ranelli, Sabrina Notarfrancisco.

The Connecticut College Theater Department offers an integrated study in drama, wherein students develop a broad knowledge of theater by balancing the study of the literatures, history, and theory of drama with an experience of living theater and the creative experience through studio work, production, and performance. The department actively uses guest artists to provide extensive residencies and workshops during which students have an opportunity to work closely with outstanding professionals in acting, directing, design, and technical theater. The varied production program is designed to offer challenging theater for the community while setting professional standards.

Fairfield University

Lynne Porter, Theatre Prog Dir
Dept. of Visual & Performing Arts
Fairfield University
1073 North Benson Road
Fairfield, CT 06824
DEPT: (203) 254-4000 x 3406
lporter@mail.fairfield.edu
admin: North Benson Rd., Fairfield, CT 06824
ADM: (203) 254-4000x2906
www.fairfield.edu/admissions/admissions.htm

3,500 Tot. Enr.; compet.
30 Majors;
Semester System
T: $24,100/$8,560 r&b
SMALL PROGRAM
fax: (203) 254-4076
www.fairfield.edu/vpa

DEGREES OFFERED

BA in Comprehensive Liberal Arts Program (38). All students participate in all areas of academics and production. Declare major in 1st or 2nd year; 2007 will grant 11 degrees.

ADMISSION & FINANCIAL INFORMATION

SAT of 1170+; GPA B+; Rank top 20% of HS or better. 49% accepted by institution. Interview encouraged with theatre faculty. Four schols. available annually to theatre majors and minors for admin. positions in Theatre Fairfield. Apply after fresh. or first full year in residence.

FACULTY AND CLASSES OFFERED

4 Full-Time, 3 Part-Time: 1 PhD, 5 MFA, 1 Prof. w/out adv. deg

A. (1/2 FT, 1 PT) Intro to Theatre-2/Y; Dramatic Lit-4/Y; Theatre

History-2/Y; Shakes-4/Y; Dramatic Criticism-1/O; Playwriting-1/Y; Production Theory-1/O.

B. (1 FT, 3 PT) Acting-3/Y; Voice/Speech-1/Y; Movemt-1/Y; Singing-2/Y; Directing-2/Y; Dance-4/Y; Voice-1/Y.

C. (2 FT) Prins. of Design-1/Y; Tech Prod'n-1/Y; Advanced Des.-2/Y; Stage Craft-1/Y; Costume Constr-1/O; Makeup-1/O; Practicum in Prod-1/Y.

D. (1/4 FT) Arts Management-1/O; B.O. Procedure-1/Y.

FACILITIES & PRODUCTIONS

MAINSTAGE: Black box, 120 seats, computerized lighting

SECOND STAGE: Studio Theatre, newly revonvated,80 seats, elect ltg

THIRD STAGE: 750 seats, prosc.theatre, comp ltg.
4 prods: 1 Fac dir, 2 Fac des, 1 Guest dir, 3-4 Guest des, 1 UG dir, 3 UG des; budget $10,000-20,000. 1-2 Fac dir/des, 1-2 UG dir/des; budg $250-500

Facility was built in 1989, includes scene shop, costume shop, prop shop, sound studio, 1 rehearsal, 1 design, 1 movement dance.

6 student-written full prod.; 12 staged readings.

Connected with Shakespeare Ventures, operates summer only. University students are eligible for internships in both Shakespeare Ventures performances and teaching opportunities. Shakespeare Ventures runs a 4-week acting workshop for actors age 10-19 in addition to producing one Shakespeare play per summer.

DESCRIPTION

Noted Faculty: Lisbeth Brailoff: Dance; Susan Haggstrom: Stagecraft; Dr. Martha S. LoMonaco: History, Theory, Criticism, Directing, Lynne Porter: Rendering & Drafting, Design, Theory, Costume, Makeup, Scene Painting; Brad Roth: Dance; Jon Leiseth: Acting, Directing.

Guest Artists: Dan Burke: Fight Choreographer; Lynne Chase: Lighting Designer; Hugh Hanson: Costume Designer; Jennifer Manzo: Costume Designer; Matt Maraffi: Scenic Designer; Doug Moser: Director; Karl Ruling: Lighting/Scenic Designer; Kevin Schneck: Scenic Designer; Kim Gill: Costume Designer; Julie Leavitt: Costume Designer; Heather Burrows: Costume Technician.

The Theatre Program at Fairfield University offers a liberal arts education balanced between the theoretical and practical aspects of the discipline. Students explore this art from the varying perspectives of performer, scholar, writer, director, designer, producer and technician. Courses stress the development of artistic abilities as well as writing and communication skills. Theatre Fairfield is the production wing of the Theatre Program, and is run on a professsional theatre model. Each year the season includes professionally directed and designed productions, performances of student-written plays, and performances by our improv troupe, On the Spot. In any given four year period we produce plays from many historical periods and styles: musicals, comedies, serious plays, period plays, contemporary works, and original plays. A board of four students chosen by competitive scholarship works closely with faculty in administering the Theatre Fairfield season. Four scholarship students are chosen each year.

National Theatre Institute at the Eugene O'Neill Theater Center (NTI)

Michael Cadman, Art Dir
NTI
305 Great Neck Rd.
Waterford, CT 06385
NTI@THEONEILL.ORG
ADMISSIONS: SAME AS ABOVE
(860) 443-7139x224
www.theoneill.org/nti

64 Total Enr.; competitive
Semester System
T: $11,200/$5,100 r&b
DEPT.: (860) 443-7139
FAX: (860) 444-1212

jroutt@theoneill.org

DEGREES OFFERED

One Semester Intensive Theatre Study (64); both NTI fall and spring fully accredited

ADMISSION & FINANCIAL INFORMATION

Completed application, required letters of evaluation, and interview. When selecting students, we look for proven ability to handle the demands of disciplined theatre work and to be a positive and a contributing member of an ensemble. Competitive, requires sufficient acting experience, 65% admitted, interview required for Grad/UG. Limited scholarship opportunites avail, distributed based on proven need. Special requirements: UG int/Grad int.

FACULTY AND CLASSES OFFERED

2 Full-Time, 16 Part-Time, 3 Staff, 14 MFA/MA; 2 Phd

A. Shakes-1/Y; Playwriting-1/Y; Other-1/Y

B. Acting-3/Y; Voice/Speech-3/Y; Movement-5/Y; Mime,Mask, Commedia, Circus-1/Y; Singing-1/Y; Directing-1/Y; Stage Combat-1/Y

C. Principles of Design-1/Y; Set Des-1/Y

FACILITIES & PRODUCTIONS

MAINSTAGE: 188 seats, computerized lighting
16 prods: 1 GA dir; 15 UG dir; 16 UG des

SECOND STAGE: 177 seats, computerized lighting
15 prods: 15 UG dir; 16 UG des

Third Stage: 145 seats, computerized lighting

60 workshopped prods by dept last 2 years.

Facility was built in 1800's and last renovated in 1990's includes prop shop, welding shop, costume shop, 4 rehearsal studios, 1 movement/dance studio, 1 design studio. 10 acre national historic site overlooking Long Island Sound has 7 bldgs used for rehearsal and performance space, housing and offices. Connected with Eugene O'Neill Theatre Center Summer Conference. O'Neill is parent company for National Theatre Institute (NTI). Students can either participate in summer courses at the O'Neill or can participate in internships with the conferences.

DESCRIPTION

Noted Faculty: Adam Bock, Playwriting; Per Brahe, Mask; Elaine Bromka, Acting with the Camera; Louis Colaianni, The Joy of Phonetics; Robert Davis, Linklater Tech; Peg Denithorne, Acting/Directing; Donna Dinovelli, Playwriting; Michael Hackett, Greek Theater; Jayne Houdyshell, Acting; Rachel Jett, Russian Movement; Gillian Lane-Plescia, Speech and Dialect; G. W. Mercier, Scene Des; Rebecca B. Taichman, Found Text in Performance; Joe Urla,

Acting

NTI is a unique and highly intensive experience. We challenge you to develop your creative instruments - body, voice, imagination and discipline. Every day. We provoke you to see and create theater in new ways. Our programs present extraordinary opportunities for theater training not otherwise available to liberal arts undergraduates. We seek students who are serious. Are you serious? Founded in 1970, this rigorous conservatory-based approach to theater training immersies the student in a diverse curriculum of theater specialties and disciplines taught by working professional and master teaching artists. Coursework is rooted in five primary elements: Acting, Directing, Playwriting, Movement & Voice, and Design. The fourteen week program is offered twice a year, in the fall and spring. Classes are held seven days a week including morning warm-ups, daytime and evening classes, and is enhanced by special workshops, guest artists, theater trips, and two weeks spent in training abroad.

Southern Connecticut State University

Dr. William R. Elwood, Chair	12,500 Total Enr.; not compet.
Department of Theatre	Semester System; ATHE
Southern Connecticut State Univ.	65 Majors
501 Crescent Street	T: $6,624/$5,824 r&b
New Haven, CT 06515	O-ST T: $15,344/$8,101 r&b
DEPT: (203) 392-6100	FAX: (203) 392-6105
www.scsu.ctstateu.edu	
ADMISSIONS: Above address	(203) 392-5644
www.southernct.edu/admissions	

MAJORS AND DEGREES OFFERED

BA in Theatre specialize in Performance, Design/Technical, Generalist, History/Literature. 2007 granted 5 UG degrees.

ADMISSION & FINANCIAL INFORMATION

High School Diploma, SAT: 1,000; 70% applicants accepted; All applicants to theatre program accepted. No audition or portfolio required. No scholarships for incoming freshmen.

FACULTY AND CLASSES OFFERED

5 Full-Time, 9 Part-Time: 3 PhD, 11 MFA/MA; 1 Prof w/o advanced degree

A. (1 FT, 5 PT) Introduction to Theatre-12/Y; Dramatic Lit-1/O; Theatre History-1/Y; Shakes-1/O; Playwriting-1/Y

B. (2 FT, 3 PT) Acting-3/Y; Voice/Speech-1/Y; Movement-2/Y; Singing-1/Y; Musical Theatre-1/Y; Directing-1/Y; Dance-1/Y

C. (1 FT, 1/2 PT) Prins of Des-1/Y; Set Des-1/Y; Cost Des-1/Y; Lighting Des-1/Y; Tech Prod-1/Y; Cost Construction-1/Y; Make-up-1/Y; Stage Mgmt-1/O

FACILITIES & PRODUCTIONS

MAINSTAGE: 1,550 seats, fly space, computerized lighting
    4 prods: 3 Fac dir, 2 Fac des, 1 Guest dir/des; budget $30,000

SECOND STAGE: 125 seats, computerized lighting
    3 prods: 1 Fac dir; 2 Fac des; 4 UG dir/des; budget $10,000

Facility was built in 1969 and in 1973, renovated in 1995; includes scene, cost. shop, classrooms.

A non-departmental, student-run organization produces 2 shows in a school year in which majors participate. 4 student-written plays have been produced by the dept in the last two years.

Connection with Long Wharf Theatre, Hartford Stage, Shubert Performing Arts Center, Goodspeed Opera, Circle in the Square and other local performance groups. Companies provide internships and employment of current students and alumni.

DESCRIPTION

Noted Faculty: Professors Elwood, Theatre History, Playwriting; Garvey, Acting, Directing; Cornwell, Lighting, Tech Theatre; Nye, Musical Theatre, Dance, Children's Theatre; Sullivan, Costume & Scene Des

Southern Connecticut State University offers a B.A. degree in theatre within the context of a liberal arts degree with particular emphasis on the following areas: theatre history, dramatic literature, playwriting, acting, directing, stage management, lighting, costume and scene design and technical theatre. Students who graduate are fully qualified to work in community theatre, regional and professional theatre and are prepared to pursue graduate study.

Trinity College

Judy Dworin, Chair	2,000 Total Enr.; compet.
Dept of Theater and Dance	Semester System
Trinity College	25 Majors
300 Summit Street	T: $36,870 R&B: $9,420
Hartford, CT 06106-3100	SMALL PROGRAM
WWW.TRINCOLL.EDU/DEPTS/THDN/	
DEPT.: (860) 297-5122	MAIN: (860) 297-2000
www.trincoll.edu	admissions.office@trincoll.ed

DEGREES OFFERED

BA in Theater & Dance (25)
Declare major in sophomore year

ADMISSION & FINANCIAL INFORMATION

30% applicants accepted. Theater and Dance Program dependent on general admission. No merit scholarships; all financial assistance awarded on the basis of need. Approximately 40% of students receive some form of aid.

FACULTY AND CLASSES OFFERED

4 Full-Time, 10 Part-Time: 10 MFA/MA, 2 Prof. w/o adv. degree; 5 Staff

A. Intro to Performance, Approaches to Performance, 20th Century Theater and Dance, European Theater, Women in Performance .

B. Acting, Voice, Directing, Dance Composition, Improvisation, Performance Art.

C. Set Design, Costume Design, Lighting Design, Technical Production.

FACILITIES AND PRODUCTIONS

MAINSTAGE: 400 seats, fly space, computerized lighting. 6 prods, Theater Fac dir/des, 2 Dance Fac dir/des, 4 UG dir/des.

SECOND STAGE: 100 seats, computerized lighting.1 Theater Fac dir/des, 6 UG dir/des.

THIRD STAGE: 60 seats, electronic lighting. 10-12 UG dir/des.

Facility was built in 1967; includes scene shop, costume shop, sound studio, video studio, 3 dance studios, 1 rehearsal studio, 2 classrooms, 1 multi-purpose space (black-box theater, gallery, reception hall, etc.)

Connection with La MaMa E.T.C. in NYC; Trinity/La MaMa Perf Arts semesters in NY, fall and spring semesters open to Trinity students and students from other schools.

DESCRIPTION

Noted Faculty: Prof. Judy Dworin: Theater/Dance Artist/Choreographer; Prof. Lesley Farlow, Theater/Dance Artist/Choreographer; Prof. Katharine Power: Assoc Academic Dean, Women's Theater and Dance historian; Mitchell Polin: Director, Performance Studies; Zishan Ugurlu: Actor and Director

Continuing Guest Artists: Blu: Lighting Designer; Michael Burke: Performance Artist; Kathy Borteck Gersten: Professional Performer, Movement Educator; Elisa Griego: Technical Designer & Director; Tony Hall: Director and Playwright; Vivian Lamb: Costume Designer; James Latzel: Lighting Designer and Production Manager; Lisa Matias: Professional Performer and Dance Educator.

Students in Trinity's Theater and Dance Department are provided with a wide selection of courses that look at the broadest spectrum of performance including history and theory, process and performance, and cross-disciplinary theater and dance studies. Students are given many opportunities to act or serve backstage functions in departmental productions taking place throughout the year. Playwriting students write their own plays, many of which are presented publicly by student directors, actors, and designers. Some students opt to do internships at companies such as the Hartford Stage Company or participate in programs like the Trinity/La MaMa Performing Arts Program in New York. In sum, theater at Trinity encourages students to take risks and develop their skills, imaginations, and intellects.

University of Connecticut

Frank Mack, Man, Dir
Dept. of Dramatic Arts
Univ. of Connecticut
802 Bolton Road, Unit 1127
Storrs, CT 06269-1127
FAX: (860) 486-3110
ADMISSIONS: 2131 Hillside Rd., U-3088, Storrs, CT 06269-3088
(860) 486-3137
www.uconn.edu

16,347 Total Enr.; h. compet.
Sem. Sys.; NAST; U/RTA
130 UG, 30 Grad Majors
T: $8,8842 UG, $22,786 O-ST
DEPT: (860) 486-4025
R&B: $6,888

FAX: (860) 486-1476
beahusky@uconn.edu

DEGREES OFFERED

BA in Theatre Studies (27); BFA in Design/Technical (23); BFA/MFA in Acting (62/9), Puppetry (11/7); MA in Production: Puppetry (6), MFA in Design-Cost., Ltg, Scenery (10), Technical (3). Declare major in fresh. year

ADMISSION & FINANCIAL INFORMATION

UG program req's. SAT/ACT; HS diploma, esssay, letters of rec., audition for actors, audition/interview for puppetry applics. Grad program req's. BA/BFA , 3.0 GPA; audition for actors, audition/interview for puppetry applics/theatre studies. Modest partial tuition scholarships for incoming students. More substantive aid available to continuing students based on demonstrated potential.

FACULTY AND CLASSES OFFERED

13 Full-Time, 1 Part-Time: 4 PhD, 9 MA/MFA, 4 Prof w/out adv. degree; 8 Staff

see website, www.drama.uconn.edu, for updated class info.

FACILITIES AND PRODUCTIONS

MAINSTAGE: 500 seats, fly space, electron. lighting. 4 prods: 1 Fac dir, 3 Guest dir, 4 Grad des; budget $7,000-14,900

SECOND STAGE: 100 seats, computerized lighting 2 prods: 2 Fac dir, 2 Grad des; budget $1,500-3,900

Third Stage:Stage Theater, 235 seats, thrust.

FOURTH STAGE: 90 seats, black box 1 Fac dir Workshop/Reading

Facility was built in 1960; includes scene shop, costume shop, prop shop, welding shop, CAD facility, video studio, dance studio, rehearsal studios, design studio, classrooms, puppetry workshop or Lab.

2 student-written play produced in the last two years.

Connection with Conn. Repertory Theatre (Equity): U-Conn students obtain professional level production experience.

DESCRIPTION

Noted Faculty: Laura Crow, Costume Design; Gary English, Scene Design; Eric Hill, Acting/Directing; Jim Franklin, Lighting Design; Bart Roccoberton, Puppetry; Karen Ryker: Acting & Voice; Tim Saternow, Scene Design; Jean Sabatine, Movement/Dance; David Alan Stern, Voice and Diction.

Guest Artists: Directors: James Warwick, Leah C. Gardiner, James Bond. Director/Choreographers; B. Peter Westerhoff, Keith Lee Grant. Choreographers: Schellie Archbold, Jayme McDaniel. Actors: William Bogert, Susanne Marley, Max von Essen, Andrew Hammond, Rob Nagle, Kristin Wold, Gray Simons, Dan Cooney, Cindy Marchionda, Elena Ferrante, Rudy Guerrero, Jayme McDaniel, Kimberly Breault, Ilene Bergerlson, Daniel Britt, June Squibb, Ron McClary, Peter-Michael Marino, Robin Aronson, Melissa Hart, Rachel Hardin, John Bisom, Alice Cannon, Ian Pfister, Allyson Turner, Jody Madaras, Kirby Ward, Camille Diamond, Jerold Goldstein, Christopher Talbert, Natasha Harper, Michael Halling, Florence Lacey, Richard Ruiz, Wendy Saver. Playwrights: Tony Kushner.

The University of Connecticut Department of Dramatic Arts and its theatre production arm, the Connecticut Repertory Theatre (CRT), combine to create an exciting center for excellence in the dramatic arts. Each year young theatre artists from across the United States choose to pursue education, training, and production experience through undergraduate study in the Department of Dramatic Arts and CRT. A division of the University of Connecticut School of Fine Arts, the Department offers comprehensive and challenging academic programs and training experiences which prepare students for professional career in the theatre and related entertainment fields including television, film, and video. The goal of the Department is twofold. First, it aims to provide the finest possible professional training through classroom and studio instruction. Second, it aims to supplement and enrich that classroom and studio training by providing outstanding opportunities for students to obtain professional level production experience through active participation in plays produced by The Connecticut Repertory Theatre.

University of Hartford

Alan Rust, Dir of
Hartt School Community Division
University of Hartford
200 Bloomfield Ave.
West Hartford, CT 06117
DEPT.: (860) 768-4742
http://www.hartford.edu/
ADMISSIONS: hartadm@hartford.edu

7,308 Total Enr.; compet.
Semester System
20 Majors
T: $$25,806/$13,000 r&b approx.
SMALL PROGRAM
FAX: (860) 768-4080
rust@hartford.edu
(860) 768-4465

DEGREES OFFERED

BA in Theatre Arts (5). Declare major in sophomore year;

ADMISSION & FINANCIAL INFORMATION

Admission to College of Arts & Sciences plus academic quality point average of 2.5, and interview req. Program accepts all applicants provided they qualify academically. Gershburg Schols. are available to jrs. and srs. majoring in drama. The most recent award of $4,000-Full. 84% of the incoming freshman class receives PAS

FACULTY AND CLASSES OFFERED

1 Full-Time, 4 Part-Time: 1 PhD, 4 MFA/MA

A. (2 PT) Intro to Theatre-4/Y; Theatre History-1/O; Shakes-2/Y; Dramatic Lit-6/X; Playwriting-2/Y; Acting for the Camera
B. (2 FT, 1 PT) Acting-4/Y;Voice/Speech-2/Y;Directing-1/O
C. (1 FT, 1 PT) Set Design-1/O; Cost. Design-1/O; Ltg. Design-1/O; Tech. Production-1/Y; Cost. Construction-1/Y; Cost. History-1/Y; Stagecraft, Applied Costuming; Lighting Des.

FACILITIES AND PRODUCTIONS

STAGE: 200 seats. 3 prods: 2 Fac dir/des, 1 Guest dir; budget $2,000-3,000 each

Several UG dir/des workshops

Mainstage facility was built in 1960, renovated in 1996; campus also has 4 other performance spaces, scene shop, cost. shop, sound studio.

Internships are available with regional organizations such as Hartford Stage, Theatre Works.

DESCRIPTION

Noted Faculty: Catherine B. Stevenson, Harvey F. Campbell ; Norma Collins, Sally Porterfield.
Guest Artists: David Watson, Tobi Silver.

The Theatre Arts program at the University of Hartford is exclusively an undergraduate, non-professionally oriented one in which theatre functions as an integral component of the College of Arts and Sciences. The program, therefore, is offered to all undergraduate students who can qualify academically, regardless of their major, and to all university personnel and faculty. The department aims to enrich the cultural experience of students and community residents by providing a broad spectrum of courses that introduces them to the theatrical expression of ideas and feelings throughout human history. The aca-

demic offerings are supplemented by a producing program that includes several fully mounted productions each year by the University Players, and by public presentations of student-directed groups such as the Directors Workshop and the Actors Studio.

Wesleyan University

John Carr, Chair
Theater Department
Wesleyan University
Middletown, CT 06459-0452
DEPT: (860) 685-2950
http://www.wesleyan.edu/theater
ADM: 275 Washington Terrace
(860) 685-3000

2,700 Total Enr.; h. compet.
Semester System
40 Majors
T: $36,806/$10,130 r&b
FAX: (860) 685-2591
jmarco@wesleyan.edu
admissions@wesleyan.edu
http://www.wesleyan.edu

DEGREES OFFERED

BA in General Theatre (40) Declare major in soph. year; 2007 granted 11 UG degrees

ADMISSION & FINANCIAL INFORMATION

SAT's: Math 710, Verbal 720, Writing 710, theatre program dependent on general admission; institution admits 27% of applicants. No special scholarships specific to theatre program.

FACULTY AND CLASSES OFFERED

7 Full-Time, 4 Part-Time: 3 PhD, 7 MFA/MA, 1 Prof w/.o advanced degree; 5 Staff

A. (2 1/2 FT, 2 PT) Intro to Theatre-1/Y; Theatre History-2/Y; Shakes-1/O; Dramatic Criticism-1/O; Playwriting-1/Y
B. (1 1/2 FT, 2 PT) Acting-4/Y; Movement-1/O; Mime, etc-1/O; Singing-X; Dance-X; Directing-2/Y
C. (3 FT) Set Design-1/Y; Costume Design-1/Y; Lighting Design-1/Y

FACILITIES AND PRODUCTIONS

MAINSTAGE: 400 seats, fly space, computerized lighting
4 prods: 2 Fac dir; 2 Fac des; 2 UG dir; 2 UG des; budget $1,200-8,000
SECOND STAGE: 130 seats, fly space, computerized lighting
12 prods: 12 UG dir; 12 UG des; budget $300-1,500
1 workshop: 1 Fac des; 1 GA dir
Facility was built in 1973, renovated in 1994; includes scene shop, cost. shop, welding shop, 2 rehearsal studios, 1 movement/dance studio, 1 design studio.
A non-departmental, student-run org. in which majors generally participate presents 22 prods/yr.

DESCRIPTION

Noted Faculty: Marcela Oteiza, Scenic Des, Media Arts/Installations; John Carr, Lighting Des, Tech Dir; Leslie Weinberg, Costume Des; Ron Jenkins, Indonesian Theater, Solo Performance; Gay Smith, Theater History & Dramaturgy; Yuriy Kordonskiy, Directing & Russian Theater; Claudia Tatinge Nacimento, Performance Studies, Brazilian Theater; David Jaffe, Acting, Producing
Guest Artists: Catherine Filloux, playwriting; Marsha Norman, playwriting; Ang Gey Pin, acting, voice, movement; Lloyd Richards, directing
Wesleyan University's Theater Department explores Theater

from both a scholarly and practical viewpoint emphasizing a world view of performance in a liberal arts context. Classes are offered in theory; history and literature of drama and theater; playwriting; criticism; costume, set and lighting design; directing and acting. Our sponsored productions reflect the diverse interests of the faculty and students, offering direct participation in creative endeavor where process, performance and understanding are equally stressed. The department produces contemporary adaptations of classical theater texts, adaptations of literary works for the stage, Latin American Theater, collaborations with the Music Department on contemporary and classical operatic works, puppet theater and the use of multi-media, solo performance and performance art. The department has two theater facilities; the Theater in the Center for the Arts, a modern highly sophisticated 400-seat space; the '92 Theater, a flexible, recently renovated, studio space. Second Stage, an extracurricular student group, has its headquarters and also sponsors productions in the '92 Theater, in cooperation with the Theater Department. Performances are also given in many alternative spaces on campus by members of the lively and diverse Wesleyan theater community.

Western Connecticut State University

Sal Trapani, Chair
Theatre Arts Department
Western Conn. State Univ.
181 White Street
Danbury, CT 06810
DEPT: (203) 837-8250
trapani@wcsu.edu
ADM: 181 White St., Danbury, CT 06810
(203) 837-9000
www.wcsu.edu/admissions

7,000 Total Enr.; competitive
Semester System
65 Majors
T: $7,000/$7,000 R&B*
O-ST T: $12,000/$7,000 R&B*
FAX: (203) 837-8912
www.wcsu.edu/theatrearts

* incl. est. cost of books

DEGREES OFFERED

BA in Theatre Arts (70)w/options: Performance, Desi/Tech; Theatre Arts Mgmt;Drama Studies; Musical Theatre. Declare major in junior year.

ADMISSION & FINANCIAL INFORMATION

Top 30% of class, SAT of 750; Int/Aud required for admission to theatre program. Some scholarships available both for incoming students and exceptional students who have been here at least one year.

FACULTY AND CLASSES OFFERED

6 Full-Time, 3 Part-Time: 4 PhD, 2 MFA

A. (2 FT, 1 PT) Intro to Theatre-2/Y; Th. History-1/Y; Shakes- 1/Y; Dramatic Lit-1/Y; Dramatic Criticism-1/Y; Playwriting-1/Y

B. (2 FT, 1 PT) Acting-4/Y; Movement-1/Y; Singing-1/Y; Directing-1/Y; Voice/Speech-2/Y; Mime/Mask-1/O; Musical Theatre-1/Y; Stage Combat-1/O

C. (1 FT, 1 PT) Principles of Design-1/Y; Set Des-2/Y; Cost Des- 1/Y; Tech. Production-1/Y; Costume History-1/Y; Stage Management-1/O; Lighting Design-2/Y; Cost Construction-1/O; Make-up-1/O

D. (1 FT) Arts Management-1/X; Marketing/Promo-1/X; BO Procedure-1/Y; Legal/Contracts-1/X

FACILITIES AND PRODUCTIONS

MAINSTAGE: 600 seats, fly space, comput. & electron. lighting.

6 prods: 4 Fac dir/des, 2 Guest Artist dir/des; budget $5,000-10,000

SECOND STAGE: 200 seats, computerized and electronic lighting. 12 prods: 4 Fac dir/des, 8 UG dir/des; budget $2,000-3,000

16 Workshops/Readings: Fac and UG dir/des; budget $300-500

Also do a yearly showcase in May on Theatre Row in NYC - use this to showcase students to the New York agent, producer, etc. Edinburgh Festival Scotland bi-yearly.

Facility was built in 1959, renovated in 1979; includes scene shop, costume shop, welding area, sound studio, video studio, dance studio, rehearsal space, classrooms.

A departmental student-run organization presents 2 productions per year in which majors participate.

5 student-written plays produced in the last two years.

Internships available with various NYC and regional theatres.

DESCRIPTION

Noted Faculty: William Walton, performance; Sal Trapani, performance, resident director Circle East; Frank Herbert, tech director

Guest Artists: William Fichtner, actor; AR Gurney, playwright; Rob DeCina, casting dir; Ron Ross, casting dir; William Smitrovich, actor; Maureen Hamill, cabaret; Robin McGhee, costumes; Randy Noojin, playwright; Amy Jones, choreographer; Jennifer Hubbard, Viewpoint; Jan Neuberger, voice.

Would you like to perform in NY, at the Edinburgh Festival, while getting many performance opportunities in a variety of styles in a variety of venues? We offer: private university education at public university prices, small classes, professional resident faculty, numerous visiting artists from NY, easy access to NY - educational and cultural opportunities in the greatest city in the world - annual showcase in NYC, biannual performances - Edinburgh Festival, participation in USITT conferences, Humana Festival, Louisville. An international reputation, having been called 'stunning' and 'transcendent' by the foreign press, quickly and quietly gaining reputation as outstanding BA theatre training programs nationally, students are trained to be creative artists and craftspeople, able to be successful in the professional world of theatre. Want exciting, dynamic program that encourages you to find your personal voice, while preparing you to enter the professional world of theatre, then Theatre Arts at WestConn is the place for you.

Yale University

Toni Dorfman, Dir of UG Studies
Theater Studies,POB 208296
Yale University, 220 York Street
New Haven, CT 06520-8296
FAX: (203) 432-1308
ADMISSIONS: 38 Hillhouse Ave.
(203) 432-9300
undergraduate.admissions@yale.edu

h. compet.
Semester System
100 Majors
DEPT.: (203) 432-1310
theater@oantheon.yale.edu

FAX: (203) 432-9392

DEGREES OFFERED

For Grad information, contact Yale School of Drama.
BA in Theater Studies (100). Declare major in sophomore year; 2001 granted 24 degrees.

ADMISSION & FINANCIAL INFORMATION

Information available through Undergraduate Office of Admissions. Special reqs. for theatre program include Aud./Int. at end of freshman year after successful completion of prerequisite course.

FACULTY AND CLASSES OFFERED

6 Full-Time, 10 Part-Time: 8 PhD, 6 MA/MFA, 2 Prof. w/o adv. degree, 1 Staff

A. (5 FT, 6 PT) Intro to Theatre-2/Y; Shakes-2/Y; Dramatic Lit-2/Y; Dramatic Criticism-2/Y; Playwriting-2/Y; Theatre History-2/Y

B. (1 FT, 4 PT) Acting-2/Y; Movement-1/Y; Directing-2/Y; Design; Dance-1/Y

FACILITIES AND PRODUCTIONS

A black box for curricular productions and many small theaters used around campus.

A non-departmental student-run org. presents 8 productions per year in which dept. majors participate. In addition to Dramat Production, there are approx. 100 student driven productions annually.

DESCRIPTION

Noted Faculty: Joseph Roach, Theater History; David Krasner, African American Theater History; Marc Robinson, Avant-Garde Theater; Donald Margulies, Playwright; Michael Tracy, Emily Coates, Movement and Dance; Reginald Jackson, Eastern Theater & Drama; Toni Dorfman, Directing/Playwright; Murray Biggs, British Drama, Shakespeare; Deb Margolin: Playwriting.

Guest Artists: Awan Amkpa, Connie Grappo, Elinor Renfield, Director

The Yale undergraduate Theater Studies major is one of the Special Majors in the Humanities, whose general purpose is to contribute to an integrated understanding of the Western cultural tradition. As a result, Theater Studies is a program designed for two kinds of students: those who wish to begin or extend their practical involvement in theater within the framework of a coherent liberal arts curriculum, and those who wish to use the study of theater to supplement wider interests in literature, languages, art, history, music, psychology, or sociology. Thus the program has the advantage of allowing students to major either in theater alone or in combination with a related major. Work in Theater Studies courses places equal emphasis on the investigation of multiple aspects of dramatic texts and on the practical application on theatrical craft within a performance context.

Yale School of Drama

James Bundy, Dean
Yale School of Drama
P.O. Box 208244
New Haven, CT 06520-8244
www.drama.yale.edu
ADMIS: Registrar, P.O. Box 208325, New Haven, CT 06520-8325
(203) 432-1507
ysd.admissions@yale.edu

200 Tot. Enr.; h. compet.
Semester System
T: $25,735/$13,000 r&b estimate
(203) 432-1505
FAX: (203) 432-8337

FAX: (203) 432-9668

DEGREES OFFERED

MFA & Certificate in Acting (47), Directing (10), Design (Scenic, Costume, Light) (27),Sound Design (10), Stage Mgmt (12), Playwriting (11), Technical Design & Production (28); MFA & DFA in Dramaturgy & Dramatic Criticism (16/8); MFA in Theatre Management (22), Technical Internship Certificate (5). Students declare major at acceptance.

ADMISSION & FINANCIAL INFORMATION

GRE required for Dramaturgy & Dramatic Criticism, Technical Design & Production, and Theater Management. All programs require application form, resume, statement of purpose, application fee, letters of recommendation, official copy of undergraduate transcript, TOEFL if applicable. Stage Mgmt: prompt/production book. Technical Design & Production: portfolio. Dramaturgy & Dramatic Criticism: 2 samples of critical writing. Playwriting: 1 original full-length or one-act play. Technical Intern: SAT scores and portfolio. 8-30% of total applics accepted, depending on program; 72 out of 1200+ to theatre program. Financial aid in the form of scholarship grants, subsidized loans, and workstudy available, based on need.

FACULTY AND CLASSES OFFERED

35 Full-Time, 43 Part-Time: 3 PhD, 41 MFA; 34 DFA, 30Prof w/out adv. degree; 50 Staff

A. (8 FT, 8 PT) Theatre History-4/Y; Shakes-3/O; Dramatic Lit-24/O; Dramatic Criticism-5/Y; Playwriting-29/Y

B. (5 FT, 13 PT) Acting-6/Y; Movement-6/Y; Singing-4/Y; Directing-10/Y; Voice/Speech-12/Y; Games/Physical Comedy/Mask-3/Y; Alexander Technique-5/Y; Stage Combat-4/Y

C. (14 FT, 11 PT) Design/Technical Design & Prod/Stage Mgmt;Principles of Design-2/Y; Cost Prod-3/Y; Tech Prod-12/Y Set Des-11/Y; Cost Des- 6/Y; Tech. Production-12/Y; Cost. History-2/Y; Stage Mgmt-9/Y; Lighting Des-6/Y; Cost Construction-3/Y; Theater Planning and Consulting-4/Y; Sound Design-12/Y; Technical Design-5/Y; Technical Management-4/Y; Sound Technology-3/Y; Prod Mgmt-4/Y; Stage Mechanization-5/Y;

D. (3 FT, 10 PT) Theater Management-12/Y; Marketing/Promo-4/Y; Legal/Contracts-3/Y; Budget/Acctng/-5/Y; Devel/Grant Writing-2/Y; Business Communication-1/Y

FACILITIES AND PRODUCTIONS

MAINSTAGE: 487 seats, fly space, stretch-wire grid,computerized lighting. and sound.
6 prods: 3 Fac dir, 4 Fac des, 3 Guest dir, 4 Guest des, 16 Grad des; budget $30,000-100,000

SECOND STAGE: 658 seats, fly space, computerized lighting and sound.
4 prods: 1 Grad dir, 3 Grad dir, 16 Grad des; budget $17,000-18,000

THIRD STAGE: up to 200 seats, flexible space, computerized lighting. and sound.
6 prods. 6 Grad dir, 3 Grad playwrights, 24 Grad des,budget-$1000

Fourth Stage: 75 seats, studio, 6 workshops, 6 Grad dir, 6 Grad playwrights.

Fifth Stage: 75 seats, cabaret, 20 prods by a Graduate student-run organization.

Yale School of Drama is comprised of six buildings, including its original facility built in1926, and a flexible 200-seat space completed in 2001. Facilities include scene shops, costume shop, prop shop, paint shop, 3 sound studios, 3 design studios, 5 rehearsal rooms, 30 classrooms, 2 computer labs and library. The Digital Media Center for the Arts includes classrooms, video studios and digital printing equipment.

Yale Repertory Theatre is the master teaching extension of Yale School of Drama, allowing students to work alongside professionals in their respective areas. At Yale Rep, acting students understudy professional actors and appear in roles; all actors graduate with their Actor's Equity Membership Card. Student scenery, costuming, lighting and sound designers assist and design at Yale Rep. Directing students assist faculty and guest directors at Yale Rep. Student dramaturgs serve as production dramaturgs to Yale Rep productions and write and edit Theater Magazine, a scholarly journal. Technical Design and Production students serve as technical directors, master electricians, sound engineers, and assistant prop masters on Yale Rep productions and write articles for the Technical Brief journal. Theater Management students fill staff positions at Yale Repertory Theatre. Stage Management students serve as stage managers and assistant stage managers under the supervision of the AEA Production Stage Manager; all stage managers graduate with their Actors' Equity Membership Card.

DESCRIPTION

Noted Faculty: Mark Bly, Playwriting; David Budries, Sound Design; Liz Diamond, Directing; Elinor Fuchs, Dramaturgy & Dramatic Crit; Jane Greenwood, Design; Doug Hughes, Directing; Peter Francis James, Acting; Ming Cho Lee, Design; James Leverett, Dramaturgy & Dramatic Crit; Benjamin Mordecai, Theater Management; Victoria Nolan, Theater Management; Eric Overmyer, Playwriting; Bronislaw Sammler, Technical Design & Prod; Catherine Sheehy, Dramaturgy & Dramatic Crit; Stephen Strawbridge, Design; Jennifer Tipton, Design; Ron Van Lieu, Acting.

Guest Artists: Avery Brooks, Actor; Culture Clash, Company; Anthony Davis, Composer; 52nd St. Project, Audience/Educational Outreach Company; Kama Ginkas, Director; Mark Lamos, Direcotr; Moscow New Generation Theatre, Company; David Rabe, Playwright; Bill Rauch, Director; Naomi Wallace, Playwright; Sam Waterston, Actor; August Wilson, Playwright.

Yale School of Drama and Yale Repertory are committed to rigorous, adventurous and passionate exploration of our art form. We embrace a global audience. Our highest aim is to train artistic leaders in every theatrical discipline-who create bold new works that astonish the mind, challenge the heart, and delight the senses. The goal of Yale School of Drama is to develop the artistry, craft, and attitudes of its students to prepare them for careers in the professional theatre. Yale School of Drama and Yale Repertory Theatre together are a unique conservatory for theatre training within the University. In each discipline of the School of Drama the aesthetics sensibility is translated into the language of the stage. The process of applying theory to professional practice is central to the School, and Yale Repertory Theatre serves as the master teacher toward this aim. Athough many graduates' paths evolve into distinctive careers in film, television, teaching, and alterna-

tive forms of theatrical production and presentation, the primary focus of training at the School of Drama is the artistry of the legitimate stage.

University of Delaware

Sanford Robbins, Chair	16,296 T. Enr.; highly compet.
Professional Theatre Training Prog	Semester System
Department of Theatre	42 Majors; ATHE
413 Academy St.	T: $8,150 R&B $7,948
University of Delaware	O-ST T: $$19,400 R&B $7,948
Newark, DE 19716	DEPT: (302) 831-2201
www.udel.edu/theatre	FAX: (302) 831-3673
admissions@udel.edu	www@udel.edu

DEGREES OFFERED

MFA in Acting (27), Technical Production (10), Stage Management (5)

ADMISSION & FINANCIAL INFORMATION

Audition for actors, interview for tech production and stage management; Grad MFA Program selects students from highly competitive national process. 6% of applicants accepted. 45 out of 1,500 applicants admitted to Graduate theatre program. No Undergraduate program

FACULTY AND CLASSES OFFERED

11 Full-Time: 7 MFA/MA, 4 Prof. w/o adv. deg.

A. (1/2 FT) Intro to Theatre-(1/Y); Th. History-1/Y; Shakespeare-1/Y; Dramatic Lit-1/Y
B. (7 FT) Acting-2/Y; Voice/Speech-2/Y; Movement-2/Y; Mime, etc.-1/Y; Singing-1/Y; Stage Combat-1/Y
C. (4 FT) Principles of Design-1/Y; Cost Design-1/Y; Set Design-1/Y; Ltg. Design-1/Y; Technical Production-2/Y; Make-up-1/Y; Stage Management.-2/Y

FACILITIES & PRODUCTIONS

Hartshorn Theatre: 200-300 seats, flexible space, computerized lighting.

Production #'s vary greatly each year

Facility built in 1930, renovated in 1989. Includes scene shop, costume shop, prop shop, dance studio, 3 rehearsal studios, 3 design studios, classrooms.

DESCRIPTION

Noted Faculty: Acting: Sanford Robbins, Jewel Walker, Leslie Reidel, Joann Browning, Steve Tague. Technical Prod: Bill Browning, Eileen Smitheimer, Stage Mgmt.: Rick Cunningham.

Guest Artists: Adrian Hall, Director; Fontain Syer, Director; Richard Ramos, Director; Peter Bennett, Director; Paul Barnes, Director; J.R. Sullivan, Director; Richard Cumming, Composer; Pat McCorkle, Casting Director; Roy Hart Theatre, Voice; Cherry Jones.

The Professional Theatre Training Program (PTTP) at the University of Delaware is distinctive in a variety of ways. Once every three years, a group of exceptionally talented students is selected for admission through an extensive search conducted throughout the United States. Because there is only one class enrolled at any one time, the faculty is able to focus its full energies on the development of each student, and the Program's time, space, and budget can be directed solely toward fulfilling the potential of this select group. This unique structure allows great flexibility and the opportunity to respond quickly to individual needs as those needs become apparent. Small classes and an emphasis on tutorial work assure that each student's development is fully addressed through maximum contact with the faculty.

DISTRICT OF COLUMBIA

The American University

Dr. Gail Humphries Mardirosian, Chair 5,000 UG & 5,000 GradTotal Enr.
4400 Massachusetts Ave.
Kreeger Building - NLO
The American University
Washington, DC 20016
DEPT: (202) 885-3439
dpa@american.edu
ADMIN:Admissions Welcome Center, 4400 Mass Ave. NW
Washington DC 20016
(202) 885-6000

competitive
50 Majors; NAST/ATHE
Semester System
T: $26,000; R&B: 12,000
FAX: (202) 885-1092
http://www.american.edu/perf-arts

www.admissions.american.edu

DEGREES OFFERED

BA in Theatre: Performance (20); Music Theatre: Performance (20); Theatre: Arts Management (5); Theatre: Technical (5). Declare major in Soph. year; 2004 granted 12 UG, 80 Grad.

ADMISSION & FINANCIAL INFORMATION

3.35 GPA, 1260 SAT, 60% admitted to inst. Audition/ interview required for admission to theatre program. Theatre program admits 25 out of 50 applicants. Theatre arts management program generally admits 18 out of 60 to grad arts management program. Financial aid through competitive application. Scholarships are given to incoming freshmen based on merit. Greenberg scholarships are given to continuing students yearly, also based on merit.

FACULTY AND CLASSES OFFERED

8 FT, 2 PT, 4 PhD, 6 MFA/MA, 2 Staff

A. (2 FT) Intro to Theatre-1/Y; Theatre History-4/Y; Shakes-2/Y; Dramatic Literature-1/X; Playwriting-1/O

B. (3 FT, 1 PT) Acting-5/Y; Voice/Speech-1/Y; Movement-1/O; Musical Theatre-2/Y; Singing-2/Y; Directing-1/O; Dance-12/Y; Film-1/O

C. (3 PT) Princ of Design-1/O; Cost Des-1/O; Set Des-1/Y; Lighting Des-1/Y; Tech Prod.-1/Y; Costume Construction-1/O; Make-up-1/O; Stage Mgmt-1/Y

D. (2 FT) Arts Management-1/Y; Marketing/Promotion-1/Y; Development/Grant Writing-2/Y; Legal: Contracts/ Copyright-1/O; Budgeting/Accounting Procedure-1/Y; Museum Management-1/O; Cultural Policy-1/O; Audience Development-1/O; Volunteer Management-1/O; Gender, Race, Management-1/O; Event Management-1/O; Arts Education-1/O.

FACILITIES & PRODUCTIONS

MAINSTAGE: 300 seats, electronic lighting
3 prods: 3 Fac dir, 3 Fac des; 5 GA des, budget varies

SECOND STAGE: 100 seats
4 prods: 3 Fac dir/4 Fac des; 1 GA dir.

Facility includes scene shop, costume shop, sound studio,1 video studio, 1 movement/dance studio, 1 rehearsal studio,1 design studio, 5 classrooms.

A student-run organization presents 4 productions per year in which majors participate.

9 student-written plays produced in the past few years.

DESCRIPTION

Noted Faculty: Gail Humphries Mardirosian, Arts Education; Caleen Sinnette Jennings, playwriting.

Guest Artists: Paul Morella, Actor, Film Acting; James Kronzer, Set Design; Russell Williams, Sound Design; Judy Simmons, Music Theatre; Earnest Thompson, Playwright; Javier Rivera, Actor/Guest Lecturer; Paul Tetrault, Artistic Director/Guest Lecturer; Tom Prewitt, Associate Artistic Director/ Guest Lecturer; David Lynch, Filmmaker/Guest Lecturer; Nick Olcott, Director/Guest Lecturer.

The program provides the core of an innovative liberal arts education for students in other disciplines. It enhances understanding of the arts. It also provides students with lifelong skills and techniques from the theatre that the students can apply to a variety of professions. In addition, the Theatre/Music Theatre Program integrates theory (cognitive skills and scholarship) and practice (experimental skills and training) in a creative process encompassing performance and production. The AU Theatre/Music Theatre program subscribes to the National Association of Schools of Theatre (NAST) values analysis, which views the arts as a center (a discipline with inherent value), as a <u>means</u>, as a <u>process</u> and as a <u>product</u>.

Catholic University of America

Gail Beach, Chair
Theatre Dept./105 Hartke
The Catholic Univ. of America
Cardinal Station
Washington, DC 20064
www.cua.edu/
www.drama.cua.edu/
ADM: 102 McMahon, 620 Michigan Ave. N.E., Wash. DC 20064
(202) 319-5305
cua-admissions@cua.edu

Tot. Enr. 6,000; competitive
Semester System
65 Majors
T: $$28,990 R/b$10,808
(202) 319-5358
FAX: (202) 319-5359

FAX: (202) 319-6533

DEGREES OFFERED

BA in Drama (65); MFA in Acting (10), Directing (2), Playwriting (1) Students declare concentration after Soph yr.

ADMISSION & FINANCIAL INFORMATION

Entire application is weighed. A particular individual score is not req. UG admits 10-15 out of 20 or 25, Grad 13-14 out of 50 applicants to theatre program. Interview or audition req. for graduate programs. Graduate fellowships are offered at various amounts after evaluation of applicant's audition, GPA, GRE and application.

FACULTY AND CLASSES OFFERED

7 Full-Time, 6 Part-Time: 5 PhD, 8 MFA/MA, 3 Staff

A. (3 FT) Intro to Theatre-2/Y; Th. History-3/Y; Shakespeare-3/YX; Dramatic Lit-3/Y; Dramatic Criticism-1/Y; Playwriting-3/Y

B. (3 FT, 5 PT) Acting-4/Y; Voice/Speech-3/Y; Movement-2/Y; Singing-X; Mus. Th-X; Directing-3/Y; Stg Combat-1/Y

C. (2, 1 FT) Principles of Design-2/YO; Set Design-1/O; Costume Design-1/O; Stage Management-1/O; Lighting Des-1/O; Cost.

Const.-1/O; Scene Painting-1/O
D. (1 PT) Budgeting/Accounting-several-X

FACILITIES AND PRODUCTIONS

MAINSTAGE: 590 seats, fly space, computerized lighting
4 prods: 3 Fac dir/des, 4 Guest des, 1 Grad dir, 1 UG des; budget $7,000-10,000

SECOND STAGE: 80 seats; computerized lighting
3 prods: 1 Guest dir, 2 Guest des, 2 Grad dir; budget $3,000-5,000

THIRD STAGE: 40 seats, black box
7 workshops/readings: 3 Fac dir, 2 Guest dir, 2 Grad dir; budget $100-500

Facility was built in 1970, Second Stage renovated in 1987; includes scene shop, costume shop, prop shop, CAD facility, video studio, 2 rehearsal studios, design studio; small theatres are used also as rehearsal space, 3 classrooms.

A non-departmental, student-run organization presents ten productions per year. 2 student-written plays produced in the last two years.

Connection with Arena Stage (Equity). Acting Internships for MFA graduate actors.

DESCRIPTION

Noted Faculty: Thomas Donahue, Design; Roland Reed, Playwriting; Susan Cohen, Alexandre Technique; Naum Panouski, Directing/Acting; Gail Beach, Costume Design; Mark Wujcik, Technical Theatre.

Guest Artists: Phillip Bosco, Acting; Tony Giordano, Directing; Michael Trautman, Movement; Kate Skinner, Acting; Marcos Martinez, Suziki Technique; Kamyar Atabai, Directing; Sergei Tcherkasky, Stanislavski Technique; David Zinder, Acting; Arthur Giron, Playwriting; SherryKramer, Playwright.

The goal of the department is to offer undergraduate and graduate programs that provide for the intellectual growth and cultural enrichment of its students and for the development of disciplined and imaginative expression in the theatre. It seeks to provide prospective teachers, actors, directors, designers, and playwrights with practical skills in their respective fields and with a sound knowledge of the history and literature of the theatre. The department strives for both academic and production excellence, believing that each depends to a great extent on the other. The undergraduate program leads to a BA degree, and the student's work and study in the theatre is coordinated with the full curriculum of a liberal arts education. The goal for undergrads is a liberal education rather than a vocational one. In its graduate programs, the objective is to bring students to advanced levels of practical proficiency in the art and to advanced levels of knowledge of and critical reflection on the history and literature of the theatre. The faculty is committed to providing both productions and academic programs of high quality.

George Washington University

Leslie B. Jacobson MFA, Chair
Dept. of Theatre & Dance
George Washington University

16,977 Total Enr.; compet.
Semester System
60 Majors

Marvin Ctr, Rm 227
800 21st Street, NW
Washington, DC 20052
www.gwu.edu/~theatre

T: $34,000/$10,000 r&b
DEPT: (202) 994-8072
ADM: (202) 994-6040

MAJORS AND DEGREES OFFERED

BA in Theatre (12), Dance (10); MFA in Theatre/Design (6), Theatre/Dance. Year to declare major not prescribed.

ADMISSION & FINANCIAL INFORMATION

SAT & ACT scores, H.S. transcript, 2 letters of recommendation including H.S. guidance councilor. 62% of applicants accepted; No special requirements for UG admission to Theatre Program; Interview required for Grad . Presidential Schols. $7,500 in annual tuition, $35,000 in four years, interview, audition req. Write Dept. of Theatre and Dance for information, application.

FACULTY AND CLASSES OFFERED

10 Full-Time: 3 PhD, 5 MFA/MA; 2 w/o advanced degree; 3 Staff

A. (1 FT, 2 PT) Introduction to Theatre-1/Y; Dramatic Lit.-4/X; Theatre History-2/Y; Shakespeare-2/O; Playwriting-2/X

B. (3 FT) Acting-5/Y; Voice/Speech-2/Y; Singing-2/X; Musical Theatre-2/Y; Directing-1/Y

C. (3 FT) Set Des-3/Y; Cost Des-2/Y; Ltg Des-2/Y; TechProd-2/Y;Cost Constr-1/Y;Cost Hist-1/Y; Make-up-1/Y; Stage Mgmt-1/O

FACILITIES & PRODUCTIONS

MAINSTAGE: 484 seats, fly space, computerized lighting
6 prods: 5 Fac/1 Guest dir; 3 Fac/Guest des, 1 UG des, 2 Grad des; budget $2500

SECOND STAGE: 50 seats, electronic lighting
2 prods: 2 Fac/UG dir/des; budget $200
Workshops/Readings, etc. budget: $200

Facility built in 1968; includes scene shop, costume shop, 3 dance studios, classroom.

Non-departmental, student-run organization presents 2 productions per year in which majors generally participate.

School is connected with two Equity Companies, Washington Stage Guild and Horizon's Theatre, where internships are available in production areas and front of house positions.

DESCRIPTION

Noted Faculty: Maida Withers, choreographer, modern dancer.

Guest Artists: John MacDonald, Artistic Director, Washington Stage Guild; Marcia Menefee, & Sara Pearson, Guest Choreographers.

The Purpose of the Bachelor of Arts in Theatre at the George Washington University is to introduce students to the principal arts and crafts of the theatre, to encourage critical understanding of these, to provide cultural enrichment, and to direct a student's specific talents toward professional training where such interest and potential warrants. The principal view of theatre taken by the program is that theatre is a vehicle for human communication and understanding. The primary function of theatre artists—directors, actors, and designers—is to interpret plays through performance. Program requirements proceed logically from these objectives. Students are required to take courses in acting, directing, costuming, theatre production, lighting, history, and dramatic literature. Additionally, students are encouraged to elect courses that develop their particular theatrical interests within the limitations of departmental and college resources. Finally, students are encouraged to relate theatre to other humanistic and scientific disciplines such as anthropology, psychology, sociology, and women's studies. Such interrelationships are at the heart of a liberal education.

Howard University

Joe W. Selmon, Chair	10,500 Total Enr.; competitive
Department of Theatre Arts	Semester System
Division of Fine Arts	154 Majors; NAST (A), ATHE
Howard University	T: $10,935
2455-6th St., NW	MAIN: (202) 806-6100
Washington, DC 20059	DEPT: (202) 806-7050

DEGREES OFFERED

BFA in Drama (79), Theatre Education (2) (Areas of Concentration: Acting, Directing, Musical Theatre, Theatre Education, Theatre Arts Administration), Theatre Technology, Dance .Arts
Declare major in freshman year; grant ~ 16 degrees.

ADMISSION & FINANCIAL INFORMATION

SAT comb. 1,000; HS diploma/GED; College prep courses; Accept 34% UG to institution; Audition/Interview required. for program; Th. program accepts 2 out of 5 applicants. Special Talent Schol., participation, acad. standing; Andrew Allen Schol., Jr./Sr. profic. in Dance, Voice and Acting, Vera J. Katz Scholarship (Directing).

FACULTY AND CLASSES OFFERED

15 Full-Time: 2 PhD, 13 MFA/MA;4 Staff

A. (3 FT) Intro to Theatre-6/Y; Th. History-3/Y; Shakespeare-X; Dram. Lit-1/Y; Dramatic Criticism-2/Y; Playwriting-2/Y; Creative Dramatics-1/Y; Th. Education-2/Y

B. (7 FT) Acting-11/Y; Voice/Speech-4/Y; Movement-8/Y; Singing-2/Y; Musical Theatre-22/Y,X; Directing-4/Y; Stage Combat-1/Y; Intro to Acting (non-major)-1/Y

C. (3 FT) Prins of Des-1/Y; Set Des- 1/Y; Ltg Des-3/Y; Tech. Production-4/Y; Cost Constr Practicum-2/Y; Cost History-2/Y; Make-up-2/Y; Stage Mgmt-1/Y; Intro to Tech. Theatre-1/Y; Sound-1/Y; Intermediate Stagecraft-1/O; Seminar/Tech Thea-1/Y

D. (3 FT) Arts Mgmt-1/Y; Mktg/Promotion-X; Devel/Grant Writing-X; Legal:Contracts/Copyright-X; Budgeting/ Accounting Procedure-X; Seminar in Theatre Admin- 1/Y; Drama Internship-1/Y

FACILITIES AND PRODUCTIONS

MAINSTAGE: 300 seats, fly space, computerized lighting
   3-5 prods: 2-3 Fac dir/des, 1 Guest dir; budget $3,500-13,000 per show

SECOND STAGE: 75 seats. 3 prods; budget $200-500; 3 stud dir readings; budget $0; various workshops/readings conducted by visiting artists; bdgt $50-1,000

Facility was built in 1960 and renovated in 1987-88; includes scene shop, costume shop, 1 dance studio, 2 classrooms.

DESCRIPTION

Noted Faculty: Al Freeman, Jr., Actor; Mike Malone, Director/ Choreographer.
Guest Artists: Debbie Allen; Phylicia Allen Rashad; Pearl Cleage, playwright; Matsemala Manaka, S. African

playwright; Rosalind Cash; Lloyd Richards, director; Giancarlo Esposito; Dawnn Lewis; Ron Milner; Woodie King; Ossie Davis; Avery Brooks; Ruby Dee; Danny Glover; Ed Hall; Robert Townsend; Spike Lee, Edward Albee and Brian Stokes Mitchell.

The Department seeks to educate the artist-scholar. In so doing, the Department espouses the following objectives: 1) to train the knowledgeable theatre artist, theorist, historian, and teacher in the theatre arts; 2) to provide theatre experience for all students in the classroom as well as in production; 3) to develop the highest quality of theatre art through understanding and practice; and 4) to investigate and perpetuate the experiences and aesthetics of Black theatre.

National Conservatory of Dramatic Arts

Ray Ficca	40 Total Enr.; not competitive
1556 Wisconsin Ave. NW	Semester System
Washington, DC 20007	T: $10,350
(202) 333-2202	fax (202) 333-1753
ncdadrama@aol.com	www.theconservatory.org
Admissions: same as above	

DEGREES OFFERED

Diploma in Conservatory Acting Program (30); Advanced Acting Program Certificate (10); declare major in first year; 2007 awarded 30 UG degrees

ADMISSION & FINANCIAL INFORMATION

HS grad, audition/interview required. Admit 9 out of 10 to Acting Program.

FACULTY AND CLASSES OFFERED

20 Part-Time: 5 MA/MFA. 15 professionals w/o advanced degree.

A. (5 PT) Dramatic Lit-10/Y; Theatre History-3/Y; Shakes-2/Y; Playwriting-1/Y

B. (10 PT) Acting-15/Y; Voice/Speech-3/Y; Movement-2/Y; Mime, etc-2/Y; Stage Combat-2/Y

C. (3 PT) Costume Des-1/Y; Lighting Des-2/Y; Tech Prod-1/Y; Stage Mgmt-1/Y; Make-up-1/Y

D. (2 PT) Arts Mgmt-1/Y; B.O. Procedure-3/Y; Marketing/Promo-1/Y

FACILITIES & PRODUCTIONS

MAINSTAGE: Black box 60 seats, computerized lighting
   6 prods: 6 Fac dir; 4 GA dir; 6 Grad dir; budget $500-1,000

3 GA dir. workshops

Facility was built in 1955, last renovated in 1999, includes scene shop, 1 movement/dance studios,2 rehearsal studios, 1 classroom.

Connected with Charter Theatre, an AEA company dedicated to the development of new works for the stage. Students can intern in technical theatre, and front of house positions. Seniors have private audition for roles and understudy parts in their mainstage season. Seniors become eligible for roles in the children's season immediately after graduation - children's season is cast exclusively from Conservatory graduates. During third year (seniors) students participate in the development of a commissioned play from first draft through two levels of developmental reading culminating in full production as the last play of their final year.

DESCRIPTION

Noted Faculty: Ray Ficca, Acting, Commedia dell'Arte; George Grant, Shakespeare; John Vreeke, Directing; David Elias, Acting & Voice; Nan Ficca, Business of Acting, Playwriting; Callie Kimball, Acting, Playwriting; Michael Kinghorn, Dramaturgy; Hope Lambert, Acting.

Guest Artists: Directors: Jeremy Skidmore, Kathleen Akerley, Jose Carrasquillo, Steven Scott Mazzola, Keith Bridges, Michael Russotto. Playwrights: Allyson Currin, Chris Stezin

The Conservatory has been successfully training actors since 1975 for careers in theatre, television and film and is the only accredited, professional actor's training studio in the Washington DC Metro area. Our programs provide individual attention, small class settings and a faculty composed of leading artists from Washington, DC, and New York. We train our actors through a full rehearsal and performance process beginning with the first semester – students complete 6 full plays in the two-year program. Those who are selected to go on to the third-year program participate in a full season of four mainstage shows under the direction of Washington's leading directors.

FLORIDA

Asolo Conservatory/ Florida State University

Greg Leaming, Director
FSU/Asolo Conservatory
FSU Center for the Performing Arts
5555 North Tamiami Trail, Sarasota, FL 34243
(941) 351-9010, x 2311

Highly competitive
Semester System
30 Majors; U/RTA, ATHE

MAJORS AND DEGREES OFFERED

Professional Actor Training Program (30) grants MFA.

ADMISSION & FINANCIAL INFORMATION

Req Aud. thru U/RTA , the Association of L.O.R.T. Based Training Programs, or in Sarasota; BA with 3.0 or GRE 1000(total); admission to Grad School of FSU. 10-12 actors selected from national audition/interview process. All students accepted into the Conservatory are on full schol., including tuition waivers, ass'tships, stipends from FSU, 8 wks. study in London, in 3rd year salary from Asolo Repertory Theatre Co.

FACULTY AND CLASSES OFFERED

6 Full-Time, 2 Permanent Adjunct

Classes in Acting, Voice/Speech/Text, Movement/Dance/Mask; Stage Combat, Acting for the Camera, professional and commercial workshops and New York showcases.

FACILITIES & PRODUCTIONS

The Asolo/FSU Conservatory is an integral part of the FSU Center for the Performing Arts, which is the home of the Asolo Repertory Theatre Company, an Equity Lort C company. The Conservatory's association with the Equity company is a keystone for both groups—neither group could exist in its present strength without the other. The Asolo Mainstage is a 500-seat house with computerized and electronic lighting. The Conservatory Theatre is a 165 seat space adjoining the Asolo Mainstage.

DESCRIPTION

Noted Faculty: Barbara Redmond, Margaret Eginton, Patricia DeLorey, Acting; Andrei Malaev-Babel, Voice; David Brunetti, Singing; Randy Spaulding, Jimmy Hoskins, Stage Movement/Dance/Mask.

The Asolo/FSU Conservatory is a 3-year professional training program culminating in a MFA in Acting degree. The program aims to train a limited number of promising candidates for careers in the professional theatre. The training is accomplished through an intensive Conservatory approach and participation in the working life of an American regional theatre. The first year of training is devoted entirely to classroom work with no public performances. During the second year of training, students perform major roles in the Asolo Conservatory Theatre Company. Second year students spend a summer in London studying British theatre. In the third year, actors become associate members of the Asolo Theatre Company and are guaranteed to appear on the LORT mainstage. All faculty are working professionals and students are continually exposed to the realities of making a career in theatre. With a total of only 30 students and six faculty in the Conservatory, individual attention to each student is possible. At the end of the training all students are eligible to join Actors Equity Association.

Eckerd College

Cynthia Totten, Chair
Theatre Dept.-CRA
Eckerd College
4200 54th Ave. So.
St. Petersburg, FL 33711
DEPT: (813) 864-8279
www.eckerd.edu/academics/theatre
tottenc@eckerd.edu
ADMISSIONS: 4200 54th Ave. So., St. Petersburg, FL 33711
(727) 864-8331/(800) 456-9009   FAX: (727) 866-2304

1,475 Total Enr.; h. compet.
14 Majors; ATHE, SETC
Semester System
T: $28,860/$8,338 r&b
SMALL PROGRAM
FAX: (813) 864-7800

DEGREES OFFERED

BA in Theatre - Performance Concentration (5), Theatre - Production/Design/Technical Concentration (1). Declare major in freshman year.

ADMISSION & FINANCIAL INFORMATION

GPA, ACT or SAT. 75% of applicants accepted by institution. Accept all to Theatre Program. Special Talent Schols. available. Letters of request for and letters of recommendation required.

FACULTY AND CLASSES OFFERED

4 Full-Time, 2 Part-Time: 4 PhD, 2 MA/MFA

A. (1 FT) Intro to Theatre-1/Y; Dramatic Lit-2/X; Theatre History-1/O; Shakes-1/X; Playwriting-1/O; Communication Arts/Persuasion-1/O; Theatre Beyond Lit-1/O; Film & Lit-1/O; Oral Interp. of Literature-1/O

B. (1 FT, 1 PT) Acting-3-4/Y; Voice/Speech-1/O; Movement-1/Y; Musical Theatre-1/O; Singing-1/O; Directing-1/O; Dance-2/Y; CAD-1/O; Mime,etc.- 1/O; Musical Theatre-1/O

C. (1 FT, 1 PT) Principles of Design-1/O; Tech Production-1/Y; Set Design-1/O; Lighting Design-1/Y; Stage Mgmt.-1/O

D. Theatre Internship-1/O; Senior Project-1/Y

FACILITIES & PRODUCTIONS

MAINSTAGE: 350 seats, electronic lighting
   3 prods: 3 Fac dir/6 UG des; $1,000-2,500

SECOND STAGE: 60-80 seats, electronic lighting
   2 prod: Fac dir/UG des; budget $1,000-1,500

Facility was built in 1970; includes scene shop, costume shop, movement/dance studio, rehearsal studio.

DESCRIPTION

Noted Faculty: Rich Rice, Play Devel.; Mark Castle, Design/Tech; Cindy Totten, Performance; Cheryl Warnock, Tech; Cindy Hennessey, Dance; Julie Empric, History of Drama.

Guest Artists: WordBRIDGE Playwrights Workshop: Kevin Kling, Actor, Playwright; Ethan Phillips, Actor; Len Berkman, Dramaturrgy; Kimberly Scott, Actor; Patrick Tovatt, Actor/Director; Tony Campisi, Actor/Director; Bill Mondy, Actor; Chuck Kartali, Actor; Joan Darling, Director-Actor; David Kranes, Dramaturg; Cathey Sawyer, Director.

Theatre at Eckerd College provides any interested student, regardless of the major, with the opportunity for artistic expression through the performing arts. This liberal arts training offers a solid background for graduate study, professional schools and apprenticeships. Theatre training can combine with other disciplines to create challenging, versatile, careers. Eckerd College Theatre sponsors two unique programs: WordBRIDGE and Avignon. In January, WordBRIDGE, a playwright is assigned a professional production team of director, dramaturg, actors, and resource artists. At the end of an intensive two-week period of readings, rehearsals, improvisations, and script analyses, each play is presented as a staged reading and its progress and process discussed. At least one WordBRIDGE play is selected for a full production during the spring. Every other summer, the department takes a production to the Festival d'Avignon, an international theatre festival in the south of France.

Florida Atlantic University ·················

Richard J. Gamble, Chair
Department of Theatre
Florida Atlantic University
777 Glades Rd.
Boca Raton, FL 33431-0991
DEPT.: (561) 297-3810
FAX: (561) 297-2180
theatre@fau.edu
ADMISSIONS: Address above.
(561) 297-3031

14,000+ Total Enr.,
   not compet
Semester System
100 Majors; ATHE
T:$756 ug; $3,558 g
O-ST T: $2,854 ug; $11,680 g
R&B: $4,160 R&B

FAX: (561) 297-2758

DEGREES OFFERED

BA in Theatre (30); BA in Acting (47) and Design/Tech(4); MFA in Acting (14), Design/Tech (1), Declare major in freshman year; granted 2 Grad, 9 UG degs.

ADMISSION & FINANCIAL INFORMATION

Inst. reqs. for UG: 3.0 GPA and SAT comb. 1000 or ACT equiv. UG generally admits 3 out of 5 applicants to theatre program. BA reqs. Aud./Int. for Act./Dir. and Portfolio/Int. for Design/ Tech. Inst. reqs. for

Grad: 3.0 GPA and GRE comb. 1000. Grad generally admits 2 out of 5 applicants to theatre program. MFA reqs. Aud./Int.All scholarships by aud, full time status, maintain 3.0 GPA.; Univ. Theatre Patron-$500-1000/term; Esther Boyer Griswold Univ. Schol. $500-1000/term; Tech Majors-Harold Burris-Meyer Schol. $300-500/term; Grad Assts. $3,500/term.

FACULTY AND CLASSES OFFERED

10 Full-Time, 5 Part-Time: 1 PhD/EdD, 7 MA/MFA, 2 Prof. w/o adv. degree; 10 Staff

A. (1 FT, 1 PT) UG: Intro to Theatre-4/Y, Dramatic Lit-2/Y, Th History-2/Y, Shakes-1/X, Playwriting-1/O; Dramatic Structure-1/Y; Grad: Dramatic Theory-2/Y, Seminar on Current Prod-2/Y

B. (3 FT, 4 PT) UG: Acting-5/Y, Voice/Spch-2/Y, Mvmt-7/Y;Make-Up-1/Y; Mime, etc.-O, Mus Th-1/O, Directing-2/Y, Stg Combat-1/O, Oral Interp-2/Y; Grad: Voice/Speech-4/Y, Mvmt-4/YO; Stg Combat-1/O, Grad Rep-2/Y, Grad Prod'n; Ind. Stud., Voice/Mvmt

C. (3 FT, 1 PT) UG: Prins of Des-2/Y, Set Des-2/Y, Cost Des-1/Y, Ltg Des-1/Y, Tech. Prod'n-1/Y, Cost Constr-1/Y, Cost Hist-1/Y, Make-up-1/Y; Grad: Prins of Design-1/Y, Set Des-1/Y, Cost Des-1/Y, Ltg Des-2/Y, Tech. Prod-1/Y, Cost Const-1/Y, Cost Hist-1/Y.

D. (1 FT) Grad: Arts Management-2/Y, other courses thru College of Business. A.M. Program is tailored to student's individual needs.

FACILITIES AND PRODUCTIONS

MAINSTAGE: 540 seats, prosc., fly space, computerized lighting
   2-5 prods; 2-3 Fac or Guest dir/des, 1-2 Grad dir/des;
   budget $20,000-25,000

SECOND STAGE: 150 seats, black box/thrust, fly space, comp. ltg. 2-5 prods: UG/Grad dir/des., budget $20-25,000.

THIRD STAGE: 70-seat black box, 2 sc. preset ligthing board.
   7-8 prods: ug & grad dir/des; budget $750-1000

The Third Stage is a departmental, student-run theatre in which all majors are encouraged to participate.

New facility (1995-96) includes 2 scene shops, costume shop & storage, props shop & storage, welding shop, dance & rehearsal studios, dressing rooms, 2 sound studios.

DESCRIPTION

Guest Artists: Tony award-winning acress Zoe Caldwell, guest artist, director & instructor; B'way actress Patricia Connolly, acting instr.; Academy Award-winning actress Olympia Dukakis, acting instr.; published scholar, Ruby Cohn, guest professor.

The Department of Theatre program at Florida Atlantic University is designed to prepare students for advanced study or for careers in the professional theatre. The program is relatively small, which provides many opportunities for hands-on work and individualized instruction. Our Emminent Scholar Program, that has brought such famous guest artists as mentioned above, and our outstanding facilities, are developing an international reputation for the Theatre Department at Florida Atlantic University.

Florida International University

Lesley-Ann Timlick, Director
Dept. of Theatre & Dance
Wertheim Performing Arts Center
11200 SW 8th St., PAC 131
Florida International University
Miami, FL 33199
www.fiu.edu~thedan
ADMISSIONS: FIU, PC140, University Park, Miami, FL 33199
ADMISSIONS: (305) 348-2363
www.fiu.edu

38,000 Total Enr.; competitive
130 Majors; Semester System
NAST
T: $2,272/$6,500 r&b
O-ST T: $9,260/$6,500 r&b
DEPT. (305) 348-2895
FAX: (305) 348-1803

FAX: (305) 348-3648
admis@fiu.edu

DEGREES OFFERED

BA in Comprehensive Theatre (60), Management (2). BFA in Acting (16), Scenic Design (2), Costume Design (2), Lighting Design (1). Declare major in soph. year; 2001 granted 10 degrees.

ADMISSION & FINANCIAL INFORMATION

SAT above 1000, GPA min. 2.5. 73% of applics. accepted by institution. Audition req. for actors, interview, portfolio for designers. Theatre program admits 7 out of 10 applicants. $31,000 in Theatre Schols. available; applic, recommendations and audition.

FACULTY AND CLASSES OFFERED

9 Full-Time, 3 Part-Time: 1 PhD, 8 MFA/MA, 2 Prof. w/o adv degree;

A. (1 1/2 FT, 1 1/2 PT) Intro to Th-2/Y; Th Hist-2/Y; Shakespeare-2/Y; Dramatic Lit-1/Y; Dramatic Criticism-1/Y; Playwriting-2/Y

B. (3 FT, 1 1/2 PT) Acting-7/Y; Voice/Speech-4/Y; Movement-4/Y; Singing-1/Y; Directing-2/Y; Dance-15/Y

C. (2 FT) Prins of Des-2/Y; Cost Des-3/Y; Tech Prod'n-1/Y; Set Des-3/Y; Ltg Des-3/Y; Stg. Mgmt.-1/Y; Cost Constr-1/Y; Make-up-1/Y

D. (1/2 FT) Arts Mgmt.1/Y

FACILITIES & PRODUCTIONS

MAINSTAGE: 240 seats, computerized lighting, fly space
    4-5 prods: 4-5 Fac dir; budget $6,000-10,000
SECOND STAGE: 150 seats, computerized lighting
    2 prods: 2 UG dir/des; budget $1,000-1,400
THIRD STAGE: 150 seats, fixed stage, computerized lighting
    6-10 Workshops/Readings: 3-5 Fac dir, 3-5 UG dir; budget $100-500
Facility was built in 1996; includes scene shop, costume shop, prop shop, sound studio, design studio.
A non-departmental, student run, producing organization presents 5 productions in a school year, in which majors participate. 8 student-written plays produced in the last two years.

DESCRIPTION

Noted Faculty: Marilyn Skow, Theatre History & Costume Design; Phillip Church, Acting; Lesley-Ann Timlick, Voice, Speech, Movement & Acting; Wayne Robinson, Acting, Movement; Tracey Moore, Voice/Movement/Acting.

Guest Artists: Tony Kushner, Playwright; Andre De Sheilds, Mark Harmon, Actors; Richard Adler, Composer; Charlie Oates, Head of Acting, UCSD/MFA; Alan Bailey, Director/Playwright; Nilo Cruz.

This excellent undergraduate theatre program covers all areas of theatre: academic, historical, performance, design and management. We offer two degrees: a BA and a BFA. The BA is a broad-based, comprehensive degree that provides our students with a strong preparation for many careers in theatre and related areas, as well as for advanced academic study in theatre. The BA is a specialized degree designed for those students with the talent and motivation to pursue careers as actors, designers, technicians, or managers. All students are admitted as BA students. Admission to the BFA, after preliminary coursework, is encouraged for those who excel in their classes and demonstrate professional potential in their area of specialization. Our program's combination of skills, training and education provides solid preparation for advanced theatre training. Our students have been admitted to prominent graduate schools including, the Yale School of Drama, NYU-Tisch, and the UCSD/La Jolla Playhouse. There are also opportunities for internships and jobs for student actors and technicians at some of the professional Miami theatres.

Florida Southern College

James F. Beck, Chairman
Florida Southern College
Buckner Theatre
111 Lake Hollingsworth Dr.
Lakeland, FL 33801-5698
jbeck@flsouthern.edu
ADMISSIONS: 111 Lake Hollingsworth Dr., Lakeland, FL 33801
Adm: (863) 680-4131
blangston@flsouthern.edu

1,659 Total Enr.; competitive
24 Majors; Semester System
T: $17,860/$6,410 r&b
SMALL PROGRAM
DEPT: (863) 680-4226
www.flsouthern.edu/theatre

www.flsouthern.edu

DEGREES OFFERED

BA in Theatre Arts: Performance (17), Technical (7).
Declare major in freshman year; 2004 granted 4 degrees.

ADMISSION & FINANCIAL INFORMATION

GPA-2.5, SAT-1000, ACT-23 scores required for admission. 85% applicants accepted to institution. Audition for actors, interview, portfolio for designers. Theatre program admits 5 out of 6 applicants. Schol. awards will be awarded on merit.

FACULTY AND CLASSES OFFERED

4 Full-Time, 4 Part-Time: 3 MFA/MA, 1 Staff

A. (1 FT, 1 PT) Intro to Th-1/Y; Dramatic Lit-X; Th Hist-2/Y; Shakespeare-2/X Playwriting-O

B. (1 FT, 1 PT) Acting-4/Y; Voice/Speech-Y; Movement-1/Y; Singing-3/Y; Directing-2/Y; Dance-2/O; Film-2/X; Musical Theatre-O; Stage Combat-O

C. (1 FT, 1 PT) Prins of Des-1/X; Cost Des-1/O; Tech Prod'n-2/Y; Stage Management-1/O; Set Des-2/Y; Ltg Des-2/Y; Cost Constr-1/O; Make-up-1/O

D. (1FT, 1 PT) Arts Mgmt.1/O

FACILITIES & PRODUCTIONS

MAINSTAGE: 336 seats, thrust, computerized lighting
    4 prods: 4 Fac dir/des, 4-5 UG des; budget $ 6,000-15,000.
SECOND STAGE: 75 seats, electronic lighting
    1 UG dir/des prods; budget $250 to $500.
Facility was built in 1970, renovated in 2000; includes scene shop, costume shop, prop shop, classrooms, rehearsal studios, design studios, video studios, CAD.
A non-departmental, student-run organization presents 1 production a year, in which department majors participate.

DESCRIPTION

Noted Faculty: Paul Bawek, Acting, Movement, Directing, Voice, Intro to Theatre; James F. Beck, Set Design, Lighting Design, Theatre History, Intro to Theatre; Mary T. Albright, Costume Design, Playwriting, Children's Theatre, Intro to Theatre.

Guest Artists: Nancy Keifer, Playwright; Ingrid MacDonald, Actress.

The goal of Florida Southern's Theatre Arts Department is to train and prepare students for a professional career in the theatre. A Theatre major at FSC has opportunities to perform major roles beginning in his or her first year at the college and design students will see their work produced on our mainstage as early as his or her sophomore year. We emphasize one on one instruction, hands on experience, individual mentoring and a high degree of professionalism. Our program is aimed at providing you with the knowledge and skills you will need to succeed at any level of theatre to which you aspire, whether it is a career as a Broadway performer, a professional designer, stage manager or technician, or further graduate study. Our aim is to see you succeed and we will give you the tools you will need to do so.

Florida State University
See ad in back of book - U/RTA

Cameron Jackson, Director
School of Theatre 239 FAB
Florida State University
Tallahassee, FL 32306-1160
ccjackson@admin.fsu.edu
Dept.: (850) 644-7257
ADMISSIONS: 329 FAB, address as above, att: Barbara Thomas
(850) 644-7234
bgthomas@admin.fsu.edu

36,683 Total Enr.; h.compet.
Semester System
490 Majors; NAST,U/RTA,ATHE
T: $3,500 ug/$5,832 grad
O-ST T: $16,440 ug/$20,976 grad
FAX: (850) 644-7408
www.theatre.fsu.edu

DEGREES OFFERED

BA in Theatre (305); BFA in Acting (35); Musical Theatre (19); MFA in Acting (30) - through Asolo Conservatory for Acting Training; Costume Des (7); Directing (3); Lighting Des (6); Professional Writing (6); Scenic Des (9); Tech Prod (10); Theatre Mgmt (11); MA in Theatre-Theatre Studies (10); MS in Theatre - Teacher Education (6); PhD in Theatre (8). Declare major in first year; 2007 granted 80 UG, 30 Grad degrees.

ADMISSION & FINANCIAL INFORMATION

Admission requirements vary annually. Florida State offers an array of scholarships to theatre students. Students are selected through a competitive application process. BFA program requires aud/int, portfolio for des. Grad des program requires int/portfolio, theatre mgmt requires int/writing samples. UG program admits 104 out of 500, Grad admits 60 out of 1,000.

FACULTY AND CLASSES OFFERED

21 Full-Time, 5 Part-Time, 5 PhD, 19 MFA/MA,2 Prof. w/out adv. degree; 19 Staff

A. (4 FT) Intro to Theatre-1/Y; Th Hist-10/Y; Shakes-3/Y; Dramatic Lit-7/Y; Dramatic Crit-3/Y; Playwriting-6/Y

B. (9 FT, 2 PT) Acting-9/Y; Voice/Speech-3/Y; Movement-9/Y;Musical Th-5/Y; Directing-7/Y; Stage Combat-2/Y; Dance -2/Y

C. (7 FT, 2 PT) Prins. of Design-7/Y-O; Set Des-8/Y-O; Cost Des-8/Y-O; Ltg Des-12/Y-O; Tech. Production-12/Y-O; Cost Construction-12/Y-O; Make-up-2/Y; Stage Mgmt-2/Y

D. (1 FT, 1 PT) Arts Mgmt-2/Y; Box Office-2/Y; Mktg/ Promo-1/Y; Devel/Grant Writing-1/Y; Contracts/Copyright- 1/Y; Budgeting/Acctg-1/Y; Leadership in Arts-1/Y

FACILITIES AND PRODUCTIONS

MAINSTAGE: 490 seats, fly space, computerized lighting
7 prods: 4 Fac dir, 1 Fac des,2 GA dir; 1 Grad dir, 26 Grad des; 1 UG des; budget $2,575-23,230

SECOND STAGE: 149 seats, fly space, computerized lighting
budget up to $600

THIRD STAGE: 189 seats, fly space, black box, computerized lighting

Facility was built in 1968; renovated in 2006 includes scene shop, costume shop, prop shop, welding shop, sound studio, CAD facility, 2 dance studios, 3 rehearsal studios, 2 design studios, resource library with multimedia stations, conference rm, and collection of 10,000+ works. .

A non-departmental, student-run organization presents 12-16 productions per year in which majors participate. 12 student-written plays produced in the last two years.

Connection with Asolo Repertory Theatre (Equity), Sarasota, FL: The Asolo Repertory Theatre is a part of Florida State University and home to the company and the Asolo Conservatory for Actor Training. The conservatory is home to FSV's MFA Acting program, based in Sarasota, FL. Additionally, graduate students in the MFA Directing program spend their second year in residence at the Asolo, working with the conservatory and AEA company.

DESCRIPTION

Noted Faculty: Colleen Muscha, Fred Chappell, Dale Jordan, Mary Karen Dahl, Geoffrey Owens, Sarah EC Maines, Kate Gelabert, Robert H. Coleman, Jean McDaniel Lickson, David Rowell, Dan Dietz

Guest Artists: Howell Binkley, Lighting Des; Jim Frangione, Acting; Joe Cacaci, Direcotry; Anthony Zerbe, Acting; John D'Aguino, Acting; John Papsideria, Casting/Aud; Burt Reynolds, Acting, Directing, Film; Robert Freedman, Theatre Mgmt; Alley Mills and Orson Bean, Acting

As one of the top-tier theatre training programs in the nation, the School of Theatre challenges its students to grow as artists and individuals as they explore the world of theatre and where they fit into it. The primary mission of the School of Theatre is to offer students a comprehensive education in theatre and to prepare emerging artists to enter the professional theatre industry. As a result, from grand-scale musicals to intimate productions, the School of Theatre provides both student artists and community audience members a diverse array of productions that explore the spectrum of our shared humanity. Florida State has an internationally recognized faculty known for their outstanding teaching, creativity, and professional experiences that daily enriches the education process. We encourage our students to dream, take chances with their dreams, and follow those dreams with the skills, knowledge and experience gained during their time at Florida State University.

Palm Beach Atlantic College

Joseph Bryan, Theatre Admissions
P. O. Box 24708
Palm Beach Atlantic College
W. Palm Beach, FL 33416-4708

DEPT: (561) 803-2417
E-mail: joseph_bryan@pba.edu
ADMISSIONS: Address above.
Toll Free: (888) 468-6722
http://www.pba.edu

2,200 Total Enr.; competitive
Semester System
55 Majors
T: $9,985 per sem.
$2,315 per sem. max. R&B
FAX: (561) 803-2424
SMALL PROGRAM
(561) 803-2000
FAX: (561) 803-2186

DEGREES OFFERED

BA/Theatre Arts in Acting/Directing (30); Drama Education (4);
Musical Theatre (7). Declare major in Soph. year..

ADMISSION & FINANCIAL INFORMATION

Min. SAT of 960 or ACT 20 scores, GPA 2.5, essay, 2 letters of recommendation; accept 71% to institut.; Req. Aud./Int., Portfolio for
designers. Talent schols. are awarded on the basis of talent, grades,
need and commitment to the department. Other aid includes institutional, state and federal.

FACULTY AND CLASSES OFFERED

2 Full-Time, 5 Part-Time: 2 PhD, 1 MFA/MA, 3 Prof. w/out adv.
  degree; 1 Staff

A. (1 PT) Intro to Theatre-1/Y; Dramatic Lit-2/X; Theatre History-2/O;
   Shakespeare-1/X; Musical Theatre History-1/O; Dance History-
   1/O; Workshop in playwriting

B. (1 FT, 4 PT) Acting-4/O; Voice/Speech-1/Y; Movement-1/Y; Singing-
   1/O; Musical Theatre-3/O; Directing-2/O; Dance-8/Y; Musical
   Theatre Repertoire-1/O; Choreography & Composition-1/O

C. (1 FT) Set Design-1/O; Costume Design-1/O; Lighting Design-1/O;
   Sound Des.-1/O; Make-up-1/Y; Sound Design-1/O

FACILITIES & PRODUCTIONS

MAINSTAGE: 220 seats, computerized lighting. 9 prods: 3 Fac dir/des, 1
  Guest dir, 1 UG dir/des budget; $6,000-8,000

SECOND STAGE: 80 seats, black box; budget $1,500-2,000
  14 Wrkshps/Readings: 1 Guest dir; 8 UG dir, 5 UG des; budget
  $500

Facility is a city historical building; includes scene shop, costume
  shop, prop shop, 3 rehearsal studios, 3 dance studios, 3 classrooms.

Dept. majors generally participate in the non-departmental, student-
  run producing organization. 6-7 productions presented per year.
  1 student-written play produced in the last two years.

Connection with Florida Stage an equity company which uses students as interns in every capacity backstage.

DESCRIPTION

Noted Faculty: Dr. Deborah McEniry, Acting, Musical
  Theatre; Dr. Eugene Hall, Theatre History, Directing,
  Church Drama; Rich Robinson, Scene and Lighting
  Design, Play Production, Stagecraft; Anna Preston,
  Dance, Dance History, Choreography; Elizabeth
  Bozic, Dance; Kasi O'Brien, Dance; Jack Pinkney,
  Costume Design.

Guest Artists: Dr. Bob Cheeseman, Director; Paulette
  Laufer, Playwright; Marni Nixon, Musical Theatre

Performer.

The purpose of the Department of Theatre of Palm Beach
Atlantic College is to offer a curriculum for theatre students who wish to become proficient actors, designers,
producers, directors, technicians, stage managers, educators, and/or church drama leaders, able to perform within the context of a given theatre production and/or program. Such skills as acting, directing, producing, designing sets, lights, costumes and makeup, based upon an
understanding of the history and literature of the theatre,
are developed in the program. Graduates of the theatre
department will effectively demonstrate capabilities in
performance and stagecraft encompassing the broad
scope of professional, educational, community, and
church-related theatre opportunities. The department
emphasizes excellence by an adherence to high academic
and performance standards and seeks to provide its students a learning environment integrated with the liberal
arts and proclaiming its dependency on and adherence to
the Christian values and heritage of Palm Beach Atlantic
College as specified in its Guiding Principles.

Rollins College

Thomas Ouellette
Dept. of Theatre and Dance
1000 Holt Ave. - 2735
Rollins College
Winter Park, FL 32789
www.rollins.edu/theater/index.htm
ADMISSIONS: 1000 Holt Ave.-2720, Winter Park, FL 32789
(407) 646-2161
www.rollins.edu/new/admissions/htm admission@rollins.edu

1,720 Total Enr.; competitive
Semester Sys, U/RTA,ATHE,SETC
74 Majors
T: $32,640/$$10,200R&B
DEPT: (407) 646-2501
FAX: (407) 646-2257
FAX: (407) 646-1502

DEGREES OFFERED

BA in Acting/Directing (30), Design-Tech (10), General (20)
Declare major in sophomore year

ADMISSION & FINANCIAL INFORMATION

Grades, test scores, recommendations, interview, course selections;
accept 48% to institution, 1 out of 2 applicants accepted to theatre
program; Req. Aud./Int. for adm. to theatre program if applying for
scholarship. Theatre Scholarships: Priscilla L. Parker Scholarship -
(based on talent/scholarship); Friend of Theatre Schol. - $1,000-
3,000 annually (based on talent/scholarship); William Webb Schol. -
$4,000 annually (based on talent/schol.) Faith Duffy - $3,000 yearly.

FACULTY AND CLASSES OFFERED

7 Full-Time: 4 PhD, 4 MFA/MA; 6 Staff

A. (2 FT) Intro to Theatre-1/Y; Dramatic Lit-1/Y; Theatre History-1/Y;
   Dramatic Criticism-1/Y; Shakespeare-1/Y, Playwriting-1/Y

B. (2 FT) Acting-4/Y; Voice/Speech-2/Y; Mvmt-2/Y; Singing-1/O; Mus
   Theatre-1/O; Stage Combat-1/O; Directing-2/Y; Dance-5/Y

C. (2 FT) Principles of Design-1/Y; Set Design-1/Y; Costume Design-
   1/O; Cost. Construction-1/Y; Lighting Design-1/Y; Make-up-1/Y;
   Stage Mgmt-1/Y; Tech Prod'n-2/Y

D. (1 FT) Arts Management-1/Y; Marketing/Promo-1/Y; Devel/Grant
   Writing-1/X; Budget/Accounting-1/X

FACILITIES & PRODUCTIONS

MAINSTAGE: 400 seats, fly space, computerized lighting
  4 prods: 4 Fac dir, 2 Fac des, 1 Guest dir, 2 Guest des;

budget $12,000-20,000

SECOND STAGE: 100 seats, computerized lighting
    4 UG dir/des prods; budget $1,000-3,000

7 Workshop/Reading: 2 Guest dir, 5 UG dir; budget $500-1,000

Facility built in 1931, renovated in 1978; includes scene shop, costume shop, props shop, CAD facil, 2 video studios, 2 rehearsal studios, design studio, dance studio, 6 classrooms.

Dept. majors generally participate in the non-departmental, student-run producing organization. 10 productions presented per year. 4 student-written plays produced in the last two years.

DESCRIPTION

Noted Faculty: Thomas Ouellette, Chair, Dr. Joseph Nassif: Directing, Criticism; Florida ACTF adjudictor W. Robert Sherry, Professor, Dir. of Dance, Fl. Dance Association; Thomas Oullette, NY and regional theatre actor & director; Spike McClure, NY University; Peg O'Keef, Ohio State University; Jesse Wolfe, Rollins, Actor's Theatre in Louisville.; D. David Charles: Improv; Kevin Griffin: Lighting Designer, Univ of Pennsylvania.

Guest Artists: Olympia Dukakis, Actor; David Weiss, Designer; Fernando Bujones, Choreographer; Edward Albee, Playwright; Dana Ivey, Actor.

The department offers a vigorous program of education in the arts and crafts of theater and dance. The student who majors in Theater Arts at Rollins College will acquire knowledge of theater history, literature, theory, criticism, management, acting, directing, stagecraft and design. All students must take a specific series of courses in the major field and participate in the production program. Students may concentrate in either performance or design/technical theater, or may elect to take a broad spectrum of courses in both areas. A student who completes the theater program is schooled in self-discipline, work skills, and knowledge to support numerous career opportunities, including the professions and all facets of the entertainment industry. Students who have specific interest in film/tv will discover that the stage is the basis for performance skills in all media.

University of Central Florida

Dr. Roberta Sloan, Chair/Art. Dir.
Dept. of Theatre
P. O. Box 162372
University of Central Florida
Orlando, FL 32816
dseay@mail.ucf.edu
DEPT: (407) 823-2862
www.cas.ucf.edu/theatre
ADMISSIONS: 4000 Central Florida Blvd, Orlando FL 32816-0111
(407) 823-3000   FAX: (407) 823-5625
http://www.ucf.edu

44,000 Tot. Enr.; h.compet.
350 Majors; ATHE
Semester System
RES. T: $$3,562 R&B $8,163
NON-RES. T: $17,763
    $8,163R&B
FAX: (407) 823-6446

DEGREES OFFERED

BA in Theatre Plus (150); BFA in Acting (60), Musical Theatre (60), Design/Tech, (50), Stage Management (48); MFA in Acting (18), Design (8), Musical Theatre (18), Theater For Young Audiences (8), Playwriting (anticipated 2006).

Declare major in freshman year; 2004 granted 25 UG degrees, 4 G degrees.

ADMISSION & FINANCIAL INFORMATION

Sliding scale 3.3-4.0; GPA/1080-1230 SAT/23-27 ACT. Audition, interview, portfolio, 3 letters of recommendation required. 70% of applics. accepted by institution. 1 out of 5 applics. admitted to theatre program; 1 out of 3 admitted to graduate program. Talent grant - not based on financial. Disney Schol.-Design/Tech candidate; Florida Theatrical-Design/Tech candidate; Academic schols through university.

FACULTY AND CLASSES OFFERED

35 Full-Time, 2 Part-Time: 6 PhD, 29 MFA/MA, 2 PT w/o advanced degrees; 11 Staff

A. (4 FT) Intro to Theatre-1/Y; Dramatic Lit. I-5/Y; Dramatic Criticism-1/Y; Theatre Hist. 2/Y; Script Analysis-1/Y; Research Methods-1/Y; Play Analysis-1/Y; Survey of Musical Theatre Dance-1/Y; Survey of Musical Theatre-3/Y; Theatre Careers-2/Y

B. (17 FT,1 PT) Acting-11/Y; Voice/Speech-8/Y; Mvmt-6/Y; Singing-8/Y; Directing-3/Y; Stage Combat-2/Y; Internship-1/Y; Mus. Theatre Acting-9/Y;Musical Theatre Cabaret-1/Y; Musical Theatre Master Class-2/Y; Musical Skills-2/X; Thesis-1/Y; Dance-9/Y

C. (12 FT) Costume Design-1/Y; Set Des-2/Y; Ltg Des-2/Y; Cost Constr-2/Y; Make-up-2/Y; Stagecraft I-III-3/Y; Sound Design-2/Y

D. (2 FT,1 PT) Arts Management-1/Y

FACILITIES & PRODUCTIONS

MAINSTAGE: 300 seats, fly space, computerized and intelligent lighting & sound. 9 prods: 6 Fac dir/des; 3 GA dir/des, 4 Grad des. Budget $6,000-$14,000.

SECOND STAGE: 125 seats, computerized lighting; 4 prods: 4 Fac dir. Budget $2,000 to $6,000

6 student showcases. Budget, $0 - $500.

Facility was built in 1982; includes scene shop, costume shop, CAD facil,props and welding shop, sound, 2 rehearsal studios, 2 movement/dance studios, 2 design studio, 6 classrooms.

OTHER FACILITIES: 329 seat Mainstage at Orlando Repertory Theatre, newly modified thrust for musical theatre. MFA to open in Spring 2006 in Daytona.

There is a non-departmental, student-run theater organization on campus that does two productions a year. Department majors generally participate.

2 student-written plays have been produced by the theatre department in the last two years.

Connected with Orlando Repertory Theatre (non-Equity); UCF Shakespeare Festival (Equity); Sepside Music Theatre (Equity); Orlando Theatre Project (Equilty).

DESCRIPTION

The Department of Theatre seeks to develop theatre artists of the highest quality by providing a select number of undergraduate students with the training, education, and experiences necessary for the successful pursuit of professional careers in theatre arts. Offering both the B.A. and the B.F.A. degrees, the Department of Theatre undertakes to develop and graduate theatre artists who are sensitive, aware, and total human beings. Through its public performance programs, the department endeavors to serve as a cultural resource for the Univer-sity, the community and the central Florida region. Striving to provide its students with a competitive edge, the department employs a faculty and staff of artists/teachers, supplemented by professional guest artists, who work intensely with students in the classroom and in production. Before graduation, BFA students are required to complete a professional theatre internship thus providing them with a unique and invaluable introduction to the real world of professional theatre.

University of Florida

Kevin Marshall, Chair	47,000 Tot. Enr: h. compet.
School of Theatre & Dance	Semester system
Nadine McGuire Theatre	174 Majors; NAST, U/RTA, ATHE
& Dance Pavilion	T: $2,630/$3,320 r&b
University of Florida	O-ST T:$12,096./$3,320R&B
P.O. Box 115900	DEPT. (352) 273-0500
Gainesville, FL 32611	FAX: (352) 392-5114

www.arts.ufl.edu/theatreanddance/index.html
ADM: 201 Criser Hall; P. O. Box 114000, Gainesville,
FL 32611-4000   (352) 392-1365;
FAX: (352) 392-2115   www.reg.ufl.edu/regadmi.htm

DEGREES OFFERED

BA in General Theatre (82),; BFA in Theatre Performance (19), Musical Th. (16), Design Tech (15); MFA in Acting (30); Design (12) Declare major in 3rd yr.; 2003-4 granted 16 UG, 15 Grad. degs.

ADMISSION & FINANCIAL INFORMATION

GPA 3.0 or 1,000 V & Q GRE. 48% of UG, 25% of Grad accepted to institution. UG BFA: req. aud. for actors, dancers, interview, portfolio for des., admit 2 out of 3 to th. program. Grad.: req. resume, aud. for actors, interview, portfolio for designers, resume; admit 12 out of 40 to th. program. Theatre Schols include; Jim Richardson Memorial Schol; M. Stoughton Theatre Schol; Ethel Ingram Theatre Schol; Judy Mason Playwriting Award; Brask Musical Theatre Award; Lawrence Baynard Hubbell Scholarship in Th. Studies; Catheryn Lombardi Scholarship. General Funding Scholarships include: Lawrence Baynard Hubbell Schol in Theatre Studies; Catheryn Lombardi Schol. Scholarship recipients selected by executive committee of the Department.

FACULTY AND CLASSES OFFERED

20 Full-Time, 9 Part-Time: 7 PhD, 17 MFA/MA

A. (1 FT) Intro to Theatre-2/Y; Dramatic Lit-1/O; Dramatic Crit-1/O; Theatre History-1/Y; Shakes-1/Y; Playwriting-1/O

B. (10 FT, 2 PT) Acting-6/Y; Voice/Speech-4/Y; Mvmt4/Y; Mus Th-5/Y; Directing-2/Y; Stg Combat-2/Y; Dance-20/Y; Mime, Mask, Commedia & Circus-1/O; Singing-2/X;

C. (7 FT, 2 PT) Prins of Des-1/Y; Cost Des-1/Y; Set Des-1/Y; Ltg Des-1/Y; Make-up-2/Y; Stage Mgmt-1/Y; Tech Prod-1/Y

FACILITIES & PRODUCTIONS

MAINSTAGE: 415 seats, fly space, computer. lighting, 8 prods, 4 Fac dir,1 Fac des, 3 Grad des, bdgt; $8,000-10,000

SECOND STAGE: 200 seats, comput. lighting, 4 prods,. 4 Fac dir/des, 3 Grad des, 1 UG des, budget $3,000-5,000

THIRD STAGE: 200 seats.

Workshops/Readings: 2 UG/Grad dir/des, 2 Grad dir/des; budget $750-1000

Mainstage was built in 1967, renovated in 2003; includes scene, costume, props, welding, CAD shops and 9 classrooms,3 movement/dance studios, 4 rehearsal studios.

A non-departmental, student-run org. presents 8 prods/yr in which majors participate. 2 student-written plays produced in last two years.

Connection with Hippodrome State Theatre. Intern possibilities, production particiaption, acting, design.

DESCRIPTION

Noted Faculty: Dr. Judith Williams, Directing/Acting; Dr. David Young, Directing/Acting; Dr. David Shelton, Directing/Acting; Tony Mata, Musical Theatre; Regina Truhart, Costume Technology; Dr. Ralf Remshardt, Dramaturgy/History; Dr. Mikell Pinkney, Directing/Diversity; Stan Kaye, Lighting and Scene Design; Paul Favini, Costume Design; Mihai Ciupe, Scene Design; Yanci Bukovec and Tiza Garland, Voice and Movement.

Guest Artists: Moira Mangiumili, Acting Style by Jeremy Whelan; Judi Ann Mason, Playwright; Paul Gallo, Lighting; Zoe Caldwell, Acting; Robert Whitehead and Miles Wilkin, Producer; Molly Pesci, Singer/Actress; Frank Wildhorn, Composer; Jelon Vieira, Choreographer; Tim Altmeyer, Voice Work; Ntozake Shange, Playwright.

At University of Florida, we educate and train artists, scholars, and teachers, and provide for its students a foundation of professionalism and dedication within a climate of diversity, discovery, and risk. We strive to develop in students and audiences an enduring passion for theatre and dance. We aim for the closest possible union between academic and applied knowledge, theory and practice, experience and reflection, within a thoroughly integrated curriculum that is sensitive to both the practical needs of an ever-changing marketplace and to the intellectual needs of the individual student. Stage and classroom are engaged in constant mutual exchange. The Department believes that the complete artist is the thinking artist who augments the mastery of concrete skills with an acute consciousness of the cultural environments and the broader realm of arts and ideas. The faculty is composed of nationally and internationally recognized practicing artists, teachers, and scholars committed to research and creative activity.

University of Miami

Vincent J. Cardinal, Chair	13,000 Total Enr.; h. compet.
Dept. of Theatre Arts	Semester System
University of Miami	150 Majors
P. O. Box 248273	T: $23,642/$7,948 R&B
Coral Gables, FL 33124	DEPT. (305) 284-4474
http://www.miami.edu/tha	FAX: (305) 284-5702
theatredepartment@miami.edu	admission@miami.edu

ADMISSIONS: P.O. Box 248025, Coral Gables, FL 33124-4616
(305) 284-4323   FAX: (305) 284-2507
www.miami.edu/admission   admission@miami.edu

DEGREES OFFERED

BA General (90); BFA in Performance (20), Musical Th (30), Design/Technical Th (3), Stage Mgmt (4), Theatre Mgmt (3) Students declare major in first year. 2001 granted 30 degrees.

ADMISSION & FINANCIAL INFORMATION

Fresh. class weighted GPA average: 3.9; SAT mid-range 1090-1270; ACT 22-28. BFA admission to theatre program requires audition/interview, portfolio for designers. Program admits 15 out of

400 applicants. Talent based schols avail from theatre dept. Audition req. Average award is $2,500.

FACULTY AND CLASSES OFFERED

15 Full-Time, 4 Part-Time: 15 MA/MFA, 2 Prof. w/out adv. degree; 3 Staff

A. (2 FT, 2 PT) Intro to Th-7/Y; Theatre History-2/Y; Dramatic Lit-2/Y

B. (9 FT) Acting-10/Y; Voice/Speech-7/Y; Movement-3/Y; Mime, etc.-2/Y; Singing-7/Y; Musical Th-2/Y; Directing-2/Y; Stg Combat-2/Y

C. (2 FT, 2 PT) Principles of Design-2/Y; Set Design-2/Y; Cost Design-2/Y; Lighting Design-2/Y; Cost Constr-1/O; Cost Hist-1/Y; Make-up-1/Y; Stage Mgmt-4/Y

D. (2 FT) Arts Mgmt-1/Y; Development-1/O; Producing on Broadway-2/Y; Non-profit Mgmt-1/Y

FACILITIES AND PRODUCTIONS

MAINSTAGE: 300-400 seats (flexible); computerized, electronic lighting 4 prods: 3 Fac dir/des, 1 Guest dir, 2 UG des; budget $20,000-30,000

SECOND STAGE: 45 seats; computerized lighting. 4 prods: 2 Fac dir, 2 UG dir, 6 UG des prod

Facility was built in 1951, last renovated in 1996; includes scene shop, welding shop, costume shop, props shop, dance studio, rehearsal studio, design studio, CAD lab.

Connection with City Theatre which is in residence in May and June. Students audition for roles or apply for technical/management internships. EMC credit availale for qualified students.

DESCRIPTION

Noted Faculty: Bruce J. Miller, Acting; Bruce Lecure, Movement and Combat; Nancy Saklad, Acting; Jon Cantor, Acting; Matt Gitkin, Acting; Clay James, Dance; N. David Williams, Singing; Kenneth Kurtz, Design; Kent Lantaff, theatre Management; Michael Barnes, Voice/Speech.

Guest Artists: George Contini, Director; Margot Moreland, Actor; Frank Wildhorn, Composer; Michael York, Actor; Stephen Schwartz, Composer; Austin Pendleton, Director, Actor; Douglas Sills, Actor; David Leong, Fight Choreographer; Wendy Wasserstein, Playwright; Vincent Liff, Casting Director.

The University of Miami offers a Bachelor of Fine Arts Conservatory, intensive training in a professional environment. Bachelor of Arts program offers a more liberal arts approach. Both programs offer specializations in performance, musical theatre, stage or theatre management, and design or technical theatre. Admission to the University required for both degrees. admission to the Conservatory requires additional application and audition or portfolio review. Courses include acting, musical theatre, dance, voice and speech, movement and stage combat as well as theatre history, technical theatre, design, directing, and management. The faculty is chosen based upon proven professional achievements in the field of theatre.

University of Miami - Musical Theatre BM

David Alt, Program Dir.
University of Miami-Musical Th Prg
Frost School of Music
P. O. Box 248165
Coral Gables, FL   33124
http://www.music.miami.edu
dalt@miami.edu
ADMISSIONS: as above
www.miami.edu/admission

650 Total Enr.; h. compet.
Semester System, NASM
30 Majors
T: $26,280/$8,300 R&B
DEPT: (305) 284-4886
FAX: (305) 284-2290

(305) 284-2241
admission@miami.edu

DEGREES OFFERED

BM in Musical Theatre (Conservatory style training) (25); BM in Musical Theatre with options (15). Students declare major in first year. 2007 anticipate granting 8 degrees.

ADMISSION & FINANCIAL INFORMATION

Fresh. class GPA minimum 3.0; SAT 1200 is average. Admission to program requires audition. Program admits 1 out of 10 applicants. Excellent talent and need-based schols vary from $15,000 to full tuition.

FACULTY AND CLASSES OFFERED

9 Full-Time: interdisciplinary arrangement between University of Miami's Frost School of Music & Theatre Arts Department.

A. Intro to Th-1/Y; Theatre History-2/Y; Shakespeare-2/Y; Playwriting-1/Y

B. Acting-8/Y; Voice/Speech-6/Y; Movement-6/Y; Mime, etc.-1/Y; Singing-8/Y; Musical Th-8/Y; Directing-2/Y; Stg Combat-2/Y; Dance-6/Y; Film-2/Y.

FACILITIES AND PRODUCTIONS

MAINSTAGE: 400 seats; computerized lighting:
6 prods: 6 Fac dir/3 Fac des.

SECOND STAGE: 40 seats; electronic lighting.
9 prods: 6 Fac dir, 3 UG prod.

THIRD STAGE: 130 SEATS; COMPUTERIZED LIGHTING.

Facility was built in 1970, renovated in 1993; includes 1 movement/dance studio, 1 design studio, 4 classrooms.

A non-department, student-run producing organization presents 2 productions per year in which majors generally participate.

City Theatre uses the performing space in the summer.

DESCRIPTION

Noted Faculty: David Alt, Voice; Mollye Otis, Voice; Kimberly Daniel deAcha, Voice; Cayce Benton, Voice; Ed Walker, Voice.

Guest Artists: Dave Clemmons, Casting; Jo Lynn Burks, Broadway musician, actor, and singer; Adam Epstein, Producer; Barry Brown, Broadway Producer, Andrew Lippa, Broadway Composer; Craig Carnella, Broadway Composer; Schmidt & Jones, Broadway Composers; Stephen Schwartz.

The Musical Theatre Program at the University of Miami's Phillip and Patricia Frost School of Music, one of the first in the United States, continues to serve as a model for others around the country. A well-rounded program, encompassing dance, singing and acting, it prepares today's students to compete as "triple threat performers."

Professional training in musical theatre is structured in a conservatory format that assures students of intensive classes in acting, singing, voice/diction, movement and dance. The goal of this highly competitive, interdisciplinary curriculum, developed in conjunction with the College of Arts and Science's Department of Theatre Arts, is to prepare students for professional performance careers - not only on the musical stage, but in non-musical dramatic theatre as well. Enhancing the program is a sequence of integrated classes in dance and movement, embracing all of the movement forms and dance techniques needed for a successful career in theatre. Each student is offered a variety of performance opportunities every semester, through a wide-ranging repertoire of plays and musicals offered at the Jerry Herman Ring Theatre in Coral Gables.

University of South Florida

Merry Lynn Morris, Advisor
School of Theatre & Dance
4202 E. Fowler Ave, TAR 230
University of South Florida
Tampa, FL 33620
DEPT: (813) 974-2701
http://www.usf.edu
ADMISSIONS: 4202 E. Fowler Ave, Ste 1036
(813) 974-3350

34,438 Total Enr.; competitive
Semester System
180 Majors; NAST, ATHE
T: $3,340/R&B $7,590
O-ST T: $$16,040 R&B $7,590
FAX: (813) 974-4122
admission@admin.usf.edu

FAX:(813) 974-9689

DEGREES OFFERED

BA in Theater Performance (95), Theatre Arts (50), Design (32). BFA in Design (3). Declare major in any. year. 2004 granted 25 UG degrees.

ADMISSION & FINANCIAL INFORMATION

GPA 3.6, SAT avg 970-1140; 20-24 composite ACTs; For scholarship info see www.theatre.arts.usf.edu/scholar.html Freshman: Recruitment schols. (#varies) apply by letter of intent and letters of rec. sent to chair. Upper Level: Nancy Cole Krewe (1), Shimberg (2), Jacqueline Britt (1), Brit (15), Playmakers Schol (1),) Talent Grants (various numbers & amounts) based on artistic and academic merit.

FACULTY AND CLASSES OFFERED

12 Full-Time, 4 Part Time: 2 PhD, 13 MFA/MA, 1 Prof. w/out adv. degree; 3 Staff.

A. (3 FT,3 PT) Intro to Theatre-2/Y; Th History-2/Y; Shakespeare-1/Y; Dramatic Lit-7/Y; Playwriting-1/Y: Dramatic Crit-2/Y

B. (4 FT,2 PT) Acting-10/Y; Voice/Speech-1/Y; Mvmt-3/Y; Mime, etc.- 1/Y; Singing-1/Y; Mus. Th-1/Y; Directing-2/Y; Stg Combat-1/Y

C. (4 FT, 1 PT) Prins of Design-2/Y; Set Des32/Y; Cost Des-3/Y; Ltg Des 3/Y; Tech. Prod'n-4/Y; Cost Construction-1/Y; Cost History-1/Y; Make-up-1/Y; Stage Mgmt-1/Y; Architectural and Decor-1/Y

FACILITIES AND PRODUCTIONS

MAINSTAGE: 552 seats, fly space, computerized lighting
7 prods: 2 Fac dir, 12 Fac des, 2 Guest dir, 1 Guest des; budget $3,000-12,000

SECOND STAGE: 125 seatsBlack Box, flex up to 250 seats, computerized lighting. budget $25-100

THIRD STAGE: 80-125 seats, electronic lighting

1 Fac dir, 1 UG dir Wkshps/Readings;
Facility was built in '59-'86, renovated in 1994/95; includes scene shop, cost. shop, prop shop, CAD fac., 1 design studios, 1 rehearsal studio, 6 classrooms.
A non-departmental, student-run organization presents 2 productions per year. 3 student-written plays produced in the last two years.

DESCRIPTION

Noted Faculty: Dr. Denis Calandra, Fassbinder Play; Dr. Patrick Finelli, Sound for the Stage; Paul Massie, British Academy Award; Nancy Cole, Christopher Steele, Directing; David Williams, G.B. Stephens, Design; Fanni Green, Robin Gordon, Performance; Bill Lorenzen, Puppetry.

Guest Artists: Matthew Francis, British Director; Sir Donald Sinden, Actor; Keith Baxter, Actor; Tim Carroll, Director; Mike Finn, Irish Playwright and Director; Mel Jessop, British Actress and Director; Jane Bertish, Britsh Acress/Director; Todd Espeland, Director; Allison Williams, Writer/Director; Sian Phillips, Actor.

Through its curriculum and production program, the School of Theatre and Dance offers seriously interested students the opportunity to prepare themselves, within a liberal arts atmosphere, for a professional career in the theatre; or to continue their studies at the graduate level. For over 30 years, our exclusively undergraduate program has prepared critically aware and skilled theatre practitioners who have used what they have learned from us and with us in theatre, film, television, and a variety of other careers. Students may graduate with a broad based theatre arts degree, or they may specialize in performance or design. Computer assisted design (CAD), playwriting, stage combat, circus skills, and musical theatre are among the many electives available. Special features: 1) BRIT Program: 6 British professionals at USF each spring; 2) Student Exchange Program with Middlesex University in London; 3) Honors Program: one year projects with faculty and guest artists.

University of West Florida

Charles Houghton, Chair
Department of Theatre
11000 University Parkway
University of West Florida
Pensacola, FL 32514-5751
theatre@uwt.edu
www.uwf.edu
DEPT: (850) 474-2146
ADMISSIONS: 11000 University Pkway, Pensacola, FL 32514
(850) 474-2230

9,136 Total Enr., competitive
Semester System
42 Majors
T: $.2,860/$6,600 R&B
O-ST T: $13,702 $6,600 R&B

SMALL PROGRAM
FAX: (850) 474-3247

www.admissions@uwf.edu

DEGREES OFFERED

BA in Theatre; BFA in Theatre: Acting, Musical Theatre.Declare major in sophomore year.

ADMISSION & FINANCIAL INFORMATION

Inst. reqs. 3.0 GPA or comb of GPA and SAT/ACT of 2.0 with 1140/25 to 2.9 with 970/20; admits 75% of freshman applicants. Aud/Interview/Portfolio review for theatre program, generally all applicants admitted. BFA Talent Schols.awarded by aud.

FACULTY AND CLASSES OFFERED

4 Full-Time,4 Part-Time: 5 MA/MFA,1 Phd, 2 Prof. w/o adv. degree, 1 Staff

A. (1 FT) Intro to Theatre-1/Y; Dramatic Lit-1/Y; Th. History-2/Y; Dramatic Criticism-1/O; Shakespeare-1/X; Playwriting-1/O

B. (3 FT, 2 PT) Acting-3/Y Voice/Speech-2/Y; Movement-1/Y; Musical Theatre-2/Y; Directing-1/Y; Singing-2/Y; Stage Combat-1/O; Dance-4/Y

C. (2 PT) Prins. of Design-1/O; Set Des-1/Y; Cost Des-1/O; Ltg Des-1/O; Cost Constr-1/O;; Make-up-1/Y; Tech Prod-1/O; Stage Mgt-1/O

FACILITIES AND PRODUCTIONS

MAINSTAGE: 426 seats, fly space, electronic lighting
4 prods: 3 Fac dir, 1 Fac des, 3 Guest des, 1 Grad dir, budget $10,000-30,000

SECOND STAGE: 120 seats, electronic lighting
3 prod: 1 Fac dir, 1 Fac des,2 UG dir, 2 UG des, budget $3,000-10,000

Facility was built in 1991; includes scene shop, costume shop, reh. studio, dance studio, Green Room,CAD, movement/dance, 3 dressing rooms, 2 classrooms, storage.

DESCRIPTION

Noted Faculty:Greg Lanier, Criticism/Shakes; Celeste Evans, Acting, History, Afro-American Theatre; Jan Savage, Acting, Directing; Joe Tomko, Acting, Directing.

Guest Artists: Chuck Wagner, actor.

The Bachelor of Fine Arts in either Musical Theatre or Acting at the University of West Florida is designed to prepare students for careers in the professional theatre or for entry into graduate programs. All students are invited to audition for university theatre productions or for the numerous student productions offered each year. In addition, the Bachelor of Arts degree gives students an excellent overall grounding in theatre.   Students wishing to teach may complete a BA in Theatre and then be certified for the K-12 classroom by completing requirements specified by the College of Professional Studies.

GEORGIA

Agnes Scott College ····························

David S. Thompson, Ph.D., Chair
Agnes Scott College
Dept. of Theatre & Dance
East College Avenue
Decatur, GA 30030
ADMISSIONS: 141 E. College Ave., Decatur, GA 30030.
(404) 471-6285
www.agnesscott.edu
dsanders@agnesscott.edu

950 Total Enr., h. compet.
Semester System
5 Majors; ATHE
T: $26,600/$9,350
SMALL PROGRAM

FAX: (404) 471-6464
admission@agnesscott.edu

DEGREES OFFERED

BA in Theatre (5) Declare major in late sophomore year. 2001 granted 1 degrees.

ADMISSION & FINANCIAL INFORMATION

Most incoming students graduate in top 10% of their high school classes. Incoming students range of SAT scores is 1130-1290, median ACT composite is 28. ASC will meet 100% of demonstated need through scholarships, loans, grants or work study. Betty Lou Houck Smith Scholarship for the rising sophomore, junior or senior chosen by the faculty who demonstrates most clearly: talent and ability as an actor, director, designer or technician; a true love of and devotion to her craft; leadership among her peers.

FACULTY AND CLASSES OFFERED

4 Full-Time, 1 Part-Time: 2 PhD, 3 MA/MFA

A. (1 FT) Intro to Theatre-1/Y; Theatre Hist-2/O; Playwriting & Screenwriting-2/Y; Dramatic Criticism-2/O; Shakes-2/YX; Dramatic Lit-4/OX

B. (1/2 FT, 2 PT) Acting-2/Y; Mus. Theatre-1/YX; Speech & Pub. Spking-1/Y; Singing (Voice)-10-YX; Directing-2/Y; Dance-15+/Y.

C. (1/2 FT) Principles of Design-2/Y

FACILITIES AND PRODUCTIONS

MAINSTAGE: 312 seats, computerized lighting
4 prods: 1 Fac dir, 2-3 Fac des, 2 UG dir, 1-2 UG des 1 Guest dir; budget $2,000-2,500. One child. show; as many one-acts as there is interest for among students. Budget for child. prod. $800-1,500

Blackfriars, a non-departmental, student-run producing organization in which majors participate, sponsors the children's production and works on all productions.

Facility was built in 1965, last renovated in 1988; includes scene shop, costume shop, design studio, 2 dance studios, 4 classrooms, dressing rooms, green room, costume-props-scenery storage, faculty offices.

DESCRIPTION

Noted Faculty: Dudley Sanders, Design, Dramatic Writing; David S. Thompson, Acting, Directing, Theatre History; Jessica Phelps West, Acting; Veronica Henson-Phillips, Public Speaking; Marylin Darling, Dance.

Guest Artists: Sally J. Robertson, Deadra Moore, Guest Directors.

As perhaps the quintessential liberal art, taking for its subject matter " what it means to be human", the study and practice of theatre at Agnes Scott promotes self-examination and self-discipline, fosters the development of artistic, analytical, critical and organizational capabilities, and stimulates the student to realize her full creative potential. The Agnes Scott curriculum in theatre integrates theory, history and practice, including foundational training in acting, directing, dramatic writing and design, and culminates in a performance project for the public. In addition, the department works closely with the volunteer student theatre organization, Blackfriars, to create a student-centered production program that encourages individual leadership and responsibility. With the Winter Theatre, an With the Winter Theatre, an intimate 310-seat auditorium with a semi-thrust stage, serving a laboratory and home, the department and Blackfriars mount two major productions and a play for children annually.

Berry College

Dr. John Countryman, Director
Theatre Program
Berry College
PO Box 490279
Mount Berry, GA 30149
THEATRE OFC: (706) 236-2263
Admis: (800) BERRY-GA

1,718 Total Enr.; competitive
Semester System
24 Majors;3 Minors, ATHE, SETC
T:*$20,570/$7,626 R&B $7,626
DEPT. (706) 236-2263
Small Program
admissions@berry.edu

DEGREES OFFERED

BA in Theatre or Musical Theatre; declare major in any year.

ADMISSION & FINANCIAL INFORMATION

85.9% of freshman applicants accepted by institution. Merit scholarships awarded based on ACT or SAT. Theatre scholarships are based on Audition/Interview; 8-10scholarships available for incoming majors and minors each year. Scholarships are renewable for 4 years; also student staff openings in theatre program.

FACULTY AND CLASSES OFFERED

3 Full-Time: 1 PhD, 3 MA/MFA, 2 PT; 1 Phd:

Theatre Practicum: Basics of Acting; Intro to Theatre; Stagecraft; Costuming & Make-up; Script Interpretation; Th. Mgmt; Senior Project; Modern and Contemporary Theatre.

Musical Theatre: Voice for the Actor; Shakes; Chekov; Modern Improv and Comedia del Arte; Intermediate Acting; Basics of Directing; Advanced Directing; Playwriting; Women and Drama; World Drama; Theatre History; History of Costume; Costume Design; Mask Making; Movement for the Stage; Modern Dance; Choreography; Children's Dance Theatre; Scene Design; Lighting Design; Prod Mgmt; Stafe Practicum; Seminar in Theatre; Special Topics/Problems.

FACILITIES AND PRODUCTIONS

MAINSTAGE: 224 seats, computerized lighting
5 prods: 3 Fac dir/des, 2 Student dir/des

SECOND STAGE: 115 seats, computerized lighting
2 Student dir/des prods. Occasional Workshops/Readings

Facility built in 1984; includes scene shop, cost. shop,prop shop, sound studio, rehearsal studio, design studio, 2 classrooms, cost/props and scene storage.

DESCRIPTION

Noted Faculty: Dr. John C. Countryman, Alice Bristow, Christian Boy, Dr. Anna Filippo, Jeanne Elkins.

Guest Artists: Heidi Cline, Director; Charlotte Headrick, Director; Hudson Adams, Actor; Eric Nielson, Guest Choreographer.

Berry College offers a BA degree of Theatre with concentrations in Musical Theatre, Theatre Performance, Costume/Scene Design. Four Faculty directed shows and numerous student productions are staged annually. Performances are presented in the E.H. Young Theatre, which houses a fully equipped 3/4 thrust main stage and studio theatre. The theatre program at Berry College is dedicated to providing the best in theatre arts training and liberal arts education. Students choosing careers strictly in theatre will find that Berry provides training and opportunities that allow them to compete effectively for jobs.

Brenau University

Dr. Ann Demling, Chair
500 Washington Street SE
Brenau University
Gainesville, GA 30501
www.brenau.edu
ademling@lib.brenau.edu
ADMISSIONS: Above
(770) 534-6100 or (800) 252-5119
www.brenau.edu

807 Total Enr.; not compet.
Semester System
25 Majors
T $17,700 R&B $8,950
SMALL PROGRAM
(770) 534-6264
wcadmissions@lib.brenau.edu
FAX: (770) 538-4306
cwhite@lib.brenau.edu

DEGREES OFFERED

BA in Theatre Arts (17). BFA in Theatre Arts, Musical Theatre Emphasis (6), Arts Management, Theatre emphasis (2). Declare major in freshman year; 2003 granted 12 UG degrees.

ADMISSION & FINANCIAL INFORMATION

SAT of 900 or ACT 19, GPA 2.3, can petition for admission if these standards not met/varies by major. 70% of applicants accepted by institution, 7 out of 10 to th. program. No special req. unless interested in scholarship. Theatre schols. available through audition: B.A. Theatre - monologues, opt. song; B.F.A. Musical Theatre: monologues and song. Recommended: bring portfolio/resume/headshot.

FACULTY AND CLASSES OFFERED

1 Full-Time, 3 Part-Time: 1 PhD/DFA, 3 MFA/MA; 3 Staff

A. (1/2 FT) Intro to Theatre-1/Y; Theatre History-2/Y; Shakes-1/X; Thesis Project-1/Y; Creative Writing-1/X

B. (1/2 FT) Acting-3/Y; Movement-1/OX; Singing-5-6/Y; Directing-2/Y; Voice/Speech-2/Y; Mime/Mask-1/O; Hist. of Musical Theatre-1/O; Opera/Opera Workshop-2/X; Public Speaking-1/Y; Oral Interp.-1/O Piano-2/X

C. (1 PT) Principles of Design-1/O; Set Design-2/O; Tech. Production-1/Y; Stage Mgmt-1/O

D. (1 PT) Arts Management-3/O; Mktng/Promo-2/X; Theatre Mgmt.-1/Y; Budget/Acct'ng-2/X

FACILITIES AND PRODUCTIONS

MAINSTAGE: 425 seats, fly space, computerized, electronic lighting. 4 prods: 2 Fac dir, 2 Guest dir; budget $10,000 (non-musical) - $50,000 (musical). This facility was built and completed 2002.

SECOND STAGE: 750 seats, electronic lighting.
1 prod: 1 UG dir; budget $500-2,000

THIRD STAGE: 250 seats, black box, computerized & electronic lighting.
2 Workshops/Readings: UG dir; budget $5000-10,000

FOURTH STAGE: 60 seat black box, electronic lighting.

Facility was built in 1978, renovated in 1999 (sound system only); includes scene shop, costume shop, CAD facil., 2 movement/dance studios, rehearsal studio, storage.

400 seat performing arts facility.

A non-departmental student-run organization presents 2-4 productions per year in which majors participate.

DESCRIPTION

Noted Faculty: Jim Hammond, Acting/General Theatre Arts; Ann Demling, Theatre History/Directing/General Theatre; Stuart Beaman, Technical Theatre/Design; Gay Hammond, Theatre For Youth, Period Acting Styles, Voice & Diction.

Guest Artists: Ken Yunker, Lighting Designer; Heidi Cline, Director; Antoinette DiPietropolo, Choreographer; Jerold Solomon, Actor; Lisa Adler, Director; Richard Garner, Director; Joseph Stell, Set/Lighting Designer; Chris Kayser, Actor; Dale Grogan, Musical Director.

The overall goal of the Theatre program is to create educated people who have a clear view of them selves and a broad awareness of the world. Our graduates are well versed in all aspects of theatre, including technical, academic and performance. The program is large enough to provide substantial grounding in all areas of theatre and small enough to offer a comfortable learning environment. Brenau Theatre is part of the Gainesville Theatre Alliance (GTA), a unique collaboration of academic, community, and professional talent. Students from Bre-nau University and Gainesville College, a two-year unit of the state university system, combine resources to offer an Associate of Arts degree from Gainesville College or a Bachelor of Arts in Theatre, a Bachelor of Fine Arts in Musical Theatre or a Bachelor of Fine Arts in Arts Management from Brenau. Courses are offered at both campuses during the first two years and at Brenau during the final two years.

Columbus State University

Tim McGraw, Int Chair
Department of Theatre
4225 University Avenue
Columbus, GA 31907-5645
DEPT: (706) 507-8400
FAX: (706) 571-4354
mcgraw_tim@colstate.edu
ADMISSIONS: Enrollment Services, Columbus State University, 4225 University Avenue, Columbus, GA 31907
www.colstate.edu   (706) 568-2035
admissions@colstate.edu

7,500 Total Enr.; not compet.
Semester System; NAST
141 Majors
T:$3,188 O ST.: $10,870
$6,014 R&B
www.theatre.colstate.edu

DEGREES OFFERED
BFA in Performance (66); Design/Tech (26); BSEdTheatre Education/Theatre for Youth (34), BA Theatre (6); Post BACC Teachers Cert (9). Declare major in freshman year; 2007 granted 7 UG degrees.

ADMISSION & FINANCIAL INFORMATION
SAT scores of at least 490 critical reading and 460 math; HS GPA of 2.50. 16 units college prep Freshman Index of 2200 or higher; 100 % of applicants accepted by institution as long as SAT scores are at or above requirements. Generally admit 10 out of 10 to theatre program. Scholarships for BFA Design/Tech, BA Theatre Arts, BFA Performance and BSEd selected by audition/interview.

FACULTY AND CLASSES OFFERED
8 Full-Time, 4 Part-Time: 2 PhD/DFA,10 MFA/MA; 4 Staff
A. (1 FT,2.5 PT) Intro to Theatre-12/Y; Theatre History-2/Y; Shakes-1/O; Dramatic Lit-2/O; Playwriting-1/O; Dramatic Crit.-O
B. (2 FT,1.5 PT) Acting-8/Y; Movement-2/Y; Singing-2/Y; Directing-4/Y; Voice/Speech-1/Y; Mime/Mask-1/O; Musical Theatre-2/Y; Dance-4/Y; Stage Combat-1/O.
C. (4 FT) Principles of Design-1/Y; Set Design-1/Y; Cost. Design-2/Y; Tech. Production-3/Y; Stage Mgmt-2/Y; Lighting Design-1/Y; Cost Construction-1/Y; Make-up-2/Y; Patterning & Draping-1/Y;

Costume Crafts-1/Y; Stage Props-1/Y; Architecture & Decor-1/Y.
D. (1 FT) Arts Management-2/Y

FACILITIES AND PRODUCTIONS
MAINSTAGE: 350 seats, computerized/electronic lighting, fly space
    5 prods: 5 Fac dir/des; budget $2,000 - $3,400
SECOND STAGE: 200 seats, computerized/electronic lighting, fly space
    10 prod: 10 UG dir/des; budget $2,000-$2,600
Third Stage: 100 seats, computerized/electronic lighting
    2 Workshop/Readings: 2 GA dir; budget $500 - $750
Facility was built in 2006 includes scene shop, costume shop, CAD facil., 1 movement/dance studios, 4 rehearsal studios, 1 design studio, 4 classrooms, lighting studio.

DESCRIPTION
Noted Faculty: Dr. Kate Musgrove, Directing; Brenda May Ito, Theatre Ed. & Theatre for Youth; Steven Graver, Costume Design & Construction; Brandon Booker, Tech Dir; Kimberly Manuel, Scene Des; Lawrence McDonald, Acting; Dr. Becky Becker, Theatre History..

Guest Artists: Barter Theatre; Chris Mixon, Second City; Rebecca McGraw, Guest Dir; Kim Garcia, Guest Costumer.

Columbus State University Department of Theatre's mission statement is to educate students in the collaborative art of theatre by preparing them for professional employment, careers in theatre education, and graduate study. The course of study teaches the craft and artistry of acting, directing, design, technical and educational theatre. The professional and energetic faculty encourages students to experiment, explore and discover in a supportive yet challenging environment. CSU productions serve as a laboratory where students practice classroom theories, test analytical skills and undertake cooperative endeavors while promoting the creative act of theatre. Theatrical seasons are selected to provide the student with the opportunity to experience plays from a range of periods/genres presented in a variety of production styles for both adult and young audiences. The CSU Department of Theatre shares its mission with the university and metropolitan communities by sharing our students' growth and development through our eclectic theatrical productions.

LaGrange College

Kim Barber Knoll, Chair
Division of Fine/Performing Arts
Department of Theatre Arts
601 Broad St.
LaGrange College
LaGrange, GA 30240-2999
DEPT: (706) 880-8266
www.lagrange.edu/academic/theatre.shtml
ADMISSIONS: Above address   (706) 880-8736
www.lagrange.edu   admission@lagrange.edu

1,058 Total Enr.; compet.
Semester System
20-25 Majors
T: $18,500/$$7,788 R&B
SMALL PROGRAM
FAX: (706) 880-8041

DEGREES OFFERED
BA in Theatre Arts,focus in Performance and Technical Theatre (20), Declare major at end of sophomore year.

ADMISSION & FINANCIAL INFORMATION

Minimum high school GPA: 2.75; SAT 1000; 70-80% of applicants admitted to institution; record of previous experience, audition/ interview, portfolio for designers req'd for admission to theatre program. Several Schols. awarded by Th. Dept. each year, auditions required. Upperclassmen auditions are near the end of Spring Semester. Fresh. scholas awarded in late Feb. or early March, student must apply and be accepted to LaGrange college. Two contrasting monologues not to exceed two min., no props or pieces with dialects. Singers have one min. to do sixteen bars of up-tempo song and a ballad (contrasting), designers have eight min. to present portfolios. For more info contact Josie Durant at (706) 880-8266..

FACULTY AND CLASSES OFFERED

3 Full-Time, 1 Part-Time: 1 PhD, 3 MFA/MA, 1 Staff

A. (1 PT) Intro to Theatre-2/Y; Drama Survey-2-3/Y; Script Analysis-1/O; Playwriting-1/O

B. (1 FT) Acting-2/Y; Movement-2/Y; Directing-1/O; Voice/Speech-1/O; Stage Combat-2/Y; Period Styles-1/O; Creative Dramatics-1-O; Special Topics-O

C. (1 FT, 1 PT) Principles of Design-1/O; Set Design-1/O; Cost Design- 1/O; Tech. Production-1/O; Costume History-1/O; Stage Mgmt-1/O; Lighting Design-1/O; Make-up-1/O; Stagecraft-1/Y

D. (1 PT) Arts Management-1/O

FACILITIES AND PRODUCTIONS

MAINSTAGE: 280 seats, fly space, elect/computerized lighting
3 prods: 2 Fac dir, 3 Fac des, 1 Guest dir, budget $6,000-10,000

SECOND STAGE: 70 seats, computerized lighting. budget $2000-3000

Facility was built in 1975, renovated black box in 2000-01; includes scene shop, costume shop, design, welding shop, dance studio, rehearsal studio, 1 classroom. Student workstations with high speed internet access. Impressive collection of stage weapons, broadswords, quarter staves, rapiers, daggers.

A non-departmental, student-run, production organization, Active Alpha Psi Omega Chapter, presents 1-2 prods. in a school yr. in which majors participate.

Connection with The Papermill Theatre in Lincoln, NH (www.papermilltheatre.org). Opportunities to work in summer theater as actors, technicians, etc. Locally and regionally there are new and ongoing opportunities for students to get hands-on experience in various professional situations. LaGrange College students have hired as professionals for improvisation, set design, lighting and sound design, singers, dancers, actors, children's theatre, stage managers, playwrights and fight choreographers.

DESCRIPTION

Noted Faculty: Kim Barber, Acting, Movement, Directing; Steven Earl-Edwards, Stage Combat, Playwriting, Management; Nathan Tomsheck, Lighting, Stagecraft, Intro to Design.

Guest Artists: Kate Warner, Guest Director; Joanna Schmink, Costume Designer; Tracy Riggs, Director; Marisabel Marratt, Scenic Designer; Karen Robinson, Guest Director; John Stephens, Guest Director; James Tolman, Scenic Designer; Joanna Schmink, Costume Designer; Jen Price, Scenic Designer; Brett Suocie, Choreographer.

The Department of Theatre Arts at LaGrange College is encompassed within the Division of Fine Arts. The Pre-Professional Program in Theatre Arts is an ensemble oriented program committed to providing a quality theatrical education for the young aspiring professional. It is searching for students who are passionate about theatre, dedicated to their art, and who understand the commitment, self-discipline, and professional approach necessary to create and maintain a quality theatrical training program. All members of the theatre faculty are practicing professionals and members of numerous unions and guilds as is appropriate for each member's area of specialization. It is our belief that, as professional educators and artists, we must keep up our professional artistic endeavors so that we may better educate our students on how to "make it" in the real world of the performing and other fine arts. In other words, we practice what we teach in both the educational and professional arenas. Each professor is expected to work outside the college in a professional venue each summer so as to help our department maintain a competitive edge with other like institutions when recruiting students.

University of Georgia

Stanley V. Longman, Head
Dept. of Drama & Theatre
University of Georgia
Athens, GA 30602-3154
(706) 542-2836
http://www.uga.edu

25,437; competitive
Semester System
189 Majors; NAST, U/RTA
T: $5,264 O-ST T:19,338
r&b $7,292
undergrad@admissions.uga.edu

DEGREES OFFERED

BA in General Drama; Film Studies, MFA in Acting, Design, Dramatic Media, Dramatic Writing; PhD in History/Theory/Criticism

ADMISSION & FINANCIAL INFORMATION

UG: 1000 base on SAT. Grad: GRE and 3.0 GPA. Grad program requires audition/interview, portfolio for designers and Dramatic Media artists. Samples of written work for playwriting and for PhD. Grad. Assist'shps are $9,462 for Masters, $10,089 for PhD students.

FACULTY AND CLASSES OFFERED

18 Full-Time: 9 PhD, 8 MFA/MA;1 Adjunct

A. (5 1/2) Intro to Theatre-2/Y; Theatre History-5/Y; Dramatic Lit-2/Y; Playwriting-5/Y

B. (3 FT) Acting-3/Y; Voice/Spch-2/Y; Mvmt-3/Y; Directing-3/Y; Acting for Camera-1/Y; Styles-1/Y

C. (6 1/2 FT) Prins of Des-2/Y; Set Des-3/Y; Ltg Des-2/Y; Tech. Prod'n-3/Y; Cost Constr.-1/Y; Cost Hist-1/Y; Make-up-2/Y; Stage Mgmt.-1/Y; CAD-1/Y; Cost. Des. for Computer-1/Y

FACILITIES AND PRODUCTIONS

MAINSTAGE: 650 seats, fly space, computerized light control
2 prods

SECOND STAGE: 280 seats, proscenium, restored historic building, 2 prods.

ALTERNATE SPACE: 100 seats, intimate house, 2 prods

ARENA STAGE: 65 seats, experimantal productions. Overall budget: $60,000.

Facility was built in 1941, renovated in 1975; includes scene shop, costume shop, props shop, welding shop, video studio, dance studio, 2 rehearsal studios, design studios, 10 classrooms, computer lab, editing studios, sound prod. studios.

DESCRIPTION

Noted Faculty: Antje Ascheid, film history; George Contini, acting; Michele Cuomo, acting; Charles B. Davis, theatre history; Richard Dunham, scenic and light design; Charles Eidsvik, film history and production; Freda Scott Giles, African-American drama; Michael Hussey, computer applications and animation; Stanley V. Longman, playwriting, theatre history; B. Don Massey, technical theatre; Richard Neupert, film history; Sylvia Hillyard Pannell, costume design and history; Ray Paolino, acting; Allen Partridge, playwriting, interactive computer; Farley Richmond, theatre of India; David Saltz, theory/criticism, computer applications.

Guest Artists: Corinne Jacker, Obie and Emmy winning playwright; Joyce Carol Oates, award winning novelist and playwright; Ann Hearn and Suzanne Ventulett, film and tv actresses; Casey Childs of Primary Stages; Nicolas Coster, actor; Victor Pisano, film producer; Monte Markham, actor/producer.

The University of Georgia aims to provide a sound liberal arts pre-professional training for its undergraduate students. The department offers both a drama and a film major. For its MFA students it offers education and training in the creative work of the various dramatic media: stage, film, television, computer applications and interactive events. On the doctoral level the emphasis is on history and theory or dramatic art.

University of West Georgia

(see ad below)

Shelly Elman, Dir. of Theatre
Mass. Comm./Theatre Arts
University of West Georgia
1601 Maple St.
Carrollton, GA 30118
DEPT: (678) 839-4700
FAX: (678) 839-4708
www.westga.edu/~theatre
ADM: Admissions, Univ. of West Georgia, Carrollton, GA 30118
(678) 839-4000
www.westga.edu

10,163 Total Enr.; compet.
Semester System
50 Majors; NAST

T: $3,460/5,182 r & b
O-ST T: $11,142/ 5,182 r & b
SMALL PROGRAM

FAX: (678) 839-4747

DEGREES OFFERED

BA in Theatre (50). Declare major in sophomore year. 2007 granted 2 UG degrees.

ADMISSION & FINANCIAL INFORMATION

GPA min-2.50; SAT CR430; Math 410; ACT E-17,M-17,C-17. Completed 16 required HS prep courses, calculated Freshman index of 2.050; No special req. for admission to theatre program. 85% accepted into theatre program. Friends of Theatre New Talent Award is given to a new intended theatre major. Candidates must apply and audition or give a portfolio presentation for faculty. Four other scholarships are awarded to returning theatre majors who have made outstanding contributions to the West Georgia Theatre Co.

FACULTY AND CLASSES OFFERED

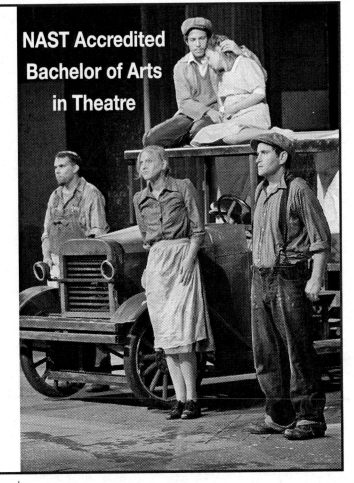

6 Full-Time, 2 PhD, 1 ABD, 3 MFA;

A. (2 FT,) Intro to Theatre-4/Y; Theatre History-2/Y; Shakes (Performance)-1/Y; Dramatic Literature-2/Y; Playwriting-1/O

B. (2 FT) Acting-3/Y; Singing-1/X; Directing-1/Y; Voice/Speech-1/X

C. (2 FT) Principles of Design-2/Y; Tech. Production-1/Y; Set Design-1/Y; Ltg. Des-1/Y; Cost. Constr.-1/Y; Cost. Hist-1/Y; Stage Mgmt.-1/O

FACILITIES AND PRODUCTIONS

MAINSTAGE: 450 seats, fly space, computerized lighting
5 prods: 4 Fac dir, 2 Fac des, 1 UG dir, 3 UG des; budget $4,000-6,000

SECOND STAGE: 120 seats, black box, computerized lighting
5 prods: 2 Fac dir, 1 Fac des, 3 UG dir, 2 UG des; budget $4,000-6,000

Workshops/Readings; budget $100-300

Facility includes sound shop, movement/dance studio, classrooms. Martha Munro, our newly restored classroom & faculty office facility houses a CAD classroom, a lighting lab and an acting/directing studio.

A non-departmental, student-run, producing organization presents Theatre Sports Troupe, 4 times/yr, majors participate. 3 student-written plays produced in the last two years.

DESCRIPTION

Noted Faculty: Tommy Cox, Scenography, Technical Direction, Musical Theatre; Amy Cuomo, AEA, Theatre History, Dramatic Lit, Interdisciplinary; Shelly Elman, AEA, Acting, Directing, Interdisciplinary; Pauline Gagnon, Playwriting, Interdisciplinary; Alan Yeong, Scenography, Costume Design, Dramatic Lit; Caleb Boyd, Dramatic Lit, Theatre History, Dramaturgy.

Guest Artists: Monica Hart, Designer; Geoffrey Williams, Director; Dr. Lundeana Thomas, Director; Scot Mann, SAFD Fight Choreographer; Rosemary Newcott, Actor, Director

The mission of the UWG theatre program is to educate and inspire students who wish to study the art of theatre. By offering a BA degree in theatre, we hope to provide students with a well-rounded education in all areas of theatre arts – production & performance (including acting, directing, and design/technical skills), literature, and history. Providing this type of education will empower individuals to seek careers in theatre, careers related to theatre, or other professions. The UWG theatre program is comprised of students from diverse backgrounds who seek careers in professional theatre, teaching, or related fields. The theatre program at UWG produces versatile graduates who are capable of working in many areas of theatre. The theatre program is currently accredited through the National Association of Schools of Theatre (NAST).

HAWAII

University of Hawaii at Manoa

Gregg Lizenbery, Chair
Department of Theatre & Dance
University of Hawaii at Manoa
1770 East-West Road

12,000 Total Enr.; not compet.
Semester System
100 Majors
T: $2,568 ug, $3,432 g

Honolulu, HI 96822
DEPT: (808) 956-2588

O-ST T: $7,200 ug, $8,160 g
Main: (808) 956-7677

MAJORS AND DEGREES OFFERED

BA in Theatre, MFA in Directing (6), Design (4), Playwriting (2), Asian Performance (6), Youth Theatre (5), Acting (6); PhD in Asian Theatre (20), Western Theatre (5) Also MA plans A (Thesis) and B (non Thesis); BA, BFA, MA, MFA in Dance. UG declare major in 2nd yr; 2000 granted 11 UG and 13 Grad degs.

ADMISSION & FINANCIAL INFORMATION

70% applicants accepted; UH acceptance req. for UG, GRE and evidence of experience and training req. for Grad; Theatre Program accepts 8 of 10 UG, 3 of 8 Grad applicants. Departmental Graduate Asst'ship in Publicity, Asian Theatre, Tech. Theatre, A-V, Costuming, Dance; Departmental Teaching Instructorships in Acting.

FACULTY AND CLASSES OFFERED

18 Full-Time: 8 PhD, 8 MFA/MA, 2 Prof. w/o degree

A. (3 FT) Intro to Theatre-1/Y; Dramatic Lit-4/O; Th History-1/Y; Dramatic Criticism-3/Y; Shakes-1/Y; Playwriting-3/Y; Film-2/Y

B. (2 FT) Acting-10/Y; Voice/Speech-1/Y; Movement-1/O; Musical Theatre-1/Y; Directing-5/O

C. (3 FT) Prins of Des-1/Y; Set Des-2/Y; Cost Des- 1/Y; Ltg Des-2/Y; Tech Prod-2/Y; Cost Constr-1/Y; Cost Hist-1/Y; Make-up-1/Y

D. Arts Management-1/O

Also: 1 1/2 FT Children's Theatre faculty (5 1/2/Y), 4 1/2 FT Dance faculty, and 3 FT Asian theatre faculty members (10/Y).

FACILITIES & PRODUCTIONS

MAINSTAGE: 630 seats, fly space, computerized lighting. 6 prods: 4-5 Fac dir/des; 1-2 Fac dir/Grad des; budget $4000-8000

SECOND STAGE: 150 seats, electronic lighting. 8-12 prods: 2 Fac dir/des; 8-10 Grad dir/des; budget $100-1000. Also 9-10 workshops/readings: Guest, UG, Grad dir; budget $0-200

Facility was built in 1963; includes scene shop, costume shop, props shop, 2 dance studios, rehearsal studio, 2 classrooms.

Non-departmental, student-run organization presents 1-2 productions per year in which majors generally participate.

DESCRIPTION

Noted Faculty: Elizabeth Wichmann-Walczak, Asian Theatre, Tamara Montgomery, Youth Th.;

Our faculty believes that the arts of theatre and dance present audiences and artists alike with valid and arresting statements of significant human experience. We expect students to gain a broad understanding of the intellectual and social bases of performance and to develop an awareness of the richness of Asian and Western theatrical cultures at the same time that they learn dedication to the disciplines of the art. The number of faculty with "international and national reputations in their fields of expertise is truly exceptional" (NAST evaluation, 1987). The Department offers exciting programs in performance training, design, history-literature-theory, youth theatre, and dance. University of Hawaii at Manoa is the premier university in the U. S. for the study of Asian theatre, including performance training in Kabuki, Chinese Opera, and South-East Asian Theatre Forms. Graduates of the Department are successful in professional theatre, film and tv industry, and hold teaching positions throughout the world.

Boise State University

Dr. Richard Klautsch, Chair
Theatre Arts Department
1910 University Drive
Boise, ID 83725-1565
DEPT: (208) 426-3957
FAX: (208) 426-1771
ADMISSIONS: 1910 University Dr., Boise, ID 83725
(208) 426-1177
bsuinfo@boisestate.edu

17,042 Tot. Enr, not compet.
Semester System, ATHE
103 Majors, NAST
T: $4,410/$5,938 R&B
O-ST T: $12,628
http://theatre.boisestate.edu
FAX: (208) 426-3765
www.BoiseState.edu

DEGREES OFFERED

BA in Theatre Arts with options in Performance (62), Design (5), Dramatic Writing (5), Directing (2), Secondary Ed. (6), Dance (8), Stage Management. Declare major in freshman year.

ADMISSION & FINANCIAL INFORMATION

Combination of H.S. GPA and ACT or SAT; request current admissions index for reference. 87% of applicants accepted by institution. Th. program admits all applicants. Brown Performing Arts Schol. and other departmental scholarships awarded on the basis of GPA, auditions and interviews; Britt Bowden Schol.- Music and Th. Depts. select nominee (community scholarship); Boise Little Theatre-selected by BLT board; Hunt Performing Arts Schol.-Music & Theatre Depts. select together with Hunt.

FACULTY AND CLASSES OFFERED

8 Full-Time,2 PhD, 5 MFA; 1 MA, 3 Staff

A. (2 FT) Intro to Theatre-1/Y; Theatre History-2/Y; Shakes-2/X; Dramatic Lit-2/Y; Playwriting-1/Y; Play Analysis-1/Y

B. (2 FT, 1 PT) Acting-4/Y; Voice/Speech-3/Y; Movement-2/Y; Dance-10/Y; Singing-1/X; Directing-2/Y; Mus. Theatre-2/O

C. (2 1/2 FT) Set Design-1/O; Cost Des-1/O; Ltg Design-1/O; Tech. Prod.-2/Y; Stage Mgmt.-1/O; Make-up-1/Y

D. (1/2 FT) Arts Mgmt.-1/O

FACILITIES AND PRODUCTIONS

MAINSTAGE: 225 seats, computerized lighting.and sound, 3 prods: 3 Fac dir, 9 Fac des, 3 UG des; budget $4,000-6,000

SECOND STAGE: 435 seats, fly space, computerized lighting 1 prod: 1 Fac dir, 3 Fac des, 1 UG des; budget $5,000-7,000

THIRD STAGE: 2100 seats, fixed stage, computerized lighting 2 Fac dir/des Workshops/Readings; budget $250-500

Facility was built in 1984; includes scene shop, costume shop. Theatre Arts Annex remodeled in 1999, holds scene and costume shops and storage.

A non-departmental, student run organization produces 2 prods. per year in which majors participate. 10 student-written plays produced in the last two years.

Connection with Idaho Shakespeare Festival and Boise Contemporary Theatre. ISF hires our students as interns in acting, stage management and running crews. We also have a close connection with Idaho Dance Theatre, in residence at Boise State. Dance majors may perform in IDT concerts.

DESCRIPTION

Noted Faculty: Phil Atlakson, Playwright and Screenwriter; Stanley Award winner; Marla Hansen,

Co-Artistic Director, Idaho Dance Theatre; Charles Fee, Artistic Dir., Idaho Shakespeare Festival.

Guest Artists: ACTER, Professionl Actors from the London Stage, one-week residency; Matt Clark, Artistic Director, Boise Contemporary Theater; Rusty Wilson, Artistic Director, Company of Fools, Hailey, ID.

The Department of Theatre Arts serves Boise State University and Idaho as the primary institution for learning about and practicing theatre arts within an active arts community and a modern urban university. It provides a variety of classes for general undergraduate education and for specialized theatre study within a liberal arts environment. It fully prepares students for advanced study on the graduate level. It provides a season of performances that educates students and offers cultural enrichment to the community at large. Finally, it interacts with the regional arts community to raise general arts awareness and it supports the growth of professional theatre for the mutual benefit of the profession and the department.

University of Idaho

David Lee-Painter
Department of Theatre & Film
University of Idaho
P.O. Box 443074
Moscow, ID 83844-3074
DEPT: (208) 885-6465
www.uitheatre.com
Adm: 1-88-88UIDAHO

12,000 Total Enr.; competitive
Semester System
140 Majors; ATHE,
USITT,KC/ACTFM,NWDC
T: $4,410/$6,424 R&B
O-ST T: $14,490/6,424 R&B
utheatre@uidaho.edu

DEGREES OFFERED

BS/BA in General Theatre (140); BFA in Acting (10), Design Tech (12); MFA in Acting (6), Directing (4), Design (8). Declare major in freshman year.

ADMISSION & FINANCIAL INFORMATION

3.0 GPA or acceptable SAT/ACT scores. 85% of applicants accepted. UG program admits all applics. (10 of 10); Grad program 5 out of 10. UG requires audition for scholarships only. Freshman schols awarded based on live aud. (or tape w/permission) portfolio and 2 letters of rec.. Grad program requires audition, interview, statement of goals, 3 letters of rec., portfolio for design.

FACULTY AND CLASSES OFFERED

10 Full-Time: 3 Performance/5 Design-Tech/1 Film/1 Directing

A. (2 FT) Intro to Theatre-2/Y; Theatre History-3/Y; Shakes-1/X; Dramatic Lit-1/Y; Dramatic Criticism-2/Y

B. (2 FT) Acting-8/Y; Voice/Speech-1/Y; Movement-1/Y; Mime, etc.-1/O; Singing-1/Y; Directing-2/Y; Stage Combat-1/Y

C. (5 FT) Prins of Design-2/Y; Set Design-2/Y; Costume Design-1/Y; Lighting Design-2/Y; Tech. Production-1/Y; Costume Construction-1/O; Costume History-1/X; Make-up-1/Y; Stage Mgmt-1/Y

D. (1 ft) Study of Film

FACILITIES AND PRODUCTIONS

MAINSTAGE: 419 seats, fly space, computerized & electronic lighting.. 4 prods: 3 Fac dir/des, 4 Guest dir, 2 Guest des, 1 Grad student dir/des; budget $1,000-2,500

SECOND STAGE: 147 seats, electronic lighting. 2-4 prods: 4 Fac dir/des; budget $200-400

THIRD STAGE: Lab Theatre, 60 seats. 4-6 prods annually

Facility was built in 1973; includes scene, costume shops, props shop, sound studio, dance studio, 1 rehearsal studios, 1 design studio, 2 classrooms. 3 student-written plays produced in the last two years.

Connection with Idaho Repertory Theatre and part of the MFA requirement (summer): Mixes guest artists with U of I students in a professional atmosphere producing 4 shows in rotating repertory format. Annual Performance Fellowship (Paid) with Oregon Shakespeare Festival, Internships w/regional and national companies.

DESCRIPTION

The University of Idaho's philosophy is aimed at training students for work in the professional theatre while at the same time providing them with a liberal arts education. Both art and craft are emphasized in the department. Individualized training is stressed as is audition preparation and portfolio development.

ILLINOIS

The Conservatory at Act One Studios

Steve Merle, Director
Act One Studios
640 N. LaSalle
Suite 535
Chicago, IL 60610
www.actone.com
smerle@actone.com

14 conserv/yr
Total Enr.; competitive
Semester System
T: $9,500
(312) 787-9384
FAX: (312) 787-3234
golszak@actone.com

DEGREES OFFERED

Certificate in Acting for those completing 2-year program.

ADMISSION & FINANCIAL INFORMATION

Audition, interview, 2 letters of recommendation required. Graduate level work, must be at least 21 years old with BA or equivalent experience. Video audition accepted. Health certificate required.

FACULTY AND CLASSES OFFERED

16 Part-Time: 9 MFA/MA, 7 prof. w/o adv deg., 5 staff

B. (16 PT) Acting-12/Y; Voice/Speech-2/Y; Movement-9/Y; Improv-2/Y; On-Camera-6/Y

FACILITIES & PRODUCTIONS

MAINSTAGE: 50 seats, computerized lighting. 2 prods: First year, guest dir, 2 prods 2nd year, 1 guest, 1 fac. dir.

Facility was renovated in 2003, includes black box theatre, 6 studios for classes & rehearsals, 2 equipped with sprung floor, 3 video equipped.

DESCRIPTION

Noted Faculty: Scott Olsen, Acting; Ted Hoerl, Meisner; Michael Gellman, Improv; Stuart Carden, Viewpoints/Movement/Growtowski; Kristen Spangler, Alexander Tech; Gretchen Sondstroem, Yoga; Matt Harding, Voice & Speech; Steve Merle, Aud Tech; Jane Alderman (CSA), Film; Oksana Fedunyszyn, Film

Guest Artists: Steve Scott, Artistic Associate Goodman Theatre; David Cromer, Director/Actor; Rondi Reed, Actor; Steppenwolf Theatre Co; Yasen Pankov, Steppenwolf Theatre Co; Austin Pendelton, Steppenwolf Theatre Co; Susan Hart & Larry Yando, Chicago Shakespeare Co

The Conservatory at Act One is a comprehensive, graduate level, 2-year professional program, designed to deepen your abilities as a creative artist preparing for a challenging career. Two 16-week terms per year. Classes meet five days per week for 13 weeks, followed by 3 weeks of rehearsal and performance. A variety of acting approaches develop truthful, spontaneous ensemble work. Immersion in voice/speech and movement develops flexible, creative vocal and physical tools. Second year study adds practical skills: on-camera work for feature film and television; audition techniques and monologue preparation. Small classes taught by practicing professionals ensure individual support. Guest Artist seminars and Guest Directors provide a connection to Chicago's vibrant professional community. A Final Showcase introduces your work to directors, agents, and casting directors. Regular exposure to both cutting edge and commercial theatre productions includes dialogue with nationally noted actors, directors, and playwrights.

Bradley University

George H. Brown, Chair
Dept. of Theatre Arts
Hartmann Center
Bradley University
Peoria, IL 61625
DEPT: (309) 677-2660
ADM: 1-800-447-6460
www.bradley.edu

5,813 Total Enr.; competitive
60 Majors; ATHE
Semester System
T: 21,200/$7,050 R&B
theatre@bradley.edu
FAX: (309) 677-2797
FAX: (309) 677-2797
admissions@bradley.edu

DEGREES OFFERED

BA/BS in Theatre Arts (34), Theatre Performance Concentration (13), Theatre Production Concentration (3), Theatre Education (8). Declare major in fresh. or soph. year; 2001 granted 9 degrees.

ADMISSION & FINANCIAL INFORMATION

Application, ACT or SAT scores, HS transcript. 89% of applics. accepted by institut. Theatre program admits 5 out of 10. No special req. for admission to th. prog. Bradley offers academic scholarships that all students may qualify for based on test scores (28 ACT or 1240 SAT) and class rank of top 10%. Theatre scholarships offered by audition and submission of Fine Arts Scholarship Application.

FACULTY AND CLASSES OFFERED

5 Full-Time, 1 Part-Time: 2 PhD, 5 MFA/MA

A. (1 FT) Intro to Th.-12/Y; Th. History-3/Y; Dramatic Lit.-3/Y

B. (2 FT) Acting-5/O; Voice/Speech-1/Y; Movement-1/O; Directing-2/Y; Stage Combat-1/O

C. (2 FT) Prins of Des-1/Y; Tech Prod'n-2/Y; Set Design-1/Y; Ltg Des-1/Y; Make-up-1/O

D. (1 PT) Marketing-1/Y; Box Office Procedure-1/Y

FACILITIES & PRODUCTIONS

MAINSTAGE: 280 seats, computerized lighting. 5 prods: 3 Fac dir/des, 2 Guest dir, 1 Guest des, 1 UG des; budget $6,000-9,000

SECOND STAGE: 70 seats, electronic lighting. 6-10 UG dir/des prods;

budget $500-600

2-4 UG dir Workshops/Readings.

Facility was built in 1909, renovated in 1979; includes scene shop, costume shop, sound studio, rehearsal studio, CAD facility, design studio, classrooms, Global Communications Center.

4 student-written plays produced in the last two years.

DESCRIPTION

Noted Faculty: James Ludwig, & Dr. Jeffrey Huberman, co-authors The Theatrical Imagination; Wm. J. Langley, Jr., Scenic & Lighting Design; Owen Collins, Technical Direction and Scenic Design; Susan Robinson, Directing; Dr. Dennis Beck, Theatre History; Thomas Glynn, Acting; Rebecca Dosen, Costume Design; Molly Sloter, Voice, Musical Direction.

Guest Artists: Marni Nixon, Robert Schenkkan, Daniel Allar, Steve Baron, Dr. Howard Stein, Pam Hill, Patrick O'Gara, August Boal, San Francisco Mime Troupe, Ann Courtney

The Department of Theatre offers academic and artistic programs that provide students with comprehensive courses in the history and theory of theatre and drama, performance studies, and production design and technology. The diversified production program offers students and faculty unique and challenging theatrical experiences that are the preserve of academic institutions and experiences available in traditional commercial venues. The major in theatre arts prepares students to pursue careers and advanced study and training in graduate programs in theatre as well as career options including, but not limited to, business, education, engineering & technology, law, and the arts. For Bradley University and its constituents the programs and productions of the Department of Theatre Arts provide a focus of discovery, creativity, and responsibility for understanding the global and multicultural diversity of human actions.

Chicago State University

Songodina Ifatunji, Arthur M. Reese, Coordinators
Chicago State University
9501 S. King Dr.
Chicago, IL 60628
(773) 995-2419
ADM: (773) 995-2513   FAX: (773) 995-3820
www.csu.edu   ug-admissions@csu.edu

DESCRIPTION

Chicago State University has an 18 credit hour minor in Theatre and a BA in Broadcast Communications. Our two full time Theatre faculty produce 6 full length mainstage shows per year. Touring Program, Program of Special Events in Music and Dance.

Columbia College

Sheldon Patinkin, Chair
Theatre Department
Columbia College
600 South Michigan
Chicago, IL 60605
spatinkin@popmail.colum.edu

10,771 Total Enr.; non-compet.
Semester System
T. $117,569/12,018 r&b.
600 Majors
(312) 344-6100
FAX: (312) 344-8077

ADM: 600 S. Michigan, 3rd Flr   (312) 344-7129
www.colum.edu   FAX: (312) 344-8024
admissions@colum.edu

DEGREES OFFERED

BA/BFA in Acting , Directing , Design; BA in Playwriting, Technical Theatre, Musical Theater Performance . Declare major in first year.

ADMISSION & FINANCIAL INFORMATION

Admit 90% of applicants. No special reqs. for theatre program. Open admissions policy. All schols. for registered Columbia students. Michael Merritt/John Murbach Award for design majors. Freshman Achievement in Theater: excellence + participation in Freshman Yr. Betty Garrett Schol.: excellence in Musical Theater, David Talbot Cox for directing majors..Only UG accepted by Admin Ofc, no graduate degree in Theatre is offered.

FACULTY AND CLASSES OFFERED

25 Full-Time, 38 Part-Time: 1 PhD, 54 MA/MFA, 8 Profs. w/o adv. degree; 4 Staff

A. (2 FT,5 PT)Dramatic Lit-1/Y; Theatre History-3/Y; Shakes-2/Y; Playwriting-2/Y; Dramatic Crit-1/Y; Community Based-1/Y, Teaching-1/Y

B. (19 FT, 27 PT) Acting-12/Y; Voice/Speech-5/Y; Movement-4/Y; Singing-2/Y; Musical Theatre-5/Y; Directing-3/Y; Stage Combat-4/Y; Improv-3/Y; Physical Theatre1/Y; Auditioning-3/Y; Dialects-2/Y; Solo Perf-2/Y; Mime/Mask-1/Y

C. (3 FT, 8 PT) Prins of Des-1/Y; Set Design-2/Y; Cost Des-2/Y; Ltg Des-2/Y; Tech. Production-4/Y; Cost Constr-2/Y; Make-up-3/Y; Stage Mgmt-1/Y; CAD-2/Y; Drafting/Rendering-3/Y

D. Arts Management-7/X; Mktg/Promo-4/X; Devel/Grant Writing-3/X; Contracts/Copyright-1/X; Budgeting/Accounting-4/X

FACILITIES AND PRODUCTIONS

MAINSTAGE: 390 seats, fly space, computerized lighting. 3 Fac dir/des, 3 Guest des, 3 UG des; budget $18,000-45,000

SECOND STAGE: 60-80 seats, computerized lighting. 2-3 Fac dir/des, 3 Guest des; 1 Guest dir, 3 UG des budget $5,000-6,000

THIRD STAGE: 60-80 seats, electronic lighting. renovated in 2002.

Workshops/Readings: 6 Fac dir,2 Guest dir, 30 UG dir, 90 UG des; budget $100-200

Facility built in the 1920s, last renovated in 2002; includes scene shop, costume shop, prop shop, CAD fac. 1 design studio, 2 dance studios, 2 rehearsal studios, make-up studio, 24 classrooms.

6 student-written plays produced in the last two years.

Connection with Second City Training School, advanced Improv/Comedy Workshop, give workshop prods at 2nd City Studio space.. Students can transfer credits between the two institutions.

DESCRIPTION

Noted Faculty Sheldon Patinkin, Directing; Fran Maggio Costume Design; David Woolley, Stage Combat; Stephanie Shaw, Solo Perfomance; Harisse Davidson, On Camera; Barbara Robertson, Auditioning; Brian Posen, Improv; David Cromer, Acting; Brian Shaw, Acting; Pauline Brailsford, Voice.

Guest Artists: Free Street, Ron Bieganski,Youth Theatre, Second City; Dan Griffiths, Physical Comedy; Alan

Arkin, Acting Director; Michael Rohd, Community-Based Theatre; Daniel Stein, Mask; Jennifer Hubbard; ViewPoints; Wilfredo Rivera, Choreography; Andrea Dymond, Director.

The Columbia College Theatre Department, like the rest of the college, requires that all faculty earn part of their living doing what they teach. The department is very much performance-oriented, with a practical and hands-on approach derived from the teachings of Stanislavsky and Viola Spolin. We also have training in the techniques of improvisation as taught at The Second City, and in Musical Theatre, which is a combined program from the theatre, music, and dance departments. Our 400-seat theater and two 80-seat studios are in almost constant operation.

DePaul University

[see listing under The Theatre School at DePaul University]

Elmhurst College

Alan W. Weiger, Dir. of Theatre
Dept. of Theatre Arts
Elmhurst College
190 Prospect Ave.
Elmhurst, IL 60126
DEPT: (630) 617-3006
www.elmhurst.edu
ADM: Above address.
FAX: (630) 617-5501

3,000 Total Enr.; competitive
15 Majors
Semester System (4-1-4)
T: $24,660/$7,124 r&b
SMALL PROGRAM
FAX: (630) 617-3740
alanw@elmhurst.edu
(630) 617-3068

DEGREES OFFERED

BA in Theatre-Professional (5), Theater Secondary Ed (4), Musical Theater (Fall 2000). Declare major in any year.

ADMISSION & FINANCIAL INFORMATION

Official HS transcript, ACT or SAT. 80% of applics. accepted by institution. Theatre program admits all applics. Interview for admission to th. prog. Theatre Scholarship -C.C. Arends Schol. Competitive Talent Award. 1/4 - 1/3 tuition remission. Top 1/3 of class, major in dept., active in productions. Apply to Dir. of Theater. Theater Assistants - paid student staff in scenery, lighting, costume, sound, paint, publicity/box office. Apply to Director of Theater in person or by letter.

FACULTY AND CLASSES OFFERED

2 1/2 Full-Time, 2 Part-Time: 1 1/2 PhD, 3 MFA/MA

A. (1 FT) Intro to Theatre-1/Y; Theatre History-1/Y; Shakespeare-1/X; Dramatic Literature-2/X; Playwriting-1/X; Avant-Garde Theater-1/O

B. (3/4 FT, 2 PT) Acting-5/Y; Voice/Speech-2/Y; Movement-1/Y; Directing-1/O; Singing-1/X; Dance-2/Y; Improv-1/Y

C. (3/4 FT) Tech Prod'n-1/O; Sound Recording-1/X

D. Arts Mgmt.-1/X; Marketing/Promotion-1/X; Legal: Contracts, etc.-1/X; Devel/Grant Writing-1/X; Budgeting/Acct'ng-1/

FACILITIES & PRODUCTIONS

MAINSTAGE: 160 seats, computerized & electronic lighting
7 prods: 3 Fac dir/des, 2 Guest dir/des, 2 UG dir/ des; budget $4-6,000

OTHER PRODUCTIONS produced in Mainstage on lesser scale:.1-3 prods: 1-2 Fac dir, 1-3 Fac des, 1-2 Guest dir/des, 1-3 UG dir, 1-4 UG des; budget $0-200

1 Fac dir Workshop/Reading.

Facility was built in 1920, renovated in 1981; includes scene shop, costume shop, prop shop, sound studio, CAD facility, dance studio, classrooms, recital hall in music dept., sound recording studio.

A non-departmental, producing org. presents 1 production/year.

2 student-written plays produced in the last two years.

Connection with Sense of Urgency. Company will produce 1-2 times per year, opening at the College before moving into Chicago. Company offers regular workshops in acting technique, scene study, monologues and theater business. Stu-dents may audition for roles and receive professional and/or college credit for design, stage management, stagecraft.

DESCRIPTION

Noted Faculty: Alan W. Weiger, Theater History, Design & Technology, Directing;Janice Pohl, Directing, Design & Tech, costuming, creative dramatics; Directing; Kristen Spangler, Voice & Movement; Aaron Johnson, voice, musical director; Lance Wilcox, (English), Dramatic Lit, Playwriting; Ted Lerud, (English), Shakespeare; Kevin Olson (Music), Musical Theater, Music Theory; Brenda Lualdi (Music), Opera, Applied Voice; Susan Moninger (Music), Vocal, Jazz, Applied Voice; Tim Hays (Music) Music Business.

Guest Artists: Ray Kasper, Audition, Directing; Bethany Alexander, Acting; Amy Kasper, Acting, Directing; Edwin Wilson, Acting, Business; Tony Noice, Acting; Lindy Loyet, Dance; Eric Appleton, Lighting Design & Technology; David Lowum, Sound Design & Technology.

The hallmark or Elmhurst College is a constructive confluence of professional preparation and a foundation in the liberal arts. The Theatre major prepares the student for entry level positions in the profession, or for further study and training. Aside from acting in productions, students also have significant opportunity to design, stage manage, and direct. The student majoring in Musical Theatre is required to complete rigorous sequences in acting, dance, and applied voice, as well as being exposed to history and literature of music, theatre, and musical theatre. The student also has the opportunity to perform in opera, straight plays, dance recitals, and ensembles such as vocal jazz, madrigals, and the improv troupe. The major in Speech/Theatre Education prepares students to become effective teachers by balancing theory and practical application, and by giving students valuable insights in the operation of extra-curricular programs in theatre and speech.

Illinois State University

Don La Casse, Director
School of Theatre
Campus Box 5700
Illinois State University
Normal, IL 61790-5700
DEPT: (309) 438-8784
dlacasse@ilstu.edu
ADMISSIONS: Campus Box 2200, Normal, IL 61761
(309) 438-2181

20,265 Total Enr.; competitive
332 Majors; Semester Sys.
NAST, U/RTA, ATHE
T: $8,039/$6,150 R&B
O-ST T: $14,730/$6,150 R&B
FAX: (309) 438-5806
www.ilstu.edu

DEGREES OFFERED

MA/MS in Theatre (12); MFA in Acting (0), Directing (5), Scene Des (11); BA/BS in Theatre Studies (44), Production/ Design (67), Performance-Acting/Dance (164), Theatre Education (57). Declare major in freshman year; 2007 granted 58 UG, 14 Grad degs.

ADMISSION & FINANCIAL INFORMATION

Average GPA 3.45, ACT 24.6. Aud/Int/Portfolio for des. req. for UG & Grad program. Approximately 40 scholarships ranging from $500-1,200 per semester. One-half in the form of tuition waivers, some with GPA requirements but all based on talent and contributions to the School of Theatre. 140 out of 170 accepted to UG theatre program, 8 out of 125 accepted to Grad program.

FACULTY AND CLASSES OFFERED

26 Full-Time, 1.5 Part-time: 8 PhD, 20 MFA/2 MA, 8 Staff

A. (8 FT) Intro to Theatre-1/Y; Theatre History-2/Y; Dramatic Lit-1/Y; Dramatic Criticism-1/Y; Playwriting-1/Y; Shakes-1/X; Intro to Black Drama-1/Y

B. (11.5 FT, 1.5 PT) Acting-7/Y; Voice/Speech-2/Y; Movement-2/Y; Musical Theatre-1/O; Directing-3/Y; Stage Combat-1/O; Dance-16/Y; Mime, etc-1/O; Acting for the Camera-1/Y; Puppetry-1/O

C. (6.5 FT) Prins. of Des-5/Y; Set Design-5/Y; Ltg Des-2/Y; Cost Constr-4/Y; Make-up-1/Y; Costume Des-3/Y; Tech Prod-2/Y; Stage Mgmt-2/Y; Sound Des-2/Y; Stagecraft-1/Y

D. Arts Management-2/Y; Creative Drama-3/Y; Cinema Studies-6/Y; Oral Interp of Lit-2/Y; Art and Society-1/Y

FACILITIES AND PRODUCTIONS

MAINSTAGE: 450 seats, fly space, computerized & electronic lighting
5 prods: 3 Fac dir,3 Fac des, 1 GA dir/des; 1 Grad dir/des

SECOND STAGE: 175 seats,fly space, computerized & electr lighting
5 prods: 2 Fac dir, 3 student dir, 5 student des

THIRD STAGE: 100 seats, black box. numerous UG dir/des prods.

Facility includes scene shop, costume shop, prop shop, welding area, sound room, CAD facility, rehearsal studio, 3 dance studios, design studio, 1 video, 8 classrooms. Facility built 2002.

Departmental student-run producing organization present 12-16 prods per year in which majors participate.

One student-written play produced in the last two years.

Connection with Illinois Shakespeare Festival (Summer, Equity). All MFA students are employed as actors or technicians. Undergraduates audition for acting roles, technicians interview for available positions.

DESCRIPTION

Noted Faculty: Calvin MacLean, Directing; Patrick O'Gara, Acting/Directing; Marian Hampton, Voice; Jack McLaughlin-Gray, Acting; J. William Ruyle, Scenic/Lighting; John Stark, Scenic; Dan Wilhelm, Costume; Sandra Zielinski, Directing/Theatre Ed; Alvin Goldfarb, History; Fergus Currie, Directing/Management;Elizabeth Mullenix, History; Cyndee Brown, Theatre Education; Kim Pererra, Acting

Guest Artists: Shozo Sato, Director,Designer; Kurt Sharp, Designer; Kathy Irvin, Director; Tim Miller, Artist in residence; Eddie O'Campo, Choreographer

To educate students in developing informed, discriminating responses to and an appreciation of the art of theatre, its literature, and its history, to educate students in all areas of theatre arts; to train individuals capable of perpetuating the art(s) of theatre, either by entering the profession or continuing with advanced graduate study; and to produce theatre art in order to assist in fulfilling the first three objectives as well as to serve the University, Bloomington-Normal, and the State of Illinois.

Illinois Wesleyan University

Nancy B. Loitz, Director
School of Theatre Arts
Illinois Wesleyan University
P. O. Box 2900
Bloomington, IL 61702-2900
DEPT: (309) 556-3195
ADM: 103 Holmes Hall, P.O.B. 2900, Bloomington, IL 61702-2900
(309) 556-3031
http://www.iwu.edu

2,000 Total Enr.; competitive
Semester System + May term
100 Majors; ATHE
T: $26,000/$6,200 R&B
FAX: (301) 556-3558
nloitz@titan.iwu.edu

(309) 556-3411
iwuadmit@titan.iwu.edu

DEGREES OFFERED

BA in Theatre Arts (21); BFA in Theatre Arts (52), Music Th. (27). Declare major in first year; 2001 granted 21 degrees

ADMISSION & FINANCIAL INFORMATION

ACT score of 25 (28 avg.) and class rank in upper 1/3; inst. accepts 45% of applicants. Audi./interview(portfolio for designers) req'd; Program admits 25 out of 100 applics. Talent awards available to entering theatre arts or music theatre majors; awards are renewable for 4 years for those who maintain "B" avg, continue to contrubute to the theatre program and maintain their major. Award is based entirely on audition or portfolio showing. Univ. also provides awards based on scholarship.

FACULTY AND CLASSES OFFERED

8 Full-Time, 7 Part-Time (includes 1 FT and 2 PT in Dance): 2 PhD, 14 MFA/MA, 1 Prof. w/o adv. degree; 1 Staff

A. (1 FT) Intro to Theatre-1/Y; Theatre History-3/O; Shakes-2/X; Dramatic Lit-1/Y; Playwriting-1/O

B. (2 FT, 2 PT) Acting-9/Y; Voice/Speech-3/Y; Movement-2/Y; Singing-2/X; Musical Theatre-4/Y; Directing-2/Y; Dance-6/Y

C. (2 FT) Prins of Des-1/Y; Set Design-1/O; Cost Des-1/Y; Ltg Des-1/O; Cost Constr-1/O; Cost Hist-1/Y; Make-up-2/Y; Stage Mgmt-1/O; Sound Design-1/Y; History of Decor-1/O

D. Box Office Procedure-1/O; Marketing/Promotion-2/X; Arts Management is a Minor Program in the University.

FACILITIES AND PRODUCTIONS

MAINSTAGE: 280 seats, fly space, computerized lighting
6 prods: 6 Fac dir; budget $3,000-6,000

SECOND STAGE: 85 seats, computerized lighting
5 Undergrad dir prods; budget $500

THIRD STAGE: 50 seats, electronic lighting
6 workshops/readings; budget $50

There is a non-departmental, student-run producing organization in which majors generally participate.

Facility was built in 1964, renovated in 1985-87; includes scene shop, costume shop, props shop, welding shop, sound studio, 2 dance studios, 2 rehearsal studios, 1 design studio, lighting lab, classrooms.

DESCRIPTION

Noted Faculty: Acting/Directing: Nancy B. Loitz, Roger Bechtel, Sandra Lindberg. Design Faculty: Marcia McDonald, Curtis Trout. Dance Faculty: Jean Kerr, Sheri Bates, Daphne McCoy, Music Theatre:Thomas Ossowski, Jeff Miller, Theatre History; Sara Freeman.

Guest Artists: John Randolph, Stacy Keach, Sr., Jack McLaughlin-Gray, Jonathan Farwell, Sheldon Harnick, James Sutorius, Ann Whitney, Tim Hardy, Plasticene.

Illinois Wesleyan's School of Theatre Arts is dedicated to undergraduate training. While the School offers pre-professional training in theatre and music theatre, it does so within the confines of a strong liberal arts university. All majors are expected to develop a broad solid base in both theatre and the liberal arts. The School of Theatre Arts is relatively small (the total of Theatre and Music majors is under 120), in order to emphasize the development of the individual student and facilitate a close relationship between students and faculty. The program includes major design opportunities on both the Mainstage and Lab Theatre seasons, as well as opportunity to act and direct. All students are encouraged to complete an internship during their four years, and most participate in May travel seminars to national and international theatre centers.

Loyola University of Chicago

Mark E. Lococo, Chair
Dept.of Theatre
Sky Building Rm. 810
6525 N. Sheridan Road
Chicago, IL 60626
(773) 508-3830
ADMISSIONS: 820 N. Michigan Ave., Chicago, IL 60611
800 262-2373
www.luc.edu

9,725 Total Enr.; compet.
Semester System, NAST(A)
120 Majors
T: $27,169 r&b:$9,930
FAX: (773) 508-8748
sgabeli@luc.edu
admission@luc.edu

DEGREES OFFERED

BA in Theatre (65)

ADMISSION & FINANCIAL INFORMATION

ACT, SAT, GPA required. Schols. are given on the basis on an audition held in Feb.

FACULTY AND CLASSES OFFERED

6 Full-Time, 8 Part-Time: 3 PhD, 3 MFA/MA; 4 Staff

A. (3 FT, 3 PT) Intro to Theatre-1/O; Theatre Hist-2/O; Shakes-X; Playwriting-1/Y; World Drama-2/Y; Modern Theatre-1/Y

B. (3 FT, 2 PT) Acting-2/Y; Voice/Speech-2/Y; Mvment-1/O; Singing-1/Y; Directing-2/Y; Dance-1/O; Stage Combat-1/O; Audition-1/Y

C. (1 FT) Prins of Des-1/Y; Set Design-1/Y; Cost Des-1/Y; Ltg Des-1/O; Stage Mgmt-1/O; Theatre Crafts-1/Y; Make-Up-1/O

FACILITIES AND PRODUCTIONS

MAINSTAGE: 299 seats, fly space, computerized lighting
    4 prods: 4 Fac dir, 12 Guest des; budget $6,000-7,500

SECOND STAGE: 45 seats. 6 prods, 4 UG dir;
    budget $400. 2 Fac dir, 2 UG dir Workshops/Readings

Facility was built in 1969; includes scene shop, costume shop, props shop, welding shop.

1 student-written play produced in the last two years.

Connection with The Playwright's Center which does new play readings at Loyola and in Chicago theatres during the school year and produces one professional show at Loyola during the summer months; non-equity, run by Loyola Theatre faculty and staff, located on campus. Students receive internship credit.

DESCRIPTION

Noted Faculty:Dr. Jack Thahey, translater; Ms. Jacqueline Fiekins, costume design; Sarah Gabel, director; Dr. Nan Withers-Wilson, Voice & Dialects; Mr. Jonathan Wilson, Directing, SSDC.

Guest Artists: Katherine Ross, Designer; Jack McGain, Designer; Ann Shanahan, Director; Alex Meadows, Designer; Chris Kris, Sound; Linda Parsons, Choreographer; Bill Underwood, Musical Director.

Loyola University chicago Theatre Department's proximity to the city of Chicago and its many theatres offers extensive opportunities for students. One of Chicago's preiere theatre critics says this, "The Chicago cliche` is different, more active, more joyous. The cliche` is all about fearlessness and flying glass and John Malkovich. The well-worn image of 'Chicago-style acting' evokes a city crammed with actors ready, willing and able to throw whole flaming chunks of 'Chicago-style' performance in an audience's face and make 'em like it." We strive to expose our students to experiences in the Chicago theatre community by bringing in professional designers, musicians, vocal directors and teachers with theatre experience. We also encourage Internships by offering credit for work done in professional theatre. Our motto is "We Illuminate the Human Spirit" and our goal is to prepare students for a future in theatre by imbuing the love of theatre into their spirits.

Millikin University

Laura Ledford, Chair
Depart. of Theatre & Dance
Millikin University
1184 West Main Street
Decatur, IL 62522
DEPT: (217) 424-6282
lledford@mail.millikin.edu
ADMISSIONS: 1184 W. Main St., Decatur, IL 62522
(217) 424-6210
www.millikin.edu

2,300 Total Enr.; competitive
Semester System
200 Majors
T: $23,250/$7,200 R&B
(217) 424-6282
FAX: (217) 424-3993

FAX: (217) 425-4669
admis@mail.millikin.edu

DEGREES OFFERED

BFA in Musical Theatre (88), Theatre-Acting (54), Directing (12), Tech/Design (21); BA in Theatre (37); Dance Minor (35), Theatre Minor. Declare major in freshman year.

ADMISSION & FINANCIAL INFORMATION

Inst. reqs. ACT 20 and top 50% of class; admit 84% of applicants. Theatre program reqs Aud. for actors; Program accepts 80 out of 300 applicants. Performance talent awards awarded through auditions; Tech/design, directing, talent awards awarded through interview process.

FACULTY AND CLASSES OFFERED

12 Full-Time, 5 Part-Time: 2 PhD, 13 MFA/MA; 1 Prof. w/o adv. degree; 4 Staff

A. (1 FT) Intro to Theatre-2/Y; Dramatic Lit-4/Y; Theatre Hist-2/Y; Dramatic Criticism-1/O; Shakes-1/Y; Theatre Seminar-4/O

B. (7 FT, 4 PT) Acting-7/Y; Voice/Spch-4/Y; Mvmt-3/Y; Mime, etc.-1/O; Singing-4/Y; Mus. Th-6/Y; Dance-7/Y; Directing-2/Y; Stage Combat-2/O; Music Theory-2/Y

C. (4 FT, 1 PT) Prins. of Des.-1/Y; Set Des.-1/O; Cost. Des.-1/O; Ltg. Des.-1/O; Cost. Hist.-1/O; Tech Prod.-1/O; Make-up-2/Y; Stage Mgmt-1/O; Stagecraft-1/Y

FACILITIES & PRODUCTIONS

MAINSTAGE: 299 seats, computerized lighting. 8 Fac dir, 13 Fac des, 3 Guest des, 7 UG des; budget $3,000-3,500

SECOND STAGE: 1,831 seats, fly space, computerized lighting 2 Fac dir, 5 Fac des, 1 Guest des; budget $6,000-7,000.

THIRD STAGE: 90 seats, black box, electronic lighting

STUDIO: 2 Fac dir prods.

Facility was built in 1901, renovated in 2006; includes scene shop, cost. shop, prop shop, welding shop, video studio, 3 dance studios, design studio, 2 classrooms.

4 student written plays have been produced in the last 2 years.

Connection with Little Theatre on the Square, an Equity theatre.

DESCRIPTION

Noted Faculty: Barry Pearson, Acting; Denise Myers, Acting & Move-ment; Laura Ledford, Voice/Acting; David Golden, Directing; Sean Morrissey, Dance/Musical Theatre; Kevin Long, Musical Theatre; Barbara Manrum, Design; Jennifer Pickard-Criswell, Theory/ Criticism; Lori Bales, Acting/Workout; Brad Criswell, Design.

Guest Artists: Kendra Bell, Costume Designer.

Our mission as teacher-artists and student-artists is to stimulate and develop, in concert with our audiences, an imaginative and honest engagement with performance as both method and subject of inquiry. As life-long learners and active participants in our communities, we explore important ideas, peoples and perspectives of the world at large, as well as the spirit and intellect of the individual, through the practice of our craft in the classroom and on the stage as disciplined theatre professionals and committed artists.

Northern Illinois University

See Ad in Back of book

Alexander Gelman, Director
School of Theatre & Dance
Northern Illinois University
PO Box 3001
DeKalb, IL 60115
(815) 753-1334
ADMISSIONS: Office of Admissions, Northern Illinois University, DeKalb, IL 60115

25,000 T. Enr.; non-compet.
Semester System; NAST
150 Majors; U/RTA, ATHE
T:$8,259 in-state, $14,409 o:st
R/b:$8,094
FAX: (815) 753-8415
admission-info@niu.edu

DEGREES OFFERED

BA in Theatre (50); BFA in Acting (50), Design/ Tech (15), Dance (40); MFA in Acting (15), Design/Tech (12). Declare major in first year; 2003 granted 31 UG, 3 Grad degrees.

ADMISSION & FINANCIAL INFORMATION

Min. ACT 18 for UG, GPA 2.8 for Grad students. Audition/portfolio and interview required for admission to Theatre Program; Program accepts 30 out of 100 UG applicants, 12 out of 100 Grad applicants. Sydney Smith Talented Scholarship Audition for Outstanding Incoming UG. Rene LeBeau Award for Outstanding Dance Performance majors. Talented Student Schol. for Acting & Design/Tech majors. Minority Student Schols.

FACULTY AND CLASSES OFFERED

17.5 Full-Time, 9 Part-Time (does not include 4 Dance): 2 PhD, 1DFA, 14 MFA/MA; 5-6 Staff MA, MFA, BFA

A. (2 FT,2PT) Intro to Theatre-1/Y; Dramatic Lit-2-3/Y; Theatre History-6/Y; Dramatic Criticism-1/O; Shakes-2/Y; Playwriting-1/Y

B. (6 1/2 FT,2 PT) Acting-13/Y; Voice/Speech-10/Y; Movement-8/Y+1/X; Singing-1/Y+6/X; Directing-8/Y; Stage Combat-1/Y; Dance-20+Y/X; Practicum-4/Y

C. (6 FT, 5 PT) Prins of Des-1/Y; Set Design-6/Y; Cost. Design- 1/Y; Ltg Des-6/Y; Technical Prod-1/Y; Cost. Construction-6/Y; Make-up-1/Y; Stage Mgmt-1/Y; Period Styles-1/Y; Computer Design-1/Y; Practicum-4/Y

D. (1/2 FT,1 PT) Arts Management-2/Y; Box Office Procedure-1/Y; Marketing/Promotion-1/Y; Legal: Contracts/Copyright-1/Y

FACILITIES & PRODUCTIONS

MAINSTAGE: 450 seats, fly space, computerized & electronic lighting. 7 prods: 16 Fac dir, 1 Guest dir, 10 Fac des, 2 Guest des, 8 Grad des; budget $6,000-25,000

SECOND STAGE: 140 seats, computerized & electronic lighting 5 prods: 2-3 Fac dir/des, 2 Grad dir, 4 Grad des, 2 UG dir, 7 UG des.; budget $200-500

THIRD STAGE: 100 seats, fixed stage; 5 workshops/readings: UG dir; budget $100

Facility was built in 1958, renovated in 1985; includes scene shop, costume shop, prop shop, sound studio, 4 dance studios, 2 rehearsal studios, design studio, 5 classrooms, lighting lab, 250 seat prosc. with no fly system. 2,000 seat road house downtown which we use once or twice a year "The Egyptian Theatre".

Connection with SummerNITE, a summer, professional (equity) producing group of Theatre at NIU. SummerNITE is university supported. Also supported by corporate gifts. Presents new plays and/or Chicago premieres. Casting restricted to AEA members & NIU Theatre students. EMC program; interns may perform understudy, work in marketing, ASM, or obtain union card through PSMing. Shows do limited tour during AY. Plans to expand production in AY.

DESCRIPTION

Noted Faculty: Alexander Gelman, Directing; Kathryn Gately, Acting; Rick Poole, Acting; Terry McClellan, Scenic Design; Christopher Markle, Directing/Acting; Deborah Robertson, Movement; Paula Frasz, Dance; Randy Newsom, Dance; Melanie Baumgartner, Costume Design.

Guest Artists: Joan Allen (Alumna), Actor; Billie Whitelaw, Actress; Curt Columbus, Directing; Luis Montero, Dance; Edward James Olmos, Actor; John Bettenbender, Jr., Director, Colin Stinton, (Alumnus), Actor, John Conklin, Designer; Tamas Fodor, (Hungary) Directing; George Bigot (France) Acting; Jean Randick, Directing

Exchange Programs:
Gaiety School of Acting in Dublin, Ireland and the
   Moscow Art Theatre School in Russia.

The School of Theatre & Dance at Northern Illinois
University provides intensive artistic and academic training for students preparing for careers in theatre and theatre
related areas. The course of study is rigorous and realis-
tic, designed to develop, challenge and broaden the skills
and attitudes of the department's highly motivated students.

Northwestern University

Rives Collins, Chairperson	12,126 Total Enr.: h. compet.
Theatre Department	Quarter System
1949 South Campus Dr.	380 Majors; U/RTA
Evanston, IL 60208	T: $35,229 r&b:$10,776
(847) 491-3170	FAX: (847) 467-2019
www.communication.northwestern.edu/theatre	
ADMISSIONS: 1801 Hinman Ave.	(847) 491-7271
lug-admission@northwestern.edu	www.northwestern.edu

DEGREES OFFERED

BS in Theatre,MA in Theatre, MFA Set Design, MFA Directing, Phd
Theatre & Drama. Declare major in 1st year; 2002 granted 91 UG
and 12 Grad degrees.

ADMISSION & FINANCIAL INFORMATION

Undergraduates can call (847) 491-7271; Graduates call (847) 491-
3170 for information. Theatre program generally admits 100 out of
700 to UG program, 26 out of 150 to Grad programs.

FACULTY AND CLASSES OFFERED

33 FT: 8 PhD, 21 MFA/MA, 4 Prof. w/out adv. degree; 2 Staff

A. (7 FT) Intro to Theatre-3/Y; Theatre History-6/Y; Shakes-2/Y;
   Dramatic Lit-6; Dramatic Criticism-6/Y; Playwriting-3/Y; Children's
   Th-1/Y; Storytelling-3/Y

B. (16 FT) Acting-11/Y; Movement-2/Y; Directing-5/Y; Voice/Speech-
   5/Y; Mime, Mask, etc.-2/Y; Musical Theatre-2/Y

C. (7 FT) Principles of Design-1/Y; Set Design-6/Y; Cost Design- 6/Y;
   Costume History-1/Y; Stage Mgmt-2/Y; Lighting Design-6/Y; Cost
   Construction- 1/Y; Make-up-1/Y; Stage Mgmt-2/Y

D. (3 FT) No courses listed.

FACILITIES AND PRODUCTIONS

MAINSTAGE A: 439 seats, thrust stage, computerized lighting
MAINSTAGE B: 369 seats, proscenium stage, electron. ltg.
BLACK BOX A: 120 seats, flexible stage, electron. ltg.
BLACK BOX B: 120 seats, electron. ltg.
PRODUCTIONS 12-13 mainstage, 6 Fac dir, 2-4 Fac des, 1 Guest dir, 2-
   4 Guest dir, 2-4 Guest des, 1 Grad dir, 18-26 Grad des, 2-10 UG
   des; budget $12,000-24,000. 32 black box; budget $100-500;
   workshops/readings budget $100-500

Facility was built in 1980; includes scene shop, costume shop, prop
   shop, welding area, 2 rehearsal studios, 2 dance studios, 1
   design studio.

Student-run organizations present 50-80 productions per year in which
   majors participate. Approx. 3 student-written plays produced per
   year - Agnes Nixon Play Festival.

DESCRIPTION

Noted Faculty: Bud Beyer, Acting; David Downs, Acting;
   Joe Appelt, Lighting; Billy Sigenfeld, Dance; Tracy
   Davis, History, Lit, Crit; Rives Collins, Child
   Drama/Theatre; Joseph Tilford, Set and Lighting
   Design; Diminic Missimi, Music Theatre; Anna
   Shapiro, Directing.
Guest Artists: Tina Landau, Director; Wendy MacLeod,
   Playwright; Pilobolus Dance Company; Shozo Sato,
   kabuki artist; Larry Yando, Actor; Tony Kushner,
   Playwright; Jeff Parry, Actor; John Cameron Mitchell,
   writer/director/actor; David Schwimmer, actor;
   Stephen Flaherty, composer.

Students who major in theatre combine a liberal arts education with intensive training in the theories and arts of
the theatre. At the heart of the program lies the idea that
the best theatre artist is the one who combines a broad
knowledge of the literature and theory of the field with
highly developed skills in its practice. The MA Theatre provides the developing scholar or theatre specialist an
opportunity to strengthen skills and knowledge beyond
the undergraduate level. The MFA Stage Design trains talented designers of scenery, costume, and lighting who
want to impact and influence the development of the
American theater and prepare to compete for positions in
theater and related performing arts professions. The MFA
Directing trains stage directors who possess strong practical knowledge of theatre practice and who demonstrate an
understanding of a range of styles and periods of dramatic literature. The PhD Theatre and Drama Program trains
outstanding students for lifetime careers in academia,
emphasizing simultaneous development of intellectual
excellence in scholarship with pedagogical skills.

Rockford College

Noel Rennerfeldt, Chairman	enrollment: 840 FT/632 PT
Dept. of Performming Arts	non-competitive
Rockford College	Semester System
5050 E. State Street	19 Majors
Rockford, IL 61108	T: $17,450
DEPT: (815) 226-4189	R&B $5630
FAX: (815) 394-5167	
ADM: same address (815) 226-4050 FAX: (815) 226-2822	
www.rockford.edu	

DEGREES OFFERED

BA in Acting/Directing (7), Technical Theatre/Design (5), Music (4);
BFA in Musical Theatre Performance (14). Declare major in sophomore yr; 2001 granted 5 UG degrees.

ADMISSION & FINANCIAL INFORMATION

UG ACT min 18, GPA min 2.5, top 50% of graduating class. Accept 8
of 10 applicants. Audition/interview required, portfolio for designers.

FACULTY AND CLASSES OFFERED

4 Full-Time, 9 Part-TIme: 1 PhD/DFA, 10 MA/MFA, 2 w/o advanced
   degree, 1 staff

A. (1 1/2 FT) Intro to Th-4/Y; Th Hist-3/Y; Shakes-5/X; Playwriting-1/Y;
   Dramatic Lit-2/Y

B. (1 1/2 FT, 8 PT) Acting-5/Y; Voice/Speech-2/Y; Movement-2/Y;
   Singing-3/Y; Musical Theatre-6/Y; Directing-2/Y; Dance-20/Y

C. (1 FT, 1 PT) Set Design-3/O; Cost Des-3/O; Ltg Des-3/O; Tech.

Prod'n-2/Y; Cost Constr-2/Y; Cost History-1/O; Make-up-1/Y; Stage Mgmt-1/Y

FACILITIES AND PRODUCTIONS

MAINSTAGE: 572 seats, fly space, computerized ltg, electronic ltg. 2 prods; 2 Fac dir, 6 Fac des; budget $3,000-5,000 per prod

SECOND STAGE: 150 seats, computerized lighting, black box
2 prods: 2 guest dir, 6 guest des; budget $3,000-5,000
4 UG dir; 12 UG designer workshops/rdgs; bgt $200-300.

Facility was built in 1969; includes scene, costume shops, 1 movement/dance studio

DESCRIPTION

Guest Artists: Second City, E. Faye Butler.

The Performing Arts department offers all Rockford College students a unique opportunity to explore dance, music and theatre as separate, but interrelated, art forms in an innovative, experimental environment where they can express themselves creatively, study the performing arts in their historical/cultural context and participate in departmental programs and productions.

Our faculty members believe in a hands-on approach of positive instruction and guidance to nurture creative and intellectual abilities. Classes are small for maximum student-teacher interaction. Some courses involve team teaching to provide a full understanding of the interrelationships of dance, music and theatre.

Juniors and seniors are urged to spend a semester in the Rockford College program at Regent's College in London, where they will have the opportunity to pursue the many cultural advantages of London and to study with an impressive variety of skilled British artists and teachers in specially designed programs.

Roosevelt University College of Performing Arts

Joel G. Fink, Dir.
The Theatre Conservatory
Chicago College of Performing Arts
Roosevelt University
430 South Michigan Ave
Chicago, IL 60605-1394
DEPT: (312) 341-3719
www.ccpa.roosevelt.edu
ADMISSIONS: Above address.
(312) 341-2162

7,500 Total Enr.; competitive
Semester System
200/32 Summer MA Majors;
ATHE
T: UG $23,750/$8-10,000 R&B
G waiver/$8-10,000 R&B
FAX: (312) 341-3814

theatre@roosevelt.edu

DEGREES OFFERED

BFA in Acting (80), Musical Theatre (85); MFA in Acting (10), MA Fast Track-Summer Program (32). Students declare major in 1st year; 2005 granted 30 UG, 20 G degs.

ADMISSION & FINANCIAL INFORMATION

2.3 GPA, ACT min. 20, SAT 960, Grad 2.7 GPA; 75% of applicants accepted to institution; Aud./Int., required for admission to Theatre Program, for both UG and Grad; Program admits 2 of 10 UG applicants, 2 of 10 Grad applicants. Theatre Award Schols are offered to many prospective students, based on aud., letters of recommendation, etc.

FACULTY AND CLASSES OFFERED

10 FT 13 PT: 3 PhD, 16 MFA/MA, 3 Prof. w/o adv. degree; 3 Staff

A. (1 FT, 3 PT) Intro to Theatre-1/Y; Dramatic Lit.-2/Y; Dramatic Theatre History-4/Y; Shakes-3/Y; Playwriting-1/Y

B. (5 FT, 5 PT) Acting-12/Y; Voice/Speech-8/Y; Movement-4/Y; Singing-8/X; Musical Th-6/Y; Directing-5/Y; Stage Combat-1/Y; Dance-12/X; Mime, mask,etc.-2/Y

C. (2 FT, 4 PT) Set Design-1/O; Cost Des-1/O; Ltg Des-1/O; Tech Production-1/Y; Make-up-2/Y; Stage Mgmt-1/Y

D. (1 FT, 1 PT) Arts Mgmt-1/O; Mktg/Promo-1/X; Devel/Grant Writing-1/X; Contracts/Copyright-1/X; Budgeting/Accounting-1/X

*Courses also taken in Depts. of English and Music.

FACILITIES & PRODUCTIONS

MAINSTAGE: 250 seats, computerized & electronic lighting; 7 prods: 5 Fac dir, 10 Fac des, 1 Guest dir, 4 Guest des; budget $1,900-5,700

SECOND STAGE: 80 seats, electron ltg. 1 Guest dir, 4 Guest des; budget $600-1,800
Workshops/Readings; budget $50

Facility was built in 1890, last renovated in 2002; includes scene shop, costume shop, rehearsal studio, classrooms, concert hall, props/furniture storage.

Internships arranged at various Chicago area theatres. Internships in acting, directing, stage management, dramaturgy and arts administration arranged at theatres such as Steppenwolf, The Goodman Theatre, Chicago Shakespeare Theatre and Lookingglass Theatre Ensemble.

DESCRIPTION

Noted Faculty: Joel G. Fink, Acting/Directing; June Compton, Dramaturgy/Asian Theatre; Luis Perez, Musical Theatre; Kestutis Nakas, Acting/Performance Art; Sean Ryan Kelley, Acting; Keland Scher, Physical Theatre/Performance Art; Christine Adaire, Voice/Speech.

Guest Artists: Dan Stetzel, Cabaret/Musical Theatre; Steve Scott, Acting; Ted Hoerl, Acting; Chuck Coyl, Stage Combat; Joe Drummond, Stage Management; Belinda Bremner, Playwriting; Catherine Head, Acting on Camera; Jane Alderman, Auditioning; Jerry Proffit, Fast Track; Lou Conte Dance Studio.

The Theatre Conservatory at Roosevelt University is located in the university's downtown Chicago campus and is the home of the acclaimed Auditorium Theatre. The Theatre Conservatory encompasses the disciplines of Theatre and Musical Theatre, and is distinctively positioned to educate and train its students in one of the country's greatest theatre cities, within walking distance from world-class arts institutions such as the Goodman Theatre, The Chicago Symphony Orchestra, The Art Institute of Chicago, Shubert Theatre, Ford: Oriental Theatre, Lyric Opera House and Chicago Theatre. Whether seeking a career in the professional theatre or a more general education, the faculty of working professionals and guest artists offers a program with a solid balance between academic courses and studio/performance work. Degrees include intensive professional B.F.A. and M.F.A. programs in Performance, as well as more general B.A. and M.A. programs. In addition, there is a summer M.A. "Fast Track" Directing program for high school teachers.

Southern Illinois University – Carbondale

Mark Varns, Chair
Department of Theater, MC 6608
1033 Communications Bldg
Southern Illinois University
Carbondale, IL 62901-6608
DEPT.: (618) 453-5741
FAX: (618) 453-7582
ADM: New Student Adms Svc., SIUC, Carbondale 62901-4710
(618) 536-4405
www.siu.edu/cwis

22,500 Total Enr.; compet.
Semester System

85 Majors; NAST
T: $4,113/$5,633 R&B
O-ST T: $7,123/$5,633 R&B
http://www.siu.edu/~mccleod/

FAX: (618) 536-4405

DEGREES OFFERED

BA in Theatre (85); MFA in Directing (2) Design/Production: Scene Design (3), Costume Design (5), Lighting Design (4); Technical Direction (2); MFA in Playwriting (4). PhD in Playwriting (2); Spch/Comm/Theatre (3). Declare major in 1st or 2nd yr; 2001 granted 12 UG and 8 G degs.

ADMISSION & FINANCIAL INFORMATION

UG top 50% class rank + comparable ACT/SAT test scores, 2.0 GPA; Grad 2.7 GPA or above. Th. prog. admission: UG accept 20 of 30; Grad portfolio, admit 5 of 30. Schols: Tuition help scholarships by applic and audition up to $1,000/semester.

FACULTY AND CLASSES OFFERED

10 Full-Time, 1 Part-TIme: 3 PhD, 8 MA/MFA; 3 Staff

A. (2 FT, 1 PT) Intro to Th-1/Y; Th Hist-2/Y; Shakes-1/O; Playwriting-3/Y; Dramatic Lit-1/Y; Dramatic Criticism-1/O

B. (3 FT) Acting-4/Y; Voice/Speech-2/Y; Movement-2/Y; Musical Theatre-2/X

C. (4 FT) Prins of Des-1/Y; Set Design-2/Y; Cost Des-2/Y; Ltg Des-2/Y; Tech. Prod'n-2/Y; Cost Constr-1/Y; Cost History-1/Y; Make-up-1/Y; Stage Mgmt-1/Y

D. Arts Management-1/O

FACILITIES AND PRODUCTIONS

MAINSTAGE: 488 seats, fly space, computerized lighting
4 prods; 3 Fac dir, 4 Fac des, 1 Guest dir/des, 7 Grad des; budget $3,500-6,000

SECOND STAGE: 100 seats, computerized lighting
10 prods: 5 Fac dir, 2 Fac des, 3 Grad dir, 8 Grad des, 2 UG dir, 6 UG des; budget $500-1,500

12 Grad dir Workshops/Readings; budget $0.

Facility was built in 1975, renovated in 2001; includes scene, costume, props shops, sound studio, rehearsal studio, design studio, lighting lab, computer graphics lab.

A non-departmental, student-run organization presents 2 prods. per year in which majors participate. 15 student-written plays produced in the last two years.

Connection with Shryock Celebrity Series and McLeod Summer Playhouse. Shryock books a number of prof. opera, dance and theatre companies each season. Students work as ushers, box office personnel, and technical crews. McLeod Summer Playhouse hires professional Directors, Designers, Actors, and also student actors and crew members.

DESCRIPTION

Noted Faculty: David Rush, Playwriting; Ronald

Naversen, Set Design; Mark Varns, Lighting Design; Kathryn Wagner, Costume Design; Anne Fletcher, History/Criticism; Susan Patrick Benson, Acting/Voice; J. Thomas Kidd, Acting; Lori Merill-Fink, Acting/Movement; Segun Ojewuy, Acting, Directing; Robert Holcombe, Tech Direction/Stage Mgmt.

Guest Artists: James Moody, Lighting Designer; Jack Parkhurt, Director; Rod Loomis, Actor, ShirleyJo Finney, Director.

The Department of Theater at Southern Illinois University at Carbondale blends scholarship and practice into an academically based theater experience preparing the student for a career in professional, educational and community based theater. The extensive production schedule in two theaters, proscenium and black box, is the laboratory extension for the academic coursework. The undergraduate BA program is designed to provide broad-based exposure to human experience and a solid foundation in basic skills of theater craft. The MFA specializations in Directing, Playwriting, Design and Production including Lighting, Costume and Scenic Design and Technical Direction provide intensive training in these areas of concentration. The PhD is an interdisciplinary degree sponsored through the Dept. of Speech Communications.

Southern Illinois University – Edwardsville

C. Otis Sweezey, Chair
Department of Theater
Campus Box 1777, UIE
Edwardsville, IL 62026-1777
DEPT: (618) 650-3111
www.siue.edu/THEATER
osweeze@siue.edu
ADM: SIUE, Box 1047, Edwardsville, IL 62026
(618) 650-2080
www.siue.edu

10,960 Total Enr.; not compet.
Semester System
68 Majors
T: $6,561/$6,780 R&B
O-ST T: $$14,402
FAX: (618) 650-3716

1-800-328-5168 x 2080
admissions@siue.edu

DEGREES OFFERED

BA, BS in Performance (24), Design/Tech (22), Dance(15), General Theater(8), Theater Education (7). Declare major in freshman yr.; 2004 granted 19 UG degs.

ADMISSION & FINANCIAL INFORMATION

The sum of the national percentile of your composite score on either SAT or ACT, and the percentile of your high school rank must equal 100 or greater. Admit 70% to institution; no spec. req's for theatre program. Departmental schols offered. Merit schol. ($500-1,000) are offered by a philanthropic support organization, Friends of Theatre and Dance. Aud. for actors, portfolio for des. for scholarship only.

FACULTY AND CLASSES OFFERED

13 Full Time: 1 Part Time, 4 PhD, 10 MA/MFA.

A. (3 ft 1 pt) Intro to Th-2/Y; Theatre Hist-1/Y; Dramatic Lit.-1/Y; Dramatic Crit.-1/Y; Playwriting-1/X

B. (6 FT) Acting-6/Y; Mvmt-1/Y; Voice/Speech-3/X; Directing-2/Y; Dance-16/Y; Musical Th.-1/X; Mime, mask, etc.-2/O

C. (3 FT) Prins. of Design-2/Y; Set Des.-1/Y; Cost. Des.-2/Y; Ltg. Des.-1/Y; Tech. Prod'n.-2/Y; Make-up-1/Y; Stage Mgmt.-1/Y

D. (1 FT) Arts Mgmt-1/Y; Box Office Procedure-1/Y; Marketing/Promotion-1/Y

FACILITIES & PRODUCTIONS

MAINSTAGE: 397 seats, fly space, comput. ltg.
  6 Prods: Fac. dir/des; budget $2-3,000

SECOND STAGE: 100-150 seats, black box, comput. ltg.
  4 Prods: 1 Fac dir, 4 UG dir/des; budget $2,000
  2 Workshops/Readings

Facility was built in 1966, renovated 1992; includes scene shop, prop shop, cost. shop, CAD facil, 2 rehearsal studios, 1 design studio.

A non-departmental, student run producing org. presents 3 productions per year in which majors generally participate. 2 student-written plays produced in the last 2 years.

Connection with St. Louis area theatres-offer internships for our students.

DESCRIPTION

Noted Faculty: Peter Bukalski, Film History & Crit; Peter Cocuzza, William Grivna, Acting & Directing; Calvin Jarrell, Dance/LaBan specialist; C. Otis Sweezey, Scene Design; James Dorethy, Design; Lana Hagan, Theatre Education; Kerry Shaul, Dance. Dr. Johanna Schmitz, Contemporary Shakespeare Performance Theory and Criticism.

Guest Artists: Dr. Lara Hanson, ,Costume Design; Chuck Harper, Acting & Directing; Michael Thomas, Dance; Beatrix Tennessen, Costume Design & Construction; Valerie Goldston, Lighting; Roger Speidel, Technical Director.

The SIUE campus spreads out over 2600 acres in Illinois, but it's only 20 minutes from downtown St. Louis, Missouri, where theatre abounds. The undergraduate program encourages students to be well-rounded theatre artists in a liberal arts setting. Affiliations with St. Louis area theatres provide an array of internships for students in both performance and technical aspects of production. The theatre education program is a new offering and will prepare students for certification in the area of theatre arts (7-12). The extensive production schedule in two theatres, proscenium and black box, is the laboratory extension for the academic classwork.

The Theatre School, DePaul University

John Culbert, Dean
The Theatre School
DePaul University
2135 N. Kenmore Avenue
Chicago, IL 60614
DEPT: (773) 325-7917
http://theatreschool.depaul.edu
Admissions: The Theatre School Admissions, 2135 N Kenmore Ave, Chicago, IL 60614-4111
(773) 325-7999
theatreadmissions@depaul.edu

23,227 Total Enr.; h. compet.
Quarter System
350 Majors
T: $23,585/9,899 r&b
O-st T: same
fax: (773) 325-7920

800-4-DEPAULx57999

DEGREES OFFERED

BFA in Cost Tech (4); BFA/MFA in Acting (120/21), BFA in Th Studies (45), Th Tech (15), Th Mgmt (11), Dramaturgy-Criticism (10), Playwriting

(14); Scene Des (14),Lighting Des (13), Costume Des (13) Costume tech (4), Stage Mgt (14), BA in Theatre Arts (55), MFA Directing (6). Declare major in freshman yr.; 2004 granted 58 UG, 10 Grad degrees.

ADMISSION & FINANCIAL INFORMATION

Min. UG req. (2.5 GPA, 1000 SAT, 20 ACT)UG: Audition for all actors/directors, Interview/portfolio review for all non-actors Grad: audition for all actors/directors. Interview for directors as well.; 3 letters of rec, photo, resume for UG & grad (all majors). Program admits 1 of 5 UG, 1 of 10 Grad apps. Limited number of scholarships available for incoming students. All applicants automatically considered.

FACULTY AND CLASSES OFFERED

21 Full-Time, 20 Part-Time: 6 PhD/DFA, 40 MFA/MA, 25 Prof. w/o adv. degree; 25 Staff

A. (5 FT, 8 PT) Intro. to Th.-38/Y; Dram. Lit.-12/Y; Th. Hist.-12/Y Dramatic Crit.-6/Y; Shakes-9/Y Playwriting-12/Y; Dramaturgy-6/Y;

B. (15 FT, 16 PT) Acting-39/Y; Voice/Speech-36/Y; Mvmt- 42/Y; Musical Th.-6/Y; Directing-18/Y; Stg Combat-6/Y

C. (7 FT,20 PT) Prins. of Des.-12/Y; Set Des.-9/Y; Cost. Des.-9/Y; Ltg. Des.-9/Y; Tech. Prod'-9/Y; Cost. Tech-12/Y; Make-up-9/Y; Stage Mgmt.-9/Y

D. Arts Mgmt-6/Y

FACILITIES & PRODUCTIONS

MAINSTAGE (SHOWCASE): 1340 seats, fly space, computerized & electronic lighting (240 dimmers), trapped stage, orchestra pit.7 prods: 6 Fac dir, 1 Fac des, 2 Guest dir/des;5 UG des. Budget: $5,000-6,500

SECOND STAGE (PLAYWORKS):70 SEATS, COMP & ELECTR LIGHTING, 6 prods:1 Fac dir, 5 Grad dir, 6 UG des

WORKSHOPS/READINGS: 14 prods: 3 Fac dir, 3 Guest dir, 8 Grad dir, 14 UG des

Facility built in 1910, renovated in 1988; includes scene, costume, prop, welding shops, sound, 3 dance, 3 rehearsal studios, 2 design studio, CAD fac., 4 video studios, 14 classrooms.

A non-departmental,student run producing organization presents 10-20 prods presented in a school year in which majors participate.

Connection with Goodman Theatre & Shakespeare on the Green (both Equity). One Grad directing major is placed in assistantship at Goodman Theatre each year. Shakespeare on the Green is the institution's professional summer outdoor theatre. Produced and directed by faculty/staff, one production is produced each summer usually involving a combination of working theatre professionals and students.

DESCRIPTION

Noted Faculty: Claudia Anderson, Voice/Speech; Linda Buchanan, Scene Design; Dexter Bullard, Acting; Nan Cibula-Jenkins, Costume Design; Dean Corrin, Playwriting; Henry Godinez, Acting; Chris Jones, Theatre Studies; Ric Murphy, Acting; Lisa Portes, Directing; Rachel Shteir, Dramaturgy.

Guest Artists: Ntozake Shange, Dramaturgy Professor; Carlos Murillo, Playwriting Prof/Guest Director; Anne Bogart; Paul Sills; Roche Schulfer, Guest Professor.

Intense. Demanding. Professional. Real. These are just a few of the words that describe The Theatre School, DePaul

University, one of America's oldest and most respected theatre training schools. Founded as the Goodman School of Drama in 1925, The Theatre School is the Midwest's oldest theatre conservatory and is recognized nationally as one of the top conservatory programs in the US. Located in the heart of Chicago's dynamic professional theatre community, our training programs emphasize learning-by-doing in a format that is intensive, highly disciplined and focused on individual development. We produce more than 200 public performances each season, featuring students in every aspect of production. Our goal is to prepare students for careers in professional theatre. And our approach works: our alumni populate the theatres of Chicago and their work can be seen on film, television, and in theatres all over the world.

University of Illinois at Chicago

Michael J. Anderson, Chair	28,000 T. Enr.; competitive
Dept. of Performing Arts, M/C 255	Semester System
U. of Ill. at Chicago	110 Majors (65 Th. Majors)
1040 W. Harrison St.	FAX: (312) 996-0954
Chicago, IL 60607-7130	www.uic.edu/depts/adpa
(312) 996-2977	T: $9,902/ $22,292 OS R&B 9,100

Admissions: 1100 SSB, MC 018, 1200 W Harrison St., Chicago, IL 60602-7161
(312) 996-4350
www.uic.edu
uicadmit@uic.edu

DEGREES OFFERED

BA in Performance (57), Directing & Design (6). BFA approved, contact department for further info.

ADMISSION & FINANCIAL INFORMATION

ACT 21 and good HS rank. 80% admitted to institution. Talent tuition waivers available. 4 out of 5 applicants admitted to UG program, for Fall, 2004 audition (performance track) or interview/portfolio (directing and design track) required for first time.

FACULTY AND CLASSES OFFERED

6 Full-Time: 1 PhD, 5 MFA, 3 Staff

A. (2 FT,) Intro to Theatre-2/Y; Theatre and Drama History-1/Y; Playwriting-1/Y; East Asian Theatre-O; Modern Theatre-O

B. (3 FT, 4+ PT) Acting-6/Y; Perf in Prod-4/Y; Voice-2/Y; Mvmt-2/Y; Directing-1/Y; Contemp Perf Tech or Investigative Collaboration-1/Y

C. (2 FT) Prins of Des-1/Y; Scene Design-1/Y; Cost Des- 1/Y; Ltg Des-O; Tech. Production-2/Y; Cost Prod- 2/Y; Cost. Des-1/Y; Make-up-O

D. (1 FT) Box Office Procedure/PR-2/Y

FACILITIES AND PRODUCTIONS

MAINSTAGE: 260 seats or more for thrust or in-the-round, fly space, computerized lighting. 4 prods; 3 Fac dir/des, 1 Guest dir, budget $1,500-3,000

SECOND STAGE: Black box up to 40 seats, pre-set lighting board, 2-4 prods, 4 UG dir prods; budget $100-500

DESCRIPTION

Noted Faculty: Jane Bagnall, Costume Design; Cynthia Blaise, Voice; Anthony Graham-White, Theatre History; William Raffeld, Performance; Liugi Salerni, Directing and Playwriting; Carl Ulaszek, Scene

Design.

Guest Artists: Valeryi Beliakvich, Artistic Director, Theatre of Moscow-Southwest;Bernard Sahlins, Cofounder, Second City.

The faculty believes students should take courses in all areas of theatre. The shift in today's theatre towards ensembles requires multi-skilled artists. Of course, students are also expected to develop skills according to their interests. For courses, productions, and internships, the program draws on Chicago's many theatres and skilled theatre specialists. In such a multi-ethnic city, there is a strong commitment to color-blind casting.

University of Illinois, Urbana-Champaign

See ad in back of book

Robert Graves, Head	35,000 T. Enr.; highly compet.
Dept. of Theatre	Semester System
Univ. of Illinois,	208 Majors; U/RTA, NAST,
Urbana-Champaign	ATHE
4-122 Krannert Center	T: $10,503 /$8,196 R&B
500 S. Goodwin Ave.	O-ST T: $$23,896/$8,196 R&B
Urbana, IL 61801	(217) 333-2371
www.theatre.uiuc.edu	FAX: (217) 244-1861

ADM: (Undergrad only–Grad apply directly to the department).
901 W. Illinois, Urbana IL 61801
(217) 333-0302
www.uiuc.edu
ugradadmissions@uiuc.edu

DEGREES OFFERED

BFA in Acting (58), Design/Management/Tech (45), Performance Studies (40); MFA in Acting (15), Design/Management/Tech (38); MA in Theatre History (3); PhD in Theatre History (10)
Declare major 1st yr.; 2002 granted 37 UG, 25 Grad degrees.

ADMISSION & FINANCIAL INFORMATION

10% of apps. accepted to institution. UG program req's aud/int/portfolio; SAT or ACT; admits 1 of 5 applicants. Grad program requires aud/int, portfolio for design; MA/PhD req. GRE; MA-one scholarly paper, Ph.D-2 schol. papers; admits 1 of 20 apps. UG-Bernard Gold Award, based on academic achvmt, theatre participation, $1,000. Talented UG Student Tuition Waiver, based on GPA and contribution to Th. Dept. Grad.- Fellowships and Assist'shps based on applic. & experience.

FACULTY AND CLASSES OFFERED

16 Full-Time, 16 Part-Time (does not include Grad Assistants): 3 PhD, 29 MFA/MA

A. (3 FT) Intro to Theatre-4/Y; Theatre History-5/Y; Dramatic Criticism-2/Y; Shakespeare-3/X; Theatre of the Black Experience-1/Y; Theatre for the Child Audience-2/Y

B. (7 FT, 5 PT) Acting-10/Y; Voice-4/Y; Mvmt- 4/Y; Mask, etc.-2/O; Mus. Th.-2/O; Stg Combat-2/O; Directing-2/Y; Oral Interp.-1/Y; Improv.-1/Y

C. (6 FT, 9 PT) Set Design-6/Y; Cost Des-6/Y; Ltg Des-2/Y; Tech Prod'n-6/Y; Cost Constr-6/Y; Cost Hist-2/Y; Make-up-1/Y; Stage Mgmt-1/Y; Property Design/Mgmt-1/Y; Sound Design-1/Y

D. (2 PT) Arts Mgmt-1/Y; Marketing/Promotion-1/Y

FACILITIES AND PRODUCTIONS

MAINSTAGE: 678 seats, fly space, computerized lighting
8 prods: 6 Fac dir, 4 Fac des, 2 Guest dir, 1 Guest des, 12 Grad

des, 8 UG des; total budget $3,000-15,000

MAINSTAGE: various seating, computerized lighting
   14 prods: 6 Grad dir, 4 Grad des, 8 UG dir, 10 UG des; budget $100-500

SECOND STAGE: Armory Free Theatre - 100 seats, black box

THIRD STAGE: 969 seats (Festival Stage), fly space, comput. ltg.

Facility was built in 1969; includes scene, costume, props, welding shop, sound studio, CAD facility, video studio, rehearsal studios, design studio, classrooms.

A non-departmental, student-run org. presents 6 prods/yr.

6 student-written plays produced in the last two years, most at the Downstate Playwright Festival.

DESCRIPTION

Noted Faculty: James Berton Harris, Costume Design; Daniel Sullivan, Directing; Henson Keys, Acting; Robin McFarquhar, Acting; Kathy Perkins, Lighting; Robert Graves, Theater History.

Guest Artists: Aquila Theater Company; Lee Blessing, Playwright; Anne Bogart, Director; Betty Buckley, Actor; Ina Marlow, Director; Allison Ford, Lighting Designer; Meredith Monk & Susan Marshall, Performance Artists; Leslie Nielsen, Actor; Charlayne Woodard, Actor.

Intensive, professional training in acting, scene design, lighting design, costume design, theatre technology, and stage management, housed in a modern five-theatre art center. The purpose of the program is to provide students with a careful balance between the many technical skills necessary in the professional theatre and the humanistic and artistic values needed to educate not simply theatre practitioners but theatre artists.

Western Illinois University

Jeannie M. Woods, Chairperson
Department of Theatre and Dance
Browne Hall #101
Western Illinois University
Macomb, IL 61455

DEPT: (309) 298-1543
theatre@wiu.edu
Admissions: 115 Sherman Hall, WIU, Macomb, Il 61455
(309)298-3157
www.student.services.wiu.edu/admissions/

13,000 Total Enr.; compet.
Semester System
105 Majors; ATHE
T + FEES: $5,439
O-ST T + FEES: $8,158
   $6,446/1yr r&b
fax: (309)298-2695
www.wiu.edu/theatre

toll free: 877-PICK-WIU

DEGREES OFFERED

BA in Acting/Directing/Production/Design (52); BFA in Musical Theatre (24); MFA in Acting/Directing/Production Design (31). Declare major in 1st year; 2001 granted 23 UG, 10 Grad degs.

ADMISSION & FINANCIAL INFORMATION

Minimum cumulative GPA of 2.5 on a 4.0 scale and ACT composite score is 20 (SAT-920).UG can aud/int for talent grants, tuition waivers and scholarships. Grad students can apply for tuition waiver and annual stipends up to $6,000. See www.wiu.edu/scholarships. No special requirements for admission to theatre program for BA. BFA/MFA aud/int/port for UG and Grad. Incoming BA students may aud or int for talent grants and tuition waivers.

FACULTY AND CLASSES OFFERED

15 Full-Time, 2.5 Part-Time: 2 PhD, 13 MFA/MA, 3 Staff

A. (2 1/2 FT) Intro to Theatre-2/Y; Theatre History-3/Y; Dramatic Lit-5/Y; Playwriting-2/Y; Shakespeare-1/O; Other-5/X

B. (10 FT, 1 PT) Acting-5/Y; Voice/Speech-7/Y; Mvmt-7/Y; Musical Th.-8/Y; Directing-9/Y; Singing-X; Stage Combat-4/Y; Acting for Camera-3/Y; Improv-1/Y; Dance-18/Y

C. (3 FT) Prins of Des-4/Y; Set Design-8/Y; Cost. Design-4/Y; Ltg. Design-6/Y; Cost Constr-2/Y; Make-up-1/Y; Stage Mgmt-1/Y; Tech Prod-4/Y; Practicum-6/Y

D. Arts Mgmt-1/O

FACILITIES AND PRODUCTIONS

MAINSTAGE: 387 seats, fly space, computerized lighting
   6 prods: 4 Fac dir, 9 Fac des, 2 Grad dir, 9 Grad des; budget $3,000-6,000

SECOND STAGE: 200 seats, electronic lighting
   budget $2,000-4,000.

THIRD STAGE: 135 seats, electronic lighting
   17 workshops/readings, 1 Fac dir, 8 Grad dir, 30 Grad des, 2 UG dir; budget $150-200

Facility was built in 1958, renovated in 1987; includes scene shop, costume shop, props shop, sound studio, welding shop, CAD facility, 2 movement/dance studios, 3 rehearsal studios, 2 design studios, 5 classrooms

There is a non-departmental, student-run producing org. in which majors participate. 17 student-written plays produced in the last two years.

Connection with Summer Music Festival at WIU and Regional Touring Theatre Company-SMT summer stock company, about 50% of company are WIU students; regional touring theatre—full semester of acting, no other classes. Mostly Grad students, some UG.

DESCRIPTION

Noted Faculty: Al Goldfarb, Theatre History; Jeannie Woods, Directing/Theatre History; Bill Kincaid, Acting; Egla Birmingham Hassam, Directing; DC Wright, Stage Combat; Carolyn Blackinton, Voice; Candace Winters-March, Dance; Heidi Clemmens, Dance; David Patrick, Scenic Des; Ray Gabica, Costume Des

Guest Artists: Michael Jerome Johnson, Actor; Michael Boatman (alum), Actor, Workshops; Laurie Eisenhower, Choreographer, Dance Residency

Undergraduate program: From their first year, students have the opportunity to work with senior faculty and get involved in 20-25 theatre, dance and musical productions. The curriculum is especially rich, with multiple courses in voice, stage combat, acting for the camera, and design and theatre technology courses. The department is large enough to offer a full range of opportunities, yet small enough to provide individual attnetion. All theatre faculty are full-time instructors with MFA, PhD or equivalent professional credentials. Graduates come away with a solid foundation for future study and professional work. Graduate Program: Western offers MFA graduate students in-depth professional training in Acting, Directing, or Costume, Lighting or Scenic Design, with professional experiences in Summer Music Theatre and Regional Touring Theatre Company. Programs are individualized to meet students needs. MFA students have opportunities to teach in the undergraduate program.

INDIANA

Ball State University

William Jenkins, Chair
Department of Theatre
Ball State University
Muncie, IN 47306
DEPT: (765) 285-8740
FAX: (765) 285-4030
ADMISSIONS: Lucina 101, Ball State University, Muncie, IN 47306
(765) 285-8300   FAX: (765) 285-1632
askus@bsu.edu

18,000 Total Enr.; compet.
Semester System
260 Th./60 Dance Majors; NAST
T: $7,258/$7,240 R&B
O-ST T: $18,326 R&B
www.bsu.edu/theatre

DEGREES OFFERED

BA and BS in Theatrical Studies (72), Design & Technology (35), Theatre Education (20); Acting (96), Musical Theatre (58), Dance (55); New Directing/Stage Mgt. degree in Fall '06. Declare major in freshman year

ADMISSION & FINANCIAL INFORMATION

Please contact Office of Admissions for information. 68% of applics accepted by institution. Dept. generally accepts 35% of students in Acting Option, and 18% in Musical Theatre. Talent Schols: audition-based; Upperclass Scholarships – application-based; Fine Arts Schols: ($1,000 per yr)- 8 scholarships awarded per year. Aud. required for Musical Theatre, Dance and Acting Options.

FACULTY AND CLASSES OFFERED

21 FT, 3 PT: 4 PhD, 16 MFA/MA, 1 Prof. w/o adv. degree; 4 Staff

A. (3 FT, 1 PT) Intro to Theatre-1/Y; Theatre History-2/Y; Shakes-1/Y; Theatre Ed.-1/Y

B. (14 FT, 1 PT) Acting-5/Y; Voice/Speech-2/Y; Singing-4/Y; Directing-2/Y; Musical Theatre Program; Dance-4/Y; Stage Combat-1/O

C. (3 1/2 FT) Prins of Des-4/Y; Set Design-2/Y; Ltg Des-2/Y; Cost Des-1/Y; Make-up-1/Y; Cost Hist-1/O; Cost Construc-1/Y

D. (1/2 FT) Arts Management-1/Y

FACILITIES AND PRODUCTIONS

MAINSTAGE: 410 seats, fly space, computerized lighting
    4 prods: 4 Fac dir, 8 Fac des, 1 Guest Dir, 1-2 Guest des, 1-4 UG des; budget $5,000-8,000

SECOND STAGE: 110 seats, computerized lighting
    3 prods:3 UG dir, 12 UG des; budget $300-500

1 major video/film project produced per year.

6 UG dir, 3 UG des Workshops/Readings; budget $100

Facility was built in 1960, renovated in 1986; includes scene shop, costume shop, prop shop, design studio, sound studio, CAD facility, 3 dance studios & facil., 3 classrooms.

4 student-written plays produced in the last two years.

DESCRIPTION

Noted Faculty: Jen Blackmer, Mgt./Directing; Karen Kessler, Directing; Dwandra Lampkin, Acting; Harold Mortimer, Voice/Musical Theatre; Wendy Mortimer, Voice/Acting; Michael O'Hara, History/Criticism; Kip Shawger, Scene Design; Hyun-Siok Kim, Costume Design; Rodger Smith, Acting for the Camera; Judy Yordon, Performance Studies.

Guest Artists: Stephanie Klapper, NY casting dir; Clair Sinnett, LA casting dir; David Shire, Broadway composer; Lindsay Crouse, LA actor; Bill Evans, Tap; Moises Kaufman, playwright; Margaret Edson, playwright.

The Mission of the Department of Theatre and Dance is to provide a pre-professional, liberal arts experience in a conservatory-style, for all students within the disciplines of acting (stage and camera), musical theatre, dance, design and technology, directing, theatrical studies, and theatre education. The department has an ethnically and culturally diverse, stylistically varied and technologically enhanced production season driven by our curriculum choices. The department encourages national, regional, community, and university partnerships that broaden the educational and professional experiences of both our students and our faculty.

Butler University

Dr. John C. Green, Chair
Theatre Department
Butler University
4603 Clarendon Rd.
Indianapolis, IN 46208
www.butler.edu/theatre
jgreen@butler.edu
ADMISSIONS: 4600 Sunset Ave.
admission@butler.edu

4,000 T Enr.; highly compet.
Semester System
85 Majors, NAST & ATHE
T: $26,070/$3,940 R&B
(317) 940-9659
FAX: (317) 940-9658

(800) 368-6852 x 9656
FAX: (317) 940-8100

DEGREES OFFERED

BA Theatre (70); BS in Arts Administration/Theatre (5). Declare major in 1st yr.

ADMISSION & FINANCIAL INFORMATION

Undergraduate program only; Minimum SAT score of 1050 or ACT score of 24 and top 1/3 of HS Class; 60% of applicants accepted; Aud/Int/Portfolio for designers req'd for admission to th. prog; accept 3 out of 4. Must apply to Jordan College of Fine Arts as well as Butler University. Audition Awards-available to incoming freshmen and transfer students. Meyer-Fitzgerald Theatre Award, based on acting ability during soph/jr. year. Daniel Warrick Outstanding Theatre Major Award, cash award to graduating senior. Workstudy also available.

FACULTY AND CLASSES OFFERED

8 FT, 5 PT; 1 Staff: 2 PhD, 7 MFA/MA, 4 Prof. w/o adv. degree, 1 staff

A. (2 FT, 2 PT) Intro to Theatre-1/Y; Dramatic Lit-2/X; Theatre History-2/Y; Dramatic Criticism-4/Y; Shakespeare-3/X; Playwriting-2/Y

B. (1 FT,5 PT) Acting-6/Y; Voice/Speech-4/Y; Mvmt-6//YX; Singing-2/X;, Directing-2/Y; Dance-6/X; Mime, etc-1/O

C. (4 FT) Prins of Des-2/Y; Set Des.-2/Y; Cost. Des.-2/Y; Ltg. Des.-2/Y; Tech. Prod'n.-2/Y; Cost Constr-2/Y; Make-up1/Y; Stage Mgmt-1/O

D. (1 FT, 1 PT) Arts Management-1/Y; Box Ofc Procedure-1/Y; Marketing/Promotion-1/Y; Legal: Contracts, etc.-1/O; Devel/Grant Writing-1/O; Budget, Acct'ng-1/O

FACILITIES & PRODUCTIONS

MAINSTAGE: (Studio Theatre) 135 seats, computerized lighting;
    3 Fac dir/des, 1 UG des prod; budget $3,000-5,000

SECOND STAGE: Theatre Lab built in 2003, 125 seats, computerized lighting

THIRD STAGE: (Clowes Memorial Hall) 2200 seats, fly space, comput. & electron. lighting

Facility was built in 1961; includes scene shop, costume shop, video studio, 3 dance studios, 2 rehearsal studios, 10 classrooms.

A non-departmental, student-run, producing org. presents 4-6 productions per year in which dept. majors participate. 8 student-written play produced in the last two years.

Connection with Indiana Repertory Theatre (Equity) and The Phoenix Theatre. Members of the company teach and direct at Butler on a regular basis. Students see approx. 15 professional theatre performances per year at these two theatres as well as meeting with members of the company for Study Days following performances. We have students doing internships and paid employment at these theatres at all times.

DESCRIPTION

Noted Faculty: Dr. John Green, Directing, Acting; Dr. Owen Schaub, History, Lighting; Diane Timmerman, Acting, Voice; Wendy Meaden, Costume, Masks, Makeup.

Guest Artists: Rob Johansen, Director, Actor, Fight Choreographer; Rockland Mers, Director; Dianne Martin, Playwright; Alissa Stamatis, Actor, Director; Barbara Dilley, Dance/Movement; Melli Hoppe, Director, Stage Movement; Joshua Friedman, Prod Supr at Indiana Rep Theatre; ELAN, Performance Art Group from Wales; Barbara Dilley, Dance, Movement; Preeti Vasudevan, Classical Indian Dance; Alessandro Fabrizi, Italian Actor/Director.

The Butler University Theatre Department provides broad-based education and training in the theatre arts within the context of a strong liberal arts tradition. Students who major in theatre are prepared for careers in theatre or to begin more intensive study of theatre at the graduate level. Along with the University's general education program, theatre students pursue course studies in acting, stagecraft, lighting, costuming, make-up, stage design and directing. Classroom study is supplemented with continuous participation in all facets of mainstage and student-directed productions. Through this work the student gains first-hand knowledge and experience in creating theatre. The Theatre Department of the Jordan College of Fine Arts has three significant strengths: its faculty, its outstanding roster of guest artists, and its students. The full-time faculty members bring to the program, not only formal graduate education, but varied professional backgrounds in the theatre and extensive experience in teaching both nationally and internationally. The roster of annual guest artists who are invited to teach and direct are drawn from the professional theatres in Indiana and from Europe. The theatre students bring not only talent but more importantly the commitment to develop that talent in innovative and outstanding theatre productions.

Franklin College

Paul M. Johnson
Dept. of Fine Arts
101 Branigin Blvd.
Franklin, IN 46131-2598
DEPT: (317) 738-8242
FAX: (317) 736-8282
http://www.franklincollege.edu
ADMISSIONS: Above address.
(317) 738-8062

1000 Total Enr.; compet.
15 Majors
Semester System
T: $21,325/$4700-6390 R&B
SMALL PROGRAM

pjohnson@franklincollege.edu
admissions@franklincollege.edu
FAX: (317) 736-6030

DEGREES OFFERED

BA in Theatre (15). Declare major in sophomore year;

ADMISSION & FINANCIAL INFORMATION

1000 SAT, 20 ACT, top 50% of graduating class and college prep classes, essay. 86% accepted to institution, generally admit all applicants to theatre program. New scholarship: Fine Arts Achievement Award available with audition/portfolio/interview, up to $6000 per year. Theatre Activity Award: avail. w/successful audition, portfolio display, or interview, $500 per year; requires involvement in 2 shows per year. Heartland Film Festival Schol: $1,000/yr., requires audition, 2.85 GPA.

FACULTY AND CLASSES OFFERED

3 Full-Time: 1 PhD, 2 MFA/MA

A. (1/2 FT) Intro to Theatre-1-2Y; Dramatic Lit-2/Y; Theatre History-1/O; Dramatic Criticism-O; Shakes-1/YX; Playwriting-1/O; Theatre of American People of Color-1/O; Film History-1/O

B. (1/2 FT, 1 PT) Acting-2/Y; Voice/Movement-2/YO; Singing-1/XY; Directing-1/O

C. (1 FT) Cost Des-1/O; Set Design-1/O; Ltg Des-1/O; Stage Management-1/O; Multimedia-1/O

D. Arts Management-1/O; Marketing/Production-3/YX; Budgeting/Accounting Procedure-3/YX

FACILITIES & PRODUCTIONS

MAINSTAGE: 125 seats, computerized lighting/sound, scene shop, costume shop light lab, sound and electrics shops, make-up and green rooms.

SECOND STAGE: Proscenium Theatre: 227 seats, computerized lighting, scene shop, sound studio, make-up room, prop and costume storage (built in 1930, renovated in 1988).

4-5 prods: 2 Fac dir, 1-2 Guest dir, 2 Fac des, 1 UG dir, 3 Guest des, 1-2 UG des; budget $2,000-4,500

4 student-written plays produced in the last two years.

DESCRIPTION

Noted Faculty: Robin Roberts, Dramatic Lit, Acting, Theatre History; Paul Johnson, Design, Mgmt; Darrell Spencer, Directing.

Guest Artists: Kate Mitchell, Costume Designer; Heather Patterson-King, Director; Rob Johansen, Fight.

Through curricular offerings and extracurricular productions, the theatre program at Franklin College aspires to develop students' appreciation of theatre as an art form by expanding their understanding of the position of theatre in society, and to develop their opportunities for participating in theatre by increasing their competence in theatrical skills and abilities. These goals are pursued both in classes, which, being small, allow individual attention by professors and in theatrical productions staged in the college's theatre season. Production is a hands-on experience for students, who have the opportunity to direct and design major productions. The program is designed primarily to give students the skills and background necessary for graduate study.

Indiana State University

Dr. Arthur Feinsod, Chair
Department of Theater
Indiana State University
540 North 7th
Terre Haute, IN 47809
DEPT: (812) 237-3342
http://www.indstate.edu/theater
ADM: ISU Office of Admission
(812) 237-2121
www.indstate.edu/admissions/index.htm
admissions@indstate.edu

8,537 T. Enr.; not compet.
Semester System
65 Majors; ATHE
T: $6,728/$6,552 R&B
O-ST T: $14,516/$4998 R&B
FAX: (812) 237-3954
tharthur@isugw.indstate.edu
www.web.indstate.edu/
FAX: (812) 237-8023

DEGREES OFFERED

BA, BS, MA, MS in Theater with Concentration in Acting, Design and Technology, Directing and Playwriting, Educational, Theatrical Dance. Declare major as Freshman, declare concentration in 3rd semester; granted 8 UG and 2 Grad degrees.

ADMISSION & FINANCIAL INFORMATION

UG: top 50% with average SAT scores; 80% applicants accepted; Theatre Program accepts 20 out of 30 UG applicants, 4 out of 7 Grad applicants. Interview required. Academic Schols awarded to students in top 10% of HS class; 10 Performing Arts Scholarships, $4400 over 4 yrs. & 3 Dept Scholarships, $1,500/ yr., all awarded on the basis of interview and letters of recommendation.

FACULTY AND CLASSES OFFERED

7 Full-Time: 2 PhD, 5 MFA/MA; 3 Staff

A. (1 1/2 FT) Intro to Theatre-1/Y; Theatre History-3/Y; Shakes-X; Dramatic Lit-3/Y; Dramatic Criticism-1/Y; Playwriting- 1/Y

B. (2 FT) Acting-5/Y; Voice/Speech-1/Y; Movement-1/Y; Singing-X; Musical Theatre-1/Y; Directing-2/Y; Stage Combat-1/O

C. (3 FT) Prins of Des-1/Y; Set Design-1/Y; Tech. Production- 1/Y; Cost Des-1/Y; Cost Constr-1/Y; Ltg Des- 2/Y; Make-up-1/Y; Stage Management-1/Y

D. (1/2 FT) Arts Management-1/Y

FACILITIES AND PRODUCTIONS

MAINSTAGE: 240 seats, fly space, computerized lighting
   8 prods: 6 Fac dir, 4 Fac des, 1 Guest dir, 3 Guest des, 1 UG dir, 1 UG des; budget $2,000-8,000

SECOND STAGE: 204 seats, computerized lighting. 8 prods:
   1 Guest dir, 3 UG dir/des, 4 Grad dir/des; budget $100-500

THIRD STAGE: 50 seats

32 workshops/readings, 24 UG dir, 8 Grad dir; budget $50-100

Facility was built in 1979; includes scene shop, cost. shop, props shop, welding shop, rehearsal studio, design studio, 3 classrooms.

Connection with SummerStage: professional actors (Equity and non-Equity), designers and technicians work directly with students & fac, produce 4 plays in rotating rep, and large-scale Cabaret.

Students act in major roles with professionals, work side by side with them in design, technical, mgmt and directing tasks. Receive small stipend.

DESCRIPTION

Noted Faculty: Chris Berchild, Directing; David Del Colletti, Design & Technology, Design; Julie Dixon, Acting; Arthur Feinsod, playwright, theater scholar, director.

The undergraduate program in the award-winning Department of Theater provides interested ISU students with a broad and solid foundation in the artistic, intellectual and practical aspects of theater through its diverse selection of courses and its many production opportunities. The program fosters a working environment – inside and outside the classroom, onstage and off – that is serious, focused, rigorous, nurturing and energetic. It encourages students to collaborate, experiment and take intitative in the development of new plays and the thoughtful reinterpretation of established ones. Directly linked to SUMMERSTAGE, a professional summer theater company, the department seeks to endow its students with a deep sense of professional ethics and standards as they create significant theater while at ISU and for the rest of their theatrical careers.

Indiana University

See ad in back of book

Jonathan Michaelsen, Chair
Dept. of Theatre and Drama
Theatre & Drama Center
Indiana University
275 N. Jordan Ave.
Bloomington, IN 47405-1101
DEPT: (812) 855-4502
http://www.iub.edu
ADMISSIONS: 300 N. Jordan Ave, Bloomington, IN 47405
(812) 855-0661
www.indiana.edu/

37,000 T. Enr.; compet.
Semester System
190 Majors; U/RTA
T: UG $6,628
O-ST T: UG $21,037
R&B: $6,676
FAX: (812) 855-4704

iuadmit@indiana.edu

DEGREES OFFERED

BA in Theatre and Drama (190); MA,MAT, PhD in Hist/Thy/Lit (13); MFA Acting/Directing (13), Cost Des (3), Lighting Des (4), Playwriting (3), Scenic Des (3), Th Tech (1). Declare major in soph. year; 2001 granted 20 UG, 10 Grad degrees.

ADMISSION & FINANCIAL INFORMATION

GPA & class rank; standardized test scores; 62% of applicants accepted; no special req's for admission to UG Th Prog., adit. 90% to th. progam. Graduate: Aud/int req'd, portfolio for des; admit 15 out of 150 Grad. Theatre Circle (Jr/Sr $1,500); McGreevey (Soph/Jr. $5,000): other $700-1,500 awards to majors demonstrating superior talent and dedication.

FACULTY AND CLASSES OFFERED

15 FT, 6 PT: 4 PhD, 9 MFA/MA, 1 Prof. w/o adv. deg; 11 Staff.

A. (4 FT) Intro to Th-2/Y; Dramatic Lit-3/Y; Th Hist- 13/Y; Dramatic Criticism-2/Y; Shakes-4/O; Playwriting-3/Y

B. (6 FT, 5 PT) Acting-7/Y; Voice/Speech-10/Y; Movement-2/Y; Singing-11/X; Mus Th-1/Y; Directing-4/Y; Mus Th-1/Y

C. (4 FT, 1 PT) Prins. of Design-2/Y; Set Design-8/Y; Cost Des-4/Y;

Ltg Des-4/Y; Technical Production-3/Y; Cost Const-5/Y; Cost Hist-1/Y; Make-up-1/Y; Stage Mgmt-1/Y

D. (1 FT) Arts Management-7/X; Box Office Procedure-1/X; Market/Promo-4/X; Legal: Contracts/Copyright-2/X; Devel/Grant/Writing-1/X; Budget/Acct'ng-1/X

FACILITIES & PRODUCTIONS

MAINSTAGE: 383 seats, fly space, computer lighting
4 Prods: 4 Fac dir, 3 Fac des, 1 Grad dir, 12 Grad des; budget $8-12,000

SECOND STAGE: 246 seats, fly space, computer ltg.
4 prods: 2-3 Fac dir, 6 Fac des, 1-2 Guest dir, 3 Guest des, 2 Grad dir; budget $8,000 avg.

Facility was built in 2001; includes scene shop, costume shop, prop shop, welding shop, video studio, sound studio, CAD facility, movement/dance studio, rehearsal studio, design studio, class-rooms. Renovation on 1941 building pending.

A non-departmental, student-run organization presents 2-4 productions per year in which majors participate. 3 student-written plays produced in the last two years.

Department produces Brown County Playhouse (in Nashville, Indiana), professional (Equity) stock theatre, in summer employing actors, designers, directors, stage managers, and staff; internships arranged with regional theatres.

DESCRIPTION

Noted Faculty: Linda Pisano, Costume; Roger W. Herzel, Rakesh Solomon, Ron Wainscott, History and Literature; Bruce Burgun, Howard Jensen, Murray McGibbon, Dale McFadden, Jonathan Michaelsen, Acting/Directing; Robert A. Shakespeare, Lighting; Robert Bovard, Technology; Fred Duer, Scene; Dennis J. Reardon, Playwriting; George Pinney, Mvmt, Musical Theatre.

Guest Artists: George C. Wolfe, Colin Teevan, Jan Clarke, Janet Allen, Jenny McKnight, Jane Alderman, Scott LaFaber, Robert Benforth, Athol Fugard, Desmond Heeley, Brian Bedford, Melinka Berberovich, Ljilana Petrovic, Joel Markus.

The undergraduate curriculum in Theatre and Drama at Indiana University is based on the belief that practical experience and classroom study are of equal and complementary value. Thus acting, directing, playwriting, design, theatre history and dramatic literature are all essential and interrelated aspects of the BA program. The graduate program at Indiana is structured for the artist or scholar who intends to pursue a professional career in the theatre and desires highly specialized training. The Department offers an MFA in Acting, Directing, Playwriting, Scene Design, Costume Design, Lighting Design, and Theatre Technology for theatre artists who have demonstrated a high degree of creative ability and technical skill. The Department also offers MA and Ph.D. programs for theatre scholars who are interested in pursuing careers in Theatre History, Theory, and Dramatic Literature.

Purdue University

Russell E. Jones, Chair
Theatre Division
Dept. of Visual & Perf. Arts
552 W. Wood Street
Purdue University
West Lafayette, IN 47907-2050
www.purdue.edu/theatre
theatre@purdue.edu
ADMISSIONS: 1080 Schleman Hall, W. Lafayette, IN 47907
(765) 494-1776

36,000 Total Enr.; compet.
Semester System
125 Majors; U/RTA, NAST, ATHE
T: $7,416/$7,530 R&B
O-ST T: $22,224/$7,530 R&B
(765) 494-3074
FAX: (765) 496-1766
www.purdue.edu/Purdue/admissions

FAX: (765) 494-0544

DEGREES OFFERED

BA in Theatre (96); MFA in Tech & Design (12), Acting (8). Declare major in soph. year; 2004 granted 18 UG, 11 Grad degrees

ADMISSION & FINANCIAL INFORMATION

Upper half of HS class, SAT or ACT req.; 85% of applics. accepted to instit.; Theatre Program accepts 8 out of 10 UG, 2 out of 12 Grad; Grad admission req's aud, interview and portfolio. Stewart Scholarship - returning undergrad, need based; 3 schols for incoming freshmen theatre majors based on theatrical involvement and academic performance. Incoming freshman scholarships: Joseph Stockdale/Ross Smith Scholarship, Theatre Merit Award, Marietta Stallard Kettelhut Scholarship.

FACULTY AND CLASSES OFFERED

11 Full-Time: 1 PhD; 10 MA/MFA; 6 Staff.

A. (1 FT) Intro to Theatre-1/Y; Theatre History-3/Y; Shakes-2/X; Dramatic Lit-3/X; Dramatic Criticism-1/Y; Playwriting-1/O

B. (4 FT) Acting-11/Y; Voice/Speech-8/O; Movement-5/O; Mime, etc.-1/O; Directing-2/Y; Stage Combat-1/O; Dance-12/O; Film-1/O

C. (5 FT) Prins of Des-2/Y; Set Design-5/Y; Tech Prod'n-4/Y; Cost Des-2/Y; Cost Constr-2/Y; Sound Studio-1/Y; Make-up-1/Y; Ltg Des-5/O; Cost Hist-1/O; Stage Mgmt-2/Y; Audio Technology-1/O; Scene Painting-1/O; Sound Des-5/O; Drafting/Rendering-3/O

D. (1 FT) Arts Management-1/O; Professional Issues-1/O

FACILITIES AND PRODUCTIONS

MAINSTAGE: 310 seats, fly space, computer & electronic lighting
4 prods: 3 Fac dir, 5 Fac des, 1 Guest dir, 9 Grad des; 2 UG des, budget $11,365-32,515

Second Stage: 105 seats, computerized/electronic lighting, 2 prods., 2 Fac dir, 4 Grad des, 3 UG des, $3,235-4,250

Workshop/readings; budget $50-200, 1 prod, 1 Guest dir

New Hall of Visual and Performing Arts spaces opened fall 2005; includes scene shop, costume shop, prop shop, sound studio, CAD facility, ,movement/dance studios, rehearsal studio, design studio and classrooms.

Students write and produce plays for Theatre Festival.

Undergraduate and graduate students have been placed for summer experiences through connections with American Players Theatre, Indiana Repertory Theatre, Tecumseh! Outdoor Drama, Texas Shakespeare Festival, and the Des Moines Metro Opera.

DESCRIPTION

Noted Faculty: Russell E. Jones, Scenic Design; Richard K. Thomas, Sound Design and Composing; Richard Stockton Rand, Acting and Movement; Kristine Holtredt, Acting; Richard Sullivan Lee, Acting/Voice; Joel Ebarb, Costume Design; Dr. Anne Fliotsos,

Theory/Criticism; Ryan Koharchik, Lighting Design; Jeff Casazza, Acting/Directing; Richard M. Dionne, Technical Direction/Stage Management.

Guest Artists: Peter Forster, Director; Daryl Stone, Costume Designer; David Swan, Director; Kate Swan, Choreographer; Katherine Burke, Director; Ryan Shively, Actor; Daniel Stein, Actor; Ross Maxwell, Playwright; Christopher R. Dunham, Scene Designer; Raul Gorizakz, Sound Technician.

The Purdue University Division of Theatre offers both undergraduate and graduate degree programs in theatre. The undergraduate program has a liberal arts focus leading to a BA degree from the University's College of Liberal Arts. By studying the many facets of this art form, students learn to apply history, art, psychology, sociology, philosophy, political/economic systems, and other disciplines toward the creation of a shared theatrical event. The graduate program is a professional training program offering an MA in acting and in design and technology. Students benefit from the continuing professional experiences of Division faculty and staff members. Undergraduate and graduate students combine classroom study and practical application in their study of theatre. The Division participates in the Kennedy Center/American College Theatre Festival, sending four productions to the regional festival since 1999. A student winner at the regional festival has competed in the national festival in Washington DC in each of the last five years, representing the areas of acting, costume design, scenic design and lighting design.

University of Evansville

John David Lutz, Chair
Dept. of Theatre
1800 Lincoln Ave.
University of Evansville
Evansville, IN 47722
www.theatre.evansville.edu
theatre@evansville.edu
ADM: Above address
www.evansville.edu/admissions
admissions@evansville.edu

2,400 Total Enr.; compet.
142 Majors; ATHE
Semester System
T: $23,710
$3,510-5,550 R&B
(812)488-2744
FAX: (812) 488-6995
(812)488-2468
FAX: (812) 474-4076

DEGREES OFFERED

BFA, BS in Performance (73), Design/Tech (27); BS in Stage Mgmt (6),Theatre Studies (11); Theatre Ed. (9).Declare degree in Freshman year; 2007 granted 39 degrees.

ADMISSION & FINANCIAL INFORMATION

Admission to the University of Evansville is based upon strength of HS curriculum, grades attained in college prep courses, SAT and/or ACT scores, counselor recommendation, and involvement in extra-curricular activities. Theatre program admits 40 out of 450. Schols avail based on a student's talent, leadership, and academic prowess. Need based grants and loans are also available to qualifying students.Special requirements for admission to theatre program for UG include aud for actors, int/port for designers, an int is required for all applicants in addition to an portfolio audition review, etc.

FACULTY AND CLASSES OFFERED

11 Full-Time; 1 PhD, 9 MFA/MA, 1 Prof w/o advanced degree; 1 Staff
A.   (2 FT) Intro to Theatre-1/Y; Dramatic Lit-2/Y; Theatre History-2/Y;

Shakes-1/Y; Dramatic Criticism-1/Y; Playwriting-1/Y;
B.   (3 FT) Acting-8/Y; Dance-4/Y; Singing-X; Directing-4/Y
C.   (5 FT) Prins of Des-2/Y; Cost Des-1/Y; Set Design-1/Y; Ltg Des-1/Y; Cost Constr-2/O; Make-up-3/Y; Stage Mgmt-1/O
D.   (1 FT) Arts Mgmt-1/Y; Box Office Procedure-2/Y; Marketing Promo-1/Y; Contracts/Copyright-1/Y; Budgeting/Acct-1/Y

FACILITIES & PRODUCTIONS

MAINSTAGE: 486 seats, computerized lighting, fly space
    4 prods: 3 Fac dir/des, 1 GA dir, 4 UG des; budget $14,000-16,000

SECOND STAGE: 127 seats, black box, electronic lighting
    2 prods: 2 UG dir, 8 UG des; budget $1,000

2 Workshop/Readings: 1 Fac dir, 1 Guest dir.

Facility was built in 1966, renovated in 1990 & 1994; includes scene shop, costume shop, prop shop, welding shop, sound studio, movement/dance studio, CAD facility, rehearsal studio, design studio.

One student written produced in the last two years.

DESCRIPTION

Noted Faculty: John David Lutz, Acting,Directing; Joseph P. Flauto, Design; R. Scott Lank, Acting,Directing; Patti McCrory, Costume Design; Chuck Meadham, Tech Director; Christia Ward, Voice & Movement; Sharla Cowden, Theatre Mgmt; Dr. Diane Brewer, Th. Hist/Dramatic Lit; Jean Nelson, Costume Shop Mgr.; Eric Ronschler, Scenic Des

Guest Artists: Lisa Rothe, Dir.; Susan Erickson, Dir; Jim Guy, Firearms; Shona Tucker, Dir; Eric Nightengale, Director; Jim Leonard, Playwright

Individual training incorporated with a broad base in liberal arts and sciences makes the University of Evansville program unique. The department has performed at the American College Theatre Festival regional events more often than any school in the nation. Eight productions have been selected to perform at the John F. Kennedy Center for the Performing Arts in Washington, D.C. Students receive training in acting, design, technical theatre, directing, playwriting, stage management, and theatre management. The mainstage theatre season includes four productions performed in a 486-seat thrust theatre. Each production is produced by a combination of students, faculty, and/or guest artists and allows advanced students an opportunity to test their skills in one of the design disciplines. The studio season includes two productions, which are performed in a black box theatre and are produced entirely by student directors, designers, and actors. Each semester a classroom project is mounted to enhance the actor/director process.

University of Indianapolis

James W. Ream, Chair
Dept. of Theatre
University of Indianapolis
1400 E. Hanna Ave.
Indianapolis, IN 46227
DEPT: (317) 788-3455
ream@uindy.edu
ADMISSIONS: Address above.
800-232- U-OF-I

4,400 Total Enr.; competitive
Semester System
50 Majors; ATHE
T: $19,540/$7,560 R&B
SMALL PROGRAM
FAX: (317) 788-3272
http://theatre.uindy.edu

DEGREES OFFERED

BA/BS in Theatre (50) concentrations in performing/directing, design/prod, teaching, theatre music. Declare major in freshman year; 2005 granted 5 UG degrees.

ADMISSION & FINANCIAL INFORMATION

Top 50%, above avg. SAT min. 800, ACT min. 20, 24 college prep courses; 90% accepted by inst. Theatre schols. based on aud. or portfolio review; Full Tuition Presidential Schol (top 5-7% of class, SAT 1270 or 29 ACT); Deans Schol (top 5-7%, SAT 1270 or ACT 29-1/2 tuition); Alumni Schols (top 15%, SAT 1100, ACT 24).

FACULTY AND CLASSES OFFERED

3 Full-Time, 6 Part-Time: 1 PhD, 6 MFA/MA; 2 Staff

A. (1 FT, 2 PT) Intro to Theatre-1/Y; Theatre History-2/Y; Shakes- 1/X; Dramatic Lit-2/X; Play Analysis-1/Y

B. (1 FT, 1 PT) Acting-3/Y; Voice/Speech-1/Y; Singing-3/X; Directing-2/Y; Movement-1/Y

C. (1 FT) Intro to Design-1/Y; Set Design-2/Y; Ltg. Design-2/Y; Tech Production-1/Y; CAD-1/Y; Make-up-1/Y; Methods-1/Y; Stage Costuming-2/Y.

FACILITIES & PRODUCTIONS

MAINSTAGE: 780 seats, computerized & electronic lighting. 3 prods; 2 Fac dir, 1 Fac des, 1 Guest dir/des; budget $4,000-8,000

SECOND STAGE: 80 seats, computerized and electronic lighting. 4 UG dir prods; budget $100-1,000

THIRD STAGE: 125 seats, black box (offsite - renovated 2000)

Facility built in 1954, renovated in 1997; includes scene shop, prop shop, costume shop, sound studio, rehearsal studio, video studio, dance studio. Annual dinner theatre is performed in main dining hall, seats 300, computerized and electronic lighting.

DESCRIPTION

Noted Faculty: Dr. Brad Wright, Acting/Directing/Th Hist/Play Analysis; James W. Ream, Des/Tech; Laura Glover, Lighting; Cate Moran, Costuming; Jen Alexander, Acting/Directing.

Guest Artists: Lynn Perkins Socey, Acting/Social Issues/Auditioning; Robert Neal, Performance/Guest Actor; Jeff Casazza, Guest Director; Rob Koharchik, Guest Designer; Michael Moffatt, Guest Designer; Curt Tofteland, Social Issues; Amber Martin, Stage Mgmt

The Department of Theatre at the University of Indianapolis provides students main stage acting, design and production opportunities. Students are also encouraged to become actively engaged in the thriving Indianapolis theatre community. The goal of the department is to develop the skills, crafts, and imaginations of its students within the liberal arts context. The curriculum encompasses the areas of acting, directing, production, scenic design, lighting, dramatic literature, theatre history, and play analysis. This broad preparation at the undergraduate level develops a foundation for any theatre specialization. Through individual attention, the faculty strives to help students acquire and develop the tools they will need in order to succeed in their future pursuits.

University of Notre Dame

Jim Collins, Acting Chair
Dept. of Film, Television and Theatre
DeBartolo Center for the Perf Arts
Notre Dame, IN 46556
DEPT: (574) 631-7054
FAX: (574) 631-3566

10,000 T. Enr.; h. compet.
Semester System
40 Majors; ATHE
T: $35,190/$9,290 R&B
ADM: (574) 631-7505
admissions@nd.edu

DEGREES OFFERED

BA in Theatre. Students declare major in soph./jr. year.

ADMISSION & FINANCIAL INFORMATION

SAT: avg. 1300, ACT: avg. 29, (class rank of 6). 35% of applicants admitted to institution. All applicants usually admitted to theatre program.

FACULTY AND CLASSES OFFERED

9 Full-Time, 1 Part-Time: 4 PhD, 4 MFA/MA; 1 Prof.w/o adv. deg.

A. (2 FT) Intro to Theatre-2/Y; Dramatic Lit-2/X; Th Hist-2/Y; Dramatic Crit-2/Y; Shakes-2/X; Playwriting-1/O

B. (1 FT, 1 PT) Acting-5/Y; Directing-2/Y

C. (3 FT) Set Design-2/Y; Costume Des-1/Y; Make-up-2/Y; Stage Management-1/Y

D. (1 FT) Marketing/Promotion-1/O.

FACILITIES & PRODUCTIONS

MAINSTAGE: 571 seats, computerized & electronic lighting. 3 prods: 3 Fac dir, 2 Fac des, 1-2 UG des or dir; budget $30,000

SECOND STAGE: 100 seats, electronic lighting. 4 prods: 4 UG dir/des; budget $300-500

Facility built in 1892, renovated in 1984; includes scene shop, costume shop, rehearsal studio, design studio, classrooms.

Non-departmental, student-run, producing organization presents 2-5 productions per year in which majors participate.

DESCRIPTION

Guest Artists: Actors from the London stage.

Notre Dame offers a major in the study and practice of theatre within a strong liberal arts context. The department had developed its program for students who seek the kind of liberal education Notre Dame has to offer. Students have stringent academic requirements (including a common freshman year) which serve as a foundation for their theatre education and help prepare them for many eventual career choices. Many students in the program will go on to further study in graduate or professional programs. The theatre program is also closely associated with a companion program in the study and practice of film and television.

Vincennes University

James Spurrier, Chair
Speech, Theatre & Dance
RSPAC-04
Vincennes University
Vincennes, IN 47591
DEPT: (812) 888-4256
jspurrier@vinu.edu
ADMISSIONS: 1002 N. First St.
800 742-9198

4,500 Total Enr.; not compet.
Semester System
30 Majors; NAST, ATHE
T: $3,400/$6,400 R&B
O-ST T: $8,525/$6,400 R&B
FAX: (812) 888-2733
www.vinu.edu
(812)888-4313
www.vinu.edu

DEGREES OFFERED

AA and AS in Theatrical Production (10); AS in Costume Construction (2), Technical Th. (6), Music Th. (9), Declare major in freshman year; 2007 granted 7 UG degrees. Cert. in Dance -1 year (3)

ADMISSION & FINANCIAL INFORMATION

HS diploma or GED; accepts 100% of applicants; Program admits all applicants. Departmental Schols-based on audition/ interview. 12 Tolson & Reed scholarships, selected by audition by May 1.

FACULTY AND CLASSES OFFERED

3 Full-Time, 2 PT: 1 PhD, 3 MFA/MA, 1 Prof. w/o adv. deg, 1 Staff

A. (1/2 FT, 1 PT) Theatre History-2/Y;Intro to Theatre-1/Y; Playwriting-1/O; World Drama-1/X

B. (1/2 FT, 1 PT) Acting-2/Y; Voice/Speech-1/Y; Dance-12/Y; Singing-5/X; Directing-1/O; Musical Theatre-2/X; Stage Combat-1/O; Music Theory-2/X

C. (2 FT) Prins of Des-3/X; Tech. Prod-1/Y; Cost Constr-2/Y; Cost Hist-1/X; Make-up-1/Y: Clothing, Tailoring & Textiles-4/X; Scene Painting-1/O; Welding-1/X

FACILITIES AND PRODUCTIONS

MAINSTAGE: 802 seats, fly space, computerized lighting
   3 prods: 3 Fac dir/des; budget $4,000-5,000

SECOND STAGE: 75 seats,computerized lighting; budget $500-$800
   2 prods: 1 Fac dir/des; 1 UG dir/des

Third Stage: 316 seats, fly space, computerized lighting
   Facility was built in 2006, includes scene shop, costume shop, welding, CAD facility, movement/dance studio, 1 design studio, 1 classroom, 1 scene/props/cost storage bldg, 2 make-up/dressing rooms.

DESCRIPTION

Noted Faculty: James Spurrier, Acting/Directing; Richard D. Holen, Scene Design/Scene Painting; Eric Margerum, Acting/Directing

Guest Artists: Hank Schob, Elizabeth Bruzzese, Craig Oldfather, Actors; Richard Burk, Stg Combat; David Gaines, Mime; Richard Rand, Mvmt/Masks; Jan Quackenbush, Playwriting; Jay Kerr, Musical Theatre

The department offers the first two years of training designed to transfer to 4-year or professional training institutions in Theatre, Cost Constr, Tech. Theatre, Dance, and, in conjunction with the Music Department, Music Theatre. The Costume Construction option is also designed as a terminal degree. Mainstage productions are limited to students only so the experience gained in performing strongly compliments the classroom training. Within a Liberal Arts setting, the student is more than adequately prepared to further his/her training after receiving the AA/AS degree. In concurrence with University policy, the department adheres to an open admission policy for anyone with a high school diploma or equivalent. Auditions are held annually for departmental scholarships. Student programs of study are developed individually and a wide range of advanced tutorial theatre electives, developmental courses, and summer internships are available.

Wabash College

Michael Abbott, Chair
Theatre Department
Wabash College
Crawfordsville, IN 47933
DEPT: (765) 361-6342
ADM: (765) 361-6448

900 Total Enr.; competitive
Semester System
15 Majors; ATHE
T: $26,350/$7,200 r&b
SMALL PROGRAM
www.wabash.edu

DEGREES OFFERED

BA in Theatre

ADMISSION & FINANCIAL INFORMATION

80-85% accepted. Fine Arts Fellowships available.

FACILITIES & PRODUCTIONS

4 Full-Time: 4 MFA; 1 Staff

A. (1 FT) Intro to Theatre-2/Y; Dramatic Lit-4/O; Theatre History-2/O; Dramatic Criticism-1/Y; Shakes-1/X; Playwriting-1/Y

B. (1 FT) Acting-2/Y; Directing-1/Y; Dramaturgy-1/Y; Film-1/Y

C. (1 FT, 1 PT) Principles of Design-1/O; Set Design-1/O; Tech. Production.-2/Y

FACILITIES & PRODUCTIONS

MAINSTAGE: 370 seats, fly space, computerized lighting
   4-6 prods: 4 Fac dir/des, 2 UG dir/des

SECOND STAGE: 100-200 seats, electronic lighting

WORKSHOPS/READINGS: 100-150 Seats, budget $400-700

Facility was built in 1968; includes scene shop, costume shop, prop shop, welding shop, sound studio, video studio, rehearsal studio, classrooms.

DESCRIPTION

Noted Faculty: James Fisher, Th. History; Dwight Watson, Playwriting & Performance; Michael Abbott, Acting, Directing, Film; James Gross, Scenic Design/Lighting.

Guest Artists: Pilobus Dance Theater, The Acting Company, Edward Albee, Mummenschanz, Mask & Mime Co., Tony Kushner, San Francisco Mime Troupe.

Each year the Wabash College Theater Department produces plays from a variety of periods and genres. Students are able to act, direct, promote and handle the technical aspects of the play. The season of plays selected by the department is chosen with careful consideration of the unique opportunities for students offered by each play. The department recommends that the student work in a variety of performance areas including acting, stage managing, set and costume construction, lighting and sound, playwriting, and directing. Through its membership in the Great Lakes Colleges Association, Wabash participates in the New York Arts Program, which is designed to provide students in the areas of communication, visual arts and theater an opportunity to spend one semester living in New York. Apprenticed to a practicing artist, students attend seminars in the arts and experience a broad range of arts events.

Clarke College

Carol Blitgen, Chair
Department of Drama
Clarke College
1550 Clarke Drive
Dubuque, IA 52001
DEPT: (563) 588-6409
carol.blitgen@clarke.edu
ADMISSIONS: 1550 Clarke Drive, Dubuque, IA 52001
(563) 588-6316
admissions@clarke.edu

1,200 Total Enr.
Semester System
16 Majors
T: $21,312/$6,574 R&B
SMALL PROGRAM
FAX: (563) 588-6789

DEGREES OFFERED

BA in Drama (non-specialized) (1).
Declare major in sophomore year. 2003 granted 3 degree.

ADMISSION & FINANCIAL INFORMATION

2.0 GPA, rank in upper 50% of class, ACT of 21 or SAT of 1000; 82% accepted to inst.; Audition, interview, portfolio for des req'd for admission to Th. Prog.; 8 out of 10 accepted to program. Renewable scholarships available to $2,000 annually based on audition, rec. of HS theatre teacher, interview.

FACULTY AND CLASSES OFFERED

3 Full-Time, 5 Part-Time: 1 PhD, 2 MFA, 2 Staff

A. (1 FT) Intro to Th-1/Y; Dramatic Lit-2/Y; Dramatic Crit.-1/Y; Th Hist-2/O; Shakes-2/O

B. (1 FT, 1 PT) Acting-2/Y; Voice/Speech-1/O; Mvmt-1/O; Singing-2/Y; Directing-1/O; Stg. Combat-1/O

C. (1 FT, 4 PT) Set Design-1/O; Cost. Design-2/O; Ltg Des-1/O; Cost Constr-2/O; Stage Mangmt.-1/O

FACILITIES & PRODUCTIONS

MAINSTAGE: 700 seats, fly space, electronic lighting
    4 prods: Fac dir; $3,500-5000
Facility built in 1928, renovated in 1981; includes scene shop, costume shop.

DESCRIPTION

Noted Faculty: Joseph Kleinbriel, Performance; Ellen Gabrielleschi, Set Design/Lighting; Dr. Carol Blitgen, Drama Lit., Th. Hist, Dir.

The Clarke College Drama/Speech Department offers a major in Drama/Speech leading to a Bachelor of Arts degree, with concentrations in costuming, technical theatre, dramatic literature/history and performance. Study of the human experience through great drama and development of practical skills in human communications prepare students to perceive, evaluate and articulate their responses to the human community. The department aims to develop in its students an aesthetic sense, analytic and critical thinking skills, communication ability, physical and affective skills, self-perception and self-presentation skills. In addition, we aim to provide a cultural context for Clarke students, to challenge them to artistic and personal risk-taking, to lifelong inquiry and self-education.

Coe College

Susan Wolverton, Chair
Theatre Arts Department
Coe College
1220 First Avenue NE
Cedar Rapids, IA 52402
theatre@coe.edu
DEPT: (319) 399-8624
ADMISSIONS: 1220 First Ave. NE, Cedar Rapids, IA 52402
www.coe.edu/admission

1,200 Total Enr.; competitive
Semester System
30 Majors
T: $23,570/$6,260 R&B
SMALL PROGRAM
www.coe.edu
FAX: (319) 399-8557

(319) 399-8500

DEGREES OFFERED

BA in Theatre Arts with emphasis in Acting, Directing, Design/Tech & General (2). Declare major in 2nd year; 2007 granted 4 degrees

ADMISSION & FINANCIAL INFORMATION

3.0 GPA, 20 ACT, 1000 SAT, top 40%. Theatre scholarships up to $2,000 annually based on merit, awards based on aud/int. No special requirements for admission to theatre program. 24 out of 30 applicants admitted.

FACULTY AND CLASSES OFFERED

3 Full-Time, 3 Part-Time; 2 PhD, 2 MA/MFA; 1 Prof. w/o advanced degree, 1 Staff.

A. (1 FT, 1 PT) Intro to Theatre-1/Y; Theatre History-1/Y; Shakes-1/O; Playwriting-2/Y; Dramaturgy-1/O; Senior Seminar-1/Y

B. (1 FT, 1 PT) Acting-3/Y; Voice/Speech-1/O; Dance-4/Y; Musical Theatre-1/O; Directing-2/Y; Movement-1/O; Advanced Directing-2/O

C. (1 FT, 1 PT) Prins of Des-1/Y; Set Des-1/O; Cost Des-1/O; Ltg Des-1/O; Intro to Tech Prod.-1/Y; Cost Constr-1/Y; Make-up-1/O

FACILITIES AND PRODUCTIONS

MAINSTAGE: 320 seats, computerized lighting
    3 prods: 2 Fac dir, 2 Fac des, 1 GA dir; budget $3,000-$6,000
SECOND STAGE: 75 seats, computerized lighting
    4 prods: 4 UG dir; 5 UG des; budget $0-$500
9 Workshops/Readings: 1 Fac dir; 8 UG dir; budget $0-100
Facility was built in 1974, renovated in 1994; includes scene shop, costume shop, CAD facility, dance studio, rehearsal studio, design studio, 3 classrooms
A non-departmental student run organization presents 8 productions per year in which majors participate. 12 student written plays have been produced in the last two years.
Connection with Theatre Cedar Rapids and Cedar Rapids Opera Theatre. Students have opportunities for internships in tech and/or acting roles.

DESCRIPTION

Noted Faculty: Susan Wolverton, MFA Design; Steven Marc Weiss, PhD, Acting, Directing; Dennis Barnett, Phd History and Acting

Guest Artists: Leslie Charipar, Director; Ellen Lewis, Playwright; Tim Miller, Artist

The Theatre Arts program at Coe College allows students to put the theories, skills, and content they learn in the classroom into practice on the stage. In the context of the liberal arts setting, students explore all aspects of theatre (Acting, Design, Directing, Dramaturgy) and are encouraged to study one of these aspects in depth. It is the mission of the program to enrich the cultural life of the college and enhance the educational experiences of all students of the college. Play auditions and entry level courses are open to all students. Student direction and design opportunities exist for majors. Theatre students take advantage of off-campus and/or internship options in New York, Chicago, Washington D.C. and London. The department also sponsors a national playwriting contest biennially which brings theatre professionals to the college to work with students, and serves to foster new work for the stage. Coe's program prepares majors for graduate study and/or professional work in theatre.

Cornell College

Mark Hunter, Chair
Dept. of Theatre & Speech
Cornell College
Mount Vernon, IA 52314
DEPT: (319) 895-4516
MAIN: (319) 895-4000
(800) 747-1112

1,200 Tot Enr.; highly compet
Block Plan
16 Majors; ACTF
T: $26,100/$6,970 R&B
SMALL PROGRAM
theatre@cornellcollege.edu
www.cornellcollege.edu

DEGREES OFFERED

BA/BS in Theatre; BS in Communications.; Th/Speech Education Certification. Declare major in sophomore year.

ADMISSION & FINANCIAL INFORMATION

Average is top 18% of class, 3.4 GPA, 50% have ACT scores of 23-28; 75% accepted; Prog. admits all applics. Schols. avail, based on academics, leadership. Merit awards in Art Music, Theatre.

FACULTY AND CLASSES OFFERED

2 Full-Time, 3 Part-Time: 4 MFA

A. (3/4 FT) Intro to Theatre-1/Y; Theatre History-4/O; Shakes-2/O; Dramatic Lit-4/OX; Playwriting-2/O; Topics course-1/O

B. (7/8 FT, 2 PT) Acting-2/Y; Musical Theatre-2/YX; Directing-2/Y; Topics course-1/O

C. (3/8 FT) Principles of Des-1/O; Tech Prod'n-1/O; Costume Construction-1/O; cr. equiv. of 1 semester hr for production work.

FACILITIES AND PRODUCTIONS

MAINSTAGE: 328 seats, limited fly space. 2 prods: 1 Fac dir/des; 1 Fac dir/UG des, 1 UG dir/des; alternate with Guest artist to direct or design; budget $3000-5000

SECOND STAGE: flexible

2-3 stud dir/des prods; budget $0-100

4-6 stud dir/des Workshops/Readings; budget 0-$25

Facility was built in 1938; includes scene shop, costume shop, dance studio, classroom.

There are informal links & internships available with Riverside Theatre in Iowa City (during the academic year), Old Creamery Theatre in Garrison, IA (summer-AEA). Summer work, internships encouraged.

DESCRIPTION

Guest Artists: Geoffrey Reeves, RSL/LAMDA; Ron Clark and Jody Hovland, Riverside Theatre.

The theatre program at Cornell College emphasizes active, hands-on participation in theatre production with-

in the context of a liberal arts education. The major includes 8 courses, including at least some exposure to acting, directing, design/tech, and history/literature. Majors are also required to participate actively in a variety of areas. The production schedule is ambitious for a small college, and all students, including non-majors, are encouraged to participate. Academic credit is available for production work; independent study opportunities are abundant. Virtually every mainstage show has at least one student designer, and mainstage directing opportunities exist. First-year students are often cast in major roles. The program is not specifically pre-professional, but many students enter professional careers or major graduate programs after graduation.

Dordt College

Jeri Schelhaas, Chair
Theatre Arts Dept.
Dordt College
Sioux Center, IA 51250
DEPT: (712) 722-6434
jschel@dordt.edu
http://www.dordt.edu.dept/ta
ADMISSIONS: 498 4th Ave. NE, Sioux Center, IA 51250
(712) 722-6080

1,500 Total Enr.; competitive
4 Majors; ATHE
Semester System
T: $19,900/$5,460 R&B
FAX: (712) 722-1185
SMALL PROGRAM

admissions@dordt.edu

DEGREES OFFERED

BA (General) in Theatre (4). Declare major in freshman or soph. year; 2003 granted 2 degrees.

ADMISSION & FINANCIAL INFORMATION

Min. 17 units of HS credits, min. GPA of 2.25, ACT score of 19 or above or SAT of 920 or above. 90% admitted to inst, 9 out of 10 to theatre program. Schols. for incoming Freshmen for majors only - Theatre Activitiy Schol, based on experience, GPA and teacher recommendation; Koldenhoven Schol. based on GPA, supporting essay; Alons Schol., based on GPA, supporting essay.

FACULTY AND CLASSES OFFERED

2 Full-Time, 2 MFA/MA; 3 Staff

A. (1 PT) Intro to Theatre-1/O; Dramatic Lit-3/Y; Dramatic Crit-1/X; Theatre History-3/Y; Shakes-1/X; Playwriting-1/O

B. (1 FT, 1 PT) Acting-3/O; Voice/Speech-1/O; Movement-1/O; Singing-2/X; Directing-1/Y; Stage Combat-1/O

C. (1 FT) Prins of Des-1/X; Set Des.-1/O; Tech Prod-1/O

FACILITIES & PRODUCTIONS

MAINSTAGE: 414 seats, computerized lighting
2 prods: Fac dir/Fac des; budget $4,500

SECOND STAGE: 120 seats, electronic lighting
3 prods: 2 Fac des, 3 UG dir, 1 UG des; budget $50-1500

1 Workshop/Reading; budget $200

Facility built in 1975, last renovated in 2000; includes scene, costume, welding shops, sound studio, CAD facility, dance studio.

6 student-written plays produced in the last two years.

Relationship with Theatre and Company & Kitchener Ontario Canada. Internships for full semester in dramaturgy, theatre management, and technical theatre. Informal relationships with Kentucky Shakespeare Festival (KY) and Creede Repertory Theatre.

DESCRIPTION

Noted Faculty: Jeri Schelhaas, Acting, Voice; April Hubbard, Directing/History.

Guest Artists: David Gaines, LeCoq Clown, Katharine Wedner, Academy for Classical Acting.

Dordt College offers a distinctive, practical Christian vision of the theatre. Our program features a core theatre program and seven areas of emphasis, each intended to develop your skills towards a particular career area. Our major is also thoroughly grounded in a liberal arts program, so that you are well prepared as a Christian artist to serve others in a wide range of settings. Our production season covers a broad range of styles and periods. Student-written and student-directed work is given the active support of the department. We are active in the ACTF, CITA, and ATHE. Student actors in our program have regularly succeeded in the Irene Ryan Acting Competition. The faculty and staff in our department are award-winning, active professionals with a wide network of contacts to serve you. Come and share in our vision!

Drake University

John Pomeroy, Chair	5,100 Total Enr.; competitive
Dept. of Theatre	68 Majors
25th & University	Semester System
Drake University	T: $19,100
Des Moines, IA 50311	R&B: $5,700 +
	$220 tech. & activities fees

DEPT: (515) 271-4031   FAX: (515) 271-2558
www.drake.edu/artsci/theatre/DrakeTheatreHomePage.html
ADMISSIONS: 2507 Univ.   (800) 44-DRAKE x 3181
www.drake.edu/du/admissions.html FAX: (515) 271-2831

DEGREES OFFERED

BA theatre (10); BFA in Theatre-Acting (26), Theatre-Design (10), Theatre-Directing (3), Musical Theatre (17), Theatre Education (2). Declare major in freshman year; 2006 granted 18 degrees.

ADMISSION & FINANCIAL INFORMATION

2.5 GPA, 21 ACT; 92% admitted to inst, 7 out of 10 to th. program. Aud/Int/Portfolio req. for schols. Usually about 10-12 talent awards are made to each freshman class. They are based on auditions and portfolio review. Video tapes may be submitted if student is unable to audition in person.

FACULTY AND CLASSES OFFERED

7 Full-Time: 2 PhD, 3 MFA/MA, 1 Prof. w/o adv. degree; 1 Staff

A. (1 FT) Intro to Theatre-1/Y; Theatre History-2/Y; Shakes-2/Y; Playwriting-1/Y

B. (3 FT) Acting-2/Y; Voice/Speech-2/Y; Movement-2/Y; Mime-1/O; Musical Th-1/Y; Directing-2/Y; Dance-3/Y; Stage Combat-1/O

C. (2 1/2 FT) Prins of Des-1/O; Set Des.-1/Y; Cost Des-1/Y; Ltg. Des-1/Y; Tech Prod-1/Y; Cost Constr-1/Y; Cost Hist-1/Y; Make-up-2/Y; Stage Mgmt-1/Y

D. (1/2 FT) no courses listed

FACILITIES & PRODUCTIONS

MAINSTAGE: 460 seats, fly space, proscenium; computerized lighting. 2 prods: 2 Fac dir/des; budget $4,000-5,000

SECOND STAGE: 125 seats, computer. & electronic lighting

6 prods: 3 Fac dir; 2-4 UG dir/des; budget $2,000-2,500

THIRD STAGE: Experimental space; 45 seats, electronic lighting

Facility was built in 1972; includes scene shop, costume shop, CAD facility, dance studio, rehearsal studio, classroom.

8 student -directed experimental pieces done last year; one student written film produced.

DESCRIPTION

Noted Faculty: Deena Conley, Acting, Directing, Th. Hist.; John Holman, Scenic, Light, Sound Des.; John Pomeroy, Technical Dir, Lighting; Josie Poppen, Costume, Make-up, Design; Clive Elliott, Acting, Voice, Directing. Michael Rothmayer, Acting, Directing; Professor: Tony Humichouser, Dance, Movement, Musical Theatre

Are you ready to act, dance, design and direct? In the Drake Theatre Arts Department students begin learning the art of theatre their first year, and we're not just talking about the classroom. With performances each year, all students have the opportunity to practice their passions, whether it be acting, directing, design or playwriting. Drake theatre enables students to design, direct, write and act in plays that are entirely student-produced.

Graceland University

Rebecca M. Foster, Coord of Theatre	1,200 Tot. Enr.; compet.
Dept. of Theatre	44 Majors
Graceland University	Sem.ester System
University Ave.	T: $17,900/$$6,000 R&B
Lamoni, IA 50140	DEPT: (641) 784-5265
mcgraw@graceland.edu	FAX: (641) 784-5480
www.graceland.edu	SMALL PROGRAM

ADM: 1 University PL., Lamoni, IA 50140
(800) 346-9208   FAX: (641) 784-5487

DEGREES OFFERED

BA in Theatre-Performance (27), Design (7), Arts and Stage Mgmt. (2), Speech and Theatre Education (5), Dramaturgy (1), Technical Directing (2). Declare major in sophomore year

ADMISSION & FINANCIAL INFORMATION

Two of the following: ACT 21/SAT 960, GPA 2.0, upper 50% of graduating class; 62% accepted to the university; 7 out of 10 to the theatre program; audition req. for actors. Student may audition for a theatre grant by performing a 2 minute monologue. Grants are awarded on financial need and individual contribution to the department.

FACULTY AND CLASSES OFFERED

2 Full-Time, 1 Part-Time:, 3 MFA/MA

A. (1/2 FT, 1/2 PT) Intro to Theatre-2/Y; Theatre History I & II-2/O; Dramatic Lit-2/O; Shakespeare-1/X; Playwriting-1/O; Trends in Contemporary Theatre-1/O

B. (1/2 FT, 1/2 PT) Intro to Acting-1/Y; Scene Analysis-1/Y; Directing I & II-1/O; Makeup, Audition Tech, Dialects, Period Styles, Senior Seminar (2 sem.)

C. (1/2 FT) Intro 2 Stagecraft-1/O; Set Des-1/O; Cost Des-1/O; Ltg. Des-1/O; Tech Prod-1/O; Make-up-1/O; Stage Mgmt-1/O; Collaboration in Theatre-1/O; Environments in the Theatre-1/Y

D. (1/2 FT) Arts Mgmt-1/O

FACILITIES & PRODUCTIONS

MAINSTAGE: 800 seats, fly space, computerized sound and lighting systems, 1 Fac dir/des prods.

SECOND STAGE: Flexible black box theatre, 150 seats, computerized sound and lighting systems, 2 Fac dir/1 Fac des production, 1 UG des production.

24 UG dir/des Workshops/Readings

Facility was built in 1983; includes scene shop, costume shop, movement/dance studio, 1 rehearsal studio, Make-up dressing room, 10 voice practice rooms, sound/computer room, 2 classrooms.

A non-departmental, student-run producing organization presents 12 prods per year in which dept. majors participate. 4 student-written plays produced in the last 2 yrs.

DESCRIPTION

Graceland University is a 4 year private, liberal arts institution located in southern Iowa. Its 1,200 students come from 44 states and 34 different countries, making Graceland a unique place to study. The theatre program is extremely active and challenges its majors to focus on process rather than product with roles and assignments given to students based on work ethic as opposed to raw talent. Students come to Graceland intent on receiving a broad theatre education during the first two years, before moving on to precise areas of concentration during the last two years. Graduates intent upon a professional theatre career have found homes at Glimmer Glass Opera Company, Utah Shakespeare Festival, American Academy of Dramatic Arts, Yale School of Drama, Center Stage, and various summer stock/repertory companies around the country. The department is committed to the education of the student as a theatre professional who is not only learned about the history, literature, and theories of theatre, but also aware of the contemporary trends in theatre, both in literature and in technology. Freshman majors begin their course of study in a unique class called Theatre Focus, where students are challenged to evaluate their views on theatre and to theorize as to the future of the art form. Those opinions are revisited during the senior year in two semester seminar courses where students are asked to write their personal manifesto of theatre. Graceland theatre is excited about their current direction and is eager to greet every student interested in theatre with a personal approach indicative of a small university.

Grinnell College

Lesley Delmenico, Chair
Department of Theatre
P. O. Box 805
Grinnell College

Grinnell, IA 50112-0805
DEPT: (641) 269-3064
ADM: www.grinnell.edu

1,300 T. Enr.; highly compet.
Semester System
26 Majors
SMALL PROGRAM
T: 30,192 r&b:8,030
ADM: (641) 269-4000
www.grinnell.edu/theatre
www.grinnell.admission.asp

DEGREES OFFERED

BA in General Theatre (26)
Declare major in sophomore year; 2001 granted 10 degrees.

ADMISSION & FINANCIAL INFORMATION

Program admits all applicants

FACULTY AND CLASSES OFFERED

4 Full-Time, 1 Part-Time; 3 PhD; 1 MFA/MA; 1 Staff

A. (1 1/2 FT) Intro to Theatre-1/Y; Dramatic Lit-1/Y; Dramatic Crit.-1/Y; Shakes-1/X; Playwriting-O

B. (2 1/2) Acting-Y; Mime, etc.-1/O; Stage Combat-1/O; Directing-1/Y; Dance-1/Y

C. (1 FT) Prins of Des-1/Y; Set Design-1/O; Ltg. Des-1/O; Cost Des-1/O; Cost. Hist-1/O; Tech Production-1/Y; Stage Mgmt-1/O; Make-up-1/O

D. Arts Mgmt.-1/O; Legal: Contracts, etc.-X; Devel./Grant Writing-X; Budget/Accounting-X

FACILITIES AND PRODUCTIONS

MAINSTAGE: 435 seats, computerized lighting
3 Fac dir, 2 Fac des prods; budget $4,500-7,000

SECOND STAGE: 128 seats, computerized lighting. 14 prods: 1 Fac dir, 2 Fac des, 12 UG dir/des; budget $4,500-7,000

8 UG dir/des Workshops/Readings; budget $150-500

Original facility built 1963, renovated in 1998; scene shop, costume shop, welding shop, CAD facility, 1 movement/dance studio, 1 rehearsal studio, 1 design studio, 2 classrooms.

A non-departmental, student-run, producing organization presents 1-3 prods. per year in which dept. majors participate. 3 student-written plays produced in the last two years.

Connection with Grinnell Productions which was set up as a semi-professional non-profit arts company, by Pip Gordon (Chair) - students have opportunity to participate in every level of production and are often stage managers, assistants, actors, technicians. 2 of our present students are interns in aaarts management with Grinnell Productions.

DESCRIPTION

Noted Faculty: Pip Gordon, Design; Ellen Mease, Dramaturgy; Lesley Delmenico, Performance Studies; Chris Connelly, Director.

Guest Artists: Wendy Knox, Director; Michael Sokolov, Director, Fight Master; Geoff Curley, Set Designer; Annie Bien, Playwright; Erin Howell Gritch, Costume Desighner; Leonard Curtis, Set Designer; Bob Sunderman, Set Designer; Becky Snider, Lighting Designer.

Grinnell is a liberal arts college and all students are expected to take in the three major divisions (Humanities, Science and Social Studies) and a variety or disciplines. Beyond this, majors acquire a general knowledge in all aspects of the arts and actively participate in performances. They are also encouraged to study one of these aspects in depth (Acting, Directing, Dramaturgy, Design) and undertake ambitious projects such as directing or designing a play. Individual or group independent projects in performance, playwriting and drama and topics of special interest (political theatre, genre study, experimental theatre) are frequently undertaken. An off-campus semester of intensive theatre training with the National Theatre Institute in Waterford, CT is available for selected students each year; Theatre students take special advantage of theatre professionals and courses during the Grinnell-in-London off-campus program each fall.

Iowa State University

Jane Cox, Director of Theatre
ISU Theatre
210 Pearson Hall
Iowa State University
Ames, IA 50011
DEPT: (515) 294-9766
jfcox@iastate.edu
ADMISSIONS: 100 Alumni Hall, ISU, Ames IA 50011
(800) 262-3810
admissions@iastate.edu

26,845 Total Enr.; competitive
Semester System
44 Majors; ATHE
T: $6,161/$6,716 R&B
O-ST T: $16,919/$6,716 R&B
FAX: (515) 294-2652
www.iastate.edu

FAX: (515) 294-2592

DEGREES OFFERED

BA in Performing Arts: Acting/Directing, Design, Dance, Theatre Studies. Declare major in fresh/soph year.

ADMISSION & FINANCIAL INFORMATION

Top 50% of grad. class, satisfactory ACT scores. 83% of applics admitted to inst.; Th. prog. generally admits all applics, Int. required. The program awards scholarships of between $500 and $1200 per year to students of outstanding promise and or achievement.

FACULTY AND CLASSES OFFERED

8 Full-Time: 2 PhD, 7 MFA/MA; 2 Staff

A. (1 FT) Intro to Theatre-2/Y; Th. Hist.-2/Y; Shakes-3/Y+X; Dramatic Lit-1-2/Y+X; Playwriting-1/Y; African American Th-1/Y

B. (4 FT) Acting-3/Y; Movement-1/O; Singing-1/Y+ Private Voice; Directing-2/Y; Voice/Speech-1/Y; Mime/Mask-1/O; Musical Theatre-2/Y; Stage Combat-1/O; Styles-1/O; Theatre For Youth-1/Y; Minority Theatre Workshop-1/Y; Touring Th. Workshop-1/Y

C. (3 FT) Principles of Design-2/Y; Cost Design-1/Y; Tech. Production-2/Y; Costume History-1/X; Stage Mgmt-1/Y; Lighting Design-1/Y; Cost Construction-1/O; Make-up-1/Y; Scene Painting-1/O

D. Arts Management-1/O

FACILITIES AND PRODUCTIONS

MAINSTAGE: 450 seats, computerized lighting
  6 prods: 6 Fac dir, 8 Fac des, 2 Guest des, 7 UG des; budget $5,000-8,000 (1 @ $40,000)

SECOND STAGE: 125 seats, computer. lighting. 4 prods: 2 Fac dir/des, 2 UG dir, 10 UG des; budget $500-1,000

Facility was built in 1974, renovated in 1994; includes scene shop, costume shop, sound studio, CAD facility, video studio, rehearsal studio, design studio, 2 dance studios, classrooms.

A non-departmental, student-run producing organization presents 4-6 prod. per year in which majors participate. 7 student-written plays produced in the last two years.

DESCRIPTION

Guest Artists: Barbara Field, Susan Gregg, Malcolm Tulip, Christopher Bayes, Dan Hurlin, Ming Cho Lee, Jennifer Tipton, Myrna Colley-Lee.

Iowa State University offers undergraduates a liberal arts education in performing arts. The core curriculum of the BA in Performing Arts explores the full range of world theatre, music and dance. Students declare an emphasis in either theatrical design, acting/directing or dance. Our students have a solid foundation in the performing arts designed to prepare them for graduate or pre-professional theatre training programs. The mainstage season of five or six productions regularly features original work commissioned by our program from playwrights both nationally and internationally recognized (Barbara Field, Karim Alrawi), Musical Theatre and Minority Theatre Workshop productions. A parallel Second Stage season allows student directors, designers and actors to explore new and challenging work. Our program engages up to five distinguished guest artists per year to work with our students and faculty. Recent graduates have gone on to work with the Oregon Shakespeare Festival, American Player's Theatre, New Mexico Repertory Theatre, Minneapolis Children's Theatre, Skylight Opera Theatre, and Wisdom Bridge Guthrie Theatre and Santa Fe Opera.

University of Iowa

Alan MacVey, Chair
Department of Theatre Arts
107 Theatre Building, U. of Iowa
Iowa City, IA 52242-1705
(319) 335-2700

20,738 Total Enr.; compet
Semester System
T:$6,293 -ST $9,465 r&b $7,250
250 Majors; NAST, U/RTA
admissions@uiowa.edu

DEGREES OFFERED

BA in Liberal Arts/Theatre (250); MFA in Acting (16), Directing (4), Playwriting (11), Design (7), Stage Management (8), Dramaturgy (3). Declare major in freshman, sophomore year; 2005 granted 40 UG, 8 Grad degrees.

ADMISSION & FINANCIAL INFORMATION

UG program admits all applic's.; Grad Program requires audition/portfolio review/play submission; admits 1 of 8 applicants. Schols available for incoming students based on ability; for continuing undergrad and grad students offered on the basis of achievement. Special scholarships available from the University for minority students.All out of state grad. students recieve financial support.

FACULTY AND CLASSES OFFERED

14 Full-Time, 6 Part-Time: 5 PhD, 4 MFA/MA, 6 Prof. w/o adv. degree; 4 Staff

A. (4 FT, 1 PT) Intro to Theatre-2/Y; Theatre History-3/Y; Shakes-3/X; Dramatic Lit-12/X; Dramatic Criticism-4/O; Playwriting-8/O; Script Analysis-2/Y; 12 academic type theatre courses on different cultures, specialized studies, etc.

B. (6 FT, 2 PT) Acting-6/Y,; Voice/Speech-3/Y; Movement-3/Y; Mime/Mask/etc.-1/O; Singing-X; Directing-2/Y; Stage Combat-2/O

C. (4 FT,3/4 PT) Prins of Des-1/Y; Set Design-5/O; Cost Des-5/O; Ltg Des-5/O; Tech Prod'n-2/Y; Cost Constr-3/O; Cost Hist-3/O; Make-up-1/Y; Stage Mgmt-2/Y; Sc Painting-1/O; Studio in Theatrical Design-1/Y

FACILITIES AND PRODUCTIONS

MAINSTAGE: 477 seats, fly space, computerized lighting. 3 prods: 3 Fac dir, 1 Fac dir, 1 Guest des; budget $15,000

SECOND STAGE: 150-190 seats, fly space, computerized lighting. 2-6 prods: 2 Fac dir/des, 0-4 Grad dir/des; budget $7,500-11,000

THIRD STAGE: 144 seats, fly space, computerized lighting, budget $7,000 to $9,000

6-20 Grad and UG dir/des prods

24-40 Grad and UG dir Workshops/Readings; budget $75-300

Mainstage facility was built in 1936, the two other theatres in 1985; scene, costume & props shops, sound studio, 4 rehearsal studios, 1 design studio, 2 classrooms, computer assisted design laboratory.

A non-departmental, student-run organization presents a production each weekend. 50 student-written plays produced in last 2 years.

Connection with Iowa Summer Rep.(A URTA Co. gives Equity points) Sponsored by department; students may audition and apply for artistic and technical staff.

DESCRIPTION

Noted Faculty: Eric Forsythe, Alan MacVey, John Cameron, Acting/Directing; Loyce Arthur, Bryon Winn, Design.

Guest Artists: Ann Bogart, Erik Ehn, Nicholas Meyer, Laurie Anderson, Mary Beth Hurt, Naomi Ilzuka. We have many guests in residence each year for periods of 1-15 weeks.

The undergraduate major in theatre rests on the belief that the best way to develop future artists is to expose them to rigorous professional practice within the framework of a liberal arts education. Workshop courses in all areas of theatre are complemented by classes in literature and history, and students are encouraged to explore a range of courses throughout the University. Dozens of productions each year provide additional opportunities to learn theatre craft and develop a personal artistic vision. The MFA programs are dedicated to the creative development of professional theatre artists. The programs in acting, directing, playwriting and design are rigorous and oriented toward the professional. The department is especially supportive of new work for the stage. Led by the Playwrights Workshop, student writers normally present at least 25 new plays each year, and 25 additional readings. The Playwrights Festival in May draws together the work of the year in a week of new plays.

University of Northern Iowa

Eric Lange,
Department Head
University of Northern Iowa
Cedar Falls, IA 50614-0371
DEPT: (319) 273-6386
Donna.crayne@uni.edu
FAX: (319) 273-6390
ADMISSIONS: Gilchrist 120, Cedar Falls, IA 50614-0018
(319) 273-2281

13,500 Total Enr.; not compet.
Semester System
103 Majors; ATHE
T: $6,190/$6,050 R&B
O-ST T: $14,282/5,260 r&b
www.uni.edu/theatre
www.uni.edu
admissions@uni.edu

DEGREES OFFERED

BA in Theatre - Performance Emphasis, Creative Drama, Theatre for Youth, Design & Prod.. Declare major in freshman year.

ADMISSION & FINANCIAL INFORMATION

Upper one-half of high school class, complete college prep curriculum; 90% accepted; Theatre program admits 8 out of 10 UG.. Activity scholarships available in varying amounts, new student auditions held first Friday of March.Competitive audition or design portfolio presentation and interview required.

FACULTY AND CLASSES OFFERED

8 Full-Time, 3 Part Time, 4 PhD, 8 MFA/MA; 1 Staff

A.   (1 FT,1 PT) Intro to Th.-1/Y; Theatre History-3/Y; Shakes-1/X; Dramatic Lit-2/Y; Dramatic Criticism-2/Y; Playwriting-1/O;

Fundamentals of Theatre-1/Y

B.   (2 FT,2 PT) Acting/Scene Study-5/Y; Voice/Speech-2/Y; Movement-2/Y; Mime, etc.-1/O; Singing-1/X; Musical Th-1/X; Directing-3/Y; Stage Combat-1/O; Dance-1/X

C.   (5 FT, 1 PT) Prins of Des-2/YO; Set Des-1/YO; Cost Des- 1/YO; Ltg Des-1/YO; Tech Prod'n-2/Y; Cost Constr-1/Y; Make-up-1/Y; Stage Mgmt- 1/Y

D.   (1 PT) Arts Management-1/O; Marketing/Promotion-2/X; Legal Contracts/Copyright-1/X

FACILITIES AND PRODUCTIONS

MAINSTAGE: 550 seats, fly space, computerized lighting
   2 prods: 2 Fac dir, 6 Fac des, 4 UG des; budget $5,000-8,000

SECOND STAGE: 125 seats, computerized lighting.
   2 prods: 2 Fac dir, 5 Fac des, 1 Grad des, 3 UG des; budget $4,000-6,000

4 Fac dir Workshop/Reading; budget $100-500

Facility was built in 1978; includes scene shop, costume shop, welding shop, CAD facility, sound studio, dance studio, rehearsal studio, design studio.

A non-departmental, student-run organization presents 4-6 productions per year in which majors participate.

DESCRIPTION

Noted Faculty: Jay Edelnant, Directing; Gretta Berghammer, Theatre for Youth; Carol Colburn, Costume Design.

Guest Artists: Kim Hines, Director; Harriette Pierce, Director; Matt Cook Anderson, Scenic Designer; Wieslaw Gorski, Playwright.

The University of Northern Iowa Dept of Theatre Program provides an intensive study of theatre within a liberal arts context. Performance and production is viewed as a studio extension of class work. Degree programs in performance and design are geared toward preparation of students to enter professional training programs. General degree programs in broad, humanities oriented approach to theatre.

KANSAS

Bethany College

Greg LeGault
Theatre Program
421 N. 1st St.
Bethany College
Lindsborg, KS 67456
(785) 227-3380x 8257
FAX: (785) 227-2860
Admission: (785) 227-3311 3380
(800) 826-2281

650 Total Enr.; not compet.
3-4 Majors
Semester System
T: $16,900/$5,500 R&B
SMALL PROGRAM
www.bethanylb.edu
legaultg@bethanylb.edu
Fax: 1-785-227-2004

DEGREES OFFERED

Theatre Minor.

ADMISSION & FINANCIAL INFORMATION

HS GPA 2.5, ACT 19, SAT combined 750. Aud/Int. req. Theatre Performance Awards: incoming students audition (live or via videotape), letters of reference, GPA. Students who remain consistently active in theatre prods/activities will be continued for add'l years.

FACULTY AND CLASSES OFFERED

1 Full-Time: 1 PhD

A. (1 FT) Intro to Theatre-1/O; Dramatic Lit-1/X; Th Hist-1/O; Shakes-1/X;

B. (1 FT) Acting-1/Y; Directing-1/O, Musical Th.-Inter-term

C. (1 FT) Design/Tech Survey-1/Y

FACILITIES & PRODUCTIONS

MAINSTAGE: 243 seats, electronic lighting
3-4 prods: 2-3 Fac dir/des; budget $2,000-6,000

SECOND STAGE: Flex seats
2-3 prods: 2-3 UG/des; budget; $200-400

Workshops/Readings; budget $200-400

Facility was built in 1974.

DESCRIPTION

Noted Faculty: Norman E. Schroder, Director.

Bethany College is, first and foremost, a four year liberal arts college. As such, this small theatre program is not structured to provide specialized theatrical training, but rather to provide a diverse theatre background within a broader liberal arts framework.

Kansas State University ··················

Kate Anderson,
  Director of Theatre
Nichols Hall 129
Kansas State University
Manhattan, KS 66506
DEPT: (785) 532-6875
FAX: (785) 532-3714
katjef@ksu.edu
ADMISSIONS: 119 Anderson
www.ksu.edu

22,700 Total Enr.; not compet.
Semester System
95 UG, 14 G Majors;
  NAST, ATHE
T: $5,250/$6,084 R&B
O-ST T: $14,336/$6,084 R&B
www.ksu.edu/sctd
kstate@ksu.edu
(785) 532-6250
FAX: (785) 532-6393

DEGREES OFFERED

BA/BS in Acting (60), Design (7), Tech Theatre (8), Stage Mgmt. (6), Theatre Mgmt (3), Drama Therapy (6); Hist/Lit (5), Declare major in freshman year; 2001 granted 18 UG, 8 Grad degrees.

ADMISSION & FINANCIAL INFORMATION

Qualified Admissions: ACT 21 or top third of class for Kansas hs grads, Out-of-State: top 50% of hs class, ACT scores; Accept 80% to inst; Th prog admits all UG applicants, 10 out of 20 Grad. Grad: req's GPA 3.0, prefer interview, letters of rec. Several Theatre Scholarships for Freshmen and transfer students. ACT of 20, audition, letters of recommendation, audition or interview for Tech/Design/Management; Must declare as Theatre Major.

FACULTY AND CLASSES OFFERED

11 Full-Time: 3 PhD, 9 MFA/MA; 2 Staff

A. (2 FT) Intro to Theatre-1/Y; Theatre History-2/Y; Dramatic Lit-4/Y; Playwriting-3/Y; Shakespeare (Literature)-1/X; Drama Therapy-3/Y.

B. (3 FT, 1 PT) Acting-4/Y; Voice-1/O; Mvmt-1/Y; Singing-2/X; Directing-2/Y; Movement-1/Y; Dance-4/Y; Mask-1/O; Shakes (Acting).-1/O; Stg. Combat-1/O; Creative Drama-1/Y

C. (5 FT) Prins. of Des.-1/Y; Set Design-2/Y; Cost. Design-2/Y; Ltg

Des-2/Y; Tech Prod'n-2/Y; Cost. Constr-1/Y; Cost. Hist-2/X; Make-up-1/Y; Stage Mgmt-1/Y; Cost. Crafts-2/O

D. (1 FT) Theatre Management-1/Y

FACILITIES AND PRODUCTIONS

MAINSTAGE: 240-280 seats, computerized lighting/sound

MAINSTAGE II: 1800 seats, fly space, computerized lighting/sound (Mainstage I & II- 5 prods; 5 Fac dir, 13 Fac des (some work on 3-4 shows), 2 Guest des; budget $5,000-20,000)

SECOND STAGE: 100 seats, computerized lighting/sound. 4 prods; 3 Grad dir, 1 UG dir, 8 UG des; budget $350-500

6 Workshops/Readings: 2 Grad dir, 4 UG dir; budget $30-50

Main facility built in 1985 (Second Stage built in 1972, Third Stage renovated in 1996); includes scene, prop, cost. shops; 3 dance studios, CAD facility, 3 rehearsal studios, design studios; 4 classrooms.

2 student-written plays produced in the last two years.

Theatre faculty assist students in finding internships w/professional theatre companies. Several faculty work with professional companies throughout the year.

DESCRIPTION

Noted Faculty: Kate Anderson, Acting; Sally Bailey, Drama Therapy; Dan Davy, Dramatic Lit; Kathy Voecks, Scenic Design, Scott Hansen, Tech Theatre; Charlotte MacFarland, Acting; Marci Maullar Management;Dana Pinkston, Costume Designer; Lew Shelton, Directing; John Uthoff, Lighting Design.

Guest Artists: Craig Benton, Actor; Victor En Yu Tan, Lighting Director; Doug Hosney, Stage Manager; Bob Trump, Costume Patterning; Danila Korogodsky, Set Design; Craig Wolfe, Lighting; Augusta Boal, Drama Therapy; Marina Raytchinova, Set Design; Simona Rybakova, Set Design; Teresa Przybylski, Set Design, Charles Smith, Playwright.

The theatre major at Kansas State University offers students a stimulating intellectual environment as well as an exciting and vital production experience while pursuing a BA, BS or MA degree. The faculty is made up of dedicated teachers and professionals who are devoted to helping the student develop skills in numerous areas of theatre including performance, design, technical production, stage management, and history/dramatic lit. KSU Theatre is one of only a handful of schools in the country to offer a drama therapy specialization. The solid liberal arts education and the extensive production opportunities offered by the program prepares students for unlimited possibilities upon graduation such as: professional internships, graduate study; immediate entry into the professional arena; or other related career options.

University of Kansas

Chuck Berg, Chair
Dept of Theatre & Film,
356 Murphy
University of Kansas
Lawrence, KS 66045
cberg@ku.edu
ADMSSIONS:
adm@ku.edu

21,353 Total Enr.; compet.
Semester System
350 Majors
T: $7,570/$7,370 R&B
O-ST T: $18,674
(785) 864-3511
FAX: (785) 864-5251
www.ku.edu

DEGREES OFFERED

BA,BGS in Film/Media(350); Theatre (125); Theatre& Film (25). MFA in Scene Design (6). PhD/MA in Film/Video (22), Theatre (24).

ADMISSION & FINANCIAL INFORMATION

UG: Appropriate HS diploma and GPA. Grad: GPA 3.2 cum; 3.5 in major. GRE: 600 verbal, 500 math, 650 analytic. Portfolio for designers. 40 out of 50 UG applicants accepted to theatre program, 12 out of 31 to Grad progrm.

FACULTY AND CLASSES OFFERED

16 Full-Time, 3 Part-Times: 12 PhD, 2 MFA/MA; 11 Staff

A. (5 3/4 FT, 2 PT) Intro to Theatre-1/Y; Dramatic Lit-2/O; Theatre History-9/Y; Dramatic Criticism-3/O; Shakes-X; Playwriting-2/Y; Dramaturgy-2/Y; Theory/Crit-6/Y

B. (4 1/2 FT) Acting-5/Y; Voice/Speech-3/Y; Movement-3/Y; Mime, etc.-1/O; Singing-X; Directing-3/Y; Asian & Oriental Mvmt & Theatre-4/Y

C. (4 FT, 1 PT) Prins of Des-2/Y; Set Des-9/Y; Cost Des-1/Y; Ltg Des-8/Y; Tech Prod'n-2/Y; Cost Constr-8/Y; Cost Hist-1/O; Make-up-2/Y

D. Management taught as an independent study.

E. (3 FT) Film Studies and Film Production; 1 T.D.

FACILITIES & PRODUCTIONS

MAINSTAGE: 1100 seats, fly space, computerized/electronic lighting. 5 prods: 5 Fac dir/des, occ. 1 Guest dir/des; budget $4000-6000

SECOND STAGE: 100+ seats, electronic lighting. 1 Fac dir/UG des, 5 UG dir/des, 2 Grad dir/UG des; budget $300-500

WORKSHOPS/READINGS: 18 UG dir, 7 Grad dir; budget $25-100

Facility was built in 1957; includes scene shop, costume shop, prop shop, video studio, rehearsal studio, design studio.

DESCRIPTION

Guest Artists: James Cullinany, director; Yaraslov Molina, Czech Designer.

Separate and distinct channels for undergraduate students provide professional actor training, a liberal arts degree, and sceneographic study. The MA is a traditional academic offering; MFA in Sceneography an interdisciplinary professional training; Ph.D. is a traditional history-theory-criticism program that also requires competence in production.

Wichita State University

Steve D. Peters, Ph.D, Chair
School of Performing Arts
Wichita State University
1845 Fairmont Street
Wichita, KS 67260-0153

14,000 Total Enr.; not compet.
Semester System
105 Majors
T: $130.40/credit hr.
O-ST T: $375.30/credit hr.

DEPT: (316) 978-3368
www.finearts.wichita.edu
ADM: (316) 978-3085

$5,440-$6,680 R&B

DEGREES OFFERED

BA in General Theatre (12); BFA in Acting (Peformance) (48), Technical Theatre/Design (15), Musical Theatre (30). Declare major in 1st-3rd year; 2001 granted 11 UG, 1 Grad degrees.

ADMISSION & FINANCIAL INFORMATION

GPA of 2.0. Theatre program admits 9 out of 10 UG and Grad applicants; UG Audition/Interview required, Grad Interview required. University Scholarships information from Financial Aid Office (316) 978-3430; 20-30 Miller Theatre Scholarships by Audition/Interview, renewable for 4 years, Add'l academic scholarships. based on GPA of 3.0 or above; 10 add'l Theatre Scholarships. awarded each spring by faculty to continuing majors; graduate assistantships.

FACULTY AND CLASSES OFFERED

9 Full-Time: 2 PhD, 9 MFA/MA, 1 Prof. w/out adv. degree; 1 Staff

A. (3 FT, 1 PT) Intro to Theatre-1/Y; Theatre History-1/Y; Dramatic Lit-1/Y; Dramatic Criticism-2/O; Playwriting-2/Y

B. (3 FT, 1 PT) Acting-4/Y; Voice/Speech-4/Y; Movement-1/O; Singing-1/Y; Musical Theatre-1/OX; Directing-2/Y; Stage Combat-1/O.

C. (3 FT) Set Design-2/Y; Cost Des-1/O; Ltg Des-2/Y; Tech Prod'n-1/Y; Cost Constr-1/Y; Cost Hist-1/O; Make-up-1/Y; Stage Management-1/Y

D. (1 FT) Arts Management-1/Y

FACILITIES AND PRODUCTIONS

MAINSTAGE: 600 seats, fly space, computerized lighting 4 Fac dir/des prods, 2 UG des; budget $8,000-20,000

SECOND STAGE: new 100 seat black box, computerized lighting.1 Fac dir, 1-2 Grad dir, 4-16 UG des; budget $900-1,200

THIRD STAGE: 540 seats, fly space, computerized lighting 1 Fac dir; musical budget $20,000-25,000

READERS THEATRE: 4 student dir prods; budget $100-250

Annual National Student Playwriting Contest, winning original plays produced for last 26 years.

Mainstage facility was built in 1936, renovated in 1965, 1980 and 1998; Second Stage built in 1999; Third Stage built in 1963, renovated in 1998; includes scene shop, costume, welding shop, prop shops, dance studio, design studio. New lighting systems in all theatres.

Semi-professional summer theatre: about 14 paid actors and designer/technicians. 3 fac/dir prod, internships, Performing Arts Academy in Theatre and Musical Theatre for high school students.

DESCRIPTION

Noted Faculty: Nyalls Hartman, Acting, Directing; Bela Kiralyfalvi, publication in Aesthetics, Dramatic Theory and Criticism; Joyce Cavarozzi, Acting, Scene Study, Styles; Judith Babnich, Acting, Voice: Feminist and Minority Theatre; Bradford Reissig, Scene & Lighting Design, Scene Painting; Betty Monroe, Cost. Design & Construction, Makeup; Marie Allyn King, Director of Musical Theatre and Opera; Linda Starkey, Associate Director of Musical Theatre.

Guest Artists: Tracy Hinkson, Director; Jane Greenwood,

Ben Edwards, Larry King, and John Lee Beatty, Designers; Cloris Leachman, Toni Gilman, Lynn Schrichte, Dick Walsbacher, Actors.

The BFA in Performing Arts program is designed to prepare students for professional careers. Production is at the very center of the program. Presenting classical, contemporary, and musical theatre as well as original scripts, the theatre has a growing reputation for quality production and academic excellence. The plays are cast at open tryouts and each year involve about 150 students in over 125 acting roles and 400 backstage jobs. WSU Theatre has sponsored a National Playwriting Competition for over 26 years and has produced the winning plays. Students get to work on original scripts wiith the authors and participate in the development. Master classes, workshops and seminars by noted professionals are held each year.

William Inge Theatre Festival ··········

Jon Sidoli, Chair
William Inge Theatre Festival
P.O. Box 708
Independence, KS 67301
(620) 332-5422

1,200 Total Enr.; n. compet.
Semester System
14 Majors

T: $1,500/$4,200 R&B
O-ST: $1,600/4,200 R&B

ADMISSIONS: 1057 WEST COLLEGE BLVD, INDEPENDENCE, KS 67301
(620) 332-5000   www.indycc.edu

DESCRIPTION
AA in Theatre Arts/Performance (12); Certificate in Tech/Playwriting (3). Declare major in first year

ADMISSION & FINANCIAL INFORMATION
Open admissions. Theatre talentships: full tuition and books. By int/aud. Playwriting scholarship: full tuition, books and additional monetary award. By submission of scripts/writing samples.

FACULTY AND CLASSES OFFERED
3 Full-Time: 2 MA/MFA; 1 Prof w/o advanced degree; 3 Staff

A. (1 FT) Intro to Theatre-4/Y; Th History-1/O; Shakes-1/O; Dramatic Criticism-O; Dramatic Lit-2/Y; Playwriting-2/Y

B. (1 FT) Acting-1/Y; Voice/Speech-1/Y; Singing-2/Y; Movement-1/Y; Directing-1/O; Stage Combat-1/O; Musical Theatre-2/Y; Mime, etc-O

C. (1 FT) Prins of Des-1/O; Set Des-1/Y; Cost Des-1/O; Tech Prod-2/Y; Ltg Des-1/Y; Stage Mgmt-1/O; Make-up-1/Y; Costume Const-1/O

FACILITIES & PRODUCTIONS
MAINSTAGE: 300 seats, computerized lighting

3 prods: 2 Fac dir; 1 Fac des; 1 GA des; 1 UG dir/des;budget $1,500

WORKSHOPS/READINGS: 4 Guest dir; budget $250

Facility was built 1970, last renovated in 2007, includes scene shop, CAD facility, rehearsal studio

A non-department student run producing organization presents 4 prods in which majors participate.

Connection with William Inge Center for the Arts (Equity), sponsor of the annual William Inge Theatre Festival. Students participate in workshops and seminars with visiting professional guest artists throughout the year; playwriting students are taught by two new

Inge Center playwrights-in-residence each semester.

DESCRIPTION
Noted Faculty: Jon Sidoli, performance; Peter Ellenstein,directing/musical theater; David Vieira, technical theater

Guest Artists: Susan Angelo, acting; Gigi Bolt, theater mgmt; Michael John Garces, directing; Stefan Haves, physical theater/clowning; Jean Kauffman, musical theater; Blake Robbins, acting; Steven Sapp, spoken word poetry; Sandy Shinner, directing; Adrienne Thompson, acting; Laurie Woolery, musical theater

The William Inge Center for the Arts Theatre Department (WICA) at Independence Community College is an intensive two-year preparatory program designed for transfer to BFA as well as BA programs. There is strong emphasis on preparing quality audition pieces. Students have been accepted to top-tier programs such as the Boston Conservatory, Theatre School at DePaul, SUNY Purchase, and the Hartt School. ICC is home of the William Inge Theatre Festival and WICA, allowing students to work with dozens of professional guest artist lecturers year-round. The Inge Festival brings to campus each spring a nationally renowned playwright and numerous professional theater artists. Previous Inge Festival playwright honorees include Stephen Sondheim, Neil Simon, Arthur Miller, August Wilson, Wendy Wasserstein, Sheldon Harnick, and many more. WICA's Professional Playwriting Certificate is a unique program for freshman and sophomores to work with accomplished playwrights. Students leave WICA having already established numerous industry relationships.

KENTUCKY

Berea College ···························

Verlaine McDonald, PhD, Chair
Dept. of English, Theatre
  & Speech Communications
CPO 2169
Berea College
Berea, KY 40404
FAX: (859) 985-3906
ADM: Office of Admissions, CPO
(859) 985-3000

1,500 Total Enr.; h. compet.
Semester System
26 Majors; ATHE, NAST
T: $776/r&b:$5,492
SMALL PROGRAM
DEPT: (859) 985-3756
verlaine_mcdonald@berea.edu
admissions@berea.edu
www.berea.edu

DEGREES OFFERED
BA in Theatre Arts (23); Declare major in Soph. yr, 2004 granted 6 degrees.

ADMISSION & FINANCIAL INFORMATION
Audition, interview, portfolio required. Sophomore review. Sat or ACT required; admission 80% from Appalachian region; 15% rest of U.S.; 5% foreign; 44% applicants accepted; Theatre program requires aud/int, admits 9 out of 10. All students on work-study/scholarship. Maximum income limitation for admission.

FACULTY AND CLASSES OFFERED
3 Full-Time: 2 PhD, 1 MA/MFA, 2 Prof. w/o adv. deg.

A. (1 FT) Intro to Theatre-1/Y; Theatre History-3/O; Shakes-2/X; Playwriting-1/O

B. (1/2 FT) Acting-2/Y; Voice/Speech-1/O; Directing-1/Y; Singing-1/X; Directing-1/Y; Dance-1/X; Mus. Th-1/XO

C. (1/2 FT) Prins of Des-1/O; Set Des-1/O; Cost Des.-1/O; Tech. Prod.-1/O; Ltg. Des-1/O; Cost. Const-1/O; Make-up-1/O

D. (1/2 FT) Arts Mgmt-1/O

FACILITIES & PRODUCTIONS

MAINSTAGE: 275 seats, computerized lighting. 4 prods: 3 Fac dir/des, 1 Guest dir, 1 UG des; budget $4,000-6,000

THIRD STAGE: 50-80 seats, black box, computerized lighting. 1 UG dir, 4 UG des prods; budget $2,000-4,000

1UG dir Workshop/Reading; budget $500-1,000

Facility was built in 1980; includes scene shop, costume shop, sound studio, design studio, rehearsal studio, classroom.

DESCRIPTION

Noted Faculty: Deborah Martin, PhD, Theatre Marketing, Acting, Directing; Albert DeGiacomo, PhD, Directing, Acting, Playwriting; Shan Ayers, MFA, Design/Technology, Theatre History

Berea College Theatre Laboratory has established Internship/ Apprenticeship relationships with several major professional theatre companies in the region; they include Horse Cave Theatre, The Lexington Children's Theatre and Jenny Wiley Theatre. There are summer-only Apprenticeships/Internships available in all areas: Production, Technical, Performance (Acting), Administration and Design. International connection: The Gate Theatre (London, UK). Stage Management Apprenticeship during the year.

The Berea B.A. theatre program has liberal arts basis and focus. The academic program is complemented by a co-curricular production program which provides students with a solidly balanced practical and theoretical approach to theatre. The production program produces quality work from a wide spectrum of the classical and contemporary canon. The college work-study program is also heavily incorporated into the academic program to further provide students with hands-on training and experience. Majors must be involved in some aspect of work-study in the theatre laboratory. Students are also encouraged to gain practical experience in theatre outside the theatre laboratory through various Internship, Apprenticeship and Study Abroad opportunities available. The combination of solid academic training, quality production work and hands on experience has enabled a large percentage of our graduates to either secure employment in professional theatre and/or acceptance into graduate programs immediately after graduation.

University of the Cumberlands

Dr. Keith Semmel, Chair
Dept of Comm & Theatre Arts
6191 College Station Dr.
Cumberland College
Williamsburg, KY 40769
DEPT.:(606) 539-4494
or 1-800-343-1609 ext 4494

1,331 Total Enr.; compet.
Semester System
16 Majors
T: $6,649 PER SEM
$3,313 R&B PER SEM
SMALL PROGRAM
FAX: (606) 539-4535

ADMISSIONS: 6178 College Station Dr.
(800) 343-1609   www.ucumberlands.edu

DESCRIPTION

BS in Theatre (5). Declare major in second year;

ADMISSION & FINANCIAL INFORMATION

18 ACT, 2.0 GPA, apps. reviewed by committee. Accept 100% to institution; No special req's. for theatre program. Contact Admissions for more info.

FACULTY AND CLASSES OFFERED

2 Full-Time: 1 PhD, 1 MA/MFA; 1 Staff

A. (1/4 FT) Intro to Theatre-1/Y; Th History-1/O; Shakes-X; Dramatic Criticism-X; Dramatic Lit-1/O

B. (1/2 FT) Acting-2/Y; Voice/Speech-X; Singing-X; Movement-X: Directing-1/O; Stage Combat-O

C. (1 FT) Prins of Des-1/O; Set Des-1/Y; Cost Des-1/O; Tech Prod'n-1/Y; Ltg Des-1/O; Stg Mgmt-1/O; Make-up-1/O

D. (1/4) no courses listed

FACILITIES & PRODUCTIONS

MAINSTAGE: 250 seats, computerized lighting. 6 prods: 3 Fac dir/des, 3 Guest dir/des; budget $5,000-7,500

WORKSHOPS/READINGS: 2 Guest dir/des

Facility was built 1999-2000; includes scene shop.

DESCRIPTION

Noted Faculty: Daniel K. Nazworth, Acting/Directing/Management; Maurice Moe Conn, Design/Technical Theatre.

Cumberland College Theatre offers a broad-based degree in order to prepare students to enter graduate study. Our objectives also include: 1) To prepare students who intend to teach drama activities in secondary schools and other community institutions; 2) to provide students with opportunities for creative development and personal expression through drama; 3) to provide a foundation for those students who may choose to seek advanced study toward a career in the performing arts; 4) to foster in students an appreciation of our cultural heritage as it is revealed through dramatic literature; and 5) to foster in students a continuing appreciation for the value and role of the theatre in our society.

Eastern Kentucky University

James R. Moreton, Coord.
Dept of English & Theatre,306 Campbell
EKU Theatre
Richmond, KY 40475-3102
DEPT: (859) 622-1315
FAX: (859) 622-5904
www.eku.edu
ADMISSIONS: SSB, CPO 54
(859) 622-2106
www.eku.edu

15,000 Total Enr.; competitive
Semester System
35 Majors
T: $5,500/$4,500 R&B
O-ST T: $14,000/$4,500 R&B
SMALL PROGRAM
james.moreton@eku.edu

FAX: (859) 622-8024

DEGREES OFFERED

BA in English w/Theatre Option (30), Theatre Teaching Option (3); Students declare major in Sophomore year. 2007 5 UG granted

ADMISSION & FINANCIAL INFORMATION

Open admissions, 18 ACT; transfer 2.0 GPA; 90% accepted by institution; Theatre program admits all applicants; Pearl Buchanan Freshman Scholarship, EKU Theatre Schol.; apply with letter and theatre resume by Apr. 1, decisions made in Spring.

FACULTY AND CLASSES OFFERED

4 Full-Time: 3 MFA, 1 MA; 2 Staff

A. (1 PT) Intro to Th-1/Y; Dramatic Lit-2/X; Th. Hist.-2/O; Shakes-1/X
B. (3 FT) Acting-4/Y; Voice/Speech-1/O; Movemt.-2/Y; Singing-X; Musical Th.-1/O; Directing-1/Y; Stage Combat-1/O
C. (2 FT) Prins of Design-1/O; Set Des.-1/O; Cost. Des.-1/O; Lighting. Des.-1/O; Tech Prod'n-1/O; Cost. Construction-1/O; Make-up-1/O; Stage Mgmt-1/O

FACILITIES & PRODUCTIONS

MAINSTAGE: 356 seats, fly space, computerized lighting. 4 prods: 3-4 Fac dir/des; 0-1 UG des; budget $2500-5000/per show

SECOND STAGE: 137 seats, electronic lighting. 1-2 UG dir/des prods; budget $50-100

Facility was built in 1972; includes scene shop, costume shop, dance studio.

DESCRIPTION

Noted Faculty: Jeffrey Boord-Dill, Keith Johnson, James R. Moreton, Homer W. Tracy (all FT).

The degree programs at Eastern Kentucky University allow for varied emphasis for the individual student. A more generalist view is stressed in the Theatre BA, which leads to graduate study in specific areas after graduation. Obviously, this course study intends to develop a strong foundation in theatre. The Teacher Education Degree Program focuses on training the Secondary School teacher.

Georgetown College · · · · · · · · · · · · · · ·

George McGee, Chair   1,407 Total Enr.; not comp.
Comm. Arts (Speech & Theatre)   Semester System
Box 258, Georgetown College   SMALL PROGRAM
Georgetown, KY 40324   (502) 863-8162
Adm. 400 E. College St.   www.georgetowncollege.edu
admissions@georgetowncollege.edu

DEGREES OFFERED

BA in Communication Arts w/ Theatre emphasis Declare major in junior year.

ADMISSION & FINANCIAL INFORMATION

See www.georgetowncollege.edu.

FACULTY AND CLASSES OFFERED

2 Full-Time: 2 MFA/MA: 1 P/T PhD

A. (1/4 FT) Intro to Th-1/Y; Th Hist-1/Y; Shakes- 1/X; Dram. Lit-1/X
B. (3/4 FT) Acting-2/Y; Voice/Speech-2/Y; Movement-1/O; Mime, etc.-1/O; Singing-2/X; Musical Theatre-1/O; Directing-1/O
C. (1/2 FT) Set Design-1/Y; Tech Prod'n-1/Y; Cost Hist-1/X

FACILITIES AND PRODUCTIONS

MAINSTAGE: 125 seats, electronic lighting

budget $2,000-2,500 per show

Facility was built in 1974; includes scene shop, classrooms.

A non-depart, student-run org. presents one production/year.

DESCRIPTION

A major in Communication Arts (Speech and Theatre) with a liberal arts background insures personal growth and achievement through varied performance opportunities, development of academic and professional skills, and potential career opportunities in diversified fields. Recognizing that each student brings a unique set of needs and abilities to the program, the department tailors a curriculum especially to enhance one's talents and stimulate one's interest. Emphasis is placed upon performance in order to allow students to expand the limits of their abilities.

Murray State University · · · · · · · · · · ·

David Balthrop, Chairman   10,110 Tot. Enr.; competitive
Dept. of Theatre & Dance, 106 FA   Semester System
Murray State University   65 Majors
P. O. Box 9   T: $9,361
Murray, KY 42071   O-ST T: $17,000
DEPT: (270) 809-4421   FAX: (270) 809-4422
www.murraystate.edu/chfa/theatre   SMALL PROGRAM
ADMISSIONS: Sparks Hall, MSU, Murray, KY 42071
(270) 809-3741   www.murraystate.edu

DEGREES OFFERED

BA/BS degrees only. Students declare major in first year. 2007 granted 5 UG degrees.

ADMISSION & FINANCIAL INFORMATION

Completion of pre-college curriculum, top half of graduating class or a 3.0 GPA, composite ACT of 18 +. 80% accepted by institution. Admit 10 out of 12 to theatre program. UG requires audition for actors, interview, portfolio for designers. Department scholarships available, selection process is by aud/int.

FACULTY AND CLASSES OFFERED

6 Full-Time, 3 Part-Time: 8 MFA/MA

A. (1 FT, 2 PT) Intro to Theatre-1/Y; Theatre History-3/Y; Playwriting-1/O; Shakes-1/O
B. (2 FT, 1 PT) Acting/Scene Study-3/Y; Voice/Speech-1/Y; Movement-1/O; Directing-2/Y; Dance-4/Y
C. (3 FT) Set Design-1/O; Cost Des-1/O; Lighting Des-1/O; Cost Constr-2/O; Make-up-1/O; Stage Management-1/O; Tech Prod-1/O
D. Arts Mgmt-1/O

FACILITIES & PRODUCTIONS

MAINSTAGE: 344 seats, computerized and electronic lighting, fly space 6-7prods: 3 Fac dir/des, 1 GA dir; 1 UG des; budget $1,000-$5,000

SECOND STAGE: 55 seats, electronic lighting
12-15 prods: 2 fac dir, 1 fac des, 1 UG des; budget $100-$500

THIRD STAGE: 1200 seats, fly space, electronic lighting,
5 prods: 5 UG dir/des Workshops/Readings; budget $0-100

Facility was built in 1975; renovated in 2005; includes scene shop, costume shop, props shop, welding shop, CAD facility, 1 movement/dance studio, 1 design studio, 1 rehearsal studio, 3 class-rooms.

A non-departmental, student-run organization presents 8-10 productions per year in which majors participate. 15-20 student-written plays produced in the last two years.

DESCRIPTION

Noted Faculty: Lissa Graham, Directing; Brent Merchinger, Design/Tech; David Balthrop, Chair; Des/History; Robert Valentine, Acting/Voice; Jonathon Awori, Acting; Maura Cravey, Design; Betty Brockway, Generalist

Guest Artists: Ross Bolen, Director; Mark Borum, Director; Chrisnelle Stause, Actor

Murray State University is an undergraduate program of 75 majors. Small classes and individualized attention are important aspects of the program. While many of our students go directly into professional areas of entertainment, we emphasize further study upon graduation. Our majors work all across the country beginning while they are attending school. They continue working professionally upon graduation.

Northern Kentucky University

Ken Jones, Chair
Dept. of Theatre & Dance
FA 205 Nunn Dr
Highland Heights, KY 41099
DEPT: (859) 572-5434
jonesk@nku.edu
ADMISSIONS: 4th Fl. AC, NKU, Highland Heights, KY 41099
(859) 572-5220

13,000 Total Enr.; not compet.
Semester System, 220 Majors
T: $3216 (2002-03)
O-ST T: $7464 (2002-03)
FAX: (859) 572-6057

DEGREES OFFERED

BA in Theatre (120); BFA in Acting/Directing (12), Management (6); Playwriting (3); Design-sound, lights, scenery, cost (10), Musical Theatre (8). Declare major in freshman year; 1999 granted 17 degrees

ADMISSION & FINANCIAL INFORMATION

SAT or ACT scores, HS/GED degree. Schol. available by auditions ea. Dec.; in-house merit schol. awarded every yr.; special scholarships for in-house students by application.

FACULTY AND CLASSES OFFERED

12 Full-Time, 13+ Part-Time: 1 PhD, 11 MFA/MA, 4 Staff

A. (2 FT, 2 PT) Intro to Theatre-18/Y; Theatre History-4/Y; Shakes-1/O; Dramatic Lit-4/Y; Dramatic Criticism-1/O; Playwriting-2/Y

B. (4 FT, 3 PT) Acting-10/Y; Voice/Speech-3/Y; Dance-30/Y; Singing-6/Y; Musical Th.-8/Y; Directing-2/Y; Stage Combat-3/Y; Mime & Commedia-1/O

C. (2 FT, 1 PT) Prins of Des-1/Y; Set Design-2/Y; Tech Prod'n-6/Y; Cost Des-2/Y; Cost Constr-4/Y; Cost Hist-2/Y; Ltg Des-2/Y;

Interviewing schools: you ask the questions!

The best way to pick a school is to visit it and see for yourself if you like the atmosphere, the people and the facilities. If that isn't possible, glean what you can from the catalogues, but don't be afraid to make a few phone calls. People connected with a good department should be enthusiastic about it and willing to talk. You should be able to get the names of some recent graduates. And if you want to know what's really happening, strike up a conversation with the departmental secretary. After all, you're investing four years of your life and perhaps as much as $120,000; you have the right to some answers before you send off that tuition check.

Ask the department:

- Who on the faculty is currently working professionally?
- Do you bring in guest directors and designers?
- Do you run a summer theatre, or encourage students to work at other summer theatres? Do you give credit for summer theatre work, or for internships with professional theaters during the school year?
- In how many productions per semester would I be involved?
- Are there any restrictions on first year students' participation in productions?
- What is the departmental casting policy?
- Are there opportunities in the department for students to direct, design, or write plays?
- Does the department encourage students to do projects on their own? Are any student productions given a budget by the department?
- Do you feel your graduates are prepared to enter the profession?
- Is there any sort of alumni network?
- What are your recent graduates doing now? Which grad schools did they get into? How many are working?

Ask their current students:

- Is the casting policy fair and even-handed?
- Have you been taught how to audition or prepare a portfolio?
- Do you feel prepared to get work once you graduate?
- Which areas do you feel are the strengths of the department? The weaknesses?
- Are the faculty members accessible to students?
- Did you get to know the guest artists they brought in?
- On how many productions have you worked since you entered the program?
- If you were looking for a program now, would you choose to come here again?

Ask their graduates:

- Are there any areas in which you feel you now have to make up for a lack of training in school?
- Did you apply to any grad schools? Were you accepted?
- Were you well prepared to start your career by the time you graduated?
- Has it been any advantage to your career that you're an alumni of this particular school?

Then ask yourself:

- Is this the program that will take me where I want to go in four years?
- Can I see myself working well in this environment?
- Do I sense a positive energy and enthusiasm in these people?

Make-up-4/Y; Stage Mgmt-1/O

D. (2 FT, 2 PT) Arts Management-1/O

FACILITIES AND PRODUCTIONS

MAINSTAGE: 320 seats, fly space, computer lighting/sound
    8 Fac dir/des prods; budget $10,000-15,000

SECOND STAGE: 140 seats, computer lighting
    2 Fac dir/UG des prods; budget $2,500

1 Fac dir Workshop/Reading

Facility was built in 1977 and renovated in 1998; includes scene, cost, prop, welding shops, 3 dance studios, sound studio, CAD facility, 1 design studio, 2 rehearsal studios, 3 classrooms.

A non-departmental, student-run, producing organization presents productions in which dept. majors participate. 4 student-written plays produced in the last two years.

Connection with Kincaid Regional Theatre, Lakes Region Summer Theatre, Ensemble Theatre(summer). Our students work professionally while still undergraduates. We are affiliated with a variety of Theatres. Company positions and internships are readily available for our students.

DESCRIPTION

Noted Faculty: Jane Green, Choreography; Ken Jones, Playwriting; Sandra Forman, Vocal Techniques; Terry Powell, Designer; Michael King, Acting; Gretchen Vaughn, Costumes; Christine Jones, Acting; Mark Hardy, Musical Theatre; Jamey Strawn, Musical Theatre.

Northern Kentucky University is an undergraduate program of 150 majors in all fields of theatre study. All the faculty are working professionals as well as professional educators. A majority of students pursue professional degree programs. As many as two thirds of our undergraduates work professionally while in school and our graduates are in all areas of theatre across the country. We have NKU students in television, film, Broadway, Regional Theatre, stock companies, theme parks and local theatres. Small classes and individual attention are strongly emphasized.

University of Kentucky

Nelson Fields, Chair
Department of Theatre
Univ. of Kentucky
114 Fine Arts Building
Rose Street
Lexington, KY 40506-0022
(859) 257-2000

30,000 competitive
106 majors, Semester sys
T: $5,314.50./yr/$4,050 r&b
O-ST T: $12,094.50./yr/$4,050 r&b
(859) 257-3297
fax: (859) 257-3042
Admission: 100 W.D. Funkhouser Bldg,
www.uky.edu/ugadmission

DEGREES OFFERED

BFA in Design Tech, Acting Concentration; BA, MA in General. Students declare major in first year; granted 30 UGrad, 5 Grad .deg.

ADMISSION & FINANCIAL INFORMATION

ACT/SAT and 2.0 required for admission. Some scholarships available for freshmen and upperclassmen.

FACULTY AND CLASSES OFFERED

11 Full-Time:4 PhD, 7 MFA;1 Staff

A. (1/2 FT) Intro to Theatre-2/Y; Theatre History-4/Y; Playwriting-1/Y

B. (4 FT) Acting-4/Y; Voice/Speech-2/Y; Movement-2/Y; Mime, etc.-1/O; Singing-X; Directing-2/Y; Stage Combat-1/O

C. (3 FT) Prins of Des-1/Y; Tech Prod'n-1/Y; Cost Constr-1/Y; Make-

up-1/Y

D. (2 FT) Arts Mgmt-2/O; Development/Grant Writing-1/O

FACILITIES & PRODUCTIONS

MAINSTAGE: 400 seats, fly space, computerized lighting
    5 prods: dir/des; budget $2000-5000

STUDIO: 2 performance spaces, 125 seat and 50 seat, 4-10 prods; grad and UG dir/des

Facility was built in 1948; includes scene shop, costume shop, rehearsal studio, classrooms.

DESCRIPTION

The Department of Theatre's strengths are intrinsically tied to the nature of our discipline. That is, as artists and scholars, we put great emphasis on a collaborative process that produces a unified work or art. Our degree programs reflect a commitment to serving the students in a process which involves them directly to the production of live theatre, as actors, critics, designers, directors, dramaturges, historians, playwrights, and technicians.

Western Kentucky University

Scott Stroot, Head
Dept. of Theatre and Dance
Western Kentucky University
One Big Red Way
Bowling Green, KY 42101
scott.stroot@wku.edu
DEPT: (270) 745-5845
Admis: One Big Red Way, Potter Hall Rm 117
ADM: (270) 745-2551

17,000 Total Enr.; compet.
Semester System
150 Majors
T: $2,376/sem; $800-1,200 R&B
O-ST T: $5,784/sem
    $800-1,200 R&B
FAX: (270) 745-5879
www.wku.edu

DEGREES OFFERED

BA in Theatre (30); BFA in Performing Arts (50).
Declare major in 2nd or 3rd year; 2004 granted 30 degrees.

ADMISSION & FINANCIAL INFORMATION

ACT 20, GPA 2.5, transfers 2.0 GPA,, inst. admits 95% of applicants; Theatre program admits all app's.Annual merit-based scholarships ranging from $150-1000.

FACULTY AND CLASSES OFFERED

8 Full-Time, 5 Part-Time: 5 PhD, 8 MFA/MA.

A. (2 FT, 2 PT) Intro to Theatre-7/Y-O; Theatre Hist-4/Y; Shakes-1/Y; Dramatic Lit-3/YX; Dramatic Criticism-4/YX; Playwriting-1/YX; Text Analysis-1/Y

B. (2 FT) Acting-6/Y; Voice/Speech-3/Y; Movement-3/Y; Singing-3/Y; Musical Theatre-2/Y; Directing-2/Y; Dance-24/Y; Audition Prep-1/Y

C. (2 FT) Set Design-2/Y; Cost Des-1/Y; Ltg Des-2/Y; Tech Prod'n-1/Y; Cost Constr-1/Y; Make-up-1/O; Stage Mgmt-1/Y

D. Arts Management-1/O; Career Seminar-1/Y; Theatre Ed-1/Y

FACILITIES AND PRODUCTIONS

MAINSTAGE: 300 seats, fly space, comput. lighting 6 prods: 5 Fac dir, 3 Fac des, 1 Guest dir, 3 UG des; budget $4,000-11,000

SECOND STAGE: 145 seats, computerized lighting. 20 prods, 20 UG dir, 20 UG des; budget $50-$100

8 WORKSHOPS; 4 FAC DIR, 4 UG DIR; $25-50

Facility was built in 1974 (renovated in 2002) includes scene shop, costume shop, sound studio, 2 dance studios, 2 rehearsal studios, design studio, 3 classrooms, career dev lab.

A non-departmental, student-run organization presents
   8 production per year in which dept. majors participate.
   3 student-written plays produced in the last two years.

Connection with Horse Cave Theatre (summer Equity company): summer internships, tech work, mgmt. Connection with Public Theatre of Kentucky, a small professional theatre in Bowling Green that uses student and faculty directors, actors, des, and techs on a consistent year-round basis.

DESCRIPTION

Noted Faculty: Clifton Keefer Brown, Dance; Dr. Pamela Walden, Dance; Dr. David Young, Acting/Children's Theatre; Tom Tutino, Scene Design; James Brown, Lighting/Sound Design; Scott Stroot, Acting/Directing; Dr. Loren Ruff, Theatre History.

Guest Artists: Bob Sigenfield, Jazz Dance; John Doyle, Director; Thomas Coash, Playwright; Dolores Whiskeyman, Playwright; Charlotte Headrick, Director; Lynnae Lehfeldt, Viewpoints (acting); Irma Del Valle, Afro-Cuban Dance.

WKU offers a 68 hour Performing Arts BFA with concentrations in acting, dance, directing, music-theatre performance, and theatre design and technology, a 42 hour BA in Theatre, designed to include a minor in another discipline, and minors in Theatre, Dance, and Performing Arts Management. All programs are designed to offer a thoughtful balance of theory and practice, featuring courses in drama, history, acting, directing, children's theatre, management, technical theatre, scenic, lighting sound and costume design, dance technique, and choreography. Our intensive production season compliments that curriculum, offering students regular and frequent opportunities to collaborate with peers, faculty and guest artists on a steady variety of theatre, music-theatre and dance productions. Career preparation is also woven firmly into our curriculum, through courses like Audition Prep Workshop, Performing Arts Career Seminar, and independent study Co-ops that allow students to earn credit working with a variety of regional and national professional arts organizations.

LOUISIANA

Centenary College of Louisiana

Robert Buseick, Head
Theatre Department
Centenary College of Louisiana
2911 Centenary Bldv.
Shreveport, LA 71134-1188
rbuseick@centenary.edu
http://www.centenary.edu
ADMISSIONS: 2911 Centenary Blvd.
admissions@centenary.edu

920 Total Enr.; competitive
Semester System
12 Majors; ATHE
T: $20,950/r&b:$7,280
DEPT: (318) 869-5074
FAX: (318) 869-5760
SMALL PROGRAM
(318) 869-5038

DEGREES OFFERED

BA in Theatre.

ADMISSION & FINANCIAL INFORMATION

85% accepted to institution. H.S. Transcript, 2.5 GPA, ACT 23 or SAT. Audition, interview for scholarships. in performance. Inquire Fin. Aid Office.

FACULTY AND CLASSES OFFERED

2 Full-Time: 2 MFA/MA, 1 Staff, 2 adjunct

A. (1 FT) Intro to Theatre-1/Y; Th History-2/Y; Dramatic Criticism-1/Y

B. (1 FT) Acting-3/Y; Movement-1/Y; Directing-2/Y

C. (1 FT) Prins of Des-2/Y; Set Design-2/O; Cost Des-1/O; Ltg Des-2/O; Tech Prod'n-2/Y; Cost Constr-1/O; Cost Hist-1/O; Make-up-1/O; Stage Mgmt-1/O

FACILITIES & PRODUCTIONS

MAINSTAGE: 200 seats, computerized lighting. 4 prods: 4 Fac dir, 3 Fac des, 1 UG des; budget $10,000-12,000

Facility was built in 1957, renovated in 1980; includes scene shop, costume shop.

DESCRIPTION

Noted Faculty: Robert Buseick, Don Hooper, Ginger Folmer.

Guest Artists: Patric McWilliams, Guest Costume Designer.

The Theatre Department offers a curriculum to serve three types of students: those who plan to attend graduate school, those who plan to teach, and those who plan to pursue a career in the profession or to use their training for vocational recreation. The Theatre Department provides cultural enrichment for the College and the community through its production schedule, representing a "Theatre With A Purpose." Participation in the productions of the department is open to any student enrolled at Centenary College.

Dillard University

Dept. of Speech Comm. & Th. Arts
Dillard University
2601 Gentilly Rd.
New Orleans, LA 70122-3097
DEPT: (504) 286-4858
ADMISSIONS: admissions@dillard.edu
1 800-216-6637

1,124 Total Enr.; competitive
Semester System
40 Majors; ATHE
T: $12,240/$$8,360 R&B
SMALL PROGRAM
FAX: (504) 286-4032
www.dillard.edu
FAX: (504) 286-4816

DEGREES OFFERED

BA in Speech Comm. and Theatre Arts (30). Declare major in freshman year.

ADMISSION & FINANCIAL INFORMATION

60% accepted to inst. Admission selected from H.S. grads, based on H.S. achievements, ACT or SAT, recs. of H.S. teachers and counselors, character and talent. Academic scholarships awarded to students with GPA 3.0+; also scholarships for freshmen and transfer students; Talent Based Scholarships, aud + GPA.

FACULTY AND CLASSES OFFERED

4 Full-Time, 1 Part-Time: 2 PhD, 2 MFA/MA, 1 PT Staff

A. (1/2 FT) Intro to Th.-1/Y; Th Hist-2/Y; Dram. Lit-2/Y; Dram. Crit-2/Y; Playwriting 1/Y; African-American Theatre/Drama-1/Y; Classical Drama-1/Y

B. (1/2 FT) Acting-2/Y; Voice/Speech-1/Y; Singing-1/Y; Movmt-1/Y; Directing-2/Y

C. (1/2 PT) Prins of Des-2/O; Set Design-2/O; Cost Des-2/O; Ltg Des-2/Y; Tech Prod'n-2/O; Cost Constr-2/Y; Cost Hist-2/O; Make-up-1/Y; Stage Mgmt-2/Y

D. (1/2 FT) Arts Mgmt-1/O; Marketing/Promotion-1/X; Legal: Contracts-1/X; Box Office Procedure-2/Y; Devel/Grant Writing-1/X

FACILITIES & PRODUCTIONS

MAINSTAGE: 250 seats, fly space, electronic lighting. 4 prods: 2 Fac dir, 1 Guest des, 1 UG dir; budget $10,000-20,000

SECOND STAGE: 100 seats. 6 UG dir/des prods; budget $100-600

WORKSHOPS/READINGS:. 5 UG dir/des, 2 Fac dir; budget $150-300

Mainstage was built in 1992; includes scene shop, design studio, video studio, rehearsal studio, classrooms.

5 student-written plays produced in the last two years.

Connection with Dashiki Theatre, Junebug Productions and Ethiopian Theatre. Internships and special arrangements are made for all areas with advanced students. Academic credits are allowed for approved professional work by students. Internships are not limited to only the professional theatres listed. Dillard students will intern at the local, state, regional and national levels.

DESCRIPTION

Noted Faculty: Dr. Alex C. Marshall, director,specialty Afro-American Th.; Mr. Gary Hyatt, Art Admin.; Dr. Doris Gavins, Public Address/Speech Communications; Christopehr Morris, Scene Designer/Technical Director.

Guest Artists: workshops: Nate Bynum, Marlon Bailey, Donold Griffin, Phillip Walker, Donna Lee Williams, Albert Bostick, Jr. Willie O. Jordan, Allen Sean Weeks, Robert Brewer, Shriff Hasan, Judi Ann Mason, James Morehead, Gerri Hobdy, Tommye Myrick, Andrea Frye, Norbert Davis, Shay Youngblood, Dollie Revis, Yvette Sirker, Willie Jordan, John Grimsley, Anthony Farve.

This program is built on educational and professional theater training in a liberal arts context. Therefore, the serious student in theater will be introduced to a tutorial approach in which a plan of study and experience is created for each student. The University theater program is designed to prepare students for advanced study and/or an entry level position in the theater profession. The Dillard University professional training program includes three areas of concentration: Performance, Theater Management and Technical Theater. The standards are high. The program requires immense energy and dedication. Students are not only trained to acquire the traditional skills necessary for advanced study and professional work, but also to develop a personal vision of the theater as a dynamic cultural force. The university theater at Dillard is dedicated to and propagated by the aspirations and culture of the Afro-American people. At the same time it will readily, and freely, and with the spirit of the creativity of all mankind, utilize any and all forces of the western heritage of that people in the arts. The faculty are all working professionals who maintain liaisons with a wide range of professional theaters and organizations.

Louisiana State University ·····················

Michael S. Tick, Chair
Dept of Theatre
Louisiana State University
Baton Rouge, LA 70803-2525
mtick1@lsu.edu
www.theatre.lsu.edu
DEPT: (225) 578-4174
UG ADMISSIONS: 110 T. Boyd Hall, LSU, Baton Rouge, LA 70803
(225) 578-1175
Grad admissions: 114 D. Boyd Hall, above
graddeanoffice@lsu.edu

30,000 Total Enr.; compet.(UG) h. competitive (Grad)
Semester System
195 Majors; ATHE,NAST
T: $4,620; O-ST T: $12,920
$7,800 r&b
FAX: (225) 578-4135
admissions@lsu.edu

DEGREES OFFERED

BA in Arts Admin (7); Design-Tech (10); Dramatic Lit/Theory/Criticism (10); Performance (12); MFA in Acting (14); Costume Tech and Design (begins 2007); Properties Tech (begins 2007); Scenic Tech and Design (begins 2007). Students declare major in freshman year; 2007 granted 18 UG, 7 Grad degrees.

ADMISSION & FINANCIAL INFORMATION

Contact admissions (see above for UG and Grad admissions contact)

FACULTY AND CLASSES OFFERED

25 FT, 5 PT: 6 PhD, 23 MFA/MA, 1 Prof w/out adv deg.; 2 Staff

A. (5 FT) Intro to Theatre-2/Y; Dramatic Lit-8/Y; Theatre History-6/Y; Dramatic Crit-8/Y; Shakes-1/O; Playwriting-2/Y; Dance History-1/Y; Black Drama & Theatre-1/Y; Women and Theatre-1/O; Drama Writing-1/O

B. (7 FT, 4 PT) Acting-12/Y; Voice/Speech-8/Y; Directing-3/Y; Dance-9/Y; Musical Theatre-1/O; Movement-8/Y; Singing-1/Y; Mime, etc-1/O; Stage Combat-1/O; Script Analysis-1/O; Performance Art-1/O;

C. (10 F) Prins of Des-4/Y; Set Des-4/Y; Cost Des-8/Y; Ltg Des-4/Y; Tech Prod-12/Y; Cost Constr-11/Y; Make-up-1/Y; Stage Mgmt-2/Y; History of Theatrical Design-1/Y; Properties Tech-6/O; Lighting Tech-3/Y; Sound Tech-3/Y

.D. (3 FT, 1 PT) Arts Mgmt-3/Y; Marketing Promo-1/Y; Dev Grant Writing-1/Y; Budgeting/Acct Procedure-1/Y

FACILITIES & PRODUCTIONS

MAINSTAGE: 415 seats, fly space, computerized lighting 3 prods: 2 Fac dir/des; 1 GA dir/des, budget $25,000-100,000.

SECOND STAGE: 300 seats, fly space, computerized lighting 3 prods: 3 Fac dir/des, budget $7,500-10,500

THIRD STAGE: 150 seats, fly space, computerized lighting 9 Prods: 2 Grad Dir; 7 UG dir/des, budget $250-500

Facility was built in 1932, renovated in 2008; includes 2 scene shops, costume shop, prop shop, welding shop, sound studio, CAD facility, 3 acting studios, 1 video studio, 2 movement/dance studios, 4 rehearsal studios, 3 design studios, 2 classrooms

A non departmental student run organization presents 3 productions in which majors participate. 1 student written play has been produced in the last two years.

Connection with a professional full-time, year-round (Equity) theatre company, Swine Palace Productions. Students have the opportunity to work alongside world-class artists in every facet of production. Many students are AEA eligible by the time they graduate.

DESCRIPTION

Noted Faculty: Leigh Clemons, Literature,Criticism, Theory; John Dennis, Acting; Femi Euba, Black Drama; George Judy, Acting; Christine Menzies, Voice/Speech; James Murphy, Production; Kristin Sosnowsky, Arts Admin; Michael Tick, Directing/Acting; Leslie A. Wade, Literature, Criticism, Theory

Guest Artists: Chris Boneau, Press Agent; Wil Calhoun, Scriptwriter; Ben Cameron, Prod Director, TCG; Ping Chong, Performance Artist; Geoffrey Kent, Fight Director; Guillermo Gomez-Pena, Performance Artist; Pilobolus Dance Theatre; Michael Rafter, B'way Musical Director; SITI Company

On the eve of our 79th season, the LSU Department of Theatre continues to achieve national and international prominence in professional training, scholarship and production. With Swine Palace, the department has distinguished itself as one of the few programs in the country that supports a full-time, year-round Equity company. While pursuing their degrees, students have the opportunity to work alongside world-class artists in every facet of production. Many students are Actor's Equity Association (AEA) eligible by the time they graduate. Our B.A. curriculum (concentration on acting, literature-history-theory, arts administration, design-technology, and theatre studies) provides rigorous comprehensive training within the framework of a liberal arts education. The M.F.A. degree (Acting) is a three-year professional training program featuring action-based work and film technique; the M.F.A. degree (scenic technology and design; costume technology and design; and properties technology) is also a three-year program. In addition to working with Swine Palace, our students support Louisiana's burgeoning film industry. To develop in students the knowledge, critical skills, and methodological approaches that will allow them to conduct research as scholars, dramaturgs, or careers in education, our highly regarded Ph.D. program (theatre history, dramatic literature, theory and criticism) attracts students from here and abroad.

Louisiana Tech University

Cherrie Sciro, Coordinator
LTU School of the Performing Arts
Box 8608 Tech Station
Ruston, LA 71272
DEPT: (318) 257-2930
FAX: (318) 257-4571
latechtheatre@yahoo.com
ADMISSIONS: P.O. Box 3178, Ruston, LA 71272-0001
(318) 257-3036

11,500 T. Enr.; competitive
Quarter System
35 Majors, ATHE
T: $4,402/$2,220 R&B
O-ST T: $8,197/$2,220 R&B
SMALL PROGRAM
http://performingarts@latech.edu
www.latech.edu/admissions

DEGREES OFFERED

BA—Generalist (35); MA—Generalist (11), emphasis in performance, tech, design, stage mgmt, arts mgmt, stage movement, playwriting. Declare major in freshman year. 2007 granted 9 UG, 5 Grad degrees

ADMISSION & FINANCIAL INFORMATION

Inst. requires one of the following: 2.0 out of 4.0 GPA, upper 50% of grad. class, 22 comp ACT; 59.4% of apps.. admitted to Univ. Th. pro-gram req's Aud./Int./Portfolios for Grad; 19 of 25 admitted to UG; 6 of 12 to Grad. Numerous scholarships for academic and perf excellence, by review of applic. and/or audition.

FACULTY AND CLASSES OFFERED

5 Full-Time, 1 PhD,4 MA/MFA

A. (1 FT) Intro to Theatre-5/Y; Dramatic Lit-2/Y; Theatre History-2/O; Dramatic Criticism-1/O; Shakes-2/X; Playwriting-2/O

B. (1 1/2 FT) Acting-7/Y; Voice/Speech-2/O; Singing-X; Stage Combat-6/Y; Directing-3/Y; Dance-6/Y

C. (1 1/2 FT) Prins of Design-2/O; Set Design-1/O; Cost. Design-1/O; Costume Constr-1/O; Ltg Des-1/O; Tech Prod-1/Y; Make-up-1/O; Stage Mgmt-2/Y

D. (1 FT) Arts Mgmt-2/Y; Marketing/Promo-1/Y

FACILITIES AND PRODUCTIONS

MAINSTAGE: 1200 seats, fly space, computerized lighting
6 prods: 1 Fac dir, 3 Grad des, 2 UG des; budget $3,000-$6,000

SECOND STAGE: 150 seats, fly space, computerized lighting
24 prods: 3 Fac dir, 1 Grad dir, 12 Grad des, 8 UG des; budget $2,000-$4,500

THIRD STAGE: 60 seats, Worshops/Readings

8 GA dir; budget $200-$500

Facility was built in 1939, last renovated in 1982; scene shop, costume shop, sound studio, props shop, 10 classrooms.

3-5 student-written plays have been produced in the last two years.

DESCRIPTION

Noted Faculty: Cherrie Sciro, Mgmt; Mark Guinn, Design/Movement; Paul Crook, Acting/Directing; Ken Robbins, Playwriting, Dianne Grigsby, Dance

Guest Artists: Jay Johnson, Ventriloquist; Brian Byrnes, Fight Master; Nigel Poulton, Fight Director & Actor; Scott Mann, Bob MacDougall, Michael Chin, Fight Directors; Jeremy Lovejoy, Guru of Sikal

The Louisiana Tech University School of the Performing Arts provides comprehensive training in the fields of music, theatre, dance, movement, playwriting, stage management, and arts management which connects the broad spectrum of historical and contemporary issues related to art and craft; and in promoting the relationship between theory and practice, prepares professionals and teachers for leadership in national and international culture and art for the twenty first century. The School is committed to providing our students with a world context for viewing and appreciating the performing arts. Every effort will be made to expose our students to the expanse of performing arts as practiced throughout the world within varied cultures. The purposes of the Department of Theatre are to educate and train artists of the theatre and to provide for its students a foundation of professionalism and dedication to their art within a climate of diversity, discovery, and risk.

Loyola University New Orleans

Georgia Gresham, Chair
Dept. of Theatre Arts and Dance
Box 165, 6363 St. Charles Ave
New Orleans, LA 70118
DEPT: (504) 865-3840
www.loyno.edu/drama/
ADMISSIONS: 6363 Charles Ave., Box 18, New Orleans, LA 70118
(504) 865-3240
http://www.loyno.edu

3,000 Total Enr.; competitive
Semester System
60 Majors; ATHE
T: $25,246/$8,252 R&B
FAX: (504) 865-2284
drama@loyno.edu

FAX: (504) 865-3383
admit@loyno.edu

DEGREES OFFERED

BA in Drama (36), Drama/Communications (29), Theatre Arts with a Minor in Business Administration (9). Declare major in freshman year; 2007 granted 11 degrees.

ADMISSION & FINANCIAL INFORMATION

Official test scores, official HS transcript, essay, resume of activities, counselor/teacher evaluation. 85% admitted to institution. Audition/Interview/Portfolio for designers. Students who are academically qualified and who wish to major in drama must audition for drama scholarships. Priority deadline is Dec. 1.

FACULTY AND CLASSES OFFERED

5 FT, 5 PT: 1 PhD, 8 MFA/MA, 3 Staff

A. (1 1/2 FT, 1 PT) Intro to Th-2/Y; Th Hist-1/Y; Shakes-1/O+1/X; Dramatic Lit-3/X; Playwriting-1/O

B. (2 FT, 4 PT) Acting-5/YO; Voice/Speech-4/Y; Movement-2/Y; Musical Theatre-1/X; Directing-1/Y; Dance-3/X

C. (2 FT) Set Design-1/O; Cost. Design-1/O; Tech Prod'n-2/Y; Ltg Des-1/O; Make-up-1/O; Arts Mgmt-1/O

*We rotate design classes. Each class offered every other year

FACILITIES AND PRODUCTIONS

MAINSTAGE: 154 seats, fly space, computerized lighting
2 prods: 1 Fac dir, 1 Guest dir; budget $2,500-5,000

SECOND STAGE: 75-80 seats, computerized lighting
2 prods: 1 Fac dir, 1 Guest dir; budget $750-3,500

8-16 UG dir/des Workshops/Readings

Facility built in 1927, renovated in 1994; includes costume shop, scene shop, acting studio, CAD facility, design studio, classrooms.

1-3 student-written plays produced in the last two years.

Internships with local theatres available. Upper class students may intern one term and summers.

DESCRIPTION

Noted Faculty: Georgia Gresham, CAD; Donald Brady, Actor; Joseph Harris, Lighting Design.

Guest Artist: John Guare, Playwright; Joanne Gordon, Director; Geoffrey Hall, Designer; Patrick McNamara, Actor; Jamie Lynn Sigler; Ricky Graham, Director; Janet Shea, Director; Perry Martin, Director and various casting directors and agents.

In keeping with its Jesuit tradition, the Theatre Arts and Dance Department of Loyola University New Orleans holds that the study of the dramatic arts is best done in the context of developing the whole person. The department provides intensive, respected theatrical training in the context of a solid liberal arts education. While it addresses the human condition through all the modes of thought, it enables the student to explore every aspect of dramatic art in a variety of courses. High caliber productions provide an extension of the classroom and an opportunity to synthesize what is learned there. The pre-professional degree is excellent preparation for further study in graduate school or entry positions in a theatre company.

McNeese State University

Charles McNeely, Interim Coord
Dept. of Performing Arts
McNeese State University
Box 92175
Lake Charles, LA 70609-5028
DEPT: (337) 475-5028
FAX: (337) 475-5063
ADMISSIONS: P.O. Box 92495
(337) 475-5146

7,500 Total Enr.; compet.
Semester System
20 Majors; ATHE
T: $2500/$4,000 R&B
O-ST T: $8640/$4,000 R&B
SMALL PROGRAM
cmcneely@mail.mcneese.edu
www.mcneese.edu

DEGREES OFFERED

BA in Theatre Arts (30). Students declare major in soph. year; 2004 granted 5 degrees.

ADMISSION & FINANCIAL INFORMATION

HS or GED diploma, 3.0 GPA, ACT 20 or SAT 940. 90% of applics. accepted. Scholarships avail, submit statement of interest, resume of performance a/o technical experience, HS GPA of 2.5, 2 letters of recommendation and interview.

FACULTY AND CLASSES OFFERED

5.5 Full Time, 2 Part-Time: 3 PhD, 3 MFA/MA, 2 Staff

A. (1/2 FT,1 PT) Intro to Theatre-1/Y; Theatre History-2/Y; Shakes-2/X; Dramatic Crit.-1/Y; Playwriting-1/O

B. (2 1/2 FT) Acting-4/Y; Voice/Speech-1/Y; Movement-1/O; Singing-2/X; Dance-2/O; Musical Theatre-1/X; Directing-1/Y; Mime, etc-1/O; Stage Combat-2/Y

C. (1 FT, 1 PT) Prins of Des-2/X; Set Design-2/Y; Cost Des-1/O; Ltg Des-2/Y; Tech Prod/n-1/Y; Make-up-1/Y

D. (1 PT) Arts Management-1/O

FACILITIES & PRODUCTIONS

MAINSTAGE: 265 seats, computerized lighting
5 prods, 4 Fac dir, 4 Fac des, 1 Guest dir, 1 Guest des, 1 UG des, budget $2,000-5,000

SECOND STAGE: 1600, electronic lighting
budget $2,000-5000

WORKSHOPS/READINGS:.2 prods, 1 Fac dir, 1 Fac des

Facility includes scene shop, costume shop, sound studio, CAD facility, dance/mvmt studio, 3 classrooms.

DESCRIPTION

Noted Faculty: Joy Pace, Voice & Diction; Charles McNeely, Acting; Lewis Whitlock, Movement/Dance; John Abegglen, Scenic/Lighting Design/Technical Theatre; Dr. Donna Jones, Theatre History/Perf Theory.

Guest Artists: Tony Kushner, Playwright; Dr. Carol Lines, Doug Burch, Actor.

Our theatre arts majors pursue a liberal arts degree

encompassing the university's core curriculum focusing upon performance, design, history, theory, and criticism of theatre. In our small program all students have opportunities to perform on stage, to design for main crews, or in production management. The program allows students to concentrate their efforts in either performance or on design and technical theatre; with the Department of Music, the student may receive a degree in musical theatre. The Theatre Arts degree bridges the humanities and arts, stresses the love of learning, the importance of asking questions, and the value of creative risk. We not only lay the foundation for continuing theatre training, but also prepare graduates for other professions that need their skills such as law, art therapy, and business.

Tulane University

Martin Sachs, Chair	10,000 Total Enr.; h. compet.
Dept of Theatre & Dance	Semester System
215 McWilliams Hall	50 Majors, USITT
Tulane University	T: $23,304/$6,710 R&B
New Orleans, LA 70118	FAX: (504) 865-6737
(504) 314-7760	www.tulane.edu~theatre

ADM: Undergraduate Admissions: Tulane Univ., 210 Gibson Hall
(504) 314-7760   FAX: (504) 862-8715
Graduate Admissions: Tulane Univ., 324 Gibson Hall
(504) 865-5100   FAX: (504) 862-5274
www.tulane.edu/

DEGREES OFFERED

BA in General Th. (14); BFA in Acting & Design/Technical Theatre (2); MFA in Design/Tech. Theatre (12). Declare major in soph. year; 2001 granted 8 UG, 1 Grad degrees.

ADMISSION & FINANCIAL INFORMATION

Requirements: (BA) GPA of 3.0, SAT min. 1050. MFA: GPA 3.0, 3.5 in major, interview required for graduate applicants, design applicants with portfolio; Every other year admit 8 applicants (odd-numbered years).

FACULTY AND CLASSES OFFERED

19 Full-Time, 7 Part-Time: 2 PhD, 12 MFA/MA; 5 Staff

A. (2 FT) Intro to Theatre-2/Y; Theatre History/Drama Lit-5/Y; Shakes-1/O; Dramatic Lit-1/Y; Th. History Special Topic Seminar-1/O; various Seminars that combine Dramatic Lit.& Criticism-2-3/Y&O

B. (3 FT, 6 PT) Acting-7/Y; Voice/Speech-4/Y; Movement-1/Y; Mime, etc.-1/O; Singing-1/X; Musical Th.-1/X; Directing-2/Y; Dance-15/Y; Th. for Social Change-1/O; Movement Stories-1/O

C. (4 FT) Prins of Des-1/Y; Set Des-3/Y; Ltg Des-3/Y; Tech Prod-3/Y; Cost Des-3/Y; Cost Constr-1/Y; Cost Hist-1/Y; Stg Mgmt-1/O; Make-up-1/O; Sound Des-3/Y

FACILITIES AND PRODUCTIONS

MAINSTAGE: 100-150 seats, computerized lighting. 4 prods: All Fac dir, 4 Fac des, 4 Grad des, 2 UG des; budget $4,200-5,000

SECOND STAGE: 30-50 seats, computerized lighting; 1-2 prods: 1-2 Fac dir; budget $800.

2 workshops/readings:. 1 Fac dir, 1 Guest dir.

Mainstage was built in 1984, offices, classrooms, shops and dance studios built in 1996. Facility includes scene shop, costume shop, sound studio, CAD facility, 4 rehearsal studios, 1 design studio, 2 classrooms.

Connection with Shakespeare Festival at Tulane (Equity) summer theatre, an adjunct function of the department. Auditions are open to students as well as production positions.

DESCRIPTION

Guest Artists: Jane Comfort Company, Performance Artist Residency; Rachel Lampert, Dance Theatre Project; Laura Edmondson, Fellowship in Playwriting; production of original script; Bryan Batt, Master Acting Class.

Departmental Philosophy: Within the liberal arts environment of Tulane, the theatre student is given the opportunity to learn about theatre in the classroom while undertaking theatre work through production and performance. Theatre training is a communal effort based upon creative interchange among skilled individuals working toward a common goal: performance. The program at Tulane introduces the student to the fundamentals of theatre as an art while giving the opportunity to develop basic skills in special areas. The department intends for initial development to center in the classroom; here the student is expected to acquire a working vocabulary, a personal method of research, and a discriminating attitude towards quality in theory and practice.

University of Louisiana Monroe

John Kelly, Director.	7,284; not compet.
TheatreWorks ULM	
Univ. of Louisiana Monroe	Semester Sys
700 University Ave	20 Majors
Monroe, LA 71209-8842	T: $3,606/$4,410 R&B
DEPT: (318) 342-1413	O-ST T:$9,559/R&B $4,410
FAX: (318) 342-7323	jkelly@ulm.edu
ADMISSIONS: Above address	(318) 362-4661
FAX: (318) 342-7323	admissions@ulm.edu

DEGREES OFFERED

BA in Theatre (20) (with emphases). Declare major in fresh. or soph. year. 2003 granted 5 UG degrees.

ADMISSION & FINANCIAL INFORMATION

High school minimum GPA of 2.0 or rank of upper 50%, ACT scores, proof of immunization. ACT comp. of 22 selective admission. The program accepts most applicants, audition/interview or portfolio/interview required for scholarships. Scholarships, talent grants, o-st waivers, work-study, emerging scholars program offered.

FACULTY AND CLASSES OFFERED

4 Full-Time: Courses in acting, directing, literatures, history, costume, make-up, scenic design, lighting, etc.

FACILITIES & PRODUCTIONS

MAINSTAGE: 750 seats, fly space, computerized lighting.

SECOND STAGE: 165 seats, computerized & electronic lighting.

THIRD STAGE: Various seats, black box, computerized lighting

Various # Workshops/Readings: UG dir/des

Facility was built in 1932/81, and was renovated in 2001-02 (mainstage currently in renovation-reopens April 2004)

Scene shop, costume shop, prop shop, welding shop, video studio, dance studio, 2 classrooms. Various shows can be scheduled for rehearsal.

4 Faculty directed prod/year, plus student directed prod, opera, and dance performances.

Department produces Paper Moon Summer Theatre (Equity). Guest Artist Contract. Students audition and interview along with professionals for available positions.

DESCRIPTION

Noted Faculty and Guest Artists not provided.

.The program features both a course of study and a production component. The course of study has three parts. The first is the liberal arts segment, consisting of a broad introduction to the arts and sciences. The second segment is composed of the core theatre courses in theatre fundamentals, play reading, acting, voice, theatre history, and communication skills. The final part of the studies program is the specialty course work created by the student and their faculty advisor. This is designed to equip the student for the career path they are developing. The production aspect of the training is conducted through the production company called Theatre Works. Noted Broadway and Hollywood artists serve as guest artists each year, enhancing the education experience of the students. The program also operates a professional summer theatre called Paper Moon Summer Theatre, which offers plays and musicals. Students can apply and audition to work side-by-side with professional actors, designers, and technicians in getting the experience needed to build a distinctive resume.

University of Louisiana at Lafayette

Buddy Himes, Interim Head	15,517; not compet.
Univ. of Louisiana at Lafayette	Semester Sys
Box 43850	95 Majors
Lafayette, LA 70504-3690	T: $1,700.85/$1,910 R&B PER SEM
DEPT: (337) 482-6357	O-ST T: $4,790/$1,910 R&B PER SEM
FAX: (337) 482-5089	SMALL PROGRAM
ADMISSIONS: P.O. Box 41210	
(337) 482-6467	
(800) 752-6553	FAX: (337) 482-1112

DEGREES OFFERED

BFA in Performing Arts. Declare major in freshman year. 2001 granted 10 UG degrees.

ADMISSION & FINANCIAL INFORMATION

Graduation from accredited high school with minimum GPA of 2.0 or min. ACT composite score of 20 or in the upper 25% of HS grad. class, 97% accepted. Limited number of competitive scholarships for freshmen and upperclassmen majoring in Performing Arts. Theatre and Dance schol. require audition and portfolio.

FACULTY AND CLASSES OFFERED

5 Full-Time, 2 Part-Time: 1 PhD, 6 MFA/MA; 2 Staff

A. (1 FT) Intro to Theatre-1/Y; Dramatic Lit-2/O; Theatre History-2/O; Dramatic Criticism-1/X; Shakes-1/X; Playwriting-1/X

B. (3 FT, 2 PT) Acting-3/Y; Voice/Speech-3/Y; Directing-2/O

C. (1/2 FT) Prins of Des-1/Y; Set Design-1/O; Cost Des-1/O; Cost Hist-1/O; Ltg Des-1/Y; Tech Prod'n-2/Y; Make-up-1/Y

D. (1/2 FT) Arts Management-1/O

FACILITIES & PRODUCTIONS

MAINSTAGE: 306 seats, fly space, computerized lighting.
3 prods: Fac dir/des, 1 Guest cost des; budget $1,500-10,000; also dance concerts.

SECOND STAGE: 135 seats, computerized lighting
2 prods: 1-2 UG dir/des; budget $200-1,000

1-2 Workshops/Readings: UG dir/des; budget $100-200

Facility was built in 1939, and was renovated (lights) in 1993, fly system in 1998; costume shop, 2 dance studios, rehearsal studio, 3 classrooms.

DESCRIPTION

Noted Faculty: Dr. Stephen Taft, Arts Admin & Directing; Lori Bales, Directing, Acting, Musical Th; Richard Gwortnay, Acting, Period Styles, Voice, History; Kenneth Jenkins, Modern Dance; Sarah Stairnska, Ballet; Cissy Whipp, Modern Dance, Jazz.

Guest Artists: Seattle Mime, Mime Troup; Celeste Miller, Performance Artist; Robert Dafford, Scenic Artist; Karla King, Cost Designer; Michael Job, Clay Jalifeno, Choreographers.

The University of Southwestern Louisiana Performing Arts Department is a pre-professional training program emphasizing the practical aspects of Theatre and Dance and the importance of process. The program encourages a multi-disciplinary approach to the Performing Arts as an avenue to personal creative exploration and growth. The department strives to integrate Theatre and Dance with elements of Architecture, Music, Drama, Visual Arts, Literature and Technology into a series of high-quality, innovative presentations to USL, the Acadiana Region and the Stage of Louisiana. By combining classroom theory and practical hands on experience, the department seeks to create imaginative, artistic graduates capable of embracing the challenges of the twenty-first century.

MAINE

Bates College

Martin E. Andrucki, Chair
Dept. of Theatre, Bates College
300 Schaeffer Theater
Lewiston, ME 04240
(207) 786-8294
admissions@bates.edu
ADMISSIONS: Lindholm House, adress above.
(207) 786-6000

1,744 T. Enr.; highly compet.
Semester System
40 Majors, ATHE
T: N/A
FAX: (207 786-8332
SMALL PROGRAM

FAX: (207) 786-6123

DEGREES OFFERED

BA in General Theatre (16) Declare major in sophomore year.

ADMISSION & FINANCIAL INFORMATION

Scores optional, distinguished HS record. Theatre program admits all applicants.

FACULTY AND CLASSES OFFERED

4 Full-Time, 4 Part-Time: 3 PhD, 3 MFA/MA; 2 Staff

A. (2 FT, 1 PT) Intro to Theatre-1/Y; Theatre History-4/Y; Shakes-2/X; Dramatic Lit-4/Y; Dramatic Criticism-1/O; Playwriting-1/Y

B. (1 FT, 2 PT) Acting-3/Y; Voice/Speech-1/Y; Movement-1/Y; Singing-1/X; Directing-1/Y; Dance-3/Y

C. (1 FT, 1 PT) Prins of Des-1/Y; Set Design-1/O; Cost Des-1/O; Lighting Des-1/O; Tech Prod. 1/O

ACILITIES AND PRODUCTIONS

MAINSTAGE: 300 seats, fly space, computerized & electronic lighting 3 prods: 2 Fac dir/des, 1 Guest dir/des, 1 UG des.; budget $1,500-8,000

SECOND STAGE: 150 seats, computerized lighting 4 UG dir/des prods.; budget $200-500

THIRD STAGE: 50 seats, electronic lighting

10 Workshops/Readings

Facility was built in 1960, renovated in 1986; includes scene shop, cost shop, dance studio, rehearsal studio, design studio, 2 classrooms.

A non-departmental, student-run org. presents 2-3 productions/yr. in which dept. majors participate. 4 student-written plays produced in the last two years.

Connection with The Public Theater: Internships in all areas.

DESCRIPTION

Noted Faculty: Martin Andrucki, Paul Kuritz, William Pope, Joshua Williamson, Marcy Plavin, Ellen Seeling.

Guest Artists: Deborah Margolin, Joan Vick, Doug Elkins, Michael Foley, Kendall Morse, Sandra Deer, Brian Flynn, Elizabeth Freydberg, Tamara Blackmer, Peter Linka, Katalin Vecsey.

Our objectives are twofold: 1) To provide comprehensive introductory training in all areas of theater for students considering a professional career in the field, giving equal emphasis to artistic training and to the study of the literature and history of the stage. This training is augmented by departmental productions of the most demanding and challenging works of both classical and contemporary

playwrights. 2) To teach theater as a liberal art in the context of a traditional liberal arts institution.

University of Maine

Marcia Douglas, Director
School of Performing Arts
Division of Theatre and Dance
5788 Class of 1944 Hall, Rm. 208
University of Maine
Orono, ME 04469-5788
www.umaine.edu/spa
ADMISSIONS: 5713 Chadbourne Hall
http://www.ume.maine.edu/~umadmit/
(207) 581-1561

9,527 Tot. Enr.; compet.
Semester System
60 Majors: ATHE, U/RTA
T: $8,330/$7,484 R&B
O-ST T: $20,540/$7,484 R&B
DEPT. (207) 581-4700
FAX: (207) 581-4701
www.umaine.ed
um-admit@maine.edu
FAX: (207) 581-1213

DEGREES OFFERED

BA in Theatre (60). Students declare major at end of 2nd year

ADMISSION & FINANCIAL INFORMATION

Official HS transcripts, results from SAT or ACT and letters of recommendation; UG admits 9 out of 10. Performing Arts Scholarship- UG.

FACULTY AND CLASSES OFFERED

4 FT, 2 PT Dance Teachers/Chor.: 2 PhD, 2 MFA/MA

A. (1 FT) Intro to Theatre-1/O; Dramatic Lit-3/Y; Theatre History-2/Y; Playwriting-1/O; Women Playwrights-1/O

B. (2 FT, 3 PT) Acting-4/Y; Voice/Speech-1/O; Movement-1/Y; Directing-4/Y; Dance-6/Y; Script Analysis-2/Y; Drama in Education-1/O; Children's Th. Prod.-1/O

C. (2 FT) Tech Prod'n-1/Y; Cost Construction-1/Y; Make-up-1/O; Topics in Theatre Tech-1/Y; Topics in Th. Design-1/Y

FACILITIES & PRODUCTIONS

MAINSTAGE: 540 seats, fly space, computerized lighting. 4 prods: 3 Fac dir/des, 1 Guest dir/des; $3500-5000

SECOND STAGE: 89 seats, computerized lighting. 3 Fac dir/des, various other productions; budget $2,000-10,000

Facility was built in 1963 (Mainstage); addition in 1996; includes scene shop, costume shop, sound studio, 2 dance studios. Supporting facilities include a 1700-seat hall.

Maine Masque, a non-departmental, student-run, producing organization presents one production per year in which majors participate.Go to www.umaine.edu/mainemasque/

DESCRIPTION

Noted Faculty: Dr. Tom Mikotowicz, Directing;Dr. Sandra Hardy, Acting; Marcia Douglas, Acting & Movement; Jane Snider, Costume Design; Chez Cherry, Set Design; Greg Mitchell, Sets/Lights.

Guest Artists: Nathaniel Packard, Light Design; Richard McPike, Costume Design.

The central mission of the Division of Theatre/Dance in the School of Performing Arts at University of Maine is to provide for the education of undergraduate students majoring in theatre and undergraduate students with a concentration in dance, as well as that of interested students from the university at large. Through the integration of academics and production, the division furthers the knowledge and appreciation of performance on campus, throughout the state, in the region, and beyond. Thus, the

Division of Theatre/Dance puts emphasis on the fact that study and activity in the classroom will support and illuminate the production program, and the production program will contribute knowledge and evidence of important application of theory to courses. Whenever possible, the division stresses research and creative activity that is multicultural, intergeneric, and interdisciplinary. In addition, significant focus is placed upon outreach activities which serve the state education system on the elementary and secondary levels through such activities as adjudication of one-act play festivals, in-house workshops and performances, career-day counseling, annual touring productions in the school and in the parks, and UM scholarships for outstanding high school students. The division offers a Bachelor of Arts in Theatre. It is our hope to prepare students for pursuing a career in theatre or dance, or applying the knowledge and values of performance to other disciplines and to their lives.

University of Southern Maine

Charles S. Kading, Chair
Department of Theatre
Univ. of Southern Maine
37 College Ave.
Gorham, ME 04038
DEPT: (207) 780-5480
www.usm.maine.edu/theater/
ADM: same address, att.: Admissions   (207) 780-5670
www.usm.maine.edu/~admit/

10,000, Total Enr; non-compet.
Semester System; ATHE
85 majors
T: check with dept
O-ST T: check with dept
FAX: (207) 780-5641

DEGREES OFFERED

BA in Acting (35), Design (10), History/Lit. (6), Oral Interpretation (4), General (30). Declare major in 2nd year; 2001 granted 10 UG degs.

ADMISSION & FINANCIAL INFORMATION

Placement by SAT scores of 950-1150, B- or above; accept all applics. to theatre program; 4 Theatre scholarships totaling approximately $2,500, selection based on GPA and individual schol. requirements.

FACULTY AND CLASSES OFFERED

9 FT, 12 PT; 2 Ph.D., 18 MA/MFA; 2 Prof. w/o adv. deg; 1 Staff

A. (2 FT) Intro. to Theatre-1/Y; Dramatic Lit.-5/Y; Th. Hist.-5/Y; Dramatic Crit.-1/Y; Shakespeare-1/O; Playwriting-2/Y

B. (4 FT, 8 PT) Acting-3/Y/O; Voice/Speech-5/Y; Mvmt.-2/Y; Mus. Th-1/O; Directing-1/Y; Dance-2/Y; Perf. Art-1/O; Creative Dramatics-1/O; Audition-1/O; On Camera Acting-2/O; Michael Chekhov Institute-1/Y

C. (3 FT, 2 PT) Prins. of Design-1/Y; Set Des.-1/Y; Cost. Des.-1/Y; Lighting Des.-1/Y; Cost. Hist.-1/Y; Cost. Construction-1/Y; Makeup-1/Y; Stage Mgmt.-1/Y; Drafting-1/O; Design Topics-1/O; Prod. Mgmt.-1/Y

D. (2 PT) Arts Mgmt.-1/Y

FACILITIES AND PRODUCTIONS

MAINSTAGE: 160 seats, computerized lighting. 6 prods: Dir-4 Fac., 1 Guest, 1 UG; Des-6 Fac., 1 Guest, 5 UG; budget $1,500-4,500 per show.

SECOND STAGE: 40 seats, electronic lighting. Used for student productions, bdgt $500-1,500; workshops $250-1,500.

A non-departmental, student-run org. presents 2 shows each year, in which majors participate; 5 student-written plays have been performed in the last 5 years.Connections with Maine State Music Theatre (Equity summer theatre); Portland Stage Company (Equity, LORT theatre); Public Theatre (Equity); students can earn 3-15 credits through interships with one of these Equity companies.

DESCRIPTION

Noted Faculty: Charles S. Kading, des/prod; William Steele, Thomas Power, act/dir/playwriting; Assunta Kent, contemp, Medieval, Asian th. hist.; Walter Stump, dir/playwriting; Wil Kilroy; Susan Picinich, cost. des/prod.; Brian Hapcic, light/sound des.

Guest Artists: John Corker, B'way Manager; Carolyn Gage, NYC playwright; Terri Gindi, NYC Mime; Avner the Eccentric, Int'l performer; Karel Wright, AEA Disney; Mala Powers, Chekhov Executrix; Diana Saing, Playwright; Lisa Dalton, Chekhov International; Shauna Kanter, Actor/Writer, London.

The Department offers a broad educational foundation in the art and craft of producing and managing theatre. Areas of concentration include Performance, Design, Technical Theatre, Playwriting, Dramaturgy, and Vocal Arts. The faculty believes that students learn by doing. Hence, along with a rigorous academic program, the Theatre Department provides a strong practicum. As an all-undergraduate program, each student has the opportunity to be cast and to do technical work on productions. We make our program accessible to non-traditional students in pursuit of their education. USM Theatre students have earned regional and national recognition through the American College Theatre Festival and national forensics competition. The Department has traveled to the Kennedy Center and on three occasions have captured national awards in performance, playwriting, and forensics. USM Theatre Majors have gone on to rewarding careers in theatre, film, and television. The Department assists students attempting to enter related job markets.

MARYLAND

Catonsville Community College

Tom Colonna, Coord.
Carl Freundel, MFA, Asst. Coord.
Dept. of Theatre & Dance
Catonsville Community College
800 South Rolling Road
Catonsville, MD 21228
DEPT: (410) 455-4591
ADMISSIONS: Above address.

10,000 T. Enr.; non-compet.
Semester System
8 Majors
T: $90-174/credit
O-ST T: $236/credit
FAX: (410) 455-5134
(301) 455-4304

DEGREES OFFERED

General Education/Emphasis on Theatre Education.
Declare major in 2nd year.

ADMISSION & FINANCIAL INFORMATION

All applicants are admitted to college, theatre program, with open-door policy for beginning level courses.

FACULTY AND CLASSES OFFERED

3 FT, 5 PT: 3 PhD, 2 MA/MFA, 1 Prof. w/o adv. degree; 7 Staff

A. (3 FT, 3 PT) Intro to Theatre-2/Y; Dramatic Lit-1/Y; Playwriting-1/Y

B. (1 PT) Acting-2/Y; Voice/Speech-X; Singing-1/Y; Dance-2/Y

C. (1 PT) Prins of Design-1/O; Make-up-1/O

D. Devel/Grant Writing-X; Budget/Acct'ng-X

FACILITIES AND PRODUCTIONS

MAINSTAGE: 350-450 seats, fly space, computerized lighting
Budget: $15,000

SECOND STAGE: 80-100 seats, electronic lighting

Facility was built in 1976; includes scene shop, costume shop, welding shop, dance studio, rehearsal studio, 3 classrooms, make-up/dressing room areas.

Majors generally participate in a non-departmental, student-run producing organization that presents 2 productions per year.

DESCRIPTION

Guest Artists: Marc Horowitz (Workshop Performance Inc.)

The theatrical program at Catonsville Community College is designed to provide the student with a foundation for further study and training at a 4-year university or college. As a full production house the CCC Theatre provides an environment in which the student can learn and practice the fundamentals of the crafts of acting and production. In acting studies, emphasis is placed on the ongoing responsibility of the actor to develop vocal and physical ability as well as the creative imagination. In production studies, attention is given to pre-production planning, design and construction of scenery and props, basic scene painting, sound reinforcement and engineering, stage management, basic lighting techniques, special effects, makeup, and mask and costuming. CCC Theatre provides for the specialized needs of the theatre major as well as providing a balanced and enriching program of study and performance serving the cultural interests of a diverse student and community population.

The Community College of Baltimore County - Essex Campus

Tom Colonna
Theatre Coordinator
The Community College of
Baltimore County
7201 Rossville Blvd.
Baltimore, MD 21237-3899
www.ccbc.md.edu
tcolonna@ccbcmd.edu
ADM: Above address

10,000 Total Enr.; not compet.
Semester System
25 Majors; NAST, ATHE
T: $113/credit/
   In-county $60 per credit
O-ST T: $168/credit
DEPT: (410) 780-6168
FAX: (410) 780-6185
www.ccbc.md.edu

DEGREES OFFERED

AA in Theatre (20); AFA in Theatre (2-year college)
Declare major in first year.

ADMISSION & FINANCIAL INFORMATION

100% accepted; Theatre program generally admits all applicants. Audition/portfolio req'd for school. Full and partial theatre scholarships based on interview/portfolio/audition.

FACULTY AND CLASSES OFFERED

7 Full-Time, 2 Part-Time: 1 PhD, 10 MFA/MA; 3 Staff

A. (3 FT, 2 PT) Intro to Theatre-1/Y; Theatre History-1/O; Shakes-1/Y; Playwriting-1/O

B. (3 FT, 1 PT) Acting-6/Y; Voice/Speech-4/Y; Singing-3/X; Musical Theatre-1/O; Directing-1/O; Dance-6/X

C. (1 FT, 1 PT) Tech Prod'n-2/Y; Make-up-1/Y

FACILITIES AND PRODUCTIONS

MAINSTAGE: 420 seats; fly space, computerized lighting.
3 prods: 2 Fac dir/des, 1 Guest dir/des; bdgt $3-5,000

SECOND STAGE: 120 seats; computerized lighting
2 UG dir prods; budget $700-1,000

THIRD STAGE: 60 seats, black box, computerized lighting
1 UG dir Workshops/Readings; budget $100-250

Facility was built in 1972, renovated in 2000; includes scene shop, costume shop, sound studio, design studio, video studio, 2 dance studios, 2 rehearsal studios.

A non-departmental, student-run org. presents 3 productions/year in which dept. majors participate. One student-written play produced in the last two years/

DESCRIPTION

The Community College of Baltimore County is the number one provider of undergraduate education and workforce training in the Baltimore metropolitan area. The multi-campus system enrolls more than half of all county residents attending undergraduate college, and its Division of Continuing Education is a leading partner for business and industry, serving more than 175 companies annually with customized employee development training.

Goucher College

Michael Simon-Curry, Chair
Dept. of Theatre
Goucher College
1021 Dulaney Valley Road
Baltimore, MD 21204-2794
DEPT: (410) 337-6410
www.goucher.edu
ADM: 8000 York Rd.
(410) 337-6100

950 Total Enr.; competitive
20 Majors; U/RTA, ATHE
Semester System
T: $31,082/$9,478 R&B
SMALL PROGRAM
Main: (410) 337-6000

(800) GOUCHER
admissions@goucher.edu

DEGREES OFFERED

BA in Theatre (6). Declare major in soph. year.

ADMISSION & FINANCIAL INFORMATION

SAT 1110, GPA 3.2. 71% of applicants accepted by institution. No specific entry req. for Theatre program, regular evaluations to stay in program. Institutional merit scholarships. ranging from $5,000 to full tuition, room and board. Selection based on SAT scores, GPA, class rank, written essays and interviews. 3 - $5,000 theatre scholarships. annually.

FACULTY AND CLASSES OFFERED

3 Full-Time: 1 PhD, 2 MFA/MA

A. (3/4 FT) Intro to Theatre-2/Y; Dramatic Lit-1/Y; Theatre History-4/O; Shakes-1/Y (team-taught w/Eng. Dept.); Playwriting-2/Y

B. (1 1/4 FT) Acting-2/Y; Voice-11/2/OYX; Movement-1/2/Y; Directing-2/O; Senior Project-2/Y; Adv. Th Workshop-1/O; TV Drama Workshop-1/O

C. (1 FT) Cost Des-1/O; Tech Production-1/Y; Set Design-1/O; Ltg Des-1/O; Applied Theatre-2/Y

D. (1 FT) Arts Management-1-2/Y; Marketing/Promotion-1/OX; Development/Grant Writing-1/OX; Budgeting/ Accounting -1/YX

FACILITIES & PRODUCTIONS

MAINSTAGE: 175 seats, computerized lighting. 5 prods: 2 Fac dir, 2-3 Fac des, 2 UG dir/des; budget $3,000-5,000

3 Workshops/Readings; 2 Fac dir, 1 UG dir; budget $100-600

Facility was built in 1991, includes scene shop, costume shop, video studio, classroom.

A non-departmental, student-run organization presents 1 production per year in which dept. majors participate. 10 student-written plays produced in the last two years.

DESCRIPTION

Guest Artists: Janet Stanford, director/teacher; Bread & Puppet Theatre.

The Theatre Department at Goucher College offers courses in acting, directing, playwriting, experimental theatre, theatre history and criticism, dramatic literature, design, and technical theatre production. The major is designed to offer a balance between the varied artistic elements of theatre and an intellectual understanding of the diverse theoretical, historical, and cultural aspects of theatre in a liberal arts context. Students are encouraged to take courses in English, dance, music, art, communication, and arts administration to complement their courses in theatre. Students have completed internships and apprenticeships at Center Stage, Dorset Theatre Festival, Berkshire Theatre Festival, American Repertory Theatre, Yale Rep, Pennsylvania Stage Company, Theatre Project, and others.

Towson University

Jay A. Herzog, Chair
Theatre Dept, Towson University
Towson, MD 21252
DEPT: (410) 704-2792
FAX: (410) 704-3914
www.towson.edu/theatre/
ADM: 8000 York Rd.
www.towson.edu

15,374 Total Enr.; compet.
Semester System
160 Majors, ATHE, NAST
T: $7,234/$7,986 R&B
O-ST T: $17,174/$7,986 R&B
admissions@towson.edu
(888) 4 TOWSON
FAX: (410) 704-3030

DEGREES OFFERED

BA or BS in Theatre Arts with tracks in Performance, Design and Production, Theatre Studies (160); MFA in Theatre (23). Declare major in 1st or 2nd yr.

ADMISSION & FINANCIAL INFORMATION

Min. 3.0 GPA, 1120 SAT; 50% of applicants accepted to institution. UG theatre program admits all applicants, Grad program 1 out of 3. Grad. req. aud/interview for actors, portfolio for designers. Recruitment Scholarships: H.S. transcript, SAT scores; letter of rec. (ie, H.S. drama teacher). Schol. for currrently enrolled theatre majors, GPA of 3.0 in theatre classes; significant contributions to Theatre Dept.; merit-based (10 different scholarships. ranging from $200-2,000).

FACULTY AND CLASSES OFFERED

12 FT, 14 PT: 3 PhD, 20 MFA/MA, 3 Prof. w/o adv. degree

A. (2 1/2 FT, 4 PT) Intro to Theatre-1/Y; Theatre History-3/Y; Dramatic Theory-1/Y; Dramaturgy-2/Y; Cultural Diversity-1/Y; Senior Thesis-1/Y; Script Analysis-1/Y; Guest Seminars-3/Y

B. (5 1/2 FT, 7 PT) Acting-10/YO; Voice/Speech-3/Y; Movement-4/Y; Mime, etc.-2/O; Musical Theatre-2/Y; Directing-2/YO; Stage Combat-1/Y; Experimental-4/Y

C. (4 FT, 3 PT) Prins of Des-2/Y; Set Design-2/Y; Cost Des- 2/Y; Tech Prod'n-2/Y; Cost Hist-2/Y; Ltg Des-2/Y; Cost Constr-1/O; Make-up-2/Y; Stg Mgmt-2/Y; Make-up-2/Y; CAD-1/Y

D. (1 PT) Self-Producing-1/O

FACILITIES AND PRODUCTIONS

MAINSTAGE: 310 seats, fly space, computerized lighting. 4 prods: 3 Fac dir/des, 1 Guest dir/des, 1 Grad des, 8 UG des; total budget approx. $5,000-7,000

SECOND STAGE: 125 seats, computer & electron. lighting. 10 prods: 1 Fac dir/des, 3 Grad dir/des, 6 UG dir/des; $200-1,500

9 Workshops/Readings: 1 Fac dir, 2 Guest dir, 3 Grad dir, 3 UG dir; budget 0-$100

Facility was built in 1972, major renovation planned for 2003-04 & 2004-05 (new 175-seat Studio Theater); includes scene shop, costume shop, dance studio, rehearsal studio, design studio, lighting lab, classrooms.

A non-departmental, student-run organization presents one production per year in which dept. majors participate. 3 student-written plays produced in the last two years.

Connection with Center Stage (Equity), Internships; Everyman (Equity), Internships; Theatre Project, Graduate Productions

DESCRIPTION

Guest Artists: Charles S. Dutton, Actor/Director; John Glove, Actor; Richard Armstrong, Voice; Kia Corthron, Playwright; Donna DiNovelli, Playwright; Theodora Skipitares, Performance Artist; Squonk Opera; San Francisco Mime Troup; Daniel Dtein, Movement.

The theatre department at Towson University is founded on the principles of collaborative artistic and academic endeavor. The undergraduate and graduate programs have distinct missions but share resources and faculty, and foster a high degree of cooperation among students. The undergraduate program provides training in all aspects of performance and production, organized around a liberal arts core curriculum. It is intentionally eclectic, including in its productions and curriculum as many styles of theatre as possible. The department maintains a policy of casting only undergraduate actors in undergraduate productions. The Master of Fine Arts in Theatre is an experimental, self-directed program focusing on the creation of original work. In the search for new forms, the graduate program includes residencies by internationally recognized guest artists. Productions are non-traditional, student-generated projects which explore interdisciplinary and cross-cultural boundaries. The department has an exchange program with the Dartington College of Art in Devon, England.

University of Maryland - Baltimore County

Lynn Watson, Chair
Dept. of Theatre
1000 Hilltop Circle
Univ. MD/Baltimore County
Baltimore, MD 21250
(410) 455-2917
FAX: (410) 455-1046
ADMISSIONS: 1000 Hilltop Circle, Baltimore, MD 21250
(410) 455-2291
www.umbc.edu/undergrad

11,711 Total Enr.; h. comp
85 Majors; ATHE
Semester System
T: $8,622
O-ST T: $17,354
$8,150 r&b
www.umbc.edu/theatre

FAX: (410) 455-1094

DEGREES OFFERED

BFA in Acting (30); BA in Acting (40), Production/Design/Tech (15).
Declare major in 1st or 2nd year; 2004 granted 14 UG degrees.

ADMISSION & FINANCIAL INFORMATION

GPA, SAT/ACT scores, class rank, strength of applicant's curriculum & other achievements considered. 74.6% admitted to institution, any student accepted to UMBC may begin the Theatre Program; audition/portfolio for merit scholarships only. Linehan Artist Scholar: compet. GPA & SAT scores, freshmen only, audition/portfolio, offers tuition, amounts vary. Fine Arts Award for freshmen and transfer students, based on audition/portfolio interview, $1,000-3,000/yr. Theatre Dept. Award: faculty evaluation after 2 semesters in program, amounts vary.

FACULTY AND CLASSES OFFERED

10 FT, 3 PT: 2 PhD, 8 MFA/MA, 1 Staff

A. (2 FT, 1 PT) Intro to Th-1/Y; Th Hist-2/Y; Shakes-1/Y; Dramatic Lit-3/Y; Dramatic Crit-1/Y; Playwriting-1/O

B. (6 FT, 2 PT) Acting-4/Y; Voice/Speech-3/Y; Movement-2/Y; Directing-1/O; Dance-1/X; Stage Combat-1/O

C. (4 FT, 2 PT) Set Des-2/Y; Tech Prod'n-2/Y; Cost. Des-2/Y; Cost. Constr-1/Y; Stage Mgmt-2/O; Ltg Des-2/Y; Make-up-1/Y; Sound Design-2/X

D. Box Office Procedure-1/Y

FACILITIES AND PRODUCTIONS

MAINSTAGE: 180 seats, computerized lighting
   3-4 Fac dir/des prods; budget $12,000-15,000
   0-1 Fac dir Workshops/Readings; budget $500-1000.
Facility built in 1968, renovated in 1999; includes scene, costume, prop shops, sound studio, CAD facility, dance studio, 2 rehrsl studios, design studio, classrooms, drafting classroom.

DESCRIPTION

Noted Faculty: Xerxes Mehta, Artistic Director of The Maryland Stage Company, former professional resident company; Wendy Salkind, Alexander Technique Teacher; Lynn Watson, Chair and Vocal Director/Coach; Alan Kreizenbeck, Theatre History and Dramatic Literature; Susan McCully, Dramaturg, Feminist Theatre.

Guest Artists: Lee Breuer, Director; Anne Bogart, Director; Tomas Kubinek, Physical Theatre; Catherine Fitzmaurice, Voice; Peggy Shaw, Actor; Evan Alexander, Scenic Designer; Craig Brown, Scenic Painter; David Gaines, Le Coq Mask; Julianne Franz, Stage Management; John Robin Midgley, English

Theatre; Vincent Lancisi, Director; Nancy Romita, Laban Movement.

University of Maryland, Baltimore County's Theatre program emphasizes the integration of research and performance. The curriculum provides students with an in-depth understanding of their chosen area of specialization and an equally expansive knowledge of dramatic history, theory and literature. Variety in theatre training is offered by awarding the B.F.A. in Acting, the only B.F.A. in Acting offered in the state of Maryland, as well as the B.A. in theatre with emphasis in acting, design/production, theatre history and literature, or a B.A. in Theatre with Secondary Education Certificate. The B.F.A. in Acting is designed for the acting student interested in an intensive performance training program leading to the pursuit of graduate study and.or experience in professional theatre. The B.A. program is designed for the student interested in a broad understanding of all areas of theatre, while maintaining a focus on acting, technical theatre, theatre history and literature, or theatre education. The core theatre courses for all programs are similar, while reflecting these differences in emphasis.

University of Maryland - College Park

See ad in back of book-U/RTA

Daniel MacLean Wagner, Chair
Department of Theatre
2810 Clarice Smith PAC-
Univ. of Maryland
College Park, MD 20742-1610
(301) 405-6676
FAX: (301) 314-9599
www.theatre.umd.edu
ADM: Office of Undergraduate Adm., Mitchell Bldg., UMCP,
  College Park, MD 20742
(301) 314-8385
www.uga.umd.edu

Total Enr 35,102 UG/6348
  Grad.; h. compet.
Semester System,ATHE, NAST, U/RTA
239 Majors
T: $7,906
O-ST T: $21,345
$8,422 R&B
thetinfo@umd.edu

FAX: (301) 314-9693
um-admit@uga.edu

DEGREES OFFERED

BA (178); MA (7); MFA (16); PhD (21). Declare major in 3rd year; 2007 granted 27 UG, 11 Grad degrees.

ADMISSION & FINANCIAL INFORMATION

CAPA and TPA scholarships available. Students selected by aud and academic eligibility. No special requirements for admission to theatre program. Grad requires portfolio for des. 50% of applicants accepted

FACULTY AND CLASSES OFFERED

16 Full-Time, 7 Part-time, 5 Phd or DFA; 8 MA/MFA; 3 Professional w/o advanced degree; 5 Staff

A. (5 FT, 1 PT) Intro to Theatre-2/Y; Theatre History-17/Y; Dramatic Criticism-1/O; Performance Study-1/O

B. (5 FT, 1 PT) Acting-12/Y; Voice/Speech-3/Y; Movement-2/Y; Musical Th.-2/Y; Directing-2/Y; Puppetry-2/Y

C. (6 FT, 5 PT) Prins of Des-5/Y; Set Design-3/Y; Cost Des-4/Y; Ltg Des-3/Y; Tech Prod-5/Y; Cost. Constr.-2/Y; Make-up-2/Y; Sound Des-2/O; Stage Properties Des-1/O

FACILITIES & PRODUCTIONS

MAINSTAGE: 652 seats, fly space, computerized lighting
2 prods: 2 Fac dir; budget $18,000-22,000

SECOND STAGE: 195 seats, computerized lighting
9 prods: 3 Fac dir, 3 Grad des, 3 UG des; budget $7,000-14,000

THIRD STAGE: 126 seats, black box, electronic lighting
7 Workshop/Readings: 3 GA dir, 2 Grad dir, 2 UG dir, budget
$500-1,500

Facility was built in 2000; includes scene shop, costume shop, paint
& prop shop, welding shop, sound studio, CAD facility, 3 rehearsal studios, 2 design studios, lighting lab, 4 classrooms.

There is a non-departmental, student-run producing organization.
Connected with the Woolly Mammoth Theatre Company and
African Continuum.

The Department is located in the Baltimore/Washington corridor, one
of the fastest growing theatre markets in the nation. There are
over sixty professional theatre companies within twenty miles of
our building. The Department hires at least one professional
director each season, and employs professional actors when
needed to support student performances. Faculty members work
professionally across the country and are on the staff of Arena
Stage, the Olney Theatre Center, Round House Theatre, and the
Studio Theatre. Our students work as understudies, apprentices,
and stage managers in professional companies.

DESCRIPTION

Noted Faculty: Daniel MacLean Wagner, Dept Chair &
Lighting Des; Heather Nathan, Assoc Chair &
History/Theory; Frank Hildy, Dir of Grad Studies &
History/Theory Architecture; Helen Huang, Dir of UG
Studies & Costume Des; Dan Conway, Head of Des &
Scenic Des; Catherine Schuler, Head of
History/Theory & History/Theory Crit; Scot Reese,
Head of Performance & Actor/Director

Guest Artists: Blair Thomas, Puppetry; Jennifer Nelson,
Jerry Whiddon, Walter Dallas and Daniel De Raey,
Directors; Jennifer Plants, Tim Getman, Keith
Johnson, David Emerson Toney and Maia DeSanti,
Acting/Performance

The Department of Theatre at the University of Maryland,
College Park offers a B.A. in Theatre. This is a liberal arts
degree intended as a foundation for further study,
although students often pursue that study while they are
working professionally. Our alumni have used the skills
learned from their experience as a theatre major in a
wide variety of jobs both inside and outside the profession. We also offer the M.A., M.F.A. in Design and Ph.D.
in Theatre and Performance Studies. These are professional training degrees designed for those pursuing a
career in academic or professional theatre. All students
take classes from a faculty with a life commitment to theatre as an art, and long professional experience with theatre as a business. For further information consult our
website at www.theatre.umd.edu

The American Repertory Theatre /
Moscow Art Theatre School

Scott Zigler, Director
Inst. for Advanced Theatre Training
American Repertory Theatre
64 Brattle Street
Cambridge, MA 02138
www.amrep.org/iatt

Highly competitive
Semester System
47 Students
T: $29,700 1st yr./
$22,900 2nd yr.
(617) 496-2000x8890
FAX: (617) 495-1705

DEGREES OFFERED

Certificate + MFA Program; Acting (35), Voice (2),
Dramaturgy (4). Declare major upon application;
1997 granted 20 certificates.

ADMISSION & FINANCIAL INFORMATION

Audition for actors, interview for dramaturgs, Generally admits 22 out
of 300 applicants.

FACULTY AND CLASSES OFFERED

15 FT, 13 PT: 3 PhD, 16 MFA/MA, 9 Prof. w/o adv. degree;
8 Staff

A. (5 FT) Intro to Theatre-2/Y; Dramatic Lit-2/Y; Th. Hist-2/Y;
Dramatic Crit.-2/Y; Shakespeare-1/Y

B. (10 FT, 12 PT) Acting-8/Y; Mvmt-4/Y; Singing-2/Y; Directing-4/Y;
Voice-4/Y; Mime/Mask, etc.-1/Y; Stage Combat-1/Y; Dance-4/Y

D. Prins of Design-2/Y

FACILITIES & PRODUCTIONS

MAINSTAGE: 500+ seats, computer & electron. lighting
8-10 prods: 2 Fac dir, 2-3 Guest dir, 4-5 UG dir.

SECOND STAGE: 100 seats, computer lighting.
10 prods: 5 Fac dir, 1 Guest dir, 4 Grad dir

THIRD STAGE: 100 seats, black box

10 Workshops/Readings: 4 Fac dir, 6 Grad dir

Facility was built in 1960; includes scene shop, costume shop, sound
studio, 2 dance studios, 2 rehearsal studios, 2 classrooms.

Connection with American Repertory Theatre, Equity theatre. Many
faculty are members of the resident company. Students may be
in company productions.

DESCRIPTION

Noted Faculty: Robert Brustein, Dramaturgy and
Dramatic Literature; Anatoly Smeliansky,
Dramaturgy; Scott Zigler, Acting; Marcus Stern,
Directing; Arthur Holmberg, Dramaturgy; Andrei
Droznin, Movement; Catherine Fitzmaurice, Voice;
Margaret Eginlon, Movement; Nancy Haufek, Voice.

Guest Artists: Dario Fo, Directing & Playwriting; Marisa
Tomei, Debra Winger, Arliss Howard, Actors; Anna
Deavere Smith, Performance Study; Robert Woodruff
and Andrei Belgrader and Andrei Serban, Directing &
Acting; David Mamet, Playwriting; Mark Setlock,
Acting.Anne Bogart.

The Institute for Advanced Theatre Training was established in 1987 by the American Repertory Theatre as a
training ground for the professional American theatre. In

1998, the Institute began an exclusive collaboration with the Moscow Art Theatre (MXAT) School. The union of the two schools has created an historic program that provides unparalleled opportunities for training and growth. The wide range of courses given by the international faculty of resident and guest artists offers students unique preparation for the multi-faceted demands of the professional theatre. Each year, approximately twenty-two students in acting, directing, dramaturgy, and special studies are admitted to the full-time, two-and-half-year program of study. Students spend the spring of their first year studying in Moscow and the rest of their time training in Cambridge at the A.R.T. Upon graduation, all students receive a certificate from Harvard University and an M.F.A. from the Moscow Art Theatre School. During the spring of their second year, acting students present their work in New York and Los Angeles. Acting students who are not members of the professional union will be eligible to join Actor's Equity by the time of graduation. With its emphases on experimental work and professionalism, the Institute attracts artists whose bold ideas, creativity, and intelligence will shape the future of the American theatre.

Amherst College

Peter Lobdell, Chair
Department of Theater & Dance
Amherst College
Amherst, MA 01002
DEPT: (413) 542-2411
Adm:PO Box 5000 Amherst, MA 01002
admission@amherst.edu

1,648 T. Enr.; highly compet.
Semester System
11 Majors; ATHE
T: $36,232/$9,420 R&B
MAIN: (413) 542-2328

DEGREES OFFERED

BA in Theater, Dance (38). Declare major in first or second year..

ADMISSION & FINANCIAL INFORMATION

SAT 1 or ACT exam and 3 SAT 2 subject tests (1 must be English); Mean SAT scores: 628 verbal/675 Math. Accept 20% to institution; no special req's. for admission to Theatre Program, dept. admits as majors all students who can complete the curriculum requirements. All financial aid is need based: no special scholarships.

FACULTY AND CLASSES OFFERED

5 Full-Time: 1 MFA/BA, 3 MFA/MA, 1 Prof. w/o adv. degree

A. (1 1/2 FT) Dramatic Criticism-1/O; Dramatic Lit.-2/Y; Shakes-2/YX; Playwriting-2/Y; Theatre History-2/O

B. (2 1/2 FT) Acting-2/Y; Movement-2/Y; Directing-2/Y; Choreog.-2/Y; Voice/Mvmt-1/Y

C. (1 FT) Prins of Des-1/Y; Set Des-2/Y; Cost Des-2/Y; Lighting Des-2/Y; Perf. Design-1

FACILITIES AND PRODUCTIONS

MAINSTAGE: 400 seats, fly space, computerized & electronic lighting. 3 prods: 2 Fac dir, 1 UG dir, 1 Fac des, 2 UG des; + 3 readings/recitals; budget $17,500

SECOND STAGE: 150 seats, fly space, computerized lighting & electronic lighting. 4 prods: 1 Fac dir, 3 UG dir, 4 UG des + 1 staged reading; budget $11,000

THIRD STAGE: 75 seats, electronic lighting. 14 prods: all UG dir/des; budget $1,000

FOURTH STAGE: 75 seats, electronic lighting. 2 prods: 1 Fac dir/des, 1

UG dir/des; budget $500

PLUS, 5-7 special topics or non-departmental productions directed by majors in department or found spaces per year; budget $500

Main stage was built in 1938, renovated 1998-99; second, third, and fourth stages built 1998; includes scene shop, costume shop, design studio, two rehearsal studios, dance studio, sound studio. In 1998-99, there were four productions (including a musical) and two staged readings of student-written plays and two plays adapted from original texts.

Several non-departmental, student-run orgs. presents 5-10 prods. per year. Dept. majors sometimes participate. 6 student-written plays produced in the last two years.

DESCRIPTION

Noted Faculty: Manuame Mukasa, Directing; Connie Congdon, Playwriting; Suzanne Palmer Dougan, Design; Peter Lobdell, Acting, Perf Making, Wendy Woodson, Dance, Performance Making, Video.

Amherst College assumes that the study of Theater and Dance is an integrated one. The historical differences are recognized but the aesthetic and theoretical similarities are stressed. In the spirit of the liberal arts education, the Department seeks to introduce the mental, physical and emotional disciplines of performance and to provide concrete experiences in the unique creativity demanded by production. Amherst encourages double-majors; many theater and dance students also major in Art, English, History, and even the sciences. Both the curriculum and the production program stress the collaborative nature of the theatrical arts. Faculty, staff and major students form the nucleus of the production team and are jointly responsible for the college's Theater and Dance season. There is a strong focus on contemporary work. The work of student playwrights, directors, choreographers, designers and performance-makers figure prominently in the department's main stage season.

Boston College

John H. Houchin,
Assoc. Prof & Chair
Theatre Dept.
Robsham Theatre Arts Center
Boston College
Chestnut Hill, MA 02467
DEPT: (617) 552-4612
ADMISSIONS: Office of Undergraduate Admission, 208 Devlin Hall
(617) 552-3100
http://infoeagle.bc.edu

11,165 Total Enr.; h. compet
Semester System
130 Majors, ATHE
T: $30,950/$10,170 R&B
SMALL PROGRAM

FAX: (617) 552-2740

FAX: (617) 552-4975

DEGREES OFFERED

We encourage more than one area of theatre study. BA in Acting (60); Directing (15); Design/Technical (15); Management (5);. Dr. Lit/History/Playwriting (10). Declare major in soph. year; 2005 granted 19 degrees.

ADMISSION & FINANCIAL INFORMATION

The midrange of SAT scores of those accepted is 1250 to 1400; 32% of apps. accepted by inst.; interview with dept. chair is highly recommended.

FACULTY AND CLASSES OFFERED

5 Full-Time, 15 Part-time: 8 PhD, 9 MFA/MA; 7 Staff

A. (2 1/4 FT, 5 1/2 PT) Intro to Theatre-20/Y; Dramatic Lit-4/Y; Dramatic Crit-2/O; Theatre History-1/O; Playwriting-2/Y; Shakespeare-1/O; American Mus. Th.-1/O

B. (3/4 FT, 4 1/2 PT) Acting-5/Y; Voice/Speech-1/Y; Mvmt-2/Y; Singing-2/X; Mus. Th.-1/X; Directing-3/Y; Dance-7/O

C. (1 FT, 1 1/2 PT) Prins. of Design-1/O; Set Design-1/Y; Cost. Des-1/2-O; Cost. History 1/2/O; Ltg. Des-1/O; Tech. Prod'n-1/Y; Cost. Constr.-1/Y; Stage Mgmt.-1/O; Scene Painting-1

D. Arts Mgmt-1/O; Marketing/promo-1/O

FACILITIES AND PRODUCTIONS

MAINSTAGE: 600 seats, fly space, computerized lighting. 16 prods: 3 Fac dir, 8 Fac des; 3 Guest des, 2 UG des; budget $4,000-9,000

SECOND STAGE: 150 seats, black box, computerized lighting 8 prods: 1 Fac dir, 3 Fac des, 2 UG dir/des; budget $700-2,000

Facility built in 1981, renovated in 1995; includes scene shop, costume shop, video studio, dance studio, design studio, classrooms.

Non-departmental, student-run orgs. present 8-12 prods per year. Staged a series of student-written works in 2004-2005.

DESCRIPTION

Noted Faculty: Stuart J. Hecht, American Theatre History, Dramaturgy, Directing; John H. Houchin, American Theatre History; Scott T. Cummings, Dramatic Literature, Criticism, Playwriting; Crystal Tiala, Set and Costume Des.Luke Jorgensen, Acting, Creative Dramatics, Children's Theatre, Boal; Patricia Riggin, Acting, Meisner; Jacqueline Dalley, Costume Design.

Guest Artists: Eric Overmyer, playwright; Chris O'Donnell, actor; Charles Mee, playwright; Ron Nicynski, producer; Paul Daigneault, artistic director; Michelle Miller, actor.

The Boston College Theatre Department–faculty and students–is committed to merging scholarship and art. We challenge ourselves to engage the dynamic and evolving experience of theatre–the vast sweep of its history, the diversity of its literature, and the ever changing contours of its criticism. We give these intellectual inquiries flesh and bone presence through an array of productions that are supported by rigorous training in acting, dance, design, playwriting, play direction and theatre technology. As students you will receive a solid foundation of skills and knowledge that prepare you to begin advanced theatre studies or embark upon a career in professional theatre or one of its sister arts. However, we are not merely a department whose goals are limited to the production of plays. We know that philosophies, economies, religions and wars are profoundly embodied in the creation, performance and reception of theatre. By acknowledging the connection between this our art and the external forces that shape it, we are thus able to use theatre as a window into history, a method of analysis and a vehicle for social change.

The Boston Conservatory

Michael Nash, Ph.D, Director
The Boston Conservatory
8 The Fenway
Boston, MA 02215
Admin (617) 912-9153
www.bostonconservatory.edu

386 Total Enr.; h. compet.
150 Majors
Semester System
T: $28,300; $10,260 ROOM
FAX: (617) 247-3159

DEGREES OFFERED

BFA, MM in Musical Theatre (142). Declare major in freshman year; ,

ADMISSION & FINANCIAL INFORMATION

40% of applicants accepted to Institution. Aud. req. for actors, UG and Grad. 4 out of 10 UG and Grad applicants admitted to program. Scholarships by audition ranking.

FACULTY AND CLASSES OFFERED

35: 17 Theatre (10 FT, 7 PT); 10 Dance (4 FT, 6 PT); 10 Voice (7 FT, 2 PT); 21 hold MFA/MA degrees.

A. (2 FT, 1 PT) Intro to Th-1/Y; Dramatic Lit-1/Y; Th Hist-1/Y; Shakes-1/Y

B. (11 FT, 4 PT) Acting-8/Y; Voice/Speech-8/Y; Movement-8/Y; Mus Th-8/Y; Singing-8/Y; Directing-4/Y

C. (2 FT, 2 PT) Make-up-2/Y; Stage Craft-2/Y

FACILITIES & PRODUCTIONS

MAINSTAGE: 400 seats. 3 prods: 3 Fac dir/des, Guest-varies

SECOND STAGE: 75 seats. 8-10 prods: various dir/des

3-4 Workshops/Readings: various dir/des

Facility was built in 1950

DESCRIPTION

Noted Faculty: Fran Charnas, Musical Theater; Neil Donohoe, Musical Theater; Jennifer Burke, Speech; Steve McConnell, Acting; Robert Ingari, Music & Mus. Theater; Robert Bouffer, Acting; Phoebe Wray, Acting, Theater History; Cathy Rand, Musical Theater, Annie Thompson, Speech; Michael Allosso, directing, Mus. Theater.

Program is an integrated curriculum of acting, music and dance. Open auditions for all performances.

Boston University

Jim Petosa, Director
Boston University
  School for the Arts
855 Commonwealth Ave. Room 470
Boston, MA 02215
(617) 353-3390
ADM: 881 Commonwealth Ave.
http://www.bu.edu

18,521 UG Enr.; compet
Semester System
230 Majors
T: $35,418/R&b $10,950
FAX: (617) 353-4363
http://web.bu.edu/CFA
admissions@bu.edu

DEGREES OFFERED

BFA in Acting (132), Stage Management (12), Independent Theatre Studies (37); BFA/MFA in Design (scene, costume, lights, sound, tech. prod.) (37); MFA in Directing (5), Theatre, Education (3). Declare major in first year; 1997 granted 38 UG, 9 Grad degrees.

ADMISSION & FINANCIAL INFORMATION

SAT, 1140-1330 (Avg.class of 1999), GPA 3.5. 50% of apps. admitted to institution. UG requires audition/interview, portfolio review for

Design, Stage Mgmt.; admits 90 of 500 applicants; Grad requires audition/interview; admits 15 of 75 applicants. Performance awards are avail. through the Theatre Arts Division to students who show exceptional preprofessional promise on their audition. Students simply need to audition and are automatically considered on that day.

FACULTY AND CLASSES OFFERED

21 FT, 10 PT: 2 Ph.D, 19 MFA/MA, 9 Prof. w/o adv. degree; 6 Staff

A. (1 FT, 2 PT) Dramatic Lit-6/Y; Dram. Crit-4/Y; Playwriting-2/Y

B. (14 FT, 5 PT) Acting-8/Y; Voice/Speech-8/Y; Movement-8/Y; Mime, etc.-2/Y; Directing-4/Y; Stage Combat-2/Y; Shakes Acting-2/Y

C. (6 FT, 2 PT) Prins. of Design-2/Y; Set Design-6/Y; Cost. Des-6/Y; Ltg. Des-6/Y; Tech. Prod'n-6/Y; Cost. Constr.-6/Y; Stage Management.-4/Y; Design Research-4/Y; Drafting-2/Y; Drawing/Painting-2/Y

D. (1 PT) Arts Management-1/Y

FACILITIES AND PRODUCTIONS

MAINSTAGE: 850 seats, fly space, computerized lighting. 3 prods: 2 Fac dir, 1 Guest dir, 3 Grad des; budget $6,000-8,000

SECOND STAGE: 100 seats, computerized lighting 4 prods: 4 Grad dir/des 4 UG des; budget $2,200-2,700

THIRD STAGE: 100 seats, electronic lighting

Facility was built in 1925, renovated in 1972 & 1981; includes scene shop, costume shop, props shop, welding shop, sound studio, 3 dance studios, 6 rehearsal studios, 4 design studios.

A non-departmental, student-run org. presents 3 prods per year.

Connection with the Huntington Theatre Company (Equity), the professional theatre in residence at BU. Intern and assistants' positions are offered in design, directing, stage mgmt, administration. Selected advanced performance majors may audition for various understudy assignments and occasional supporting roles. An average of 24 advanced students work with HTC each season. Students also have opportunities to observe professional preparations, performances, and special demonstrations and to engage in colloquy with artists and staff.

DESCRIPTION

Noted Faculty: Jacques Cartier, Directing; Paula Langton, Voice/ Speech; William Young, Acting; Marianne Verheyen, Costume Des; Scott Bradley, Sharon Perlmutter, Scene Design (PT).

Guest Artists: Maria Aitken, Claire Bloom, Caroline Eves, Ralph Funicello, William Hurt, Pat McCorkle, Mark Redanty, Campbell Scott, Irene Worth, Mary Zimmerman.

The Boston University School of Theatre Arts offers professional training for talented, highly-motivated students who wish to prepare for a career in the theatre. This training, conducted by a resident faculty drawn from the professional ranks and augmented by guest artists, emphasizes the collaborative nature of theatre while it encourages each student's individual growth. In each area a carefully structured sequence of courses provides students with the knowledge, skills, command of craft, and understanding of professional practice that will allow them to assume active and creative positions in the theatre. At each step in the student's development, classroom experience is related to appropriate performance and production experience. In addition to the intensive

studio courses, undergrads have the opportunity to take one liberal arts course per semester, and additional elective opportunities are available on the advanced level. Continuation in all programs is based on professional review by the faculty. The School's graduate programs are highly selective and, in addition to rigorous programs of study, offer valuable internship opportunities with HTC and other theatres throughout the country.

Brandeis University

Chair, Theater Arts
Theater Arts Program
P. O. Box 9110 MS 072
Brandeis University
Waltham, MA 02454-9110
www.brandeis.edu/theater
theater@brandeis.edu
ADM: UG: MS003, above addr.
Adm: Grad. School, GSAS, MS 031
UGweb: www.brandeis.edu/admissions
Gradweb:www.brandeis.edu/gsas

3,304 Total Enr.; h. compet
Semester System
60 Majors; ATHE
T: $35,702/$9,908 r&b
DEPT: (781) 746-3340
FAX: (781) 736-3408
www.brandeis.edu
UG: (781) 736-3500
Grad: (781) 736-3410

DEGREES OFFERED

BA in Theatre Arts (68);MFA in Acting (26); Design (21). Declare major in soph. year

ADMISSION & FINANCIAL INFORMATION

Audition, portfolio review, writing samples, call Admissions for specific requirements; Univ. accepts 43% to institution; UG Th. program admits through Admissions office, not dept. Anyone can major, SAT,ACT, TOEFL. Grad prog. req's dramatic writing sample for playwrights/dramaturgs, critical/literary writing sample for dramaturgs, interviews and auditions for acting applicants, submission of portfolios for design applicants. Audition for actors; interview/portfolio/review for designers,TOEFL. Grad: tuition remission (in part or full) and possible stipend to majority of MFA candidates.

FACULTY AND CLASSES OFFERED

11 FT, 11 PT: 1 PhD, 9 MFA/MA, 12 Prof. w/o adv. degree; 7 Staff UG & Grad combined.

A. (1 FT, 2 PT) Theater Hist.-2/Y; Dramatic Lit-18/YX; Playwtg-1/O; Shakes-2/X; Introl to Theatre-2/Y

B. (5 FT, 3 PT) Acting-15/Y; Voice/Speech-13/Y; Stage Combat-4/Y Movement 9/Y; Singing-2/Y; Directing-2/O; Improv-1/Y

C. (5 FT, 6 PT) Stage Mgmt.-1/Y;Cost Des-13/Y; Set Des-12/Y; Ltg Des-9/Y; Tech Prod'n-5/Y; Cost Constr-9/YO; Scene Paint-10/Y;Sound-1/Y; Principles of Des-15/Y

FACILITIES AND PRODUCTIONS

MAINSTAGE: 748 seats, fly space, computerized lighting. 1 prods: 1 Fac dir, 1 Grad des; budget $8,000-14,000

SECOND STAGE: 165 seats; computerized lighting. 5 prods: 2 Fac dir, 3 Guest dir, 3 Grad des; budget $2,000-3,000

THIRD STAGE: 120 seats; electronic lighting, 5 workshops/readings, 5 prods, 1 fac dir, 2 Grad dir, 3 Grad des, 2 UG dir/des; budget $50-300

Facility was built in 1965, last renovated in 1991; includes scene shop, costume shop, prop shop, sound studio, welding, CAD fac-dance studios, rehearsal studios, design studio, classrooms, costume shops, electrical shop, light lab, paint area, study carrells, 8 dressing rooms, paint area, costume/prop spray booth area.

Several non-departmental, student-run organizations present 8-10 productions/yr in which majors sometimes participate. 10 major student-written productions, 2 major and several workshops produced in the last 2 yrs.

Connection with New Repertory Theater (equity operates during school yr) in Newton, MA. Third-year graduate actors and designers are given parts or design opportunities with The New Rep. A touring company tours local schools with another production.

DESCRIPTION

Noted Faculty: Janet Morrison, Acting; Marya Lowry, Voice/Acting; Susan Dibble, Movement; Nancy Armstrong, Singing; Karl Eigsti, Design; Robert O. Moody, Scene Painting; Debra Booth, Design; Jennifer Von Mayrhauser, Costume Des.; Denise Loewenguth, Cost. Construction; Arthur Holmberg, Dramatic Lit/Theory.

Guest Artists: Trezana Beverly, Director; Gordana Maric, Acting; Zanko Tomic, Acting; Clinton Turner Davis, Director; Jeff Mousseau, Director; Constance McCashin, Acting; Candice Brown, Director; Wesley Savick, Director.

The MFA Professional Theater Training Program at Brandeis focuses on the center of the theatrical experience: the human being. While encouraging experimentation and adventure, we stress the development of a solidly rooted technique, asking actors and designers to investigate roles, scenes, and spaces-and their own creative impulses - with honesty and intelligence. The BA in Theater Arts includes courses in theater history, dramatic literature, and theory, as well as courses in directing, playwriting, design, technical theater, stage management, and acting - voice, speech, movement, stage combat, and improvisation. The program combines intensive classroom training by a resident faculty of active professionals-augmented by guest instructors-with continual practical experience. Six major and several studio productions are mounted each year, directed by distinguished visiting professionals or faculty. Plays are chosen to provide maximum integration between classroom and stage for students in all areas.

College of the Holy Cross

Edward Isser, Chair
Department of Theatre
College of the Holy Cross
1 College Street
Worcester, MA 01610-2395
DEPT: (508) 793-3490
www.holycross.edu
ADMISSIONS: College of the Holy Cross, 1 College St., Worcester, MA 01610
(508) 793-2443
www.holycross.edu (see Admissions webpage)

2,700 Total Enr.; h. compet.
Semester System
31 Majors; ATHE, NAST
T: $34,630/9,960 r & b
SMALL PROGRAM
FAX: (508) 793-3030

DEGREES OFFERED

BA in Theatre (31). Students declare major in any year; 2007 granted 8 degrees.

ADMISSION & FINANCIAL INFORMATION

Generally, top 20% of high school class. Standardized test results are optional. No special requirements for admission to theatre program.

FACULTY AND CLASSES OFFERED

6 FT, 4 PT: 3 PhD/DFA, 6 MFA/MA, 3 Staff

A. (2 FT) Dramatic Lit-2/Y; Theatre History-3/Y; Shakes-1/Y; Film Studies-2/Y

B. (2 FT,4 PT) Acting-6/Y; Voice/Speech-1/Y; Mime, etc.-1/O; Singing-2/X; Directing-2/Y; Dance-8/Y

C. (2 FT) Principles of Design-1/Y; Set Des-1/O; Cost Des-1/Y; Lighting Des-1/O; Costume Constr-1/O; Stage Mgmt-1/Y

FACILITIES & PRODUCTIONS

MAINSTAGE: 220 seats, computerized lighting
2 prods: 2 Fac dir, 8 Fac des, budget $20,000-30,000

SECOND STAGE: 75 seats,
5-8 prods: 5-8 UG dir/des; budget $0-500

Facility renovated in 2005 includes costume, scene shop, 2 movement/dance studios, design studio, CAD facility, 2 rehearsal studios, 2 classrooms, green room/majors lounge.

A non-departmental, student-run, producing organization presents 2 productions per year in which majors participate.

Connected with Redfeather Theatre at Holy Cross, operates summer only. Redfeather runs the Worcester Summer Shakespeare Festival. There are 8 internships (for both acting and crew) available each summer. Undergrads routinely have lead roles in productions alongside Equity and professional actors.

DESCRIPTION

Noted Faculty: Kaela San Lee, Dance; Steve Vineberg, Dramatic Lit, Film Studies; Lynn Kremer, Voice, Scene Study; Edward Isser, Directing, Shakespeare; Timothy Smith, Acting; William Rynders, Design; Kurt Hultgren, Costume Design.

Guest Artists: Andrea Caspari, Puppetry; Eric Culver, Music Direction; Jere Shea, Voice; Bartlett Sher, Directing; Rinde Eckert, Performance; I Wayan Dibia, Gamelan and Balinese Dance

The Theatre major is a rigorous program for the liberal arts student, providing a thorough foundation for those who may choose professional training or graduate studies. The major offers pre-graduate school preparation equal to that of any undergraduate institution in the country. There are five full-time and one part-time faculty in theatre, three part-time faculty in dance, and a full-time costume designer. The number of majors is limited in order to provide for daily formal and informal contact between faculty, staff and students. Practical experience is provided through a professionally directed and designed, fully mounted, full-length theatrical production each semester. Auditions are open to the entire college community. All majors are encouraged to participate in each production; they are not, however, guaranteed roles. There are also numerous studio productions, and a variety of end-of-semester class projects in dance, acting, directing and playwriting.

Emerson College

Melia Bensussen,Interim Chair
Department of Performing Arts
120 Boylston Street
Boston, MA 02116-4624
DEPT: (617) 824-8780
auditions@emerson.edu
Admin info:
www.admission@emerson.edu

3,402 Total Enr.; competitive
Semester System
450 UG, 40 G Majors; ATHE
T: $22,144/R&B $9828
FAX:(617) 824-8799
www.emerson.edu
(617) 824-8600
fax:(617) 824-8609

DEGREES OFFERED

BFA in Acting, Dance/Theatre, Musical Theatre, Production/Stage Management, Theatre Design/Tech; BA in Theatre Education and Theatre Studies (performance and non-performance emphasis); MA in Theatre Education.

ADMISSION & FINANCIAL INFORMATION

Competitive; selection is based upon applicants' academic record, recommendations, writing competency, and standardized test scores. Also consider personal qualities as seen in extracurricular activities, community involvement, and demonstrated leadership. Candidates for Performing Arts programs are required to submit a resume of theatre-related activities and either audition or interview, or submit a portfolio or essay. More than 65% of the student body receives financial aid, typically packaged in awards that combine grant and scholarship, loan, and college work-study. Merit scholarships are awarded on academic credentials and range from $4,000 to half-tuition.

FACULTY AND CLASSES OFFERED

15 FT, 16 PT: 5 PhD, 21 MA/MFA, 5 Prof. w/o adv. degree; 9 Staff

Department core courses: Languages of Stage; Stagecraft Labs; World Drama, and choice among performance and dramaturgy offerings. Major-specific classes include: Acting (44 credits in movememt, improv, scene, ensemble, and studio); Musical Theatre (32-34 credits in movement, improv, scene, ensemble, dance, voice, and studio); Dance (32 credits in dance theatre, composition and technique courses); Design/Tech (32 credits in fundamentals, theory/practice, and production assignments); Stage Management (28 credits in arts/stage management, directing, production projects, internship); Theatre Education (24-32 credits in education, psychology, teaching certification).

FACILITIES AND PRODUCTIONS

MAINSTAGE: Historic 1,200-seat Cutler Majestic Theatre (renovated in 2003); digital lighting and sound, fly space, wired for broadcast.

SECOND STAGE: 208-260 seat Tufte Theatre #1; 3/4 thrust-flexible, digital lighting and sound, tension grid, wired for broadcast, wheelchair accessible (backstage and audience).

THIRD STAGE: 115 seat Greene Theatre; end stage, digital lights and sound, wired for broadcast.

The Tufte Performance and Production Center (11 stories, constructed in 2003) includes rehearsal and performance space, costume and scene shop, classrooms, design/tech center, and television studios with editing and control rooms.

Students participate in 8-10 fully staged theatre, dance, and musical theatre productions (budget $20,000-$50,000) and an additional 50 productions (budget $500-$7500) produced by faculty, guest directors, and students.

DESCRIPTION

Noted Faculty: Maureen Shea, directing/acting; Rhea Gaisner, acting; Kathleen Donohue, acting; Robbie McCauley, acting; Mark Cohen, acting; Ken Cheeseman, acting; Dossy Peabody, acting; Stephen Terrell, musical theatre; Scott Wheeler, musical theatre; Janet Talsey Craft, dance; Timothy Jozwick, design; Mary Ellen Adams, design; Harry Morgan, design; Melia Bensussen, production; Bonnie J. Baggesen, production; Robert Colby, theatre education; and artist-in-residence Amelia Broome Silberman, Sarah Hickler, and Susan Main.

Guest Artists/Master Classes: Brian Dennehy, actor; Whoopi Goldberg, actor; Peter Sellers, director; Kathleen Turner, actor; Kevin Bright, producer; Henry Winkler, actor/producer; Jane Alexander, actress; Anthony Clark, comedian.

The Department of Performing Arts at Emerson offers students a well-rounded college education (with rigorous training at its center) while enabling them to develop expertise in clearly defined specialty areas. Although our comprehensive educational goals differ from traditional conservatories, Emerson students are nonetheless prepared for professional outcomes or further training. Faculty teach rigorous training sequences designed to improve creative talents and reach students' fullest potential. An Emerson education allows for both immersion in an effective training environment—for actors, designers, musical theatre performers, playwrights, or directors—and freedom to grow and develop through a rich college curriculum within an institution specializing in communication and the arts.

Mount Holyoke College

Vanessa James, Chair
Dept. of Theatre Arts
Mount Holyoke College
South Hadley, MA 01075
DEPT: (413) 538-2832
ADM: 50 College St., So. Hadley, MA 01075
MAIN: (413) 538-2118
admission@mtholyoke.edu

2,149 Total Enr.; h. compet.
20 Majors; ATHE
Semester System
SMALL PROGRAM
theatre@mtholyoke.edu

FAX: (413) 538-2838
T:$35,940/R&b $10,520

DEGREES OFFERED

BA in Theatre Arts (7). Declare major in sophomore year

ADMISSION & FINANCIAL INFORMATION

No special requirements for admission to theatre program.

FACULTY AND CLASSES OFFERED

4 FT, 1 FT Guest Artist: plus guest artists in directing, performing art, arts management.

A. (2 FT) Intro to Theatre-2/Y; Th History-1/Y; Dramaturgy-1/O; History Seminars-1/Y

B. (2 FT) Acting-3/Y; Directing-2/Y

C. (1 FT) Cost Des-1/Y; Set Des-1/Y; Ltg Des-1/Y; Art Direction for Film and Television-1/O

D. (1 PT) Lighting Design-1/O; Tech Theatre-1/O; Cost. Constr-1/O; Cost. Hist-1/O; Make-up-1/O

FACILITIES & PRODUCTIONS

MAINSTAGE: 192 seats, fly space, computerized lighting
4 + prods: 2 Fac dir, 12 Fac des, 1 Guest dir, 2 Guest des, 1 UG dir, 2 UG des; budget $5,000

15 (approx.) UG dir/des Workshops/Readings

BLACK BOX: 30 seats

Facility was built in 1968, includes scene shop, costume shop, prop shop, welding shop, design studio, dance studio, rehearsal studio, classrooms.

Student-run Free Theatre presents original works and scripted plays.

DESCRIPTION

Noted Faculty: Vanessa James, Costume/Set Design; Joyce Devlin, Acting; Roger Babb, Acting.

Guest Lecturer: Paula Alekson

Northeastern University

[Has not been updated from 9th edition]

Janet Bobcean, Chair	12,376 Total Enr.
Department of Theatre	Quarter System; ATHE
337 Ryder Hall	100 Majors; NETC,
ACTFNortheastern University	T: $32,149, r&b:$11,010
360 Huntington Avenue	ADM: (617) 373-2000
Boston, MA 02115	DEPT: (617) 373-2244
admissions@neu.edu	www.northeastern.edu/

DEGREES OFFERED

BA and BS in Theatre Generalist Program (28), Acting Concentration (15), Production and Design (2). Students declare major in 1st year;

ADMISSION & FINANCIAL INFORMATION

Requirements for admission to univ. vary according to program; all students accepted to Univ. are admitted to Th prog; interview at end of each year to remain in program. Max. financial aid $12,900/yr., average freshman award $6,825. Write to Financial Aid, Initial Year Unit, for info. Dept of Theatre annual award for majors only: The Blackman Scholarship. Write to Janet Bobcean, Chair, for information.

FACULTY AND CLASSES OFFERED

4 Full-Time, 7 Part-Time; 1 Staff

A. (2 FT, 1 PT) Intro to Theatre-1/Y; Dramatic Lit-4/Y; Theatre History-3/Y; Dramatic Crit-1/Y; Shakes-XY; Playwriting-1/Y

B. (3 FT, 4 PT) Acting-4/Y; Voice/Speech-1/Y; Movement-1/Y; Singing-XY; Musical Theatre-2/O; Directing-1/O; Stage Combat-1/O

C. (1 FT, 2 PT) Prins of Des-2/O; Set Design-2/O; Cost Des-1/O; Ltg Des-2/O Tech Prod'n-1/O; Cost Constr-1/O; Costume History-1/O; Make-up-1/Y; Stage Mgmt- 1/O

FACILITIES & PRODUCTIONS

MAINSTAGE: 1,100 seats, fly space, computerized lighting
1 prods: 1 Fac dir, 1 UG des; budget $6,000-8,000

SECOND STAGE: 100 seats, fly space, computerized lighting
3 prods: 3 Fac dir, 3 Guest des; budget $3,000-6,000

THIRD STAGE: 40 seats, electronic lighting

3 UG dir/des Workshops/Readings; budget $100-500

Facility was built in 1967, renovated in 1988; includes scene shop, costume shop, video studio, 2 movement studios, 2 rehearsal studios, design studio, 1 classroom, 1 lighting lab. All of the studios are classrooms plus one studio is our third stage.

Non-departmental, student-run, organization presents 3 productions per year in which majors participate.

DESCRIPTION

Noted Faculty: Janet Bobcean, Chair and Producer; Ed Bullins, Playwright; Dr. Nancy Kindelan, Directing, Dramaturgy, Dramatic Literature; Del Lewis, Acting and Directing; Theodore Janello, Technical Director.Thomas Keating, Acting

At Northeastern University, the undergraduate theatre major will be introduced to the total theatre experience, then elect one of three concentrations: Theatre Generalist, Performance or Production. The curricula allow the student to obtain the background for advanced study on a graduate level or for a career in the professional theatre. The classroom and stages are viewed as laboratories where theory is tested in rehearsal and performance (experiential learning). Theatre majors are encouraged to express individual creative and interpretive impulses and, with the support of a faculty advisor, are often able to perform a variety of projects of their own initiation in acting, directing, playwriting, design, performance. The difference between the B.A. and B.S. degree is one of flexibility, where the B.A. requires more College core courses and the B.S., more theatre or elective courses. Opportunity exists for the student to have a dual major in such areas as Education, American Sign Language, Music Industry, and other areas, to be announced.

Salem State College

See ad next page

William Cunningham	4,900 Total Enr.;not competitive
Theatre & Speech Comm Dept	163 Majors; NAST
Salem State College	Semester System
352 Lafayette St.	T: $5,500/$3,242-6,030 R&B
Salem, MA 01970	O-ST T: $11,600/$3,242-6,030 R&B
(978) 542-6291	FAX: (978) 542-6291
wcunningham@salemstate.edu	
ADMISSIONS: Address above.	
(978) 542-6200	www.salemstate.edu

DEGREES OFFERED

BA in Performance or Technical (117); BA Theatre Secondary Education (6); BFA in Performance (38), Design (4), Technical (3), and Stage Management (3). Declare major in freshman year; 2004 granted 28 degrees.

ADMISSION & FINANCIAL INFORMATION

Min. 2.51 GPA, SAT 920. 80% of applicants accepted by institution. Theatre program admits 50 out of 70 applicants. Presidential Arts Schol-audition and interview, covers in-state tuition only, does not include college fees.

FACULTY AND CLASSES OFFERED

9 Full-Time, 4 Part-Time:, 10 MFA/MA; 1 Prof. w/o adv degree, 2 Staff

A. (1FT, 1PT) Intro to Theatre-1/Y; Dramatic Lit-6/Y; Theatre Hist-2/Y; Shakes-2/Y; Dramatic Criticism-1/Y; Playwriting-2/Y

115

B. (4 FT, 1 PT) Acting-6/Y; Voice/Speech-3/Y; Movement-2/Y; Mime, etc.-1/Y; Directing-1/Y; Stage Combat-1/Y

C. (4 FT) Prins of Des-1/Y; Cost Des-1/O; Tech Prod'n-2/O; Set Design-2/Y; Ltg Des-2/Y; Cost Constr-2/Y; Stage Mgmt-2/Y; Make-up-1/Y.

FACILITIES & PRODUCTIONS

MAINSTAGE: 725 seats, fly space, computerized lighting. 5 prods: 3 Fac dir, 4 Fac des, 1 Guest des, 2 UG dir/ 4UG des; budget $8,000-15,000

SECOND STAGE: 90 seats, computerized lighting. 4 prods: 2 Fac dir, 4 Fac des, 2 UG dir, 4 UG des; budget $5,000-8,000

Workshops/Readings; 3 prods,1 Fac dir, 2 UG dir/des; budget $100-750

Facility was built in 1956, renovated in 2002; includes scene shop, costume shop, sound studio, CAD facil, video studio, dance studio, design studio, 4 classrooms.

A non-departmental, student-run organization presents 5 productions per year. Dept. Majors participate. 5 student-written play produced in the last two years.

Summer Theatre at Salem and student group, Student Theatre Ensemble, uses the facility during the summer.

DESCRIPTION

Noted Faculty: Celena Sky April, Voice/Styles; Tatsuya Aoyagi, Movement/Acting; David Allen George, Acting/Styles; William Cunningham, Playwright/Directing/History; James J. Fallon, Scenic Lighting; Whitney White, Lighting/Scenic; Peter Zachari, Directing; Thomas Luddy, History; Christopher Morris/Technical.

Guest Artists: Molly Trainer, Costume Design, Dominic Donadio, Automated Lighting.

The Theatre program seeks to instill within students an awareness of theatre as a significant educational and spiritual force. We engage in the pursuit of educational excellence through innovation, tradition, and technology and serve as an artistic, cultural and educational resource. We provide theatre education and training of the highest quality within a liberal arts setting, fostering personal and artistic development. We strive to achieve this through excellence in the classroom and in the production process, with a strong program to production link and artistic excellence in productions. The BA (39 credits in theatre) is designed to provide students with a theatrical worldview, a foreign language and a minor that is supportive of their major career aspirations. The BFA (66 credits in theatre, 15 credits in dramatic literature) program provides students with a high level of competency, specialized knowledge and extensive experience in preparation for a professional career in theatre.

Smith College

Kiki Gounaridou, Chair
Theatre Department
Mendenhall Center for the Perf Arts
Smith College
Northampton, MA 01063
DEPT: (413) 585-3204
ADMISSIONS: 7 College Lane
admission@smith.edu

3,000 +/- Total Enr.; h. compet.
Semester System
45 Majors; ATHE
T: $32,320/$10,880 R&B
FAX: (413) 585-3229
kgounari@email.smith.edu
(413) 585-2523
www.smith.edu

DEGREES OFFERED

BA in Theatre (45); MFA in Playwriting (3). Declare major in soph. year. 2007 granted 16 UG, 3 Grad

ADMISSION & FINANCIAL INFORMATION

SAT; requirements vary according to program. MFA in Playwriting requires interview and writing sample. Grad admits 5 of 20 applics.

FACULTY AND CLASSES OFFERED

9 FT, 4 PT: 3 PhD, 6 MFA/MA, 9 Staff

A. (3 FT) Theatre History-2/Y; Dramatic Lit-3/Y; Dramatic Criticism-1/Y; Playwriting-4/Y; Shakes-XY

B. (3 FT, 4 PT) Acting-6/Y; Voice/Speech-2/Y; Mime, etc. -1/O; Directing-4/Y; Movement-1/O; Dance-XY

C. (3 FT) Principles of Design-1/Y; Set Design-3/Y; Ltg Des-3/Y; Cost. Design-3/Y; Costume Constr-1/Y; Make-up-1/Y; Tech Prod-1/Y; Stage Mgmt-1/Y

D. B.O. Procedure-1/Y

FACILITIES AND PRODUCTIONS

MAINSTAGE: 461 seats, fly space, computerized lighting
4 prods: 1 Fac dir/des; 1 GA dir/des; 2 UG dir/des; budget $5,000

SECOND STAGE: 220 seats, fly space, computerized lighting
1 prods: 1 UG dir/des; budget $5,000

Third stage: 50 seats
8 prods: 8 UG dir; budget $1,000

Facility built in 1968, last renovated in 2001, includes scene shop, costume shop, props shop, welding shop, sound studio, movement/dance studio, rehearsal studios, design studio, classrooms, theatre and music library, non-print resources, computer facilities for design.

A non-departmental, student-run organization presents 4 productions per year in which dept majors participate. 2 student-written plays have been produced in the last two years.

DESCRIPTION

Noted Faculty: Kiki Gounaridou, Chair, Theatre History; Ed Check, Set Design; Kiki Smith, Costume Design; Nan Zhang, Lighting Design; Len Berkman, Playwriting/Dramatic Lit; Andrea Hairston, Playwriting/Dramatic Lit; John Hellweg, Acting/Directing; Ellen W. Kaplan, Acting/Directing; Paul Zimet, Acting/Directing

Guest Artists: Anna Deavere Smith, Venya Smekhov, Elaine Bromka, Holly Derr, Emily Mann, Tina Shepard, Pearl Cleage, Deborah Lubar

The Theatre Department explores all aspects of Theatre Studies: Theatre History, Dramatic Literature, Dramatic Theory and Criticism, all aspects of Theatre Design, Acting, Directing, and Playwriting. Theatre courses explore both western and non-western theatre traditions, as well as African-American, Asian, Native, and feminist theatres.

Tufts University

Barbara W. Grossman, Chair
Dept. of Drama & Dance
Tufts University
Medford, MA 02155
DEPT : (617) 627-3524
FAX: (617) 627-3803
ADMISSIONS: Tufts University, Medford, MA 02155
www.tufts.edu

4,500 Total Enr.
Semester System
20 Majors; ATHE, ASTR
T: $35,842/$5,220 R&B
MAIN: (617) 628-5000
www.tufts.edu/as/drama

(617) 627-3170

DEGREES OFFERED

BA in Drama. Declare major in sophomore year; 2005 granted 12 degrees. (Also M.A. and Ph.D. in Drama; 2005 granted 3 degrees.)

ADMISSION & FINANCIAL INFORMATION

Univ. requires SAT I or ACT and 3 SAT IIs, letters of recom, essays. No special requirements for theatre program. Univ. admits 28% of applicants.

FACULTY AND CLASSES OFFERED

12 FT (includes Dance), 7 PT: 8 PhD, 9 MA/MFA, 2 BA, 4 Staff

A. (4 1/2 FT, 2 PT) Dramatic Lit/Theory-5+/Y; Theatre History-2+/Y; Shakes-1+/Y; Screenwriting-2/Y; Theater and Film-3+/Y.

B. (3 1/2 FT, 4 PT) Acting-6+/Y; Movement-2+/Y; Modern Dance-1+/Y; Creative Process-1/Y; Directing-2/Y; Kathak-1/Y; West African Dance-2/Y; Public Speaking-3+/Y.

C. (4 FT, 1 PT) Prins of Design-1/Y; Theatre Tech-1/Y; Stage Engr-1/Y; Set Design-2/Y; Cost Des-2/Y; Ltg Des-2/Y; CAD-1/Y; 3-D Des-2/Y; Stage Mgmt-1/Y; Makeup-1/Y.

FACILITIES AND PRODUCTIONS

MAINSTAGE: 216 seats, Balch Arena Theater, computerized lighting, flexible space
3 Fac dir and Fac or UG des, 1 Fac choreograph, 3 UG dir/des; bdgt $2,000-10,000

7+ UG dir/des workshops on the mainstage; budget $150-500

Facility built in 1991; includes scene shop, costume shop, sound studio, dance studio, 2 rehearsal studios, design studio; alternative spaces on campus used for student productions.

Majors often participate in and lead student drama organizations that present 12-15 productions annually on the mainstage (not including dance performances) and elsewhere on campus. The groups produce musicals, new plays, improv comedy, sketch comedy, mime, children's theater and dance pieces.

DESCRIPTION

Noted Faculty: Laurence Senelick, Dramatic Literature & Theory, Theatre History, Film Studies; Downing Cless, Dramatic Literature & Theory, Acting & Directing; Barbara W. Grossman, Theatre History, Dramatic Lit, Crit, Director; Claire Conceison, Theatre History, Asian & Asian American Theatre, Performance Studies; Don Weingust, Shakespeare Studies, Dramatic Literature & Theory, Theatre History, Acting; Sheriden Thomas, Acting & Directing; Alice Trexler & Daniel McCusker, Dance; Margo Caddell,

Lighting Design; Ted Simpson, Scene Design.

Guest Artists: Elaine Bromka, actor; Nora Chipaumire, dancer/choreographer; Laura Harrington, playwright; Meng Jinghui, director, playwright; Dan Kwong, actor/playwright; Manjula Padmanabhan, playwright; Christopher Vasquez, performance artist; Paul Zaloom, performance artist.

Tufts University is ranked high among drama programs at private liberal arts colleges by the Gourman Report. We believe theatre is inherently multidisciplinary, creating unique windows to various worlds of human knowledge. Our proximity to Boston/NYC allows students easy access to outstanding performing arts, including the A.R.T. in Cambridge. Majors take courses in acting, directing, design, film studies, theatre history, dramatic literature and theory, technical theater and dance. An active production season complements the coursework so that artistic and critical skills can be applied and understood in the context of performance. The 2007-2008 season includes *Big Love, Rosencrantz and Guildenstern are Dead, and The Alarm Clock* (a new Chinese play), student-directed/designed shows, workshops, showcases, and dance concerts. We value the insights our majors gain from taking courses in other departments, and students often double-major. Minors in drama, dance, or drama and dance are also available, as are study-abroad conservatory programs. Our integrated curriculum prepares students for top graduate schools/professional training programs (A.C.T., Brown, Columbia, Juilliard, NYU, Yale) and two-thirds of our alumni have careers in theatre arts specialization. Alumni include professional directors, writers, designers, and actors on film/TV (*The Simpsons, American Beauty*), Broadway (*Caroline, or Change, Cats, Rent, Spamalot*), and off-B'way (*I Love You, You're Perfect, Now Change*).

University of Massachusetts

Harley Erdman, Assoc. Prof.	19,823-UG Total Enr.; compet.
Department of Theater	Semester System
Room 112, Fine Arts Center	230 Majors
University of Massachusetts	NAST, ATHE
151 President's Dr. OFC 2	T: $9,921/R&B $7,274
Amherst, MA 01003-9331	O-ST T: $18,144/r&b $7,274
DEPT: (413) 545-3490	FAX: (413) 577-0025

www.umass.edu/theater
ADM: Adm. Center, UMass, Amherst MA 01003
(413) 545-0222   www.umass.edu/umhome/admissions

DEGREES OFFERED

BA in Theater (230), includes broad-based study of dramaturgy, acting, design.. Declare major by 1st or 2nd year; 2004 granted 40 UG, 4 Grad degs.

ADMISSION & FINANCIAL INFORMATION

22% of apps. accepted by institution. Avg. SAT: c: 1125; avg. class rank: top third. Interview, portfolio for Grad applicants. Chancellor's Talent Award. cost of tuition, given to jrs., srs., must be resident of MA, full time student, maintain 2.5 GPA and a major avg. of at least 2.8, a series of basic level theater courses must have been completed. Candidates who are eligible for the award are selected by faculty based on such factors as involvement in the dept. and achievement.

FACULTY AND CLASSES OFFERED

10 FT, 1 PT:4 PhD/DFA, 5 MFA/MA, 2 Prof. w/o adv. degree;7 Staff

A. (3 FT, 1 PT) Intro to Th-1/Y; Dram. Lit-5/Y; Shakes-1/Y; Playwriting-1/O;

B. (3 FT) Acting-4/Y; Voice/Speech-2/Y; Mvmt-1/Y; Mime, etc-1/O; Singing-1/X; Musical Th-1/O; Directing-2/Y

C. (4 FT) Prins of Design-1/Y; Set Des-2/Y; Cost Des-2/Y; Ltg Des-2/Y; Tech Prod-11/Y; Stage Mgmt-1/O

FACILITIES AND PRODUCTIONS

MAINSTAGE: 560 seats, fly space, comput. lighting. 5 prods: 1 Fac dir, 2 Fac des, 3 Guest des, 3 Grad dir, 7 Grad des, 1 UG dir, 3 UG des, budget $3000-5000

SECOND STAGE: 90 seats. 4 prods: 1 Fac dir, 3 Fax des, 4 Guest des, 1 Grad dir, 3 Grad des, 2 UG dir (independent student production by theater majors, not part of season), 1 UG des; budget $12-14,000

Workshops/readings 20+ budget $10-50.

Facility was built in the 1970's; includes scene shop, costume shop, 1 dance studio, rehearsal studio, 4 classrooms.

A non-departmental, student-run organization presents 4 productions per year, majors sometimes participate. 1 student written play presented in the last two years.

DESCRIPTION

Noted Faculty: Milan Dragicevich, Acting; Harley Erdman, Dramaturgy; June Gaeke, Costume Design; Gilbert McCauley, Directing; Julie Nelson, Acting/Movement/Voice; Julian Olf, Dramaturgy/Playwriting; Penny Remsen, Lighting Design; Miguel Romero, Scenic Design.

Guest Artists: Nora Amin, Performer/Writer; Constance Congdon, Playwright; Tsidii LeLoka, Singer/Performer; Bill Pullman, Actor; Mark Stanley, Lighting Designer; Theatre De La Jeune Lune, Acting Troupe; Alice Tuan, Playwright; Billy Dee Williams, Actor; Greg Allen, Director.

The University of Massachusetts Department of Theater offers a liberal arts undergraduate program and a professional graduate program in directing, design, and dramaturgy. Undergraduates are expected to encounter all the arts of the theater; premature specialization is not encouraged. Graduates of the B.A. program are accepted by leading professional programs including NYU, Washington, Texas, Rutgers, Temple, North Carolina and others. M.F.A. graduates include actor Bill Pullman, playwright Constance Congdon, dramaturg John Dias, and director Greg Leaming. Our production philosophy combines theory and practice.

Wellesley College

Nora Hussey, Dir. of Theatre	2,500 Total Enr. (women's coll.)
Alumnae Hall, WCT	8 Majors; competitive
Wellesley, MA 02481	Semester System
DEPT: (781) 283-2029	T: $32,000 $10,000 R&B
FAX: (781) 283-3625	SMALL PROGRAM

nhussey@wellesley.edu
ADMISSIONS: 106 Central St. Wellesley, MA 02481
(781) 283-2270   FAX: (781) 283-3678

www.wellesley.edu

DEGREES OFFERED
BA with a major in Theatre - not a specific discipline
Declare major in 2nd year; 2007 granted 6 degrees.

ADMISSION & FINANCIAL INFORMATION
HS record, class rank, test scores, letters of rec., essays, interview.
Ruth Nagel Jones Fund-based on financial need and talent.

FACULTY AND CLASSES OFFERED
2 Full-Time, 4 Part-Time: 6 Prof. w/o adv. degree; 1 Staff

A.   Shakespeare-1/O; Dramatic Criticism-1/Y

B.   (2 FT) Acting-3/Y; Directing-1/Y; Independent Study 3/Y

C.   (1 PT) Set Design-1/Y

FACILITIES & PRODUCTIONS
MAINSTAGE: 1000 seats, fly space, computerized lighting
    3 Fac dir prods; budget $8,000-10,000

SECOND STAGE: 100 seats, computerized lighting
    12 UG dir prods; budget $1,000-3,000

3 Workshops/Readings; budget $100-500

Facility was built in 1993, includes scene shop, sound studio, movement/dance studio, rehearsal studio, classrooms.

A non-departmental, student-run organization presents 10-12 productions per year in which dept. majors participate. 2 student-written plays produced in the last two years.

Connection with Wellesley Summer Theatre, Boston Playwright's Theatre. The summer company is in its ninth year and is a critically acclaimed addition to the Boston theatre scene. Students are in the company and fill any number of roles and staff positions. Three productions are presented and all positions are salaried. Students work with seasoned professionals and are an integral part of the resident company.

DESCRIPTION
Guest Artists: Actos from the London stage; Company of Women workshop, Lois Roach, Playwright's Director; Billie Whitelaw, Beckett Actress; Kate DeVore, Speech, "Acter" Group; David Perry, Shakespeare; John Kane, Actor.

Theatre at Wellesley College is open and inclusionary of all interested students not just majors. The thrust of the program is enhancing and developing the individual progression of each performer regardless of their career plans. Our productions are designed by theatre professionals and male roles are filled by members of the Boston theatre Community. Thus students are working with individuals who may have far more wide range experiences. The director of theatre is a professional who maintains a career outside of Wellesley as well as within it.

MICHIGAN

Alma College

Joe Jezewski, Director of Theatre
Heritage Center
Alma College
Alma, MI 48801

1,400 Total Enr.; h. compet.
Semester System
40 Majors
T: $23,688; $7,774 R&B

DEPT: (989) 463-7262   FAX: (989) 463-7277
www.alma.edu/departments/theatredance
jezewski@alma.edu   admissions@alma.edu
ADMISSIONS: Admissions, 614 W. Superior St., Alma, MI 48801
(800) 321-ALMA   FAX: (989) 463-7057
www.alma.edu

DEGREES OFFERED
BA in Acting (23), Design/Tech (12), Dance (12)
Declare major in 2nd year; 2005 granted 12 UG degs.

ADMISSION & FINANCIAL INFORMATION
GPA 3.0 and ACT 22 (avg. GPA 3.6 with 25.7 Act); 66% of applicants admitted to institution; Th. program admits all UG applicants. Performance scholarship in theatre of $1,000 to $2,000 and distinguished trustee theatre scholarship of $3,000 - full tuition renewable each year, theatre scholarships. awarded on basis of aud/interview. Numerous other scholarships awarded on basis of academic record.

FACULTY AND CLASSES OFFERED
7 Full-Time, 2 Part-Time: 1 PhD, 6 MFA/MA; 3 Staff

A.   (2 FT) Theatre History-3/O; Shakes-2/X; Dramatic Lit-4/X; Dramatic Criticism-1/X; Playwriting-2/O

B.   (3 FT, 1 PT) Acting-4/Y; Movement-2/Y; Singing-4/X; Dance-6/Y; Directing-4/Y; Voice/Speech-2/O; Musical Theatre-1/X

C.   (2 FT) Prins of Des-1/Y; Cost Des-2/O; Tech. Prod'-2/Y; Cost Hist-1/O; Stage Mgmt-1/Y; Lighting Des-2/O; Cost Construction-1/O

D.   (1 PT) Arts Management-1/O; Box Ofice Procedure-1/Y.-1/O

FACILITIES AND PRODUCTIONS
MAINSTAGE: 190 seats, computerized lighting. 4 prods: 2 Fac dir, 3 Fac des, 1 Guest dir, 1 UG dir; budget $3,000-7,000

SECOND STAGE: 500 seats, computerized lighting

Facility was built in 1993, includes scene shop, costume shop, welding shop, 1 dance studio, 1 reh. studio, 1 design studio.

Five student-written plays have been produced in the last two years.

DESCRIPTION
Noted Faculty: Joe Jezewski, Acting & Directing; Kristeen Crosser, Scene & Lighting Design; Tina Hartley, Costume Design; Carol Fike, Dance; Thomas Morris, Dance; Ione Saroyan, Acting.

The Alma College Theatre Department stresses theatre as an aesthetic study of the human condition. Founded upon the reality of doing, the department uses the Meisner technique to explore the craft of acting and to build within students a firm foundation upon which they may continue their studies or leap into the professional theatre world. Our design program emphasizes the use of lights, sound and sets to enhance the discoveries within a story, and much of our training is a hands-on practicum within theatrical productions. While many of our students choose to continue their studies in MFA programs, a large number have found homes within the professional theatre world, working as actors, designers and stage managers. Additionally, we have introduced classes to explore the craft of playwriting, inspiring many of our students to carve out their own stories using the ritual of theatrical production.

Eastern Michigan University

Ken Stevens, Artistic Director
Dept of Comm. & Theatre Arts
103 Quirk
Eastern Michigan University
Ypsilanti, MI 48197
DEPT: (734) 487-1220
emu.theatre@emich.edu
www.emich.edu/public/cta/cta.html
ADMISSIONS: Pierce Hall, EMU, Ypsilanti MI 48197
(800) 468-6368
www.emich.edu/admissions/admissions.html

24,700 Total Enr.; competitive
Semester System
105 Majors, ATHE
T: $4200/$5600 R&B UG
O-ST T: $13,200/$5600 R&B UG
FAX: (734) 487-3443

DEGREES OFFERED

BA/BS/MA in Theatre Arts (74) Arts Mgmt. (24), Musical Theatre (minor) (20), MA/MFA in Theatre for the Young (7). Declare major in 2nd year; 2004 granted 14 UG and 11 Grad. degs.

ADMISSION & FINANCIAL INFORMATION

In 2001, average incoming freshman had a 3.13 GPA and a 21+ ACT score. Sliding scale for FTIAC admission. UG: GPA 2.5, Grad: 3.0, ACT & SAT scores; 65-70% of applicants admitted to institution; Th. program admits all UG applicants, 15 out of 25 Grad. applicants; Interview required for Grad. applicants. 15-25 scholarships available for UG, $500-$1500. Acting, Musical Theatre by audition, tech theatre and front of house by interview and portfolio, Both require letters of rec.

FACULTY AND CLASSES OFFERED

9 Full-Time: 4 PhD, 5 MFA/MA; 3 Staff

A. (3 FT) Intro to Theatre-3/Y; Theatre History-3/Y; Shakes-1/O; Dramatic Lit-2/Y; Dramatic Criticism-2/Y; Playwriting-2/O; Audition-1/Y; Mus. Th. History-1/Y

B. (5 FT) Acting-5/Y; Movement-1/Y; Singing-3/X; Directing-3/Y; Voice/Speech-4/Y; Mime/Mask-1/O; Musical Theatre-2/Y

C. (2 FT) Prins of Des-2/Y; Cost Des-2/Y; Tech. Prod'-2/Y; Cost Hist-2/Y; Stage Mgmt-2/O; Lighting Des-2/O; Cost Construction-2/Y

D. (1 FT) Arts Management-1/Y; Marketing/Promotion-1/Y; Contracts/Copyright-1/Y; Personal Mgmt.-1/O; Dev./Grant Writing-1/O

FACILITIES AND PRODUCTIONS

MAINSTAGE: 411 seats, fly space, computerized lighting
4 prods: 3 Fac dir/des, 1 Guest dir; budget $5,000-11,000

SECOND STAGE: 201 seats, computerized lighting. 3 Fac dir,
2 Fac dir, 1 Grad. dir/des prods.; budget $1,000-5,000

THIRD STAGE: 50 seats, electronic lighting

Workshops/Readings: 12 UG dir/des, 4 Grad dir/des; budget $50-150

Facility includes scene shop, costume shop, welding area, 2 video studios, 1 dance studio, 8 classrooms.

Six student-written plays produced in the last two years.

Connection with Purple Rose Theatre Company (Equity). A number of students go on to participate in the apprentice program there, with option to earn Equity card. One faculty member is a regular company member. Arts Management interns are placed with several companies including Attic Theatre, Barn Theatre, Meadowbrook, Purple Rose, Cherry County Playhouse, Tibbits Opera House, Boarshead Theatre, Red Barn Theatre and Midland Center for the Performing Arts.

DESCRIPTION

Noted Faculty: Wallace Bridges, member Actors Equity Association; Terry Heck Seibert, member Actors Equity Association, Acting/Assoc. Artist, Purple Rose Theatre Company; Ken Stevens, Director of Theatre, Producer, E. Ray Scott, Michigan Artist Award-winner.

Guest Artists: Ben Vereen, Tony Award-winning performer; Gillian Eaton, Actor/Director; Augusto Boal, Director/Theorist/Writer; Nancy Uffner, Stage Manager; Antoine McKay, Actor.

The Theatre programs at EMU reflect commitment to liberal arts education with pre-professional training. Programs are designed to include 3 learning segments: 1. The breadth of knowledge required to adequately frame the world's humor, passion and ideas from which drama is born. 2. The Focused Studies segment combines major and minor programs from the core of the theatre experience. 3. The Career and Individual Studies segment provides training needed to become a competent practitioner of theatre.

Henry Ford Community College

George Popovich, Dir. of Theatre
Performing Arts Department
Henry Ford Community College
5101 Evergreen Road
Dearborn, MI 48128
DEPT: (313) 845-6478
MAIN: (313) 271-2750
popovich@hfcc.net

15,000 Total Enr.; non-compet.
Semester System
15 Majors
T: $$60 - $115 per cr. hr.
O-ST T: $120 per cr. hr.
SMALL PROGRAM
http://hfcc.net

DEGREES OFFERED

AA in Theatre (25). Declare major in first year.

ADMISSION & FINANCIAL INFORMATION

Open admissions policy; college admits 100% of applicants; theatre program admits all applicants. Tuition grants available, on merit basis.

FACULTY AND CLASSES OFFERED

1 FT, 3 PT: 1 PhD, 2 MA/MFA; 1 Prof. w/o adv. degree; 1 Staff

A. (1 FT) Intro to Theatre-4/Y; Theatre History-1/O; Drama Lit-6/X

B. (1 PT) Acting-8/Y; Voice/Speech-3/X; Mvmt-1/O; Mime, etc.-3/O; Musical Th-1/O; Stg Combat-1/O; Directing-1/Y

C. (1 PT) Prins of Design-1/Y; Cost Des-1/O; Ltg Des-1/Y; Tech Prod'n-1/Y; Cost Constr-1/Y; Make-up-1/Y; Stage Mgmt-1/O; Set Des-1/Y; Cost. Hist.-1/O

FACILITIES AND PRODUCTIONS

MAINSTAGE: 400 seats, fly space, electronic lighting
4 prods: 3 Fac dir/des, budget $3,500-5,000

Facility was built in 1980; includes scene shop, costume shop, prop shop, classrooms.

DESCRIPTION

Henry Ford Community College offers the Associate in Arts degree in Theatre with an area of concentration in Theatre. This degree program is designed to provide a sound basis for understanding the theory and practice of the theatrical arts and opportunities for experience through a curriculum of pre-professional training in theory, performance, and production. Students who desire to major in theatre and intend to complete courses in a 4- or 5-year college or university can complete their first 2 years of work at HFCC. (Theatre majors should check the curriculum guide sheets of transfer institutions to be certain of the transferability of courses to those institutions.) It is expected that all students electing to major in theatre will complete a minimum of 21 credits in theatre. It is desirable that students intending to major in theatre begin their work in theatre in their freshman year in order to complete the recommended core requirements during the freshman and sophomore years. HFCC has just added (2001) a fantastic virtual reality theatre training program: visit http://theatre.hfcc.net for info.

Hope College Theatre

Daina Robins, Chair
Hope College Theatre Dept
DeWitt Ctr, #18093
Holland, MI 49422-9000
www.hope.edu/academic/theatre

3,015 Total Enr.; compet.
Semester System
21 Majors; NAST (A)
DEPT: (616) 395-7600
FAX: (616) 395-7180
T: $22,430/$6,982 R&B

ADM: 69 E. 10th St., Holland, MI 49423
(800) 968-7850
admissions@hope.edu

(616) 395-7130

DEGREES OFFERED

BA in Theatre (21); Declare major soph. or junior yr; 2006 granted 11 deg.

ADMISSION & FINANCIAL INFORMATION

Top 30% of class, ACT-middle 50% (22-28), SAT-middle 50% (1060-1290), Avg. GPA 3.75. Accept 89% to institution. No special req's for theatre program. Distinguished Artist Awards, up to 12/yr @ $2500 each, awarded on basis of audition or portfolio & interview.

FACULTY & CLASSES OFFERED

5 Full-Time, 2 Part-Time: 1 PhD, 6 MA/MFA; 11/2 Staff

A. (1/2 FT) Intro to Theatre-1/O; Th Hist-3/Y; Shakes-1/X; Playwriting-1/O

B. (1 1/2 FT, 2 PT) Acting-5/Y; Singing-X; Directing-2/Y; Musical Th-2/Y; Dance (full major curriculum)-X

C. (3 FT) Prins of Des-1/Y; Set Design-1/O; Cost Des-1/O; Ltg Des-1/O; Tech Prod'n (Cost, Ltg, Sound, Scenery)-2/Y; Stg Mgmt-1/Y; Make-up-1/O

FACILITIES AND PRODUCTIONS

MAINSTAGE: 500 seats, fly space, computerized lighting.
4 Prods.: 4 Fac dir; 3 Fac des, 1-2 UG des; budget $5-6,000

SECOND STAGE: 80 seats, computerized lighting; budget $2-3,000
Workshops/Readings, budget $100-500

Facility built in 1971, renovated 1997; scene, welding, cost shops, mvmt/dance studio, sound studio, video studio, design studio, seminar room, classrms.

A non-departmental, student-run organization produces 3 plays/year, majors participate. 3 student-written plays produced in the last two years.

Hope Summer Repertory Theatre is a semi-professional company with Equity Guest Artists which operates at the facility in the summer. Acting, Design, and Stage Mgmt. internships available as well as paid staff positions.

DESCRIPTION

Noted Faculty: John Tammi, Directing, Acting, Playwriting, Th. History; Richard Smith, Scenography, Cinema; Perry Landes, Ltg & Sound Des; Michelle Bombe, Cost. Des.; Daina Robins, Acting, Directing.

Guest Artists: Directors: Nathan Allen, Jon Cranney, Sean Dooley; Designers: Erik Alberg, Devon Painter; Actors: Tom Tammi; Guest Residencies: Don Finn, Kevin Kling, Curt Tofteland.

A major in theatre generally serves one of the following purposes: 1. More intensive study in this particular discipline as the emphasis within the student's liberal arts education; 2. Preparation for graduate work leading to an MA, MFA, PhD or DFA degree in theatre; 3. Preparation for work in a non-commercial field of theatre such as community theatre; 4. Preparation for advanced training leading to a career in the professional theatre.

Michigan State University

George F. Peters, Chair
Department of Theatre
Michigan State University
149 Auditorium Building
East Lansing, MI 48824
(517) 355-6690
theatre@msu.edu
www.msu.edu/

35,821 Total Enr.; compet
Semester System; ATHE
135 Majors
T: $9,862 r&b $6,094
O-ST T: $$22,450
FAX: (517) 355-1698
http://msu/theatre/unit

DEGREES OFFERED

BA in Theatre (147); MA in Theatre (4); MFA in Acting (6), Production Design (6). Declare major in junior year.

ADMISSION & FINANCIAL INFORMATION

Univ. acceptance, GRAD: GPA 3.0, GRE, TOEFL-580 overall with no subscores below 55; no special requirements for UG theatre program; Aud./Int./Portfolio for designers required for Grad theatre program; theatre program admits all UG applicants, 15 out of 30 of Grad applicants. Creative Arts Scholarship - by Audition.

FACULTY AND CLASSES OFFERED

8 Full-Time: 2 PhD, 6 MA/MFA; 5 Staff

A. (2 FT) Intro to Theatre-1/X; Dramatic Lit-5/X; Theatre History-5/Y; Dramatic Crit.-1/Y; Shakes-2/X;

B. (3 FT) Acting-8/Y; Voice/Speech-2/Y; Movement-5/Y; Directing-3/Y

C. (3 FT) Prins of Des-2/Y; Set Des-2/Y; Cost Des-2/Y; Ltg Des-2/Y; Tech Prod'n-1/Y; Cost Constr-2/Y; Cost. Hist-1/Y; Make-up-2/Y

FACILITIES AND PRODUCTIONS

MAINSTAGE: 2200 seats, fly space, computerized lighting. 4 prods: 4 Fac dir, 3 Fac des, 1 Grad des; budget $3,000-6,000

SECOND STAGE: 600 seats, fly space, computerized lighting
4 prods: 2 Fac dir, 2 Grad dir, 4 Grad des; bdgt. $500-800

THIRD STAGE: 600 seats, fly space

2 Fac dir workshops/readings

Facility was built in 1982; includes scene shop, costume shop, props shop, sound studio, dance studio, rehearsal studio, design studio, classrooms. Other facilities include Arena Theatre, Studio Theatre, Outdoor Theatre.

Majors generally participate in a non-departmental, student-run producing organization that presents 6-8 productions per year. 3

student-written plays produced in last two years.

Connection with Boarshead Theatre, an Equity theatre. Perform with Equity actors, professional director, master classes.

DESCRIPTION

Noted Faculty: Dixie Durr, Dance; Gretel Geist, Cost Des, Make-Up; Kirk Domer, Light and Set Design; Marcus Olson, Acting; Frank Rutledge, Theatre History, Directing; Georg Schuttler, Theory & Criticism, Directing; Lynette Overby, PhD, Dance, Theatre Education, Julia Lenardon, Voice, Acting.

The purposes of the Michigan State University Theatre Department are to offer theatrical experiences of professional caliber to the MSU student, to offer various levels of training to prepare some students for careers in theatre, and to provide opportunities for many students to perform in all aspects of this art as an expressive and social outlet. It is also the intent of the department to provoke and sustain interest in the theatre as a source of truth and insight into the human condition; to preserve and investigate further the theatre's historical traditions, and to present new plays and reflect the present condition of society.

Michigan Tech University

Roger Held
Visual & Performing Arts
Michigan Tech University
1400 Townsend Drive
Houghton, MI 49931-1295
(906) 487-2067
fax: (906) 487-1841
www.fa.mtu.edu

6500 Total Enr.
competitive
Semester System
38 Majors, ACTF
T: $8,271/6,840 r & b
o-st: $20,040
fineart@mtu.edu

Admissions: Michigan Tech Univ, 1400 Townsend Drive, Houghton, MI 49931
(906) 487-2335   (888) 688-1885
mtu4u@mtu.edu

DEGREES OFFERED:

BA in Theatre and Entertainment Technology; Sound Design; BS in Theatre and Entertainment Technology; Audio Production and Technology. Students declare major in first year. 2007 granted 2 degrees

ADMISSION and FINANCIAL INFORMATION:

Average ACT composite: 25.1, Math: 26.2, English: 23.7, Average HS GPA: 3.50, Also accept SAT scores. Special requirements for admittance to theatre program is audition for actors, portfolio for designers.

FACULTY AND COURSES OFFERED:

6 Full-Time, 1 1/2 Part-Time; 2 Phd/DFA, 4 MA/MFA; 1 Prof. w/o advanced degree; 1 Staff
A. (1 FT, 1/2 PT) Intro to Theatre-O; Dramatic Lit-2/Y; Theatre History-2/Y; Shakes-1/X
B. (3 FT, 1/2 PT) Acting-2/Y; Voice/Speech-2/Y; Singing-1/Y; Musical Theatre-1/O; Directing-1/O; Stage Combat-1/O; Dance-1/O; Presentation Skills-2/Y; TV/Film-2/Y; Movement-O
C. (2 FT, 1/2 PT) Principles of Des-2/Y; Set Design-1/Y; Costume Des-1/O; Lighting Des-1/Y; Tech Prod-2/Y; Costume Constr-1/Y; Stage Mgmt-1/O; Make-up-1/O; Audio Tech-2/Y; Sound Des-2/Y
D. Marketing the Performer-1/O; Portfolio Presentation-1/Y

FACILITIES AND PRODUCTIONS:

Mainstage: 1100 seats, fly space, computerized and electronic lighting
4 prods: 4 Fac dir; budget $3,000-12,000
Second Stage: 200-300 seats, computerized and electronic lighting
Projects in video, radio, media arts

A non-departmental, student-run producing organization presents 2 productions per year. 6 student-written plays have been produced in the last two years.

Northern Michigan University

Dr. James A. Panowski,
Director of Theatre
Forest Roberts Theatre
Northern Michigan University
Marquette, MI 49855
(906) 227-2553
www.nmu.edu/theatre

9,000 Total Enr.; competitive
www.nmu.edu
Semester System
40 Majors
T: $6,708/$7,220 R&B
O-ST T: $10,644/$7,220 R&B
SMALL PROGRAM

DEGREES OFFERED

BA and BS in Theatre. Declare major in second year

ADMISSION & FINANCIAL INFORMATION

Theatre program admits all applicants to the program.

FACULTY AND CLASSES OFFERED

4 Full-Time: 3 PhD, 1 MFA
A. (1 FT) Intro to Th-1/Y; Th Hist-1/Y; Shakes-1/O; Modern Drama-1/Y; Playwriting-1/X; Special Topics in Drama-1/O
B. (2 FT) Acting-1/Y; Voice/Diction-1/Y; Mvmt/Stg Combat-1/O; Singing-1/X; American Musical Theatre-1/Y; Directing-1/Y; Auditions-1/Y; Directing Practicum-2/Y; Field Studies-1/Y.
C. (1/2 FT) Set Design-1/Y; Cost Des-1/O; Ltg Des-1/Y; Make-up-1/Y; Stg Mgmt-1/O; Stagecraft-1/Y; Methods of Design Presentation-1/O; History of the Physical Stage-1/O; Stage Properties- 1/O
D. (1/2 FT) Theatre Management-1/Y

FACILITIES AND PRODUCTIONS

MAINSTAGE: 525 seats, fly space, computerized lighting. 5 prods: 5 Fac dir/des; budget $10,000-20,000
SECOND STAGE: 125 seats, electronic lighting, flexible black box. 9 stud dir/des prods; budget $100-200
Facility was built in 1964; includes scene shop, costume shop.

DESCRIPTION

Noted Faculty: James Panoski, Dir, Mus. Th.; Victor Holliday, Design; Shelley Russell-Parks, Voice, Mvmt, Acting, Stg. Combat; Paul Truckey, Acting; Kim Hegmegee, Technical Director.

Guest Artists: Nicholas Pennell, Trent Arterberry, Pat Hingle, William Leach, Glenn Farnham, Frank Hartenstein, Edward Albee, Milan Stitt, Barry McGregor.

A liberal arts-professional program designed to prepare the student to seek further professional training in recognized MA or MFA programs or by internships with professional theatre companies. Maximum opportunities are offered for involvement in both the theoretical and practical aspects of the theatrical arts. All students are required to participate each semester in a jury presentation, scheduled and critiqued by the theatre faculty. Juries are evaluated on a "pass/fail" basis and are not reflected in student's academic transcripts. Students who fail two consecutive theatre juries at a given level may be dropped from the major. All theatre majors are required to have at least one field studies experience as part of their program. Only the New York Field Studies, the Stratford Summer Tour, or a comparable substitute approved by the theatre faculty will fulfill this requirement. The Audition class prepares students for the realities of finding work in theatre, be it in the performance, design/technical, or management area. Casting for all productions is open, with equal consideration given to Theatre majors and to interested non-theatre students in the hope of fostering an appreciation for the theatrical arts among the total college community. The Mildred and Albert Panowski Playwriting Award allows students the chance to work with an original script, with the playwright in residence for the week of the production. Students generally specialize in performance or design/tech, but all students are encouraged to have an understanding of at least the basics of all the production areas.

Oakland University

Kerro Knox, Program Head
Theatre Program
Dept. of Music, Theatre & Dance
Oakland University
Rochester, MI 48309-4401
DEPT: (248) 370-2030
FAX: (248) 370-2041
www.otus.oakland.edu/mtd
ADMISSIONS: Above address
www3.oakland.edu

13,701 Tot. Enr., compet.
80 Majors; NAST
Semester System
T: $$7,202/$6,670 R&B
O-ST T: $16,788

SMALL PROGRAM
mtd@oakland.edu
(248) 370-3360
OUinfo@oakland.edu

DEGREES OFFERED

BA in Performance Arts-Theatre Performance (25), Theatre Production (23), Musical Theatre (32). Declare major in freshman year. 2003 granted 13 degrees.

ADMISSION & FINANCIAL INFORMATION

GPA 2.50. 78% of applics admitted to instit. 8 out of 10 admitted to th. prog. Scholarships. for incoming freshmen & transfer students through aud/interview or portfolio/interview. Audition Days in Feb., March before Fall entrance to the univ. Call (248) 370-2035 for information. Once in the program, current students not already on schol. may apply for a merit schol.which may be available.

FACULTY AND CLASSES OFFERED

4 FT 9 PT: 1 PhD, 5 MFA/MA, 7 Prof. w/o adv. degree; 2 Staff

A. (1/2 FT, 2 PT) Intro to Theatre-1/Y; Dramatic Lit-3/X; Theatre History-3/Y; Shakes-1/O; Playwriting-2/Y
B. (3 FT, 4 PT) Acting-4/Y; Voice/Speech-2/O; Mvmt-3/Y; Mus Th-3/Y; Mime, etc.-1/O; Singing-5/Y; *Dance-3/Y; Directing-2/Y; Stg Combat-1/O; Stage Dialects-1/O (*though 5 semesters of voice and 3 semesters of dance are required of music theatre majors, our combined dept. has full programs in dance and vocal performance so many other classes in the dept. can be used for electives in dance and singing.)
C. (1 1/2 FT, 3 PT) Set Design-1/O; Cost Des-1/O; Tech Prod'n-2/Y;

Set Design-1/O; Ltg Des-1/O; Cost Constr-1/Y; Cost Hist-2/O; Make-up-1/Y; Stg Mgmt-1/Y

FACILITIES & PRODUCTIONS

MAINSTAGE: 80-160 seats, black box, computerized lighting.
 3 prods: 2 Fac dir, 2 Fac des, 1 Guest dir/des, 3 UG des; budget $11,000-14,000
SECOND STAGE: 80 seats, black box, computerized lighting
 3 prods: 1 Fac dir, 2 UG dir, 7 UG des; budget $6,000-8,000
THIRD STAGE: 425 seats, fixed stage. 1 production children's theatre in spring term.
7 UG dir Workshops/Readings; budget $200
Facility was built in 1970; includes scene shop, costume shop, CAD facility, 2 movement/dance studios, rehearsal studio, design studio, make-up room, classrooms.
Connection with Meadow Brook Theatre. Equity (Lort C) theatre, Apprenticeships (PG), Internships (UG), occasional hiring as actors and or technicians. Faculty hired as actors or designers.

DESCRIPTION

Noted Faculty: Michael Gillespie, Alexander Technique; Karen Sheridan, Head of Theatre, Acting; Kerro Knox 3, Scenic and Lighting Design; Thomas Suda, Acting, Intro to Theatre Leslie Littell, Costume Design

Guest Artists: Kitty Dubin, Playwriting; Thomas Mahard, Acting; John Manfredi, Combat; Lynnae Lehfeldt, Voice, Acting; Beth Guest; Acting.

The Theatre Program at Oakland University is designed to train well-rounded theatre artists and to promote critical and creative thinking in students pursuing the study of Theatre in a strong liberal-arts setting. The NAST accredited program operates within a dynamic multi-disciplinary Department of Music, Theatre and Dance providing students access to excellent working faculty and instruction in each of these arts. The program encourages students to become actively involved in a broad range of courses and production activities and offers the opportunity to concentrate in Theatre Performance, Theatre Production, or Musical Theatre. Students receive the personal attention of a dedicated faculty have additional opportunities to work with and be taught by the professional staff of Meadow Brook Theatre located on campus. Many graduates of Oakland's Theatre Program go on to pursue graduate training and/or professional careers in Musical Theatre, Theatre Performance and Production.

Olivet College

Arthur Williams, Dir. of Theatre
Dept of Arts & Communication
Olivet College
Olivet, MI 49076
DEPT: (269) 749-7246
awilliams@olivetnet.edu
ADM: Office of Admissions

1060 Total Enr; Non-compet.
Semester System
10 Majors; ATHE
T: $18,648/$6,346 R&B
SMALL PROGRAM
admissions@olivetcollege.edu
(269) 749-7635

DEGREES OFFERED

BA in Theatre, Speech Secondary Teaching. Declare major in sophomore year.

ADMISSION & FINANCIAL INFORMATION

HS Grad, GPA of 2.6 or better, w/college prep courses, ACT or SAT, HS transcripts; No special req's. for admission to Th Program.

FACULTY AND CLASSES OFFERED

1 FT, 3 PT: 1 PhD, 1 MFA, 1 MA; 1 BA
Acting-3/Y; Intro to Theatre-2/Y; Public Speaking-2/Y; Oral Interpretation-1/Y; Prod (tech)-2/Y; Prod(acting)-2/Y; Intro to Oral Comm-2/Y; Dramatic Lit-1/Y.

FACILITIES & PRODUCTIONS

MAINSTAGE: 150 seats
4 prods: 2 dir/des, 1 UG dir/des; budget $5,000
Facility was built in 1946, renovated in 1989; includes scene shop, costume shop, props shop.
Theatre is also used by local community theatre, in which students participate.

DESCRIPTION

Theatre at Olivet College is dedicated to the liberal arts philosophy, providing educational growth for all students in cultural understanding, arts appreciation, arts expression, aesthetics, personal expressiveness, and oral communication. The theatre major is designed to prepare students for advanced training and study at graduate level, careers in stage performance or in technical theatre, and teaching careers in elementary or secondary schools; and to provide enhanced ability for artistic expression and communication, as elements of the program combine classroom study, research, stage performance and stagecraft.

University of Michigan

Prof. Erik Fredricksen
Dept. of Theatre and Drama
University of Michigan
2550 Frieze Building
Ann Arbor, MI 48109-1285
DEPT: (734) 764-5350
ADMISSIONS:: UG 2290 Moore Bldg., U Mich, Ann Arbor, MI 48109-2085 (734) 764-0593
http://www.music.umich.edu/

35,000 Tot. Enr.; h. compet
Trimester System
134 Majors, ATHE
T: UG $10,341; G N/A
O-ST T: $30,154; R&B:$8,230
(734) 647-2297
FAX: (734) 763-5097
theatre.info@umich.edu

DEGREES OFFERED

BA in Theatre Concentration (14); BFA in Performance (75), Production Design (24); BTA in Theatre Arts (20); Declare major in freshman yr

ADMISSION & FINANCIAL INFORMATION

UG: GPA of 3.0, SAT 1000, ACT 24. Audition, interview, portfolio req'd for UG. Th. program generally admits 50 out of 200 UG. UG: Merit awards made to continuing students based on faculty rankings of majors:academic record, demonstrated commitment to the program, prod'n or perf. skills.

FACULTY AND CLASSES OFFERED

16 FT, 12 PT, 5 PhD, 8 MA/MFA, 3 Prof. w/o adv. degree; 3 Staff
A. (3 FT, 1 PT) Intro to Th.-2/Y; Th. Hist.-4/Y; Shakes-2/X; Playwriting-4/Y; Dramatic Lit.-2/Y; Dramatic Crit.-1/X; Th. & Film-1/Y
B. (7 FT, 2 PT) Acting/Scene Study-12/Y; Voice/Speech-4/Y; Movement-4/Y; Singing-1/X; Musical Th.-3/X; Directing-3/Y; Stage Combat-2/Y
C. (5 FT, 9 PT) Prins of Des-2/Y; Set Design-5/Y; Cost Des-4/Y; Ltg Des-4/Y; Tech Prod'n-8/Y; Cost Constr-3/Y; Costume History-2/Y; Make-up-2/Y; Stg Mgmt-3/Y; Mask-Making-1/O; Dye Workshop-1/O; Model-Making-1/O; Millinery-1/Y
D. (2 PT) Arts Management-2/Y

FACILITIES & PRODUCTIONS

MAINSTAGE: 1,400 seats, fly space, computerized & electronic lighting. 5 prods: 4 Fac dir, 5 Fac des, 1 Guest dir/des, 4 Grad des, 2 UG des
SECOND STAGE: 650 seats, electronic lighting. 12-15 UG dir/des prods.
THIRD STAGE: 150 seats, electronic lighting
Facility includes scene shop, costume shop, prop shop, welding shop, sound studio, 3 movement/dance studios, 5 rehearsal studios, 2 design studios, 7 classrooms, computer sites.
A non-departmental, student-run prod. org. presents 20-25 productions per year in which dept. majors participate.
Connection with Purple Rose Theatre (Chelsea, MI): founded by actor Jeff Daniels. Many of our students, designers and faculty are cast in his productions, design, and conduct classes at the Purple Rose.

DESCRIPTION

Noted Faculty: Actors: Erik Fredricksen (Chair), founder of SAFD, John Neville-Andrews, Actor and Director, Drama Desk Award; Philip Kerr, Actor/Director, Joseph Jefferson Award; Mark Lamos, Director; Lucille Lortel Award; OyamO, Playwright.
Guest Artist: Hal Cooper, Hollywood Director; Christine Lahti, Actress; Michele Shay, Actress, Director; Ann Bogart, Director; Holly Hughes, Performance Artist; Stuart Duke, Lighting Designer; Russell Metheny, Scenic Designer.

University of Michigan theatre students have all the advantages of attending a first-class university, while enjoying the more intimate atmosphere of the Department of Theatre and Drama. The BFA in Performance offers a concentration in performance (acting, movement, voice and stage combat) or in directing, and also provides solid liberal arts education through required and elective courses. The BFA in Design & Production takes a very strong direction into the field of design, technical production and stage management. Students are encouraged to further their training at various performance festivals and camps or to work in regional theatre. The Bachelor of Theatre Arts (BTA) provides a well-rounded and substantive theatre education, allowing students flexibility in developing a minor concentration.

University of Michigan - Flint

Dr. Lauren Friesen, Chair
Dept. of Theatre & Dance
University of Michigan-Flint
Flint, MI 48502-1950
DEPT: (810) 762-3230
lfriesen@umflint.edu
ADM: 245 University Pavilion
http://www.umflint.edu/
admissions@umflint.edu

5,600 Tot. Enr.; compet
Semester System
65 Majors
T: $7,067
O-ST T: $13,780
FAX: (810) 762-3687
(810) 762-3300
FAX: (810) 766-6630
umflint.edu/departments/theater-dance

DEGREES OFFERED

BA Comprehensive Degree (46); BFA in Acting (4); Teacher Certification; TCP Speech. Students declare major in any year; 1999 granted 10 UG degrees.

ADMISSION & FINANCIAL INFORMATION

BFA generally admit 1 out of 3 applicants. BFA by audition only, after completion of 30 hrs./no more than 65 hrs. Carl & Sarah Morgan Trust, Chancellor's Schol. & Theatre Dept Schol-all by on-site audition, awarded yearly, renewable, awards up to cost of in-state tuition.

FACULTY AND CLASSES OFFERED

6 FT, 6 PT, 1 PhD, 6 MA/MFA, 1 Prof. w/o adv. degree; 3 Staff

A. (1 FT) Intro to Theatre-7/Y; Theatre History-5/Y; Shakes-2/YX;Dramatic Lit-1/Y; Dramatic Crit-1/X; Playwriting-1/Y

B. (3 FT, 4 PT) Acting-2/Y; Voice/Speech-2/Y; Movement-2/Y; Singing-1/Y; Musical Theatre-2/Y; Directing-1/Y; Stage Combat-1/O; Mime, etc. -1/O; Dance-12/Y

C. (2 FT, 2 PT) Prins of Des-1/Y; Set Design-1/O; Cost Des-1/Y; Ltg Des-2/Y; Tech Prod'n-4/Y; Cost Constr-2/Y; Make-up-1/Y; Stg Mgmt-1/Y

FACILITIES & PRODUCTIONS

MAINSTAGE: 410 seats, fly space, computer. lighting. 4 prods: 3 Fac dir, 6 Fac des, 1 Guest dir, 3 UG des; bdgt. $6-7,000

SECOND STAGE: 50-90 seats, black box. 2 UG dir, 4 UG des prods.; budget $100-300

Facility built in 1976; includes scene shop, costume shop, sound studio, movement studios, design studio, classrooms.

Several student-written plays produced in the last two years, including KC/ACTF, 1999 National Short lay Winner.

DESCRIPTION

Noted Faculty: Carolyn M. Gillespie, Acting/Directing; Scott Dahl, Set Design/Design Theory; Lauren Friesen, Theatre History/Playwriting; Carolyn Gillespie, Acting/Directing; Doug Mueller, Lighting Design/Stagecraft; Jan Sage, Acting/Musical Theatre; Danielle Sorum,Dance; Ann Dasen, Costume Design.

Noted Faculty: Wole Soyinka, Playwriting Residency; Kristen Nuienhuis, Stage Mgmt Seminar.

The Theatre Department at the University of Michigan-Flint encourages students to discover resources within themselves. Within the liberal arts context, we offer training in the areas of theatre history, literature, acting, directing, production design, technology, stage management and dance. Our program balances the practical with the theoretical. Our students confront the realities of performance; they act and learn how to act; they direct and learn directing; they design and learn practical creativity; they manage and learn effective communication; and they dance and learn to master grace and motion. Most importantly, they work daily with a strong faculty who encourage the combination of solid academic discipline with practical professional theatre experience. Every member of our faculty is a working professional. We look with pride to graduates who are working and studying as playwrights, actors, directors and designers, and those who are applying their skills to such diverse careers as law, advertising, television, film, education, etc. Solid training in liberal arts and the skills they mastered in our pro-

gram—effective communication, creative problem-solving, self-discipline, independent thinking and action—have opened doors and prepared them well for today's challenges.

Wayne State University

Dr. Blair V. Anderson, Dept/Chair
Theatre Department
Wayne State University
4841 Cass, Ste. 3225
Detroit, MI 48202-3489
DEPT: (313) 577-3508
FAX: (313) 577-0935
ADM: (313) 577-3577
admissions@wayne.edu

32,000 T. Enr.; highly compet.
Semester System
150 Majors
NAST, U/RTA, ATHE
T: $7,844/$16,595 o st
r&b $6,702
www.theatre.wayne.edu
FAX: (313) 577-7536
www.wayne.edu

DEGREES OFFERED

BFA in Acting (100), Technical Design (25); MFA in Acting (18), Costume Design (5), Scenic Design (8), Lighting Design (4), Th. Mgmt (8), Stage Mgmt. (3). Declare major in soph. year; 2001 granted 20 UG, 20 Grad degrees.

ADMISSION & FINANCIAL INFORMATION

UG req's.: 3.0 GPA or ACT score of 21 or SAT of 940 (min. 500 verbal and 440 math); 70% accepted. Theatre program requires Aud for UG scholarships, Aud for BFA, Aud/Int for Grad, portfolio review for technical theatre, writing and publicity skills for MFA in Mgmt; 100% UG accepted (with attrition rate of 50%), Grad program accepts 20 out of 300 applicants. MFA Th. Prog. - Full tuition, medical benefits, plus over $10,000 Stipend. Various half-tuition scholarships - BFA students.

FACULTY AND CLASSES OFFERED

15 FT, 7 PT: 6 PhD, 14 MFA/MA, 2 Prof. w/out adv degree; 6 Staff

A. (2 1/2, 1 PT) Intro to Theatre-2/Y; Dramatic Lit-2/Y; Dramatic Criticism-1/Y; Playwriting-1/Y

B. (6 1/2 FT, 3 PT) Acting-6/Y; Voice/Speech-6/Y; Movement-4/Y; Directing-1/Y; Dance-1/Y

C. (5 FT, 1 PT) Prins of Des-4/Y; Set Design-4/Y; Cost Des-2/Y; Ltg Des-4/Y; Costume Hist.-1/Y; Make-up-2/Y; Stg Mgmt-2/Y

D. (1 FT, 2 PT) Arts Mgmt-1/Y; Box Office-1/Y; Marketing/ Promo-1/Y; Development/Grant Writing-1/O; Budgeting/ Accounting-1/O; Legal: Contracts-1/O

FACILITIES AND PRODUCTIONS

MAINSTAGE: 534 seats, fly space, computerized & electron. lighting. 7 prods: 2 Fac dir/des, 5 Fac dir/Grad des; budget $3,000-5,000

SECOND STAGE: 1170 seats, fly space, computer & electron. lighting.. 5 prods: 1 Fac dir/des, 4 Fac dir/Grad des; budget $2,500-4,500

THIRD STAGE: 112 seats, black box, fixed stage. 4-5 prods: 2 Fac dir/Grad des,, 3 Grd dir/UG des

10-15 prods. per year student produced.

Scene shop, costume shop, 2 movement studios, 3 rehearsal studios.

Connection with Hilberry Repertory Theatre.

DESCRIPTION

Noted Faculty: Blair Anderson, James Thomas, Lavinia Hart, Jerry Cleveland, Thomas Schraeder; Nira Pullin, Larry Kaushansky, John Woodland, Joe

Calarco.

Guest Artists: Barry MacGregor, John Broome, Antonio Cimolino, Colm all from Stratford Festival; Felix Cochran, Designer; Danny Newman, Audience Development; Jose Quintero, Director, Lloyd Richards; Ruben Santiago Hudson, Sergei Barkhin.

The underlying philosophy of the Department of Theatre is a production-oriented, learning-by-doing approach that has shaped its programs on both the graduate and undergraduate levels. Undergraduates have actual design and stage management as well as performance opportunities in at least nine fully-realized productions and a touring troupe annually. The Hilberry Repertory Company is the only graduate company of its kind in the United States. Established in 1963, the company is based on the principle that he most effective kind of theatre training is the production of classic plays in a rotating repertory system. The unique Hilberry program offers graduate degree candidates the opportunity to gain both educational training and practical work experience simultaneously. In a typical season Hilberry students are involved in more than 115 performances of seven plays before an audience of over 45,000 people. The PhD in Theatre at Wayne State University is designed to train the scholar/director through a unique combination of a traditional academic approach and continuous hands-on opportunities in teaching and directing.

Western Michigan University

Dr. Joan Herrington, Chair	25,000 Total Enr.; compet.
Department of Theatre	Semester System
Western Michigan University	175 Majors; ATHE; NAST
1903 W. Michigan Ave.	T: $8000/$5000 R&B
Kalamazoo, MI 49008-5308	O-ST T: $16,000/$5000 R&B
DEPT: (269) 387-3220	FAX: (269) 387-3222
www.wmich.edu/theatre	
ADMISSIONS: Above address.	(269) 387-3220
www.wmich.edu	

DEGREES OFFERED

BA in Performance (87), Design/Tech (36), Arts Mgmt (3), Stage Mgmt (4). BFA in Music Theatre Performance (39), Declare major in freshman year; 2004 granted 33 degrees.

ADMISSION & FINANCIAL INFORMATION

Requires ACT test scores, GPA, academic transcripts. UG admits 1 out of 5 applicants. Audition, interview and portfolio for designers, proof of admission by Univ. Schols. range from one-time only awards of $500 to $6,000. Awarded by audition/interview process.

FACULTY AND CLASSES OFFERED

9 Full-Time, 4 Part-Time: 3 PhD, 6 MFA/MA, 3 Staff (MFA's)

A. (2 FT, 2 PT) Intro to Theatre-1/Y; Th. History-3/Y; Shakes-1/X; Dramatic Lit-2/Y

B. (5 FT, 1 PT) Acting-6/Y; Singing-8/YX; Dance-8/YX; Directing-2/Y; Voice-1/Y; Musical Th.-4/Y; Movement-4/Y

C. (3 FT, 1 PT, 2 Staff) Styles of Des-1/Y; Drafting-1/Y; Set Design-2/Y; Cost Des-2/Y; Ltg Des-2/Y; Tech Prod-1/Y; Cost Constr-1/Y; Make-up-1/Y; Adv. Design-1/O

D. (1 FT, 1 Staff) Arts Management-1/O; Stage Mgmt-1/Y

FACILITIES AND PRODUCTIONS

MAINSTAGE: 550 seats, computerized lighting. 8 prods: 3 Fac dir, 1 Guest dir; 3 UG des total budget $7-8,000

SECOND STAGE: 350 seats, fly space, computerized ltg.. 7 prods: 3 Fac dir, 1 UG dir, 3 UG des; budget $700-1000

THIRD STAGE: 115 seats, black box, computerized

10 UG dir Workshops/Readings; budget $100

Facility was built in 1968, renovated in 1994; includes scene shop, costume shop, props shop, sound studio, CAD facility, 1 movement studio, 2 rehearsal studios, 1 design studio, 3 classrooms, Conference Room-Library, Arts Mgt Suite, 2 green rooms

4 student-written plays have been produced in the last two years.

DESCRIPTION

Noted Faculty: Joan Herrington, scholar/writer; VanWashington, actor (film,tv,stage); James Daniels, actor (film,tv,stage).

Guest Artists: Reuben Santiago-Hudson, Tina Landau, Leon Ingulsrud, Yvette Heyliger; Susan Zeder; Ellen Lauren; Alice Ripley; David Jacques; Brigitte Jaques; Lizzie Ingram.

The philosophy and thrust of the Western Michigan University Department of Theatre is to prepare undergraduate students for more intensive training offered by the nation's top MFA/PhD programs by exposing them to a well-rounded liberal arts theatre training program and to prepare BFA's in Music Theatre for the profession.

MINNESOTA

College of St. Catherine

Kathleen Skinner, Admi	*12,000 Total Enr.; not compet.
Theatre Dept.	Semester System
	T:$24,338/R&b$6,088
College of St. Catherine	21 Majors; ATHE
2004 Randolph Ave.	(651) 690-6680
St. Paul, MN 55105	SMALL PROGRAM
ADMISSIONS: Address above. (651) 690-8850	
www.stkate.edu -	

Combined Theatre Dept. w/ University of St. Thomas in St. Paul
* Total enrollment of both Institutions.

DEGREES OFFERED

Both CSC and UST combined: BA in Performance (21), History/Theory, Education with certification in Theater/Dance (1). Declare major in soph. year. 2002 granted 8 degrees.

ADMISSION & FINANCIAL INFORMATION

ACT or SAT, H.S. Transcript. Only women admitted to College of St. Catherine. After completing core curriculum, students may petition to major in Theater. Acceptance is the norm. See University of St. Thomas listing for further information on joint Theatre Program.

Gustavus Adolphus College

Steven Griffith, Chair
Dept. of Theatre and Dance
Gustavus Adolphus College
800 W. College Ave.
St. Peter, MN 56082
griffith@gac.edu
www.gac.edu
ADMISSIONS: same address
admission@gac.edu

2,500 Total Enr.; competitive
Semester System
35 Majors; ATHE
T: $28,125/$6,775 r&b
SMALL PROGRAM
DEPT: (507) 933-7353
FAX: (507) 933-7041
(507) 933-8000
FAX: (507) 933-7041

DEGREES OFFERED

BA (35); There are not separate programs; students may focus on acting, design, directing, or dance.Declare major in sophomore year; 2001 granted 6 degrees.

ADMISSION & FINANCIAL INFORMATION

Avg. ACT 25, SAT 1110; 75% from top 1/4 of HS class; college admits 80% of applicants; no special requirements for theatre program. Evelyn Anderson Theatreand Dance Scholarships-applicants complete an application, a video, and an interview.

FACULTY AND CLASSES OFFERED

3 FT, 2 PT (+ 3 dance faculty): 2 PhD, 3 MA/MFA; 2 Staff

A. (1 FT) Intro to Theatre-1/Y; Dramatic Lit-1/X; Theatre History-1/Y; Shakes-X; Dramatic Criticism-X; Playwriting-1/O; Theatre in Society-1/O; Dramatic Theory-1/O

B. (1 FT) Acting-3/Y; Movement-1/O; Directing-2/Y; Dance-8/Y

C. (1 FT, 2 PT) Prins of Des-1/Y; Set Des-1/O; Cost. Des-1/O; Ltg Des-1/O; Cost Constr-1/O

D. (FT) Arts Management-1/O

FACILITIES AND PRODUCTIONS

MAINSTAGE: 270 seats, computerized lighting. 4 Fac dir, 2 Fac des, 1-2 Guest des, 2-3 UG des; bdgt $2,500-6,000

SECOND STAGE: 50 seats, computerized lighting. 4-6 prods: UG dir; budget $50-100

6 Workshops./Readings: 2 Fac dir, 4 UG dir

2 Dance Concerts: 2 Fac dir, 4 UG dir

Facility was built in 1971; includes scene shop, costume shop, sound studio, design studio, rehearsal studio, classrooms.

DESCRIPTION

Noted Faculty: Robert Gardner, Acting/Directing; Michele Rusinko, Chair, Dance; Amy Seham, Acting/Directing; Steve Griffith, Design; Terena Wilkens, Stagecraft; Sue Guniess, Maria Gomez Tierney, Dance.

Guest Artists: Yuri Belov, Clowning; Michael Ferrell, Choreog.; Dennie Gordon, Television/Film; Sarah Hauss, Choreog.; Lee Breuer, Director; David Horn, Lighting Des; K.J. Holmes, Performance, Improvisation Artist; E.E. Balcos, Choreog.; Rich Hamson, Costume Designer; Michael Croswell, Sound Designer; Nyna Ramey, Design; Cynthia Freet, Design; Shenandoah Shakespeare Express, Performance.

The Department of Theatre and Dance at Gustavus Adolphus College broadly educated future theatre and dance artists and educators. The Department also pro-vides artistic experiences for the wider Gustavus community. Within a supportive liberal arts context, theatre majors acquire foundational skills in acting, design, and directing while dance majors study dance composition as well as ballet and modern dance technique. Both theatre and dance students examine the history, theory, and literature of their disciplines and work to develop their own identities as artists. Through classes and production, non-major students also develop as performers and experience the richly varied ways in which theatre and dance artists interpret life. All members of the Gustavus community - students, faculty, and staff - enjoy the diverse, challenging, entertaining series of plays and dance concerts produced by the department each year.

Minnesota State University—Mankato

Dr. Paul J. Hustoles, Chair
Dept. of Theatre and Dance
201 Performing Arts Center
Minnesota State Univ, Mankato
Mankato, MN 56001
(507) 389-2118
www.MSUTheatre.com
ADMISSIONS: www.mnsu.edu

14,000 Total Enr.; compet.
Semester System
125 Majors, ATHE
T: $2,920/$3,672 R&B
O-ST T: $5,834/$3,672 R&B
FAX: (507) 389-2922
paul.hustoles@mnsu.edu
1 (800) 722-0544
FAX: (507) 389-5114

DEGREES OFFERED

BFA in Acting (12); Musical Theatre (12); Design Technology (20); BA or BS in Theatre Generalist (50); MFA in Acting (3), Musical Theatre (2); Directing (3), Design (Scene, costume, lights) (5); MA Generalist (2). Declare major in freshman year; grant 20 UG, 5 Grad degrees.

ADMISSION & FINANCIAL INFORMATION

HS rank in top 50% or ACT score; 80% accepted to inst; no special req. for UG; accept all UG applics to Th. Program; Grad program admits 6 out of 24 apps, requires aud/int for actors, portfolio for designers. Selected Grad applicants are invited on campus for a full day interview process. Freshman Talent Grant avail. through aud/int. The Dept. gives a departmental scholarships by application, prior residency req'd.

FACULTY AND CLASSES OFFERED

12 FT, 1 PT: 3 PhD, 9 MFA/MA, 1 (PT), 2 staff

A. (1 FT) Intro to Th-1/Y; Th Hist-3/Y; Shakes-2/X; Dramatic Criticism-1/O; Theatre of Diversity-1/O

B. (3 1/2 FT, 2 PT) Acting-10/Y; Voice/Spch/Dialects-3/Y; Mvmt- 3/Y; Singing-10+/Y; Mus Th-1/Y; Directing-3/Y; Stg Combat-1/Y; Audition Methods-1/Y; Practicum, etc-Y; Touring Th-1/Y

C. (4 1/2 FT) Set Design-3/Y; Tech. Prod.-2/Y; Cost. Design-3/Y; Cost. Constr.-1/Y; Cost. History-1/Y; Ltg Des.-3/Y; Stage Mgmt-1/Y; Make-up-2/Y; Sound Design-2/Y; Practicum-Y

D. (1 FT) Arts Management-1/O; Marketing, Promo-X; Devel/Grant Writing-X; Budget/Acct'ng-X; Careers in Theatre-1/Y

FACILITIES AND PRODUCTIONS

MAINSTAGE: 529 seats, fly space, computerized lighting. 6 prods: 8 Fac dir, 10 Fac des, occs'nal Guest dir/des, 1-2 UG des, 5 Grad des, 5 UG des; budget $6,000-30,000

SECOND STAGE: 250 seats, black box, computerized lighting.. 4 prods: 1 Fac dir, 1-2 Fac des, 2-3 Grad dir, 8-10 Grad des, 1-2

UG dir, 7-9 UG des UG dir/des, 3-4 Grad dir, 5-6 Gr des; bdgt $800-2,000

THIRD STAGE: 70 seats, black box. 15 prods: 5 Grad dir, 10 UG dir; budget 0-$100

TOUR: 1 prod: 1 Grad dir/des, 1 UG des

4 student-written plays produced in the last two years.

Facility built in 1967, new 250 seat black box theatre in 2000; includes scene shop, costume shop, prop shop, welding shop, sound studio, CAD facility, video studio, 2 dance studios, 2 rehearsal studios, 2 design studios, 4 classrooms.

Connected with Highland Summer Theatre, a professional non-Equity summer stock company in its 41st season. Four productions in nine weeks, students may audition for acting company; often hired for tech and management positions. Occasional design opportunities.

DESCRIPTION

Noted Faculty: Paul J. Hustoles, Acting/Directing/History; David McCarl, Costume Design; Julie Kerr-Berry, Dance; Randy York, Theatre Tech; Steve Smith, Lighting Design; Paul Finocchiaro, Acting, Dance; George Grubb, Sound Design; Brad Garner, Dance.

Guest Artists: Tom Woldt, Director; John Paul, Designer; E.J. Sudkoviak, Actor; Mike Croswell, Designer; Tony Nation, Actor; Kurt Sharp, Designer; Michael Lonergan, Director; Curt Enderle, Designer.

The Department of Theatre and Dance at Minnesota State University, Mankato firmly believes in preparing the practicing theatre artist through intense theoretical and experiential training. There is a heavy production schedule in all theatrical styles with an emphasis on popular genres. The undergraduate degree program is advanced training in both the academic and practical aspects of Theatre Arts based upon a strong and varied Liberal Arts education. Students may specialize in the BFA but are encouraged to try all aspects of production. The MA program is designed for the academician and as further preparation for the PhD. The MFA degree is designed as professional preparation in Acting, Musical Theatre, Directing or Design. Major production responsibilities, a core of theatre history, theory and literature and a professional internship are integral to the program.

Minnesota State University - Moorhead

David Wheeler, Dept. Chair
Jim Bartruff, Director of Theatre
Dept. of Speech & Theatre
Center for the Arts
Minnesota State Univ.-Moorhead
Moorhead, MN 56563
DEPT: (218) 236-2126
www.mnstate.edu/speech
ADMISSIONS: 1104 7th Ave. S.
(218) 236-2161

7,000 Total Enr.; compet.
Semester System
68 Majors
T: $9,116 R&B
O-ST T: $465 per cred
SMALL PROGRAM
FAX: (218) 236-4612

dragon@mnstate.edu
www.mnstate.edu/admissions

DEGREES OFFERED

BS in Speech/Theatre Teaching (12); BA in Theatre Arts: Acting (52), Directing (10), Design/Tech (6) AA Dance Minor (15).
Declare major in soph. year; 2001 granted 10 UG degs.

ADMISSION & FINANCIAL INFORMATION

Admission: HS rank top 50% or ACT; univ. admits 85% of applicants. Theatre program admits all UG applicants; Delmar J. Hansen Schol.: 64 credtis, GPA of 3.0, dept. contributions. Mark R. Lulac: Soph. or Jr., good acad. standing, contribution. Carol Gaede: Less than 64 credits, GPA of 3.0, contributions. Freshman Talent: Entering freshmen, application.

FACULTY AND CLASSES OFFERED

5 FT, 2 PT: 2 PhD, 5 MA/MFA; 3 Staff

A. (1 FT) Intro to Theatre-1/Y; Dramatic Lit-3/O; Theatre History-2/Y; Shakes-1/X; Playwriting-1/O

B. (3 FT) Acting-2/Y; Voice/Speech-2/Y; Movement-2/Y; Singing-1/X; Musical Th-1/O; Directing-2/Y; Stage Combat-1/O; Dance-3/Y

C. (1 FT,1 PT) Prins of Design-1/Y; Set Design-2/O; Ltg Des-1/O; Tech Prod'n-2/Y; Make-up-1/O

D. (1 PT) Arts Management-1/O

FACILITIES AND PRODUCTIONS

MAINSTAGE: 900 seats, fly space, computerized lighting. 9 prods: 4 Fac dir,4 Fac des, 5 UG dir, 5 UG des; budget $8,000-30,000

SECOND STAGE: 320 seats, fly space, computerized lighting. 8 prods: 3 Fac dir, 1 Fac des, 5 UG dir/7 UG des; budget $5-12,000

Workshop/Readings-budget $50-500.

Facility was built in 1963 & 1980; last renovated in 1990; includes scene, costume, welding shops, sound studio, CAD facility, 2 video studios, 2 dance studios, rehearsal studio, design studio, 4 classrooms; also Weld Auditorium (500 seats), music industry studio, recording studio.

Connection with professional summer theatre company: Straw Hat Players Summer Theatre Co.is a 40 year-old stock operation that presents 4 major productions in a 10-week summer season. We hire a company of 30+ each year, including some Equity guest artists. MSUM students are given the opportunity to be hired as company members and may also obtain credit. We encourage all theatre majors to participate in at least 2-3 seasons of Straw Hat Players; the casting is open and talented students work and act beside experienced professionals. We also provide qualified students with design and administrative opportunities.

DESCRIPTION

Noted Faculty: James Bartruff, Acting/Directing; David Wheeler, Theatre Historian; Roray Hedges, Design; Craig Ellingson, Directing/Choreography.

Guest Artists: Dirs: Brant Pope, Dan Yurgaitis. Actors: Jim Baker, Jan Maxwell, Laurie Barger, Peter Halverson, Jerry VerDorn.

At Minnesota State University - Moorhead , we are dedicated to the training and development of the undergraduate theatre student. Our emphasis on a solid foundation in liberal arts and our "mentor" approach to teaching, combined with one of the country's most active and successful university performance schedules, provides each student with a quality education in all of the theatrical arts. Our academic season has 26,000 paid admissions per year. At MSU, each student's classroom study is continually augmented with numerous assignments in acting, directing, technical theatre, and theatre management. Every summer, our students join forces with top-notch professionals in our Straw Hat Players summer stock theatre program to produce 4-6 plays and musicals for a regional audience of 16,000 patrons. If you are looking for a department that combines the personalized attention of a small college with the production resources of a major university, then look no further than Moorhead State University. And remember our liberal scholarship programs and tuition reciprocity agreements make us one of the best values in higher education. Spread your artistic wings at MSU! Come Play with us!

St. Cloud State University

Eva Honegger, Chair
Dept. of Theatre, Film Studies
 & Dance
PAC 202
St. Cloud State University
720 Fourth Ave. South
St. Cloud, MN 56301-4498
DEPT: (320) 308-3229
www.stcloudstate.edu
ADMISSIONS: 720 4th Ave. So., St. Cloud, MN 56301
877-654-7278 toll free

16,000 Total Enr.;
 competitive
Semester System
26 Major, NAST, ATHE
T:$5,633/$4,942 R&B
O-ST T: $10,920/$4,942 R&B
SMALL PROGRAM
FAX: (320) 308-2902

scsu4u@stcloudstate.edu

DEGREES OFFERED

BA in Theatre (3). Students declare major by soph. year. 2007 anticipate 3 UG degrees granted

ADMISSION & FINANCIAL INFORMATION

Top 50% of HS or ACT composite score of 25; Accept 86%; admits 9 out of 10 UG to program; application and participation in productions required.

FACULTY AND CLASSES OFFERED

4 FT: 2 PT; 5 PhD, 1 MFA/MA; 2 Staff

A. (1 FT) Intro to Theatre-1/Y; Dramatic Lit-2/Y; Theatre History-2/O; Shakes-2/X; Playwriting-2/X

B. (1 FT, 2 PT) Acting-3/Y; Voice/Movement-2/Y; Directing-2/Y; Musical Th-1/O; Dance-12/O; Dance Minor

C. (2 FT) Prins of Des-1/Y; Set Des-1/O; Cost Des-1/O; Ltg Des-2/Y; Tech Prod-1/O; Cost Constr-1/O; Make-up-1/O; Stage Mgmt-1/O

FACILITIES & PRODUCTIONS

MAINSTAGE: 425 seats, fly space, computerized & electronic lighting
  3 prods: 3 Fac dir; 4-6 Fac des; 2-4 UG Des; budget $5,000-7,000

SECOND STAGE: 175 seats, black box, computerized & electron lighting.
  3 prods: 2 Fac dir; 2-4 Fac des; 1 UG dir; 2-4 UG des; budget $5,000-$7,000

Facility was built in 1968; includes scene, costume, sound studio, video studio, dance studio, rehearsal studio, 2 classrooms, script library.

A non-departmental student-run producing organization presents 1-2 productions per year in which majors participate. Connected with professional Theatre l'Homme Dieu during the summer. Students audition or present porfolios for work in summer theatre.

DESCRIPTION

Noted Faculty: (Theatre) Jeffrey Bleam: Costume Des, Costume Tech, Directing, History; David R. Borron: Lighting, Scenic and Sound Design, Tech Theatre; M. Kate Sinnett: Acting, Directing, Voice, Movement, Dramatic Literature; Brenda Wentworth: Acting, Directing, History, Dramatic Lit and Theory. (Film Studies) Brad Chisholm: Film History, Film Theory; Philippe Costaglioli: International Film; Eva Honegger: Film Prod; Christopher Jordan: Film and Culture. (Dance) April Sellers: Modern; Tracy Vacura: Ballet.

St. Cloud State University is an accredited institutional member of the National Association of Schools of Theatre. Our faculty is committed to providing the most comprehensive undergraduate theatre education in Minnesota, with particular emphasis on student opportunities to direct, choreograph and design. Theatre students at SCSU complete a BA degree that balances rigorous academic coursework with extensive studio experience. This degree prepares students to pursue careers in the professional theatre or to continue their education at the graduate level. We also offer a minor and major in film studies and a minor in dance, areas that have become increasingly relevant to students who seek careers in the dramatic arts. Interested students should contact us through our website. Our faculty members will gladly answer your questions about our program.

Saint Olaf College

Brian Bjorklund, Chair
Dept. of Theatre
Saint Olaf College
1500 St. Olaf Ave.
Northfield, MN 55057-1098
DEPT: (507) 646-3240
glimsdal@stolaf.edu
ADMISSIONS: Admissions,1520 St. Olaf Ave.,Northfield, MN 55057
(507) 646-3025

3,000 Total Enr.; competitive
Semester System
SMALL PROGRAM
65 Majors, NAST, ATHE
T/R&B: $38,500
FAX: (507) 646-3949
www.stolaf.edu/depts/theatre

www.stolaf.edu/admissions

DEGREES OFFERED

BA in Theatre (65). Students declare major in any year.

ADMISSION & FINANCIAL INFORMATION

Req's.: Graduation from accredited high school with at least 4 years of English or literature, 4 years of Social Studies or history, 3-4 years of college prep. math, 3-4 years of college prep. science, 2-4 years of foreign language; Adjusted G.P.A. of 3.3 or higher. Essay, 2-4 recommendation letters, ACT/SAT test scores; No special req's. for admission to Theatre Program; Admit all to program.

FACULTY AND CLASSES OFFERED

4 FT, 2PT: 2 PhD, 3 MFA/MA; 1 professional without advanced degree; 2 Staff

A. (1 FT, 1 PT) Intro to Theatre-2/Y; Dramatic Lit-X; Theatre History-2/Y; Shakes-1/O; Playwriting-2/O

B. (2 FT) Acting-3/Y; Voice/Speech-2/O; Movement-1/O; Singing-X; Musical Theatre-1/O; Directing-2/Y; Stage Combat-1/O; Dance-X

C. (1 FT, 1 PT) Prins of Des-1/Y; Set Des-1/Y; Cost Des-1/Y; Ltg Des-1/Y; Sound Des-1/Y

D. Arts Management-X; Marketing/Promotion-X

FACILITIES & PRODUCTIONS

MAINSTAGE: 348 seats, fly space, computerized/electronic lighting. 3 prods: 3 Fac dir/1 Fac des; 2 UG des; budget $5,000-5,800

SECOND STAGE: 120 seats, computerized/electronic lighting. 2 prods: 1 Fac dir, 1 UG dir/ 2UG des; budget $1,500-1,900

Facility was built in 1919, last renovated in 1979; includes scene, costume, props shop, welding shop, sound, 1 movement/dance, CAD facility, 1 design studio, 2 classrooms.

A non-departmental, student run producing organization presents 8 to 12 productions a year, in which department majors generally participate. Three student-written plays were produced in the last two years.

DESCRIPTION

Noted Faculty: Gary Gisselman, Artist-in-Residence and Artistic Director.

Guest Artists: Nayna Ramey, Designer; Peter Moore, Instructor; Emil Herrera, Instructor; Gwendolyn Schwinke, Instructor; Kevin Kling, performer and playwright; Vincent Delaney, playwright.

The activities and skills necessary for learning about and making theatre are well suited to learning about and contributing to lives of worth and service. The basic theatre activity is making things: play scripts, sets, costumes, characters and the complete works of which these are a part. The theatre skills are leading, following, reading, writing, talking, drawing, building, acting, performing and making arrangements. We place these skiiklls in the service of our conception of theatre as a way of knowing. Our courses, along with the rest of the college curriculum, develop an appreciation of the need for moral choice, an imagination of the constructs and examines alternatives, and an understanding of creativity as a reality in the world and an agency of community and change. We think of the program as a kind of laboratory for a serious and productive life.

Southwest Minnesota State University

Dr. Ray Oster, Director
Theatre Program,
  Dept. of Fine Arts
Southwest Minnesota State Univ.
Marshall, MN 56258
Theatre Prog: (507) 537-7103
oster@southwest.msus.edu
www.southwest.msus.edu/programs/THTR1
FAX: (507) 537-7014
ADMISSIONS: www.southwest.msus.edu/Admission/
(800) 642-0684

3,500 Total Enr.; not compet.
Semester System
SMALL PROGRAM
30 Majors, U/RTA
KC/ ACTF, USITT
T: $6,455
R&B:$5,500

shearerr@southwestmsu.edu

FAX: (507) 537-7154

DEGREES OFFERED

BA in Theatre(20), Radio/TV (40). Declare major usually in 1st or 2nd year; 2004 granted 5 degrees.

ADMISSION & FINANCIAL INFORMATION

80% accepted to institution; Theatre program admits all applicants to program. Scholarships: Letter to Ray Oster, above.

FACULTY AND CLASSES OFFERED

3 MFA/MA

A. (1 FT) Intro to Theatre-3/Y; Theatre History-2/Y; Shakes-2/X; Dramatic Lit-1/O; Playwriting-1/O

B. (1 FT) Acting-4/Y; Voice/Speech-4/Y; Directing-2/YO

C. (1 FT) Set Design-1/Y; Cost Des-1/Y; Ltg Des-1/Y; Cost Constr-1/Y; Cost Hist-1/Y; Make-up-1/Y

FACILITIES AND PRODUCTIONS

MAINSTAGE: 330 seats, fly space, computerized lighting. 3 prods: 2 Fac dir/des, 1 Guest dir, 1 Grad des; budget $5,000-6,000

SECOND STAGE: 200 seats, black box, 4 student dir/des prods; budget $500-1,000

Facility was built in 1967, renovated in 1993; includes scene shop, costume shop, sound studio, video studio, dance studio, rehearsal studio, design studio.

Majors generally participate in a non-departmental, student-run drama club that presents 3 productions per year in studio theatre.

DESCRIPTION

Noted Faculty: Nadine Schmidt, Acting/Directing; Ray Oster, Tech. Dir/Scene Design; Sheila Tabaka, Costume/Director.

Guest Artists: Warren Bowles, Guest Director; Robert Patrick.

Southwest Minnesota State University supports an active theatre program that produces three Mainstage theatre productions each year, along with numerous studio productions. All shows are cast from the entire student body regardless of their major and with an emphasis on total student involvement. The Studio Theatre also provides students an opportunity to produce new and experimental theatre. The theatre staff consists of three full-time faculty members who have all worked in professional theatre and are dedicated to continuing the tradition of excellence that SMSU Theatre has enjoyed in the past. A three-time winner of the American College Theatre Festival, SSU Theatre provides students the opportunity to perform in a broad spectrum of plays from classic to modern, with practical experience in tv as well.

University of Minnesota

Judy Bartl, Prog Dir.
580 Rarig Center
330 21st Ave. S.
Minneapolis, MN 55455
theatre@umn.edu
(612) 625-6699
http://umn.edu/theatre
**Grad, highly competitive; UG, not competitive
ADMISSIONS: (Undergrad) 240 Williamson
(612) 625-2008 or 1-800-752-1000
http://admissions.tc.umn.edu/
ADMISSIONS: (Grad) 309 Johnson
Grad site www..grad.umn.edu

32,113 Total Enr., **
Semester System
300 Majors; NAST, U/RTA
RES T: 9,885
NON-R T: UG $13,885
$7,062 r&b
FAX: (612) 625-6334

FAX: (612) 626-1693
admissions@tc.umn.edu
(612) 625-3014

DEGREES OFFERED

BA in Theatre Arts (240); *MA/PhD in Theatre Arts (27); MFA in Directing (0), Design/Technology (11). *Students admitted on an MA/PhD track-we do not offer an MA-only degree. BFA in Acting (62). Declare major in freshman year; 2004 granted 70 UG, 7 Grad degs.

ADMISSION & FINANCIAL INFORMATION

8% of applicants accepted to inst. BA theatre program admits all applics; BFA in Acting program admits from national audition; Grad admits 8-10 out of 75, requires aud/int, portfolio for designers, writing samples for MA/PhD; on-campus aud. for MFA dir. GRE req. for all Grad programs, min. 3.0 GPA. Approx. $50,000 in scholarships. available for both Grad and UG on a yearly competitive basis. Students apply and are selected by the faculty based on the various criteria of the scholarship.

FACULTY AND CLASSES OFFERED

22 FT, 20 PT: 7 PhD, 12 MFA/MBA, 13 Prof. w/out adv. degree

A. (4 1/2 FT, 1 PT) Intro to Theatre-1/Y; Theatre History-2/Y; Shakes-2/O; Dramatic Lit-2/Y; Playwriting-2/Y; Black Th. Hist-2/O; Historiography-1/O; Dramaturgy-1/O; Drama & the Media-1/Y; Actor/Director Collaboration-1/O; Hist/Theory Western Th-6/O (6 course seq. req. PhD);

B. (6 1/2 FT, 15 PT) Acting-4/Y; Voice/Speech-2/Y; Movement- 1/Y; Mime/Mask/Commedia/Circus-1/O; Singing-1/Y; Musical Th-1/Y; Directing-4/Y; Stage Combat-1/Y; Acting for the Camera-1/Y; Career Preparation-1/Y; Dance (separate program in this dept.)

C. (4 FT, 3 PT) Set Design-3/YO; Cost Des-3/YO; Ltg Des-4/YO; Cost Constr-1/O; Make-up-1/O; Stg Mgmt-2/Y; Technology Courses-2/Y; Sound Design-1/O; Design Composition/Collaboration-1/O; Drawing/Rendering/Scene Painting for the Designer-2/Y; Lighting Tech-1/O; Sound Tech-2/O; Audio Engineering-1/O; Digital Audio-1/O; Multimedia-1/O.

D. (1 PT) Arts Management-1/O; Marketing/Promo-1/O; Development-1/O

FACILITIES AND PRODUCTIONS

MAINSTAGE: 466 seats, fly space, computerized & electronic ltg
5 prods: 2 Fac dir, 4 Fac des, 7 Guest dir, 1 Guest des, 2 Grad dir, 9 Grad des, 5 UG des; budget $1,500-10,000

SECOND STAGE: 421 seats, fly space, computerized & electronic lighting. 12 prods: 3 Grad dir, 5 Grad des, 9 UG dir, 12 UG des; budget; $3,000

THIRD STAGE: 196 seats, fixed stage, computerized & electronic lighting.

Facility built in 1973, ongoing renovation; includes scene, costume, props shops; sound, design studios, 2 dance studios. New dance bldg., opened March '99, includes performance space seating 125, 1 classroom, 2 addn'l dance studios. New showboat on Mississippi at St. Paul. Summer operation seating 200- opens 2002.

A departmental, student-run producing organization presents 5-7 productions per year in the 4th theatre (blackbox) in which dept. majors participate. at least 5 student written plays have been produced in Summer New Works Series. In addition, the MA/PhD students run a theatre organization called Crisis Point: Theatre of Danger and Opportunity.

Connection with Guthrie Theater (Equity). The BFA-Acting program is a joint program with the Guthrie Theater. Internships available for both graduate and undergraduate students at the Guthrie, Penumbra Theatre, Children's Theatre, Theatre de la Jeune Lune, among others. The Penumbra Theatre also accepts internships for graduates.and sponsors the August Wilson Fellowship for 1MA/PhD student every 2 years.

DESCRIPTION

Noted Faculty: Lou Bellamy, Artistic Dir. Penumbra Theatre, Directing & Acting; Matt LeFebvre, Cost.

Design; Martin Gwinup, Sound Design & Technology; Michel Kobialka, Hist/Theory; Stephen Kanee, Directing; C. Lance Brockman, Sc. Des./Painting; Elizabeth Nash, Voice; Barbara Reid, Actor; Neksandra Volska, Directing; Sonja Kuftinec, History/Theory; Kari Margolis, Acting/Directing.

Guest Artists: Kent Stephens, Illusion Theatre, Director; Michael Brindisi, Chanhassen Dinner Theatre, Director; Peter Moore, Director, Combat; Kira Obolensky, Playwright; Michael Sommers, Puppetry; Charles Nolte, Director; Jill Dolan, PhD Lecture Series; Janelle Reinelt, PhD Lecture Series; Dijana Milosevic, PhD Lecture Series.

The University of Minnesota Department of Theatre Arts and Dance undergraduate BA degree program offers a liberal arts education with strong preparation for concentrated training at the graduate level through the study of both the theoretical context and the practice of live dramatic performance. Coursework embraces theatre as a group art, an art in which individual excellence is often fully realized only in collaboration with other artists. Students are encouraged to test classroom experiences under the pressure of public performance in the laboratory of the University Theatre on both the undergraduate and the graduate level. Graduate degree programs seek to produce artists and scholars of the highest calibre, preparing them for careers in professional and/or academic theatre and related artistic fields. Professional internships are available for both graduate and undergraduate students in the very active Twin Cities professional theatre community.

University of St. Thomas

Theatre Dept.
University of St. Thomas
2115 Summit Ave.
St. Paul, MN 55105-1096

*12,000 Total Enr.; not compet.
Semester System
21 Majors; ATHE
(651) 690-6700
SMALL PROGRAM
T: $26,274/$7,312 r&b

ADMISSIONS: Office of Admissions, Mail #32F-1, UST, St. Paul, MN 55105-1096
(800) 328-6819
www.stthomas.edu
admissions@stthomas.edu
www.stthomas.edu - see website for current tuition/R&B fees
Combined Theatre Dept. w/ College of St. Catherine in St. Paul
* Total enrollment of both Institutions.

DEGREES OFFERED

Both CSC and UST combined: BA in Performance (21), History/Theory, Education with certification in Theater/Dance (1). Declare major in soph. year.

ADMISSION & FINANCIAL INFORMATION

No special requirements. UST is co-ed. Students accepted into Theater major as sophomores provided they are in good standing academically.

FACULTY AND CLASSES OFFERED

3 FT, 1 PT: 1 PhD, 3 MFA/MA; 2 Staff

A. (1 FT) Intro to Theatre-1/Y; Dramatic Lit-3/Y; Th Hist-3/Y; Shakes-2/X; Dramatic Criticism-1/O; Film History-4/Y

B. (1 FT) Acting/Scene Study-2/Y; Directing-2/Y; Dance-1/O; Film

Making-1/O

C. (1 PT) Prins of Des-1/O; Tech Prod'n-1/Y

D. (1 FT) Directing/Film Studies

FACILITIES & PRODUCTIONS

MAINSTAGE: 240 seats, fly space, electronic lighting. 2 prods: 2 Fac dir/des

SECOND STAGE: 230 seats, fly space, electronic lighting. 2 prods: 2 Fac dir/des

Facility was built in 1970's, renovated in 1980's; includes scene shop, costume shop, video studio, dance studio, classrooms.

One student-directed play produced in the last two years.

Informal ties to several local companies.

DESCRIPTION

Noted Faculty: Amelia Howe Kritzer, Theater History, Dramatic Literature; JoAnn Holonbek, Acting, Creative Dramatics; Jon Leiseth, Directing, Acting.

Guest Artists: Jennifer Allton, Stage Combat.

The Joint Dept of Theater is intended to provide education in the history, theory, and practical arts of theater, as well as performance opportunities for all students, within the context of the liberal arts.

Winona State University ••••••••••••

Prof. David Bratt, Chair
Dept. of Theatre & Dance
P .O. Box 5838
Winona State University
Winona, MN 55987-5838
DEPT: (507)457-5230
dbratt@winona.edu
ADMISSIONS: Above address.
www.winona.edu

Tot. Enr: 7,000; compet.
25 Majors; NAST, ATHE
Semester System
T: $6,324/$5,060 R&B
O-ST T: $10,800/$6,060 R&B
FAX: (507) 457-5481
SMALL PROGRAM
(507) 457-5100

DEGREES OFFERED

BA Theatre (25). Declare major in first or second year; 2004 granted 5 degrees.

ADMISSION & FINANCIAL INFORMATION

ACT 21 or top 50% of HS class, 80% of applicants accepted by institution, all applicants accepted to theatre program. Scholar-ship of $800, by audition, apply with resume, 2 letters of rec., apply by 4/15.

FACULTY AND CLASSES OFFERED

3 Full-Time: 1 PhD, 3 MFA/MA; 2 Staff

A. (1 FT) Intro to Theatre-1/Y; Dramatic Lit-2/Y; Th Hist-1/Y; Shakes-2/YX; Dramatic Criticism-1/Y; Playwriting-1/YX; Modern Drama-1/YX; Play Analysis-1/Y

B. (1 1/2F T) Acting-3/Y; Voice/Speech-1/Y; Movement-1/Y; Singing-1/YX; Directing-2/Y; Dance Courses-Y

C. (1 FT) Prins of Des-1/Y; Tech Prod'n-1/Y; Set Design-1/O; Ltg Des-1/O; Stg Mgmt-1/Y; Design Project-1/Y; CAD-1/O

FACILITIES & PRODUCTIONS

MAINSTAGE: 420 seats, fly space, computerized lighting
3 prods: 2 Fac dir/des; budget $10,000

SECOND STAGE: 75-125 seats, computerized lighting
5 prods: 1 Fac dir/des, 1 UG dir/des; budget $3,000-4,500

Facility built in 1969; includes scene shop, costume shop, sound studio, dance studio, classrooms. CADD lab/equipment.

A non-departmental, student-run organization presents 3-4 productions per year in which majors participate.

DESCRIPTION

Guest Artists: Martha Connerton & Monica Maye, "performance art" production; dance/movement- Urban Bushwomen, Dance Compass, and individuals such as Kari Margolis, James Sewell, Joe Chuvela, Kim Nofzinger, Lou Fencher.

The liberal arts major in theatre balances cognitive, creative, and practical classes which integrate the study of theory and history with performance. We aim to develop kinesthetic, cognitive, and creative understanding as well as skill—perception, imaginative problem-solving, concentration, and respect for craft—which are important to original work in all fields. The dance minor helps students regardless of major, to enhance the integration of their bodies and minds and to tap their creative potentials through the art of movement.

MISSISSIPPI

Mississippi University for Women ••••

William G. Biddy, Chair.
Mississippi Univ. for Women
P. O. Box W-70
Columbus MS 39701
DEPT: (601) 329-7260
ADM: (601) 329-7106
www.muw.edu

2,080 Total Enr.; compet.
Semester System
10 Majs; ATHE, SETC, ACTF
T: $4,209/$4,819 R&B
O-ST T: $10,723/$4,819 R&B
SMALL PROGRAM
admissions@muw.edu

DEGREES OFFERED

BA in Fine Arts (Theatre Emphasis) (18). Declare major in fresh/soph. year.

ADMISSION & FINANCIAL INFORMATION

ACT 16, SAT scores accepted, call for details; univ. admits 87% of applicants, no special reqs for theatre program. Theatre scholarships given to declared theatre majors in the Spring semester of each year, based on GPA and dept. participation. Univ. scholarships. are available for students with ACT 21 and above.

FACULTY AND CLASSES OFFERED

2 FT, 1/2 PT: 2 MA/MFA; 1/2 Prof. w/o adv. deg; 1 Staff

A. (1/2 FT) Intro to Theatre-1/Y; Dramatic Lit-2/OX; Theatre History-2/O; Shakes-1/X; Playwriting-1/O

B. (1/2 FT, 1/2 PT) Acting/Scene Study-2/Y; Voice/Speech-1/Y; Movement-1/O; Singing-2/X; Musical Theatre-1/O; Dance-4/Y

C. (1/2 FT) Prins of Des-1/O; Set Des-1/O; Cost Des-1/O; Ltg Des-1/O; Tech Prod-1/O; Cost Hist-1/O; Make-up-1/O; Stg Mgmt-1/O

D. (1/2 FT) Arts Management-1/O

FACILITIES AND PRODUCTIONS

MAINSTAGE: 300 seats, fly space, computerized lighting. 3 prods: 1 Fac dir/des, 1 Guest dir, 1 UG dir, 5 UG des; bdgt $1-6,000

SECOND STAGE: 60 seats, electronic lighting. 3-9 prods (number varies based on Directing class enrollment and student-proposed prods): UG dir/des; budget $0-100;

2 UG dir/des Workshop/Reading

Facility was built in 1976; includes scene shop, costume shop, dance studio, rehearsal studio, 5 classrooms.

DESCRIPTION

The nation's first public college for women, Mississippi University for Women opened its doors 15 years ago to men as well. Since its founding in 1884, MUW has maintained a distinguished reputation for academic excellence. Part of the Division of Fine and Performing Arts, the MUW Theatre Program collaborates with the areas of dance and music in both coursework and productions. The program offers a BA in Fine Arts with a Theatre Emphasis, and its hallmark is a rigorous production schedule, individual attention throughout the training process, and first-rate production values. MUW Theatre students acquire a broad understanding of theatre as a liberal art, a strong sense of self, and the competitive skills with which to pursue professional or graduate work. The placement rate for graduates since 1990 in professional theatre and graduate programs has been 100%. The MUW Theatre program is designed for the serious student with the desire to work in a company atmosphere.

University of Southern Mississippi

Louis Rackoff, Chair
USM Theatre & Dance
118 College Dr. #5052
Univ. of Southern Mississippi
Hattiesburg, MS 39406-0001
DEPT: (601) 266-4994
www.usm.edu/theatre
ADMISSIONS: 118 COLLEGE DR #5166, Hattiesburg, MS 39406
(601) 266-5000
www.usm.edu/admissions

35,845 Tot Enr.; Compet.
Semester System
200 Majors; NAST
T: $2,297/$1,328 R&B
O-ST T: $3,014/$1,699 R&B
FAX: (601) 266-6423
theatre@usm.edu

FAX: (601) 266-5148

DEGREES OFFERED

BA in General Theatre; BFA in Performance, Design/Tech; MFA in Performance, Directing, Scenic Design, Costume Design, Light/Sound Design. Declare major in second year.

ADMISSION & FINANCIAL INFORMATION

College prep curriculum with a 3.2 high school GPA, SAT score of 770 or ACT score of 16. Theatre service award scholarships and out-of-state audition/interview; UGs enter program as pre-theatre majors and apply for either the BA or BFA plans. Aud/Int required for scholarship consideration. Aud for Grad actors, portfolio for Grad des. 10 out of 10 UG applicants are generally admitted to theatre program, 4 out of 10 Grad applicants admitted.

FACULTY AND CLASSES OFFERED

7 Full Time; 2 PT 9 MFA/MA

A. Intro to Theatre-1/Y; Theatre Hist-2/Y; Shakes-1/O; Dramatic Lit-2/YX; Playwriting-1/O

B. (3 FT, 2 PT) Acting-12/Y; Voice/Speech-2/Y; Movement-3/Y; Mime, etc-2/Y; Singing-2/Y; Musical Th-2/Y; Directing-3/Y; Stage Combat-3/Y; Dance-8/Y

C. (4 FT) Prins of Des-1/Y; Set Des-3/Y; Cost. Des-4/Y; Lighting Des-3/O; Cost. Constr.-2/O; Make-up-2/Y; Stage Mgmt-1/O

FACILITIES AND PRODUCTIONS

MAINSTAGE: 275 seats, thrust, fly space, computerized & electronic lighting
15 prods: 3 Fac dir/des, 2 Grad dir, 5 Grad des, 2 UG des; budget $3,500-7,500.

SECOND STAGE: 500 seats, prosc., computerized lighting
3 prods: 3 Grad dir/des, 6 UG des; budget $500-1,000

THIRD STAGE: 150 seats, black box, computerized & electronic lighting

Workshops/Readings: 18 prods: 6 Grad dir, 6 UG dir/des.

Plus summer season of three plays in rep.

Facility built in 2001, includes scene shop, costume shop, sound studio, CAD facility, mini prosc. for classes (seats 75).

Dept has produced 3 student-written plays in the last 2 years.

We operate our summer rep season as a professional company, although students get credit as well as stipends for their participation.

DESCRIPTION

Noted Faculty: David Stellhorn, Production; Monica Hayes, Acting; Robin Aronson, Acting/Voice; Sean Boyd, Acting/Movement; Stephen Judd, Scene Design; Larry Mullican, Costume Design; Mike Post, Lighting/Sound; Luois Rackoff, Directing

Guest Artists: Ty Burrell, Actor; Patrick Ryan Sullivan, Actor; Gregory Thornton, Actor; James Moriarty, Composer; Patrick Benson, Director

The theatre program at Southern Miss is committed to preparing students for careers in professional or academic theatre. The University of Southern Mississippi is an accredited institutional member of the National Association of Schools of Theatre (NAST). With a nationally recognized program, a highly qualified faculty, a state-of-the-art facility, a vigorous production program, and individualized attention to our students, we offer a first-rate theatre education. Members of the faculty have worked professionally in New York, London, California, Chicago and elsewhere, and are fully dedicated to preparing students for success. Undergraduate studies in theatre at southern Miss combine all the advantages of a liberal arts education with intensive training in the skills of the profession. The graduate program at Southern Miss is focused on preparing students for a career in theatre. The training is specialized and rigorous, with an emphasis on individual attention and practical application.

MISSOURI

Avila University

Dr. Charlene Gould
Director of Theatre
Avila University
11901 Wornall Rd.
Kansas City, MO 64145
ADM: 1-800/GO AVILA

1,800 Total Enr.; not compet.
Semester System
50 Majors
T: $8,650/$2,750 R&B
DEPT: (816) 501-2411

DEGREES OFFERED

BFA in Acting, Producing/Directing, Technical Theatre, Musical Theatre; BA in Theatre, Theatre Education.

ADMISSION & FINANCIAL INFORMATION

Requirements for freshmen-20 ACT, 2.5 HS GPA; Requirements for transfers-GPA of at least 2.0 in at least 24 cr. hrs. of college work. The institution accepts 60% of applicants. An audition and interview is required for acceptance into the Theatre Program.

FACULTY AND CLASSES OFFERED
3 FT, 4 PT: 1 PhD, 5 MFA

A. (1/2 FT, 1/2 PT) Introduction to Theatre-Y; Theatre History-O; Shakespeare-O; Dramatic Literature-O; Playwriting-O; Dramatic Criticism-O

B. (1/2 FT, 2PT) Acting/Scene Study-Y; Voice/Speech-O; Movement-Y; Mime, etc-Y; Singing-Y; Musical Theatre-Y; Directing-O; Stage Combat-Y; Dance-Y

C. (1 FT, 1/2 PT) Principles of Des-Y; Set Design-Y; Cost Des-Y; Ltg Des-Y; Tech Prod-Y; Cost Constr-Y; Make-up-O; Stage Mgmt-O

D. Arts Mgmt-O; Box Ofc Procedure-Y; Marketing/Promo-O; Development/Grant Writing-O; Budgeting/Acctg Procedure-O

FACILITIES AND PRODUCTIONS
MAINSTAGE: 450 seats, fly space, thrust stage
    4 prods: 2 Fac dir, 2 Guest dir, 4 UG des

SECOND STAGE: 30 seats
    4 prods: 4 UG dir/des; .

Facility was built in 1974; includes scene shop, costume shop, props shop, video studio, dance studio, 2 classrooms. Children's Theatre travelling troupe, master classes.

DESCRIPTION

Noted Faculty: Charlene Gould, Directing, Theatre History, Dramatic Criticism; Jason Harris, Technical Director; Bill Warren, Acting & Stage Combat; Robert Foulk, Acting, Stage Management; Gene Mackey, Acting/Theatre History/Children's Theatre.

The Theatre Program at Avila University, totally undergraduate in nature, is based primarily on direct experience in the classroom, studio, and stage. Students are trained for professional careers, graduate programs, and teacher education. A liberal arts foundation is the basis of the Theater program, which offers both BA and BFA degrees.

Central Missouri State University

Dr. Richard Herman, Chair
Theatre Dept
Central Missouri State Univ.
113 Martin
Warrensburg, MO 64093
DEPT: (660) 543-4020
tilden@cmsu1.cmsu.edu
ADMISSIONS: WDE 1401, CMSU
(660) 543-4290

12,000 Tot. Enr.; not compet.
Semester System
120 Majors
T: $166/hr; O-ST: $320/hr
R&B: $2,400/yr.
FAX: (660) 543-8006
www.cmsu.edu/theatre

FAX: (660) 543-8517

DEGREES OFFERED
BA in General Theatre; BFA in Acting, BFA in Design/ Technology; BS in Theatre-Teacher Education; MA in General Theatre.; 2003 granted 18 UG degrees.

ADMISSION & FINANCIAL INFORMATION
ACT score of 20 or above. UG program admits all applics; Grad program admits 1 of 3 applics. Theatre Achievement Award - students must audition or present portfolio, send letter of recommendation and

rank in upper one half of graduating class.

FACULTY AND CLASSES OFFERED
6 Full-Time: 2 PhD, 3 MFA, 1 MA

A. (3 FT) Intro to Theatre-1/Y; Theatre History-2/Y; Shakes-1/X; Dramatic Literature-1/Y; Dra Criticism-1/Y; Playwriting-1/O

B. (2 FT) Acting-2/Y; Voice/Speech-1/Y; Movement-1/Y; Mime, etc.-1/O; Singing-1/X; Musical Theatre-1/X; Directing-2/Y; Stage Combat-1/Y

C. (2 FT) Principles of Design-1/Y; Set Design-1/Y; Costume Design-1/Y; Lighting Design-2/Y; Technical Production-1/Y; Costume Construction- 1/Y; Costume History-1/Y; Make-up-1/Y; Stage Management-1/O; Drafting- 1/Y

D. Arts Management-1/Y

FACILITIES AND PRODUCTIONS
MAINSTAGE: 442 seats, fly space, computerized lighting
    5 Fac dir/des prods; budget $4,000

SECOND STAGE: 80 seats, black box

12 UG dir/des; budget $750

Variety of Fac, UG and Guest dir workshops/readings.

14 student-written plays produced in the last two years.

Facility was built in 1971, renovated in 1988; includes scene shop, costume shop, welding shop, prop shop, sound studio, technology classroom.

Connection with Central Missouri Repertory (summer): Students can be cast or fill major design responsibilities. The season incudes 2 in-house productions and a children's touring show.

DESCRIPTION

Guest Artists: Kip Niven, Auditioning; Jeanne Beechwood, Directing; Eugene Stickland, Playwright; Kevin Willmont, Playwright; Janet Ulrich Brooks, Actress; Thurston James, Properties; Richard Rand, Mask Acting; Paige O'Hara, Musical Theatre; Rick Sordelet, Fight Direction.

The Central Missouri State University Theatre Department is dedicated to the individual growth and preparation of its students. The thrust is primarily toward the undergraduates. With the option of three separate degrees, students are provided the avenues to pursue careers in teaching, the specialization of the professional theatre, or a broad-based liberal arts education. The faculty is continually concerned with the students academically and personally and devotes considerable time to advisement.

Culver-Stockton College

Haidee Heaton, Ph.D., Head
Theatre Department
Culver Stockton College
Canton, MO 63435
DEPT: (573) 288-6434
www.culver.edu
hheaton@culver.edu

865 Total Enr.; competitive
Semester System
34 Majors
T: $23,700/R&B INCL
FAX: (573) 288-6617
SMALL PROGRAM
admissions@culver.edu

DEGREES OFFERED
BA/BFA in Theatre-Performance (11), Theatre Design (6); BFA in Arts Management (15), Musical Theatre (begins Fall 2007); BSE in Theatre Ed (2). Declare major in freshman year; 2007 granted 8 UG degrees.

ADMISSION & FINANCIAL INFORMATION

ACT-18 min, GPA-2.5 min; top 1/3 of class, reviewed individually on case by case basis. 35% of applicants accepted by institution. 8 out of 10 UG admitted to theatre program. Departmental talent grants. Required aud, int, portfolio a/o aud tape.

FACULTY AND CLASSES OFFERED

6 1/2 FT, 1 PT: 1 PhD, 2 MFA/MA, 1 Prof. w/o adv. degree; 1 Staff

A. (1 1/2 FT) Intro to Th.-1/Y; Th. Hist-2/Y; Shakes-X; Playwriting-1/O; Advanced Playwriting-1/O

B. (1 FT,1 PT) Acting/Scene Study-2/Y; Voice/Speech-2/Y; Musical Theatre-2/O; Movement-1/O; Singing-X; Directing-1/Y; Dance-2/Y; Advanced Directing-1/O

C. (1 1/2 FT) Principles of Des-1/Y; Set Design-1/O; Costume Design-1/O; Lighting Des-1/O; Technical Prod-1/O; Make-up-1/O; Costume Construct-1/O; Advanced Design in set, lights, costumes, make-up-4/O

D. (2 1/2 FT) Arts Management-1/O; Box Ofc Procedure-1/O; Marketing/Promo-1/O; Devel/Grant Writing-X; Contracts/Copyrights-X; Budgeting/Acct Procedure-X

FACILITIES AND PRODUCTIONS

MAINSTAGE: 900 seats, fly space, computerized lighting
5 prods: 5 Fac dir/des; 5 UG des; budget $1,000-3,000

SECOND STAGE: 240 seats; computerized lighting
6-7 prods: 6-7 UG dir/des;budget $0-$150

2-6 Workshops/Readings: 2-6 UG dir/des; budget $0-150

Facility was built in 1968; last renovated in 2007; includes scene, costume shops, props,9 practice rooms, movement/dance, 3 rehearsal studios, 4 classrooms

A non-departmental student-run organization presents 2-6 prods per year in which majors participate. 2 student written plays have been produced in the last two years.

DESCRIPTION

Noted Faculty: Haidee Heaton, Ph.D. Acting, Directing, Voice, Musical Theatre; S. Kent Miller, M.F.A. Design, Arts Mgmt, Tech, Directing,; Jeffrey Kellogg, M.F.A. History, Playwriting, Costuming, Arts Mgmt, Directing; Carol Matheison, PhD., Voice

Guest Artists: Actors: Jane Lind, Michael Boatman, Michael Brainard, James Kiberd, George McDaniel, Steve Vinovich

Culver-Stockton College is a small liberal arts college. Our BA in Theatre provides a well-rounded education. Our BSE in Theatre Education offers preparation for professional work or graduate study. Our BFA's in Theatre and Arts Management are intended as pre-professional degrees and prepare students for graduate study. We offer a new BFA in Musical Theatre beginning in Fall 2007. We find and encourage each student's strength by early involvement as Freshmen both on stage and behind-the-scenes. Students have the opportunity to take advanced courses in their areas of interest.

Lindenwood University

Ted Gregory, Dir. of Theatre
Dept. of Performing Arts
Lindenwood University
209 S. Kingshighway

14,000 Total Enr.; compet.
Semester System
125 Majors
T: $12,400/$6,200 R&B

St. Charles, MO 63301
tgregory@lindenwood.edu
ADMISSIONS: Address above.
www.lindenwood.edu

DEPT: (636) 949-4966
FAX: (636) 949-4910
(636) 949-4949

DEGREES OFFERED

BA in Arts Mgmt, Performing Arts, Theatre, Speech/Theatre Teacher Cert; BFA in Acting, Directing, Design/Tech, Theatre, Performing Arts; MA,MFA in Theatre. Declare major in first or second year; 2007 granted 10 UG and 8 Grad degrees.

ADMISSION & FINANCIAL INFORMATION

ACT 20, 2.5 HS GPA; 75% of applicants accepted by institution, Special requirements for BFA only: UG aud/int and portfolio for designers. Grad aud/int/portfolio/writing sample. 7 out of 10 admitted to UG, 5 out of 10 admitted to Grad MA, 3 out of 10 to MFA. Scholarships and talent grants are available. Criteria for these awards vary. Contact Department Chair for specific details.

FACULTY AND CLASSES OFFERED

7 Full-Time, 6 Part-Time, 3 PhD/DMA, 8 MA/MFA, 2 Prof /o advanced degree, 2 Staff

A. (2.25 FT) Intro to Th-1/Y; Dramatic Lit-2/Y; Theatre Hist-1/Y; Shakes-1/X; Playwriting-OX

B. (2 1/2 FT, 5 PT) Acting/Scene Study-8/Y; Voice/Speech-1/Y; Movement-1/Y; Singing-6/X; Musical Theatre-2/Y; Directing-4/Y; Stage Combat-1/O; Dance-8/Y

C. (2 FT) Prins of Des-2/Y; Set Des-2/Y; Cost Des-2/Y; Ltg Des-2/Y; Tech Prod-1/Y; Cost Constr-3/Y; Make-up-2/Y; Stg Mgmt-2/Y

D. (1/4 FT, 1 PT) Arts Mgmt-1/Y; Marketing/Promotion-1/X; Development/Grant Writing-1/X; Contracts/Copyright-1/X; Budgeting/Accounting Procedure-4/X

FACILITIES AND PRODUCTIONS

MAINSTAGE: 300 seats, computerized lighting
6 prods: 4 Fac dir; 1 GA dir; 1 Grad dir
SECOND STAGE: 75 seats, computerized lighting
12 prods: 2 Grad dir; 10 UG dir.
THIRD STAGE: 700 seats, computerized lighting
Workshops/Readings: 2 Fac dir

2 student-written plays in the past two years.

New facility in 2008 includes scene shop, costume shop, video studio, movement/dance studio, rehearsal studio

Connection with Hot City Theatre (Equity), Utah Shakespeare, Opera Theatre St.Louis, Shakespeare Festival of St. Louis. Connection offers internships and employment opportunities as professional actors, with opportunity to earn Equity Membership Candidacy (EMC), as well as paid technical positions.

DESCRIPTION

Noted Faculty: Ted Gregory, Acting, Directing, Arts Mgmt; Larry Quiggins, Playwriting, Children's Theatre, Puppetry, Improv; Janet Strzetec, Musical Theatre Direction, Ballet, Choreography; Donnell Walsh, Technical Design; Marsha Parker, Directing, Period Styles, Dramatic Lit; Cynda Galikin, Costume Design

Guest Artists: Gerome (Gerry) Vogel, Stage Movement and Voice; Peter Bezemes, Casting Director; Bill Grivna, Acting for the Camera; Susan Miller,

Playwriting; Jeremy Sher, Suzuki Movement; Judith Newmark, Playwriting; Edward Caulfield, Theatre Mgmt; Carrie Houk, Acting for Film; Marcus Bugler, Dance.

Lindenwood University - with a 180 year history in Arts training - prides itself on preparing students to enter into professional theatre. Our Alumni work in some of the most prestigious theatres in the world. Guided by a professional faculty, students learn in an environment of development through professional practice which is essential to the educational/training process. Students not only participate in an active theatre season that boasts an average of 20 productions a year, but also are eligible to serve in professional internships. The new 133,000 square foot Performing Arts Center, slated for completion in fall 2008, will provide a venue for professional and students productions unparalleled in the Midwestern region.

Missouri Southern State College

Dr. Jay E. Fields
Department of Theatre
MO. Southern State College
Joplin, MO 64801
DEPT: (417) 625-9393
FAX: (417) 625-3136
ADM: (417) 782-6772
www.mssu.edu

6,000 Total Enr.; competitive
Semester Systems
60 Majors; ATHE
T: $4,240; O-ST T: $8,290
R&B: $4,720
SMALL PROGRAM
FAX: (417) 659-4429
admissions@mssu.edu

DEGREES OFFERED

BA in Theatre-acting, directing, design; BSE-education, with teaching fields in theatre and speech (8 total)

ADMISSION & FINANCIAL INFORMATION

ACT of at least 18, upper half of graduating class. 75% of applicants accepted to institution; 15 out of 25 apps. accepted to program. Academic Patron schols awarded; Full Theatre schols (tuition, R&B); Student Ass't. awarded for work in dept.; audition/interview req'd for theatre scholarships. Aud./interview required if financial aid is desired.

FACULTY AND CLASSES OFFERED

4 FT, 3 PT: 2 PhD, 2 MFA/MA, 2 Staff

A. (2 PT) Intro to Theatre-16/Y; Deamatic Crit.-1/X; Dramatic Lit-1/X; Theatre History-2/O; Shakes-1/O; Playwriting-1/O

B. (2 FT, 1 PT) Acting/Scene Study-3/O; Voice/Speech-1/O; Movement- 1/O; Directing-2/O; Mus. Th.-1/O; Stage Combat-1/O

C. (2 FT) Prins of Des-2/O; Set Design-1/O; Cost Des-1/O; Ltg Des-1/O; Tech Prod'n-1/O Cost Constr-1/O; Cost Hist-1/O; Make-up-1/O; Stg Mgmt- 1/O, Sound Design-1/0

FACILITIES & PRODUCTIONS

MAINSTAGE: 2,000 seats, fly space, computerized & electronic lighting.. 4 prods: 3 Fac dir, 2 Fac des, 1 Guest des, 1 UG dir/des; budget $1,000-3,000

SECOND STAGE: 200 seat, computerized lighting. 2 prods: 1 Fac dir/des, 1 UG dir/des

Workshops/Readings: 1 Fac dir, 1 UG dir/des; budget $500-800

Mainstage was built in 1980, new Second Stage built in 1999; includes scene shop, costume shop, video studio, rehearsal studio, classrooms.

DESCRIPTION

Noted Faculty: Dr. Jay E. Fields, Dr. Alex Pinkston.

Guest Artists: Dr. David Weiss from University of Virginia.

Students at Missouri Southern State College pursue a variety of occupations upon completion of their theatre degree. Probably one third become high school teachers (BSE in Education with Teaching Fields in speech and Theater), some go on to grad school (looking for a job in professional theater). Probably a little more than half find jobs in areas other than theatre but jobs for which the theatre has trained them well: sales, public relations, etc. The department is strong in children's theatre, presenting two children's productions per year and busing in 12,000-15,000 children each season.

Missouri Valley College

Diana Malan, Chair
Department of Theatre
Missouri Valley College
500 E. College St.
Marshall, MO 65340
DEPT: (660) 831-4215
maland@moval.edu
www.moval.edu
ADMISSIONS: Above Address

1,425 Total Enr.; not competitive
Semester Systems
25 Majors
T: $$15,450/$5,850 r&b
SMALL PROGRAM
FAX: (660) 831-4039

admissions@moval.ed
(660) 831-4114

DEGREES OFFERED

BA/BFA in Theatre, with concentrations in Musical Theatre(BFA), Performance (BFA), Technical (BFA), General Theatre (BA), Speech & Theatre Ed (BS). Declare major in sophomore year.

ADMISSION & FINANCIAL INFORMATION

Composite ACT score of 18; 20 cumulative GPA, top half class rank. 76% of applicants accepted to institution. Fine and performing arts scholarship are available: must apply and audition. Auditions for actors, auditions and portfolios for designers required for theatre program, 8 out of 10 apps. accepted to program. Schols based on individual basis on talent and need, selected through auditions and applics.

FACULTY AND CLASSES OFFERED

1 PhD, 4 MFA/MA

A. (1/4 FT) Intro to Theatre-1/Y; Dramatic Lit-1/X; Theatre History-2/O; Shakes-1/X; Dramatic Crit-1/X; Playwriting-1/Y

B. (2 1/2 FT) Acting/Scene Study-4/Y; Voice/Speech-1/Y; Movement-1/Y; Singing (Choir, Applied Voice)-6/Y; Directing-2/O; Mus. Th.-2/Y; Mime, Mask, etc.-1/X; Dance-5/Y; Stage Combat-1/O; Film-1/X

C. (3/4 FT) Prins of Des-1/Y; Set Design-1/O; Cost Des-1/Y; Ltg Des-2/O; Costume Construction-1/O; Stage Management-1/O; Make-up-1/Y

D. (1/8 FT) Box Office Procedure-1/O; Marketing/Promo-2/X; Budget/Acct'ng-2/X;

FACILITIES & PRODUCTIONS

MAINSTAGE: 270 seats, computerized/electronic lighting. 4 Fac dir/ 1 Fac des prods; budget $1,500-2,500

SECOND STAGE: 100 seats

Facility built in 1977; renovated in 2001; includes scene shop, costume shop, prop shop, video studio, mvmt/dance studio, rehearsal studio, TV studio, radio station.

A non-departmental, student-run org. presents productions each year in which dept. majors participate.

A festival of original student written plays will be held in April '06.

Connection with Arrow Rock Lyceum Theatre (summer only). Students have the opportunity to serve internships for the professional theatre, and are hired for a variety of positions.

DESCRIPTION

Noted Faculty: Diana Malan, Musical Theatre/Music; Geoffrey Howard, Acting, Directing, Design; Tiffany Howard, Acting, Directing, Costuming; Holly Lampe, Dance, Choreography; Judy Ransom, Music; Susan Dittmer, Voice (speech)

Guest Artists: Ron Yuval, Workshops and Performance, Musicantica, Workshops and Performance.

Missouri Valley College productions allow students to integrate theatre theory and practice. Casting for all productions is based upon ability; therefore, any student is eligible to audition for any production. First year students typically perform in mainstage production. Mabee Theatre is an extended apron facility which provides for proscenium, thrust, and arena configurations. Other production and storage facilities are located in Mabee and Morrison Hall. The department currently offers specializations in Musical Theatre, Performance, Speech Communication and Design/Technical. A major in Speech and Theatre Education is also offered. Multiple levels of instruction in ballet, modern, tap and jazz and choreography are available, leading to a minor in dance. The Music Department also has several choral groups in which theatre students with musical abilities figure prominently. Show Choir does two major concerts in the Spring of each year. Two dance showcases are also included in the season.

Northwest Missouri State University

Dr. David Oehler, Chair	6,800 Total Enr.; compet.
Dept. of Comm, Theatre & Languages	Trimester System
Northwest Missouri State Univ.	50 Majors; ATHE, USITT,KC-ACTF
800 University Dr.	T: $5,500/$6,100 R&B
Maryville, MO 64468	O-ST T: $9,400/$6,100 R&B
commtha@nwmissouri.edu	SMALL PROGRAM
www.nwmissouri.edu/dept/ctl	
DEPT: (660) 562-1279	FAX: (660) 562-1411
ADMISSIONS: Above address.	(660) 562-1562
admissions@nwmissouri.edu	FAX: (660) 562-1121
www.nwmissouri.edu/admissions	

DEGREES OFFERED

BA in Theatre (general) (5); BS in Tech/Design (15), Performance (15); BSEd in Education (15). Declare major in first year; 2007 granted 12 degrees.

ADMISSION & FINANCIAL INFORMATION

GPA=2.0, ACT=21; No special requirement for admittance at Freshman level. Admittance to major is made at sophomore level through written and oral exam. Theatre program requires aud/interview/portfolio for scholarships. Scholarships are available in performance and design/tech areas and are available for BA, BS and BSEd majors. Website provides details.

FACULTY AND CLASSES OFFERED

6 FT: 2 PhD, 4 MFA, 2 grad. assist.

A. (1 FT) Intro to Theatre-1/Y; Dramatic Lit-1/X; Theatre History-3/Y; Shakes-1/X

B. (2 FT) Acting/Scene Study-4/Y; Voice/Speech-1/O; Directing-1/Y; Movement-1/O; Mime, etc-1/O; Musical Theatre-1/X; Dance-6/X; Singing-4/X; Creative Dramatics-1/O

C. (2 FT) Set Des-1/O; Cost Des-1/O; Ltg Des-1/O; Tech Prod-2/Y; Make-up-1/Y; Costume Construct-1/Y

D. (1 FT) Marketing-Promo-1/X;Budgeting/Acctg Procedure-1/X

FACILITIES AND PRODUCTIONS

MAINSTAGE: 1,000 seats, fly space, computerized lighting

SECOND STAGE: 600 seats, fly space, computerized lighting

THIRD STAGE: 75 seats, computerized lighting

12 shows per year, 4 of which are faculty directed, 8 student directed, majors and non-majors participate.

Facility was built in 1984; includes scene, costume, props shops, sound, rehearsal, design studios, 2 classrooms, 1 Movement, welding, CAD.

DESCRIPTION

Majors within the Department of Communications, Theatre and Languages provide students with the theory and practice necessary to enable them to pursue careers in education, business and industry, and communication and theatre professions, or to continue on to graduate school. All of the majors within the department provide both a theoretical understanding of their field as well as the opportunity for hands-on experience in order to establish competency in the discipline. Departmental programs support the University's other key quality indicators by developing the student's competencies in : 1) communication, 2) problem solving, 3) critical/creative thinking, 4) self-directed learning, 5) personal development, 6) team work/team leading, 7) multiculturalism. Student organizations within the department provide students with additional opportunities to learn by doing, to learn from each other, and to network with professionals in their field.

Southeast Missouri State University

Dr. Kenn Stilson, Chair	10,000 Total Enr.; compet.
Dept. of Theatre & Dance	Semester System
One University Plaza MS 2800	75 Majors, ATHE, KC/ACTF, ACDF
Southeast Missouri State Univ	T: $4,215/$5,500 R&B
Cape Girardeau, MO 63701	O-ST T: $7,290./$5,500.R&B
DEPT: (573) 986-6818	SMALL PROGRAM
kstilson@semo.edu	
www.semo.edu/theatreanddance	dept fax: (573)986-6175
ADMISSIONS: (573) 651-2590	FAX: (573) 651-5936
www.semo.edu	

DEGREES OFFERED

BA in Theatre (25); BS in Speech & Theatre Education (15); BFA in Acting/Directing (30); Design/Technology (12); Dance (20). Declare major in first year; 2007 granted 15 UG degrees.

ADMISSION & FINANCIAL INFORMATION

GPA: 2.0 , ACT of 18+; have met core curriculum of classes; 90% of applicants admitted to inst; Th program admits 4 out of 5 applicants. Numerous individual scholarships and assistships, contact Chair for application and to set up interview a/o audition-Mar 15th deadline.

FACULTY AND CLASSES OFFERED

9 FT, 4 PhD, 5 MFA/MA; 4 Staff

A. (1 FT) Intro to Theatre-1/Y; Theatre History-2/Y; Shakes-2/X; Dramatic Lit-1/Y

B. (5 FT) Acting-6/Y; Movement-1/Y; Directing-2/Y; Voice/Speech-1/Y; Singing-4/Y; Dance-12/Y; Musical Th.-1/Y; Stage Combat-2/Y

C. (3 FT) Tech. Production-2/Y; Lighting Design-2/Y; Cost Construction-1/Y; Make-up-1/Y; Principles of Design-1/Y; Costume Design-2/Y; Set Design-2/Y; Stage Mgmt-1/Y

FACILITIES AND PRODUCTIONS

MAINSTAGE: 950 seats, fly space, comp/electronic lighting
6 prods, 4 Fac dir, 12 Fac des, budget 10,000-25,000

SECOND STAGE: 250 seats, comp./electronic lighting
4 prods: 2 Fac dir,2 Fac des, 2 UG dir, 4 UG des; budget $500-1,000.

1 Fac workshops/readings; budget $100-250

State-of-the-Art facility opens in July 2007 includes scene shop, costume shop, design studio, CAD, 2 movement/dance, 3 rehearsal, 6 classroom.

1-2 prods by student run org in school year. Dept majors participate. 1student written play has been done by dept in last two years.

DESCRIPTION

Noted Faculty: Robert W. Dillon, Jr., Acting/Directing/Theatre History; Dennis C. Seyer, Scenic Design/Directing; Phil Nacy, Lighting, Sound Design; Kenn Stilson, Acting/Directing/Literature; Marc Strauss, Dance/Choreography; Hilary Peterson, Dance/Choreography; Lees Hummel, Musical Theatre/Choreography; Judith Farris, Musical Theatre/Voice; Rhonda Weller-Stilson, Scenic Design/Costume Design.

Guest Artists: Nana Shineflug, Chicago Moving Company; Miami City Ballet; Don Garner, Actor/Playwright; Dallas Children's Theatre; Paul Taylor Dance; Nigerian Talking Drum Ensemble.

The Department of Theatre and Dance offers students an intensive training program in the development of an informed appreciation of the performing arts within the context of a liberal arts education designed to prepare students for advanced educational programs, internships, and the professional performing arts market. The Department offers two degrees for students who are interested in pursuing a profession in theatre and dance. The BFA (Design/Tech; Acting/Directing; Musical Theatre or Dance) is an intensive specialist degree that consists of a thorough study of the aesthetic, cultural, and historical contexts of the theatre and dance disciplines. Students must audition/interview for admittance into this program and make sustained progress-both academically and artistically-to maintain candidacy. The BA (Theatre) and BS (Theatre & Speech Education) are equally important but more general degrees that are well suited for education majors or students who plan to choose a minor or double-major.

Missouri State University

Mark Biggs, Dept Head
Dept. of Theatre & Dance
901 S. National Ave
Southwest Missouri State U.
Springfield, MO 65804-0095
(417) 836-4400
www.missouristate.edu
ADM: (417) 836-5517

16,234 Total Enr.; not compet.
Semester System
245 Majors
T: $179-206 per cred/R&B:$5,416
O-ST T: $349 per credit hour
R&B:5,416
FAX: (417) 836-4234
smsuinfo@smsu.edu

DEGREES OFFERED

BA in Liberal Arts (15); BFA in Performance (95), Design/Tech (35), Musical Theatre (60); BSE in Speech/Theatre Education (40).. Declare major in freshman year.

ADMISSION & FINANCIAL INFORMATION

Selection index is 96 which is the sum of class rank percentile and ACT or SAT percentile. Aud req., portfolio for designers.
24 Scholarships avail. by audition.

FACULTY AND CLASSES OFFERED

18 Full-Time: 2 PhD, 16 MFA/MA; 8 Staff

A. (2 FT) Intro to Theatre-1/Y; Theatre History-4/Y; Shakes-2/X; Dramatic Lit-3/X; Dramatic Criticism-1/X; Playwriting-2/X

B. (6 FT) Acting-6/Y; Movement-2/Y; Dance-15/Y; Directing-2/Y; Musical Theatre-6/X; Stage Combat-1/Y; Voice/Speech-2/Y

C. (5 FT) Prins of Design-1/Y; Set Design-1/Y; Cost Des-1/Y; Lighting Design-1/Y; Cost Constr.-1/Y; Make-up-1/Y; Stage Mgmt-1/Y

FACILITIES AND PRODUCTIONS

MAINSTAGE: 475 seats, fly space, computerized lighting. 6 prods:
6 Fac dir, 4 Fac des, 2 UG des; budget $2,500-8,000

SECOND STAGE: 400 seats, electronic lighting
4 prods: 2 Grad dir, 2 UG dir, 4 UG des; budget $500-2,000

THIRD STAGE: 100 seats, black box, computerized lighting

Facility was built in 1968, renovated in 1995; includes scene, costume shops, sound studio, rehearsal, dance studios.

DESCRIPTION

Noted Faculty: Jodi Kanter, Performance Studies; George Cron, Acting Combat; Sharon Ellis, Children's Theatre; Michael Mauldin, Classical Acting Style; James Woodland, Acting/Musical Theatre; Robert Little, Scenic Design.

Guest Artists: Kathleen Turner, Actor; Jack Laufer, Actor; Kip Niven, Actor, Musical Theatre; Dan Ettinger, Scenic Designer; Jeff Wirth, Improvisation.

Programs in the department are intended to give students a foundation for professional work as performers, designers, choreographers and directors to move into regional theatres or pursue graduate studies. Former students are working in many capacities in the industry throughout the nation. Graduates who have completed the teaching certification program are working in secondary schools throughout the states. The highly noted Summer Tent Theatre is a time for students to immerse themselves in creating and performing in a semi-professional company.

Stephens College

Beth Leonard, Dean
School of Performing Arts
Stephens College
Columbia, MO 65215
DEPT: (573) 876-7194
bleonard@stephens.edu

700 Total Enr.; competitive
Semester System
102 Majors
T: $21,730/$8,240 r & b
MAIN: (800) 876-7207
www.stephens.edu/apply

DEGREES OFFERED

BFA in Theatre Arts (98); Theatre Mgmt (1); Theatrical Costume Design (3); Dance (related major in Sch of Perf Arts). Declare major in 1st year; 2007 granted 29 degrees.

ADMISSION & FINANCIAL INFORMATION

Minimum 2.7 GPA, 21 ACT (1500 New SAT). Special requirements for admission to theatre program are only for male apprenticeship program & technical theatre. Accept all applicants to theatre program. Awards offered to students interested in BFA in TA or TM or a BA in TA. For consideration, students must submit a video of two auds selections & two songs (if they sing). Awards in theatrical design also available. Must submit a resume & complete an interview.

FACULTY AND CLASSES OFFERED

9 Full-Time: plus guest artists

A. (1 1/2 FT) Theatre History-2/Y; Shakes-1/Y; Dramatic Lit courses - 3-5/XY
B. (8 FT) Acting/Scene Study-6/Y; Voice/Speech-2/Y; Movement-1-2/Y; Private Voice; Musical Theatre-2/Y; Directing-2/Y; Senior capstone course for actors, on working in the theatre
C. (4 1/2 FT, 1/2 PT) Set Des-2/Y; Cost Des-2/Y; Ltg Des-2/Y; Tech Prod'n-2-3/Y; Cost Constr- 2/Y; Cost Hist-1/XY; Make-up-2/Y; Stg Mgmt-2/Y; Rendering-2/Y; Sc Painting-1/Y; Des Practicums.

FACILITIES & PRODUCTIONS

MAINSTAGE: 314 seats, fly space, computerized lighting. 6 prods: 3-4 Fac dir/des, 2-3 Guest dir/UG des; budget $3000-6000

SECOND STAGE: Black Box. 4-5 prods: 4-5 UG dir/des, includes 8 1-Acts directed by advanced directing students; budget $300-500

Facility includes scene shop, costume shop, prop shop, movement/dance, rehearsal studio, classrooms.

A non-departmental, student-run organization presents 4 productions per year in which majors participate.

Connected with Okoboji Summer Theatre. Our students curriculum is for 3 years and 2 summers. 1st summer is an intensive workshop and classroom program on campus. The 2nd summer is spent at Okoboji Summer Theatre. Students work w/ professionals to produce 9 plays in 10 weeks, receive credit in acting, tech prod, theatre promotion and mgmt. We are a women's college. Male roles are played by hired company of actors and faculty. Professional designers are members of the company.

DESCRIPTION

Guest Artists: Lee Blessing, Playwright; Carol Estey, NY Director; Jennifer Martin, Movement Coach, Missouri Repertory Theatre; Annie Potts, Film Star; Bethany Rooney, TV Director; R.J. Visciglia Jr., Hollywood Director/Producer

The theatre arts program offers intensive training in acting, scenic, costume and lighting design, technical theatre, directing, and stage management. The faculty includes professional actor-teachers, designers, and management staff. Theatre arts operates two production facilities on campus, presenting ten productions each year. Two summer programs afford additional theatre experience and college credits, the Stephens Summer Theatre Institute (on campus) and the Okoboji Summer Stock Theatre at Spirit Lake, Iowa. (see description under "Facilities & Productions")

University of Missouri - Columbia

Clyde Ruffin, Chair
Dept. of Theatre
129 Fine Arts Center
U. of Missouri-Columbia
Columbia, MO 65211
DEPT: (573) 882-2021
ADMISSIONS: 230 Jesse Hall
(573) 882-7786

26,000 Total Enr.; compet
Semester System
80 Majors; ATHE
T: $4956; O-ST T: $13,500
R&B: $5374
http://www.theatre.missouri.edu

www.missouri.edu

DEGREES OFFERED

BA in Performance (55), Design/Tech (10), Writing For Performance (15) MA/PhD in History, Theory, Dramatic Lit (15). Declare major in Soph. year; 2006 granted 15 UG, 4 Grad degrees.

ADMISSION & FINANCIAL INFORMATION

ACT score; class rank and HS core course work; all accepted to UG theatre prog.; Grad program admits 3 out of 15 apps; 27 scholarships av. $1,000 per year awarded to Soph., Jr. & Sr.'s.

FACULTY AND CLASSES OFFERED

10 Full-Time, 1 Part-time: 5 PhD, 5 MFA; 7 Staff

A. (2 FT) Intro to Theatre-1/Y; Dramatic Lit-1/Y; Th. History-1/Y; Dramatic Criticism-1/Y; Playwriting-4/Y
B. (3 FT) Acting/Scene Study-3/Y; Voice/Speech-2/Y; Movement-1/Y; Musical Th-1/Y; Directing-2/Y; Movement-1/Y
C. (3 FT,1 PT) Prins of Design-1/Y; Set Design-1/Y; Cost Des-1/Y; Lighting Des-1/Y; Tech Prod'n-1/Y; Cost. Construction-1/Y; Make-up-1/Y; Stage Mgmt-1/Y

FACILITIES & PRODUCTIONS

MAINSTAGE: 276 seats, Proscenium, fully equipped. 4 prods: 4 Fac dir/des, 2 Grad des; 10 UG des budget $3,000-6,000

SECOND STAGE: 100 seats, black box. 4 prods: 2 Fac dir, 2 Fac des, 1 Grad dir, 2 Grad des; 1 UG dir; 12 UG des budget $500-2,000

Workshop/Readings-5 workshops, 1 Grad dir, 2 UG dir, 2 fac dir

Facility was built in 1960, renovated in 1996; includes scene shop, costume shop, welding shop, sound studio, CAD facility.

8 student-written plays produced in the last two years.

DESCRIPTION

Noted Faculty: Suzanne Burgoyne, Th. History, Directing; David Crespy, Playwriting; Jim Miller, Cost. Design, Mucical Th., Acting; Clyde Ruffin, African-American Drama, Acting, Voice; Pat Atkinson, Sc., lighting. Design, Th. Architecture; Kerri Packard, Cost. Design & Constr.; Dean Packard, Sound Design, Stage Mgmt., Scene Design; Cheryl Black, Acting, Th. History; Heather Carver, Playwriting, Performance Studies.

Guest Artist: Playwrights: Edward Albee, John Guare, Lanford Wilson, Lynn Nottage, Toni Press-Coffman,

Mac Wellman; Actor: Robert Loggia.

The Department of Theatre offers the BA degree, which allows students to make theatre the foundation of their liberal arts education. The undergraduate curriculum meets the needs of those who want a strong liberal arts education while specializing in performance, design/tech, or writing for performance. While the department remains committed to a broad-based, stimulating liberal arts education promoting skills in critical thinking and communication, its programs also prepare students who want a career in the professional theatre to enter that field or to pursue graduate studies leading to a professional theatre career. Our MA and PhD programs are designed to develop the artist/scholar's capacity for research, teaching and creative achievement. Students enter an exciting, demanding and highly selective program on the campus of a learning-centered research university ranked as one of the foremost institutions of its kind in the country.

University of Missouri - Kansas City

Tom Mardikes, Chair,	9,383 Total Enr.; compet.
UMKC Theatre	Semester System
Univ. of Missouri-Kansas City	41 Majors; NAST, U/RTA
4949 Cherry St.	T: $7,946 in-st/R&b $7,046
Kansas City, MO 64110	O-ST T: UG $18,602
www.umkc.edu/theatre	(816) 235-2702
theatre@umkc.edu	FAX: (816) 235-6562
ADM:: Admissions, 5100 Rockhill Rd., K.C., MO 64110	
(816) 235-1111	FAX: (816) 235-5544
www.umkc.ecu/admissions	

DEGREES OFFERED

BA in General Theatre (41); MA in Theater History, Lit and Playwriting (8); MFA in Acting (32), Design/Technology (50). Declare major in first-third year.

ADMISSION & FINANCIAL INFORMATION

19% of apps. accepted by institution. UG admits all applicants; Grad requires aud/int/portfolio; admits 31 out of 300 applicants. MFA and MA scholarships apply through dept. aid is awarded on the basis of audition and portfolio presentation.

FACULTY AND CLASSES OFFERED

12 FT, 6 PT: 3 PhD, 8 MFA/MA, 1 Prof. w/o adv. degree; 2 Staff

A. (2 FT) Intro to Theatre-8/Y; Theatre History-6/Y; Shakes-1/O; Dramatic Lit-4/Y; Dramatic Criticism-4/Y; Playwriting-2/Y

B. (5 FT) Acting-14/Y; Voice/Speech-8/Y; Movement-8/Y; Mime,etc.-8/Y; Singing-1/Y; Musical Th-1/O; Stage Combat-1/Y

C. (7 FT) Prins. of Design-6/Y; Set Design-4/Y; Cost. Design-8/Y; Ltg Des-6/Y; Sound Des; Tech Prod'n-3/Y; Cost. Constr-4/Y; Sound Des-1/Y; Cost. History-2/Y; Make-up-2/Y; Stage Mgmt-2/Y

FACILITIES AND PRODUCTIONS

MAINSTAGE: 700 seats, fly space, computerized lighting.. 3 prods: 1 Fac dir/des or guest dir/des; budget $12,500

SECOND STAGE: 170 seats, computerized lighting 3 Fac dir/des prods; or guest dir/des budget $9,900

THIRD STAGE: 200 Seats, computerized lighting, Community based, 3 fac dir/des or guest dir/des

2 Workshops/readings: Fac/grad dir/des; budget $9,100

Facility was built in 1979; includes scene, cost, prop, welding shops, sound studio, dance, rehearsal studios, design studio, classrooms.

Connection with Missouri Repertory Theatre (Equity): with opportunities to work in professional theaters side-by-side with nationally and internationally famous theater artists as part of training.

DESCRIPTION

Noted Faculty: Louis Colaianni, Voice Training; John Ezell/Gene Friedman, Scenic Design; Felicia Londre, Th. Hist; Jennifer Martin, Movement; Victor Tan, Lighting Design; Dale AJ Rose, Perf Training; Tom Mardikes, Sound; Lindsay Davis, Costume Design; Barry Kyle, Acting/Directing.

Guest Artists: Kristin Linklater, Santo Loquasto, Sarah Barker, Ralph Koltai, Fiona Shaw, Jeff Davis, Pat McCorkle, Ian McNeil, faculty from Dell Arte School of Physical Theatre in residence; Barry Kyle.

The Department of Theater offers a wide spectrum of theater training. At the undergraduate level, the theater major receives a solid liberal arts background in theater. The MA Degree prepares playwrights, dramaturgs and theatre historians. The main thrust of the MFA programs is the preparation of professional actors and designers for careers in regional theatres of the United States. The training is performance and production oriented. The special arrangement by which UMKC Theatre and the Missouri Repertory Theatre co-exist, interrelate, and support each other provides a set of ideal opportunities for those who are preparing for a life in the professional theater.

Washington University

Robert K. Henke, Chair	10,000 Total Enr.; h. compet.
Performing Arts Dept.	Semester System
Campus Box 1108, 1 Brookings Dr	49 Majors; U/RTA, ATHE
Washington University	T: $34,500/$11,632 R&B
St. Louis, MO 63130-4899	(314) 935-5858
www.padarts.wustl.edu	pad@artsci.wustl.edu
ADM: CB 1089, One Brookings Dr., St. Louis, MO 63130	
(314) 935-6000	www.admissions.wustl.edu
admissions@wustl.edu	

ADMISSION & FINANCIAL INFORMATION

Part 1 and 2 of Wash. U. application form, teacher & counselor recommendations, ACT or SAT scores. Univ. accepts 6% of applicants. Worseck Dance Schol. is available to dancers based on financial need, dance accomplishment, and commitment to the field of dance. Must submit video, recommendations, personal statement of previous dance experience and future expectations/objectives.

FACULTY AND CLASSES OFFERED

20 FT, 5 PT: 5 PhD, 17 MA/MFA, 3 Prof. w.out adv. degree; 5 Staff

A. (8 FT, 1 PT) Intro to Theatre-1/Y; Dramatic Lit-5/Y; Dramatic Crit-5/Y; Theatre History-7/Y; Shakes-2/Y; Black Th. Wkshp-2/Y; Playwriting-5/Y

B. (8 FT, 2 PT) Acting/Scene Study-6/Y; Voice/Speech-4/Y; Movement-2/Y; Mime. etc.-3/Y; Musical Th.-1/Y; Singing-XY; Directing-4/Y; Dance-40/Y; Film & Media-18/Y

C. (4 FT, 1 PT) Prins of Design-4/Y; Set Design-4/Y; Cost Des/Constr-2/Y; Ltg Des-2/Y; Tech Prod-3/Y; Cost. History-2/Y; Make-up-1/Y;

Stg Mgmt-1/Y

D. (1 PT) Arts Mgmt-1/O; Marketing/Promo-XY; Budget/Accounting-XY

FACILITIES AND PRODUCTIONS

MAINSTAGE: 656 seats, fly space, computerized & electronic lighting
   3 prods: 3 Fac dir/des, 3 Guest des; budget $15,000-20,000

SECOND STAGE: 120 seats, computerized & electronic lighting
   3 prods.: 3 Fac dir, 2 Fac des, 2 UG des, budget $3,000-5,000

Facility was built in 1973; includes scene, cost., CAD facil, video & editing studio, 3 dance studios, rehearsal studio, design studio, classrooms.

Majors generally participate in non-departmental, student-run productions as well.

DESCRIPTION

Noted Faculty: Henry I. Schvey, Theatre Studies; Robert K. Henke, Theatre Studies; Mary-Jean Cowell, Dance; William J. Paul, Film Studies; Carter W. Lewis, Playwright; Jeff Smith, Film Studies; Jeffrey Matthews, Acting; Anna Pileggi, Acting/Movement; Christine O'Neal, Ballet; Bonnie Kruger, Cost. Des.

Guest Artists: Ann Bogart, Director; Carlos Fittante, Dancer; Harold Ramis, Actor/Director; David Dorfman, Dancer; Jane Lapotaire, Actor; Elizabeth Franz, Actor; Michael Shamberg, Producer/Director; Zoe Caldwell, Actor; Isaburoh Hanayagi, Dancer; Patrick Suzeau, Dancer.

The Performing Arts Department at Washington University is made up of three divisions — drama, film and dance — and is firmly dedicated to the importance of the performing arts within the context of a liberal arts education. Departmental offerings combine a strong emphasis on performance in our excellent facilities with a highly disciplined approach to the study of the arts and their interrelationships. Washington U's Performing Arts Department prides itself on offering the talented undergraduate a creative blend of practical training and intellectual rigor that can be scarcely matched elsewhere. Our classes are taught by a combination of distinguished scholars and working professionals, which allows the undergraduate an opportunity to achieve the highest performance standards while attaining a first-rate background in the liberal arts.

Webster University

Dorothy Marshall Englis, Chair
Conservatory of Theatre Arts
Webster University
470 E. Lockwood Ave.
St. Louis, MO 63119
marshado@webster.edu
www.webster.edu/depts/finearts/theatre/
ADMISSIONS: Address above
(314) 968-6991

20,964 worldwide; h.compet.
Semester System
150 Majors; ATHE
T: $19,330/$8,220 r&b
(314) 968-6929
FAX: (314) 963-6102

www.webster.edu

DEGREES OFFERED

BA in Directing (6); BFA in Regional Theatre/Musical Theatre (75), Stage Mgmt. (23); Design (Lighting, Scenery, Costume, Makeup, Sound) (36); Technical Theatre (Technical Direction, Costume Construction, Scene Painting) (10). Declare major in 1st yr.; 2004 granted 20 UG degrees.

ADMISSION & FINANCIAL INFORMATION

Min. 2.5 GPA, upper 50% class range, ACT 21, SAT 1000. Univ. admits 65% of applicants. Aud/interview/portfolio req. for admission to theatre program. 20 out of 100 applicants admitted to theatre program. 1st yr. Schols are based on GPA & test scores, endowed scholarships awarded by faculty available 3rd & 4th yrs.

FACULTY AND CLASSES OFFERED

16 FT, 20 PT, 22 MA/MFA, 1 PhD, 13 Prof. w/o adv. deg.

A. (1 PT) Intro to Theatre-1/Y; Dramatic Lit-2/Y; Theatre History-2/Y; Shakes-1/Y

B. (7 FT, 5 PT) Acting-8/Y; Voice-10/Y; Mvmt-12/Y; Mus Th-4/Y; Singing-8/Y; Directing-4/Y; Stg Combat-2/Y; Dance-40/Y; Mask, etc. 2/Y; Voice-10/Y; Other-4/Y

C. (9 FT, 14 PT) Prins of Design-2/Y; Set Design-4/Y; Costume Des-4/Y; Ltg Des-4/Y; Tech Prod-18/Y; Cost Constr-6/Y; Make-up-4/Y; Stg Mgmt-8/Y; Other-4/Y

FACILITIES AND PRODUCTIONS

MAINSTAGE: 499 seats, fly space, computerized lighting. 2 prods: 1 Fac dir, 1 GA dir, 2 UG des; bdgt $12,000-14,000

SECOND STAGE: 125 seats, computerized lighting
   4 prods, 2 Fac dir, 1 GA dir, 1 UG dir, 2 UG des; budget $3,-6,000

Third Stage: 125 seats, computerized lighting

Facility was built in 1966, renovated in 2001; includes scene, costume, props, welding, sound, CAD facility, 3 movement/dance, 4 rehearsal studios, 1 design studio, 10 classrooms.

Connection with Repertory Theatre of St. Louis (Equity-operates during school year). Students participate as actors, crew members, dramaturgees, director assistants, production assistants, design assistants, stage management personnel, technical support overhire. Faculty can be hired as actors, designers, vocal/movement/voice coaches. Rep staff teach conservatory classes a/o mentor students.

Connection with OperaTheatre of Saint Louis (operates summer only). Students can be hired as technical support staff. Opera staff teach conservatory classes a/o mentor students.

DESCRIPTION

Noted Faculty: Peter Sargent, Lighting and Stage Mgmt; Bruce Longworth, Acting, Voice & Speech, Shakespeare; Byron Grant, Musical Theatre.

Guest Artists: Paul Barnes, Andrea Urice, David Caldwell, Directors; Marie-Ann Chiment, Designer.

Students in the Department of Theatre and Dance have been selected for their talent and ability to be trained for a career in Theatre. It is expected that students and faculty together have made a willing commitment to expand themselves to the fullest in the hard work and discipline that is necessary to excel. The faculty has been selected to bring the finest of training to the Conservatory. It is our mission to train our future colleagues to become visionaries, creators and leaders of the next generation of American professional theatre. Our students will: possess skills within their area of expertise; demonstrate an effective working process; be disciplined theatre practitioners; understand the value of the ensemble; be able to realize the potential of their imagination; experience theatre production in professional and learning environments; be prepared to get work.

William Woods University

Joe Potter, Art Dir

Dept. of Fine & Performing Arts
William Woods University
Fulton, MO 65251
DEPT: (573) 592-4281
ADM: One University Ave.
www.williamwoods.edu
admissions@williamwoods.edu

1,162 Total Enr.; competitive
Semester System
35 Majors
T: $16,140/r&b:$6,400
SMALL PROGRAM
FAX: (573) 592-4574
(573) 592-4221
FAX: (573) 592-4574

DEGREES OFFERED

BA in Theatre (18), Radio/TV (10); BFA in Radio/TV (5)
Declare major in second year.

ADMISSION & FINANCIAL INFORMATION

Admission based on a combination of ACT/SAT scores, class rank, references and GPA; Aud/int req'd for theatre prog, accept 5 out of 8. Auds for actors, resume, two recs. Awarding of schols is based on grades, talent potential and need. Interviews are held for technicians at which time a portfolio review and interview are scheduled. Technicians are expected to submit a resume and at least two letters of rec.

FACULTY AND CLASSES OFFERED

2 Full-Time; 2 MFA/MA, 2 Prof. w/out adv. degree; 2 Staff.

A. (1/2 FT) Intro to Theatre Arts-1/Y; Theatre History-2/O; Dramatic Lit-1/O; Shakespeare-X

B. (1/2 FT) Acting/Scene Study-2/Y; Voice/Speech-1/Y; Movement-2/Y; Singing-2/Y; Directing-1/O; Musical Th.-1/O; Stage Combat-1/O

C. (1/2 FT) Prins of Des-1/O; Set Design-2/Y; Cost Des-1/O; Ltg Des-2/Y; Tech Prod'n-5/Y; Cost Constr-2/Y; Make-up-1/O; Stg Mgmt-1/O

D. (1/2 FT) Arts Management-1/O

FACILITIES AND PRODUCTIONS

MAINSTAGE: 1,250 seats, fly space, computerized lighting.
    4 prods: Fac dir/des, Guest dir/des; budget $3,000-4,000

SECOND STAGE: 282 seats, computerized lighting.
    4 prods: Fac & Guest dir/des; bdgt $3,000-4,000

3 UG dir/des Workshops/Readings; budget $0-500

A non-departmental, student-run, producing org. presents 3-4 productions per year in which dept. majors participate.

DESCRIPTION

Noted Faculty: Joe Potter, Christian West, Designers.

Guest Artists: Todd Potter, Designer; Dick Godwin, Scenic Artist/Des; Ted Shackelford, Actor; Harlan Brownlee, Choreog.

The primary goal is to educate students in theatre and radio/television. The university provides balanced academic and laboratory training, with an emphasis on developing Performers/Technicians through the small faculty/student ratio. Students are afforded the opportunity to study 14-16 weeks with working professionals in either New York City or Los Angeles. Graduates from our program have been accepted in graduate schools across the US as well as entering the profession in various positions.

MONTANA

Montana State University

Walter Metz, PhD., Chair
Media & Theatre Arts POB 173350
Montana State University
Bozeman, MT 59717-3350
DEPT: (406) 994-2484
FAX: (406) 994-6214
ADMISSIONS: 212 MONTANA Hall

11,000 Total Enr.; compet.
Semester System
310 Majors; ATHE
T: $5,749; $6,780 r&b
O-ST T: $16,274; $6,780 r&b
mta@montana.edu
(406) 994-4371

DEGREES OFFERED

BA in Media & Theatre Arts Motion Picture/Video/Theatre (310). Declare major freshman year.

ADMISSION & FINANCIAL INFORMATION

Must either be Montana resident or in top 50% of high school class; Motion Picture/Video/Theatre program admits 3 out of 4 apps. Advancement to 2nd yr. classes requires 2.75 GPA on departmental courses; 3.0 for 3rd yr. courses. Audition scholarships awarded end of January; also Presidential Scholarships and other competitive awards given at the same time.

FACULTY AND CLASSES OFFERED

12 FT, 1 PT; 4 PhD., 9 MFA/MA; 4 Staff

A. (1 PT) Intro to Th-1/Y; Shakes-1/O; Dramatic Lit.-1/O; Dramatic Crit-1/O; ThHistory-1/Y; Shakes-1/O; New Directions/Theatre-1/Y; Film History2/Y; Scriptwriting-1/Y; Playwriting-1/X.

B. (1 FT, 2 PT) Acting-2/Y; Voice/Speech-1/X; Movement-1/Y; Directing-2/Y; Mime, Mask, etc.-1/O; Film Production-1/Y; TV Studio Prod.-1/Y

C. (1 FT, 1 PT) Prins of Des-1/O; Ltg Des-1/Y; Tech Prod'n-1/O; Set Des-1/Y; Stage Mgmt-1/O; Film Prod. Mgmt-1/O; Topics in Design/Construct-1/Y

D. Film Prod. Management-1/O

FACILITIES & PRODUCTIONS

MAINSTAGE: 411 seats, fly space, computerized ligthing. 2 Fac dir/des, 1 Guest dir/des; 2 UG dir/des; $2,500-5,000

SECOND STAGE: 120 seats, computerized lighting.

2 UG dir/des prods., may be add'l events; budget $500-1000

Facility was built in 1940, renovated in 1954; includes scene shop, costume shop, sound studio, rehearsal studio, classrooms, complete facilities for motion picture/video/television prodction.

Connection with Montana Shakespeare in the Parks, a professional touring company which trvels to 50-some sites each summer, and is an outreach program of Montana State University. Students may do internships as actors/actresses, technical crew, and management.

DESCRIPTION

Noted Faculty: Dennis Aig, Film Direction; Stephanie Campbell, Acting; Joel Jahnke, Directing; Bill Neff, Film Directing; Walter Metz, Film and Theatre History/Theory/Criticism; David Scheerer, Film

Direction; Ronald Tobias, Scriptwriting; Tom Watson, Tech Theatre; David Koester, Sound; Cindy Stillwell, Camera.

Guest Artists: Bill Dance, Dora Lanier, Jeff Meyer, John Dahl, Shelley Fabres, Mike Farrel, Scott Seiffert, Robert McDonough.

Theatre at Montana State University is within an unusual program that provides students the opportunity for stage production in conjunction with an integrated curriculum in Motion Picture/Video/ Theatre Production. In the upper-division classes, students may elect a concentration in "Dramatic Stage Production". The program is designed to emphasize production opportunities in stage and screen. The unique facilities for production at Montana Stage University, and the fact that the faculty integrates strengths in theatre with Motion Picture/Video Production, provides a unique atmosphere to learn in an exciting arts community located in one of America's most beautiful locales.

The University of Montana

Mark Dean, Chair
Department of Drama/Dance
32 Campus Dr, MFA102
The University of Montana
Missoula, MT 59812-8136
(406) 243-4481
(406) 243-5726 (fax)

13,600 Total Enr.
competitive
Semester System
161 Majors; NAST, U/RTA
T&F: $4,978
O-ST T&F: $14,484

DEGREES OFFERED

BA in Drama (98), Dance (23); Drama Education (20); BFA in Acting (44), Design/Technology (22), Dance (15); MA in Theatre (2); MFA in Acting (4), Directing (2), Design/Technology (2). Declare major in 1st or 2nd year; 2006 granted 30 UG, 7 G degrees.

ADMISSION & FINANCIAL INFORMATION

2.5 GPA in-state or 22 ACT (920 SAT) or top 50% of class; out-of-state 2.5 GPA or 22 ACT, college prep. Accept 79% to inst; Audition/Portfolio (Grads only). Th program accepts all UG, 2 out of 3 Grad applics.

FACULTY AND CLASSES OFFERED

13 FT, 5 PT: 2 PhD, 11 MA/MFA, 6 Staff

A. (1 FT,2 PT) Th Appreciation-1/Y; Dr Lit-1/O; Th Hist-2/Y; Shakes-X; Playwriting-1/Y; Indep Study in Th Hist-2/O and Drama Lit-2/O

B. (5 FT, 3 PT) Acting-9/Y; Voice/Speech-4/Y; Movement-4/Y; Musical Theatre-1/Y; Directing-3/Y; Stage Combat-1/O

C. (4 FT) Principles of Des-1/Y; Set Design-4/Y; Cost Des-2/Y; Ltg Des-4/Y; Tech Prod-4/Y; Cost Constr-2/Y; Cost Hist-2/Y; Make-up-1/Y; Stg Mgmt-1/Y; Make-up-1/Y;

D. (4 FT, 2 PT) Dance

FACILITIES & PRODUCTIONS

MAINSTAGE: 499 seats, fly space, computerized & electronic lighting. 5 prods: Fac/Guest/Grad dir/des; budget $4,000-10,000

SECOND STAGE: 290 seats, fly space, computerized & electronic lighting. 6 prods: Fac/Guest/Grad dir/des; budget $1,000-6,000

THIRD STAGE: various # seats, computerized & electronic lighting

Facility was built in 1984; includes scene, costume, props shops, sound studio, 2 dance studio, 2 reh studios, design studio, classroom.

Connection with the Montana Repertory Theatre, which evolved from student company to a professional Equity company 26 years ago; 1 show tours extensively throughout the West, 1 show tours nationally. Students in the drama program are selected as acting and technical interns; faculty and guests direct and design.

DESCRIPTION

The University of Montana has a strong tradition of excellence in the liberal and professional arts. Its professional schools, including the School of Fine Arts and the Department of Drama/Dance, provide in-depth training in a context of developing and investigating human values. We are a small university with an emphasis on the individual and personal attention. Our mission is to provide quality professional training in theatre and dance for those students seeking to work and teach in the performing arts. We also strive to provide the highest quality educational and professional theatre and dance experiences and leadership for the community, state, and region.

NEBRASKA

Nebraska Wesleyan University

Jay Scott Chipman,
Director of Theatre
Nebraska Wesleyan University
5000 St. Paul
Lincoln, NE 68504-2794
DEPT: (402) 466-2395
jsc@nebrwesleyan.edu
ADM: 5000 Saint Paul Avenue
FAX: (402) 465-2179
admissions@nebrwesleyan.edu

11,864 Total Enr.; competitive
Semester System
25 Majors; ATHE
T: $20,252 includes R&B:$5,340
SMALL PROGRAM
FAX: (402) 465-2179

(402) 465-2218
www.nebrwesleyan.edu

DEGREES OFFERED

BA in Theatre Arts (10); BA in Communication and Theatre Arts (4); BFA in Theatre Arts (11). Students declare major fresh. or soph. year; 2001 granted 7 UG degrees.

ADMISSION & FINANCIAL INFORMATION

Required: ACT 19; top 50% of high school class; 75% accepted by inst. Theatre participation schol. by applic. aud/interview or portfolio review.

FACULTY AND CLASSES OFFERED

4 FT, 1 PT: 1 PhD/DFA, 4 MFA/MA

A. (1 FT) Intro to Th-1/Y; Dramatic Lit-2/Y; Th Hist- 2/Y; Shakes-1/X; Playwriting-1/O; Script Analysis-1/Y

B. (3 FT, 1 PT) Acting-4/Y; Voice/Speech-1/Y; Mvmt-1/Y; Singing-4/X; Directing-2/Y; Mus. Th-1/Y; Perf. of Lit-1/Y; Prof. Prep for Theatre-1/Y; Internship-1/Y

C. (2 FT) Prins of Des-1/YX; Set Design-1/Y; Cost Des-1/Y; Ltg Des-1/Y; Tech Prod'n-1/Y; Cost Constr-1/Y; Make-up Design-1/Y; Stg Mgmt-1/O; Advanced Make-up-1/Y; Practical Problems-7/Y

D. Arts Management-1/O; Mktn'g/Promo-1/X

FACILITIES & PRODUCTIONS

MAINSTAGE: 300 seats, fly space, computerized lighting
    6 prods: 5 Fac dir/des, 1 UG dir/des; budget $1,200-1,500

SECOND STAGE: 100 seats, black box, computerized lighting. 12 prods:

1 Fac dir/des, 11 UG dir/des prods.; budget $25-200

Facility built in 1982; includes scene, costume shops, props shop, rehearsal, costume library, properties library, 2 classrooms.

A non-departmental, student-run, producing org. presents 10-15 productions per year in which dept. majors participate.

3 student-written plays produced in the last two years. 1 student written musical produced in last two years.

DESCRIPTION

Noted Faculty: Jack Parhust, Acting & Directing.

The Nebraska Wesleyan University Theatre Arts program provides courses of study as well as produced activities to prepare majors for careers in theatre and to provide aesthetic education for students engaged in becoming educated in the liberal arts. Coursework in Theatre Arts includes study of theatre history, criticism, performance, directing and theatre design and technology, taught in lecture, studio and workshop formats. Each university season includes a carefully developed series of productions that represent diverse scope, style, and form. The BFA major provides the opportunity for specialized training in a selected area relating to theatre arts and is designed to prepare students for graduate study or a professional career in theatre. Self-designed emphasis areas may include: acting, directing, design, musical theatre, creative writing, arts management, and public relations. The BA major prepares students for graduate study in theatre and/or for professional study in preparing for law, ministry or teaching. It emphasizes cultural understanding, aesthetic sensitivity and creative skill.

University of Nebraska - Lincoln

Paul Steger, director
Todd Cuddy, Admission Coordinator
Johnny Carson School of
Theatre and Film
215 Temple, 12th & R Sts.
Box 880201
University of Nebraska
Lincoln, NE 68588-0201
DEPT: (402) 472-2072
www.unl.edu/TheatreArts
ADMISSIONS: University of Nebraska-Lincoln, Temple Building.
(800) 472-8800   theatrearts@unl.edu

22,268 Tot Enr.; UG not comp

Semester System; G compet.
113 Majors
NAST, U/RTA, ATHE
T: $6,292;
$6,308 R&B
O-ST T.: $16,312
FAX: (402) 472-9055

DEGREES OFFERED

BA in Performance (85), Production (3), BA in Th. Studies (0); BFA in Design/Tech (10); MFA in Acting (8), Design/Tech (7).
Declare major in jr. year; 2001 granted 10 UG, 8 Grad degrees.

ADMISSION & FINANCIAL INFORMATION

90 - 100% of UG apps. accepted to inst. Grad reqs. 4 units of English, 4 Math, 3 Social Studies, 3 Nat. Sci, 2 Foreign Lang., ranked 50th percentile or higher or ACT 20 or SAT of 950. UG theatre prog admits all applicants, (MFA) prog admits 6 of 10 applics; aud/int, portfolio for des/dir req'd. Freshman schols by aud; contact Shirley Mason. Upperclass scholarships from soph. yr. on; based on GPA and involvement, contact Julie Hagemeier.

FACULTY AND CLASSES OFFERED

16 FT, 3 PT: 5 PhD, 12 MFA, 2 Prof. w/out Adv. Degree; 4 Staff
A. (4 FT, 2 1/2 PT) Intro to Th-1/Y; Theatre History-2/Y; Shake-speare-

1/O; Dramatic Lit-1/Y; Dramatic Criticism-2/O; Playwriting-2/Y

B. (5 FT) Acting-5/Y; Voice/Speech-2/Y; Mvmt-2/Y; Singing-X; Musical Th-1/Y; Directing-2/Y; Stage Combat-1/O; Dance-X

C. (5 FT,1/2 PT) Prins of Des-X; Set Design-2/Y; Cost Des- 2/Y; Ltg Des-2/Y; Tech Prod-2/Y; Cost Constr-2/Y; Cost Hist-1/Y; Make-up-1/Y; Stage Mgmt.-1/Y; Rigging-1/O; Rendering-1/O; Architecture-1/O

D. (2 FT) Film & New Media-8/YO

FACILITIES AND PRODUCTIONS

MAINSTAGE: 323 seats, fly space, computerized lighting. 6 prods: 5 Fac dir, 4 Fac des, 15 Grad des, 5 UG des; budget $7,000-10,000

SECOND STAGE: 200 seats, computerized lighting 6 prods: 5 UG dir, 1 Grad dir, 6 UG des; budget $100-200

THIRD STAGE: 240 seats, black box, computerized lighting

Facility was built in 1907, last renovated in 1980; includes scene shop, costume shop, props shop, welding shop, sound studio, video studio, CAD facility, dance studio, 2 rehearsal studios, design studio, classroom, Lied Center for Performing Arts.

Majors generally participate in a non-departmental, student-run org. that presents 6 productions per year. 8 student-written plays produced in the last two years.

Connection with Nebraska Repertory Theatre (summer, Equity): Formed in 1968, NRT hires Equity actors, with the remainder of the cast local professionals and upper-level students. Faculty members and guest artists (SSDC & USAA) design and direct. Graduate students often design. Undergraduate and graduate students act as technicians and managers.

DESCRIPTION

Noted Faculty: Tice L. Miller, History/Criticism; Jeffery Elwell, Playwriting; William Grange, History/Criticism; Charles O'Connor, Scenic Design; William Kenyor, Lighting Design; Stan Brown, Voice; Harris Smith, Movement; Virginia Smith, Acting/Directing.

Guest Artists: Janis Martin, Costume Design; Rob Urbinati, Directing; David Wiles, Acting; David Ackroyd, Acting; Brant Pope, Directing; Lew Hunter, Film; Anthony Rapp, Acting/Musical Theatre; Joseph M. Gallo, Acting.

The Department of Theatre Arts at University of Nebraska-Lincoln is committed to the philosophy that prospective practitioners must be provided with thorough training and practical experience in order to develop fully their skills and talents for employment in professional, university/college, community, or high school settings. The department remains fully aware of its obligations to other important constituents: those wishing preparation for careers in related fields; those liberal arts students wishing to enhance their education through theatre experiences; and those members of the broader community who look to UNL for cultural enrichment.

University of Nevada - Las Vegas

See ad in back of book

Charles O'Connor, Chair
Dept of Theatre
University of Nevada, Las Vegas
4505 S. Maryland Parkway
Box 455036
Las Vegas, NV 89154-5036
theatre@ccmail.nevada.edu
ADMISSIONS: UNLV STUDENT ENROLLMENT & FINANCIAL SERVICES, BOX 451021, LAS VEGAS, NV 89154-1021 (702) 895-3443
undergraduate.recruitment@unlv.edu

21,853 Tot. Enr., compet.
181 UG, 49 G Majors; NAST, U/RTA, ATHE, USITT
T: $4,077; R&B: $8,857
O-ST T: $14,887
(702) 895-3666
FAX: (702) 895-0833

DEGREES OFFERED

BA in Senior Adult Theatre (20), theatre minor toward BA (19); BA/MFA in Design/Tech (34) Performance (100); MFA in Directing (2), Playwriting (8); MFA in Stage Mgmt (2); BA/MA in Theatre Studies (27). Students declare major in second year. 2004 granted 83 UG, 24 Grad degrees

ADMISSION & FINANCIAL INFORMATION

GPA 2.75 min., ACT & SAT req. for admission to instit; min. 2.75 GPA for acceptance to theatre program. 59 % of applics. accepted by inst.; 10 out of 10 UG, 17 out of 49 Grad admitted to program except every third year for Performance Conservatory Program which generally admits 10 out of 40. Specific Grad requirements available online. Transfer students must aud. for performance or D/T. Schols: Nevada Millennium. DeVos Drama (by audition), Birdman Family (need-based). Jim Brennan Design (D/T). John Hartzell Technology (D/T). Albert Kaye Trust. George Sidney. John Tarang (Acting for the Camera) & John Tarang (Stage Management).

FACULTY AND CLASSES OFFERED

15 FT, 17 PT: 2 PhD, 11 MFA/MA, 2 Prof. w/o adv deg; 4 Staff

A. (1 FT, 6 PT) Intro to Theatre-23/Y; Theatre Hist-14/Y; Shakes-4/Y; Playwriting-12/Y; Play Structure-4/Y; Research-4/Y; Gay Plays-8/Y; Women's Plays-2/Y; Senior Adult Theatre Course-6/Y; Dramaturgy-2/Y; Dramatic Lit-X; Dramatic Crit-X.

B. (5 FT, 12 PT) Acting/Scene Study-57/Y; Voice/Speech-12/Y; Movement-12/Y; Mime, etc-2/Y; Mus Th-6/Y; Directing-4/Y; Stage Combat-3/Y; Dance -2/Y; Improv-4/Y; Stand Up Comedy-4/Y; Singing-X; Film-X.

C. (5 FT, 4 PT) Cost Des-6/Y; Tech Prod'n-10/Y; Scenic Design-6/Y; Ltg Des-6/Y; Stage Mgmt 4/Y; Make-up-2/Y; Entertainment Visualization-2/Y; Sound Des.-6/Y; Design Seminar-2/Y; Principles of Design-X; Costume Constr.-X

D. (1 FT, 2 PT) Legal: Contracts/Copyrights.-4/Y; Marketing/Promotion-2/Y; Graduate Seminar-2/Y; Special Topics (varies)-6/Y; Arts Mgmt-X; B.O. Procedure-X; Development Grant Writing-X; Budgeting/Accounting Procedure-X

FACILITIES & PRODUCTIONS

MAINSTAGE: 550 seats, fly space, computer lighting. 7 prods: 5 Fac dir, 5 Fac des, 2 Guest dir, 1 Guest des, 14 Grad des, budget $2000-19,200

SECOND STAGE: 120 seats, fly space, electronic lighting. 5 prods: 3 Guest/Grad dir, $1,000-2,150

THIRD STAGE: 99 seats, fly space, electronic lighting; 3 prods, 3 Guest/Grad dir.

2 Workshop/Readings, 2 Fac dir, budget up to $2,000.

Facility built in 1963, renovated in 1995, includes scene, costume shops, CAD facility, prop shop, welding shop, 5 rehearsal studios, 1design studio, 7 classrooms, 1 video studio, 3 movement/dance studios. Bldgs/classrooms on UNLV campus.

8 student-written plays produced in the last two years.

The Nevada Conservatory Theatre (Lort-affiliate candidate) engages national and international theatre professionals in all disciplines to work alongside the most advanced students from the UNLV Department of Theatre. It is a leading theatre in Las Vegas and Southern Nevada. It enriches, strengthens, and challenges the cultural and artistic life of the city and strives to be the state's premiere theatre. It seeks the most advanced level of artistic achievement and to become a renowned regional theatre in America.

DESCRIPTION

Noted Faculty: Dr. Ann McDonough, writer; Joe Aldridge, Tech Dir; Robert Brewer, Musical THTR & NCT Artistic Dir; Nate Bynum, Film actor; Glenn Casale, Director; KC Davis, Playwright; Brackley Frayer, Lighting Des; Michael Lugering, Perf/Mvmnt; Charles O'Connor, Tech; Shannon Sumpter, Stage Mgt.

Guest Artists: G.W. Bailey, Judy Jean Berns, Jeff Craggs, Sally Struthers, James Sutorius, Equity Actors; Paul Barnes, Deanna Duplechain, Directors; Jack Gaughan, Musical Director; Walter Klappert, Lighting Designer; Xu-Zheng He, Scenic Designer.

The BA degree in Theatre allows the student to pursue & integrate the theory and practice of theatre with an intellectual discipline of performing and visual art to develop a knowledge of the craft and technique while participating in the cultural enrichment through productions. The Senior Adult Theatre Program invites participation of students in all aspects of Department productions. Nevada students 62 and over may register for six credit hours per semester at no cost. The MA program is a selected course of work designed to supplement/complete a student's study in the field of theatre while becoming familiar with professional standards, methods of research, and modes of thought in preparation for advancement in the teaching profession or further study at the doctorate level. The MFA is a program in Design/Technology, Directing, Performance, Playwriting, or Stage Management that disciplines, fosters, and encourages an integrated and collaborative approach to theatre while providing comprehensive and specialized training to advancec talent and craft for entry into theatre careers.

University of Nevada - Reno

Dr. Gordon Zimmerman, Chair
Theatre Department #0228
University of Nevada
Reno, NV 89557
DEPT: (775) 784-6839
FAX: (775) 784-1175
www.unr.edu/nevadarep

16,000 total enr. not competitive
Semester System
70 Majors
T: $109.25/credit
O-ST T: $4,955/sem
GZimm@unr.edu

ADMISSIONS: Mail stop 0120, UNR, Reno, NV 89557
(775) 784-4700 www.ss.unr.edu/admissions

DEGREES OFFERED

BA in Theatre (63); BFA in Performance, Technical (7) Declare major in first year. 2007 granted 7 degrees.

ADMISSION & FINANCIAL INFORMATION

ACT/SAT scores, 2.5 HS GPA, $40 application fee, official transcripts. Th. program admits all applicants. Dept. schol. avail. to upper division students who have made outstanding contributions to the program.

FACULTY AND CLASSES OFFERED

7 FT, 2 PT: 2 PhD/DFA, 7 MA; 9 Staff

A. (1 FT) Intro to Theatre-3/Y; Theatre History-2/Y; Playwriting-1/O

B. (2 FT, 2 PT) Acting-4/Y; Voice/Speech-1/Y; Directing-2/Y

C. (4 FT) Prins of Des-1/O; Cost Des-1/Y; Tech Prod-1/Y; Set Design-1/O; Ltg Des-1/O; Cost Constr-1/O; Make-up-1/Y

FACILITIES & PRODUCTIONS

MAINSTAGE: 260 seats, fly space, computerized lighting
    3 prods: 3 Fac dir/des; budget $5,000-10,000

SECOND STAGE: variable seats, computerized lighting
    2 prods: 2 Fac dir/des; budget $5,000-10,000

2 Fac dir Workshop/Reading

Facility was built in 1965/1987, includes scene shop, costume shop, rehearsal studio, design studio, 2 classrooms, sound studio, CAD.

A departmental, student-run organization presents 4 productions in which majors generally participate. 1 student-written play has been produced in the last two years.

DESCRIPTION

The small but very active program allows undergraduates excellent opportunities for both performance and technical experience. Based on a liberal arts curriculum, the program enables the student to prepare for a wide variety of career options including professional goals and advanced training at the graduate level. The departmental philosophy maintains that practical experience is vital for the training of any theatre artist.

NEW HAMPSHIRE

Dartmouth College

Peter Hackett, Dir.	5,700 Total Enr.; h. compet.
Department of Theater	Quarter System
Box 6204	12 Majors; NAST, U/RTA
Hopkins Center	T: $33,501/$9,840 r & b
Dartmouth College	(603) 646-3104
Hanover, NH 03755	fax (603) 646-1757

department.of.theater@dartmouth.edu
www.dartmouth.edu/~theater
Admissions: Box HB6016   (603) 646-2875
www.dartmouth.edu/apply   admissions.office@dartmouth.edu

DEGREES OFFERED

BA in Theater(25). Declare major in sophomore year; 2007 granted 2 UG degrees.

ADMISSION & FINANCIAL INFORMATION

SAT score required. 15% of applicants accepted by institution. No special requirements to theatre program.

FACULTY AND CLASSES OFFERED

6 FT, 10 PT: 3 PhD, 9 MFA/MA, 4 Prof. w/o adv. degree; 6 Staff

A. (2 FT,3PT) Intro to Theatre-1/Y; Dramatic Lit-1/O; Theatre History-7/Y; Dramatic Criticism-1/O; Shakes-3/X; Playwriting-3/Y

B. (2 FT, 3 PT) Acting-5/Y; Voice/Speech-1/Y; Movement- 2/Y; Directing-2/Y; Dance-3/Y; Musical Theatre-1/O; Singing-2/X

C. (2 FT,4 PT) Set Des-2/Y; Cost. Des-2/Y; Ltg Des-2/Y; Tech Prod-2/Y; Cost. Constr-1/O; Stg Mgmt-1/O

Dartmouth College is connected to New York Theatre Workshop, which is in residency during the summer. Students serve as assistants.

FACILITIES & PRODUCTIONS

MAINSTAGE: 480 seats, fly space, computerized/electronic lighting
    3 prods: 2 Fac dir/des; 1 GA dir/des; budget $7,000-7,500

SECOND STAGE: 181 seats, computerized lighting.
    12 prods: 12 UG dir/des; budget $300-$500

Workshop/Readings: 1 UG Dir

Facility was built in 1963, renovated in 1995; scene shop, costume shop, dance studio, 2 rehearsal studios, design studio, 2 classrooms, carpentry shop.

A non-departmental, student-run organization presents 5 productions per year in which majors participate. 13 student-written plays have been produced in the last two years.

Connected with the New York Theater Workshop (summer only) in residence, students serve as assistants.

DESCRIPTION

Noted Faculty: Peter Hackett, Director; Jamie Horton, Director; Georgi Alexi-Meskhishvili, Designer; Daniel Kotlowitz, Designer; Joe Sutton, Playwright

Guest Artists: Jerry Zaks, Director; Pavel Dobrusky, Designer, Carol MacVey, Director

The Theater program is dedicated exclusively to undergraduate students. Since there is no graduate theater program at Dartmouth, undergraduate students do not compete with graduate students for casting and production opportunities. In contrast with many other theater programs, virtually all roles onstage, and all production assignments backstage, are filled by undergraduates. All courses are taught by faculty members; no graduate assistants are used. Students may major in theater with a concentration. A Modified Major is also available, in which theater is combined with another area, such as English, Government, Psychology, etc. In addition, The New York Theater Workshop is in residency in the summer through the Theater Department.

Keene State College

Daniel Peterson, Chair	4,800 Total Enr.; competitive
Dept. of Theatre & Dance	Semester System
Keene State College	120 Majors
229 Main Street	T: $6,180
Keene, NH 03435-2405	O-ST T: $13,730
DEPT: (603) 358-2162	MAIN: (603) 358-2276
admissions@keene.edu	www.keene.edu

DEGREES OFFERED

BA in Theatre Arts with concentrations in Acting/Directing, Design/Tech Theatre, Dance and Critical Studies. Declare major end of Soph. year. There is also a BA in Film Studies with concentrations in Film Production, Film History/Criticism.
For more information on Film, contact the department.

ADMISSION & FINANCIAL INFORMATION

College prep curriculum, SATs; 79% accepted; program generally admits all applicants. (1) 2 annual theatre talent scoharships. (1 Theatre and Dance, 1 Film). $2,400 each renewable for 4 yrs. total; audition, submission of film, video, or design work, + recommendations; (2) Various academic scholarships/loans; scholarship criteria are academic potential, past performance, need, recommendations.

FACULTY AND CLASSES OFFERED

Theatre and Dance: 7 FT, 3 PT: 1 PhD, 5 MFA/MA, 1 Prof. w/o adv. degree. Film Studies: 2.5 faculty (halftime with Womens' Studies), 4 PT: 1 PhD, 1 ABD, 1 MFA

A. (5 FT) Intro to Theatre-1/Y; Theatre Hist/Drama Lit-3/Y

B. (3 FT, 2 PT) Acting-4/Y; Voice/Speech-1/Y; Mvmt-1/Y; Musical Th-1/O; Directing-2/O; Modern Dance-11/Y

C. (2 FT, 1 PT) Prins of Des-1/Y; Set Des-1/O; Cost Des-1/Y;Ltg Des-1/O; Tech Prod.-2/Y; Cost. Sonstr-1/Y; Make-up-1/Y; Sc Pntg-1/O; Draft-1/O

FACILITIES & PRODUCTIONS

MAINSTAGE: 571 seats, fly space, computerized lighting. 3 Fac dir/des, up to 4 UG dir/des, occas. Guest dir/des; bdgt $3,250 avg. (includes annual Dance Concert)

SECOND STAGE: Black Box 80-120 seats, computerized lighting

1 Fac dir/des;bdgt $2000; every 2 yrs, up to 10 student dir/des 1-acts.

Facility was built in 1981; includes scene shop, costume shop, 2 dance studios (1 in Student Center), classroom, band and choral rehearsal rooms, gallery area, 20 practice modules.

DESCRIPTION

Our program is dedicated to a comprehensive course of study, balancing theory and practice with a liberal arts education. As artists and teachers, our primary focus is to encourage and guide our students with their individual journey as they experience and appreciate the world and themselves through theatre, dance and file. The Keene State College Theatre, Dance and Film major accommodates disciplines that, while separate, are also related. Options offer opportunities to prepare for careers in a variety of fields involving contact with the public, either directly or through the arts and the media. The Theatre Arts option balances theoretical with applied course work. Students may specialize in Acting/Directing, Dance, or Design/Technical Theatre. While some graduates go on to further study or work in professional theatre, others choose careers in such areas as personnel, counseling, advertising, public relations, or sales.

New England College

Glenn Stuart,
Assoc. Prof. of Theatre
Theatre Department
New England College
Henniker, NH 03242
DEPT: (603) 428-2454
gstuart@nec.edu
ADM: 89 Bridge St.
(603)428-2223
(800) 521-7642

1,000 Total Enr.; compet.
Semester System
30 Majors/minors
T: $23,936
SMALL PROGRAM
FAX: (603) 428-7230

admission@nec.edu
www.nec.edu

DEGREES OFFERED

BA in Theatre, Minor in Theatre. Declare major in first or second year; 2007 graduated 6 students with theatre degree and 5 with minor in theatre.

ADMISSION & FINANCIAL INFORMATION

2.7 GPA, SAT optional. 83% of applicants admitted to institution; 100% admitted to theatre program.

FACULTY AND CLASSES OFFERED

3 FT, 2 PT: 1 PhD/DFA, 4 MFA/MA; 1 instructor w/o adv. degree

A. (1 FT) Intro to Theatre-2/Y; Theatre History-2/Y; Shakes-1/Y; Dramatic Criticism-1/Y; Dramatic Theory-1/Y; Dramaturgy-1/O; Playwriting-2/YO

B. (1 FT, 1 PT) Acting-4/Y; Movement-1/Y; Directing-2/Y

C. (1 FT) Tech Prod-4/Y; Production-2/Y; Design-4/O

FACILITIES AND PRODUCTIONS

MAINSTAGE: 102 seats, computerized lighting. 2 Fac dir/des prods.; budget $3,000-6,000

SECOND STAGE: 50-60 seats, computerized/electronic lighting . 2-4 UG dir/des prods; budget $400-600

Facility was built in 60's, renovated in 2001; includes scene shop, costume shop.

A non-departmental, student-run organization presents 2-4 productions per year, in which majors/minors participate. Open Door Theatre: One summer production by company composed of current students, alumni, and associates of Theatre Dept.

DESCRIPTION

The major in theatre at the New England College is designed to provide students with a solid foundation in the craft and art of theatre through both theoretical and practical principles. The philosophy of the Theatre Department stresses the relationship between a Liberal Arts education and training students for possible career paths in the theatre or further study in graduate programs. The theatre department is a teaching theatre, in that the mainstage productions in the fall and spring are utilized in the curricula of appropriate courses, thus providing a laboratory in which the students can study and analyze the difficult process of producing high caliber theatre.

Plymouth State University

Jonathan Santore, PhD.
Chair
Dept. of Music, Theatre & Dance
MSC 37
Plymouth State Univ.
Plymouth, NH 03264
DEPT: (603) 535-2232
jsantore@plymouth.edu
ADMISSIONS: Russell House (MSC52), PSU, Plymouth, NH 03264
(800) 842-6900
FAX: (603) 535-2714
www.plymouth.edu/mtd/theatre

3,200 Total Enr.; competitive
Semester System
65 Majors; ATHE
T: $6,180/$8,030 R&B
O-ST T: $13,730/$8,030 R&B
SMALL PROGRAM
FAX: (603) 535-2645

DEGREES OFFERED

BA in Theatre Arts with options (65); Contract Option (15), Acting Option (25), Design/Tech Option (10); Musical Th. Performance Option (15); BA Music + BS Music Ed (80), Dance Minor (15). Declare major in sophomore/junior year.

ADMISSION & FINANCIAL INFORMATION

GPA 2.0, SAT 900; 60% accepted; 9 out of 10 applicants accepted to Th Prog; audition/interview/portfolio for designers, recommendations, resume. 4 theatre talent grants and 2 musical theatre grants, audition/portfolio plus interview. Talent grants are $2,000/yr. 10-12 other scholarships avail. to continuing students based on academic achievement, involvement in production and need.

FACULTY AND CLASSES OFFERED

4 FT, 2 PT: 1 PhD, 5 MFA/MA; 3 Staff

A. (1 FT) Intro to Theatre-1/Y; Dramatic Criticism-1/O; Dramatic Lit-4/Y; Theatre History- 3/Y; Shakes-2/X; Playwriting-2/O;

B. (1 1/2 FT, 1 PT) Acting-5/Y; Movement-2/Y; Singing-4/Y; Mus Th-2/Y; Directing-1/O; Dance-5/Y

C. (1 1/2 FT, 1 PT) Prins of Des-1/Y; Cost Des-1/O; Set Des-2/Y; Ltg Des-1/O; Tech Prod'n-1/Y; Cost Constr-1/Y; Make-up-2/Y; Stg Mgmt-1/Y; Tech Topics-6/Y

FACILITIES & PRODUCTIONS

MAINSTAGE: 660 seats, fly space, computerized lighting. 3 prods: 1 Fac dir, 2 Fac des, 1 Guest dir, 2 Guest des, 1 UG dir, 2 UG des; budget $6,000-20,000

SECOND STAGE: 180 seats, computerized lighting. 4 prods: 1 Fac dir, 2 Fac des, 1 Guest dir, 2 Guest des, 2 UG dir, 2 UG des; budget $4,500-10,000

THIRD STAGE: 20-40 seats, black box, computerized lighting.

8 Workshops/Readings: 3 Fac dir, 1 Guest dir, 2 UG dir, 3 UG des; budget $100-300

The Rep Company offers 4-10 workshops.

The new Silver Cultural Arts Center opened in 1992. Scene shop, costume shop, CAD facility, 6 classrooms. Recital hall, 180 seats, computerized lighting, Dolby recording.

The Plymouth Players, a student-run organization presents productions in which majors participate. 4-5 productions presented in a school year. 6 student-written plays produced in the last two years.

Connection with North Country Center for the Arts which operates in the summer. Students often have the opportunity for employment with this company. One of our faculty members works as a casting consultant and many others have directed, designed and acted with NCCA and continue to do so.

DESCRIPTION

Noted Faculty: Paul Mroczka, History, Lit., Dramatic Writing; Elizabeth Cox, Acting, Voice + Diction, Directing; Matthew Kizer, Matthew Braur, Design/Tech; Michael Littman, Acting.

Guest Artists: John Ambrosone, Designer; Marla Blakey, Choreographer; John R. Briggs, Director, Writer, Composer; Kevin Gardner, Director; Jane Stein, Designer; Liza Williams, Designer; Pontine Movement Theatre, Actors, Directors, Designers, Writers.

The Department of Music and Theatre at Plymouth State University is the fastest growing department on campus. Despite this fact we still emphasize individualized attention. The Theatre Arts major, which in the past four years has grown from twelve to over sixty majors, offers a B.A. with newly instituted options in Acting, Musical Theatre Performance, Design/Tech and Contract (self-design). Theatre Arts majors are given many opportunities to act, design, direct, etc. Emphasis is on classroom study and training and its application in production. In the past three years we have had a 90% success rate with selected graduates being accepted into advanced training programs and many more of our graduates found work in professional venues. Students graduate with a well-rounded education and at least one area of specialization. As our major grows so too do advanced opportunities for our students both on and off campus.

University of New Hampshire

Deborah Kinghorn, Assoc Prof
Dept of Theatre & Dance
Paul Creative Arts Center
UNH, 30 College Road
Durham, NH 03824-3538
DEPT: (603) 862-2919
nancy.pearson@unh.edu
ADMISSIONS: Grant House, Garrison Ave., Durham, NH 03824
(603) 862-1360
admissions@unh.edu

13,506 Total Enr.; compet.
Semester System
138 Majors; NAST, U/RTA, ATHE
T: $10,401/$7,584 R&B
O-ST T: $22,851/$7,584 R&B
FAX: (603) 862-0298
www.unh.edu/theatre-dance
www.unh.edu/admissions

DEGREES OFFERED

BA in Theatre: Emphasis offered in: General (14); Youth Drama (6); Theatre Ed (13); Dance (25); Musical Theatre (42); Acting (39); Tech (14). Students declare major in any year. 2007 granted 32 degrees.

ADMISSION & FINANCIAL INFORMATION

72% of applics. accepted by institution. Th. & Dance Dept. admits all pending acceptance by Admissions. Solid B average; college prep, 4 yr. math + English, 3+ yr. lab science, 2+ yr social science, foreign lang; SAT 1120 (563 V/569 M). On average, $79,000 is available to Theatre & Dance majors. Some scholarships are merit based, some are need based, and some are fellowships in which students receive money towards tuition in return for working for the department.

FACULTY AND CLASSES OFFERED

10 FT, 2 PT: 1 PhD/DFA, 10 MFA/MA, 6 Prof. w/out adv degree; 1 Staff.

A. (1 1/2 FT) Intro to Theatre-1/Y; Th. Hist-4/Y; Shakes-1/Y; Playwriting-1/O

B. (3 1/2 FT, 2 PT) Acting-4/Y; Voice/Speech-2/Y; Movement-2/Y; Singing-O; Musical Th.-6/Y; Directing-3/Y; Dance-11/Y

C. (4 1/2 FT) Prins of Design-2/Y; Set Design-2/Y; Cost Des-3/Y; Ltg Des-1/Y; Tech Prod-2/Y; Cost Constr-1/Y; Make-up-1/Y; Stage Mgmt-1/Y

D. (1/2 FT) Arts Mgmt-1/Y

FACILITIES AND PRODUCTIONS

MAINSTAGE: 688 seats, fly space, electronic lighting
    11 prods: 4 Fac dir; 5 Fac des, 2 GA des; budget $8,500-$13,000

SECOND STAGE: 160 seats, electronic lighting
    9 prods: 2 Fac dir, 5 Fac des, 2 GA des; budget $3,500-$4,500

Facility was built in 1960's, renovated in 2000; includes scene, costume shops, sound, design studios, 2 movement/dance studios, lighting studio, 2 dressing rooms, green room, 4 classrooms

A non-departmental, student-run producing organization presents 5 productions in which majors participate.

DESCRIPTION

Noted Faculty: Carol Lucha Burns, Mus. Th.; David Richman, History, Shakespeare/Honors; Gay Nardone, Jazz, Tap, Modern, Trapeze, Aerial, Circus Art, Composition; Larry Robertson, Ballet, Choreography; Joan Churchill, Design, Scenic Paint, Rendering; David Ramsey, Stagecraft, Mgmt, Sound, Light; David Kaye, Directing, Acting, Playwriting; Raina Ames, Youth Drama, Secondary Ed, Special Ed, Makeup; Deb Kinghorn, Voice, Movement, Acting, Directing; Sarah Marschner, Intro, Theatre History.

Guest Artists: Mary Gallagher, Playwright; Marianne Plunkett, Musical Theatre; Bobby Peaco, Musical Writing, Accompanying, Directing; Helen Baldassare, Musical Cabaret; Eddie Riechert, Director, Musical Theatre; Janie Howland, Scenic Designer; Eberhand Scheiffele, Psychotherapist/Psychodramatist; Lindsey McDonald, Costume Designer; Brian Swasey, Choreographer; Linette Miles, Choreographer.

University of New Hampshire Theatre/Dance is one of the largest, most varied undergraduate programs in the northeast. Liberal Arts BA Degree and Theatre major/minor (acting, musical theatre, general theatre, design/technical theatre, dance, secondary ed, special ed, youth drama) are all valuable in the pursuit of graduate studies and career paths. Some receive their undergrad and master's degree (MAT) with teaching certification in secondary/elementary ed, a 5-yr. plan. Productions, cast through auditions, are not limited to upperclassmen or majors. Annual opportunities include 7 mainstage faculty-directed productions, 40+ performances to 10,000+ patrons; 20 + student-produced/performed plays, improv, musical theatre, dance, puppetry, youth drama, 1-Acts; 3 touring productions, 150+ performances to 60,000+ people. Paid theatre positions and performance/tech credits: touring, internships, scholarships, practicum, work-study. No audition is required to enter Theatre program. Alumni work throughout the world: theatre, film, television, music, dance, management, design, teaching, touring, etc. and receive international acclaim/employment in London, on-off Broadway, and Hollywood.

Drew University

Daniel LaPenta, Chair
Theatre Arts Department
Drew University
Madison, NJ 07940-1493
DEPT: (973) 408-3627
ADM: (973) 408-4000
http://www.drew.edu

1,500 Total Enr. h. compet.
Semester System
50 Majors; ATHE
T: $34,790/ $9,476 R&B
SMALL PROGRAM
theatre@drew.edu
cadm@drew.edu

DEGREES OFFERED

BA in Theatre Arts (50). Declare major in any year. 2003 granted 14 degs.

ADMISSION & FINANCIAL INFORMATION

HS record, SAT or ACT scores, essay, recs. Admit 100% to th. prog. President's Schol. in the Arts has additional req's beyond those to get into the school. Contact admis. office for details. Various other scholarships

FACULTY AND CLASSES OFFERED

6 FT, 7 PT: 1 PhD, 11 MFA/MA, 1 Prof. w/o adv deg.

A. (2 FT,3 PT) Intro to Th.-1/Y; Text Analysis-2/Y; Theatre History-3/Y; Shakes-2/Y (English Dept.); Dramatic Lit-1/Y; Playwriting-3/Y

B. (2 FT, 4 PT) Acting-6/Y; Voice/Speech-2/Y; Movement- 3/Y; Directing-4/Y; Musical Theatre-1/Y (Music Dept.)

C. (2 FT) Prins of Des-2/Y; Set/Ltg/Cost-3/Y; Tech Prod-2/Y

FACILITIES AND PRODUCTIONS

MAINSTAGE: Black Box Theatre/Dorothy Young Center for Arts (opened, Jan 2003): 130-180 seats, computerized lighting. 5 prods, 1 fac/4 UG dir, 5 UG des. Budget $250-600.
    F.M. KIRBY SHAKESPEARE THEATRE: 310 SEATS, COMPUTERIZED LIGHTING, 5 PRODS, 5 UG DIR/DES. BUDGET $250-600.

Second Stage: Directing Lab/Young Center for the Arts. 78 seats, computerized lighting. 12-15 staged readings, UG dir/written.

Formal internships with Shakespeare Theatre of NJ and Playwrights Theatre of NJ (both Equity and close to campus). Also NYC/Metro NJ "Theatre Semester" program.

DESCRIPTION

Noted Faculty: Jim Bazewicz, design; Cheryl Clark, dance; Daniel LaPenta, directing; Buzz McLaughlin, playwriting; Rosemary McLaughlin, history of theatre; Joe Patenuade, acting/directing.

Guest Artists: Chris Ceraso (Ensemble Studio Theatre, John Pietrowski (Playwrights Theatre of NJ).

The curricular and production programs of the Theatre Arts Department are built upon these basic principles: 1) Studying theatre in the context of a liberal arts education. A well-rounded education is a necessity for the development of any artist. 2) Giving our students a broadly-based theatrical training. Our curriculum provides them with a solid grounding in the theory, history and practice of all of the theatrical arts. 3) Involving students creatively in all areas of our production program. Our teaching philosophy is that the best way to learn theatre is by doing. The integration of classroom learning with "on the boards" practical experience is critical to the overall educational process, so our production program is organized to offer our students numerous opportunities in acting, directing, playwriting, design, stage management and technical theatre. 4) Creating a learning environment that is collaborative and supportive. We see theatre not as the work of individuals but as the collaborative, creative effort of a group of dedicated artists striving together for a common goal. We believe in the primary importance of and so emphasize the developmental process, while realizing that the "product" of performance in front of an audience is an element of that process.

Kean University

Prof. Holly Logue, Chairperson	12,000 Total Enr.; compet.
Dept. of Theatre	90 Majors; NAST
School of Visual & Perf Arts	Semester System
Kean University	T: $8,000
1000 Morris Ave	O-ST T: $11,000
Union, NJ 07083	DEPT: (908) 737-4420
theatre@kean.edu	FAX: (908) 737-4425

www.kean.edu/theatre-dept/welcome.html
ADM: Admissions Office, Kean University, Union, NJ 07083
(908)737-7100
www.kean.edu/kean_admissions/index.html

DEGREES OFFERED

BA in Theatre (56); Theatre Ed (19); BFA in Performance (10); Design Tech (5) Declare major in soph. yr; 2007 granted 13 degs.

ADMISSION & FINANCIAL INFORMATION

69% of applicants accepted to university. SAT. 1100 combined, H.S. GPA 2.75. Theatre program admits 6 out of 10. Special requirements for admission to theatre program include audition (actors),interview, and portfolio. 8 scholarships for theatre majors are available, ranging from $1000 to full tuition waivers. Info available at www.kean.edu

FACULTY AND CLASSES OFFERED

6 FT, 11 PT: 1 PhD,16 MFA; 1 Staff

A. (1 FT, 1 PT) Intro to Theatre-1/Y; Theatre History-2/Y; Shakes-2/Y; Playwriting-2/Y; Dramatic Lit.-3/Y, Dramatic Crit.-O

B. (3 FT, 8 PT) Acting-6/Y; Voice/Speech-1/Y; Movement-2/Y; Singing-3/Y; Directing-1/Y; Dance-6/Y; Musical Theatre-1/O; Stage Combat-1/O

C. (2 FT, 1 PT) Cost Des-1/O; Set Design-1/O; Tech Prod-1/Y; Cost. Constr-1/O; Cost Hist-1/O; Stage Mgmt-1/Y; Make-up-1/O; Ltg Des-1/O; Scene Painting-1/O

D. (1 PT) Arts Mgmt-1/O

FACILITIES & PRODUCTIONS

MAINSTAGE: 956 seats, fly space, computerized and electronic lighting
    4 prods: 4 Fac dir/des; budget $10,000-50,000

SECOND STAGE: 225 seats, computerized and electronic lighting
    7 prods: 2 Fac des, 5 GA dir, 3 GA des, 2 UG dir; budget $100-2,500

THIRD STAGE: 99 seats, black box, computerized and electronic lighting.
    2 Workshops/Readings: 2 Fac dir, 1 GA des; budget $0-$1000

Facility was built in 1965, renovated in 2006, includes scene, cost, prop shops, sound studio, CAD facil., video studio, 1 dance studios, 1 rehearsal studios, 2 classrooms, welding shop

Dept. majors generally participate in a student-run producing organization that presents 1-2 prods. per year. 1-2 student-written plays produced in the last two years.

Connection with Premiere Stages (Equity-summer and school year) and includes student internships, EMC opportunities, performance opportunities, master classes, boot camp, co-productions with Dept of Theatre.

DESCRIPTION

Noted Faculty: Holly Logue, Acting, Musical Theatre, Directing; Dr. E. Teresa Choate, Theatre History & Lit, Dramaturgy; Nadine Charlsen, Set/Light Design, Stage Management; Karen L. Hart, Costume Design & Production; Ernest W. Wiggins, Voice & Speech, Acting;Rachel Evans, Theatre Education, Creative Drama, TYA

Guest Artists: Olympia Dukakis, Actor; Ray Wills, Actor; Daphne Rubin Vega, Performer; Louis Zorich, Actor; Lee Blessing, Playwright; Sebastian Bach, Performer; Rick Dennis, Designer; Kim Zimmer, Actor; AC Weary, Director; Barb Taylor, Prop Designer; Linda and David Laundra, TV Director/Producers

Accredited by the National Association of Schools of Theatre, Kean University's Department of Theatre mirrors the university's mission to provide a core educational foundation based on the traditional liberal arts. The Department of Theatre seeks to engender lifelong artistic appreciation by providing cultural and educational experiences for the student body, the university, and surrounding communities. We are also deeply committed to exploring cultural diversity through learning about oneself and the human condition and learning about world cultures, past and present. In addition, our major curriculum is designed to educate theatre students to enter the professional realm of theatre or advanced graduate studies. Our production program serves as an indispensable laboratory for both the core liberal studies and the intensive professional studies of our major curriculum.

Montclair State University

Dr. Jane T. Peterson	16,000 Total Enr.; compet.
Department of Theatre and Dance	Semester System
Montclair State University	265 Majors; NAST, ATHE
Upper Montclair, NJ 07043	T: $6,026/$6,718 r & b
DEPT: (973) 655-4217	O-ST T: $11,382/$8,888 r & b
FAX: (973) 655-7717	www.montclair.edu

petersonj@mail.montclair.edu
Admissions: Office of Admissions, Montclair State Univ, above
(973) 655-4444
undergraduate.admissions@montclair.edu

DEGREES OFFERED

BA in Theatre Studies (115); BFA in Acting (65), Prod/Design (35) Musical Theatre (50). Declare major in freshman year. 2007 granted 40 UG, 5 Grad

ADMISSION & FINANCIAL INFORMATION

SAT 1000+, B avg in h.s. work, refs; 20% accepted; Th Prog requires Aud for actors, Portfolio for designers in BFA Acting & Musical Theatre and BA Theatre Studies. Graduate need Interview for MA Theatre: concentrations in Theatre Studies, Arts Mgmt, Prod/Stage Mgmt. UG generally admit 1 out of 20 to theatre program, Grad admit 1 out of 3.

FACULTY AND CLASSES OFFERED

12 FT, 13 PT: 2 PhD/DFA, 22 MFA/MA, 1 Prof. w/o adv. degree;2 Staff

A. (2 1/2 FT, 3 PT) Intro to Theatre-2/Y; Theatre History-3/Y; Shakes-2/Y; Dramatic Lit-2/Y; Dramatic Criticism-3/Y; Playwriting-1/Y; Dramaturgy-1/O

B. (5 1/2 FT,4 PT) Acting-10/Y; Voice/Speech-4/Y; Movement- 4/Y; Musical Th-8/Y; Directing- 2/Y; Stage Combat-1/Y; Dance-3/Y; Singing-3/Y

C. (3 FT,3 PT) Principles of Des-1/Y; Set Des-1/Y; Cost. Des-1/Y; Ltg Des-1/Y; Tech. Prod.-2/Y; Cost. Constr-1/Y; Make-up-1/Y; Stage Mgmt- 1/Y; Prod Mgmt-1/Y; Drawing and Rendering-1/Y; Drafting-1/Y

D. (1 FT, 3 PT) Arts Management-2/Y; Marketing/Promo-1/X; Development/Grant Writing-1/Y; Budgeting/Accounting Proc-2/Y; Contracts/Copyright-1/X

FACILITIES AND PRODUCTIONS

MAINSTAGE: 500 seats, fly space, computerized & electronic lighting
    2 prods: 2 Fac dir, 1 Fac des, 1 Guest des, 1 UG des

SECOND STAGE: 200 seats, computerized & electronic lighting
    4 prods: 1 Fac dir/des, 2 GA dir, 1 GA des, 1 Grad dir, 2 UG des

THIRD STAGE: 1 prod: 1 Fac dir, 1 UG des workshop/readings

Various facilities including 2 scene shops, costume shop, welding shop, sound studio, 4 dance studios, 3 rehearsal studios, 2 design studios, classrooms.

A non-departmental, student-run producing organization presents 5 prods per year in which majors generally participate. 1 student-written play has been produced in the last two years.

DESCRIPTION

Noted Faculty: Dr. Suzanne Trauth, Acting; Jorge Cacheiro, Directing/Acting; Clay James, Musical Theatre; J Wiese, Scene Design; Debra Otte, Costume Design; Dr. Jane Peterson, History/Lit; Susan Kerner, Directing

Guest Artists: Luis Santiero, Playwriting; Brenda Gray, Lighting; Lisa Brenner, Dramaturgy; Diane Zaremba, Voice; Ruth Clark, Movement; John Basil, Acting

The Department of Theatre and Dance is a vibrant, growing department that offers professional-training BFA degrees in acting, musical theatre, and production/design, all within a liberal arts university. The more broadly based BA in Theatre Studies focuses on collaborative creation of original works. The seven main stage productions each year are in one of four venues: the new state-of-the-art 500-seat Kasser Theatre, a 200 seat black box, a 50 seat experimental theatre and the 1000 seat Memorial Auditorium. Student-generated productions, workshops and other performance opportunities are part of the Theatre in the Raw series. Accredited by both the National Assoc of Schools of Theatre (NAST) and the National Assoc of Schools of Dance (NASD), Montclair State University offers the best of both worlds: an excellent, affordable education on a beautiful suburban campus that is only 12 miles from NYC, the theatre capital of the world.

Rowan University

Phillip Graneto, Chair
Dept. of Theatre & Dance
Rowan University
201 Mullica Hill Road
Glassboro, NJ 08028
DEPT: (609) 256-4034
http://www.rowan.edu

8,430 Total Enr.; competitive
Semester System
80 Majors; ATHE
T: $10,068/$9,092 R&B)
N-R T: $17,376
MAIN: (609) 256-4030
admissions@rowan.edu

DEGREES OFFERED

BA in Theatre Arts with tracks in Perf, Design/Tech, Th. Ed, BA in Child. Drama. NAST approved.. Declare major by 2nd year; grant (on the average) 13 degrees/yr.

ADMISSION & FINANCIAL INFORMATION

Class rank top 40%, SAT min. 550 math, 550 verbal, 16 c.u., min. GPA 2.5. Admission to Th. Program req's audition, interview for tech & child drama specialization; admits 5 out of 10 applics.

FACULTY AND CLASSES OFFERED

9 FT, 8 PT: 2 PhD/DFA, 7 MFA/MA; 2 Staff

A. (2 1/2 FT) Intro to Theatre-1/Y; Theatre History-2/Y; Shakes-2/X; Dramatic Lit-1/Y; Playwriting-1/O; Contemp. World Theatre-1/y; Seminar-1/Y; Senior Project-1/Y

B. (2 1/2 FT) Acting-3/Y; Voice/Speech-1/Y; Mvmt-Y; Singing-2/X; Musical Th.-1/O; Directing-1/Y; Jazz Dance-1/O; Musical Th Dance-1/O; Directing II-1/O; Advanced Acting-1/O; Reader's Th-1/O; Creative Dramatics-1/Y; Internship-3/O

C. (3 FT) Prins of Design-2/X; Tech Prod'n-2/Y; Lighting-1/O; Make-up-1/2/Y; Cost Des-1/2/Y; Set Design-1/O; Cost Hist-1/Y; Children's Theatre-1/Y; Cost Constr-1/Y

D. Arts Management-1/O

FACILITIES AND PRODUCTIONS

MAINSTAGE: 425 seats, fly space, computerized lighting. 4 prods: 4 Fac dir/des; budget $4000-8000.

SECOND STAGE: 70 seats, computerized lighting. 5 prods: UG dir/des; budget $500-800.

1-2 Workshops/Readings: Fac dir; budget $100

Facility was built in 1924, last renovated in 1990; scene, costume, props shops, video studio, 2 dance, rehearsal studio, design studio, new spaces under design to open 2007.

Majors generally participate in non-departmental, student run prod'ns, approx. 7 /yr. Several student-written plays produced in last 2 yrs.

DESCRIPTION

Noted Faculty: Joseph Robinette, Playwright; Phillipp Graneto, Carolyn O'Donnell, Acting; Bartholomew Healy, Design; Paule Turner, Melanie Stewart, Dance.

Guest Artists: Peter Clerke, Director; Michael Duke, Writer/Director; Stuart Vaughan, Director/Teacher.

Our liberal arts programs in theatre and child drama are designed for students excited by theatre and intent upon developing the discipline necessary to function in an increasingly complex society. We believe that true learning is centered in excitement; that students who love theatre will make it a vital center for a broad education leading to a variety of careers including performance, teaching, and graduate study. We offer degree programs in either theatre or child drama, with minors available in dance, or design/technical theatre. Elementary or secondary teaching certification requires at least one extra semester of study. If you would like time to explore a variety of possibilities, to expand your knowledge of yourself and the world around you, to develop your skill in written and oral expression, then our BA programs are right for you. A secure future depends upon a secure sense of self. In our changing world college graduates change careers many times, but logic, literacy and discipline are skills that will last a lifetime.

Rutgers University - Camden

Martin Rosenberg, PhD., Chair (On leave 2007-2008)

Julianne Baird, Ph.D, Acting Chair
Dept. of Fine Arts/Theatre
Rutgers University/Camden
Camden, NJ 08102
DEPT: (856) 225-6176
www.finearts.camden.rutgers.edu

3,300 Total Enr.;competitive
Semester System
10 Majors
T: $20,376.80 r&b incl
O-ST T: $29,545.30 r&b incl.
SMALL PROGRAM

DEGREES OFFERED

BA in General Theatre (10). Declare major in first or second year.

ADMISSION & FINANCIAL INFORMATION

Inst. requires 1060 SAT; theatre program admits all applicants.

FACULTY AND CLASSES OFFERED

3 Full-Time: 3 MFA/MA

A. (1 FT) Intro to Theatre-4/Y; Theatre History-2/Y; Dramatic Lit-1/Y; Playwriting-1/O

B. (1 FT) Acting-2/Y; Voice/Speech-1/Y

C. (1 FT) Prins. of Des-1/O; Set Des-1/O; Cost Des-1/O; Ltg Des-1/O; Tech Prod-1/Y: Cost Constr-1/O; Make-up-1/O; Stage Management-1/Y

FACILITIES AND PRODUCTIONS

MAINSTAGE: 663 seats, fly space, Computerized & electronic lighting. 4 Fac dir prods.

SECOND STAGE: 80 seats, electronic lighting. 2 Fac dir prods.

Facility built in 1972, includes scene, cost shops, rehearsal studio, sound studio, 6 classrooms.

DESCRIPTION

Noted Faculty: Prof. Jospeh A. Walker, playwright, whose play The River Niger won 1973 Tony, OBIE, Drama Desk, John Gassner, Outer Critics Circle, etc; alwo awarded 1995 National Black Theatre Festival's "Living Legend" award.

The overall objective of the program in theater arts is to develop students in two ways. First, as an integral part of a liberal arts education, its courses will sharpen insights, perceptions, and creative thought processes in the area of dramatic thinking. Second, the theater curriculum will provide students with the rigorous training of an artistic discipline. The value of this process lies in the direct expression of oneself as an instrument—emotional, physical, and vocal. Students in the theater program realize their education in a fully personal sense, through complete theoretical, laboratory, and experiential work.

Rutgers University - New Brunswick

Julianne Baird, Chair
Theatre Arts Department
2 Chapel Drive
Rutgers University
New Brunswick,
　NJ 08901-8527
DEPT: (732) 932-9891 x 10
UG ADM: (732) 445-3770

40,000 Total Enr.; h. compet.
Semester System
257 Majors;
T: $20,376.80 r&b incl
O-ST T: $29,545.30 r&b incl.
www.rutgers.edu/
FAX: (732) 932-1409
GRAD ADM: (732) 932-7711

DEGREES OFFERED

BFA in Acting (64), Design (25), Production (26); MFA in Acting (50), Design (16), Directing (7), Playwriting (4), Stage Management (5). Declare major as an applicant for the BFA program, sophomore year for BA program, as applicant for MFA program.

ADMISSION & FINANCIAL INFORMATION

Aud/Int./Portfolio req. for MFA & BFA; SATs req. for BFA & BA; Theatre program admits 32 of 500 UG, 32 of 300 Grad applics. UG: One $600 schol plus several academic scholarships Grad: Levin Schol for incoming students, $1,000-2,000 ea. 60+ teaching assistantships (1 semester).

FACULTY AND CLASSES OFFERED

Grad:13 FT, 28 PT; UG: 9 FT, 15 PT.

A. (5 FT, 2 PT) Dramatic Lit-3/Y; Dram. Crit.-2/Y; Playwriting-6/Y; Intro to Th-3/Y; Theatre His/Theory-2/Y; Theatre Theory-1/Y; Internships-4/Y.

B. (7 FT, 2 PT) Acting-17/Y; Voice/Speech-17/Y; Movemt/Combat-6/Y; Movement-5/Y; Directing-13/Y; Dance-4/Y; Act Perf-6/Y; Stg. Combat-2/Y; Auditioning-2/Y; Style Study-2; Singing-2/Y; Dir Prod-6/Y.

C. (6 FT, 22 PT) Prins of Des-6/Y; Set Design-9/Y; Cost Des-10/Y; Ltg Des-14/Y; Tech Prod'n-9/Y; Cost Constr-9/Y; Cost Hist-8/Y; Make-up-1/Y; Stg Mgmt-10/Y; Drawing Practicum-2/Y; Architecture & Design-2/Y; Architecture & Decor-2/Y; Watercolor-2/Y; Drawing-2/Y; Props-Y; Stage Craft-2/Y.

D. (2 FT) Arts Management-4/Y

FACILITIES & PRODUCTIONS

MAINSTAGE I: 335 seats prosc., fly space, computerized lighting 7 prods: 4 Fac dir, 10 Grad des, 2 UG des; budget $10,000-13,000

MAINSTAGE II: 335 seats, 3/4 thrust; 3 prods, 1 Guest dir 2 Grad dir 5 Grad des, 4 UG des; budget $8,000.

THIRD STAGE: 75 SEATS, ELECTRONIC LIGHTING; 18 PROD, 18 GRAD DIR, 10 GRAD DES, 8 UG DES; BUDGET $4,000.

Facility includes fully equipped scene shop, costume shop, costume teaching shop, props shop, welding shop, sound studio, CAD facility, 1 movement/dance studio, 7 rehearsal studios, 2 design studios, state-of-the-art lighting lab.

3 non-departmental, student-run organization present prods in which majors participate.

DESCRIPTION

Noted Faculty: William Esper, Lloyd Richards, Barbara Marchant, Deborah Hedwall; Acting; Amy Saltz, Pamela Berlin, Israel Hicks; Directing: David Murin, Vickie Espisito, F. Mitchell, Donn Michael Miller, Design: Jan Leys, Danielle Luccardo, Movement:

Patricia Norcia, Nancy Mayans, Voice and Speech: Avery Brooks.

Guest Artists: Mason Gross Presents: F. Murray Abraham, Kevin Kline, Samuel E. Wright; Directors: Philip Minor, Joseph Brancato, John Going, Pierre Lefevre, and William Woodman. Master classes by Pierre Lefevre; Masques: Nancy Curtis, Paul Lazar, Ernie Losso, Video; Noel Behn, Playwriting, Mark Weiss, Lighting.

The Rutger's Theater Company, production program of the Theater Arts Dept, is designed to compliment the curriculum of the four major theater disciplines comprising our professional training programs, The fundamental mission of the department is to train and develop professional artists in Acting, Design, Directing and Playwriting. The program is meant to provide professional level experience in public productions solely for students in the professional training programs. Participation in actual productions is an important part of any serious professional training program and is in effect an extension of studio class work and not a substitute for it. Technical skills are mastered through assiduous and strenuous work with master teachers in the studio and the tested and enriched by constant participation in actual productions.

Seton Hall University

Pete Reader, MFA, Chairman
Dept. of Communication
Seton Hall University
400 S. Orange Avenue
South Orange, NJ 07079
DEPT: (973) 761-9474
MAIN: (973) 761-9000
www.shu.edu

6,000 Total Enr.; competitive
Semester System
400 Majors
T: $27,850/$10,828 R&B
readerpe@shu.edu
FAX: (973) 275-2144
thehall@shu.edu

DEGREES OFFERED

BA in Theatre Studies and Performance. Students declare major in soph. yr.

ADMISSION & FINANCIAL INFORMATION

Minimum high school GPA: 2.8, SAT of 1000 combined. 70% of applicants admitted to institution; Theatre program generally admits 6 out of 8 applicants. Dept. workstudy program, new $1,000 scholarship available.

FACULTY AND CLASSES OFFERED

4 Full-Time: 1 PhD/DFA, 3 MFA/MA, 1 staff carpenter

A. (2 FT) Intro to Theatre-1/Y; Theatre History-1/Y; Shakes-1/Y; Dramatic Lit-2/Y; Dramatic Criticism-1/Y; Playwriting-1/Y

B. (1 FT) Acting-2/Y; Voice/Speech-1/Y; Mus. Th-1/Y; Film-1/Y

C. (1 FT) Set Design-1/Y; Ltg Design-1/Y

FACILITIES AND PRODUCTIONS

MAINSTAGE: 425 seats, computerized and electronic lighting. 7 prods: 7 Fac dir/des; budget $4,000 to $6,000.

SECOND STAGE: 100 seats, computerized lighting. 5 UG dir/des; budget $300-500;

2 Workshop/Reading, UG dir/des.

Facility was built in 2005; includes scene shop. Other facility includes a theatre-in-the-round.

A non-departmental student-run organization presents 6 productions per year in which dept. majors participate.

2 student written plays have been produced by the department in the last two years.

Connection with Celtic Theatre Co., which presents four productions per school year. Advanced acting students are encouraged to participate. The performance space is used by the Summer Theatre Program.

DESCRIPTION

Noted Faculty: James P. McGlone, PhD, History; Raymond Miranda, MFA, Musical Theatre; Dierdre Yates, MFA, Acting; Pete Reader, MFA, Design.

Seton Hall University is 30 minutes from Broadway. It will be opening a new performing arts center in conjunction with the village of South Orange. Small class sizes means close mentoring in the craft of theatre. Theatre will be an experience, not just an education.

NEW MEXICO

The College of Santa Fe

Thomas Salzman, Chair
Performing Arts Department
Greer Garson Theatre Center
The College of Santa Fe
1600 St. Michael's Dr.
Santa Fe, NM 87505
ADMISSIONS: (505) 473-6133
www.csf.edu

1,400 Total Enr.; compet.
Semester System
100 Majors; ATHE
T: $20,000/$6,000 R&B
DEPT: (505) 473-6439
FAX: (505) 473-6016
FAX: (505) 473-6127
admissions@csf.edu

DEGREES OFFERED

BA in Theater Management (3); BA/BFA in Acting (66), Design/Tech/Stg Mgmt (25); BFA in Music Theatre (18). Students declare major upon entering.

ADMISSION & FINANCIAL INFORMATION

Requirements: ACT-21 or SAT-1000, GPA 2.5; 80% accepted to institution. Aud/int req'd for admission to th prog; accept 30 out of 125. Schols, $1-4,000 avail based on audition/interview GPA, test scores.

FACULTY AND CLASSES OFFERED

7 FT, 8 PT: 7 MFA/MA, 8 Prof. w/o adv. degree

A. (1 FT, 2 PT) Intro to Theatre-1/Y; Theatre History-3/Y; Shakes-2/X; Playwriting-1/O; Dramatic Lit.-2/X

B. (2 FT, 3 PT) Acting-6/Y; Voice/Speech-2/Y; Movement-3/Y; Musical Theatre-2/Y; Directing-1/Y; Stage Combat-1/O

C. (3 FT) Prins of Des-1/Y; Set Design-5/Y; Cost Des-3/Y; Ltg Des-3/Y; Tech Prod'n-3/Y; Cost Constr-2/Y; Make-up-1/Y; Stg Mgmt-2/Y; Drawing, Drafting, CAD, Scenic Painting-Y

D. (1 FT) Arts Mgmt-2/Y; Marktg-2/X; Bdget/Actg-2/X; Contracts-1/X

FACILITIES & PRODUCTIONS

MAINSTAGE: 500 seats, fly space, computerized lighting. 4 prods: 4 Fac dir, 3 Fac des, 1 UG des; budget $7,000-12,000

SECOND STAGE: 100 seats, electronic lighting. 6 prods: 1 Fac dir, 5 UG dir, 6 UG des; budget $200-500

6 Fac or Guest dir Workshops/Readings: budget $50-200

Facility was built in 1965, renovated in 1985; includes scene, costume shops, sound, dance, rehearsal studio, classrooms, recording and video studios, computer lab, music practice rooms, art studios.

4 student written plays have been produced in the last four years.

DESCRIPTION

Noted Faculty: David Minkoff, scenic design; Peter Zapp, acting; Clare Davidson, directing; Gail Springer, voice, movement; Cheryl Odom, costume design; George Johnson, TD, lighting design; Campbell Martin, Dance.

Guest Artists: Carol Burnett, Actor; Theatre Grottesco; Philip Burton; Martin Markinson, producer; Jose Rivera, playwright; Jon Jory, director; Judith Malina, director, theatre founder, Howard Korder, playwright.

The department's objective is to provide students with a practical and theoretical background and discipline for further professional training in the various areas of theatre. The department is intensive in its demands on students in terms of time and productivity within an overall liberal arts educational environment. Every attempt is made to allow students to develop sufficient skill and understanding and demonstrate their potential for graduate school/conservatory training and career success. The department offers a major in theatre (performance, design, technical/management) as well as a minor in dance. Practicing professional guest artists from America and abroad are brought in for workshops, seminars, teaching, and directorial projects/assignments in the three disciplines. Mainstage and studio productions, recitals, and directing class projects provide students with abundant production experience. In the junior year selected students have the opportunity to broaden their experience while earning credits toward their degree through programs of study in London and NYC.

University of New Mexico

Susan Pearson, Chair	25,000 Tot. Enr.; compet.
Theatre Arts	Semester System
Fine Arts Center, Rm. 1412	195 Majors; NAST, ATHE
University of New Mexico	T: $4,570
Albuquerque, NM 87131	O-ST T: $14,942
DEPT. (505) 277-4332	R&B: $6,800
FAX: (505)277-8921	
www.unm.edu/~theatre	theatre@unm.edu
ADMISSIONS: Office of Admissions, Student Services Center 150	
(505) (505) 277-2446	FAX: (505) 277-6686
www.unm.edu	apply@unm.edu

DEGREES OFFERED

BA in Theatre (28), Dance (13); BFA in Dance (6); MA in Theatre-Concentrations: Directing, Theatre Education; MFA in Dramatic Writing.. Declare major in soph. year.

ADMISSION & FINANCIAL INFORMATION

Minimum high school GPA: 2.25 w/ACT; 91.2% of freshmen, 50.4% of Grad. applicants admitted to institution. UG req. audition/portfolio, Grad req. interview. For admission information contact Theatre Dept. Theatre scholarships/grants are available with various requirements, write for details.

FACULTY AND CLASSES OFFERED

13 FT, 5 PT: 6 PhD/DFA, 7 MFA/MA, 2 Prof. w/out adv. degree; 3 Staff

A. (4 1/2 FT) Intro to Theatre-2/Y; Theatre History-2/Y; Shakes-2/X; Dramatic Lit-1/Y; Dramatic Criticism-3/Y; Playwriting-6/Y; Perf.

Theory-1/Y

B. (3 1/2 FT, 5 PT) Acting-10/Y; Movement-6/Y; Directing-2/Y; Voice/Speech-6/Y; Mime/Mask-1/Y; Musical Theatre-2/Y; Stage Combat-1/O; Children's Th.-1/Y; Creative Drama-1/Y

C. (5 FT) Prins of Design-2/Y; Cost Des-2/Y; Set Des-3/Y; Tech Prod.-2/Y; Cost Hist-1/Y; Stage Mgmt-1/O; Ltg Des-3/Y; Cost Constr-2/Y; Make-up-1/Y

FACILITIES AND PRODUCTIONS

MAINSTAGE: 410 seats, fly space, computerized lighting. 12 prods: 12 Fac dir/des

SECOND STAGE: 110 seats, black box, computerized lighting. 32 prods: 1 Fac dir, 12 Grad dir, 3 UG dir, 16 UG des

4 Guest dir workshops/readings

Facility built in 1966, renovated in 1996; includes scene shop, costume shop, prop shop, welding shop, sound studio, design studio, CAD facility, 6 dance studios, design studio, 4 classrooms.

DESCRIPTION

Noted Faculty: David Jones, author, Great Directors at Work; John Malolepsy, scenic/ltg des, Nuestro Pueblo, Teatro Nacional de Caracas; Susan Pearson-Davis, Pres., AATE, Editor, Wish in One Hand Spit in the Others: A Collection of Plays by Susan Zeder.

Guest Artists: Dance: Mac Wellman, Len Jenkin, Mark Medoff, Elizabeth Streb, Christian Swensen, Marco Antonio Silva. Anne Bogart, Directing; Danny Hoch, Performance Artist; Jim Glavan, Mask Design; Augusto Boal, Theatre Artist; Steve Smith, Director of Clown College; Tony Church, Director Shakespeare Workshop; Issac Chocron, Venezuelan Playwright.

The University of New Mexico's Department of Theatre and Dance offers the state's most comprehensive—and only nationally accredited—undergraduate and graduate degree programs. Fostering artistic activity which embraces the cultural diversity of the Southwest, Mexico and other Latin America countries, the department supports outreach, touring, and programming in the public schools. Through teaching and production activities the department provides a creative professional atmosphere and prepares students for further training on the graduate level, and in the wider world. We view theatre as a powerful perspective from which to understand the traditional issues of liberal education. Because the writer is often the catalyst in the creative process, we committed to creating a one million dollar endowment for our playwriting program to support faculty, program activities and a new MFA degree in Dramatic Writing. Overall, the faculty strives to provide an environment that allows for the development of personal vision in the arenas of classroom, studio and stage.

Adelphi University

Nicholas Petron, Chair
Theater Program
Dept of Performing Arts
One South Ave, POB 701
Adelphi University
Garden City, NY 11530-0701
FAX: (516) 877-4926
ADMISSIONS: Levermore Hall, Room 114
(516) 877-3050

6,002 Total Enr.; compet.
Semester System
138 Majors
T: $18,000
O-ST T: $27,000
DEPT: (516) 877-4930
petron@adelphi.edu

FAX: (516) 877-3039

DEGREES OFFERED

BFA in Theatre (Acting) (50), Design/Tech (12). 2000 granted 20 UG degrees.

ADMISSION & FINANCIAL INFORMATION

80% of applicants admitted to institution; Theatre program generally admits 4 out of 10 applicants; aud/int/portfolio req. Talent awards based on audition or design/tech interview.

FACULTY AND CLASSES OFFERED

6 Full-Time, 3 Part-Time: 1 PhD, 7 MFA/MA; 5 Staff

A. (1 PT) Intro to Theatre-1/O; Theatre Hist.-2/Y; Shakes-2/Y

B. (1 FT) Acting-2/Y; Movement-2/Y; Directing-1/Y; Voice/Speech-2/Y; Dance-2/Y; Manhattan Production-1/Y

C. (1 FT) Principles of Design-1/Y; Cost Design-1/Y; Set Design-1/Y; Tech. Production-1/Y; Costume History-1/Y; Stage Mgmt-1/Y; Lighting Design-1/Y; Cost Construction-1/Y; Make-up-1/Y; Scene Painting-1/Y; Scene Painting II-1/Y

D. (1 FT) No courses listed

FACILITIES AND PRODUCTIONS

MAINSTAGE: 334 seats, fly space, computer & electronic lighting
3 prods: 3 Fac dir/des budget $4,000.

SECOND STAGE: 62 seats, electronic lighting.
2 prods: 2 Fac dir/des; budget $200

Facility built in 1973, renovated in 1992; includes scene shop, costume shop, prop shop, welding shop, sound studio, 1 design studio, 4 dance studios, 3 rehearsal studios, 3 classrooms.

A new Performing Arts Center is being built and will be open Fall 2008-will house 3 theatres, Black Boxes, classrooms, rehearsal spaces, scene shop, Green rooms, costume shop, etc.-all state-of-art.

DESCRIPTION

Noted Faculty: Frank Augustyn, Dance.

Guest Artists: Stanley Kauffmann, Drama Critic, Brian Rose, Jacques Burdick.

Performing arts majors may choose concentrations in acting, design/technical theater, or dance to prepare for a lifetime of practice in drama, music, and dramatic movement. Adelphi's programs offer a unique blend of theatrical practice—the skills, crafts and attitudes necessary to succeed in the performing arts—with the tradition of liberal learning through which each new generation of creators and critics reinterprets and revitalizes these arts. To this end, the Department of Performing Arts offers programs leading to a B.F.A. degree in dance and a B.F.A. degree in theater arts with specializations in acting and design/technical theater.

Alfred University

Lisa Lantz, Chairperson
Div of Perf Arts, Alfred Univ.
1 Saxon Drive
Alfred, NY 14802-1232
(607) 871-2562
www.alfred.edu
ADMISSIONS: 1 Saxon Dr., Alfred, NY 14802-1205
(607) 871-2115
admissions@alfred.edu

2,246 Total Enr.; h.compet.
Semester System
20 Majors; ATHE
T: $23,162/$10,384 R&B
FAX: (607) 871-2587
Performs@alfred.edu

FAX: (607) 871-2198

DEGREES OFFERED

BA in Theatre (20), BA in Fine Arts-Performance Art (40)
Declare major in any year; 2001 granted 12 degrees.

ADMISSION & FINANCIAL INFORMATION

SAT or ACT, SAT II writing test, essay & applic. 84% of applicants accepted to inst., all to Th. prog. Perf Arts Scholarship Competition (Aud. in Spring); open to all disciplines in Perf. Arts (Theatre, Dance, Music).

FACULTY AND CLASSES OFFERED

5 FT, 5 PT: 5 PhD, 3 MFA, 2 Prof. w/out adv. degree; 1 Staff

A. (1 FT, 2 PT) Intro to Theatre-2/Y; Theatre History-2/O; Shakes-4/X; Dramatic Lit-2/X; Dramatic Criticism-2/X; Playwriting-1/Y

B. (3 FT, 1 PT) Acting-5/Y; Voice/Speech-X; Movement-2/Y; Singing-5/Y; Dance-5/Y; Directing-2/Y; Tai Chi-2/O

C. (1 FT, 2 PT) Set Design-1/Y; Cost Des-1/O; Ltg Des-1/Y; Tech Prod'n-2/Y; Cost Constr-1/O; Make-up-1/O; Stg Mgmt-1/O;

D. Marketing/Promo-X; Legal: Contracts/Copyright-X.

FACILITIES AND PRODUCTIONS

MAINSTAGE: 445 seats, fly space, computerized lighting. 2 prods:
2 Fac dir, 1 Fac des, 1-2 UG des; budget $1,500-3,500

SECOND STAGE: 200 seats, computerized lighting. 6 prods: 2 Fac dir, 1 Fac des, 4 UG dir, 4-6 UG des; bdgt $1,5-3,500.

A non-departmental, student-run producing org. presents 2-3 productions per year in which dept. majors participate.

Facility built in 1996; includes scene, costume shops, sound studio, dance studio, rehearsal studio, design studio, classrooms.

DESCRIPTION

Noted Faculty: J. Stephen Crosby, Becky Prophet, Sean O'Skea, Chase Angier, Choreographer. Luanne Clarke-Crosby, Voice.

The Alfred program guides students in the exploration of the breadth and depth of theatre as an art form and as a means of human expression. In the context of integrated liberal arts learning, the student learns his or her craft in the areas of acting, directing, design, etc. while discovering theatre as a way of thinking about our world, both past and present. The Alfred program prepares the student to move directly into a variety of professional theatre occupations or to enter graduate schools and other advanced programs.

American Academy of Dramatic Arts

Dino Scopas, Director
The American Acad. of Dramatic Arts
120 Madison Avenue
New York, NY 10016
(212) 686-9244 x313
www.aada.org
ADMISSIONS: Address above.

Enr: 314; compet.
Semester System; NAST
95 Majors
T: $18,500.
Fax: 212-685-8093
dscopas@ny.aada.org
800-463-8990

DEGREES OFFERED

AOS in Acting; Certificate in Advanced Studies in Actor Training for those who complete the 3rd year.

ADMISSION & FINANCIAL INFORMATION

Must have HS diploma or equivalent; Audition/Interview, two recommendations, health certificate and transcripts required; 150 out of 500 applicants accepted to prog. Merit and need-based scholarships.

FACULTY AND CLASSES OFFERED

7 FT; 21 PT: 2 PhD, 5 MFA/MA, 21 Prof. w/o adv. degree
A. Theatre Hstory 2/Y; Shakespere styles-2/Y
B. (7 FT, 21 PT) Acting 16-Y; Movement-4/Y; Voice/Speech-4/Y; Stage Combat-1/Y; Career Mgmt-1/Y; Vocal Prod-4/Y; Acting for Camera-6/Y; Make-up- 1/Y

FACILITIES AND PRODUCTIONS

MAINSTAGE: 170 seats, electronic lighting 9 Fac dir, 1 Fac des, 6 GA Dir, 1GA Des, budget $1,800-2,500

SECOND STAGE: 169 seats, electronic lighting 12 prods, 8 Fac dir, 1 Fac des, 4 GA dir; budget $1,800-2,500

THIRD STAGE: 122 seats,fly space, electronic lighting, 12 prods, 7 Fac dir, 1 Fac des, 5 GA dir; budget $1,800-2,500

Facility is housed in a landmark building, built in 1905. Last renovated 2006, Facility includes a video studio, 7 rehersal studios, music room, conference room, 11 admin offices, 3 faculity offices, library, scene, costume, prop shops, sound studio, 2 dance studios, student and faculty lounges, and classrooms.

Academy students are constantly working on performance projects throughout the first two years, culminating in fully produced "senior plays" at the end of the 2nd year. The Third Year "Academy Company" program is offered to 22-28 selected graduates. Emphasis is on advanced personalized development of each actor through performance of plays in Academy theatres, combined with career guidance and showcasing. 12-16 productions are mounted by professional directors between Aug.–Feb., attended by agents, casting directors and potential employers of actors.

DESCRIPTION

Noted Faculty: Jacqueline Bartone, Tim Demonic, Michael Donaghy, Todd Peters, Janis Powell, Jacqueline Solotar, Tracy Trevett

Guest Artists: Jonathan Bolt, Paul Blankenship, Stephan Hollis, Liza Millianzzo, Barbara Rubin, Robert Tunstall, Jack Wann

Founded in New York in 1884, the Academy was the first school in America to provide professional education for actors. The Academy remains dedicated to that single purpose: training actors. Every course and activity, including the intrinsic liberal arts components, is related to the development of the actor. Academy training involves the student intellectually, physically and emotionally—stressing self-discovery and self-discipline and encouraging individuality. Underlying Academy training are the beliefs that an actor trained to work on the stage is best prepared to face the challenge of film and television acting; and that students must constantly be tested in the practical arena of theatre performance. The soundness of the Academy's approach is reflected in the achievements of its alumni, a diverse body of professionals unmatched by any other institution. For the serious, well-motivated student who is ready to make a commitment to acting and to concentrated, professional training, the Academy offers more than a century of success, a well-balanced, carefully structured curriculum and a vital, dedicated and caring faculty. In 1974, the Academy opened a west coast campus, now in its new permanent home: American Academy of Dramatic Arts Hollywood, 1336 N. La Brea Avenue, Hollywood, California. (See listing under California for further information.) Transferring between the two branches is permitted.

The American Musical and Dramatic Academy

LA and NYC (also listed in CA)

David Martin, Artistic Director
AMDA, 2109 Broadway
New York, NY10023
ADMISSIONS: (212) 787-5300
800-367-7908

800 Total Enr.; competitive
Semester Sys; NAST
T: $24,240/yr./H:$6700/yr.
FAX: (212) 799-4623
www.amda.edu

California Address 6305 Yucca St. LA 90028 (Call NYC campus for information) 1-323-469-3300 Fax 323-469-3350

DEGREES OFFERED

Certificate in Theatre (Musical Theatre and Acting). Declare major at Application and Audition.

ADMISSION & FINANCIAL INFORMATION

Adm. reqs-Applicants to AMDA include graduating HS seniors, college transfer students and college graduates. Applicants are required to submit application, $50 fee, all transcripts from HS and college, 2 ltrs of recommendation, student essays and to audition to be considered for acceptance to the school. A 2.5 QPA from HS is required. 50-55% of applicants are accepted. Scholaships are available. Scholarships are determined by audition and application. Scholarships offered for 2 yr program and open to first year students. Auditions are held monthly on campus in NY and LA as well as throughout the US and Canada. Auditions have been held in the following cities: Atlanta, Boston, Chicago, Cleveland, Columbus, Dallas, Denver, Houston, Kansas City, Las Vegas, LA, Minneapolis, Nashville, NY, Phoenix, Portland, Raleigh, SF, Seattle, St. Louis, Tampa, DC, Calgary, Montreal, Toronto and Vancouver. See Website for further information.

FACULTY AND CLASSES OFFERED

150 faculty of professional artists and accompanists. Part-Time: 6 PhD, 30 MFA/MA, the remaining with B.A.'s and/or professional training and certificates; 35 Staff

CURRICULUM FOR THE INTEGRATED PROGRAM: Musical Theatre I, II, III

(Techniques, Performance Styles and Scene Work), Acting I, II, III (Scene Study and Technique, Scene Study and Rehearsal Projects), Theatre Dance I, II, III, Ballet I, II, III, Tap I, II, III, Jazz I, II, III, Voice Production and Speech I, II, III, Voice I, Individual Voice II, III, IV, Musicianship I, Musicianship/Sight Singing, II, Fourth Semester: Performance Project, Career Seminars, Aud. Portfolio Workshop, Musical Th. Prep. for Auds, Monologues and Cold Readings for Auds, Dance Combinations for Auds, Acting for Film and Television Workshops.

CURRICULUM FOR THE STUDIO PROGRAM:: Acting I, II (Techniques and Resources), Acting I, II (Scene Study), Voice Production and Speech I, II, III, Theatre Movement I, II, III, Stage Combat I, II, III), Improvisation I, II, III, Masterpieces of the Stage, I, II, Heroic Acting I, Acting for Film and TV II, III, Shakes, Singing Technique and Jazz Dance (electives) I. 4th semester: Performance Project, Career Seminars, Aud. Workshops, Monologues and Cold Readings for Auds., Auditioning for Film and TV; Dialects, Singing Techniques or Stage Combat (electives).

FACILITIES AND PRODUCTIONS

AMDA -NY has two locations in the upper West Side of Manhattan: the Ansonia location is at 2109 B'way at West 73rd St and the other location is at 211 West 61st St at Amsterdam Ave. Both locations in NY have a mainstage theatre, private voice studios, dance studios, rehearsal studios, scene shops, costume shops, prop rooms and classrooms. There are 12 studio spaces and mainstage theatre at West 73rd St. location and 22 studios and a mainstage theatre at the 61st St. location. These locations are a short 12 blocks apart.

AMDA-LA is located on two acres in historic Hollywood, the campus is one block north of the intersection of Hollywood Blvd & Vine at 6305 Yucca Street. there is a mainstage theatre and 9 studios which include private voice studios, dance studios, rehearsal studios, scene shop, prop room, and classrooms. There is also housing and parking on campus. AMDA provides housing for all who request it in both NYC and LA.

IN 2002-03 THERE WERE 35 FACULTY DIRECTED PRODUCTIONS FOR STUDENTS IN MUSICAL THEATRE AND ACTING. ALL IN HOUSE PRODUCTIONS SERVE AS GRADUATION PERFORMANCES TO WHICH OUTSIDE PEOPLE ARE INVITED.

DESCRIPTION

The creation of the American Musical and Dramatic Academy in 1964 marked a new era in the training of performers for the American Theatre. AMDA, as it has come to be known, was the first school to address the critical need for training in both acting and musical theatre. Today, the versatile performer is the rule, not the exception. Respected actors move from the legitimate stage to the musical stage, from modern plays to the classics, and from the live theatre to film and television. AMDA graduates have successful careers and habe been doing this for 40 years. Continuing with this vision AMDA has opened a second campus in LA to provide opportunities to students who wish to study in the two entertainment centers of the US. AMDA's 2 Training Programs, the Integrated Program and the Studio Program are carefully planned to prepare the student for a career in the performing arts. The focus is proactical rather than academic and is rigorous and requires. strong discipline.   The Integrated Program is designed to prepare the student to work as an actor, singer and dancer in the professional theatre as well as in film and television. The Studio Program is deisgned to prepare the student to work as an actor in the pro-

fessional theatre, film and television. Each program is offered in both locations and is 4 semesters of training. Upon completion of the 1st year students return to the 2nd year by invitation only. Fulfillment of all course requirements entitles the student to a Certificate of Theatre. AMDA offers a joint degree program leading to a BFA in Musical Theatre for Integrated students and a BA for Studio students with New School University in NYC.

Barnard College

Patrica Denison, Interim Chair	2,000 Total Enr.; competitive
Dept. of Theatre,	30 Majors; ATHE
Fifth Floor Milbank Hall,	Semester System
3009 Broadway	T: $33,726
Barnard College	(212) 854-2080
New York, NY 10027	www.barnard.edu/theatre

DEGREES OFFERED

BA in Theatre: focus in Acting/Directing, Design/Tech, History/ Theory/Criticism (10). Declare major end of soph. year.

ADMISSION & FINANCIAL INFORMATION

No special requirements for admission to theatre program.

FACULTY AND CLASSES OFFERED

7 FT, 8 PT: 1 PhD, 7 MFA/MA, 2 prof. w/o advanced degree; 1 Staff. "Please refer to our website for faculty and course information."

FACILITIES & PRODUCTIONS

MAINSTAGE: 190 seats, computerized lighting. 3 Fac dir/des, 6 approx. UG dir/des prods.; budget $60-6,000

SECOND STAGE: 50 seats. 4 UG dir/des prods; budget $1,200
2 UG dir Workshops/Readings

Facility was renovated in 1993, includes scene shop, costume shop, movement/dance studio, classrooms.

A non-departmental, student-run organization presents 2 prods. per year, majors sometimes participate. 6 student-written plays produced in the last two years.

DESCRIPTION

Noted Faculty: Denny Partridge, Amy Trompelter, Patricia Denison, Steve Friedman, Ben Bush, Andy Gale, Kat Kavanagh, Caroline Kavg, Shawn Garrett.

Guest Artists: Joseph Mydell, Actor; Lilene Mansell/Liz Himelstein, Voice/Speech workshops; Allen Suddeth, Stage Combat, Choreog. for Production; Maria Aitken, High Comedy Wkshp; Mark Wing-Davey, Acting; Judith Pearce, Flutist, Composer.

Theatre is the art form which brings together all the arts. The Barnard Theatre Department seeks to introduce students to the many aspects of theatre separately and in combination with equal respect for the theoretical and the practical. Theatrical production at Barnard is closely related to coursework: performance is the defining event of the art form. Courses in theatre history, design, playwriting, dramatic literature, acting, directing and critical theory all lead to understanding how live theatre is created and how it is experienced by both its makers and its spectators. Theatre is the most social of the arts and its successful realization requires collaboration among theatre workers and between spectator and performer. Students are required to collaborate in class and in production and to become conversant with several aspects of the work. There is also the expectation that students will participate fully as audience members for department productions.

Binghamton University

John E. Vestal, Chair
Theater Dept POB 6000
SUNY - Binghamton Univ
Binghamton NY13902-6000
DEPT: (607) 777-6968
FAX: (607) 777-2489
ADMISSIONS: P.O. Box 6000
http://theatre.binghamton.edu

12,000 T. Enr.; highly compet.
Semester System
64 Majors
T: UG $4,350/$8,967 R&B
O-ST T: $10,610/$8,967 R&B
jvestal@binghamton.edu
(607) 777-2456

DEGREES OFFERED

BA in Acting/Directing (48);Technical/Design (13); Dance (3). Declare major in any year; 2007 granted 15 UG, 2 Grad degrees.

ADMISSION & FINANCIAL INFORMATION

UG: GPA 91, SAT 1200 and class rank, GRE's req'd for MA admis; inst. admits 40% of applics; 3 out of 4 UGs admitted to th program; Grad: aud./int. req. if student does not meet normal standards, apply on talented student program; 3 out of 5 Grad applics admitted. Awards & scholar. available after soph. year.

FACULTY AND CLASSES OFFERED

8 FT, 4 PT: 3 PhD/DFA, 7 MA/MFA, 2 Prof w/o adv. degree

A. (1 FT, 1 PT) Intro to Theatre-1/Y; Theatre History-1/Y; Dramatic Criticism-1/Y; Dramatic Lit-1/Y; Shakespeare-1/Y; Playwriting-1/O.

B. (5 FT, 1 PT) Acting-10/Y; Voice/Speech-2/Y; Movement-2/Y; Directing-1/Y; Dance-12/O; Musical Theatre-2/Y

C. (2 FT, 2 PT) Prins of Des-1/Y; Set Des-2/Y; Lighting Des-1/Y; Tech Production-2/Y; Cost Construct-1/Y; Stage Management-1/Y; Costume Des-1/Y; Make-up-1/Y; Scene Paint-1/Y.

D. Marketing/Promotion-1/Y.

FACILITIES AND PRODUCTIONS

MAINSTAGE: Concert Theatre - 1200 seats, fly space, computerized lighting. 8 prods: 3 Fac dir/des, 1 Guest dir/des

SECOND STAGE: D.A. Watters Theatre - 600 seats, fly space, computerized lighting. 4 prods: 3 Fac dir/des, 1 Guest dir/des.

THIRD STAGE: Chamber Hall - 140 fly space, computerized lighting 2 prod: 1 Fac dir/des; 1 Guest dir/des.

STUDIO A: 148 seats as arena and 118 as thrust, computerized lighting

STUDIO B: 133 seats, premanent thrust stage. Computerized lighting

Studio A & B: 13 prod: 1 Fac dir/des, 5 Grad dir/des, 7 UG dir/des.

Facility was built in 1985; includes scene shop, costume shop, 2 dance, 4 rehearsal studios, design studio.

DESCRIPTION

Noted Faculty: John Bielenberg, Scene Design; John E. Vestal, Lighting Design; Don Boros, History, Theory; Tom Kremer, Ann Brady and Theodore Swetz, Acting and Directing; Fred Weiss, Acting, Directing and Dance, Barbara Wolfe, Costume des/const;

Guest Artists: Doug Hall, Chicago, Rocky Horror Pic

Show, Burt Scott, des- Chicago; John Hood, des-Rocky Horror Pic Show.

Binghamton University Theatre Department produces 4 main stage productions per year. Additionally, they produce between 4 and 13 studio productions depending on the number of graduate student and upper level student directors. The undergraduate program is considered "pre-professional," preparing students in a strong liberal arts context for advanced training in MFA programs or professional schools. Extensive production and performance opportunities have always been our hallmark. The MA program generally leads to MFA or PhD programs elsewhere or to teaching careers at the secondary level.

Circle in the Square Theatre School

E. Colin O'Leary,Exec Dir
Circle in the Square Theatre School
1633 Broadway
New York, NY 10019-6795
(212) 307-0388
www.circlesquare.org

90 Tot. Enr.; highly compet.
Semester System
NAST
T: $10,500-10,750
FAX: (212) 307-0257
circleinthesquare@att.net

DEGREES OFFERED

Professional Workshop in Acting, certificate granted (45), Musical Theatre Workshop certificate (45).

ADMISSION & FINANCIAL INFORMATION

Inst. admits 10-20% of applicants. Audition, interview and 2 letters of recommendation, headshot/resume, application required. Martha Schlamme Scholarship Award to second-year student who demonstrates outstanding talent in singing interpretation; The Nikos Psacharopolos Merit Scholarship to second-year student who demonstrates outstanding talent in acting combined with a constant devotion to the dramatic arts.

FACULTY AND CLASSES OFFERED

23 Part-Time: 3 PhD, 6 MFA/MA, 14 Prof w/o adv. deg; 3 Staff

A. (1 PT) Shakes-1/Y; Classical Text-1/Y; Dramatic Lit-1/Y

B. (22 PT) Acting-7/Y; Voice/Speech-4/Y; Movement-2/Y; Mime/Mask, etc.-3/Y; Singing-7/Y; Musical Th-1/Y; Stage Combat-2/Y; Alexander Technique-1/Y; Music Theory-2/Y; Prof Orient-1/Y; GA seminars-2/Y; Dance-2/Y

Note the Acting classes are 4 Acting Technique, 1 Contemporary Scene Study, 1 Scene Study Workshop, 1 European/Chekhov Scene Study

FACILITIES AND PRODUCTIONS

MAINSTAGE: 700 seats, fly space, computerized lighting
5 prods: 4 Fac dir, 1 GA dir

2 Workshops/ Readings, fac dir

Facility was built in 1974; last renovated in 2005,costume shop, prop shop, 8 rehearsal studios, 8 classrooms

Connected with Circle in the Square Theatre (Equity). Circle in the Square Theatre School is housed in the Circle in the Square Broadway Theatre. The students are able to observe rehearsals, see performances for free, meet with Broadway cast members and students perform their student projects on the Broadway stage.

DESCRIPTION

Noted Faculty: "All faculty are practicing professionals."

B. H. Barry, Fight Choreographer; Jacqueline Brookes, Actress;Terese Haydon, Actress; Alan Langdon, Director; Edward Berkeley, Director;Bill Reed, Voice Teacher; Sara Louise Lazarus, Director; Albert Stephenson, Choreographer; Moni Yakim, Movement Director; Maria Tucci, Actress

Guest Artists: Mari Lyn Henry, Independent Casting Director; Joanna Gleason, Actress; Gregory Abels, Director; Ralph Zitto, Director; Brian O'Neil, Actor/Author; John Bolger, Actor; Barbara Garrick, Actress; Allen Miller, Director; Kevin McGuire, Actor/Director; Alfred Molina, Actor

The Circle in the Square Theatre School was founded in 1961. Its primary objective is to train actors for the professional theatre. This is accomplished in intensive Workshop programs for carefully selected young actors and actor/singers. Each program, whether acting or musical theatre, is structured and designed to develop style and technique with primary emphasis on the development of both the physical and intellectual aspects of successful interpretation of a role. We deal with both the traditional and experimental aspects of professional theatre. We believe strongly in an eclectic curriculum in order to expose students to various acting styles and to different viewpoints on those styles. Our intention is that actors trained at the Circle in the Square Theatre School will have the range and ability to perform all styles and forms of theatre, and that their talents can be easily adapted to the area of film and television as well.

City University of New York Graduate School

Marvin Carlson, Chair	3,300 T. Enr.; highly compet.
PhD Program in Theatre	Semester System
365 Fifth Ave.	4 Majors; ATHE
CUNY-Graduate School	T: $2,860/ost $560 per credit
New York, NY10016-4309	DEPT: (212) 817-8870
theatre@gc.cuny.ed	SMALL PROGRAM
FAX:212-817-1538	www.gc.cuny.edu/
WWW.GC.CUNY.EDU/ADMIN_OFFICES/ADMISSIONS/INDEX.HTM	

DEGREES OFFERED

PhD in Theatre.

ADMISSION & FINANCIAL INFORMATION

GPA, letters, statement, GRE (or TOEFL), writing sample required: 30-40% accepted; Grad program admits 35 out of 100 applicants. A limited amount of financial aid is available to entering and matriculated students. Merit for enrolled students is gauged by past performance, for entering students by transcripts and GRE scores.

FACULTY AND CLASSES OFFERED

5 Full-Time, 17 Part-Time: 22 PhD; 2 Staff

A. (5 FT, 17 PT) Dramatic Structure-1/Y; Theatre Historiography-1/Y; Seminars in National Theatre-7/O; Theatre Theory-2/Y; Seminars in Comp. Drama-1/O; Research & Bibliography-1/Y; Film Seminars-3/Y

DESCRIPTION

Noted Faculty: Marvin Carlson, Daniel Gerould, Jonathan Kalb, Judith Milhous, David Savran, Pamela Sheingorn, Alisa Solomon.

The City University of New York Ph.D. Program in Theatre prepares students for teaching, research, writing, dramaturgy, and related occupations. The program is generally acknowledged to be among the foremost in the country for the distinction and range of its faculty. Its alumni have made substantial contributions in theatre scholarship and have assumed positions of leadership in the academic and professional community. The Martin E. Segal center is involved in a wide range of research and publication projects, including a translation project and publishes three journals: The Journal of American Drama and Theatre, Western European Stages, and Slavic and East European Performance. The Program has strong international ties and interests, and has specific exchange ties with major research institutes in France and Germany.

Cobalt Studios

(see Summer Theatre Dir/Summer Training Prog)

Rachel Keebler, President	6-8 Total Enrol.; compet.
PO Box 79, 134 Royce Rd.	Semester system, 2 yr prog
White Lake, NY 12786	T: $6,500/$3,500 R&B
(845) 583-7025	SMALL PROGRAM
FAX: (845) 583-7025	mail@cobaltstudios.net
www.fcc.net/cobaltstudios	cobaltstudios@fcc.net

ADMISSION INFORMATION

2 year Scenic Artist Training Program, must be HS grad.min, 3 letters of rec. with application; overnight interview with portfolio required for acceptance. Accept 6 out of 10 applicants.

DEGREES OFFERED

2 year program - Certificate in Scene Painting

FACULTY

2 Full-Time; 4-6 Guest Instructors; 2 Staff

FACILITIES

Secluded farmhouse on 28 acres of fields and woods accommodates students and guest artists. Painting studio w/ painting deck, class space, paint mixing room, library, drafting facilities, and student lounge and lockers.

DESCRIPTION

Noted Faculty & Guest Artists: Rachel Keebler, Howard Jones; C. Lance Brockman, Bob Moody, Susan Crabtree, Nels Christianson, Donna Wymore and Kimb Williamson.

The emphasis at Cobalt Studios is on the training talented artists in the skills of scenic painting and in the communication, management, and administrative skills necessary for any team endeavor. While some training will necessarily involve demonstration and lectures, the curriculum is heavily weighted toward practicum and lab projects. The "hands on" approach is the hallmark of Cobalt Studios' Scenic Artist Training Program. The program operates on a full time academic schedule, form Sept to May for two years. It is designed for the student who seriously wants to become a scenic painter, or wants to be as proficient a painter as they are a designer. Graduating students look forward to steady exciting work as Scenic Artists, whether in theatre, movies, or interiors, from regional theatres to scenery studios. This resident 40 hr/wk program balances the student's time: 50% classwork and commission work, concentrating on creating painters ready for the workforce. Other programs include: Summer Scene Painting, Month at Cobalt, Specialty Seminars: Painted Marble & Woodgrain, etc.

Colgate University

Adrian Giurgea
Colgate University Theater
13 Oak Drive, Dana Arts Center
Hamilton, NY 13346
DEPT: (315) 228-7639
agiurgea@mail.colgate.edu
ADMISSIONS: Office of Admissions
www.colgate.edu/offices/admission/

2,750 Tot. Enr.; h. compet.
Semester System, ATHE, U/RTA
16 Majors
T: $29,940/$7,155 R&B
FAX: (315) 228-7002
www.colgate.edu
(315) 228-7401
FAX: (315) 228-7544

DEGREES OFFERED

BA Theater Major/Minor (16). Students declare major in soph. year.

ADMISSION & FINANCIAL INFORMATION

Strong academic record, standard testing, recommendation, personal essays, extra curricular involvement. Scholarships not specific to theatre majors, need based. No special requirements for admission to theater program.

FACULTY AND CLASSES OFFERED

6 FT Fac., 2 PhD, 4 MFA/MA, 1 Staff

A. Theatre History-1/Y; Shakes-1/O; Dramatic Criticism-1/O; Dramatic Lit-3/Y; Playwriting-1/Y

B. (1 1/2 FT) Acting-2/Y; Singing-XO; Directing-1/Y; Voice/Speech-1/Y; Children's Theater-1/Y

C. (2 FT) Cost Des-1/Y; Tech Prod-1/O; Set Design-2/Y; Lighting Des-1/O; Stagecraft-1/Y

FACILITIES & PRODUCTIONS

MAINSTAGE: 336 seats, computerized lighting. 8 prods: 3 Fac dir, 2 Fac des, 5 UG dir, 5 UG des; b $5,000-8,000.

SECOND STAGE: 90-100 seats, 4 prods, 1 UG dir/des; bdgt $1,000-3,000.

Facility was built in 1965, renovated in 2001; includes scene, cost. shops, 2 rehearsal/dance studios, 5 classrooms.

Non-departmental, student-run organization present 6-7 prods. per year in which majors participate. Student-written plays produced each year.

DESCRIPTION

The goal of the major is to combine a thorough grounding in basic performance and technical skills with a wide-ranging exposure to the literature, including plays and theoretical writings, and to offer choices that allow for deeper, more advanced involvement in specific areas of specialization, e.g. acting/directing, playwriting, history/criticism, design, technical theater. Although the course of study is not based on a conservatory model, remaining instead within a broader Liberal Arts framework, it will nevertheless provide a solid preparation for further study in graduate or professional school.

Columbia University

Steven Chaikelson, Chair
2960 Broadway, MC 1807
Columbia University
School of the Arts
New York, NY 10027
www.columbia.edu/cu/arts/
ADMISSIONS: 2960 Broadway, MC 1803
(212) 854-2134
admissions-arts@columbia.edu

h. competitive
Semester System
92 Majors
T: $38,812/$20,000 R&B
DEPT: (212) 854-3408
FAX: (212) 854-3344

(212) 854-1309

DEGREES OFFERED

MFA in Acting, (49), Directing (19), Playwriting (22), Dramaturgy (22), Management (20) Stage Mgmt.

ADMISSION & FINANCIAL INFORMATION

Admission based on 2 written pieces, transcripts, work samples, resumes, references. Auditions for actors and directors, interviews for all others are required. 15% accepted to institution, 44 out of 350 admitted to theatre program. The top choice in each area is awarded a schol. Based on talent.

FACULTY AND CLASSES OFFERED

10 Full-Time, 18 Part-Time: 1 PhD, 8 MFA/MA; 3 Staff

A. (3 FT, 4 PT) Dramatic Lit-1/X; Th. History-2/Y; Dramatic Crit.-2/Y; Dramatic Lit-4/X; Shakes-2/X; Playwriting-4/Y

B. (5 FT, 6 PT) Acting-4/Y; Movemt-1/Y; Mime/Mask-1/Y; Direct'g-4/Y; Voice/Speech-4/Y; Stage Combat-1/Y; Mime, etc.-1/Y

C. (2 PT) Prins of Des.-1/Y; Set Design-1/X; Lighting Des.-1/X

D. (8 PT) Box Ofc. Procedure-1/Y; Mktg/Promo-2/Y; Devel/ Grant Writing-2/Y; Contracts/Copyrights-2/Y; Budgeting/ Accounting-1/Y

FACILITIES & PRODUCTIONS

MAINSTAGE: 99 seats, computerized & electronic lighting. 7 prods: 1 Fac dir, 6 Grad dir; budget $1,000-1,500

SECOND STAGE: 99 seats, computerized lighting. 10 prods: 3 Fac dir, 7 Grad dir.

Workshops/Readings: budget $25-100

Facility built in the 1800's, renovated 1998; includes scene shop, costume shop, prop shop, 1 rehearsal studio, 1 classroom.

DESCRIPTION

Noted Faculty: Andrei Serban, Anne Bogart, Robert Woodruff, Directing; Arnold Aronson, History; James Leverett, Dramaturgy; Victoria Bailey, Barry Groves, Gerald Schoenfeld, Management; Kristin Linklater, Acting; Eduardo Machado, Playwright

Guest Artists: Linda Winer, Elinor Fuchs, Robin Wagner, Tina Landau, Arby Ovanessian, Vjacheslav Dolgatchev.

The Oscar Hammerstein II Center for Theatre Studies, named for the renowned alumnus, playwright, and lyricist, and under the directorship of Andrei Serban, coordinates degree programs in theatre arts and all aspects of theatre production at Columbia University through the School of the Arts. The Hammerstein Center is a unique operation, dedicated to preparing artists for the theatre profession, as well as training students in all aspects of theatre art and research.

Cornell University

Kent Goetz, Chair
Dept. of Theatre, Film & Dance
430 College Ave.
Cornell University
Ithaca, NY 14850
www.arts.cornell.edu/theatrearts
theatre@cornell.edu
Admissions: 349 Pine Tree Road Ithaca, NY 14853

13,562 Tot. Enr.
Semester System
70 Majors
T: $34,781/$11,190 r&b
(607) 254-2700
FAX: (607) 254-2733
admissions@cornell.edu

DEGREES OFFERED

BA in Theatre, Film and Dance. Declare major in sophomore year; 2001 granted 33 UG degrees.

ADMISSION & FINANCIAL INFORMATION

SAT 1150 or higher - top 5% of class, 10% of applicants admitted to institution. Theatre program has no special requirements.

FACULTY AND CLASSES OFFERED

32 Full-Time: 8 PhD, 14 MFA/MA, 10 prof. w/o adv. degree

A. (5 FT) Intro to Theatre-2/Y; Dramatic Lit-6-8/Y; Theatre History-8/Y; Shakes-2/Y; Dramatic Criticism-3/Y; Playwtg-2/Y

B. (5 FT) Acting-6/Y; Voice/Speech-1/Y; MusicTh-1/Y; Direct-2/Y

C. (10 FT) Prins of Des-2/Y; Cost Des-2/Y; Tech Production-2/Y; Cost Hist-2/Y; Set Design-2/Y; Ltg Des-2/Y; Cost Construction-2/Y; Make-up-1/Y; Stg Mgmt-2/Y

D. (2 FT) no courses listed

FACILITIES & PRODUCTIONS

MAINSTAGE: 476 seats, fly space, computerized lighting. 6 prods: 5 Fac dir, 6 Fac des, 1 Guest dir/des, 1 UG des; budget $4-18,000

SECOND STAGE: 170 seats, computerized lighting. 4 prods: 4 UG dir/des; budget $200-1,000. 4 Workshops/Readings: 1 Fac dir, 2 Guest dir, 1 Grad dir; budget $1,000-6,000.

Facility built in 1989, includes scene shop, costume shop, prop shop, welding shop, 4 video studios, 4 rehearsal studios, 3 movement/dance studios, design studio, 4 classrooms.

2 student-written plays produced in the last two yrs. 6 professional actors perform in production alongside students; all roles open cast.

DESCRIPTION

Noted Faculty: David Feldshuh, dir/ perf; Marilyn Rivchin, film prod;
    J. Ellen Gainor, th hist; David Bathrick, theatre history; Joyce Morgenroth, dance.
Guest Artists: Norman Ayrton, director; Paul Wonseck, design; Gabrielle Barre, acting, film & dance; Albert Reid, choreography; David Gordon, Pick-Up Company, dance; Penny Metropol, director; Limon Dance Co.; Prof. Kenny Bowman, teacher dance/theatre; Meridith Monk, dance series; Dance Alloy, dance series; Kim Hines, director.

The Department of Theatre Arts is a University-wide department. Students from all areas of the campus enroll in its classes, perform on its stages, and attend its productions. The department's broad appeal is in part due to the fact that the performing arts are an outlet for self expression and an avenue to one's own creativity. At the center for Theatre Arts, any student can explore his or her own relationship to performance through the study of history, criticism, literature, acting, directing, design, improvisation, choreography, filmmaking, theatre technology, playwriting, and dance technique. The department offers some eighty courses each semester and a season of 4-6 plays, three student-faculty dance concerts, and 2-3 visiting dance companies each year. Additional performance opportunities include the Student Laboratory Theatre Company, dance classroom concerts, play readings, Black Box Series and the Cornell Theatre Outreach program.

Fordham University

Matthew Maguire, Chair
Fordham Univ. Theatre Program
Lincoln Center Campus
113 W. 60th St. Room 423
New York, NY 10023
www.fordham.edu/theatre
ADMISSIONS: 113 W. 60th St., NY, NY 10023
(212) 636-6710
enroll@fordham.edu

7,701 Total Enr.; h. compet.
Semester System
150 Majors
T: $32,354/$12,300 R&B
DEPT: (212) 636-6303
FAX: (212) 636-7003

FAX: (212) 636-7002

DEGREES OFFERED

BA in Theatre (150). Four pre-professional tracks: Performance Track (52 credits); Production/Design (52 credits); Playwriting (52 credits); Directing (52 credits). There is also a Theatre minor (32 credits). Declare major in soph. yr.

ADMISSION & FINANCIAL INFORMATION

GPA, SATs. Th. Dept. admits 10% of applicants. Audition/ Interview. Top theatre candidates receive special financial aid consideration. Other scholarships are academically based.

FACULTY AND CLASSES OFFERED

8 Full-Time, 14 Part-Time: 16 MFA/MA, 6 Prof. w/o adv. degree

A. (1 1/3 FT, 3 PT) Intro to Theatre-1/Y; Theatre History-5/Y; Shakes-2/Y; Playwriting-4/Y; Asian Theatre-1/O; Theatre and Social Action-1/O; Irish Theatre-1/O; Multicultural Th-1/O; Theatre & Visual Arts-1/O

B. (3 1/2 FT, 9 PT) Acting-6/Y; Voice/Speech-3/Y; Movement-3/Y; Mime/Mask, etc.-1/O; Musical Theatre-2/Y; Directing-4/Y; Occasional stage combat, mask, etc. workshops done by guest artists

C. (3 FT, 2 PT) Prins of Des-1/Y; Set Des-1/Y; Cost Des-2/Y; Ltg Des-1/Y; Tech Prod-1/Y; Cost Constr-1/Y; Cost Hist-1/O; Make-up-1/O; Stg Mgmt-1/O

D. (1/2 FT) Arts Mgmt-1/O; Mktng/Promo-1/X; Legal: Contracts, etc-1/X; Devel/Grant Writing-1/X; Budget/Accounting-1/X

FACILITIES & PRODUCTIONS

MAINSTAGE: 200 seats, computerized lighting. 4 prods: 2 Fac dir, 4 Fac des, 2 Guest dir, 4 Guest des; bdgt $10-15,000

SECOND STAGE: Black Box, 75 seats, computerized lighting. 15 prods: 5 Guest dir, 10 UG dir; budget $100-500.

THIRD STAGE: White Box stuido theatre, flex seats, electronic ltg.

10 Workshops/Readings: 5 Guest dir, 5 UG dir; budget $0-100

Facility was built in 1968, renovated in 1999; includes scene shop, costume shop, props shop, dance studio, rehearsal studio, design studio, classrooms.

A non-departmental, student-run producing org. presents 2 productions per year in which dept. majors participate. 16 student-written plays produced by the dept. in the last 2 years.

Students have the opportunity to audition for the Fordham Summer Theatre Institute in Orvieto, Italy. Participants study the actor's work with physical actions with international master teachers.

DESCRIPTION

Noted Faculty: Lawrence Sacharow, Director of Theatre Program, directed Edward Albee's Pulitzer Prize-winning play Three Tall Women; Marian Seldes, Acting; Steven Skybell, Acting/Shakespeare; Matthew Maguire, Acting & Playwriting; Eva Patton, Acting; Elizabeth Margid, Directing; Morgan Jenness, Theatre History; Chad McCarver, Lighting Design; Michael Massee, Set & Cost. Design; Diane Carter, Technical Theatre; Tim Zay, Tech Theatre.

Professionals (past 2 years): Fiona Shaw, Actor; Edward Albee, Playwright; Betty Buckley, Acting; Karin Coonrod, Director; Olympia Dukakis, Actor; John Guare, Playwright; Tony Kushner, Playwright; Lloyd Richards, Playwright; Ellen Stewart, Founder, La MaMa, ETC; Rosemarie Tichler, Producing Director, The Public Theatre/NYSF, among many others.

The Fordham University Theatre Program at New York City's Lincoln Center Campus has become one of the most outstanding Liberal Arts theatre training programs in the country. What makes Fordham unique is the opportunity to receive first rate pre-professional training in addition to a B.A. degree. Students study with some of the most outstanding theatre professionals in the business on a campus located in the heart of New York City, just blocks away from the Broadway and Off-Broadway theatre districts. Entrance into the performance track is by audition only. Entrance into the production/design, playwriting, and directing tracks are by interview only. Study abroad programs available as well as many opportunities to intern with leading New York theatre, film and television venues. Senior showcase for agents and casting directors. Each student's growth and progress is carefully monitored by an alert and nurturing faculty. Website: www.fordham.edu/theatre.

Genesee Community College

Director	3,400 Total Enr.; n. compet
Fine & Performing Arts	25 Majors; ATHE, ACTF
One College Road	Semester System
Genesee Community College	T: $$7,515
Batavia, NY14020-9704	O-ST T: $$12,995
DEPT: (716) 345-6802	SMALL PROGRAM
mkmorrison@genesee.edu	FAX: (716) 345-6815
ADM: 1 College Road, Batavia, NY 14020	
(716) 345-6800	www.genesee.suny.edu

DEGREES OFFERED

AA in Theatre Arts (25), Certificate in Musical Theatre. Declare major in freshman year.

ADMISSION & FINANCIAL INFORMATION

H.S. degree or GED, ACT scores (mean 18-19), 95% admitted to university. Theatre program admits all applicants. Special Talent Award in Performing Arts - top 20% of graduating class; Batavia Players Scholarship - to outstanding freshman. Robert W. Hunter Performing Arts Scholarship-top 20% of graduating class.

FACULTY AND CLASSES OFFERED

2 Full-Time, 4 Part-Time: 6 MFA/MA; 3 Staff

A. (1/2 FT) Intro to Theatre-2/Y; Dramatic Lit-1/Y; Th Hist-2/Y
B. (1/2 FT, 2 PT) Acting-2/Y; Voice/Speech-1/Y; Movement-2/Y; Musical Th.-1/Y; Children's Theatre-1/Y
C. (1 FT) Prins of Design-1/Y; Costume Des-1/Y; Tech Prod'n-2/Y; Lighting Des-1/O; Make-up-1/O

FACILITIES & PRODUCTIONS

MAINSTAGE: 328 seats, fly space, computerized lighting. 4 prods: 3 Fac dir/des, 1 UG dir/des.; budget $1,000-5,000

SECOND STAGE: 1 UG dir/des; budget $500

Facility was built in 1991, includes scene shop, costume shop, welding shop, CAD facil, movement/dance studio, rehearsal studio, classrooms, dressing rooms, computerized box office.

A departmental, student-run organization co-sponsors 3 productions per year in which majors participate.

Students with appropriate experience can direct on the mainstage. The student producing group has the opportunity to produce in alternate spaces.

DESCRIPTION

Noted Faculty: Marcia K. Morrison, Performance Studies, served on national and regional boards for ATHE and ACTF, and on International Advisory Board to 4th International Women Playwrights Conference; Ann Reid, Musical Theatre, member of SAG, Equity, ASCAP and Dramatist Guild.

Guest Artists: Independent Eye- Improvisation Techniques; Steve Vaughan, Stage Combat; Kathleen Baum, Meyerhold Movement Techniques; National Circus Project.

Why come to GCC? There are a number of reasons. First, it's extremely affordable. There are also tuition scholarships available, such as the Special Talent Award Program and the Batavia Players Award for Excellence in Theatre Arts, for qualified high school seniors. Secondly, we are an award-winning program with a new theatre facility equipped with state-of-the-art lighting and sound equipment. Thirdly, because we're a SMALL PROGRAM, you'll be an important part of the decision-making team for each of our four yearly productions and have lots of opportunities to practice and refine your acting skills. Finally, you'll be exposed to a number of visiting guest professionals and be encouraged to intern at professional theatre companies in nearby Rochester and Buffalo.

Hofstra University

Jean Dobie Giebel, Prof of Drama	8,000 Total Enr.; compet.
Dept. of Drama & Dance	Semester System
118 Hofstra University	200 Majors; ATHE
Hempstead, NY 11549-1180	T: $26,600/$9,000 R&B
DEPT: (516) 463-5444	FAX: (516) 463-4001
ADM: Admissions Center, above	(516) 463-6700
www.hofstra.edu	hofstra@hofstra.edu

DEGREES OFFERED

BA in Drama; Dance; BFA in Performance, Production
Declare major in freshman year; 2006 granted 40 degrees.

ADMISSION & FINANCIAL INFORMATION

Req's: B avg,1000+ comb. SAT's. BA prog. can be elected by students, BFA programs selective based on 2 semester's GPA plus aud/int. Presidential Schol; Activity Grant for Theatre: Awarded on basis of audition/interview to freshmen, renewable on basis of leadership and activity in dept.

FACULTY AND CLASSES OFFERED

11 FT, 5 PT, 2 PhD, 1 DFA, 8 MFA, 2 Staff

A. (1 1/2 FT, 1 PT) Intro to Th.-2/sem.; Th. History-1/Y; Shakes-2/XY; Dram. Lit-2/Y; Play Analysis-1/Y; Styles-2/Y

B. (3 1/2 FT, 3 PT) Acting-8/Y; Voice/Speech-4/Y; Movement- 4/Y; Singing-XY; Directing-2/Y

C. (3 FT, 1 PT) Prins of Des-1/Y; Set Design-1/O; Scenic Painting-1/O;Sound-1/O; Props-1/O; Cost Des- 1/O; Ltg Des-2/Y: Tech Prod'n-4/O; Cost Constr- 1/O; Cost Hist-1/O; Make-up-1/Y; Stage Mgmt-1/O

FACILITIES AND PRODUCTIONS

MAINSTAGE: 1,134 seats, fly space, hydraulic pit, lighting/sound/rigging
2 Fac dir/des prods; budget $8,000-20,000

SECOND STAGE: 200 seats, 2-story black box, lighting/sound
3 Fac dir/des prods; budget $2,000-6,000

THIRD STAGE: 99 seats, lighting/sound. Occasional workshops/ readings: Fac and UG dir/des; budget $50-200

Mainstage built in 1958, renovated in 2003; new Black Box opened 2006; renovated teaching facilities 2007 includes 2 scene shops, craft room, costume shop, sound studio, light lab, 3 dance studios, 2 movement studios, 2 des studios, 5 classrooms.

2 student-run organizations present 4 productions per year in which majors participate.

Internship with Equity theatres Ensemble Studio Theatre (Lit. Mgmt, A.D.)and Signature Theatre (Production Assistant).

DESCRIPTION

Noted Faculty: Acting/Dir: Peter Sander, Jean Dobie Giebel, James Kolb, Royston Coppenger, Cindy Rosenthal; Voice/Movement: Ilona Pierce, Robert Westley; Design: David Henderson, Rych Curtiss.

Guest Artists: Directors: Gus Kaikkonen, Charles Repole, Edward Cornell, Clay Fullum, Ken Mitchell; Actors: Lainie Kazan, Robert Stattel, Ben Hammer, Kenneth Marks.

The goals of the Hofstra University Drama Department are to provide students with a thorough background in theatre within a strong liberal arts context. This includes practical training and experience; professionally oriented craft classes in performance and/or production, and a broad range of performance opportunities in a spectrum of plays including an annual Shakespeare production.

Hunter College

Jonathan Kalb
Department of Theatre
Hunter College
695 Park Avenue
New York, NY 10021
DEPT: (212) 772-5148 /9
jkalb@hunter.cuny.edu
ADMISSIONS: 695 Park Ave., NY, NY 10021   (212) 772-4486
admissions@hunter.cuny.edu

15,805 Total Enr.; compet.
Semester System
150 Majors; ATHE
T: $4,349/$3,250 r&b
O-ST T: $8,989/$3,250 r&b
FAX: (212) 650-3584

DEGREES OFFERED

BA in Theatre (150); MA in Theatre (50). Declare major in Soph. year; 2001 granted 30 UG, 9 Grad degs.

ADMISSION & FINANCIAL INFORMATION

75% of applics admitted to institution. Theatre Program admits 100% of all UG applicants, 8 out of 10 Grad applicants; Roberts Graduate Fellowship, incoming student, GRE & grades; Teaching Assistantships; Playwriting Awards.

FACULTY AND CLASSES OFFERED

9 Full-Time, 14 Part-Time + 4 Teaching Assistants: 7 PhD, 9 MA/MFA, 2 Prof. w/o adv. deg; 2 Staff

A. (5 FT, 5 PT) Intro to Theatre-28/Y; Dramatic Lit-2/Y; Theatre History-6/Y; Dramatic Criticism-2/Y; Playwriting-4/Y

B. (3 FT, 5 PT) Acting-2/Y; Voice/Speech-1/Y; Movement-2/Y; Mime/Mask, etc.-1/Y; Musical Th.-1/O; Directing-5/Y

C. (2 FT, 3 PT) Prins of Des-4/Y; Set Des-1/O; Cost. Des-1/O; Ltg Des-1/O; Tech Prod-1/O; Make-up-1/O; StgMgmt-1/O

D. (1 PT) Arts Management-1/O

FACILITIES & PRODUCTIONS

MAINSTAGE: 110 seats, computerized lighting
4 Fac dir prods; budget $5,000-9,000

SECOND STAGE: 650 seats, fly space, computerized lighting
1 prod.: 1 Fac dir, 1 Grad dir, 2 UG dir; budget $11,000. Workshops/Readings: 2 Fac dir; budget $300-500

Facility was built in 1890's, renovated in 1998; includes scene shop, costume shop, rehearsal studio.

A non-departmental, student-run, org. presents 4 prods/yr in which majors participate. 10 student-written plays produced in the last 2 yrs.

DESCRIPTION

Noted Faculty: Arthur Kopit, Tina Howe, Playwriting; Eric Bentley; Stanley Kauffmann, Dramatic Literature.

Guest Artists: Ruby Dee.

The Department of Theatre studies stage production, the history and theory of theatre and drama, the relationship between text and performance, and commonalities and divergences between theatre and film. Theatre courses include acting, playwriting, directing, history, theory, design, production, children's theatre, and creative drama. The curriculum was developed with an emphasis on professional standards within a liberal arts context. The theatre major requires courses in practical hands-on work, as well as study of theoretical, critical, and historical approaches to theatre, interdisciplinary courses include acting, lighting and design for theatre, film and television, adaptation for theatre and film, and comparative aesthetics. Students pursuing a major in theatre must work on theatre productions as part of their requirements for graduation. Advanced undergraduate playwrights may have their work produced by Hunter Playwrights. Many students who graduate from the theatre program work as actors, directors, stage managers and designers. Some of our students continue their creative study in conservatory or MFA programs. Others continue their education in history and theory as MA or PhD students. Graduates who concentrate in developmental drama frequently enter the field as teachers and directors of theatre in education. The department maintains associations with major theatre institutions. Students have opportunities for placements as interns and apprentices with various professional group.

Ithaca College

Lee Byron,
  Chair & Dir. of Theatre
Department of Theatre Arts
Ithaca College
201 Dillingham Center
Ithaca, NY 14850-7293
theatrearts@ithaca.edu
ADMISSIONS: 100 Job Hall, Ithaca College, Ithaca, NY 14850
(607) 274-3124   FAX: (607) 274-1900
www.ithaca.edu/admissions

6,000 Total Enr.; compet
Semester System
280 Majors; NAST
T: $28,670/$10,728 R&B
DEPT: (607) 274-3345
FAX: (607) 274-3672
www.ithaca.edu/theatre

DEGREES OFFERED

BA in Drama (102); BS in Theatre Arts Management (37); BFA in Acting (54), Theatrical Production Arts (54), Musical Theatre (40). Declare major in 1st year; 2006 granted 65 degrees.

ADMISSION & FINANCIAL INFORMATION

Based on HS record, personal recommendations. 56% accepted to inst; Audition for actors admission to Theatre Program, interview/portfolia for designers & tech. Interview for BA Drama and BS Theatre Arts Mgmt. Accepts 150 out of 1200 applicants. Ithaca Premier Talent Scholarship, $16,000 maximum, eligibility based on talent. Additional scholarships available in 2nd, 3rd and 4th yr. based on application.

FACULTY AND CLASSES OFFERED

18 Full-Time, 6 Part-Time: 3 PhD/DFA, 18 MFA/MA, 3 Prof. w/o adv. degree; 5 Teaching Staff.

A. (2 FT) Intro to Theatre-1/Y; Th. Hist.-2/Y; Shakes-1/YX; Dramatic Lit-2/YX; Dramatic Criticism-4/Y; Playwriting-1/O; Dance His-1/O; Intro to Dance-1/Y.

B. (9 FT, 4 PT) Acting-7/Y; Voice-5/Y; Mvmt-2/Y; Singing-4/YX; Dir-2/Y; Dance-20/Y; Dialects-1/Y; Dance Comp-1/O; Acting General-4/Y; Mime, etc.-1/O; Musical Th-2/Y; Styles of Acting-2/Y.

C. (6 FT, 3 PT) Prins of Des-1/Y; Set Des-4/Y; Ltg. Des-4/Y; Tech Prod'n-5/Y; Cost Des-4/Y; Cost. Hist-2/Y; Stage Mgmt.-1/O; Cost. Constr-2/Y; Make-up-1/Y; CAD-1/Y; Sound Des-4/Y; Theatre Prod-2/Y; Drafting-1/Y; Stage Craft-1/Y; Hist of Cost Decor-2/Y

D. (1 FT, 1 PT) Arts Mgmt-1/Y; Marketing/Promo-1/Y; Budget/Acctng-2/O; Th Arts Mgmt.-2/Y.

FACILITIES AND PRODUCTIONS

MAINSTAGE: 525 seats, fly space, computerized lighting. 6 prods: 6 Fac dir, 7 Fac des, 16 UG des prods; budget $6,000-25,000

SECOND STAGE: 270 seats, computerized lighting.

THIRD STAGE: 60 seats, black box, computerized. lighting

8 UG dir, 8 UG des Workshops./Readings, budget: $100-250.

Facility built in 1967, last renovated in 1990; includes scene, cost shops, CAD facility, sound studio, 2 dance studios, 2 design studio, lighting lab/studio.

A non-departmental student-run organization presents prods in which dept majors participate. 12 student-written plays produced in the last two years.

There is no formal connection with a professional company however, many students have opportunity to work with the summer Hangar Theatre and the year-round Kitchen Theatre.

DESCRIPTION

Noted Faculty: Our resident and adjunct faculty are all active theatre professionals.

Guest Artists: Joe Calarco, dir.; Terrence Mann, dir/actor; Christopher D'Amboise, choreographer; Phil Reno, mus. dir.; Jason Robert Brown, composer; Paul Gallo, light des; Tony Meola, sound des; Mark Price, actor; Catherine Fitzmaurice, voice/text specialist; Frank Wood, actor.

The Department of Theatre Arts at Ithaca College offers a powerful combination of intensive classroom and performance experiences that has made it one of the most effective and highly respected training programs in the nation. The department's goal is to prepare its students for careers in the theatre and entertainment industry. This is a highly selective program, staffed by a faculty whose unique combination of academic and professional theatre experience enables them to provide for the focused, personalized instruction that is the key to successful theatrical training.

The Juilliard School

James Houghton,
Richard Rogers Dir of Drama Division
The Juilliard School
60 Lincoln Ctr. Plaza
New York, NY 10023-6588
DEPT.: (212) 799-5000 x 251
ADMISSIONS: Above address.
www.juilliard.edu

Highly competitive
Semester System
483 tot. / 84 Division Majors
T: $27,150
R&B $10,740l
FAX: (212) 875-8437
(212) 799-5000 x 223
admissions@juilliard.edu

DEGREES OFFERED

BFA in Acting; Also four-year diploma course in Acting. Also graduate-level, non-degree programs in Playwriting (1 yr. fellowship) and Directing (3 year fellowship).

ADMISSION & FINANCIAL INFORMATION

2-3% accepted by institution. Requirements for acting program: HS diploma or equivalent; college grads encouraged to apply; Admission is based primarily on in-person audition; admitting 18 out of 1,000 applicants. 2 candidates are selected for the Directing Program based on application/interview; up to 4 candidates are selected for Playwriting Program based on application/ interview. Scholarships are widely available based primarily on financial need.

FACULTY AND CLASSES OFFERED

30 FT, 6 PT: 4 PhD, 6 MFA/MA, 12 Prof. w/o adv. degree; 5 Staff

Comprehensive actor training program; complete catalogue available on request.

FACILITIES & PRODUCTIONS

MAINSTAGE: 206 seats; 5 prods + rep, professionally dir/des

SECOND STAGE: 70 seats

5 professionally directed productions for students in their third and fourth year of training.

Facility built in 1968; includes scene shop, costume shop, props shop, sound studio, dance studio, rehearsal studio, classrooms.

There are informal connections with The Acting Company (which grew out of the Juilliard Program), and the Shakespeare Theatre in Washington D.C.,(whose Artistic Dir. is the Dir. of Drama at Juilliard).

DESCRIPTION

Noted Faculty: Michael Kahn, Acting; Andrei Beigrader, dir. of Directing Program; Christopher Durang & Marsha Norman, co-dirs of Playwriting Program; Ralph Zito, Voice & Speech; Moni Yakim, Movement; Richard Feldman, Acting; Robert Williams, Voice & Speech.

Guest Artists: Earle Gister; Mercedes Reuhl; LisaGay Hamilton; Edie Falco; Brenda Blethyn; Laura Linney; Patrick Stewart; Val Kilmer; Kevin Kline; Judi Dench; Kevin Spacey; Sir Ian McKellan; Fiona Shaw.

In four years, students acquire the skills they need for both classical and contemporary acting styles. The training that they receive emphasizes intuition and spontaneity as well as discipline and intellectual development. Imagination and empathy are part of it. So are the careful study of voice and movement. All the courses are related to each other; none is optional. The Drama Division has become one of the most respected training programs for actors in the English-speaking world. Founded by John Houseman, it follows guidelines established by the renowned teacher-director Michel Saint-Denis. Actors trained at Juilliard are well prepared to join established repertory companies, many of which recruit new members at the school. In 1993 the Drama Division inaugurated its Playwriting Program, currently led by Christopher Durang and Marsha Norman. The Directing Program under the leadership of Andrei Belgrader began in 1995

London Dramatic Academy

Fordham University, NY (see listing page 293)

Long Island University - C. W. Post Campus

Dr. Cara Gargano, Chair
Department of Theatre & Film
L. I. U./C.W. Post Campus
Brookville, NY 11548
DEPT: (516) 299-2353
cgargano@liu.edu
ADM: 720 Northern Blvd. LIU/CW Post Campus, Brookville NY 11548
(516) 299-2900
800-LIU-PLAN

11,000 Total Enr.; compet.
Semester System
75 Majors, ATHE
T: $11,685 UG/$478 cred. G
$4,170 room/$2,290 board
FAX: (516) 299-3824
enroll@cwpost.liu.edu

DEGREES OFFERED

BA in Theatre (18); BFA in Acting (40), Production & Design (10); Arts Mgmt/Theatre (5); MA in Theatre (7) Declare major in 1st year; 2007 granted 10 UG, 3 Grad degrees

ADMISSION & FINANCIAL INFORMATION

UG requires audition/interview, 1000 SAT, 80 avg; Admits 26 of 150 UG applicants; Grad requires aud./interview - portfolio for designers; Admits 6 of 30 applics. Theatre scholarships through audition/application AFTER acceptance to the program.

FACULTY AND CLASSES OFFERED

5 Full-Time, 12 Part-Time: 2 PhD, 10 MFA/MA; 5 Staff

A.　(1 FT,1 PT) Intro to Th-2/Y; Th Hist-3/Y; Shakes-1/Y; Dramatic Lit-1/Y; Dramatic Criticism-1/Y; Playwriting-2/Y

B.　(2 FT, 5 PT) Acting-8/Y; Voice/Speech-3/Y; Movement- 2/Y; Singing-3/X; Musical Theatre- 2/Y; Directing-2/Y; Stage Combat-1/O; Dance-5/Y

C.　(1 FT, 4 PT) Prin. of Design-1/Y; Set Design-2/Y; Cost. Design-2/Y; Ltg Design-2/Y; Tech Prod-1/Y; Cost. Constr.- 2/Y; Make-up-1/Y; Stage Mgmt-1/Y

D.　(1 FT, 2 PT) Arts Mgmt-2/Y; Box Office-1/Y; Marketing/Promotion-1/Y; Contracts/Copyright-1/Y; Budgeting/Accounting-1/Y; Development/Grant Writing-1/Y

FACILITIES AND PRODUCTIONS

MAINSTAGE: 120-140 seats 5 prods: 2 Fac dir, 3 GA dir, 8 GA des.3 Grad des, 1 UG des; budget $8,000-15,000

SECOND STAGE: 50-90 seats
3 prods: 3 Grad dir, 3 UG des; budget $200-400

Workshop/readings: 2 prods: 2 Fac dir; budget $100

Facility built in 1962, includes scene shop, costume shop, prop shop, CAD facility, 1 Video studio,1 movement/dance studio, 1 design studio, 1 rehearsal studio, 5 classrooms.

A non-departmental, student-run organization presents 2 productions per year in which majors participate.1 Student written play produced in last 2 years.

DESCRIPTION

Noted Faculty: Maria Porter; Acting, Suzuki; Rick DesRochers, Theatre History, Dramaturgy

Guest Artists: Victor Maog, Director; Niklas Anderson, Designer; Dyana Kimball, Director.

30 miles from Manhattan. The BFA is a pre-professional, process-based and performance oriented program operating within a liberal arts college. Intensive training and significant performance opportunities in area of concentration. All degree programs are coordinated with the Post Theatre Company, which is committed to challenging theatre and international experience.

Marymount Manhattan College
See ad above

Mary Fleischer, Chair
Theatre Arts Department
Marymount Manhattan College
221 East 71 St.
New York, NY 10021
David Mold, Dir. of Th. Admissions
theatre@mmm.edu
ADM: Above address
(212) 774-0767
marymount.mmm.edu

1,800 Total Enr.; competitive
430 Majors; ATHE
Semester System
T: $19,638/$12,090 r&b
FAX: (212) 774-0770
DEPT: (212) 774-0760

1-800-MARYMOUNT or
FAX: (212) 517-0448
admissions@mmm.edu

DEGREES OFFERED

BFA in Acting (120), BA Theatre Arts (320): concentrations in Theatre Performance (215), Design & Production (26), Writing for the Stage (17), Th. Studies (15), Directing (32); Producing & Management (30). Students declare major in 1st yr. 2006 granted 92 degrees.

ADMISSION & FINANCIAL INFORMATION

1140 SAT, "B +" avg., other factors considered. 65% accepted. Auds, int. for actors; int. & portfolio for design, directing, playwriting. Th. program admits 1 out of 3. Competitive Merit Schols ($500-4,000/yr.) awarded in Acting & Th. Arts each year to graduation provided student maintains req. GPA. Scholarships awarded based on audition or portfolio and interview and academic achievement.

FACULTY AND CLASSES OFFERED

15 FT, 65 PT: 10 PhD, 59 MFA/MA, 12 w/o adv. degree; 2 Staff
A.   (4 FT, 17 PT) Intro to Theatre-1/Y; Dramatic Lit.-7/Y; Dramatic Crit-

1/O; Theatre History-2/Y; Shakes-1/Y; Playwriting-6/Y; Other-3/Y

B.   (8 FT, 34 PT) Acting-14/Y; Voice/Speech-4/Y; Mvmt-2/Y; Mus Th-7/Y; Directing-3/Y; Mime, etc-2/O; Singing-2/Y; Stg Combat-1/O; Dance-3/Y; Film-4/X

C.   (3 FT, 11 PT) Principles of Des.-1/Y; Cost Des-4/Y; Set Design-5/Y; Ltg Des-5/Y; Stg Mgmt-2/Y; Costume Constr-1/O; Make-up-1/O; Design for Directing & Choreog.-1/O; Stagecraft-6/Y

D.   (3 PT) Arts Mgmt-3/Y; Teaching Methods for Theatre-1/O.

FACILITIES & PRODUCTIONS

MAINSTAGE: 249 seats, fly space, computerized lighting. 4 prods: 4 Fac dir, 3 Fac des, 3 Guest des, 5 UG des; budget $8,000-11,000

THIRD STAGE: 60 seats, black box; 27 UG dir, 20 UG des prods

Facility was built in 1975, renovated in 1998; includes scene shop, costume shop, sound studio, video studio, movement studio, rehearsal studio, classrooms. Off Campus: Students perform and take selected classes off campus.

Non-depart., student-run organizations present 6-10 productions per year in which approx. 20% of majors participate.

Approx. 20 student written plays presented in the last 2 yrs.

DESCRIPTION

The Theatre Arts programs at Marymount Manhattan College provide professional training combined with a strong liberal arts education in an independent college setting on Manhattan's Upper East Side. The BA in Theatre and BFA in Acting programs offer men and women individualized attention and a strong faculty advisement program. Studio classes are limited to 12 students; qualified students may take on substantial projects and roles beginning in the first year. Internships are offered in a variety of settings (B'way, Off and Off-off B'way, dance, film, video) and develop experience and a potential employment network in the NYC performing arts community. Students are encouraged to pursue a minor from a wide variety of fields including arts management, musical theatre and from liberal arts departments such as literature, international studies, or psychology; double majors are also possible combined with the BA in Theatre.

Nazareth College

Dr. David M. Ferrell, Chairman
Theatre Arts Dept.
Nazareth College
4245 East Ave.
Rochester, NY 14618-3790
DEPT: (585) 389-2785
admissions@naz.edu

2,148 Total Enr.; competitive
Semester System;, USITT
36 Majors; ATHE, ECTC
T: $22,834/9,402 r&b
SMALL PROGRAM
MAIN: (585) 389-2525

DEGREES OFFERED

BA in Theatre Arts, may concentrate in Acting and Tech Theatre but do not receive a special degree. Declare major junior year.

ADMISSION & FINANCIAL INFORMATION

GPA, B avg. preferred, SAT & ACT above avg. preferred. 70% accepted, audition, interview, portfolio for designers, theatre program admits 10-12 out of 15 applicants. Theatre scholarships, through auditions and interviews (incl. portfolios) College merit scholarships based on above average GPA and test scores on a competitive basis.

FACULTY AND CLASSES OFFERED

4 Full-Time: 1 PhD, 3 MFA/MA; 1 Staff with MFA

A. (1 FT, 1 PT) Intro to Theatre-2/Y; Dramatic Lit-1/Y; Th Hist-3/O; Shakes-2/X; Playwriting-1/O; Amer. Musical Th-1/O; Film-1/O

B. (1 FT) Acting-3/O; Voice/Speech-2/O; Movement-2/O; Musical Theatre-1/O; Singing-1/X; Directing-1/O

C. (1 FT, 1 PT) Cost Des-1/O; Tech Prod'n-2/O; Cost Hist-1/O; Set Design-1/O; Ltg Des-1/O; Cost Constr-1/O; Make-up-1/O; Stg Mgmt-1/O; Styles-1/O

FACILITIES & PRODUCTIONS

MAINSTAGE: 1153 seats, computerized lighting. 4 prods: 2 Fac dir/des, 1 UG des; budget $4,000-7,000

SECOND STAGE: 100 seats, computerized lighting. 4 prods: 1 Fac dir/des, 1 Guest dir/des; budget $1,800-2,500

5 UG dir/des Workshops/Readings

Facility was built in 1967; includes scene shop, costume shop, 2 rehearsal studios, design studio, 2 classrooms.

A non-dept, non-producing student-run organization works with Theatre Dept. shows. Majors generally participate.

Some paid work for students with a touring performing arts center, presenting such groups as Mummenshanz, Lynn Redgrave, Emmy Gifford Theatre, etc.: 12 groups total.

DESCRIPTION

Noted Faculty: Dr. David M. Ferrell, theatre hist, directing; Ken Canfield, design/tech; Linday Reading

Korth, acting, directing; Yuanting Zhao, costuming.
Guest Artists: Maria Sanguedolce, dir; Crystl Balazar, musical director; Meggins Kelley choreog.

The Theatre Department of Nazareth College is firmly rooted in a Liberal Arts tradition and espouses the philosophy that training in the theatre is as valuable a preparation for life and for a variety of alternate careers as any liberal art. The program introduces students to all phases of theatre arts, both on stage and backstage, providing a balanced background in theatre history, analysis and directing, along with studio courses in acting, stagecraft and design. Simultaneously, the department provides serious preparation for further study and work towards a theatre career. Therefore, the objective is a broad but thorough preparation in the important academic and production areas of theatre arts integrated within a liberal arts setting where various modes of critical thinking, problem solving and written analysis are employed. The study of theatre exists and thrives appropriately within this context while enriching the cultural life of the campus with a diverse array of theatrical productions.

Neighborhood Playhouse
School of Theatre

Harold G. Baldridge, Exec. Dir.
Neighborhood Playhouse .
  School of Theatre
340 E. 54th St.
New York, NY 10022
www.neighborhoodplayhouse.org
Admis: as above

110 Total Enr.; h. competitive
Semester Sys., NAST
T: $12,900
(212) 688-3770
FAX: (212) 906-9051
hgb340@aol.com

DEGREES OFFERED

2 yr certificate program in Dramatic Arts. No degree offered (95); Six-week summer session certificate program (50).

ADMISSION & FINANCIAL INFORMATION

HS grad., interview req., three letters of reference, photo. Must be 18 yrs. old. Limited scholarships to 2nd year returnees. 35 % of applicants accepted.

FACULTY AND CLASSES OFFERED

2 FT, 15 PT, 1 Ph.D., 4 MFA/MA, 10 Prof. w/o adv. deg.

A. (1 FT) Th. Hist.-2/Y; Shakes-1/Y

B. (1 FT, 15 PT) Acting-2/Y; Voice/Speech-2/Y; Movement-3/Y; Singing-1/Y; Stage Combat-1/Y; Musical Theatre-1/Y

FACILITIES & PRODUCTIONS

MAINSTAGE: 100 seats, electronic lighting, 3 prods: $20,000-25,000.

Facility was built in 1947, last renovated in 1965; includes scene shop, 1 dance studio, rehearsal studio, classrooms.

Two student-written plays have been produced in the last two years.

Three productions are presented in the school year, dept majors generally participate.

DESCRIPTION

Noted Faculty: Richard Pinter, Head of Acting Dept.: trained to teach by Sanford Meisner.

The Neighborhood Playhouse School of the Theatre - "where The Meisner Technique was born."

New Actors Workshop

George Morrison, Mike Nichols, Paul Sills	55 Tot. Enr.; compet.
New Actors Workshop	Semester System
259 West 30th Street, 2nd Fl.	10 Majors
New York, NY 10001	T: $10,900
(212) 947-1310	SMALL PROGRAM
www.newactorsworkshop.com	FAX: (212) 947-9729
	newactorsw@aol.com

DEGREES OFFERED

Certificate or MA in Acting in conjunction with Antioch Univ.

ADMISSION & FINANCIAL INFORMATION

Accept 30% to institution; H.S. degree req.; Aud/Int. req.;
SLM Career Training loans available to qualifying certificate students. Federal loan available for MA students.

FACULTY AND CLASSES OFFERED

3 FT, 9 PT: 1 PhD, 3 MFA/MA, 8 Prof. w/o adv. degree; 1 Staff

Courses: Acting Technique, Scene Study, Improvisation, Movement Improvisation, Speech, Voice, Alexander and Kinetic Awareness.

FACILITIES & PRODUCTIONS

3 studios for classes, rehearsals and performances, extensive library of plays and theatre related volumes.

MAINSTAGE: 70 seats, electronic lighting.

Weekly improv perfs. Story Theatre production with guest directors (2nd year). Scene evening (1st year). Continuing support of graduates includes professional guidance, rehearsal & performance space below cost and continuing access to Mr. Nichols' master class. Several companies have been formed by graduates. It is this kind of independent, self-generated artistic activity that the three founders hoped to nurture when they first conceived of the school.

DESCRIPTION

Noted Faculty: George Morrison, Professor Emeritus, SUNY @Purchase, scene study and acting technique (8 hours per week); Mike Nichols, weekly master class as schedule permits.

Guest Artists: David Mamet, Elaine May, Meryl Streep, Gene Hackman, Charles Marowitz, Michael Shurtleff, Brian Bedford, Shira Piven, Diane Paulus, Stanley Tucci.

Several factors distinguish us from other training programs. Our balance between improvisational theatre training and Stanislavski-based, scripted scene work enhances your flexibility. You learn to shift easily from one set of craft requirements to an entirely different one: from performing a well-formed, entertaining, improvised scene in front of an audience to performing carefully rehearsed and repeatable character work. Working alternately in these two disciplines prepares you to function effectively in any performance situation. Our small size creates an intimacy that facilitates your growth as an actor. Our continuity of instructors permits a gradual deepening of teacher-student rapport. Our curriculum gives you access to the newest discoveries in actor training, many of which are unique to the Workshop. Our understanding of and focus on the creative process increases your capacity to surprise yourself. Our supportive, respectful environment allows you to feel safe to explore personal boundaries.

The New School For Drama

Robert LuPone, Dir	208 Total Enr.; compet.
151 Bank Street	Semester System
New York, NY 10014	
(212) 229-5859	T: $15,350+
University Admissions, 79 Fifth Avenue, 5th Floor New York, NY 10003	
www.newschool.edu	studentinfo@newschool.edu
Adm. 877.528.3321	

DEGREES OFFERED

MFA in Dramatic Arts with concentrations in Acting (155), Directing (24), Playwriting (29). Declare major upon application.

ADMISSION & FINANCIAL INFORMATION

Candidates are invited to audition based on application submissions, portfolio, and/or writing sample(s). 75% receive invitations to audition/interview. 40% of those invited are admitted. Scholarships available based on candidate's overall admission rank.

FACULTY AND CLASSES OFFERED

47 Part-T: 6 PhD, 10 MA/MFA, 27 Prof. w/o adv. degree; 9 Staff
A. (7 PT) Theatre History-3/Y; Playwriting-4/Y
B. (37 PT) Acting-12/Y; Movement-6/Y; Alexander Technique-6/Y; Voice-10/Y; Directing-3/Y.
C. (3 PT) Principles of Design-2/Y; Set Design-1/Y; Lighting Design-2/Y

FACILITIES AND PRODUCTIONS

Classes and performances are held in the newly-renovated Westbeth Theatre Centre on Bank Street in the Greenwich Village neighborhood.

DESCRIPTION

Noted Faculty: Directing: Lloyd Richards, Gene Lasko, Arthur Storch, Elinor Renfield; Playwriting: Laura Maria Censbella, Neal Bek, Lee Blessing; Acting: Sam Schacht, Elizabeth Kemp, Barbara Poitier, Stage Design: Tony Walton; Lighting Design: Don Holder.

Craft Seminar (seen on television as "Inside the Actors Studio"Selected Guests: Paul Newman, Arthur Penn, Alec Baldwin, Sidney Lumet, Shelly Winters, Arthur Miller, Stephen Sondheim, Sally Field, Dennis Hopper, Robert Redford, Sydney Pollack, Ellen Burstyn, Jessica Lange, Christopher Walken, Mark Rydell, Nathan Lane, Anjelica Huston, Neil Simon, Glenn Close, Holly Hunter, Christopher Reeve, Mike Nichols,William Dafoe, Billy Crystal, Harvey Keitel, Shirley MacLaine, Eli Wallach, Anne Jackson, Lauren Bacall, Anthony Hopkins, Danny Glover, Jack Lemmon, Kathy Bates, Gene Hackman, Robert DeNiro, Susan Sarandon, Laurence Fishburne, Sean Penn, Stephen Spielberg, Tom Hanks, Michael Caine, Meryl Streep, Kevin Spacey, Harrison Ford, Richard Dreyfuss, Spike Lee, Ed Harris, Mike Myers, Francis Ford Coppola, Vanessa Redgrave, Phillip Seymour Hoffman, Edward Norton and Ian McKellan..

Actors Studio Drama School is a three-year MFA in Dramatic Arts. The famous "system" described in Constantin Stanislavski's three historic books: An Actor Prepares, Building a Character, and Creating a Role modified by Stanislavski himself and subsequent generations of dramatic artists, serves as a template for the three years of this program. The School treats all the aspects of the dramatic arts as a unified process with a central methodology and a common language. The three disciplines - acting, writing, and directing - train side-by-side in the First Year, while playwrights and directors are also being trained in their own crafts. These First-Year directing and playwriting classes enable them to fulfill the demands that will be made in the Playwrights and Directors Unit, which begins with the first sessions of the Second Year. In the Second Year, all three disciplines move onto parallel tracks, and in the Third, the three reconverge to create a repertory company, unified by the common language and craft they have learned in their three years together. Since this Drama School is unique among degree-granting institutions in having a parent institution like The Actors Studio, we take advantage of that special relationship with the Observer privileges accorded our students. This permits our students to attend the Studio's closed-door sessions on 44th, a very rare privilege for which professional and foreign applicants must apply and often wait years.

New York City College of Technology

David B. Smith, Dir.
Entertainment Technology
300 Jay St., Rm. V411
New York City College
Brooklyn, NY 11201
www.citytech.cuny.edu
ADMISSIONS: Above address.
(718) 260-5588

12,400 Tot. Enr.; not compet.
Semester System
93 Majors
RES. T: $3,600
DEPT: (718) 260-5588
FAX: (718) 260-5591
admissions@citytech.cuny.edu
FAX: (718) 260-5591

DEGREES OFFERED

Bachelor of Technology in Ent. Techn. (72). Program is 9 years old. Anticipated total enrollment for all four classes is 120. Declare major in freshman year. Certificate programs in sound, lighting, scenery and show control.

ADMISSION & FINANCIAL INFORMATION

HS or GED; 80% admitted to inst.; 35 out of 55 applicants admitted to program. SAT encouraged.

FACULTY AND CLASSES OFFERED

9 Full-Time, 7 Part-Time: 2 PhD, 6 MFA/MA; 1 Staff

A. (1 FT) Intro to Theatre-1/Y; Th. Hist.-1/Y; Shakes- 1/Y; Dramatic Lit-2/Y; Dramatic Criticism-1/X; Playwriting-1/X; Play Analysis-1/Y

B. (2 FT, 3 PT) Acting-2/Y; Movement-1/X; Singing-1/Y; Directing-1/X; Voice/Speech-4/Y; Musical Theatre-1/X

C. (5 FT, 4 PT) Prins of Design-1/Y; Cost Design- 1/Y; Tech. Prod'n-13/Y; Cost Hist-1/Y; Stage Mgmt-1/Y; Lighting Design-3/Y; Cost Construction-1/Y; Make-up-1/Y; Sound-3/Y; Auto Cad-2/Y; Electronics-1/Y; Metalworking-2/Y; Internship-1/Y

D. (1 FT) Marketing/Promo-1/X; Legal: Contracts/Copyright-1/X; Development-1/X; Budget/Accounting-1/X; Industrial Management-1/Y

FACILITIES AND PRODUCTIONS

MAINSTAGE: 900 seats, fly space, computer & electron. lighting
　　7 prods: 6 Fac dir, 4 Fac des, 1 Guest dir, 2 Guest des, 3 Grad des, 2 UG des; budget $10-15,000

SECOND STAGE: 200 seats, fly space, electron. lighting
　　5 prods: 4 Fac dir, 1 Fac des, 1 Guest dir, 2 Guest des, 3 Grad des, 4 UG des; budget $1,000-5,000

THIRD STAGE: 100 seats, black box, computer lighting
　　6 prods: 4 Grad dir, 2 UG dir Wkshops, Readings; budget $50-500

Facility was built in 1986, renovated in 1997; includes scene, cost., prop shops, welding shop, sound studio, CAD facility 1 video studio, 1 dance studio, 1 rehearsal studio, 2 design studios, 18 classrooms, motion control and stage rigging lab, lighting lab, engineering lab.

A non-departmental student-run organization presents 2 productions per year in which majors participate.

Internships with technical theatre businesses in NYC. Students work with suppliers, manufacturers, rental houses, scene shops, rigging companies and Off-B'way theatre productions in credit-bearing internships. Theatre production is also required with the Brooklyn Center for the Performing Arts at Brooklyn College.

DESCRIPTION

Noted Faculty: Charles Scott, Lighting Technology; David Smith, Sound Design; Tim MalDonado, Model-Making; Eileen Fisher, Play Analysis; Mark Horowitz, Auto Cad; Elliot Colchamiro, Structural Analysis; Frank DeZego, Theater Studies; John Huntington, Entertainment Control Systems; Norma Lee Chartoff, Scene Design, Painting.

Guest Artists: Brendon Quigley, Vari Lites; Craig North, Director; Alex Bartlett, Costume Designer.

The Entertainment Technology Program at City Tech (the only one of its kind in the Northeast) will teach you how things work, why they work, and will provide hands on training in a multi-million dollar lab facility. You will study the scientific and technical principles that are the "behind the scenes" framework for the illusion that is created in any theatrical venue, from window displays to Broadway, theme parks, concerts, film and television. City Tech recognizes the dynamic nature of the field and provides the specialized course work required in a variety of professional careers. Study lighting technology, sound, show control, shop operations, metalworking, mechanics and rigging, electronics, props, painting, AutoCAD, plastics, and much more. Combine these courses with a liberal arts core, theater history and literature, and design classes offered through Brooklyn College and you will be the most sought after candidate for jobs in all technical aspects of the entertainment industry.

Professional Theatre Internships

Performance ★ Arts Management ★ Technical ★ Education

Opportunities to work side-by-side with professionals in performance, technical theatre, arts management and theatre education for a semester or a full year. Earn academic credit while fulfilling your requirements for graduation. Gain training, experience, preparation, and resumé credit unattainable in a classroom. Summer and part-time internships also available.

Call Arlene Leff, Intern Program Director at 518-274-3573 or go online to www.nysti.org

The New York State Theatre Institute (outside Albany, NY) is a professional theatre with an educational mission that has performed around the world, across the state, and both on and off broadway.

PHOTO LEFT: Scene from NYS Theatre Institute Production *American Soup*: L to R: Gary Lynch, Sam Crevatas*, John McGuire, Shannon Johnson, Kay Koch*, Christine Boice Saplin, Ron Komora, Jennifer Walczak*. * 2006-07 interns

PHOTO RIGHT: Interns Scott Herrington and Sarah Koblenz working as assistant stage managers for NYSTI's rehearsal of *Magna Carta*.

New York State Theatre Institute
See ad Above

Arlene Leff,
  Program Director
37 First St.
Troy, NY 12180
DEPT: (518) 274-3573
aileff@nysti.org

Competitive
Semester System
T: $300 fee/find own R&B
MAIN: (518) 274-3200
FAX: (518) 274-3815
http://www.nysti.org

DEGREES OFFERED

We validate credits from other institutions. We are a professional theatre company.

ADMISSION & FINANCIAL INFORMATION

Accept 70% to institution; requires application, recommendation, interview; Program generally admits 2 out of 3 applicants. Course offering at SUNY at Albany & Russell Sage College; financial aid and work/study available.

FACULTY AND CLASSES OFFERED

We offer work and classes in arts management, technical theatre and performance. We have a variety of professional guests; most of the 35 staff members have at least undergraduate degrees; some have MFAs and other graduate degrees.

FACILITIES & PRODUCTIONS

MAINSTAGE: 1400 seats, computerized ltg.; budget varies. Main-stage Facility includes costume shop, rehearsal space, classrooms. Various other locations in Albany & Troy provide rehearsal and dance studios, classrooms, administrative offices, production shops, storage space, design, sound studios.

DESCRIPTION

Noted Faculty: Comes from productions as well as staff; various teachers from among season's guest artists.

The New York State Theatre Institute Internship program of study is full-time; however, part-time internships, designed according to the student's academic program, are also available. The intern functions as an auxiliary staff member, receiving academic credit instead of a salary. Each intern and his or her Institute staff mentor design an individual contract of work to be completed and evaluated, after it is approved by the intern's home campus. The semester's work assignments include some or all of the following activities: Crew Work—interns receive hands-on experience working on Institute's full-scale professional productions; Classwork—classes are held throughout the semester; Residencies—students do research and design lesson plans and serve as teacher aides in the classroom on residences; Performance—interns are cast in roles in Institute productions at the discretion of the director.

New York University-
The Steinhardt School

Note: N.Y.U. has two separate listings:: The Steinhardt School of Education and Tisch School of the Arts

Chair: Lawrence Ferrara
Program Directors: Philip Taylor, Educational Theatre,
William Wesbrooks, Music Theatre;
Brann Wry, Performing Arts Administration

NYU The Steinhardt School	1,200 T. Enrol. for Dept.
Dept. of Music &	highly compet.
Performing Arts Professions	Semester System; 200 majors
35 West 4th St., 7th Fl.	UG T:$35,283; G:$17,615t
	$11,780 r&b
New York, NY 10003	FAX: (212) 995-4043
DEPT: (212) 998-5424	www.nyu.edu/education

ADM: UG: Office of Undergrad. Adm., 22 Washington Sq. N.,
NY, NY 10011-9191 (212) 998-4500
G: School of Ed., Grad Admissions, 82 Washington Sq. E., 2nd Fl
NY, NY 10003-6680　　(212) 998-5030
admissions@nyu.edu　　grad.admissions@nyu.edu

DEGREES OFFERED

Educational Th. in High Schools: BS, MA (95), Educational Th. in Colleges: MA (35), Educational Theatre: PhD, EdD (30); Performing Arts Admin.: MA (50), Music Theatre-Vocal Performance: BM (120), MA (30). Music Performance: BM (150), MA (70), PhD (15); Music Tech: BM (60), MA (40); Music Compostion: BM (25), MA (15), PhD (6); Music Business: BM (150), MM (60); Drama Therapy: MA (25); Music Therapy: MA (46), DA (7).

ADMISSION & FINANCIAL INFORMATION

Varies somewhat, depending on program. Applics. accepted on the basis of predicted success in the program: academic record, standardized test scores, recs, pers. stmt, GRE for doctoral applicants in Educational Th. Scholarships awarded as part of a total fin. aid package based on merit, need. Audition required for Music Theatre; relevant experience required for grad. programs.

FACULTY AND CLASSES OFFERED

DEPT: 27 FT, 200 PT; 14 FT PhD; 13 FT MA/MFA; 41 PT PhD; 105 PT MA/MFA; 54 PT w/o adv. deg.

Courses vary according to program. May include: Intro to Th.; Th. Hist., Shakespeare, Dramatic Lit, Dramatic Crit., Playwriting, Acting, Directing, Mime/Mask, Musical Theatre, Stage Combat, Dance, Singing, Voice/Speech, Prins. of Des, Cost. Design, Set Design, Ltg Design, Tech. Prod'n; Arts Mgmt, Finance, Accounting, Marketing, Law, Development.

FACILITIES AND PRODUCTIONS

EDUCATIONAL THEATRE:

MAINSTAGE: 133 seats, computerized lighting 4 prods: 3 Fac des, 3 Guest des, 1 Grad dir

SECOND STAGE: 70 seats, computerized lighting. 2 prods: 1 Fac dir/Guest des prod.; 1 student dir.

Additional venue: Provincetown Playhouse

MUSIC THEATRE:

MAINSTAGE: 900 seats, computerized lighting & sound, orchestra pit. 2 Prods: Fac. dir, budget $100,000.

SECOND STAGE: 300 seats, computerized lighting. 4 Prods: Dir - 2 Fac., 1 Guest, 1 Grad; Des 9 Guest, budget $30,000 - $45,000.

THIRD STAGE: 130 seats, comp. ltg. 2 prods: fac. dir/guest des.;

budget $20,000

FOURTH STAGE: 50 seats, 3 workshps/rdgs., budget $1,000-$2,000

Other facilities: scene, cost., prop shops, sound studio; 3 movement/dance studios, 3 rehearsal studios, 10 classrooms.

Connections with: North Shore Music Theatre; Goodspeed Opera House; Virginia Opera; Sacramento Light Opera Paper Mill Playhouse. All Equity companies; internships for students.

DESCRIPTION

Noted Faculty (in all programs) include: Ralph Lee, Nellie McCaslin, Laurie Brooks, Catherine Russell, Meg Bussert, William Wesbrooks, Dianna Heldman, Grant Wenaus, Greg Ganakas, Carolann Page, Linda Shelton, Timothy A. McClimon, Patricia Iacorelli, Duncan Webb, John Koprowski.

Guest Artists include: James Urquart, David Booth, Cecily O'Neil, Ellis Jones, James Still, Rives Collins, Stephen Schwartz, Marvin Hamlisch, Fred Ebb, Betty Comden, Adolph Green, Susan Stroman, Douglas Carter Beane, Nello McDaniel, George Wolfe, Michael Kaiser, Jake Heggie, Sheldon Harnick, Faith Prince.

The Program in Educational Theatre has one of the largest worldwide enrollments of graduate students in the field. Established in 1966, the initial mission of the Program was to bring the two fields of education and theatre together – in the classroom, workshop, studio and stage. This mission has broadened to include the investigation and scholarship of educational theatre, which includes dramatic play and drama education, creative and developmental drama, applied theatre and aesthetic education. The Program promotes knowledge in the creation and performance of art, the analysis and critique of art, the contribution of art and culture to humankind. There is a large outreach and community service of the Program where youngsters and adults engage directly with the power of theatre in their daily lives. Throughout the year, the community experiences storytelling events and other performances which enable audiences to understand more closely what it means to live together in peaceful and challenging times. Audience members are invited to participate dramatically in the productions and to directly interrogate the issues raised. The faculty is recognized as world leaders in their discipline and has published formative texts which have been used in educational settings, and cultural and community contexts across the globe. The undergraduate (BS) and graduate programs (MA & PhD) provide comprehensive education in all aspects of educational theatre from preschool through higher education, as well as for arts organizations and government departments, and professional and outreach theatres. Graduates assume major career posts within educational and applied settings in the US and abroad. The Program is committed to praxis, the idea that transformative education is powered by a critical ability to reflect on action. Action, Reflection, Transformation (ART) is at the center of the Program's mission. And this praxis is occurring within a city where there is an eclectic range of activity, a city with a beat and an edge, the heart of where educational theatre is happening.

Music Theatre at NYU's The Steinhardt School of

Education offers the finest music-based training for a career in music theatre. An internationally recognized academic institution, NYU is among the very few schools in the country to offer both UG and G programs in music performance focusing on music theatre. Through ongoing relationships with the musical and theatrical communities of New York as well as regional and stock companies across the country, we provide professional opportunities for music theatre students Our faculty draws heavily from the Broadway community so students can learn from and develop professional relationships with leading music theatre figures. Frequent lectures, master classes, seminars, and internships further enrich the curriculum. With the professional connections and training they have received, our graduates have gone on to Broadway, national and international tours, and regional productions as actors, conductors, music directors, musicians, composers, lyricists, stage managers, and casting directors.

The Master's program in Performing Arts Administration was founded in 1971 and is one of the oldest arts management programs in the country. The program educates prospective and practicing administrators for positions with outstanding arts organizations in th8is country and abroad, including theaters. It does this with a combination of courses, specifically designed for arts administrators, in the areas of the environment of arts administration, development for the arts, marketing the performing arts, law and the arts, statistics, and business courses in economics, accounting, behavioral science, and marketing, which are offered through NYU's Leonard N. Stern School of Business. In addition, the program emphasizes the acquisition of executive skills in the areas of organizational assessment, career planning, and executive presentation through periodic workshops offered only to students enrolled in the master's degree program. Internships with leading arts managers are a required part of the program of study and enhance course work.

New York University - Tisch School of Arts

Tisch School of the Arts, NYU
721 Broadway, 8th Fl.
New York, NY 10003

(212) 998-1900
ADMISSIONS: UG: 22 Washington Sq. No., NY, NY 10003
(212) 998-4500
admissions@nyu.edu

2,800 T. Enr.; highly compet.
Semester System; 950 Majors
T: UG $38,722/r&b $11,780.00
   G:$18,354/r&b $11,780.00
www.nyu.edu/tisch

FAX: (212) 995-4902
grad.admissions@nyu.edu

DEGREES OFFERED

Dance: BFA (75), MFA (30); Design for Stage and Film: BFA (10), MFA (75); Grad Acting: MFA (50); Drama Undergraduate: BFA in Theatre (acting, musical theatre, directing and tech. prod'n) (1,400); Dramatic Writing: BFA (200) and MFA (40). MFA Graduate Musical Th. Writing (0). Students declare major upon application.

ADMISSION & FINANCIAL INFORMATION

Appls accepted on the basis of predicted success in the program: academic record, standardized test scores, recs, pers. stmt, Aud./Port. Aud./Int. req'd for Acting and Dance Program, portfolio/Int. for Design/Tech., portfolio for Dramatic Writing Program. Schols awarded as part of a total fin. aid package based on merit, need. Due to the number of applicants, early application is strongly recommended.

FACULTY AND CLASSES OFFERED

Dance: 7 FT, 14 PT Faculty; Design: 9 FT, 5 PT Faculty; Grad Acting: 6 FT, 17 PT Faculty; Drama: UG: 18 FT, 142 PT Faculty; Dramatic Writing Program: 7 FT, 36 PT Faculty. Graduate Musical Theatre Writing: 6 FT, 45 PT

Dance courses include: Ballet, Modern, Pointe, Men's Class, Partnering, Dance Theory & Composition, Acting, Improvisation, Dance History, Music Theory & Composition, Musical Lit.

Design courses include Set Design, Costume Design, Lighting Design, Art Direction for Film and Television.

Grad Acting courses include: Acting, Voice/Speech, Movement, Mime, Singing, Stage Combat.

Drama, UG courses include: Intro to Th., Th. Studies (British, European, U.S., African-American, Feminist, Post-Colonial, Latin American, Asian), Theory, Shakes, Th Hist, Drama Therapy. Acting, Directing, Design, Production.

Dramatic Writing courses include: Th Hist, Shakes, Contemp. Amer. Playwrights, Video, Film Script Analysis, Poetry/Fiction, Acting, Directing, Characterization, Dialogue, Storytelling, Masterclasses in playwriting and screenwriting.

Graduate Musical Theatre Writing Program writing courses include: Writing Workshop, The American Musical, Theatre/ Music Theatre, Crafts of Musical Theatre, Producing for Theatre, Master classes in bookwriting, lyrics and music.

FACILITIES AND PRODUCTIONS

Dance:

MAINSTAGE: 200 seats, 5 dance studios, 15-20 productions/year.
Design for Stage and Film:

Scene, costume, props, welding shops; 3 design studios; CAD facility. Dept. majors generally design productions for G Acting, Dance, and UG Drama productions.

Grad Acting:

MAINSTAGE: 200 seats, computerized & electronic lighting; 2 prods: 1 Fac dir/Grad des, 1 Guest dir/Grad des.

SECOND STAGE: 80-100 seats, computerized & electronic lighting. 3 prods: 1 Fac dir/Grad des, 2 Guest dir/Grad des

THIRD STAGE: 80 seats, electronic & computerized lighting; 4 prods

Drama, UG: (over 150 productions/year)

MAINSTAGE: 99 seats, computerized lighting 6 prods: 1 Fac dir/des, 9 Grad des, 4 Guest dir, 6 UG des

SECOND STAGE: 72 seats, computerized lighting. 1 Fac dir, 3 Guest dir, 6 Guest des, 2 Grad des, 1 UG des prods

THIRD STAGE: 49 seats, electronic lighting

30 UG dir/des workshops/readings

Studio Theatre: 39 seats, electronic lighting. 40 directing projects

Scene, costume shop, props shop, sound studio, 5 rehearsal studios, design studio.

Dramatic Writing:

MAINSTAGE: 80 seats, electronic lighting
6 prods: 6 Guest dir/des

Graduate Musical Theatre Writing:

BLACKBOX: 70 seats, electronic lighting

2 seminar rooms, 6 practice rooms, recording studio.

Approx. 11 readings w/Guest dirs.

DESCRIPTION

Noted Faculty include: Zelda Fichandler, Liviu Ciulei, Woodie King, Jr., Paul Sills, Carrie Robbins, Paul Steinberg, Eduardo Sicangco, Tina Howe, Alfred Uhry.

Guest Artists have included: Mark Morris, Doug Varone, Twyla Tharp, Ann Reinking, William Forsythe, Bill T. Jones, Patricia Birch,
Arthur Laurents, Richard Schechner, Ping Chong, Judith Malina, Andre Gregory, Eduardo Machado, Liz McCaan, Terrance McNally, Arthur Miller, Gil Wechsler, Bruce Myers, Augusto Boal, Ivica Boban.

The Graduate Acting Program is a professional training program that prepares students for the profession. It recognizes that performance careers include work in film and television, and we acknowledge such acting demands in our training. But essentially we deal with serious theatre performance, with the awareness that serious theatre artists are capable of handling all kinds of performance. First-year work deals with the acting instrumenT: voice, body, emotions, intellect. Second-year students learn to master the progression from scene work to full performance; third-year work involves advanced workshops and performance projects.

The Department of Dance offers an intensive program for students committed to entering the profession as dancers or choreographers. It provides a full range of technical training and, for those interested in choreography, a solid base for creative work.

The Department of Design for Stage and Film seeks to instill in each student designer an acute awareness of scenery, lighting and costume for theatre, film and television. A student may specialize in one of more of these areas, but also gains a strong sense of the totality of the discipline. Student designers observe professionals at work in theatres, design studios and shops, as well as in film and tv studios. The department also prepares students for union examination.

The Department of Drama, Undergraduate, is an intensive program combining professional theatre training with liberal arts studies. Com-prehensive areas of study are: Acting, Musical Theatre, Directing, and Theatre Production (design, production, and management). Students spend three days per week in one of eight professional training studios located in New York City. The other two days students are on campus taking academic courses in theatre studies and liberal arts. Admission to the program is based on a two part evaluation: artistic and academic. Artistic reviews are held in New York and several other cities.

The Department of Dramatic Writing is an intensive, professional undergraduate and graduate training program in writing for stage, screen, and television. The program's aim is to educate writers who are equipped to originate and develop scripts in all the above media. The Department, whose faculty includes some of the most active and respected professionals in their fields, represents a diversity of styles concurrent with its philosophy, which encourages the individual voice.

The Graduate Musical Theatre Writing Program. Guided by a resident faculty and guest teachers drawn from major artists in the field, students collaborate on new material to gain experience with a variety of styles and approaches. From the traditional book musical to innovative forms of musical theatre, they participate in ongoing writing workshops and tutorials emphasizing craft, artistic communication and storytelling in music, lyrics and book.

Niagara University

Sharon Watkinson, Ph.D.
Theatre Studies Program
Niagara University
Niagara, NY 14109
sw@niagara.edu
WWW.NIAGARA.EDU

2,800 Total Enr.; competitive
Semester System; U/RTA, ATHE
92 Majors
T: $21,400/$9,300 R&B
DEPT: (716) 286-8480
FAX: (716) 286-8495

ADMISSIONS: Bailo Hall, Niagara Univ, NY 14109
(716) 286-8700   www.niagara.edu
admissions@niagara.edu

DEGREES OFFERED

BFA in Performance/Acting (78); Design/Tech (9); General (5). Declare major in 1st year; 2007 granted 20 degrees.

ADMISSION & FINANCIAL INFORMATION

SAT 500-reading, 500-math, GPA-B average, Act 20-21; 80% accepted to institution.. Interview/interview/portfolio required for admission to theatre program, necessary to be considered for scholarship; generally admit 35 out of 65. 8 Theatre Merit Scholarship ($5,350 each) based on aud, academic background & financial need.

FACULTY AND CLASSES OFFERED

9 Full-Time, 10 Part-Time: 2 PhD/DFA, 17 MFA/MA; 2 Staff

A. (1 FT, 1 PT) Intro to Theatre-1/Y; Theatre Hist-4/Y; Dram Lit-4/Y; Dramatic Criticism-1/Y; Shakes-1/Y; Playwriting-1/O.

B. (4 FT, 9 PT) Acting-8/Y; Voice/Speech-2/Y; Mime/Mask,etc.-4/Y; Singing-4/Y; Directing-1/Y; Stage Combat-3/Y; Dance-8/Y

C. (3 FT) Prins of Des-1/Y; Cost Des-1/Y; Ltg Des-1/O; Cost Constr-1/Y; Make-up-2/Y; Stage Mgmt-1/O; Set Des-1/O.

FACILITIES & PRODUCTIONS

MAINSTAGE: 155 seats; computerized lighting

26 prods: 6 Fac dir/des; 20 UG dir;. budget $5,000-7,000

SECOND STAGE: 150 seats, computerized lighting

2 prods: 2 Fac dir/des; budget $3,000-4,000

Facility was built in 1972, renovated in 1998; includes scene shop, cost. shop, prop. shop, sound studio, 2 movement/dance studio, 3 rehearsal studios,

2 student-written plays have been produced in the last two years.

Noted faculty: Sharon Watkinson, Ph.D., Chair, History, Dramatic Lit, Criticism; Brother Augustine Towey, CM,Ph.D., Directing; Neil Casey, Acting; Brendan Powers, Acting; Douglas Zschiegner, Acting and Directing; Maureen Stevens, Costume Design; Marilynn Deighton, Costume Tech; Eric Appleton, Set and Light Des; Terri Filips, Dance

Guest Artists: John Kander, Debra Monk, Joe DiPietro, Armand Schultz, Gemzie DeLappe

DESCRIPTION

Niagara University Theatre Studies combines a conservatory training approach to teaching performance skills with a full undergraduate liberal arts education. The program is basically designed to prepare students for professional careers in theatre as well as being a foundation for graduate study if the student so chooses. The program comprises a full curriculum in performance as well as a full curriculum in the history, literature, and criticism of theatre. Part of its philosophy is devoted to the fact that students learn theatre by doing theatre, and therefore the University Theatre produces approximately 8 to 10 major productions and 20 to 25 one-act productions per year.

Pace University

Ruis Woertendyke, Chair/Dir
Dept. of Performing Arts
PACE University
1 Pace Plaza
New York, NY 10038
DEPT: (212) 346-1352
ADMISSIONS: Above address
www.pace.edu

8,030 Tot. Enr.; compet.
Semester System
150 Majors
T: $30,158/$10,280 r&b
theater@pace.edu
FAX: (212) 346-1681
(212) 346-1225
infoctr@pace.edu

DEGREES OFFERED

Degree: BFA in Theater (51); BA in Theater Arts (20), Music Th (28), Design/Tech (6), Mgmt. (3), Directing (2). Students declare major in fresh. year.

ADMISSION & FINANCIAL INFORMATION

SAT: 1100, (V450-550, M460-580). GPA 2 - 2.9 or higher. 1 out of 4 accepted to theatre program. Audition for actors. Int/Portfolio, 2 letters of recommendation for designers. President's and Dean's schols are avail. to academically deserving students.

FACULTY AND CLASSES OFFERED

6 FT, 18 PT: 2 PhD, 13 MFA/MA, 9 Prof. w/out adv. degree.

A. (1 FT, 2 PT) Intro to Theatre-2/Y; Theatre History-5/Y; Dramatic Lit-2/X; Shakes-2/X; Playwriting-1/Y; Dramatic Critism-1/Y.

B. (3 FT, 3 PT) Acting-8/Y; Voice/Speech-2/Y; Singing-9//Y; Musical Th.-3/Y; Directing-1/Y; Stage Combat-1/O; Dance-3/Y; Movement-2/Y.

C. (1 FT, 4 PT) Prins of Des-2/Y; Cost Des-1/Y; Set Des-1/Y; Lighting Des-1/Y; Tech Prod-2/Y; Make-up-1/Y; Stage Mgmt-1/Y; Cost. Const.-2/Y.

D. (1 PT) Arts Mgmt-1/Y.

FACILITIES & PRODUCTIONS

MAINSTAGE: 655 seats; fly space, computerized lighting. 2 prods: 2 Fac dir/des; budget $4,000-7,000

SECOND STAGE: 72 seats, black box, electron. lighting. 22 prods: 2 Fac dir/des, 20 UG dir/des; budget $100-3,500

Facility was built in 1969, renovated in 1996; includes scene shop, cost. shop, sound studio, video studio, 1 movement, 1 rehearsal studio, 6 classrooms

30 student-written plays produced in the last two years.

Pace University and National Actors Theatre (NAT) have entered into a five year agreement where NAT will hold its theatrical performances, rehearsals, box office, and educational outreach programs at the University's Michael Schimmel Center for the Arts. NAT will also offer acting, production, and administrative internships for students. Qualified Pace students may audition for parts and will be considered for paid positions within NAT, and NAT staffers will also be available to teach courses at Pace. NAT presented its first production at Pace in October 2002, *The Resistible Rise of Artuo Ui* starring Al Pacino.

DESCRIPTION

Noted Faculty: Dr. Ruis Woertendyke, Director, Actor, Playwright; Christopher Thomas, Designer; Dr. Lee Evans, Music; Amy Rogers, Music Th.; Anjali Vashi, Acting, Movement, Voice; Paul Guzzone, Music, Management; Charles Maryan, Acting; Erica Gould, Acting; Audrey Koran, Stage Mgmt.; Anne Lommel, Design; Scott C. Parker, Technical Theatre.

Guest Artists: Student forums with William Windom; cast of NAT's *Arturo Ui* including Tony Randall, John Goodman, Steve Bucemi, Bill Crudup, Chazz Palminteri. Workshops: The Business of Acting, TVI Actor's Studio; The Alexander Technique, Claudia Peyton; Strasberg Workshop, Susan Grace Cohen; Grotowski Workshop, Zenon Kruszelnicki.

The Theatre Program at Pace University is dedicated to building foundations with both theory and extensive performance practice that will prepare the undergraduate student for a working lifetime in the theatre. We believe in nurturing the student through an accessible faculty and small classes that allow for extensive individual training. The often difficult transition from school to a career is eased through internships and direct faculty involvement in New York professional theatre. Further, our "Professionals in Theatre" series brings our students into direct contact with established and emerging working practitioners. Graduating students are presented to agents and casting directory in an annual showcase. Designers, directors, and actors who choose to continue with graduate study are individually counseled in building their portfolios and honing their audition skills.

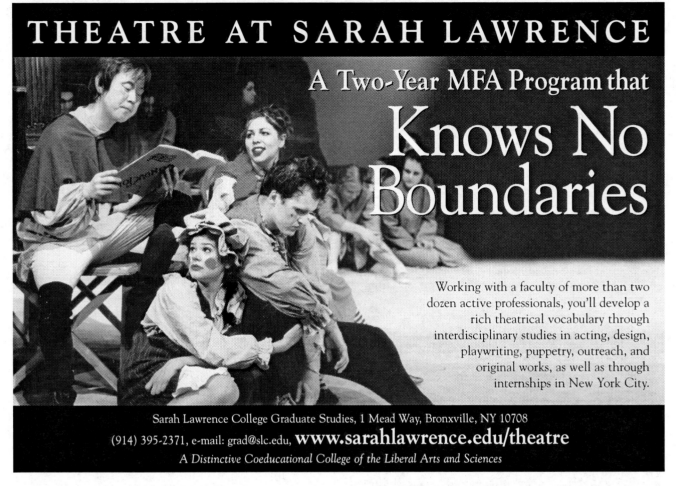

THEATRE AT SARAH LAWRENCE

A Two-Year MFA Program that

Knows No Boundaries

Working with a faculty of more than two dozen active professionals, you'll develop a rich theatrical vocabulary through interdisciplinary studies in acting, design, playwriting, puppetry, outreach, and original works, as well as through internships in New York City.

Sarah Lawrence College Graduate Studies, 1 Mead Way, Bronxville, NY 10708
(914) 395-2371, e-mail: grad@slc.edu, **www.sarahlawrence.edu/theatre**
A Distinctive Coeducational College of the Liberal Arts and Sciences

Sarah Lawrence College

See ad Above

John Dillon, Director
Sarah Lawrence College
Graduate Studies, One Mead Way
Bronxville, NY 10708-5999
DEPT: (914) 395-2430
www.sarahlawrence.edu
ADMISSIONS: Above address.
FAX: (914) 395-2664

1,408 Total Enr.; h. compet.
Semester System
24 Majors
T: 1st year $23,520/2nd yr. $11,760
FAX: (914) 395-2664

(914) 395-2510
slcadmit@mail.slc.edu

DEGREES OFFERED

MFA in Theatre

ADMISSION & FINANCIAL INFORMATION

Applicants who demonstrate serious motivation to study advanced theatre are encouraged to apply. See our website:www.sarahlawrence.edu. The Theatre faculty invites qualifing applicants for a required on-campus interview. Prospective graduate students are strongly urged to spend time meeting faculty and students and sit in on workshops. Based on the application and interview, the theatre faculty makes its decisions. Deadline for MFA in Theatre is January 15. International students unable to come for interview should contact the Office of Graduate Studies to make special arrangements. All financial aid is need-based.

FACULTY AND CLASSES OFFERED

25 Part-Time: 9 MFA/MA, 16 Prof. w/o adv. deg; 6 Staff

A. Intro to Theatre 1/Y, Shakes-2/X; Dramatic Lit-2/X; Dramatic Crit-3/Y; Playwriting-5/Y; Theatre Education-1/Y; Contemporary Theatre-1/Y, Period Styles 1/O

B. Acting-3/Y; Voice/Speech-4/Y; Movement-1/Y; Musical Theatre-1/Y; Mime, etc.-1/Y; Singing-1/Y; Directing-3/Y; Dance-1/Y; Alexander-1/Y; Comedy Styles and Workshops-2/Y; Improv-2/Y; Acting for the Camera-1/Y

C. Cost Des-2/O; Set Design-2/Y; Ltg Des-1/Y; Cost Constr-2/Y; Tech Production-1/Y; Play to Screen-1/Y; Practicum-1/Y; Puppetry-1/Y; Sound Design-2/Y., Scene Painting-1/Y

D. Arts Management 1/O

FACILITIES & PRODUCTIONS

MAINSTAGE: 170 seats, flyspace, computerized lighting. 5 prods: 2 Fac dir, 1 Fac des, 1 Guest dir/des, 1 Grad dir, 2 Grad des, 1 UG dir/des; budget $2,000-7,000

SECOND STAGE: 120 seats, fly space, computerized lighting. 7 prods: 1 Fac dir/des, 1 Guest dir, 3 Grad dir/des, 2 UG dir, 3 UG des; budget $1,000-5,000

THIRD STAGE: 80 seats, fly space, computerized lighting. 17 prods: 2 Fac dir, 2 Guest dir, 8 Grad dir, 6 Grad des, 5 UG dir, 11 UG des; budget $50-2,000

Facility was built in the mid-1960's and renovated in the mid-1980's; includes scene shop, costume shop, sound studio, design studio, 2 movement/dance studios, 3 rehearsal studios. Fourth theatre space is a 60 seat black box, outdoor performance space w/30 seats.

A non-departmental, student-run, producing org. presents 10 prods. per year in which dept. majors participate.

The Theatre Program mounts 25-30 prods./year, ranging from staged readings of original student work to full prods. of student and faculty written plays and published wks. An equally divided number of faculty, undergrad, and grad students direct and design all productions.

Connection with Ensemble Studio Theatre (Equity) in NYC. Internships, readings, job opportunities, casting. Connections to many other NYC theatres incl: Ubu Rep, Cocteau, La Mama, The Kitchen, etc. and most off and off-off B'way houses and to The Shubert Organization.

Outside Programs; Theater students may be invited to participate in outside programs, including: London Theatre Tour; La MaMa, Umbria International; The Ensemble Studio Theatre; Annual Summer Conference Playwriting Retreat.

DESCRIPTION

Noted Faculty: Edward Allan Baker, Playwright; Kevin Confoy, Directing; John Dillon, Directing; Christine Farrell, Comedy; Dan Hurlin, Performance Art; Shirley Kaplan, Acting, Directing; Cassandra Medley, Playwright; Dave McRee, Directing; Carol Pelletier, Costume Design; Stuart Spencer, Theatre History, Playwright.

Guest Artists: Ernest Aruba, Actor,Director; Michael Early, Actor; June Ekman, Alexander Technique; Amlin Gray, Playwright; Tom Lee, Set Designer; Greg Macpherson, Lighting Design; Doug MacHugh, Film Actor; David Neuman, Dancer; Fanchon Schier, Improvization; Sterling Swann, Stage Combat.

The Graduate Program in Theatre offers an advance study of theatre that is interdisciplinary, collaborative, comprehensive and practical in nature. It is a two-year program, leading to a Master of Fine Arts degree. Like the college at large, the graduate theatre program empahsizes an individualized learning process.

The program offers wide-ranging opportunities for students to learn by doing. Stdents may participate in internships or fieldwork in New York City theatres. They may also work in theatre outreach programs in the surrounding community and its schools. In addition there are multiple production opportunities available for graduate students.

School for Film and Television

	Total Enr: 107 FT, 1224 PT
School for Film and Television	T: $21,800
39 West 19th St.	90 Majors; NAST
New York, NY 10011	Trimester System
(212) 645-0030	FAX: (212) 645-0039
www.filmandtelevision.com	888.645.0030
ADM: Above address	(212) 645-0030 x 772

DEGREES OFFERED

2 Year Conservatory Program Certificate (125). Part time Professional Studies Div. 2001 granted 35 certificates.

ADMISSION & FINANCIAL INFORMATION

HS graduate, C average, 2 letters of rec. showing commitment to goals: SAT Verbal Scores preferred. 35% admitted to instit.; audition/interview required. Schols: Selected locations and thespian festivals; several times a year on campus-call for dated; awarded on basis of talent or talent and need.

FACULTY AND CLASSES OFFERED

42 Part-Time; 33 MA/MFA, 9 Prof. w/out adv. degree

A. (2 PT) Film Genres-1/Y; Throughline of Action; Script Analysis-1/Y

B. (36 PT) Acting-19/Y; Movement-4/Y; Voice/Speech-9/Y; The Business of Acting-1/Y; Improvisation-5/Y; Aud for Film & TV-2/Y; Prins of Preparation-1/Y; Situation Comedy-1/Y; Agents & Casting Dirs-3/Y; Prof. Dirs. Days-1/Y; Prof. Reel & Presen-tion-1/Y; Commericial Print-1/Y; Daytime Drama Workshops-1/Y

FACILITIES AND PRODUCTIONS

Facility built in 1986, renovated in 1995; 7 video studios, movement/dance studio, 2 rehearsal studios, editing equipment: 1 3-cam setup, 2 2-camera setup, 6 1-camera setups.

MAIN STUDIO: 1 Guest Artist dir/des production budget $40,000-50,000

SECOND STAGE: 10 Fac dir, Guest des prods; budget $300-500 3-4 Guest dir Workshops/Readings

The Showcase Reel results in Actors entering the industry with a fully-produced and edited tape of their work. So when asked for a Sample Reel they have one. This end-of-year production is our big budget item for our second year. It is the equivalent of Graduation Plays at our sister conservatories.

DESCRIPTION

Noted Faculty: Roy Steinberg, Director; JoAnn Secarick, John O'Commel Director; Heidi Latsky, Choreographer/Dancer; Larry Silverberg - Actor/Teacher; Alice Spivak, Actress.

Guest Artists: Arista Balronis, Casting; Tex Beha, Talent Manager; Howard Meltzer, Casting; Alison Renzel, CBS Daytime; Flo Rothacker, Film Agent; Peter James, Dir. of Photo-Movies; Jeff Moroni, Calif. Talent Mgr.; Carrie Morgan, Agent.

The School for Film and Television is a 2-year conservatory training program designed for the student actor who wishes to pursue a professional film and television career. Grounded in the belief that "good acting is good acting" no matter the medium, this intense program stresses the development of solid acting technique throughout the program. FIRST YEAR consists of three semesters of the Meisner acting technique, Improvisation, Movement, Voice, Film Studies, Acting for the Camera, and one end of year small theater production. The SECOND YEAR focuses on all aspects of on-camera work with ten different on-camera technique classes. There are also 9 courses emphasizing the development of audition and marketing skills designed to aid the actor in career advancement. At the end of the second year, students are filmed in a professional studio under the guidance of a professional director and crew for later presentation in an industry-wide showcase.

Siena College

Ralph Blasting, PhD, Dean
    Theatre Program
Siena College
Loudonville, NY 12211
(518) 783-2381
FAX: (518) 783-2381
ADMISSIONS: 515 Loudon Rd., Loudonville, NY 12211-1462
(518) 783-2423
www.siena.edu

2,800 Total Enr.; competitive
Semester System
25 Majors; ATHE
T: $22,685/$8,875 R&B
SMALL PROGRAM
www.siena.edu/theatre

FAX: (518) 783-4293
admit@siena.edu

DEGREES OFFERED

BA in Creative Arts (5); Cert. in Theatre (20). Students declare major in freshman or sophomore year.

ADMISSION & FINANCIAL INFORMATION

Based on SAT or ACT, Solid B in college prep program, interview recommended, high school transcripts, guidance counselor recommendation required (60% accepted); Interview required for admission to Th Program. No theatre merit scholarships; Fin. Aid in theatre granted through federal work study program (need based) and 4-5 $1,000 salaried positions in office and tech areas, selected on ability.

FACULTY AND CLASSES OFFERED

2 Full-Time, 4 Part-Time: 6 MFA/MA; 2 Staff

A. (1 FT, 2 PT) Intro to Theatre-1/Y; Dramatic Lit-3/X; Theatre History-3/Y; Playwriting-2/O

B. (1 FT, 1 PT) Acting-3/Y; Voice-1/Y; Movement-1/Y; Singing-2/Y; Musical Th.-1/Y; Directing-1/Y; Directing Practicum-1/Y

C. (1 PT) Set Des-1/O; Costume Des-1/O; Lighting Des-1/O; Tech Prod-1/Y; Make-up-1/O; Practica in Design, Technology, Management, 1/Y each.

D. Internships

FACILITIES & PRODUCTIONS

MAINSTAGE: 310 seats, computerized lighting. 4 prods: 3 Fac dir, 3-4 Fac des, 1 Guest dir, 1-4 Guest des; budget $3,000-7,500

Workshops/Readings: 1 Fac dir, 2 UG dir, 6 UG des; budget $0-500

Facility was built in 1955, renovated in 1976; includes scene shop, costume shop, rehearsal studio, 1 classroom.

DESCRIPTION

Noted Faculty: Gary Maciag, Directing, Theatre History; Mahmood Karimi-Hakak, Acting, Directing, Cindy Brizzell, Acting, Theatre History.

Guest Artists: David Hopes, Playwright; Jim Farrell, Playwright; Kyle Pulliam, Lighting Design.

The Theatre Program, a certificate program in the Siena College Department of Creative Arts, offers students the opportunity to pursue a formal 24-credit curriculum in theatre studies. The Theatre Program aims to acquaint students with the theory, history and aesthetics of the dramatic event; strives to develop an appreciation of theatre as a complex artistic expression of humankind's struggle to understand itself; works to develop first-hand experience with those essential skills necessary to create theatre: acting, directing and design. Students earning a certificate in the Theatre Program may choose to pursue careers as drama directors and educators in the secondary school system, as theatre practitioners, or might choose to deepen their understanding and appreciation of the art form through graduate study. Students enrolled in the Theatre Certificate Program have the option of choosing an internship with a professional theatre organization in acting, directing, scenery, costumes, lighting, sound or management.

State University of New York - Buffalo State College

Donna McCarthy, Chair
Dept. of Theatre
221 Donald Savage Building
1300 Elmwood Avenue
Buffalo, NY 14260-5030
DEPT: (716) 878-6416
www.buffalostate.edu/theater
ADM: See above
www.buffalostate.edu/admissions

11,220 T. Enr.; compet.
Semester System
67 majors, NAST
T: $2,650/$4,157 R&B
O-ST T: $5,780/4,157 R&B
FAX: (716) 878-4409
mccartde@buffalostate.edu
(716) 878-5519

DEGREES OFFERED

BA in Theatre (67). Students declare major in 1st or 2nd year. 2007 granted 15 degrees.

ADMISSION & FINANCIAL INFORMATION

Admission requrements A combination of high school grade average, class rank, SAT or ACT and recommendations. Institution generally accepts 46 percent of applicants. Theatre program generally admits 1 out of 2 applicants to the program. Two schols, $1,000 each annually, for incoming freshmen; one for actors (audition requried) and one for production (essay required).

FACULTY AND CLASSES OFFERED

5 Full-Time, 3 Part-Time: 7 MFA/MA, 1 Prof. w/o adv. degree; 1 Staff

A. (.5 FT, 2 PT) Intro to Theatre-1/Y; Dramatic Lit-2/X; Theatre History 2/Y; Shakes Lit-2/X; Playwriting-1Y; Period Styles-1/O

B. (2.5 FT, 1 PT)Acting-4/Y; Voice/Speech-2/Y; Movement-2/Y; Singing 1X; Stage Combat-1/O; Dance-1/O; Directing-2/Y

C. (2 FT) Set Des-2/Y; Cost Des-2/O; Ltg Des-1/O; Tech Prod-1/Y; Cost Constr-2/O; Make-up-1/O; Practicums-4/Y; Scene Painting-1/Y

D. (1 PT) Arts Management-1/O

FACILITIES & PRODUCTIONS

MAINSTAGE: 400 seats, fly space, comput. lighting
    2 prods: 1 Fac dir, 3 Fac des, 1 GA dir, 3 GA des, 1 UG des; budget $7,000-10,000

SECOND STAGE: 100 seats, comput. lighting
    1 prod: 1 Fac dir, 2 FAc des, 1 UG des; budget $5,000-7,000

9 workshop/readings: 3 Fac dir, 4 GA dir, 2 UG dir

Facility was built in 1964 and last renovated in 2003; includes scene shop, costume shop, CAD facility, 2 movement/dance studios, 2 rehearsal studios, 1 design studio, 1 classroom, computer lab and makeup studio.

A non-departmental, student-run organization co-produces productions with the department.

Three student written play workshops were produced in the last two years.

Connection with Studio Arena Theatre, an Equity company that operates during the school year; offers acting internships in mainstage season (non-speaking roles); internships in all production areas.

DESCRIPTION

Noted Faculty: Drew Kahn, Acting; Donn Youngstrom, Directing/Theater History; Gerry Trentham, Voice and Movement; Carol Beckley, Set Design; Donna McCarthy, Costume Design.

Guest Artists: Andre Deshields, Acting/Directing; Tom Fontana, TV Writer/Producer/Playwright; Vince Cardinal, Playwright; Shaun McLaughlin, TV Producer.

The Buffalo State Theater Program is dedicated to developing the intellectual growth, creativity, aesthetic appreciation, professional preparedness, and character of its students by combining rigorous training with a liberal arts education that engenders a lifelong appreciation for the performing arts. Learning in this program is a collaborative experience that embraces professional standards in the studio, in the classroom and in production. The program is committed to attracting a diverse body of talented students. We strive to prepare students who will actively participate in a global community that encompasses the theater, film, television and entertainment industries.

Accredited by the National Association of Schools of Theatre (NAST), Buffalo State's Theater Department offers all that students need to succeed in a wide variety of theater careers. With access to hands-on internships, top-notch facilities, personalized attention, guest artists and a mutli-disciplinary curriculum, theater students immerse themselves in their work, working side-by-side with faculty and fellow students to mount productions and gain valuable real-world experience.

State University of New York – Fredonia
See ad

Dr. James Ivey
Rockefeller Arts Center
SUNY/College at Fredonia
Fredonia, NY 14063-1136
(716) 673-3596
FAX: (716) 673-3621
www.fredonia.edu/department/theatre/index.htm
admissions.office@fredonia.edu
ADMISSIONS: Fenner House, SUNY Fredonia, Fredonia, NY 14063
(716) 673-3251   FAX: (716) 673-3249

5,000 Total Enr.; competitive
Semester System
140 Majors; NAST, ATHE
T: $5,425/$8,350 R&B
O-ST T: $11,802/$8,350 R&B
theatre@fredonia.com

DEGREES OFFERED

BA in General Studies (52); BFA in Acting (21), Musical Theatre (37); Production/Design (30). Declare major in first year; 2002 granted 25 degrees.

ADMISSION & FINANCIAL INFORMATION

Quality of academic prep, academic achievement, SAT; admits 40%. BA students admitted by acceptance to college/BFA by aud/interview/portfolio; admit 4 out of 10 BFA.

FACULTY AND CLASSES OFFERED

9 FT, 3 PT: 1 PhD, 8 MFA; 3 Staff

A. (1 FT) Intro to Theatre-1/Y; Th. Hist-2/Y; Shakes-2/X; Script Analysis-1/Y; Playwriting-1/O

B. (3 FT) Acting-8/Y; Voice-4/Y; Movement-2/Y; Singing-1/X; Directing-2/Y; Mus. Th-1/O; Stage Combat-1/O

C. (4 FT) Set Design-2/Y; Cost Des-2/Y; Ltg Des-2/Y; Cost. Construction-2/Y; Cost. History-1/Y; Make-up-2/Y; Stage Mgmt-1/O; Intro to Tech-2/Y; Pattern Drafting-1/Y; Rendering-3/Y; Sc. Painting-2/Y; Stagecraft-2/Y; Scene Painting-2/Y; Dyeing-1/Y

D. (1 PT) Arts Management-1/Y

FACILITIES AND PRODUCTIONS

MAINSTAGE: 400 seats, fly space, computerized lighting. 4 prods: 3 Fac dir/des; 1 Guest dir/des; budget $6,300-8,300

SECOND STAGE: 200 seats; computerized lighting. 2 prods: 2 Fac dir/des; budget $2,300-2,500

4 UG dir/des Workshops/Readings; budget $500

Facility was built in 1968; includes scene shop, costume shop, sound studio, design studio, CAD facil, 1 movement/dance studio, 3 rehearsal studios.

Majors generally participate in a non-departmental, student-run organization that presents 4 productions per year.

DESCRIPTION

Noted Faculty: Curtis Phillips, Professional Resident Designer; Mary Charbonnet, Equity Actress in Residence; Paul Mockovak, Musical Theatre Specialist and Choreographer; Carol Blanchard-Rocheleau, Costume Designer; Stephen Rees, Technical Direction; James Ivey, Theatre History; Todd Proffitt, Sound and Lighting Design; Ted Sharon, Voice and Movement.

Guest Artists: Judith Ivey, Actress; Tony Kushner, Playwright; Carol Hall, Composer/Lyricist; Ted Sluberski, Cast.ing Dir

It is the mission of the Department of Theatre and Dance at SUNY Fredonia to provide training for students of theatre within the framework of the liberal arts education. The Bachelor of Fine Arts degree program is limited to those students who demonstrate excellence or the potential for excellence in performance and/or production design. It is designed for those students who enter college with a firm idea of their professional goals. We provide the opportunity for experimentation and growth so that students are able to stimulate and release their imaginative and creative energies while developing a respect for the technical and craft skills to be mastered. The faculty and staff are comprised of professional resident artists who work closely with students in a production-oriented program. The theatre program is an accredited member of the National Association of Schools of Theatre and adheres to the standards set forth by NAST.

State University of New York – Geneseo

Jack Johnston, Director
School of the Arts
One College Circle
SUNY Geneseo
Geneseo, NY 14454
johnston@geneseo.edu
www.geneseo.edu

5,300 Total Enr.; h. compet.
Semester System
Res. T: $4,440/$5,930 R&B
Non-Res. T: $9,340/$5,930 R&B
Dept: (585) 245-5841
FAX: (585) 245-5826

ADMISSIONS: Erwin Hall, One College Circle, Geneseo, NY 14454
(585) 245-5571   FAX: (585) 245-5550

DEGREES OFFERED

BA in Theatre. Declare major in junior year; 2004 granted 9 degrees.

ADMISSION & FINANCIAL INFORMATION

High School Average: 93% unweighted, SAT: c.1290. Th. program admits 2 out of 3 applicants; audition for actors, interview/portfolio for designers. Four merit scholarships $1,000 ea., annually, for meritorious continuing students.

FACULTY AND CLASSES OFFERED

6 Full-Time, 1 Part-Time: 3 PhD/DFA, 4 MFA/MA

A. (2 1/2 FT,1/ 2 PT) Intro to Theatre-2/Y; Theatre History-4/Y; Play Analysis-2/Y; London Th. Seminar-1/Y; Experimental Th-1/O; Th. Seminar-1/O

B. (1 1/2 FT,1/ 2 PT) Acting-4/YO; Directing-2/YO; Voice/Speech-1/O; Theatre Practicum-1/Y; Creative Dramatics-1/O

C. (2 FT) Principles of Design-1/Y; Set Design-2/O; Cost Design-1/O; Tech. Production-3/YO; Costume History-1/Y; Stage Mgmt-1/O; Lighting Des-2/O; Cost Constr-1/O; Make-up-1/O; Stage Elec. & Sound-1/O; Scene Painting-1/O; Theatre Practicum-1/Y

D. Arts Management-1/O

FACILITIES AND PRODUCTIONS

MAINSTAGE: 404 seats, fly space, computerized & electronic lighting. 2 prods: 2 Fac dir, 4 Fac des, 2 UG des; budget $7,550-8,200

SECOND STAGE: 150 seats, electronic lighting. 5 prods: 1 Fac dir, 4 Fac des, 4 UG dir, 1 UG des; budget $3,800-5,350

Facility built in 1967; includes scene, cost., prop shops, sound studio, CAD facility, 2 dance, 1 design studio, 1 classroom.

A non-departmental student-run organization presents 3 productions per year in which majors participate.

DESCRIPTION

Noted Faculty: Dr. Melanie Blood, Director; Dr. Leah

Garland, Director; Johnnie Ferrell, Designer; Dr. Randy Kaplan, Director; Crystal Ferrell, Adjunct Lecturer; Adam West, Designer; Steven Stubblefield, Designer.

Guest Artists: Roy Kift, Playwright.

The primary educational objective of SUNY-Geneseo's School of the Arts is to provide highly qualified majors with artistic and academic opportunities sufficient in scope and excellence to qualify them for admission to well-regarded, professional graduate programs or professional applications.

State University of New York –New Paltz

Frank Trezza, Chair
Dept. of Theatre Arts
SUNY College at New Paltz
New Paltz, NY 12561
DEPT: (845) 257-3865
FAX: (845) 257-3882

7,70 Total Enr.; compet.
Semester System
110 Majors, NAST
T: $2,175/$3,900 & up R&B
O-ST T: $5,305/$3,900 & up R&B
www.newpaltz.edu/theatre

ADMISSIONS: Office of Undergraduate Admissions, SUNY New Paltz, 1 Hawk Drive, New Paltz, NY 12561
(845) 257-3200   FAX: (845) 257-3209
www.newpaltz.edu/admissions

DEGREES OFFERED

BS in Theatre Arts (103); BA in Theatre Arts (7); BFA in Scenography (0); Declare major in freshman yr. 2001 granted 30 UG degrees.

ADMISSION & FINANCIAL INFORMATION

College Prep, SAT's, GPA and other; 43% of applics. accepted by institution; 45 out of 100 applicants admitted to theatre program. Audition, for actors, interview for design/tech, portfolio for designers. Bruce Bennett Schol. by faculty selection on merit; John Morrow/Vera Rushforth Irwin Schol., faculty selection on merit and need.

FACULTY AND CLASSES OFFERED

9 FT, 5 PT: 2 PhD, 9 MFA/MA, 2 Prof. w/o adv. degree; 1 Staff

A. (2 FT, 1 PT) Intro to Theatre-1/Y; Theatre History-2/Y; Dramatic Lit-2/Y; Playwriting-X

B. (3 FT, 4 PT) Acting-6/Y; Movement-1/Y; Singing-2/Y; Directing-2/Y; Voice/Speech-2/Y; Mus. Th-5/Y; Stage Combat-1/O; Dance-5/Y

C. (3 3/4 FT) Principles of Des-1/Y; Set Des-3/Y; Cost Des-2/Y; Cost History-1/Y; Stage Mgmt-1/Y; Lighting Design-2/Y; Cost Construction-3/Y; Make-up-2/Y

FACILITIES AND PRODUCTIONS

MAINSTAGE: 374 seats, fly space, comput. & electronic ltg.. 4 prods: 4 Fac dir, 16 Fac des; budget $12,000-20,000

SECOND STAGE: 175 seats, computerized & electronic lighting. 2 prods: 2 Fac dir, 8 Fac des; budget $5,000-10,000

THIRD STAGE: 50 seats, black box, electronic lighting

Workshops/Readings: Fac dir/UG dir; budget $200-3,000

Facility built in 1961, renovated in 1994; includes scene shop, costume shop, CAD facility, 2 large rehearsal studios, 2 dance studios, 1 design studio, 3 classrooms, outdoor summer stage.

A non-departmental student-run organization presents 2-3 productions per year in which majors participate.

DESCRIPTION

Noted Faculty: Beverly Brumm, Acting/Directing; Simone Federman, Acting/Directing; Kate Ingram, Acting/Directing; Yoav Kaddar, Dance; Max Lydy, Technical Direction; Christine McDowell, Costume Design; Joseph Paparone, Acting/Directing; Liming Tang, Scenic Design; John Wade, Lighting Design.

Guest Artists: Michael Badalucco, Actor; John Turturro, Actor; Scott Cohen, Actor; Dan Grimaldi, Actor; Michael Williams, Actor; Todd Thaler, Casting Agent; Gillian Farrell, Lecturer, Actor, Scholar; Julie Regan, Professor/Lecturer.

The mission of the Department of Theatre Arts is to provide professionally-oriented training in theatre within the humanistic context of a liberal arts education. To achieve this, the faculty offers students an environment based on professional theatre models. Much of the curriculum involves hands-on training, and all students are required to develop fundamental skills in many areas of theatre: acting, stagecraft, lighting, costumes and production. Our training is pre-professional in intention: students choose a concentration in Performance or Design/Technical and complete course sequences in preparation for moving to the next level upon graduation. This may mean employment in the profession - stage, film, or television, enrollment in graduate school, professional internships, more advanced professional training, or exploration of other professional alternatives. The Department also offers a BFA in Scenography to selected qualified students. Students are encouraged to make their own theatre collaboratively, through writing, directing, ensemble groups, production teams. As a department, we value creative community.

State University of New York –Oswego

Mark Cole, Chair
Dept. of Theatre
Tyler Hall
SUNY/College at Oswego
Oswego, NY 13126
DEPT: (315) 312-4883
www.oswego.edu/theatre
ADMISSIONS: 211 Culkin Hall
www.oswego.edu
admiss@oswego.edu

7,046 Total Enr.; competitive
Semester System
81 Majors
T: Annual $5,434/$9,470 R&B
O-ST. T: $11,694/$9,470 R&B
FAX: (312) 312-3394

(315) 312-2250
FAX: (315) 312-3260

DEGREES OFFERED

BA in Acting/Directing (36), Technical Theatre/Design (24). Declare major by junior year; 2003 granted 15 degrees.

ADMISSION & FINANCIAL INFORMATION

Average GPA 87.5, SAT 1050, ACT 23; inst. admits 62% of applicants; special admission to theatre program is available thru Aud./Portfolio; theatre program admits all accepted by the inst. Schols: $1,500 Schol for Tech Theatre: applic, resume, 3 letters of rec; inst. has over 40 general schols ($100-1,000), apply Fin. Aid Office.

FACULTY AND CLASSES OFFERED

9 FT faculty & prof. staff; 7 MA/MFA, 1 BA; adjuncts as needed

A. (1/2 FT) Intro to Theatre-2/Y; Dramatic Lit-2/X; Theatre History-5/Y; Dramatic Criticism-1/O; Shakes-2/X; Playwriting-2/X; Women and Theatre-1/O

B. (3 FT) Acting-6/Y; Voice/Speech-3/Y; Mvmt-1/Y; Singing-3/X; Musical Th.-1/X; Directing-2/Y

C. (2 FT, 3 PT) Prins of Des-1/O; Set Des-2/Y; Cost Des-1/O; Ltg Des-2/Y; Tech. Prod-2/Y; Cost Constr-1/Y; Cost Hist-1/Y; Make-up-1/Y; Stg Mgmt-1/O; Sound Des-1/O; Photog & Spec Effects-1/O; Stg Electronics-1/Y; Computers for the Th-1/O; Drafting-1/O

D. (1/4 FT) Arts Management-1/O

FACILITIES AND PRODUCTIONS

MAINSTAGE: 525 seats, fly space, computerized lighting. 3 prods: 3 Fac dir/des, 2 UG dir/des; budget $3,000-10,000

SECOND STAGE: 110 seats, electronic lighting. 1 prods: UG dir/des; budget $2,000-5,000

Workshop/Readings: 1 Fac dir/des, 20 UG dir/des;bdgt $0-100

Facility was built in 1968; scene shop, costume shop, sound studio, design studio, 3 classrooms; all facilities are available from other depts. and are used by theatre majors.

Dept. majors generally participate in four mainstage productions, smaller student projects.

DESCRIPTION

The Theatre Department at SUNY-Oswego offers a BA in Theatre with individual concentrations in acting, directing, design, technical production, theory and criticism. The program offers introductory, intermediate, and highly specialized advanced course work in all areas while maintaining a strong adherence to the spirit of a liberal arts education. In addition to 4 major productions during the academic year featuring the classics, contemporary drama, and musicals, the department sponsors numerous smaller-scale activities such as Reader's Theatre, dance, student workshop scenes, and student written 10 minute play fest. In recent years, visiting artists presented workshops in movement, dance, wigs & make-up, soft sculpture & mask making, and planning and maintaining a career in the arts. The department maintains a large, active, and helpful alumni network ranging from regional theatre to Broadway, including TV and film.

State University of New York – Purchase

Gregory Taylor, Interim Dean
Conservatory of Theatre Arts
 & Film
Purchase College, SUNY
735 Anderson Hill Road
Purchase, NY 10577
www.purchase.edu

3,300 Tot. Enr.; highly compet.
Semester System
T: $5,709
O-ST T: $11,969
DEPT: (914) 251-6831
ADM: (914) 251-6300

DEGREES OFFERED

BFA in Acting (65) BFA, MFA in Stage Design/Theatre Tech w/ focus in Set Des, Ltg Des, Cost Des, Tech Dir., Directing/ Stage Management (120); BFA Dramatic Writing (50)

ADMISSION & FINANCIAL INFORMATION

Audition, Interview and/or Portfolio Review, "B" H.S. avg., SAT 1000, 2.0 transfers. Acting Program admits 20 out of 1,200.

FACULTY AND CLASSES OFFERED

8 Full-Time, 16 Part-Time: 7 MFA, 6 Prof. w/o adv. deg; 2 Staff

A. (1 PT) Theatre History-1/Y; Dramatic Criticism-1/Y

B. (5 FT, 1 PT) Acting-2/Y; Voice/Speech-2/Y; Movement-2/Y; Mime, etc.-1/Y; Stage Combat-1/Y

C. (3 FT, 14 PT) Prins of Des-2/Y; Cost Des-3/Y; Tech Prod'n-3/Y; Set Design-3/Y; Ltg Des-3/Y; Cost Constr-2/Y; Make-up-1/Y; Stage Mgmt-3/Y; Scene Painting-2/Y; Sound Design-1/Y

FACILITIES & PRODUCTIONS

MAINSTAGE: 1,500 seats, computerized lighting. 5 prods: 3 Fac dir, 2 Guest dir; budget $5,000-9,000

SECOND STAGE: 800 seats, computerized lighting

THIRD STAGE: 500 seats, computerized lighting

2 Fac dir/Guest des Workshops/Readings; budget $500 (Studios-$2,000)

Facility built in 1975; includes scene shop, costume shop, prop shop, welding shop.

DESCRIPTION

Noted Faculty: Acting: A. Lawrence Kornfeld, Eulalie Noble, A. Dean Irby, Joan Potter; Design/Technology: Daniel Hanessian, Thom Kelly, Dennis Parichy, Brian MacDevitt, Kenneth Posner; Dramatic Writing: Howard Enders.

Guest Artists: Sherry Stringfield, Kevin Spacy, Stanley Tucci, Actors; Lloyd Richards, Director; Franco CoLavecchia, Set/Cost. Des; Ina Mayhew, Prod. Des; Gene O'Donnovan, Prod. Man.; David Gallo, Set Des.; Tony Ealton, Set/Cost Des.

The Division of Theatre Arts and Film provides students of high motivation and talent with professional training and cultural background needed to prepare them for careers in theatre and film, and awards the BFA degree. The faculty are working professionals and the program is designed to train young would-be professionals in a student mentor relationship. The Design/Technology Program places major emphasis on studio/classroom training under the guidance of established working professionals. The following options are available as areas of specialization: set design, lighting design, costume design, technical direction and stage direction and stage management. Purchase offers a two- and three-year Master of Fine Arts program for professional training in theatre design/technology and prepares students for a professional career that equips the designer and technical director for today and the future.

State University of New York–Stony Brook

Nick Mangano, Chair
Department of Theatre Arts
SUNY at Stony Brook
Stony Brook, NY 11794-5450

DEPT: (631) 632-7300
enroll@stonybrook.edu

14,847 Total Enr.; competitive
Semester System
80 Majors; ATHE, NAST (A)
T:$5,758/r&b 8,870
O-ST T: $12,018
ADM: (631) 632-7300
www.stonybrook.edu

DEGREES OFFERED

BA in Theatre (55); MA in Theatre (5); MFA in Dramaturgy (12) Declare major in 3rd year.

ADMISSION & FINANCIAL INFORMATION

Based in part on SAT and GPA; 50% accepted; Theatre program requires GRE and sample of writing for Grad applicants; Program admits 5 out of 5 UG, 2 out of 5 Grad applicants.

FACULTY AND CLASSES OFFERED

7 Full-Time, 6 1/2 Part-Time: 4 PhD, 4 MFA/MA; 4 1/2 Staff

A. (2 FT, 3 PT) Intro to Theatre-1/Y; Theatre History-3/Y; Shakes-1/O; Dramatic Lit-1/O; Dramatic Crit-1/O; Playwriting-1/O

B. (4 FT, 4 PT) Acting-3/O; Voice/Speech-1/Y; Movement-1/Y; Singing-X; Directing-2/O; Dance: Ballet, Jazz, Tap, Modern-7/Y; Mask-1/O

C. (2 FT, 1 PT) Prins of Des-3/Y; Set Design-3/Y; Cost. Design-1/O; Ltg Des-1/Y; Tech. Production-2/Y; Cost. Construction-2/O; Cost. History-1/O; Make-up-1/O; Stage Mgmt-1/O

D. (1/2 PT) Marketing/Promotion-1/Y

FACILITIES AND PRODUCTIONS

MAINSTAGE: 225 seats, computerized lighting
    3 Prods: 3 Fac dir, 3 Fac des, budget $2,500-4,000

SECOND STAGE: 225 seats, computerized lighting
    2 Fac dir, 1 Fac des, 1 Grad des; budget $2,500-4,000

THIRD STAGE: 75 seats, computerized lighting. 5 Workshops/Readings: 4 Grad dir/des; 1 UG dir/des; budget $500

Facility was built in 1978; includes scene shop, costume shop, props shop, video studio, dance studio, 3 rehearsal studios, 2 design studios, 2 classrooms; electonic classroom lab. for tech in arts.

DESCRIPTION

Noted Faculty: Jonathan Levy, Playwriting: John Lutterbie, Theory & Hist.; Michael Zelenak, Dramaturgy; Theresa Kim, Asian Theatre.

Guest Artists: Ping Chong & Co, Holly Hughes, Charles Marowitz, Aquilla Theatre Company.

For those who want to be near New York without having to live in the City, the Theatre Arts Department at Stony Brook focuses on developing theatre practitioners who understand the process of making theatre today and tomorrow. The curriculum places special emphasis on developing a company work ethic, exploring the relationship between interactive technologies and the theatre arts. Students train for careers in the theatre profession, but also develop career goals in other fields, such as law, medicine, business and the media industry.

Suffolk County Community College

Charles Wittreich, Chair
Theatre Arts Department
Suffolk County Community College
Selden, NY 11784
DEPT: (631) 451-4163
FAX: (631) 451-4601
www.sunysuffolk.edu/academics/dept/theatre/index.asp

22,000 Total Enr.; not compet.
Semester System
63 Majors
T: $2,990
O-ST T: $5,980
wittrec@sunysuffolk.edu

ADMISSIONS: 533 COLLEGE RD, SELDEN, NY 11784

(631) 451-4022
www.sunysuffolk.edu

www.sunysuffolk.edu
FAX: (516) 451-4094

DEGREES OFFERED

AS in General Theatre Sequence, Acting Sequence, Technical Sequence also Automated Lighting and Stage Rigging Cert Declare major in first year; 2007 granted 12 UG degrees.

ADMISSION & FINANCIAL INFORMATION

College placement test. Performance based scholarships awarded each May. Shirley Cox - all around excellence; RJ Shakespeare - excellence in classical performance; Harriette Novick - excellence in contemporary performance. Special requirements for actors - audition at end of semester through "Evening of Scenes".

FACULTY AND CLASSES OFFERED

7 Full-Time, 2 Part-Time: 7 MFA/MA; 2 Staff

A. (1 PT) Intro to Theatre-1/Y; Theatre History-2/Y; Shakes-1/X; Dramatic Lit-1/X

B. (2 FT, 1 PT) Acting-3/Y; Stage Combat-1/Y; Voice-1/X; Mvmnt-2/X; Singing-1/X; Oral Interpretation-1/X

C. (4 FT) Prins of Design-1/Y; Cost Constr.-1/Y; Stage Craft-1/Y; Lighting Craft-1/Y; Sound Craft-1/Y

D. (1 FT) no courses listed

FACILITIES AND PRODUCTIONS

MAINSTAGE: 450 seats, comput. lighting, modern sound system
    4 prods: 4 Fac dir/des; budget $10,000-20,000

SECOND STAGE: 100 seats, comput. ltg, modern sound system
    2 prods: 2 Fac dir/des; budget $10,000-20,000

Workshop/Readings - 1 Fac dir/des; budget $500-3,000

Facility built in 1969, renovated in 1999; includes scene shop, costume shop, sound studio, CAD facility, 3 classrooms.

DESCRIPTION

Guest Artists: Brian MacDevitt, Lighting Designer; Adrienne Thompson, Actress; Charlie Wittreich, Designer ; Edward Haynes, Scenic Designer; Barrie Ingham, Actor; Patty Cohenour & Matt Loney, Actors/Singers; Marie Danvers, Actor/Singer; Roger Reese, Actor.

The goal of the Department of Theatre is to provide a nurturing yet disciplined environment that is rich in academic exposure and rigorous in its practical application. We are committed to the general education of students and to training them in the skills and disciplines of professional theatre practice, the outcome of which prepares our students for a successful transition to baccalaureate and/or professional training programs. The department provides an academic and artistic environment for both majors and non-majors in which they will develop intellectual and artistic skills. We afford students the opportunity for creative thinking, problem solving and exploration in an atmosphere that values artistic integrity, understands failure as well as success and respects cultural heritage. Through personalized mentorship by faculty and staff, students will master individual skills through classroom and production work to create collaborative works of art. The department provides high quality theatrical productions that offer entertainment to the Suffolk County community and bring distiction to the College.

Syracuse University

Timothy Bond, Prod Artistic Dir
Drama Dept.
Syracuse University
Syracuse, NY 13244
DEPT: (315) 443-2669
FAX: (315) 443-9846
ADM: 200 Crouse Hinds Hall, Syracuse, NY 13244
(315) 443- 3611
www.syracuse.edu/orange

15,000 Total Enr.; h. compet.
305 Majors; ATHE
Semester System
T: $31,686/$10,940
www.vpa.syr.edu/drama
www.syracuse.edu

FAX: (315) 443-4226
orange@syr.edu

DEGREES OFFERED

BFA in Acting (41), Musical Th. (20), Design/Tech (8), Stage Mgmt. (4); BS in Drama (10). Declare major in first year.

ADMISSION & FINANCIAL INFORMATION

Average profile: 3.0 GPA, 1200 SAT, College preparatory level curriculum. 62% of applicants accepted to inst. Audition for actors, portfolio for designers. Theatre program admits 2 out of 10 UG applicants (Grad Program on hiatus, no new students are being accepted at this time). Schols: Founders $10,000/yr; Chancellor $8,000/yr; Dean's $6,000/yr.

FACULTY AND CLASSES OFFERED

14 FT, 16 PT: 2 PhD, 19 MFA/MA, 8 Prof. w/o adv.deg; 35 Staff

A. (1 FT, 5 PT) Intro to Theatre-2/Y; Dramatic Lit-2/Y; Theatre History-4/Y; Shakes-2/O; Dramatic Criticism-2/Y; Playwriting-1/Y

B. (9 FT, 7 PT) Acting-18/Y; Voice/Speech-5/Y; Mvmt-2/Y; Mime,etc.-3/O; Musical Th-5/Y; Singing-2/Y; Directing-3/Y; Stg Combat-1/Y; Dance-7/Y; Sight Singing-2/Y; Acting for non-Majors-5/Y; Audition-2/Y

C. (2 FT, 4 PT) Prins of Des-2/Y; Cost Des-2/Y; Tech Prod'n-1/O; Cost Hist-1/O; Set Design-3/O; Ltg Des-4/Y; Cost Constr-2/O; Make-up-1/Y; Stg. Mgmt-2/Y; Drafting-1/Y; Th. Crafts-2/Y; CAD-1/Y

D. (1 FT) Arts Management-1/O; Budget, Acct'ng-1/O

FACILITIES & PRODUCTIONS

DRAMA DEPT MAINSTAGE: 200 seats, computerized lighting. Various prods: Faculty directed. Drama majors only as cast members UG des; bdgt $5,000-20,000

SYRACUSE STAGE MAINSTAGE: (LORT THEATRE) 500 seats, computerized lighting. Various prods: Prof. Directors. Drama majors in some roles. Prof. Designers; bdgt $10,000 - $30,000

THIRD STAGE: 60 seats, black box, electronic lighting. Various Fac dir, UG dir/des Workshps/Readings; budget $50-200

CABARET SPACE: Sutton Pavilion, 100 seats.

Facility built in 1965, major additions in 1980 & 1992; includes scene, costume, prop shops, welding shop, 2 movement/ dance studios, 5 rehearsal studios, 3 classrooms, design studio, CAD -lab, music practice rooms, 500 seat Archbold Theatre- Home of Syracuse Stage.

A non-departmental, student-run org. presents 2 prods/yr in which majors participate. 6 student-written plays produced in the last two years.

Connection with Syracuse Stage (LORT Equity). Acting and musical theatre majors may participate in professional shows in the following ways: performing in age-appropriate roles with the Equity actors, participating in the understudy program, and auditioning for the co-production between Syracuse Stage and the Department. (In the 2003-2004 season, it was *Big River*).

Professional staff members serve as adjunct professors and design students regularly assist the professional guest designers.

DESCRIPTION

Noted Faculty: Gerardine Clark, Acting/ Playwriting; Rodney Hudson, Acting/Musical Theatre; Elizabeth Ingram and Malcolm Ingram, Acting/Voice/Verse; Marie Kemp, Musical Theatre/Acting; Craig MacDonald, Acting/Mask; Bob Moss, Directing; Anthony Salatino, Dance/Movement; David Wanstreet, Dance; Maria Marrero, Design Tech.

Guest Artists: Aaron Sorkin, Playwriting; Pearl Cleage, Playwriting; Marion McClinton, Directing; Brian O'Neil, Acting as a Business; Arielle Tepper, Producer; Taye Diggs, Acting; Elizabeth Franz, Acting, August Wilson, Playwriting. Cherry Jones, Acting; Alice Ripley, Musical Theatre; Tim Douglas, Directing.

The major thrust of the Department of Drama at Syracuse University is to prepare the undergraduate student for a career as a performer, designer/technician or stage manager in theatre (and television/film). The actor training is based on the teachings of Stanislavsky and the voice training is based on the work of Kristin Linklater. Musical theatre students participate in all acting classes in addition to their dance classes, voice lessons, and music performance classes. Acting students have an opportunity to take dance and musical performance classes on a space-available basis. Design/technical students and stage management students have several opportunities to design and stage manage during their undergraduate experience. Because Syracuse Stage, a professional LORT theatre, shares the 4-theatre complex with the Department, there are many opportunities for drama students to attend equity productions and to meet and work with professionals. Through a generous gift from Arielle Tepper, the Department has opened the Tepper Center for Careers in Theatre to help students make the transition from college to the professional world.

University at Albany / SUNY

J. Kevin Doolen, Chair
Department of Theatre
Performing Arts Center 262
University at Albany/SUNY
1400 Washington Ave.
Albany, NY 12222
www.albany.edu/theatre
jkdoolen@albany.edu
ADM. (518) 442-4200

16,751 Total Enr.; competitive
Semester System
61 Majors; ATHE
T: UG $3,400, G $5,100
O-ST T: UG $8,300, G $8,416
DEPT: (518) 442-4200
FAX: (518) 442-4206
ADMISSIONS: UAB 101
www.albany.edu

DEGREES OFFERED

BA in General Theatre and Drama (35), Concentration in Theatre (33); MA in General Theatre and Drama (10). Declare major in 2nd year; 2001 granted 14 UG, 4 G degs. Transfers from 2 year and 4 year programs accepted.

ADMISSION & FINANCIAL INFORMATION

Academic evaluation weighing GPA, SAT or ACT, and rank in class; Means: 88 GPA, 1120 SAT, top 20% of class for enrolling freshmen; inst. admits 60% of applicants; Theatre Program accepts all UG applicants, 3 out of 5 Grad applicants.

FACULTY AND CLASSES OFFERED

9 Full-Time, 7 Part-Time: 4 PhD, 9 MFA/MA; 1 Staff
A. (2 1/2 FT, 2 PT) Intro to Theatre-1/Y; Theatre History-6/Y; Shakes-2/X; Dramatic Lit-7/Y; Playwriting-2/Y,2/X
B. (2 1/2 FT, 3 PT) Acting-9/Y; Voice/Speech-5/O; Movement-5/O; Directing-2/Y
C. (3 FT) Prins of Des-2/Y; Set Design-2/O; Cost Des-2/Y; Ltg Des-2/Y; Tech. Production-3/Y; Cost Constr-2/Y; Cost Hist-1/Y; Make-up-1/Y; Drafting-1/Y; Stg Mgmt-1/O; Sound Design-1/O

FACILITIES AND PRODUCTIONS

MAINSTAGE: 500 seats, fly space proscenium, computer & electronic lighting
2 Fac dir/Guest des prods; budget $3,000-10,000

SECOND STAGE: 150 seats, fly space, electronic lighting. 2 prods: 2 Fac dir/des, 1 Grad dir/UG dir; budget $1500-3500

THIRD STAGE: 198 seats, arena, electronic, computer lighting

FOURTH STAGE: flexible seating, electronic, computerized lighting

Facility built in 1968; includes scene, costume shop; 2 classrooms.

Dept. majors regularly participate in a non-departmental, student-run producing organization that presents 4-8 productions annually.

Formal Internship with New York State Theatre Institute, Troy, NY. Informal connection with Capital Repertory Theatre (Equity)and StageWorks in Hudson, NY (Equity): Some students are hired on a part-time basis and some continue full-time after graduation.

DESCRIPTION

Noted Faculty: J. Kevin Doolen, directing, acting; Mark Dalton, acting, directing; Eszter Szalczer, theatre history; Andi Lyons, lighting design, theatre technology, Janet Sussman, costume design, Adam Zonder, technical; Ken Goldstein, set design; James Farrell, playwright, dramaturg, literary advisor; Jackie Roberts, acting, directing.

Guest Artists: Richard Schechner, Director/scholar; Ruby Dee, Actress; Wallace Shawn, Playwright; Elizabeth Wong, Playwright; Ingrid Sonnichsen, Actor, Director, Shakespearean specialist; Bea Terry, Director; Gretchen Michelfeld, Voice Coach, Actress; Jeffrey Mousseau, Director; Sara Schatz, Casting Director; David Bunce, Fight Choreographer; Peter Sellars, Director; Marvin Carlson, theatre history; Anna Manahan, acting; Fintan O'Toole, theatre criticism; Can-dace Taylor, dialects, acting; ACTER (A Center for Theatre, Edu-cation and Research -Shakespeare) Jane Arden, Lara Bobroff, David Horovitch, Michael Thomas, Timothy Watson, David Acton, Henrietta Bess, Peter Forbes, Peter Lindford, Biddy Wells.

The University at Albany Department of Theatre is dedicated to providing our students with a broad-based foundation in the history, theory, and practice of theatre arts and dance. At its core, the study and practice of theatre thrives on collaboration and active learning. It promotes the synthesis of literature, theory, science, technology, and art. As a visual, textual and performing art form, theatre provides an ideal focus for a liberal arts education. Our courses cultivate the intellectual and creative growth of our students, leading them toward self-knowledge and understanding of the arts of diverse cultures from the past and present. Simultaneously, we challenge our students to envision and nurture the arts of the future. Our studio and departmental presentations illuminate and integrate course material, encourage process-oriented experimentation and creative risk, and develop informed audiences attuned to the diversity and power of the arts.

University at Buffalo/SUNY Buffalo

Robert Knopf, Chair
Dept. of Theatre & Dance
285 Alumni Arena
State University of NY @ Buffalo
Buffalo, NY 14260-5030
DEPT: (716) 645-6898 ext. 1334
www.cas.buffalo.edu/depts/theatredance
ADM: 17 Capen Hall, University @ Buffalo, Buffalo, NY 14260
(716) 645-6900   ubadmit@buffalo.edu
http://admissions.buffalo/edu/

27,000 T. Enr.; h. compet.
Semester System
282 majors,
T: $4,350/$7,526 R&B
O-ST T: $5,966/7,526 R&B
FAX. (716) 645-6992

DEGREES OFFERED

BA in Theatre (115), Dance (67); BFA in Acting (19),Music Theatre (33) Dance (16) Design/Tech (12). Declare major in 1st yr.; 2007 granted 58 degrees.

ADMISSION & FINANCIAL INFORMATION

Creative and Perf. Arts scholarship - academic grades/audition. No special requirements for acceptance to theatre program, acceptance to UB.

FACULTY AND CLASSES OFFERED

18 Full-Time, 12 Part-Time: 4 PhD, 22 MFA/MA, 4 Prof. w/o adv. degree; 5 Staff

A. Intro to Theatre-1/Y; Dramatic Lit-4/Y; Theatre History 2/Y; Shakes Lit-1/Y; Playwriting-2/Y; Special Topics-1/Y

B. Acting-8/Y; Voice/Speech-2/Y; Movement-1/Y; Mime, etc.-1/Y; Singing (Musical Theatre major); Stage Combat-1/Y; Dance-8/Y; Directing-2/Y; Special Topics-2/Y

C. Principles of Des-4/Y; Set Des-2/Y; Cost Des-2/Y; Ltg Des-2/Y; Tech Prod-3/Y; Cost Constr-1/Y; Stage Mgmt-1/Y; Studio Courses-2/Y; Make-up-1/O

D. Arts Management-1/Y

FACILITIES & PRODUCTIONS

MAINSTAGE: 1850 seats, fly space electronic & comput. lighting Budget $10,000-15,000

SECOND STAGE: 380 seats, fly space, comput. & electronic lighting Budget $1,500-10,000

THIRD STAGE: 10-150 seats, electronic & computerized lighting; Workshops/Readings budget $1,000-3,000

Facility was built in 1993; includes scene shop, costume shop, props shop, welding shop, sound studio, 3 dance studios, 4 design studios, centrally scheduled classrooms. 4 add'l theatre/recital hall performance spaces - used occasionally. Seating range 20-700.

A non-departmental, student-run organization presents 5 productions in which majors and non-majors occasionally participate. Connection with Irish Classical Theatre Co.; Shakespeare in Delaware Park; Jewish Th., "Musical Fare". Faculty members are Founding/Artistic Directors. Directors will cast from student population as well as Equity and professional actors. Internships available.

DESCRIPTION

Noted Faculty: Kazimierz Braun, International Director, Playwright, Scholar; Stephen Henderson, Broadway Actor; Tom Ralabate, International Ballroom Dance Champion, Jazz; Vincent O'Neill, Artistic Director; Saul Elkin, Artistic Director; Robert Knopf, Director, Scholar; Catherine Norgren, Costume Designer.

Guest Artists: Elliot Caplan; MarshaMilgrom Dodge; Daniel Pelzig; Erica Gould; Jessica Blank; Doug Varone, Dance Residency; John Plumpis, Timon "Lion King."

The Department of Theatre and Dance offers majors in each discipline, a minor in theatre, and a combined major , a major in any discipline, or combined with another discipline. We respect the differences between each major while emphasizing that which they share in common. We seek to develop disciplined, creative, articulate, and versatile individuals whose impact on their art and the world is positive and enriching. All study/performance is encouraged with full access for theatre majors to all dance courses for which they are qualified, and vice versa. Our 51 million dollar Arts Center brings together Theatre, Dance, Music, Visual Arts, and Media Studies in a variety of performance spaces with state-of-the-art design/technology capabilitires and a full production staff.

Wagner College

Gary Sullivan, Chair
Wagner College Theatre
631 Howard Ave.
Wagner College
Staten Island, NY 10301
DEPT: (718) 390-3223
ADMISSIONS: 1 CAMPUS RD.
www.wagner.edu

2,000 Tot. Enr.; compet.
Semester System
125 Majors; USITT, SETC
T: $29,500
$8,900 R&B
FAX: (718) 390-3323
(718) 390-3411
FAX: (718) 390-3105

DEGREES OFFERED

BA in Musical Theatre Perf. (100), Acting (10), Technical Design (5), Generalists (10), Arts Admin, concentration in theatre.
Declare major in fresh/soph year.

ADMISSION & FINANCIAL INFORMATION

Admission requirements SAT min. 1020-1170, solid B-GPA; 70% of applicants accepted to inst. Theatre program generally admits 48 out of 100 applicants; audition/interview/portfolio. Both theatre schols and scholastic schols. available.

FACULTY AND CLASSES OFFERED

6 FT, 6 PT: 6 MA/MFA, 6 Prof. w/o adv. deg; 3 Staff.

A. (1 FT, 1 PT) Intro to Th-1/Y; Th Hist-2/Y; Mus Th. Survey-2/Y; Shakes-1/Y; Dramatic Lit.-2/Y; Dram. Crit.-1/O; Playwriting-1/O

B. (3 FT, 3 PT) Acting-2/Y; Dance-2/Y; Singing-2/X; Directing-2/Y; Voice/Speech-2/Y; Mime-1/O; Musical Th-2/Y; Stage Combat-1/O

C. (1 FT, 2 PT) Prins of Design-1/Y; Set Design-1/Y; Ltg Des-1/Y; Make-up-1/O; Stage Mgmt-1/Y; Cost Des-1/Y; Cost Hist-1/Y; Cost Constr-1/O; Tech. Production-1/Y

D. (1 FT) Arts Management-1/O; Box Ofc. Procedure-1/O.

FACILITIES AND PRODUCTIONS

MAINSTAGE: 400 seats, fly space, comp. lighting. 4 prods: 3 Fac dir/Guest des, 1 Fac des./Guest dir; bdgt $10-40,000

SECOND STAGE: 70 seats, black box. 3 prods: 2 Fac dir, 1 Guest dir; budget $0-5,000WORKSHOPS: 2 prod: 2 Guest des; budget $0-500

Facility built in 1928, last renovation 1995; includes scene, prop shops, CAD facility, dance studio, design studio, classrooms, part time use of cabaret space. One student-written play produced in last 2 yrs.

The Department presents 4 main stage productions yearly, lavishly produced, 3 of which are musicals, to a Season Subscription Audience. Each production runs 2-3 weeks. Additionally, we produce 5-6 Studio Theatre productions (classics, experimental, new works). Also we have an annual Dance Concert or Recital + One Act Play Marathon, approx. 250 roles available yearly.

DESCRIPTION

Noted Faculty: Lewis Hardee, Musical Th/Hist; Christopher Catt, Dir/Acting & Movement; Elizabeth Terry, Director/Acting & Voice; John Jamiel, Director/Acting & Voice; Phil Hickox, TD/Design; Gary Sullivan, Director/Communication; Rusty Curcid, Dan Knechtges, Choreography/Dance.

Guest Artists: We have about 8-10 Guest Artists/year as Directors/ Choreog of Main Stage and occasionally Studio productions; and to give Workshops. Drew Harris, Richard Sabelico, Broad-way Dir/Choreogs; Francis Rousel, Clown/Mvmt Workshops; Evaly Baron, Broadway credits, Musical Theatre Workshops.

Wagner College theatre offers an intense four year liberal arts program with a theatre orientation leading to a BA in Theatre. The play production program specializes in Musical Theatre, and is highly competitive, but also offers Acting, Dance, Directing, and Design and Technical Applications. The Department offers 4 Main Stage productions yearly, 3 of which are musicals, for a total of 40-50 performances yearly, to a season subscription audience. A vigorous Studio Theatre and Dance program offers 30 additional public performances yearly. Graduates have a proven record of successfully competing with comparable institutions in the professional job market and for entry into graduate programs. Importantly, the Department strives to promote the attributes of good citizenship and human values, desirable and essential to the communal occupation and art that is Theatre, and to the Human family.

NORTH CAROLINA

Appalachian State University

Ray Miller, Chair	14,000 T. Enr.; h. compet.
Dept. of Theatre & Dance	Semester System
Appalachian State Univ.	100 Majors; ATHE, NAST
Boone, NC 28608	T: $4,241/$5,900 r&b
DEPT: (828) 262-3028	O-ST T: $$13,983/$5,900 r&b
FAX: (828) 265-8694	
www.theatre.appstate.edu	2sutheatre@appstate.edu
ADMISSIONS: (828) 262-2120	FAX: (828) 262-3296
admissions@appstate.edu	

DEGREES OFFERED

BA in General Theatre (56), Th. Performance (16), Design/ Technology (8); BS Teaching Theatre (20). Declare major in sophomore year.

ADMISSION & FINANCIAL INFORMATION

SAT min. 1,100; GPA 3.5; accept 20% into institution; Audition, Interview, Portfolio for designers. Th. program admits all applicants; Dept. schols, $1,000/yr. renewable; resume, transcript, GPA, recs.

FACULTY AND CLASSES OFFERED

9 Full-Time, 5 PT: 3 PhD, 10 MFA/MA; 3 Staff

A. (2 FT, 5 PT) Intro to Theatre-1/Y; Theatre History-3/Y; Shakes-2/X; Dramatic Lit-1/Y; Playwriting-1/Y

B. (4 FT, 4 PT) Acting-4/Y; Voice-3/Y; Mvmt-1/Y; Directing-2/Y; Stage Combat-1/Y; Perf. of Lit-3/Y; Children's Th-1/Y; Creative Drama-2/Y; Singing-X; Film-4/Y

C. (3 FT) Prins of Des-1/Y; Set Design-1/O; Cost Des-1/O; Ltg Des-1/O; Tech Prod-1/Y; Cost Constr-1/Y; Cost Hist-X; Make-up-2/Y; Stage Mgmt-1/Y

D. (1 PT) Arts Management-1/Y

FACILITIES AND PRODUCTIONS

MAINSTAGE: 335 seats, computerized lighting. 4 Fac dir, 5 Fac des, 2 UG des prods; budget $10,000-15,000

SECOND STAGE: 125 seats, computerized lighting. 19 prods: 1 Fac dir/UG des, 18 UG dir/des; budget $100-1,000

Facility built in 1938, renovated in 1994; includes scene shop, cost. shop, dance, rehearsal studios, design studio, 2 classrooms.

8 student-written plays produced in the last two years.

Connection wih Blowing Rock Stage Company. Internships in stage management, production, dramaturgy, opportunities for acting, co-productions. Also associated with Horn in the West, summers, which uses student actors, tech, and dancers.

DESCRIPTION

Guest Artist: Robby Benson, Acting for Camera and Screenwriting; Glenn Bruce, Acting for Camera, Screenwriting; Gary Walker, Film; Bill Pivetta, Film.

Appalachian State University Theatre offers a broadly based liberal arts education in theatre. Students are prepared to teach theatre with K-12 certification or are prepared for further study in theatre either in graduate school, professional schools, or as apprentices in professional companies. Students are encouraged to study and participate in all aspects of theatre training and production. Students in the BA program are allowed to select one of three concentrations: performance, design/tech or general theatre. The theatre offers an active and varied production program; students are given opportunities to direct, design, stage manage, and work in promotional and business areas as well as act in a variety of plays in three theatres and on tour.

Campbell University

Dept. of Theatre Arts	2,500 Tot Enr.; H
P. O. Box 21	Semester System
Buies Creek, NC 27506	30 Majors; ATHE
DEPT: (910) 893-1495	T: $18,850/$6,300 R&B
FAX: (910) 893-1515	SMALL PROGRAM
www.campbell.edu	
ADMISSIONS: P. O. Box 546, Buies Creek, NC 27506	
(910) 893-1290	adm@mailcenter.campbell.edu

DEGREES OFFERED

BA in Theatre Arts (20), Drama & Christian Ministry (10). Declare major sophomore year.

ADMISSION & FINANCIAL INFORMATION

Inst reqs. ACT & SAT scores; th program admits all apps, no special reqs. Brenda Holland Scholarship, based on performance and academics.

FACULTY AND CLASSES OFFERED

2 FT, 1 PT, 3 MA/MFA

A. (1 FT) Intro to Theatre-1/Y; Theatre History-2/Y; Shakes-1/X; Dramatic Lit.-1/O; Playwriting-1/O; Theatrical Production in a Church Environment 1/O

B. (1 FT) Acting/Scene Study-4/Y; Voice/Speech-2/Y; Directing-2/Y; Dance-2/X; Movement-1/X; Singing-3/X; Stage Combat-1/O; Puppetry-1/O

C. (1 PT) Set Des-1/O; Cost Des-1/O; Ltg Des-1/O; Make-up-1/O; Stg Mgmt-1/O; Principals of Design-2/O; Tech Production-1/O; Costume Construction-1/O

FACILITIES AND PRODUCTIONS

MAINSTAGE: 400 seats, fly space, computerized lighting. 4 Prods: 3-4 Fac Dir/Des, 1-2 UG Dir/Des.

Facility was built in 1985. Includes scene, costume, CAD facility, 1 movement/dance studio.

DESCRIPTION

Noted Faculty: Georgia Martin, Performance, E. Bert Wallace, Playwriting/Dramaturgy

Guest Artists: Doug Berkey, Masks/Mime.

Cambell University is a Christian institution dedicated to a liberal artrs philosophy. The Department of Theatre Arts offers courses of study both in general theatre as well as drama ministry. We see human vocation as living by faith under grace, with no conflict between the life of faith and the life of inquiry. The Department operates within a Christian liberal arts framework: training students in the theatre arts while providing a well-rounded overall education.

Catawba College

Woodrow Hood, Chair
Theatre Arts Dept.
Catawba College
Salisbury, NC 28144
DEPT: (704) 637-4440
wbhood@catawba.edu
ADMISSIONS: 2300 W. Innes, St., Salisbury, NC 28144
(704) 637-4402

1,250 Tot Enr.; competitive
Semester System
120 Majors; ATHE
T: $18,000/$6,000 R&B
FAX: (704) 637-4207
www.catawba.edu

FAX: (704) 637-4222
admissions@catawba.edu

DEGREES OFFERED

BA in Musical Theatre (50) Theatre Arts (50); BS in Theatre Admin (4); BFA in Musical Theatre (8); Design (4); Performance (4)Declare major first year; 2007 granted 35 degrees.

ADMISSION & FINANCIAL INFORMATION

SAT of 1100 + essay, minimum 3.0 GPA, 80% of applicants admitted; 30 out of 100 applicants admitted to theatre program, special requirements are audition (actors), interview, and portfolio for designers. Scholarships for theatre are awarded by audition.

FACULTY AND CLASSES OFFERED

14 Full-Time, 2 Part-Time: 2 PhD, 12 MA/MFA; 2 Staff

A. (1 FT, 1 PT) Intro to Theatre-1/Y; Dramatic Lit-1/Y; Dramatic Crit-1/Y; Theatre History-2/Y; Shakes-5/Y; Playwriting-1/Y

B. (4 FT, 1 PT) Acting-7/Y; Voice/Speech-8/Y; Movement-1/Y; Singing-8/Y; Musical Th-10/Y; Directing-2/Y; Stage Combat-1/Y; Dance-4/Y;Mime, etc-3/O

C. (5 FT) Prins of Des-2/Y; Set Des-2/Y; Cost Des-2/Y; Ltg Des-2/Y; Tech Prod-3/Y; Cost Constr-2/Y; Make-up-2/Y; Stg Mgmt-1/Y

D. (2 FT) Arts Mgmt-8/Y; Marketing/Promo-8/Y; Budgeting/Acct-O; Contracts/Copyright-1/Y; B.O. Proced-O; Development/Grant Writing-O

FACILITIES AND PRODUCTIONS

MAINSTAGE: 1500 seats, fly space, computerized lighting
6-7 prods: 6-7 Fac dir/des; budget $4,000-9,000

SECOND STAGE: 250 seats, computerized lighting
12 prods: 12 UG dir; 10 UG des; budget $1,000-2,000

THIRD STAGE: 100 seats, black box, computerized lighting
4 Workshop/Readings: 2 Fac dir; 2 UG dir; budget $50-$100

Facility built in 1964, last renovated in 2005, includes scene, costume shops, prop shop, welding shop, CAD Facility, sound studio, dance studio, rehearsal studio, 2 design studios, 5 classrooms.

A non-departmental student-run organization presents 2-4 prods per year in which majors participate. 4 student-written plays have been produced in the last two years.

Department is connected to 10 professional companies.

DESCRIPTION

Noted Faculty: Woodrow Hood, History/Acting/Playwriting; Dayna Anderson, Acting, Directing; Elizabeth Homan, Acting/Directing; David Pulliam, Set Design; Chris Zink, Design; Missy Barnes, Musical Theatre; Joe Falocco, Acting/Literature; Eric Abbott, Costumes; Linda Kesler, Mgmt; Jeff Chase, TD

Catawba College Theatre Arts ranked amongst the top 10 in the nation regularly by the Princeton Review: Recent grads work on Broadway and around the country at professional, equity companies. Long established relationships with multiple professional companies. Study theatre abroad in England, Japan, Italy, France and others. Internships available in NY, London, and others. Virtually 100% of graduates work professionally or attend graduate school after graduation. Large production season offers multiple casting and design opportunities for students. Large Music Theatre program. No graduate program means all shows are acted and staged by undergraduates. Intimate college environment in an authentic community atmosphere.

Davidson College

Ann Marie Costa, Chair
Dept of Theatre
P. O. Box 7141
Davidson College
Davidson, NC 28035-7141
DEPT: (704) 894-2361
ancosta@davidson.edu
ADMISSIONS: P. O. Box 7156, Davidson, NC 28035-7156
(704) 894-2230
www.davidson.edu

1,700 Tot Enr.; compet.
Semester System
12 Majors; ATHE
T: $25,903/$7,371 R&B
SMALL PROGRAM
FAX: (704) 894-2463

admission@davidson.edu

DEGREES OFFERED

BA in Theatre (17). Declare major in sophomore year; 2006 granted 7 degrees.

ADMISSION & FINANCIAL INFORMATION

30% of applicants accepted, no special reqs for theatre program.

FACULTY AND CLASSES OFFERED

4 FT; 2 PT; 2 PhD; 4 MA/MFA; 3 Staff

A. (1/2 FT) Intro to Theatre-2/Y; Theatre History-1/Y; Shakes-1/X; Playwriting-1/O

B. (2 1/2 FT) Acting/Scene Study-4/Y; Directing-2/Y; Movement-1/Y

C. (1 FT; 1 PT) Prins of Des-1/Y; Set Des-1/Y; Lighting Des-1/Y; Stage Management-1/O

D. (1PT) Arts Management-1/Y

FACILITIES AND PRODUCTIONS

MAINSTAGE: 569 seats, fly space; computerized, electronic lighting; 2 prods, 2 Fac dir/des prods; budget $1,000-5,000

SECOND STAGE: 289 seats, computerized, electronic lighting, 2 prods, 1 Fac dir, 2 Fac des prods, 1 Guest Art Dir; budget $250-600

Third stage: 100 seats, computerized, electronic lighting.

6 UG Direct and 2 UG Design Wkshop/Readings; budget $50-150

Facility was built in 1960, renovated in 2002; includes scene shop, costume shop, movement/dance studio.

Non-departmental student run producing organization presents 3-4 prods in which department majors participate.

Connection with Actor's Theatre of Charlotte (guest artist contracts with Equity). Students often intern in stage management, admin. and design. Also, acting internships are available.

DESCRIPTION

Noted Faculty: Dr. Joseph Gardner, Design/Hist; Prof. Ann Marie Costa, Performance/Directing; Dr. Sharon Green, Hist/Scholar/Contemporary Play Analysis; Prof. Jack Beasley. Visiting Professors: Scott Ripley and Mark Sutch.

Guest Artists: Penny Fuller, Actress; Steve Umberger, Dir; Keith Martin, Dir; Mark Eisman, Playwright; RSC, 2 week residency; Rebecca Cairns, Costumer; Irene Fornes, Playwright; Terry Loughlin, Actor; Robert Moss, Art Dir, Syracuse Stage.

Davidson College is a liberal arts institution known for its academic rigor and highly selective admissions standards. The Theatre program offers a range of courses balanced between theoretical and practical knowledge. Courses at all levels are heavily subscribed, testifying to the quality of classroom instruction. Complementing the curriculum is an active production program which includes both faculty-directed and student-directed work. Many students in classes and production are non-majors; the relatively small size of the institution (1,700) encourages participation by many students regardless of major. The theatre faculty gives qualified students special assistance in securing internships, preparing for regional and national auditions, and applying for graduate studies. In 2002 Davidson College built the Duke Family Performance Hall, a state-of-the-art theatre facility which houses our two mainstage productions.

Duke University

John Clum, Director
Dept of Theater Studies
206 Bivins Bldg, Box 90680
Duke University
Durham, NC 27708
DEPT: (919) 660-3343
www.duke.edu/web/theaterstudies/
ADMISSIONS: Office of UG Adm., Box 90586, Durham, NC 27708
(919) 684-3214   www.admissions.duke.edu

Total Enr. 6,200; h. comp.
Semester System
40 majors; NAST, ATHE, U/RTA
T: $34,202/$9,500 R&B
theater@duke.edu

DEGREES OFFERED

BA in Theater Studies. 2006 granted 10 degrees. Declare major in sophomore year.

ADMISSION & FINANCIAL INFORMATION

Inst. accepts 10%; top 10% HS, average ACT 29-32, SAT 600-690 verbal, 660-750 math. No special requirements for acceptance. Optional supplementary materials may be submitted.

FACULTY AND CLASSES OFFERED

11 FT; 4 PT; 10 PhD; 13 MA/MFA; 1 MBA; 1 Prof. w/out adv. degree; 3 Staff

A. (4 1/2 FT, 9 PT) Intro to Th-1/Y; Shakes-2/Y; Dramatic Lit-10/Y; Playwriting-4/Y; Dramatic Crit-1/O

B. (4 1/2 FT, 1 PT) Acting-5/Y; Directing-2/Y; Voice/Speech-1/Y; Musical Theatre-1/Y; Voice/Body Gesture-1/Y; Production/Workshop/Lab-6/Y

C. (1 FT, 1 PT) Lighting Des-1/Y; Costume Des-1/Y; Set Des-1/Y

D. (1 FT) Arts Management-2/Y

FACILITIES AND PRODUCTIONS

MAINSTAGE: 620 seats, fly space, computerized lighting. 1 Prod, Fac. dir/des, budget $8,500-9,000

SECOND STAGE: 120 seats, computerized lighting. 2 Prod, 2 Fac dir/des, 1 UG des; budget $7,500-8,000

THIRD STAGE: 100 seats; 2 Workshops/Readings; Fac Dir/Des, UG Des, budget $200-300

Facility includes scene, costume, prop, CAD Fac, movement/dance, 1 rehearsal, 2 design and 3 classrooms.

NEW THEATER STUDIES STUDIO- built in 2003. Includes new costume and scene shop, design studio and seminar room.

Student-run producing organizations generally present 6 productions per year in which dept. majors participate. 10 student-written plays produced in last 2 years.

Connection with Theater Previews at Duke (AEA). This is the professional arm of the Dept of Theater Studies. A laboratory for the professional development and production of new plays and musicals on Duke's campus, Theater Previews gives students opportunities to work with playwrights, composers, actors, directors, designers, managers, and technicians and to participate in the creation of a new work of theater. Guest professionals from all over the country converge on campus to write, develop, and rehearse the works in progress.

DESCRIPTION

Noted Faculty: John Clum, Lit; Jody McAuliffe, Lit, Directing; Jeff Storer, Acting, Directing; Neal Bell, Playwriting, Screenwriting;

Emanuel Azenberg, Producer; Zannie Voss, Theater Management; Daniel Foster, Lit; Michael Malone, Screenwriting.

Guest Artists: Wilson Milam, Derek McLane, Sutton Foster, Yusef El Guindi, Nick Hornby, Brian Charles Rooney, Maureen McGovern, Jim Findlay, Ari Fliakos, Gore Vidal, Susan H. Schulman, Chris Noth, Michael Learned, Charles Durning.

Combining respect for history with immersion in contemporary issues, and intellectual engagement with creative expression, the Dept of Theater Studies offers students a variety of opportunities to study and practice theater. The faculty view theater as a form of human expression, shaped by social, economic, technological, personal, and artistic forces. Courses are designed to give majors a broad background necessary for advanced professional or scholarly work and to offer non-majors the opportunity to deepen their understanding and appreciation of the theater. Guiding the work of the faculty is the belief that the theater is a collaborative art form that reaches out to other disciplines. Courses in dramatic literature and the theater arts are complemented by productions of plays, past and present. This combination of academic coursework and production experience is a hallmark of the department's approach. Its courses and productions are open to all undergraduates..

East Carolina University

John Shearin, Director
School of Theatre & Dance
East Carolina University
Greenville, NC 27858
DEPT: (252) 328-6390
theatre-dance@ecu.edu
ADM: ECU, Greenville, NC 27858
(252) 328-6640

20,000 Total Enr.
Semester; not compet.
200 Majors
T: $2,986/10,000 r&b
O-ST T: $12,642/10,000 r&b

www.ecu.edu/admissions

DEGREES OFFERED

BA in Theatre Arts (30); BFA in Prof. Acting (60), Design & Production (30), Stage Management (5), Dance Performance (60), Dance Education (40), Musical Th (60), Theatre Ed (15); Declare major in sophomore year; 2004 granted 30 degrees.

ADMISSION & FINANCIAL INFORMATION

Contact area co-ordinator by email, names for scholarship information available on website. Auditions for Prof. Acting & Musical Theatre in spring of freshman or sophomore year.

FACULTY AND CLASSES OFFERED

15 Full-Time, 17 MFA/MA. Catalog available on line.

FACILITIES AND PRODUCTIONS

MAINSTAGE: 600 seats, fly space, 5 prods (see website)

Facility built in 1960, completely renovated in 1982; scene, cost, props shops, CAD Fac, 1 Video Studio, 3 Movement/Dance studios, paint shop, black box theatre.

Connection with the ECU/Loessin Summer Theater, an Equity company; gifted students are hired on an individual basis to work both backstage and as actors.

DESCRIPTION

Noted Faculty: John Shearin, Donald Biehn, Joseph Carow, Michael

Tahaney, Robert Alpers.

Guest Artists: Pat Hingle, Ryan Hilliard, Joseph Kolinsky; Dancer-choreographers - Eddy Ocampo, Thomas Bell, Gabriel Masson, Martin Kravitz.

The mission of the Theatre and Dance Department is twofold: BFA programs—to prepare actors, dancers production technicians and teachers to work professionally upon graduation, and a BA - to offer basic liberal arts experience as a foundation for further training. Theatre majors obtain experience in the basics of performance production: acting, stage scenery, voice and articulation, theatre history, lighting, costuming, movement, and audition preparation.

Elon University

Fredrick J. Rubeck, Chair
Dept. of Performing Arts
Campus Box 2800
Elon University
Elon, NC 27244
rubeck@elon.edu
www.elon.edu/perarts
ADMISSIONS: CAMPUS BOX 2700, Elon, NC 27244
(800) 334-8448
admissions@elon.edu

4,956 Total Enr.; h.compet.
130 Majors
Semester System
T: $22,166/$7,296 R&B
DEPT: (336) 278-5600
FAX: (336) 278-5609

www.elon.edu/admissions

DEGREES OFFERED

BFA in Music Theatre (75), Acting (50)); BA in Design & Prod (18); Theatre Studies (25) Declare major in freshman year; 2007 granted 35 UG degrees.

ADMISSION & FINANCIAL INFORMATION: 40% admitted by institution,3.6 GPA, mid SAT 1720-1960; audition/interview for actors; interview, portfolio for designers; Theatre prog. admits 32 out of 300 applicants. A number of performance based scholarships are available. The entrance audition qualifies each student for consideration.

FACULTY AND CLASSES OFFERED

8 1/2 FT, 2 1/2 PT: 1 PhD, 12 MFA/MA,2 Staff

A. (1 1/2 FT, 1/2 PT) Intro to Theatre-1/Y; Th Hist-2/Y; Shakes-1/O Dramatic Lit-2/Y

B. (4 FT, 1 PT) Acting-10/Y; Movement-2/Y; Singing-pvt/Y; Directing-1/Y; Voice/Speech-4/Y; Dance-27/Y; Stage Combat-1/O; Musical Th.-3/Y; Mime, etc-1/O

C. (3 FT, 1 PT) Set Des-1/Y; Ltg Des-1/Y; Make-up-1/Y; Stage Mgmt-1/O; Cost Des-1/O; Tech Prod-1/Y; Cost Constr-1/Y

FACILITIES AND PRODUCTIONS

MAINSTAGE: 572 seats, fly space, computerized & electronic lighting
     4 prods: 4 Fac dir, 14 Fac des, 2 GA des; budget $2,500-15,000

SECOND STAGE: 100 seats, electronic lighting
     17 prods: 6 Fac dir, 12 Fac des, 11 UG dir, 30 UG des; budget $500-1500

THIRD STAGE: 125 seats, computerized lighting

Facility was built in 1988, black box renovated in 2006; includes scene, costume shops, 4 rehearsal studios, 1 design studio, 3 dance studio, 2 classrooms.

DESCRIPTION

Noted Faculty: Catharine McNeela, Music Theatre; Frederick J.

Rubeck, Acting; Richard P. Gang, Acting/Dir; Linda Sabo, Music Theatre; Dale Becherer, Design; Bill Webb, Lighting Design; Jane Wellford, Dance; Shouze Ma, Dance (Modern); Nina Wheeler, Jazz.

Guest Artists: Master Classes: Scott Bradley, Des; Dave Clemmons, Casting; Andrew Lippa, Jason Robert Brown, Ricky Ian Gordon

Elon University Department of Performing Arts provides conservatory style training in a liberal arts setting. We offer BFA degrees in Music Theatre and Acting; and BA degrees in Theatre Studies and Theatrical Design & Production. We strive to achieve the following: To thoroughly prepare students for a career in the performing arts or for graduate study with the following specialties: Music Theatre - to train performers skilled in voice, theory, acting and dance; Acting - to train performers skilled in performance, voice for the actor, movement and a broad range of acting technique and style; Theatre Studies - to prepare a theatre generalist experienced in performance, theory, design and production, and to foster an appreciation of all aspects of the art form; For Design & Production - to train students in technical production, scenic, lighting and costume design. We train all majors not only for the art but also for the business.

Greensboro College

David Schram, Chair
Theatre Department
Greensboro College
815 W. Market St.
Greensboro, NC 27401-1875
http://theatre.gborocollege.edu
DEPT: (336) 272-7102 x 242
ADMISSIONS: Above address
(800) 346-8226

1,300 Total Enr.; compet.
53 Majors
Semester System
T: $17,670/$7,400 R&B
O-ST: $19,470/$7,400 R&B
theatre@gborocollege.edu
FAX: (336) 217-7235

www.gborocollege.edu

DEGREES OFFERED
BA, BS in Acting (28); Design/Technical (13), Theatre Education (2), Stage Dir/Mgmt. (5); Costume (5) Declare major in freshman year; 2007 granted 10 degrees.

ADMISSION & FINANCIAL INFORMATION
SAT, GPA, class rank; 60% of applicants admitted to institution; aud, interview, portfolio for designers, directors & stage mgrs; Th. prog. admits 4 out of 10 apps. One full scholarship (Haley Scholarship) to incoming student each year. All theatre majors on scholarship ($2,500-$7,500) by aud/portfolio review and interview.

FACULTY AND CLASSES OFFERED
4 FT, 9 PT: 1 PhD/DFA, 10 MFA/MA, 2 Prof. w/o adv. degree

A. (2 PT) Intro to Theatre-1/Y; Th Hist-1/Y; Shakes-1/X; Dramatic Lit-2/X; Dramatic Crit-1/O; Playwriting-1/Y

B. (1 1/3 FT, 4 PT) Acting-8/Y; Movement-2/Y; Singing-8/Y; Directing-3/Y; Voice/Speech-2/Y; Stage Combat-1/O; Musical Th.-1/O

C. (2 1/3 FT, 2 PT) Principles of Des-4/Y; Costume Des-5/Y; Tech Prod-5/Y; Stage Mgmt-3/Y; Lighting Des-1/Y; Make-up-1/Y

D. (1 PT) Arts Mgmt-1/Y

FACILITIES AND PRODUCTIONS
MAINSTAGE: 789 seats, fly space, computerized lighting
    4 prods: 1 Fac dir, 2 Fac des, 1 GA dir; 2 UG dir; budget $5,000-10,000

SECOND STAGE: 119 seats, computerized lighting
    7 prods: 2 Fac dir, 5 UG dir, 4 UG des; budget $500-2,500

Facility was built in 1928, renovated in 2000; includes scene, costume shops, CAD facility, 1 movement/dance; 2 rehearsal studio, 1 design studio

Connected with the Berkshire Theatre Festival (Equity), guaranteed opportunities for actors to be in the acting internship program. Guaranteed opportunity for directors, stage managers and theatre manager to intern at BTF. Paid opportunities for designer/Tech and costumers to work at BTF.

DESCRIPTION
Noted Faculty: John Saari, Design/Tech; Robin Monteith, Acting; David Schram, Directing; John Heil, Tech Dir; Ashley Hyers, Alexander Tech; Dan Seaman, Theatre Educ; Marion Seaman, Costume; Richard Whittington, Theatre Mgmt; Kim Moore, Playwriting; Kathy Keating, Drama Lit

Guest Artists: Paul Owen, Scenic Des; Stephen DuBay, Lighting; Stephanie Holladay, Acting; Katy Brown, Acting; E. Gray Simons, Acting; James Langer, Acting; Katharine Hagner, Stage Mgmt

Greensboro College Theatre Department offers a Bachelor of Arts and a Bachelor of Science degree in Theatre with emphases in Acting for the Stage, Costuming, Stage Directing/Management, Theatre Education, and Theatre Design and Technical Theatre. First Year Students get acting roles and tech jobs right away; there are no graduate school students at GC. An incoming student will work immediately - hard and long hours to prepare you for the profession. The theatre program produces main stage, second stage, and student directed and designed shows. Most theatre majors work in professional theatre every summer. Graduates attend MFA theatre programs throughout the country and work in professional theatre and the television entertainment, and education fields. We are the ONLY college theatre program that has an affiliation with the nationally renowned Berkshire Theatre Festival in Massachusetts. Students attend the acting apprenticeship program, work as technicians, and intern as assistant directors and assistant stage managers at BTF. We were the ONLY college/university theatre program selected to perform at the prestigious Skena-Up International Student Theatre and Film Festival in Pristina, Kosova in November, 2006. The Theatre Department received a $2 million gift in a matching fund drive ($4 million total) to improve facilities and hire faculty and guest artists.

Guilford College

Jack Zerbe, Chair
Dept. of Theatre Studies
Guilford College

800 W. Friendly Ave.
Greensboro, NC 27410
DEPT: (910) 316-2341
admission@guilford.edu

1,202 Total Enr.; competitive
Semester System
28 Majors; ATHE
T:$24,470/$6,860 r&b
T: $10,270
SMALL PROGRAM
MAIN: (910) 316-2000
www.guilford.edu

DEGREES OFFERED
BA in Theatre Studies (30). Declare major in 1st or 2nd year.

ADMISSION & FINANCIAL INFORMATION

Inst. admits 67% of applicants. ACT/SAT, GPA. Inst. scholarships: honors scholarships. awarded thru admissions process; Dana Scholarships to outstanding upperclassmen through faculty committee.

FACULTY AND CLASSES OFFERED

3 Full-Time, 1 PT: 3 MA/MFA; 2 Staff

A. (1 FT) Intro to Theatre-1/Y; Dramatic Lit-4/O; Theatre History-2/O; Shakes-2/OY; Playwriting-1/O

B. (1 FT) Acting-4/YO; Voice/Speech-2/YO; Directing-2/YO;Auds-1/O

C. (1 FT, 1 PT) Prins of Des-2/Y; Tech Prod'n-1/O; Make-up-1; Stg Mgmt-1/Y; Ltg Des.-1/O; Set Design-1/O; Ltg Tech-1/Y; Props - 1/Y; Cost Maint.-1/Y

D. Marketing/Promotion-1/Y; Box Office-1/Y; House Management-1/Y

FACILITIES AND PRODUCTIONS

MAINSTAGE: 150-200 seats, computerized lighting. 3 Fac dir/des prods (0-1 Guest dir/des); budget $10,000-12,000

Facility was build in 1975; scene shop renovated in 1990; includes scene shop, 2 rehearsal studios, 1 classroom.

Dept. majors generally participate in a non-departmental, student-run producing organization that presents 2 productions per year.

DESCRIPTION

Noted Faculty: April Soroko, design; Lee Soroko, acting, stage combat, lit; Jack Zerbe, act/dir, hist, lit.; Robert Elderkin, tech. prod/sound des.

Guest Artists: (classes, workshops, production) Edward Albee, playwright; Tony Escher, playwright, Sidney Poitier, actor.

The Theatre Studies Department cultivates the capacity of students to create and appreciate theatre that explores and illuminates the human condition. The course of study seeks to produce creative artists with intellectual acuity, refined craft, and a heightened appreciation for theatre as an instrument of social change. We nurture individuals who want to make a difference in the world by taking constructive action through the art form of theatre. The program offers both majors and non-majors the chance to experience the collaborative process by which actors, designers, directors, scholars, and technicians interpret a playscript and translate a shared vision of its meaning into the medium of theatrical production. Classes develop the skills essential to that process: critical thinking; research methods; intuitive reasoning; communication; project planning and time management; problem-solving; team work; leadership. The integration of theory and practice is fundamental to the program, as it is to successful theatre, and the conceptual learning of formal course work is therefore augmented by laboratory work in the form of theatrical productions. Productions are chosen with attention to the developmental needs of the current student population. In a four-year period, students will experience a broad range of styles and periods of dramatic literature in performance.

Lees-McRae College

Janet Barton Speer, Director
Div of Performing Arts
Lees-McRae College
Banner Elk, NC 28604
DEPT: (828) 898-8840
admissions@lmc.edu
pasrecruitment@lmc.edu

939 Total Enr.; competitive
Semester System
92 majors/minors
T, R&B: $19,940
MAIN: (828) 898-5241
www.lmc.edu

DEGREES OFFERED

BA/BS in Musical Theatre, Theatre Arts, Th. Arts Education (K-12), Arts Ministry, Dance. Declare major in 1st year.

ADMISSION & FINANCIAL INFORMATION

Inst. requires SAT/ACT, GPA, teacher rec., class rank, activities; theatre program requires audition for scholarships.

FACULTY AND CLASSES OFFERED

8 Full-Time: 2 PhD, 6 MFA/MA; 2 Staff & 2 Adjunct

A. (1 1/2 FT) Intro to Th-1/Y; Th History-1/Y; Shakes-2/Y; Playwriting-1/Y; Hist. of Musical Th-1/O; Hist. of Mod World Drama-1/O

B. (3 FT) Acting-4/Y; Voice/Speech-1/Y; Movement-8/Y; Singing-12/Y; Musical Theatre-2/0; Directing-2/Y

C. (1 FT) Set Design-1/Y; Cost Des-1/O; Ltg Des-1/Y; Tech Prod'n-5/Y; Cost Constr-1/O; Cost Hist-1/O; Make-up-1/O; Stg Mgmt-1/O

D. (1/2 FT) Theatre Management and Publicity-1/O

FACILITIES AND PRODUCTIONS

MAINSTAGE: 815 seats, computerized lighting. 8 prods: 6 Fac dir, 1 Guest dir, 1 student dir, 2 Fac des, 2 Guest des, 1 student des; budget $1500-3000

SECOND STAGE: 50 seats. 1 Fac dir/des prod; budget $300-1000,

10 Guest dir Workshops./Readings; budget $100-500

Facility was built in 1964; facility includes scene, costume, props shops, dance studio, rehearsal studio, design studio, classrooms.

Connection with Lees-McRae Summer Theatre. Students work in acting, set construction, lighting, props, box office, costumes, publicity. Faculty also helps students aud. for other summer comps.; 100% of students who audition are placed in summer theatre jobs.

DESCRIPTION

Noted Faculty: Dr. Janet Barton Speer; Steve Parrish, Mus Th; Michael Hannah, Costumes, History and Directing; Jim Taylor, Voice; Kacy Crabtree, Dance; David Dawson, Tech, Design; Paul Adamson, Keyboard; Stacy Burgess, Clogging, various guest artists.

At Lees-McRae College, a small school with a "family" atmosphere, students are allowed to excel. Freshmen and sophomores are given immediate performance and technical opportunities. The Division of Performing Arts at Lees-McRae provides students with a sound academic program that includes studies in history, theatre literature, critical thinking, writing skills, and vocal technique. Students also study acting, dance, piano, voice, directing, theatre management, and technical theatre.

Lenoir Rhyne College

Mia Self, Artistic Dir.
School of Comm. & Literature
Lenoir-Rhyne College
Hickory, NC 28603
DEPT: (828) 328-7162
FAX: (828) 328-7163
ADMISSIONS: P. O. Box 7227, Lenoir-Rhyne College, Hickory, NC 28603
(800) 277-5721   (828) 328-7300
FAX: (828) 328-7378
admission@lrc.edu   www.lrc.edu

1,550 Total Enr.; not compet.
Semester System
23 Majors; ATHE
T: $10,345 PER SEM
$3,910-$4,810 R&B PER SEM
SMALL PROGRAM

DEGREES OFFERED

BA in Theatre (19), Theatre-Education (1), Theatre-English (1), Theatre-English Education (1). Declare major in 1st year; 2001 granted 7 degrees.

ADMISSION & FINANCIAL INFORMATION

Inst. reqs. SAT, GPA, class rank, activities; Th. program admits all applics. Playmaker Th. Scholarships - $1,000, awarded by audition.

FACULTY AND CLASSES OFFERED

2 Full-Time, 1 Part-Time: 2 PhD, 3 MA/MFA

A. (1/2 FT) Intro to Theatre-2/Y; Dramatic Lit-3/X; Theatre History-2/Y; Shakes-1/X; Playwriting-1/O

B. (1/2 FT, 1 PT) Acting/Scene Study-3/Y; Voice/Speech-1/O; Directing-1/O

C. (1 FT) Set Des-1/O; Cost Des-1/O; Ltg Des-1/O; Tech Prod-1/Y; Cost Constr-1/O; Make-up-1/O; Stg Mgmt-1/O

FACILITIES AND PRODUCTIONS

MAIN STAGE: 180 seats, computerized lighting. 2 Fac dir/des prods; budget $1,500-2,500

SECOND STAGE: 1500 seats, fly space, computerized lighting 1 UG dir/des prod; budget $500-1,000

Mainstage was built in 1982; facilities include scene, costume shops, sound, video studios, dance rehearsal studios, design studio, classrooms.

Majors participate in a non-departmental, student-run producing organization that presents 1 production per year.

DESCRIPTION

Guest Artists/Visiting Teachers: Max Howard, actor; Ron Aulgur, actor; Jerry Stubblefield, playwright; Mike Farrel, actor; Fred Nash, video performer; Rafael Lopez-Barrantes, vocal coach.

Lenoir-Rhyne College is an institution of the Lutheran Church. The primary concern of the college is to liberate mind and spirit, clarify personal faith, foster physical wholeness, build a sense of community, and promote responsible leadership for service in the world. The Theatre Arts program is housed in the Department of Art, Theatre Arts and Communication. Arts study at Lenoir-Rhyne is grounded in the liberal arts tradition and tailored to fit a student's individual needs. Theatre students pursue course work in dramatic theory, history, and literature as well as various studio courses in all phases of production work (performance, stage and camera, scenography, stage technology, and management). Supplementing class work is an ambitious production program involving 3 mainstage shows, a student laboratory. Full-time staff instruct and produce for stage and television. Visiting artists and practicing professionals teach during limited residencies and workshops. Internship programs with regional theatres; career counseling and portfolio review; semester abroad; programs in England and theatre arts workshops in New York; honors program and teacher certification are available; successful job placement and graduate school entrance.

Livingstone College

Chair
Theatre Arts Dept.
Livingstone College
Salisbury, NC 28144
DEPT: (704) 216-1849
ADM: 701 West Monroe St., Salisbury, NC 28144
(800) 835-3435   (704) 216-1217
www.livingstone.edu

1,200 Total enr.; competitive
16 Majors; U/RTA, ATHE
Res. T:$10,278.90
$5,641.10 R&B
SMALL PROGRAM
FAX: (704) 216-1217

DEGREES OFFERED

BFA in Acting (10), Tech. Theatre(3), Th. Mgmt.(3)
Declare major in 1st yr

ADMISSION & FINANCIAL INFORMATION

GPA and SAT for inst. admission; Theatre Prog. req's aud./portfolio/int., recommendations. Accept 50% to inst., 10 of 80 apps. to Th. prog.

FACULTY AND CLASSES OFFERED

4 FT, 3 PT; 2 Ph.D., 2 MA/MFA; 1 Prof. w/o adv.deg.

A. (2 FT) Intro. to Th.-1/Y; Th. Hist.-2/Y; Shakes.-1/X; Dram. Lit.-1/Y; Drama Crit.-1/Y; Playwriting-5/Y

B. (2 FT, 1 PT) Acting-12/Y; ?Voice/Speech-2/Y; Mvmt.-2/Y; Singing-10/X; Directing-2/Y; Dance-2/X

C. (1 PT) Prins. of Des.-3/Y; Cost., Set., Ltg. Design-2/Y; Tech prod.-2/Y; Cost. Hist.-2/Y; Stg. Mgmt.-3/Y; Cost. Constr.-2/Y; Makeup-2/Y

D. (1 PT) Arts Mgmt.-2/Y; Box Office Prodceure-2/Y; Mktg/Promo-2/Y; Development-2/Y; Accting-2/Y

FACILITIES AND PRODUCTIONS

MAINSTAGE: 400 seats, computerized lighting. 4 prods, Fac. dir/des; budget $1-8,000

SECOND STAGE: 400 seats, fly space. 2 prods, UG dir, Guest & UG des; budget $500-1,000

THIRD STAGE: 50 seats, black box. 4 wkshop/rdgs, 1 fac dir, 1 Guest dir, 2 UG dir/des; bdgt.$0-50

Facility was built in 1972, renovated 1980; includes scene shop, cost. shop, prop shop, reh. studio.

Two student-written plays produced in the last 2 years.

In the process of connecting with a prof. company.

DESCRIPTION

Noted Faculty: Dr. H.D. Flowers, II, Acting/Dir/Black Theatre; Dr. Eddie P. Bradley, Playwriting.

Guest Artists: Tracy Peterson, Voice; Gregory Carlee, Tech.

The Theatre Arts program is designed to provide students with a study of the theoretical, historical and literary aspects of Theatre, practical fulfillment with specific advanced training in aspects of Theatre production. The program of study will lead to the B.F.A. degree.

Concentrations in performance, art administration and tech. theatre are designed to produce professionals who will have skills, knowledge and aptitudes to become successful with inter-cultural settings. The student majoring in Theatre Arts will be prepared to pursue professional careers in theatre and to perform successfully in para-professionial and graduate school programs in theatre. The intent of the Theatre Arts program is to nurture and develop students to their fullest potential.

Mars Hill College

H. Neil St. Clair, Chair
Theatre Arts Department
Mars Hill College
100 Athletic St
Mars Hill, NC 28754
DEPT. (828) 689-1462
nstclair@mhc.edu
ADMISSIONS: P. O. Box 6768
(800) 543-1514
www.admissions@mhc.edu or www.mhc.edu

1,000 Total Enr.; competitive
Semester System
36 Majors; NAST
T: $18,812/$7,000 R&B
SMALL PROGRAM
FAX: (828) 689-1272
www.mhc.edu

FAX: (828) 689-1272

DEGREES OFFERED

BA in Th. Arts (18); BFA in Musical Th. (18). Declare major in freshman year; 2006 granted 8 degrees.

ADMISSION & FINANCIAL INFORMATION

SAT 800, ACT 17, GPA 2.0. Admit 85% into inst. Admit 8 out of 10 to theatre programs. 25 Th. Arts Scholarships. ($1000-3000/yr.) Aud. req., awarded on basis of promise as a performer and acceptable academic work. Aud required for BFA Musical Th.

FACULTY AND CLASSES OFFERED

3 1/2 FT, 1/2 PT: 3 1/2 MA/MFA, plus Music and Dance faculty for Musical Theatre, who belong to other Depts.; 1 Staff

A. (1/2 FT) Intro to Th-1/Y; Dramatic Lit-3/Y; Th Hist-3/Y; Shakes-1/X; Playwriting-1/O

B. (1 FT) Acting-3/Y; Voice/Speech-3/Y; Mvmt-1/O; Singing-8/Y; Directing-2/Y; Dance-4/X; Stage Combat-1/O; Musical Th-8/Y

C. (1/2 FT, 1/2 PT) Prins of Des-1/Y; Set Des-1/O; Cost Des-1/O; Ltg Des-1/O; Make-up-1/O; Stg Mgmt-1/O

FACILITIES AND PRODUCTIONS

MAINSTAGE: 166 seats, computerized lighting
    4 Fac dir/des; budget $1,000-2,000

SECOND STAGE: 1800 seats, fly space, computerized lighting
    2 UG dir/des prods; budget: up to $300-500

Facility was built in 1918, renovated in 1985; includes scene shop, costume shop, props shop, 2 video studios, 1 dance studio, rehearsal studio, design studio, theatre library.

Connection with Southern Appalachian Repertory Theatre (summer). SART is a professional, non-Equity (occasional Equity Guest artists) company under the aegis of the Dept. of Theatre Arts, Mars Hill College; many students get their first professional experience on campus (onstage and backstage). Students may be employed by the company or serve as apprentices.

DESCRIPTION

Noted Faculty: Neil St. Clair, Director.

The aims of the Department of Theatre Arts at Mars Hill

College are four-fold: 1) to prepare students for careers in the field; 2) to provide opportunities for non-majors to participate in theatre 3) to provide cultural experiences for the campus and community; and 4) to complement the work of other departments in the college. Our small program affords all students opportunities to perform onstage and backstage which is the basis for our competency based curriculum. To graduate, students must demonstrate competence in three areas: 1) dramatic literature/criticism, and theatre history; 2) technical theatre and design; 3) performance. It is our intent to work individually with students to challenge them and help them develop to their fullest potential.

North Carolina Agricultural & Technical State University

Dr. Brenda S. Faison
1601 East Market Street
NC Ag. & Tech. State Univ.
Greensboro, NC 27411
DEPT. (336) 334-7852
Frankie@ncat.edu
www.ncat.edu/

Highly competitive
Semester System
73 Majors; NAST (A), ATHE
T: $3,000
O-ST T: $11,651
FAX: (336) 334-4741

DEGREES OFFERED

BFA in Acting (68), Theatre Technology (5). Declare major in freshman year.

ADMISSION & FINANCIAL INFORMATION

SAT min 800; 2.5 GPA; Accept 85% into inst; Aud req. for Acting majors for acceptance into program, Portfolio/int. for Tech major; Accept 60% into Th Program; Tuition remission scholarships avail for out-of-state students; Th. Prog. offers ten scholarships ($250-$1,000/yr.).

FACULTY AND CLASSES OFFERED

5 Full-Time, 1 Part-Time: 1 PhD, 5 MFA/MA; 2 Staff

A. (1 FT, 1 PT) Intro to Theatre-4/Y; Dramatic Lit-2/Y; Theatre History-1/Y; Shakes-1/Y; Playwriting-1/O

B. (3 FT, 1 PT) Acting-8/Y; Voice/Speech-6/O; Movement- 2/Y; Singing-2/X; Musical Theatre-1/O; Directing-2/Y

C. (2 FT, 1 PT) Prins of Des-1/Y; Set Des-1/Y; Cost Des-1/Y; Ltg Des-1/Y; Tech Prod'n-1/Y; Cost Constr-1/Y; Cost Hist-1/Y; Make-up-1/Y; Stage Mgmt-1/Y

D. (1 FT) Arts Mgmt-1/Y; Box Office Procedure-1/Y; Marketing/Promotion-1/Y; Budgeting/Accounting Procedure-2/O

FACILITIES & PRODUCTIONS

MAINSTAGE: 372 seats, fly space, computerized lighting. 5 prods:
    4 Fac dir/des, 1 Guest dir, 1 stud des; budget $2,500-10,000

SECOND STAGE: 100 seats, computerized lighting. 2 Fac dir,
    1 Guest dir/des, 5 stud dir/des, 7 stud dir; budget $500-2,000

3 workshops/readings: 1 Fac dir/des, 2 student dir/des; budget $50-250

Facility was built in 1970, renovated in 1996; includes scene shop, costume shop, sound studio, video, rehearsal , design studios.

DESCRIPTION

Noted Faculty: Holds offices in national organization panel presenting workshop conductor.

Guest Artists: Practicing professional actresses, actors, managers and designers are frequent visitors to this campus.

The Theatre Department offers the BFA degree in acting and theatre technology. The programs are designed to prepare students for entry level positions in professional theatre and/or advanced study. All curriculums are professional oriented within a liberal arts context. The department presents four major productions annually and, numerous studio works. The theatre division premiers annually new productions from the black experience.

North Carolina Central University

Dr. Johnny B. Alston, Chair
Dept. of Theatre
North Carolina Central Univ.
Durham, NC 27707
DEPT: (919) 530-6242
FAX: (919) 530-5117
WWW.NCCU.EDU/ARTSCI/DRAMA/DRAMA.HTM
ADMISSIONS: North Carolina Central University, Undergraduate Admissions, P.O. Box 19717, Durham, NC 27707
(919) 530-6298 or (877) 667-7533
admissions@nccu.edu

7,727 Total Enr.; compet.
Semester System
73 Majors; NAST, U/RTA, ATHE
T: $3,666//$7,706 R&B
O-ST T: $13,410/$7,706 R&B

DEGREES OFFERED

BA in Theatre (73). In May of '05 will grant 10 undergraduate degrees.

ADMISSION & FINANCIAL INFORMATION

SAT 700 in-state, 750 out-of-state; ACT: 1400 in-state, 1600 out-of-state, G.P.A. 2.0.
There are no special requirements for admission to theatre program, although there are semester observations. Scholarships are awarded based on student auditions. The program generally admits 8 out of 10 applicants.

FACULTY AND CLASSES OFFERED

6 FT, 2 PT: 3 Ph.D, 5 MFA/MA, 3 Staff

A.   (3 FT) Intro to Th-2/Y; Dramatic Lit-3/Y; Th. Hist-2/Y; Playwriting-1/Y Shakespeare-1/Y

B.   (2 FT, 1 PT) Acting-3/Y; Voice/Speech-1/Y; Movement-1/Y; Directing-2/Y; Dance-1/X; Mus Th.-1/O

C.   (1 FT) Prins of Des-1/Y; Set Des-1/Y; Cost Des-1/Y; Ltg Design-1/Y; Tech Production-2/Y; Cost Construct-1/O; Stage Mgmt-1/Y

D.   (1 PT) Arts Mgmt-1/Y; Marketing/ Promo-1/X; Devel/Grant Writing-1/X; Budget/Accounting Procedure-1/X

FACILITIES AND PRODUCTIONS

MAINSTAGE: 319 seats, fly space, computerized & electronic lighting. 3 prods: 3 Fac dir./des.; budget $750-2,000

SECOND STAGE: 50 seats, computerized lighting. 3 prods: 1 Guest dir./des., 2 UG dir./des; budget $25-50.

Workshop/Reading: 1GA dir/des; budget $250-500.

Facility built in 1976, last renovated in 1995; includes scene, costume, sound studio, video studio, rehearsal studio, design studio, and prop, scenery and costume storage.

A non-departmental, student-run producing organization offers one production a year, in which departmental majors generally participate.

Two student-written plays were produced in the last two years.
Connected with Long Leaf Opera, which operates during the school year and shares facilities and production/performance personnel.

DESCRIPTION

Noted Faculty: W. Randolph Umberger, Theatre History, Management & Playwriting; Linda K. Norflett, Theatre Literature & Performance Studies; Johnny B. Alston, Technical Theatre, Literature & Criticism; Karen Dacons-Brock, Speech, Vocal & Performance Studies.

Guest Artists: Samm-Art Williams, TV/Film Producer; Woodie King Jr., Producer/Director; Daphne Reid, Actress; Juanita Bethea, Actress; Clarise Taylor, Actress; Thalmus Rasulala, Actor; Micki Grant, Actress & Playwright; Ivan Dixon, Actor, TV/Film Director; Ruby Dee, Actress; Larry Leon Hamlin, Founder and Executive Producer, National Black Theatre Festival.

The mission of the Department of Theatre is to provide a stimulating academic and artistic environment, which advocates the pursuit and acquisition of knowledge and skills, emphasizing the interdependence of theatre with our culturally diverse world of ideas and actions. We have a proud heritage of equal opportunity for all students, embracing a full spectrum of social and cultural orientations. The Department further advocates excellence in the personal and professional development of our students as they prepare to become proficient leaders of tomorrow.

North Carolina School of the Arts

See ad following page
Gerald Freedman, Dean
School of Drama
NCSA, P. O. Box 12189
Winston-Salem, NC 27117-2189
DEPT: (336) 770-3238
FAX: (336) 770-3369
ADMISSIONS: 1533 South Main St.
(336) 770-3290
www.ncarts.edu

1,065 Total Enr.; h. compet.
Trimester System
98 Majors
T: $3,224/$2,145 R&B
O-ST T: $14,654/$6,431 R&B

FAX: (336) 770-3370
admissions@ncarts.edu

DEGREES OFFERED

Diploma/BFA in Acting (91), Directing (7). Declare major in freshman year; 2004 granted 22 degrees.

ADMISSION & FINANCIAL INFORMATION

SAT or ACT scores, transcripts, personal audition/interview, 2 letters of recommendation, resume, application, application fee.; number admitted to inst. varies by dept. & discipline. 30-32 out of app. 500 applics. to acting program, 14 out of approx. 25 to design program. Th. Prog. requires aud/int/portfolio for designers. Grad requires portfolio for designers. Merit awards granted based on the audition performance and demonstrated potential.

FACULTY AND CLASSES OFFERED

16 FT, 7 PT: 7 MFA/MA, 7 Prof. w/o adv. degree; 3 Staff

A.   (2 FT, 1 PT) Intro to Th-1/Y; Dramatic Lit-4/O; Th. Hist-3/Y; Dramatic Crit-3/Y; Playwriting-O; Shakespeare-2/Y

B.   (14 FT, 6 PT) Acting-6/Y; Voice/Speech-4/Y; Movement (phys. improv, period & style, ballroom, circus, physical training-7/Y; Mime, etc.-4/Y; Singing-3/Y; Directing-3/Y; Mus Th.-3/Y; Stage Combat-3/Y; Dance:Jazz/Tap/Modern-3/Y; Intro to Biz/Audition technique (on & off camera)-1/Y

C.   Prins of Des-8/Y; Set Des-8/Y; Cost Des-7/Y; Ltg Design-8/Y;

Tech Production-4/Y; Cost Constuct-4/Y; Cost Hist-6/Y; Make-up-6/Y; Stage Mgmt-8/Y

D. Arts Mgmt-1/Y; Box Office Procedure-1/Y; Marketing/ Promo-1/Y; Devel/Grant Writing-1/Y; Legal: Contracts/ Copyright-1/Y; Budget/Accounting Procedure-1/Y

FACILITIES AND PRODUCTIONS

MAINSTAGE: 1300 seats, fly space, computerized & electronic lighting. 5 prods: 2 Fac dir, 3 Guest dir, 2 Grad des; budget $5,000-18,000

SECOND STAGE: 370 seats, fly space, electronic lighting. 3 prods: 3 Fac dir, 2 Guest dir, 3 Grad des, 2 UG des; budget $1,500-3,000

THIRD STAGE: 200 seats, black box, computerized & electronic lighting. 6 Workshops/Readings: 3 Fac dir, 3 Guest des, 3 Grad des, 2 UG des; budget $250-500

FOURTH STAGE: 100 seats, black box, computerized & electronic lighting.

Facility built in 1988; includes scene, costume, props shop, welding shop, sound studio, CAD facility, design studios, classrooms, wig & make-up shop. DeMille Theatre seats 250.

Intensive Arts Projects: Approx. 4 (one acts only, minimal prod. support)

DESCRIPTION

Noted Faculty: Matthew Bulluck, Acting; Dale Girard, Combat, Acting; Greg Walter, Singing, Musical Theatre.

Guest Artists: Benny Sato Ambush, Professional Director; Laura Henry, Meisner expert, On Camera Acting Coach; Donald Saddler, Broadway Director, Choreographer; Kevin Stites, B'way Musical Dir/Conductor; Daniel Swee, Lincoln Center Theatre Casting Dir.; Jordan Thaler, NY Shakespeare Festival Casting Dir.; Nikki Valco, Television Casting Director for Frazier; Mandy Patinkin, Actor; Joe Mantello, Film & Broadway Director, Alumnus; Mary Louise Parker, Actress, Alumnus; Terence Mann, Actor, Alumnus; Arthur Laurents, Playwright.

The School of Drama is committed to training talented young men and women to be exciting, experienced, accomplished professional actors and actresses. The School responds to a definite need in the profession for actors to be technically well-equipped and versatile, as well as creatively inspired. This vital fusion of talent and skill is the concern of the highly qualified professional faculty, which gives close personal attention to each student's development and goals. The School of Drama affirms classical values in its training process. An actor graduating from the Drama School will possess a finely honed technique and an artistic sensitivity, capable of discerning standards of quality and integrity. As part of this process, the faculty supports the pursuit of courses in the Division of General Studies in order to provide an artistically and culturally diverse environment that nurtures and develops the whole person. Above all, the actor will be grounded in a behavior that is ethical, disciplined and responsible.

University of North Carolina - Chapel Hill

A. McKay Coble, Chair
Department of Dramatic Art
CB# 3230, Ctr for Dram Art
University of North Carolina
Chapel Hill, NC 27599-3230
DEPT: (919) 962-1132
www.drama.unc.edu
ADM: CB #2200, Jackson Hall
FAX: (919) 962-3045
unchelp@admissions.unc.edu

24,501 T. Enr.; h.compet.
Semester System
100 UG Majors; 25 Grad.
T: $5,340
O-ST T: $20,988
R&B: $7,696

(919) 966-3621
www.unc.edu/admissions

DEGREES OFFERED

BA in Dramatic Art (100); MFA in Acting (10), Costume Production (7), Technical Direction (4). Declare major end of soph. yr.; 2001 granted 25 UG, 8 Grad degrees.

ADMISSION & FINANCIAL INFORMATION

Admit 20% UG applicants to inst.; 1200 SAT/top 10% of HS class. Admit all UG applics. to UG th. program, 1 out of 15 applicants to Grad program with Aud. Several scholarships. avail. to continuing students awarded by merit. All drama majors are eligible, no applic. prossess. FAF for financial aid due by Mar 1; some Teaching Ass'tships available.

FACULTY AND CLASSES OFFERED

15 FT, 4 PT, 1 Prof. w/out adv. deg: 3 PhD, 15 MFA/MA; 24 Staff (G denotes Grad courses)

A.　(4 FT, 1 PT) Intro to Th-3/Y; Dramatic Lit-5/Y; Th. Hist. & Lit.-6/Y; Shakes-1/Y; Beg. Playwriting-1/Y; Adv. Playwriting-1/Y

B.　(6 FT, 1 PT/4 FT, 1 PT-G) Acting-5/Y+3/Y G; Voice/Speech-2/YO+2/YO G; *Movement-2/YO+3/Y G; Directing-1/Y (1 FT); Reh. Perf.-3/Y G; *Movement includes Mime, Mask, Commedia, Circus, Combat, Alexander Technique.

C.　(5 FT, 1 PT UG/2 FT, 2 PT-G) Prins of Design-2/Y+1/Y G; Set Des.-2/YO+1/YO G; Cost Des.-2/YO; Ltg Des.-2/YO; Tech Prod-1/Y, 2/YG; Cost Constr-10/Y, 2/YG; Cost History-2/Y+ 2/YG; Stage Mgmt-1/Y; Prof. Th. Lab-2/Y.

D.　(1 PT) Arts Management-1/Y

FACILITIES AND PRODUCTIONS

MAINSTAGE: 499 seats, thrust stage; Equity Company; six prods; guest and resident directors and designers; budget approx. $1,400,000.

SECOND STAGE: 75-200 seats, variable configuration.

THIRD STAGE: 283 seats, proscenium

21 UG prods: 2 Fac dir, 19 UG dir/des prods

4 G prods; 4 Fac dir, 6 UG des; biudget $500-4,000

Facility was built in 1978, expanded in 1998; includes scene, costume, props shops, welding shop, sound studio, dance, rehearsal studios, design studios.

Connection with PlayMakers Repertory Company (Equity, LORT). Graduate students directly benefit. Some opportunity for undergrads.

DESCRIPTION

Noted Faculty: Adam Versenyi, Dramaturgy, Theatre History & Lit; David Hammond, Directing & Acting; Bobbi Owen, Costume History & Design; Bonnie Raphael, Voice and Speech; Raymond E. Dooley, Acting; Craig Turner, Movement for the Actor; Judy Adamson, Costume Production.; Michael Rolleri, Tech Prod.

Guest Artists: Drew Barr, Directin; Laszlo Martin, Directing; Nagle Jackson, Directing; Alan Armstrong, Costume Design; Narelle Sissons, Scenic Design; Bill Clarke, Design; Trazana Beverly Acting and Directing; Phil Monat, Lighting Design; Peter West, Lighting Design.

In the context of liberal arts studies, Dramatic Art students at UNC at Chapel Hill have the opportunity to learn about theatre in the classroom and to practice their craft in productions. The presence of PlayMakers Repertory Company gives students opportunities to associate with and learn from theatre professionals active in the regional and commercial theatre. In this BA program the student acquires a broad basis for understanding and appreciating theatre as a cultural and artistic process, while developing basic skills in the various facets of theatre. The Professional Actor Training Program at UNC-Chapel Hill is a 3-year graduate program leading to a MFA degree, organized in a conservatory structure and closely affiliated with PlayMakers Rep., the LORT/Equity theatre associated with the University and located on the campus. Students work with this company during all 3 years of their training, progressing from understudy and "walk-on" assignments to significant roles. MFA in Costume Technology is designed to develop the skills and attitude of a costume in the professional theatre. Students work with PRC to produce 6 shows per season; emphasis in courses is on technical skills. Technical Production courses give students the comprehensive knowledge needed to be effective and creative technical directors and technicians. PRC serves as a laboratory.

University of North Carolina - Greensboro

Lorraine Shackelford, Dir
Theatre Dept.
201 Taylor Building, UNCG
University of North Carolina
　at Greensboro
Greensboro, NC 27412
DEPT: (336) 334-5576
ADMISSIONS: 1000 Spring Garden, Greensboro, NC 27412
undergrad_admissions@uncg.edu
(336) 334-5243

13,000 Total Enr.; compet
Semester System
282 Majors; NAST , ATHE
www.uncg.edu
T: $4,029/$6,051 R&B
O-ST T: $15,297/$6,051 R&B
FAX: (336) 334-5100

FAX: (336) 334-3009

DEGREES OFFERED

BA in Drama (78); BFA/MFA in Acting (93/6), Design (37/11); BFA in Theatre Ed (48) MFA in Directing (3), Theatre for Youth (4); M.Ed. in Theatre Edu. (2). Declare major in sophomore.

ADMISSION & FINANCIAL INFORMATION

Accept 25% of applicants to institution. UG: Aud/Int/Port conducted after 2 semesters in the program, admit 50 of 75 applicants; Grad: Aud/Int/Port required, admit 25 of 100 applicants. Scholarships: MFA Students: Barrett: Theatre for Youth; England: Theatre. BFA: Middleton (Jr. Theatre major); Taylor (Freshman Theatre Major). MFA or BFA: Burns (Musical Theatre) Selection by faculty committees.

FACULTY AND CLASSES OFFERED

14 Full-Time: 2 PhD, 12 MFA; 5 Staff

A. (1 FT) Intro to Theatre-6/Y; Theatre History-2/Y; Shakes-2/X; Dramatic Lit-2/Y; Dramatic Criticism-1/Y; Playwriting-1/Y

B. (7 FT, 2 PT) Acting-12/Y; Voice/Speech-4/Y: Mvmt-2/X; Mime, etc-2/Y; Singing-X; Directing-4/Y; Children's Theatre-4/Y

C. (4 FT, 1 PT) Prins of Des-1/Y; Set Des- 4/Y; Cost Des-2/Y; Ltg Des-3/Y; Tech Prod'n-4/y; Cost Constr-3/Y; Cost Hist-1/X; Make-up-2/Y; Stg Mgmt-1/Y

D (1 FT) Arts Management-1/Y

FACILITIES AND PRODUCTIONS

MAINSTAGE: 500 seats, fly space, computerized lighting. 7 prods: 4 Fac dir, 2 Fac des, 1 Guest des, 3 Grad dir, 7 Grad des, 6 UG des; budget $1,000-8,000.

SECOND STAGE: 2,000 seats, fly space, computerized lighting. 2 Fac dir, 1 UG dir prods.; budget to $17,000

THIRD STAGE: 140 seats; also 75-seat black box. 2 Fac dir, 1 UG dir Readings/Workshops

Facility built in 1969, renovated in 1996; includes scene, costume shops, CAD facility. 1 student-written play produced in last two years.

Connection with North Carolina Theatre for Young People, during the school year.

DESCRIPTION

Noted Faculty: Dr. Robert C. Hansen, Theatre Hist; Rachel Briley, Th. for Youth; Alan D. Cook, Directing; Deborah L. Bell, Cost.; James M. Wren, Acting; Cynthia Barrett, Acting, Dialects; John Gulley, Directing, Acting; Randall J. McMullen, Scene Des; Dr. Marsha M. Paludan, Acting, Movement; John Wolf, Ltg. Des.

Guest Artists: Tony Walton, Award Winning Designer; Playwright Ed Simpson; Director Preston Lane; Broadway Actor Jay Winick; Director Andrew Tsubaki.

University of North Carolina at Greensboro Theatre offers both strong liberal arts and strong pre-professional training in all areas of theatre at the graduate and undergraduate level. Our academic program is supported by an extensive and intensive productions program that affords students the opportunity to work in all facets of theatre production. The program has an outstanding reputation within the state and southeast region of the country.

University of North Carolina - Pembroke

Dr. Chet Jordan, Dir. of Theatre
Givens Performing Arts Center
University of NC at Pembroke
Pembroke, NC 28372-1510
DEPT: (910) 521-6289
FAX: (910) 521-6552
www.uncp.edu/theatre
ADM: PO Box 1510, Pembroke, NC 28372-1510
(910) 521-6262
www.uncp.edu/admissions

5,100 Total Enr.; not compet.
Semester System
14 Majors; ATHE
T: $3,507/$5,800 R&B
O-ST T: $12,767/$5,800 R&B
SMALL PROGRAM
jordan@uncp.edu

FAX: (910) 521-6497
admissions@papa.uncp.edu

DEGREES OFFERED

BA in Liberal Arts (74), Musical Theatre. Declare major in sophomore year.

ADMISSION & FINANCIAL INFORMATION

Standard N.C. min. adm. req. - 17 ACT, 820 SAT. Accept 79% to

institution, 9 out of 10 to Th. Program; no special req's for Theatre Program. Theatre majors are provided first opportunity to work in Performing Arts Center events, road shows, etc. for minimum wage. Several technical assistantships available to those who have worked events in the theatre.

FACULTY AND CLASSES OFFERED

5 Full-Time, 2 Part-Time: 3 PhD, 4 MFA/MA; 2 Staff

A. (1 FT) Intro to Theatre-1/Y; Dramatic Lit-2/Y; Theatre History-2/O; Shakes-1/Y; Native American Theatre-1/O

B. (2 FT, 2 PT) Acting-3/Y; Voice/Speech-2/Y; Directing-1/O; Singing-4/Y; Stage Combat-Y/O; Musical Theatre Hist-1/O; Musical Prod-1/O; Stage Dance-1/O

C. (2 FT) Prins of Des-1/O; Set Des-1/O; Ltg Des-1/O; Tech Prod-1/O; Make-up-1/O; Cost Des-1/O; Stg Mgmt-1/O; Stagecraft-1/O; Play Prod'n-4/Y

D. (1/2 FT) Arts Mgmt-2/O

FACILITIES & PRODUCTIONS

MAINSTAGE: 1,675 seats, fly space, computerized lighting. 2 prods.: 2 Fac dir/des, 1 Guest des; budget $3,000-16,000

SECOND STAGE: 49 seats, computerized lighting. 4 prods; 1 Fac dir/des, 3 UG dir, 1 UG des; budget $0-3,000
1 Workshop/Reading; budget $0-1,000

Facility was built in 1977, renovated in 2001; includes scene shop, costume shop, props shop, welding shop, sound studio, rehearsal studio, CAD facility, classroom, green room, dressing rooms w/showers (1M, 1W).

DESCRIPTION

Noted Faculty: Dr. Chet Jordan, History & Directing; Dr. Kay McClanahan, Voice; Mr. Holden Hansen, Acting; Mr. Travis Stockley, Musical Th; Mr. David Underwood, Design; Mr. Gary Tremble, Tech Th.

Guest Artists: Ms. April Metz, Makeup Specialist; Mr. David Thaggard, Director.

The University of North Carolina at Pembroke Dept. of English, Theatre and Languages offers a theatre program grounded in the liberal arts. Our curriculum includes three groups: general education courses, theatre courses and electives. We provide classroom and practical experience for all of our undergraduate students through our theatre classes, our production program and our participation int the road show theatre events which also use our facilities. Our program focuses on developing the technical strengths of our students and in preparing them for graduate school. Our greatest strength is that we provide a program personalized to each student with experiences tailored to their interests be they in acting, design, directing or other technical areas.

University of North Carolina - Wilmington

Paul Castagno, Chair
Dept. of Theatre
601 S. College Road
University of North Carolina
Wilmington, NC 28403-3297
DEPT: (910) 962-3446
ADM: (910) 962-3243

11,000 Total Enr.; compet.
Semester System
75 Majors; ATHE
T: $3,180/$4,000 R&B
O-ST T: $6,855/$2,000 R&B
castagnop@uncw.edu
FAX: (910) 962-2110

DEGREES OFFERED

BA in Theatre; Concentration Areas: Acting, Projects, Design; 2007 granted 25 degrees.

ADMISSION & FINANCIAL INFORMATION

HS diploma, 1150 SAT or ACT; overall "C" average on all work attempted, 4 units English, 3 units math, 2 units soc. studies, 3 science, 2 foreign lang, GED if out of school 2 full years. Aud/Int for actors, portfolio for designers. Th. program admits 3 out of 5 applics. $1000 scholarship; other schol through university.

FACULTY AND CLASSES OFFERED

8 Full-Time, 3 Part-Time: 4 PhD, 4 MFA; 1 Staff

A. (2 FT) Intro to Theatre-2/Y; Theatre History-2/Y; Dramatic Criticism-2/O; Playwriting-1/X

B. (2 FT, 3 PT) Acting-4/Y; Directing-2/Y; Voice/Speech-1/Y; Movement-1/Y; Singing-1/X; Musical Theatre-1/O

C. (3 FT) Prins. of Des-1/Y; Set Des-2/Y; Cost Des- 1/Y; Ltg Des-1/Y; Tech Prod-1/Y; Cost Constr-1/Y; Cost Hist-1/Y; Make-up-2/Y

D. (1 PT) Box Office. Procedure-1/Y

FACILITIES & PRODUCTIONS

MAINSTAGE: 295 seats, brand new 34 million dollar facility; fly space, computerized & electronic lighting. Fac dir/des prod.; budget $4,000-5,000 per show.

SECOND STAGE: 124 seats, computerized lighting Fac dir/des, 1 UG dir/des prods.; budget $3,000-4,000

Facility was built in 2007; includes scene, cost., prop, welding shops, CAD facility.

A non-departmental, student-run organization presents 1-2 prods. per year in which dept. majors participate.

DESCRIPTION

Guest Artists: Pat Hingle, Film Production; Gary C. Eckhart, USA Scene Design, working with Directors.

The UNCW Department of Theatre Program, based on a liberal arts philosophy of undergraduate education, emphasizes a well-rounded theatre background with production participation utilized to exercise classroom skills. The curriculum is comprised of a required core providing a foundation of basic theatre studies and an area of selected theatre courses for personal interest and development. The strength of this theatre program is its marvelous new facility and personal attention; the faculty is able to concentrate on a personalized training experience. Involvement in each aspect of Department of Theatre productions is required of all theatre students.

Wake Forest University

Mary Wayne-Thomas, Chair
Dept of Theatre and Dance
Box 7264, Reynold Station
Winston-Salem, NC 27109
DEPT: (336) 758-5294
www.wfu.edu/Theatre
ADM: Box 7305, Winston-Salem, NC 27109
(336) 758-5201
www.wfu.edu

6,453 T. Enr.; highly compet.
Semester System
26 Majors; ATHE,U/RTA,ACTF
T: $34,330/$9,500 R&B
FAX: (336) 758-5668
theatre@wfu.edu

FAX: (336) 758-4324
admissions@wfu.edu

DEGREES OFFERED

BA (General)(Major & minor) in Theatre (26), Dance (minor only) (3). Declare major in soph. yr.

ADMISSION & FINANCIAL INFORMATION

70% in top 10% of graduating class; middle 50% SAT I 1250-1390; High school perf., scores, extracuriculars, essays and recommendations considered. Accept 40% to inst.; no special req. for theatre program. Incoming freshmen may apply for the Presidential Schol in Theatre by audition, interview, portfolio & academic performance. Theatre is one of 9 categories offered; 20 sholarships valued at $11,200/yr. are awarded each year. Junior and senior theatre majors may apply for the Jordan Scholarship, valued at $2,500/yr. Freshman may apply for Collins Scholarship valued at $1500.

FACULTY AND CLASSES OFFERED

8 FT, 1 PT: 4 PhD, 5 MFA/MA; 3 Staff

A. (4 FT) Intro to Theatre-9/Y; Theatre History 2/Y; Shakes-1/X; Dramatic Lit-1/Y; Playwriting-1/O

B. (4 FT) Acting-4/Y; Dynamics of Voice/Movement-2/Y; Movement-2/Y; Mime, etc.-1/Y; Singing-2/X; Directing-1/Y; Dance-6/Y; Musical Theatre-1/X

C. (3 FT) Set Des-1/Y; Cost Des-1-Y; Ltg Des-1/Y; Make-up-1/Y; Intro to Des. & Prod-1/Y

D. (1/2 FT) Theatre Mgmt-1/O

FACILITIES AND PRODUCTIONS

MAINSTAGE: 344 seats, fly space, computerized lighting 4 Fac dir/des, 1 UG des prods; bdgt $2-10,000

ARENA STAGE: 124 seats, computerized lighting. 6 UG dir/des prods; bdgt $100-1,000.

10 Guest/UG workshops/readings; budget $0-100

Facility was built in 1976; includes scene shop, costume shop, dance studio, rehearsal studio, computer lab, 2 classrooms, digital art + music labs.

Majors frequently participate in a non-departmental, student-run producing organization that presents 2 productions per year. 2 student-written play produced in the last 3 years.

DESCRIPTION

Noted Faculty: Sharon Andrews, Acting, Directing; Jon Christman, Design; J.K. Curry, Theatre History; Brook Davis, Acting, Directing; J.E.R. Friendenberg, Mgmt; Cindy Gendrich, Acting, Directing; Nina Lucas, Dance; Frank Ludwig, Design; Mary Wayne-Thomas, Design.

Guest Artists: Alphonso Armada, Playwright; Rosemary Harris; Tim Miller, Performance Artist; Kathleen Baum, Teacher; Penelope Niven, Biographer; Philip Rose, Producer; Dennis Krasnick, Director; Romulus Linney, Author.

Wake Forest's Department of Theatre and Dance offers courses in the history, theory and practice of theatre arts. The University Theatre's productions provide a wide range of cocurricular activities for theater majors, minors and other theater participants. Wake Forest is committed to the liberal arts; its theater studies develop a solid foundation in performance, design, production techniques as well as in theater history, theory and literature. The faculty encourages study abroad and conducts annual study trips to London and less frequent trips to New York City. Each school year the University Theater presents four Mainstage productions in the 344-seat proscenium Mainstage Theatre. Theatre students produce numerous studio plays in the Ring Theatre, a 124-seat arena theater. Famed designer Jo Meilziner served as the theatre consultant on these two well-equipped stages.

Western Carolina University

Susan Brown-Strauss, Head
Dept of Sage and Screen
Western Carolina University
114C Stillwell
Culowhee, NC 28723
(828) 227-3963
www.wcu.edu/as/ctd/theatrearts

6,200 Total Enr.; not compet.
36 Majors; ATHE, USITT
Semester System
T: $4,871/$4,902 R&B
O-ST T: $14,454/$4,902
SMALL PROGRAM

DEGREES OFFERED

BA in Acting; BFA in Acting. Declare major in 2nd year.

ADMISSION & FINANCIAL INFORMATION

Min 700 SAT, top 50% of hs class; Theatre program admits all applicants. Audition, portfolio for scholarships.

FACULTY AND CLASSES OFFERED

4 Full-Time, 1 Part-Time: 3 PhD, 2 MFA/MA

A. (1 FT) Intro to Theatre-2/Y; Dramatic Lit/Criticism-2/Y; Theatre History-2/Y; Shakes-2/X

B. (1 FT, 1 PT) Acting-4/Y; Singing-1/Y; Directing-2/Y; Stage Combat-1/O; Voice/Speech-1/O

C. (2 F.PT) Prins of Design-1/Y; Cost Des-1/Y; Set Design-1/Y; Ltg Des-1/Y; Cost Constr-1/Y; Make-up-2/Y; Tech Prod.-2/Y

FACILITIES & PRODUCTIONS

MAINSTAGE: 460 seats, fly space, computerized lighting. 8 prods: 4 Fac dir, 3-4 Fac des, 0-1 UG des prods; budget $6-8,000

SECOND STAGE: 140 seats, electronic lighting.
2-3 UG dir/des prods; budget $1,000-2,000

Facility was built in 1936, renovated in 1988; includes scene, cost shops, welding shop, design studio, 2 classrooms.

DESCRIPTION

Noted Faculty; Steve Ayers, Acting.

The Department's proximity to the NC and GA film and TV industry has provided excellent opportunity for faculty and students alike. Over 20 students have had film roles and production work in the past 5 years. Susan Brown-Strauss, costume and scenic design, received recognition by USITT in the 1994 juried Design Exposition.

NORTH DAKOTA

North Dakota State University

Dr. Paul Lifton, Theatre Arts
Division of Fine Arts
P.O. Box 5691
North Dakota State University
Fargo, ND 58105-5691
(701) 231-7932
Paul.Lifton@ndsu.edu
ADMISSIONS: Ceres Hall 124
800-488-6378

12,000 Tot. Enr.; non-compet.
Semester System
55 Majors; NAST
T: $2,410/$2,968 R&B
O-ST T: $5,934/$2,968 R&B
FAX: (701) 231-2085

FAX: (701) 231-8802

www.ndsu.edu   nuadmiss@plains.nodak.edu

DEGREES OFFERED

BA, BS, BFA in Acting/Dir. (8); BA, BS in Design/Tech (7); BA in Th. Hist./Literary/Criticism. 2001 granted 4 UG degs.

ADMISSION & FINANCIAL INFORMATION

21 ACT, 2.5 GPA req. for admission; 95% of applicants admitted to inst. and 100% to theatre program. F.G. Walsh Talent Grant, Johnson Talent Grant, Lyddon Award, A.G. Arnold Scholarship for Theatre Arts, J & S. Ozbun Scholarship for Fine Arts. Amounts vary from $200-600. Presidential scholarships. for freshmen also avail. (dependent on funding) - $500-750. All scholarships. awarded on basis of academic & artistic record, promise of future achievement in Theatre Arts program and/or past commitment of time and talent to the program.

FACULTY AND CLASSES OFFERED

5 Full-Time: 2 PhD, 3 MA/MFA

A. (1 FT) Intro to Theatre-1/Y; Dramatic Lit-1/Y; Theatre History-2/Y; World Theatre 1/Y; Shakespeare-1/X; Script Analysis-1/Y

B. (2 FT) Acting-3/YO; Movement-2/O; Singing-X; Dance-3/YO; Directing-3/YO; Voice/Speech-2/O; Mime, etc-1/Y; Musical Theatre-1/O; Stage Combat-1/Y; Business of Acting-1/Y

C. (1 FT) Prins of Design-1/Y; Cost Design-1/O; Ltg Des-1/O; Make-up-1/Y; Stage Mgmt-2/O; Tech Prod-2/Y; Portfolio Review-1/O; History of Dress & Decor-2/O

FACILITIES AND PRODUCTIONS

MAINSTAGE: 380 seats, electronic lighting. 3-4 prods: 3 Fac dir/des, 1 UG des; budget $750-6,000

SECOND STAGE: 200 seats, electronic lighting. 1-2 prods: UG dir/des; budget $75-150

THIRD STAGE: Campus Auditorium, 990 seats, computerized lighting. 6 Workshops/Readings: Fac, Guest, UG dir.; budget $1,500-3,000

Facility was built in 1968, last renovated in 1978; includes scene, cost shops, video studio, movement/dance, rehearsal studios, design studio, 1 classroom, 125 seat recital hall, small apron cinema theatre.

DESCRIPTION

Noted Faculty: Don Larew, Design; Dr. Paul Lifton, Th. Hist/Crit, Act/Dir; Lori Horvik, Act/Dir, Stage Mgmt., Audition, Lit; Dr. Pam Chabora, Act/Dir, Voice, Mvmt, Audition; Mark Spitzer, Tech Th; Rooth Varland, Make-Up Design, Costumer.

Guest Artists: Kottakkal Sasidharan Nair (Indian Kathakali dancer and dance teacher. Served as choreographer and movement coach for production of Sanskrit play, The Recognition of Sakuntala, Fall 2006).

North Dakota State University Dept. of Theatre Arts is dedicated to the highest standards of excellence in both its academic and its performance/technical theatre programs. Its energies are committed to fostering student creativity in all areas of the theatre discipline—design, performance, directing, management—and to helping students in the process to gain better insights into themselves and the world around them. Regular trips to Boston and NYC equip student majors to succeed in the business of theatre. Our Theatre Arts program is NAST accredited and has been a vital and important part of the curriculum and student activities at NDSU for over 75 years.

University of North Dakota

Kathleen McLennan, Chair
Dept of Theatre Arts
Box 8136
University of North Dakota
Grand Forks, ND 58202
DEPT: (701) 777-3446

12,000 Total Enr.; not compet.
Semester System
40 Majors; NAST, ATHE
T: $2428/$2,654 R&B
O-ST T: $5,952/$2,654 R&B
ADM: (701) 777-3821

DEGREES OFFERED

BA in Liberal Arts (19); BFA in Performance (12), MA in General
Lit./Crit/History (14). Declare major in 2nd year; 2001 granted 7 UG,
7 Grad degrees.

ADMISSION & FINANCIAL INFORMATION

Req. HS Grad, SAT or ACT. Accept 100% into institution; Aud/Int or
portfolio req. for BFA, open admission to BA; accept 4 of 5 to
BFA;Multiple awards from $300 to $3000 based on audition, rec.
interview.

FACULTY AND CLASSES OFFERED

6 Full-Time, 1/2 PT: 2 PhD, 41/2 MFA/MA; 1 Staff

A. (2 FT) Intro to Theatre-Y; Dramatic Lit-Y; Theatre History-Y;
Dramatic Criticism-Y; Shakes-Y; Playwriting-Y

B. (2 FT, 1/2 PT) Acting-Y; Voice/Speech-Y; Mvmt-Y; Mime, etc-X;
Singing-X; Musical Th-Y; Directing-Y; Stage Combat-Y; Dance
(tap, jazz, ballet, modern).

C. (2 FT) Prins of Des-Y; Set Des-Y; Cost Des-Y; Ltg Des-Y; Tech
Prod-Y; Make-up-2/Y; Stg Mgmt-O; Cost Constr-Y; Make-up-Y

D. Arts Mgmt-O; B.O. Procedure-X;Marketing/Promo-O;
Development/Grant Writing-X; Legal-X

FACILITIES & PRODUCTIONS

MAINSTAGE: 365 seats. 4 prods: 4 Fac dir, 3 Fac des, 1 Grad/des;
budget $2,000-4,000

SECOND STAGE: 1-200 seats. 15 prods: 5 Grad dir/des, 10 UG dir/des;
budget $100-500

4 Workshops./Rdgs: 1 Fac dir, 3 Grad dir; budget $0

Facility built in 1963, last renovated in 1993; includes scene shop, costume shop, welding shop, props shop, sound studio, dance studio,
2 rehearsal studios, CAD design studio, classroom.

4 student-written plays produced in the last two years.

DESCRIPTION

Noted Faculty: Dr. Kathleen McLennan, Dept Chair, His/Lit/American
Theatre/Playwriting; Dr. Mary Cutler, Acting, Voice, Dramatic
Lit/Criticism, Oral Interpretation, Feminist Theory, Musical
Theatre; Patricia Downey, Movement & Dance; Dr. Jim Williams;
Dir, Mus. Th, Dramatic Lit/Criticism, Perf Theory; Gaye Burgess,
Acting, Voice, Movement, Musical Theatre, Choreography; Brad
Reissis, Scenic/Lighting Des, Scene Painting; Tracey Lyons,
Costume Des and Construction; Loren Liepold, TD, Sound Des.

The Department of Theatre Arts at the University of North
Dakota is recognized as a leading program of theatre art
for the state, and indeed for most of the region. The Dept
achieved National Accreditation in 1986, an honor it continues to hold. The diversified and highly qualified faculty includes experts skilled in acting, directing, design,
playwriting, history and literature. Students graduating

from UND in Theatre Arts have sought and achieved a
variety of employment opportunities. Several have been
able to find consistent work as actors, directors, designer
and technicians; many have gone on for advanced
degrees and are teaching at some of the finest colleges
and universities in the nation.

OHIO

Baldwin-Wallace College

Peter Landgren, Director
Conservatory of Music
275 Eastland Rd.
Baldwin-Wallace College
Berea, OH 44017
DEPT: (440) 826-2385
FAX: (440) 826-3239
ADMISSIONS: Conservatory Admission Office
(866) BW- MUSIC
admission@bw.edu

3,625 T. Enr.; compet.
145 Majors; Sem. System,
NASM
T: $22,404
$7,358 R&B
Conservatory

FAX: (440) 826-3239
www.bw.ed

DEGREES OFFERED

BM in Musical Theatre (40), Vocal Performance (25); BA in Theatre
(50), Dance (20), Arts Management (20). Declare major 1st yr.
Liberal Arts, 2nd yr. BA.

ADMISSION & FINANCIAL INFORMATION

College and Conservatory Applics. req. 2.8 GPA, ACT (21-26) or SAT
scores (1000-1200), HS transcript, counselor and teacher rec. 81%
of applics. accepted to college, 50% to Conservatory. UG eligible for
all academic scholarship offered by the College. Students working
toward the Bachelor of Music degree as a musical th. major are eligible for the Griffiths Scholarship, a talent scholarship offered by the
Conservatory based on the audition.

FACULTY AND CLASSES OFFERED

26 FT, 32 PT (Conservatory): 15 PhD, 27 MFA; 14 Prof. w/out adv.
degree

A. (2 FT) Intro to Th-1/Y; Th History-2/Y; Shakes-2/Y; Dramatic Lit-
4/Y; Dramatic Criticism-1/O; Playwriting-1/O

B. (24 FT, 1 PT) Acting-9/Y; Mvmt-2/Y; Singing-8/Y; Mus Th-8/Y;
Directing-2/Y; Voice-2/Y; Stage Combat-1/O; Dance-8/Y

C. (1 FT, 1 PT) Prins of Des-2/Y; Set Des-1/Y; Cost Des-1/O; Ltg Des-
1/Y; Tech Prod'n-1/Y; Cost Hist.-1/O; Make-up-1/O; Stg Mgmt-
1/Y

D. (1 FT) Arts Mgmt-2/Y; Mkting-Promo-1/O; Legal: Contracts/
Copyright-1/O

FACILITIES AND PRODUCTIONS

MAINSTAGE: 550 seats, fly space, computerized lighting. 9 prods: 3
Fac dir, 4 Fac des, 1 Guest Actor, 1 UG dir; budget $12,000-
19,000

SECOND STAGE: 140 seats, computerized lighting. 3 prods: 1 Fac
dir/des, 1 UG dir: budget $2,000-8,000

THIRD STAGE: 650 seats, fixed stage.
1 Fac dir Workshop/Reading; budget $100-400

Facility built in 1968; includes scene, costume shops, 2 move-
ment/dance studios, 20 classrooms, 100 seat chamber hall, 650
seat recital hall, 52 practice rooms w/ pianos.

Connection with Great Lakes Theatre Festival, (Equity). a professional regional theatre. Musical Theatre majors earn EMC weeks as understudies. In summer, students often audition for Cain Park and Porthouse Theatre.

DESCRIPTION

Noted Faculty: Resident Dir. Great Lakes Theatre Festival; Sophie Ginn-Paster, Singer; Neal Pool, Director/Actor; Janiece Kelly-Kiteley, Choreog/Dancer; Nancy Maier, Musical Coach; Larry Hartzell, Conductor; Stuart Raleigh, Conductor; Nanette Canfield, Singer/Actress.

Guest Artists: Jason Robert Brown, Composer; Dale Rieling, Conductor; Donna McKechnie, Actress; Lynn Taylor Corbett, Broadway Director/Choreographer; Janet Watson, Broadway Choreographer; Bob Cline, NY Casting Director; Paulette Haupt, Artistic Director; National Music Theatre Conference; Jack Lee, Broadway Music Director.

The Bachelor of Music Degree in Musical Theatre is a pre-professional degree designed for the student who wishes to pursue a career in musical theatre. The program provides intense study in the areas of music, theatre and dance. All three areas collaborate in the fall musical, winter opera, and spring musical performed in concert. Professional guest artists are a crucial part of the degree and participate by giving master classes, professional dance calls, and in performance with students. Off campus opportunities include working for various Cleveland theatres: Great Lakes Theatre Festival, Cleveland Playhouse, Cleveland Opera, Playhouse Square and Cain Park. Students are coached for regional combined auditions and gain summer employment in theatres around the country. A senior showcase is presented in New York for agents, casting directors, directors and producers each Spring at the April Actors Presentation, organized by the Actors Center in New York.

Bowling Green State University

Ronald E. Shields, PhD., Chair	15,000+ T. Enr.;
Theatre & Film Department	Semester System
338 South Hall	70 Majors; NAST, ATHE
Bowling Green State University	T: UG $9,044
Bowling Green, OH 43403-0180	
theatre@bgnet.bgsu.edu	O-ST T: UG $$16,352
www.bgsu.edu/departments/theatrefilm	6,880 r&b
DEPT: (419) 372-2222	FAX: (419) 372-7186
rshield@bgnet.bgsu.edu	
ADMISSIONS: Office of Admissions, McFall Center	
(419) 372-2478	FAX: (419) 372-6955
admissions@bgnet.bgsu.edu	

DEGREES OFFERED

BA, BAC, MA & PhD in Theatre. Declare major in sophomore year;

ADMISSION & FINANCIAL INFORMATION

Req. for Grad: GRE, writing samples, 3 letters of rec.; Accept 80% to institution; accept 10 out of 12 UG, 25 out of 40 Grad applics to program; Grant in Aids for Acting, Technical, Forensics; Audition on campus in March; apply for application form at BGSU Theatre Office (419) 372-2222.

FACULTY AND CLASSES OFFERED

9 Full-Time, 5 Part-Time: 9 PhD, 3 MFA; 5 Staff

A. (4 FT, 6 PT) Intro to Th-12/Y; Th History-2/Y; Shakes-1/O; Dramatic Lit-2/Y; Dramatic Criticism-3/Y; Playwriting-1/Y

B. (2 FT) Acting-4/Y; Movement/Voice-1/Y; Mus Th-1/Y; Directing-2/Y

C. (3 FT) Prins of Design-2/Y; Set Design-1/O; Cost Des-1/O; Ltg Des-1/Y; Cost Constr-1/O; Make-up-1/O; Stg Mgmt-1/O

D. (1 PT) Arts Mgmt-1/O

FACILITIES AND PRODUCTIONS

MAINSTAGE: 609 seats, fly space, proscenium
3-4 Fac dir/des prods; budget $6,000-10,000

SECOND STAGE: 258 seats, electronic lighting, proscenium
4 prods: 1 Fac dir, 3 Grad dir, 4 Grad des; budget $600-800

THIRD STAGE: 70-80 seats. 2 Grad dir/des, 2 UG dir/des
Workshops/Readings; budget $200

Facility built in 1915, renovated in 1970's; includes scene, costume, props shops, 3 rehearsal studios, design studio, classrooms.

Generally 3-4 student-written plays produced during Shorts Festival.

DESCRIPTION

Noted Faculty: Steven Boone, Lighting Design; Bradford Clark, Scenic Design; Lisa Lockford, Acting; Michael Ellison, Musical Theatre; Margaret McCubbin, Costume Design; F. Scott Regan, Theatre for Young Audiences; Ronald Shields, Performance Studies; Lisa Wolford, Cultural Diversity.

UNDERGRADUATE: The Theatre Department is committed to the humanistic values of studying live theatre both in the classroom and on stage with academic rigor, dedication to artistic excellence and sensitivity to significant learning opportunities. Each undergraduate degree program is academically and artistically rigorous, challenging each student in the classroom and on the stage to stretch intellectually and artistically and to grow as a creative person. Approximately 300 students annually participate in the production program. Special programs offered to undergraduate students are the Treehouse Troupe, Humanities Troupe, Huron Playhouse, and the Forensics Team.

GRADUATE: The goal of the program is to enhance the knowledge, research and writing skills, and artistic ability of students to enable them to function effectively as scholars, teachers, and artists. The MA degrees are designed to relate basic ideas in theatre history, theory and criticism to creative production in an effort to prepare students for futures in education, professional training or further graduate study. The PhD is a terminal degree for those students planning careers as faculty members in higher education. It is clearly an academically oriented degree that is focused on the student's ability to do teaching, research, and writing in an area of specialization.

Case Western Reserve

Ron Wilson, Chair,	9,000 Total Enr.; h. compet
Dept. of Theatre Arts	Semester System
Case Western Reserve Univ.	45 Majors; ATHE
10900 Euclid Ave.	T: $32,638/$10,260 r&b
Cleveland, OH 44106-7077	
DEPT: (216) 368-4868	MAIN: (216) 368-4868

FAX: (216) 368-5184   ksg@po.cwru.edu
admission@case.edu

DEGREES OFFERED

BA in General Th., Acting, Directing, Dramatic Writing, Design/Tech Th (45); MFA in Acting (8). Declare major in freshman year.

ADMISSION & FINANCIAL INFORMATION

Req. HS Trans. incl. GPA and Rank; SAT or ACT scores; rec's.; Accept 70% into institution, no special reqs for UG admission to theatre program; audition., interview for scholarship only. Grad: 8 out of 1,000 applicants. admitted every two years, with Aud./Int. Tuition, Stipend, Scholarship, Creative and Minority scholarship

FACULTY AND CLASSES OFFERED

7 FT, 5 PT: 1 PhD, 10 MFA, 1 Prof. w/out adv deg.; 4 Staff

A. (2 1/2FT, 2 PT) Intro to Theatre-2/Y; Dramatic Lit-2/Y; Theatre History-2/Y; Dramatic Crit-2/Y; Shakes-2/X; Playwriting-2/O; Screenwriting-1/O

B. (3 1/2 FT, 3 PT) Acting-12/Y; Voice/Speech-5/Y; Movement-5/Y; Mime, Mask, etc.-2/O; Directing-2/Y; Stage Combat-1/O

C. (1 FT) Prins of Des-1/Y; Set Design-4/Y; Tech Prod.-1/Y; Ltg Des-1/Y; Cost Des-1/Y; Cost Constr-1/Y; Stg Mgmt-1/Y; Make-up-1/O

FACILITIES & PRODUCTIONS

MAINSTAGE: 152 seats, fly space, computerized lighting. 6 prods: 3 Fac dir, 1 Guest dir/des, 1 Grad dir; budget $3,000-5,000

SECOND STAGE: 40 seats, computerized lighting. 2 prods: 2 Fac dir; budget $0-125

Facility was built in 1897, last renovated in 1995; includes scene, costume, dance studio, design studio, classroom.

A non-departmental, student-run organization presents 2 productions/year, in which majors participate. 3 student-written plays have been produced in the last two years.

Connection with The Cleveland Play House (Equity). Undergraduates have had administrative internships and performed in small roles. Graduate students begin work at the Play House in their first year and continue through their third year.

DESCRIPTION

Noted Faculty: Ron Wilson, Chair, Acting, Movement; John Orlock, Playwriting; Catherine Albers, Acting; Shanna Beth McGee, Voice; Jerrold Scott, Speech; David Colacci, Acting; Russ Borkski, design; Joseph Fahey, History, Theory.

Guest Artists: Jane Gabbert, Commercial Class; Drew Fracher, Stage Combat; Janine Thompson, View Points; Denise Gabriel, Movement; Jairo Cuesta, Grotowski; Geoff Bullen, Shakespeare Texting (RADA); Paul Fouquet, Auditioning and MFA Showcase.

Case Western Reserve's Department of Theater Arts offers an experiential education within the Acting Degree Program. This area of study provides a training and production structure that invites participation not only of the undergraduate major, but of all interested non-majors throughout the university community. The department offers a challenging Bachelor of Arts degree which balances performance and theory, as well as carefully structured professional actor training program leading to a Master of Fine Arts degree. The MFA Graduate Acting Program is housed at the Cleveland Play House Facility:

all ensemble performances and classes. The Case/Cleveland Play House partnership is committed to giving the MFA Acting Students a full professional experience. In the first year of study the graduate actors are in intensive classes, and ensemble productions at the Cleveland Play House; in the second year, along with performance opportunities in ensemble productions, the graduates continue their formal involvement with the Play House with understudy and staged reading experiences; third year graduates work as professional interns at the Play House acting as cast in understudy, staged reading and mainstage performance situations.

Denison University

Peter Pauze, Chair
Dept. of Theatre   2,100 Total Enr.; competitive
Denison University   Semester System
Granville, OH 43023   50 Majors; ATHE
DEPT: (740) 587-6231   T: $32,160/$9,420 R&B
FAX: (740) 587-5755   SMALL PROGRAM
www.denison.edu/theatre   pauze@denison.edu
ADM: Office of Admissions, Denison University, above
(740) 587-6276   FAX: (740) 587-6306
www.denison.edu/admissions   admissions@denison.edu

DEGREES OFFERED

BA in Theatre (50) Declare major in sophomore year; 2007 granted 13 degrees.

ADMISSION & FINANCIAL INFORMATION

Median of accepted students: SAT: 1270, ACT: 27. 38% applicants accepted to institution. Accept all UG applics. to th. prog., no special req for UG prog. Theatre scholarships, merit and need-based, are awarded after the first year to selected students.

FACULTY AND CLASSES OFFERED

5 FT, 1 PT: 1 PhD, 5 MA/MFA; 6 Staff (+2 non-teaching)

A. (1 FT) Intro to Th-2/Y; Theatre History-4/Y; Dramatic Criticism-1/O; Dramatic Lit-1/Y; Shakes-1/O; Playwriting-3/O

B. (2 FT) Acting-5/Y; Voice/Speech-1/O; Directing-2/O; Movement-2/Y; Mime, etc.-1/O; Stage Combat-1/O

C. (2 FT, 1 PT) Principles of Des-1/Y; Set Des-1/O; Cost Des-2/O; Ltg Des-1/O; Tech Prod-1/O; Make-up-1/O; Cost Constr-1/O

FACILITIES AND PRODUCTIONS

MAINSTAGE: 198 seats, computerized lighting/sound
4 prods: 3 Fac dir, 2 Fac des, 1 GA dir/des; 1 UG des; budget $5,400-$6,400

SECOND STAGE: 125 seats, computerized and electronic lighting
3 prods: 3 UG dir/des; budget $200-400

Mainstage facility was built in 1956, last renovated in 1995; includes scene, costume, prop, welding shops, CAD facility, sound studio, 2 classrooms.

A non-departmental, student-run producing organization presents 2-3 prods in which majors participate. 2 student-written full length plays and 5 one-acts are produced by student organization in the last two years.

DESCRIPTION

Noted Faculty: Peter Pauze, Theatre Studies, Scenic &

Lighting Des, Playwriting; Cynthia Turnbull, Costume Des, Creative Dramatics; Robert Gander, Directing, Acting; John Sipes, Acting, Directing, Movement, Stage Combat; Mark Evans Bryan, Theatre History, Lit, Theory, Playwriting; Andrew Johns, Tech Theatre

Guest Artists: Elizabeth Norment, Actor; Jorge Ignacio Cortinas, Playwright; Holly Cate, Director; Dale Ricardo Shields, Director; Melissa Bell, Dialect Coach; Mary Sykes, Lighting Des; Jeff Stone, Composer & Sound Des; Brad Steinmetz, Scenic Des; Tatjana Longerot, Costume Des; Mark Sorensen, Costume Des

The Denison University Department of Theatre offers a broad-based liberal arts education, emphasizing historical, social, and theoretical study, along with studies in the various arts of theatre. We encourage our majors to complement their theatre studies with challenging work in other disciplines. Many of our students choose to double major, or to pursue a major and a minor. The major in theatre is designed to aid the serious student in developing his or her artistic, creative, and intellectual potential; understanding fundamental principles of theatre arts; making practical application of those principles in stage production; developing analytical skill, facility in problem-solving, historical perspective, and appreciation of aesthetic form; and developing a sound basis for graduate study in theatre. Our majors are encouraged to spend at least one semester in off-campus study. Many are placed in NYC with professional training programs or as assistants to theatrical directors, producers and designers.

Hiram College

Richard Hyde, Chair	1,200 Total Enr.; competitive
Theatre Arts	Semester System
Hiram College	15 Majors; ATHE
PO Box 67 Rt. 700	T: $24,215/$7,990 R&B
Hiram, OH 44234	SMALL PROGRAM
DEPT: (330) 569-5211	MAIN: (800) 362-5280
www.hiram.edu	(330) 569-3211

DEGREES OFFERED

BA in Theatre Arts (20). Declare major in Junior year; 2001 granted 2 degrees.

ADMISSION & FINANCIAL INFORMATION

H.S. transcript, ACT, SAT, college prep. curriculum, application. 75 % of apps. admitted to institution. No special scholarship for Theatre Arts majors, but significant scholarship ranging from $3,000-12,000/yr.

FACULTY AND CLASSES OFFERED

3 Full-Time, 1 Part-Time: 1 PhD, 3 MFA/MA; 1 Staff

A. (1 FT) Intro to Theatre-2/Y; Dramatic Lit-1/O; Theatre History-1/Y; Shakes-1/X; Playwriting-1/X; Modern Drama-1/Y; American Drama-1/Y; Chinese Drama & Dance-1/O

B. (2 FT, 1 PT) Acting-1/Y; Voice/Speech-1/O; Movement-1/O; Singing-1/X; Directing-1/O; Dance-4/Y; Topics in Dance-1/Y

C. (1 FT) Prins of Des-1/O; Set Design-1/O; Cost Design-1/O; Ltg Des-1/O; Tech. Prod.-1/Y; Cost Construction-1/Y; Cost History-1/O; Make-up-1/Y; Stg Mgmt-1/Y

D. (1/3 FT) Arts Management-1/O; Box Office Procedure-1/O; Marketing/Promotion-1/O

FACILITIES & PRODUCTIONS

MAINSTAGE: 560 seats, computerized lighting. 2 Fac dir/des, 2 UG dir prods; budget $3,000-3,300

SECOND STAGE: 100 seats. 3 prods; 3 UG dir, 1 UG des; budget $200-450

Facility built in 1936, last renovated in '77; includes scene, costume shops, dance, rehearsal studios, design studio, 4 classrooms.

A non-departmental, student-run producing organization presents 3-4 productions per year in which dept. majors usually participate.

DESCRIPTION

Noted Faculty: Richard Hyde, Directing/Acting; Robert D. Moeller, Design/Tech; Erica Eufinger (Repertory Project), Dance; Elizabeth Bauman, Costumer/Acting; Ellen Summers, Shakespeare.

A major in Theatre Arts at Hiram College is designed to provide students with a historical, theoretical, and practical basis in theatre. The application of theory to practice is one of the basic teaching principles. Practical and theoretical courses are interrelated so that modern creative practice is grounded in comprehensive study of the history of the theatre, dramatic literature, and related areas. All majors must participate in at least two productions each year. The Theatre Arts Department requires students to participate in theatre productions and assist faculty directors and designers. Students apply their knowledge and training under performance conditions. Two major productions are presented each year; student directors, actors, and technicians work with faculty members on a variety of creative and artistic efforts throughout the year in addition to major productions. The department offices and theatre are located in Bates Hall.

Kent State University

Cindy Stillings, Interim Dir	20,846 Total Enr.; compet.
School of Theatre & Dance	Semester System, NAST
Kent State University	275 Majors
P. O. Box 5190	T: UG $7,950, G $8,460
Kent, OH 44242-0001	O-ST T: UG $15,380,
	G $15,890
	R&B: $3,800/2-person dorm
(330) 672-2082	FAX: (330) 672-2889
theatre@kent.edu	www.theatre.kent.edu
ADMISSIONS:P.O. Box 5190, Kent State Univ, OH 44242	
(330) 672-2444	FAX: (330) 672-2499
www.kent.edu/admissions	TYDD: (330) 672-3148

DEGREES OFFERED

BA in General Theatre (175); BFA in Design/Tech (14), Modern Dance (30), Musical Theatre (30). New in 2005: certificate in Entertainment Arts and Technology (4). Declare major in freshman year.

ADMISSION & FINANCIAL INFORMATION

ACT, SAT scores, hs. transcript. 87% admitted to Kent campus. BA no special req. Musical Theatre requires audition; MFA Acting requires audition. Design/Tech requires interview and portfolio. BFA require aud/int for actors, portfolio for design/tech. Graduate program generally admit 18 out of 190.

FACULTY AND CLASSES OFFERED

13 FT, 4-7 PT: 4 PhD, 12-15 MFA/MA, 1 Prof w/out adv. degree; 5 Staff

A. (3 FT, 2 PT) Intro to Th-2/Y; Th Hist-5/Y-O; Shakes-2/O; Dramatic Criticism-1/Y; Playwriting-2/Y

B. (5 FT) Acting-5/Y; Voice-3/Y; Mvmt-3/Y; Dir-1/Y; Mus. Th.-4/Y; Singing-2/Y; Stage Combat-1/O

C. (6 FT) Prins of Design-5/Y; Set Des-2/Y; Cost Des-2/Y; Ltg. Des.-2/Y; Tech. Prod.-2/Y; Cost Const-3/Y; Make-up-1/Y; Stage Mgmt-1/O

D. Devel/Grant Writing-1/O

FACILITIES AND PRODUCTIONS

MAINSTAGE: 525 seats, fly space, computerized & electronic lighting. 4 prods: 4 Fac dir, 1 Fac des, 3 Grad des, 4 UG des; budget $4,500-7,000.

SECOND STAGE: 190-225 seats, computerized lighting. 4 prods: 4 Fac. dir/des, 2 Grad des, 2 UG des; budget $500-1,000.

THIRD STAGE: 60 seats, black box, electronic lighting

Facility was built in 1950 & 1980, last major renovation in 1990; includes scene (incl. welding shop), costume, props shop, sound studio, dance studio, CAD facil, computer lab, reh. studio, des studio, 1 classroom.

A departmental, student-run producing org. presents 5 productions per year in which majors participate. 2 student-written plays have been produced by dept. in the last two years.

Porthouse Theatre Company is an Equity theatre which shares resources and a resident staff with the Kent State School of Theatre and Dance. Students from across the country have the opportunity to work side-by-side with professional actors, directors and designers at this professional summer theatre.

DESCRIPTION

The School of Theatre and Dance at Kent State University provides students with liberal and professional education preparing them for careers in the performing arts as artists, scholars, and educators. The School's production season serves as the primary laboratory for the development of student artistic expression and technique. As performing arts, theatre and dance reflect and communicate cultural values and identities intrinsic to human existence. As such, the study of theatre and dance is central to the humanities curriculum.

Miami University-Oxford

Elizabeth Reitz-Mullinex, Chair
Dept. of Theatre
131 Center for Perf. Arts
Miami University
Oxford, OH 45056
DEPT: (513) 529-3053
www.muohio.edu/theatre
ADMISSIONS: Campus Ave. Bldg
(513) 529-2531

16,000 Total Enr.; h. compet
85 Majors; ATHE, NAST (A)
Semester System
T: $7,665/$6,342 R&B
O-ST T: $16,389/$6,342 R&B
FAX: (513) 529-4048
mullener@muohio.edu
admission@muohio.edu
FAX: (513) 529-1550

DEGREES OFFERED

BA in Theatre; MA in Theatre.

ADMISSION & FINANCIAL INFORMATION

UG prog. req's interview and demonstration of creative work. The Dept. of Theatre and School of Fine Arts offers several scholarships to incoming students based on talent.

FACULTY AND CLASSES OFFERED

11 Full-Time, 2 Part-Time: 6 PhD, 5 MFA/MA; 3 Staff

A. (4 FT, 1/2 PT) Intro to Theatre-2/Y; Dramatic Lit-3/Y; Theatre History-3/Y; Playwriting-2/Y; Th. Appreciation-1/Y

B. (2 FT, 1/2 PT) Acting-3/Y; Voice/Speech-2/Y; Movement-2/Y; Directing-2/Y; Dance-X

C. (2 1/2 FT) Prins of Des-1/Y; Set Design-1/Y; Cost Des-1/Y; Tech Prod-1/Y; Ltg Des-1/Y; Make-up-2/Y; Stg Mgmt-1/Y

D. (1/2 FT) Theatre Management-O

FACILITIES & PRODUCTIONS

MAINSTAGE: 374 seats, fly space, computerized lighting 4 prods: 4 Fac dir, 3 Fac des, frequent student des; budget $5,000-8,000

SECOND STAGE: 113 seats, computerized lighting. 2 prods: 2 Grad dir, frequent student designers; budget $300-500

"First Stages": Facilities vary; 10-5 prods. per yr. includes student-directed one-acts; "Scripts Out of Hand": Weekly readings of new student-written scripts.

Facility was built in 1970; includes scene, cost, prop shops, 1 rehearsal studio, design studio.

2 student-written plays produced in the last two years.

DESCRIPTION

Noted Faculty: Directors: Ann Elizabeth Armstrong, Martin J. Bennison, William Doan, Howard A. Blanning, Designers: Lin Conaway, Gion DeFrancesco, Jay Rozema.

Our primary mission is to enable our undergraduate students to reach their fullest potential in their chosen professional fields. Central to achieving that are the development and production of theatrical works, and the study of theatre and drama in its literary, historical, aesthetic and cultural aspects. Additionally, the production of theatrical works enables us to have an impact on the liberal education learning environment at Miami University by serving as a cultural resource for out audiences in the university and in the community at large. We are committed to a continuously developing comprehensive curriculum devoted to the highest standards of artistic and academic excellence. Our success will result in graduates of recognized accomplishment.

Oberlin College

Paul Moser, Chair
Theatre and Dance Program,
Warner Center, Oberlin College
Oberlin, OH 44074
DEPT: (440) 775-8152
www.oberlin.edu/thedance
ADMISSIONS: 101 N. Professor St.
college.admissions@oberlin.edu
(440) 775-8411

2,500 Total Enr.; competitive
49 Majors; ATHE
Semester System
T: $36,282/$9,280 R&B
FAX: (440) 775-8340
www.oberlin.edu

FAX: (440) 775-6905

DEGREES OFFERED

BA, Majors in Theatre, Dance and Interdisciplinary Performance
Five Year Double Degree Program: BA (major in Theater); BA of
Music from Conservatory. Declare major in soph. year.

ADMISSION & FINANCIAL INFORMATION

Admission to Oberlin is academically competitive: based on Test
scores, GPA, etc. Auditions for enrollment into acting technique
classes. Work assistantships for tech, office and management positions. Non-departmental aid is available as loans, work-study and
scholarships.

FACULTY AND CLASSES OFFERED

3 FT Theatre Faculty, 3 PT, 6 Production/Design Staff/Instruc-tors; 1
DFA; 11 MFA's

A. (1 FT) Theatre History; Dramatic Lit; Avant-Garde/Non-Literary;
   Playwriting; Film

B. (2 FT, 1 PT) Acting 1-3; Shakespeare; Voice/Movement; Black Arts

C. (1 FT) Design and Production (in Costume, Scenic, Lighting and
   Sound); Stage Management

D. Puppetry; Collaborations; Performance Studies

E. Dance (Modern, Ballet, Contact and African)

F. Singing at Oberlin's Conservatory of Music; Opera Theater
   Prograam

G. Senior Directing Projects; London Semester; and Honors
   Program

FACILITIES & PRODUCTIONS

MAINSTAGE: 501 seats, fly space, computerized lighting. 3 prods: 2
Fac dir/des, 1 Fac dir/UG des; budget $3,000-4,500

SECOND STAGE: 75 seats, electronic lighting. 6 prods: 1 Fac dir, 5 UG
dir, 6 UG des; budget $200-400
2 Guest dir/des Workshops/Readings; budget $0-150

Facility built in 1953, includes scene, costume, prop shops, 3
rehearsal studios, design, sound studios, 3 classrooms. The
Warner Center, houses dance and rehearsal studios and a 200
seat perf. facility.

Several non-departmental, student-run organization present numerous productions per year in which department majors generally
participate. Student-written plays are produced every year.

DESCRIPTION

Noted Faculty: Roger Copeland, Th. crit.; Paul Moser,
Matthew Wright, Caroline Jackson-Smith, dirs;
Michael Grube, scene des.; Jen Groseth, Light/Sound
designer; Chris Flaharty, costume designer. Several
guest artists each year.

The Oberlin College Theater and Dance Program offers
courses for majors and non-majors and sponsors a wide
range of productions and events. the theater Major puts
equal stress on artistic and academic pursuits. The curriculum is designed to offer a solid liberal arts background while preparing students for graduate study or
professional work. Program is very supportive of student
directed theater, and encourages interdisciplinary and
experimental work.

Ohio State University

Mark Shanda, Chair/Prof
Department of Theatre
The Ohio State University
1849 Cannon Dr.,
1089 Drake Union
Columbus, OH 43210
http://theatre.osu.edu
DEPT: (614) 292-5821
ADM: 3rd Fl. Lincoln Tower, 1800 Cannon Dr.
(614) 292-8925 UG
(614) 292-9444 Grad/Prof/Intl

59,091 Total Enr.; competitive
Quarter System; NAST,U/RTA
185 Majors
T: $2,136/6,792 R&B
O-ST T: $5,855/6,792 R&B
theatre@osu.edu

FAX: (614) 292-3222
http://www.osu.edu

DEGREES OFFERED

BA in General Th. (185); MA/Ph.D. in Hist/Lit/Crit (22); MFA in Acting
(10), Design (11). Declare major in any year. 2007 granted 50 UG, 9
Grad degrees.

ADMISSION & FINANCIAL INFORMATION

Use ACT, SAT, GRE, & GPA; no special req. for adm. to UG program, admit all UG; Aud./Int., portfolio for des. req. for Grad admission; req. 3.0 GPA for MFA programs; MA, PhD req GRE regardless
of GPA.   Special scholarships available to theatre majors:
Scholarships for UG are available. Applications are due in the spring
with awards applied to autumn quarter tuition.

FACULTY AND CLASSES OFFERED

16 Full-Time, 2 Part-Time: 7 PhD, 11 MFA/MA, 9 staff

A. (6 FT, 1 PT) Intro to Th-3/Y; Th Hist-6/Y; Dramatic Lit-3/Y; Dramatic
   Crit-3/Y; Playwriting-1/Y; Shakespeare-1/Y

B. (5 FT, 1 PT) Acting-4/Y; Voice/Speech-6/Y; Movement-6/Y; Singing-
   X; Directing-2/Y; Dance-X; Mime, etc.-2/O; Music Th-2/O; Stage
   Combat-1/O

C. (5 FT) Princ. of Design-2/Y; Cost Design-2/Y; Set Design-6/Y;
   Lighting Des.-6/Y; Tech. Prod.-2/Y; Cost Constr.-2/Y; Make-up-
   1/Y; Stage Mgmt-1/Y

D. Theatre Mgmt-1/O; Outreach-3/Y; Arts Mgmt-X;
   Marketing/Promo-X; Contracts/Copyrights-X; Develop/Grant
   Writing-X; Budgeting/Acctg-X

FACILITIES AND PRODUCTIONS

MAINSTAGE: 600 seats, fly space, computerized/electronic lighting
3 prods: 1 Fac dir, 2 Fac des.; 2 GA dir, 1 GA des, 7 Grad des, 3
UG des; budget $7,200-$10,700

SECOND STAGE: 250 seats, fly space, computerized/electronic lighting;
3 prods: 2 Fac dir., 1 GA dir., 6 Grad des, 3 UG des; budget,
$5,100-$6,300

THIRD STAGE: 70 seats, fly space, computerized/electronic lighting
9 workshops/readings: 1 Fac dir, 1 GA dir,5 Grad dir, 4 Grad des,
2 UG dir, 3 UG des; budget $800-$1,850

Facility was built in 1970, renovated in 2006; includes scene shop,
costume shop, prop shop, welding shop, sound studio, 1 video
studio, 1 movement studio, 3 rehearsal studios, 1 design studio,
3 classrooms, 1 computer lab.

A non-departmental, student-run organ. presents 5 prods/yr. in which
majors participate.

12 student written plays in last 2 years.

DESCRIPTION

Noted Faculty: Mark Shanda, Chair and Technical

Theatre; Dr. Stratos Constantinidis, Critical Theorist; Dr. Lesley Ferris, Director; Dan Gray, Scenic Design; Dr. Anthony Hill, African-American Studies; Kristine Kearney, Costume Design; Dr. Joy Reilly, Senior Theatre; Mary Tarantino, Lighting Design; Jeanine Thompson, Movement; Dr. Alan Woods, Historian

Guest Artists: Alexandru Berceanu, Peter Cutts, and Karen Coe Miller, Directors; Harry Elam, Jr., and Margo Jefferson, Writers; The Neo-Futurists Company; Ann Bogart & Siti Company; Madeleine Sobota, Lighting Des; Carlyle Brown and Robbie McCauley, Playwrights

The Ohio State University Department of Theatre is dedicated to the education and training of the theatre artists and scholars wherein intellectual rigor informs creative choices. Undergraduates explore the wide field of theatrical scholarship and practice, while graduate students focus on deepening their skills, expanding their vision, and articulating the results of their research either in production or in print.

Ohio University

See ad in back of book

Robert St. Lawrence, School of Theater
307 Kantner Hall
Ohio University
Athens, OH 45701
DEPT: (740) 593-4818
FAX: (740) 593-4817
ADMISSIONS: Chubb Hall (740) 593-4109 ; FAX: (740) 593-0560

20,000 Total Enr.; compet.
Quarter System
110 Majors; NAST, U/RTA
T: UG $5,000/$5,000 R&B
O-ST T: UG $10,000/$5,000 R&B
www.ohio.edu/theater

DEGREES OFFERED

BFA in Theater, Honors Tutorial College, Performance, Playwriting, Production Design & Tech, Mgmt ; MA in Theater, Th History & Crit; MFA in Directing, Playwriting, Production Design & Technology, Prof. Actor Training. Declare major end of freshman yr.

ADMISSION & FINANCIAL INFORMATION

3.0 GPA; Accept 67% to institution; no special req. for UG program, accept all applics to UG program; Aud/Int./Portfolio req. for Grad for admission into program; Accept 50 out of 250 Grad to program. Many endowed scholarship are offered and awarded on a nomination/voting basis by faculty and staff.

FACULTY AND CLASSES OFFERED

21 FT, 2 PhD, 19 MFA/MA, 6 Staff

A. (4 FT) Intro to Theatre-4/Y; Dramatic Lit-6/Y; Theatre History 14/Y; Dramatic Criticism-4/Y; Shakes-6/X; Playwriting-8/Y

B. (7 FT, 2 PT) Acting-21/Y; Voice-13/Y; Movement-13/X; Mime, etc.-1/O; Singing-8/X; Music Th-3/O; Directing-10/Y; Stage Combat-1/Y

C. (4 FT) Prins of Des-2/Y; Set Design-11/Y; Cost Des- 6/Y; Ltg Des-7/Y; Tech Prod'n-5/Y; Cost Constr-1/Y; Costume History-2/Y; Make-up-3/Y; Stage Mgmt- 2/Y; Properties of Special Effects-1/Y

D. (1 FT) Arts Management-2/Y; Marketing/Promotion-1/Y

FACILITIES & PRODUCTIONS

MAINSTAGE: 268 seats, fly space, computerized lighting. 5-6 prods: 3 Fac dir/des, 1 Fac dir/Guest des, 2 Grad dir/Guest des, 1 Grad dir/des; budget $8,000

SECOND STAGE: 252 seats, fly space, electronic lighting. 6 Grad dir/des; budget $400

THIRD STAGE: 75 seats, black box, comput & electronic lighting. 24 Workshops/Readings: 6 UG dir, 15 Grad dir; budget $150

Facility built in 1950, renovated in 1992; includes scene shop, costume shop, props shop, sound studio, CAD facility, dance studio, 2 rehearsal studios, design studio, 2 classrooms, electrical shop, drafting studio, publicity office, box office.

The graduate programs in Acting and Directing expect third-year students to spend at least two quarters in internships with LORT professional companies. Most 3rd-year acting students have a year-long internship at the Cincinnati Playhouse in the Park. Other possible internships: McCarter, Milwaukee Rep, Actors Theater of Louisville, The Guthrie, Steppenwolf; directing interns frequently work in England with the National Theatre and similar companies.

In the summer, Ohio University maintains its Monomoy Theatre, a non-Equity summer stock company on Cape Cod in Chatham, MA. This theatre is primarily staffed and cast from O. U. theater students.

DESCRIPTION

Noted Faculty: Ursula Belden, Designer; Dennis Delaney, Director; Hole Cole, Costume Designer; William Condee, Scholar/Dramaturg; William Fisher, Actor/Director; Charles Smith, Playwright.

Guest Artist: Designers: Ming Cho Lee, Kirk Bookman, Michael Cesario, Drew Fracher, stage combat; Kristin Linklater, voice; Fan Yi-Song, mvmt; Guest Artists: Michael Lincoln, Michael Spencer, Astrid Hilne, Judith Malina, Michael Sims, Andrew Jackness, Linda Carmichael Rose, Amiri Baraka, Milan Stitt, Herbert Blau.

The undergraduate programs of the Ohio University School of Theater seek to train students in the professional disciplines of the theater, while providing a strong base of educational exploration. Students showing exceptional progress are encouraged to enter the professional theater; many others are guided toward further study and training. The graduate programs in Acting, Directing, Design and Playwriting are devoted to training and preparing students for fulfilled careers in the professional theater. The School of Theater demands intense, practical performance programs leading to internships with professional theaters in the final year. Students completing the professional programs are expected to be fully ready to enter the professional world.

Ohio Wesleyan University

Dr. Bonnie Milne Gardner
Dept. of Theatre & Dance
Chappelear Drama Center
Ohio Wesleyan University
Delaware, OH 43015-2370
(740) 368-3845
thtrdnce@owu.edu

1,900 Total Enr.; competitive
40 Majors; ATHE
Semester System
T: $29,870/$7,700 R&B
SMALL PROGRAM
FAX: (740) 368-3858
http://theatre.owu.edu

DEGREES OFFERED

BA in Theatre (33), Dance Theatre (3), Educational Theatre (4). Declare major in sophomore year; 2007 granted 8 degrees.

ADMISSION & FINANCIAL INFORMATION

Avg. SAT of 1200, avg. ACT 26, avg. GPA 3.3. Admit 63% of applicants to institution. No special req. for admission to th. program. Th. scholarship applicants submit portfolio or audition by Feb 15; awards are based on both talent, experience, and academics.

FACULTY AND CLASSES OFFERED

4 Full-Time, 6 Part-Time: 5 PhD, 5 MFA/MA; 3 Staff

A. (1 FT, 2 PT) Intro to Theatre-1/Y; Dramatic Lit-5/Y; Theatre History-5/Y; Dramatic Criticism-1/Y; Playwriting-2/Y; Shakespeare-1/Y

B. (2 FT, 2 PT) Acting-4/Y; Voice/Speech-1/Y; Movement-1/Y; Musical Theatre-1/O; Directing-1/Y; Singing-X; Dance-5/Y

C. (1 FT, 2 PT) Prins of Des-1/Y; Tech Production-2/Y; Set Design-1/Y; Ltg Des-1/Y; Make-up-1/Y; Stage Mgmt-1/Y; Costume Constr-1/Y; Costume Des-1/O

D. Arts Management-1/O; Marketing/Promo-1/X; Budget/Accounting-1/X

FACILITIES & PRODUCTIONS

MAINSTAGE: 400 seats, fly space, electronic lighting

     3 Fac dir; 2 Fac des, 1 GA des; budget $3,000-15,000

SECOND STAGE: 130 seats, electronic lighting

     6 prods: 2 Fac dir, 1 Fac des, 4 UG dir/des; budget $1,500-5,000

2 Workshop/readings: budget $150-200

Facility was built in 1972, renovated in 1998; includes scene shop, costume shop, prop shop, sound studio, CAD facility, movement/dance studio, rehearsal studio, design studio, storage, 2 classrooms

A non-departmental, student-run organization presents 1-2 productions per year in which dept. majors participate. 20 student-written plays produced in the last two years.

DESCRIPTION

Noted Faculty: D. Glen Vanderbilt, Design; Bonnie Milne Gardner, Theatre History, Lit, Playwriting; Elane Denny-Todd, Acting, Movement, Voice; Edward Kahn, Directing, Theatre History, Theory; Tim Veach, Dance; Katie Teuchtler, Dance

Guest Artists: Kia Corthern, Playwright; Rob Johnson, Designer; Hijinks Dance Company; Parallel Exit Theatre Company; Kenyon Farrow, Actor, Author; High Wire Theatre Company; Julie Iezzi, Movement Specialist.

The goals of the Department of Theatre & Dance are to provide a liberal arts education, to provide pre-professional training, to provide a cultural environment for the community, and to provide opportunities for creative and research activities. The department produces a balanced season of classical and contemporary plays and performances. Internships in NYC are available for semester credit.

Otterbein College

Dr. John Stefano, Chair
Dept. of Theatre & Dance
Otterbein College
Westerville, OH 43081
DEPT: (614) 823-1657

3,000 Total Enr.; competitive
Quarter System
98 Majors, NAST, ATHE
T: $25,065/$7,149 R&B
(614) 823-1898

jstefano@otterbein.edu   www.otterbein.edu
Office of Admissions, 1 Otterbein College
(614) 823-1500   FAX: (614) 823-1200
uotterb@otterbein.edu

DEGREES OFFERED

BFA in Acting (22), Musical Theatre (28), Design/Tech (22), Musical Theatre/Dance (6); BA in Theatre (20).
Declare major in freshman yr.

ADMISSION & FINANCIAL INFORMATION

Completed applic. form & $20 fee, official copy of current H.S. transcript, GPA, class rank, ACT or SAT scores; inst. Int/aud, portfolio for designers req.; admit 30 of 225 apps. to theatre program. Dept. Talent Grants based on audition and resume or portfolio review and interview for design/tech.

FACULTY AND CLASSES OFFERED

8 FT, 2 PT: 1 PhD, 7 MFA/MA, 1 Prof. w/o adv. degree; 4 Staff

A. (1/2 FT, 1 PT) Intro to Theatre-3/Y; Dramatic Lit-1/X; Dramatic Crit-1/X; Theatre History-3/Y; Shakes-2/YX; Playwriting-2/X

B. (3 1/2 FT, 1 PT) Acting-10/Y; Voice/Speech-3/Y; Mvmt-1/Y; Singing-3/YX; Mus Th-1/Y; Directing-2/Y; Stage Combat-1/Y; Dance-7/Y

C. (4 FT) Prins of Des-1/Y; Set Design-1/Y; Cost Des-1/Y; Ltg Des-1/Y; Technical Production-3/X; Cost Constr-1/Y; Make-up-1/Y; Stage Mgmt-1/Y; Electrics-1/Y; Welding-1/Y

D. (1 PT) Arts Management-1/X; Marketing/Promo-3/X; Devel/Grant Writing-1/X; Budget/Acct'ng-1/X

FACILITIES AND PRODUCTIONS

MAINSTAGE: 1,100 seats, fly space, computerized & electronic lighting. 6 prods: 5 Fac dir, 13 Fac des, 1 Guest dir, 11 Guest des, 2 UG des; budget $5,800-19,950

SECOND STAGE: 250 seats, computerized lighting. 6 UG dir/des Workshops/Readings; budget $500

Mainstage built in 1951, renovated in 1962; includes scene, cost shops, video, dance, design studios, CAD facility, classrooms, two dance/acting spaces in addition to formal dance studio.

Connection CATCO (Columbus's major Equity theatre). Offers opportunities for auditions for selected roles to our Junior and Senior Theatre students.

DESCRIPTION

Noted Faculty: John Stefano, Acting, Musical Theatre; Chris Kirk, Acting, Directing; Ed Vaughan, Acting, Movement; Dennis Romer, Acting; Dana White, Light Design/Technology; Rob Johnson, Design Technology, CAD; Greg Bell, Design Technology, Welding; Stella Kane, Dance, Musical Theatre; Cathryn Robbins, Costume Design, Make-up; Mask Making.

Guest Artists: Jonathon Putnam, TV/Film; Robert Behrens, Stage Combat; Judith Daitzman, Lighting Designer; Glen Vanderbilt, Set & Lighting Designer; Stephanie Gerckens, Set Designer; David Zyla, Costume Designer; Dick Block, Set Designer; Paul Karicki, Sound Design; Matt Kari, Set Designer.

Otterbein College Department of Theatre and Dance offers a special combination of pre-professional training to students preparing for a career in acting, musical theatre, musical theatre dance or design/technology through an intensive BFA degree program ad for careers in stage management through an intensive BFA degree program and for careers in stage management through the BA degree. Students wishing to continue their studies are fully prepared for entry into graduate school. The senior year ten-week internship helps students make the transition from college to the professional theatre. Through the BFA and Ba degrees and the Integrative Studies program, Otterbein College undertakes to develop and graduate theatre artists who are sensitive and aware human beings. In addition to the regular six-production winter season, we also offer a three-production summer theatre in our second space. Professional guest directors and designers augment the work of the experienced faculty in bringing quality theatre to an audience of over 30,000 people each year.

University of Akron

Neil Sapienza, Actg Dir.	not compet.
School of Dance, Theatre & Arts Admin.	Semester System
University of Akron	(330) 972-7890
Akron, OH 44325-1005	FAX: (330) 972-7892

ADMISSIONS: Univ. of Akron Admissions, Akron OH 44325-2001
(330) 972-7100　　　　　　(330) 972-7022
www.uakron.edu/dtaa

DEGREES OFFERED

BA in Theatre Arts (24); MA in Theatre Arts (modular summer program); MA in Arts Admin. Declare major in freshman year; 2001 granted 6 Grad degrees.

ADMISSION & FINANCIAL INFORMATION

No special requirements for UG, Grad requires interview/portfolio for designers.

FACULTY AND CLASSES OFFERED

5 Full-Time, 4 Part-Time: 2 PhD, 3 MFA/MA

A. (1 FT, 1 PT) Intro to Theatre-1/Y; Theatre History-1/Y; Dramatic Lit-1/Y; Dramatic Criticism-1/O

B. (2 FT, 2 PT) Acting-3/Y; Movement-2/Y; Singing-2/Y; Directing-2/Y; Voice/Speech-1/Y; Musical Theatre-2/O; Dance-X

C. (2 FT, 1 PT) Principles of Design-2/O; Cost Design-2/O; Stage Mgmt-1/O; Lighting Design-1/O; Make-up-1/Y

D. (1 FT) Arts Management-1/Y; Legal: Contracts etc.; Devel/ Grant Writing-1/O

FACILITIES AND PRODUCTIONS

MAINSTAGE: 250 seats, fly space, computerized lighting

SECOND STAGE: 100 seats, computerized lighting
　　3 Fac dir/des prods

THIRD STAGE: 50 seats

Workshops/Readings: 1 Grad dir/des, 2 UG dir/des; budget $300

Facility built in 1955/1976; includes scene shop, costume shop, CAD facility, rehearsal studio, design studio, 3 classrooms.

A departmental student-run organization presents 3 productions per year in which dept. majors participate. 2 student-written plays produced in the last two years.

DESCRIPTION

Noted Faculty: Adel Migid, Resident Designer, Coordinator, Production/Design Technology; Durand Pope, Coordintor, Arts Admin; James Slowiak, Coord, Theatre Arts Grad Prog, K-12 licensure,Resident Director, Acting, Voice, Movement; Susan Speers, PhD, Resident Director, Acting.

Guest Artists: New World Performance Laboratory, Twyla Tharp, David Auburn, Michey Birnbaum.

University of Cincinnati College Conservatory of Music

R. Terrell Finney, Jr., Head	35,180 Total Enr.; h. compet
OMDA	Quarter System
University of Cincinnati	240 Majors; NAST, U/RTA
College Conservatory of Music	T: UG $9,399, G $11,661
P. O. Box 210003	O-ST T: UG $23,922
Cincinnati, OH 45221-0003	G $21,495
	$8,286 R&B
DEPT: (513) 556-5803	FAX: (513) 556-3399
www.uc.edu/ccm	finneyt@ucmail.uc.edu
ADMISSIONS: as above	
(513) 556-9479	FAX: (513) 556-1028
www.ccm.uc.edu/admission	woolstpf@ucmail.uc.edu

DEGREES OFFERED

BFA in Dramatic Performance (48), Musical Th. (67), Th. Design/Prod'n (72); MFA in Th. Dir. (3), Cost Design (5), Scenic Design (5), Stage Mgmt (2), Make-up & Wig Design (5), Sound Design (4), Lighting Des (7), Technical Prod (2); MA/MBA in Arts Admin. (20). Declare major in freshman year; 2007 granted 37 UG, 25 Grad degs.

ADMISSION & FINANCIAL INFORMATION

UG and Grad theatre programs require aud, interview, portfolio review for Des/Prod; no Grad acting; UG admits 110 out of 744, Grad admits 44 out of 130. Talent-based scholarships are awarded based on audition/faculty recommendation. Academic scholarships - Cincinnatus

FACULTY AND CLASSES OFFERED

24 FT, 13 PT: 2 PhD, 28 MFA/MA, 7 Prof. w/o adv. degree; 9 Staff

A. (1 FT, 1 PT) Intro to Theatre-1/Y; Theatre History-3/Y; Shakes-3/X; Dramatic Lit-X/Y; Dramatic Crit.-4/O; Playwriting-X/Y

B. (12 FT, 5 PT) Acting-21/Y; Voice/Speech-12/Y; Movement-12/Y; Mime, etc.-3/Y; Musical Th-15/Y; Directing-10/Y; Stage Combat-3/Y; Dance-21/Y; Singing-15/Y; Mus Th Perf. Group-3/Y; Acting for the Camera-1/Y; Cabaret Techniques-1/Y; Characterization & Repertory-2/Y; Aud Tech-2/Y; Script Analysis-1/Y

C. (8 FT, 5 PT) Prins of Design-1/Y; Set Design-16/Y; Cost Design-9/Y; Ltg Des-12/Y; Tech. Prod.-12/Y; Cost Constr-10/Y; Costume History-1/Y; Make-up-14/Y; Stg Mgmt-11/Y; Stage Props-1/Y; Sound Des-12/Y; Drafting-2/Y

D. (2 FT, 2 PT) Arts Mgmt-1/Y; Box Offc. Procedure-1/Y; Marketing/Promo-1/Y; Devel/Grant Wrt'ng-1/Y; Budget/Devel-1/Y; Legal: Contracts/Copyright-1/Y

FACILITIES AND PRODUCTIONS

MAINSTAGE: 740 seats, fly space, computerized lighting
　　6 prods: 5 Fac dir, 8 Fac des, 10 Grad des; budget $59,000-77,000

SECOND STAGE: 380 seats, fly space, computerized lighting.
6 prods: 3 Fac dir, 6 Fac des, 3 Grad dir, 20 Grad des, 4 UG des; budget $40,000-$72,000

THIRD STAGE: 135 seats, black box, computerized lighting
6 Workshops/Readings: 3 Fac dir, 3 Grad dir; budget $200-5,000

Facility was built in 1967, renovated in 1999; includes scene, cost shops, props shop, sound studio, CAD facility, 2 video studios, 3 dance studios, 1 design studio, 6 rehearsal studios. State-of-the-Art theatre design center opened in January 1997. New studio theatre opened April '99.

5 student written plays produced in last 2 years.

DESCRIPTION

Noted Faculty: A. Berg, Musical Theatre; N. Mangano, Directing; S. Waxler, Tech Dir; T. Umfrid, Set Des; C. Hatcher, Sound; M. Kay, Stage Mgmt; R. Hess, Dramatic Perf; R. DalVera, Vocal Prod; D. Mogle, Costumes; J. Gage, Lighting; K. Yurko, Wigs and Makeup

Guest Artists: Peter Filichia, Critic; Jim Wilhelm, Agent; Richard Powers, Choreographer; Melissa James Gibson, Playwright; Jose Rivera, Playwright; Tony Martinelli, Entertainment Marketing; Craig Carnelia, Composer & Vocal Coach; Gary Krasny, Agent; Alum Broadway Actors - Musical Theatre; Ellen McLaughlin, Playwright; Athol Fugard, Playwright; Cooper Thornton, Actor

The University of Cincinnati College - Conservatory of Music provides professional, conservatory-style training to BFA and/or MFA students in acting, musical theatre, directing and theatre design and production. Theatre programs complement one another and students also draw upon resources of other divisions at CCM (Voice, Dance, Electronic Media) to enhance educational opportunities. While the training is conservatory-style, CCM is not a private conservatory. It is a component college of the University of Cincinnati, and academic courses are taken through other UC colleges. The BFA degrees in Theatre Design and Production, Musical Theatre, and Dramatic Performance are all separate theatre programs with their own degree requirements. CCM training is designed for those students who know specifically that they wish to study a particular area of theatre in depth. It is not designed for the student who wishes to pursue general theatre studies. Acceptance to all degree programs is highly competitive and is by audition/interview only. Member NAST, U/RTA.

University of Toledo

Holly Monsos, Chair
Dept. of Theatre & Film
University of Toledo
Toledo, OH 43606-3390
DEPT: (419) 530-2202
www.theatrefilm.utoledo.edu
SIONS: 2801 W. Bancroft Ave., Toledo, OH 43606
(419) 530-8700
http://www.utoledo.edu

21,000 Tot. Enr.; non-compet.
Semester
140 Majors; ATHE, USITT
T: $7,927; O-ST T:$16,739
R&B: $$8,990
FAX: (419) 530-8439   ADMIS-
enroll@utnet.utoledo.edu

DEGREES OFFERED

BA in Theatre (50), Film (120). Declare major in first year; 2005

granted 15 degrees.

ADMISSION & FINANCIAL INFORMATION

HS graduate; 85% of applicants accepted by instit.; no special reqs. for theatre program. $30,000+ awarded annually in scholarships for UG. Contact department for more information.

FACULTY AND CLASSES OFFERED

9 Full-Time, 8 Part-Time: 3 PhD, 14 MA/MFA; 4 Staff

A. (1 FT, 3 PT) Intro to Th-5/Y; Th Hist-2/Y; Shakes.-2/O; Dramatic Lit-1/X; Dramatic Crit.-1/O; Playwriting-2/Y; Screenwriting-2/Y

B. (4 1/2 FT, 3 PT) Acting-3/Y; Voice/Speech-2/Y; Movement-3/Y; Musical Th-1/O; Directing-2/Y; Mime, Mask, etc.-1/O; Stage Combat-1/O

C. (3 FT, 2 PT) Set Design-2/Y; Cost Des-1/Y; Ltg Des-1/Y; Tech Prod'n-2/Y; Cost Constr-2/Y; Make-up-1/O; Stg Mgmt-2/Y

D. (1/2 FT) Arts Management-1/O; Mktng/Promo-1/O; B.O. Procedure-2/Y

FACILITIES AND PRODUCTIONS

MAINSTAGE: 200 seats, fly space, computerized & electronic lighting. 5 prods, 4 Fac dir, 1 Guest dir; budget $2,500-10,000

SECOND STAGE: 100 seats, black box, comput. lighting. 2 prods: 1 Fac dir, 1 UG dir, budget $500-2,500

Workshops/Readings: 4 prods, 2 Fac dir, 1 Guest dir, budget $0-100

Facility was built in 1975, renovated in 1985; includes scene shop, cost shop, sound studio, welding, CAD facility, video studio, dance/movement studio, rehearsal studio, design studio, classrooms.

DESCRIPTION

Noted Faculty: Sue Ott Rowlands, Chair, Acting, Directing; James Hill (Chair), Design; Tammy Kinsey, Film Production; Elspeth Kydd, Film Studies; Holly Monsos, Design; Kirby Wahl, Acting; Cornel Gabara, Acting; Dan Watermeier, Theatre Studies; Charles Williams, Design; Jakyung Seo, Design; Dyrk Ashton, Film Studies.

Guest Artists: Jaroslav Malina, Designer; Bina Sharif, Actress, Director; Judy Chesnut, Designer.

The Department of Theatre and Film at University of Toledo offers a B.A. in Theatre and a B.A. in Film. Our programs provide opportunities for undergraduate students to study theatre an film/video in a unique integrated curriculum that prepares the theatre/film artist for a future in the liberal and performing arts. The department's programs combine historical and critical study with practical work in performing, directing, playwriting, design, technical theatre, and film making. To complement the classroom and studio, the department produces a balanced season of classical and contemporary plays. Additionally, we produce independent film and video work. Because we are a unique, integrated undergraduate-only department, students are given many opportunities to produce, act, direct and design on department productions in theatre and film/video. Students choose majors and minors in theatre and/or film. Current initiatives include numerous international guests and collaborations. Department embraces diversity in student body and production season.

Wright State University

Dr. W. Stuart McDowell, Chair
Dept of Theatre Arts, 3640 Col Glenn Hwy
Wright State University
Dayton, OH 45435-0001
DEPT: (937) 775-3072
FAX: (937) 775-3787
ADM: E148 Student Union
(937) 775-5700

17,000 Tot. Enr.; not compet.
Quarter System
350 Majors
T: $7,278 + R&B
O-ST T: $14,004 + r&b
www.cola.wright.edu/dept/th/html
www.wright.edu

DEGREES OFFERED

BA in Theatre Studies (50), Motion Picture History, Theory, Criticism (14); BFA in Acting and Acting/Musical Theatre emphasis (76), Design/Theatre Technology/Stage Mgmt (37), Dance (41), Motion Picture Production (9), MP History (14). Declare major in freshman year. 2002 granted 25 degrees.

ADMISSION & FINANCIAL INFORMATION

2.5 GPA. Admit 35-40 out of 200+ to Th. Prog. Audition for actors; /Interview/ Portfolio for designers req. for admission to program. Theatre Talent scholarship based on interview and audition; returning students can apply for Theatre Merit Scholarship For additional information contact Victoria Oleen, (937) 775-3072 or victoria.oleen@wright.edu

FACULTY AND CLASSES OFFERED

10 1/2 FT, 8 PT: 4 PhD, 10 MFA/MA, 6 Prof. w/o adv. degree; 7 Staff

A. (1/2 FT, 1 PT) Intro to Theatre-3/Y; Theatre History-2/O; Dramatic Lit-3/O; Shakes-1/Y

B. (6 FT, 8 PT) Acting-12/Y; Voice/Speech-9/Y; Movement-9/Y; Singing-12/Y; Directing-1/Y; Musical Th-6/Y; Stage Combat-2/Y; Mime, etc.-1/O; Dance-12/Y

C. (4 FT) Prins of Des-3/Y; Set Design-1/Y; Cost Des- 1/Y; Ltg Des-1/Y; Tech Prod'n-18/Y; Cost Constr-18/Y; Make-up-1/Y; Stg Mgmt-1/Y

FACILITIES AND PRODUCTIONS

MAINSTAGE: 375 seats, fly space, computerized/electronic lighting; 5 Fac dir, 11 Fac des, 4 Guest des, 2 UG des prods.

SECOND STAGE: 60-100 seats; computerized/electronic lighting; 3 Fac dir, 9 UG des prods

THIRD STAGE: 92 seats, computerized/electronic lighting

Facility was built in 1974, last renovated in 2002; includes scene shop, costume shop, prop shop, welding shop, sound, CAD, video studios, 3 dance studios, 1 reh. studio, 1 des studio, 5 classrooms.

There is not an official affiliation, but faculty direct, design and perform with The Human Race Theatre Company; also provides some acting opportunities for students. Students need dept. permission to accept outside acting jobs. Selected full-time dance majors have the opportunity to be members of Dayton Ballet II and Dayton Contemporary Dance Company II which is an official affiliation.

DESCRIPTION

Noted Faculty: Acting: Sandra Crews, D'Arcy Smith, Bruce Cromer, Dr. Mary Donahoe, Joe Deer, Greg Hellems, Sheila Ramsey. Design Tech: Bart Blair, Don David, Matt Benjamin, Pam Knauert Lavarnway. Motion Pictures; Dr. Charles Derry, Russell Johnson, Dr. William Lafferty, Jim Klein, Julia Reichert.; Dance:

Tong Wang, Gina Walther, Teressa McWilliams.
Guest Artists: Design: Ken Billington, Michael Amico. Acting: Ricky Ian Gordon, Tina Landau, Jason Robert Brown, Judy Blazer, Michael John La Chiusa, Shirley Jones, Kate Mulgrew, Victoria Clark, Austin Pendleton, Pat McCorkle, Tom Jones, Ted Neely.

The Wright State University Department of Theatre Arts is a comprehensive department offering 4 BFA and 2 BA degree programs for undergraduate students exclusively. The BFA programs are in Acting and Acting/Musical Theatre emphasis, Design/Technology, Stage Management, Dance, and Motion Pictures Production. The BA programs are in Theatre Studies and in Motion Pictures Production, Theory & Criticism. The BFA programs are dedicated to professional training within a University environment. While each BFA major curriculum is intensely structured, general education requirements are maintained. The objective of each BFA program is to prepare students for professional employment. Admission to the BFA programs in Acting/Musical Theatre and Dance are by audition only. All transfer students audition for acceptance and placement. Each program follows a plan of selective retention based upon student's progress, yearly evaluations and interviews, auditions, and presentations. Each BFA program culminates with an additional senior project or professional internship.

Youngstown State University

Dr. Frank Castronovo,
   Dir. of Theater
Dept. of Communications & Theater
Youngstown State University
Youngstown, OH 44555
DEPT: (330) 941-3631
FAX: (330) 941-1851
www.fpa.ysu.edu/theater/
ADM: One University Plaza
enroll@ysu.edu

12,000 Tot. Enr.; not compet.
Semester System

80 Majors
T: $6,697/$6,490 R&B
O-ST T: $12,205/$6,490 R&B
SMALL PROGRAM
www.ysu.edu
(330) 941-2000
FAX: (330) 941-1658

DEGREES OFFERED

BA in Theater (27); BFA in Theater (42), Musical Theater (11). Declare major in sophomore; 2000 granted 6 UG degrees.

ADMISSION & FINANCIAL INFORMATION

Ohio residents: Open to high school graduates, ACT required; Non-residents: H.S. Graduate, upper 2/3 of class, ACT 17 or combined SAT of 820. Admit 7 out of 10 to theatre program; aud/interview/portfolio for des. req. of B.F.A. degree applicants; BA in theater req. no auditions. University Theater Awards - 4 @ $1800, aud/interview; Beecher Awards-16 @ $1,000, audition/interview.

FACULTY AND CLASSES OFFERED

5 Full-Time, 4 Part-Time: 2 PhD/DFA, 6 MFA/MA; 2 Staff

A. (1 FT, 2 PT) Intro to Theatre-1/Y; Theatre History-2/Y; Shakes- 1/X; Dramatic Lit-2/Y; Dramatic Criticism-1/O

B. (1 FT, 2 PT) Acting-4/Y; Movement-1/Y; Singing-8/X; Directing-2/Y; Musical Theatre-1/Y; Stage Combat-1/Y; Dance-4/Y

C. (2 FT) Principles of Design-1/O; Cost Design-1/O; Tech. Production-1/O; Costume History-1/O; Stage Mgmt-1/O; Lighting Design-1/O; Cost Construction-1/O; Make-up-2/O

FACILITIES AND PRODUCTIONS

MAINSTAGE: 400 seats, fly space, computerized lighting
    4 prods: 4 Fac dir/des; budget $3,000-5,000

SECOND STAGE: 180 seats, black box, electronic lighting
    2 prods: 2 UG dir/des; budget $750-1,500

Facility was built in 1976, renovated in 1999; includes scene shop, costume shop, sound studio, CAD facility, 2 video studios, 1 dance studio, 1 rehearsal studio, 1 design studio.

2 student-written plays produced in the last two years.

DESCRIPTION

Noted Faculty: Frank Castronovo, PhD, Dramatic Literature & His-tory; Dennis Henneman, PhD, Acting, Directing, Stage Combat; Jane Shanabarger, MA, Costume Design, Make-up; John Murphy, MFA, Scenic & Lighting Design.

Guest Artists: Claire Bloom, Actor; Mark Routh, Broadway Producer; Paul Miller, B'way Lighting Designer (Titanic, On The Town); Great Lakes Theater Company; Merce Cunningham, Dancer/ Choreographer; Dick Smith, Makeup Artist;Kate Mulgrew, Actor; Alden Quinn, Actor.

Philosophy: Youngstown State University is dedicated to balanced undergraduate training in theater arts. Our degree programs reflect our commitment to providing students with a maximum amount of practical training and experience in on-stage and backstage work, plus a broad-based general education to meet the needs of a rapidly changing society. The B.A. in Theater is a solid liberal arts degree, where students sample widely from studies in history, philosophy, natural and social sciences, comparative cultures and foreign language, while developing special skills in theater production. The B.F.A. in Theater or Musical Theater is designed to provide much more intensive practical theater training specifically in preparation for careers in the performing arts. It is available by audition/interview only, and retention is subject to yearly progress review. In both degree programs, our majors can expect a very favorable student/faculty ratio, with a great deal of personal attention, and a high degree of involvement in our active production season. Educationally, we favor the mentor approach to theater training, and upper-class students will find themselves doing much of their production work by independent studies contracted with a faculty advisor. YSU theater graduated have been highly successful in finding positions in professional, community and educational theater, as well as in graduate study.

OKLAHOMA

Northeastern State University

Robyn Magee Pursley, Coord.
Theatre Dept
Shawnee Street Theater
Northeastern State Univ.
Tahlequah, OK 74464
DEPT: (918) 456-5511 x 3600
ADM: (918) 456-5511 X 2000

9,000 Total Enr.; competitive
Semester System
50 Majors
T: $126/cr. hr; O-ST T: $310.60/cr. hr
R&B: $1,656
SMALL PROGRAM
ARAPAHO.NSUOK.EDU/~THEATRE

DEGREES OFFERED

BA in Speech/Ed Speech. Declare major in sophomore year.

ADMISSION & FINANCIAL INFORMATION

HS GPA 2.70 or higher, and ranked in upper 50% of graduating class, or ACT 20 or higher. No special req. to program, program admits 50% of applics. Regents Fee Waivers, Scholarships.

FACULTY AND CLASSES OFFERED

3 1/2 Full-Time, Several Adjuncts: MFA/MA

A. (1 FT) Intro to Th; Hist of Th; Acting; Playwriting
B. (1 FT) Stagecraft; Design; Lighting; Auditions
C. (1 1/4 FT) Costume; Makeup; Stage Movement; Child. Th.

FACILITIES AND PRODUCTIONS

MAINSTAGE: 1056 seats, fly space, comput. & electronic lighting.
    1 prods: 1 Fac dir; budget $5,000

SECOND STAGE: 150 seats
    4 prods. 3 Fac dir, 1 UG dir; 4 UG des; budget $8,000

THIRD STAGE: 200 seats, undergoing renovation.
    Occasional workshops/readings.

Facility was built in 1950's, renovated in 1994; includes scene, costume, props, welding shops, sound, video, dance, rehearsal studios, classrooms.

Connection with River City Players, a summer music-variety show and with Olde-Time Mellerdrama. Students audition for acting and off-stage work and are given preference in hiring.

DESCRIPTION

Guest Artists: Norman Lloyd, Rilla Askew, Rob Inglis.

The Theatre major is offered as part of the Department of Communication and Theatre presenting practical training in the arts for teachers (BA in Education) and for the professional (BA). Emphasis is placed on a broad based education in all aspects of theatre arts and the allied arts to offer potential teachers, actors, designers and technicians the broadest possible experience. The program is hands-on, providing ample opportunities for student directors and designers, as well as performers and playwrights.

Oklahoma City University

Don Childs, Director
Speech and Theatre Dept
Oklahoma City University
2501 N. Blackwelder
Oklahoma City, OK 73106-1493
DEPT: (800) 633-7242x5121
ADMISSIONS: 2501 N. Blackwelder
1 800-633-7242x5050

2,100 Total Enr.; competitive
Semester System
50 Majors; ATHE, AATE
T: $20,800/$6,550 R&B
SMALL PROGRAM
www.okcu.edu
uadmissions@okcu.edu

DEGREES OFFERED

BA in Theatre (Theatre Perf, Music & Dance (25), General Theatre (20); BS in Tech Theatre (5); BA or BS in Speech/ Drama Cert.; MA in Theatre; Theatre for Young Audiences; Technical Theatre Costume Design; Tech Theatre Scene Design. Declare major in fresh year.

ADMISSION & FINANCIAL INFORMATION

Min. GPA 2.5 or better, min. score of 20 on ACT or 950 SAT and/or class rank in the upper 1/2 of graduating class. Accept 80% to institution; No special req. for UG theatre program; international student are tested -English. Grad applics require interview. Theatre Talent: (1) audition at OK HS, aud day in Jan; (2) at OCU; (3) send video aud; (4) send video of a play in which you had a role.

FACULTY AND CLASSES OFFERED

5 FT, 8 PT: 2 PhD, 3 MFA/MA, 5 Prof. w/o adv. degree; 12 Staff. (incl Comm Studies)

A. (1 FT,3 PT) Theatre History-1/O; Shakes-1/X; Modern Drama-1/X; Dramatic Lit-1/Y; Dramatic Crit-1/Y; Playwriting-1/O; Child Th-1/Y; Play Anal-1/Y; Creative Drama-2/Y; Multi-cultural Th-1/O

B. (1 FT, 3 PT) Acting-3/Y; Voice/Speech-1/Y; Singing-2/X; Musical Theatre-2/X; Directing-2/Y; Dance-4/X; Movement-1/O; Oral Interpretation-1/Y; On-camera acting-2/Y; Fencing-2/X

C. (2 FT, 2 PT) Prins of Des-1/O; Set Des-3/Y; Cost Des-1/O; Ltg Des-2/Y; Cost Constr-2/O; Make-up-3/Y; Tech Prod'n-1/O

D. Arts Mgmt-1/X; Contracts/Copyright-1/X; Budget/Acct'ng-1/X

FACILITIES AND PRODUCTIONS

MAINSTAGE: 256 seats, electron. lighting.
  6 prods: 4 Fac dir; 2 Guest dir, budget $150

SECOND MAINSTAGE: 1089 seats, fly space, computerized lighting. 6 prods, 1 Grad dir, 5 UG dir; budget $4,000

Various # Workshops/Readings: budget $100-150.

Facility was built in the 1950's, last renovated 2003-05, includes scene, cost, prop, sound studio, video studio, 7 movement/dance studios,2 rehearsal studio, 2 classrooms.

1 student written play prod in the last 2 years.

DESCRIPTION

Oklahoma City University Theatre offers undergraduate and graduate degrees, and teaching certification. Theatre Performance-Triple Threat majors take at least six acting classes - including on-camera acting - as well as voice and dance classes, all leading to a BA degree and the ability to be a triple threat! Theatre majors can choose an emphasis in acting, directing, children's theatre, teaching — even playwriting is available — resulting in a BA degree. Technical Theatre majors take classes in drawing, stagecraft, lighting, design, and play analysis for a BS degree. Graduate degrees include a MA in Theatre, Theatre for Young Audiences, Technical Theatre Costume Design, and Technical Theatre Scene Design. Oklahoma City University has one of the only college theatre programs that presents a six-show main stage season, houses a resident touring company, and has a paid professional costume designer, scene designer, and support staff.

Oklahoma State University

Judith Cronk, Acting Chair
Department of Theatre
121 Seretean Center
Oklahoma State University
Stillwater, OK 74078
DEPT: (405) 744-6094
www.theatre.okstate.edu
ADMISSIONS: 324 Student Union, Stillwater, OK 74076
(405) 744-6858

29,000 Total Enr.; compet.
Semester System
67 Majors; NAST, ATHE
T: $1,850/$3,100 R&B
O-ST T: $5,000/$3,100 R&B
FAX: (405) 744-6509
Judith.Cronk@okstate.edu
http://osu.okstate.edu.admissions

DEGREES OFFERED

BA in Theatre (42); BFA in Theatre (25); MA in Theatre (12). Declare major in soph. year. 2006-7 granted 28 UG, 4 Grad (MA)degrees.

ADMISSION & FINANCIAL INFORMATION

Admit 95% of applicants., ACT 22 or hs SAT 1020 or GPA of 3.0 and rank in top 1/3 of class. No special reqs. for UG admission to theatre program; Interview req. for Grad. admission to program; Accept 10 out of 10 UG, 3 out of 4 Grad to program. Freshman scholarships awarded on basis of audition & academic performance. Upper classmen scholarship awarded on basis of academic performance and service/special merit.

FACULTY AND CLASSES OFFERED

12 Full-Time: 1 PhD, 7 MFA; 4 Staff

A. (1 FT) Intro to Theatre-1/Y; Theatre History-2/Y; Dramatic Criticism-1/Y; Shakes-2/X; Dramatic Lit-1/Y

B. (4 FT) Acting-5/Y; Voice/Speech-2/X; Mvmt-2/Y; Directing-2/Y;Dance-4/Y; Stage Combat-2/Y

C. (3 FT) Prins of Des-1/Y; Set Des-1/Y; Cost Des-1/Y; Ltg Des-1/O; Cost Constr-1/Y; Make-up-1/Y; Stage Mgmt.-1/Y; Tech Prod-1/Y

D. (1 FT) Arts Mgmt-1/Y

FACILITIES & PRODUCTIONS

MAINSTAGE: 598 seats, fly space, computerized & electronic sound. 4 prods: 4 Fac dir, Fac, Guest, UG des; budget $6,000-12,000

SECOND STAGE: 110 seats, computerized and electronic lighting 4 Grad dir/UG des, fac, UG dir prods; budget $1,200-1,500 2 Grad or UG dir Workshops/Readings; budget $150

Facility was built in 1970, renovated in 1999; scheduled additional renovation 2007 includes scene shop, costume shop, welding shop, prop shop, sound studio, CAD facility, 2 rehearsal studios, 1 design studio, 2 classrooms.

DESCRIPTION

Noted Faculty: Heidi Hoffer, Design, Scenic Art;Judith Cronk, Costume Design;Jessica Maerz, History, Crit; Peter Westerhoff, Dir, Dance; Lloyd Caldwell, Acting, Movement, Stage Combat; Matthew Tomlonovich, Acting,Voice, Movement.

Guest Artists: Rich Larson, Designer; Kevin McCurdy, Stunt Coord; Herb Blau, Dir; Chuck Leider, Costume Design; Rocco Dal Vera, Voice; Wes Studi, Actor; Brad Greenquist, Actor; Tony Wolf, Movement Spec; Rachel Bown-Williams, Fight Dir; Miodrag Tabacki, Designer; Bob Bovard, Designer.

Oklahoma State University's Department of Theatre stresses professional theatre training within the context of a strong liberal arts education. We emphasize a strong generalist theatre foundation with individual emphasis in Acting or Design/Technology. Audition skills and development are a central part of our program for all students. The professionally active faculty takes an individualized approach with each student. Master of Arts students take an intellectually challenging course of study, which still allows for an emphasis in acting, directing, or history literature and criticism. Thesis and creative component options are available. Overseas study opportunities are available.

IT'S ABOUT YOU @ **ORU**

Oral Roberts University

See ad

Laura L. Holland, MFA Chair
Communication Arts Dept
Oral Roberts University
7777 South Lewis
Tulsa, OK 74171
(918) 495-6870
Fax: (918) 495-7394
lholland@oru.edu
Admissions: above
http://admissions.oru.edu/index

5,000 Total Enr.; competitive
100 Majors; ATHE
Semester System
T: $17,000/annual
$7,000 fees/annual
SMALL PROGRAM

(918) 495-6518

DEGREES OFFERED

BA in Comm Arts Educ (4); Communication Arts Drama (8) Dance-Performance (begins Fall 2007); Musical Theatre (begins Fall 2007); BS in Drama-Television-Film Perf (40); BS in Worship Arts (48) Declare major in freshman year; 2007 granted 15 degrees

ADMISSION & FINANCIAL INFORMATION

Vocal auditions are required for admission into Musical Theatre Program and the Worship Arts Program. Anyone interested must contact the Oral Roberts University Music Dept for audition appointment at: 918-495-7500. The Dance program has an audition requirement to be admitted into the program. Audition information and registration forms are on line at: http://oru.edu or contact the Communication Arts Department at 918-495-6861. Theatre program admits all applicants. Theatre internships available (scenic and costume shop, props, lighting, makeup, publicity and box office). Four $1,000 freshman scholarships awarded through audition.

FACULTY AND CLASSES OFFERED

3 Full-Time, 2 Part-Time: 2 PhD, 6 MFA/MA, 2 w/o advanced degrees, 3 staff

A. (1 FT, 1 PT) Intro to Th-1/Y; Theatre History-2/Y; Shakes-1/X; Playwriting/Scriptwriting-2/Y; Sketchwriting for Church-1/Y; Acting for the Camera

B. (1 FT, 1 PT) Acting-4/Y; Musical Theatre; Movement/Dance; Directing-1/Y

C. (1 FT) Cost Des-1/Y; Tech Production-1/Y; Set Des-1/Y;Make-up-1/Y

FACILITIES & PRODUCTIONS

MAINSTAGE: 900 seats, fly space, computerized lighting, electronic lighting. 6 prods:
   3 Fac dir/des; 30 UG dir/des; bdgt $6,000-10,000
   24 UG dir/des Workshops/ Readings. Four student-written one act plays were produced in the last two years.
Facility built in 1970; includes scene, cost, movement/dance studios, rehearsal studio, classrooms.

DESCRIPTION

The drama division of the Communication Arts Dept. 1) provides a foundation on which one can build experiences in professional, semi-professional or amateur dramatic production 2) develops the intellectual, aesthetic and creative potential of students through drama as a liberal arts study and 3) prepares students for graduate study in theatre.

University of Oklahoma

Tom Huston Orr, Dir, School of Drama
James Garner, Chair
Producer-University Theatre
Univ. of Oklahoma
729 Elm Ave, Hester Hall 165
Norman, OK 73019
www.ou.edu/finearts/drama

20,000+ Total Enr.
Semester System
75 Majors; NAST
(405) 325-4021
FAX: (405) 325-0400
thorr@ou.edu

DEGREES OFFERED

BFA in Performance (60), Design/Tech (10), Dramaturgy, Stage Mgmt, Theatre Tech; MA in Drama (10); MFA in Directing (6), Design (4) 2001 granted 38 UG, 6 Grad degrees.

ADMISSION & FINANCIAL INFORMATION

Aud., HS GPA of 2.5 req. for UG program; Audition/Interview, UG GPA of 3.0 req. for Grad program.

FACULTY AND CLASSES OFFERED

9 Full-Time, 5 Part-Time; 2 PhD, 10 MFA/MA; 4 Staff

A. (1 FT, 1 PT) Intro to Theatre-1/Y; Theatre History-2/Y; Dramatic Literature-1/Y; Dramatic Criticism-1/O; Shakes-2/X; Playwriting-2/O; Dramaturgy Seminar-1/O

B. (4 FT, 2 PT) Acting-7/Y; Voice/Speech-3/Y; Movement-2/Y; Directing-2/Y; Stage Combat-1/O; Acting for Camera-1/Y

C. (4 FT, 2 PT) Prins of Des-2/Y; Set Design-1/Y; Cost Des- 1/Y; Lighting Des-1/Y; Cost Constr-1/Y; Stage Management- 1/Y; Stagecraft-1/Y

FACILITIES & PRODUCTIONS

MAINSTAGE: 600 seats, fly space, computerized lighting
6 prods: 5 Fac dir/des, 1 Guest dir/Fac des; budget $8,000
SECOND STAGE: 204 seats; 4 prods: 1 Fac dir/des, 3 Grad dir/UG des; budget $1,500
Facility includes scene, costume, props shops, sound studio, 3 dance studios, 3 rehearsal studios, design studio, 5 classrooms.

DESCRIPTION

Noted Faculty: Tom Huston Orr, Dir, Acting; Mike Buchwald, Costume Des, Tech/Design; Tonia Campanella, Acting; Rena Cook, Voice/Diction; Karen Craig, Theatre Hist/Dramaturgy; Steven A. Draheim, Lighting Des; Matthew E. Ellis, Movement; Michael D. Fain, Theatre Tech, Tech Dir; Kae Koger, Theatre Hist/Dramaturgy; Judith Pender, Acting/Dir, Grad Liaison; Diana Rodriguez, Costume Instr; George Ryan, Sound Des; Christopher Sadler, Stage Mgmt; Susan Shaughnessy, Acting/Dir; Michael Sullivan, Scene Des.

Guest Artists: Charlie Pollock, Adam Kulbersh, Timothy Mooney, Thomas Keating, Ian Ricketts, Ken Kercheval, Larry Drake, Performance; Joel Ferrell, Directing; Andrew Wade, Rocco DalVera, Jane Boston; Gillianne Kayes, Voice; Louis Broome, Colleen Curran, Michael Wright, Sheila Rinear, Playwriting; Lenora Inez Brown, Dramaturgy; Paul Horpedahl, Alex Hutton, Bob LaValle, Design.

The University of Oklahoma's School of Drama is a professional program which strives to prepare students for careers in Theatre. As a vital artistic education unit within a major university, the School of Drama believes that the student experience should include areas of investigation beyond the narrowly focused instruction that characterizes most non-university affiliated professional training programs in the performing arts. Through the classroom and the laboratory of public production we seek to educate and train theatrical artists, craftspeople and audiences.

University of Tulsa

David Cook, Chair & Prof of Theatre
Theatre Dept.
University of Tulsa
600 South College Ave
Tulsa, OK 74104-3189
david-cook@utulsa.edu
ADMISSIONS: Above address.
www.utulsa.edu

4,200 Total Enr.; compet.
Semester System, ATHE
60 Majors
T: $21,650/$7,052 R&B
(918) 631-2566
FAX: (918) 631-5155
(918) 631-2307

DEGREES OFFERED

BA in Theatre (Acting, Design, Playwriting) (9); Musical Theatre (6); Arts Mgmt (7). Declare major in soph year; 2007 granted 22 UG degrees.

ADMISSION & FINANCIAL INFORMATION

Act 24-30, SAT 1100-1400, top 30% of class, 3.0 GPA, Aud/portfolio; scholarships available for all specialties (performance, design, tech, playwriting). Accept 50% to inst; Aud/Int/Portfolio. scholarship avail

FACULTY AND CLASSES OFFERED

7 FT, 7 PT: 1 PhD, 7 MFA/MA, 6 Prof. w/out adv. degree; 3 Staff

A. (1 1/2 F) Intro to Th.-1/Y; Dramatic Lit-2/Y; Th. History-4/O-Y; Dramatic Crit.-1/O; Shakes-1/O; Playwriting-2/O-Y; Screenwriting-2/O-Y

B. (1/2 FT, 3 1/2 PT) Acting-3/O-Y; Voice/Speech-1/Y; Movement-1/Y; Singing-1/Y;Mime, etc-1/O; Dance-6/Y; Styles of Acting-1/O; Directing-1/O; Dialects-1/O

C. (4 FT) Principles of Des-1/Y; Set Des-2/Y; Cost Des-1/Y; Ltg Des-2/Y; Cost. Constr.-1/O; Cost. Hist-1/Y; Make-up-1/O;Patterning-1/O; Stage Management-1/Y

D. (1 FT, 2 PT) Arts Management-6/Y

FACILITIES & PRODUCTIONS

MAINSTAGE: 400 seats, fly space, computerized lighting
5 prods: 4 Fac dir/des, 1 GA dir/des; budget $5,000-15,000
SECOND STAGE: 100 seats, computerized lighting
2-3 prods: 1 Fac dir/des, 1/2 UG dir/des; budget $50-500
1 Workshop/Reading: 1 Fac dir/des; budget $50-$200
Facility was built in 1975, renovated in 2005; includes scene shop, costume shop, 2 movement/dance studios, CAD Facility, design studio, rehearsal studio, 3 classrooms.

DESCRIPTION

Noted Faculty: David Cook, Theatre History, Literature, Criticism, Directing; Lisa Wilson, Acting, Voice, Movement, Directing; Susan Barrett, Scenic, Lighting Des, Stage Mgmt; Michael Wright, Playwriting, Screenwriting; Ashley Bellet, Costume & Scenic Des; Curt Selby, Tech Theatre & Scene; Gail Algeo, Dance

Guest Artists: Paul Pearson, Director; Ken Spence, Director; Lee Blessing, Sarah Hammonds, Soo Jin Le,

Paul Shoulberg, Elaine Avila, Playwrights; Crista Wolfe, Costumer; Niki McDonald, Scene Painting; Michael Riha, Scene Design

The University of Tulsa Department of Theatre emphasizes professional training and the majority of our graduates pursue careers in the profession; however, a quality, balanced curriculum is available for the student who desires to teach and/or pursue graduate work. The BA in Theatre (approximately 42 hours) can be designed to emphasize performance, design, playwriting, tech or generalist. The BA in Musical Theatre (60 hours) is performance-oriented. Theatre majors take dance and private voice every semester. Study abroad is available.

OREGON

Oregon State University

Charlotte Headrick, Assoc Chair,	15,000 Total Enr.; compet.
Theatre Arts Division	Quarter System
Dept. of Speech Communication	20 Majors
141 Withycombe Hall	T: $5,829/$7,566 R&B
Oregon State University	O-ST T: $17,598/$7,566 R&B
Corvallis, OR 97331-6709	(541) 737-2853
www.oregonstate.edu/dept/theatre	FAX: (541) 737-4443

ADM: Admissions, Oregon State University, Corvallis, OR 97331-2106
(541) 737-4411   (800) 291-4192

DEGREES OFFERED

BA/BS in Speech Communication with option in Theatre Arts; TA students may concentrate in Acting/Directing (20), Design/ Technical (10), General Education (6); MA in Interdisciplinary Studies requires TA and 2 additional disciplines. Declare major in fresh/soph year.

ADMISSION & FINANCIAL INFORMATION

HS Grad., 3.0 GPA, college prep. curric., SAT or ACT; Accept 75% to inst; Accept all to Th program; Interview, application. See office of Fin. Aid for Inst. scholarship; Th Arts faculty selects from applications of students in program one schol/yr in amt. of one term in-state tuition, on basis of contrib. to program, acad. perf & promise, and financial need. Work study available.

FACULTY AND CLASSES OFFERED

5 Full-Time, 1/2 Part-Time PT: 2 PhD, 4 MFA/MA

A. (1 FT, 1/2 PT) Intro to Theatre-1/Y; Dramatic Lit-5/O; Th. His-tory-3/O; Dramatic Crit.-1/O; Shakes-2/O; Playwriting-4/O; Shakespeare-2/O; Playwriting-4/O; Seminar in Irish Lit./Sem in Cont. Brit. Drama-1/Y; Mulitcultural Am. Theatre-1/Y

B. (1/2 FT) Acting-4/Y; Oral Interp.-3/YO

C. (3 FT) Prins of Des-1/O; Set Des-1/Y; Cost Des-1/Y; Ltg Des-1/O; Tech Prod-2/Y; Cost. Constr.-1/Y; Cost. Hist-1/O; Make-up-1/Y; Stage Mgmt-1/O

D. (1/3 FT) Arts Management-1/O

FACILITIES & PRODUCTIONS

MAINSTAGE: 362 seats, computerized lighting. 4 Fac dir/des prods; budget $6,280-8,665

SECOND STAGE: 125 seats, computerized lighting. 11 UG dir/des; budget $50-100. Faculty dir Workshops/Readings; budget $25-400

Plus Summer Th. Festival Faculty designed & directed, Mainstage.

Facility was built in 1991 (Mainstage) & 1996 (Second stage);

includes scene shop, costume shop, Prop shop, rehearsal studio, design studio. 8 student-written plays produced in the last two years.

DESCRIPTION

Guest Artists: Jonathan Miller, lecturer; John Doyle, British Director; Jim Edmondson, Dan Kremer, Prof. Actors.

Theatre Arts at Oregon State University is under the College of Liberal Arts; its productions are perceived as contributions to the cultural atmosphere of the University and the community at large, as well as opportunities for practical application of skills, theories, and concepts presented and developed in the theatre arts courses. The major is designed as a liberalizing experience for the student, developing not only practical skills and creativity as a theatre artist and craftsperson, but also a better understanding and clearer perception of his/her place in the world community. Theatre studies are approached in two categories: the history, theory, criticism, and literature of the theatre; and the practical applications, including performance and technical and design skills. Graduate studies are possible through the Master of Arts in Interdisciplinary Studies program.

Reed College

Craig D. Clinton, Chair	1,200 Total Enr.; h. compet.
Theatre Department	Semester System
Reed College	16 Majors
3203 S. E. Woodstock Blvd.	T: $34,530/$9,000 R&B
Portland, OR 97202	SMALL PROGRAM

DEPT: (503) 777-7357
ADMISSIONS: 3203 S.E. Woodstock Blvd., Portland, OR 97202
(503) 777-7511 or 800 547-4750
www.reed.edu   admission@reed.edu

DEGREES OFFERED

BA in Theatre, Literature-Theatre, Dance Theatre
Declare major in junior year; 2004 granted 12 degrees.

ADMISSION & FINANCIAL INFORMATION

Inst. requires test scores, GPA, admissions essay, letters of recommendation; no special reqs for theatre program. Check with Admissions for specific info.

FACULTY AND CLASSES OFFERED

4 Full-Time: 1 PhD, 3 MFA/MA

A. (1 FT) Intro to Theatre-1/Y; Theatre History-2/Y; Dramatic Lit-4/X; Dramatic Crit-1/X; Shakes-2/X; Playwriting-1/Y

B. (1 FT) Acting-2/Y; Directing 2/Y; Dance-3/X

C. (2 PT) Set Design-1/Y; Cost Des-1/Y; Cost Constr-1/O; Cost Hist-1/O; Ltg Des-1/Y; Make-up-1/Y

FACILITIES AND PRODUCTIONS

MAINSTAGE: 150 seats.
6-10 prods: 2 Fac dir/des, 4-8 stud dir/des; budget $350-2,500

SECOND STAGE: 50-70 seats

Facility was built in 1963, last renovated in 2001; includes costume shop, rehearsal studio, 2 classrooms. New Theatre Annex includes two rehearsal studios, scene shop.

DESCRIPTION

The Reed College Theatre Department offers a broadly based program in theatre in a liberal arts context. Graduates have been accepted into leading advanced-degree programs.

Southern Oregon University

Chris Sackett, Chair
Dept. of Theatre Arts
Southern Oregon University
Ashland, OR 97520
DEPT: (541) 552-6689
www.sou.edu/theatre
ADMISSIONS: 1250 Siskiyou Blvd. Ashland OR 97520
(541) 552-6411
www.sou.edu

5,023 Total Enr.; competitive
Quarter System
155 Majors; ATHE
T: $3,204/$5,484 R&B
O-ST T: $9,402/$5,484 R&B
FAX: (541) 552-6429

FAX: (541)552-8403
admissions@sou.edu

DEGREES OFFERED

BA & BS in General Theatre Arts (100); BFA in Acting (20), Directing (5), Costume Design (8), Scene Design (8), Sound (3), Stage Stage Lighting (10), Stage Management (10). Declare major in soph. yr. 2000 granted 17 degrees.

ADMISSION & FINANCIAL INFORMATION

1010 SAT, 2.75 GPA, 21 on ACT; Accept 80%; all UG admitted for BA/BS; aud/interview/portfolio for des. required. Depart-mental and privately sponsored scholarship are awarded for achievement and academic merit by a Scholarshop Committee consisting of Theatre Arts faculty and student members.

FACULTY AND CLASSES OFFERED

9 Full-Time, Part-Time: 1 PhD, 6 MFA/MA; 2 Staff.

A. (1 FT, 1/2 PT) Intro to Theatre-1/Y; Dramatic Lit-3/Y; Theatre History-3/Y; Dramatic Criticism-3/Y; Shakespeare-2/Y; Playwriting-1/Y

B. (2 FT, 1/2 PT) Acting-8/Y; Voice/Speech-2/Y; Movement-2/Y; Singing-1/Y; Directing-2/Y; Dance-2/Y

C. (1 1/2 FT) Prins of Des-1/Y; Set Design-4/Y; Cost Des-4/Y; Ltg Des-2/Y; Tech Prod'n-3/Y; Cost. Constr.-4/Y; Cost. History-1/Y; Make-up-2/Y; Stg Mgmt-1/Y; Sound-2/Y; Th. Foundations-1/Y

D. (1/2 FT) no courses listed

FACILITIES & PRODUCTIONS

MAINSTAGE: 300 seats, fly space, computerized lighting. 3 prods: 3 Fac dir, 2 Fac des, 1 Guest des; budget $7,000-12,000

SECOND STAGE: 100 seats, electronic lighting. 2 prods: 1 Fac dir, 1 UG des prods; bdgt $1,000-2,500

Facility was built in 1982; includes scene shop, costume shop, props shop, welding shop, CAD facility, dance studio, design studio, make-up room and a large lobby that services both venues and can be used as a dance/movement or rehearsal studio.

Ashland is the site of one of the most successful regional repertory theatres in the U.S., the Tony Award-winning Oregon Shakespeare Festival. The Dept of Theatre supplement its faculty. The faculty recommends students for internships at OSF.

DESCRIPTION

Noted Faculty: Dale R. Luciano, Dept. Chair; Dennis Smith, Directing/Acting; Craig Hudson, Scenic Design; Ellen Dennis, Costume Design; Chris Sackett, Technical Director; Maggie McLellan, Acting/Movement/Speech.

The Department of Theatre Arts at Southern Oregon University is the only state institution in Oregon that offers the pre-professional BFA degree, and the SOU campus has been designated by the Oregon University System as a center of excellence in the fine and performing arts. The objective of the Theatre Arts Department is to train undergraduates who possess the temperament and talent to successfully pursue careers in professional theatre. In its production program, the Department attempts to approximate the working conditions of professional theatre, to make the transition to actual work in professional theatre a smooth one. Dedicated to creating opportunities for students to apply their knowledge and skills in practical ways, the Department not only supplies performance opportunities for students but also mounts productions that are often designed and executed predominantly by students.

University of Oregon

John Schmor, Head
Dept. of Theatre Arts
University of Oregon
Eugene, OR 97403-1231
DEPT: (541) 346-4171
FAX: (541) 346-1978
http://theatre.uoregon.edu
ADMISSIONS: Office of Admissions, 1217 University of Oregon, Eugene, OR 97403-1217
(541) 346-3201 or 1-800-BE-A-DUCK
http://admissions.uoregon.edu

20,000 Total Enr.; Not comp UG
h. competitive Grad
158 Majors + 14 grad students
Quarter System
T: $6,168/$7,848
O-ST T: $19,332
R&B: $7,848

uoadmit@uoregon.edu

DEGREES OFFERED

BA General/Comprehensive (158); MA in General/Comprehensive (5) MFA in Costume Design (2), Scenic Design (2); PhD in Comprehensive (5) Declare major in any year.

ADMISSION & FINANCIAL INFORMATION

No specific requirements. For Grad students, personal statement, writing sample, transcripts, three letters of recommendation. Theatre program admits all undergraduate, 8 out of 40 Grad applicants. Portfolio req'd for Grad designers. 18 scholarships for sophomores, juniors and seniors, 5-7 for grads. Selected by academic merit, participation in productions, average about $1,000 per year.

FACULTY AND CLASSES OFFERED

8 Full-Time: 7 PhD, 1 MFA/MA, 4 staff

A. (3 1/2 FT) Intro to Theatre-1/Y; Dramatic Lit-5/Y; Theatre History-3/Y; Shakes-3/X; Playwriting-1/Y; Script Analysis-2/Y; Devising-1/Y.

B. (1 1/2 FT) Acting-6/Y; Voice/Speech-1/Y; Directing-1/Y; Singing-1/X; Dance-X; Film-X

C. (2 1/2 FT) Prins of Des-3/Y; Cost Des-2/Y; Set Des-2/Y; Ltg Des-1/Y; Cost Constr-2/Y; Make-up-1/Y; Stg Mgmt-1/O; Tech Production-1/Y

D. (1/2 PT) Development/Grant Writing-1/X; Arts Management-X; Marketing/Promotion-X; Budgeting/Accounting Procedure-X

FACILITIES & PRODUCTIONS

MAINSTAGE: 370 seats, fly space, computerized & electronic lighting. 3

prods: 3 Fac dir, 2 Fac des, 4 Grad des; bdgt $10,000-20,000

SECOND STAGE: 80 seats, computerized lighting. 3 prods: 3 Grad dir, 6 Grad des, 1 UG des; budget $8-1,500

THIRD STAGE: 50 seats

Workshops/Readings: 3 Grad, UG dir/des; budget $0-100

Facility was built in 1949, renovated in 1975; includes scene shop, costume shop, CAD facility, 4 classrooms.

A non-departmental, student-run organization presents 12 productions per school year in which majors participate. 9 student-written plays produced in the last two years; one student-devised piece per years is produced by the department, led by one faculty member.

The department runs a children's theatre program in the summer.

DESCRIPTION

Noted Faculty: Robert Barton, Acting, Voice; Alexandra Bonds, Costume Design; Joseph Gilg, Acting, Directing; Jerry Hooker, Scenic Design; Jeffrey Mason, American Theatre, Playwriting; Grant McKernie, Theatre & Culture; Janet Rose, Technical Director, Lighting Design; John Schmor, Performance Theory, New Practices, Devising; Jack Watson, Theatre History, Directing.

Guest Artists: Kirk Boyd, Oregon Shakespeare Festival; Rob Urbanati, Director; William Mastrosimone, Playwright.

Theatre Arts at Oregon offers a humanistic and liberal-arts education. Some courses, pre-professional in nature, provide vocational competence in teaching and in some aspects of commercial theater. Others are focused on the study of theatre as a means of understanding the human condition. Many students continue their studies to obtain MA/MFA or PhD degrees at various institutions throughout the country. Others use their liberal-arts background to pursue vocational opportunities in a wide variety of fields that require excellent skills in communication and organization. Throughout the program, a balance between performance and academic study is our goal, for performance without context is as meaningless as is knowledge of drama without the ability to actuate it in performance.

University of Portland

Dr. Larry Larsen, Theatre
University of Portland
5000 N. Willamette Blvd.
Portland, OR 97203
DEPT: (503) 943-7228
FAX: (503) 943-7805
www.up.edu

3,000 Tot.Enr. competitive
40 majors; NAST, ATHE
Semester System
T: $27,890/$8,300 R&B
SMALL PROGRAM
www.up.edu
admissio@up.edu

DEGREES OFFERED

BA in Acting (38), Design/Tech (5); BS in Th Mgmt (2). Declare major 1st or 2nd yr.

ADMISSION & FINANCIAL INFORMATION

Avg. GPA 3.45; Avg. SAT 1150; avg. ACT 24. Int/Port. for Grad applicants. Th. prog. admits 2 out of 4 UG, 2 out of 10 Grad applicants. Scholarships from $500-$2,000, separate from other University Awards. Awarded based on audition/interview or portfolio/interview. University-wide scholarship up to $5,000.

FACULTY AND CLASSES OFFERED

4 FT, 3 PT: 1 PhD, 5 MFA/MA, 1 Prof. w/o adv. deg

A. (1 FT, 1 PT) Intro to Theatre-1/Y; Dramatic Lit-2/Y; Dramatic Criticism-2/Y; Theatre History-2/Y; Shakespeare-Y/X; Playwriting-1/O

B. (2 FT,1 PT) Acting-3/Y; Voice/Speech-1/O; Movement-1/Y; Musical Theatre-1/Y; Directing-2/Y; Dance-3/Y; Voice/Speech-1/O; Stage Combat-1/O

C. (2 FT) Prins of Des-2/Y; Cost Des-3/Y; Set Design-2/Y; Ltg Des-2/Y; Cost Constr-1/O; Make-up-1/Y; Stage Mgmt-1/O

D. (1 PT) Arts Management-1/O; Marketing/Promotion-1/Y; Legal: Contracts/Copyright-1/Y

FACILITIES & PRODUCTIONS

MAINSTAGE: 300 seats, fly space, computerized lighting. 4 prods: 2 Fac dir, 3 Fac des, 1 Guest dir, 1 Grad dir/des; budget $3,000-5,000

SECOND STAGE: 50 seats.
4 prods: 2 Grad dir/des/ 2 UG dir/des; budget $250-750

Facility was built in 1973, renovated in 1997; includes scene shop, costume shop, design studio, rehearsal studio.

2 student-written plays produced in the last two years.

Connection with Mock's Crest Productions. Summer Gilbert and Sullivan Company.

DESCRIPTION

Noted Faculty: John Kretzu, Joanne Johnson, Allen Nause; Michael Griggs, Dave Demke, Beth Harper, Rebecca Becker.

The Drama program at University of Portland sees itself as strongly supporting the mission of the department and the University. The program at the University of Portland is dedicated to providing broad-based generalist foundation for undergraduate and graduate students with the knowledge, skills, and opportunities necessary for establishing a life-long association with the theatre. Furthermore, its aim is to demonstrate a strong commitment to teaching and learning in a personal, energetic, interactive, liberals arts environment. This is done by offering a broad-based curriculum of theatre courses that provides a common knowledge base and skill level. Beyond that, the program provides advanced course work in areas of specialization that prepare the students for a myriad of career and educational options. Finally, the program provides a variety of production opportunities open to the entire campus student community. Students are encouraged, mentored, and supervised in these productions, where they are challenged to use their academic background and technical training in the real laboratory of the live theatre.

Willamette University

Susan Coromel & Chris Harris
  Assoc. Chairs
Dept. of Theatre
Willamette University
900 State St.
Salem, OR 97301
wutheatre@twillamette.edu

1,855 Tot. Enr.; compet.
Semester System
33 Majors
T: $31,865/$7,570 r&b
DEPT: (503) 370-6222
theatre-faculty@willamette.edu
www.willamette.edu/cla/theatre

ADMISSIONS: OFFICE OF ADMISSIONS AT above address

(503) 370-6303　　　libarts@willamette.edu
www.willamette.edu/admission

DEGREES OFFERED

BA in Acting Emphasis, Design Emphasis, Performance Emphasis.
Declare major in sophomore year

ADMISSION & FINANCIAL INFORMATION

No specific minimum GPA or test score figures. See
www.willamette.edu/admission/information/answers click on 'requirements'. Aud/int/portfolio for scholarship - merit based scholarship
offered to applicants with a serious commitment to theatre. Students
must complete the scholarship form, two references, an audition (2
monologues), a portfolio (for design students), and an interview with
the faculty.

FACULTY AND CLASSES OFFERED

4 Full-Time, 2 Part-Time: 1 PhD/DFA; 3 MFA/MA; 1 Staff (MBA)

A.　(1 FT) Intro to Theatre-1/Y; Theatre History-3/Y

B.　(1 FT, 2 PT) Acting-5/Y;Movement-1/Y; Directing-2/Y; Dance-9/Y;
　　Voice/Speech-1/Y; Stage Combat-1/O; Singing-X

C.　(1 FT) Principles of Des-1/O; Set Des-3/O; Cost Des- 1/O;
　　Lighting Des-1/O; Cost Construction-1/O; Make-up-2/O; Stage
　　Craft-2/Y

D.　(1 FT) Arts Mgmt-1/O

FACILITIES AND PRODUCTIONS

MAINSTAGE: 250 seats, computerized lighting

　　3 prods: 2 Fac dir, 1 GA dir

SECOND STAGE: 125 seats, computerized lighting

　　1 prod: 1 Fac dir

Facility renovated in 1978; includes scene, cost shops, cost.
　　storage, video studio, design studio, rehearsal, dance studio, 2
　　classrooms.

DESCRIPTION

Noted Faculty: Jonathan Cole, Historian/Director;
　　Christopher L. Harris, Scene Design; Bobby Brewer-
　　Wallen, Costume Design; Susan Coromel, Acting;
　　Virginia Belt, Dance.

Guest Artists : John Parnham, Make-Up artist, Special
　　Effects; Stephanie Timm, Playwright; Tom Butler,
　　Director; Jen Raynak, Sound Design; Susan Vaslev,
　　Musical Director; Hal Logan, Sound Design;
　　Gabrielle Brewer-Wallin, Director; Philip Cuomo,
　　Actor; Luba Zarembinska, Director; Michael Griggs,
　　Actor; Patryk Czaplicki, Asst Director; Stefan
　　Puchalski, Hurdy Gurdy

The Theatre Department at Willamette University is a
vital part of the university in its exploration of human
values and creativity, enabling students to understand
themselves, their society and environment. Students
majoring in theatre are provided with a broad range of
experiences in all areas of the discipline. They gain creative awareness, historical perspective and practical skills
which can be applied both in careers in the professional
theatre and to numerous other fields, especially ones
which require collaboration and imaginative communication. Working with visiting guest artists, the Theatre
Department, seeks to provide the opportunity for students
to be involved in undergraduate theatre of the highest

artistic quality. Our production program is conceived on
the basis that during the student's four years on the
Willamette campus, opportunities will be given to participate in performances that will serve to ignite a student's
love of the creative process of theatre. We seek to stretch
the creative boundaries of all artists in our department;
faculty, guest artists, staff and students alike.

PENNSYLVANIA

Arcadia University

Mark Wade, Director
450 S. Easton Rd.
Arcadia University
Glenside, PA 19038
www.arcadia.edu
DEPT: (215) 572-2986
FAX: (215) 517-2599
ADM: Above address

2,800 Total Enr.; compet.
Semester System
37 Majors
T: $27,800/$9,980 R&B
SMALL PROGRAM
www.arcadia.edu
admiss@arcadia.edu
(215) 572-2900

DEGREES OFFERED

BA in Theater Arts and English (60); BFA in Acting & Musical
Theatre. Declare major in freshman year.

ADMISSION & FINANCIAL INFORMATION

SAT 1080. No special req. for adm. to theatre program. 65% of apps
accepted by institution. 6 out of 10 apps. admitted to theatre prog.
Theatre Scholarship Challenge, Shakespeare Award, Charlotte
Cushman Award.

FACULTY AND CLASSES OFFERED

4 Full-Time, 6 Part-Time: 2 PhD, 7 MFA/MA; 1 Staff

A.　(2 FT) Intro to Th-1/Y; Th Hist-1/O; Shakes-1/Y; Dramatic Lit-1/Y;
　　Dramatic Crit-1/O; Playwriting-1/Y

B.　(1 FT, 4 PT) Acting-2/Y; Voice-2/Y; Movement-2/Y; Mime, etc.-2/Y;
　　Singing-2/X; Mus. Theatre-1/O; Directing-1/Y; Stage Combat-2/Y

C.　(2 PT) Prins of Des-1-Y; Set Des-1/O; Costume Des-1/Y; Cost
　　Hist-1/O; Cost Construct-1/O; Make-up-1/O; Stage
　　Management.-1/O

D.　(1 FT) Arts Mgmt-1/O; Marketing/Promotion-1/X; Devel/ Grant
　　Writing-1/X; Legal: Contracts, etc.-1/X; Budgeting/ Accounting
　　Procedure-1/X

FACILITIES AND PRODUCTIONS

MAINSTAGE: 150 seats, fly space, computerized lighting.
　　12 prods: 3 Fac dir, 4 Fac des, 1 Guest dir, 4 Guest des; budget
　　$8,000-10,000

Mainstage facility was built in 1959, renovated in 2001; includes
　　scene shop, costume shop, prop shop, CAD facility, video studio,
　　dance studio, reh. studio, 6 classrooms.

2 student-written plays have been produced by the dept. in the last
　　two years.

DESCRIPTION

Noted Faculty: David Bassuk (MFA), Directing; Clista
　　Townsend (MFA), Acting; Ashley McLaurin (MFA),
　　Stage Management; Janet Pilla (MFA), Dance and
　　Movement; Jennifer Christensen (MFA), Voice and
　　Speech; Ian Rose (BFA), Stage Combat.

Guest Artists: Laila Swanson (MFA), Stage and Costume

Design; Susan Wilder (MFA), Acting and Directing; Mike Lemon (MA), Audition Technique; Quinn Bauridel, Lecoq Technique.

The entertainment industry in this country has grown into a major economic force and studies in theater are fundamental to careers in television and film today. The goal of this program is to provide our students and the marketplace with a rigorous four-year sequential course of study in acting, the speaking and singing voice, speech, movement for actors, dramatic literature. In addition there are offerings in acting and directing for the camera, stage combat, dance, performance improvisation, mask, make-up, and audition technique. Theater Arts majors also participate actively in the life of the College through four faculty directed productions a year. Our curriculum is designed to provide students with significant knowledge and proficiency in a broad body of skills and information appropriate for general professional entry into the field of acting. The reality of the profession is that actors need to be able to "project themselves believably in word and action into imaginary circumstances" be those circumstances Shakespearean in scope, or corporate - as in a McDonald's commercial. Acting Students need flexible technique that will support their work in large theaters or in front of a camera and microphone. They need to be familiar with the various opportunities that are available in which to ply their trade. The Theater major also benefits from a proximity to Philadelphia's cultural community, through internships at local theater and opera companies, as well as local film companies and television stations. The Theater Arts major is enriched by Arcadia University's extensive offerings through Center for Education Abroad (CEA). The Program at Goldsmith's College (England) is especially recommended for Theater Arts majors interested in taking a semester abroad. Theater students have also taken advantage of the London Internship Program. One such student worked as a literary department intern at the Royal Court Theater, another worked on three productions at the Bush Theater.

Bucknell University

Robert Gainer, Chair
Dept. of Theatre and Dance
Bucknell University
Lewisburg, PA 17837
DEPT: (570) 577-1235
gainer@bucknell.edu
Admissions: Admissions, Bucknell University, Lewisburg, PA 17837
ADM: (570) 577-1101

3,638 Total Enr.; h. compet.
Semester System
12 Majors
T: $32,592, $6,872 R&B
FAX: (570) 577-3501
www.bucknell.edu

DEGREES OFFERED

BA in General Theatre Major (19), Minor (8), Dance (10).
Declare major in sophomore year. Granted 8 degrees in 2004.

ADMISSION & FINANCIAL INFORMATION

Interview (encouraged, not req.), audition for actors. 35 percent of applicants accepted by institution. 1 scholarship for summer research, selected by faculty committee decision.

FACULTY AND CLASSES OFFERED

7 Full-Time: 1 PhD, 6 MFA

A.   (1 FT) Intro to Th-1/Y; Th Hist-3/Y; Dramatic Lit-1/Y

B.   (1 FT) Acting-3/Y; Directing-1/Y; Dance-12/Y

C.   (3 FT) Prins of Des-1/Y; Set Des-2/Y; Cost Des-2/Y; Lighting Des-1/Y; Cost Construction-1/Y; Make-up-1/Y; Tech Production-1/Y; Sound Design-1/Y; Computer Aided Design-1/Y

D.   (2 FT) Dance

FACILITIES AND PRODUCTIONS

MAINSTAGE: 483 seats, fly space, computerized lighting
5 prods: 2 Fac dir, 1 UG dir, 3 Fac des; budget $2,000-6,000

SECOND STAGE: flexible-200 seats, computerized lighting

Mainstage facility built in 1956, renovated in 1997; facilities include scene shop, 1 design studio, CAD facility, costume shop, 1 dance studios, 2 rehearsal studios, 2 classrooms.

A non-departmental, student-run org. presents 8 prods/year in which majors participate.

2 student-written plays have been produced by the dept. in the last two years.

DESCRIPTION

Noted Faculty: Robert Gainer, Acting, Directing, Chair of Dept.; Gary Grant, Th Hist., Theory, Directing; Heath Hansum, Technical Direction, Lighting; Elaine Williams, Scene and Costume Design; Paula Davis, Costume Des. and History.

Dance Faculty: Er-Dong Hu, Dance Technique and Theory, Director of Dance; Kelly Knox, Dance Technique and Theory.

Guest Artists: Barry Kur, Vocal Coach; Meredith Monk, Performance Artist; Edward Herrmann, Actor; Ping Chong, Performance Artist; Bernardo Solano, Playwright; Graciela Danielle and Sean Curran, Guest Choreographers.

Directed by a professional faculty, the department of theatre and dance at Bucknell offers opportunities in all phases of the dramatic arts. Courses in all aspects of theatre arts constitute a major or minor program for students who elect theatre as a focal point for their liberal arts education. The theatre program presents a balanced season of plays from various periods, as well as forays into nontraditional theatrical modes. Students have a wide range of opportunities. Not only do they make up the cast and crews of each production, they also have a voice in the program's administration. Each year, selected students direct or design major productions in collaboration with the theatre's professional staff. Cocktail Theatre series presents several one-act plays, directed and produced entirely by students in a studio theatre setting. The department also offers a dance minor program led by a professional faculty. Two mainstage dance performances are offered each year, as well as a Choreographer's Showcase, in collaboration with the Bucknell Dance Company. Theatre and dance are joined at Bucknell to enrich and illuminate the students' sense of self, to offer professional direction, and to instill an appreciation of artistic expression, basic to the human experience.

California University of Pennsylvania

Dr. Michael J. Slavin, Chair
Department of Theatre & Dance
California Univ. of Pennsylvania
250 University Ave, Box 16
California, PA 15419-1394
DEPT: (724) 938-4220/4221
slavin@cup.edu
ADMISSIONS: Dixon Hall, Rm 201
www.cup.edu

6,500 Total Enr.; competitive
Semester System
45 Majors; NAST (pndg) ATHE
SMALL PROGRAM
T: $5,254/$5,128 r&b
O-ST T: $8,408/$5,128 r&b
FAX: (724) 938-1587
(724)938-4404
FAX: (724) 938-4564

DEGREES OFFERED

BA in Theatre (45), Dance (5). Declare major in 1st year; 2006 granted 6 UG degrees.

ADMISSION & FINANCIAL INFORMATION

Inst. reqs. 2.5 GPA, 900 comb. SAT; inst. admits 75% of applicants; no special req. for theatre program; UG admits all to program. Board of Governor-4 yr full-tuition (instate only), 6 other scholarships ranging from $250-1000. Special out-of-state tuition rate, 150% of instate tuition for out-of-state theatre majors.

FACULTY AND CLASSES OFFERED

5 1/2 Full-Time: 2 PT, 3 PhD, 2 MA/MFA;1 Prof w/o adv deg, 3 Staff

A. (1/2 FT) Intro to Th.-1/Y; Dramatic Lit-2/O; Th. Hist.-2/O; Dram. Crit.-1/O; Shakes.-1/O; Playwriting-1/OX

B. (2 FT,2 PT) Acting-3/Y; Voice-3/Y; Dance-8/Y; Singing-1/X; Directing-1/O

C. (2 FT,) Cost. Des.-1/O; Lighting Des.-2/Y; Tech Prod-1/Y; Cost. Constr-1/O; Make-up-1/Y; Princ of Des-1/Y; Set Des-2/Y

D. (1 FT) Arts Mgmt-1/OX

FACILITIES AND PRODUCTIONS

MAINSTAGE: 625 seats, fly space, computerized lighting.. 7-8 prods: 6 Fac dir, 5 Fac des, 1 Guest dir/des; budget $20,000-25,000

SECOND STAGE: 50 seats, black box, computerized lighting. 2-3 Guest dir/des; budget $100-1000

Workshop/Readings budget $100-200

Facility was built in 1959: the auditorium/theatre renovation began in May '06 through August '07. Includes scene shop, costume shop, prop shop, sound booth, video studio, dance studio, rehearsal studio, classrooms. Second Stage is black box area for Freshman shows.

A non-departmental, student-run, producing org. presents productions in which majors are required to participate.

3 student written plays have been produced in the last 2 years.

Connection with West Virginia Public Theatre. West Virginia Public is primarily a professional summer stock company who will use students as interns in prod and performance areas.

DESCRIPTION

Noted Faculty: Mrs. Donna Anthony, Dance; Mr. Malcolm Callery, Design; Mr. William O'Donnell, Design; Dr. Michele Pagen, Acting, Directing, Voice and Speech/Interp; Dr. Michael Slavin, Acting, Child Drama, Lit, Th Hist.

Guest Artists: Miss Soili Arvola, Mr. Andrew Drost, Mr. Leo Ahonen, Miss Cheryl Giannini, Mr. Stephane Andre, Mr. Ajay Bhandaram, Mr. Matthew

Winnegge, Mr. Craig Salstein.

California University Department of Theatre offers an academically-based, performance oriented program designed to meet the vocational, pre-professional, recreational and cultural needs of our students, faculty, staff, and community. Currently in force is a reduction in tuition for out-of-state students who choose to major in theatre. Tuition is at 150% of the in-state rate. Freshmen students get involved immediately in our annual all-freshman production offered each fall.

Carnegie Mellon University

Elizabeth Bradley, Head, School of Drama
College of Fine Arts 106
5000 Forbes Ave.
Carnegie Mellon University
Pittsburgh, PA 15213
(412) 268-2392
ADM: WH101, 5000 Forbes Ave. Pittsburgh., PA 15213
(412) 268-2082 (UG)
undergraduate-admissions@andrew.cmu.edu

8,500 T. Enr.; compet.
Semester System
270 Majors; CCTTP
T: $35,984/$9,350 r&b
www.cmu.edu/cfa/drama
FAX:(412) 621-0281
www.cmu.edu

DEGREES OFFERED

BFA in Acting (64), Musical Theatre (35); BFA/MFA in Design (78), Directing (22), PTM (Production Technology & Mgmt) (36); MFA in Dramatic Writing (11). Declare major in 1st year.

ADMISSION & FINANCIAL INFORMATION

SAT 2, GRE not req. for UG, TOEFL req. for int'l students. Theatre Dept.: requires audition, interview, and portfolio; Design: portfolio required for admission; 65% of applicants accepted. UG admits 50 out of 1000, Grad 25 out of 150 apps. Grad must submit one full length and one one-act play for MFA dramatic writing.

FACULTY AND CLASSES OFFERED

32 FT, 7 PT: 5 PhD, 16 MA/MFA, 13 Staff

A. (4 FT) Intro to Theatre-2/Y; Dramatic Lit-4/Y; Theatre History-6/Y; Shakes-1/Y; Playwriting-7/Y; His. of Art-2/Y; His. of Clothing-2/Y; His. of Arch & Decor-2/Y

B. (18 FT, 2 PT) Acting-10/Y; Voice/Speech-14/Y; Movement-7/Y; Mime, etc.-2/Y; Singing-8/Y; Mus Th-6/Y; Directing-11/Y; Dance-13/Y; Stage Combat-1/O; Improv-3/Y; Camera Lab-2/Y; Piano-6/Y

C. (10 FT, 3 PT) Prins of Design-4/Y; Set Design-4/Y; Cost Des-4/Y; Lighting Des-6/Y; Tech Prod'n (Structure/Machinery)-16/Y; Cost Constr.-4/Y; Make-up-2/Y; Stage Mgmt-2/Y; Drawing/Drafting-4/Y; Sound-4/Y; Scene Painting-3/Y; Computer Application-2/Y; Des/Dir-1/Y; Welding/Elec-3/Y

D. (2 PT) Community Outreach-2/Y; Arts Mgmt-Y

FACILITIES AND PRODUCTIONS

MAINSTAGE: 420 seats, fly space, computerized lighting. 4 prods: 2 Fac dir, 2 Guest dir, 2 Grad des, 2 UG des; bdgt. $11,000

SECOND STAGE: 100-120 seats, comput. lighting. 9 prods: 4 Grad dir, 3 Grad des, 5 UG dir, 6 UG des; budget $500

THIRD STAGE: 80-100 seats, comput. lighting, bdgt. $175

8 Workshops/Rdgs: 8 Grad dir, 2 Grad des

Facility built in 1999; includes scene, cost, props, welding shops, sound studio, CAD facility, 2 dance studios, 3 rehearsal studios, video studio, 3 design studios, 11 classrooms

There is a non-dept., student-run producing organization which produces 2-3 productions each year. Dept. majors rarely participate. 8 student-written plays have been produced in the last two years.

DESCRIPTION

Noted Faculty: Barbara Anderson, Cletus Anderson, Design. Michael Olich, Design; Brian Johnston, Th. Hist.

Guest Artists: John Van Burek, Dir.; Ken Sawyer, Dir.; Bill C. Davis, Playwright; Richard Pilbrow, Lighting; Susan Tsu, Costume; Paul Talewell, Costume.

Carnegie Mellon offers a BFA program designed to prepare students for entry into the profession directly upon graduation. A conservatory approach, the training is four years of intensive, in-depth study of the chosen area (i.e. acting, design, etc.) while providing a strong core understanding of theatre in general. The MFA degree offers students a 3 year individualized program. A serious concentration in the chosen field (scenery, costume, lighting, directing, writing, production) is geared towards helping each student find his/her own voice as an artist. All productions (up to 25 in various venues) are fully created by students with the exception of 4 faculty or guest directors for the mainstage. Top professionals in all areas are brought in throughout the year to work with and network with our students.

Chatham University

Lisa Rose Weaver
Dept of Theatre
Woodland Road
Chatham College
Pittsburgh, PA 15232
DEPT: (412) 365-1167
stevenson@chatham.edu
admissions@chatham.edu

630 Total Enr.; competitive
10 Majors
Semester System
T: $25,216/$7,892 r&b
SMALL PROGRAM
FAX: (412) 365-1505
MAIN: (412) 365-1100
www.chatham.edu

DEGREES OFFERED

BA in Theatre. Declare major in soph. year.

ADMISSION & FINANCIAL INFORMATION

Each candidate is reviewed on an individual basis. 86% of applicants admitted to institution. Special requirements for scholarship applicants only. Theatre scholarship awarded each fall to an incoming first year student. Audition/interview necessary.

FACULTY AND CLASSES OFFERED

1 Full-Time, 1 1/2 Part-Time: 1 PhD, 1 1/2 MFA/MA

A. (1 FT) Intro to Theatre-1/Y; Dramatic Lit/Criticism/History-3/O; Playwriting-1/O; Special Topics-1/YO

B. (1 FT) Acting-2/Y; Directing-1/Y; Special Topics Seminar-1/O; American Theatre-1/O

C. (1 1/2 PT) Design for the Stage-1/O

FACILITIES & PRODUCTIONS

MAINSTAGE: 285 seats, electronic lighting. 2 prods: 2 Fac dir/des; budget $2,000-3,000

SECOND STAGE: 75 seats, computerized lighting. 2-3 prods: 1-2 Fac dir/des; budget $500-700

Main Stage built in 1973, Studio in 1991; includes costume shop.

DESCRIPTION

Noted Faculty: Mark Philip Stevenson, Acting, Directing; Chris Howard, Tech Director.

Guest Artists: Joan Wagman, Dance.

The Chatham College Theatre Program offers students the opportunity to explore the various theatre arts within the context of a liberal education. Courses in acting, directing, and technical theatre are complemented by a sequence of theatre history/dramatic literature and playwriting courses. As Chatham is an institution committed to the education of women, the theatre program has designed its courses and production schedule in accordance with this commitment.

Clarion University of Pennsylvania

Marilouise Michel, Chair
Theatre
Clarion University of PA
Clarion, PA 16214
DEPT: (814) 226-2284

6,000 Total Enr.; competitive
Semester System
8 Maj., 4 Min.; ATHE
T: $6,866/$5,808 r&b
O-ST T: $12,043/$5,808 r&b

DEGREES OFFERED

BA in Theatre; BFA Theatre: Acting, Theatre: Design/Technical, Musical Theatre. Declare major in soph. year.

ADMISSION & FINANCIAL INFORMATION

Accept 75% to inst., based on overall applic., college entrance exam, board test or ACT. Aud., portfolio (for designers). 80% accepted to program. Cheri Aharrah Reid Memorial or Daniel Preuhs Talent Scholarship-send app. to Dept. Chair; add'l scholarships and work study programs - contact CUP admissions.

FACULTY AND CLASSES OFFERED

4 Full-Time; 4 MFA/MA

A. (3 FT) Intro to Theatre-2/Y; Dramatic Lit-2/X; Theatre History-1/Y; Dramatic Criticism-2/X; Shakes-2/Y

B. (3 FT) Acting-2/Y; Voice/Speech-2/Y; Movement-2/Y; Singing-4/X; Directing-1/Y; Musical Theatre-1/Y

C. (1 FT) Prins of Des-1/Y; Cost Des-1/O; Lighting Des-1/Y; Technical Production-1/Y; Cost Constr-1/O; Make- up-1/O; Stage Mgmt-1/O

FACILITIES & PRODUCTIONS

MAINSTAGE: 1600 seats, fly space, computerized lighting. 4 Fac dir, Fac/stud des prods; budget $2,000-5,000

SECOND STAGE: 200 seats, computerized ltg; budget $1,-2,000

Facility was built in 1970; includes scene, costume shops, rehearsal & design studios, 5 classrooms. Video studio across street. Annual fac/student choreog/des dance concert; 2 student-produced, student-dir projects, many have been student-written, including a musical.

A non-departmental, student-run, organization also presents one production per year in which majors participate.

Summer theatre produces 3 musicals in rep on campus and at Cook Forest Sawmill Center for the Arts.

DESCRIPTION

The Bachelor of Fine Arts Degree Program in Theatre at Clarion University provides professional training in acting and in design/technical theatre for a select group of students who, by reason of talent and motivation, appear likely to succeed in the highly competitive world of professional theatre. While continuous professional employment in the field of theatre can never be assured, graduates of this program may reasonably expect to present impressive credentials. Our faculty views theatre not only as a craft but also as an art form which can provide valid and arresting statements of significant human experience. The theatre is more than an art form; it is a way of life. Students must learn a discipline and responsibility in the use of this art. The "total theatre person" is one who knows the theatre art and has personal integrity of the true artist to go along with it. Students are therefore expected to have or to develop a broad interest in the arts and humanities and to acquire a wide knowledge of the relation of theatre to these and to other intellectual and creative activities.

DeSales University

John Bell
Performing and Fine Arts Dept.
2755 Station Ave.
DeSales University
Center Valley, PA 18034-9568
(610) 282-1100 x 1247
John.Bell@desales.edu
Admissions: above

1,400 Total Enr.; competitive
Semester System
320 Majors
 PA Shakespeare Festival
T: $23,000/$8,750 R&B
FAX: (610)282-2240
www.desales.edu
(610) 282-4443

DEGREES OFFERED

BA in Acting/Directing (90), Design/Tech (20); Theatre Education (10); Musical Theatre (25); Declare major in first year. 2007 granted 70 UG degrees.

ADMISSION & FINANCIAL INFORMATION

GPA 3.0, B avg, SAT comb. 900-1100+; inst. admits 65%; aud/int. required for th. program, accept 45 out of 120 applicants. Talent scholarships by audition/interview; Mullin Scholarship by faculty nomination. DeSales Angel Grants by faculty nomination.

FACULTY AND CLASSES OFFERED

14 Full-Time, Dance addl 3, TV/Film addl 3; 2 Part-Time: 1 PhD, 14 MFA/MA; 6 Staff

A. (1.5 FT, 1 PT) Intro to Theatre-1/Y; Th. History-2/Y; Shakes-1/Y; Dramatic Lit-3/Y; Dramatic Crit-1/Y; Senior Seminar-1/Y

B. (4 FT, 1 PT) Acting-9/Y; Voice/Speech-1/Y; Movement-1/Y; Singing-3/Y; Musical Theatre-2/Y; Directing-2/Y; Dance-4/Y; Acting for Camera-2/Y; Shakespeare Tour-1/Y; Stage Combat-1/O

C. (3 FT) Principles of Des-1/Y; Set Des-1/Y; Cost Des-1/Y; Lighting Des-1/Y; Tech Prod-1/Y; Cost Constr.-1/Y; Make-up-1/Y; Scene Painting-1/Y; Stagecraft-1/Y; Stage Mgmt-1/Y

D. (1 FT) Box Office Procedure-1/Y

FACILITIES AND PRODUCTIONS

MAINSTAGE: 473 seats, fly space, computerized lighting
   4 prods: 4 Fac dir, 3 Fac des, budget $6,000-12,000
SECOND STAGE: 200 seats, computerized lighting
   3 prods: 2 Fac dir, 1 UG dir, 9 UG des; budget $1,500-3,500
THIRD STAGE: 100 seats, electronic lighting
   1-2 prods: 1-2 Fac dir; budget $150 - $1,000
Facility was built in 1981, superbly maintained; includes scene, cos-

tume, props, welding shops; sound, design studios; 2 dance studios; 3 rehearsal studio, CAF Facility, 3 classrooms

1 student-written play has been produced by student organization in the last two years.

Connection with Pennsylvania Shakespeare Festival at DeSales Univ., Equity, summer only. Faculty design/direct for festival. Students may be actors, technical or mgmt interns, paid position plus housing.

DESCRIPTION

Noted Faculty: Wayne Turney, Acting, Directing; John Bell, Musical Theatre; Anne Lewis, Acting; Steven Dennis, Acting; Will Neuert, Scenic Design; Dennis Razze, Directing, Musical Theatre; Patrick Mulcahy, Acting.

Guest Artists: Keith Gonzales, Design, Scenic Teaching; Eric Haugen, Lighting Des; Christine Neghenbon, Choreography; Matt Pfeiffer, Guest Director.

The DeSales University Theatre program endeavors to give its students a solid foundation in all areas of theatre. The program is set within a liberal arts context. The liberal arts requirements help the student to understand the moral, philosophical, and political context in which every artist practices. The University and the Theatre, Dance and TV/Film Programs encourage the student to develop a perspective that fosters the Christian Humanist way of life. All theatre students are required to take a basic set of courses in theatre, but each student chooses an area of specialization in either Acting, Directing, Musical Theatre, Design/Tech, or Theatre Education. The challenging production program includes four main stage production, an arena stage children's theatre production, three second stage productions, two dance concerts, and 40 studio theatre productions each year, and provides each student with numerous opportunities for practical experience in all areas of theatre. Theatre majors are required to work in some capacity on every Mainstage production.

Dickinson College

Todd Wronski, Chair
Theatre & Dance, Box 1773
Dickinson College
Carlisle, PA 17013-2896
DEPT: (717) 245-1239
www.dickinson.edu/departments/drama
ADMISSIONS: P. O. Box 1773, Carlisle, PA 17013
(800) 644-1773
www.dickinson.edu/admit@dickinson.edu

2100 Total Enr.; h. compet.
Semester System
15 Majors; ATHE
T: $32,100/$8,000 r&b
FAX: (717) 245-1145

FAX: (717) 245-1442

DEGREES OFFERED

BA in Theatre Arts (Acting/Directing, Dance, Literature , Theatrical Design emphasis) (15). Declare major in sophomore/junior year; 2003 granted 9 degrees.

ADMISSION & FINANCIAL INFORMATION

H.S. record (GPA, course selection, rank), recommendations, essay, activities, test scores. Accept 45% to institution; no special req's for program. Academic merit scholarships are available.

FACULTY AND CLASSES OFFERED

4 FT, 1/2 PT: 3 PhD/DFA, 1 MFA/MA, w/o adv. degree; 2 Staff

A. (1 FT) Intro to Theatre-1/Y; Dramatic Lit-5/OX; Theatre History-1/Y; Shakes-3/Y; Playwriting-X

B. (2 FT, 1/2 PT) Acting-2/Y; Voice/Speech-1/O; Movement-1/Y; Singing-3/X; Directing-2/Y

C. (2 FT) Prins of Des-1/Y; Technical Production-1/Y

FACILITIES & PRODUCTIONS

MAINSTAGE: 228 seats, computerized lighting & sound. 3 Fac dir/des prods; budget $4,000-6,000

SECOND STAGE: 6 UG dir/des prod; budget $500-1,000
Variable # of Workshops/Readings

Facility was built in 1964, renovated 1990 + 2000; includes scene, cost shops, sound studio, dance studio. New black box theatre opened 9/97.

A non-departmental, student-run organization presents 2 productions (improv. comedy)/year in which majors participate. 2 student-written productions, and 3 readings produced in last 2 years.

The department arranges performance and production internships at a number of theatres, on an on-going basis, as well as paid student internships involving international performance.

DESCRIPTION

Noted Faculty: Jim Lartin-Drake, Sherry Harper-McCombs, Design; Karen Lordi, Todd Wronski, Directing, Acting; Amy Ginsburg, Dance.

Guest Artists: Robert Hobbs, Vincent Patterson, Rebecca Frederick, Robert Klingelhoefer, Twyla Tharp, Susan Soetaert.

Ours is a program designed to place the study of theatre within a broad-based approach to education. Opportunities are available for both non-majors and majors, with an intensive, integrated sequence of study for those wishing to major. A minor is also offered. The major is designed around a curriculum, the successful completion of which would allow competitive application to excellent graduate programs in a suitable specialty, or that would facilitate entry into the profession through an apprentice program with a regional professional theatre. Focus areas within the major include acting/directing, dramatic literature, and dance. In addition to our formal classroom learning, the department sponsors an extensive production program of student-acted productions under faculty/professional direction and a series of student produced laboratory productions. International perspective is important in this program. Departmental productions have recently been presented in Edinburgh, Scotland; Victoria, British Columbia, Berlin, Germany, Arezzo, Italy; and Norwich, England. Our department also offers an "inter-arts" major in Dance and Music.

Franklin & Marshall College

Lynn M. Brooks, Chair
Dept. of Theatre, Dance & Film
Franklin & Marshall College
Box 3003
Lancaster, PA 17604-3003
DEPT: (717) 291-4017
TOLL FREE: (877) 678-9111

1,800 Total Enr.; h. compet.
Semester System
30-35 Majors; U/RTA, ATHE
T: $45,604 incl. r&b
O-ST T: $246 per unit
ADM: (717) 291-3951
FAX: (717) 291-4389

www.fandm.edu   admission@fandm.edu

DEGREES OFFERED

A major in Theatre, Dance and Film can choose a concentration in Acting, Design, Dance or Film. All must have a background in Dramatic Literature. Students may also major in another field and have a minor in Theatre Dance, or Film Media Studies. Declare major in soph. year; 2001 granted 15 UG degrees.

ADMISSION & FINANCIAL INFORMATION

Most students rank in the top 25% of HS class with average SAT scores for verbal 510-620 and math 560-670; 65% of applicants admitted to institution; Theatre program generally admits all applicants, no special requirements. Merit is recognized for outstanding students with a variety of special skills and talents.

FACULTY AND CLASSES OFFERED

8 Full-Time: 5 PhD, 3 MFA/MA

A. (2 FT) Intro to Theatre-2/Y; Theatre History-2/Y; Shakes- 2/Y; Dramatic Lit-5/Y; Dramatic Criticism-1/O; Playwriting-1/O; Design-3/Y; Film-6/Y; Dance-6/Y

B. (3 FT) Acting-5/Y; Movement-1/Y; Singing-1/Y; Directing-2/Y; Voice/Speech-2/Y; Musical Theatre-1/O; Stage Combat-1/Y

C. (2 FT) Set Design- 1/Y; Costume History-1/Y; Lighting Design-1/Y; Cost Construction- 1/Y

FACILITIES AND PRODUCTIONS

MAINSTAGE: 200 seats, computerized lighting. 4 prods: 3 Fac dir, 4 Fac des, 1 Guest dir; budget $5,000-8,000

SECOND STAGE: 80 seats, computerized lighting. 4-6 Grad dir/des prods; budget $200-1,000

THIRD STAGE: 80 seats, computerized lighting

Facility includes scene shop, costume shop, 1 video studio, 1 dance studio, 1 design studio.

A non-departmental student-run organization presents 3 productions per year in which majors participate.

DESCRIPTION

Noted Faculty: Lynn Brooks, Julie Brody, dance; Dirk Eitzen, film/video; Dorothy Lovise, playwriting; Donald McManus, acting, directing, dramatic lit. ; Virginia West, cost. design; John Whiting, scene/lighting design, theatre mgmt, production.

Guest Artists: Scott Segar, Designer, director, actor; Billie Whitelaw, Beckett muse; Akiro Matsui, Noh actor/dancer; Lori Bellilove, Isadora Duncan dance specialist; Jose Greco, Spanish dance artist; London Small Theatre Company, Aquilla Producions.

The course of study in the Department of Theatre, Dance and Film at Franklin & Marshall College offers the opportunity for a major or minor, with a choice of area concentration in acting, design, dance, or film and media studies. Core courses explore theatre across geography and chronology, as well as across disciplines and approaches. Upper-level courses include focus on particular periods and playwrights, on selected themes, on discipline-based theory, and on advanced production work in areas of concentration. Active production work in design, directing, or performance is required and credited. Graduates have gone on to such fields as performing, directing, playwriting, teaching, choreography, arts journalism, dance/movement therapy, physical therapy, television production, and filmmaking.

Indiana University of Pennsylvania

Barbara Blackledge, Chair	14,000 Total Enr., compet.
Dept. of Theater & Dance	Semester System
104 Waller Hall	110 Majors; NAST
Indiana Univ. of PA	T: $2,453/sem/2,581 r&b
Indiana, PA 15705-1087	O-ST T: $6,133/sem/2,581 r&b
DEPT: (724) 357-2965	FAX: (724) 357-7899
barb.blackledge@iup.edu	www.arts.iup.edu/theater
ADMISSIONS: 117 Sutton Hall, Indiana, PA 15705	
(724) 357-2230	800-442-6830
admissions-inquiry@iup.edu	www.iup.edu/admissions-and-aid

DEGREES OFFERED

BA in Theater (95); Music-Theater (10), Dance Arts (5)
Declare major in freshman year; 2007 granted 25 degrees.

ADMISSION & FINANCIAL INFORMATION

Aud/interview for actors/portfolio for designers required for admission to theatre major; admits 20 out of 60 applicants admitted to theatre program, 50% of applicants accepted by instit. SAT or ACT; transcripts with grades and courses taken, class rank, recommendation, extra curricular activities. Theatre by the Grove Talent Scholarships - aud and recommendation; Provost Scholarships - SATof 1000+, PA resident and audition & recommendation.

FACULTY AND CLASSES OFFERED

10 FT: 2 PhD, 8 MFA/MA; 3 Staff

A. (3 FT) Intro to Th-8/Y; Dramatic Lit-4/Y; Th Hist-4/Y; Dramatic Crit-2/Y; Shakes-1/O; Playwriting-1/Y

B. (3 1/2 FT) Acting-4/Y; Voice/Speech-1/Y; Movement-1/Y; Directing-2/Y; Mime, etc-1/O; Mus Th-2/Y; Stage Combat-1/O; Dance-10/Y; Intro to Dance-2/Y; Improv-1/O; Choreography-1/O; Audition Tech-1/O; Acting for the Camera-1/O; Dance Prod-1/O; Stage Dialects-1/O; Singing-1/Y

C. (3 FT) Prins of Des-1/Y; Set Design-1/O; Cost Des-1/O; Lighting Des-1/O; Tech Prod-3/Y; Cost Constr-2/Y; Make-up-1/Y; Stage Mgmt-1/O; Scene Painting-1/O; CAD/Tech Drawing-1/O; Sound Des-1/O; Props-1/O; Costume Crafts-1/O; Puppetry-1/O

D. (1/2 FT) no courses listed

FACILITIES & PRODUCTIONS

MAINSTAGE: 220 seats, computerized & electronic lighting
6 prods; 4-6 Fac dir, 3-6 Fac des, 1-2 GA dir/des, 0-1 UG dir, 1-3 UG des; budget $3,000-5,500

SECOND STAGE: 70 seats, computerized lighting.
25 prods: 0-2 Fac dir, 0-1 Fac des, 23-25 UG dir, 25 UG des; budget $100-500

THIRD STAGE: 1500 seats, fly space, computerized lighting
6 prods: 1-2 Fac dir, 3-5 UG dir; budget $0-100

Facility was built in 1930, renovated in 1989; includes scene shop, cost. shop, props shop, welding shop, sound studio, CAD facility, 2 dance studios, reh. studio, classrooms, 2 dressing rooms, green room, set/props/costume storage.

10+ student-written plays produced in the last two years.

Connected with Keystone Music Theater, operates summer only, students can get acting, tech or management internships

DESCRIPTION

Noted Faculty: Tom Ault, Historian Renaissance and Indian Theater; Barb Blackledge, Shakespeare Performance; Jason Chimonides, Playwright; Rick Kemp, Devised Theater; Patrick McCreary, Theater Consultant

Guest Artists: Matko Srsen, Director; Michael Hood, Director; Mark Hamberger, Costume Des; Jeremy Rolla, Light Des

The IUP Department of Theater and Dance is dedicated to both theater and dance as collaborative and highly disciplined fine arts that demand an education that offers an extended view of the world as a part of a liberal and humanistic education. Successful students develop an artistic sensibility and a disciplined work ethic, skills necessary in most endeavors. The department is committed to:

1.) Providing comprehensive course work, from introductory through advanced levels of study, in all major areas of theater and dance. 2.) Providing diverse production opportunities at all academic levels to develop students as artists by developing proficiency in one or more of the areas of playwriting, research, performance and production while stimulating intellectual growth. 3.) Establishing a work ethic of collaboration, personal discipline and respect. An integrated program achieves these goals, combining academic rigor, variegated production experiences and allowing for both breath and depth of learning.

Kutztown University

Prof. Roberta L. Crisson, Chair	8,200 Total Enr.
Department of Speech Communication and Theatre	Semester System
	61 Majors; ATHE
Kutztown University	T: $7,898/$2,600 r&b
Kutztown, PA 19530-1610	O-ST T: $13,252/$2,600 r&b
DEPT: (610) 683-4560	FAX: (610) 683-4659
www.kutztown.edu	crisson@kutztown.edu
ADMISSIONS: Admissions House, Kutztown Univ.	
(610) 683-4472	

DEGREES OFFERED

BA in Theatre (61). Declare major in freshman/sophomore year; 2004 granted 10 degs.

ADMISSION & FINANCIAL INFORMATION

Req.: ACT, SAT, V-380, M-400; DDS Program: PGA 1.80-1.99; Minority Admission: GPA 2.0; Accept 70% to institution; open admissions. Department scholarships-$250-500, based on need, GPA. Artistically talented-full tuition waiver, based on department recommendation, need, GPA.

FACULTY AND CLASSES OFFERED

6 Full-Time: 1 PhD, 5 MFA/MA

A. (1 1/2 FT) Intro to Th.-Y; Dramatic Lit-2/X; Th. Hist.-5/Y; Shakes-3/X; Playwriting-1/X; Script Analysis-1/O

B. (2 1/2 FT) Acting-5/Y; Voice/Speech-1/Y; Mvmt-1/Y; Singing -X; Mus. Th. -1/Y; Directing-2/Y; Stage Combat-2/Y; Dance-X

C. (2 FT) Prins of Des-1/Y; Set Design-1/O; Cost Des-1/Y; Lighting Des-1/O; Tech Prod-1/O; Cost Constr-1/Y; Make-up-1/Y; Stg Mgmt-1/O; Adv. Design Proj.-1/O

D. Marketing/Promo-X; Box Office Procedure (Independent Study)-Y

FACILITIES & PRODUCTIONS

MAINSTAGE: 170 seats, computerized lighting
   2 prods: 2 Fac dir, 2 Fac des; budget $5,000-10,000

SECOND STAGE: 97 seats, fixed stage, electronic lighting. 1 Fac dir/des,
   2 UG dir, 4 UG des

Workshop/Reading; budget $1,000-1,500

Facility built in 1930, renovated in 1985; includes scene shop, costume shop, CAD facility, sound studio, 6 classrooms.

Non-departmental, student-run organizations present 2-4 productions per year in which majors may participate.

DESCRIPTION

Noted Faculty: Prof. James N. Brown & Prof. Roxane Rix, Equity actors & specialists in stage combat & Alba emoting, respectively.

Guest Artists: Joan Roberts, Actress, original cast of Oklahoma!; Jan Robertson, Conductor, Jekyll & Hyde, Garth Fagan.

Objectives of the Speech Communication & Theatre Department of Kutztown University: 1) To provide for the general education of the undergraduate so that the student, regardless of major, will understand the aesthetic dimension of human experience to the degree necessary to appreciate theatre. 2) To provide in-depth studies for students wishing to be prepared for advanced study in Theatre and/or successful in theatrical careers, and for those students wishing to teach at the elementary or secondary level. 3) To provide for the cultural enrichment of the University and surrounding community via presentation of dramatic events by guest artists and department personnel on-campus, and the presentation of off-campus events.

Lafayette College

Suzanne Westfall, Dir. of Theatre
Williams Center for the Arts
Lafayette College
Easton, PA 18042
(610) 330-5326

www.lafayette.edu

2,381 Total Enr.; h. compet.
ATHE
Semester System
T: $33,811/$10,377 r&b
Fax: 610-330-5606
SMALL PROGRAM
admissions@lafayette.edu

DEGREES OFFERED

BA in English, Concentration in Drama/Theatre; Minor in Theatre. Declare major in sophomore year.

ADMISSION & FINANCIAL INFORMATION

SAT/ACT scores. 36% accepted to institution.

FACULTY AND CLASSES OFFERED

4 Full-Time, 4 Pt-Time: 4 PhD, 3 MFA/MA, 1 Prof. w/o adv. deg

A. (3 FT) Intro to Theatre-1/Y; Dramatic Lit-2/Y; Shakes-3/Y; Dramatic Criticism-1/O; Playwriting-1/O

B. (1 FT, 2 PT) Acting-2/Y; Voice/Speech-1/Y; Singing-1/X; Dir-1/O

C. (3 PT) Tech Prod'n-1/Y

FACILITIES & PRODUCTIONS

MAINSTAGE: 400 seats, fly space, computerized lighting
   2 prods: 2 Fac dir/des; budget 6,000-8,000

SECOND STAGE: 100 seats
   4 prods: 1 Fac dir/des, 1 UG dir/des; budget $3,000-5,000

6 Guest dir/des Workshops/Readings; budget $100-2,500

Facility built in 1983; includes scene shop, prop shop, classrooms.

A non-departmental, student-run org presents 1 prod. per year.

DESCRIPTION

Noted Faculty: Ian Smith, Drama; Suzanne Westfall, Perf; Michael O'Neill, Dir; Richard Kendrick, Des.

Guest Artists: Ping Chong and Company; ACTER (from London); John Kane, RSC; Pilobus; American Repertory Theatre; Philip Glass; P.S. 122; Asian Repertory Company; Charles Busch, Danny Hoch, Urban Bush Women, Bread & Puppet Theatre.

Lafayette College Theatre offers a unique approach to theatre training through courses, productions, and guest artists. Some students opt to major in English with a concentration in Drama/Theatre. Most theatre students, however, elect courses in theatre and do independent study in theatre. Lafayette's theatre program presents four major productions each year; in addition, students work closely with guest artists and artists-in-residence at the Williams Center for the Arts. Special features of the Lafayette program include interim theatre classes in London and New York, and program support for student design and directing projects.

Lehigh University

Augustine Ripa, Chair
Theatre Department
Zoellner Arts Center
420 E. Packer Ave.
Lehigh University
Bethlehem, PA 18015
ADMISSIONS: 27 Memorial Dr. W.
(610) 758-3100

6,500 Total Enr.; h. compet.
Semester System
25 Majors; NAST, ATHE
T: $35,310/$9,340 r&b
DEPT: (610) 758-3640
FAX: (610) 758-6543
www.lehigh.edu
FAX: (610) 758-4361

DEGREES OFFERED

BA in Theatre. May concentrate in Acting/Directing, Design/Technical, History/Literature or General Theatre Studies. Declare major in sophomore year; 1998 granted 8 degrees.

ADMISSION & FINANCIAL INFORMATION

Require SAT, 3 Ach. Tests, 16 cr. of college prep; Accept 50% to inst; accepts all to program; DEPT: offers Baker and Williams Scholarships; Univ. offers Nat'l Merit scholarship, Trustee scholarship, etc.; based on need, merit, extracur. activity.

FACULTY AND CLASSES OFFERED

6 FT, 8 PT: 11 MFA/MA, 1 PhD, 3 Prof w/out adv. degree; 1 Staff

A. (1 FT, 2 PT) Intro to Theatre-1/Y; Dramatic Lit/Theatre History-2/Y, 2/X; Shakes-2/X; Playwriting-1/O

B. (3 FT, 2 PT) Acting-5/Y; Voice/Speech-4/X; Movement-1/Y; Singing-4/X; Directing-3/Y; Dance-3/Y

C. (3 FT, 5 PT) Prin of Des-1/Y; Set Des-2/Y; Lighting Des-2/Y; Cost. Des-2/Y; Costume-1/Y; Make-up-1/Y; Scene Painting-2/Y; Sound Design-2/Y; Drafting-1/Y; Stagecraft-1/Y

D. House Management-1/Y; Press & Public Relations-1/Y; Marketing-3/X; Contracts/Copyright-1/X; Devel, Grant Writing-3/X; Budgeting/Accounting Procedure-1/X

FACILITIES & PRODUCTIONS

MAINSTAGE: 300 seats, fly space, electronic lighting. 4 prods: 2 Fac dir/des, 1 Guest dir/des, 1 UG dir/des; budget $2,-3,500

THIRD STAGE: 100 seats, black box, computer & electronic lighting.

Mainstage facility (Zoellner Arts Center) was built in 1997. Facility includes scene shop, costume shop, design studio, CAD facility, sound studio, 2 rehearsal studios.

A non-departmental, student-run producing org. presents 1 production per year in which majors particiapte. 1 student-written play produced in the last two years.

Connection with Touchstone Theatre, Professional non-AEA.

DESCRIPTION

Noted Faculty: Drew Francis, Scene Des./Scene Painting; Erica Hoelscher, Costume Design; Kashi Johnson, Acting/Movement; Jeffrey Milet, Light Design; Pam Pepper, Acting/Directing; Augustine Ripa, Acting Directing.

Lehigh University's Department of Theatre is one of five NAST-accredited undergraduate programs in Pennsylvania. The BA in theatre offered by the Department of Theatre constitutes one of the several major arts concentrations in the College of Arts and Science. Yet Lehigh students from all walks of academic life participate in theatre courses and production activity. In this light we are more than a major program in our College; we are a service in the highest sense to the overall goals of the University. Theatre stands with disciplines such as philosophy, classics, or music, concerned with educating a central core of majors while exerting a humanizing and liberalizing influence on students from all of Lehigh's Colleges. The major in theatre provides a comprehensive understanding of the theory and practice, literature, and history of the theatre, preparing the most serious students to gain acceptance to reputable graduate programs; because some theatre majors will earn their living in areas outside of theatre after college, the theatre major is constructed so as to allow students to add a second major, and minor programs in theatre will satisfy the interests of students in curricula too rigid to allow a second major in theatre. The theatre department mounts a full production program annually.

Muhlenberg College

Charles Richter, Dir of Theatre
Theatre Arts
Muhlenberg College
Baker Ctr for Arts 2400
Allentown, PA 18104
DEPT: (484) 664-3330
ADMISSIONS: Office of Admissions, above address
(484) 664-3200
www.muhlenberg.edu

2,000 Total Enr.; h. compet.
Semester System
190 Majors; ATHE
T: $30,715/$7,025 r&b
FAX: (484) 664-3031
richter@muhlenberg.edu

FAX: (484) 664-3234

DEGREES OFFERED

BA in Acting (135), Tech/Design (15), Dance (60), Directing (20); Stage Management (10); Performance Studies (10). Declare major in sophomore year; 2006 granted 50 UG degs.

ADMISSION & FINANCIAL INFORMATION

SAT score: 1200+ comb. GPA B+ avg. (3.5); Accept 35% to inst.; no special req's. for admission to theatre program. There are talent Scholarships for entering theatre majors, aud required. Students must audition in person or send a video with two monologues no more than five minutes total. An optional song can also be included. No accents, characters.

FACULTY AND CLASSES OFFERED

13 FT, 10 PT; 2 PhD, 14 MFA/MA, 6 Prof. w/o adv. deg.; 8 Staff

A. (3 FT, 2 PT) Intro to Theatre-1/Y; Dramatic Literature-6/Y+O; Theatre History-2/Y; Shakes-3/Y; Playwriting-1/O

B. (4 FT, 1 PT) Acting-6/Y; Voice/Speech-2/Y; Singing (private lessons every term); Directing-3/Y; Dance-13/Y; Mus Th-1/O

C. (3 FT, 1 PT) Prins of Des-2/Y; Set Des-2/Y; Lighting Des-2/Y; Cost Des-2/Y; Cost History-1/Y; Make-up-1/Y; Sound Des-1/Y

D. (4 FT, 8 PT) Dance

FACILITIES & PRODUCTIONS

MAINSTAGE I: 392 seats, computerized lighting. 6 prods: 3 Fac dir, 7 Fac des, 1 Guest dir, 5 Guest des, 2 UG dir, 3 UG des; budget $10,000-40,000

MAINSTAGE II: 340 seats, computerized lighting. 20 UG dir/des prods; budget $10,000-20,000

THIRD STAGE: 150 seats, black box, computerized lighting.

3 UG dir Workshops/Readings; budget $100.

Facility was built in 1976, new Theatre Center ($10 million facility) opened Fall '99; includes scene shop, costume shop, prop shop, sound studio, 2 dance studios, 2 rehearsal studios, 3 classrooms.

2 student-written plays produced in the last two years.

There is a connection with Muhlberg Summer Music Theatre Festival. Operated by the department, professionals direct and design all productions. Students play leading roles and work in the ensemble alongside Equity guest artists. Students also have technical staff and stage mgmt. positions. Everyone, students included, are paid for their work with the company.

DESCRIPTION

Noted Faculty: Holly Cate, Francine Roussel, Troy Dwyer, Constance Case, Acting; Charles Richter, Dir./Hist; Tim Averill, Curtis Dretch, Design; Karen Dearborn, Dance; Liz Covey, Costumes; Shelly Oliver, Tap Dance; James Peck, Directing, Theatre History; Beth Schachter, Acting/Directing, Theatre History.

Guest Artists: Dennis Parichy, Lighting; Brighde Mullins, Playwright; James Ryan, Playwright, John Ramsey, Actor; Mac Wellman, Playwright; John McKernon, Lighting.

We offer quality theatre training in the context of a broad liberal arts education. All performance and design teachers are highly regarded working professionals. The program focuses on the individual creative growth of each student. Students can concentrate in one area or study any combination of acting/directing/design or dance. The small size of the department allows for close student-faculty interaction. The production program is very well funded by the college, has received numerous awards from ACTF and enjoys wide popular and critical acclaim. Students may study abroad in our program run in cooperation with the University of London. Students can double major in a second field and non-majors are welcomed to participate in the production program. First-year students are encouraged to audition for, and are cast in, mainstage productions. With strong offerings in dance and an excellent vocal training program in the music department, Muhlenberg offers fine training in Musical Theatre. Each year a fully staged musical is mounted as part of the production program. There are also studio productions of musicals and operas.

Northampton Community College

Ron Heneghan,	8,000 Tot. Enr.; not compet.
Theatre	Semester System
Department of Theatre Arts	40 Majors
Northampton Comm. College	T: $103/credit hr. in county
3835 Green Pond Rd.	T: $223/credit hr. out-of county
Bethlehem, PA 18020-7599	O-ST T: $331/credit hr.
	r&b: $5,536
DEPT: (610) 861-5316	FAX: (610) 861-4167
nroberts@northampton.edu	SMALL PROGRAM

ADMISSIONS: Office of Admissions, above address
(610) 861-5500   FAX: (610) 861-4560
adminfo@northampton.edu

DEGREES OFFERED

AA (2 yr. college) Theatre (48). Declare major in freshman year.

ADMISSION & FINANCIAL INFORMATION

Open enrollment; admit 97%, 90% accepted to th. prog., audition required. Aud for actors, Portfolio for des. Actors Scholarship Fund for students going on to major in theatre at 4-year college. Students must have a B or better GPA and acted in 4 or more major productions while at NCC. Maximum monetary amount given per student is $1,000.

FACULTY AND CLASSES OFFERED

2 FT, 2 PT; 4 MA/MFA; 1 Staff

A. (1/2 FT, 1 PT) Intro to Theatre-1/Y; Dramatic Literature-1/Y; Shakes-1/X; Th. Portfolio-1/Y

B. (1 1/2 FT) Acting-2/Y; Voice/Movement-2/Y; Directing-1/Y

C. (1 PT) Technical Theatre-1/Y; Stage Craft-1/Y

FACILITIES & PRODUCTIONS

MAINSTAGE: 350 seats, thrust, computerized lighting. 2 prod: 2 Fac dir, 2 Fac des; budget $10,000

SECOND STAGE: 100-125 seats, black box, computerized lighting. 2 prods: 2 Fac dir/des, 2 Guest dir, budget $6,000

Workshops/Touring: 1 Fac dir/des; 20 UG dir/des, budget $100-2,500

Facility was built in 1972, renovated in 2002; includes scene shop, costume shop, sound studio, 1 video studio, 3 classrooms. On-campus dorms and aprtments available.

DESCRIPTION

Noted Faculty: Norman Roberts, Acting/Directing; Ronald Heneghan, Voice and Movement, Literature; Vicki Neal, Scenic/Lighting.

Guest Artists: Bethany Nauroth, Director; Tom DiGiovanni, Pianist; D. Polly Kendrick, Costumer

The curriculum is designed for acting/directing majors and design/technical theatre majors, but will serve as the first two years for theatre education majors. as well. NCC Theatre is production-oriented, with two fully produced productions in the fall and two in the spring, a tour production to local high schools, workshop productions at our branch campus and student directed one-acts. Productions are performed in the college's 350 seat main theatre, 100-125 seat Lab Theatre, and in created and found spaces all around the college, Monroe campus, and throughout the Lehigh Valley. Guest directing by program alumni, returning to display their newly acquired university training and guest designing by highly qualified free-lance artists, is well established at Northampton. Upon successful completion of the program, students will be awarded an Associate in Arts degree in Theatre and be ready to transfer to the university of their choice. Temple University, University of Iowa, University of Missouri at Kansas City, Westchester University and Montclair State College are examples of institutions at which our graduates have recently excelled. Significant production work is required of theatre majors via the practicum components of all theatre courses. Auditioning for productions is required.

Pennsylvania State University ··········

Dan Carter, Director	41,000+ Total Enr.; compet.
School of Theatre	Semester System; 172 Majors;
103 Arts Building	37 Grad
Pennsylvania State University	NAST, U/RTA, ATHE
University Park, PA 16802-2900	T: UG $11,646, G $13,224
DEPT: (814) 865-7586	O-ST T: UG $22,194/G $24,064
Fax: (814) 865-5754	
dhc4@PSU.EDU	www.theatre.psu.edu

ADMISSIONS: UG: 201 Shields Bldg., Univ. Park, PA 16802
Grad: 114 Kern. Bldg., Univ. Park, PA 16802
UG: (814) 865-5471   G: (814) 865-1795   www.psu.edu

DEGREES OFFERED

BA in Liberal Arts (111); BFA in Musical Theatre (47), Design (49), Stage Management (18); MFA in Acting (19), Costume (6), Directing (5), Scene Design (5). Declare major in 1st year; 2007 granted 36 UG, 12 Grad degs.

ADMISSION & FINANCIAL INFORMATION

UG based on interview, aud/portfolio, HS record, and SAT or ACT; Grad students audition, present portfolio & interview; Theatre prog. admits 74 out of 294 UG appl and 15 out of 500 Grad. Two $1000 scholarships for entering freshmen, given in the name of Gallu; based on academic achievement in HS, talent, potential for a career in theatre, and need; Students apply in writing and decisions are made by the Director in assoc. with an UG scholarship committee.

FACULTY AND CLASSES OFFERED

27 FT, 1 PT: 3 PhD, 19 MA/MFA, 6 Prof. w/o adv. degree; 14 1/4 Staff

A. (3 FT) Intro to Theatre1/Y; Dramatic Lit-2/Y; Theatre History-2/Y; Playwriting-1/Y

B. (14 FT, 1 PT) Acting/Scene Study-11/Y; Voice/Speech-4/Y; Movement-5/Y; Mime-1/Y; Musical Th.-5/Y; Directing-4/Y; Stage Combat-1/Y; Dance-12/Y

C. (10 FT) Prins of Des.-3/Y; Set Des.-6/Y; Cost Des.-6/Y; Lighting Des.-3/Y; Tech Prod'n-6/Y; Cost Constr.-5/Y; Stage Mgmt-2/Y; Make-up-1/Y

FACILITIES AND PRODUCTIONS

MAINSTAGE: 450 seats, fly space, computerized & electronic lighting. 19 prods: 5 Fac dir, 1 GA dir, 8 Grad des, 5 UG des; budget $8,000-17,000

SECOND STAGE: 250 seats, computerized & electronic lighting. 5 prods: 1 Fac des., 3 Grad dir, 1 Grad des; budget $2,500-4,000

THIRD STAGE: 150 seats, computerized & electronic lighting.

Workshops/Readings: budget $500

Pavillion in 1960, renovated 1990, Playhouse built in 1963, Downtown Theatre 2003; includes scene, cost, props, welding shops; sound studio, 2 design studios; 3 dance studios, 2 rehearsal studios; classrooms, paint shop, dye room, CAD lab, lighting lab, storage shop, dressing rooms.

There is a student-run producing organization that presents 30 productions per year. Dept majors generally participate.

Connection with Pennsylvania Centre Stage, an Equity theatre serving as the professional arm of the School of Theatre, offers numerous opportunities for Penn State students as well as students from schools nationwide. In addition to professional resident and guest artists, we engage students in all areas including company, stage and production management. Acting internships which accrue equity candidacy points are also offered.

DESCRIPTION

Noted Faculty: Jim Wise, Acting; Jane Ridley, Acting; Mark Olsen, Movement; Charmian Hoare, Voice; Barry Kur, Voice; William Schroder, Costume/Scenic Design; Suzanne Elder, Costume Technology

The educational philosophy of Penn State's undergraduate theatre program is that theatre study must combine experience in production and performance with a broad base in theory and practice. The BA program provides study and experience in all areas of theater, and students may concentrate their studies in one or more areas of interest, such as acting or dramaturgy. This program prepares students to enter the profession, further their study in graduate school, or enter related fields such as teaching, law and communications. The BFA program is a four-year professional training program for students interested in theatre design and technology, stage management, or musical theatre. The philosophy underpinning MFA training at Penn State is simple: Start with the very best candidates and aggressively seek to enhance the unique qualities in each student we accept. Actors, designers, and directors study with highly skilled professionals and then have ample opportunity to translate the studio experience into theatre reality. Through this combination of studio learning and practical experience, and under the guidance of master artists/teachers who are committed to theatre training, students learn to find their own "artistic voice". A distinctive component of our MFA programs is the extensive international program which offers each of our students the opportunity to study abroad on three separate occasions throughout their time with us.

Point Park College

Ronald Allan-Lindblom, Dean
Point Park College
Conservatory of Performing Arts
201 Wood St.
Pittsburgh, PA 15222

1200 Tot. Enr; compet.
Semester System; ATHE
275 Majors
T: $18,990/$8,440 r&b
DEPT: (412) 392-3450

FAX: (412) 392-2424
ADMISSIONS: Above address.
(412) 392-3430

www.pointpark.ed
uenroll@pointpark.edu
FAX: (412) 392-3902

DEGREES OFFERED

BA, BFA, MFA in Acting (75); BA or BFA in Musical Theatre (180); BA, BFA in Technical Theatre & Design (40); BA, BFA in Stage Mgmt (15). Declare major in freshman year.

ADMISSION & FINANCIAL INFORMATION

SAT 950 or ACT 20, 2.5 GPA and audition. Aud/Interview Portfoio for UG, Aud/Interview for Grad. Theatre program admits 1 out of 4 UG and 1 out of 10 Grad applicants. Talent schols and apprenticeships avail. through audition process, academic schols offered through admissions office.

FACULTY AND CLASSES OFFERED

8 FT, 9 PT: 1 PhD, 6 MFA/MA, 2 Prof. w/o adv deg; 3 Staff

A. (1 1/2 FT,1 1/2 PT) Intro to Theatre-1/Y; Theatre History-2/Y; Shakes-2/Y; Playwriting-1/O; Dramatic Lit-2/Y; Dramatic Crit-1/O

B. (5 1/2 FT, 6 1/2 PT) Acting-6/Y; Movement-4/Y; Singing-8/Y; Directing-2/Y; Voice/Speech-6/Y; Mime/Mask-4/Y; Musical Theatre-6/Y; Dance-8/Y; Stage Combat-2/Y

C. (1 FT, 1 PT) Prins of Design-2/Y; Set Design-2/Y; Cost Des-4/Y; Tech. Prod-8/Y; Costume Hist-2/Y; Stage Mgmt-2/Y; Lighting Des-2/Y; Cost Constr-2/Y; Make-up-1/Y;

FACILITIES AND PRODUCTIONS

MAINSTAGE: 480 seats, fly space, computerized lighting. 4 prods: 1 Fac dir/des, 3 Guest dir/des; budget $17,000-25,000

SECOND STAGE: 285 seats. 4 prods: 4 Fac dir, 1 Fac des, 3 Guest des; budget $5,000-7,000

THIRD STAGE: 90 seats, black box, fixed stage. budget $500-1,000

Facility was renovated in 2000; includes scene shop, costume shop, prop shop, CAD facility, dance studio, design studio, rehearsal studio, classrooms.

Connection with Pittsburgh Playhouse Rep Company an Equity company, operates during school yr. Students invited to audition based on Production needs.

DESCRIPTION

Noted Faculty: John Amplas, Acting, Voice & Speech; Shirley Barasch, Musical Theatre Techniques, Private Voice; Jack Allison, Rehearsal & Performance, Musical Theatre Techniques; Sandra Greciano, Singing for Actors, Musical Theatre Techniques, Private Voice; Rich Keitel, Acting, Voice & Speech; Miriam Kelly, Voice & Speech; John Shepard, Acting, Directing; Shirley Tannenbaum, Acting, Voice & Speech; Robin Walsh, Acting, Voice and Speech.

Guest Artists: Jack Allison, Director/Musical Th; Michael Rupert, Director/Actor; Richard Rossi, Music Director; Scott Wise, Choreographer; Cicely Berry, Voice & Speech; Wade Russo, Musical Theatre; Albert Poland, Auditioning; Larry Meyers, Director.

From backstage to center stage, Park Point College has been providing the arts with talented, well-trained performers and technicians-many who are in touring productions, on Broadway, television, or on the silver screen. All of the training occurs in professional classes, scene and costume shops, and in three theaters of the

Playhouse: The Rockwell Theatre, The Hamlet Street Theatre and The Theatre Downstairs. This sixty year old facility is staffed by instructors, designers, artisans, front of house, box office and public relations personnel who supervise students in a full range of theater operations from designing to managing to acting. Faculty, production staff and students intensively work in classes and rehearsals seven days a week involving twelve subscription productions. There are also opportunities for theatre majors to specialize in other programs from stage and arts management to teaching certification for elementary Children's theatre and secondary schools.

Seton Hill University

Terry Brino-Dean, Director
Seton Hill Univ. Theatre
1 Seton Hill Drive, POB 492F
Greensburg, PA 15601
DEPT: (724) 830-0300
www.setonhill.edu
brinodean@setonhill.edu
ADMISSIONS: (800) 826-6234
admit@setonhill.edu

1,800 Total Enr.; competitive
38 Majors, ATHE
Semester System
T: $23,180/7,230 r&b
FAX: (724) 830-4611
SMALL PROGRAM

FAX: (724) 830-1294

DEGREES OFFERED

BA in Theatre Performance (14), Technical Theatre (8), Theatre Arts (4),Music/Theatre (10), Theatre/Business (4); Declare major in soph year; 2006 granted 6 degrees.

ADMISSION & FINANCIAL INFORMATION

HS diploma and transcript, SAT or ACT score. Audition for actors; interview, portfolio for des. 80% accepted to inst. 4 out of 5 to theatre prog. Scholarships available: Eight 4-yr. $3,000-6,000/per, also $12,000 - $24,000 total. All based on past academic performance, past artistic experience, and aud. or portfolio review.

FACULTY AND CLASSES OFFERED

2 FT, 6 PT: 1 PhD, 4 MFA/MA, 3 Prof. w/o adv. degree; 2 Staff

A. (1 FT) Intro to Theatre-1/Y; Dramatic Lit-2/O; Th History-2/O; Shakes-1/X, 1/O; Playwriting-1/O

B. (1 FT, 3 PT) Acting-4/Y; Voice/Speech-2/Y; Mvmt-1/O; Mime, etc.-1/O; Singing-8/X; Directing-2/Y; Dance-5/Y, Music Th.-1/O; Stage Combat-1/O; Film-1/O.

C. (3 PT) Tech Prod-1/Y; Set Design-1/Y; Cost Des-1/O; Lighting Des-1/O; Cost. Constr-1/Y; Make-up-1/Y; Sound Des-1/O; Stage Mgmt-1/O

D. Arts Mgmt-1/X; Mktg/Promo-2/X; Legal: Contracts/Copyright-1/X; Development/Grant Writing-1/X; Budgeting/Accounting Proc.-4/X

FACILITIES & PRODUCTIONS

MAINSTAGE: 132 seats, computerized lighting. 4 prods: 3 Fac dir, 13 Fac des, 1 Guest dir; 3 UG des,budget $3,000-4,000 per prod

SECOND STAGE: 60 seats, electronic lighting. 8 prods: 8 UG dir, 30 UG des; budget: $100-200

12 Workshop/Readings, 2 fac dir./10 UG dir.

Facility includes scene shop, costume shop, sound studio, dance studio, CAD facility, video studio, rehearsal studio, design studio, classrooms. New facilities under construction,opening 2008-9.

There is no non-departmental, student-run organization. 10 student-written play readings were held in the last two years.

The performance space is used in the summer by Apple Hill Playhouse and Stage Right for camps and conferences.

DESCRIPTION

Noted Faculty: Dr. Terry Brino - Dean, ,Theatre History & Theory, Directing, Acting, Sound Design; Karen Glass, Scene Des, Lighting Des, Th. Tech; Ken Clothier, Scene Design, Lighting Design, Sound Design, Technical Direction; Denise Pullen, Acting, Directing, Playwriting, Voice and Speech, Movement; Susan O'Neill, Costume Des/Construction; Ta Mara Swank, Dance; Joseph Domencic, Musical Direction, Stage Movement, Voice.

Guest Artists: Directors: Ron Siebert, Shawn Sturnick, Kathryn Moroney; Fight Dir: Shaun Rolly; Musical Director: Jim Overly, Joe Domencic.

The Seton Hill Theatre Program values personalized instruction within the contexts of the liberal arts, selective admission and intimate size. The Theatre Program offers a B.A. degree in Theatre Arts. Students may also choose an emphasis. The Theatre Performance Emphasis is designed for those seeking careers as professional performers, preparing them for MFA conservatory programs and professional competition. The interdisciplinary Music/Theatre Emphasis is demanding and stringent. Students entering it should be highly motivated and in excellent health. The interdisciplinary Technical Theatre Emphasis is designed for those seeking careers in a wide range of technical fields. It prepares students for MFA design programs or professional intern or apprentice positions. The interdisciplinary Theatre/Business Emphasis is designed for students seeking careers in the administrative and commercial aspects of the entertainment industry. The new Seton Hill University Performing Arts Center replaces all current facilities and will open in the 2008-2009 year.

Swarthmore College

Allen Kuharski, Chairman
Dept of Theater
500 College Ave.
Swarthmore College
Swarthmore, PA 19081
DEPT: (610) 328-7794
ADM: (610) 328-8152
admissions@swarthmore.edu

1,500 Total Enr.; h. compet.
16 Majors; ATHE, LMDA
Semester System
T: $34,884/$10,816 r&b
akuhars1@swarthmore.edu
FAX: (610) 690-6837
SMALL DEPT
www.swarthmore.edu

DEGREES OFFERED

BA in Theater (12-16). Declare major in spring of 2nd year.

ADMISSION & FINANCIAL INFORMATION

High Boards, high rank in class, wide talents & interests. Theater dept admits all applicants.

FACULTY AND CLASSES OFFERED

4 FT, 8 PT: 4 PhD, 6 MFA/MA, 2 Prof. w/o adv. degree

A. (1 FT, 1 PT) Intro to Th.-2/Y; Th. History-1/Y; Playwriting-1/Y; Performance Theory-1/Y; Prod Dramaturgy-1/Y

B. (3 FT) Acting-7/Y; Directing-2/Y

C. (1 FT) Intermediate Scenography-1/Y; Advanced Scenography-1/Y; Lighting. Design-1/Y; Set Design-1/Y; Costume Des-1/Y

FACILITIES & PRODUCTIONS

MAINSTAGE: 350 seats, fly space, computerized lighting
extra curricular, student-run prods.; budget $500-3,500; dept, fac dir prod each spring: budget $6,000. Guest art perf, 1-2/yr; budgeted at $10,000-30,000.

SECOND STAGE: 120 seats, black box, computerized lighting
Classes only (acting, directing, playwriting); budget $100-5,000 work prods. associated w/ classwork.

Facility was built in 1991; includes scene shop, costume shop, CAD facility, 2 movement/dance studios, design studio, cinema, 2 classrooms. Mainstage converts: proscenium/thrust.

A non-departmental, student-run organization presents 6-12 productions per year in which DEPT: majors participate.

Connection with People's Light & Theatre Co. & Pig Iron Theatre Company. Pig Iron: non-equity, year 'round, all alums, internships, in residence during the summer. People's Light: LORT D, year 'round, various faculty, 2 alums currently on staff.

DESCRIPTION

Guest Artists: SF Mime Troupe, Holly Hughes, Sotigui Kouyate, Silesian Dance Theatre Qi Shu Fang Peking Opera Company, Joseph Chaikin, Peggy Shaw.; Ridge Theater Co; Bread & Puppet Theater; Provisorium & Kompania (Lublin, Poland).

Special Visiting Faculty: Sue-Ellen Case., Jacek Luminski; Kofi Anyidoho.

The Department of Theater at Swarthmore College regards theater as a range of processes for making works of art in collaboration with other people. All our courses are sited in production process; we teach dramaturgy, not criticism or literature; all play production is a part of course work. Courses in acting, directing, design & production dramaturgy use ensemble methods as their model. Majors usually work at a paid job in the Department of Theater, which is conceived as an arts organization producing a theater curriculum. Each class, during junior and senior years, forms a company which produces a "season" of ensemble theater projects. The Department of Theater is closely connected to the profession (both academic and commercial), but aims to be of broad educational benefit regardless of a student's vocational plans. We believe that Theater is an excellent liberal arts major, a way of organizing what we learn about an increasingly diverse world, and a place to experience and practice the arts of making moral choices in a productive life. The Department of Theater supports a special semester-abroad program for theater and dance students in Poland, and cooperates with programs in the UK and Russia. A new foreign study initiative for theater and dance students in India is under discussion. Roughly 50% of Theater Department graduates have gone on in some aspect of the performing arts via internships, graduate schools and professional conservatories, and paid professional work. Graduates of the Department are also active in television and film production. Those not going on in the arts have entered the fields of law, medicine, engineering, business administration, and education.

Temple University
See ad in back of book
Roberta Sloan, Chair   30,000 Total Enr: not compet

Theater Dept.
Temple University
1301 W. Norris St.
Philadelphia, PA 19122-6075
DEPT: (215) 204-8414
www.scat.temple.edu/theater
ADM: 1301 W. Norris, St., Phila, PA 19122-6075
(215) 204-8414
tuadm@temple.edu

180 Majors; NAST, U/RTA
Semester System, ATHE
T: $10,180/8,231 r&b
O-ST T: $18,224/8,231 r&b
plunked@temple.edu
theater@temple.edu

FAX: (215) 204-2566
www.temple.edu

DEGREES OFFERED

BA in Theater; MFA in Acting , Directing , Design (Scene, Lighting, Costume)). Declare major in 1st, 2nd, or 3rd yr.

ADMISSION & FINANCIAL INFORMATION

Requires completed University Adm. Process. Th program admits any UG who qualifies for university admission, selects a limited number of Grad appl at U/RTA audtions. Paul Randall Scholarship - $1,000- Soph. or Jr. based on exhibited talent and need; Paul Hutton internship - $1,000- based on internship proposal and demonstrated talent; Benzwie Scholarship- $ varies -playwriting; Wing Scholarship - incoming student who intends to specialize in acting, need based, must apply and be eligible for financial aid; Temple Theaters Alumni Scholarship- $2,000 to incoming freshman or transfer, based on talent and high GPA; Domenic Spagnola Award-$500 to graduating theater major who has participated in at least one of Temple Theaters mainstage productions and has at least a 2.75 GPA.

FACULTY AND CLASSES OFFERED

13 FT, 12 PT: 18 MFA/MA, 5 Staff

UNDERGRADUATE COURSES

A. (3 FT, 2 PT) Intro to Th-4/Y; Dramatic Lit-4/Y; Th History-6/Y; Shakes-XY; Playwriting-2/Y

B. (7 FT, 6 PT) Acting-8/Y; Voice-4/Y; Mvmt-4/Y; Mus. Th 1/O; Directing-2/Y; Stage Combat-2/Y

C. (4 FT, 1 PT) Prins of Des-2/Y; Cost Des-4/Y; Tech Prod'n-4/Y; Cost Hist-4/Y; Set Des-4/Y; Lighting Des-4/Y; Cost Constr-4/Y; Make-up-1/O; Stg Mgmt-2/Y

GRADUATE COURSES

A. (3 FT) Dramatic Lit-2/Y; Shakes-Text Analysis-2/Y; Play writing-3/Y; Workshop-2/Y; Video Studio-2/X; Project in Acting-2/Y

B. (6 FT, 3 PT) Acting-4/Y; Voice/Speech-8/Y; Movement-4/Y; Singing-4/Y; Stage Combat-4/Y; 3rd Year-Tutorials in Acting, Voice, Speech, Movement, Singing-Y

C. (4 FT) Prins of Des-1/Y; Cost Des-3/Y; Tech Prod'n-3/Y; Cost Hist-2/Y; Set Design-6/Y; Lighting Des-6/Y; Cost Constr-2/Y; Make-up-1/Y; Hist. Mod. Scenic Des. -1/Y; Drawing & Rendering-1/Y; Scene Painting-1/Y

FACILITIES & PRODUCTIONS

MAINSTAGE: 452 seats, fly space, comput. & electron. lighting.
3 prods: 1 Fac dir/des, 2 Grad dir, 8 Grad des; budget $9,500-16,000

SECOND STAGE: 83 seats, flexible, computer. & electronic lighting
3 prods: 1 Fac dir, 2 Grad dir/9 Grad des; budget $5,000-12,000.

8 Workshops/Readings: 2 Guest dir, 2 Grad dir, 4 UG dir; budget $0-500

Facility was built in 1968; includes scene shop, costume shop, sound studio, CAD facility, light lab, rehearsal studio, design studio, 4 classrooms.

A non-departmental, student-run, producing organization presents one production per year in which dept. majors generally participate. Approx. 15 student-written, one-act plays produced in the last two years.

DESCRIPTION

Noted Faculty: Martin Dallago, Assoc. Chair, Technical Production and Stage Mgmt.; Neil Bierbower, Costume and Scene Design; Dan Boylen, Chair, Scene Design; Kevin Cotter, Acting and Directing; Kathy Garrinella, Movement and Dance; Robert Hedley, History, Literature, Playwriting and Directing; Curt Senie, Head, Graduate Design Program, Lighting Design; Donna Snow, Head, Graduate Acting Program, Voice and Acting; Kimika Williams-Witherspoon, Theater Arts and Playwriting.

The Theatre Department of Temple University's objective is to develop a student artist's creative, cognitive and communicative skills while introducing him or her to the many opportunities in theater as a profession. We train our students for careers in acting, theatrical design, directing, stage-management and technical theater among others. The Temple Theaters production program is a powerful extension of our classroom and studio work. It affords our undergraduate and graduate actors, designers and technicians the opportunity to practice and refine their craft in a setting conducive to learning. Our Alumni work in all aspects of entertainment, including on Broadway, in regional theaters, film, television and on National and World Tours in a wide variety of positions.

University of the Arts

Gene Terruso, Dir. Sch. of Th. Arts
The University of the Arts
320 S. Broad Street
Philadelphia, PA 19102
DEPT: (215) 717-6450
gterruso@uarts.edu
ADM: address as above
http://www.uarts.edu

2,000 Total Enr.; h. compet.
Semester System
215 Majors
T: $27,220, r: $6,600

FAX: (215) 717-6364
(215) 717-6038
admissions@uarts.edu

DEGREES OFFERED

BFA in Acting (100), Musical Theatre (62), Applied Theatre Arts (44); Des/Tech (9). Declare major in freshman year.

ADMISSION & FINANCIAL INFORMATION

Inst. reqs. standarized test scores, secondary school record, recommendations, personal essay, artistic presentation/audition. Audition for actors and Musical Theatre majors, interview and portfolio for designers and Applied Theatre Arts majors are required.Program admits 20% of applicants; admits 1 out of 8. Two Theatre Alliance Scholarships are available for freshmen. Applied Theatre Arts majors and Musical Theatre majors. Presidential and Merit scholarships are available to all majors. At the junior level, the Gary Wheeler Scholarship is available to actors, the Jac Lewis Scholarship for Design-Tech majors and the Laurie Beechman Schlarship for Musical Theatre Majors.

FACULTY AND CLASSES OFFERED

16 FT, 31 PT: 4 PhD, 20 MFA/MA; 15 Prof.w/o adv. degree, 4 Staff
A. (1 FT, 3 PT) Th. History-6/Y; Dramatic Lit-10/X; Into to Th-1/Y;

Dramatic Crit-3/X; Shake-2/X; Playwriting-2/X; Script Analysis-4/Y

B. (10 FT, 28 PT) Acting-11/Y; Speech-6/Y; Movement-8/Y; Mask, etc.-2/Y; Singing-8/Y; Musical Theatre-9/Y; Directing- 2/Y; Stage Combat-8/Y; Dance-8/Y

C. (4 FT) Tech Prod-4/Y; Make-up-2/Y; Princ. of Des.-1/Y; Set Des.-1/Y; Costume Des.-1/Y; Light Des.-1/Y; Costume Const.-2/Y; Stage Mgmt-2/Y; Sound-1/X; Foundations of Des.-4/X

D. (2 FT) Marketing/Promotion-1/Y; Legal Contracts/Copyright-2/Y; Arts Mgmt-1/Y; Box Office-1/Y

FACILITIES & PRODUCTIONS

MAINSTAGE: 1700 seats, fly space, computerized lighting. 2 prod, Fac dir; budget $10,000

SECOND STAGE: 230 seats. 6 prods; 4 Fac dir/des, 2 guest dir, 2 UG dir, 4 Grad dir; budget $7,000

THIRD STAGE: 75 seats. 17 Workshops/Readings; 10 fac dir, 7 guest dir, 1 guest des; budget $1,000

Facility built in the 1920's, last renovated in 1980s; includes costume shop, props shop, sound studio (School of Music), 4 dance studios, 5 rehearsal studios, classrooms.

A dept.-sponsored, student-run production org. presents an evening of student-written plays each year.

Informal professional relationship with Wilma Theatre Company, Arden Theatre, and Hedgerow Theatre and The Harold Prince Musical Theatre can lead to internship.

DESCRIPTION

Noted Faculty: Gene Terruso, Acting/Dir; Johnnie Hobbs, Jr., Acting/Dir; Charlie Gilbert, Musical Th.; Jennifer Childs, Audition Techniques; Irene Baird, Acting; Jiri Zizka, Acting on Camera; Aaron Posner, Dir.; Charles Conwell, Stage Combat.

The BFA in Theater Arts at The University of the Arts is a highly focused, conservatory-styled program committed to training the actor by developing the skills, attitudes, and craft required for a career in the professional theater. The curriculum is concentrated in the acting studio, with training in voice, movement, dance, speech, improvisation, masks, combat, music, mime, history, literature, script analysis, and directing to support work done in the studios. Rehearsals and performances ranging from solo pieces to full-scale productions supplement the actor's studio training. The Musical Theater program provides integrated training in theater, music and dance, with equal emphasis on history, current practice, and the future of musical theater. Through its relationship with Philadelphia's Harold Prince Theatre, it offers students opportunities for professional contact and experience.

University of Pittsburgh

Bruce McConachie, PhD, Chair
Department of Theatre Arts
1617 Cathedral of Learning
University of Pittsburgh
Pittsburgh, PA 15260
DEPT: (412) 624-6568
FAX: (412) 624-6338
refocus@pitt.edu

34,003; competitive
Semester System
70 Majors; NAST
T: UG $7,868; All r&b: $6,470
Grad $10,726
O-ST T: UG $16,676
Grad $21,312
www.pitt.edu/~play

admiss: Alumni Hall, 4227 Fifth Ave, Pgh,PA 15260
ADM: (412) 624-7488 (UG)   www.pitt.edu~oafa (UG)
Grad use dept phone/website

DEGREES OFFERED
BA in Theatre Arts (70); MFA in Perf. Pedagogy (3); MA/PhD in Hist/Lit/Crit (2); MA Hist/Lit/Crit (2); PhD Hist/Lit/Crit (15). Declare major in soph year; 2004 granted 20 UG, 3 Grad degrees.

ADMISSION & FINANCIAL INFORMATION
UG: SATI or ACT, transcripts; Grad: GPA's, Ltrs of recommendation, Statement of Purpose, Writing Sample, GRE scores. Accept 54% to institution; No special req. for UG program. Aud. req. for MFA program, Int. for MA, PhD; accept 6 out of 22 Grad. No entry scholarships for UG (Katz Award; Buell Whitehill Award, Pittsburgh Playhouse Scholarship, and the Don Brocket Mem'l Scholarship - all offer small monetary awards for upperclass students in theatre arts). Grad: tuition remission, TA/TF/GSA stipends, misc research fellowships offered throughout univ to upper level grad students.

FACULTY AND CLASSES OFFERED
9 Full-Time, 3 Part-Time: 6 PhD, 9 MFA/MA; 3 Prof. w/o adv deg, 9 Staff

A. (4 1/2 FT) Intro to Theatre-3/Y; Dramatic Lit-4/Y; Th. History-4/Y; Dramatic Crit.-1/Y; Shakes.-2/Y; Playwriting-2/Y; Drama/Perf in the Classroom-1/X; Grad. Seminars, Various Topics-3/Y

B. (7 1/2 FT, 1 PT) Acting-/4-Y; Voice/Speech-2-O; Movement-2-O; Mime, etc-1/O; Musical Theatre-1/O; Directing- 4/Y; Intro to Performance-1/Y

C. (2 1/2 FT, 2 PT) Prins of Des-1/Y; Set Design-2/Y; Cost Des-2/Y; Lighting Des-2/Y; Technical Production-3/Y; Cost Constr-2/Y; Cost Hist-1/O; Make-up-1/O; Stage Mgmt-1/Y; Scene Painting-1/O

D. (1/2 FT) Arts Mgmt-1/Y

FACILITIES & PRODUCTIONS
MAINSTAGE: 500 seats, fly space, electronic & comput. lighting. 2 Fac dir/des, budget $7,000-10,000

SECOND STAGE: 150 seats, electronic & comput. lighting. 2 prods; 2 Grad dir/des, budget $3,000-5,000

THIRD STAGE: 110 seats. comput. lighting, 8 prod; 2 Grad dir, 6 UG dir, 8 UG des. Workshops/Readings; budget $475-600

Facility built in the late 1920's, renovated in 2003, includes scene shop, costume shop, dance studio, design studio, prop shop, rehearsal studio, classrooms. Computer lab w/sound & lighting programs. State-of-the-art mainstage sound system, also used for sound classes.

Two original and 4 adaptations of student-written plays produced in the last two years.

We have connection with Pittsburgh Irish & Classical Theatre, UnSeam'd Shakespeare Co., Pgh Musical Theatre, Friday Night Improvs, Dog & Pony, Pittsburgh Playback Theatre,Attack Theatre. Each connection varies with each company and ranges from donated audition and rehearsal space to reduced performance & shop rental fees to donated dramaturgical services. Students are given a wide range of opportunities from free specialty workshops to free specialty performance courses for credit to special casting consideration and tech and production job opportunities.

DESCRIPTION
Noted Faculty: Bruce McConachie, Hist/Theory/Dir.; Attillio Favorini, Shakes; Kathleen George, Playwriting; W. Stephen Coleman, Act/Dir; Lynne Conner, Playwriting/Dramaturgy/Dance Hist; Don Mangone, Costume Design, Make-up; Melanie Dreyer, Acting/Directing; Annmarie Duggan, Light Des,. Mgmt.

Guest Artists: Holly Thuma, Actor/Teacher; Nona Girad, Actor/Dir/Des/Teacher; Eleana Alexandratos, Actor/Teacher; Julie Ray, Des/Teacher

The Department holds a firm conviction that theory and practice, academic and creative work, and educational and professional theatre must be integrated for a successful program of theatre education. We likewise share the conviction that the study, practice, and experience of the art of theatre directly aid the power of imagination, and our understanding of our place in the world. The practice of theatre is an ongoing exploration of the potency of human expressivity, and the experience of theatre is the occasion for the focusing of values and the celebration of community. Productions presented to the public—and roles assigned to students herein—are selected in line with the three-fold objectives of the Department: 1. To provide the widest possible spectrum of educational training opportunities to the theatre artists 2. To give as many students as possible a direct experience of the theatre as the occasion for self-development and artistic expression and 3. To contribute to the cultural life of the University and the community by presenting "classic" drama along with contemporary plays and musicals, as well as various ethnic and intercultural productions.

Villanova University

Rev. Richard G. Cannuli, OSA Chair   8,000 Total Enr.; competitive
Theatre Department   Semester System
800 Lancaster Avenue   52 Grads; ATHE
Villanova University   T: $33,474/$9,810 r&b
Villanova, PA 19085   DEPT: (610) 519-4760
theatre.villanova.edu/   FAX: (610) 519-6800
ADM: Above address   (215) 519-6000   FAX: (610) 519-6800
gotovu@villanova.edu

DEGREES OFFERED
MA in Theatre (with concentrations) (52).UG minor only.

ADMISSION & FINANCIAL INFORMATION
3.0 GPA, BA, 3 recs, exper. desirable, GRE's required; Accept 80% to inst., 25 out of 30 to grad program; Acting Scholarships by audition; Ass'tship. in costume, set, PR, & research by interview; University offers minority fellowships.

FACULTY AND CLASSES OFFERED
9 FT, 3 PT: 5 PhD, 7 MFA/MA; 7 Staff

A. (3 FT, 1 PT) Intro to Theatre-6/Y; Th History-2/Y; Shakes-1/O; Dramatic Lit-2/Y; Dramatic Criticism-2/Y; Playwriting-1/Y

B. (3 FT, 5 PT) Acting-24/Y; Voice/Speech-2-O; Movement-1/O; Directing-2/Y; Mime, etc.-1/O; Musical Th-2/O; Dance-4/Y

C. (4 PT) Set Des-1/Y; Lighting Des-1/Y; Cost Des-1/Y; Cost Constr-1/Y; Tech. Prod.-1/Y

FACILITIES AND PRODUCTIONS

MAINSTAGE: 185 seats, computerized lighting. 4 prods: 3 Fac dir, 2 Fac des, 1 Guest dir, 4 Guest des; budget $7,000-10,000

Built in 1970, renovated 1982; scene shop, prop shop, cost shop, 2 rehearsal studios.

A non-departmental, student-run, producing organization presents 2 productions per year.

DESCRIPTION

Noted Faculty: Joe Walker, Tony-award winning playwright, and Bruce Graham, playwright (both PT); Michael Hollinger, Playwright.

Guest Artists: Jaqienka Zych-Drweski, director; Michael Lupu, dramaturg; Bob Chapra, Feldenkrais movement expert; Ntozake Shange, playwright; Barry Kur, voice/dialect coach; Stanislav Gorka, voice/movement instructor, Heinz-Uwe Haus, director.

The MA in Theatre is a combination scholarly and practical program of study. It is for the student to deepen his or her understanding of the scope and content of world theatre and drama, from classic to contemporary, from East to West, as well as to enrich his or her skills in artistic areas. While stabilizing the student in the fundamentals of research necessary for a theatre professional, the program provides experience in each of the component crafts of the theatre culminating, in the final semester of study, in a selected artistic area. The knowledge and practice achieved in attaining the degree thus provide crucial tools for the developing theatre practitioner, educator or scholar.

Wilkes University

Ms. Teresa Fallon, Director of Theater
Dorothy Dickson Darte Center
Wilkes University
Wilkes-Barre, PA 18766
DEPT: (570) 408-4417
ADM: 800-537-4444
Fax: (570) 408-4904

3,100 Total Enr.; competitive
Semester System
30 Majors;ATHE
T: $24,080/$10,100 R&B
SMALL PROGRAM
(570) 408-4400
www.wilkes.edu

DEGREES OFFERED

BA in Theatre/Performance (25), Mus.Th. (5). Declare major in 1st year.

ADMISSION & FINANCIAL INFORMATION

Inst. reqs. 2.00 GPA, SAT comb. 800 or greater, admits 80% of applicants; th prog req's. Aud./Int., admits 8 out of 10 applicants. 4 Th. Scholarships based on aud/int, SAT, class rank, fin. need.

FACULTY AND CLASSES OFFERED

2 FT, 1 3/4 PT: 2 MA/MFA, 1 Prof. w/o adv. deg, 1 Staff.

A. (1/2 FT) Intro to Theatre-2/Y; Dramatic Lit-2/Y; Theatre History-2/Y; Dramatic Criticism-2/Y; Shakes-X; Playwriting-X

B. (1/2 FT, 1 PT) Acting-4/Y; Voice/Speech-2/Y; Directing-2/Y; Singing-X

C. (1FT,1/2 PT) Set Des-1/Y; Lighting Des-1/Y; Tech Prod'n-2/Y; Make-up-1/O

FACILITIES AND PRODUCTIONS

MAINSTAGE: 486 seats, fly space, computerized lighting. 6 prods: 3 Fac dir/des, 3 student dir/des; budget $2,500-6,000

SECOND STAGE: 91 seats, computerized lighting
3 UG dir prod; budget $1,000-2,000

3 student dir workshops/readings

Facility built in 1964, renovated in 1995; includes scene, cost, welding shops, sound, dance, rehearsal studios,.

Dept. majors generally participate in a non-departmental, student-run producing organization that presents 1 production per year.

Some faculty connected with Bloomsburg Theatre Ensemble.

DESCRIPTION

Noted Faculty: Meritorious awards in Directing, Excellence in Stage Lighting and Irene Ryan nominations from ACTF.

Guest Artists:Adam Hill, dir. of Adam Hill Studios in L.A. and Bobby Zammeroski, prof. actor in Boy's Life with Robert DeNiro, both worked on Sniper, by playwright-in-residence Bonnie Bedford; campus production, moved to NYC.

The Theatre Division of the Department of Music, Theatre and Dance at Wilkes University is designed to develop the skills, crafts, and imagination of its students within the liberal arts context. The program is a strong pre-professional curriculum in the major, distributed in the areas of acting, directing, dramatic literature, theatre history, and scenography. Options in Scene Design, Music Theatre and a Dance minor are also available.

York College of Pennsylvania

Dr. Jim McGhee
Director of Theatre
English & Humanities Dept.
York College of PA
York, PA 17405-7199
(717) 815-1401
ADM: 411 Country Club Road, York, PA 17403
(717) 849-1600
www.ycp.edu

5,000 Total Enr.; competitive
10 Majors; ATHE
Semester System
T: $5,790/$4,100 R&B
jmcghee@ycp.edu

(717) 549-1607

DEGREES OFFERED

BA in Theatre (12). Declare major in 1st or 2nd year.

ADMISSION & FINANCIAL INFORMATION

Upper half, 950-1000 SAT min. Inst. admits 50% of applicants. Theatre program admits all applicants. Trustee Honor scholarship-full tuition, GPA/SAT/Competition; Pres. -1/2 yr. tuition, GPA/SAT; Dean's-1/3 yr. tuition, GPA/SAT; Valedictorian/ Salutatorian, 1/2 yr/ tuition GPA/SAT.

FACULTY AND CLASSES OFFERED

A. (1/3 FT, 1 PT) Intro to Theatre-1/Y; Dramatic Lit-2/O; Th History-1/Y; Shakes-1/Y; Dramatic Criticism-1/Y; Playwriting-1/O

B. (1/3 FT,1 PT) Acting-2/Y; Directing-1/O; Mime, etc-1/O

C. (1/3 FT) Principles of Des-1/O; Set Des-1/O; Costume Des-1/O; Lighting Des-1/O

FACILITIES & PRODUCTIONS

MAINSTAGE: 700 seats, fly space, computerized & electronic lighting
SECOND STAGE: 130 seats, computerized lighting
6 prods: 1 Fac dir/des; 5 UG dir/des; budget $2,000-2,500
Facility new in 2008; includes scene shop, costume, shop, prop

shop, sound studio, video studio, classrooms.

10-12 student-written plays have been produced in the last two years.

DESCRIPTION

Noted Faculty: James McGee, Modern Drama, History of Theatre, Scene/Lighting Des, Directing; Rachel Snyder, Acting; Monica Barion, Intro to Theatre.

The Theatre major at York College has developed significantly in quality and content over the last few years. The Theatre major offers students opportunities to act, design, direct, write, and participate in the management of student-run productions. Our purpose is to produce graduates with a broad background in the liberal arts and intensive experience in a variety of productions. In the past few years we have done plays by O'Neill, Shakespeare, Wycherley, Mastrosimone, Mamet, Beckett, and Shepard as well as musicals by Sondheim, Lerner and Lowe, and Rodgers and Hammerstein. Some of our graduates have gone directly into professional acting, others are aspiring, and others opt for graduate study.

RHODE ISLAND

Brown University

John Emigh, Dir of Grad Program
Dept. of Theatre, Speech & Dance
Box 1897, Brown University
Providence, RI 02912
DEPT: (401) 863-3283
www.brown.edu/departments/theatre_speech_dance
spencer_golub@brown.edu
ADM: Box 1876, Brown Univ.
admission_undergraduate@brown.edu   FAX: (401) 863-9300

6,500 Total Enr.; h. compet.
Semester System
39 Majors; ATHE
T: $36,342/$9,606 r&b
FAX: (401) 863-7529

(401) 863-3283

DEGREES OFFERED

BA in General Theatre Concentration (39); MA in Theatre and Performance Studies (10); PhD in Theatre and Performance Studies (2 admissions/yr). Declare major in 2nd year; 2001 granted 14 UG, 4 Grad degrees.

ADMISSION & FINANCIAL INFORMATION

Inst. admits 20% of applicants; UG program accepts all enrolled students, Grad accepts 2 out of 95 applics; interview optional; writing sample. Over 50% of students on fin. aid, 1/3 on direct scholarship based on need.

FACULTY AND CLASSES OFFERED

12 1/2 FT, 4 PT: 7 PhD, 9 MFA/MA, 2 Prof. w/out adv degree; 3 Staff (most Staff also teach)

A. (4 FT, 1 PT) Th Hist-12/YO; Shakes-X; Dramatic Lit-X; Dramatic Criticism/Theory-1/O; Playwriting-1/Y+X; Dramaturgy-1/Y

B. (5 FT, 1 PT) Acting/Directing-6/YO; Voice/Speech-4/YO; Movement/Dance-1/O; Musical Theatre-1/O; Singing-1/O; Dance-10/YO

C. (3 FT, 2 PT) Cost Des-2/Y; Lighting Des-2/YO; Cost Constr-1/Y; Tech. Production-1/Y; Cost Hist-1/Y; Stage Mgmt-1/O

D. (1/2 FT) Arts Mgmt-1/O

FACILITIES AND PRODUCTIONS

MAINSTAGE: 350 seats, fly space, computer & electronic lighting 8 prods: 6 Fac dir/des, 2 UG dir/des; budgt $7,000-10,000 (All prods. considered Mainstage).

SECOND STAGE: 200 seats, fly space, computerized & electronic lighting

THIRD STAGE: 120 seats, computerized & electronic lighting

Mainstage built in 1931, renovated in 1993, second stage in 1898, renovated in 1982; include scene, cost shops, prop shop, sound studio, dance studio, 2 rehearsal studios, 4 classrooms, library.

Dept. majors generally participate in a non-departmental, student-run organization that presents 30 productions per year. 10 student-written plays produced in the last two years.

Connection with two Equity companies: Rites and Reason, housed at Brown, interacts with DEPT. program in new plays, acting, technical work; Trinity Repertory Co.; students have played roles, served as interns in dramaturgy and management. Professional Summer Theatre. New Play Festival; internships; some employment. 2 Trinity personnel have appointments on Brown faculty.

DESCRIPTION

Noted Faculty: Don B. Wilmeth, Th Hist (Emeritus); Spencer Golub, Russian Th; Dir/Act: John Emigh, Non-Western Performance; Lowry Marshall, Acting; Elmo Terry-Morgan, Playwriting; Julie Strandberg, Michelle Bach-Coalibaly, Dance; Rebecca Schneider, Performance Studies; Patricia Ybarra, Latin American Theatre; Nancy R. Dunbar, Barbara Tannenbaum, Speech; Phillip Contic, Costume; Eugene Lee, Design; Michael McGarty, Design.

The undergraduate academic and production programs at Brown combine to offer the student vital experiences in one of humankind's major artistic traditions within the context of a liberal arts education. The Department offers a concentration program in Theatre Arts, and students from throughout the University are encouraged to take classes and to participate in all Departmental activities. Academic offerings combine the study of dramatic literature, performance history, and dramatic, theatrical, and rhetorical theory with the opportunity to take practicum courses in the various theatre arts. Interdepartmental and intercultural study is encouraged. An essential aspect of the program is the engagement of the student in performance, with over 50 theatre and dance productions offered each year. Along with courses stressing scholarship and research, courses are available from the Freshman year onwards in acting and directing, playwriting, dance and technical direction and design. The MA program is primarily designed as a pre-PhD degree in Theatre and Performance Studies. MFA degrees in Acting and Directing are offered through the Brown/Trinity Rep Graduate Consortium. There is also an MFA professional training degree in Playwriting offered through the Graduate Program in Creative Writing of the English Dept. students interested in that program should contact Prof. Paula Vogel.

Brown University / Trinity Rep Consortium

Stephen Berenson,	58 Total Enr.;
Chair of MFA Programs	h. compet.
Spencer Golub,	Semester System; ATHE
Chair of Dept. of Theatre,	46 Acting Majors
Speech and Dance	6 Directing; 6 Ph.D.

Brown Univ./Trinity Rep Consortium T: $35,500
201 Washington Street   (401) 521-1100 x 271
Providence, RI 02903   FAX: (401) 751-5577
ADM: c/o Jill Jann, Consortium Administrator
c/o Trinity Rep, 201 Washington St., Providence, RI 02903
(401) 521-1100x271   FAX: (401) 751-5577
jjann@trinityrep.com   www.brown.edu
www.trinityrep.com

DEGREES OFFERED

MFA in Acting (46), Directing (6); PhD in Theatre and Performance Studies (6).

ADMISSION & FINANCIAL INFORMATION

For Actors and Directors: Program requires Bachelor's degree, private audition in New York, Chicago, San Francisco, or Providence. Applic, photo and resume, college transcripts, personal statement, letters of recommendation req'd. Full and partial Scholarships are awarded at the time of acceptance, based on financial need, past performance and evidence of potential success in the program. The program generally admits 20 out of 400 applicants.

FACULTY AND CLASSES OFFERED

18 FT, 8 PT: 4 PhD, 12 MFA/MA, 10 Prof. w/o adv. deg

A. (6 FT, 2 PT) Intro to Theatre 2-Y; Dramatic Lit-2/Y; Dramatic Criticism-2/Y; Theatre History-2/Y; Shakespeare-4/Y; Playwriting-6/Y

B. (9 FT, 6 PT) Acting/Scene Study-7/Y; Voice/Speech-6/Y; Movement-6/Y; Singing-6/Y; Directing-6/Y; Dance-6/Y; Mus. Th-2/Y; Stage Combat-1/Y; Performance Studies-2/Y; Performance Theory-2/Y; Non-Western Performance-2/Y; Solo Performance-1/Y; Alexander Technique-6/Y; Africana Performance-2/Y

C. (3 FT) Prins of Design-6/Y

FACILITIES AND PRODUCTIONS

MAINSTAGE: 700 seats, computerized lighting, fly space

SECOND STAGE: 300 seats, computerized lighting

THIRD STAGE: 400 seats, computerized lighting

Facility includes scene shop, prop shop, welding shop, sound studio, 7 rehearsal studios, 1 design studio.

15 one-acts, 12 full-length.

Connection with Trinity Rep Company (Equity). Students generally have extensive experience on the mainstage in various sized roles, as understudies, and as assistant directors. Equity card awarded at graduation.

DESCRIPTION

Noted Faculty: Stephen Berenson, Acting; Stephen Buescher, Physical Theatre; Curt Columbus, Directing, Dramaturgy; Spencer Golub, Theatrical Modernism and Theory; Thom Jones, Voice/Speech; Brian McEleney, Acting; Kevin Moriarty, Directing; Rebecca Spencer, Performance Studies; Paula Vogel, Playwriting.

Guest Artists: Kate Burton, Actress; Eric Bogosian,

Writer and Actor; Pat Collins, Lighting Designer; Craig Handel, Stage Combat; Danny Hoch, Writer and Actor; Arnold Mungioli, Casting Director; Charles Strouse, Writer and Composer; Jeanine Tesori, Composer and Lyricist; Coppelia Kahn, Gender Studies; Wadda C. R'os-Font, Hispanic Studies.

The Brown University/Trinity Rep Consortium was established in 2002. This highly competitive program provides three-year professional training under the auspices of an Ivy League University and Rhode Island's Tony Award-winning theatre company. The M.F.A. curriculum offers a rigorous technical training program taught by a resident faculty, supplemented by guest artists from the professional and academic arenas. The primary focus in the actor training is in developing technically skilled, versatile actors capable of working in the variety of styles demanded by contemporary theatre. Directors are given the opportunity to develop their own vision, creating new work as well as rediscovering existing texts. Doctoral candidates will develop sophisticated conceptual and critical skills learned in and applied to historical and theoretical contexts, along with practical performance-based knowledge. Students have the opportunity to work as actors, directors and dramaturgs on Trinity Rep mainstage productions. Brown University offers Consortium students all its excellent resources.

Providence College

Dr. Wendy Oliver	3,700 Total Enr.; competitive
Theatre Dept, River Ave	Semester System
Providence College	25 Majors
Providence, RI 02918	T: $26,780
DEPT: (401) 865-2206	MAIN: (401) 865-2535
E-MAIL: MCOPPA@PROVIDENCE.EDU	

DEGREES OFFERED

BA in Theatre, also Minor. Declare major in freshman or soph. year; 2007 granted 6 UG degs.

ADMISSION & FINANCIAL INFORMATION

Accept 35-40% to institution; no special req's. for theatre program; accept all to program; Blackfriars scholarship, renewable for 4 years, based on aud. and application etter.

FACULTY AND CLASSES OFFERED

5 Full-Time, 2 Part-Time: 2 PhD, 4 MFA; 2 FT Staff

A. (2 FT) Intro to Theatre-1/Y; Dramatic Lit-4/YX; Th Hist- 1/Y; Dramatic Criticism-1/O; Shakes-2/YX; Playwriting-1/Y

B. (4 FT) Acting-4/Y; Voice/Speech-1/Y; Movement/Dance- 6/YO; Singing-2/Y; Musical Th.-1/O; Directing-1/Y; Oral Interp.-1/Y

C. (1 FT, 1 PT) Prins of Des-1/X; Set Design-2/O; Cost Des-1/Y; Lighting Des-1/O; Tech Prod'n-1/O; Th Mgmt-1/O; Script Analysis-1/Y

FACILITIES & PRODUCTIONS

MAINSTAGE: 275 seats. 4 prods: 3 Fac dir/des, 1 Student dir/des; budget $8,000-10,000

SECOND STAGE: 100 seats

2 new theatres in Fall, 2004.

Workshops/Readings: vary

New facility 2004; includes scene, costume, props shops, dance studio, rehearsal studio, classrooms, publicity office.

Roger Williams University

Dorisa Boggs, Coordinator	4361 FT day Enr.
Theatre Department	Semester System
Roger Williams University	35 Majors; NETC,ATHE,USITT
One Old Ferry Road	T: $25,394/$10,943 r&b
Bristol, RI 02809-2921	SMALL PROGRAM
DEPT:(401) 254-3626	Main: 1 800-458-7144
FAX: (401) 254-3634	dboggs@rwu.edu
www.rwu.edu	admit@rwu.edu

DEGREES OFFERED

BA in Performance Track or, Design Track.

ADMISSION & FINANCIAL INFORMATION

All individually evaluated. Inst. accepts 79% of applicants; program admits 38 of 49 applicants. Miglietta Schol: By aud/int, for freshmen; Paolino Theatre/Arts Schol: Excellence in theatre, upperclasspersons; Whitcomb Schol: Excellence, combined with need, all students.

FACULTY AND CLASSES OFFERED

3 FT, 5 PT: 1 PhD, 5 MFA/MA; 2 Staff

Art of the Theatre,Modern Theatre and Drama,Acting I & II,Theatre of Shakespeare (London),Design for the Theatre,Contemporary European Theatre, Production (London), Musical Theatre Workshop, Acting Workshop (London), History of the Theatre I & II, Seminar in Design (London), Intermediate Design, History of European Art and Architecture (London), Directing, Cultures in Contact (London), Drama in Production, Contemporary Drama, Theatre Practicum, Asian Drama and Dance, Acting Studio, Theatre for Young Audiences, Design Studio Senior Topics, Drama Theory and Criticism

FACILITIES AND PRODUCTIONS

MAINSTAGE: 200 seats, computerized lighting
　　4 Fac dir/des prods; budget $15,000

Facility built in 1895, renovated in 1986; includes scene shop, costume shop, dance studio, rehearsal studio, seminar room.

A non-dept, student-run org. presents 6-12 productions/yr.

Internships available at many local professional theatres.

DESCRIPTION

Guest Artists: James Roose-Evans, a professional director in London, teaches our Acting Workshop in London.

In addition to making an artistic and cultural contribution to campus life through frequent and varied productions of plays, the theatre program aims to give its students a broad perspective on theatre art. This is achieved in several ways: the opportunity to study theatre crafts and to develop theatre skills; study of theatre in the context of our basic cultural traditions; optional participation in the semester-long London Theatre Program, an unusual opportunity to see some of the world's finest theatre while living overseas; the chance to work for a professional company, before graduation, as a theatre intern; and a good deal of practical experience in most phases of theatre through the university's Main Season and less formal Studio theatre productions.

University of Rhode Island

Paula McGlasson, Dept of Th.	12,000 Total Enr.; compet.
Fine Arts Center	100 Majors
University of Rhode Island	Semester System
Kingston, RI 02881	T: $5,600/$7,518 r&b
www.uri.edu/theatre	O-ST T: $19,356/$14,268 r&b
DEPT: (401) 874-5921	FAX: (401) 874-5618
paulam@uri.edu	
ADMISSIONS: Green Hall	(401) 874-7100
FAX: (401) 874-5523	uri@admit.uri.acc.uri.edu

DEGREES OFFERED

BFA in Design/Tech (15), Acting (60), Theatre Mgmt (15), Directing (10). Declare major in sophomore year.

ADMISSION & FINANCIAL INFORMATION

GPA, SAT, Lts of recommendation. Accept 75% to institution, admit 6 out of 10 to program; no special req. for UG. BFA program requires faculty review/evaluation annually. Univ awards Centennial Scholarship; eight $500 theatre Merit scholar, two $500 theatre endowment awards, four $500 Pezzullo scholar.; two $1000 freshman theater scholarships.

FACULTY AND CLASSES OFFERED

5 FT, 12 PT: 13 MFA/MA, 1 FT Prof. w/o adv. deg, 3 PT Prof. w/o adv. deg., 4 Staff

A.　(1 FT, 2 PT) Intro to Theatre-4/Y; Th Hist-5/Y; Shakes-2/Y; Playwriting-1/O; Script Analysis-4/Y

B.　(2 FT, 6 PT) Acting-8/Y; Voice/Speech-8/Y; Movement-5/Y; Singing-1/Y; Mus. Th-1/O; Directing-3/Y; Stage Combat-1/Y; Dance-1/Y.

C.　(1 FT; 3 PT) Prins of Design-1/Y; Costume. Design-2/Y; Lighting Des-2/Y; Tech. Production-2/Y; Cost. Construction-2/Y; Cost. History-2/Y; Make-up-1/Y; Stg Mgmt-2/Y

D.　(1 FT, 1 PT) Arts Management-1/Y

FACILITIES AND PRODUCTIONS

MAINSTAGE: 550 seats, fly space, computerized, electronic lighting. 2 prods: 2 Fac dir/des, 1 Guest dir, 2 Guest des; budget $30,000-50,000

SECOND STAGE: 250 seats, computerized, electronic lighting. 2 prods: 1 Fac dir, 1 Fac des, 0-2 Guest dir, 3 Guest des, budget $15,000-20,000

THIRD STAGE: 80 seats, 4 workshops/readings: 4 UG dir

Facility was built in 1970, renovated in 1987; includes scene shop, costume shop, props shop, sound studio, welding shop, dance studio, rehearsal studio, design studio, classrooms.

DESCRIPTION

Noted Faculty: Bryna Wortman, acting/directing; David T. Howard, cost. des; Christian Wittwer, light/scene des.; Alan Hawkridge, acting/dir; Paula McGlasson, acting, stage mgmt

Guest Artists: Tony Estrella, acting/dir; Ed Shea, script analysis; Craig Handel, stage combat; Lila Kane, singing for musical th; Claudia Traub, voice/movement; Steven Pennell, Theatre History.

The Theatre Department at University of Rhode Island is firmly committed to creating a professional production model as the laboratory for classroom/studio learning. The Department produces a wide range of "classics"—

Greek to Modern Drama, but is particularly committed to the development of new work. As part of a research institution, the Department produces at least one full length new play as a major production each year. In addition, there are numerous readings of new work. Faculty include widely published scholars and theatre professionals who continue to work in theatres outside of the institution.

SOUTH CAROLINA

College of Charleston

Todd McNerney, Chair	11,000 Total Enr.; competitive
School of the Fine Arts	Semester System
College of Charleston	140 Majors; ATHE
Charleston, SC 29424	T: $7,234/$4,496 r&b
DEPT: (843) 953-6306	O-ST T: $16,800/$6,714 r&b
FAX: (843) 953-8210	
ADMISSIONS: 66 George St.	(843) 953-5670
www.cofc.edu	FAX: (843) 953-6322

DEGREES OFFERED

BA in Theatre Concentration in Performance (105); in General Theatre (5); Costume (5); Set/Lights (15); Theatre for Youth (10) Declare major in freshman year; 2007 granted 40 degrees.

ADMISSION & FINANCIAL INFORMATION

GPA 3.6, mid range SAT 1100-1300 or comparable ACT. 60% of applics admitted to instit. Several scholarships of varying amounts awarded each yr. to selected entering th. majors. To be considered, students contact the DEPT. in the fall semester to secure an audition date on campus. Students present either 2 monologues or portfolio of technical experience.

FACULTY AND CLASSES OFFERED

12 FT, 11 PT: 3 PhD, 15 MFA/MA, 5 Prof. w/o adv. deg; 3 Staff

A. (2 FT, 5 PT) Intro to Theatre-1/Y; Th History-2/Y; Dramatic Criticism-1/Y; Playwriting-4/Y;Shakes-2/X

B. (7 FT, 6 PT) Acting-5/Y; Voice/Speech-1/Y; Movement-1/Y; Musical Theatre-2/Y; Singing-2/Y; Directing-1/Y; Dance-7/Y; Stage Combat-1/O; Career Development-1/Y; Acting Shakes-1/O

C. (3 FT) Principles of Des-1/Y; Set Design-1/Y; Cost Des-1/Y; Lighting Des-1/Y; Tech Prod-1/Y; Cost Constr-1/Y; Make-up-1/Y; Stage Mgmt-1/O

D. Arts Mgmt-3/X; Development/Grant Writing-1/X; Marketing/Promo-1/X

FACILITIES & PRODUCTIONS

MAINSTAGE: 310 seats, fly space, computerized & electronic lighting
  5 prods: 5 Fac dir, 10 Fac des, 5 UG des; budget $8,000-$11,000

SECOND STAGE: 106 seats, computerized lighting
  8 prods: 2 Fac dir/des, 6 UG dir, 20 UG des: budget $750-6,000

Third Stage: 106 seats,
  3 UG dir Workshops/Readings; budget $0-500

Facility was built in 1979 and recently renovated, includes scene shop, costume shop, sound studio CAD facility, design studio, dance studio, 2 rehearsal studio,3 classrooms.

A non-departmental, student-run organization presents 3-6 productions per year in which majors participate. A series of ten minute plays every year and short plays fully produced.

DESCRIPTION

Noted Faculty: Susan Kattwinker, Theatre History; Brent Laing, Intro; Mark Landis, Script Analysis; Allen Lyndrup, Directing; Todd McNerney, Acting; Janine McCabe, Costuming; Tricia Thelen, Scenery; Joy Vandervort-Cobb, Acting; Laura Turner, Theatre for Youth; Evan Parry, Acting

Guest Artists: Recent guest speakers: Paul Weidner, Directing; Robert Carter, Dance; Marianne Chellis, Vocal Tech; Jamie Smithson, Acting; Jack Landry, Acting. Recent productions: Take Me Out, King Lear, Wedding Band, The Tempest, Metamorphoses, Blue Surge and Cabaret.

The Theatre Department at the College of Charleston promotes a love of learning, a desire for excellence and professional behavior in its students and faculty through balanced attention to coursework and production experience. All students are encouraged to seek practical experience in productions. The Department strongly supports the ideal of liberal education promoted at the College. We believe that by liberally educating our theatre majors in the humanities, sciences, and languages as well as in a comprehensive theatre specialty, we produce superior theatre practitioners. The Department is home to the largest solely undergraduate program in the state and is a host venue for Spoleto Festival, USA and for Piccolo Spoleto. Students have opportunities not only to work with professionals affiliated with these festivals, but also to perform in a series of works, which focuses on our Department's students, faculty, and alumni.

Converse College

John Bald, Chair	1,100 Total Enr.; competitive
Converse College	Semester System
580 E. Main St.	8 Majors
Spartanburg, SC 29302-0006	T: $23,344/$7,190 r&b
DEPT: (864) 596-9067	SMALL PROGRAM
FAX: (864) 596-9211	ADM: Above address
(800) 766-1125	FAX: (864) 596-9225
www.converse.edu	info@converse.edu

DEGREES OFFERED

BA in Theatre (8). Declare major in sophomore year.

ADMISSION & FINANCIAL INFORMATION

GPA 2.8, SAT 980, ACT 20. 76% of applics admitted to instit. No special req's. for program; admit 9 out of 10 to th. program. Hayward Ellis Scholarship: Aud/Interview; Hazel B. Abbott Scholarship: Faculty Award.

FACULTY AND CLASSES OFFERED

3 FT, 1 PT: 3 MFA, 1 MA

A. (1/2, 1/3 FT) Intro to Theatre-1/Y; Th Hist-2/O*; Dramatic Lit-1/O*; Dramatic Crit-1/O*; Playwriting-1/O*

B. (1 1/3 FT, 1/2 PT) Acting-3/Y; Voice/Speech-2/Y; Movement-2/O; Mime, etc.-1/O; Dir-1/Y; Stage Combat-1/O; Dance-7/Y

C. (1/2, 1/3 FT) Princ of Des-1/O*; Set Design-1/O*; Cost Des-1/O*; Cost Construction-1/O*; Lighting Des-1/O*; Tech Prod'n-2/O*; Make-up-1/O*; Stg Mgmt-1/O

D. (1/2 PT) Arts Mgmt-1/O*

*Classes offered in alternate years.

FACILITIES & PRODUCTIONS

MAINSTAGE: 279 seats, computerized lighting
    3 Fac dir/des prods; budget $5,000-8,000

SECOND STAGE: 75 seats, black box, computerized lighting
    4 UG dir/des prods: budget $200-300. 2 Workshops/Readings: 1
    Fac dir, 1 Guest dir; budget $0-500

Facility was built in 1896, renovated in 1997; includes scene shop,
    CAD facility, dance studio, design studio.

2 student-written plays produced in the last two years.

DESCRIPTION

Noted Faculty: John Bald, Design, History; Steven Hunt,
    Directing, Acting; Mary Nicholson, Youth Theatre,
    Arts. Mgmt.; Jennifer Scanlon, Dance, Dance History.

Guest Artists: Steve Chicurel, Voice for the Musical
    Theatre.

The Department of Theatre at Converse College provides opportunities which enable students to develop their skills and talents in theatre arts and to foster a better understanding of the contribution that live theatre makes to the process of educating the whole person in a liberal arts environment. Through the availability of experiences in a number of areas, students will find a wide variety of challenges and means of expression. The program of study places emphasis on the aesthetic and practical decisions inherent to these areas, thereby strengthening the student's general intellectual capabilities and maturation as an artist. By the time of graduation, theatre majors should demonstrate basic competencies in each area of theatre and should be able to compete successfully for positions in graduate school and in the professional job market.

Presbyterian College

Lesley J. Preston, Chair	1,049 Total Enr.; compet.
Dept. of Theatre Arts	Semester System
Presbyterian College	12 Majors; ATHE
101 Harper Center	T: $26,320/$8,148 r&b
Clinton, SC 29325	SMALL PROGRAM
DEPT: (864) 833-8383	FAX: (864) 833-8600
lpreston@presby.edu	
ADMISSIONS: Smith Administration Building, 503 S. Broad	
(864) 833-8230	FAX: (864) 833-8481
www.presby.edu	admissions@presby.edu

DEGREES OFFERED

BA in General (2), Acting/Directing (6), Design/Technical (2).
Declare major in soph. year

ADMISSION & FINANCIAL INFORMATION

Reqs GPA min. 2.5, SAT min. comb. 1000; inst. admits 60% of applicants; interview req'd, 80% admitted to theatre prog. Competitive scholarships, to full tuition, selected by app, int.

FACULTY AND CLASSES OFFERED

2 Full-Time: 1 PhD, 1 MA/MFA; 1 Staff

A. (1/2 FT) Intro to Th-4/Y; Th Hist-1/every 2Y; Shakes-1/YX;
    Playwriting-1/YX

B. (3/4 FT) Acting-2/Y; Voice/Speech-2/Y; Directing-1/every 2Y;
    Musical Theatre-1/OX

C. (3/4 FT) Prins of Design-1/YX; Set Design-1/every 2 Y; Cost Des-
    1/O; Lighting Des-1/every 2 Y; Tech. Production-2/Y; Make-up-
    1/Y

D. (1 PT) Arts Mgmt-1/O

FACILITIES AND PRODUCTIONS

MAINSTAGE: 150 seats, computerized lighting
    3 prods: 2 Fac dir/des, 1 UG des; budget $5,000
    8 student dir/des Workshops/Readings; budget $500

Facility built in 1993, includes scene, costume, props shop,
    sound studio, design studio, 2 rehearsal studio, 2 classrooms.

DESCRIPTION

Noted Faculty: Miriam Ragland, Acting/Directing; Lesley
    Preston, Design/Technology.

Guest Artists: Myra Green Schaffer, Richard K. Blair,
    Directors.

The theatre program at Presbyterian College is a liberal arts rather than a professional program, although we insist on professional quality work. The department works to see that the theater program touches in some way almost every student on campus. It believes that theater is just as beneficial to the math or physics major as to the theater arts major. Indeed, the department has students from many departments who work in the theater program.

University of South Carolina

Jim Hunter, Chair	25,140 Total Enr.; compet
Theatre and Dance	Semester System
USC, Columbia, SC 29208	95 Majors; NAST, U/RTA
www.cas.sc.edu/thea	hunter@sc.edu
DEPT: (803) 777-4288	FAX: (803) 777-6669
ADMISSIONS: USC Graduate School, Byrne Center.	
(803) 777-4243	FAX: (803) 777-2973
Admissions: UG	
(800) 868-5872	Fax: (803) 777-0101

DEGREES OFFERED

BA in Theatre (95), MFA in Design (13), Acting (15), Directing (3), MA in Theatre (6). Declare major in first year.

ADMISSION & FINANCIAL INFORMATION

UG College official transcript, Report of GRE or Miller Analogies. BA program admits all applics; Grad program requires audition/interview/portfolio for designers.

FACULTY AND CLASSES OFFERED

17 FT, 3 PT: 2 PhD, 14 MFA/MA; 8 Staff

A. (2 FT, 2 PT) Intro to Theatre-1/Y; Th Hist-4/Y; Shakes-1/Y; Dramatic
    Lit-2/O; Dramatic Criticism-2/Y; Playwriting-1/Y

B. (8 FT, 1 PT) Acting-8/Y; Voice/Speech-3/Y; Mvmt-4/Y; Dir-2/Y;
    Stage Combat-1/O; Dance-10/Y

C. (7 FT) Principles of Des-2/Y; Set Design-4/Y; Cost Des-4/Y;
    Lighting Des-4/Y; Tech Prod-4/Y; Cost Constr-3/Y; Cost His-1/Y;
    Make-up-2/O; Stg Mgmt-1/O; Computer Design-1/Y; Thea
    Safety-1/O; Scene Painting-2/Y; Architecture Hist-1/Y

FACILITIES AND PRODUCTIONS

MAINSTAGE: 395 seats, fly space, computerized lighting. 3 prods: 2 Fac dir, 1 Fac des, 1 Guest dir, 2 Grad des; budget $5,000-10,000

SECOND STAGE: 312 seats, computerized lighting. 3 prods: 2 Fac dir, 1 Guest dir, 3 Grad des; budget $5,000-10,000

THIRD STAGE: 99 seats, electronic lighting.

Facility renovated in 1989, includes scene shop, costume shop, props shop, dance studio, rehearsal studio, design studio.

Connection with Milwaukee Repertory, Shakespeare Theatre in Washington (Equity, school year): The Department's MFA program has active internship with these two theatres. MFA students are required to complete a professional internship at one of these theatres or another approved by the graduate faculty.

DESCRIPTION

Noted Faculty: Steven Pearson, acting; Jim Hunter, des; Nic Ularu, des.

Guest Artists: Directors: Paul Mullins, Bob Leonard Actors: Helen Arey, Scott Mann; Designer: Michael Phillipi.

The BA program prepares the student for either further study in the area of theatre or for careers in multiple professions which share the disciplines developed in the study of theatre: research, developing alternate viewpoints, self confidence in public situations, and working with others on a shared goal within a given time frame. The MAT program is primarily designed for those seeking preparation for a terminal degree. The MAT degree program is appropriate also for those experienced and certified secondary school teachers who wish intensive academic specialization in theatre. The Master of Fine Arts programs prepare designers, actors and directors to assume responsible roles in the profession. A well coordinated series of classes and production projects moves the student through progressively more demanding material. All MFA programs culminate with internships at outstanding theatres such as the Shakespeare Theatre in Washington D.C. or the Milwaukee Repertory Theatre and the Alliance Theatre in Atlanta among others.

Winthrop University

Andrew Vorder Bruegge, Chair
Dept. of Theatre and Dance
Winthrop University
115 Johnson Hall
Rock Hill, SC 29733

6,500 Total Enr.; not competitive
163 Majors; NAST, NASD
Semester System
theaterdance@winthrop.edu
DEPT: (803) 323-2287
T: $8,756//$5,352 r&b

FAX: (803) 323-2560   O-ST T: $16,150/$5,352 r&b
www.winthrop.edu/VPA/theatre_&_dance/default.htm
ADMISSIONS: Office of Admissions, above address
800-WINTHROP   admissions@winthrop.edu
www.winthrop.edu/admissions/default.htm

DEGREES OFFERED

BA in Theatre Performance (58); in Theatre Design/Tech (14); Theatre Education (18); Dance Performance (43); Dance Education (27). Declare major in first year; 2007 granted 32 degrees.

ADMISSION & FINANCIAL INFORMATION

SAT 800 min., top 50% of HS class; college prep. curriculum; 70%

admitted to inst. Theatre program admits all. Dean's Meritorious Scholarship-$200-500; out-of-state waiver by audition; Producers Circle Scholarships - $200-$500; out-of-state waiver-by application.

FACULTY AND CLASSES OFFERED:

7 Full Time, 6 Part Time: 1 PhD/DFA; 13 MA/MFA

A. (2 FT, 1 PT) Dramatic Lit-1/Y; Theatre History-2/Y; Dramatic Crit-1/O; Shakespeare-1/X; Playwriting-2/Y
B. (2 FT, 3 PT) Acting-3/Y; Voice/Speech-1/Y; Movement-2/Y; Singing; 1/Y; Directing-2/Y; Dance-4/Y
C. (3 FT, 1 PT) Principles of Des-1/Y; Set Design-1/Y; Costume Des-1/Y; Lighting Des-1/Y; Tech Prod-1/Y; Costume Constr-1/Y; Stage Mgmt-1/Y; Make-up-1/Y
D. (1 PT) Marketing/Promo-1/Y; Box Office Procedure-1/Y

FACILITIES & PRODUCTIONS

MAINSTAGE: 334 seats, fly space, computerized lighting 4 prods: 4 Fac dir/des prods; budget $3,000-5,000

SECOND STAGE: 89 seats, computerized lighting. 6 prods: 6 UG dir/des; budget $250

Facility built in 1920, renovated in 1994; includes scene, cost shop, CAD facility, 2 movement/dance studios, rehearsal studio, design studio, 2 classrooms.

A non-departmental student-run producing organization presents 2 productions per year in which majors participate. 2 student-written plays have been produced by the dept in the last two years.

DESCRIPTION

The Department of Theatre and Dance, as one of three departments within the College of Visual and Performing Arts at Winthrop University, is committed to fostering each individual student's aesthetic, intellectual and creative development within the context of a liberal arts education. Through class instruction, private coaching, consultation and performance, the department advocates both theoretical and creative explorations to achieve significant understanding of the social, political, historical and technological aspects of theatre and dance. Within a broad production and curricular repertoire lies a commitment to collaborative ensemble an interarts explorations of issues relevant to contemporary society. The Department of Theatre and Dance encourages and supports the active participation of its students and faculty in festivals, competitions, and conferences which provide further opportunity for creative and scholarly development, professional leadership and cultural enrichment.

SOUTH DAKOTA

University of South Dakota

Dept. of Theater
University of South Dakota
414 East Clark St.
Vermillion, SD 57069-2390
(605) 677-5418

7,000 Total Enr.; competitive
Semester System
59 Majors; NAST, ATHE
*T: UG $11,211 incl. r&b

FAX: (605) 677-5988   *O-ST T: UG $12,667 incl. r&b
www.usd.edu/cfa/Theatre
theatre@usd.edu   R&B: $2,600 approx.
ADM: 1-877-COYOTES   FAX: (605) 677-6723

www.usd.edu/admissions   admiss@usd.edu
*Various Tuition rates for MN reciprocity, IA & NE and Western UG Exchange. See website for full details

DEGREES OFFERED

BFA Theatre Specialization (34) - All first year theatre majors enter this spec; BFA Acting Specialization (9) - Aud/int for entrance into this spec in spring of 2nd yr; BFA Des/Tech Specialization with emphasis in Scene Des, Costume Des, Light Des, Light & Sound Des, or Technical Theatre (3) - Port/int for entrance into this spec in spring of 2nd yr; BA/BS in Theatre as a Double major (3); MA in Theatre; MFA Directing Specialization (6); MFA Des/Tech Specialization with emphasis in Scene Des, Costume Des, Light & Sound Des, or Tech Theatre (4).

ADMISSION & FINANCIAL INFORMATION

UG: must rank in the top 60% of their HS grad class, OR achieve an ACT composite score of 18 or above or SAT I score of 870 or above, OR earn a GPA of at least 2.6 on a 4.0 scale in all HS courses; Complete the following required courses with a cumulative grade point avg of "C" or higher (2.0 on a 4.0 scale); 4 yrs of English, OR ACT English sub-test score of 18 or above, OR AP English score of 3 or above; 3 yrs of Advance Math (adv math includes algebra or any higher level of math), OR ACT Math sub-test score of 20 or above, OR AP calculus score of 3 or above; 3 yrs of Laboratory Science (lab science includes biology, chemistry, physics, or other approved science courses in which there is a weekly lab period sched), OR ACT Science Reasoning sub-test score of 17 or above, OR AP Science score of 3 or above; 3 yrs of Social Science, OR ACT Social Studies/Reading sub-test score of 17 or above OR AP Social Studies score of 3 or above; 1/2 yr of Fine Arts (will increase to 1 yr for Fall 2005 admissions), OR AP Fine Arts score of 3 or above. At the time of admission, it is expected that students will have basic keyboarding skills and have had experience in using computer word processing, database and spreadsheet packages and in using the Internet or other wide area networks. These expectations may be met by HS course work or demonstrated by some other means. Incoming students assessed and found deficient in this area may be required to complete specific computer skills courses. 100% of Theatre applicants accepted into program upon being accepted in the Univ. The Promise Scholarship promises a min of $1,000/yr in scholarship assist, renewable for a total of 4 yrs, is available to all first-time, full-time freshmen students who attend the Vermillion campus and have an ACT score of at least 24 (or SAT SCORE of 1100). In order to continue receiving the scholarship, students must average 30 cr hrs/yr and maintain a GPA of 3.2 or higher. Theatre Freshman Talent Scholarships range from $400-1200 and applicant must aud/int (on campus, if possible); Various endowed scholarships are available to sophomore-senior theatre majors who have demonstrated excellence in the classroom, prod season participation; Must have a 2.5 cum GPA and 3.0 Theatre GPA.

GRAD: A signed and dated appl form with a $35/non-refundable fee; 3 ltrs of recommend; Hold potential for successful completion of the program and for positive contribution to the field; Have submitted 2 final transcripts showing grad date and Baccalaureate deg in Theatre from and inst with full regional accreditation for the degree; A min UG grade point avg of 2.7; GRE score for MA only; MFA Directing spec appl must submit a written statement of directorial approach to a full-lengh, published playscript to include analyses of action, major characters, char relationships, language, and setting; should note major directorial problems; and should present an approach to staging. Submission of promptscripts from prev directed prod a/o an acting aud may aid evaluation. MFA Des/Tech spec appl must submit a

porfolio emphasizing the areas of spec to incl photographs (slides a/o prints), rough sketches, finished renderings, and draftings; Costume sketches should be swatched, and lighting designers should incl 4/5 lighting plots; All pieces marked with the applicant's name, the name of the play, and whether it was realized in prod; Assistantships are avail.

FACULTY AND CLASSES OFFERED

8 Full-Time, 2 PhD, 6 MFA/MA; 1 Staff

A. (3 1/2 FT) Intro to Theatre-1/Y; Film Appre-1/Y; Th Hist-4/Y; Shakes-2/XY

B. (3 1/2 FT) Acting-7/Y; Voice/Speech-3/Y; Mvmt-3/Y; Directing-4/Y; Stg Combat-2/Y

C. (1 1/2 FT) Scene Des & Scene Paint-3/Y; Cost Des & Cost Constr-3/Y; Lighting Des-3/Y; Make-up-1/Y; Stage Mgmt-1/O; Tech Prod.-6/Y; Sound Des-2/Y

D. (1 1-/2 FT) Arts Mgmt-X

FACILITIES AND PRODUCTIONS

MAINSTAGE: 470 seats, prosc, fly space, computerized & electron. lighting, 4 prods: 2 Fac dir/des, 2 Grad dir, 2 Grad des budget $3,000-6,000

SECOND STAGE: 80 seats, black box, computerized & electronic lighting.. 2 prods: 2 Grad dir, 2 Grad des, 2 UG des; budget $0-150

Facility built in 1975; includes 3000 sq ft scene shop,2000 sq ft costume shop, prop shop, sound/light studio, dance studio, design studio, computer lab, 2 classrooms.

Maintains a close assoc with the Black Hills Playhouse: Founded by Warren M. Lee in 1946, Dean of the College of Fine Arts; Internships are possible; many USD students and faculty-artists may be hired to work in all areas; join with other theatre professionals, students, and teachers form across the nation for intensive seasons of high-quality, summer-stock theatre.

DESCRIPTION

As its mission, the Department of Theatre at The University of South Dakota prepares the student for a career in the theatre and encourages personal and creative growth. It does this by providing a comprehensive humanistic education, supplemented by intensive craft training, in which classroom study and practical experience are of equal and complementary value. The Department promotes excellence in education, research, and service; explores new questions, techniques and practices in theatre; and inspires students to become life-long learners who contribute to their respective discipline and profession while enhancing the cultural life of their community.

TENNESSEE

Austin Peay State University

Mike Gotcher,
  Chair
Dept of Comm. & Theatre
Austin Peay State University
P. O. Box 4446
Clarksville, TN 37044
DEPT: (931) 221-7378
www.apsu.edu

7,000 Total Enr.; compet.
Semester System
30 Majors; ATHE
T: $5,238/$5,510 R&B
O-ST T: $15,514/$5,50 R&B
SMALL PROGRAM
ADM: (800) 844-APSU
admissions@apsu.edu

DEGREES OFFERED

BA, BS & MA in Theatre (24), BA, MA in Theatre Education (1)
Declare major in sophomore year.

ADMISSION & FINANCIAL INFORMATION

2.75 GPA, 19 ACT; 90% of applicants admitted to institution; theatre program generally admits all applicants. Perf. schols are awarded on the basis of acting or technical expertise, academic record, and willingness to work. Interested students should contact the dept by Jan. to apply for Scholarships The process includes an aud/interview or portfolio.

FACULTY AND CLASSES OFFERED

13 Full-Time, 1 Part-Time: 9 PhD, 4 MFA/MA; 1 Staff

A. (1 1/2 FT, 1/2 PT) Intro to Theatre-2/Y; Theatre History-2/O; Shakes-1/X; Dramatic Lit-1/Y; Playwriting-1/Y

B. (1 FT, 1/2 PT) Acting-3/Y; Singing-1/X; Directing-1/O

C. (1 FT) Principles of Design-1/Y; Tech. Production-1/O; Topics in Tech. Theatre-1/O

D. (1/2 FT) Arts Management-1/O; Legal: Contracts, etc.-1/X

FACILITIES AND PRODUCTIONS

MAINSTAGE: 196 seats, fly space, new computerized lighting. 4 prods: 3 Fac dir, 2 Fac des, 1 Guest dir; budget $3,000-4,000 (opps. for students to dir/des w/approval from th. coordinator)

SECOND STAGE: Various seating

Outreach/perf., workshops/readings; Fac and Grad dir

Facility built in 1974, renovated in 1994; includes scene, costume, prop shops, sound, video studios, dance studio, classrooms.

A non-departmental student-run organization presents 4 productions per year in which majors participate.

10-15 student-written plays produced in the last two years.

Connection with Center Stage, non-Equity prof. summer theatre; productions give students an opportunity to participate in several weeks of intensive daily activity in a rewarding combination of master classes and live performances. Professionals, college students, and paid apprentices work together in a pleasant, productive setting.

DESCRIPTION

Noted Faculty: Dr. Ivan Joe Filippo Honors: post doctoral fellowship to Yale University, National Endowment for the Humanities, Seminar on the American Playwright; Distinguished Professor Award, APSU; Certificate of Outstanding Service to Minority Students. Producer: Center Stage (1987-1993). Cowriter, Belly Up to the Bard, and evening of entertainment.

Guest Artists: Dr. Howard Stein, former dean of the Yale School of Drama; Robert Wilson, performance artist; Ron Foreman, movement, pantomime.

Austin Peay's theatre program offers students a foundation for further study and training in acting and technical theatre. Interested students can also obtain a degree and experience in teaching theatre at the secondary grade level. All students within our department major in Communication Arts; degrees differ only by "concentrations" in Mass Communications, and/or Theatre. A "BA" differs from a "BS" by the fact that the "BA" students take two years of a foreign language. Since Austin Peay is a Liberal Arts institution, our theatre program provides a balance between the scholarly study of theatre and its practical application. Participation in theatre production is viewed as co-curricular, and students who are interested in acting have opportunities to perform in a variety of production types and acting styles over the course of a student generation (4 to 5 years). Those students interested in technical theatre have the opportunity to gain hands-on experience in their preferred area of specialization, be it lights, set, costumes or management.

Rhodes College

McCoy Theatre
Rhodes College
2000 North Parkway
Memphis, TN 38112
DEPT: (901) 843-3834
http://jilg.theater.rhodes.edu/theater.htmls/mccoy.html
ADMISSIONS: 2000 N. Parkway (901) 843-3700
adminfo@rhodes.edu FAX: (901) 843-3719
www.rhodes.edu adminfo@rhodes.edu

1,687 Total Enr.; h. compet.
Semester System
20-25 Majors; ATHE
T: $27,108/$7,108
SMALL PROGRAM
FAX: (901) 843-3406

DEGREES OFFERED

BA in Theatre (5). Declare major in sophomore year.

ADMISSION & FINANCIAL INFORMATION

Avg. Scores-SAT 1184. ACT 27; GPA 3.5; Min. 16 academic units, incl. 4 Eng., 3 Math, 2 For. Lang.; Accepts 72% to institution; no special req's. for theatre program; Fine Arts Award by audition or portfolio.

FACULTY AND CLASSES OFFERED

4 Full-Time, 1 Part-Time: 1 PhD, 5 MFA/MA; 1 Staff

A. (1 FT, 1 PT) Intro to Theatre-1/Y; Th Hist-2/Y; Dramatic Lit-1/Y; Playwriting-1/Y; Shakespeare-2/YX

B. (1 FT, 1/2 PT) Acting-3/Y; Voice/Speech-1/X; Movement-2/Y; Directing-1/Y; Singing-1/X; Musical Th-1/O

C. (1 FT, 1/2 PT) Prins of Des-1/Y; Set Des-1/Y; Lighting Des-1/Y; Stg Mgmt-2/Y; Tech Prod.-1/Y; Cost Des-1/Y

D. (1 FT) Arts Management-1/Y; Box Office Procedure-1/Y

FACILITIES & PRODUCTIONS

MAINSTAGE: 150 seats, computerized lighting. 4 prods: 2 Fac dir/des, 2 Fac des/Guest dir; budget $3,375

Facility was built in 1982; includes scene shop, costume shop, Renovation 2006-2007

DESCRIPTION

Guest Artists: Greasy Joan Company, Aquila, Core Ensemble; Harold Leaver, Actor/Director; Brad Shelton, Actor/Director; M. Whittles, Movement/Actress; Dina Facklin, Improv Artist, Pat McKenna, Improv Artist.

The Rhodes College Department of Theatre offers courses of instruction that are designed to develop an understanding of theatre as integral part of the society in which it exists. The courses are grounded in the belief that the liberal arts curriculum should give the highest priorities to the teaching of principles and concepts and that skills are valuable only if they are integrated components of a thorough understanding of those underlying principles and concepts. A major in Theatre provides the basis for further study in graduate school, professional theatre training, or in almost any area of public relations or arts management.

University of Memphis

Robert A. Hetherington, Chair	20,562; competitive
Dept of Theatre & Dance	Semester System
University of Memphis	97 Majors; NAST, USITT, SETC
144 Theatre Comm Bldg.	T: UG $5,520, G $6,708
Memphis, TN 38152-3150	O-ST T: UG $16,598, G $17,786
DEPT: (901) 678-2523	$6,100 R&B
theatrelib@memphis.edu	FAX: (901) 678-1350
www.memphis.edu/theatre	
ADM: (901) 678-2101	FAX: (901) 678-3053
www.memphis.edu	

DEGREES OFFERED

BFA in Design & Technical Prod (20), Performance (Acting) (69), MFA in Directing (5), Design & Tech Prod'n (9). Declare major in 2nd year; 2004 granted 5 Grad degrees.

ADMISSION & FINANCIAL INFORMATION

UG reqs. ACT min. 20 or SAT 930, HS GPA min. 3.0 for guaranteed admis; admits 76%. Aud./Portfolio req'd for UG, Grad req. Interview/Portfolio. UG aud. req'd. each semester to continue in program; Accept 1 out of 3 UG, 1 out of 4 Grad. 3 Talent schols are avail ea. yr. for incoming BFA students, aud/interview req., full tuition fee waiver. Other schols from $200-400 to current majors.

FACULTY AND CLASSES OFFERED

13 FT, 12 PT: 1 PhD, 12 MFA/MA; 5 Staff (2 professional, 2 adm. professional, 1 clerical)

A. (3 1/2 FT, 8 PT) Intro to Theatre-1/Y; Dramatic Lit-2/Y; Th. His-tory-2/Y; Dra Criticism-1/Y; Shakes-1/O; Playwriting-3/Y

B. (3 1/2 FT, 4 PT) Acting-8/Y; Voice/Speech-4/Y; Movement-5/Y; Mime, etc.-2/Y; Directing-6/Y; Stg Combat-1/Y; Dance- 15/Y; Oral Interp-1/Y

C. (3 1/2 FT) Prins of Des-1/Y; Set Design-4/Y; Cost Des-3/Y; Lighting Des-3/Y; Tech Prod'n-8/Y; Cost Constr-2/Y; Costume History-1/Y; Make-up-1/Y; Stg Mgmt-1/Y

D. (1/2 FT) Arts Management-2/Y

FACILITIES & PRODUCTIONS

MAINSTAGE: 324 seats, fly space, computerized lighting. 4 prods: 3 Fac dir, 6 Fac des, 1 Grad dir, 9 Grad des, 1 UG des; budget $4,000-10,000

SECOND STAGE: 100 seats, computerized lighting. 1 Fac des, 2 Grad dir, 5 Grad des, 2 UG des prods; budget $2-4,000

THIRD STAGE: 50+ seats, electronic lighting

15 Workshops/Readings: 3 Guest dir, 9 Grad dir, 3 UG dir

Facility was built in 1966; includes scene shop, costume shop, Computer Design Lab, 2 dance studios, design studio, 12 class-rooms.

Connection with Playhouse on the Square; Faculty designers have designed shows; MFA designers and directors have presented work as part of their degree; some BFA graduates have intern-ships.

DESCRIPTION

Noted Faculty: Robert Hetherington, Directing; John McFadden, Lighting and Sound Design; Gloria Baxter, Directing, Narrative Theatre; Susan Chrietzberg, Movement Studies; Stephen Hancock, Playwriting; Anita Jo Lenhart, Voice; Reggie Brown, Acting; Dave Nofsinger, Set Design; Holly Lau, Dance Education.

Guest Artists: Ellen McLaughlin, Kathleen Chalfant, Ursula Payne, Tiffany Mills Dance Company, Rennie Harris Pure Movement, Claire Porter, Sue Hogan, Scott McKowen, Jeanine Thompson, Roscoe Lee Browne, Anthony Zerbe, Robert Fetterman, Dana Nye; Dennis Krausnick, Shakespeare & Co Director; Ellen McLaughlin, Kathleen Chalfant, Scott McKowan, Jeanine Thompson, Ming Cho Lee, Dana Nye, David Diamond, Jason Robert Brown, Eric Schaeffer.

The University of Memphis provides opportunity for theatre education and training through BFA and MFA degree programs. Our programs provide students with a set of professional standards, attitudes, and competencies which will allow them to function productively in the theatre profession. The BFA degree is a professionally oriented degree specifically designed for students whose certain interests and abilities strongly suggest the potential for pursuing careers in theatre. The degree program provides students with the opportunity to concentrate upon studies in performance or in design and technical production. The MFA degree is a terminal degree designed for the student who has made the decision to pursue seriously a professional career in theatre. The principal objectives are the development of artistic and technical skill, conceptual understanding, personal style and vision, creativity, and professional competencies which are evidenced by a body of practical work.

University of the South

Peter Smith, Chair	1,400 Total Enr.; competitive
735 University Ave.	Semester System
University of the South	25-30 Majors; ATHE
Sewanee, TN 37383-1000	T: $30,000/$8,000 r&b
pesmith@sewanee.edu	
DEPT: (931) 598-1226	FAX: (931) 598-3264
ADM: (931) 598-1238	FAX: (931) 598-1145

DEGREES OFFERED

BA in General Theatre (50). Declare major in second year; 2007 granted 10 degrees.

ADMISSION & FINANCIAL INFORMATION

1260 SAT; GPA-3.3; Accepts 50% to institution; no special req's. for theatre program; program admits all applicants; university-wide scholarship req's. interview, essay, GPA & SATs (highly competitive).

FACULTY AND CLASSES OFFERED

4 Full-Time, 4 Part-Time: 2 PhD, 6 MFA/MA; 2 Staff

A. (1 1/2 FT, 1/2 PT) Intro to Th-1/Y; Th Hist-1/Y; Shakes-1/Y; Playwriting-1/Y

B. (1 1/2 FT, 1 PT) Acting-3/Y; Voice/Speech-1/Y; Movement-3/Y;

Directing-1/Y; Singing-1/Y; Dance-3/Y; Mime, etc. -1/Y

C. (2 FT, 2 1/2) Prins of Des-1/Y; Cost. Des-1/Y; Cost. Hist-1/O; Set Design-1/Y; Lighting Des-1/Y; Tech. Production-1/Y; Costume Des.-1/Y; Make-up-1/O

FACILITIES AND PRODUCTIONS

MAINSTAGE: 200 seats, computerized lighting. 8 prods: 4 Fac dir/des, 20 UG dir/des; budget $5-10,000

SECOND STAGE: 1,000 seats, comput.erized lighting; 1 prods., 1 fac. dir; 7 UG dir, 3 UG des.; budget $500

THIRD STAGE: 50 seats, black box, computerized lighting
1 Fac dir, 7 UG dir, 8 UG des prods
6 Guest dir Workshops/Readings; budget $250

Facility was built in 1998; includes scene shop, costume shop, dance studio, design studio, sound studio, CAD facility, 2 rehearsal studios, classroom.

A non-departmental, student-run organization presents 3-4 productions per year in which majors occasionally participate. 2 student-written plays produced in the last two years.

DESCRIPTION

Noted Faculty: Peter Smith, Act/Dir; David Landon, Acting; Dan Backlund, Design; John Piccard, Design & Technology; Phoebe Pearigen, Dance; Jennifer Matthews, Costume.

Guest Artists: Danny Hoch, Writer/Performer; Joseph Mydell, Actor; Paul Bonin-Rodriguez, Writer/Actor/Dancer.

The University of the South department of Theatre Arts offers the student a background in all areas of theatre within a liberal arts setting. The department expects its majors to gain knowledge and experience by active participation in the production program of the university theatres. Thanks to the generous bequest of Tennessee Williams, the department annually invites to campus guest artists who combine their work as performers with creative work as writers. The heart of the program is the newly constructed Tennessee Williams Center, a state-of-the-art multiform theatre.

University of Tennessee

Blake Robison, Dept. Head
Department of Theatre
206 McClung Tower
University of Tennessee
Knoxville, TN 37996-0420
www.clarencebrowntheatre.org
cbt@utk.edu
FAX: (865) 974-4867
ADMISSIONS: 800 Andy Holt Tower., Knoxville, TN 37996
(865) 974-2184   admissions@tennessee.edu

20,619 Total Enr.; compet.
Semester System
75 Majors, ATHE, LORT, TCG
T: $5,864;
O-ST T: UG $17,130
r&b: 6,358
DEPT: (865) 974-6011

DEGREES OFFERED

BA in Theatre; MFA in Performance & Des. Declare major in soph year; 2004 granted 14 UG, 11 Grad degs.

ADMISSION & FINANCIAL INFORMATION

Req.: ACT 25, average GPA 3.4; Accept 65-70% to institution; Req. for theatre program — assoc with College of Arts & Sciences & Intro to Theatre (prerequisite); Aud/Int. req. for Grad program; Accept all UG, 12 out of 40 Grad applicants to program; Fred Fields. Scholarships include the Emily Mahan Faust Fellowship for grad students; Clarence/Marion Brown Career Development Award for a graduating grad; William Desmond, Performing Arts UG/Grad; Robert & Mary Culver for UG; Opening Night Club for UG, Upperclassmen, Grad; Carl A. Vines Jr. (alternates with English every fiscal year) for UG; Dr. & Mrs. David Shea Theatre Movement/dance for Jr/Sr and/or 2nd/3rd year Grad; Ralph Frost for UG or Grad; Davd A. York for UG; and Ellis Mayes for UG.

FACULTY AND CLASSES OFFERED

12 FT, 3 PT, 24 Staff, 4 Artists in Residence

A. (2 1/2 FT) Intro to Theatre-1-Y; Dramatic Lit-2/Y; Th Hist-4/Y; Dramatic Criticism-1/Y; Shakes-2/X

B. (4 1/2 FT, 3 PT) Acting-4/Y; Singing-X; Mus. Th-1/X; Directing-1/Y

C. (6 FT) Prin of Des-1/Y; Set Des-4/Y; Cost Des- 4/Y; Lighting Des-4/Y; Tech Prod-1/O; Cost Constr-4/Y; Cost Hist-1/O; Make-up-1/O; Stg Mgmt- 1/O

FACILITIES & PRODUCTIONS

MAINSTAGE: 585 seats, fly space, computerized lighting. 6 prods: 1 Fac dir, 3 Guest dir, 2 Grad dir, 3 Fac cost des, 3 Grad cost. des, 1 Fac scene des, 3 Guest scene des, 1 Grad scene des, 4 Fac lighting. des, 1 Guest lighting des, 1 Grad lighting des

SECOND STAGE: 350 seats, computerized lighting. 1 prod: 1 Grad/Fac dir, 1 cost des, 1 Grad scene des, 1 Fac lighting. des

THIRD STAGE: 125 seats, computerized lighting. 6 Workshops/ Readings: 1 Fac dir, 1 Guest dir, 2 UG dir, 4 UG des, 2 Grad dir, 2 Grad scene des, 6 Grad lighting. des; budget $100-500

Facility built in 1970 and 1951; includes scene, cost, prop shops, welding shop, sound studio, design studio, classrooms, electric shop and computer design studio.

A non-departmental, student-run organization presents 3-4 productions per year in which majors participate. Theatre students at U.T. have the opportunity to see great performances by great actors, and to interact and share in informal workshop experiences with distinguished performers and designers of the Clarence Brown Company. Many students serve in CBC productions as actors, stage managers, designers and technicians.

DESCRIPTION

Guest Artists: Frank Hanig, Dir/Des; Paul Barnes, Dir; Jaroslav Malina, Scenic Des; Jeff Modereger, Scenic Des; Petr Matasek, Puppetry Des; Beverly Emmons, Light Des; Alan Timar,Dir; Penny Remsen, Light Des; Veronika Nowag-Jones, Dir; Martin Pakledinaz, Cost. Des.

The mission of the department is to provide quality undergraduate and graduate programs in theatre. The BA degree is designed to build a foundation for further study and training. Although undergraduate education is in the liberal arts, extensive course offerings in theatre and drama are available to students majoring in theatre. The department provides professional training programs leading to a MFA degree—a three year course of study for students with demonstrated ability in their chosen area of concentration. Undergraduates and students in the MFA Program have the opportunity to learn, develop and demonstrate their craft by working in all three producing components of the program. Gifted undergraduates and candidates for the MFA degree also have the opportunity, through participation in Clarence Brown Theatre Company productions, to earn their first professional credits.

University of Tennessee at Martin

Douglas Cook, Chair
Dept. of Visual & Theatre Arts
102 Fine Arts Bldg.
Univ. of Tennessee at Martin
Martin, TN 38238
DEPT: (731) 587-7400
ADM: 200 Hall Moody Adm. Bldg.
(731) 587-7020
admitme@utm.edu

5,600 Total Enr.; not compet.
Semester System.
76 Majors
T: $4,932/$5,641 R&B
O-ST T: $14,528/$5,641 R&B
FAX: (731) 587-7415
www.utm.edu
FAX: (731) 587-7029

DEGREES OFFERED

BFA in Fine & Performing Arts (76) with concentration in: Art, Art Education (K-12), Graphic Design, Theatre. Declare major in soph. year

ADMISSION & FINANCIAL INFORMATION

Accept all applics to theatre program. No special requirements Gala for the Arts Scholarship Letter of applic and audition. $1,500 - one yr.

FACULTY AND CLASSES OFFERED

3 FT: 1 PhD, 2 MFA/MA; 2 Staff

A. (1 FT) Intro to Theatre-2/Y; Th Hist-2/Y; Playwriting-1/O

B. (1 1/2 FT) Acting-3/Y; Voice/Speech-2/Y; Singing-2/X; Directing-1/Y; Dance-6/Y

C. (1/2 FT) Set Design-1/O; Lighting Design-1/O; Cost Construction-1/O; Make-up-1/O

FACILITIES & PRODUCTIONS

MAINSTAGE: 469 seats, fly space, electronic lighting.
    2 prods: 2 Fac dir/des

SECOND STAGE: 99 seats, electronic lighting.
    1 prods: 1 Fac des, 1 UG dir

Facility built in 1970, renovated in 1995; includes scene, cost shops, video studio, movement/dance, rehearsal studio, computer lab, dance studion w/performing space, classrooms.

5 student-written plays produced in the last two years.

DESCRIPTION

Noted Faculty: Douglas Cook, Design; Melanie Hollis, Acting; Ken Zimmerman, Acting/Directing, Alix M. Gausline, Dance.

Guest Artists: Melanie Hollis.

The faculties of Visual and Theatre Arts are devoted to the pursuit of excellence in their disciplines. Emphasis is placed on the development of the individual student as an artist. Programs of study are studio-based and oriented toward production and performance. Students are given ample opportunity for performing. Theatre students participate in the productions of University of Tennessee at Martin's Vanguard Theatre. Dancers perform with the UTM Dance Ensemble. The Fine Arts Building contains rehearsal studios, classrooms, and two performing spaces, The dance studio, located in the Physical Education Building, features a stage complete with light-

ing and other technical support. Graduates of the B.F.A. program may choose to enter professional life as an artist, designer, or teacher. An impressive number of these students are accepted into advanced study in the finest graduate schools in the nation. Whatever the specific objectives, graduates benefit from a solid core of basic training taught by artist/teachers.

Vanderbilt University

Jon & Terryl Hallquist,
    Co-Directors
Vanderbilt University Theatre
2301 Vanderbilt Place
VU Station B, P.O. Box 1
Nashville, TN 37235-0001

6,300 Tot enr; highly compet.
Semester System
30 Majors
T: $34,414
DEPT: (615) 322-2404

DEGREES OFFERED

BA or BS in Theatre Arts (30). Declare major in sophomore year; 2004 granted 12 degrees.

ADMISSION & FINANCIAL INFORMATION

Accept 50% to institution; SAT's, GPA, letters of rec. and essays; no special req. for theatre program. No theatre program scholarships offered; inst. scholarship based on academic merit; contact fin. aid office.

FACULTY AND CLASSES OFFERED

6 Full-Time: 3 PhD; 3 MA/MFA; 1 Staff

A. (2) Intro to Theatre-4/Y; Th Hist-2/Y & Dr. Lit-4/Y; Shakes-peare-1/Y; Playwriting-1/Y; Film Study-3/Y; Th in London-1/Y

B. (2) Acting-3/Y; Directing-1/Y; Independent studies in Acting & Directing-2/Y

C. (2) Set Design-1/Y; Cost Des-1/Y; Lighting Des-1/Y; Independent Studies in Design-1/Y; Production-1/Y

FACILITIES AND PRODUCTIONS

MAINSTAGE: 350 seats, computerized lighting. 4 prods: Fac dir/des; budget $5,000-10,000

5 Workshops/Readings, UG dir/des.; budget $50-100

Facility was built in 1976; includes scene, costume, prop shops, design studio, classroom.

A student-run, non-departmental producing org. presents 2 additional shows per year, with some majors participating.

DESCRIPTION

Guest Artists: Karl Malden, Fiona Shaw, Irene Corey, Joan MacIntosh, Olympia Dukakis, Eva Marie Saint, Jeff Hayden.

Our goal at Vanderbilt University Theatre is to expose the liberal arts student as a generalist to all the aspects of theatre at an introductory level. We recognize that further study in a specific area is necessary but that the solid foundation received at VUT will readily prepare them for future training. Many of our alumni have gone on to pursue graduate work or internships with professional theatres.

TEXAS

Abilene Christian University

Adam Hester, Chair
ACU Theatre
WPAC 123, Box 27843
Abilene, TX 79699
DEPT: (325) 674-2021
www.acu.edu/theatre
FAX: (325) 674-6887
ADM: ACU Box 2900
(800) 460-6228

4,700 Total Enr.;compet.
Semester System
88 Majors; TCG, CITA, TNT, SWTA
SMALL PROGRAM
T: $25,000/$6,000 r&b
hestera@acu.edu

info@admissions.acu.edu

DEGREES OFFERED
BA in General Theatre (2), Theatre Ministry (0); BFA in Acting (33), Directing (8), Design/Tech (13), Musical Theatre (19). Declare major in freshman year; 2007 granted 11 degrees.

ADMISSION & FINANCIAL INFORMATION
ACT-20, SAT-960 without writing portion, transcript, 2 letters of recommendation, GPA 2.0 to transfer. Accept 53% to inst; aud/int/portfolio req'd for theatre prog; admit up to 12 out of 90. Auditions and Interviews are held by appointment. Pat and Arradel Powell Scholarship Fund, Charleton Heston Family Theatre Scholarship Fund for the Performing Arts, Fred Barton Scholarship Fund, Shakespeare Festival Scholarships, and many more

FACULTY AND CLASSES OFFERED
6 FT: 6 MA/MFA; 2 Staff

A. (1 1/2 FT) Intro to Theatre-1/Y; Th Hist-2/O; Shakes-1/Y; Period Styles-1/O; Dramatic Lt-2/X; Dramatic Crit-1/O; Playwriting-1/O

B. (2 1/2 FT) Acting-3/Y; Movement-1/Y; Directing-3/Y; Voice-1/Y; Mus. Th.-1/O; Dance-4/Y; Singing-4/Y; Stanislavski-1/Y; Senior Showcase-1/Y; Film Appreciation-1/Y

C. (1 1/2 FT) Principles of Design-1/O; Set Design-1/O; Cost Des-2/O; Lighting Des-1/O; Tech Prod-1/Y; Stage Mgmt-1/O; Cost. Constr-1/Y; Make-up-1/O

D. (1/2 FT) Arts Mgmt-1/O; Box Office Procedures-1/Y

FACILITIES AND PRODUCTIONS
MAINSTAGE: 325 seats, fly space, comput. & electronic lighting
   4 prods: 3 Fac dir, 2 Fac des, 1 UG dir, 2 UG des; budget $3,000-6,000
SECOND STAGE: 2,200 seats, comput. & electronic lighting
   1 prod: 1 Fac dir, 2 Fac des; budget $20,000
THIRD STAGE: 150 seats, comput. lighting
   2 prods: 1 Fac dir, 2 Fac des, 1 GA dir/des; budget $0-$2500
New space built in 2003; movement/dance studio, rehearsal studio, 2 classrooms; scene, costume, scene and prop shops located in different space
One non-dept, student-run producing organization.

DESCRIPTION
Guest Artists: Adam Hester, Acting, Directing; Michael Fernandez, Playwriting, Script Analysis, History; Dawne Swearingen, Movement, Period Styles; Gary Varner, Set/Light Design, Children's Theatre, Improv; Sandy Freeman, Costume Design; Donna Hester, Educational Theatre

Guest Artists: Justin Boccitto, Dancer, Master Tap Class; Shauna Kanter, Director, Voice Theatre; Katie Eason, Dance; Carmen Beaubeaux, Actor; Nan Gurley, Actor; Robert Langdon Lloyd, Actor; John Shea, Agent, Frontier Booking; Mona Slomsky, Tara Rubin Casting

The Abilene Christian University Department of Theatre is committed to providing quality training and opportunity for the disciplined theatre artist in a nurturing environment that models Christian values. The department provides pre-professional training for students seeking a career in the theatre.

Angelo State University

Bill Doll, PhD, Dir. of Theatre
ASU Station #10895
Angelo State University
San Angelo, TX 76909-0895
Dept: (325) 942-2146
FAX: (325) 942-2033
www.@angelo.edu
ADMISSIONS: ASU Station #11014, San Angelo TX 76909
(325) 942-2185
www.angelo.edu

6,500 Total Enr.; compet.
Semester System
60 Majors
T: $2,000/$4,000+/- R&B
O-ST. T: $7,000/$4,000+/- R&B
SMALL PROGRAM

FAX: (325) 942-2078
admission@angelo.edu

DEGREES OFFERED
BA in Drama, any specialization (38); Drama w/secondary Ed. Certification (22). Declare major in any year; 2006 granted 15 degrees.

ADMISSION & FINANCIAL INFORMATION
SAT 1030, ACT 23; top 1/2 of HS class. Accept 94% to inst; interview/portfolio for designers required for theatre prog; Admit 8 out of 10 to theatre prog. Carr Performing Arts Scholarships - a competitive audition/application process; Departmental scholarships by aud/interview; Drama Endowed Scholarships by aud/interview. Totals $600-4,000/yr.

FACULTY AND CLASSES OFFERED
2 Full-Time: 1 PhD, 1 MFA/MA; 2 1/2 Staff

A. (1/2 FT) Intro to Theatre-1/Y; Th Hist-2/O; Dramatic Lit-1/O; Dramatic Criticism-1/O; Playwriting-1/O

B. (1/2 FT) Acting-3/Y; Voice/Speech-1/O; Directing-1/O

C. (1/2 FT) Prins of Des-1/O; Set Design-1/O; Cost Des-1/O; Lighting Des-1/O; Tech Prod'n-1/O; Costume History-1/O; Cost. Constr-1/O; Make-up-1/O; Stage Mgmt-1/O

D. (1/2 FT) Arts Mgmt-1/O

FACILITIES AND PRODUCTIONS
MAINSTAGE: 419 seats, fly space, comput. lighting. 2 prods:
   2 Fac dir, 8 Fac des prods; budget $3,000-10,000
SECOND MAINSTAGE: 180 seats, fly space, computerized lighting.
   4 prods: 4 Fac dir, 16 Fac des; $3,000-5,000
Mainstage built in 1948, renovated in 1976; Second Stage built in 1976; includes scene, costume, prop shops, CAD facility, classrooms.
Two student-written play produced in the last two years.

DESCRIPTION
Noted Faculty: Bill Doll, Theatre, Creative Studies, Fine

Arts, Acting/Directing; James Worley, Directing, Management, Design.

Guest Artists: Bill Erwin,Randy Barkee

The Department of Drama at Angelo State is committed to providing a general knowledge of theatre within a liberal arts education. The program is a mixed academic/production concept, with six produced mainstage productions per year, utilizing students from all undergraduate levels on-stage, in technical areas, and front-of-house responsibilities, and four student directed productions. All technical/house student management positions are paid positions. The program is designed as a foundation for professional or educational theatre careers. Students may specialize in production fields or prepare through generalized experience. ASU has an extraordinary Modular Theatre which is perhaps the most flexible theatre space possible for training in various acting styles and challenges in design opportunities.

Baylor University

Stan Denman, Chair	13,000 Total Enr.; compet.
Baylor Theatre	Semester System
P. O. Box 97262	100 Maj; ATHE,NAST,SWTA,ETAS
Baylor University	T: $24,490/$7,526 R&B
Waco, TX 76798	MAIN: (254) 710-1011
DEPT: (254) 710-1861	http://www.baylor.edu/theatre
Admin: (254) 710-3435	

DEGREES OFFERED

BA in Theatre Arts (20); BFA in Performance (65), Design (15);MFA in Directing (6). Declare major in freshman year.

ADMISSION & FINANCIAL INFORMATION

Top half of class, and/or Avg 24 on ACT, 1100 on SAT for full acceptance. Conditional acceptance may be granted for lower scores. Accept 74% to inst; audition/interview req. for admission into program; Limited Scholarships set aside for entering freshmen or transfers in performance or technical fields. Most dept. scholarships req. the student be present for two full semesters before being eligible.

FACULTY AND CLASSES OFFERED

13 Full-Time, 4 PhD, 9 MFA/MA; 1 professional w/o advanceed degree, 8 Staff

A. (4 FT) Theatre Appreciation-1/Y; Theatre History-3/Y; Mast Works-1/Y; Th & Christianity-1/Y; Dramaturgy-1/Y; Org & Dev-1/Y

B. (6 FT) Non-major Acting-1/Y; Acting-5/Y; Voice/Movement-5/Y; Realism-3/Y; Audition-1/Y; Shakes-2/Y; Mask-1/Y; Improv-1/Y; Children's Theatre-1/Y; Dance-4/Y; Mus Th-1/Y; Singing-1/Y; Directing-4/Y; Senior Showcase-1/Y

C. (4 FT) Drafting-1/Y; CAD/CAM-1/Y; Th Drawing-1/Y; Scene Painting-1/Y; Makeup-1/Y; Stage Mgmt-2/Y; Set Des-4/Y; Costume Des-4/Y; Lighting Des-3/Y; Sound Des-2/Y; Prod Lab-4/Y; Prod Des-1/Y

FACILITIES AND PRODUCTIONS

MAINSTAGE: 350 seats, proscenium stage, fly space, computerized lighting.. 2 Fac dir/des, budget $5,000-18,000

SECOND MAINSTAGE: 250 seats, fly space, computerized lighting. 3 Fac dir/des; budget $3000-12,000,10 Grad dir/des, 2 UG dir/des

Blackbox: 90 seats, computerized lighting, 4 Grad dir, 1 UG des; budget $1,500-5,000.

Workshops/Readings; $0-500

Facility built in 1981; includes scene, costume shops, sound studio, dance studio, rehearsal studio, design studio, 2 classrooms.

DESCRIPTION

The mission of the Department of Theatre Arts is to prepare students for theatre arts related fields by integrating excellence in traditional scholarship and artistic creativity with a Christian worldview. The mission of the Baylor Theatre is to act as a cultural laboratory which engages the university, the larger community of artist scholars, and the world. The vision of the Department of Theatre Arts is inextricably connected to Baylor's ambitious 2012 Vision. Whereas the UG program in theatre arts now stands as one of the top ranked programs in the US, the theatre arts faculty envisions Baylor Theatre as being one of the leading academic theatre institutions in the country by the year 2012, in both graduate and UG theatre training. The theatre arts faculty and staff are committed to the students, to the unversity, and to the worthiness of reaching this vision without surrendering its foundational beliefs in scholarship and artistry enriched by a Christian worldview.

College of the Mainland

Director	4,000 Total Enr.; non-compet.
College of the Mainland	Semester System
Arena Theatre	20 Majors
1200 Amburn Road	T: $242-638 per cred
Texas City, TX 77591	SMALL PROGRAM
(409) 938-1211 ext 345	FAX: (409) 938-0022
www.com.edu	

DEGREES OFFERED

AA in TheatreArts/Drama (20)

ADMISSION & FINANCIAL INFORMATION

Inst. reqs SAT, ACT, TSAP or local entrance exam; admit 8 out of 10 to program. Scholarships liberally awarded to most theatre majors. Audition/interview for scholarship

FACULTY AND CLASSES OFFERED

2 Full-Time, 3 Part-Time: 1 PhD, 4 MA/MFA; 1 Staff

A. (1 FT) Intro to Theatre-1/Y

B. (1 FT, 1 PT) Acting-3/Y

C. (2 PT) Tech Production-1/Y

FACILITIES AND PRODUCTIONS

MAINSTAGE: 248 seats, computerized lighting. 6 Fac dir, 3 Fac des, 2 Guest dir, 3 Guest des, 6 UG dir/des; budget $4,000-15,000

SECOND STAGE: 500 seats, fly space, computerized lighting

THIRD STAGE: 100 seats, electronic lighting.

Facility was built in 1970, last renovated in 1991; includes scene shop, costume shop, prop shop, rehearsal studio, classrooms.

A student-run producing organization presents 6 prods. per year in which majors participate. 2 student-written plays produced in the last two years.

College of the Mainland Arena Theatre-25 years of continuous operations, 119 performances a year with a subscription audience approaching 2,000.

DESCRIPTION

Noted Faculty: Jack Westin, Mark A. Adams, Tom King.

Guest Artists: J. Newton White, Thom Guthrie, Kelly Babb.

Theatre at College of the Mainland has two components, the Community Theatre and Academic Theatre programs. The Community Theatre, a part of the college's commitment to continuing community education, produces 6-9 plays annually chosen from a wide variety of classics, comedies, dramas, and musicals. With almost 2000 season subscribers, most of the 100 performances each year are sold out. Casting is done from a pool of actors drawn from a large geographical area—actors who appreciate the high quality of productions and wish to have the experience of working in a community theatre setting with strong educational ties. Auditions are open to everyone. Workshops are offered periodically in Acting, Stage Combat, Auditioning, etc. The fully accredited Academic Theatre program can lead to transfer to a 4-year college or to an Associate of Arts degree. Students have the opportunity of performing in the community theatre productions as well as productions specifically for students.

Collin College

Dr. Brad Baker, Chair of Theatre
Quad C. Theatre
2800 E. Spring Creek Pkwy.
Collin College
Plano, TX 75074-3300
FAX: (972) 881-5103
bbaker@ccccd.edu

26,000 Tot. Enr.; not compet.
Semester System
60 Majors; ATHE
T: $1,100; O-ST T: $3,000
DEPT: (972) 881-5679
www.collintheatrecenter.com

DEGREES OFFERED

AA in Theatre. Declare major in freshman year; 2004 granted 10 degrees.

ADMISSION & FINANCIAL INFORMATION

High school diploma or equivalency; 100% of applicants admitted to institution; Apply to Chair of Theatre by May 1st, auditions will be arranged. Theatre program admits all applicants; Contact department for scholarship info.

FACULTY AND CLASSES OFFERED

9 FT, 7 PT: 1 PhD, 11 MFA/MA, 4 Staff

A. (2 FT, 6 PT) Intro to Theatre-1/Y; Th History-2/Y; Shakes- 1/Y; Dramatic Lit-1/Y

B. (4 FT) Acting-4/Y; Movement-1/Y; Singing-2/Y; Directing-1/Y; Voice/Speech-1/Y; Mime/Mask-1/Y; Musical Theatre-2/Y; Stage Combat-1/Y; Dance-X

C. (2 FT, 1 PT) Principles of Design-3/Y; Set Des-2/Y; Cost Design-2/Y; Tech. Production-2/Y; Stage Mgmt-1/Y; Lighting Design-1/Y; Cost Construction-2/Y; Make-up-1/Y

D. (1 FT) Marketing/ Promo-1/O

FACILITIES AND PRODUCTIONS

MAINSTAGE: 345 seats, fly space, computerized & electronic lighting
   3 prods: 3 Fac dir; budget $1,000-20,000

SECOND STAGE: 120 seats, computerized & electronic lighting
   2 prods: 1 Fac dir, 1 GA dir; budget $500-10,000

THIRD STAGE: 50 seats, black box, computerized & electronic lighting
   4 Workshops/Readings: 1 Fac dir, 3 UG dir; budget $0-500

Facility built in 1988; includes scene, costume shop, welding area, sound, dance and rehearsal studio, make-up studio, box office, classrooms, experimental theatre.

2 student-written plays produced in the last two years.

DESCRIPTION

Noted Faculty: Brad Baker, Gail Cronauer, Craig Erickson, Robin Armstrong, Shannon Kearns-Simmons, Sandra Snyder

Guest Artists: Bryan Woffard, Laura McMeley, Rosemary Andress, Rene Moreno, Matthew Tomlanovich, K. Callan, Michael Urie, Joanne Zipay

The Collin College Theatre program offers a 2-year curriculum of theatre study including acting, directing, playwrighting, voice, scenic and lighting design, costuming, makeup, theatre history, dramatic literature, marketing, as well as specialty courses in circus skills, stunt work and stage combat. Collin is committed to preparing students for further undergraduate study in theatre. Collin annually presents a 7-8 play season, including: world and regional premieres with the playwrights in residence; revivals of classic plays; award-winning student-written productions. Students taught by Collin faculty have gained employment with major theatres and related companies nationwide, as well as in motion pictures such as Natural Born Killers, Philadelphia, Nobody's Fool, Interview with the Vampire, JFK, Mississippi Burning, Jacob's Ladder, Bull Durham, The Alamo and others.

Hardin-Simmons University

Larry Wheeler, PhD., Dept. Head
Theatre Dept.
Box 14864
Hardin-Simmons University
Abilene, TX 79698-4864
DEPT: (325) 670-1511
www.hsutx.edu
ADM: Box 16050

2,500 Total Enr.; not compet.
8 Majors; ATHE
Semester System
T: $580/sem. hr.
$1139 - $1353 R per sem.
SMALL PROGRAM
FAX: (325) 677-8351
(325) 670-1206

DEGREES OFFERED

BA in Theatre (13), B.B.S. in Theatre (2). Declare major in freshman year.

ADMISSION & FINANCIAL INFORMATION

SAT 990, ACT 21, GPA; 50% accepted to inst; Th program admits all; Scholarships based on need and aud/int (held in Spring), GPA, rec's.

FACULTY AND CLASSES OFFERED

2 Full-Time: 1 PhD, 1 MFA/MA; 7 Staff

A. (1 FT, 1 PT) Intro to Theatre-1/Y; Dramatic Lit-1/Y; Th Hist-2/O; Shakes-1/X

B. (1 FT, 1 PT) Acting-2/Y; Voice/Speech-1/Y; Stage Combat-1/O; Directing-1/Y; Dance-1/Y; Creative Dramatics-1/Y

C. (1 FT, 1 PT) Cost Des-1/O; Tech Prod'n-1/Y; Set Des-1/O; Ltg Des-1/Y; Cost Constr-1/O; Make-up-1/O; Stage Mgmt-1/Y

D. (1 FT, 1 PT) Arts Management-1/O

FACILITIES & PRODUCTIONS

MAINSTAGE: 1900 seats, fly space, computerized lighting. 4 Fac dir/des prods.; budget $2,000-2,500

SECOND STAGE: 300 seats, fly space, computerized lighting. 4 UG dir/des prods.; budget $200-300

THIRD STAGE: 100 seats, black box, electronic lighting

Facility was built in 1961, renovated in 1993; includes scene shop, costume shop.

DESCRIPTION

Noted Faculty: Larry Wheeler, PhD., Design; Melissa D. Green

The Dept of Theatre at Hardin-Simmons University gives students the opportunity to combine practical and theoretical knowledge of the theatre in the classroom and on the stage. It is the goal of the department to prepare theatre artists who can effectively express themselves as directors, performers, designers, and teachers. Courses in the Department of Theatre lead to a Bachelor of Arts or Bachelor of Behavioral Sciences degree and a wide exposure to the scope of world theatre. In addition to the beginning courses of introduction to theatre, stagecraft, and acting, a variety of advanced courses prepare the student for all phases of theatre production. These include stage design, theatre management, theatre history, and directing. The Department of Theatre also produces three to four major productions a year in the Van Ellis Theatre. The range of plays selected for production includes musicals, serious dramas, and comedies from all periods and styles in the world of theatre. Student-directed one-act plays are produced in the spring also. In addition to these performance opportunities, the department has an improvisational theatre troupe that performs for campus and civic organizations.

KD Studio

T.A. Taylor	110 Total Enr.; compet
Dir. of Education	Semester Syst., NAST
KD Studio	15-month program
2600 Stemmons, #117	T: $10,750
Dallas, TX 75207	(214) 638-0484
www.kdstudio.com	FAX: (214) 630-5140

DEGREES OFFERED

AAA in Acting Performance (98); Musical Theatre (12). Declare major 1st year. 2001 granted 65 degrees.

ADMISSION & FINANCIAL INFORMATION

HS completion or GED, personal interview/audition; inst. admits 80% of applicants, 8 out of 10 admitted to theatre program.For scholarship info, contact above.

FACULTY AND CLASSES OFFERED

22 PT: 1 PhD, 12 MFA/MA/MS, 9 Prof. w/o adv. degree; 18 Staff
  NOTE: S denotes offered each semester

A. (4 PT) Intro to Theatre-1/S; Shakespeare-1/S

B. (18 PT) Acting-1/S; Voice/Speech-1/S; Movement-1/S; Singing-1/S; Musical Theatre-1/S; Stage Combat-1/S; Mime/Mask-1/S; Dance-1/S

FACILITIES & PRODUCTIONS

MAINSTAGE: 135 seats, electronic lighting
  3 prods: 3 Fac dir

Second Stage: 150 seats, computerized lighting
  1 prod: 1 UG dir

2 Workshop/Readings: 2 UG dir

Facility built in 1965, last renovated in 2000;1 video studio, 2 dance studio, 2 rehearsal studios, 10 classrooms, library, casting.

DESCRIPTION

Noted Faculty: Michael Serrecchia, Rene Moreno, John Davies, Linda Leonard, Paula Morelan, Lynn Ambrose

Guest Artists: Kevin Costner, Janine Turner, Ned Beatty, Martin Jurow, William Hickey, Steve Raulback, Tim Roth, Rich Jaffa.

KD Studio, Actors Conservatory of the Southwest, exists as a bridge between educational and professional acting. A great percentage of the program is aimed at developing camera acting skills as well as stage acting. Faculty are involved as industry professionals concurrent with their teaching duties. Students receive up-to-the-minute advice/instruction in succeeding professionally. As a conservatory, our 14-month program focuses on acting. Every course offered is aimed at increasing the student actor's knowledge of the craft of acting and professional potential. Approved by Texas Education Agency. Texas Higher Education Coordinating Board. Accredited by National Association of Schools of Theatre.

St. Edward's University

Ev Lunning, Artistic Dir.	
Mary Moody Northern Theatre	3,000 Total Enr.; not compet.
3001 South Congress	70 Majors, U/RTA
St. Edward's University	Sem. System
Austin, TX 78704-6489	T: $11,075 per sem.
DEPT: (512) 448-8486	$2,911-$4,098 R&B per sem.
	www.stedwards.edu
ADMISSIONS: Above address.	(512) 448-8500
(800) 555-0164	FAX: (512) 464-8877
seu.admit@admin.stedwards.edu	

DEGREES OFFERED

BA in Theatre, Acting Emphasis (60), Theatre Design Emphasis (5), Theatre, Arts Admin. Emphasis (5) Declare major in freshman year; 1997 granted 12 degrees.

ADMISSION & FINANCIAL INFORMATION

Top 50% of class, ACT 19; SAT 1000; review extracurricular and community activities. 75-80% of applics admitted to inst. No special req. for admission to theatre program, 9 out of 10 admitted to th. program. Applics for the Freshman class have the opportunity to audition for merit schols the first weekend in March.

FACULTY AND CLASSES OFFERED

5 FT, 8 PT: 1 PhD, 4 MFA/MA, 3 Prof. w/out adv. degree; 2 Staff

A. (1 FT, 1 PT) Intro to Theatre-1/X; Dramatic Lit-1/X; Th Hist-2/Y; Shakes-2/Y

B. (2 FT, 4 PT) Acting-4/Y; Voice/Speech-2/Y; Mus Th-1/Y; Singing-

4/X; Directing-1/Y; Dance-4/Y

C. (1 FT, 2 PT) Set Des-1/Y; Cost Des-1/Y; Lighting Des-1/Y; Tech Prod'n-1/Y; Cost Constr-1/Y; Make-up-1/Y; Stg Mgmt-1/O

D. (1 FT, 1 PT) Arts Mgmt-1/Y; Marketing/Promo-1/X; Budget/Accounting-1/X

FACILITIES & PRODUCTIONS

MAINSTAGE: 180 seats, computerized lighting. 6 Fac dir, 4 Fac des, 1 Guest dir, 23 Guest des, 1 UG des; budget $1,000-3,000

Facility built in 1972; includes scene, cost, reh studio, classrooms.

Connection with Mary Moody Northern Theatre, which operates under U/RTA Equity contract. MMNT employs several guest artists a year. Students who appear in productions with Equity guest artists earn candidacy points. It is possible for students to be eligible for equity memberhip on graduation.

DESCRIPTION

Noted Faculty: Dr. Melba Martinez, PhD, Performance Theory.

Guest Artists: Ev Lunning, Jr., Louis A. Rigler, Eddie Mekka, Rod Arrants, Actors; Michael Costello, Director; Thomas C. Parker, Actor; Sheila Marie Gordon, Actor; Hank Hehmsoth, Music Director; Scott Thompson, Director; Amparo Garcia, Director.

We recognize the responsibility of providing our students with the basic training, education and experience necessary for the pursuit of careers in professional educational or community theatres. Second, we recognize the responsibility of providing our students with the knowledge and abilities to lead full, rewarding and productive lives. We seek to develop artists who are sensitive, aware human beings. Our program is grounded in classroom training mixed with production experience. We invite guest artists from professional theatre, film and television to work with faculty and students in production. We offer direct opportunities for observation and association with working professionals before graduation. Because of our URTA contract with Actors' Equity Association, students who complete the Membership Candidate Program are eligible to join Equity upon graduation.

Sam Houston State University

Penelope A. Hasekoester, Chair
Dept.of Theatre & Dance
Sam Houston State University
Huntsville, TX 77341-2297
drm_pah@shsu.edu
www.shsu.edu/~drm.www/
ADMISSIONS: P.O. Box 2418, SHSU, Huntsville, TX 77341-2418
www.shsu.edu/~adm.www
(936) 294-1828

14,500 Total Enr.; compet.
27 Majors, Sem. System
T: $50 PER CREDIT HR.
O-ST T: $328 PER CREDIT
DEPT. (936) 294-1329
FAX: (936) 294-3898

FAX: (936) 294-3758

DEGREES OFFERED

BFA in Musical Theatre (40), Acting & Directing (100), Design & Technical Theatre (35), Secondary Teaching Certification (15) Declare major in first year; 2004 granted 21 degrees.

ADMISSION & FINANCIAL INFORMATION

Upper 1/4 of graduating class, no minimum on ACT or SAT; 19 ACT or 930 SAT if 2nd 1/4 of graduating class; 22 ACT or 1030 SAT if 3rd 1/4 of grad class; 25 ACT or 1140 SAT if 4th 1/4 of grad class;

Theatre Scholarships available for new students through auditions and interviews-Humphreys, freshman & transfers; Charles Schmidt, perform. & grades; Kevin J. Dodson, perform. & grades; Departmental, perf. & grades; Wm Brown Endowment, perform. & grades; Erica Starr, musical thr-perf. & grades; Katie & E. Don Walker Scholarship, Nicholson-Bozeman Scholarship, perf. & grades.

FACULTY AND CLASSES OFFERED

8 Full-Time: 2 PT; 1 PhD, 7 MFA/MA; 3 Staff

A. (1 FT) Intro to Theatre-1/Y; Th Hist-2/Y; Shakes-1/X; Dramatic Criticism-1/Y; Playwriting-1/Y

B. (3 FT 2 PT) Acting-6/Y; Voice-2/Y; Mus Th-2/Y; Directing-2/Y; Film-1/O; Singing-X; Dance-X

C. (3 FT) Cost Des-2/Y; Tech Prod'n-2/Y; Set Design-1/Y; Lighting Des-2/Y; Cost Constr-1/Y; Make-up-2/Y; Stg Mgmt-1/Y

D. (1 FT) Box Office Procedure-1/Y; Dev/Grant Writing-X; Budgeting/Acctg-X

FACILITIES & PRODUCTIONS

MAINSTAGE: 396 seats, fly space, computerized lighting. Budget $3,000-5,000

SECOND STAGE: 100 seats, computerized lighting; budget $0-100 2 Workshops/Readings; 1 Fac dir, 1 guest dir; budget $0-100

Facility built in 1976, last renovated in 2002; includes rehearsal studio, 2 classrooms; Other facilities include a mainstage and showcase stage.

A non-departmental, student-run organization presents 2 productions per year in which dept. majors participate. 2 student-written plays produced in the last two years.

DESCRIPTION

Noted Faculty: Penelope Hasekoester, MFA Acting, Scriptwriting, Stage Mgmt, Improv, Theory & Crit; Tom Prior, MFA Speech, Directing; Thomas Soare, PhD, History, Appreciation; Maureen V. McIntyre, Acting, Directing, Kristina Hanssen, Costume Design, Make-up, Costume History; Don Childs, Lighting Design

Guest Artists: Mark Ramont, Director; Keith Caldwell, Actor; Dave Clements, Auditioning; Ann James, Acting; Jeff Lane, Acting.

The Theatre Program at Sam Houston State University is committed to a superior undergraduate education in theatre. A strong theoretical background is balanced with active practical participation which results in quality training, a good resume or portfolio, and helpful professional contacts. This preparation for the commercial or educational theatre provides a student with a variety of career choices upon graduating. A theatre major at Sam Houston first studies each area of the theatre to gain substantial knowledge of acting, technical theatre, costume and scenic design, stage makeup, history, criticism, and directing. From that background, a person can specialize in one of these areas with additional course work in drama, as well as in shows every semester. As they develop expertise in areas of their primary interest, they may design lights, sets, costumes and makeup for major productions. Guest productions and professional visitors provide students additional contacts with other people in professional theatre. Prospective students comparing both quality and cost of various universities will find our program especially attractive.

Southern Methodist University

Cecil O'Neal, Chair
Theatre Division
1164 Owens Art Center
Southern Methodist University
Dallas, TX 75275
FAX: (214) 768-1136
ADM: P.O. Box 750356, Dallas TX 75275-0356
http://www.smu.edu/meadows/

11,152 Total Enr.; h. compet.
Semester Sys.; 138 Majors
NAST, U/RTA, ATHE
T: $27,400/10,825 r&b
DEPT: (214) 768-2558
coneal@smu.edu
(214) 768-4326

DEGREES OFFERED

BFA in Theatre Studies (52); BFA/MFA in Acting (66) (12), MFA in Design/Directing (8). Declare major by end fresh. yr; 2004 granted 29 UG, 7 Grad degrs.

ADMISSION & FINANCIAL INFORMATION

SAT 1050+, ACT 27-28; GPA (avg.) 3.3; Inst accepts 70-75% of apps; Aud/Int/Portfolio required for UG & Grad; Accept 30-35 out of 900 UG, 10 out of 600 Grad; various artistic scholarships available, by audition.

FACULTY AND CLASSES OFFERED

10 FT 12 PT: 4 PhD, 14 MFA/MA, 4 w/o adv. degree; 3 Staff

A. (2 FT, 1 PT) Intro to Theatre-2/Y; Th Hist-2/Y; Dramatic Criticism-1/O; Dramatic Lit-1/O; Playwriting-4/Y

B. (5 FT, 4 PT) Acting-14/Y; Voice-10/Y; Mus Th-1/Y; Movement-16/Y; Singing-2/Y; Directing-8/Y; Stage Combat-2/Y; Improv-2/Y; Auditions-2/Y

C. (3 FT, 7 PT) Make-up-2/Y; Stg Mgmt-4/Y; Scene Painting-2/Y

FACILITIES AND PRODUCTIONS

MAINSTAGE: Bob Hope Th, 392 seats, prosc., fly space, comput.lighting. 4 prods: 4 Fac dir, 5 Fac des, 6 Guest des, 1 Grad des; budget $10,000-15,000

SECOND STAGE: Greer Garson Theatre, 386 seats, 3/4 thrust stage, computerized lighting . 4 prods: 2 Fac dir, 1 Fac des, 7 Guest des, *3-5 UG dir; budget $3,000-8,000.
* one slot is a 3-play rep. slot for student work.

THIRD STAGE: Margo Jones Theatre, 125 seats, black box, fly space, computerized lighting. 20+ UG dir Workshops/ Readings; budget 0-$300

Facility includes scene shop, costume shop, classrooms/rehearsal studios (spaces combined).

10 student-written plays produced in the last two years.

Connections with Dallas Theater Center (Eq.), Kitchen Dog Theatre (non-Eq.) Faculty are in company; students are cast.

DESCRIPTION

Noted Faculty: Claudia Stephens, Russell Parkman, Steve Woods, Design; Michael Connolly, Acting; Bill Lengfelder, Sara Romersberger, Movement; Rhonda Blair, Critical Studies; Cecil O'Neal, James Crawford, Leslie Brott, Acting; Gretchen Smith, Playwriting, Critical Studies; Virginia Ness Ray, Ashley Smith, Voice.

Guest Artists: Deb Margolin, Actress/Writer/Performance Artist; Patricia Richardson, Actress; Mark Medoff, Playwright; Caridad Svich, Playwright; Paula Vogel, Playwright; Mary Gallagher, Playwright; Jose Rivera, Playwright; Drew Fracher, Fight/Combat Specialist; Carl Forsman, Richard Foreman, Leah Gardiner,

Directors; Ming Cho Lee, Design; Henry Woronicz, Acting/Directing.

Our rigorous, professionally-tracked theatre curriculum is grounded in a substantial liberal arts education. Students prepare for an engagement with theatre and the broader world by intensively studying acting, directing, playwriting, critical studies, design and/or stage management, while completing significant general studies. Our faculty is active professionally, and we regularly host guests from the profession and the academy. Our staff and facilities are first-rate. We seek intelligent, passionate students who will make theatre that celebrates our relationships and connections with each other and meet the highest standards of excellence and creativity in theatre and performance. We seek students who reflect the diversity of our culture. Representative alumni include Oscar-winner Kathy Bates; Pulitzer-winner Beth Henley; Tony-winners Debra Monk, John Arnone, and Scott Warra; Garland Wright, Regina Taylor, Steve Tobolowsky, Patricia Richardson, and Powers Booth.

Southwestern University

Rick Roemer, Chair & Art Dir
Theatre
Southwestern University
1001 E. University Ave.
Georgetown, TX 78626
DEPT PHONE/FAX: 863-1422
ADM: (512) 863-1200
PO Box 770 Georgetown, TX 78627-0770
admission@southwestern.edu

1,200 Total Enr.; h. compet.
Semester System
50 Majors; ATHE
T: $25,740/$8,440 R&B
SMALL PROGRAM
roemerr@southwestern.edu
FAX: (512) 863-9601

http://www.southwestern.edu

DEGREES OFFERED

BFA in Design & Technology (3), Acting (12), Musical Theatre; BA in Theatre (35). Declare major in sophomore year.

ADMISSION & FINANCIAL INFORMATION

Most admitted students rank in the top 10% of their HS class and avg. over 1200 on SAT. 72% of applics admitted to inst.; Th prog admits 12 out of 30; req's aud/interview/portfolio. Aud./portfolio req'd for scholarships

FACULTY AND CLASSES OFFERED

6 FT: 3 PhD, 3 MFA/MA; 2 staff: Technical Director, Master Electrician

A. (1 FT) Intro to Theatre-1/Y; Theatre History-2/Y; Shakes-1/X; Dramatic Lit-1/Y; Dramatic Criticism-2/Y; Playwriting-1/O

B. (2 FT) Acting-5/Y; Movement-1/Y; Singing-1/X; Directing-2/Y; Voice/Speech-1/Y; Musical Theatre-3/Y; Dance-4/Y; Alexander Technique-1/Y.

C. (3 FT) Prins of Des-1/Y; Set Des-2/Y; Cost Des- 1/Y; Lighting Des-2/Y; Cost Construction-1/Y; Make-up-1/Y; Stage Mgmt-1/Y

D. Arts Mgmt-1/O

FACILITIES AND PRODUCTIONS

MAINSTAGE: 840 seats, fly space, comput. & electronic lighting 4prods: 2 Fac dir, 3 Fac des, 1 GA dir; 1 UG dir/des; budget $3,000-6,000

SECOND STAGE: 325 seats, fly space, computerized & electronic lighting. 3 prods: 3UG dir, 3 UG des; budget $500-1,500

THIRD STAGE: 75 seats, black box, electronic lighting.

Facility built in 1993; includes scene shop, costume shop, prop shop, sound studio, CAD facility, dance studio, design studio, rehearsal studio, classrooms.

A non-departmental, student-run organization produces 3 productions a year in which majors generally participate.

Two student-written plays produced in the last two years.

DESCRIPTION

Noted Faculty: Rick Roemer, Acting, Directing, Musical Theatre; Kathleen Juhl, Alexander Technique, Performance Studies; Sergio Costola, Th. History, Dramatic Literature/Criticism; John Ore, Lighting Design; Kerry Bechtel, Cost Des, Cost Constr; Desiderio Roybal, Scenic Des., Scene Painting.

Guest Artists: Elena Aaroz, Directing; Dennis Whitehead, Musical Director; Tony Kushner, guest lecturer.

The Theatre Department provides students with a solid and comprehensive critical, historical and artistic education in theatre performance, design, playwriting, literature and theory. An important focus of the curriculum is on the detailed study of theatre as a cultural and artistic phenomena that has flourished in many different forms and contexts throughout the world. Students are trained rigorously and practically in both the intellectual foundations and in the arts and crafts of the theatre. The Department places importance on enhancing the cultural and intellectual life of the Southwestern University and central Texas communities through presenting thought-provoking, challenging and entertaining theatrical productions. While presenting theatre to the public is a vital activity of the department, the curriculum and production program has been designed to encourage students to become intelligent, insightful and compassionate theatre artists, technicians, managers, scholars and teachers. The Department is dedicated to teaching theatre as a vital academic discipline within a liberal arts context where the student theatre artist and scholar begins to develop a life-long passion and commitment to being an advocate for the arts.

To that end, the Theatre Department offers a comprehensive plan of study that focuses on performance, design, playwriting, history, literature and theory. This foundation provides a student of the theatre with the option to focus on a specialized area of professional theatre training (BFA) or a solid, comprehensive plan of theatre study (BA). The BFA is intended to serve only those seeking an intensive program of theatre studies. Options: BFA (musical theatre); BFA (design/technology); BFA (acting). The BA is intended to serve those wishing to acquire a general liberal arts degree which can lead to work in a wide variety of fields in graduate schools or combined with Southwestern's education courses, can lead to teacher certification. BA (liberal arts education); BA (liberal arts education/teacher certification).

Stephen F. Austin State University ····

Scott Shattuck, Director
Theatre Department, Box 6090
Stephen F. Austin State Univ.
75962
DEPT: (936) 468-4003

12,000
150 Majors, NAST, ATHE
T: $5,232/Nacogdoches, TX
O-ST T: 13,482/ $6,544 R&B

FAX: (936) 468-7601
www.finearts.sfasu.edu/theatre   shattucksh@sfasu.edu
ADMISSIONS: SFA Station Box 13051   (936) 468-2504
admissions@sfasu.edu   (800) 259-9732
www.sfasu.edu   FAX: (936) 468-3849

DEGREES OFFERED

BA in Theatre-General (40), Theatre-Teacher Certification (40); BFA in Acting/Directing (60), Design/Tech (20);American Theatre Arts (22).

ADMISSION & FINANCIAL INFORMATION

1st Quarter - No minimum scores; 2nd Quarter - SAT: 850, ACT: 18; 3rd Quarter - SAT: 1050, ACT: 23; 4th Quarter - SAT 1250, ACT:28. Theatre program admits all UG. Auditions req. for scholarships. Please contact the Dept. of Theatre for additional information.

FACULTY AND CLASSES OFFERED

9 1/2 Full-Time: 3 PhD, 6 MFA/MA; 3 Staff

A. (2 1/2 FT) Intro to Theatre-8/Y; Dramatic Lit-1/2/YX; Th Hist-3/Y; Shakes-1/X; Dramatic Criticism-2/Y; Playwriting-1/Y

B. (3 FT) Acting-3/Y; Voice/Speech-2/Y; Movement-2/Y; Singing-1/X; Directing-2/Y; Dance-6/X; Mus. Th-1/Y; Stage Combat-1/Y

C. (1 1/2) Prins of Des-1/Y; Cost Des-2/Y; Tech Prod'n-2/Y; Costume History-1/Y; Set Design-2/Y; Lighting Des-2/Y; Cost Constr-1/Y; Make-up-2/Y; Stg Mgmt-1/Y

D. (1/2) No courses listed.

FACILITIES & PRODUCTIONS

MAINSTAGE: 1,100 seats, fly space, computer & electronic lighting. 7 prods: 6 Fac dir, 1 Guest dir; budget $4,000-6,000

SECOND STAGE: 75 seats, electronic lighting. 8 prods, 8 UG dir; budget $0-500

THIRD STAGE: 100 seats, black box, electron lighting. 12 UG dir Workshops/Readings; budget $100-3,000

Facility built in 1984; includes scene shop, costume shop, prop shop, welding shop, CAD facility, movement/dance studio, design studio, 2 rehearsal studios, 6 classrooms, green room, dressing rooms, dye room, laundry, scenic, cost, props storage.

A non-departmental, student-run, producing org. presents 20 productions per yr. in which dept. majors participate. 4-5 student-written plays produced in the last two years.

Connection with Milwaukee Repertory Theatre, Theatre Three, Climb, Dallas Children's Theatre Center, Arizona Theatre Co. We offer professional internships with over 120 nationally recognized theatres, including the five listed above.

DESCRIPTION

Noted Faculty: C.W. Bahs, Directing, Theory/Crit., Hist; Alan Nielson, Playwriting, Theory & Criticism, History; Allen Oster, Acting, Dialects, Speech & Voice; R.C. Jones III, History; Angela Bacarisse, Costume Design; Shari Watterston, Lecturer; Tomy Matthys, Scenic Design, Lighting Des.; Playwright-in-Residence Jack Heifner; Juanita Finkenberg, Movement.

Guest Artists: Wilfred Harrison: United Kingdom, Actor, Director, Playwright; Terry Long, Director, Actor; Richard Rehse, Director; Michael Ouimet, Actor; Susan Arnold, Actor; Jean Waldera/Laura Gordon/Thomas Dalton/Stephanie Cozart.

The SFA theatre program is dedicated to the training of those students who are interested in the theatre profession (performance, design, or technical theatre), teacher certification, or simply desire a major strongly based in a liberal arts tradition. The department provides an atmosphere in which young artists/students are nourished and their talents developed by an outstanding and committed faculty. The Department provides a comprehensive curriculum which will allow students to pursue a wide range of career options.

Sul Ross State University

Dona Roman,Dir.
Dept. of Fine Arts &
  Communications
Box C-43
Sul Ross State University
Alpine, TX 79832
DEPT: (915) 837-8220
FAX: (915) 837-8376
admissions@sulross.edu

2,600 Total Enr.; non-compet.
25 Majors;
Semester System
T: $4,336/$4,260 R&B
O-ST T: $12,586/$4,260 R&B
SMALL PROGRAM
MAIN: (915) 837-8050
www.sulross.edu

DEGREES OFFERED
BA in General Th (20), Th Ed. w/ Cert. (5), MEd (2)
Declare major in soph. year.

ADMISSION & FINANCIAL INFORMATION
Inst reqs. ACT 20, SAT comb. 920, or top 1/2 half HS class; admits 90% of applicants; no special reqs for theatre program. Academic, course, and talent schols available, for further info contact Adm Office; selection based on merit and departmental or group/sponsor rec.

FACULTY AND CLASSES OFFERED
4 Full-Time: 1 PhD, 3 MA/MFA; 5 Staff

A. (1 1/2 FT) Intro to Theatre-3/Y; Dramatic Lit-3/X; Th Hist-2/O; Dramatic Criticism-1/O; Shakes-1/X; Playwriting-1/O

B. (1 1/2 FT) Acting-4/Y; Voice/Speech-2/Y; Singing-3/X; Musical Th-2/Y; Directing-2/O; Mvmt-1/O; Stg Combat-1/O; Child. Th.-2/Y

C. (1/2 FT) Tech Prod'n-4/Y; Cost Constr-1/O; Make-up-1/O

D. (1/2 FT) Arts Management-1/O

FACILITIES AND PRODUCTIONS
MAINSTAGE: 702 seats, fly space, computerized lighting. 7 prod: 4 Fac dir,1 Grad dir,3 ug dir,6Fac des,1ug des;bdgt $750-4,500

SECOND STAGE: 125 seats, electronic lighting.
  3 ug dir/des prods.; budget $200-500

THIRD STAGE: 400 seats, computerized lighting
  4 Workshops./Readings: 2 Fac dir, 2 ug dir, 4 ug des.

Facility built in 1930, last renovated in 1980 & 1993; includes scene, costume shops, sound, video, 3 rehearsal studios, 4 classrooms.

A non-departmental student-run organization produces 2 plays/year in which majors participate.

DESCRIPTION
The Sul Ross Theatre Program is designed to give the student opportunities in a wide range of dramatic experi-

ences. This general foundation will afford the Drama major many valuable experiences in all aspects of theatre with which s/he can pursue many career choices: educational theatre, theatre management, community theatre or graduate school. The theatre student is guaranteed an opportunity to act, direct, design, stage manage, choreograph and learn in a year-long theatre program that produces many stage productions as well as radio theatre performances.

Texas A & M University

Theatre Dept Head
Theater Arts Program
Texas A&M University
152 John R. Blocker Bldg.
College Station, TX 77843-4248
DEPT: (979) 845-2588
MAIN: (979) 845-2621

36,580 Total Enr.
Semester System
50 Majors, U/RTA, ATHE
T: $7,335/$7,660 R&B
O-ST T: $15,675./$7,660 R&B
www.tamu.edu
admissions@tamu.edu

DEGREES OFFERED
BA Basic Theatre Degree (75) Declare major in freshman year.

ADMISSION & FINANCIAL INFORMATION
If top 10% HS, no min. SAT/ACT; If first quarter HS, SAT min 1000, ACT min 24; If 2nd qtr HS, SAT min 1100, ACT min 27; 3rd & 4th qtr, SAT min 1200, ACT 29; no special reqs. for theatre program; $500-2500 annual awards based on merit (academic/performance), 2 letters of recomm. reqd.

FACULTY AND CLASSES OFFERED
8 Full-Time,4 PhD, 3 MFA, 1 MA

A. (3 FT) Intro to Theatre-1/Y; Dramatic Lit-2/X; Th Hist-3/Y;

B. (3 FT) Acting-3/Y; Voice/Speech-1/Y; Directing-1/Y

C. (2 FT) Prins of Des-1/O; Set Des.-1/O; Cost Des.-1/Y; Lighting Des-1/O; Cost. Constr-1/O; TechProd-2/Y; Cost Hist-1/O;Make-up-1/Y

FACILITIES & PRODUCTIONS
MAINSTAGE: 250 seats, computerized lighting. 4 prods: Fac or Guest Artist dir, 2 Fac or Guest Artist des, 2 UG des; budget $3,000-8,000

SECOND STAGE: 60 seats

3-5 prods: 1 Fac dir/des, 4 UG dir/des; budget $500-1,500

Facility built in 1972; includes scene, costume, props shop, computer lab, rehearsal studio, design studio, classrooms.

A non-departmental, student-run prod. org. presents 2 prods. per year in which DEPT. majors participate. 3 student-written plays produced in the last two years.

DESCRIPTION

Theater is one of the oldest and most widespread forms of cultural activity; its uniquely broad compass includes the whole the liberal and fine arts. The mission of the program in Theater Arts at Texas A&M University is to insure that this essential cultural heritage is adequately represented in meeting the educational, research, and service obligations of the College of Liberal Arts. To carry out this mission, we are dedicated to four major objectives: (1) To provide a broad humanistic education, centered on the study of Theatre Arts, which also can prepare those students with plans for a career in theater for more advanced study. (2) To offer to all students opportunities for creative development and personal expression through theatrical productions. (3) To produce high-quality theatrical performances for the benefit and enrichment of the entire University community. (4) To support continued and intense faculty involvement in professional artistic work, scholarly research, and creative activity, including the exploration of both current and historical possibilities for theatrical expression as well as the creation of new methodologies and art forms.

Texas A & M University - Commerce

John Hanners, Head	5,263 Total Enr.; competitive
Mass Media, Comm &	35 Majors
Theatre Department, PO Box 3011	ATHE, SWTA, TETA
Texas A&M Univ.- Commerce	Semester System
Commerce, TX 75429-3011	T: $5,190/$6,340
(903) 886-5336	O-ST T: $13,440/$6,340
FAX: (903) 468-3250	John_Hanners@tamu-commerce.edu
ADMISSIONS:PO Box 3011	(903) 886-5081
FAX: (903) 886-5888	www.tamu-commerce.edu

DEGREES OFFERED

BA, BS, MA, MS in Acting (25), Design (8), Theory/Crit (10). Declare major any year.

ADMISSION & FINANCIAL INFORMATION

SAT or ACT, upper 50% of class. 85% accepted to inst. Inter-view, portfolio for designers req. for Grad. program. Theatre program admits 14 out of 21 UG, 8 out of 15 Grad. applicants. Scholarships from univ. and foundations, selected by faculty.

FACULTY AND CLASSES OFFERED

8 Full-Time: 4 PhD, 4 MFA/MA; 1 Staff

A. (3 FT) Intro to Theatre-1/Y; Dramatic Lit-1/O; Th Hist-4/Y; Shakes-2/X; Dramatic Criticism-1/O; Playwriting-2/Y

B. (2 1/2 FT) Acting-4/Y; Voice/Speech-3/Y; Movement-1/X; Singing-1/X; Directing-2/Y; Dance-5/X

C. (2 FT) Prins of Des-2/Y; Cost Des-1/O; Tech Prod'n-2/Y; Set Design-1/Y; Lighting Des-1/Y; Make-up-1/O

D. (1 1/2 FT) Arts Management-1/O

FACILITIES & PRODUCTIONS

MAINSTAGE: 304 seats, fly space, computerized lighting. 4 prods: 3 Fac dir, 4 Fac des, 1 UG dir; $4,000-7,500

SECOND STAGE: 100 seats, computerized lighting. 6 prods: 1 Fac des, 2 Grad dir, 3 Grad des, 4 UG dir, 2 UG des; budget $500-1,500

THIRD STAGE: 1,700 seats, fixed stage, electron lighting. Workshops/Readings: budget $150

Facility built in 1978, renovated 1997; includes scene, costume shops, sound studio, video studio, classrooms.

3 student-written plays produced in the last two years.

DESCRIPTION

Noted Faculty: James T. Anderson, Playwriting, Anne Bomar, Acting, Intro, Oral Interp, Voice & Phonetics; Gary Burton, Design and Technical Theatre; Bethany Banister, John Hanners, History, Criticism, Acting.

Guest Artists: Andy Fitch, Designer, Tina Fitch, Director,

Lisa Vollrath, Costume, Jerry Biggs, Actor.

Texas A&M University-Commerce prepares students for careers in Theatre, film and television and in teaching, particularly at the college level. Students go on to professional careers in theatre, film and tv (the department houses a fully operational radio-television division with a broadcasting studio and two radio stations), teach at the secondary, junior college and university levels. The department houses a professional troupe: Cricket City Improv. Former students have appeared in dozens of films, including Tender Mercies, Lonesome Dove, Silverado and many tv dramas. Others have founded theatres such as the world famous Trinity Rep in Providence, Apple Street, Inc; the Kitchen Dog theatre and others. It is a rigorous program with a strong reputation for turning out theatre professionals and educators.

Texas State University-San Marcos

John Fleming, Chairman	26,500 Total Enr.; compet.
Dept. of Theatre & Dance	Semester System
Texas State Univ.	330 Majors
601 University Drive	T: $3,000
San Marcos, TX 78666-4616	O-ST T: $7,000/$6,000 R&B
DEPT: (512) 245-2147	www.theatreanddance.txstate.edu

DEGREES OFFERED

BA in General Theatre (40); BFA in Acting (60), Design/Tech (40), Performance & Production (100), Musical Theatre (20), Teacher Certification (40); MA in History/Criticism (8), Directing (8),Playwriting (4). Declare major in soph. year; 2006 granted 80 UG & 8 Grad degrees.

ADMISSION & FINANCIAL INFORMATION

ACT of 22 or SAT of 900, lower if in top 10% or next 15% of class; 35% of apps admitted to inst; Th prog admits all applicants to UG, 4 out of 5 to G; GRE & GPA for Grad admission. James. G. Barton Scholarship: ACT or SAT, letter of rec. Theatre Alumni Scholarship: GPA, participation, letters of rec. Fine Arts Scholarship: GPA, Rotary Club Scholarship: GPA.

FACULTY AND CLASSES OFFERED

16 Full-Time: 6 PhD, 11 MFA/MA, 1 Prof. w/o adv. degree

A. (2 1/2) Theatre History-2/Y; Shakes-2/X; Dramatic Lit-2/Y; Dramatic Criticism-2/Y; Playwriting-1/Y

B. (7 1/2 FT) Acting/Scene Study-12/Y; Movement-2/Y; Singing-4/X; Directing-3/Y; Voice/Speech-3/Y; Musical Theatre-5/Y

C. (3 FT) Prins of Design-1/Y; Set Des-2/Y; Cost Design- 1/Y; Cost Hist-1/Y; Ltg Des-2/Y; Cost Const-1/Y; Make-up-1/Y

FACILITIES AND PRODUCTIONS

MAINSTAGE: 350 seats, fly space, comput. & electronic lighting. 5 prods: 5 Fac dir, 1 Fac des; budget $7,000-10,000

SECOND STAGE: 80 seats, electronic lighting. 4 Grad dir prods; budget $300-500

Facility built in 1971; includes scene, cost shop, sound studio, 2 rehearsal studios, 5 classrooms, computer drafting lab.

A departmental student-run organization present 3-4 full length plays and 6 short plays per year

Three student-written plays produced in the last two years.

DESCRIPTION

Noted Faculty: Laura Lane, Acting; Chuck Ney, Michael Costello, Acting and Dir; Michele Ney, Scene Design; Sheila Margett, Costume Des; Darren McCroom, Light Des; John Fleming, Theatre History & Playwriting; Richard Sodders, Dir; Chuck Pascoe, Children's Theatre; Debra Charlton, Shakespeare & Dramaturgy.

Guest Artists: Artist in Residence, Eugene Lee, member of SAG, AFTRA, Equity. David Nancarrow, Pip Gordon, Light Des; Catherine Fitzmaurice, Voice; Richard Brestoff, Dorothy Lyman, Anthony Chisholm, Acting; GW Edwards, Romulus Linney, Playwriting; Richard Isaackes, Scene Des; Joe Luis Cedillo, Playwriting and Dramaturgy.

Since 2001, Texas State has sent at least one student each year to the Kennedy Center as a National Finalist in The American College Theatre Festival. We also do an annual Showcase in NY for agents and casting directors, and have a Study Abroad Program with the Royal Shakespeare Institute. While maintaining its strong reputation for training teachers, the Department of Theatre at Texas State University prepares students for work in all areas of the discipline. Our graduates are active in professional theatre from coast to coast. Those who have become successful on the stage and in film return to the campus to conduct workshops and to share their experiences with current students. The theatre faculty are determined to provide a stimulating and creative environment in which students may deepen their aesthetic experience as well as their knowledge of theatre skills and principles.

Texas Tech University

Frederick B. Christoffel, Chair
Dept. of Theatre & Dance
Texas Tech University
P. O. Box 42061
Lubbock, TX 79409-2061
DEPT:: (806) 742-3601
fred.christoffel@ttu.edu   FAX: (806) 742-1338
ADMISSIONS: MS 45015 100 West Hall, Lubbock TX 79409-5015.
(806) 742-3661   FAX: (806) 742-0355
www.ttu.edu   admissions@ttu.edu

22,851 Total Enr.; not compet.
102 Maj; ATHE, SWTA, TETA
Semester System, ACDFA
T: $6,783/$7,846
O-ST T: $15,123/$7,846

DEGREES OFFERED

BA in Theatre Arts (57), Dance (26); BFA in Acting/Directing (7); Design Tech (2); MA in Theatre Arts (1); MFA in Theatre (24); PhD in Fine Arts (interdisciplinary) (30). Declare major in sophomore year;

ADMISSION & FINANCIAL INFORMATION

SAT or ACT, class rank, GPA, GRE. Letters of rec., writing sample, statement of purpose for MA, MFA, PhD. 74% of applics accepted by instit. Audition, portfolio for designers req. for UG program, Interview, portfolio req. for Grad program. Theatre program admits 20 out of 25 UG, 10-15 out of 20 Grad. applicants. Scholarships from College of Visual & Performing as well as DEPT: Scholarships Selection for latter are GPA, service to dept, need, recommendation, field of study. Grad students may also apply for Teaching Assistantships.

FACULTY AND CLASSES OFFERED

10 FT: 6 PhD, 4 MFA/MA, 3 Prof. w/out adv. degree; 4 Staff

A. (2 FT) Intro to Theatre-2/Y; Th Hist-7/Y; Shakes-X; Dramatic Criticism-5/Y; Playwriting-3/Y; Cinema-1/Y

B. (3 FT) Acting-11/Y; Voice/Speech-2/Y; Movement-2/Y; Directing-4/Y; Dance-14/Y; Mus Th.-X; Singing-X

C. (2 FT) Prins of Des-1/O; Cost Des-2/O; Cost Const-1/Y; Set Des-3/Y; Lighting Des-3/Y; Make-up-1/Y; Stage Mgmt-1/O

D. (1 FT) Arts Management-4/Y; Marketing/Promo-2/Y; Development-1/O

E. (2 FT) Dance

FACILITIES & PRODUCTIONS

MAINSTAGE: 398 seats, fly space, computerized lighting. 5 prods: 5 Fac dir, 3 Fac des, 3 Grad des, 1-2 UG des; $3,000-5,000

SECOND STAGE: 98 seats, computerized & electronic ltg. 12 prods: 8 Grad dir, 4 Grad des, 4 UG dir/des; budget $200-400

Facility built in 1966, renovted 1984; includes scene, costume shops, CAD facility, 1 dance studio, 1 design studio.

12 student-written plays produced in the last two years.

Connection with Angel Fire Summmer Theatre (New Mexico). Opportunity to direct, act and stage manage the productions that originate in our summer season and then travel to Angel Fire, NM.

DESCRIPTION

Noted Faculty: Norman A. Bert, Playwriting; Frederick. B. Christoffel, Th. Des & Planning, Stage Craft; Jonathan Marks, Dir; Linda Donahue, Th Mgmt; David Williams, Th. History, Theory, Criticism; Bill Gelber, Acting; Andrea Bilkey, Light & Sound; Melissa Merz, Costume.

Guest Artists: Respondents: Jack Adler, Richard Hamburger, Carole Brandt, Carlos Morton, Carlos Morton, C. Lee Turner, Stephen Peters. Max Bondar, Dancer, Elizabeth Kendall, Debra Sayle-Senchak, NJ Ballet, Dancer.

The Department of Theatre and Dance at Texas Tech University provides solid academic education and pre-professional theatre training in a production-intensive atmosphere. Concentrations are available in acting/directing, design/tech, playwriting, history/criticism, and theatre management. The department produces 5 faculty-directed plays and a dance show annually in its 400-seat, proscenium arch, main-stage theatre and 4 student-directed shows in its summer repertory season of 3 to 5 student-directed plays. Alumni of the department go on to further graduate work or directly into professional careers. Graduates of the programs work as professional actors, designers, and stage managers on both coasts and in regional theatre around the country; they alsowork in other entertainment-related careers such as film producers, casting directors, talent agents, and dance companies; they also work as theatre and dance professionals in public schools, dance studios, amusement parks, fitness centers, and universities.

University of Dallas

Patrick Kelly, Chairman
Drama Department
University of Dallas
1845 E. Northgate Dr.
Irving, TX 75062-4799
DEPT: (972) 721-5061

1,180 Total Enr.; h. compet.
Semester System
55 Majors; ATHE
T: $21,819/$7,614 R&B PER SEM
SMALL PROGRAM
FAX: (972) 721-5302

drama@udallas.edu   www.udallas.edu/drama/
ADMISSIONS: 1845 E. Northgate Dr. Irving, TX 75062-4736
(972) 721-5266   FAX: (972) 721-5017
www.udallas.edu   unadmis@acad.udallas.edu

DEGREES OFFERED

BA in Drama (50). Declare major in junior year;
2004 granted 19 degrees.

ADMISSION & FINANCIAL INFORMATION

Avg. SAT-1120; Avg. ACT-26-27; top half of class. Accept 85% into inst; no special req's. for th. prog. Wide spectrum of fin. asst. Substantial Theatre Schols are available. Awarded based on participation in auditions scheduled annually in Feb.

FACULTY AND CLASSES OFFERED

5 Full-Time, 3 MFA/MA

A. (1 1/2 FT) Dra Lit-2/Y; Th Hist-2/Y; Shakes-4/X; Playwtg-1/O
B. (1/2 FT, 1 PT) Acting-2/Y; Singing-2/X; Directing-2/Y; Mime, mask-1/O
C. (2 FT) Prins of Des-1/Y; StageCraft-1/Y; Make-up-1/O

FACILITIES & PRODUCTIONS

MAINSTAGE: 80 seats, computerized lighting. 17 prods: 2 Fac dir/des, 15 UG dir/des; budget $2-4,000.

Theatre was built in 1972, renovated in 1989; includes scene, cost, prop shops, rehearsal studio.

4 student-written plays produced in the last two years.

Connection with Dallas Theater Center. Positions from volunteer scene shop assistants to management interns to assistants to artistic and managing directors are regularly filled by U.D. drama students.

DESCRIPTION

Noted Faculty: Patrick Kelly, Director, History; Judith French Kelly, Literature, TV Producer; Mary McClung, Design, Production; Tristan Decker, StageCraft, Lighting; Chamblee Ferguson, Acting.
Guest Artists: William Gaskill, Director.

The established and effective sequence of courses at the University of Dallas provides the necessary theoretical grounding through theatre history, acting, the study of plays, interpretation directing, tech theatre and criticism. Concurrently, University Theater productions of classic plays supply a continuing practical arena in which specific challenges of actual performance test and expand the classroom's theory. Graduates of the program, having completed graduate school or professional training (often in the most competitive settings), are meeting with success in the varied fields of acting, directing, design, tech production, management, actor-training, film, radio and television, and elementary and secondary school teaching. The classical examination of the aesthetic of theater combines with the application of modern production practice to make the UD Drama graduate an educated professional rather than a trained specialist, a theater person whose insight, originality and imagination have been developed along with his basic skills.

University of Houston

Steven W. Wallace, Dir.
School of Theatre
University of Houston
133 Wortham
Houston, TX 77204-4016
DEPT: (713) 743-3003
FAX: (713) 743-2648
ADMISSIONS: Office of Admissions 212 E. Cullen Building
Houston, TX 77204.   (713) 743-1010
/www.uh.edu   admissions@uh.edu

27,400 Total Enr.; not compet.
Semester System
191 Majors; ATHE
T: $$6,909/$6,418 R&B
O-ST T: $15,159/$6,418 R&B
sjudice@uh.edu

DEGREES OFFERED

BA in Theatre (90); MA/MFA in Acting (48), Directing (49), Costume Design (2), Scene Design (2), Lighting Design (2), Playwriting (1), Declare major any year

ADMISSION & FINANCIAL INFORMATION

UG- ACT, SAT, GPA. Graduate-GRE, GPA. Accepts 80% to institution; 100% UG, 85% Grad; very few Drama Scholarships, write for info.

FACULTY AND CLASSES OFFERED

10 Full-Time: 2 PhD, 5 MFA/MA, 1 Prof. w/o adv. degree; 8 Staff

A. (2 FT) Intro to Th-1/Y; Th Hist-2/Y; Dra Crit-1/Y; Playwtg-3/Y
B. (3 FT) Acting-5/Y; Voice/Speech-1/Y; Movement-2/Y; Mime, etc.-2/Y; Directing-3/Y; Stage Combat-2/Y
C. (3 FT) Set Design-1/Y; Cost Des-1/O; Lighting Des-1/Y; Costume History-1/Y; Make-up-1/Y; Stage Mgmt-1/O; Musical Theatre

FACILITIES & PRODUCTIONS

MAINSTAGE: 566 seats, fly space, computerized lighting. 8 prods: 3 Fac dir/des, 1 Fac dir/Guest des; budget $7,000-12,000
SECOND STAGE: flexible seating, computerized lighting. 1 Fac dir prod; budget $7,000-9,000. 4-5 Workshops/ Readings, Fac and Grad dir, Grad des; budget $2-3,000

Facility was built in 1977; includes scene shop, costume shop, sound studio, rehearsal studio.

A non-departmental, student-run, producing organization presents 4-8 productions per year, in which majors generally participate.

Connection with Alley Theatre, a professional, Equity company; graduate students can do internships there, co-produce.

DESCRIPTION

Noted Faculty: Edward Albee teaches 2 classes each spring; Stuart Ostrow teaches two musical theatre classes in the fall and one in the spring, Sir Peter Hall teaches one semester per year.

The University of Houston School of Theatre basic philosophy is that it serves as a pre-professional program, designed to prepare students for either further conservatory work, allied fields or the profession itself. It assumes the position that production work is co-curricular and that fully professional theatre projects must co-exist with the curricular program. We currently produce Houston Shakespeare Festival and Children's Theatre Festival, the former on an Equity letter of agreement, among other professional projects in support of this view.

University of the Incarnate Word

Bryn Jameson, Chair
Dept of Theatre
4301 Broadway/CPO #66
Univ. of the Incarnate Word
San Antonio, TX 78209-6397
www.uiw.edu
jameson@uiwtx.edu
ADMISSIONS: Univ. of the Incarnate Word, 4301 Broadway, San
Antonio, TX 78209
FAX: (210) 829-3921

4,000 Tot. Enr.; compet.
58 Majors; NAST, ATHE
Semester System
T: $13,400/*$4,780 (dbl) R&B
DEPT: (210) 829-3810
FAX: (210) 283-5026

(210) 829-6005
www.uiw.edu/adm

DEGREES OFFERED

BA in Theatre Arts (58). Declare major in freshman year;
2004 granted 11 degrees.

ADMISSION & FINANCIAL INFORMATION

SAT 850+, ACT 18+, GPA 2.0 min.; 81% accepted to inst; Th. prog
admits 95%; THAR Performance Scholarships range from $500-
4,000/yr, renewable for up to 4 yrs, selected by aud/port review.

FACULTY AND CLASSES OFFERED

4 FT, 2 PT: 3 PhD, 3 MFA/MA, 1 profession without advanced
   degree; 1 Staff

A. (2 PT) Intro to Theatre-2/Y; Dramatic Lit-3/O; Dramatic Crit-1/O;
   Th Hist-2/Y; Shakes-1/X; Playwriting-1/O

B. (2 FT) Acting-4/Y; Voice/Speech-2/O; Movement-1/Y; Singing-4/X;
   Directing-1/Y; Dance-8/X; Musical Th-2/X; Stage Combat-1/O

C. (2 FT) Principles of Design-1/Y; Cost Des-1/O; Tech Prod'n-1/Y;
   Stage Management-1/O; Set Des-1/O; Lighting Des-1/O; Cost
   Constr-1/Y; Make-up-1/O

D. Arts Management-1/O.

FACILITIES & PRODUCTIONS

MAINSTAGE: 270 seats, fly space, electronic & computerized lighting:
   2-4 Fac dir, 4-8 Fac des, 1 Guest dir, 2 Guest des, 2-4 UG des;
   budget $10,000-$13,000.

SECOND STAGE: 75-100 seats, electronic lighting: 2-4 Fac dir, 4-8 Fac
   des, 1-2 GA dir, 4-8 GA des; 1-2 UG dir, 4-8 UG des; budget
   $3,000-5,000

Workshops/Readings: 1-2 UG dir, 2-4 UG des; budget $1,000-2,000

Facility built in 1980, renovated in 1997; includes scene shop, cost.
   shop, prop shop, welding shop, CAD facility, mvmt/dance studio,
   rehearsal studio, design studio, 3 classrooms.

A non-departmental, student-run producing org. presents 1 production
   per year in which dept majors participate.

One student-written play produced in the last two years.

DESCRIPTION

Noted Faculty: Dr. Robert Ball, Acting/Directing/Theatre
   Hist.; Margaret Mitchell, Costume Design, Costume
   History & Construction; Bryn Jameson, Acting,
   Directing, Voice; Donald Fox, Set and Light Des

Guest Artists: Arnulfo Maldonado, Scene Design;
   Melissa Gaspar, Light Design; Robin Payne, taught
   Voice Master Class, Director; Rene Garza, Sound
   Design; Halka, Performance Art, taught workshop;
   David Maj, taught puppetry workshop.

The Department of Theatre Arts at the University of the
Incarnate Word provides its majors with a strong foundation in the performing arts, enabling them to pursue
educational and professional opportunities in theatre.
Students learn different aspects of theatre and their relationships to each other in a diverse environment. We
support our university's mission by fostering in all students a life-long appreciation for creativity, and by
enriching the cultural, intellectual and spiritual lives of
our community through our production season. The
department's courses are closely tied to its production
season, wherein students have ample opportunity to
apply what they've learned in department courses.
Although our faculty has numerous professional theatre
credits, participate in international design exhibitions,
and publish well-respected scholarship, they put teaching first. Students find the faculty very accessible.

University of North Texas

Dr. Lorenzo Garcia, Chair
Dept of Dance and Theatre
PO Box 310607
University of North Texas
Denton, TX 76203
(940) 565-2211
data@unt.edu

30,000+ Total Enr.; not comp.
Semester System
275 Majors
T: $4,000/$5,250 R&B
O-T: $9,500/$5,250 R&B
FAX: (940) 565-4453
www.unt.edu

DEGREES OFFERED

BA in Theatre (267); BFA in Des/Tech (1), Musical Th. (6),
Performance (2). Declare major in any year. 2004 granted 25
degrees.

ADMISSION & FINANCIAL INFORMATION

Sliding scale compares HS class rank and SAT/ACT scores.
Students scoring lower than 950 SAT/20 ACT or in bottom quarter
of class subject to individual review. Audition & interview required for
theatre program. Portfolio for design. Four scholarships available for
theatre majors. Distribution is competitive based on GPA,
audition/portfolio and interview. Audition process in January for following school year.

FACULTY AND COURSES OFFERED

13 FT, 4 PT: 4 PhD, 10 MA/MFA, 5 Staff

A. (2 FT, 2 PT) Intro to Th-1/Y; Th Hist-2/Y; Dramatic Criticism-2/O;
   Playwriting-1/Y; Shakes-1/Y; Dramatic Lit-1/Y

B. (4 FT, 1 PT) Acting/Scene-1/Y; Voice/Speech-1/Y; Movement-1/Y;
   Music Th-1/Y; Directing-2/Y

C. (3 FT) Princ of Des-3/O; Set Des-1/O; Costume Des-1/O; Light
   Des-1/O; Costume Construc.-1/Y; Stage Mgmt-2/Y

D. (4 FT, 1 PT) Dance

FACILITIES AND PRODUCTIONS

MAINSTAGE: 478 seats, fly space, computerized lighting
5 prods: 4 Fac dir, 10 Fac des, 1 GA dir, 5 UG des; $2,000-10,000.
SECOND STAGE: 175 seats, fly space, electronic lighting
1 prod: 1 UG dir, 4 UG des; budget $200-500

Facility last renovated in 2001 now includes scene, costume, prop
and welding shops, sound studio, CAD facility, 3 movement studios,
2 rehearsal studios, 1 design studio, 1 classroom.
There is a non-dept student-run producing organization. They present 1-2 productions each school year. Dept. majors generally participate in this organization.

No connection with a professional theatre company but informal connections resulting from ongoing faculty/staff provide outside employment with area professional theatres.

DESCRIPTION

Noted Faculty: Barbara C. Cox, Costume Des; Dr. Lorenzo Garcia, Theatre for Youth, Theatre Ed; Dr. B. Donald Grose, Theatre History; Dr. Andrew Harris, Theatre History & Criticism, Playwriting; Marjorie Hayes, Acting & Directing; Sally Vahle, Acting; Dr. Timothy Wilson, Movement; Mario Tooch, Tech Dir; Dr. Mary Lynn Babcock, Movement and Dance

Guest Artists: Joel Ferrell, Dir; Rudy Eastman, Dir; Ed Brazo, Choreographer; Dr. Ralph Culp, Dir; Kerry Kreiman, Choreographer, Frank Barrow, Betty Ann Barrow, Dirs.

The University of North Texas, the College of Arts and Sciences and the Dept of Dance and Theatre promotes excellence by preparing students to find meaning within their lives as a result of actively engaging in dance/theatre scholarship, research, teaching, practice, and production. The theatre program at the University of North Texas offers a broad spectrum of education that prepares students for a full understanding of theatre in today's world. At the same time, the high standard of excellence maintained by the department guarantees a depth of study and a level of achievment adequate to prepare the student for a professional or academic career. With a faculty actively engaged in the professional aspects of their field, who are also scholars dedicated to working with students, the breadth of the program offers the opportunity to explore theatre in a broad context or to concentrate on a particular area.

University of Texas at Austin

See ad in back of book-U/RTA

Robert N. Schmidt, Interim Chair	48,000; competitive
Dept. of Theatre & Dance	Semester System
College of Fine Arts	400 Majors; NAST
University of Texas at Austin	T: $1,246 per cr. hr./per sem.
Austin, TX 78712	O-ST T: $3,988 per cr. hr./per sem.
DEPT: (512) 471-5793	FAX: (512) 471-0824
ADM: (512) 475-7399	www.utexas.edu

DEGREES OFFERED

BA in Theatre & Dance (227); BFA in Dance (26), in Th Studies (50); MFA in Directing (5), Playwriting (4), Acting (15), Design (18), Drama and Theatre for Youth (17), Theatre Tech (3); MA in Teacher Training (1); MA/PhD in Theatre Hist/Crit (29). Declare major in any year.

ADMISSION & FINANCIAL INFORMATION

TX Res: Top 10% of class, SAT 900 or ACT 22. Non Res.: SAT 1200 or ACT 29. Admit 3 out of 10 Grad apps. Aud/int/port. for theatre program. Merit Scholarships to UG and Grad majors; incoming & continuing students.

FACULTY AND CLASSES OFFERED

25 FT, 17 PT: 12 PhD, 22 MFA/MA, 8 Prof. w/o adv. degree, 8 Staff

A. (4 FT, 4 PT) Intro to Th.-2/Y; Th. History-3/Y; Dramatic Criticism-2/Y; Dramatic Lit-2/Y; Playwriting-5/Y

B. (5 FT, 5 PT) Acting-8/Y; Mvmt-4/Y; Directing-8/Y; Voice/ Speech-8/Y

C. (7 FT, 1 PT) Prin of Des-2/Y; Set Des-3/Y; Cost. Des-2/Y; Lighting Des-2/Y; Tech Prod-2/Y; Cost Const-2/Y; Cost Hist-1/Y; Make-up-1/Y; Stg Mgmt- 1/Y

D. (5 FT, 6 PT) Dance

FACILITIES & PRODUCTIONS

MAINSTAGE: 500 seats, fly space computerized lighting. 2 prods: 2 Fac dir, 1 Fac des, 1 Guest des: budget $7,000-8,000

SECOND STAGE: 200 seats, electronic lighting 3 prods: 3 Grad dir/des, 1 UG des; budget $200

THIRD STAGE: 150 seats, electronic lighting. 20 Workshps/ Readings: 10 UG dir, 10 Grad dir; budget $25-50

Facility built in 1964, renovated in 1976; includes scene shop, costume shop, welding shop, props shop, sound studio, video studio, 4 dance studios, 5 rehearsal studios, 2 design studios, 5 classrooms.

A non-departmental, student-run, producing organization presents 4 productions per year, in which majors generally participate. 20 student-written plays produced in the last two years.

Connection with Actors Repertory of Texas (Equity). Through internships, students will have opportunities to work with professional theatre artists of the highest quality.

DESCRIPTION

Noted Faculty: Oscar Brockett, Charlotte Canning, th hist/crit; Richard Isackes, David Nancarrow, Susan Tsu, Robert Schmidt, design; Coleman A. Jennings, Suzan Zeder, creative drama; Michael Bloom, directing; Sharon Vasques, dance.

Guest Artists: Anatoly Smeliansky, The Acting Company, Pina Bausch, Mabou Mines, Mel Shapiro, Romulus Linney, Paula Vogel.

The Department of Theatre & Dance exist as a community of artists and scholars committed to excellence and artistic/intellectual freedom. Through a laboratory for teaching, research, and creative endeavor, we promote innovation and risk-taking in a nurturing and collaborative environment. While preserving and honoring the diverse traditions of the past and present, we seek to shape the future by challenging ourselves and our society to consider the ever changing nature and function of performance.

University of Texas - El Paso

Dr. Joel Murray, Chair	19,800 Total Enr.; compet.
Dept of Theatre, Dance & Film	Semester System
University of Texas/El Paso	100 Majors; ATHE
500 W Univ Way, FFA 371D	
El Paso, TX 79968	T: $4,000
www.utep.edu/theatre	dept: (915) 747-5146
fax: (915) 747-5438	
adm: Academic Services Bldg, Room 102, El Paso, TX 79968	
(915) 747-5890	www.academics.utep.edu

DEGREES OFFERED

BA in Theatre/Design minor in Film; BFA in Dance; Music Theatre. Declare major in 1st year; 2000 granted 4 UG, 1

Grad degrees.

ADMISSION & FINANCIAL INFORMATION

UG req. 21-22 high academic prep. credits, be in the upper half of grad. class or a min. of 920 on SAT or a 20 composite score on the ACT. Accept 85% to inst. Accept all UG theatre arts majors. Interview required for Grad.

FACULTY AND CLASSES OFFERED

13 Full-Time,3 PhD, 10 MFA/MA; 4 Staff

A. (6 FT) Intro to Th-1/Y; Dramatic Crit-X; Th Hist-3/Y; Playwriting-2/O; Dramatic Lit-X; Shakes-X

B. (3 FT) Acting-6/Y; Voice/Speech-1/Y; Musical Theatre-X; Movement-1/Y; Singing-X; Directing-2/Y; Dance-10/Y; Stage Combat-1/Y

C. (3 FT) Principles of Des-1/Y; Set Design-2/Y; Cost Des-2/Y; Tech Prod-3/Y; Lighting Des-2/Y; Cost Constr-2/Y; Make-up-1/Y

D. (1 FT) Box Office Procedure-1/Y

FACILITIES & PRODUCTIONS

Mainstage: 389 seats, fly space, computerized lighting
   4 prods: 4 Fac dir; budget $1,000-2,000

Second stage: 99 seats
   2 prods:2 Fac dir, 1 Fac des, 1 GA dir/des; 1 Grad dir/des; 4 UG des; budget $500

Workshops/Readings: 1 UG dir

Facility built in 1975; includes scene, cost, prop shops, movement/dance, rehearsal, design studios, 3 classrooms, film room.

A non-departmental, student-run producing organization presents various productions in which majors generally participate.

DESCRIPTION

Noted Faculty: Joel Murray, Playwriting, Acting and Directing; Mitch Baker, Costume Des; Ross Fleming, Scene Design; Eric Cope, Lighting Des; Sheila Skaff, FilmStudies; Greg Taylor, Musical Theatre; Adriana Dominquez, Creative Drama

Guest Artists: Donn Finn, Adriana Garza Cortazar, Jorge Huerta

The regionally and nationally recognized Department of Theatre, Dance, and Film at the University of Texas-El Paso offers BA and MA degrees in theatre, a BFA in Musical Theatre, a BFA in Dance, as well as minors in theatre, dance , and film. The faculty and staff are recognized educators and award-winning professionals who put their students first. We focus on developing complete artists, balancing professional training and academics. The department has a very active and high quality production program where students have garnered many significant awards and honors. Students have many opportunities to practice and study as designers, playwrights, actors, directors, choreographers, dancers, and filmmakers. Department faculty and staff are also actively involved in scholarly research, publication, and have distinguished reputations in many highly regarded professional organizations. There have been many new developments in our production and academic programs, including new outstanding faculty, curriculum, community outreach, and technical theatre. Please contact us for information regarding our production and academic programs.

University of Texas - Pan American

Dr. Salma Ghanem, Chair
University Theatre
Communications Dept.
Univ. of Texas-Pan American
Edinburg, TX 78541
(956) 381-3583
ghanem@upta.edu
ADMISSIONS: 1201 W. University, Edinburg, TX 78541
(210) 381-2206
admissions@panam.edu

15,076 Total Enr.; compet.
Semester System
60 Majors; ATHE, TETA
T: $$3,848.
O-ST T: $10,448
R&B: $5,930
FAX: (956) 381-2187
www./www.utpa.edu

DEGREES OFFERED

BA in Production (30), Performance (30), Management (7), Design (7), Teacher Ed (6); MA in Communication/Drama
Declare major in 2nd year.

ADMISSION & FINANCIAL INFORMATION

ACT - 20 or above; SAT 930 or above; upper half of class; no special req's. for theatre program; Grad reqs 600 GRE or 2.75 GPA in UG theatre classes; University scholarships readily avail through Fin. Aid Ofc.; Dept scholarships based on 2.6 min GPA.

FACULTY AND CLASSES OFFERED

6 Full-Time, 2 Part-Time: 5 PhD, 3 MFA/MA; 1 Staff

A. (1 FT, 1 PT) Intro to Theatre-1/Y; Dramatic Lit-2/Y; Th. His-tory-2/Y; Dramatic Criticism-1/Y; Shakes-2/Y; Playwriting-1/Y

B. (2 FT, 1 PT) Acting-8/Y; Voice/Speech-2/Y; Movement-8/Y; Singing-8/Y; Musical Theatre-1/Y; Directing-2/Y

C. (2 FT) Prin of Des-3/Y; Set Des-1/Y; Cost Des-1/O; Lighting Des-1/Y; Tech Prod'n-3/Y; Cost Constr-1/O; Make-up-1/O; Stage Mgmt-1/Y

D. (1 FT) Arts Management-1/Y

FACILITIES & PRODUCTIONS

MAINSTAGE: 297 seats, computerized lighting. 9 prods: 8 Fac dir/des, 1 Guest dir/des; budget $1,000-6,000

SECOND STAGE: 99 seats, computerized lighting. 18 Prods: 2 Fac dir/des; 1 Grad dir/des, 15 UG dir/des. 2 Grad dir/des Workshops./Readings

Facility built in 1985; includes scene, costume, props, welding shops, sound, video, dance, rehearsal studios, 10 classrooms.

Pan American Summer Stock Theatre (PASS Theatre) presents 3-4 plays each June and July, casting participants in the Summer Theatre Workshop, an intensive course in theatre production. Pan American Summer Television (PAST) films a full-length made-for-TV movie during the second half of the summer. Post production work occupies most of the rest of the year. Students in the workshop are used for many of the roles and all of the production work.

DESCRIPTION

Guest Artists: Gerald Freedman, Great Lakes Theatre Fest.; Robert Benedetti; Mari Lyn Henry, ABC casting director; Milcha Sanchez Scott, Playwright.

The University of Texas-Pan American Communications Department offers a broad-based undergraduate degree with specializations in the areas of theatre (including television), journalism, and speech. The University Theatre, the production arm of the department, produces at least 8 major productions annually and sponsors student productions, readings, and special workshops in addition. Theatre students are able to actively work in television production, which is part of their specialization. The department has produced 9 full-length made-for-television motion pictures, with all production work done by students. Guest artists and lecturers are brought in to work directly with students. A working relationship exists with several professional theatres. The faculty and staff of the University Theatre see the department as a pre-professional training program in theater and television; many UTPA graduates have been accepted to outstanding graduate schools and professional training programs. Production excellence and hard work are stressed within a program small enough to meet personal needs. NAST accredited website www.panam.edu.

UTAH

Brigham Young University · · · · · · · · · ·

Rodger Sorensen, Chair	29,158 Total Enr.
Theatre & Media Arts	Semester System
D-581B HFAC	309 Majors; NAST, ATHE
Brigham Young University	LDS: $3,060; $4,650 R&B
Provo, UT 84602	Non-LDS: $4,600; $4,650 R&B
rodger_sorensen@byu.edu	
DEPT: (801) 378-6645	FAX: (801) 378-5988
ADM: A-153 ASB, Provo, Utah 84602	
(801) 378-2507	FAX: (801) 422-0005
admissions@besmart.com	

DEGREES OFFERED

BA in Theatre Studies (76), Theatre Ed (38), Media Arts (98); BFA in Acting (22), Musical Dance Theatre (75). Declare major in 1st year; 2001 granted 55 UG, 3 Grad degrees.

ADMISSION & FINANCIAL INFORMATION

Avg. Act-27, avg. GPA 3.7; inst. admits 73% of applicants; UG prog req. aud, applic, pre-req. classes, sample paper, play reviews, generallly admits all to UG prog; Grad prog reqs portfolio review, writing sample, generally admits 7 out of 10. Talent awards based on applic, port. and/or aud., scholarship and/or leadership.

FACULTY AND CLASSES OFFERED

22 FT, 39 PT: 8 PhD, 13 MFA/MA, 2 Prof. w/o adv. deg; 11 Staff

A. (4 FT, 4 PT) Intro to Theatre-1/Y; Th Hist-2/Y; Shakes-2/Y; Dramatic Lit-2/Y; Dramatic Criticism-3/Y; Playwriting/ Screenwriting-6/Y; Pedagogy-1/Y

B. (5 FT, 4 PT) Acting-13/Y; Voice/Speech-5/Y; Movement-1/Y, Musical Theatre-6/Y; Directing-8/Y; Stage Combat-1/Y; Dance-1/Y; Theatre for Young Audiences-3/Y; Puppetry-1/Y

C. (4 FT, 8 PT) Prins of Des-2/Y; Set Design-9/Y; Cost Des-4/Y; Lighting Des-5/Y; Tech Prod'n-3/Y; Cost Constr-5/Y; Cost Hist-1/Y; Make-up-4/Y; Stg Mgmt-2/Y; Sound-1/Y; Properties-1/O

D. (1 PT) Arts Management-1/Y; Box Office Procedure-1/Y; Marketing/Promo-1/Y

FACILITIES AND PRODUCTIONS

MAINSTAGE: 612 seats, fly space, computerized lighting. 33 prods: 5 Fac dir, 9 Fac des, 1 Grad dir, 4 Grad des, 14 UG des

SECOND STAGE: 250 sets, computerized lighting. 17 prods: 2 Fac dir, 1 Fac des, 1 Grad dir, 2 Grad des, 11 UG des

THIRD STAGE: 150 seats, computerized lighting

Facility built in 1964; includes scene, costume, props shops, video, design studios, classrooms, make-up & paint rooms.

1 student-written play produced in the last two years.

DESCRIPTION

Noted Faculty: Harold Oaks, Child Drama; Bob Nelson, Dramatic Theory/Crit; Eric Samuelsen, Playwriting; Eric Fielding, Design & Tech; Janet Swenson, Costume Design.

Guest Artists: Ragnar Henriksen, Film Director/Producer; Gareth Armstrong, Actor; Claire Bloom, Actress; Teresa Love, Children's Th. Dir/Producer; Susanna Bloch, Acting Theorist; Toralv Maurstad, Actor; Sterling VanWagennen, Film Producer and Academic; Judd Funk, Exec. Vice President of Business & Legal Affaris New Line Cinema.

The BYU theatre program is designed to educate the student in a basic foundation of dramatic literature, theatre history, performance skills as both actor and director, and techniques in all areas of theatre design technology and production. Recognizing the need to enrich people's lives through theatre and media arts, the department seeks excellence in the study and practice of these arts by stressing rigorous scholarship, high artistic standards, and Christian behavior. The department (1) educates broadly in the best liberal arts tradition; (2) develops disciplined scholars, artists, and educators; ad (3) prepares articulate, thinking, caring individuals who will effectively serve their professions, their communities, and their church.

Dixie State College · · · · · · · · · · · · ·

Brent Hanson, Director	6,000 Total Enr.
Theatre Department	Semester System
Dixie College	40 Majors
225 South 700 East	RES T: $95.50 per cr. hr.
St. George, UT 84770	NON O-ST T: $386 per cr. hr.
DEPT: (435) 652-7792	SMALL PROGRAM
FAX: (435) 656-4001	hanson@cc.dixie.edu
ADMI.: Student Service Center, 2nd Fl. (435) 652-7590	
www.explore.dixie.edu/apply-now.html	FAX: (435) 656-4005

DEGREES OFFERED

AS or AA in Theatre Performance (12), Technical Theatre (3) Declare major in freshman year.

ADMISSION & FINANCIAL INFORMATION

Req. SAT or Dixie College Achievement Test, applic.; Open-entry; no special req's. for admission to th. program; Accept 100% to program. Special Scholarships avail; audition req'd.

FACULTY AND CLASSES OFFERED

3 Full-Time: 1 PhD, 2 MFA/MA

A. (1 FT) Intro to Theatre-2/4; Dramatic Lit-1/3; Theatre History-1/3; Dramatic Criticism-2/4; Shakes-2/3

B. (1 FT) Acting-2/2; Voice/Speech-2/2; Singing-3/3; Musical Theatre-1/3; Directing-1/1

C. (1 FT) Principles of Design-1/3; Set Des.-1/3; Cost Des.-1/3; Lighting Des.-1/3; Tech Prod.-1/3; Cost Constr.-1/3; Stage Mgmt-

FACILITIES & PRODUCTIONS

MAINSTAGE: 512 seats, fly space, computerized lighting.
  4 Fac dir/des prods

SECOND STAGE: 200 seats, electronic lighting
  4 Fac dir, 3 Fac des, 2 Guest dir, 5-8 UG dir/des

THIRD STAGE: 1200 seats, fly space, computerized lighting
  2 Fac dir Workshops/Readings

Main- and Second Stages built 1963, Third Stage built in 1986.
  Facility includes scene shop, costume shop, props shop, sound
  studio, rehearsal studio, classrooms.

DESCRIPTION

In each of the Fine Arts Division areas—music, art, speech
communications, and theatre arts—basic courses are
directed toward developing in students an understanding
and sound standards of appreciation for the arts, our
artistic heritage, and our contemporary art and life. In all
areas, students may elect to major or minor, and courses
are taught which provide a strong subject matter and
experience background. The depth and breadth of our
programs in art, music, speech communications, and theatre arts, all of which aim to evaluate, sensitize, and
refine the individual, is a source of pride to an outstanding faculty. Musical Theatre is a specialty of Dixie College,
and cooperation and interaction between Theatre and
Music Departments creates a delightful opportunity to
blend experiences in music and theatre. Also, the close
interrelationship of speech experiences and training with
theatre is emphasized in providing thorough development
of the actor's vocal instrument.

Southern Utah University

Shauna Mendini , Chair	6,048 Total Enr.
Dept. of Theatre Arts & Dance	Semester System
Southern Utah University	177 Majors; U/RTA
351 West Center St.	NAST Candidate
Cedar City, UT 84720	T:$3,796/$4,442 r&b,
(435) 586-7746	O-ST $11,326/o-st:$4,442
mendini_s@suu.edu	ACTF Participant
adminfo@suu.edu	www.suu.edu

DEGREES OFFERED

BA/BS in Acting/Directing (75), Des/Tech (36), Education (24); Dance
(42); MFA in Arts Admin (4). Also a minor in Th. Arts. Declare major
in any year.

ADMISSION & FINANCIAL INFORMATION

No audition required for admittance. Audition for scholarship avail.

FACULTY AND CLASSES OFFERED

15 FT, 11 MFA/MA, 2 PhD, 1 GA; 1 Staff

A. Inside the Art of Theatre-1/Y; Th. Styles Hist-1/Y; Th. Hist-1/Y;
    Classic Th-1/Y jTh. Hist II-1/Y; Realism, Post Realistic and
    Contemp Th-1/Y; Th for Elem. Ed-1/Y

B. Acting I-1/Y; Acting II-1/Y; Acting Styles I: Modern-Contemporary-
    1/Y, Acting Styles II: Musical Th-1/Y, Acting Styles III: Classical
    and Shakes-1/Y, Acting Styles IV: Studio Intensive - Masks-1/Y,

Aud Prep-1/Y, Dir I-1/Y, Directing II: Methods Approach-1/Y,
Directing II: Lab-1/Y; Portfolio-1/Y, Prod Mgmt-1/Y

C. Design Anal-1/Y, Stage Rendering-1/Y, Collaborative Approach to
    Des-1/Y, Cost Des-1/Y, Lighting Des-1/Y, Scenic Des-1/Y, Stage
    Makeup-1/Y, Stagecraft-1/Y, Cost Const-1/Y, Drafting for Theatre-
    1/Y, Portfolio-1/Y, Prod Mgmt-1/Y

D. Arts Admin.-O & MFA: Principles of Arts Admin-1/Y; Prof Writing
    & Comm-1/Y, The Arts & Society/Govt Relations-1/Y, Marketing
    the Arts I-1/Y, Fund Devel for Arts Admin-1/Y,Practices &
    Principles of Visual Arts-1/Y, Planning for Arts Admin-1/Y,
    Leadership Training & Devel-1/Y, Human Resource Mgmt-1/Y,
    Board Relations-1/Y Legal Aspects of a Fine Arts Organization-
    1/Y, Marketing the Arts I-1/Y, Practices & Principles of Arts
    Organization-1/Y

FACILITIES AND PRODUCTIONS

MAINSTAGE: 1,000 seats, fly space, computerized lighting, audio and
  pit motion control.

SECOND STAGE: 740 seats, fly space, computerized lighting, audio &
  pit motion control.

Black Box: Flexible

Minimum 6 prod each season; Fac/Student Dir.ectors & Designers
  vary

Facility includes scene shop, costume shop, sound studio, dance
  studio, classrooms.

Connection with 2000 Tony Award Winning Utah Shakespearean
  Festival (summer) and Burch Mann's American Folk Ballet.

DESCRIPTION

To provide a nurturing and challenging educational environment, which celebrates our history, propels us toward
our future, and excels in practical application of theatrical and dance techniques. A rich diversity of idioms, theatrical disciplines and technologies combine with an
ever-changing array of production opportunities and per-
sonalizd mentoring by all of our faculty and staff. Central
to our focus as a department is superior teaching; our
classroom encompasses the studio, the stage and the
technical laboratory. To build, pebble upon pebble, by
more and better programs, faculty, and facilities, a rising
arch of knowledge for our students through which the
river of their and our artistic influence will flow across the
community, region, and country, so that the national
recognition of their talents may enrich all society.

University of Utah

Dr. Bob Nelson, Chair	28,619 Tot.Enr.;
Theatre Dept, Rm 206	Semester System
240 S. 1500 E.	200+ Majors
University of Utah	T: $1,964/sem
Salt Lake City, UT 84112-0170	O-ST T: $6,113/sem
(801) 581-6448	

DEGREES OFFERED

BA in Th. Studies (80); BFA in Acting (70), Production/Design (30),
Stage Mgmt. (20); Declare major in freshman year.

ADMISSION & FINANCIAL INFORMATION

ATP Program requires audition, interview; admit 3 out of 10 performance applicants.

FACULTY AND CLASSES OFFERED

10 Full-Time, 15 Part-Time: 4 PhD, 22 MFA/MA; 5 Staff

A. (1 FT) Intro to Th-4/Y; Th. Hist-6/Y

B. (3 FT, 6 PT) Acting-9/Y; Voice/Speech-7/YO; Movement- 3/Y
Singing-2/X

C. (2 FT, 3 PT) Prins of Des.1/Y; Set Des.-5/Y; Cost Des.-3/Y; Lighting
Des.-3/Y; Make-up-2/Y; Stage Mgmt- 2/Y

FACILITIES AND PRODUCTIONS

MAINSTAGE: 130 seats, computerized lighting: Babcock Theate
4 prods: 2 Fac dir/des, 2 Guest dir/des

SECOND STAGE: 60 seats, computerized and electronic lighting

Studio 115: 7 prods: Fac dir/des, 2 UG dir/des

Mainstage facility built in 1962, Studio 115 in 1974; facilities include
scene, costume, props shops, sound studio, video studios,
dance, rehearsal, design studios, 13 classrooms.

Pioneer Theatre Company (Equity, school year): Students have
opportunities to perform (by audition), occasionally to work on
lighting and costume, and to serve as acting interns.

DESCRIPTION

Noted Faculty: Sandra Shotwell, Gage Williams, Jerry
Gardner, Sarah Shippobotham, Xan S.Johnson, Tim
Slover.

The Department of Theatre BFA programs offer excellent
pre-professional training; and the BA in Theatre offers a
broad liberal education program in theatre. One of the
advantages the professional programs offer to students is
the opportunity for wide experience in productions annually. The department offers the opportunity to work with
professional performers, directors and designers on the
main stage season and to earn both credit and stipends.
Additionally, several Pioneer Theatre Company professional staff members in design/technical theatre teach
their specialty to theatre students. The faculty also
includes specialists in voice, movement, dialects, singing
and stage management. There are two theatre spaces so
students have the opportunity to learn all aspects of theatre from first hand experience. Spectacular training is
strengthened by solid academic work in history, playwriting, dramatic literature and criticism from noted schol-
ar/teachers.

Utah State University

Colin Johnson, Head
Department of Theatre Arts
Utah State University
UMC-4025
Logan, UT 84322-4025
DEPT. (435) 797-3046
Colin.Johnson@usu.edu
ADMISSIONS: 1600 Old Main Hill, USU, Logan 84322-1600
(435) 797-1107   FAX: (435) 797-4077
/www.usu.edu   admit@cc.usu.edu

12,779 Total Enr.; compet.
Semester System
85 Majors
T: $4,133/$$4,580 R&B
O-ST T: $12,011/$4,770 R&B
FAX: (435) 797-0086

DEGREES OFFERED

BA in General Th. (5); BFA in Acting (30), Design/ Technical Theatre
(15), Theatre Education (20); MA/MFA Graduate (6); (Nondeclared)
(10). Declare major in freshman year.

ADMISSION & FINANCIAL INFORMATION

University score of 85 or above (request/refer to catalogue). Accept
80% to institution; UG program req's. aud./int., portfolio for designers; Grad req's interview, portfolio. Accept 20 out of 25 UG, 2 out of 5
Grad. Admission to specific degree programs (BFA) at end of freshman yr. Talent Award Tuition (In-state). Scholarships awarded by
application and audition or interview.

FACULTY AND CLASSES OFFERED

10 Full-Time, 2 Part-Time: 3 PhD, 9 MFA/MA; 5 Staff

A. (1 FT, 21/2 PT) Intro to Th.-1/Y; Th History-2/Y; Shakes-2/X;
Dramatic Lit-1/Y + 2/X; Dramatic Crit-1/Y; Playwriting-2/Y; Intro to
Film-1/Y; Performances Lit/Storytelling-4/Y; Creative
Drama/Child. Th.-1/Y+1/O

B. (4 FT, 1 1/2 PT) Acting-7/Y; Voice/Speech-3/Y; Movement- 4/Y;
Musical Th.-1/O; Directing-2/Y; Stage Combat-1/O; Dance-3/Y;
Singing-X

C. (2 FT) Prins. of Des-1/Y; Set Des.-2/Y+1/O; Cost Des.-1/Y;
Lighting Design-2/Y; Tech Prod.-1/Y+1/O; Costume Construction-
2/Y; Cost Hist-1/Y; Make-up-1/Y; Stg Mgmt-1/Y; Scenepainting-
1/Y; Costume Design-2/Y; Theatre Sound-1/O

D. Arts Management-1/O

FACILITIES AND PRODUCTIONS

MAINSTAGE: 700 seats, fly space, computer. lighting. 4 prods: 4 Fac
dir, 3 Fac des, 1 Grad des; budget $600-6000

SECOND STAGE: 384 seats, fly space, computerized lighting.
4 prods: 2 Fac dir, 1 Fac des, 2 Grad dir, 1 Grad des, 2 UG des;
budget $800-2,000

THIRD STAGE: 90 seats, black box, electronic lighting. 4 Work-
shops/Readings: 1 Fac dir, 2 Grad dir, 1 Grad des, 1 UG dir,
3 UG des; budget $100-400

Facility built in 1967; includes scene, costume, props shops, dance
studio, 2 rehearsal studios, design studio, 3 classrooms.

4 student-written plays produced in the last two years.

The Old Lyric Repertory Company (Equity) produces 4 plays in rotating rep each summer. Full company members receive $2,500-
2,700 honorarium plus 4 semester credits; for upper division &
graduate students; five undergraduate internships available.
Graduate students are required to work with the OLRC or another
company for at least one summer.

DESCRIPTION

Guest Artists: Anne Bogart, SM,Actors form The Britsh
Stage: Amy Tribbey, Wendy Dale Young, David Carey
Foster, Robert Gretta, Fred Willecke, Actors; Leigh
Selting, Actor/Director;Beverly Emmons, Mitch Dana,
Lighting; Regina Cate, Costumes; Ann Benson, Ron
Ranson, John Lee Beatty, Scenery.

A primary objective of Utah State University's Theatre
Arts Department is to model a high level of professionalism and quality to students regardless of the venue in
which they choose to practice their craft and art: professional, regional, community, or educational theatres.
Every graduate is expected to gain a solid foundation in
all aspects of the discipline and to train extensively in a
specialization. This means that the acquisition of skills
and knowledge from the classroom be applied directly in
the studio and stage in a highly collaborative environment. A core of five courses in acting, technical practice,

play analysis, directing, and theatre history is required of everyone. This is complemented by a series of diverse practicums on production crews as well as a curriculum of academic courses which include theatre history, dramatic literature, playwriting, costume history, and so forth. The department offers four areas of specialization for undergraduates: design/tech theatre, performance, theatre education, and a general theatre studies degree. The MFA graduate program specializes in design/tech theatre and directing. Our students are readily accepted into advanced degree programs at major universities and conservatory programs, and education majors have a very high placement percentage.

VERMONT

Bennington College

Dance/Drama Coordinator
1 College Drive
Bennington, VT 05201
(802) 440-4547
ADMISSIONS: (800) 833-6845
admissions@bennington.edu

600 Total Enr.; competitive
Semester System
T: $36,800
R&B: $9,380
FAX: (802) 440-4550
www.bennington.edu

DEGREES OFFERED
BA Individualized for each student through ongoing planning process, MFA in Fine Arts

ADMISSION & FINANCIAL INFORMATION
Two essays, two recommendations, transcripts; the interview is treated with particular seriousness. We welcome additional work, e.g. a critical paper, tape, or poetry. Portfolio welcome. Merit-based financial aid available. 65% of applicants offered admission.

FACULTY AND CLASSES OFFERED
10 Full-Time; 3 FT Staff

A. (1 FT) Dramatic Lit-2/Y/X; Theatre History-2/Y; Shakes-2/Y; Dramatic Criticism-2/Y; Playwriting-4/Y

B. (4 FT) Acting-10/Y; Voice/Speech-1/Y; Movement-4/Y; Singing-2/Y; Directing-4/Y; Masks-1/O; Opera-1/O; Dance-10/Y; Film-2/Y; Musical Theatre-2/O

C. (5 FT) Costume Design-4/Y; Set Design-4/Y; Lighting Des-4/Y; Stg Mgmt-3/Y

D. Individual tutorial on various subjects-8/Y

FACILITIES & PRODUCTIONS
MAINSTAGE: 200 seats, computerized lighting, flexible seating.
2 prods: 1 Fac dir/UG des; budget $2,000-5,000

SECOND STAGE: 100 seats, computerized lighting
4-6 prods: 6 UG dir/des; budget $400-800

THIRD STAGE: 75 seats, electronic lighting
5 UG dir/des Workshops/Readings; budget $50

Facility built in 1975, minor renovations on-going; includes scene shop, costume shop, welding shop, video studio, 2 movement/dance studios, 2 rehearsal studios, 2 design studios.

Student-run org. supports independent work. 4 student-written plays produced in the last two years.

Students may have the opportunity to assist faculty in theri professional work.

DESCRIPTION

Noted Faculty: Kathleen Dimmick, Michael Giannitti, Kirk Jackson, Dina Janis, Daniel Michaelson, Jean Randich, Jennifer Rohn, Sue Rees, Gladden Schrock.

Guest Artists: Roberta Levitow, Mac Wellman, Len Jenkin, Theresa Rebeck, Steve Mellor, Didi O'Connell, Quincy Long, Stephen Guirgis, Malcom Ewen

Bennington's drama program embraces the breadth and depth of the theatrical medium. The emphasis on learning by doing under the guidance of artist-mentors, the opportunity to pursue one's passion in theatre as the heart of an education rather than as an extra-curricular activity, and the interdisciplinary and collaborative nature of the drama discipline uniquely position Bennington College at the forefront of undergraduate theatre education. In order to achieve this goal, faculty input and curricular offerings provide vitality, context, depth, and breadth. There is a strong relationship between work done in drama classes and work done on productions, and there are regular opportunities for students to work with faculty directors (either on productions or in workshop situations.) Guest artists are an additional vital component of the program, to bring diversity, infuse new energy, and provide additional opportunities for students. Additional course offerings by Bennington's renowned dance and music faculty are also available.

Green Mountain College

See ad next page
Jennifer Baker, VPA Chair
Visual and Performing Art
Green Mountain College
One College Circle
Poultney, VT 05764
DEPT: (802) 287-8290
GEN: (800) 287-8000

729 Total Enr.
Semester System
26 Majors
T: $24,565/$8,982 R&B
SMALL PROGRAM
nassiveraj@greenmtn.edu
www.greenmtn.edu

DEGREES OFFERED
B. A. in Interdisciplinary Studies: Performing Arts, Minor in Theatre Arts

ADMISSION & FINANCIAL INFORMATION
No minimum GPA or "cut-off" scores. We want to understand the student's academic history in the context of the entire application portfolio. Various packages available including need-based monies as well as merit awards and other self-help funding. Refer to web site for current financial aid and scholarship information.

FACULTY AND CLASSES OFFERED
2 PT: 1 PhD, 1 MFA/MA,

A. Theatre History 1/O; Playwriting 1/O, Modern Drama 1/O, Contemp. Drama 1/X; Theatre Audience 1/O; Screen Writing; Independent Study

B. Acting 2/O; Voice/Speech; Directing; Creative Dramatics; Performance Theatre Workshops

DESCRIPTION
Noted faculty: John Nassivera, Paula Mann.

Green Mountain College prepares students for productive, caring, and fulfilling lives by taking the environment as the unifying theme underlying its academic and co-curricular programs. This innovative interdisciplinary approach to liberal arts education is grounded in the institution's strong tradition of effective teaching and mentoring, and is complemented by a diversity of community-oriented campus life opportunities. Through a wide range of liberal arts and career-focused majors, the college fosters the ideals of environmental responsibility, public service, global understanding, and lifelong intellectual, physical, and spiritual development.

Middlebury College

Douglas Sprigg, Chair Th. Prog.
Dept. of Theatre &, Dance
Middlebury College
Middlebury, VT 05753
(802) 443-5601
www.middlebury.edu

2,406 Total Enr.; h. compet.
Semester System
70 Majors
T: N/A
SMALL PROGRAM
admissions@middlebury.edu

DEGREES OFFERED

BA in Acting/Directing (22), Design/prod (3), Dance (5), Film (4). Declare major in second year.

ADMISSION & FINANCIAL INFORMATION

Accept 15% to institution; No special req's. for admission to program; admit all applicants to program; "Need-blind" admission policy; students are admitted w/o regard for need. All admitted students who are eligible for Financial Aid receive it.

FACULTY AND CLASSES OFFERED

4 FT, 3 PT: 3 PhD, 3 MFA/MA, 1 Prof. w/o adv. degree, 4 Staff

A. (3 FT) Intro to Theatre-1/Y; Theatre History-1/O; Shakes-1/X; Dramatic Lit-5/Y; Playwriting-2/Y

B. (3 FT, 1/3 PT) Acting-4/Y; Voice/Speech-1/Y; Mvmt-1/Y; Dir-2/Y

C. (2 FT) Prins of Des-1/Y; Set Design-2/Y; Costume Design- 1/O; Lighting Des-2/Y; Tech Prod'n-2/Y; Cost Hist-1/O

FACILITIES AND PRODUCTIONS

MAINSTAGE: 360 seats, fly space, computerized lighting. 6 prods: 2 Fac dir/des, 2 UG dir/des; budget $4,000-6,000

SECOND STAGE: 200 seats, computerized lighting. 6 prods: 3 Fac dir/des, 1 UG dir/des; budget $2,000-4,000. 17 Workshops/Readings, 1 Fac dir, 12 UG dir, 4 UG des

Mainstage built in 1958, second stage in 1991; includes scene shop, costume shop, welding shop, sound studio, rehearsal studio, dance studio, classrooms.

A non-departmental, student-run org. presents 6-12 prods. per year. 4 student-written plays produced in the last two years.

Connection with Potomac Theatre Project, (Equity). 4-10 students perform with professional summer company Washington, DC. Students also work in tech and mgmt capacities, are paid a small stipend.

DESCRIPTION

Theatre Faculty: Act/Dir, etc: Douglas C. Sprigg, Richard Romagnoli, Cheryl Faraone, Claudio Medeiros, Dana

Yeaton; Design: Mark Evancho, Jule Emerson.

Guest Artists: Joseph Chaikin, Jean-Claude van Itallie, Bob Lu Pone, B.H. Barry, Alan Wade, Oliver Ford Davies, Paul Zimet, Anne Bogart.

Designed to encourage creativity, artistic excellence, and a vigorous exploration of the current and historical possibilities for theatrical expression, the theatre program guides students towards an integrated understanding of all aspects of the theatrical experience while sharpening their creative skills as actors, directors, designers, and playwrights.

St. Michael's College

Dr. Susan Summerfield, Chair
Department of Fine Arts
St. Michael's College
Winooski Park
Colchester, VT 05439
DEPT: (802) 654-2448
ADMISSIONS: c/o Jerry Flanagan

1,700 Total Enr.; competitive
Semester System
35 Majors; ATHE
T:$29,695 R&B:$7,460
SMALL PROGRAM

(802) 654-2541

DEGREES OFFERED

BA in Fine Arts/Theatre (8). Declare major in 1st or 2nd year.;

ADMISSION & FINANCIAL INFORMATION

Avg. SAT 1035, Rank in class 77th percentile, GPA B+; Accept 43% to inst.; th program admits all applicants Paulin scholarship by audition.

FACULTY AND CLASSES OFFERED

4 Full-Time: 3 MFA, 1 PhD

A. Intro to Theatre-1/Y; Theatre History-2/Y; Shakes-1/Y; Dramatic Lit-3/Y; Playwriting-1/Y

B. Acting-3/Y; Voice/Speech-3/Y; Singing-1/O; Directing-2/Y; Dance-12/Y

C. Prins of Design-1/Y; Set Design-1/Y; Costume Design-1/Y; Technical Prod'n-3/Y; Cost History-1/Y

FACILITIES & PRODUCTIONS

MAINSTAGE: 366 seats, fly space, computerized lighting
    2 Fac dir/des prods; budget $3,000-10,000

SECOND STAGE: 60 seats, electronic lighting
    5-10 UG dir/des prods: budget $0-1,000
    2 Fac dir/des Workshops/Readings; budget $0-150

Facility was built in 1975; includes scene shop, costume shop, prop shop, sound studio, 3 classrooms.

A non-departmental, student-run producing org. presents 2 prods. per year in which department majors participate. 6 student-written plays produced in the last two years.

Connected with St. Michael's Playhouse, an Equity (CORST-Z) Company operated by members of theatre faculty. Students work as interns or rotating crew, EMC credit, opportunity to audition for appropriate roles, produce childrens theatre presentation.

DESCRIPTION

Noted Faculty: Kirk Everist, History; Peter Harrigan, Directing, Acting, Costumes; Cathy Hurst, Acting, Directing, Voice; John Devlin, Set, Lights, Sound Design.

The theatre program at St. Michael's College is adminis-

tratively within the Fine Arts Department, along with Music and Art. This union provides for easy, productive cooperation among the three areas. In the theatre, the philosophy is to provide a broad base exposure in theatrical arts in a liberal arts setting. The department is small, but supplemented by non-majors in production, and by other departmental course work (as in English; Shakespeare; Genres Dramas; ETV; Radio; and Business courses). Our faculty directed productions are few in number in order to provide more time for character development and individual working with students, which has led to critically acclaimed productions (and participation in ACTF).

University of Vermont

Jeff Modereger, Chair
Department of Theatre
Royall Tyler Theatre
University of Vermont
116 University Place
Burlington, VT 05405-0102
DEPT: (802) 656-2095
www.uvm.edu/theatre
ADMISSIONS: 194 So. Prospect St. Burlington, VT 05405
(802) 656-3370

10,800 Total Enr.; competitive
Semester System; NAST, U/RTA
...ATHE
72 majors, 58 minors
T + R&B: $17,500
O-ST T + R&B: $32,500
FAX: (802) 656-0349
jeffrey.modereger@uvm.edu

admissions@uvm.edu

DEGREES OFFERED

BA in Theatre w/emphasis in Performance (45): Design/Production (23); or History/Criticism (4) plus major concentration for College of Education and Social Sciences. Declare major in 2nd year; 2007 granted 14 degrees.

ADMISSION & FINANCIAL INFORMATION

Minimum HS course requirements. Generally admit all theatre program applicants

FACULTY AND CLASSES OFFERED

7 Full-Time, 5 Part-Time: 1 PhD, 10 MA/MFA; 1 prof. w/o advanced degree; 4 Staff

A. (1 FT, 2 PT) Intro to Th-1/Y; Theatre History-2/Y; Shakes-1/Y; Dramatic Lit-2/Y; Dramatic Crit-1/Y; Playwriting-2/Y

B. (3 FT, 3 PT) Acting-3/Y; Voice-1/Y; Movement-1/Y; Directing-2/Y; Singing-1/Y; Dance (Dept of Dance)-3/X

C. (3 FT) Principles of Des-3/Y; Set Design-2/Y; Lighting Des-1/Y; Cost Construct-3/O; Costume Design-1/Y; Make-Up-1/O; Stage Mgmt-1/Y; Scene Painting-1/O; Tech Prod-1/Y

FACILITIES & PRODUCTIONS

MAINSTAGE: 300 seats, fly space, computerized/electronic lighting
    4 prods: 3 Fac dir/des, 1 UG dir/des (fac des may supervise student des); budget $20,000-$32,000

Facility built in 1901, renovated 1972; includes scene shop, costume shop, sound studio, 2 rehearsal studios, 2 design studios, 2 classrooms. Black Box & proscenium in other building.

A non-departmental, student-run producing organization presents 1-2 productions in which majors generally participate.

Connection with Vermont Stage Company - Equity and operates during the school year - student experience includes: lighting design, electricians, scenic design, carpenters, stage managers, costume design, wardrobe, and acting.

DESCRIPTION

Noted Faculty: Jeff Modereger, Scene Des/Painting; Martin Thaler, Costume Des/Constr; Peter Jack Tkatch, Acting, Voice; Sarah Carleton, Acting, Movement; Lynne Greeley, Dramatic Analyis,Theatre History; John Forbes, Lighting Des/Stage Mgmt; Greg Ramos, Directing, Theatre Diversity

Guest Artists: Brett Smock, Director; Dawn Wagner, SM

The B.A. in theatre program at University of Vermont is designed to give the student a well integrated and practical experience of theatrical history, theory, and production in a liberal arts setting. Students study acting, costuming, lighting, scenery, dramatic analysis, and history, and choose an area of emphasis in design/tech or performance or history. Small class size allows individual attention. The Dept. of Theatre produces three mainstage productions each year which includes opportunities to hire professionals to work along side the student population. In addition, there is the opportunity for students to pursue the teaching of theatre through an affiliation with the University's College of Education and Social Sciences. Graduates have gone on to study in professional or graduate theatre schools, to teach and direct theatre activities in schools, and to work in the professional theatre and related fields.

VIRGINIA

Barter Conservatory at Emory & Henry College

Biliana Stoytcheva-Horissian, Chair
Dept. of Theatre
Barter Conservatory at
  Emory & Henry College
P. O. Box 947
Emory, VA 24327
DEPT: (276) 944-6667
ADMISSIONS: Office of Admissions, P.O. Box 10, Emory, VA 24327.
(276) 944-6657
www.ehc.edu

1,060 Total Enr.;compet.
Semester System
10 Majors; ATHE
T: $22,320/$7,670 R&B
SMALL PROGRAM

FAX: (276) 944-6259

FAX: (276) 944-6657

DEGREES OFFERED
BA in Acting (5), Playwriting (2), Production (2), Musical Theatre (3), Directing (4). Declare major in freshman year; 2001 granted 5 UG degrees.

ADMISSION & FINANCIAL INFORMATION
GPA-2.5, SAT 1040, ACT: 21. Theatre Grants: Open to theatre majors only. Call 800-848-5493 for information. Student prepares one 2 minute memorized monolgue, fills out theatre grant form, letter of rec from teacher, schedules appointment. No special req. for admissions to theatre program.

FACULTY AND CLASSES OFFERED
2 Full-Time, 5 Part-Time: 3 PhD, 4 MFA/MA

A. (1 PT) Intro to Theatre-3/Y; Theatre History-2/Y; Shakes-1/X; Dramatic Lit-1/Y; Playwriting-1/Y

B. (2 FT, 2 PT) Acting/Scene Study-2/Y; Voice/Speech-1/O; Movement-1/O; Mime/Mask, etc-1/O; Singing-2/X; Directing-2/Y; Mus. Theatre-1/O; Stage Combat-1/O

C. (1 PT) Prins of Des-1/Y; Set Des-1/Y; Lighting. Des-1/Y; Cost Des-1/O; Tech. Prod'n-1/O; Cost Hist-1/O; Stage Mgmt-1/O;

Cost Const-1/O; Make-up-1/O

D. (1 PT) Arts Management-1/Y; Box Office Procedure-1/O; Marketing/Promo-1/O

FACILITIES AND PRODUCTIONS

MAINSTAGE: 600 seats, electronic lighting. 4 prods: 2 Fac dir/des, 1 Guest dir/des, 1 UG dir/des; budget $5,000

SECOND STAGE: 140 seats, fly space, computerized lighting 1 prod: Fac dir/des; budget $3,000

Facility was built in 1961, renovated in 1996; includes scene shop, costume shop, prop shop, welding shop, rehearsal studio, design studio, classrooms.

A non-departmental student-run organization presents 1 production per year in which dept. majors generally participate.

1 student-written play produced in the last two years.

Connection with Barter Theatre, (Equity). Full connection. Barter professionals teach at Emory and Henry and selected students will work at Barter Theatre their senior year.

DESCRIPTION

Noted Faculty: Dr. Kate Musgrove, Directing & Management; Richard Rose, Producing Artistic Director of Barter Theatre; Dr. John Hardy, Playwright & Associate Artistic Dir. of Barter Theatre; Cheri Prough, Properties Master & Scene Designer of Barter Theatre. Guest Artists: Evelyn Baron, Acting/Musical Theatre, Visiting Faculty, NYU; Mike Ostroski, Professional Actor, Theatre Marketing.

The Barter Conservatory at Emory & Henry College is a joint venture between the Department of Theatre at Emory & Henry College, one of the Southeast's most respected colleges, and the Barter Theatre, the second oldest active theatre in the U.S. and the State Theatre of Virginia. The conservatory is intended to offer students pre-professional training who are interested in making theatre their career, whether that be in acting, directing, musical theatre, playwriting, or theatre production. This is one of the most unique and student oriented theatre programs in the country. Not only will they be instructed by full-time Emory & Henry faculty, but also will have the opportunity to take classes with Barter professionals in acting, playwriting, history, and design. Academically sound students of talent and promise will be able to audition and interview at the end of the sophomore year for the conservatory.

College of William and Mary

Steve Holliday, Chair
Dept. of Theatre, Speech
  & Dance
College of William & Mary
P. O. Box 8795
Williamsburg, VA 23187-8795
DEPT: (757) 221-2660
www.wm.edu/theatre
ADMISSIONS: Office of Admissions, above address.
(757) 221-4223
www.wm.edu/admission

5,734 Total Enr UG; 2,000 G;
  h. compet.
Semester System
60 Majors; ATHE, USITT, SETC
T: $9,164/$6,066 R&B
O-ST T: $26,725/$7,385 R&B
FAX: (757) 221-2636
seholl@wm.edu

FAX: (757) 221-1242
admiss@wm.edu

DEGREES OFFERED

BA Theatre (92), minor Theatre (1) or Dance (114). Declare major in late soph. year.

ADMISSION & FINANCIAL INFORMATION

Middle 50% for SAT 1270-1420 on SAT's; GPA-top 10 percent of graduating class, most advance coursework available, extracurricular activities. Institution admits 25 % out of state, 40-50 % in state. Approx $21,500 available for student studies and student run productions.

FACULTY AND CLASSES OFFERED

14 Full-Time, 6 Part-Time: 5 PhD, 15 MFA/MA; 3 Staff

A. (2 1/2 FT) Intro to Theatre-1/Y; Theatre History-2/Y; Playwriting-3/Y

B. (7 FT, 4 PT) Acting/Scene Study-3/Y; Movement-1/Y; Singing-3/Y; Directing-1/Y; Dance-8/Y; Voice/Speech-5/Y; Mime/Mask-1/O; Musical Theatre-3/Y; Stage Combat-1/O

C. (4 FT, 2 PT) Prins of Des-1/Y; Set Des-2/Y; Cost Des-1/Y; Tech. Prod'n-2/Y; Stage Mgmt-1/O; Lighting Des-2/Y; Cost Const-2/Y; Make-up-1/Y; Theatre Management-1/O; Sound Des-1/O

D. (1/2 FT) Arts Management-1/O; Mktg Promo-X; Contract/Copyright-X; Budgeting/Acctg Procedures-X

FACILITIES AND PRODUCTIONS

MAINSTAGE: 763 seats, fly space, computerized lighting. 4 prods: 4 Fac dir; budget $5,000-16,000

SECOND STAGE: 150 seats, fly space, computerized lighting 4 UG dir; budget $50-600

THIRD STAGE: 100 seats, black box, computerized lighting

Facility was built in 1957, renovated in 1987; includes scene shop, costume shop, 6 classrooms, 1 dance studio, 1 deesign studio, 2 rehearsal studios, CAD facility, lab space, green room, men's and women's dressing rooms, on- & off-site costume & properties storage.

A non-departmental student-run organization presents 7 productions per year in which dept majors generally participate.

20 student-written plays produced in the last two years.

Connection with Virginia Shakespeare Festival, which offers internships which students may apply for in all areas of theatre. The festival is run in department space during the summer by a faculty member.

DESCRIPTION

Noted Faculty: Richard Palmer, History, Criticism; Patricia Wesp, Costumes; Steve Holliday, Design; Michael Mehler, Design; Dorothy Chansky, History & Criticism; Laurie Wolf, History & Criticism; Elizabeth Wiley, Acting; Joan Cavaler, Dance; Christopher Owens, Directing; Denise Damon-Wade, Dance.

Guest Artists: Gary Green, Musical Theatre; Sarah Jones, Performance; David Doersch, Directing, Stage Combat; Brenda Rosseau, Costumes; Shana Burns, Design; Peppe Ostensson, Movement; Lois Weaver, Solo Performance; Gregg Hillman, Lighting.

William and Mary offers an exclusively undergraduate liberal arts theatre program where students work closely with faculty in productions and in over thirty courses. A well-equipped 763 seat proscenium theatre and two black box theatres house a full-production schedule, supplemented in the summer by the Virginia Shakespeare Festival, all of which enjoy strong campus and community support. Because of the College's high admission standards, talented and bright undergraduates have opportunities to perform, design, direct, and write not usually encountered elsewhere until graduate school. The department is small enough to provide personal attention but large enough to offer multiple instructors in all specialties. Diversity is encouraged with all students taking basic courses in acting, play production, design, theatre history and literature, and directing. Classes in theatre average fifteen students. Advanced work provides pre-professional training, and graduates regularly enter the top graduate professional training programs.

Ferrum College

H. Wayne Bowman, Chair
Performing and Visual Arts Division
Ferrum College
Ferrum, VA 24088
DEPT: (540) 365-4338
FAX: (540) 365-4213
ADMISSIONS: 215 Ferrum Mtn., Ferrum VA 24088
(540) 365-4290
www.ferrum.edu

1,060 Total Enr.; not compet.
Semester System
11 Majors
SMALL PROGRAM
$20,885, $6,900 R&B
wbowman@ferrum.edu

FAX: (540) 365-4266
admissions@ferrum.edu

DEGREES OFFERED

BA in Dramatic and Theatre Arts (3); BFA in Dramatic and Theatre Arts (3). Declare major in any year.

ADMISSION & FINANCIAL INFORMATION

HS grades, activities, SAT considered. Program admits all applicants. Performing Arts Schols - videotape explaining desire and experience in children's theatre and HS grades. Drama Schol - recommendations and HS grades.

FACULTY AND CLASSES OFFERED

2 1/8 Full-Time, 1 Part-Time: 1 PhD, 1 MFA/MA

A. (1/8 FT) Intro to Theatre-1/Y; Th Hist-2/O; Dramatic Lit-2/O; Shakes-1/X; Playwriting-1/O

B. (1 1/4 FT) Acting-3/Y; Voice/Speech-2/Y; Directing-1/O; Dance-8/X; Singing-2/X

C. (3/4 FT) Prins of Des-1/O; Tech Prod'n-2/O

FACILITIES AND PRODUCTIONS

MAINSTAGE: 252 seats, electronic lighting 2 Fac dir/des prods; budget $1,000

SECOND STAGE: Flexible 50-150 seats, electronic lighting 2-15 Prods: UG dir/des; budget $100

Facility was renovated in 1984; includes scene shop, costume shop, dance studio, movement/dance.

Connection with Blue Ridge Dinner Theatre (summer) holds open auditions for its eight week run. Students may audition, many employed, some develop into lower management positions.

DESCRIPTION

Noted Faculty: R. Rex Stephenson, author 8 published and 17 produced plays, Artistic Director Jack Tale Players, BRDT, CSC; H. Wayne Bowman, guest director at several regional theatres; Jody D. Brown, regular presenter at Shakespeare Conferences both national and international.

Guest Artists: Nellie McCaslin, Children's Theatre, Joe Wray, Guest Actor; Dean Gates, Emmy Winner; Jon Cohn, DC Actor; Willette Thompson, SAG Actress.

Students in the drama program receive experience to reinforce the course work through productions, large and small. The BA and BFA programs in Dramatic and Theatre Arts emphasize process drama. The program attempts to give the student basic knowledge and competency as a performer, audience, historian, technician, theorist, and teacher. There are also opportunities for the student and advisor to create a highly individualized program of study. Focusing on the needs of students for academic and career preparation, the program offers various disciplines within educational theatre: recreational drama, play writing, children's theater, production, creative drama, and theatre management. Students are also prepared to enter into graduate programs. Internship experience is encouraged either in Ferrum's own summer theater program or any one of the many summer theatre groups across the country.

George Mason University

Dept. of Theatre
College of Visual and
  Performing Arts
George Mason University
4400 University Drive
Fairfax, VA 22030-4444
DEPT: (703) 993-2192

18,221 Total Enr.; compet.
100 Majors; ATHE
Semester System

T: $6,840/R&B:$7,020
O-ST T: $19,728/$7,020
MAIN: (703) 993-1120

DEGREES OFFERED

BA in Theater (35). Declare major in freshman or soph. year.

ADMISSION & FINANCIAL INFORMATION

Middle 50%, SAT avg. 1100, avg. H.S. GPA 3.24. Several scholarships avail. for VA residents.

FACULTY AND CLASSES OFFERED

10 FT, 4 PT, 1 PhD, 2 DFA, 10 MFA/MA, 1 prf. w/o adv. degree; 2 Staff

A. (2 1/2 FT, 2 PT) Intro to Theatre-1/Y; Dramatic Lit-4/Y; Theatre History-2/Y; Shakes-4/OX; Dramatic Criticism-1/O; Playwriting-4/Y; Dramaturgy-1/O

B. (2 1/2 FT, 6 PT) Acting-14/Y; Voice/Speech-2/Y; Movement-2/Y; Musical Theatre-1/O; Singing-O; Directing-3/Y; Stage Com-bat-1/Y; Alexander Technique-1/Y; Audition Techniques-1/Y

C. (4 PT) Prins of Des-1/O; Cost Des-1/O; Tech Prod-2/Y; Set Des-1/O; Lighting Des-1/O; Make-up-1/O; Stg Mgmt-1/Y; Puppetry-1/O

D. (1 PT) Arts Management-1/O; Marketing/Promotion-2/X; Budgeting/Accounting Procedure-2/X; Literary Mgmt.-1/O

FACILITIES & PRODUCTIONS

MAINSTAGE: 520 seats, fly space, computerized lighting. 2 prods: 1 Fac dir/des, 1 Guest dir/des, 2 UG des; budget $2-4,000

SECOND STAGE: 200 seats, computerized lighting. 2 prods: 1 Fac dir/des, 1 Guest dir/des, 2 UG des; budget $1,-2,500
  Many Fac/UG dir/des Workshops/Readings; budget $0-100

Facility built in 1989; includes scene, cost, welding shops, video studio, 3 mvmt/dance studios, rehearsal studio, design studio.

A faculty-directed student-run org. presents 7 prods/yr, 1 student-written play and many student-written readings produced by the dept. in the last 2 years.

Theatre of the First Amendment, Equity company, operates during school year. Its artistic director, Rick Davis, also teaches in the department, and many faculty work as TFA artists. Students also work as asst's to all principal artists, as ASM's, tech crew, understudies, and are eligible for casting subject to Equity restrictions. Students may earn EMC credit for roles in TFA productions. In the past two seasons approx. 12 students have had roles in TFA productions.

DESCRIPTION

Noted Faculty: Act/Dir: Rick Davis, Edward Gero, Kaiulani Lee, Clayton Austin, Technical Theater; Heather McDonald, Playwriting; Voice/Spch; Paul D'Andrea, Dramatic Lit.

Guest Artists: Directors: Dianne McIntyre, Shozo Sato, Lynnie Raybuck; Tom Prewitt, James Konzer, Ann Gibson, Jason Rubin, Tony Cisek, Set Designers; Brad Waller, Stage combat; Susan Martin Cohen, Alexander Technique.

The Department of Theatre in the College of Visual and Performing Arts offers a B.A. degree in Theater. The course of study stresses the breadth and rigor of the liberal arts ideal in the belief that such study, combined with serious practical training and experience, offers the best preparation for a life in the theater. Participation in Theater Division productions is expected of all declared majors. Up to two practicum credits can be awarded for satisfactory completion of four production assignments in the major (i.e. faculty or guest-directed) productions or on T.F.A. productions.

Hampton University

Dr. Karen Ward, Chair
Hampton Players & Company
Dept. of Fine & Performing Arts
Hampton University
Hampton, VA 23668
ADMISSIONS: (757) 727-5000
www.hamptonu.edu

5,500 Total Enr.; compet.
Semester System; 83 Majors
T: $14,026/$7,084 R&B
SMALL PROGRAM
DEPT: (757) 727-5402
FAX: (757) 727-5095
FAPA@hamptonu.edu

DEGREES OFFERED

BA in Comprehensive Art (7) Graphic Design (65); Theatre Performance (9); Theatre Technical and Theory (2). Declare major in freshman/sophomore year.

ADMISSION & FINANCIAL INFORMATION

Minimum high school GPA: 2.0, 920 combined SAT; 20 math, 20 verbal ACT. All applicants admitted to program. No special requirements.

FACULTY AND CLASSES OFFERED

4 Full-Time: 1 PhD, 3 MFA/MA; 3 Staff

A. (2 FT) Intro to Theatre-1/Y; Theatre History-1/Y; Shakes-1/X; Dramatic Literature & Criticism-1/Y; Playwriting-1/Y; Scriptwriting-1/X

B. (5 FT, 1 PT) Acting-2/Y; Singing-4/Y; Directing-2/Y; Voice/Speech-3/Y; Dance-2/Y

C. (3 FT) Cost Design- 1/Y; Tech. Production-1/Y; Cost

Construction/Make-up-1/Y; Technical Workshops-2/Y

D. (1 FT) Box Office Procedure-1/Y

FACILITIES AND PRODUCTIONS

MAINSTAGE: 365 seats, computerized lighting
　　3 prods: 3 Fac dir, 6 Fac des

TOUR:: 1 Fac dir, 2 Fac des prods.

Facility was built in 1965, renovated in 1996; includes scene, costume shops, sound studio, dance studio, state-of-the-art recording studio.

DESCRIPTION

Noted Faculty: Dr. Karen Ward, Criticism and Acting; Jerry Cleveland, Acting & Directing; Maurice Halfhide, Costume and Make-up; Curtis Otto, Scenography and Lighting.

Our theatre majors receive a strong liberal arts foundation in preparation for a wide variety of career opportunities. We have a diverse and demanding curriculum with two tracks including performance and technical theatre. We are an educational theatre, committed to exposing our students and community to all types of theatre in their historical and theoretical contests. Our productions serve as a laboratory for the objective teaching of drama and offer practical experience in theatre management, production, acting, directing, design and criticism. We have developed theatre dedicated to and propagated by the aspirations and culture of the African-American people, but also resilient enough to incorporate and interpret the best of world drama, whatever the source.

James Madison University

William J. Buck, Director
School of Theatre and Dance
James Madison University
MSC 5601
Harrisonburg, VA 22807
DEPT: (540) 568-6342
FAX: (540) 568-7858

15,000 Total Enr.; compet
Semester System
195 Majors, NAST, NASD
T: $3,145/$3,248 R&B/SEM
O-ST T: $8,118/$3,248 R&B
www.jmu.edu/theatre
ADMISSIONS: www.jmu.edu

DEGREES OFFERED

BA in Theatre (120), Musical Theatre (35), Dance (45)
Declare major in any year; 2001 granted 25 degrees.

ADMISSION & FINANCIAL INFORMATION

Mean SAT (1172), most freshmen rank in top 1/3 of HS class; admit 5 out of 10 applicants to theatre program, admission to th prog requires aud/int, portfolio. Scholarships avail after admission, students can apply for scholarships each spring.

FACULTY AND CLASSES OFFERED

13 Full-Time, 4 Part-Time: 4 PhD, 9 MFA; 6 Staff

A. (2 FT) Intro to Theatre-1/Y; Dramatic Lit-2/Y; Theatre History-1/Y; Shakes-2/X; Playwriting-2/Y

B. (4 FT) Acting-4/Y; Voice/Speech-1/O; Movement-1/Y; Musical Theatre-1/Y; Directing-1/Y; Stage Combat-1/O

C. (4 FT) Prins of Des-1/Y; Set Design-1/Y; Costume Design-1/Y; Lighting Des-1/Y; Technical Prod'n-2/Y; Cost Constr-1/Y; Cost History-1/Y; Stage Mgmt-1/O

D. (1 PT) Arts Management-X

FACILITIES & PRODUCTIONS

MAINSTAGE: 330 seats, fly space, computerized & electronic lighting. 4 Fac des, 7 Fac dir, 4 UG des prods.; budget $1,500-6,000

SECOND STAGE: 150 seats, computerized & electronic lighting.
　　15 prods: 20 UG dir; budget $200-2,000
　　10 UG dir Workshops/Readings; budget $100-200

Facility built in 1962, renovated in 1990; includes scene, cost shops, welding shop, sound, dance, rehearsal studios, design studio, classrooms.

A non-departmental, student-run, organization presents productions in which majors often participate. 8 student-written plays produced in the last two years.

DESCRIPTION

The James Madison University School of Theatre and Dance is organized to contribute to the general education of all students and to prepare majors for entry level positions or for further graduate study. The programs provide a broad-based education in the theory, history and practice of theatre and dance. The program stresses a humanistic, liberal arts education rather than a professional orientation to theatre. In addition to performance elements, students study theatre history, aesthetics, and dramatic theory and literature. The program offers both a major and minor in theatre and dance. Students participate in the production activities and can gain credit through the theatre practicum course. The JMU Theatre presents a season of four mainstage productions, while the Experimental Theatre provides numerous opportunities to direct, design and perform. Recent JMU graduates have gained employment with professional theatres, as well as major television and film companies. Undergraduates regularly work in professional summer theatres and theme parks.

Longwood University

Dr. Gene Muto, Coordinator,
Theatre Program
201 High Street
Longwood University
Farmville, VA 23901
DEPT: (434) 395-2643
theatre@longwood.edu
ADMISSIONS: Above address
www.longwood.edu/theatre

4,370 Total Enr.; compet.

Semester, 50 Majors, NAST
T: $3,795/$3,029 R&B
O-ST T: $7,630/$3,029 R&B
SMALL PROGRAM
FAX: (434) 395-2680
(800) 281-4677 #2
FAX: (434) 395-2332

DEGREES OFFERED

BA in Theatre Ed (12), Theatre (20), BFA in Th. Des & Tech (10), Acting (9). 2006 granted 7 degrees BA in Theatre.

ADMISSION & FINANCIAL INFORMATION

GPA 3.0 min-transfer, 3.3 freshmen, 1085 SAT (Act 23 if necessary). 71% of applicants admitted to institution, 73% admitted to theatre program. No special req's. for admission to Th. program. Scholarships avail based on merit and/or need after one semester.

FACULTY AND CLASSES OFFERED

4 FT, 1 PT, 1 PhD, 4 MFA; 3 Staff

A. (1 FT, 1 PT) Intro to Th-2/Y; Th Hist-2/Y; Shakes-1/O; Dra Lit-2/Y; Playwriting-1/O; Theatre Aesthetics-1/Y

B. (1 FT) Acting-4/Y; Voice/Speech-3/YO; Mvmt-3/Y; Directing-1/Y; Singing-X; Dance-X

C. (2 FT) Set Design-2/Y; Cost Des.-2/Y; Lighting Des-2/Y; Tech Prod.-3/Y; Costume Construction-2/Y; Make-up-1/Y; Stage Mgmt-1/Y;Props-1/O; Drafting-1/O; Scene Painting-1/O; Fashion History-1/O; Elements of Design-1/Y

FACILITIES AND PRODUCTIONS

MAINSTAGE: 400 seats, fly space, computerized lighting
4 prods: 2 Fac dir, 1 Guest dir, 1 UG dir, 2 UG des; budget $42,000

SECOND STAGE: 75 seats, computerized lighting
4 prod: 2 UG dir/des;budget varies

Facility built 1951, scheduled for renovation in 2008; incl. scene, costume shops, dance, rehearsal studio, design studios, computer lab.

DESCRIPTION

Noted Faculty: Gene Muto, Directing, Th. History, Dramatic Lit.; Pam Arkin, Acting, Voice & Mvmt, Creative Dramatics; Melissa Panzarello, Costumes, Make-Up, Props; Eric Koger, Tech Th., Scene & Light Des, SM.

Guest Artists: Bread & Puppet Theatre, Dah Theatre - Yugoslavia, Alabama Shakespeare Festival.

In order to provide a cohesive body of knowledge in performance art, Longwood Theatre is committed to excellence in teaching, advancement of knowledge, and cultural enrichment. The program is designed both to prepare students for professional careers and to serve as a foundation for further study and training. To this end, Longwood offers two degrees in Theatre: The B.A. in Theatre; and the Pre-professional Track, leading to the B.F.A. for Theatre Practitioners. 1) The B.A. Degree: With the broad array of theatre courses, Longwood students have the opportunity to achieve a traditional and holistic view of the world through the study of literature, performance art, and technological development. B.A. students will be prepared for careers in Education and Applied Theatre, and for graduate study. 2) The B.F.A. Degree: A faculty and staff of theatre historians, theoreticians, and professional artists mentor students who desire pre-professional training in Design/Technology and Acting. Entrance to this program is selective and competitive. Students undergo analysis and evaluation each semester.

Mary Baldwin College ···········

Paul Menzer, Prog Dir.
Department of Theatre
Dr. Frank Southerington, Dir.
MLitt/MFA
Mary Baldwin College
Staunton, VA 24401
DEPT: (540) 887-7189
ADM: (540) 887-7000
http://www.mbc.edu

1,563 Total Enr.; competitive
Sem. + May Term; 14 Majors, 51
Grad students
shakespeare@mbc.edu
T: $22,730/$6,470 R&B
SMALL PROGRAM
FAX: (540) 887-7189
tsouther@mbc.edu
admit@mbc.edu

DEGREES OFFERED

BA in Theatre and Drama (14), Arts Management—Theatre (2), MLitt

and MFA in Shakespeare and Renaissance Lit. in Performance (51). Declare major in soph. year.

ADMISSION & FINANCIAL INFORMATION

SAT or ACT, HS transcript. Interview recommended; 80% of applicants admitted to inst. No special req's. for Th. prog., but int. recommended. Baldwin Schol based on SAT & GPA; Bailey Scholarship competition. GRE and aud./interview required for graduate students. 60% of applicants admitted.

FACULTY AND CLASSES OFFERED

5 Full-Time, 4 Part-Time: 4 PhD, 4 MFA/MA; 1 Staff

A. (1 FT, 2 PT) Intro to Theatre-3/Y; Th History-2/Y; Shakes-1/YX; Dramatic Lit-5/Y; Playwriting-1/O; London Theatre- 1/O

B. (1/2 PT) Acting-3/Y; Voice/Speech-3/Y; Movement-2/YX; Mime, etc.-1/YX; Singing-4/YX; Musical Theatre-1/OX; Directing-2/O

C. (1/2 FT) Set Design-1/Y; Cost Des.-1/Y; Lighting Des-1/Y; Intro to Prod'n-1/Y; Tech Prod.-1/Y; Costume Const-1/Y; Make-up-1/O; Stage Mgmt-1/Y; Indep. study in all areas-4/Y

D. (2 PT) Arts Mgmt-3/Y; Marketing-3/YX; Development-1/Y; Accounting Procedure-6/YX; Public Relations-2/YX; Personnel Mgmt-1/YX; Computer Applics-1/O; Advert-2/YX

E. 36 courses at the graduate level

FACILITIES AND PRODUCTIONS

MAINSTAGE: 120 seats, computerized lighting. 5 prods: 2 Fac dir/ des, 1 Guest dir/Fac des, 1 Guest dir/student des, 1 student dir/des; budget $2,000

SECOND STAGE: 232 seats, electronic lighting

BLACKFRIARS PLAYHOUSE: The only modern replica of Shakespeare's winter theatre, in conjunction with Shenandoah Shakespeare International Shakespearian Scholars for graduate program.

2 Guest dir prods; budget $1,500-separate budget for MLitt/MFA

Facility built 1930, renovated 1984; incl. scene, costume, props shops, video, dance studios, 6 classrooms, computer labs.

DESCRIPTION

Guest Artists:Shenandoah Shakespeare, Timothy Mooney.

Mary Baldwin College offers an undergraduate liberal arts degree with majors in theatre or arts management (theatre). The training is deliberately broad, which we view as the best preperation for careers in the theatre. All female acting roles and production responsibilities are reserved for students, providing the experience that enables students to enter and succeed in graduate school or the profession, following graduation. Our extensive internship program also enhances students' professional training. Mary Baldwin offers an Mlitt/MFA in Shakespeare and Renaissance Literature in Performance in partnership with Shenandoah Shakespeare. The only replica of Shakespeare's Blackfriar's Playhouse in the world is the laboratory and performance space for the students as they study the literature, performance, history, art, and theatrical conventions of the period. Guest professors include Andrew Gurr, Giles Block, Tiffany Stern and Tina Packer. The program is firmly grounded in the liberal arts tradition combining scholarship with practical experience.

Old Dominion University

Christopher Hanna, Dir. of Theatre	17,500 Total Enr.; compet
Dept. of Theatre Arts & Comm.	Semester System
Old Dominion University	40 Majors; NAST
5215 Hampton Blvd.	T: $6,000(avg.)/R&B fees vary
Norfolk, VA 23529	O-ST T: $16,500 (avg.)
www.odu.edu	R&B fees vary
channa@odu.edu	SMALL PROGRAM
DEPT: (757) 683-3838	FAX: (757) 683-4700
ADM: 108 Rollins Hall	(757) 683-36385
	FAX: (757) 683-3255

DEGREES OFFERED

BA in Theatre (40); BFA in Acting—instituted Spring '02.
Declare major in sophomore year; 2001 granted 5 UG degs.

ADMISSION & FINANCIAL INFORMATION

SAT 1050, GPA 3.20, exception allowed. Theatre majors compete for $1,000 support awards through audition or portfolio review at the start of each academic year.

FACULTY AND CLASSES OFFERED

3 Full-Time, 2 Part-Time: 1 PhD, 3 MFA/MA; 3 Staff

A. (1 FT) Intro to Theatre-6/Y; Dramatic Lit-4/X; Theatre History-2/O; Shakes-2/X+1/O; Playwriting-2/X

B. (2 FT, 2 PT) Acting-8/Y; Voice/Speech-2/Y; Mvmt-1/O; Dance-1/Y; Singing-2/X; Musical Th-1/X; Directing-1/Y; Stage Combat-1-O

C. (1 FT) Prins of Des-1/O; Set Design-1/O; Lighting Des- 1/O; Tech Prod'n-1/Y; Cost Construction-1/O; Make-up-1/O; Video Production-2/Y; Cost Hist-1/O; Stage Mgmt-1/O

FACILITIES & PRODUCTIONS

MAINSTAGE: 300 seats, fly space, computerized lighting. 2 prods: 1 Fac dir, 2 Fac des, 1 Guest dir, 2 Guest des, 2 UG des; budget $5,000-8,000

SECOND STAGE: 90 seats, computerized lighting. 2 prods: 1 Fac dir, 2 Fac des, 2 Guest des, 1 UG dir, 2 UG des; budget $500-2,000. 2 Workshops/Readings: 2 Fac dir/des, 2 Guest des, 2 UG des; budget $500-2,000

Facility was built in 1950, renovated in 1985; includes scene shop, CAD facility, video studio, design studio, 3 dance studios, rehearsal studio.

Two student-written plays produced in the last two years.

Virginia Stage Company, Equity. Internship opportunities in all areas, including mainstage performance opportunities.

DESCRIPTION

Noted Faculty: Christopher Hanna, Acting & Directing; Antonio Zarro, Camera Acting & Filmmaking; Brian Silberman, Playwriting.

Guest Artists: Leon Ingulsrud, Director; Mark Olson, Masks; Bonnie Raphael, Shakespeare Text; Deborah Bell, Costumes; Geralo Swarz, Director.

Old Dominion University theatre differs from many university programs by giving students the opportunity to be involved in production throughout all years of study and in all capacities. The faculty works with every student in individualizing a course of study, range of production responsibilities, and a professional internship opportunity that addresses that student's specific interests, talents, and career goals. Emphasis is placed simultaneously on attaining the practical tools that lead to successful job placement and on developing an informed context for creative decision making that characterizes serious artistic pursuit.

Radford University

Carl H. Lefko, Chair	9,000 Total Enr.; competitive
Dept. of Theatre	Sem. System; NAST
Box 6969	82 Majors; ATHE, SETC
Radford University	T: $5,746/$6,218 R&B
Radford, VA 24141	O-ST T: $13,494/$6,218 R&B
DEPT: (540) 831-5012	FAX: (540) 831-6313
clefko@radford.edu	
ADMISSIONS: Radford University, Box 6903	
(540) 831-5271	ruadmiss@radford.edu

DEGREES OFFERED

BA (22), BS (60) in Theatre (Acting, directing, perf, design, tech) Declare major in freshman/sophomore year; 2004 granted 16 degrees.

ADMISSION & FINANCIAL INFORMATION

Avg. SAT-1000, avg. GPA-3.3 and above; accept 70% to inst.; departmental interview recommended, but not req.; 80% admitted to theatre program; schols avail in all areas, based on theatre experience, commitment to the major, strong work-ethic, GPA of 2.8 and above, audition and application required.

FACULTY AND CLASSES OFFERED

7 FT, 1 PT, 7 MFA, 1 Prof w/out adv. degree

A. (4 FT) Intro to Theatre-1/Y; Theatre History-2/Y; Dramatic Lit-2/Y; Playwriting-1/Y

B. (1 FT) Acting-5/Y; Voice/Speech-2/Y; Movement-1/X; Directing-2/Y; Stage Combat-1/O

C. (3 FT) Set Design-2/Y; Costume Design- 2/Y; Costume History-1/Y; Lighting Des-2/Y; Make-up-4/Y

D. (1 FT) Arts Mgmt-1/Y

FACILITIES AND PRODUCTIONS

MAINSTAGE: 500 seats, fly space, computerized & electronic ltg. 3 prods: 3 Fac dir, 2 Fac des, 1 UG dir; bdgt $5,000-8,000

SECOND STAGE: 100 seats, computerized & electron. lighting 3 UG dir/des prods; budget $500-1,000

Facility was built in 1926, renovated n 1991; includes scene shop, costume shop, prop shop, sound studio, video studio, dance studio, CAD lab.

A non-departmental, student-run producing org. presents 1 play per yr. in which DEPT: majors participate. 3 student-written plays produced by DEPT: in the last two years.

Connection with Mill Mountain Theater. Opportunities for apprentices and interns on a regular basis.

DESCRIPTION

Noted Faculty: Jennifer Juul, Acting; History & Lit; CW. David Wheeler, Light Des, Tech; Anthony Guest, Acting, Stage Combat; Carl Holland Lefko, Design; Theodore McKosky, Film, Sound; Wesley Young, Performance, Directing; Monica Weinzapfel, Costuming

Guest Performers: Matthew Ashford, Actor; Kyle T. Heffner, Actor; Sally Struthers, Actor

Curricula at Radford University lead to bachelor of arts and science which are designed around liberal arts core. In addition to theatre as a general background, concentrations of acting, directing, technical theatre or history and literature are required. A challenging variety of performance opportunities, including major studio, children's theatrical productions for the campus and community and the general public are mounted. A variety of areas such as technical theatre, cinematic arts, makeup, acting,costume, scenic, lighting design and construction are among those studied. We also have study tours to New York and abroad, usually scheduled during summer sessions or semester breaks. Professional internships are available to students through departmental liaisons with Mill Mountain Theatre of Roanoke, Virginia.

Shenandoah University

Thomas Albert, Chairman	2,500 Total Enr.; competitive
Music Theatre/Theatre	Semester System
Shenandoah University	180 Majors
1460 University Ave	T: $11,020/term
Winchester, VA 22601	R&B: $3,995/term
talbert@su.edu	
ADM: (800) 432-2266	FAX: (540) 665-4627
www.su.edu	

DEGREES OFFERED

BFA in Music Theatre (116), Theatre for Youth (10); BA in Acting (36), Scenic/Lighting Design (10), Directing (2), Cost. Design (5) Declare major in freshman year; 2001 granted 28 degrees.

ADMISSION & FINANCIAL INFORMATION

GPA 2.5, SAT 1,000; Accept 60%; Req. by Theatre Program: Aud. for Performance; Audition/Portfolio review req. for design/tech.; Accept 1 out of 4 applicants to program; Talent Scholarships by audition or portfolio for designers.

FACULTY AND CLASSES OFFERED

16 1/2 FT, 7 PT; 7 PhD; 10 MFA/MA; 2 Prof. w/o adv. degree; 2 1/2 Staff

A. (1/2 PT) Dramatic Lit-2/X; Theatre History-2/Y; Shakes-1/X

B. (12 FT, 5 PT) Acting-11/Y; Voice/Speech-2/Y; Mvmt-4/Y; Singing/Private Study-Y; Directing-4/Y; Mus Th-3/Y; Childs Th-2/Y; Dance-16/Y; Showmakers/Childrens Tour-2/Y; Music Theatre Ensemble-2/Y; Creative Dramatics-1/O

C. (5 FT) Prins of Design-2/Y; Set Des.-2/O; Cost Des.-2/O; Lighting Des.-2/Y; Tech Prod-1/Y; Cost Constr.-2/Y; Cost Hist.-2/O; Make-up-1/Y; Stage Mgmt-1/O; Scenic Art-2/O; Stage Props-1/O; Stage Lighting-1/Y; Sound-2/Y; Graphic Arts for Design-2/O; Cost Rendering-2/O

D. (1 PT) Arts Mgment-2/X; Marketing- 2/X; Development-1/X; Legal: Contracts/Copyright-2/X; Accounting Procedure-3/X

FACILITIES & PRODUCTIONS

MAINSTAGE: 632 seats, fly space, computerized lighting. 6 prods: 6 Fac dir, 16 Fac des, 2 UG des prods; budget $4-6,000

SECOND STAGE: 175 seats, computerized lighting. 4 prods: 4 Fac dir, 4 Fac des, 6 UG des prods; budget $1,500-2,000 55 Workshops/Readings; UG dir/des

Facility built in 1998; includes scene, costume shop, sound studio, 2 dance studios, 2 rehearsal studios, design studio, media center/midi-recording studio, CAD facility.

Shenandoah Summer Music Theatre, professional stock company, produces 4 musicals in 10-wk season using Shenandoah University facilities, budget and maintenance services. En-rolled students and alumni are given first chance at auditions for company members, interns and staff positions before open auditions. Equity Guest Artists often join the company. It is an intensive production experience, rehearsing one show while performing another.

DESCRIPTION

Guest Artists: Robert Duval, Actor; 10 Equity Guest Actors per summer season, divided amongst the 4 shows.

Theatre at Shenandoah University is a way of life. Extensive classroom experience and intensive production work are combined to develop the young pre-professional theatre artist. Students are encouraged to audition and be cast in productions starting immediately. Each discipline—the BFA in Music Theatre, the BA (BFA pending) concentrations of acting, directing, scenic and lighting design and costume design—are intensive in their specialty and in all areas of theatre. 85% of alumni are working in their fields. Those students who have chosen graduate school have gone to the school of their choice with assistantships and fellowships.

University of Mary Washington

Gregg Stull, Chair, Th. Program	4,000 Total Enr.; compet.
Theatre & Dance	Semester System
University of Mary Washington	42 Majors
1301 College Ave.	T: $6,084/$6,244 R&B
Fredericksburg, VA 22401-5300	O-ST.T: $15,964/$6,244 R&B
gstull@umw.edu	www.umw.edu/cas/theatre
(540)654-1980	FAX: (540) 654-1083
ADM: UMW, 1301 College Ave., Fredericksburg, VA 22401	
(540) 654-2000	
www.umw.edu/admissions	

DEGREES OFFERED

BA in Theatre Arts (37). Declare major in sophomore year. Granted 15 degrees in 2004.

ADMISSION & FINANCIAL INFORMATION

GPA of 3.0, SAT between 1650 - 1980. Accepts 60% into inst. Scholarships are available to students active in the program on an application basis.

FACULTY AND CLASSES OFFERED

6 Full-Time, 2 Part-Time: 1 PhD, 6 MFA/MA

A. (2 1/2 FT, 2 PT) Intro to Theatre-1/Y; Theatre History-2/O; Shakes-2/X; Dramatic Lit-2/Y; Dramatic Crit-1/X; Playwriting-1/O

B. (1 FT) Acting-3/Y; Movement-1/Y; Singing-2/X; Directing-2/Y; Dance-7/Y; Film-1/X; Voice/Speech-1/Y; Musical Theatre-2/O

C. (1 1/2 FT) Prins of Des-1/Y; Set Design-1/Y; Cost Des.-1/O; Lighting Des.-1/Y; Cost Construction-1/O; Make-up-1/O; Stage Mgmt.-1/O; Stagecraft-2/Y; Stage Painting-1/O; Theatre Crafts-1/O; Fashion History-1/O; Fabric Painting & Dyeing-1/Y;

Patterning-1/O.

D. (1/2 FT) Arts Management-1/Y; Marketing & Promotion-1/X; Budgeting/Accounting Procedure-1/X

FACILITIES AND PRODUCTIONS

MAINSTAGE: 295 seats, fly seats, computerized lighting. 4 prods: 2 Fac dir, 3 Fac des, 1 Guest des; budget $25,000-50,000

SECOND STAGE: flexible seating, computerized lighting. 4 prods, 4 UG dir, 12 UG des.

Facility built 1955, last renovated in 1994; includes scene shop, dye room, costume shop, prop shop, CAD facility, 2 dance studios, 2 rehearsal studios, 2 design studios, 8 classrooms, and a Black Box studio.

There is a non-departmental, student-run producing organization that presents 3 dance programs per year.

2 student written plays were produced in the last 2 years.

DESCRIPTION

Noted Faculty: Gregg Stull, Acting, Directing, Management; Helen Housely, Theatre History & Voice; Julie Hodge, Scene & Lighting Design; Kevin McCluskey, Costume Design; Jill Mitten, Literature; David Hunt, Scene & Lighting Design.

Guest Artists: Nancy Robinette, Acting; Martin Desjandins, Sound Design; J. Christopher Dalen, Choreographer; Christopher Wingert, Musical Dir

Whether you intend to work professionally, work in a related field or pursue professional or graduate training, the liberal arts education you receive at the University of Mary Washington will prepare you for your future. Our flexible major program allows you to concentrate in the area of theatre in which you have the greatest interest, as well as pursue a double major or obtain a teaching license, if you wish. Our students have excellent opportunities beginning in their first year. You can explore your potential in class or on the stage, in the design studio or costume shop. Whether your interest is acting, scene design, stage management, sound design, directing, playwriting, dramaturgy, costume construction, scenic technology or theatre management, the Department of Theatre and Dance has a place for you!

University of Richmond

Walter Schoen, Chair, Th. Program
Modlin Center for the Arts
University of Richmond
Richmond, VA 23173
(804) 289-8592
ADM: 28 Westhampton Way, Richmond, VA 23173
(804) 289-8640
http://theatre.richmond.edu

3,751 Total Enr.; h. compet.
Semester System
16 Majors
T: $42,500 TOTAL
FAX: (804) 287-1841
FAX: (804) 287-6003

DEGREES OFFERED

BA in Theatre Arts. Declare major in sophomore year.

ADMISSION & FINANCIAL INFORMATION

SAT I (1220-1370) & SAT II, (Writing & math subject tests). Accepts 45% into inst, admits all apps to Th. Prog. Scholarships by audition (tape or in person) or portfolio. 1 partial scholarship offered each year. Aud in Jan. or Feb., application on website.

FACULTY AND CLASSES OFFERED

8 Full-Time: 1 PhD, 6 MFA/MA; 2 Staff

A. (2 FT) Intro to Theatre-1/Y; Theatre History-1/Y; Shakes-1/Y; Dramatic Lit-1/YX; Playwriting-1/O

B. (3 FT) Acting-2/Y; Directing-1/O; Dance-5/Y; Stage Combat-1/O; Musical Th-1/O

C. (2 FT) Prins of Des-1/Y; Set Design-1/Y; Cost Des.-2/Y; Cost Hist-1/O; Lighting Des.-1/O; Make-up-1/Y; Stage Mgmt.-1/O; Tech Prod'n-1/Y

D. Arts Management-1/Y

FACILITIES AND PRODUCTIONS

MAINSTAGE: 500 seats, computerized lighting, digital sound system. 4 prods: 3 Fac dir, 1 Fac des, 1 Guest dir/des; budget $8,000-25,000

SECOND STAGE: 150 seats, black box, computerized lighting 3 student dir/des prods. 3 Guest Workshops./Readings

Facility built 1996; includes scene shop, costume shop, classroom, rehearsal studio.

Department majors generally participate in a non-departmental, student-run producing organization that presents 4 productions per year.

DESCRIPTION

Noted Faculty: W. Reed West, III, Technical Dir./Instructor; Walter Schoen, Instructor/Director; Dorothy Holland, Instructor/Director; Myra Daleng, Instructor/Dance Director; Anne Van Gelder, Instructor/Asst. Dance Director

The University of Richmond's Theatre Program seeks to maintain high academic standards while producing each season four mainstage events. This is a liberal arts program, with basic instruction offered in all areas of theatre. Small classes as well as a full production schedule provide opportunity for much individual interaction between students and professors and also important production responsibilities. We stress Communication, Collaboration, Discipline, Leadership and Professionalism. Theatre major requires 37 hours distribution among History/Theory, Performance, Technical Theatre/Design We stress the interrelationship of theatrical arts with other disciplines such as English, Modern Languages, History and, yes, Physics. Majors are expected to obtain practical—and crucial—experience in actual theatre production. Independent Study is available for selected majors to design mainstage productions, to direct studio theatre productions. The Program also offers a Theatre Arts minor requiring 22 hours. UR's Theatre Program, by promoting creativity, discipline, a cultured mind, and the ability to work with other people, is superior training for any non-theatre career that might be pursued by a liberal arts graduate.

University of Virginia

Tom Bloom, Chair
Dept. of Drama
U. of Virginia
PO Box 400128
Charlottesville, VA 22904
(804) 924-3326

17,500 Total Enr.; h. compet.
Semester System
ATHE, NAST, U/RTA, SETC
75 Majors (UG)
T: $17,764
O-ST T: $35,644

tab4p@virginia.edu

DEGREES OFFERED

BA in Drama (25); MFA in Acting (8), Set Design (2), Costume Design (3). MFA in Lighting Design (2), Theatre Technology (4) Declare major in second year; 2005 granted 25 UG degs.

ADMISSION & FINANCIAL INFORMATION

UG admission, highly competitive; University admits 34% of applicants. Req. SAT: 1260/1330, GPA: NA, 2 Achievement tests; Grad admission, competitive; No special req's. for UG Th program, accepts all; Grad req's. Aud./Int., admits 17 out of 100. UG Scholarships, Jefferson Scholarship & Ecoles Scholarship; Grad-various Scholarships/fellowships/assistantships.

FACULTY AND CLASSES OFFERED

15 Full-Time, 3 Part-Time: 3 PhD, 14 MFA/MA; 4 Staff

A. (3 FT) Intro to Th-1/Y; Th History-7/Y; Shakes-2/O; Dramatic Lit-2/Y; Playwriting-6/Y

B. (5 FT, 1/2 PT) Acting-5/Y; Voice-3/Y; Movement- 1/Y; Mime,etc.-2/O; Singing-X; Directing-11/Y; Oral Interp-1/Y; Stage Combat-2/Y

C. (3 FT) Prins of Des-2/Y; Set Design-4/Y; Costume Design-6/Y; Lighting Des-2/Y; Tech Prod-6/Y; Cost Constr-6/Y; Cost History-2/Y; Make-up-2/Y; Stage Mgmt-1/Y

D. (1 FT) Arts Management-1/Y; Marketing/Promotion-1/Y

FACILITIES AND PRODUCTIONS

MAINSTAGE: 595 seats, fly space, computerized lighting.4 prods: 3 Fac dir/des, or 1 Guest dir/des, or 2 Grad dir/des; budget $4,000-7,000

SECOND STAGE: 200 seats, computerized lighting. 6 prods: Mostly student directed; budget $500-1,000 24-30 Workshops/Readings: UG dir/des; budget $100

Facility was built in 1974; includes scene, costume, props shops, 2 rehearsal studios, design studio, 5 classrooms.

A non-departmental, student-run organization presents 10-20 one-act productions per year in which majors participate. 4 student-written plays produced in the last two years.

Heritage Repertory Company (Equity/U/RTA, Guest Artist), a resident company of professional theatre artists from across the country, offers students acting and directing internships, tech and front of house positions, by aud/interview. EMC points available.

DESCRIPTION

Noted Faculty: Robert Chapel, John Frick, Doug Grissom, Lavahn Hoh, Richard Warner, Gwen West, Kate Burke, Lee Kennedy, Tom Bloom, Betsy Tucker.

Guest Artists: Ann Hould-Ward, Joanne Akalaitis, Anne Bogart, Tina Shepard, Bill Irwin.

Rooted in the liberal arts tradition, the undergraduate program emphasizes collaboration and risk-taking in educating students to be "people of the theatre." Students are required to take courses in all areas of the theatre, acting, directing, design, literature and history. The M.F.A. is a three-year conservatory program with an academic component, with enrollment once every three years. Its mission is to train people for a career as a professional actor, director, or designer.

Virginia Commonwealth University

David S. Leong, Chair
Department of Theatre
Virginia Commonwealth Univ.
922 Park Avenue
Box 842524
Richmond, VA 23284
(804) 828-1514

21,260 Total Enr.; compet
Semester System, NAST
235 UG, 42 G Majors
T: UG $6,196/
O-ST T: UG $18,572
r&b: $7,567l
Fax: (804) 828-6741

ADM: UG: Univ. Enrollment Services, UG Admissions, 821 W. Franklin St., Richmond, VA 23284   theatre@vcu.edu
Grad: 901 W. Franklin St., P.O. Box 843051, Richmond, VA 23284
www.vcu.edu/ugrad/   ugrad@vcu.edu

DEGREES OFFERED

BFA in Performance (159), Theatre Education (23), Design/Tech (45), SM (8); MFA in Costumer Des (2).
MFA in theatre Pedagogy with emphasis in Acting/Directing, Voice and Speech, Movement and Stage Combat, Theatre History, Literature and Criticism, Scene or Costume Design. 2004 granted 30 UG, 10 Grad Degs.

ADMISSION & FINANCIAL INFORMATION

GPA 3.0+; SAT 1050+, audition/portfolio and interview required; Accept 75 out of 200 to UG program. Send for application, above address.

FACULTY AND CLASSES OFFERED

14 FT, 3 PT, 3 PhD, 8 MFA/MA, 6 Staff

A. (2 FT) Intro to Theatre-2/Y; Theatre History-2/Y; Shakes; Dramatic Lit-2/Y; Dramatic Criticism; Playwriting

B. (8 FT, 1 PT) Acting-6/Y; Voice/Speech-4/Y; Movement-4/Y; Directing-2/Y; Physical Acting and Stage Combat-1/Y; Acting for the Camera; Audition-1/Y

C. (4 FT, 4 PT) Stagecraft; Cost Construct-1/Y; Set Design; Costume Design-2/Y; Lighting Des-1/Y; Hist of Costume; Make-up-2/Y; Stage Mgmt-2/Y; Drawing-4/Y; Scene Des-1/Y

D. Business of Theatre-1/Y

FACILITIES AND PRODUCTIONS

MAINSTAGE: Hodges Theatre: 256 seats, 3/4 round; ltd. fly space, computerized & electronic lighting. 4 prods: 2 Fac dir/des, 2 dir by third-year grad students; budget $10,000-20,000 per prod.

SECOND STAGE: Shafer Street Playhouse: 150 seats, proscenium, computerized & electronic lighting. 2 studio productions directed by second-yr grad students; budget $100-5,000 per production

Numerous workshops, scenes and special productions offered

The Performing Arts Center was built in 1980. Includes Hodges Theatre, scene shop, costume and prop storage, dance studio, design computer room, 2 classrooms, faculty offices.

Shafer Street Playhouse will be renovated in summer 1999 and will include: theatre, 2 acting and 1 directing studio, scene design studio, make-up studio, small conference room, and student offices.

Theatre VCU has a cooperative and collaborative agreement with Theatre Virginia, a LORT theatre, providing internships for students in every area, acting, assistant directing, SM, design, and technical. Students can earn points toward their Equity card. Guest artists frequently lecture at Theatre VCU.

DESCRIPTION

Noted Faculty: David S. Leong, Chairman and Producer, Physical Acting and Stage Combat; Gary C. Hopper, Assistant Chair/ Director of Undergraduate Studies, Theatre History; Janet Rodgers, Director of Voice and Speech; Marvin Sims (Head of Performance), Kelly Morgan, Monica Benton-Palmer and Joe Sampson, Acting and Directing; Aaron Anderson, Voice and Movement, Acting and Stage Combat; Liz Hopper, Head of Stage Design, Costume Design; Ron Keller, Scene Design; Lou Szari, Lighting Design; Joy Paoletto, Alexander Technique; Maggie O'Donnell, Stage Management.

Guest Artists 2003-04: Patti d'Beck, Choreographer; Frank Bluestein, Teacher; Avner Eisenberg, Clown; Susie Cordin, SM; Lynn Thomson, Dramaturg; Randy Mercer, Hair, Wig, Make-up; Shozo Sato, Dir; Michele Shay, Dir.

BFA degrees are offered in Performance, Design, SM and Theatre Ed. MFA degrees are offered in Theatre Pedagogy. Theatre Pedagogy majors emphasize voice and speech, voice and movement, movement, acting/directing, theatre history, literature and criticism, scene design or costume design. The programs are designed for the student who plans a career in any area of the professional theatre or who intends to teach theatre at the university/college or secondary school level. Students are guided in an area of specialization as well as in the fundamentals of artistic decision making. The student will develop a communictive ability through which he/she may participate fully in the creative process of theatre.

Virginia Tech

Patricia A. Raun, Head
Dept. of Theatre Arts
203 Performing Arts Bldg.
Virginia Tech
Blacksburg, VA 24061-0141
DEPT: (540) 231-5335
www.theatre.vt.edu
ADMISSIONS: 104 Burruss, Blacksburg, VA 24061-0202
(540) 231-6267
VTADMISS@vt.edu

24,000 Total Enr.
Semester System
133 Majors; NAST, ATHE
T: $5,450/$4,700 R&B
O-ST T: $17,406/$4,700 R&B
FAX: (540) 231-7321
praun@vt.edu
ttp://www.vt.edu/admissions.html

DEGREES OFFERED

BA in Theatre Arts (120); MFA in Costume Des (3), SM (3), Light Des (2), Scene Des (3), Tech Dir (1). Declare major in 1st-3rd year; 2004 granted 25 UG, 9 Grad degrees.

ADMISSION & FINANCIAL INFORMATION

No min. but entering class typically avgs. SAT 1100 to 1290 range, top 10% of class, Audition/interview/portfolio review for available scholarships. Theatre program admits 1 out of 3 UG applicants, 1 out of 4 Grad apps.

FACULTY AND CLASSES OFFERED

14 FT, 2 PhD, 11 MFA/MA, 1 Prof. w/o adv.degree; 4 Staff

A. (3 FT) Intro to Theatre-2/Y; Theatre History-2/Y; Shakes-3/OX; Dramatic Lit-2/Y; Dramatic Criticism-O; Playwriting-2/Y

B. (4 FT) Acting-2/Y; Voice/Speech-3/Y; Movement-3/Y; Mime, etc.-1/O; Singing-1/O; Musical Th.-1/OX; Directing-2/Y; Stage Combat-1/O; Dance-1/Y

C. (5 FT) Prins of Design-2-3/Y; Set Design-2/Y; Costume Design-3/Y; Lighting Des-2/Y; Tech Prod'n-3/Y; Costume Construction-1/Y; Make-up-1/Y; Stage Mgmt-1/Y

D. (2 FT) Arts Management-2/Y; Marketing/Promo-1/O; Box Office-1/O; Dev and Grant Writing-O; Legal Contracts/Copyright-O; Budgt. Procedure-1/X

FACILITIES AND PRODUCTIONS

MAINSTAGE: 460 seats, fly space, computerized/electron lighting. 5 prods: 4 Fac dir, 3-6 Fac des, 1 GA dir/des, 1-2 Grad des; budget $8,000-28,000

SECOND STAGE: 230 seats, fly space, computerized & electronic lighting. 5 prods: 2 Fac dir, 4 Fac des, 1 GA dir, 1 Grad dir, 4 Grad des, 1 UG dir/des; budget $1,000-4,000.

THIRD STAGE: 60-120 seats, electronic lighting.

8 Workshops/Readings: 1 Fac dir, 1 Fac des, Occasional GA dir, 2 Grad dir, 4 Grad des, 5 UG dir, 6 UG des; bdgt $50-200

Mainstage facility built in 1993: includes scene shop, costume shop, props shop, sound studio, CAD facility, dance studio, rehearsal studios, design studio, classrooms.

There is a non-dept student-run organization that presents two shows per year. 6 student written plays have be written by the dept.

Affilitated with AEA theatres, Arena Stage, Mill Mountain Theatre, Barter Theatre and others operating through the school year. Informal connection with opportunities for internships and auditioning for roles.

DESCRIPTION

Noted Faculty: Tony Distler, Donald A. Drapeau, Bob Leonard, Randy Ward, John McCann, John Ambrosone.

Guest Artists: Ping Chong, Molly Smith, Ben Cameron, Jack Young, Andrew Wade, Benny Ambush, Emsa Lakovich, Gertrude Stein Repertory Theatre, Seret Scott.

The Department of Theatre Arts offers a balanced approach to the study of theatre by providing a strong liberal arts orientation to the exploration of the history, literature, and practice of theatre, and by having an active production program in which students can participate and develop performance and production skills. Internships with professional theatres and advanced course work are available to those students who wish to pursue more focused study. 15-20 productions each year allow students to develop marketable theatre skills. The success of the program is due primarily to the close working relationship between the students and the faculty of teacher/artists who have worked professionally. The low student/teacher ratio makes it possible for students to receive individual attention and guidance. The faculty is supported by one of the finest theatre facilities in the East. A 500-seat, fully equipped modern proscenium theatre, a 210-seat thrust stage theatre, and a totally flexible "black box" theatre allow the student to experience a variety of approaches to theatre production.

WASHINGTON

Central Washington University

Scott R. Robinson, Chair
Theatre Arts Dept.
Central Washington University
400 E University Way
Ellensburg, WA 98926
robinsos@cwu.edu
www.cwu.edu/~theatre
DEPT: (509) 963-1273
ADMISSIONS: 400 E University Way, above
Toll free 866-298-4968

10,435 Total Enr.; competitive
106 Majors
   42 grads; ATHE
Quarter System
T: $1,464 UG/$2,104 Grad
O-ST T: $4,449 UG/$4,704 Grad

FAX: (509) 963-1767

886-CWU-4YOU

DEGREES OFFERED

Degrees in Performance, Design/Technology, Theatre Management, Education/Youth Theatre, General Studies; Theatre Production. Declare major in 1st or 2nd year; 2007 granted 24 UG degrees, 14 Grad.

ADMISSION & FINANCIAL INFORMATION

GPA avg 3.22, SAT avg 1000, ACT avg 20. Admitted through admissions index using all scores. 68% applicants are accepted by institution. 98 out of 100 UG applicants admitted to theatre program; 95 out of 100 admitted to Grad.Application required for specializations. Graduate level see Grad office. Out of state tuition waivers available at Department. Also housing, talent and study abroad scholarships from Dept.

FACULTY AND CLASSES OFFERED

7 FT, 5 PT, 1 PhD, 8 MFA/MA, 2 prof. w/o advanced degree, 6 Staff

A. (1 1/2 FT) Intro to Theatre-1/Y; Dramatic Lit-5/Y; Dramatic Crit-1/Y; Th Hist-3/Y; Shakes-2/Y; Playwriting-2/Y

B. (2 1/2 FT) Acting-6/Y; Movement-3/Y; Singing-3/Y; Directing-2/Y; Dance (in dept)-1/Y; Stage Combat-3/Y; Dance-12/X

C. (3 FT, 3 PT) Prins of Des-1/Y; Cost Des-1/O; Tech Production-1/Y; Set Design-1/O; Lighting Des-1/O; Cost Construction-2/Y; Make-up-1/Y; Stage Mgmt-1/Y

D. (2 PT) Arts Managment-1/O; Marketing/Promo-1/O

FACILITIES & PRODUCTIONS

CENTER STAGE: 750 seats, fly space, computerized lighting and sound, digital sound

   4 prods: 2-3 Fac dir, 6-12 Fac des, 1 GA dir, 1-2 GA des, 1 Grad dir; budget $3,000-12,000

SECOND STAGE-OFF CENTER: 240-310 seat black box theatre, computerized and electronic lighting

   5 prods: 2-3 Fac dir, 6-12 Fac des, 1-2 GA des, 3 UG dir/des; budget $2,000-8,000

Workshops/Readings: 4 prods: 1 Fac dir, 3 UG dir/des; budget $50-1,000

Facility was built in 1930; renovated in 2003, includes scene shop, costume shop prop shop, welding shop, sound studio, CAD facility, 1 video studio, 2 movement/dance studio, 2 rehearsal studio, 1 design studio,2 classrooms. Other facilities: small black box, 50 seat capacity.

A non-departmental, student-run organization presents one production per year in which majors generally participate. 8 student

written plays have been produced in the last two years.
Connected with Central Theatre Ensemble which operates during the school year.

DESCRIPTION

Noted Faculty: Terri Brown, Musical Theatre, Lit; Brenda Hubbard, Acting, Directing; Michael Smith, Acting, Voice; George Bellah, Movement, Combat; Elise Forier, Playwright, Education; Scott Robinson, Cost Des, Tech; Christina Barrigan, Lighting Des; Wesley Van Tassel, Shakespeare, Marketing

Guest Artists: Scott Warrender, Playwright; Ronn Campbell, Sound Des; Kat McMillian, Designer.

A perfect choice for the theatre artist, the General Studies emphasis allows you to become the kind of well-rounded theatre artist, with the greatest of flexibility, who can go on to a focused study in graduate school or a variety of careers in the field. Design and Technology students take a solid core of classes and participate in a wide range of production opportunities and rapidly become the backbone of the program – realizing designs in all areas. Four years of acting classes culminate with concentrated study and practice in the performance of classic theatre, as well as film and television acting. Voice training, singing lessons, dance, stage movement and combat, and other specialty classes round out your thorough preparation for a career in performance. The Musical Theatre minors are designed for students who aspire to a career at the secondary school level or professionally. Unprecedented hands-on opportunities for you in Education K-12. By graduation time students will have directed a play; planned and built a major set piece; sewed costumes; hung lights; written a script; created and implemented a lesson plan for a classroom; designed a program of theatre arts study for a specific population – and more.

Cornish College of the Arts

Richard E.T. White, Chair
  Theater Dept
Cornish College of the Arts
1000 Lenora St.
Seattle, WA 98121
www.cornish.edu/theater
www.cornish.edu
admissions@cornish.edu

789 Total Enr.;
  competitive
Semester System
144 Th Majors; 37
Perform. Prod. majors
T: $24,100
DEPT: (206) 726-5151
FAX. (206)726-1011

DEGREES OFFERED

Theater: BFA and Certificate in Theater - Emphasis in Acting, Original Works, Performing Arts. Performance Production: BFA in Performance Prod (Scenic/Costume/Lighting/Sound/Stage Mgmt/Tech). Declare major 1st year.

ADMISSION & FINANCIAL INFORMATION

HS Transcript or GED; Application; $35 fee; Accept 75%; 3.5 to theater program. Dept req's: Aud/Port/Int; Scholarships based on combined GPA & Audition Ranking for new students, combined GPA & Faculty Eval for continuing students. See website for more info.

FACULTY AND CLASSES OFFERED

16 FT, 23 PT: 18 MFA/MA, 21 Prof. w/o adv. degree; 8 Staff

A. (2 1/2 FT) Theater History-3/Y; Shakes-2/Y; Dramatic Lit-2/Y; Playwriting-2/Y; Original Works-4/Y

B. (8 FT, 16 PT) Acting/Scene Study-12/Y; Voice/Speech-8/Y; Mvmt-10/Y; Clown-2/Y; Singing-2/Y; Directing-2/Y; Stage Combat-2/Y; Dialects-2/Y; Dance-2/4, YX; Dance for Actors-2/Y

C. (1 FT, 7 PT) Prins of Design-2/Y; Set Design-4/Y; Cost Design-4/Y; Lighting Des-4/Y; Tech Prod'n-4/Y; Costume Constr-1/Y; Sound Design-4/Y; Make-up-2/Y; Stage Mgmt-2/Y; Scene Painting-1/Y; Video Techniques-2/Y

FACILITIES & PRODUCTIONS

MAINSTAGE: 100 seats, computerized lighting & sound. 4-6 prods: 4 Fac dir/des; 2 Guest dir/UG des; budget $6,000-14,000

SECOND STAGE: 210 seats, computerized lighting and sound. 7-8 prods: 3 Fac dir, 4 Guest dir; 4 Fac des, 4 Guest/UG des budget $500-3,000

THIRD STAGE: 35 seats, computerized lighting. 20 Guest/UG dir Workshops/Readings; budget $100-300

Also perform 1-2 classical prods in outdoor venues in spring.

New facility was built in 2003; 1 video studio, 3 movement/dance studios, 2 rehearsal studios, 2 design studios and 8 classrooms.

Students must produce a senior thesis project: many are original works, and some have been subsequently presented at local theatres. Professional internships have included Seattle Repertory Theatre, Intiman Theatre, ACT Theatre, Seattle Opera, Oregon Shakespeare Festival, Steppenwolf Theatre, Milwaukee Repertory Theatre, Seattle Shakespeare Co., Empty Space Theatre, New City Theater, Deutsches Opera Berlin and other professional theatres.

DESCRIPTION

Noted Faculty: Richard E. T. White, Theater Chair, Directing; Dave Tosti-Lane, Perf Prod Chair, Sound Des; Kathryn Mesney, Acting; Timothy McCuen Piggee, Text; Robin Lynn Smith, Acting; Hal Ryder, Shakespeare; Ellen Boyle, Voice, Yoga; Robert Macdougall, Movement, Stage Combat; David Taft, Movement, Clown; Mame Hunt, Playwriting; Karen Gjelsteen Set Design; Roberta Russell, Lighting Design; Ron Erickson, Costume Design.

Guest Artists: Jodi Rothfield, CSA, Casting Director; Rita Giomi, Guest Director; Stephen Wadsworth, Seattle Opera/Seattle Rep; Stephen LeGrand, Sound Design; Laurie Anderson, Original Works; Jessica Blank and Eric Jensen, Playwriting; Rober LePage, Original Works; Jeff Perry, Acting; John Dillon, Directing; The Improbable Theatre, Visual Theatre; Barbara Cook, Music Theatre; Carey Wong, Set Design.

The Cornish Theater Department's mission is to help you develop your own creative voice within the broad and embracing art form that is the theater, and to actively connect your work with the world around you. The Theater Department's educational tracks ground you in a fundamental understanding of techniques that will be of use to you whether your goals are in regional theater, television, film, improvisation of multi-disciplinary experimental work. Our intent is to present you with a range of possible skills to fill your theater artist's "toolbox" while providing you with a stimulating learning environment within which you can develop a vision of yourself as an independent artist with a unique creative voice and a

viable, coherent process for approaching your work. Your education will be founded on a dynamic relationship to the history of the craft and an intellectually ambitious exploration of the conditions of the world around you. As a Cornish Theater graduate you should be physically and vocally flexible and powerful, critically astute and articulate, and in command of a wide variety of techniques applicable to a range of theatrical styles. In addition, you should be able to work effectively within an ensemble for a goal larger than yourself, and to present yourself and your personal aesthetic with clarity and confidence.

The Cornish Theater Dept. provides you with an education that can help you develop an emotionally and physically healthy as well as intellectually challenging approach to the art of theater. Whether your goals are to perform, direct or generate original work, you will participate in an educational process that:

− Values and promotes both personal and artistic trowth

− Places an equal emphaiss on the acquistions of technical skills and the develpment of ethics and aesthetics

− Actively engages the department in partnerships with the Seattle and national professional theater community, so you can take advantage of the widest range of learning opportunities

− Provides a continuous forum for students and faculty to engage in generative and cross-disciplinary creative work

With an education based in the essentials of both personal development and breadth of professional experience, you will be prepared to create a place for yourself in the world as an artist, citizen and innovator.

Lower Columbia College

Donald A. Correll, Theatre Dir
Lower Columbia College
1600 Maple St.
Longview, WA 98632
DEPT: (360) 422-2682
FAX: (360) 422-2509
dcorrell@lcc.ctc.edu
ADMISSIONS: Above address
(360) 422-2370
www.lowercolumbia.edu/Common/getting-started

2,400 Total Enr.; non-competitive
Quarter System
ATHE
T: $3,012
O-ST T: $3,734
www.lowercolumbia.edu

DEGREES OFFERED

AA Theatre (12). 2007 granted 6 degrees.

ADMISSION & FINANCIAL INFORMATION

HS diploma. No special requirements for admission to program. Audition for actors, portfolio for designers. Reiniger Scholarships; Lee Foundation Scholarships, Selected application, theatre experience and interview.

FACULTY AND CLASSES OFFERED

1 Full-Time, 1 Part-Time; 1 MFA/MA; 1 prof. w/o advanced degree

A. Intro to Th-Y; Shakes-O

B. (1/2 FT) Acting/Scene Study-Y; Voice/Speech-Y; Mime, etc.-Y; Movement-Y; Singing-X

C. (1/2 FT, 1 PT) Principles of Des-Y; Set Design-Y; Cost Design-O; Lighting Des-Y; Tech Production-Y; Costume Construction-O; Stage Mgmt-Y

FACILITIES & PRODUCTIONS

MAINSTAGE: 87 seats, fly space, computerized lighting.
 3 prods: 3 Fac dir; budget $5,000-6,000

Currently performing at Pepper Theatre in Columbia Theatre while new facility is being built.

DESCRIPTION

Noted Faculty: Donald A. Correll, Acting, Dir, Movement, Masks

Guest Artists: Mary Rayon, Costume Des

Be as professional as you can be. This is how the college theatre program operates. To be a professional demands discipline and commitment. The college performance program is used as a tool to help students understand how essential it is to be prepared, to take chances, to try new ideas and to learn from each production and class that students are involved in. Drama students are involved in all areas of theatre from onstage to back stage. This requirement of self-discipline is to prepare students for entry into a four-year school, conservatory or into the community.

Skagit Valley College

Department Head	2,500 Total Enr.; not compet.
Theatre & Drama	Quarter System
Skagit Valley College	15 Majors; ATHE
2401 E. College Way	T: $73.20 per credit
Mount Vernon, WA 98273	O-ST T: $90.60 per credit
DEPT: (360) 416-7723	SMALL PROGRAM

ADMIN: 2405 East College Way, Mount Vernon, WA 98273
(360) 416-7697   admissions@skagit.edu
www.scagit.edu

DEGREES OFFERED

AA only.

ADMISSION & FINANCIAL INFORMATION

Asset test for placement, no admission test req'd; open enrollment based on space; 12 Theatre Scholarships/yr., $600 ea, by aud; also local, WA scholarships

FACULTY AND CLASSES OFFERED

1 Full-Time, 1/2 PT: 1 MFA/MA; Staff

A. (1/4 FT) Intro to Theatre-1/Y; Shakes-1/Y; Dramatic Lit-1/Y; Playwriting-1/O

B. (3/4 FT) Acting-2/Y; Voice/Speech-1/Y; Movement-1/Y; Singing-2/X; Musical Theatre-1/X; Directing-2/Y; Stand-up Comedy-2/Y

C. Set Design-1/O; Lighting Des-1/O

FACILITIES & PRODUCTIONS

MAINSTAGE: 218 seats. 5 prods: 3 Fac dir/des, 1 Guest dir/Fac des, 1 UG dir/Fac des; budget $500-1,500

Facility was built in 1952, last renovated in 1986; includes scene shop, sound studio, rehearsal studio, classrooms.

DESCRIPTION

Noted Faculty: Steven Craig, Designer/Tech. Director

The training received at Skagit Valley College is intended as a foundation for continued training. The training is pre-

professional in nature and yet serves a population of both majors and non-majors. Students transfer to 4-year institutions, primarily in the state of Washington for the BA or BFA in Theatre. Our program stresses the collaborative nature of the theatre. Actors and directors are trained to trust each other and to work together toward common goals. Script analysis, development of a coherent rehearsal process and method for pre-rehearsal preparation, and study of the Stanislavski system are a major part of the students' work. Technique classes and production work (a minimum of 3 per year, including one Shakespeare) combine to give each student a strong basis for further study. A special emphasis is placed on the development and production of new plays.

University of Washington

See ad in back of book-U/RTA

Prof. Sarah Nash Gates, Exec. Dir.	38,788 T Enr.; highly compet
School of Drama	Quarter System
University of Washington	250 Majors; U/RTA
Box 353950	T: UG $5,985, G $8,818
Seattle, WA 98195-3950	O-ST T: UG $21,283
DEPT: (206) 543-5140	G $20,641
FAX: (206) 543-8512	$5-6,000 R&B

www.depts.washington.edu/uwdrama
uwdrama@u.washington.edu

DEGREES OFFERED

BA in Drama (Liberal Arts) (250); MFA in Acting (30), Directing (4), Design (18); PhD in History, Theory (9) Declare major 2nd or 3rd year; 2004 granted 65 UG, 20 Grad degrees.

ADMISSION & FINANCIAL INFORMATION

Contact school for institutional admission req's (based on GPA & test scores); UG Theatre program admits all applicants, after pre-req's completed.; Grad admits 1 out of 10 applicants; program req. aud/int plus portfolio (design), paper (PhD). Contact for information.

FACULTY AND CLASSES OFFERED

19 FT, 10 PT: 5 PhD, 11 MFA/MA, 3 Prof w/out adv. degree; 19 Staff

A. (4 FT, 1 PT) Intro to Theatre-3/Y; Theatre History-6/Y; Dramatic Criticism-3/Y; Shakespeare-1/Y; Drama Lit-3/Y

B. (9 FT, 5 PT) Acting-12/Y; Voice/Speech-3/Y; Mvmt-3/Y; Singing-3/Y; Directing-9/Y; Stg Combat-3/Y

C. (6 FT, 3 PT) Prins of Des-3/Y; Set Design-11/Y; Cost Des-6/Y; Lighting Des-8/Y; Tech. Production-6/Y; Costume Constr-6/Y; Cost History-1/Y; Make-up-3/Y; Stage Mgmt- 3/Y

FACILITIES AND PRODUCTIONS

THRUST: 208 seats, electronic lighting; built 1948, under renovation 2007-2008

ARENA STAGE: 160 seats, computerized lighting; built '40, renov. '91

END STAGE: 224 seats, computerized lighting; built '74, renov. '96.

PROSC. STAGE: 1200 seats, fly space, computerized lighting; built '74

MAINSTAGE - ALL THEATRES: 8 prods: 4 Fac dir, 3 Guest dir, 4 Grad dir, 1 Fac des, 2 Guest des, 7 Grad des; budget $1,000-4,000

OPERA STAGE: 2 prods; 2 Fac dir, 1 fac des, 1 Grad des Workshops/Readings; 3 Guest dir, 25 Grad dir,

20 Grad des, 5 UG des; budget $0-25

Facilities include scene, costume, prop, welding shops; sound studio, 3 dance studios, 6 rehearsal studios, 1 design studio, 1 light lab, paint shop, 4 classrooms.

A non-departmental, student-run org. presents 4-6 productions per year in which department majors participate.

Connection with Utah Shakespearean Festival, Seattle Rep, Seattle Children's Theatre, ACT, and others; Internships in acting, management, stage management, design, and crafts. Actors employed as well as designers.

DESCRIPTION

Noted Faculty: Acting: Andrew Tsao, Mark Jenkins, Jon Jory. Design: Robert Dahlstrom, Geoff Korf, Thomas Lynch. History: Barry Witham, Thomas Postlewait, Odai Johnson. Criticism: Sarah Bryant-Bertail.

Guest Artists: Directors; Aaron Posner, Corey Madden, Leonid Anisimov, Mark Weil. Design: Ming Cho Lee, Dennis Millam. History/Criticism: Herb Blau, Steve Wilmer, Oscar Brockett. Acting: Keith Hitchcock, R. Hamilton Wright, KJ Sanchez.

Graduate Programs: To provide advanced training which prepares theatre artists and scholars to make significant contributions in theatre performance, production, and scholarship. Undergraduate Program: To provide undergraduate students with a well-rounded Drama major as a means to enriched artistic expression, as a foundation for further study, and for the cultivation of essential life skills: Teamwork, communications, critical thinking, and imagination.

Western Washington University

Gregory L Pulver, Chair	11,476 Total Enr.; h. compet.
Theatre Arts Dept.	Quarter System; NAST
519 High St./Perf. Arts Ctr. 395b	160 Majors; ATHE, U/RTA
Western Washington University	T:$5291/$7,090 R&B
Bellingham, WA 98225-9108	O-ST T. $16,365/$7,090 R&B
DEPT: (360) 650-7310	FAX: (360) 650-7648
ADMISSIONS: WWU, 200 Old Main, Bellingham, WA 98225-9009	
(360) 650-3440	FAX: (360) 650-7369
admit@wwu.edu	www.wwo.edu

DEGREES OFFERED

BA in Theatre Arts (various concentrations) (150), English/ Theatre Education (10). Declare major in any year; 2001 granted 18 UG, 4 Grad degs.

ADMISSION & FINANCIAL INFORMATION

2.0 GPA, but exceptions are accas. made based on add'nl activities; % of apps. accepted to inst. varies; Interview/Portfolio req. for Th. Program plus a number of prerequisite courses; Accept 10 out of 12 UG to program; 3 out of 4 Grad. 7 Scholarships specific to Theatre Dept; application, 2 rec. letters to qualify, reviewed by fac. committee. Award winners will be notified mid-April.

FACULTY AND CLASSES OFFERED

9 FT, 3 PT: 7 MFA/MA, 2 Prof. w/out adv. deg; 4 Staff

A. (4 1/3 FT) Intro to Th-1/Y; Dramatic Lit-7/Y; Th Hist-2/Y; Shakes-2/X; Dramatic Crit-1/Y; Playwriting-5/Y

B. (1 1/2 FT, 2 PT) Acting-9/Y; Voice-2/O; Mime, etc.-1/O; Movement-1/Y; Musical Theatre-3/Y; Singing-5/X; Directing-5/Y; Dance-11/Y

C. (2 5/6 FT, 1 PT) Principles of Des-1/Y; Set Design-4/Y; Cosume Des-3/Y; Lighting Des-3/Y; Tech Prod'n-2/Y; Cost Hist-2/Y; Make-up-2/Y; Stage Mgmt-1/Y

D. (1/3 FT) Arts Management-1/O

FACILITIES & PRODUCTIONS

MAINSTAGE: 1,087 seats, fly space, computerized lighting 12 Fac dir/des prods; $25,000-50,000

SECOND STAGE: 200 seats, computerized lighting. 44 prods: 2 Grad dir/des 20 UG dir/des; budget $6,000-8,000

THIRD STAGE: Various seats, black box, computerized lighting. 4 Guest dir/des Workshops/Readings; budget $700-1,000

Facility built in 1951, renovated in 1995; includes scene shop, costume shop, prop shop, rehearsal studio, design studio, 2 classrooms. Largest costume collection and storage on the west coast.

A non-departmental, student-run, producing org. presents 2-3 prods. per year in which majors generally participate.

30+ student-written plays produced in the last two years.

DESCRIPTION

Noted Faculty: Thomas E. Ward, Theatre Management; Roger Germain, Scenic Design; Mark Kuntz, Educational Drama; Victor H. Leverett, Costume Design; James. E. Lortz, Acting; Perry F. Mills, Playwriting; Maureen E. O'Reilly, Direction; Lee H. Taylor, Lighting Design.

Guest Artists: Chuck Harper, Actor/Director; Actors: Barbara Eden, Michael Learned, Lawrence Pressman, G. Valmont Thomas; PJ Sirl, Actor/Combat Specialist; Directors:Jose Jorgero, Sandy Wilson, Allen Bartolik, Ruber Van Kempen, Bob Goodman; cast & crew of The X-Files; Poltergeist, The Legacy, The Sentinel; Dr. Nike Imoru, University of Hull, England; Second City Comedy Troupe; Rebecca Wells, Novelist/Actress; Mark Dean, Lighting Designer; Bryan Tyrell, Brian Willis, Playwrights; Joan Carson, Director for Film and Television; Michelle Allen, Casting Director.

The Theatre Arts Department at Western Washington University offers a M.A. and a B.A. in Theatre Arts. These degrees combine academic study with practical work on theatre productions. The Theatre Arts Department strives to prepare the student to be a broad based theatre artist while encouraging the student to explore creative activities in any area of the student's choice. The student will also learn to recognize the value of diversity in the theatre while exploring their creative spirit.

Whitworth College

Dr. Rick Hornor, Chair,	2,600 Total Enr.; competitive
Theatre Department	Semester System
Whitworth College	30 Majors; ATHE
300 W Hawthorne Road	T: $23,850/$3,816 R&B
Spokane, WA 99251-0305	DEPT: (509) 777-3707
FAX: (509) 777-4592	www.whitworth.edu
ADMISSIONS: (509) 777-1000	

DEGREES OFFERED

BA in Performance (10); Technical Theatre (3); Community-based

Theatre (2); General Theatre (15). Declare major in sophomore year; 2007 granted 7 degrees.

ADMISSION & FINANCIAL INFORMATION

GPA 3.50, SAT 1100, ACT 25; Accept 9 out of 10 to program; Theatre program scholarships awarded to incoming freshmen based on audition. Contact theatre department for information.

FACULTY AND CLASSES OFFERED

3 Full-Time, 2 Part-Time: 2 PhD, 3 MFA/MA; 1 Staff

A. (3 FT) Intro to Theatre-1/Y; Dram Lit-1/O; Th Hist-2/O; Shakes-1/X; Performance & Social Change-1/O; Community Arts-1/Y; Performance Theory-1/Y

B. (3 FT) Acting-2/Y; Voice-2/Y; Mime, etc.-1/O; Musical Theatre-1/O; Directing-1/Y; Dance-3/Y; Movement-1/O; Story Theatre-1/O

C. (1 FT) Prins of Des-1/X; Set Design-1/Y; Lighting Design- 1/Y; Tech Production-1/Y; Make-up-1/O; Mask Making-1/O; Costume Des-1/O

D. Arts Mgmt-1/X; Marketing/Promo-1/X; Budgeting/Acctg Proced.-1/X

FACILITIES & PRODUCTIONS

MAINSTAGE: 1,000 seats, computerized lighting & sound 2 Fac dir/des prods; $3,000-5,000

SECOND STAGE: 135 seats, electronic lighting. 6 prods: 5 Fac dir, 1 UG dir; budget $75-100. 4 Fac dir Workshops/Readings; budget $200-800

Facility was built in 1960, renovated in 1995; includes scene shop, dance studio, rehearsal studio (Mainstage and Second Stage serve as teaching stations).

Graduates have been hired in tech and box office areas and graduate schools in acting and technical theatre.

DESCRIPTION

Guest Artists: Brenda WongAoki, Chris Harrold, Tom Key, Diane Ferlotte, Harris Smith.

The faculty of the Department of Theatre is convinced that the study of theatre is historically rooted in the liberal arts and is perceived as a legitimate academic endeavor. This conviction is reflected in the design of the curriculum, which insists that students study theory and understand the dynamics of the literature. This prepares students to understand and experience a "sense of the other," which is essential to good performance. The confidence, creativity, discipline, and reflection that are learned in this course of study afford students a discovery of self, which is in keeping with the student development goals of the college. Beyond preparation for advanced professional study, the department offers to all students opportunities to develop communication skills, confident stage presence, and exposes them to the cultural, historical, moral, and artistic dimensions of dramatic literature, which are important components of a Christian liberal arts education.

WEST VIRGINIA

Marshall University

Lang Reynolds, Chair
Dept. of Theatre,
One John Marshall Dr.
Marshall University
Huntington, WV 25755-2242
DEPT: (304) 696-7184
FAX: (304) 696-6582
ADMISSIONS: Dir. of Admissions, above address.
www.marshall.edu
admissions@marshall.edu

9,723 Total Enr.;
not compet.
Semester System
55 Majors
T: $10,642/$6,492 R&B
O-ST T: $17,546/$6,492 R&B
reynoldsh@marshall.edu
800-642-3463
FAX: (304) 696-3135

DEGREES OFFERED

BFA in Performance, Design/Technology. Declare major in any year.

ADMISSION & FINANCIAL INFORMATION

89.9% of applicants accepted by inst. 2.0 or 17 ACT or 680 SAT. No special req. for Th. Prog., admits all applicants Three Scholarships for continuing students are decided upon by the faculty based on the students' work in previous semesters. Some other scholarships and stipends available.

FACULTY AND CLASSES OFFERED

5 Full-Time, 4 Part-Time

A. (1 FT) Intro to Theatre-2/Y; Theatre History-2/O; Shakes-2/X&O; Dramatic Lit-X; Dra Criticism-1/O; Playwriting-1/Y

B. (2 FT) Acting-5/Y; Voice/Speech-2/Y; Movement-1/Y; Singing-X; Musical Theatre-2/Y; Directing-2/Y; Dance-4/Y

C. (2 FT,1 PT) Set Design-2/Y; Cost Des-1/O; Lighting Des-2/Y; Tech Production-3/Y; Costume Constr-1/O; Cost Hist-1/Y; Make-up-1/Y; Stage Management-1/O

FACILITIES & PRODUCTIONS

MAINSTAGE: 543 seats, fly space, computerized lighting. 4 prods: 4 Fac dir/des, 1 UG des; budget $5,000-17,750

SECOND STAGE: 230 seats, computerized lighting. 3 prods: 2 Fac dir/des, 1 Guest dir, 1 UG des; budget $3,000-6,000

THIRD STAGE: 100 seats, black box, electronic lighting Workshops/Readings, 2 Fac dir, 3 UG dir, 1 UG des; budget $0-500

Facility built in 1992; includes scene, cost shops, props shop, sound studio, CAD facility, 2 dance studios, reh. studio, 2 classrooms, box office suite, greenroom, 8 dressing rooms, theatre archives.

DESCRIPTION

The Department is composed of a number of academicians who have worked or currently do work in professional theatre as actors and designers. We prepare our students for graduated training programs or professional theatre. A large percentage of our former students are involved in both. As an undergraduate program, opportunities abound for eager students to actually do the "stuff" on stage for the public.

West Virginia University

Margaret McKowen, Assoc. Prof
Division of Theatre & Dance
PO Box 6111
West Virginia University
Morgantown, WV 26506
DEPT: (304) 293-4841x3121
FAX: (304) 293-2533
margaret.mckowen@mail.wvu.edu

20,590 Total Enr.; not compet.
Semester Sys; 143 Majors
NAST, U/RTA, ATHE
T: $4,722
O-ST T: $14,600
$6,826 R&B
www.wvu.edu/~ccarts

ADMISSIONS: PO Box 6201 (304) 293-2124
www.arc.wvu.edu go2wvu@mail.wvu.edu

DEGREES OFFERED

BA in Visual/Perf Arts (23); BFA/MFA in Acting (70), Design/ Tech (40); BFA in Puppetry/Creative Dramatics (10).

ADMISSION & FINANCIAL INFORMATION

46% of applicants accepted. Aud/int/portfolio req'd for Grad Th Program, GPA 2.0 for UG. Students who graduated w/i last 5 years or whose expected graduation date was w/i the past 5 years must submit ACT or SAT scores. Accepts all UG, 8 out of 65 Grad. There are full tuition waivers and endowed cash awards that are given to students based solely on talent. We hold auditions and portfolio reviews with an interview/application process.

FACULTY AND CLASSES OFFERED

16 FT, 2 PT, 1 PhD, 18 MFA/MA; 1 Prof w/o adv. degree, 4 Staff

A. (3 FT, 1 PT) Intro to Theatre-6/Y; Theatre History-4/Y; Shakes-1/Y; Dramatic Criticism-1/O; Dramatic Lit-3/Y; Playwriting-2/Y; Grad Seminar-1/O

B. (6 FT, 3 PT) Acting-8/Y; Voice/Speech-6/Y; Movement-6/Y; Singing-1/O; Directing-2/Y; Dance-6/Y; Mime/Mask, etc-1/O; Musical Th-1/O; Stage Combat-1/O; Fencing-1/O

C. Prins of Design-2/Y; Set Design-3/Y; Cost Des-3/Y; Lighting Des-3/Y; Cost Construct-3/Y; Make-up-2/Y; SM-1/Y; Tech Prod-5/Y; Sound Seminar-1/Y; CAD-2/Y; Rendering-2/O; Model bldg-2/O; Costume Crafts-2/Y; Props-2/Y; Scene Painting-2/Y

D. Arts Mgmt-1/X

FACILITIES & PRODUCTIONS

MAINSTAGE: 1380 seats, fly space computerized lighting. 6-8 prod. 7 Fac dir, 4 Fac des, 1 GA dir/des, 8 Grad des, 8 UG des; budget $2,500-15,000

SECOND STAGE: 220 seats, computerized lighting. 1-3 prod. 1 Fac dir/des, 1 UG des. budget $500-1,000

THIRD STAGE: 80 seats

Facility built in 1962, last renovated 2003-04; includes scene, costume, props & welding shops, CAD facility, 3 Mvmt/dance studios, 5 rehearsal studio, 2 design studio, 10 classrooms.

4 student-written plays produced in the last two years.

Our connection with a variety of AEA, summer and year-round theatres includes West Virginia Public Theatre, American Contemporary Theatre, Unseamed Shakespeare Company, Jean Cocteau Rep, Arkansas Rep. Opportunities for internships in SM and directing, ass't design work, and performance internships.

DESCRIPTION

Noted Faculty: Frank Gagliano, Playwriting; Phillip Beck, Acting; Joshua Williamson, Light Des; Jay Malarcher, Th Hist; Theresa Davis, Acting; Margaret McKowen, Costume Des, William Winsor, Scene Des; Jerry McGonigle, Acting; Joann Spencer-Siegrist, Puppetry.

Guest Artist: Michael Bogdanov, Writer; Robert Leigh, Dir; Gerald Leiss, Actor; Jackie Arrington, Draper; Barbara Bell, Draper; Fred Noel, SM; Robin Walsh, Actor; Laura Smiley, Art Dir; Tony Stragis, Designer; Ed Herendeen.

The goal of the West Virginia University Division of Theatre is the preparation of students for professional work in the theatre (either commercial or academic). We pride ourselves on the close personal attention given each student in small classes taught by some of the best teachers in the field. Indeed, teaching and individual guidance are our most important mission. Emphasis is placed on the enhancement of a solid undergraduate BFA education, founded on a sound humanities base plus the essential craft/art skills necessary for a successful career or as preparation for graduate studies. Graduate MFA students follow curriculum tracks in Acting and Design leading to professional employment. BFA and MFA programs in Acting provide intensive studio training in Acting, Voice, Movement and Text Analysis. Similar training is provided for students in Design/Tech, with professional preparation being emphasized at the graduate level. A BFA program is also offered in a unique Puppetry/Creative Dramatics emphasis. BA programs are available in Theatre for students with wider theatre interests. The Division maintains its tradition of encouraging the production of new works in its Laboratory Theatre productions.

WISCONSIN

Carroll College

Tom Bruno, Program Head
Theatre Arts Dept.
Carroll College
Waukesha, WI 53186
DEPT: (262) 524-7304
FAX: (262) 524-7139
ADMISSIONS: Admissions Dept. at above address
(262) 524-7220
ccadmin.cc.edu

2,300 Tot. Enr.; competitive
20 Majors, ATHE

SMALL PROGRAM
T: $17,020/$5,500 R&B
tbruno@cc.edu

FAX: (262) 524-7139
jwiseman@ccadmin.cc.edu

DEGREES OFFERED

BA in Theatre Arts, Acting/Directing Emphasis (17), Tech & Design Emphasis (3), Th. Arts Minor (7). Declare major in 1st or 2nd year.

ADMISSION & FINANCIAL INFORMATION

ACT or SAT scores are viewed as well as high school curriculum, GPA and class roank. 85% of applics are accepted by institution. Th. program admits 7 out of 10. Sainsbury-Steinmetz Th Schols -$1,000 annually for actors; $2,500 for actors with Spanish/Russian as first language; $2,500 for theatre design/tech students. Scholarships competitive, req. aud/int/portfolio; renewable annually for four years.

FACULTY AND CLASSES OFFERED

2 Full-Time, 1 Part-Time: 2 MFA/MA, 2 Prof. w/o adv. degree

A. (1/2 FT) Intro to Theatre-2/Y; Dramatic Lit-1/O; Th Hist-2/O

B. (1/2 FT) Acting-3/Y; Directing -1/O; Movement-1/X; Singing-1/X; Dance-1/X; Stage Combat-1/O

C. (1 FT, 1 PT) Prins of Des-1/Y; Tech Prod-1/Y; Set Design-1/O; Costume Design-1/O; Lighting Design-1/O; Costume Const.-1/O; Make-up-1/Y

D. Arts Mgmt-1/O

FACILITIES & PRODUCTIONS

MAINSTAGE: 244 seats, fly space, computerized lighting. 2 prods.: 4 Fac des, 2 Guest dir, 3 Guest des. prods; budget $3,200-8,000

SECOND STAGE: 50 seats: 1 Prod: 1 Guest dir, 1 UG dir, 4 UG des prods; budget $150-500

Workshops: 1 UG dir, 1 UG des.

Facility was built in 1979, renovated in 1996 and 2007; includes scene shop, costume shop, prop shop, dance studio, rehearsal studio, design studio, 2 classrooms, outdoor stage.

We interact with various theatres from the former Soviet Union, England and Central America, Uzbeckistan; Vakhtangov Theatre, Moscow; Teatro Sol Del Rio, El Salvador; Theatre La Fraqua, Honduras with artist and performance exchanges; we are also affilitated with the Up With People International Touring Program.

Project Create, a summer theatre camp, uses the performance space in the summer.

DESCRIPTION

Noted Faculty: Tom Bruno, Acting, Directing, History; Cecelia Mason Kuenn, Costume Design; Scott M. Boyle, Technical Direction, Design, Set and Lights.

Guest Artists: Maria Bonilla, University of Costa Rica Theatre Department; Brian Parsons, Univ. of Hull, England; Raeleen McMillan, Co-founder Renaissance Theatre Company; Drew Brhel, Director; Rob Goodman, First Stage Children's Theatre; Ed Morgan, Director; Jane Flieller, In Tandem Theatre; Bret Hazelton, Milwaukee Rep Theatre.

The Carroll College Theatre Arts Department founded in 1896, represents one of the Midwest's first programs combining theatre and the liberal arts. Today, the department focuses upon providing undergraduates with a solid core of theatre study with emphasis in acting, direction, technical theatre, design, or theatre arts/theatre education minor programs. The Carroll Players are noted for their international tours, having become the first North American University or College to tour Central America with performances (January, 1996; May, 1998). The Players also toured productions to various Republics of the former Soviet Union (January, 1995; May 1997. Theatre artists and companies from these regions of the world are brought to the campus. An affiliation with Up With People, the international touring program extends the opportunity for international experiences. The nearby Chicago and Milwaukee theatre centers supply production artists, workshop leaders, and intern opportunities. Graduates combine other major fields in their studies with about 60% entering the theatre careers; 40% a myriad of other professions.

Lawrence University

Richmond Frielund, Chair
Dept. of Theatre Arts
Lawrence University
P.O. Box 599
Appleton, WI 54912-0599
DEPT: (920) 832-6747
ADM:FRIELUNR@LAWRENCE.EDU
P.O. Box 599, Appleton, WI 54912
800 227-0982
www.lawrence.edu/admissions/

1,200 Total Enr; h. compet
21 Majors, ATHE
Trimester System
T/$29,376/$6,822 R&B
SMALL PROGRAM
FAX: (920) 832-6633

FAX: (920) 832-6782

DEGREES OFFERED

BA in Theatre (with area of emphasis in Performance, Design, or Hist/Lit/Crit) (21). Declare major in junior year; 2001 granted 12 degrees.

ADMISSION & FINANCIAL INFORMATION

Typical profile: Top 20% of class, GPA 3.6, ACT 26, SAT 1250 (no set requirements). 60% of applicants accepted to inst. Offer merit scholarships based on audition or technical theatre portfolio, competition essay and meeting our academic profile. Typical past recipients have academic profiles meeting or exceeding a 3.7 GPA/ACT 24/SAT 1100/top 10% rank. Scholarships range from $5,000-10,000/yr. and are renewable with maintenance of a 3.0 GPA. All merit awards are offered without regard to financial need.

FACULTY AND CLASSES OFFERED

3 FT, 3 PT: 1 PhD, 4 MFA/MA, 1 Prof w/out adv. degree

A. (1 FT) Intro to Theatre-1/Y; Dramatic Lit-7/OX; Th Hist-3/Y; Shakes-1/X; Dramatic Criticism-1/O; Playwriting-1/O

B. (1 FT, 1 PT) Acting-3/X; Voice/Speech-1/Y; Movement-1/Y; Singing-3/X; Musical Th-1/X; Dance-3/YO; Directing-2/YO

C. (1 FT, 2 PT) Prins of Des-2/YO; Set Design-2/O; Cost Des-1/O; Tech Prod-1/Y; Set Design-2/O; Lighting Des-1/O; Make-up-1/Y; Stage Management-1/O; Sound Des-1/O

FACILITIES & PRODUCTIONS

MAINSTAGE: 500 seats, fly space, computerized lighting. 4 Fac dir/des prods, 1 (alternative) Guest Dir, 3-8 Guest des; budget $5,000

SECOND STAGE: 200 seats, computerized lighting 3-8 UG dir/des prods; budget $1000

Facility was built in 1958; includes scene shop, costume shop, design studio.

A non-departmental, student-run organization presents one musical production every other year in which department majors participate. Two student-written plays produced in the last two years.

DESCRIPTION

Noted Faculty: Richmond Frielund, Design, Tech; Kim Instenes, Costume, Make-Up; Debra Loewen, Dance, Movement; David Owens, Design, Tech, Sound; Kathy Privatt, Acting, Literature and History, Theory; Timothy X. Troy, Directing-Plays, Operas, Musicals, Acting, Script Analysis; Fred Gaines, (Emeritus), Playwright, Intro to Theatre.

Guest Artists: Eric Appleton, Lighting Design; Tye Dobeck, Costume Desing. Residencies: Guthrie Theatre, Wild Space Dance Co., Actors from The London Stage.

Students arrive at Lawrence with a wide variety of theatre experiences and nearly as wide a set of expectations. Many have had a high-school experience of working in theatre productions. Some see their college years as the first step toward a career in theatre. Others see theatre as a rewarding extracurricular activity, and they hope to continue enjoying that involvement. To meet the interests of the first group, the Department of Theatre and Drama has designed a curriculum that allows the student to deepen his or her general knowledge of the field while beginning the process of specialization within a particular focus area. To meet the expectations of the second group, the department produces a wide variety of plays and musicals and sponsors a theatre club that actively participates in visits to some of the professional theatre companies in the area.

Marquette University

Phylis Ravel, Artistic Dir/Chair
Dept. of Perf Arts
Marquette Univ.
13th & Clybourn Sts.
Milwaukee, WI 53233
FAX: (414) 288-7048
www.marquette.edu/comm/dept/thar.html
ADMISSIONS:
www.marquette.edu/admissions

12,000 Total Enr.;compet
Semester System
65 Majors
T: $26,270/$8,880 R&B
DEPT: (414) 288-7505
phylis.ravel@marquette.edu
(414) 288-5558
carlos.garces@marquette.edu

DEGREES OFFERED

BA in Performing Arts (concentrations in Performance, Design, Technical) Declare major in freshman year; 2006 granted 17 degrees.

ADMISSION & FINANCIAL INFORMATION

Mean class rank 77 percentile; middle 50% SAT 1060-1250, ACT 23-28, HS GPA 3.0; Accept 88% to inst.; no special req's for admission to Theatre Program; Admit all UG, Performance scholarship $10,000 & $2,000, auditions for incoming Freshmen each February. $10,000 scholarship for Design/Tech.

FACULTY AND CLASSES OFFERED

5 Full-Time, 6 Part-Time: 7 MFA, 2 Prof. w/out adv. degree

A. (1 FT, 2 PT) Intro to Theatre-1/Y; Th Hist-1/Y; Shakes-1/X; Dram Lit-2/X; Dramatic Crit-2/X; Playwriting-1/Y; Play Analysis-1/Y

B. (2 FT, 3 PT) Acting-5/Y; Voice/Speech-2/Y; Movement-3/Y; Directing-2/Y

C. (3 FT) Prins of Des-1/Y; Set Design-1/Y; Cost Des-2/Y; Lighting Des-1/Y; Tech. Production-1/Y; Costume Construction-1/Y; Cost Hist-2/Y; Make-up-1/Y

FACILITIES AND PRODUCTIONS

MAINSTAGE: 226 seats, fly space, computerized & electronic lighting. 5 prods: 3 Fac dir/des, 2 Guest dir, 1 Guest des; 2 student des - $3,000 for dramas, $20,000 for musicals

SECOND STAGE: 89 seats. Class projects, student directed workshops and projects - $100 budget

THIRD STAGE: 40 seats, black box, 4 to 6 workshops, $100 budget

Facility was built in 1961, annual maintenance and renovation when necessary. Building includes theatre, scene and costume shop, conference room, dance/acting/black box studio, faculty offices, box office. Television studio and other classrooms in main Comm building. Strong relationship with all professional theatres in the Milwaukee area for both performers, designers and technicians.

DESCRIPTION

Noted Faculty: Phylis Ravel, Artistic Director, Chair; Debra Krajec, Directing, Costume; John Schneider, Playwrights, Disciplines of Movement, Scene Study, Acting for Non-Majors, Play Analysis; Maureen Kilmurry, Shakespeare, Career Preparation, Voice and Movement, Voice and Speech; Roxanne Kess, African Dance, Modern Dance, History of Dance, Choreographer; Connie Petersen, Basic Costume Tech, Advance Costume Tech, Make-up, Shop Mgr; Stephen Hudson-Mairet, Scenic Design, Theatre History, Theatre Appreciation, Scenographic Techniques, CAD Design; Chester Loeffler-Bell, Stagecraft, Lighting Des, Prod Mgr, Shop Mgr; Patrick McGilligan, Film as Art, Hollywood and the Blacklist, The films of Altman, the films of Clint Eastwood; Paul Salsini, History of the Musical of America.

Guest Artists: Patrick Sutton, Gaiety School of Acting, Directing; Martin Sheen, the actor and social justice; George Drance, Ben Munisteri, the Ben Munisteri Dance Project; Andrea Smith of the Bill T. Jones/Arnie Zanes Company; David Neuman of the Advanced Beginner Group; Robert Benedetti, Acting Coach; Jack Forbes Wilson, Musical Director; Michael Wright, Chamber Theatre.

The curriculum of the theatre major at Marquette University is dedicated to the idea that the study of theatre outside the context of cultural traditions is essentially meaningless. At the same time we insist upon the careful and disciplined integration of curriculum with actual stage production of plays. Such an integration differentiates education from mere training. An education at Marquette University with a major in theatre therefore combines knowledge and skill, stressing performance under disciplined standards. Marquette students work regularly with Equity companies while completing successfully a demanding curriculum of courses not only in theatre, but also in philosophy, languages, history, and literature.

University of Wisconsin - Eau Claire

Terry Allen, Dir of Theatre
Dept. Theatre Arts
UWEC Theatre #305
Univ. of Wisconsin
Eau Claire, WI 54702-4004
DEPT: (715) 836-2284
www.uwec.edu/Academic/Mus-The/theatre/index.html
ADM: (715) 836-5415
www.uwec.edu/Admin/Admissions

10,000 Total Enr.; compet
Semester System
54 Majors, 45 minors
T: $4,900/$3,133 R&B
O-ST T: $9,600/$3,133 R&B
allentj@uwec.edu
FAX: (715) 836-3952
eiask.uwec@uwed.edu

DEGREES OFFERED

BA/BS in Comprehensive Th. Arts (25), Theatre-Liberal Arts (19); BA in Theatre Education, Secondary/Middle (10); Declare major in first year.

ADMISSION & FINANCIAL INFORMATION

Test scores, ACT/SAT, GPA. 70% of applics accepted by institution. No special req. for admission to Th Program. Program admits 7 out of 10 applicants Some freshman scholarship money is available, to apply send letter of application, resume, and 2 letters of recommendation.

FACULTY AND CLASSES OFFERED

5 Full-Time: 3 PhD, 2 MFA/MA; 3 Staff

A. (1 FT) Intro to Theatre-1/Y; Theatre History-1/Y; Dramatic Lit-1/O; Theatre of Holocaust-1/O

B. (2 FT) Acting-3/O; Voice/Speech-1/O; Movement-1/O; Singing-1/X; Mus. Th.-1/Y; Directing-1/Y; Dance-6/Y; Stage Combat-1/O

C. (1 1/2 FT) Set Des.-1/O; Cost. Des.-1/2-O; Lighting. Des.-1/O; Tech.Prod.-1/O; Cost.Const.- 1/Y; Cost. Hist.-1/2-O; Make-up-1/O; Mask Design-1/O; CAD Design-1/O

D. (1/2 FT) Arts Management-1/O; Touring Theatre-1/Y

FACILITIES AND PRODUCTIONS

MAINSTAGE: 368 seats, fly space, computerized lighting.
   3 Fac dir/des prods; budget $6,000-9,000

SECOND STAGE: 600 seats, fly space, computerized lighting
   1 Fac dir/des prods; budget $9,000-11,000

THIRD STAGE: 200 seats, fixed stage, computerized lighting 1 Fac & 25
   UG dir/des workshops/readings; budget $5,000-6,000

Facility was built in 1953 and 1970, renovated in '87 & '99; includes
   scene shop, costume shop, design studio, 1 video studio, 1
   dance studio, CAD facility, 2 classrooms.

DESCRIPTION

Noted Faculty: Dr. Terry Allen, Director of Theatre,
   Acting, Directing, Playwriting, Theatre of the
   Holocaust; Richard F. Nimke, Acting, Dram Lit,
   History and Music Theatre; Dr. Mitra Sadeghpoar,
   Voice; Kevin Gawley, Scenic Design, Lighting Design,
   Technical Theatre; Dr. Cheryl Starr, Theatre
   Education, Costume Des/Tech; Dr. Toni Poll-
   Sorenson, Dance.

Guest Artists: The Department brings in professionals for
   workshops on a regular basis and takes trips to professional theatre production in Minneapolis,
   Madison, Milwaukee, and Chicago.

The Theatre Area of the Department of Music and Theatre
Arts at University of Wisconsin-Eau Claire is a Liberal Arts
training program that prepares students for numerous
positions in and out of theatre after graduation. All of our
students are well trained in ALL areas of theatre. We
believe that a Liberal Arts background best prepares students to cope both in and out of the Art form of Theatre.
Students are exposed to a wide range of production experiences. Qualified students will often take on major design
and production roles in our main bill productions.
Freshmen, minors, and non-theatre students are all eligible to audition for our productions. Theatre majors also
have options in music (voice) and in dance. Five major productions and up to 25 student productions are done each
year so there are many opportunities available. The community of Eau Claire also offers numerous theatre experiences as well as a beautiful safe environment.

University of Wisconsin - Green Bay

Laura Riddle, Chair of Theatre
Dept. of Theatre
Univ. of Wisconsin-Green Bay
2420 Nicolet Dr.
Green Bay, WI 54311-7001
DEPT: (920) 465-2441
ADM: SS1200, above address.
www.uwgb.edu

5,661 Total Enr.; competitive
Semester System, 90 Majors
T: $5,716
O-ST T: $13,190
riddlel@uwgb.edu
FAX: (920) 465-2890
(920) 465-2111
admissns@uwgb.edu

DEGREES OFFERED

BA in Performance (24), Theatre Studies (38), Design/Technical
Theatre (20), Musical Theatre (8).Declare major in fresh/soph.

ADMISSION & FINANCIAL INFORMATION

GPA 2.5, ACT 23, SAT 1070, top 45% of class. Incoming and returning student scholarships, aud/interview req.

FACULTY AND CLASSES OFFERED

6 FT, 1 PT: 6 MA/MFA, 2 Staff

A. (1 FT) Intro to Theatre-1/Y; Dramatic Lit-3/O; Theatre History-
   3/O;NY/London Theatre-1/O

B. (2 FT) Acting-3/Y; Voice/Speech-2/Y; Directing-2/Y; Dance-12/Y;
   Audition-1/Y; Singing-4/Y;

C. (3 FT) Cost. Des.-1/O; Set Design-1/O; Cost. Construct-1/Y;
   Lighting Des-2/Y; Tech. Prod-1/Y; Make-up-1/O; Stage Mgmt-1/Y;
   CAD-1/O

D. (1 PT) Arts Mgmt-1/Y; Marketing/Promo-1/Y; Dev/Grant Writing-
   1/Y; Budgeting/Acctg-1/Y

FACILITIES AND PRODUCTIONS

MAINSTAGE: 475 seats, fly space, computerized lighting. 4 prods:
   4 Fac dir, 7 Fac des, 5 UG des; budget $6,000-20,000

SECOND STAGE: 99 seats, computerized lighting
   2 prods: 2 UG dir, 6 UG des prods; budget $100-500
   1 UG dir Workshop/Reading; budget $50

Facility was built in 1970; includes scene studio, costume studio,
   CAD facility, 2 dance studios, rehearsal studio.

Connection with The Weidner Center for the Performing Arts, a state-
of-the-art facility which is a touring house on the University campus. Facilities include a 2000 seat proscenium theatre and 2 studio spaces. Students have the opportunity to work on touring
productions and to work as Interns in Production and
Administration.

DESCRIPTION

Noted Faculty: Jeffrey Entwistle, Design; Kaoime Malloy,
   Design; R. Michael Ingraham, Technical Theatre.

Guest Artists: Shifra Werch, Designer; Rachel Rockwell,
   AEA; Amy McKenzie, Acting Teacher; Aquila Theatre,
   Performance Worshop and workshops with the com-
   panies of Ragtime, Rent, Alvin Ailey.

The Theatre Program at the University of Wisconsin-Green
Bay is committed to a solid background in the Theatre Arts
within the context of a Liberal Arts foundation. Students
study all areas of Theatre and then specialize in
Performance/Directing or Design/Technical theatre.
Laboratory involvement in Mainstage and Studio productions is a vital extension of the classwork and undergraduates at all levels are strongly involved. The Weidner
Center offers unique opportunities for students to see professional touring companies as well as the opportunity to
work backstage on these productions and to engage in
workshops and seminars with visiting artists. UWGB theatre graduates typically go on to internships and graduate
programs in acting, directing, design and technical theatre. Students also find gainful employment in professional theatre by working in resident companies, children's
theatre, summer stock and television and commercial
fields.

University of Wisconsin - La Crosse

William T. Clow, Chair
Dept. of Theatre Arts
153 Center for the Arts
University of Wisconsin
La Crosse, WI 54601
DEPT: (608) 785-6701
clow.will@uwlax.edu

8,300 Total Enr.; h. competitive
Semester System
50 Majors; ATHE
T: $9,465 - R&B included
O-ST T: $19,511 - R&B INCLUDED
Fax: (608)785-6720
www.uwlax.edu/theatre

ADMISSIONS: 115 Main Hall, 1725 State Street, La Crosse, WI 54601

ADM: (608) 785-8939   admissions@uwlax.edu
www.uwlax.edu/admissions

DEGREES OFFERED

BA/BS in Theatre Arts: Performance, General Emphasis, Design/Technical, or Theatre Management; Theatre Arts & Music: Music Theatre. Declare major in any year; 2005 granted 12 UG degrees.

ADMISSION & FINANCIAL INFORMATION

HS class rank in upper 25 % with a composite ACT score of 23 or rank in upper 30 % of class with a composite ACT score of 26; Admission to Musical Theatre program requires audition. Scholarships include Toland Scholarship, Helen Leide Fund, Tinapp/Joyce Scholarship; Frederick Fund, Children's Theatre Scholarship & Next Stage Scholarship. Scholarships in the theatre arts are awarded for scholastic achievement, theatre participation and financial need.

FACULTY AND CLASSES OFFERED

6 Full-Time, 1 Part-Time: 1 PhD, 5 MFA; 1 Staff

A. (1 FT) Intro to Theatre-1/Y; Theatre History-4/Y; Shakespeare-1/X; Dramatic Criticism-1/Y; Playwriting-1/O.

B. (1 FT, 1 PT) Acting-4/Y; Directing-1/O; Singing-1/Y; Dance-5/X; Musical Theatre-4/Y

C. (2 FT) Prins of Design-1/O; Set Design-2/O; Cost Des-1/O; Lighting Des-1/O; Tech. Prod-4/Y; Make-up-1/O; Stage Management-1/O; Costume Construction-1/O.

D. (1 FT) Arts Mgmt-1/O; Marketing/Promotion-1/O; Other-1/O.

E. (1FT) Voice & Diction; Movement.

FACILITIES AND PRODUCTIONS

MAINSTAGE: 426 seats, fly space, computerized lighting
    6 prods: 4-5 Fac dir/25 Fac des; 0-1 GA dir., 10 UG des; budget $5,000-10,000

SECOND STAGE: 110 seats, flexible thrust, computerized lighting.
    2 Prods.; 2-4 UG dir prods; budget $500-1,000

Facility built in 1974, last renovated in 1999; includes scene shop, costume shop, sound studio, CAD facility, dance studio, design studio, classroom.

A non-departmental, student-run producing organization presents two to four productions a year in which theater majors generally participate.

Two student-written plays were produced in the last two years.

The program is connected with Summer Stage, a semi-professional, local regional troupe with occasional Equity guest artists which operates in the summer only.

DESCRIPTION

The Department of Theatre Arts at the University of Wisconsin-La Crosse is an innovative and challenging theatre arts program that provides diverse opportunities for academic study and practical experience in all aspects of theatrical performance and production. The Theatre Arts program provides students with the tools necessary to function as complete artists and self-realized individuals, combining theatrical training with strong liberal arts curriculum. The Theatre Arts Major and Minor allows students to experience all aspects of theatrical production while giving them the opportunity to receive advanced and undergraduate training in performance, music theatre, design/technical theatre, theatre management, or general theatre studies. Our low student-to-faculty ration guarantees attention to students on an individual basis. In addition to our full-time faculty, the department frequently brings guest artists/teachers to campus from professional and educational theatres. The university and the department offer Study Abroad Programs which have enabled theatre students to spend a semester abroad studying and experiencing world theatre. In addition to scholarships, part-time employment in theatre is available through such areas as scenery or costume construction, properties, lighting, sound, or house management and publicity.

University of Wisconsin – Madison

Michael Vanden Heuvel, Chair
Dept of Theatre & Drama
Univ. of WI-Madison
6173 Vilas Hall,
821 University Ave.
Madison, WI 53706-1497
DEPT: (608) 263-3934
drama@macc.wisc.edu
www.wisc.edu
ADM: UG: U of WI./Madison, 716 Langdon St., Madison WI
    53706-1481   (608) 262-3961 http://apply.wisconsin.edu
Grad- U. of WI/Madison, 228 Bascom Hall, 500 Lincoln Dr.,
    Madison, WI 53706   (608) 262-2433 FAX: (608) 265-9505
http://www.wisc.edu/grad.eapp/

30,055 Total Enr.; h. compet.
Semester System; NAST
170 Majors;
NAST, U/RTA, ATHE, USITT
T: 8,808/$7,574 r&b
O-ST T:21,438/$7,574 r&b
FAX: (608) 263-2463
email: gradsec@theatre.wisc.edu
onwisconsin@admissions.wisc.edu

DEGREES OFFERED

BA in Theatre & Drama (73), Theatre & Drama - Acting Specialist (48); MA in Theatre Research (3); MFA in Acting (9), Design & Tech (10), Directing (2); PhD in Theatre Research (22). Declare major in soph/jr year.

ADMISSION & FINANCIAL INFORMATION

Test scores, GPA, GRE; 66% admitted to inst., UG theatre program generally accepts all, Grad accepts 1 out of 3. Aud. req'd for BA Acting Specialist program; Portfolios for Grad design students, interviews, auditions for actors.

FACULTY AND CLASSES OFFERED

15 Full-Time: 2 PT, 7 PhD, 10 MA/MFA; 4 Staff

A. (6 FT, 1 PT) Intro to Theatre-1/Y; Dramatic Lit-16/Y/O/X; Theatre History-10/Y/O; Dramatic Criticism-9/Y/O/X; Shakes-2/O; Playwriting-1/O

B. (5 FT) Acting-6/Y; Voice/Speech-3/Y; Movement-3/Y; Mime,etc-1/O; Musical Theatre-1/O; Directing-4/Y; Stage Combat-O; Dance-O; Asian Stage Discipline-4-Y/O; Singing-O

C. (4 FT) Prins of Des-1/Y; Set Des-2/Y/O; Cost Des-2/Y; Lighting Des-3/Y/O; Tech. Prod-11/Y/O; Cost Constr-5/Y/O; Stage Mgmt-1/Y; Makeup-1/O

D. (1 PT) Arts Mgmt-O; B.O. Proc-O; Marketing/Promo-O; Dev/Grant Writing-O; Legal-O; Budgeting/Acctg-O

FACILITIES AND PRODUCTIONS

MAINSTAGE: 321 seats, computerized/electronic lighting
    9 prods, 5 Fac dir, 3 Fac des, 2 Guest dir, 2 Guest des, 2 Grad dir, 2 Grad des, 2 UG des, budget $1,000-10,000

SECOND STAGE: 150-200 seats, computerized/electronic lighting
    2-4 prods, 2 Grad dir, 2 Grad des; budget $0-200

Facility built in 1970, last renovated in 2000, includes scene, costume, prop shop, welding shop, CAD facility, 4 rehearsal studios, 2 des studio, light lab, 10 classrooms.

There is a non-departmental, student-run organization in which majors generally participate.

1 student written play have been produced in the last two years.

Connection with Milwaukee Rep Theatre-observership in design (mentorship); American Players Theatre-some acting students intern there; Madison Rep Theatre-stage management students often get practicum experience.(AEA operating during school year)

DESCRIPTION

Noted Faculty: Sally Banes, Theatre Research/Dance-History; Patricia Boyette, Acting; Aparna Dharwadker, Dramatic Literature and Asian Indian Theatre; Dennis Dorn, Theatre Technology; Linda Essig, Lighting Design; David Furumoto, Kabuki Theatre Movement Marna King, Costume Design; James S. Moy, Theatre History & Theory; Herbert Parker, Acting; Michael Peterson, Dramtic Literature and Theatre Criticism; KAren Ryker, Acting/Voice; Robert Skloot, American & British Drama/Theatre of Holocaust; Michael Vanden Heuvel, Theatre Research; Joseph Varga, Scene Design; Paul Dennhart, Scting and Movement; Norma Saldivar, Directing; Manon Van de Water, Theatre for Youth.

Guest Artists: Mark Stanley, Lighting Designer (NYC Ballet); Laura Forti, Director; Roseanne Sheridan, Acting Teacher (American Players Theatre); Vijay Tendulkar, Playwright; Vicki Smith, Set Designer.

The Department of Theatre and Drama/University Theatre is a collaborative community of artists and scholars–faculty, staff and students–aiming to achieve the highest level of excellence in their teaching and learning, research and creative endeavors, and outreach to the community and the state. In our teaching we aim to prepare our undergraduates for a lifetime of successful engagement with the theatre. We provide an intellectual, practical and experiential knowledge of the performing arts, a working knowledge of the craft, discipline, and critical thinking it requires, and a deep appreciation for the collaborative art of the theatre. We aim to prepare our graduate students for successful 21st century careers in the theatre as both practitioners and scholars and so provide focused, professionally oriented study of theatre practice and scholarship. Through production and scholarship we aim to excite, entertain, pose questions, challenge assumptions, and critically examine values and beliefs. Our production programs and theatre spaces serve as the instructional laboratory for our classroom and studio work as well as providing an interface with the communities that make up our audiences.

University of Wisconsin - Milwaukee

Bruce Brockman, Chair.
Dept. of Theatre & Dance
P. O. Box 413
Univ. of Wisconsin
Milwaukee, WI 53201
DEPT: (414) 229-3048
FAX: (414) 229-2728
http://www3.uwm.edu/arts/home.cfm

28,000 Total Enr.; competitive
Semester System
193 Majors
T: UG $3,989/G $6,065
R&B: $4,850
R&B: $2,942

ADMISSIONS: www.uwm.edu
UG: (414) 229-2222   Grad: (414) 229-6569

DEGREES OFFERED

BA in Theatre (148); BFA in Theatre (45)

ADMISSION & FINANCIAL INFORMATION

UG - top half of HS class, ACT 21. Grad GPA of 2.5, UG admits 1 out of 40, G 1 out of 20. PTTP Scholarships, applic; based on talent and need.

FACULTY AND CLASSES OFFERED

14 FT, 5 PT: 1 PhD, 5 MFA/MA, 13 Prof. w/o degree; 3 Staff

A. (1 FT, 5 PT) Intro to Th-1/Y; Th History-2/Y; Dramatic Lit-1/Y; Shakes-X

B. (3 FT, 1 PT) Acting-9/Y; Voice/Speech-6/Y; Movement-6/Y; Stage Combat-2-Y; Directing-1/Y; Dance-X

C. (7 FT, 3 PT) Prins of Des-2/Y; Tech. Production-6/Y; Costume Construction-6/Y; Cost History-3/Y; Make-up-1/Y; Stage Mgmt-6/Y

D. (1 FT) Arts Management-1/O; Market'ng/Promo-X; Devel/Grant Wrt'ng-X; Budgeting/Acct'ng Procedure-X

FACILITIES AND PRODUCTIONS

MAINSTAGE: 550 seats, fly space, computerized lighting. 4 prods: 2 Fac dir, 6 Fac des, 2 Guest dir, 6 Guest des; budget $6,000-17,000

SECOND STAGE: 100 seats, computerized lighting. 2 prod: 2 Fac dir, 6 Fac des, 2 Guest dir, 6 Guest des; budget $2,000-8,000

THIRD STAGE: 80 seats, black box, electronic lighting.

Facility was built in 1968, renovated in 1997 (lighting); includes scene shop, costume shop, props shop, welding shop, sound studio, CAD facility, dance studio, 2 rehearsal studios, design studio, classrooms.

A non-departmental, student-run producing organization presents 4 plays per year in which department majors participate.

The PTTP enjoys a strong working relationshop with professional theatre companies and schools here and aborad, including the Milwaukee Repertory Theater, Milwaukee Chamber Theatre, Utah Shakespearean Festival, Shanghai Theatre Academy, Toi Whakaari New Zealand Drama School, The Univeristy of Goteborg in Sweden and the Arts Institute on Bournemouth in England. Student internships and exchanges with these institutions take place on a regular basis, as do faculty exchanges and guest artist residencies.

DESCRIPTION

Noted Faculty: Michelle Lopez, Voice and Speech; Bill Watson, Acting; Corliss Phillabaum, Theatre History and Criticism; Jeffrey Lieder, Costume Crafts, Tailoring and Millinery; Pamela J. Rehberg, Pattern-Making, Draping and Costume History; Stephen R. White, Production Management; Christopher J. Guse, Scenery and Rigging; R.H. Graham, Drafting and Design; Sandry J. Strawn, Stage Properties; LeRoy Stoner, Lighting.

Guest Artists: Victor Becker, Designer; William Brown, Director; David Frank, Acting Teacher; Lisa Harrow, Acting Teacher; Rosemary Ingham, Designer; Lou Salerni, Director; John Sipes, Director and Movement Teacher; Michael Tracy, Movement Teacher; Ann Wrightson, Designer.

University of Wisconsin - Parkside

Dean R Yohnk, Chair & Art Dir
Theatre Arts Dept.
900 Wood Road Box 2000
Univ. of Wisc.-Parkside
Kenosha, WI 53141
(262) 595-2352
yohnk@uwp.edu
ADMISSIONS: Above address
www.uwp.edu/admissions

4,800 Total Enr.; competitive
Semester System
50 Majors, U/RTA, ATHE
T: $6,000; $3,500 R&B
O-ST T:$9,000; $3,500 R&B
FAX: (262) 595-2271
www.uwp.edu/theatre
(262) 595-2355

DEGREES OFFERED

BA in Theatre Arts (generalist) with professional training concentrations in Acting, Music Theatre, Direction and Mgmt, Des and Tech, Arts Admin, Theater Education.

ADMISSION & FINANCIAL INFORMATION

Admission to the Theatre Arts program is by interview and audition only. Prospective majors must have a minimum ACT score of 20, and minimum GPA of 2.5, and be in the upper 50% of their class in order to schedule an interview or audition. Thomas Newman NY Trip Scholarship, Stage Club Talent Scholarships selected by faculty and staff based on service, leadership, artistic and academic success and potential. 75% applicants accepted by institution, 20 out of 50 UG admitted to theatre program.

FACULTY AND CLASSES OFFERED

6 FT, 1 PT: 1 PhD, 5 1/2 MFA/MA, 1/2 Prof. w/o advanced degree

A. (1 1/2 FT) Intro to Th-1/Y; Th History-2/Y; Dramatic Lit-2/Y; Shakes-1/Y; Playwriting-2/O

B. (1 1/2 FT) Acting-8/Y; Voice/Speech-2/O; Movement-2/O; Singing-2/Y; Musical Theatre-4/O; Stage Combat-2/O; Directing-2/Y; Dance-8/Y

C. (3 FT, 1/2 PT) Prins of Des-1/Y; Set Design-2/O; Cost Des-2/O; Lighting Des-2/O; Tech. Production-2/Y; Costume Construction-2/O; Make-up-5/Y; Stage Mgmt-2/Y

D. (1/2 PT) Arts Management-6/Y; Marketing/Promo-2/Y

FACILITIES AND PRODUCTIONS

MAINSTAGE: 685 seats, fly space, computerized & electronic lighting. 2 Fac dir, various Fac des prods; budget $6,000-9,000

SECOND STAGE: 90 seats, computerized & electronic lighting. 2 Fac dir, 1 Fac des, variouse UG dir, 1 UG des; budget $2,000-4,000

Facility was built in 1973; includes scene shop, costume shop, CAD facility, dance studio, rehearsal studios, 12 classrooms.

Connection with Fireside Playhouse (Equity) and Rocky Mountain Rep (Equity/Summer). Opportunities for Tech Prod at Fireside, Performance & Production at Rocky Mountain.

DESCRIPTION

Noted Faculty: Dr. Dean Yohnk, Directing, Playwriting; Jamie Cheatham, Acting, Directing; Skelly Warren, Scenic, Lighting Des; Judith Tucker-Snider, Costume & Make-up Des; Keith Harris, Scenic & Lighting Des; Michael Clickner, Tech Prod, Directing; Kimberly Instenes, Costume Des; Gale Childs-Daly, Directing, Text Coaching; Carol Cianelli, Voice & Diction

Guest Artists: Our program maintains extensive profes-

sional theatre partnership with the Milwaukee Repertory Theatre, The Fireside Theatre, and the Great River Shakespeare Festival. Frequent guest artist residencies and internships occur with these professional companies.

The UW-Parkside Theatre Arts Department is proud to offer the following special features:

Incredible location in the heart of America's leading theatre community: 220 professional theatres in Chicago and Milwaukee are less than 60 miles from campus. Countless theatrical, cultural, and entertainment opportunities are just a short drive or train ride away. Professional theatre connections and internships: Our primary goal is to prepare you for a fulfilling career in the professional theatre. We believe that it is essential for you to continuously 'connect' with theatre professionals while you are a student here. We are very proud of our very successful active partnerships with the Milwaukee Repertory Theatre and the Fireside Theatre, and we actively encourage our students to participate in valuable job shadowing experiences, guest artist residencies, and internship opportunities offered in cooperation with one of our professional theater partners. Our program has a very comprehensive program in place to provide each student with regular feedback on their progress and development as a student and as an artist. Twice each year we meet with each student individually to discuss, review, and access their growth and development – and to assist each individual in setting clear goals for the future.

University of Wisconsin - River Falls

Robin Murray, Chair
Dept. of Theatre Arts
410 S. 3rd St.
Univ. of Wisconsin
River Falls, WI 54022
DEPT: (715) 425-3791
FAX: (715) 425-0654
ADMISSIONS: uwrf.edu

6,000 Total Enr.; Compet.
Semester System
40 Majors; ATHE
T: $2,600/$2,700 R&B
O-ST T: $6,700/$2,700 R&B
SMALL PROGRAM

(715) 425-3500

DEGREES OFFERED

BS in Theatre Arts (40), Mass Comm. (30), Speech Comm (30). Students declare major in 2nd year; 2006 granted 12 degrees.

ADMISSION & FINANCIAL INFORMATION

HS rank upper 40% or ACT 22, no special reqs for theatre program. $400 scholarship for new student; $1000 SYSE scholarship for returning student; applic. & merit.

FACULTY AND CLASSES OFFERED

5 Full-Time: 2 PhD, 3 MA/MFA

A. (1 FT) Intro to Theatre-2/Y; Dramatic Lit-1/O; Theatre History-3/O; Shakes-1/X; Playwriting-1/O

B. (1 FT) Acting-2/Y; Voice/Speech-2/O; Directing-2/O; Dance-2/X

C. (2 FT) Prins of Design-1/Y; Set Design-1/O; Cost Des-1/Y; Lighting Des-1/O; Tech. Production-1/O; Costume Construc-tion-1/O; Cost Hist-1/Y; Make-up-1/O; Stage Mgmt-1/O

D. Arts Management-1/O

FACILITIES AND PRODUCTIONS

MAINSTAGE: 300 seats, fly space, computerized lighting. 3 prods: 3

Fac dir, 1 Guest dir/des, 1 UG dir/des; budget $3,000-5,000

SECOND STAGE: 100 seats, computerized lighting. 2 prods: 1 Fac dir/des, 1 UG dir/des; budget $500-1,500

Facility was built in 1972, includes scene, costume shops, sound, video studios, 2 rehearsal studios.

Department majors generally participate in a non-departmental, student-run producing organization that presents 1 production per year.

DESCRIPTION

The University of Wisconsin-River Falls Theatre Program offers students the advantages of a small, personalized educational program within easy access to a large metropolitan area. The theatre faculty is readily accessible and makes a strong commitment to the individual development of each student. The Minneapolis/St. Paul theatre community, home to over 100 vital theatre companies, is only 27 miles away. The theatre program is designed to expose students to all aspects of theatre. Students are also encouraged to pursue advanced courses in areas of special interest. Many opportunities exist for students to apply skills learned in class, in studio, and lab productions. Advanced students may be provided with opportunities to design or direct on main stage for academic credit, and they may pursue internships with metropolitan area arts organizations, also for academic credit. Internships are arranged individually, and can be tailored to meet the needs and objectives of the student.

University of Wisconsin - Stevens Point

Kenneth W. Risch, Chair
Dept. of Theatre & Dance
Univ. of Wisc/Stevens Point
1800 Portage St.
Stevens Point, WI   54481
DEPT: (715) 346-4429
www.uwsp.edu/theatre-dance
ADMISSIONS: UWSP Admissions Office, Rm. 102, Student Services Ctr, UW-Stevens Point, Stevens Point, WI 54481-3897
(715) 346-2441
www..uwsp.edu/admit/admiss.htm

8,612 Total Enr.; h. compet.
Semester System
145 Majors; ATHE, NAST (A)
T: $5,787$4,932 R&B
O-ST T: $15,380/$4,932 R&B
FAX: (715) 346-4794
www.uwsp.edu

FAX: (715) 346-2441
admiss@uwsp.edu

DEGREES OFFERED

BA/BS in Theatre Arts (37), Dance (43); BFA in Musical Theatre (29), Design/Tech (14), Acting (22). Declare major in freshman year; 2004 granted 25 degrees.

ADMISSION & FINANCIAL INFORMATION

HS cumulative GPA of 3.25 or above and ACT score of 21 or higher (SAT I of 990) or class rank in top 25% or ACT 21 (SAT I of 990) or higher and rank in top 50%. Th. program requires audition for dancers, actors; interview/essay for BA/BS, portfolio for designers. Theatre program generally admits 40 out of 120-150. Annual scholarship awarded to incoming students, one each: Acting, Dance, Design/Tech, Music Theatre; $500-1000; audition and interview required.

FACULTY AND CLASSES OFFERED

12 FT, 1/2 PT: 1 PhD, 11 MFA/MA, 1 w/o adv. degree; 2 Staff

A. (1 FT) Intro to Theatre-1/Y; Dramatic Lit-2/Y; Th History-2/Y; Shakes-2/X; Playwriting-1/O; Survey of Asian Th.-1/O; Script Analysis-1/Y; Survey of Musical Theatre I, II-2/Y

B. (8 FT, 1/2 PT) Acting-9/Y; Voice/Speech-3/Y; Singing-4/Y; Mus Th-3/Y; Directing-2/Y; Stage Combat-1/Y; Dance-24/Y + 9/O; Acting for the Camera-2/O

C. (3 FT) Principles of Des-1/Y; Set Design-2/Y; Cost Des- 2/Y; Lighting Des-2/Y; Tech Production-1/O; Costume Construc-tion-3/Y; Make-up-1/Y; Stg Management-1/O; Scene Paint-ing-1/O; Intro to Th. Tech-1/Y; Computer Aided Design-1/O

D. Arts Mgmt-X; Box Ofc.-X; Marketing/Promotion-X; Legal: Contracts/ Copyright-X; Box Office Procedure-X; Devel./Grant Writing-X; Budgeting/Accounting-X

FACILITIES & PRODUCTIONS

MAINSTAGE: 377 seats, fly space, computerized lighting.4 prods: 4 Fac dir, 7 Fac des, 7 UG des; budget $2-4,000 per show

SECOND STAGE: 150 seats, computerized lighting. 4 prods: 3 Fac dir/des, 1 UG dir, 8 UG des; budget $1,000-3,000

Facility was built in 1970, renovation/expansion in 2005; includes scene shop, costume shop, 2 dance studios, 2 rehearsal studios, CAD facility, design studio, 2 classrooms, state-of-the-art computer-assisted design lab.

A non-departmental, student-run, organization presents 3 productions per year in which dept. majors participate.

One student-written play and one faculty-written play produced in the last two years.

DESCRIPTION

Noted Faculty: Dance: Susan Gringrasso, Jeannie Hill, Joan Karlen. Theatre History/Playwriting: Kyle Bostian. Acting/Dir: Kenneth Risch, Stephen Trovillion Smith. Musical Theatre: Alan Shorter, Roger Nelson. Design: Stephen Sherwin (Scenic); Susan Sherwin (Costume); Gary Olsen (Lighting).

Guest Artists: Randy Winkler, Choreographer for *Children of Eden*; Residencies: Argentine choreographer, Margarita Bali; Aquila Theatre Company; River North Chicago Dance Company.

It is the goal of the University of Wisconsin-Stevens Point Department of Theatre and Dance to prepare our majors to enter the theatre arts profession and/or to pursue further training in performance, design, technology, and/or theory. To accomplish this, the Department seeks to give our majors, through both theory and practical experience, a solid foundation in the basic skills required of a professional in the field. These skills include those required of artistic understanding and perception, creative craftsmanship, and personal humanistic development. While increasing our majors' ability to perform as theatre professionals with a keen understanding of, and practical experience in, their chosen field, the Department emphasizes the need for majors to be sensitive, perceptive, responsible, dedicated, and creative human beings.

University of Wisconsin - Whitewater

Marshall Anderson, Chair
Univ. of Wisconsin-Whitewater
800 West Main St.
Whitewater, WI 53190-1790
DEPT: (262) 472-1566
FAX: (262) 472-2808
ADMISSIONS: Above address.

10,500 Total Enr.; compet.
Semester System
91 Majors; NAST
T: $2,920/$1,710 R&B
O-ST T: $9,200/$1,710 R&B
andersom@uww.edu
(262) 472-1440

uwwadmit@uww.edu   FAX: (262) 472-1515

DEGREES OFFERED

BA in General Theatre (34); BFA in Performance(26), Design/Tech (16), Stage Management (4), Mgmt/Promotion (2); BSE in Theatre (9). Declare major in first year; 2006 granted 28 degrees.

ADMISSION & FINANCIAL INFORMATION

Top 50% of HS class or comb. HS class & ACT/SAT ranks of 100 or above & completed req'd academic unit pattern. Accept 95% to institution; Th Prog. admits all students eliglble to enter university. Various schols available for incoming freshmen as well as upper classmen in theatre; general scholarships also avail. through Financial Aid Office; theatre scholarships determined by committee of theatre faculty in April of each year.

FACULTY AND CLASSES OFFERED

7 Full-Time, 4 Part-Time: 2 PhD, 6 MFA/MA; 1 Staff

A. (1 FT, 1 PT) Intro to Theatre-1/Y; Dramatic Lit-5/Y; Dramatic Crit-1/Y; Th History-5/Y; Shakes-2/X; Playwriting-1/X

B. (2 FT, 1 PT) Acting-4/Y; Voice/Speech-1/Y; Movement-1/Y; Singing-1/X; Dance-10/Y; Mime, mask, etc.-1/Y-O; Musical Theatre-O; Directing-2/Y; Stage Combat-O; Film-O

C. (3 FT, 1 PT) Prins of Des-1/Y; Set Design-2/Y; Cost Des-2/Y; Lighting Des-2/Y; Tech Prod'n-1/Y; Cost Construction-2/Y; Make-up-1/Y; Stage Mgmt-1/Y

D. (1 FT, 1 PT) Arts Management-4/Y; Marketing/Promotion-2/Y

FACILITIES & PRODUCTIONS

MAINSTAGE: 412 seats, computerized lighting. 6 prods: 5 Fac dir, 10 Fac des, 1 Guest dir; 11 UG des; budget $3,000-7,000/show

SECOND STAGE: 160 seats, computerized lighting.

Facility built in 1971, renovated in 2002; includes scene, costume, prop, CAD facility, video studio, 2 dance studio, 2 rehearsal studio, design studio, 3 classrooms.

A non-departmental, student-run, organization presents 1 production per year in which department majors participate.

One student-written play produced in the last two years.

UWW's own Summerland Theatre uses the performance space in the summer.

DESCRIPTION

Noted Faculty: Marshall Anderson, Design, Technical, Costume; Jim Butchart, Acting, Directing; Tom Colwin, Design/Technical - scenery, lights; Charles "Skip" Grover, Acting, Directing, History, Theatre Education; Angela Iannone, Acting; Robin Petterson, Dance, Performance Art; Megan Matthews, Management, Promotions; Sarah Altermatt, Management, Promotions; Steve Chene, Technical Direction, Lights; Barbara Grubel, Dance; Denise Ehren, Costume.

Guest Artists: Simone Ferro, Dance; Jim Fletcher, Stage Combat; Montgomery Davis, Directing; Jenny Wanasek, Directing; Jan Erkert, Dance.

The University of Wisconsin-Whitewater Theatre/Dance Department is committed to a hands-on, learn-by-doing approach to learning. Guided by faculty advisors, students can take advantage of numerous opportunities to perform, design, direct, choreograph and work as technicians and managers. The academic-year season consists of four mainstage plays, a mainstage dance concert and a children's play that tours throughout the region. In addition, students produce numerous one-act plays and other production projects. During the summer, students have the opportunity to participate in the three-play Summeround season as well. UW-Whitewater's location near Milwaukee, Madison and Chicago also allows students to pursue individualized internships with area arts organizations for academic credit.

Viterbo University

Rick Walters, Chair
Theatre Arts Department
900 Viterbo Drive
Viterbo College
La Crosse, WI 54601
skhauser@viterbo.edu

1,600 Total Enr; competitive
Semester System
70 Majors; ATHE
T: $9,085 per sem
$2665-$4080 R&B per sem
DEPT: (608) 796-3760
FAX: (608) 796-3736

ADM: 900 Viterbo Drive, La Crosse, WI 54601
(608) 796-3010   (800)VITERBO
FAX: (608) 796-3020   www.viterbo.edu

DEGREES OFFERED

BFA in Acting (26), Design/Tech (13), Directing/Management (2), Music Theatre (25), Arts Management (7); BA in Theatre Education (2); BS in Theatre Education (2). Declare major in freshman year; 2001 granted 5 degrees

ADMISSION & FINANCIAL INFORMATION

ACT 24, GPA 3.0, inst. accepts 80%; admission to theatre prog. requires: audition/interview/portfolio, resume, 2 recs; program admits 1 out of 2 applicants In addition to academic merit scholarships ($2,500-6,000/yr), majors may also audition for $1,000/year talent scholarship

FACULTY AND CLASSES OFFERED

8 Full-Time: 1 PhD, 7 MFA/MA, 4 Staff

A. (2 FT) Intro to Theatre-2/Y; Theatre History-2/Y; Shakes-1/X; Dramatic Lit-4/Y; Dramatic Criticism-2/O; Playwriting-1/O

B. (3 FT) Acting-4/Y; Voice-3/Y; Movement-2/Y; Musical Theatre-8/Y; Directing-2/Y; Singing-8/Y; Oral Interp-1/O

C. (2 FT) Prins of Des-12/Y; Set Design-21/O; Cost Des-21/O; Lighting Des-1/O; Tech. Production-2/O; Cost Constr-1/O; Cost History-1/Y; Make-up-2/Y; Stage Mgmt- 1/O

D. (1 FT) Arts Management-2/Y

FACILITIES AND PRODUCTIONS

MAINSTAGE: 1,100 seats, fly space, computerized & electron. ltg. 2 prods: 2 Fac dir/des, 1 Guest dir/des; budget $2,000-10,000

SECOND STAGE: 145 seats, black box, computerized and electronic lighting. 3 prods: 3 Fac dir, 1 Fac des, 2 UG des; budget $50-100. 4-8 Workshops/Readings: 3 Fac dir, 1-4 UG

Facility built in 1970, renovated in 2000; includes scene, costume, and props shop; dance, rehearsal, studios, classrooms.

2-4 student-written plays produced by department in the last two years.

DESCRIPTION

Guest Artists: Active professionals brought in each year in acting, design, directing, playwriting, etc. Also performing arts series brings Broadway tours and international performing artists.

The mission of the Viterbo College Theatre program is to educate and train students as theatre professionals within a liberal arts context. We believe that a solid liberal arts curriculum is essential for the growth and development of the whole human artist—body, mind and spirit. To this end, students receive a thorough and comprehensive exposure to all areas of theatre, including literature, history, design, acting, directing and management. Students are also ensured opportunities to become actively involved with the theatre productions activities of our thriving department. Because we are dedicated to providing students a well-rounded balance of both academic and production opportunities, we limit class and departmental size to allow for personal, hands-on opportunities and learning experiences. Approx. 90% of our theatre graduates since 1990 are currently working professionals in theatre or are completing advanced degrees at institutions of higher learning.

WYOMING

Casper College

Tom Empey, Dir. of Theatre
Casper College
125 College Drive
Casper, WY 82601
DEPT: (307) 268-2216
FAX: (307) 268-3020
ADM: AD-128, 125 College Drive, Casper, WY 82601
(307) 268-2458

4,000 Total Enr.; non-compet.
Semester System
60 Majors; NAST, ATHE
T: N/A
O-ST T: N/A
www.caspercollege.edu

(307) 268-2611

DEGREES OFFERED

AA in Acting (25), Dance (15), Tech (8), Musical Theatre Performance (5); Theatre Ed. (3). Declare major in freshman year.

ADMISSION & FINANCIAL INFORMATION

Inst. reqs ACT, HS diploma, 2.0 GPA, admits 90% of applicants; theatre program reqs Aud./Int./Portfolio, admits all applicants. Theatre Activity Scholarships - full tuition selected by audition (acting, dance, musical theatre) or portfolio review (tech).

FACULTY AND CLASSES OFFERED

5 FT, 1 PT: 5 MA/MFA, 1 Prof. w/o adv. degree; 1 Staff

A. (1 FT) Intro to Th-4/Y; Dramatic Lit-2/Y; Shakes-1/X; Dance History-1/Y; Theatre His.-1/O

B. (2 FT, 2 PT) Acting-6/Y; Voice/Speech-2/Y; Movement-1/Y; Music Voice-10/X; Dance-20/Y.

C. (2 FT, 1 PT) Lighting Des-1/O; Tech. Production-2/Y; Costume Construction-1/Y; Make-up-2/Y

FACILITIES AND PRODUCTIONS

MAINSTAGE: 419 seats, computerized lighting
    5 prods: 5 Fac dir/des; budget $8,000-$25,000

SECOND STAGE: Black Box, 150 seats, computerized lighting, 2 Fac Dir, Fac/UG des prod.; budget $1,000-$10,000

THIRD STAGE: Dance performance, 120 seats, computerized lighting, 2-4 Fac dir., Fac/UG des prod.; budget $300-$1,000

FOURTH STAGE: Student lab, 44 seats, electronic lighting, 1-4 Fac/UG Dir., UG des; budget $100-$500

The facility was renovated in 2003 and now includes: scene shop, costume shop, 2 dance studios, make-up lab, classrooms, CAD facility.

DESCRIPTION

Noted Faculty: Tom Empey, Theatre History; Richard Burk, Acting/ Movement/Voice; Jodi Youmans-Jones, Dance; Douglas Garland, Costume Design.

Guest Artists: Anthony Zerbe, Actor; Kurt Stamm, Dir/Choreographer; Dr. Jerry Henderson, Dir.; Mark Medoff, Playwright; Keema Jamal, Dancer; Ricardo Iznaola, Composer.

The Department of Theatre and Dance at Casper College offers 2-year Associate of Arts Degrees in Acting, Dance, Technical Theatre, Theatre Education and Musical Theatre Performance. The program is designed to prepare students to transfer to 4-year programs in their chosen field. Built on a strong production foundation, Casper College offers coursework equivalent to the fist two years in a university. With the recent addition of a Dance major in the past two years, and the introduction of a Musical Theatre Performance major beginning fall 2001, Casper College has one of the most comprehensive programs residing in a 2-year institution. The Department of Theatre and Dance at Casper College is accredited by the National Association of Schools of Theatre (N.A.S.T.)

University of Wyoming

Dr. Rebecca Hilliker, Chair
Theatre & Dance Dept
Dept 3951, 1000 E. Univ. Ave
Laramie, WY 82071-3951
DEPT: (307) 766-2198
ADM: (800) 342-5996
kirisk@uwyo.edu

12,700 Total Enr.; compet
110 Majors
Semester System
T: $2,808/$4,744 R&B
O-ST T: $8,280/$4,744 R&B
FAX: (307) 766-2197
www.uwyo.edu

DEGREES OFFERED

BA, BFA in Acting, Design Tech, Playwriting, Dance; BA in Theatre/English joint degree. All degrees offered also w/certification to teach if desired.

ADMISSION & FINANCIAL INFORMATION

GPA out of state 2.5; ACT/SAT scores that are "acceptable"; 95% of applicants admitted to inst. Theatre program admits all applicants. Full tuition Theatre and Dance scholarships offered through audition/interview/videotape. Deadline is Jan 30.

FACULTY AND CLASSES OFFERED

11 Full-Time: 2 PhD, 9 MFA/MA; 4 Staff

A. (3 FT) Intro to Theatre-1/Y; Dramatic Lit-2/O; Theatre History-2/O; Shakes-2/X; Playwriting-2/Y

B. (5 FT) Acting-5/Y; Voice/Speech-2/Y; Movement-2/Y; Mus. Th.-1/O; Directing-2/Y; Stage Combat-2/Y; Dance-20; Acting for Camera

C. (3 FT) Prins. of Design-2/Y; Cost Des-2/Y; Tech Production-2/Y; Set Design-2/Y; Lighting Des-2/Y; Cost Construction-1/O; Make-up-1/Y; Stage Management-1/X

FACILITIES & PRODUCTIONS

MAINSTAGE: 384 seats, fly space, computerized lighting
    6 prods: 4-5 Fac dir/des, 1 UG des; budget varies

SECOND STAGE: 130 seats, computerized lighting
   1-2 prods: 1-2 Fac dir/des, 1 UG des; budget varies

THIRD STAGE: 1800 seats, fly space, computerized lighting
   Many Fac dir/des Workshops/Readings

FOURTH STAGE / FILM STUDIO: 200 seats

Facility was built in 1972, renovated in 2001, new addition of Acting Studio 2000; includes scene shop, costume shop, prop shop, 2 movement/dance studios, rehearsal studio, design studio, 2 classrooms, mainstage, studio theatre.

A non-departmental, student-run organization presents 4-5 productions per year in which DEPT: majors participate. 8-10 student-written plays produced in the last two years.

Wyoming Summer Theatre, a professional, non-union, summerstock, now in its 40th season, recruits up to 16 students nationally each summer; stipend-$300/wk.

DESCRIPTION

Noted Faculty: Acting: Leigh Selting, Lou Anne Wright. Directing: Rebecca Hilliker. Playwriting: William Missouri Downs. Scene Design: Casey Kearns. Costume Design: Lee Hodgson. Lighting Design: Larry Hazlett. Dance: Marsha Fay Knight, Margaret Wilson. Tech Dir: Mike Earl.

Guest Artists: Actors from the London Stage, Mala Powers, Chekhov; Wilfred Harrison, BBC Actor; Actors from RSC; Tony Church, Nat'l Theatre Conservatory; John Basil, American Globe Theatre; Dale Anthony Girard, Soc. of American Fight Directors.

The study of theatre provides students with a broad understanding of the art of theatre appropriate to theatre's position as a fine art in a liberal arts college. The study of theatre is considered to provide a basis for more specialized theatre study in a graduate or professional school. The liberal arts education in theatre together with extensive experience in the production program also provides the foundation for a professional career in theatre, motion pictures, or television for those individuals with special desires and abilities. Secondary teaching certification in theatre can be obtained though this program of study.

Western Wyoming College

Jamie Young, Dir. of Theatre
Western Wyoming College
2500 College Dr.
Rock Springs, WY 82901
WWW.WWCC.WY.EDU/XTHEATRE
DEPT: (307) 382-1729
FAX: (307) 382-1887
ADM: 2500 College Drive, Rock Springs, WY 82901
307) 382-1600
www.wwcc.wy.edu

2,500 Total Enr.; not compet
60 Majors
Semester System
T: $1,828/$3,412 R&B
O-ST T: $4,804*/$3,412 R&B
SMALL PROGRAM
jyoung@wwcc.wy.us
FAX: (307) 382-7665
*reduced tuition for Western States Exchange

DEGREES OFFERED

AFA in Musical Theatre (35); Technical Theatre (12); AA in Musical Theatre (10); Technical Theatre (3); Theatre (0). Declare major in first year; 2007 granted 15 degrees.

ADMISSION & FINANCIAL INFORMATION

Open admission; 100% of applicants admitted to institution. Theatre program admits all applicants. 95% of students are on scholarship. Excellent academic scholarships are available for everyone with a 2.5 GPA and 19 ACT/1350 SAT or better. Additionally theatre scholarships are plentiful. Theatre scholarships are granted after a successful audition/interview process.

FACULTY AND CLASSES OFFERED

7 FT, 3 PT: 1 PhD, 5 MFA/MA; 4 prof. w/o advanced degree,20 Staff

A. (2 FT, 1 PT) Intro to Theatre-1/Y; Theatre History-3/Y; Shakes-1/X; Playwriting-1/O

B. (3 FT, 1 PT) Acting-4/Y; Musical Theatre-8/Y; Singing-6/Y; Directing-1/Y; Dance-13/Y

C. (1 FT, 1 PT) Prins of Design-1/Y; Set Design-1/Y; Lighting Des-1/Y; Make-up-1/Y; Costume Des-1/Y; Costume Constr-1/Y; Tech Prod-1/Y; Costume Des-1/Y

D. (1 FT) Arts Mgmt-1/Y; Box Office Procedure-1/Y; Marketing/Promo-1/Y; Development/Grant Writing-1/Y; Budgeting/Accounting Procedure-1/Y

FACILITIES & PRODUCTIONS

MAINSTAGE: 521 seats, fly space, computerized & electron lighting
   4 prods: 3 Fac dir, 2 Fac des, 1 GA dir, 2 GA des; budget $11,000-18,000

Facility built in 1988; includes scene shop, costume shop, prop shop, welding shop, sound studio, CAD facility, movement/dance studio, design studio, classrooms.

A non-departmental student-run producing organization presents 1-2 productions (summer) in which some majors participate.2 full length musicals have been produced by the department in the last two years.

DESCRIPTION

Noted Faculty: Jamie Young, Musical Theatre; Amy Critchfield, Technical Theatre; Deirdre MacDonald, Dance; Martha Holloway, Music

Guest Artists: Rob Lauer, Playwright, Lyricist; Sam Cardon, Composer; Randy Mugleston, Lighting Des; Fritha Pengelly, Choreographer; Lisa Niedemeyer, Choreographer; Mara McEwan, Performer; Emily Bunning, Performer

Western's Theatre program is built upon three guiding principles: A) Nourish the individual student in a safe emotional and physical environment by striving for unity and synergy. B) Provide talented and dedicated students guaranteed opportunities in a Theatre modeled after the professional world. C) Collaborate with students and faculty who strive for excellence in course work and production. The curriculum is carefully crafted to educate and train well-rounded, proactive, ethical, and organic theatre artists. Western has Musical Theatre (a composite study of Theatre, Dance and Music), Technical Theatre, and General Theatre programs. All of this work is a pleasure in the extremely well-equipped, multi-million dollar, state -of-the-art theatre facility. Why Western? 1) Small class sizes and personal attention. 2) Guaranteed performance and technical opportunities every year for every student. 2) Guaranteed performance and technical opportunities every year for every student. 3) Quality education. 4) Friendly and safe environment. 5) More affordable tuition. 6) Fun!!! 7) Hard and rewarding work. 8) Great scholarships. 9) Paid internships.

Concordia University

Edward Little, Chair
Theatre Department
Concordia University
7141 Sherbrooke West
Montreal, Quebec CN H4B 1R6
DEPT: (514) 848-2424 ext.4747
http://theatre.concordia.ca
ADMISSIONS: 1455 de Maisonneuve Boulevad West,
   Montreal, Qc, H3G 1M8
(514) 848-2668
http://websis.concordia.ca/admissionsinfo.htm

26,000 Total enr.
Sem. System; 172 Majors
T: N/A
OUT OF QUEBEC: T: N/A

FAX: (514) 848-4525
carolpl@alcor.concordia.ca

FAX: (514) 848-2621

DEGREES OFFERED

BFA in Major in Theatre (41), with specializations Theatre Performance (51), Theatre & Development (39); Design for the Theatre (36); Playwriting Specialization (5); Theatre Minor (13). Declare major on entry; 1999 granted 66 degrees.

ADMISSION & FINANCIAL INFORMATION

Audition, interview, portfolio, and min. univ. entrance requirements; accept 44% to institution; accept 4.4 out of 10 to program. Canadian and permanent residents are eligible. Contact the Financial Aid and Awards Office. (514) 848-3507.

FACULTY AND CLASSES OFFERED

9 FT, 13 PT: 4 PhD; 8 MA/MFA; 10 Profs. w/o advanced degree; 10 Staff

A. (2 1/2 FT) Intro to Th-2/Y; Th Hist-4/Y; Drama Lit.-1/O; Drama Crit-1/O; Playwriting-1/Y; Women Playwrights-1/O; Solo Playwriting-1/O

B. (2 1/2 FT) Acting-6/Y; Mvmt-2/Y; Singing-1/Y; Directing-1/Y; Voice-2/Y; Mime, etc.-1/Y; Mus Th-1/O; Stage Combat-1/O; Dance-1/X; Drama for Human Devel-2/Y; Popular Th-1/Y; Stories & Storytelling-1/Y; Drama Therapy-1/O; Drama for Special Populations-1/Y; Drama Experiences for Children-1/O; Th for Young Aud's-1/O

C. (4 FT, 1 PT) Prins of Des-2/Y; Set Des-1/O; Cost Des-1/O; Lighting Des-1/O; Tech. Prod.-1/O; Cost Constr.-1/O; Stage Mgmt-1/Y; Cost Hist-1/X; Portfolio Devel-1/O; Prod'n-4/Y; Sc. Painting-1/Y

D. (1 PT) Marketing/Promo-1/O

FACILITIES & PRODUCTIONS

MAINSTAGE: 380 seats, fly space, computerized & electronic lighting. 5 Prods; 1 Fac dir, 1 Fac des; 4 Guest dir, 4 UG des; budget $2,500-9,000

SECOND STAGE: 420 seats, computerized & electronic lighting 6 Prods; budget $200-1,500

THIRD STAGE: 90 seats, black box, electronic lighting. 8 Workshops/Readings, all UG dir; no budget.

Facility built in 1966, renovated in 1982; includes scene, costume, prop shops, design studio, 5 rehearsal studios.

A non-departmental, student-run, producing org. presents six productions per year in which majors participate.

Six student-written plays produced in last 2 years.

DESCRIPTION

Noted Faculty: Ralph Allison, Commedia Dell'Arte; Kit Brennan, Playwriting; Ana Cappelluto, Gene Gibbons, Theatre Design; Gerry Gross, Directing; Nancy Helms, Music Theatre; Ted Little, Social Drama; Eric Mongerson, Lighting. Design; Philip Spensley, Th. Hist.

Guest Artists: Bryan Doubt, Lib Spry, Diane Roberts, Robert Astle, Joel Miller.

The Theatre Department at Concordia University offers students an opportunity to explore theatre as an art form and instrument for social change. The programme provides students a basic grounding in design, playwriting, management nd performance and serves as preparation for advanced studies. It also allows individuals who wish to focus on drama within the context of human development to study educational, rehabilitative and therapeutic aspects of theatre. The Department welcomes autonomy and personal creativity in its students while encouraging initiative and collaboration. reflecting the realities of modern theatre, it also prepares students for self-employment and entrepreneurial roles within the Canadian theatre milieu.

McGill University

Drama Program, Dept. of English
853 Sherbrook St. West
McGill University
Montreal, Quebec, CN H3A 2T6
DEPT: (514) 398-6559
FAX: (514) 398-6336
www.arts.mcgill.ca/programs/english/english.html
ADM: 845 Sherbrook St. W., Montreal Quebec Canada H3A 2T5
(514) 398-3910
www.mcgill.ca/applying

21,000 Tot. Enr, competitive
46 majors, 28 minors;
Semester System; U/RTA
Province students: $3,189.70
Non Province $ 6,562.30
Non-Canada: 29115,300.10
r&b:N/A

FAX: (514) 398-4193

DEGREES OFFERED

BA in English (Drama & Theatre Option). Declare major in 1st of 3-year, 2nd of 4-year program; (10 Drama & Theatre).

ADMISSION & FINANCIAL INFORMATION

High scores 1st 3 yrs. of high school, h.s. diploma or equivalent; 47% accepted by inst. Theatre program admits all applicants. There are a variety of entrance and other scholarships available. For more information, phone the office of Student Aid (514) 398-6013/6014.

FACULTY AND CLASSES OFFERED

5 FT, 1/2 PT: 4 PhD, 2 MFA/MA, 1 PT prof. w/out adv. degree; 1 Staff

A. (3 1/2 FT) Intro to Theatre-1/Y; Dramatic Lit-8-10/Y; Theatre History-2+/Y; Shakes-2+/Y

B. (1 FT) Acting-3/Y; Directing-2/Y; Theatre Laboratory-2/Y

C. (1/2 FT, 1/2 PT) Stage Scenery & Lighting-1-2/O; Costuming for the Theatre-1-2/Y

FACILITIES & PRODUCTIONS

MAINSTAGE: 309 seats, fly space, computerized lighting. 2-3 prods: generally Fac dir/des, opportunities for exceptional students.

SECOND STAGE: 60 seats, electronic lighting 30 prods: generally student-run

Facility was built in 1926, renovated in 1992; includes scene shop, costume shop.

Two non-dept, student-run orgs present 14 prods/yr., majors participate. 20 student written plays received readings in past two years.

DESCRIPTION

Noted Faculty: Catherine Bradley, Sean Carney, Leanore Lieblein, Patrick Neilson, Denis Salter, Myrna Wyatt Selkirk.

Guest Artists: Alexandre Marine, Bryden MacDonald, Directors; John Denning, Rene-Daniel Dubois, Gail Hanrahan, Gordon McCall, Visiting Speakers.

McGill's Drama and Theatre Program, established in 1969, is one of three options within the Department of English, and offers both majors and honours degrees. Drama and Theatre is studied as a Liberal Arts Subject, with particular emphasis on its historical and theoretical context. Students select Drama and Theatre courses from extensive offerings in dramatic literature, performance theory, and theatre history. The program offers practical courses in costume, set and lighting design, acting, directing and stagecraft. All practical courses are taught by professionally trained faculty. Although some students have gone on to careers in theatre, the Drama Program does not attempt to provide professional theatre training. Rather, it encourages its students to develop a clear understanding of what professionalism means in the practice of theatre; an understanding which provides an excellent foundation for a wide variety of careers.

University of Windsor

Prof. Lionel Walsh, Director	16,000 Tot. Enr.;
School of Dramatic Art	competitive
401 Sunset Ave.	Semester System;
University of Windsor	ATHE
Windsor, Ontario, Canada N9B 3P4	342 Majors
email: drama@uwindsor.ca	CN T: contact dept
DEPT: (519) 253-3000x2804	US: $5,000 (NAFTA tuition)
FAX: (519) 971-3629	www.uwindsor.ca/drama

ADMS: Registrar's Office, 401 Sunset, Windsor, ONT, CA N9B 3P4
(519) 253-3000 x 3315   uwindsor.ca/registrar

DEGREES OFFERED

BFA-Acting (77); BA (Honours) Drama in Education & Community (101), Drama/Communication Studies (68), Dramatic Art (96). Declare major in first year; 2004 granted 84 UG.

ADMISSION & FINANCIAL INFORMATION

From U.S.A., 2.75 G.P.A.; the institution also looks at SAT scores. Audition for BFA actors; interview for drama in education and community; Theatre program generally admits 100 out of 300 applicants. Frances Hyland Entrance Scholarship awarded to a student based on audition

FACULTY AND CLASSES OFFERED

14 FT, 9 PT: 3 PhD, 10 MFA/MA, 10 Prof. w/out adv deg; 6 Staff

A. (4 FT, 2 PT) Intro to Theatre-3/Y; Dramatic Lit-8/O; Theatre History-3/Y; Shakes-2/X; Playwriting-O; Dramatic Crit-O

B. (7 FT, 6 PT) Acting-17/Y; Voice/Speech-3/Y; Movement-5/Y; Singing-2/O; Directing-3/Y; Dance-1/Y; Film-6/O; Mime, Etc.-O; Musical Theatre-O; Stage Combat-O.

C. (3 FT) Principles of Design-1/Y; Set Design-3/Y; Lighting. Design-2/Y; Cost Design-2/Y; Costume Constr.-1/Y; Tech. Production-2/Y; Stage Mgmt-2/Y

D. (1 PT) Arts Management-1/Y; Budget/Accounting Procedure-2/O

FACILITIES & PRODUCTIONS

MAINSTAGE: 319 seats, computerized lighting. 6 prods: 4 Fac dir, 4 Fac des, 2 Guest dir, 2 Guest des; budget $15,000-25,000

Second Stage: 100 seats, computerized lighting

Facility built in 2003, includes scene shop, costume shop, prop shop, welding shop, sound studio (at Univ., not part of facility), dance studio, 3 video studios, 4 classrooms, 1 rehearsal studio.

A non-departmental, student-run orgs presents 4 to 6 productions a year, majors participate. 2 student written plays produced in past two years.

Connection with Stratford Festival of Canada, in Stratford, Ontario. Summer courses offered at The Festival in Text and Shakespeare in Performance.

DESCRIPTION

Noted Faculty: Prof. William Pinnel, Scenic Design, Directing; Prof. Bernie Warren, Drama in Education; Prof. Brian Taylor, Acting, Directing; Prof. Brian Rintoul, Acting.

Guest Artists: Norma Bowles, Artistic Director; Rod Ceballos, Actor, Director; Jonathan Fox, Artistic Director; Rick Kish, Actor, Singer, Director; Ellen Lauren, Actor; James Luce, Actor, Director; Jackie Maxwell, Artistic Director, Director; Lenard Petit, Actor, Director; Mike Shara, Actor.

Boasting the newest theatre school facility in Canada, The School of Dramatic Art offers degree programmes for students interested in careers in professional theatre as actors, directors, stage managers, and designers, as well as those interested in becoming classroom teachers, theatre arts teachers, or theatre for social action specialists working with community-based organizations. Relatively small classes, most of which are practically oriented, and easy access to professors make possible the kind of personalised attention and individualised approach to development that fosters artistic growth, scholarship, and an unforgettable university experience. Accomplished theatre professionals and educators are part of the dedicated teaching faculty at the School of Dramatic Art. Guest Artists serve as visiting professors, directors, and artists in residence. Our theatre company, University Players, produces six fully mounted productions annually; workshop productions are mounted by faculty and students in our state-of-the-art Studio Theatre.

UNITED KINGDOM

London Academy of Music and Dramatic Art

Peter James, Principal	250-300 Total Enr.
LAMDA	h. Competitive
155 Talgarth Road	T: SEE WEBSITE
London W14 9DA, UK	enquiries@lamda.org.uk
ADMISSIONS: above	www.lamda.org.uk

TEL: +44 20 8834 0500   FAX: +44 20 8834 0501
www.lambda.org.uk
Affiliate of UK's Conservatoire for Dance and Drama

DEGREES OFFERED

BA (Hons) Acting-3 year course (28); BA (Hons) Acting-2 year course (26); Dip HE Stage Management & Technical Theatre (20); LAMDA Classical Acting-one year diploma (25-40); LAMDA Classical Acting-single semester (45); Foundation Course-one year (30); Directing, Movement Director, Designer, Musical Director and Repetiteur; LAMDA Summer Courses. Please see website above for further info

ADMISSION & FINANCIAL INFORMATION

Entry to the academy is by audition and/or interview. As the training is vocational, there are no specific academic pre-requisites. There is no college-owned housing. Some LAMDA scholarships are available. Awards and scholarships are allocated at the academy's discretion. There is no application procedure prior to being offered a place.Audition required for actors, interview for stage mgmt an technical theatre course.

FACULTY AND CLASSES OFFERED

Acting: The Two or Three Year Acting Course: BA (Hons) Professional Acting, accredited by the National Council for Drama Training (NCDT) and validated by the University of Kent at Canterbury. Disciplines include: Acting and Improvisation; Voice, including the speaking of Poetry; Movement, including Period Movement; Singing, including Choral and Solo; Textual Interpretation and Analysis; Alexander Technique; Physical Theatre (including Mask, Clown, Bouffon and Melodrama); Stage Combat; Dance, including Tap, Jazz, Flamenco, Historic; History of the Industry

During the training, students might expect to experience a variety of performance styles including: Greek; Shakespearean and Jacobean; Restoration; 19th century Russian Naturalism; 20th & 21st century plays; Music Theatre; A Play-Making process.

Technical-Two-year Stage Mgmt & Technical Theatre Course: Dip HE; Foundation Course-one year; Classical Acting Courses; Post-Graduate One Year Diploma Courses for Directors, Theatre Designers; Musical Directors & Repetiteurs and Movement Instructors. 2 to 8 week Summer Workshops*These courses include an excursion to the Royal Shakespeare Company at Stratford-upon-Avon, as well as visits to performances at London theatres.

FACILITIES & PRODUCTIONS

MAINSTAGE: 120 seats, fly space, electronic lighting
    13 Prods

Second Stage: 80 seats, Black Box Studio, electronic lighting
    13 prods

Facility was built in 1963, renovated in 1992; includes scene, cost, welding shops, sound, video, CAD studios, movement/ dance studio, 10 rehearsal studios, library, common room/ canteen, armory, a number of smaller class rooms and teaching spaces.

Four collaborations between students and a professional playwright and director-The LAMDA Long Project. . 2 student-written rehearsed readings produced in the last two years.

There is no official connection, but our students have constant contact with the industry. In July 2006, our final year students presented two plays at the Royal Court Theatre as part of the courts' 50th anniversary celebrations.

DESCRIPTION

Noted Faculty: Peter James, Principal, Director; Colin Cook, Vice-Principal, Director; Rodney Cottier, Head of Acting/Stage Combat; Penny Cherns, Acting; Yvonne Morley, Voice; Jennifer Tatam, Music; Anne Durman, Movement; Rob Young, Head of Stage Mgmt, Technical Theatre; John Link, Acting

Guest Artists: Mark Ravenhill, Playwright; Conor Mitchell, Composer, Playwright; Van Badham, Playwright; Kathryn Hunter, Director; Thea Sharrock, Director; Josie Rourke, Director; Peter Morris, Playwright; Richard Bullwinkle, Designer

"At LAMDA, we are proud to offer a classical training for the modern actor, stage manager or theatre technician." Peter James, Principal.

The institutions that combined to form LAMDA date from 1861, making the Academy the oldest of its kind in the UK, with a long-established and international reputation for excellence. An affiliate of the UK's prestigious Conservatoire for Dance and Drama, LAMDA's continuing success derives from its ability to adapt its traditional teaching to the tumultuous changes taking place in today's entertainment industry. While we truly believe that drama needs no more than 'bare boards and a passion', we are acutely aware that acting in the contemporary world often takes place in more technological circumstances. LAMDA is dedicated to helping actors, directors, stage managers, and theatre technicians acquire the necessary skills to meet the highest demands in contemporary theatre, film and television. Our alumni include: Jim Broadbent; Brian Cox; Swoosie Kurtz; John Lithgow; David Suchet; Donald Sutherland and Janet Suzman.

London Dramatic Academy
Fordham University, New York
See Ad

Richard Digby Day, Art. Director	Semester System
c/o Savina Antal	20-25 Majors; ATHE
Walsh Library, Ste 039	T:$15,200/$5,800
Fordham University	room per semester/no board
Bronx, NY 10458	UK Tel: 00-44-207-242-7004
lda@fordham.edu	UK Fax: 00-44-207-831-7185
Admissions: (718) 817 3464	www.fordham.edu/lda
londoncentre@fordham.edu	

Full application including essay, references and interview required; 60 % of applicants accepted by institution.

Curriculum includes: British Theatre Acting: Practical Shakespeare; Acting; British Theatre, now and then: British Theatre History, Dramatic Literature, Theatre Discussion; Movement and Stage Combat, Alexander Technique, Historical Dance, Movement, Physical Theatre, Stage Combat; Voice Training for Actors, Speech, Voice, Dialect

Master classes have included: Imelda Staunton, Jeremy Irons, Michael Sheen, Dame Judi Dench, Ian McKellan, Jim Broadbent, Derek Jacobi, Michael Frayn

The study abroad (London) programme sponsored by Fordham University, Bronx, NY.

At the London Dramatic Academy the faculty has one principal aim: it is to introduce you, in an exciting and practical way, to the crafts that have made British Theatre, over the centuries, the most vital in the western world. We want you to have a challenging, vibrant and unforgettable semester here in London. We work together to that end. LDA was founded over 30 years ago by instructors from the Royal Academy of Dramatic Art at the request of Marymount College of Tarrytown, NY. Since 2003, it has been under the aegis of Fordham University, which has given it a renewed sense of energy and purpose.

London International Film School

Mike Leigh, Chair/Ben Gibson, Director
The London International Film School
24 Shelton Street
London, WC2H 9UB Great Britain
www.lfs.org.uk

MAIN: 020 7240 0168
DEPT: 020 7836 9642
FAX: 020 7497 3718

film.school@lfs.org.uk

DEGREES OFFERED
MA in Film-Making, MA in Screenwriting

ADMISSION & FINANCIAL INFORMATION
Minimum age 20 yrs. Students are expected to be mature and self-motivated and will generally possess a degree or other tertiary level qualification, or may otherwise be accepted in cases of special ability or experience. Avg. age 24.

COURSE INFORMATION
MA in Filmmaking Program commences each January, April, and September. Intensive two-year, full-time practical course teaching skills to professional levels. All students work on one or more films in each of the six terms and are encouraged to interchange unit roles termly to experience different skill areas. The technical formats of the termly films are specified, growing more complex and demanding of student's abilities until, in the fifth term, a 35mm colour drama is shot on student-constructed sets. In the final term, the format is unspecified and students organise their productions in a way more closely reflecting commercial film practice. Approximately half each term is spent in film-making, half in practical instruction, seminars. workshops, tutorials, scriptwriting and film analysis. Faculty consists of permanent and visiting professionals.

FACILITIES & PRODUCTIONS
2 viewing rooms, 2 shooting stages, 2 rehearsal stages, 15 cutting rooms; 16mm and 35mm Panavision, Arriflex and rostrum cameras, Nagra recorders, Steenbeck editing machines, U-matic video.

DESCRIPTION
Established for over 40 years, the School is constituted as an independent, non-profit making, educational charity and is a member of NAHEFV and CILECT - respectively the national and international federations of film schools. Graduates have achieved leading positions in film and television industries world-wide and include Les Blair, Don Boyd, Bill Douglas, Mark Forstater, Danny Huston, John Irvin, Mike Leigh, Michael Mann, Horace Ove and Franc Roddam.

The London Dramatic Academy is a challenging 14 week programme, offered in both Fall and Spring, that provides a practical, intensive and wide ranging introduction to British acting styles – from Shakespeare to Stoppard.

For more information see www.fordham.edu/LDA. To request a brochure call the Fordham University Study Abroad Office at 212 636 7714 or contact The London Dramatic Academy, 22 Brownlow Mews, London WC1N 2LA UK

"A theatre programme that was beyond expectation, words or thanks"

Study abroad at
The London Dramatic Academy

Mountview Academy of Theatre Arts

Ralph Richardson Memorial Studios
Paul Clements, Principal
Kingfisher Place, Clarendon Road
London N22 6XF, Great Britain
DEPT: (+44)208 8801 2201
enquiries@mountview.ac.uk
ADMISSIONS: Above address
9216
enquiries@mountview.ac.uk
www.mountview.ac.uk

301 Total Enr.;
h.compet.
Trimester system; ELIA
T: please enquire
FAX:(+44)0208 8829 0034
www.mountview.ac.uk
ADM:(+44)0208 8826

FAX:(+44)208 8829 0034

DEGREES OFFERED

3 yr BA in Performance, Acting and Musical Theatre Options; 2 yr BA in Tech Theatre; Post Grad: 1 yr MA in Performance; 1 yr Post Grad Diploma in Tech Theatre; 1 yr Post Grad in Theatre Directing.

ADMISSION & FINANCIAL INFORMATION

Audition for Performance students; Interview for Technical Theatre students. For the BA (Hons) courses the Academy normally requires standard qualifications. However the Academy recognises that talent/skill cannot always be measured by conventional academic achievement and welcome applications form people (particularly mature applicants) without standard entry qualifications.

CLASSES OFFERED

Acting and Text, Singing, Dance & Movement, Voice & Speech, Music Theory, Song Presentation, Performance Projects, Microphone Technique, Radio Technique, Alexander Technique, TV Technique, Stage Combat, Audition Technique, Improv, Lighting and Sound, Lighting Design, Board Operation, Sound Design, Electrics, CAD, Tech Drawing, Metalwork, Wood turning, Set Design, Prop Making, Scenic Painting, Printing, Dyeing, Costume Making, Score Reading, Theatre History, Risk Assessment, Building a Character, Approach to Text, Text into Performance, Voice, Verse, Sight Reading, Dance and Movement, Acting for the Camera, plus lectures and seminars providing practical knowledge required to begin work as an actor.

FACILITIES AND PRODUCTIONS

Mountview has two sites: The Wood Green Complex and 104 Crouch Hill, situated in the London Borough of Haringey and well placed for easy access to West End Theatres, fringe venues and London nightlife. Wood Green Complex: is where most of the training and rehearsal work for Performance, Technical and Directing students take place. Productions are presented throughout the year. Venues include Mountview's own Judi Dench Theatre (60 seats) and the Mountview Theatre (100 seats) plus studio theatre facilities are available at the Ralph Richardson memorial Studios. Mountview also presents productions in other London venues.

DESCRIPTION

Noted Faculty: Paul Clements, Principal & Dir of Acting Courses; Paul Sabel, Dir of Musical Theatre Courses; Francesca Greatorex, Dir of Tech Theatre Courses; Amir Korangy, Head of Postgraduate Studies; Rick Lipton, Head of Voice; Sam Spencer-Lane, Head of Movement & Dance.

Guest Artists: Kevin Spacey, Richard E. Grant, Mike Leigh, Anthony Sher, Vanessa Redgrave, Bazil Meade, Lynn Redgrave, Anne Skates.

Founded in 1945, Mountview is recognised as one of the UK's leading Academies of Theatre Arts, attracting students from all over the world, offering an extensive and stimulating training for those interested in pursuing a Performance Directing or Technical Theatre career. The courses are structured to give students a thorough grounding in all aspects of their craft. The curricula are constantly updated to match the ever-changing needs of the profession and this has been borne out by the widespread success of graduates in virtually every area of the performing arts. The employment record of Mountview's graduates is enviable with our ex-students working in all media in Britain and abroad. Mountview also offers superb after-care services to all graduates. Mountview is passionately committed to releasing the individuality, skills and flair of each student in his or her chosen field of study.

how to use the index

This index is an alphabetical listing of all the schools in this edition which charts the degrees offered by each institution. In using this index, please note:

The first column is the page number of the institution's listing so that you may easily get more information.

The chart uses the following symbols to show which degrees are offered in each area by the institution:

① AA (Associate Arts)
● AS (Associate Science)
② BA (Bachelor of Arts)
● BS (Bachelor of Science)
③ BFA (Bachelor of Fine Arts)
④ MA (Master of Arts)
● MS (Master of Science)
⑤ MFA (Master of Fine Arts)

⑥ PhD (Doctor of Philosophy)

● Certificate (or Diploma, not an accredited academic degree; if followed by "AEA" it means an Equity card is earned.)

The areas of study are as follows, found at the head of each column in the chart:

GENERAL - includes all general degrees in Drama, Theatre Arts, Theatre Studies, etc., without further specialization.

ACTING - Acting, Performance

DIRECTING - Directing

DESIGN - Scenic, Lighting, and/or Costume Design

PRODUCT/TECH - Theatre Production, Technical Theatre, Production Management; also Set or Costume Construction

STAGE MANGMNT - Stage Management

PLAYWTG/DIRECTING - Playwriting, Dramaturgy

HISTORY/CRITICISM - Theatre History, Dramatic Criticism, Theatre Criticism, Theory

THEATRE MANGMNT - Theatre Management

THEATRE EDUCATION - Theatre Education, Teaching Theatre

MUSICAL THEATRE - Musical Theatre

CHILDREN's - Children's Theatre, Child Drama, Creative Dramatics

NOTE: When preparing this index, the question arose as to how we might distinguish between a situation where the institution offers a degree in various different theatre areas, and a situation where the degree offered is a general one, such as Drama or Theatre Arts, with specializations or concentrations in several areas. It was decided that no distinction should be made in this index, and, in either case, no degree (BA, MA, etc) is noted under each area of specialization. It is up to the user, once having noted a particular school's offering in one's area of interest, to determine whether one can obtain a degree in that area, or if the degree is generalized, with a concentration in that area.

Also, if areas were combined, as often happened with "Design/Tech" and less frequently with "Acting/Directing," the degree symbol appears in both columns. Again, the user must determine the exact area of the degree by referring to the listing.

alphabetical index of schools and degrees granted

	PAGE	GENERAL	ACTING	DIRECTING	DESIGN	PRODUCT/TECH	STAGE MANGMNT	PLAYWTG/DIRECTING	HISTORY/CRITICISM	THEATRE MANGMNT	THEATRE EDUCATN	MUSICAL THEATRE	CHILDREN'S	OTHER
Abilene Christian University	244	②	③	③	③	③						③		②Th. Ministry
Act One Studios Conservatory	66		●											
Adelphi University	155		③		③	③								
Agnes Scott College	59	②												
Alabama Shakespeare Festival	1		⑤				⑤			⑤				See ad back of book
Alfred University	156	②	②		②	②								
Alma College	119		②	②	②									② Dance
American Acad. of Dramatic Arts (NY)	156		①●											
American Acad. of Dramatic Arts (CA)	11		①●											
American Conservatory Theater	12		⑤											
American Musical & Dramatic Academy NY	156		③⑤	⑤	③⑤	③⑤		⑤		③⑤			●	
American Musical & Dramatic Academy CA	12		●③⑤	⑤	③⑤	③⑤		⑤		③⑤			●	
Moscow Art Theatre School	109													
Amer. RepertoryTheatre Institute @ Harvard	109		●AEA	●				●						● Voice
American University	47	②	②		②	②			②	②			②	② Speech/Voice
Amherst College	110	②												② Dance
Angelo State University	244	②	②		②	②					②			
Appalachian State University	185	②	②								❷			
Arcadia University	217	②	③								②	③		

A-1

alphabetical index of schools and degrees granted

KEY: ①: AA ●: AS ②: BA ❷: BS ③: BFA ④: MA ❹: MS ⑤: MFA ⑥: PhD ●: certificate

School	Page	General	Acting	Directing	Design	Product'n Tech	Stage Mangm't	Playw'tg	History/Criticism	Theatre Mangm't	Theatre Educat'n	Musical Theatre	Children's	Other
Arizona State University	7	②												
Asolo Conservatory •see Florida State University	50													See ad in back of book
Auburn University	1	②	③		③	③				③				
Auburn University @ Montgomery	2	②	②											
Austin Peay State University	239	②❷④									②④			
Avila University	133	②	③	③		③					②	③		
Baldwin-Wallace College	199	②								②		③		②Dance
Ball State University	78	②❷	②❷		②❷	②❷					②❷	②❷		②❷Dance See ad
Barnard College	157	②	②	②	②	②			②					
Barter Conservatory @ Emory & Henry Coll.	264		②	②				②				②		
Bates College	104	②												
Baylor University	245	②	③	③⑤④	③	③								
Bennington College	261	②												Individualized degree
Berea College	93	②												
Berry College	60	②												
Bethany College	90	②										②		
Binghamton University	158		②	②	②	②								②Dance
Boise State University	65	②	②	②	②	②	②				②			②Dance
Boston College	110		②	②	②	②	②		②	②				
Boston Conservatory	111											③④		
Boston University	111	③	③	⑤	③⑤	③⑤	③				⑤			③Indep. Stud.
Bowling Green State University	200	②④⑥	③				③							
Bradley University	66	②❷	②❷			②❷					②❷	③		
Brandeis University	112	②	⑤	⑤	⑤			⑤						
Brenau University	60	②③	③									③		
Brigham Young University	258	②④	③							③	②	③		②Media Arts
Brown University	233	②④⑥	⑥											
Brown University, Trinity Rep Consortium	234	⑤⑥	⑤⑥	⑤										②Dance
Bucknell University	218	②												
Butler University	78	②								●				
California Institute of the Arts	13		③⑤		③⑤	③⑤				③⑤				
California State Polytech. University	14	②	②	②	②	②								②Dance
California State-Bakersfield	14	②												
California State-Dominguez Hills	15	②	②		②	②								②Television Arts
California State-Fresno	15	②	②		②	②					②			②Dance
California State-Fullerton	16	②	②⑤	②	②⑤	②⑤		②			②	③		②Dance

KEY: ①: AA ②: AS ❶: BA ❷: BS ③: BFA ④: MA ❹: MS ⑤: MFA ⑥: PhD ●: certificate

School	Page	General	Acting	Directing	Design	Product/Tech	Stage Mangm't	Playwrt'ng	Directing	History/Criticism	Theatre Mangm't	Theatre Education	Musical Theatre	Children's Theatre	Other
California State-Long Beach	17	②	②⑤		②⑤	②					⑤				
California State-Northridge	17	②④													
California State-Sacramento	18	②④		②											
California State-Stanislaus	18	②	②	②		②									
California University of Pennsylvania	219	②													②Dance
Campbell University	185		②			②					②				②Drama/Christ.Min
Carnegie Mellon University	219		③⑤	③⑤	③⑤	③⑤				③⑤	③⑤		③		
Carroll College	279	②	②	②	②	②						②			Theatre Arts Minor
Case Western Reserve	200	②	②⑤	②	②	②									
Casper College	288	①	①			①							①		
Catawba College	186	③	③		③	③				❷					Dance
Catholic University of America	47	②	⑤	⑤						⑤		②③	②		
Catonsville Community College	105	①													
Centenary College of Louisiana	98	②													
Central Connecticut State University	38	②③	③		③	③									②③Dance
Central Missouri State University	134	②❷④	③		③	③				❷		❷			
Central Washington University	274	②④	②		②	②				②④		②		②	
Chatham University	220	②													
Chicago State University	67														②RadioTV
Circle in the Square Theatre School	158		●										●		
City University of NY - Grad School	159	⑥			③										
Clarion University of Pennsylvania	220	②③	③			③							③		
Clarke College	85	②													
Cobalt Studios	159														●Scene Paint.
Coe College	85	②	②	②	②										
Colgate University	160	②													
College of Charleston	236	②	②		②	②								②	
College of Performing Arts • see Roosevelt University															
College of the Holy Cross	113	②													
College of the Mainland	245	①	①												
College of St. Catherine	126	②	②									②			●Theatre/Dance
College of Santa Fe	153	②③	②③	②③	②③	②③			⑤			③			
College of William & Mary	264	②	②		②③	②									Minor - Dance
Collin College	246	①													
Columbia College	67	②③	②③	②③	②③	②									
Columbia University	160		⑤	⑤				⑤		⑤			②		

alphabetical index of schools and degrees granted

KEY: ①: AA ●: AS ②: BA ●: BS ③: BFA ④: MA ●: MS ⑤: MFA ⑥: PhD ●: certificate

School	PAGE	GENERAL	ACTING	DIRECTING	DESIGN	PRODUCT'N TECH	STAGE MANAGM'N	PLAYWT'G DIRECTING	HISTORY CRITICISM	THEATRE MANAGM'N	THEATRE EDUCAT'N	MUSICAL THEATRE	CHILDREN'S	OTHER
Columbus State University	61	②	③		③	③					②		②	
Comm. College of Baltimore County-Essex	106	①												
Concordia University	290	③	③		③			③			③			Theatre Minor
Connecticut College	39	②												
Conservatory at Act One Studios, The	66													2 year Cert in Acting
Conservatory of Music • see Univ. of Cincinnati														
Converse College	236	②												
Cornell College	86	②❷									●			② Communic.
Cornell University	161	②												② Film, Dance
Cornish College of the Arts	274	③●	③●		③●	③	③							③ ● Original Works
Culver-Stockton College	134		②③		②③				②③		②			② Comm
Cumberland College-Univ of the Cumberlands	94	❷												
Dartmouth College	146	②												
Davidson College	186	②												
Dell'Atre Int'l School of Physical Theatre	19	⑤												● Acting/Physical Th.
Denison University	201	②	③		③	③								
dePaul University, The Theatre School	75	③②	③⑤	⑤	③	③	③	③	③	③				
DeSales University	221	②	②	②	②	②								② Th. Comm/Dance/TV-Film
Dickinson College	221	②	②	②	②				②					② Dance
Dillard University	98	②	②											② Speech/Comm
Dixie College	258		①			①								
Dordt College	86	②	③											
Drake University	87	②	③	③	③	③					③	③		
Drew University	149	②												
Duke University	187	②												
East Carolina University	188	②	③		③	③	③				③	③		③ DancePerf/Ed
Eastern Kentucky University	95	②	③								②			
Eastern Michigan University	120	②❷④								②④❷		②④❷	④⑤	
Eckerd College	50	②	②	②	②	②								
Elmhurst College	68	②	②③		②	②					②	②		②Theatre/Speech
Elon University	188	②③	②③	②	②	②						③		
Emerson College	114	②	③		③	③	③		③	③	②④	③		③Dance
Emory & Henry College see Barter Conservatory														
Fairfield University	39	②												
Ferrum College	265	②③	②⑤											
Florida Atlantic University	51	②	②⑤		②⑤	⑤②								

alphabetical index of schools and degrees grant...

KEY: ①: AA ❶: AS ②: BA ❷: BS ③: BFA ④: MA ❹: MS ⑤: MFA ⑥: PhD ●: certificate

School	Page	General	Acting	Directing	Design	Production Tech	Stage Mangmnt	Playwtg/Directing	History/Criticism	Theatre Educatn	Theatre Mangmnt	Musical Theatre	Children's	Other
Florida International University	52	②	③		③						②			
Florida Southern College	52	②	②		③	②								see ad, back of book
Florida State University/Asolo Conservatory	50	②④⑥	③⑤	⑤	③⑤	⑤				⑤	⑤	③⑤		see ad, back of book
Florida State University School of Theatre	53	②	③⑤	⑤	③⑤	③⑤				⑤	⑤	③⑤		see ad, back of book
Fordham University	161	②												
Franklin College	79	②												
Franklin & Marshall College	222		②		②									② Film ② Dance
Genesee Community College	162	①										●		
George Mason University	266	②												
George Washington University	48	②			⑤									②⑤Dance
Georgetown College	95													② Comm Arts
Globe, The Old / University of San Diego	19	⑤											see ad	
Goucher College	106	②	②	②	②									
Graceland University	87		②	②	②	②	②			②				
Greensboro College	189	②②	②②	②②	②②	②②	②②			②②				② VisualPerf. Arts see ad
Green Mountain College	261	②	②											
Grinnell College	88	②												
Guilford College	189	②												
Gustavus Adolphus College	127	②	②	②	②									② Dance
Hampton University	266	②	②	②	②	②			②					
Hardin-Simmons University	246	②②												
Harvard University	109													
Henry Ford Community College	120	①												
Hiram College	202	②	③			③								
Hofstra University	162	②	③		③									
Hope College	121	②	③	③		④								
Howard University	49	③	③	③	③	③				③	③	③		③ Dance
Humboldt State University	20	②	④			④								
Hunter College	163	②④												
Illinois State University	68	②④❷④	②④❹	②④❷④	②②⑤	②②④	②②④			②②	②②④			②② Dance
Illinois Wesleyan University	69	②③	②⑤❷	⑤								③		
Indiana State University	80	②④❷④	②④❹	②④❷④	②④❷④		②④❹			②④❷④	②④❷④			②②④ Dance
Indiana University	80	②	⑤	⑤	⑤		⑤		④⑥					see ad, back of book
Indiana University of Pennsylvania	223	②	②	②	②									② Dance minor
Iowa State University	89	②	②	②	②									②Dance
Ithaca College	164	②	③	③	③	③					❷	③		

A-5

alphabetical index of schools and degrees granted

KEY: ①: AA ❶: AS ②: BA ❷: BS ③: BFA ④: MA ❹: MS ⑤: MFA ⑥: PhD ●: certificate

School	PAGE	GENERAL	ACTING	DIRECTING	DESIGN	PRODUCT TECH	STAGE MANGMNT	PLAYWTG/DIRECTING	HISTORY/CRITICISM	THEATRE MANGMNT	THEATRE EDUCATN	MUSICAL THEATRE	CHILDREN'S	OTHER
James Madison University	267	②										②		② Dance
Juilliard School	164	②	③	●				●						
Kansas State University	91	②	②❷	●	②❷	②❷	②❷		②❷	②❷				②❷ Drama Therapy
KD Studio	247		①											see ad
Kean University	150	②	③		③	③								
Keene State College	146	②	②	②	②	②			②					② Film, Dance
Kent State University	202	②	③		③	③						③		③ Mod Dance, ● Ent arts/tech
Kutztown University	223	②												
Lafayette College	224	②												② English w/Theatre Concent.
LaGrange College	61	②	②											
Lawrence University	280	②	②	②	②				②					
Lees-McRae College	190	②❷	②	②	②	②					②❷	②❷		②❷ Dance, Ministry
Lehigh University	224	②	②	②	②	②			②					
Lenoir-Rhyne College	191	②									②			② Th Arts/Eng
Lindenwood University	135	②	②③⑤	③⑤	③⑤	③⑤				②	②	③		
Livingstone College	191		③							③				
London Academy Music & Dramatic Art	291	●	●	●	●	●			●					● Music Direction
London Dramatic Acad (Fordham Univ)	292													
London International Film School	293													●④ Film
Long Island University- C. W. Post	166	②④	③		③	③								
Longwood University	267	③	③		③	③					②			
Los Angeles Theatre Academy @ LA City College	21		①●		①●	①								
Louisiana State University	99	②⑥	⑤		②	②			②⑥					
Louisiana Tech University	100	②④												
Lower Columbia College	275	①												
Loyola-Marymount University	22	②												
Loyola University of Chicago	70	②												
Loyola University - New Orleans	101	②								②				②Comm
Lyon College	9	②												
McGill University	290	②												② English
McNeese State University	101	②	②	②	②	②								
Marquette University	281	②	②		②	②								
Marshall University	278		③		③	③								
Mars Hill College	192	②												
Mary Baldwin College	268	②	②							②		③		⑤ Lit
Marymount Manhattan College	166	②	②③	②	②	②		②	②	②				see ad

A-6

Alphabetical Index to Theatre Programs & Degrees Granted

KEY: ①: AA ②: BA ❷: BS ③: BFA ④: MA ❹: MS ⑤: MFA ⑥: PhD ●: certificate

School	Page	General*	Acting	Directing	Design	Prod'n Tech	Stage Mgmt	Playwrtg	History/Crit	Theatre Mgmt	Theatre Educ	Musical Theatre	Children's	Other
Metropolitan State College of Denver	34	②												②Speech/Comm
Miami University @ Oxford, OH	203	②④												
Michigan State University	121	②④	⑤		⑤									
Michigan Tech University	122	②				❷								
Middlebury College	262		②	②	②	②								②Dance, Film
Millikin University	70	②	③	③	③	③						③		② Dance
Minnesota State University @ Mankato	127	②④❷	②❷⑤	②❷⑤	②❷⑤	②❷								❷ Speech ① Dance minor
Minnesota State University @ Moorhead	128	②	②	②	②	②					❷			
Mississippi University for Women	132	②												
Missouri State College	138		②	②	②	②					❷			❷ Speech
Missouri Valley College	136	②③	②	②	②						②❷	②❷		❷ Speech Ed.
Montana State University	142				②	②								② Media/Film/Video
Montclair State College	150	②	③	③	③	③								④Communic.
Mount Holyoke College	114	②												
Mountview Academy of Theatre Arts	294		②●	●		●	●					●		②Dance
Muhlenberg College	225	②	②	②	②	②	②							
Murray State University	95	②❷												
National Conservatory of Dramatic Arts	49		●											
National Theatre Conservatory	35		●⑤											
National Theatre Inst (NTI)	40													
Nazareth College	167	②												
Nebraska Wesleyan University	143	②③												②Communic.
Neighborhood Playhouse School of Theatre	167		●											6 week summer session
New Actors Workshop	168		④											
New England College	147	Non-degree												
New School for Drama	168	⑤	⑤					⑤						
N.Y.C. College of Technology	169					❷								
New York State Theatre Institute	169													
New York University-The Steinhardt School	171									④	❷④⑥	②④⑥		④ Drama/Music Therapy
New York University-Tisch School of Arts	172	③	③⑤		③⑤			③⑤				③		③⑤Dance
Niagara University	173	③	③		③	③								
North Carolina Ag & Tech State University	192	③	③		③	③								
North Carolina Central University	193	②	③											
North Carolina School of the Arts	193		③	③										
North Dakota State University	198		②❷③	②❷③	②❷	②❷			②					See Ad.
Northhampton Community College	226	①												

A-7

alphabetical index of schools and degrees granted

KEY: ①: AA ❶: AS ②: BA ❷: BS ③: BFA/④: MA ❹: MS ⑤: MFA/⑤: MS ⑥: PhD ●: certificate

School	PAGE	GENERAL	ACTING	DIRECTING	DESIGN	PRODUCT TECH	STAGE MANGMNT	PLAYWRTG	HISTORY/CRITICISM	THEATRE MANGMNT	THEATRE EDUCATN	MUSICAL THEATRE	CHILDREN'S	OTHER
Northeastern State University	210	②												② Speech/Speech Ed
Northeastern University	115	②❷	②❷	❷	②❷	②❷					②			
Northern Arizona University	7	②	②		②	②					②			
Northern Illinois University	71	②	③⑤	③	③⑤	③⑤					③	③		③Dance
Northern Kentucky University	96	②	③	③	③			③		③		③		
Northern Michigan University	122	②❷												
Northwest Missouri State University	137	②	❷	❷	❷	❷					❷			
Northwestern University	72	②④⑥	②③	⑤	⑤			⑤						
Oakland University	123	②				②						②		
Oberlin College	203		②											② Dance, Music
Occidental College	22		①	①	①			①	①					
Ohio State University	204	②	⑤	⑤	⑤	⑤			④⑥					See ad in back of book
Ohio University	205	③④	③⑤	⑤	⑤	⑤		⑤③	④	②				See ad in back of book
Ohio Wesleyan University	205	②								②	②			② Dance
Oklahoma City University	210	②④			④	❷④					②❷		④	②❷ Spch. Comm
Oklahoma State University	211	②④												
Old Dominion University	269	②	②③								②			
Olivet College	123	②												
O'Neill National Theatre Institute	40	●	❷											❷ TV & Film
Oral Roberts University	212	②❷	❷	②	②	②					②			
Oregon State University	214	②❷	②❷	②❷	②❷	②❷					②❷			④Interdisciplinary
Otterbein College	206	②	③		③	③						③		③ Dance
Pace University	173	②③		②	②	②				②		②		
PCPA TheatreFest	23	●	●	②		●								
Palm Beach Atlantic College	54	②	②	②	②	②					②	②		
Pennsylvania State University	226	②	⑤	⑤	⑤	③⑤	③				②	③		See ad in back of book
Plymouth State University	148	②									②❷Music	②		Dance Minor
Point Park College	227	②	②③⑤	②③	②③	②③	②③					②③		
Pomona College	23	②	②	②	②							②		
Presbyterian College	237	②	②	②	②	②								
Providence College	234	②	②		②									
Purdue University	81	②	⑤	⑤	⑤	⑤								
Radford University	269	②❷	②❷	②❷	②❷	②❷								
Reed College	214	②												②Dance/Theatre ②Lit/Theatre
Rhodes College	240	②												
Rockford College	72	②	②	②	②	②						③②		

alphabetical index of schools and degrees granted

KEY: ①: AA ②: BA ❷: BS ❸: BFA ④: MA ❹: MS ⑤: MFA ⑥: PhD ●: certificate

School	PAGE	GENERAL	ACTING	DIRECTING	DESIGN	PRODUCT TECH	STAGE MANGMNT	PLAYWTG	DIRECTING	HISTORY/CRITICISM	THEATRE MANGMNT	THEATRE EDUCAT'N	MUSICAL THEATRE	CHILDREN's	OTHER
Roger Williams University	235														
Rollins College	54	②	②	②	②	②									
Roosevelt Univ.- College of Performing Arts	73	②	③⑤	⑤									③		Fast track Summer Program See ad
Rowan University	151	②												②	
Rutgers University-Camden	152	②													
Rutgers University-New Brunswick	152		③⑤	⑤	③⑤	③	⑤	⑤							
St. Cloud State University	129	②													
St. Edwards University	247		②	⑤	②					②					
St. Michael's College	263	②													
Saint Olaf College	129	②													
Salem State College	115		②③		②③	②③									see ad
Sam Houston State University	248		③	③	③	③						③	③		
San Diego State University	24	②	②		②⑤	⑤					②	②	⑤	②	② Design-TV/Film
San Francisco State University	25	②④			⑤										
San Jose State University	25	②④									②	②	②		②Radio,TV, Film
Santa Clara University	26	②													②Dance
Sarah Lawrence College	175	③⑤													see ad
School for Film & TV	176		●Film/TV												
Seton Hall University	153	②	②	②											
Seton Hill University	228	②	②	②	②	②			②		②		②		
Shenandoah University	270		②	②	②	③						③	③	③	
Siena College	177	●													② Creative Arts
Skagit Valley College	276	①						②⑤	②						
Smith College	117		②	②	②	②			②						
Sonoma State University	27	②	②	②	②	②									②Dance
Southeast Missouri State University	137	②	③	③	③	③			②		❷				❷Speech ③Dance
Southern Arkansas University	9	②													
Southern Connecticut State University	41	②	②	②	②	②		⑤⑥	②						⑥Sp/Comm/Th
Southern Illinois University-Carbondale	74	②⑥	②❷	⑤	⑤	⑤									
Southern Illinois University-Edwardsville	74	②❷	③⑤	②②	②②	②②				②②		②②			② ❷Dance
Southern Methodist University	249	③	③⑤	⑤	⑤	③				③					See ad in back of book
Southern Oregon University	214	②❷	③	③	③	③	③								
Southern Utah University	259		②②	②②	②②	❷❷				⑤	⑤	②②			②Dance,Minor Th. Arts
Southwest Minnesota State University	130	②	③		③										
Southwestern University	249	②	③	③	③	③							③		②TV,Radio
State Univ. of New York (S.U.N.Y.)-Albany	183	②④	②④												

alphabetical index of schools and degrees granted

KEY: ①: AA ❶: AS ②: BA ❷: BS ③: BFA ④: MA ❹: MS ⑤: MFA ⑥: PhD ●: certificate

School	PAGE	GENERAL	ACTING	DIRECTING	DESIGN	PRODUC TECH	STAGE MANGMNT	PLAYWRTNG/DIRECTING	HISTORY CRITICISM	THEATRE MANGMNT	THEATRE EDUCATN	MUSICAL THEATRE	CHILDREN'S THEATRE	OTHER
S.U.N.Y.-Binghamtom • see Binghamton Univ.	158													
S.U.N.Y.-Buffalo State	177	②												
S.U.N.Y.-Buffalo • see University at Buffalo	184													
S.U.N.Y.-Fredonia	178	②	③		③	③						③		See ad
S.U.N.Y.-Geneseo	179	②												
S.U.N.Y.-New Paltz	179	②❷			❸									
S.U.N.Y.-Oswego	180		②	②	②	②								
S.U.N.Y.-Purchase	180	②④	③	③⑤	③⑤	③⑤	③⑤	⑤						
S.U.N.Y.-Stony Brook	181	②④						⑤						
Stephen F. Austin State University	250	②③	③	③	③	③					②			
Stephens College	139	①	③		③	③						③		
Suffolk County Community College	181	①												
Sul Ross State University	251	②									②④			
Swarthmore College	228	②												
Syracuse University	182		②③	⑤	③	③	③					③		
Temple University	229	②	⑤	⑤	⑤									
Texas A&M University	251	②												See ad in back of book
Texas A&M @ Commerce	252		②②④❹	②②④	②②④				②②④❹					
Texas State University at San Marcos	252	②	③	④③	④③	④③			④		③	③		
Texas Tech University	253	②④⑤⑥	⑤	③	③	③			③	③				② Dance
Theatre School at dePaul Univ	75	②③	⑤	③⑤	③	③	③		③	③				
Towson University	107	②❷⑤	②②		②②	②②								② Dance
Trinity College	41	②												
Trinity Repertory Conservatory/Brown Univ	234	②④⑥	⑤ ●	⑤ ●										
Tufts University	117	②④⑥												
Tulane University	102	②	③		③	③⑤								
University of Akron	207	②												
University of Alabama- Birmingham	2	②	②	②	②	②								
University of Alabama-Tuscaloosa	3	②	⑤	⑤	⑤	⑤	⑤			⑤				②Dance
University of Alaska-Anchorage	5													
University of Alaska-Fairbanks	6		②	②	②	②								
University at Albany - S.U.N.Y.	182	②④												
University of Arizona	8	②③④	③	③	③⑤	③⑤					③	③		②Dance
University of Arkansas-Fayetteville	10	②	⑤	⑤	⑤			⑤						
University of Arkansas-Little Rock	10	②												② Dance

A-10

alphabetical index of schools and degrees offered

KEY: ①: AA ❶: AS ②: BA ❷: BS ③: BFA ④: MA ❹: MS ⑤: MFA ⑥: PhD ●: certificate

School	Page	General	Acting	Directing	Design	Production Tech	Stage Mangmnt	Playwriting	History/Criticism	Theatre Mangmnt	Theatre Educate	Musical Theatre	Children's Theatre	Other
University of the Arts	230	③	③	③	③	③				③		③		②③ Dance
University at Buffalo S.U.N.Y.	184	②③	③		③							③		②⑤ Dance ⑥ Perf
University of California-Davis	28	②	⑤	⑤	⑤									
University of California-Irvine	28	②⑥	⑤	⑤	⑤	⑤	⑤							
University of California-Los Angeles	29	②⑥	⑤	⑤	⑤	⑤		⑤						②③Film/TV
University of California-Riverside	30	②	⑤	⑤	⑤			⑤						
University of California-San Diego	31	②⑥	⑤	⑤	⑤	⑤	⑤	⑤						② Dance
University of California-Santa Barbara	31	②	③	②	②				④②⑥					
University of Central Arkansas	11	②❷												
University of Central Florida	55	②	③⑤	③⑤	③⑤	③	③	⑤				③⑤	⑤	see ad back of book
U. of Cincinnati-Col. Conservatory of Music	207	③⑤	⑤	③⑤	③⑤	③⑤	⑤			④⑤	③⑤	③		
University of Colorado @ Boulder	35	②③④⑥												
University of Colorado @ Denver	36	②③												
University of Connecticut	42	②	③⑤	③⑤	③⑤	③④								③④⑤Puppetry
University of Dallas	253	②												
University of Delaware	46		⑤		⑤	⑤	⑤							
University of Denver	37	②												
University of Evansville	82	②❷	❷③	❷③	③	③			❷	❷				
University of Florida	56	②	③⑤	⑤	③⑤	③						③		
University of Georgia	62	②	⑤	②	⑤		⑤		⑥					⑤Dram. Media,②Film
University of Hartford	43	②												
University of Hawaii- Manoa	64	②④	⑤	⑤	⑤	⑤	⑤						②③④⑤ Dance	⑤⑥Asian, ⑥ WstTh
University of Houston	254	②	④⑤	④⑤	④⑤	④⑤		④⑤						
University of Idaho	65	②❷	③⑤	⑤	③⑤	③								
University of Illinois-Chicago	76		②③	②③	②③									
University of Illinois-Urbana-Champaign	76		③⑤	⑤	③⑤	③⑤			④⑥	③⑤				See ad back of book
University of the Incarnate Word	255	②												
University of Indianapolis	82	②❷	②❷	②❷	②❷	②❷					②❷	②❷		
University of Iowa	89	②	⑤	⑤	⑤		⑤	⑤						
University of Kansas	92	②❷④⑥	④⑤	④⑤	⑤	⑤						②❷		②❷④⑥Film/Video
University of Kentucky	97	②④	③	⑤	③	③								
University of LaVerne	32	②	②	②				②			②			
University of Louisiana @ Lafayette	103	③												
University of Louisiana @ Monroe	102	②												
University of Maine-Orono	104	②												
University of Mary Washington	270	②												

alphabetical index of schools and degrees granted

KEY: ①: AA ●: AS ②: BA ❷: BS ③: BFA ④: MA ❹: MS ⑤: MFA ⑥: PhD ●: certificate

School	PAGE	GENERAL	ACTING	DIRECTING	DESIGN	PRODUCT. TECH	STAGE MANGMNT	PLAYWRTG / DIRECTING / MANGMNT	HISTORY CRITICISM	THEATRE MANGMNT	THEATRE EDUCATN	MUSICAL THEATRE	CHILDREN'S	OTHER
University of Maryland-Baltimore County	108	⑤⑥	②③		②	②			④					See ad in back of book
University of Maryland-College Park	108	②	②		②⑤	②			④					See ad in back of book
University of Massachusetts	118		②					②						
University of Memphis	241		③	⑤	③⑤	③⑤	③							
University of Miami	56	②	③		③	③	③			③		③		BM in Musical Theatre
University of Miami-Musical Theatre	57													
University of Michigan	124	②	③		③	③	③							
University of Michigan-Flint	124	②	③								●			● Speech
University of Minnesota	130	②⑥	③	⑤	⑤									see ad, back of book
University of Missouri-Columbia	139	②	②		②	⑤		②	④⑥					
University of Missouri-Kansas City	140	②	⑤		⑤	⑤		④	④					
University of Montana	143	②④	③⑤		③⑤	③⑤								②③Dance ⑤Media
University of Montevallo	3	②❷③												
University of Nebraska-Lincoln	144	②	⑤②	⑤	③⑤	③②⑤		⑤						
University of Nevada-Las Vegas	145	②⑤④	②⑤	⑤	⑤②	⑤②	⑤							
University of Nevada-Reno	145	②	③			③								
University of New Hampshire	148	②	②		②	②					②	②	②	②Dance
University of New Mexico	154	②④						⑤						②③ Dance
University of North Alabama	4	②❷												
University of North Carolina-Chapel Hill	194	②	⑤	⑤	⑤	⑤								
University of North Carolina-Greensboro	195	②	③⑤	⑤	③⑤						③		⑤	
University of North Carolina-Pembroke	196	②	②	②	②							②		
University of North Carolina-Wilmington	196	②	②	②	②									
University of North Dakota	198	②	③	⑤	③	③			④					
University of North Texas	255	②	③		③	③						③		
University of Northern Colorado	37	②	②		②	②					②	②		
University of Northern Iowa	90		②		②	②							②	
University of Notre Dame	83	②					③							
University of Oklahoma	213	④③	③	⑤	③⑤	③	③							
University of Oregon	215	②⑥			⑤	⑤								
University of the Pacific	33	②	⑤									②		
University of Pittsburgh	230		⑤						⑥④			②		
University of Portland	216		②		②	②				❷				
University of Rhode Island	235		③	③	③	③				③				
University of Richmond	271	②												
University of St. Thomas	131		②		②				②		②			●Dance

alphabetic Index of schools & degrees granted

KEY: ①: AA ❶: AS ②: BA ❷: BS ③: BFA ④: MA ❹: MS ⑤: MFA ⑥: PhD ●: certificate

School	PAGE	GENERAL	ACTING	DIRECTING	DESIGN	PRODUCT. TECH	STAGE MANGMNT	PLAYWRT'G	DIRECTING	HISTORY/CRITICISM	THEATRE MANGMNT	THEATRE EDUCAT'N	MUSICAL THEATRE	CHILDREN'S THEATRE	OTHER
University of San Diego (The Old Globe)	19	⑤													
University of the South	241	②													
University of South Alabama	5	②③													
University of South Carolina	237	②④	⑤	⑤	⑤										
University of South Dakota	238	②❷③④	③	⑤	③⑤	③⑤									
University of South Florida	58	②	②		②③							②			
University of Southern California	33	②	③		⑤	③		⑤		②					②Oral Interp.
University of Southern Maine	105	②	②		②					②					
University of Southern Mississippi	133	②	③⑤	⑤	③⑤	③⑤									See ad in back of book
University of Tennessee-Knoxville	242	②⑤	⑤		⑤										②③ Dance, Art Ed., Art, Graphic Des.
University of Tennessee-Martin	243	②③													②③Dance
University of Texas-Austin	256	②③	⑤	⑤	⑤	⑤		⑤		④⑥		④	⑤		②③Dance
University of Texas-El Paso	256	②④	②④	②④	②④			②④		②④			③		Minor in Film,theatre, dance, ③Dance
University of Texas-Pan American	257	④	②	②	②	②					②	②			See ad in back of book
University of Toledo	208	②	③												②Film
University of Tulsa	213		②		②			②					②		
University of Utah	259	②	③		③	③						③			see ad
University of Vermont	263	②	②		②	②		②		②					
University of Virginia	271	②	⑤	⑤	⑤	⑤		⑤							
University of Washington	276	②③	⑤	⑤	⑤	⑤				⑥					
University of West Florida	58	②③	③										③		see ad
University of West Georgia	63	②	②		②										see ad
University of Windsor	291	②	③		③	②						②			②Communic.
University of Wisconsin-Eau Claire	281	②❷	②		②	②③						②			
University of Wisconsin-Green Bay	282	②	②	②	②	②							②		
University of Wisconsin-La Crosse	282	②❷	②❷	②	②❷						②❷	②❷	②❷		②❷Music
University of Wisconsin-Madison	283	③②	②⑤	⑤	⑤	⑤									④⑥Theatre Research
University of Wisconsin-Milwaukee	284	②	⑤	⑤	⑤	⑤	⑤								⑤Cost. Prod.
University of Wisconsin-Parkside	285	❷	②	②	②	②	②								
University of Wisconsin-River Falls	285	❷													② Comm, Spch
University of Wisconsin-Stevens Point	286	②❷	②③	②③	②③	②③	③						③		②❷Dance
University of Wisconsin-Whitewater	286	②	③	③	③	③	③					BS Ed.			
University of Wyoming	288	②③❷	③	②③	②③	②③		②③				②			②③Dance
Utah State University	260	②④⑤	③	③	③	③						③			
Vanderbilt University	243	②❷													

alphabetical index of schools and degrees granted

KEY: ①: AA ❶: AS ②: BA ❷: BS ③: BFA ④: MA ❹: MS ❹: MFA ⑤: PhD ●: certificate

School	PAGE	GENERAL	ACTING	DIRECTING	DESIGN	PRODUCT'N TECH	STAGE MANGM'T	PLAYWTG/DIRECTING	HISTORY/CRITICISM	THEATRE MANGM'T	THEATRE EDUCAT'N	MUSICAL THEATRE	CHILDREN'S THEATRE	OTHER
Villanova University	231	④												
Vincennes University	83	①❶				❶						❶		●Dance
Virginia Commonwealth University	272	②	③⑤	⑤	⑤③	③⑤	③⑤		⑤		③			
Virginia Tech	273	②			⑤	⑤	⑤		⑤					
Viterbo College	287	②❷	③	③	③	③			③	③	③			
Wabash College	84	②												
Wagner College	184	②	②		②	②			②	②		②		
Wake Forest University	197	②												②Dance Minor
Washington University	140	②												②Dance, Film
Wayne State University	125	③⑤	⑤③		⑤③		⑤		⑤					
Webster University	141	③		②	③	③	③					③		
Wellesley College	118	② indep.												
Wesleyan University	43	②												
West Virginia University	278	②	③⑤	⑤	③⑤	③⑤								③Puppetry
Western Carolina University	198	②	②③											
Western Connecticut State University	44	②			②⑤									
Western Illinois University	77	②	②⑤	②⑤										
Western Kentucky University	97	②	③											③ Perf. Arts
Western Michigan University	126	②	②		②	②	②		②	②		③		
Western Washington University	277	②								②				
Western Wyoming College	289											①		
Whitworth College	277	②												
Wichita State University	92	②	③		③	③			②	②		③		
Wilkes University	232	②	②							②		②		
Willamette University	216	②	②	②	②									
William Inge Theatre Festival	93	①	①			●	●							
William Woods University	142	②												②③Radio/TV
Winona State University	132	②												
Winthrop University	238	②	②		②	②				②				② Dance/w teach cert
Wright State University	209	②	③		③	③	③		②			③		③Dance ②③ Film
Yale University	44	②												
Yale University School of Drama	45	●⑤	●⑤	⑤	⑤⑤	●	⑤	●	⑤					
York College of Pennsylvania	232	②												
Youngstown State University	209	②③	③									③		

A unique collection of graduate training programs in all fields of theatre
Acting | Design | Directing | Stage Management | Technology | Theatre Management

URTA

In 2008:
University/Resident Theatre Association
National Unified Auditions/Interviews

New York: January 26-30
Chicago: February 2-6
Las Vegas: February 8-10

For 2009 dates: Contact URTA

urta.com
Where to go to get there.

For other programs/services, visit U/RTA's website:
www.urta.com

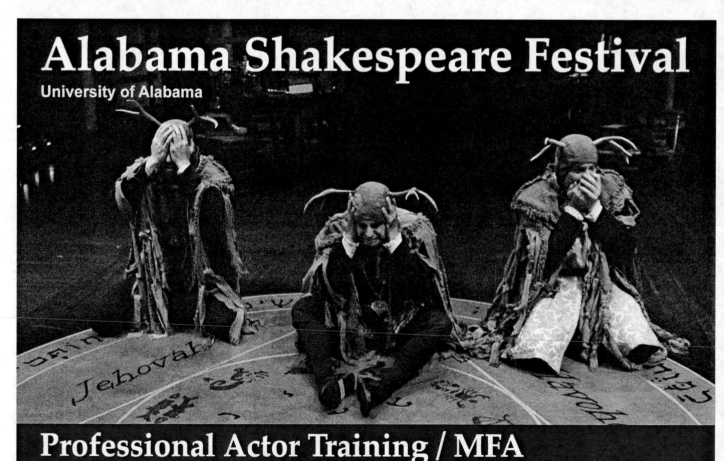

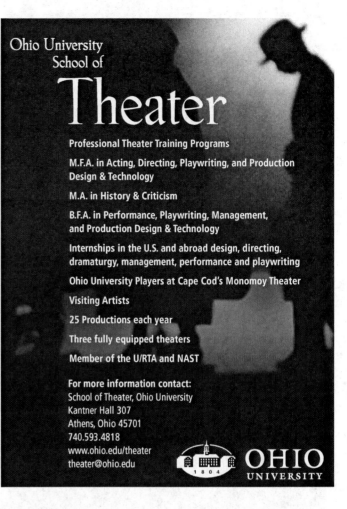

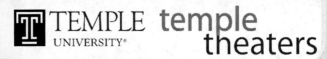

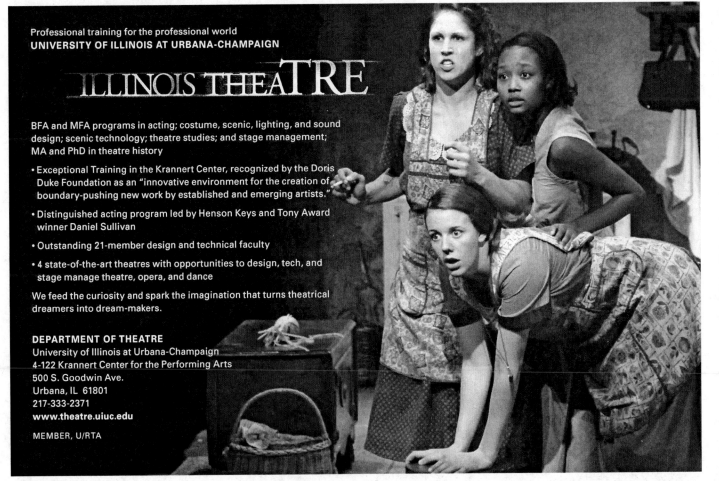

THEATRE DIRECTORIES

Qty

	Summer Theatre Directory 2008	$29.50
	Directory of Theatre Training Prog, 11th Ed.	$39.50
	Stars in Your Eyes...	$16.95
	Regional Theatre Directory 2007-08	$29.50
	Student's Guide to Playwriting Oppor. 3rd Ed	$23.95
	Special Reports each	$ 7.50
	Showbiz Bookeeper	$22.95
	Mailing Labels STD, RTD, DTTP each	$45.00

		Subtotal	$
Media Mail	**Priority or UPS**		
1 bk - $7.50	$10.75		
2-3 bks $9.00	$11.50		
4+ bks - UPS rates		S/H=	$
		Total=$	

☐ Check or M.O.(payable to **Theatre Directories Inc.**)

☐ Please bill my credit card: _____

    3 or 4 digit security code: _____ Zip on Credit Card: _____

                                Exp. Date: _____ / _____

☐ Please Invoice: Purchase Order # _____

Name/Institution: _____

Address 1: _____

Address 2: _____

City: _____ State: _____ Zip: _____

Phone: _____ email: _____

Mail to: Theatre Directories Inc, PO Box 159, Dorset, VT 05251

www.theatredirectories.com

Phone: 802 867 9333 Fax: 802 867 2297 email: info@theatredirectories.com